A HISTORICAL LINKAGE

THE TIMETABLES OF™ HISTORY

FOURTH EDITION

OF PEOPLE AND EVENTS

BERNARD GRUN

A TOUCHSTONE BOOK
Published by Simon & Schuster
New York London Toronto Sydney

TOUCHSTONE
Rockefeller Center
1230 Avenue of the Americas
New York, NY 10020

Revised Touchstone Edition 2005

Published by arrangement with F.A. Herbig Verlagsbuchhandlung

Previously published in German by F.A. Herbig Verlagsbuchhandlung

Manufactured in the United States of America

3 5 7 9 10 8 6 4 2

Library of Congress Cataloging-in-Publication Data

Grun, Bernard, 1901–1972.
The timetables of history : a historical linkage of people and events /
Bernard Grun.—4th ed.
p. cm.
"A Touchstone book."
"Based on Werner Stein's Kulturfahrplan."
Includes index.
ISBN-13: 978-0-7432-7003-8
ISBN-10: 0-7432-7003-7
1. Chronology, Historical—Tables. I. Stein, Werner, 1913– Kulturfahrplan. II. Title.

D11.G78 2005
902'.02—dc22 2005049766

PUBLISHER'S NOTE

(THIRD EDITION)

The Timetables of History is a direct translation of much of the material that appears in the original great work on which it is based, *Kulturfahrplan (The Culture Timetables),* a spectacular success in Germany ever since its creator, Werner Stein, produced it in 1946. In the intervening years between then and now, it has been updated several times and in its various editions has sold in the millions of copies.

Obviously an English-language version of this fascinating and prestigious work was eminently desirable, but for more than twenty years the difficulties appeared to be so great as to make a translation impracticable, both from an editorial and an economic standpoint.

Fortunately, in the late 1960s a man emerged who was not only eager to tackle the task but ideally equipped to accomplish it. Bernard Grun, born in the Czech part of the old Austro-Hungarian monarchy and educated in law and philosophy at the universities of Prague and Vienna, had by then been settled in London for decades. An eminent musicologist, he was almost as well-known as a historian with an encyclopedic talent and turn of mind. Completely bilingual in German and English, he could translate, delete, revise, and add fresh material, so that a new volume would emerge that would be a pertinent and useful one for the English-language reading public. Additionally, to make sure that sufficient emphasis was given to American topics, the manuscript was then turned over to an American scholar, Wallace Brockway, whose authority and experience both in history and in compiling encyclopedic works were very similar to Mr. Grun's.

Sadly, after several years of work on the project, both men died before the first edition of this book could be printed and published, and this was a source of deep regret to all of us. We are grateful to a number of people for their help in checking, rounding off, updating, and completing what had been left unfinished, and in this connection acknowledgments are due to Helen Barrow, Sophie Sorkin, and Elise Sachs. Special acknowledgments go to Laurence Urdang and his firm, who did a superb job for the first two editions, and to Market House Books, who saw to the complete expanding of this new, updated edition.

—Peter Schwed, 1991

NOTE TO FOURTH EDITION

We acknowledge Frauke Hoppen of Buchverlage Langen Müller, the German Book Office, and Lilian Friedberg for their work on this fourth edition.

FOREWORD

BY DANIEL J. BOORSTIN

"Time," wrote the famous American philosopher-idler Henry David Thoreau, "is but the stream I go fishing in." Each of us—with the help of parents, grandparents, friends, teachers, historians, and others—goes fishing in that stream. And we usually come up with what we knew, or strongly suspected, was already there. One of the purposes of this book is to make it possible for us to go fishing and come up with some surprises.

At a glance, *The Timetables of History* can give us a feel for the fluidity and many-sidedness of past experience. Here we plainly see that the historian's neat categories parse experience in ways never found among living people. While, even in this volume, the authors have found it necessary to separate events into political, cultural, artistic, and scientific categories, when we cast our eye across any page we see how overlapping, interfusing, inseparable, and arbitrary are all such separations. Often the most interesting—and most surprising—are the miscellaneous items which the authors list in the last right-hand column under "Daily Life." Precisely because these items are commonplace in their time, precisely because they were so obviously in the foreground of the experience of non-historians, historians have been reluctant to give them the dignity of "history."

For people in the past, just as for us, experience has had no academic neatness. The miscellany on every page of this book can help remind us of this neglected first principle of history. For example, 1776, the year of the United States' Declaration of Independence, was also the year of publication of the first volume of Gibbon's *Decline and Fall of the Roman Empire* and of Adam Smith's *Wealth of Nations;* the year of the death of the Scottish philosopher David Hume; the year when Fragonard made one of his best-known paintings and when the English landscape painter John Constable was born; the year of Mozart's Serenade in D Major, K. 250 (the "Haffner"), of Cook's third voyage to the Pacific, and of military ski competitions in Norway. Or 1927, the year when Lindbergh flew the Atlantic, was also the year when Trotsky was expelled from the Communist Party, when *Show Boat* opened in New York, when Sigmund Freud published *The Future of an Illusion* and Thornton Wilder *The Bridge of San Luis Rey,* when Pavlov did his work on conditioned reflexes, Al Jolson starred in the epoch-making "talkie" *The Jazz Singer,* the German economic system collapsed, and the Harlem Globetrotters basketball team was organized. Which of these items was most vivid to anyone living in Western Europe or America at the time must have depended on where that person lived, and on his education, interests, social class, and prejudices. On every page of this book, then, we see clues to how polychromatic and how iridescent is the experience of any age.

A number of peculiarities in our thinking and teaching have made "chronology"—the study of the arrangement of events in time—seem less interesting than it really is.

First is the time-cliché. This is the notion that history mainly consists of certain "key" dates—"1066 and All That!" Dates, then, seem the rigid skeleton of history, which historians flesh out. And early Anglo-American history would be all that happened between "1066" (The Norman Conquest) and "1776" (The American Revolution). "Crucial dates," we are told, are the Landmarks of History. But if we teach history as chronology the landmarks overshadow the landscape.

It is not surprising, then, that the unwilling student thinks of history as little more than lists of numbers (and names) to be memorized. A more profound consequence, for those of us who did our homework and learned the lists, was to shape—or rather pervert—our notions of human experience in the long past. History was not a broad stream of many eddies, but a neat and narrow road with sharp turns, unambiguous starting points, and clearly marked dead ends. Roman civilization "ended" when Alaric and the Visigoths sacked Rome in 410 A.D. Then the Dark Ages "began." Favorite examination questions asked: When did the Renaissance commence? Was it with the birth of Petrarch in 1304? or of Shakespeare in 1564? A sophisticated student was one who had become adept at marshaling and juggling dates to mark off one or another sharply bounded expanse of time.

Such a date-oriented history was inevitably a story of sudden beginnings and instant endings. The great eras and grand movements of history seemed to arrive with fanfare and to depart with formal valedictory. People who lived "in advance of their age" were "prophets." The past was peopled with figures of transition "wandering between two worlds, one dead, the other powerless to be born." It was such thinking that led an imaginative student to describe Dante (1265–1321) as "the Italian poet who had one foot in the Middle Ages, and with the other saluted the rising star of the Renaissance."

While these time-clichés pervert our view of the *pro-*

cesses of history, another peculiarity of our date-oriented thinking perverts our view of the *experience* of history. Against this malady *The Timetables of History* may be a mild corrective. For we have been trained to think of the past as a *sequence,* and to think of history as consequences. We learn about the American Revolution because a great nation came out of it. Among its other consequences we may count the French revolutions of 1789 (1830?, 1848?) and too, indirectly, the Paris Commune of 1871, the Russian Revolution of 1917, and the myriad anti-colonial revolutions of our age. We have been so overwhelmed and dazzled by this sequence-oriented view of the past that we have failed even to notice what we have been missing–History as Experience!

One of the obvious features of the experience that fills *our* lives every day is that we never can know what will flow out of it. But the historian is the scientist of hindsight. Since he knows (or thinks he knows) how it all turned out, he is preoccupied with the question: What chain of events made it come out that way? On the other hand, we, the people, live in a world of the contemporary. We see ourselves dominated by the events that happen at one time–in *our* time. We are charmed and enticed, and threatened by the uncertainties of the future. The historian in his library and at his leisure can focus in turn on one kind of event after another–the political, the economic, the intellectual. He has the opportunity to sort out origins and consequences. But the citizen is the simultaneous target of all sorts of events. These *Timetables of History,* then, can remind us of how numerous and how diverse are the events which make up the experience of living men and women.

Another effect of our common way of viewing the historical past is to reinforce our habits of thinking in ways that make us feel at home where we already are. We actually use our chronology to narrow our historical vision. We do this, for example, when we make the birth of Jesus the turning point of historical dating. The signs of A.D. and B.C. proclaim the central importance of an event which is actually believed to be central by only a small proportion of mankind. The cumbersome designation of early events by a subtractive system of B.C. simply adds to the problem of finding our bearings in strange and ancient societies. Muslims, naturally enough, date their events A.H. *(Annus Hegirae)* from the crucial event in the history of *their* religion.

All such ways of looking at chronology inhibit our thinking about the whole human past. In addition, the decimal system and the celebration of centuries and their multiples induce us to give the fluid past an unnatural neatness and rigidity. Among the ancient Jews, a "jubilee" when slaves were manumitted and debts were forgiven was celebrated every fifty years. Then the Roman Catholic Church began the practice of proclaiming a Holy Year (generally once every 25 years, when special privileges were given by the Church for pilgrimage to Rome, and there was an unusual jubilee indulgence), the first of which was proclaimed by Pope Boniface VIII in 1300. Since the rise of the historical profession in Western countries this slicing of the past into "centuries" has dominated us in ways difficult to overestimate. At first a hundred years was described as "a century of years." Then by the middle of the seventeenth century the word "century" itself had come to mean a period of 100 years. Ever since then the units of academic instruction and scholarship have been wrapped in parcels, each 100 years long.

Scholars will surely dispute some of the dates offered here. While the authors of this volume have conscientiously aimed at precision and accuracy, they would be the first to caution the reader. *The Timetables of History* is a stimulus and an eye-opener for everyman's exploration of the past. This book should be the starting point, and not the conclusion, of some new questions for us to ask about the past.

The reader should be reminded, too, that much of the contemporaneity of happenings all over the world revealed in these *Timetables* was itself beyond the consciousness of people living at the time. The events and achievements that are contemporary by the calendar are not contemporary in experience unless people know of them. During nearly all history, communications have been limited, slow, and desultory. We must therefore be wary of assuming that because different events occurred in the same year they were *known* to contemporaries at about the same time. For example, Adam Smith's *Wealth of Nations* (probably the first comprehensive treatment of political economy in a Western language) had first been delivered as lectures in Glasgow, was first published in Britain in 1776, and did not appear in an American edition until 1789. It was not translated into French or German until 1794. The writings of John Locke, which were first published in England in the late seventeenth century, and were frequently referred to by the authors of the Declaration of Independence and the Constitution, remained scarce on American shores throughout the eighteenth century. One of the more tantalizing questions for the historian is how, when, and where knowledge of an event occurring in one place reached other parts of the earth.

In many cases this inability to communicate promptly, so that people in one part of the earth remained ignorant of some of the contemporaneity revealed in these *Timetables,* has been a crucial fact shaping the course of history. And there are a number of familiar examples in the history of the United States. If James Monroe, President Thomas Jefferson's special envoy, and Robert R. Livingston, then the United States Minister in Paris, had been able to consult President Jefferson about the urgent and surprising terms that Napoleon offered in 1803 for the sale of the whole of Louisiana, Jefferson and the Congress of the United States might have balked. Both the history and the boundaries of this nation might then have been quite different. These envoys' inability to keep their President currently informed forced them to strike a bargain on their own. Faced not with the question but with their answer, Jefferson put his constitutional scruples behind him, and the Congress ratified what they would not have initiated.

Similarly, Andrew Jackson's reputation as a military hero was in no small part due to the lack of communications. At the famous Battle of New Orleans on the morning of January 8, 1815, General Andrew Jackson, then commander of the American army in the Southwest, repulsed a superior British force, which lost more than 2,000 men, at a cost of only 71 Americans. So he "saved" New Orleans and the Mississippi Valley from a British invasion. But this battle had no effect on the outcome of the war with Britain, because the peace terms had been settled two weeks earlier by the Treaty of Ghent (signed December 24, 1814), a fact which neither Jackson nor his British opponents knew. If communications had been speedier, the battle might have been forestalled, and Andrew Jackson would never have been given the opportunity to become "The Hero of New Orleans"—with consequences for American politics and the rise and demise of "Jacksonian Democracy" on which we can only speculate.

Among the crucial features of our human experience, then, we must count not only the vast range of events and achievements that make up a contemporary life, but the accessibility of the events and achievements of one place to people living elsewhere. Contemporaneity—as a quality not of the calendar but of living human experience—is a relative and variable term. It depends not only on what happens when and where, but on who knows what, when, and where. Among the grand changes in human experience few have been more drastic than our changing and suddenly enlarging sense of the contemporary. In the most recent times we can begin to take it for granted that dominant events and achievements which occur in a particular year enter the experience of larger and larger numbers of people in that very year, or even on the very day of their occurrence.

The calendar of dates and the reach of experience come closer and closer together. To millions of citizens in our Televised States of America, an increasing number of events are known (and of course many are actually seen and heard) at the moment when they happen. This flood of confused contemporaneity has itself become a dominant and bewildering feature of life in our time.

As we read *The Timetables of History* for the years before the late twentieth century, we should not forget that we are seeing "contemporary" events as only God could have seen them. And so we can discover what men of the Pre-Television Age were missing about life in their own time. The horizontal columns show us the interesting coincidences and the surprising range of events and achievements of mankind in each era.

Another reminder—and a caution—to all users of this book. The focus of the authors' views is Western Europe and the Americas. While relevant events in Africa, Asia, and elsewhere are not intentionally omitted, the authors have made no effort to survey the historical events of those parts of the world. The reader should be aware that *Timetables* for those other parts would be at least as copious and no less interesting. If there is no logical justification for this limitation of the book, there is ample human justification. Western civilization alone offers an exhausting enterprise of chronology. Werner Stein, Bernard Grun, Wallace Brockway, and their helpers have given us a wealth of facts about a considerable part of the human story.

We hope that the reader and the browser will find here most of the items that he would expect to find. But, except for the more familiar and more obvious items in politics and the arts, the authors' choice has been personal. For there really is no such thing as a "correct" or complete selection of items for inclusion in such a volume as this. Much of the interest, and most of the stimulus and the usefulness of these *Timetables* must come from the unexpectedness and even from the arbitrariness of the authors' interests. The inquiring reader will be grateful to these authors for awakening him to kinds of events and achievements which he had never even thought of looking up.

This fantastic miscellany can help us see what we thought we already knew in a lively new perspective. And it can also open our vision to vistas of human experience that we never thought of as "history" but which enrich our understanding of the whole human past and of ourselves.

ACRONYMS

European Monetary Union (EMU)
European Monetary System (EMS)
European Currency Unit (ECU)
European Space Observatory (ESO)
Commonwealth of Independent States (C.I.S.)
O.S.C.E (Organization for Safety and Security in Europe)—after 1991
C.S.C.E. (Council for Security and Cooperation in Europe)—until 1991
O.E.C.D (Organization for Economic Co-operation and Development)
RWE (Rhine Westphalia Electric Works)
R.A.F. (Red Army Faction)
World Health Organization (W.H.O.)
DGB Association of German Trade Unions
DGB (German Trade Union Association)
FDGB (Federation of German Trade Unions)
G.D.R. (Germ. Dem. Rep.)
F.R.G. (Fed. Rep. of Germany)
World Wildlife Fund (W.W.F.)
European Economic Area (EEA)
E.F.T.A. (European Free Trade Association)
A.S.E.A.N. (Association of Southeast Asian Nations)
Asian-Pacific Economic Cooperation (A.P.E.C.)
OPCW (Organization for the Prohibition of Chemical Weapons)
BDA (German Architects Assoc.)
I.L.O. (International Labor Organization)
General Agreement on Tariffs and Trade (GATT)
bovine growth hormones (BGH)
E.S.A. (European Space Agency)
International Labour Organization (I.L.O.)
U.N.I.C.E.F. (United Nations International Children's Fund)
United Nations Educational, Scientific and Cultural Organization (U.N.E.S.C.O.)
U.N. Food and Agriculture Organization (F.A.O.)
CASTOR (Casks for Storage and Transport of Radioactive Material)
International Olympic Committee (I.O.C.)
Union of European Football Associations (U.E.F.A.)
Federation of International Football Associations (F.I.F.A.)
International Space Station (I.S.S.)
European Southern Observatory (ESO)
Very Large Telescope Array (VLT)

Austrian Political Parties:
Social Democratic Party (ÖVP)
Austrian People's Party (SPÖ)
Freedom Party (FPÖ)

German Political Parties:
CDU—Christian Democratic Union
CSU—Christian Social Union
SPD—Social Democratic Party
FDP—Free Democratic Party
B 90/Greens

Misc. Other Political Parties
African National Congress (A.N.C.)
Chinese Communist Party (CCP)
Islamic Salvation Front (FIS)
Kurdish Labor Party (PKK)

THE TIMETABLES OF HISTORY

	A. HISTORY, POLITICS	B. LITERATURE, THEATER	C. RELIGION, PHILOSOPHY, LEARNING
-5000 to -4001			
-4000 to -3501	End of Paleolithic period along Mediterranean coastline Sumerians settle on the site of city of Babylon Babylonian influence predominant in Mediterranean regions of Asia (to –2000)	Sumerian writing, done on clay tablets, shows about 2,000 pictographic signs Earliest Babylonian omen tablets	
-3500 to -3001	Height of Sumerian civilization Neolithic period in western Europe (to –1700) Bronze Age in Bohemia King Menes the Fighter unites Upper and Lower Egypt 1st and 2nd dynasties in Egypt (Archaic period to –2800)	Sumerian wedge-shaped (cuneiform) writing, the earliest known	
-3000 to -2501	Semitic tribes occupy Assyria in northern part of the plain of Shinar and Akkad Phoenicians settle on Syrian coast, with centers at Tyre and Sidon Neolithic settlements in Crete Height of Danubian culture Beginning of the period of the "Sage Kings" in China Old Kingdom of Egypt, 3rd to 6th dynasty (–2815 to –2294) Beginning of early dynastic period of Mesopotamia (to –2350) Zoser, king of 3rd Egyptian dynasty (–2780 to –2720) Gilgamesh, legendary king of Uruk (Erech) (c. –2750) Cheops, king of 4th Egyptian dynasty (–2700 to –2675) Egyptians invade Palestine as reprisal for attacks on trade caravans Mis-anni-padda, king of Ur, first recorded ruler in Mesopotamia	Sumerian poetry, lamenting the death of Tammuz, the shepherd god; also first epic tales of Gilgamesh (see –1200, Gilgamesh Epic) Sumerian cuneiform writing reduces pictographs still in use to about 550 Pepi's papyrus, "Instructions to a Son," one of earliest preserved literary documents	Sumerian chief deities are Mother Goddess Innin and her son Tammuz; similar divinities are worshiped by Egyptians, Hittites, Phoenicians, and Scandinavians Pharaoh, the god-king in Egypt Major religious festival in Sumeria celebrates victory of god of spring over goddess of chaos
-2500 to -2001	Settlement of Aramean nomads from Euphrates area and of Semitic Canaanite tribes in Palestine Yao dynasty in China (to –2300) Lugalzaggisi, king of Uruk, defeats the Lagash empire and becomes "King of the Countries" (–2400 to –2350) Sargon, first king of Akkadian dynasty, defeats Lugalzaggisi, creates a vast Semitic empire in Mesopotamia, and calls himself "King of the Four Quarters" (–2350 to –2100) Shun dynasty in China (–2300 to –2205) Naramsin, ruler of Babylon (–2270 to –2233) First of the Hsai dynasties in China (–2200 to –1760) Egypt ruled by the Hyksos, "Shepherd Kings" (–2200 to –1700) Dynasty of Pharaohs in Egypt (–2200 to –525) End of Old Kingdom and beginning of Middle Kingdom of Egypt, 11th and 12th dynasties (–2100 to –1700) Abraham leaves Ur in Chaldea (c. –2100) Disappearance of city of Agade; end of Akkadian civilization in Mesopotamia	The first libraries in Egypt Script changes from Sumerian style (horizontal, left to right) to Semitic style (vertical, right to left) Epic poetry in Babylonia celebrates re-creation of the world In Egyptian literature, lamentations and skepticism about meaning of life	The snake and the bull are religious symbols in early Minoan culture on Crete Isis and Osiris cult in Egypt (resurrection from death) Ishtar is worshiped as goddess of love

D. VISUAL ARTS	E. MUSIC	F. SCIENCE, TECHNOLOGY, GROWTH	G. DAILY LIFE	
		The Egyptian calendar, regulated by sun and moon: 360 days, 12 months of 30 days each	Earliest cities in Mesopotamia (carbon-test dated)	**-5000 to -4001**
White painted pottery in Egypt and southeastern Europe Multi-colored ceramic ware originating in Russia reaches China	Harps and flutes played in Egypt	Copper alloys used by Egyptians and Sumerians; smelting of gold and silver known	Cretan ships predominant in Mediterranean First year of Jewish calendar –3760 Disastrous floods in Mesopotamian region	**-4000 to -3501**
Sumerian temple of Janna at Eridu erected Temple at Al Ubaid and tomb of Mes-Kalam-Dug built near Ur, Chaldea White temple at Uruk built	Lyres and double-clarinets played in Egypt	Earliest known numerals in Egypt First date in Mayan chronology is –3372 Potter's wheel used in Mesopotamia	Masons and smiths become craftsmen Wheeled vehicles in use in Sumeria Linen is produced in Middle East Economy of Sumerian cities is based on agriculture and husbandry Plowing, raking, and manuring in Egypt	**-3500 to -3001**
Brick temples with colored pillars in Uruk, Sumeria Earliest Trojan culture Glass beads in Egypt First terraced tower temples in Mesopotamia Rock carvings of Pharaoh Semempsis at Sinai Cheops Pyramid at Gizeh and "Ship of Re" to transport soul of king to immortality The Great Sphinx of Gizeh	The Chin. court musician Ling-lun cuts the first bamboo pipe	Sumerian medicine discovers the healing qualities of mineral springs Weaving loom known in Europe Beginning of systematic astronomical observations in Egypt, Babylonia, India, and China Egypt introduces calendar of 365 days without adjustments –2772 Great wall of Uruk, with 900 towers, is built Cheops Pyramid conforms in layout and dimensions to astronomical measurements Sumerian numerical system based on multiples of 6 and 12 Probable date of manufacture of first iron objects	Wrestling becomes the first highly developed sport Oil-burning lamps used by Sumerians First reports of domesticated dogs in Egypt Sumerians grow barley, bake bread, make beer; metal coins begin to replace barley as legal tender Lake dwellings in middle Europe Metal mirrors used in Egypt	**-3000 to -2501**
Indus civilization in India (to –1500) Early Minoan period in Crete Dolmen period of Scandinavian Neolithic Age (to –2200) Building of Sakkara pyramids Height of Sumeric-Akkadian art Painted and black pottery in China	Chin. music has five-tone scale	Egyptians discover use of papyrus Potter's wheels and kilns used in Mesopotamia Egyptian ships import gold from Africa Map of Babylonia Bow and arrow used in warfare Equinoxes and solstices determined in China; lunar year of 360 days changes to variable sun-moon cycle	The oldest pictorial representation of skiing: carving on a rock, found at Rodoy, southern Norway The earliest Egyptian mummies First domesticated chickens in Babylon African Pygmies appear at the Egyptian court Important agricultural developments in Malaya Hsai dynasty introduces tithe system with annual distribution of fields Foundation of Memphis Indications that cotton is cultivated in Peru	**-2500 to -2001**

	A. HISTORY, POLITICS	B. LITERATURE, THEATER	C. RELIGION, PHILOSOPHY, LEARNING
-2000 to -1501	The Hittites, Indo-European tribes from Asia Minor, join together in one single kingdom Egyptians in control of Crete and the Aegean Islands The Greeks begin to move from the shores of the Caspian Sea toward the eastern Mediterranean (-2000 to -1000) The Jomon people settle in Japan Sesostris I of Egypt extends influence to Nubia The Hittites attack and plunder Babylon Sesostris III (-1887 to -1849) invades Canaan Hammurabi, king of Babylonia, reunites kingdom (18th century B.C.) Shang dynasty in China (-1760 to -1122) Beginnings of Persian Empire (-1750 to -550) Social unrest in Egypt Hittite attacks on Syria Teutonic settlements in southern Norway The Hyksos drive the Egyptians south and form a kingdom in the Nile Delta (17th century B.C.) End of Middle Kingdom Decline of Babylonian Empire under Hammurabi's son, Samsuiluna Liberation of Egypt from Hyksos rule by Amosis I marks beginning of New Kingdom (-1575 to -1200) Cecrops, according to tradition, first king of Attica in Greece 18th dynasty brings Egypt to height of its power and achievements Amenhotep I (-1555 to -1530) Thutmose I (-1530 to -1515) Queen Hatshepsut, wife of Thutmose II, rules for Thutmose III until his coming of age in -1480	Egyptians use alphabet of 24 signs The "Story of Sinuhe," oldest form of a novel, written in Egypt Beginning of Semitic alphabet First Hittite cuneiform inscriptions First of seven periods of Chinese literature (to -600)	Marduk becomes god of Babylon Stonehenge, England, is center of religious worship Hammurabi, king of Babylon, sets laws of kingdom in order and provides first of all legal systems The "Book of the Dead," collection of religious documents of the 18th Egyptian dynsty Thutmose I of Egypt builds first tomb in Valley of Kings
-1500 to -1001	The Phrygians migrate from Thrace to Asia Minor Chiapa de Carzo, earliest known settlement in Mexico Thutmose III (-1480 to -1450) extends Egyptian empire along eastern Mediterranean, to banks of Euphrates, and to upper Nile Under the peaceful reign of Amenhotep III (-1420 to -1385) Egyptian trade and culture flourish The Phoenicians reach Malta Amenhotep IV (Pharaoh Ikhnaton, -1385 to -1358) builds new residence in Amarna; attempts revolutionary changes in army and priesthood, later annulled by Tutankhamen 19th dynasty (Seti I, Ramses II and III, -1350 to -1200) moves seat of government to Memphis, reestablishes pre-Ikhnaton status King Shalmaneser I establishes Assyrian supremacy; founds first city of Nimrud The Israelites, led by Moses, leave Egypt, reach Canaan Phoenicians become the predominant trading power in Mediterranean area 20th dynasty in Egypt (-1200 to -1090); decline of power begins Crossing of the Jordan by the Israelites Destruction of Troy during Trojan War (-1193, sixth level) Nebuchadnezzar I, king of Babylon (-1146 to -1123) Chou dynasty succeeds Shang dynasty (-1122 to -480) Tiglath-pileser I (-1116 to -1077) founds Assyrian Empire and fortifies it against migrating peoples from the north; conquers Babylon Ethiopia becomes independent power The Dorians conquer the Peloponnesus 21st dynasty in Egypt (-1090 to -945); civil war under Ramses XI Abolition of monarchy in Athens; Medon becomes first *(contd)*	"Upanishad" tradition in India (hymns of the Rigveda) Primitive Greek alphabet at Cnossus Ikhnaton's "Hymns to Aton" and correspondence with neighboring states in Amarna archives Library in Hittite capital has tablets in eight languages First mention of Israelites in Egyptian victory hymn Gilgamesh Epic is recorded (-1200) First Chin. dictionary, with 40,000 characters	Vedic religion assigns different powers to the separate deities of the heavens, the air, and the earth Ikhnaton (Amenhotep IV) of Egypt destroys the old gods and sets up Aton, the sun god, as only god (-1385); this monotheistic religion is short-lived; his successor, Tutankhamen, reinstates the earlier deities Moses receives the Ten Commandments on Mount Sinai Age of the "Judges" elected from 12 Israelite tribes

D. VISUAL ARTS	E. MUSIC	F. SCIENCE, TECHNOLOGY, GROWTH	G. DAILY LIFE	
Middle Minoan period in Crete Bronze Age in Britain Huangho culture in China The oldest palace at Mycenae Elaborate royal tombs in Middle Europe First palace of Minos at Cnossus, Crete, built Great Labyrinth of Egypt built by Amenemhet III Earliest beginnings of the building of Stonehenge, near Salisbury, Wiltshire, England Bronze Age in western Europe Late Minoan period in Crete (to –1400)	Reports of first trumpets being played in Denmark Religious dances in Crete Percussion instruments added to Egyptian orchestral music	Babylonia uses highly developed geometry as basis for astronomic measurements; knows signs of the zodiac Egyptians use knotted rope triangle with "Pythagorean" numbers to construct right angles Minos palace has light and air shafts, bathrooms with water supply Irrigation system in Egypt utilizes Nile floods Code of Hammurabi includes guidelines for medical practices (including eye surgery) and permissible fees Decimal system in Crete Water dam in India built of polished marble Edwin Smith Papyrus describes medical and surgical practices Mercury used in Egypt Four basic elements known in India: earth, air, fire, and water	Babylon becomes capital of the empire due to the shift in the course of Euphrates River Trade routes spread from eastern Mediterranean through Europe Contraceptives in use in Egypt Horses are used to draw vehicles Code of Hammurabi defines criminal laws, lines of inheritance	**-2000 to -1501**
Beginning of blooming of Cretan-Mycenaean culture (to –1200) The famous Cretan terracotta vases Shang culture in China Ganges civilization in India (to –400) Middle Mycenean culture Beginnings of Bronze Age in Scandinavia Ornate terrace temple of Queen Hatshepsut at Deir-el-Bahri; her life and travels recorded in elaborate sculptures "Cleopatra's Needle," obelisk from the reign of Thutmose III (see A.D. 1819 and 1878) Tapestries made in Egypt Amarna culture shows softer, more natural lines Head of Nefertiti, painted limestone sculpture of Ikhnaton's wife Beehive Tomb at Mycenae: the treasury of Atreus War memorial in Egypt shows Syrian soldier with Egyptian wife and son Tutankhamen's body embalmed and placed in sarcophagus of wood and gold Great temple of Abu-Simbel, Nubia The Lion Gate at Palace of Minos, Mycenae Troy excavation shows city described in Iliad at sixth level (total nine levels, dating from –3500 to Roman rule) Elaborate bronze sculptures in China *(contd)*	Mural in Thebes shows female musicians entertaining at festive gathering Hittites have religious dances; instruments include guitar, lyre, trumpet, tambourine Court dances in Egypt accompanied by harp music	Obelisks in Egypt serve as sun dials Intricate clock, measuring flow of water, found in tomb of Amenhotep III Possible existence of a first "Suez Canal" Mathematical permutations and "magic squares" known in Chin. mathematics Advanced knowledge of shipbuilding in Mediterranean and Scandinavian countries Properties of Pythagorean triangle theory also known in China Beginning of true Iron Age in Syria and Palestine Height of sun in relation to incline of polar axis measured in China	Kikkuli of Mitanni writes the first treatise on horse breeding and training Leprosy in India and Egypt Foundation of Corinth Memphis becomes Egyptian capital in place of Thebes Regulations concerning the sale of beer in Egypt Extensive export and import trade in Egypt Silk fabrics in China Labor strike in Thebes Widespread robbery of royal tombs in Egypt; thieves are brought to trial Prohibition decreed in China The Phoenicians import tin from mines in England	**-1500 to -1001**

	A. HISTORY, POLITICS	B. LITERATURE, THEATER	C. RELIGION, PHILOSOPHY, LEARNING
-1500 to -1001 contd	archon Saul becomes first king of Israel (−1002 to −1000) and is defeated by Philistines		
-1000 to -901	Phoenicians, established at Tyre, continue westward expansion into Cyprus and western Mediterranean; found colonies on west coast of Morocco; early link of Asiatic and Greek civilization Ionians, dispossessed from their homeland in Greece, found 12 cities on west coast of Asia Minor, among them Miletus and Ephesus, which later unite in Ionian Confederacy Accession of David as king of united kingdom of Judah and Israel (−1000 to −960), with Jerusalem as capital; returns Ark of Covenant and Decalogue to city King David is succeeded by his son, Solomon (−960 to −925), who builds Yahweh Temple in Jerusalem; under his rule, country reaches height of its civilization Political unification of Attica under rule of Athenian kings Peking in existence 22nd dynasty of Egypt (−945 to −745) begins with Sheshonk I (to −920) Division of Hebrew kingdom into Israel and Judah (−933) King Solomon dies (−933), succeeded by his son Rehoboam I as king of Judah (to −917), and by Jeroboam I as king of Israel (to−907) Sheshonk I of Egypt conquers and pillages Jerusalem Adadnirari II of Assyria makes peace with Babylon	Greek script, based on old Semitic-Phoenician characters with addition of vowels, uses only capital letters (to −800) Chin. script fully developed Hebrew alphabet, as opposed to earlier Semitic alphabets, developed (see −2000 to −1501) Cuneiform writing in Urartu, Babylonia Beginning of Hebrew literature: Song of Deborah, later collected in Song of Songs	Classic paganism in full bloom in Greece (chaos spawns Uranus and Gaea–heaven and earth–from whom descend the Titans, later vanquished by Zeus, Hera, Poseidon, Demeter, Apollo, Artemis, Ares, Aphrodite, Athena, Hermes, Hephaestus, and others) Pantheistic religion develops in India (Brahminism and Atmanism) teaching identity of self, transmigration of soul; caste system In China, rational philosophy of Chou dynasty gains over mysticism of earlier Shang (Yin) dynasty
-900 to -801	Phoenicians settle in Cyprus Assurnasirpal II, king of Assyria (−883 to −859) Samaria (formerly Sichem) rebuilt as capital of Israel in −879, destroyed by Sargon II in −722 Shalmaneser III, king of Assyria (−859 to −824) Dorians conquer city of Corinth Queen Samuramat of Assyria (−811 to −807), the legendary Queen of Semiramis 23rd dynasty of Egypt (−800 to −730) in dual reign with 22nd	Victory stele for King Mesa of Moabs at Dibon (eastern Jordan) among earliest samples of Hebrew script and language "Iliad" and "Odyssey," the Greek epics traditionally ascribed to Homer Leather scrolls with translations of Old Babylonian texts into Aramaic and Greek represent link beteen early clay tablets and Greek papyrus	The earliest Jewish prophets Samaria becomes religious center of Israel The prophet Elijah fights against worship of Baal and has Queen Athalia, who supports it, killed The bull, the bull's horns, other animals often shown with wings, and a winged sun are worshiped in most countries of the eastern Mediterranean
-800 to -701	Greeks settle on coast of Spain In Crete, rivalry develops between ancient city-states Etruscans move into Italy, bringing urban civilization of high order Amaziah, king of Judah, defeated by Israel, is killed in Judean rebellion King Joas of Israel (−801 to −787) Foundation of city of Rome (traditional date is −753) Greeks begin to settle in southern Italy, found Messina and Syracuse in Sicily Spartans found Taranto in southern Italy The nobility of Attica settles in Athens Celts move into England Jeroboam II, last important ruler of Israel (−784 to −744) Tiglath-pileser III of Assyria (−746 to −727) subjugates Syria and Philistia *(contd)*	Oldest Chin. poems contained in the "Book of Songs" Egyptian fable "Battle between Head and Belly" Syrian language changes from Phoenician to Aramaic Hesiod, Greek poet from Boeotia known for "Theogony" (creation of the world and gods of mythology), "Works and Days" (an educational poem), and "Shield of Heracles" Start of collection of "Sayings of Solomon"	A woman reigns as high priest in Thebes Apollo is worshiped at Delphi Legendary laws of Lycurgus at Sparta Prophets Amos, Hosea, and Isaiah fight religious and social abuses in Israel Isaiah's teachings of the coming of the Messiah; he predicts fall of Assyria (d. −701) Hesiod defines the five classic ages: Golden (paradisical), Silver (godless), Bronze (art and warfare), Heroic, and Iron; he names the nine Muses *(contd)*

D. VISUAL ARTS	E. MUSIC	F. SCIENCE, TECHNOLOGY, GROWTH	G. DAILY LIFE	
Mexican Sun Pyramid in Teotihuacan (age verified by carbon tests) Monumental tower temples in Assur Beginning of Olmec culture in Mexico				**-1500 to -1001 contd**
Brush and ink painting in China (lacquer painting practiced since early ages) Temple of Hera, oldest remaining temple in Olympia, Greece Temple in Jerusalem has main aisle with vestibule, three-storied wings; Phoenician architects collaborate Geometric art designs on Greek artifacts Gold vessels and jewelry in use in northern Europe	Professional musicians sing and play at religious ceremonies in Israel; same instruments still in use today	Fabric dyes made from purple snails and staining with alum practiced in Mediterranean area Water supply system through reinforced subterranean tunnels built in Jerusalem Indian lunar year has 360 days adjusted at random to coincide with solar year Chin. textbook of mathematics includes planimetry, proportions, "rule of 3" arithmetic, root multiplication, geometry, equations with one and more unknown quantities, theory of motion Earliest use of iron in Greece Evidence in Sierra Nevada and California of huts built by Pinto Indians, using wood interwoven with reeds and covered with loam Chaldeans use water-filled cube for measuring time, weight, and length King Adadnirari II of Assyria starts new chronology (verified in connection with solar eclipse of June 15, 763 B.C.)	Beginning of mass migration of Germanic peoples Wigs are used by aristocratic Egyptians and Assyrians The caftan is worn in Israel Molded and embossed jewelry and utensils in use in northern Europe First verified date of poppies grown in Egypt (–950)	**-1000 to -901**
Assurnasirpal II of Assyria rebuilds capital city Kalach (Nimrud) and new ornate palace with highly descriptive bas-relief friezes Royal palace and Ishtar Temple rebuilt at Nineveh Bronze doors and black obelisk at palace in Balawat are evidence of highly developed metal and stone sculpture		Iron and steel production in Indo-Caucasian culture Beginning of verified Chin. historical chronology (–841)	Favorite royal sport in Kalach is hunting from chariots (Nimrod legend of royal hunter) Sandstone stele at Nimrud palace describes imported and native fauna and flora Carthage founded as trading center with Tyre (–813)	**-900 to -801**
Arts and crafts flourishing in Asia Minor: metal sculpture, especially finely carved griffons, used as furniture legs; carpet weaving, embroidery, rock carving Greek art adapts and stylizes plant and flower ornaments from Asian art, later adopted by the Romans Ivory carving practiced in Egypt, Phoenicia, and Samaria Construction of royal palace at Nineveh is begun Art forms in Assyria become more naturalistic *(contd)*	Five-tone and seven-tone scales in Babylonian music Earliest recorded music, a hymn on a tablet in Sumeria, written in cuneiform In Greece, music is part of daily life; choral and dramatic music develops; *(contd)*	Homer refers to highly developed battlefield surgery Etruscans use hand cranks Sledges with rollers in use for heavy loads In India, medicine becomes divorced from priesthood; medical training uses anatomical models Etruscans introduce horse-drawn chariots to Italy Babylonian and Chin. astronomy understands planetary movements; new calendar confirmed Spoked wheels and horseshoes in use in Europe (Hallstatt culture) Assyrians use animal bladders as *(contd)*	Assyrian clothes almost the same for men and women First recorded Olympic Games –776 (possibly existing since –1350); celebrated every fourth year, they feature horse racing, wrestling, boxing, Pentathlon, running; women not admitted as spectators In Greece, crafts and trade flourish, farmers starve *(contd)*	**-800 to -701**

	A. HISTORY, POLITICS	B. LITERATURE, THEATER	C. RELIGION, PHILOSOPHY, LEARNING
-800 to -701 contd	First Messenian War: Sparta gains hegemony in Greece Sargon II of Assyria conquers the Hittites in northern Syria, the Chaldeans in Urartu, and Samaria (end of kingdom of Israel) Numa Pompilius, fabled second king of Rome (–715 to –672), adds Jan. and Feb. to Romulus' 10-month calendar Babylonian rebellion against Assyrian rule (end of Kalach/Nimrud as royal residence) King Sennacherib of Assyria (–705 to –681) defeats Egypt and Judah at Altaku		superseding the earlier three: Contemplation, Memory, Song; his philosophy: to work is man's duty
-700 to -601	Under harsh reign of Sennacherib, Nineveh is regarded as symbol of tyranny and bloody suppression Manasseh, king of Judah (–690 to –638) Assyrians destroy Babylon and divert Euphrates to cover site of city Second Messenian war Annual election of Areopagites (members of judicial court) in Athens Judah submits to Assyria; fabled King Candaules of Lydia deposed, succeeded by Gyges (–682 to –652) Assyrians destroy Memphis and Thebes Scythian raiders in Syria and Palestine Solon, Athenian law giver and statesman (–640 to –560) Josiah, king of Judah (–638 to –608) Chaldean general, Nabopolassar, seizes Babylonian throne, declares independence from Assyria Medes, Babylonians, and Scythians destroy Nineveh; end of Assyrian Empire, which is divided among its conquerors Nebuchadnezzar II makes Judah tributary; beginning of Babylonian Captivity (The Lamentations of Jeremiah) Nebuchadnezzar II defeats Egyptian army under Necho II	Egyptian hieroglyphs are adapted to demotic script Kallinos, earliest known Greek lyricist (preserved: battle hymn) Archilochus, Greek lyricist and author of fables, raises iambic to art form Library at Nineveh contains poetry, educational texts, instructions for grammatical translation of Sumerian texts into a Semitic language Tyrtaeus and Mimnermus, Greek poets, write elegies, love and war songs Stesichorus of Sicily, known as creator of heroic ballad Alcaeus, Greek author of political, love, and war songs Sappho of Lesbos, Greek poetess Beginning of second period of Chin. literature (to –200) Indian Vedas, a collection of religious, philosophical, and educational writings, completed	In Greek religion, the worship of Apollo and Dionysus (later named Bacchus) and mysticisms such as Orphism gain acceptance In India, Brahminic religion defines six stages of the transmigration of the soul Jeremiah predicts the fall of Judah Thales of Miletus, Greek philosopher (–624 to –545) King Josiah revives Yahweh worship in Jerusalem First written laws of Athens by Draco Zoroaster, founder of Persian religion (–630 to –553) "Graffiti" by Greek soldiers in Nubia show good elementary education Anaximander of Miletus, Greek philosopher (–611 to –546) Lao-tse, Chinese philosopher, b. –604

D. VISUAL ARTS	E. MUSIC	F. SCIENCE, TECHNOLOGY, GROWTH	G. DAILY LIFE	
Etruscan art forms appear in Tuscany	period of itinerant singers (Rhapsodes)	swimming aids in warfare Romulus, first king of Rome, divides year into 10 months	First iron utensils Solar eclipse of Sept. 6, –775 is first authenticated date in Chin. history	**-800 to -701 contd**
King Essarhaddon rebuilds Babylon First Doric columns in Peloponnesus Stone architecture and monumental sculptures in Greece, also color sketches First Ionic columns on Samos Limestone and marble used in construction of temples in Greece; design of houses becomes more ornate Acropolis in Athens is begun; Doric style and life-size sculptures of women become popular Nebuchadnezzar sponsors Babylonian art and architecture; builds fortress; first use of colored glazed bricks on Ishtar portals Marduk temple in Babylon (Tower of Babel) begun	New art forms for songs; flute and lyre popular as accompanying instruments Seven-string lyre is introduced Terpander writes for solo voice with instruments Arion, Greek composer and poet, introduces strophe and antistrophe	King Sennacherib's garden in Nineveh palace has rare plants and animals; planting space and irrigation channels blasted from rock Progress in water installations; Jerusalem has subterranean water tunnels; Sennacherib builds aqueduct; Nineveh has bucket wells King Assurbanipal's famous library, with over 22,000 clay tablets, covers history, medicine, astronomy, astrology; movement of planets and signs of zodiac are recorded Water clocks in Assyria Kaleus is first to sail through Straits of Gibraltar (Pillars of Hercules) Glaucus of Chios invents soldering of iron Pharaoh Nechos of Egypt starts canal between Nile and Red Sea	King Sennacherib's mountain climbing is first mention of alpine sports Hesiod's poem "Works and Days" mentions cultivation of barley, wheat, legumes, grapes, olives, figs; also husbandry of horses, cattle, goats, sheep, pigs Foundation of Ostia near Rome by the Etruscans Ornamental weaving in Greece Coins in Lydia made of electrum (gold-silver alloy) Nineveh important trading center as shown by documents in library about sales, exchange, rentals, leases, loan interest, mortgages Foundation of Paestum, southern Italy, and Massilia (Marseilles)	**-700 to -601**

	A. HISTORY, POLITICS	B. LITERATURE, THEATER	C. RELIGION, PHILOSOPHY, LEARNING
-600 to -501	Mayan civilization in Mexico (authenticated by carbon tests in 1956) Nebuchadnezzar II burns Jerusalem (–581) The Phoenicians in Corsica Croesus, last king of Lydia (–561 to –546), overthrown by Cyrus the Great of Persia in –547 Cyprus under Egyptian rule Peisistratus usurps government in Athens; known as tyrant, but also introduces the great musical and theatrical Dionysia; upon his death in –527, his sons, Hippias and Hipparchus, continue tyranny until overthrown in –510 by Cleisthenes Amasis II of Egypt (–569 to –526), friend of Polycrates of Greece, furthers trade with Greece; patron of the arts Cyrus II, the Great, of Persia (–553 to –529) conquers Lydia, the Medes, and Babylonia, transforming Persia into vast empire; in –536 he frees Jews from Babylonian Captivity and aids their return to Israel Cyrus II is succeeded by his son Cambyses II (–529 to –522), who conquers Egypt and has himself crowned Pharaoh Darius I (–522 to –485), his successor, divides empire into 20 provinces (satrapies), introduces far-reaching reforms including a common currency, regular taxes, a standing army Servius Tullius, last king of Rome but one: fortifies city and establishes class system based on property (–578 to –534) Themistocles, Athenian statesman and general (–525 to –459) Xerxes, future king of Persia (–485 to –465), b. –519 Rome declared a republic; last king, Tarquin the Proud, expelled; Lucius Junius Brutus and Collatinus become first consuls Cleisthenes introduces sweeping democratic reforms in Athens –510 Etruscans defeat Romans; the legends of Horatius Cocles and Mucius Scaevola	Oldest extant Lat. inscriptions Anacreon, Greek poet (–580 to –495) The "Fables" of Aesop, a former Phrygian slave Greek poet Thespis has first public performance of a tragedy based on hymn to Dionysus The impoverished poet Hipponax of Ephesus invents "lame" iambics as form for his political satires Aeschylus, Greek dramatist (–525 to –456) Cratinus, Greek author of comedies (–520 to –421) Building of theater at Delphi Epicharmus of Megara, Sicily (–550 to –460), writes early comedies and farces	Age of the "Seven Wise Men of Greece" (Thales, Pittacus, Bias, Solon, Cleobulus, Periander, Chilo) During the Babylonian Captivity of the Jews, many books of the Old Testament, based on word-of-mouth traditions, are first written down in Hebrew After first conquest of Jerusalem by Nebuchadnezzar, the prophet Ezekiel is exiled to Babylon; Jeremiah flees to Egypt, d. –585 Solon's laws promulgated in Athens (repeal of debtor's bondage; limited land ownership; class system for citizens involving army service and paying of taxes; rule by nine archons from highest class; council of 400 from third class, popular vote) Height of influence of oracle at Delphi and its priestess Anaximenes of Miletus, Greek philosopher and pupil of Anaximander (–586 to –526) Pythagoras, philosopher and mathematician (–581 to –497) Mahavira Jina (Vardhamana) founds Jainism in India; first known rebel against caste system Kung Fu-tse (Confucius), Chin. philosopher (–551 to –479) Siddhartha (Gautama Buddha, called Sakyamuni), founder of Buddhism (–550 to –480) Xenophanes founds school of philosophy Public libraries in Athens Buddha leaves his home to devote himself to philosophy and asceticism, preaches his first sermon in deer park of holy city of Benares (–521) Buddha's "Inspiration" Parmenides, Greek philosopher, b. –515 Completion of Temple of Jupiter Optimus Maximus, called the Capitol, in Rome –509 In Confucius, Buddha, Zoroaster, Lao-tse, the Jewish prophets, the Greek poets, artists, philosophers and scientists, the sixth century B.C. reaches a zenith of human wisdom and achievement
-500 to -451	Pericles of Athens b. –500 (d. –429) Sardinia captured by Greeks, Phoenicians, and Carthaginians –500 High point of Etruscan political power and civilization in Italy c. –500 Decline of Chin. feudal state under Chou dynasty begins The Ionians revolt from Persia under Histiaeus and Aristagoras, tyrants of Miletus, –500 Ionian War (–499 to –494); ends with capture of Miletus Sardis burned by Athenians –499 Tarquin defeated and killed at Battle of Lake Regillus –498 Latin League, under leadership of Rome in Latium, directed against Etruscans; secession of the plebeians; creation of the tribunate –494 Miltiades flees to Athens –493 Romans conquer the town of Corioli; their general, Gaius *(contd)*	In Palestine the Aramaic language begins to replace Old Hebrew Pratinas introduces the satyr play in Athens c. –500 Sophocles, tragic dramatist, b. –496 (d. –406) Anacreon, Greek poet, d. –495 (b. –580) Dionysus' theater in Athens –493 Aeschylus' first *(contd)*	Beginning of historical writing in Greece (Hecataeus and Dionysius of Miletus) Heraclitus: "Concerning Nature" (fire as center of creation and dissolution) (–500) "Ramayana," ancient Hindu poem (c. –500) Anaxagoras, Greek philosopher from Asia Minor, b. c. –500 (d. c. –428) Pythagoras, philosopher and scientist of Samos, d. –497 (b. –581) Greek civilization in Rome Empedocles, Greek philosopher, b. –490 (d. –430) Zeno of Elea, disciple of Parmenides, called by Aristotle the founder of dialectic, b. –490 Protagoras from Abdera, Greek philosopher, *(contd)*

D. VISUAL ARTS	E. MUSIC	F. SCIENCE, TECHNOLOGY, GROWTH	G. DAILY LIFE	
Greek art becomes independent of foreign influences, develops own style and form; archaic frontal style makes room for contrapost; sculptures as personification of majesty and divinity become more humanized, representing idealistic forms, athletic ideals; draped garments in sculpture, later copied in Persian art; architecture develops from severe Doric to more graceful Ionic; first caryatids in Greek temples Shwe Dagon Pagoda built in Burma Peisistratus builds Hecatompedon (sacrificial temple) in Athens Evidence of Thracian influence in lower Danube region through find of gold treasures at Valci Tran Temple of Artemis at Ephesus (Asia Minor), one of seven wonders of ancient world (destroyed by Herostratus in –356, later rebuilt in original form) La Tène culture in Europe Temple of Apollo at Corinth Temple of Olympian Zeus at Athens Temple of Ceres at Paestum Temple of Jerusalem is rebuilt Bas-relief of Darius records victory over nine Median kings in pictures and three languages Romans adopt arched ceilings and squared temple foundations from Etruscan architecture	Pythagoras is said to have introduced the octave in music Modes in music Pindar, Greek composer and poet (–520 to –447) Indian vina, two hollow gourds connected by strings and bamboo reed, is considered origin of all hollow string instruments	Water system built by Eupalinus, on Samos, three-quarter-mile-long tunnel started simultaneously at both ends T. Priscus builds first Roman stone bridge First reliably recorded circumnavigation of Africa by Phoenicians, ordered by Pharaoh Necho of Egypt; started from Red Sea and lasting three years Sun dial (gnomon) in use in Greece and China Prediction of solar eclipse (by Thales of Miletus) is presumed to be first in occidental astronomy Nebuchadnezzar II builds palace with terrace gardens in Babylon (presumed to be the legendary "Hanging Gardens," one of seven wonders of the world); a tunnel more than half a mile long, connecting the palace and the Temple of the Sun, traverses the Euphrates below the river bed Greek philosophers adopt theory of earth as a disk covered by dome of sky, or as floating free in spherical sky Theodorus of Samos credited with invention of ore smelting and casting, water level, lock and key, carpenter's square, and turning lathe Roman lunar year has 10 months of varying lengths (later 12 months) Babylonian astronomy begins to conform to present reckonings; lunar year has 354 days regulated into 12 months alternating between 29 and 30 days Anaximander d. –546; taught that all life develops from amphibians First water supply system in Athens has nine pipes leading to main well Thales of Miletus d. –545; he knew that a magnet attracts iron and that amber, when rubbed, becomes magnetic; the "Thales Proposition" (triangles over the diameter of a circle are right-angled) is oldest theory of occidental mathematics Alcmaeon of Croton, Greek anatomist, discovers difference between veins and arteries, also connection between brain and sensing organs Darius I uses pontoon bridge across Bosphorus during warfare	Position of Greek women in civil rights declines First reports of the introduction of papyrus into Greece Olive tree brought to Italy by Greek settlers Cyrus of Persia establishes regular courier service by messengers on horseback Tightly fitting leather clothes worn in Persia Greek women take over men's short chiton as long dress of their own Banking business practiced in Babylon Milo of Crotona, legendary athlete, crowned six times at Olympic Games in –536 First Persian coin with picture of ruler (previously: owl in Greece, tortoise in Lydia) Darius founds city of Persepolis (razed –494); explores Indian coast	**-600 to -501**
Erection of the Theseum, Athens (c. –500) Phidias, Greek sculptor, b. c. –500 (d. c. –435) "Treasury of the Athenians," Delphi –500 Building of first Temple of Saturn, Rome (c. –498) Amun temple at El Charge, Egypt Vouni Palace, Cyprus, erected by Doxandrus –494 Temple of Ceres, Cosmedin –493 Hypostyle Hall of Xerxes at Persepolis –485 Temple of Castor and Pollux, Rome –484 *(contd)*	Pindar begins to write his odes –500 Zenith of Greek choral music (c. –500) Main Greek musical instruments: aulos, cithara, lyre Further development of Greek musical theory through Pythagoras	Hecataeus (c. –549 to c. –486) mentions India in his writings Indian surgeon Susrata performs cataract operations c. –500 Alcmaeon, Greek physician, discovers Eustachian tubes c. –500 Babylonian astronomer Naburiannu determines length of lunar month (–500) Hanno the Carthaginian travels down the western coast of Africa c. –500 Development of technology and agriculture in China Hippocrates, Greek physician, "Father of Medicine," b. –460 Long walls from Athens to Piraeus finished –456 (begun –461)	Dams are being constructed in India Coins used as legal tender Viticulture in Italy and Gaul (wooden barrels serve for preservation) Ball games in Greece Series of disastrous earthquakes at Sparta (c. –465) *(contd)*	**-500 to -451**

	A. HISTORY, POLITICS	B. LITERATURE, THEATER	C. RELIGION, PHILOSOPHY, LEARNING
-500 to -451 contd	Marcius, receives the surname Coriolanus -493 Darius I demands tribute of earth and water from Greece -492 Coriolanus banished from Rome -491 Persian Wars (-490 to -449): Persian army defeated by Greeks under Miltiades at Marathon -490; Spartans under King Leonidas defeated by Persians at Thermopylae -480; Athens is burned by Xerxes I, the Acropolis destroyed -480; Athenians destroy Persian fleet at Battle of Salamis -480; Greeks under the Spartan general, Pausanias, defeat Persians at Plataea -479; Cimon, son of Miltiades, campaigns against the Persians (-477 to -449); he destroys the Persian army and navy at the Battle of the Eurymedon -466; Persians, finally defeated at Salamis in Cyprus, recognize in the Peace of Callias the independence of the Greek cities -449 Miltiades, in disgrace, d. -488 Gelo becomes tyrant of Syracuse -485 Darius I of Persia d. -485; Persian decline begins Xerxes I, king of Persia (-485 to -465) Aristides banished -483 Themistocles builds navy, founds Athenian sea power -483 The Carthaginians, under Hamilcar Barca, defeated by Gelo of Syracuse at Himera in Sicily -480 Persians capture and destroy Babylon -479 Walls of Athens rebuilt, Piraeus harbor fortified -478 Aristides, opponent of Themistocles, founds Delian League c. -478 Beginning of Athenian ascendancy c. -477 Legendary death of the 306 Roman Fabii in battle with Etruscan forces -477 Themistocles banished -471 The plebeians in Rome choose their own tribune -471 Nicias, Athenian statesman and general, b. -469 (d. -413) Xerxes I assassinated -465; succeeded by his son Artaxerxes I (to -424) Democracy in Syracuse -465 Cimon banished (-462 to -454) Pericles' rise in Athens begins -462 Themistocles d. -459 (b. -525) Cincinnatus becomes Roman dictator and rescues army surrounded by the Aequi -485 War between Athens and Corinth -458 Achaea joins Athenian alliance -454 Greeks in Egypt defeated by Megabyzus -454 Three Roman senators sent to Athens to study the laws of Solon -451	success as tragic dramatist -484 Euripides, tragic dramatist, b. -484 (d. -406) Hiero, tyrant of Syracuse, calls the Greek poets Aeschylus, Pindar, and Bacchylides to his court -478 Phrynichus: "Phoenissae," a tragedy about the Persian Wars (c. -475) Aeschylus: "The Persians," tragedy (-472) Aeschylus introduces a second actor, in addition to the protagonist and the chorus, in his tragedy -471 Sophocles introduces a third actor; defeats Aeschylus for the prize in tragedy -468 Simonides of Keos, Greek poet, d. -468 (b. -556) Aeschylus: "Prometheus Bound" -460 Aeschylus: "Oresteia" -458 Aeschylus d. -456 (b. -525)	b. -485 (d. -415) The Greek Herodotus, "Father of History," b. -485 (d. -424) Heraclitus, Greek philosopher, d. -483 (b. -544) Buddha d. -480 (b. -550) Confucius, Chin. philosopher, d. -479 (b. -551) Vardhamana, Indian pre-Buddhist reformer, d. -477 Socrates, Athenian philosopher, b. -470 (d. -399) Democritus, Greek philosopher, b. -460 Ezra, Hebrew scribe, goes to Jerusalem to restore the laws of Moses -458
-450 to -401	Alcibiades, Greek politician and general, b. -450 (d. -404) Tarentum, important Greek trading city in Italy, subdued by Rome -450 Beginning of Indian empire: Magadha, "cradle of Buddhism" Assembly of the Roman plebeians is given the right to share in making laws Etruscan predominance on the Ital. peninsula declining Marseilles flourishes as western Europe's portal to Greek and Etruscan civilization Cimon of Athens d. -449 Administration of Roman exchequer passes into the hands of quaestors -447 Revolt of Megabyzus, Persian satrap of Syria -447 Athenians defeated at Coronea by Boeotians -447 30-year truce (-445 to -415) between Athens and Sparta Wall of Jerusalem reputed to have been built by Nehemiah and Ezra *(contd)*	Aristophanes, later known as master of the Old Comedy in Greece, b. c. -450 (d. c. -387) Bacchylides, Greek poet, d. c. -450 Sophron of Syracuse initiates mime as a dramatic form -450 The Periclean Age blooms: Anaxagoras, Protagoras, Empedocles, and Socrates as philosophers; Sophocles and Euripides as tragic poets; Crates, Cratinus, and Aristophanes as comedy authors; Thucydides, Herodotus, and Xanthus as historians; Phidias and Polygnotus as artists Sophocles: "Antigone" -443 Euripides: "Medea" -431 *(contd)*	The Decemvirs codify Roman laws in a form known as the Twelve Tables -450 The Torah becomes the moral essence of the Jewish state Consecration of the completed Parthenon -438 Plato b. -427 (d. -347) Herodotus, historian, d. -424 (b. -485) Thucydides exiled from Athens -424 Protagoras, Greek philosopher, d. -415 Diogenes b. c. -411 *(contd)*

D. VISUAL ARTS	E. MUSIC	F. SCIENCE, TECHNOLOGY, GROWTH	G. DAILY LIFE	
Classical period of Greek pottery Greek theater of Syracuse Marble temple of Apollo at Delphi (c. –478) "Victorious Charioteer" of Delphi (early Greek bronze) c. –478 Micon and Polygnotus, Greek painters, flourish Polyclitus, Greek sculptor, b. c. –465 (d. c. –420) Building of Temple of Zeus, Olympia (c. –460)			Soldiers and judges of Athens receive regular salaries (–462)	**-500 to -451 contd**
Temple of Theseus built at Athens (c. –450) Rebuilding of the Acropolis, Athens, designed by Ictinus and Callicrates; much of the sculpture by Phidias (–448 to –433) Temple of Poseidon at Cape Sunium (c. –445) Phidias: "Elgin Marbles" from the Parthenon c. –440 (now in the British Museum) Bust of Pericles by Cresilas –439 Temple of Apollo in Rome –431 Polyclitus, Greek sculptor, d. c. –420 (b. –465) Erechtheum completed on the Acropolis at Athens (c. –407)	Pindar, Greek musician and poet, d. –447 (b. –520)		Aspasia, mistress of Pericles, rules Athenian society (c. –450) Celtic settlements in the British Isles Carrier pigeons used in Greece The population of Greece consists of two million citizens and one million slaves; in Athens there are 50,000 citizens and 100,000 slaves The plague in Athens (–430 to –423) The Spartans use chemicals in warfare (charcoal, sulfur, and pitch) Hippodamus of Miletus builds *(contd)*	**-450 to -401**

	A. HISTORY, POLITICS	B. LITERATURE, THEATER	C. RELIGION, PHILOSOPHY, LEARNING
-450 to -401 contd	Lex Canuleia permits intermarriage between patricians and plebeians in Rome (–445) Pericles elected Athenian general in –443 for 15 years Pericles takes Samos –440 Judean law forbids marriage between Jews and aliens –440 Pericles founds the colony of Thurii in southern Italy (c. –440), Herodotus being one of its citizens Plebeian revolt in Rome: Lucius Quinctius Cincinnatus appointed dictator –439 Amphipolis on the north Aegean coast colonized by Athenians –437 Pericles' "Funeral Oration" –431 (as recorded by Thucydides) Peloponnesian War between Athens and Sparta (–431 to –404) Pericles d. –429 (b. c. –500); succeeded by Cleon and Nicias Xerxes II becomes king of Persia –424, is assassinated two months later, and is succeeded by Darius II (d. –405) Peace of Nicias between Athens and Sparta (for 50 years) –421 Epaminondas of Thebes b. –420 (d. –362) Renewed war between Athens and Sparta –415 Athenians invade Sicily and besiege Syracuse –415 Alcibiades, accused in his absence of sacrilege–mutilation of the Hermae–goes over to Spartans –415 Athenian army in Sicily destroyed –414 Athenian general Nicias executed after the Sicilian disaster –413 Coup d'état in Athens: power transferred to people's assembly –411 Alcibiades returns to Athens –411 The Athenians capture Byzantium –408 Athens rejects Sparta's peace offer –406 Spartan navy under Lysander destroys Athenian navy at Aegospotami –405; end of Peloponnesian War The Medes try without success to throw off Persian rule –408 In the war against Carthage, Dionysius I (–430 to –367) becomes tyrant of Syracuse –406 Darius II, king of Persia (since –424), d. –405; succeeded by Artaxerxes II (to –359) Alcibiades murdered in exile, by order of Sparta –404 Restitution of Athenian democracy; Thrasybulus expels the 30 tyrants –403	Aristophanes: "The Clouds," satirical comedy –423 Cratinus, Greek comedy author, d. –421 Aristophanes: "The Peace," comedy –421 Euripides: "The Trojan Women" –415 Aristophanes: "The Birds," comedy –414 Euripides: "Iphigenia in Aulis," tragedy –407 Euripides d. –406 (b. –484) Sophocles d. –406 (b. –496) Aristophanes: "The Frogs" (–405)	Plato becomes the pupil of Socrates (–407 to –399)
-400 to -351	Retreat of the Ten Thousand under Xenophon: Greek army successfully withdrawn after defeat at Cunaxa –400 Carthaginians occupy Malta –400 End of Indian civilization in Mexico Etruscan city of Veii captured by Romans after 10-year siege –396 The Carthaginians destroy Messina –396 Coalition of Athens, Thebes, Corinth, and Argos against Sparta –395 Spartan general Agesilaus defeats allied troops at Coronea –394 Gauls from northern Italy under Brennus capture Rome, sack it, and withdraw ("Vae victis") –390 Peace of Antalcidas: Greek cities in Asia Minor surrender to Artaxerxes II M. Manlius Capitolinus, accused of royal ambitions, is thrown from the Tarpeian rock –384 The 30th dynasty in Egypt (–380 to –343), last native house to rule the country Massacre of the Spartan tyrants at Thebes by Pelopidas and Epaminondas –379 *(contd)*	Aristophanes d. c. –387 (b. c. –450) Etruscan actors stage the first theatrical performances in Rome –365	The "Five Books of Moses" (Pentateuch) receive their definite form Socrates d. –399 (b. –470) Plato: "Apologia" (in defense of Socrates) –396 Eucleides, a pupil of Socrates, founds the Megarian school of philosophy, which has a Socratic basis Thucydides, Greek historian, d. –395 (b. –460) Meh Tih, Chin. philosopher, d. c. –390 Plato: "Symposium" –387 Aristotle, Greek philosopher, b. –384 (d. –322) Demosthenes, Greek statesman and orator, b. –384 (d. –322) Plato: "Phaedon," on what Socrates said on his last day Xenophon: "Anabasis" –371 *(contd)*

D. VISUAL ARTS	E. MUSIC	F. SCIENCE, TECHNOLOGY, GROWTH	G. DAILY LIFE	
			town and harbor of Rhodes −407	**−450 to −401 contd**
Praxiteles, Greek sculptor, b. −400 (d. −330) Etruscan bronze statue of Mars −400 Temple of Concordia built in Rome −366 Tomb of Mausolus completed (the first mausoleum) −351	Trumpet-playing competitions in Greece	Hippocrates of Cos, Greek physician, d. −377 (b. −460)	Use of catapults as weapons of war Rome rebuilt after the Gallic invasion −387 City walls built around Rome −377 The Greek Herostratus sets fire to the Temple of Artemis in Ephesus −356	**−400 to −351**

	A. HISTORY, POLITICS	B. LITERATURE, THEATER	C. RELIGION, PHILOSOPHY, LEARNING
-400 to -351 contd	Battle of Leuctra: Thebans under Epaminondas defeat Sparta -371 The first plebeian elected to office of consul in Rome -366 Marcus Furius Camillus, Roman general and dictator, d. -365 Epaminondas, Theban general, killed in the Battle of Mantinea -362 Cappadocia becomes a kingdom under Ariarathes I -360 Philip II of Macedon (-352 to -336) Accession of Artaxerxes III in Persia -359 Alexander the Great, son of Philip II of Macedon, b. -356 (d. -323) Building of the first wall in China, against the Huns c. -356		Democritus of Abdera, the "laughing philosopher," d. c. -360 Xenophon, Greek historian, d. c. -354 (b. c. -430) Demosthenes delivers his first "Philippic" against Philip II of Macedon -351
-350 to -301	Phoenician cities Sidon, Tyre, Aradus, and Byblus secede from Persia c. -350 The Gauls leave southern France and settle in northern Italy c. -350 Etruscan power on the decline c. -350 Revolt of the Jews against Artaxerxes III in Persia c. -350 Trade agreement between Rome and Carthage -348 Philip of Macedon takes Olynthus -348 Philip II joins with Thebans in -343 in the "Sacred War" against the Phocians The First Samnite War (-343 to -341) Persians reconquer Egypt -343 Philip defeats the Greeks at Chaeronea -338 Assassination of Artaxerxes III of Persia, accession of Arses -338 Philip of Macedon assassinated at Aegae (-336); succeeded by Alexander the Great (to -323) Assassination of Arses of Persia; accession of Darius III Codomannus -336 Alexander destroys Thebes -335 Alexander campaigns against Persia: he defeats Darius at Issus -333, conquers Tyre and Jerusalem -332, and defeats Darius at Gaugamela -331 Alexander occupies Babylon, Susa, and Persepolis -330 Darius III of Persia murdered -330 The Spartans under Agis defeated by Antipater of Macedon -330 Alexander marries Bactrian princess Roxana -328 Alexander invades India -327 Renewal of war between Rome and the Samnites (-327 to -304) Roman army defeated by the Samnites at Caudine Forks -321; Samnites defeated by the Romans at Luceria -320; Samnites defeated by Rome at Vadimonian Lake -310; Rome conquers the Etruscan town of Perusia (Perugia) -309; end of Second Samnite War -304 Alexander extends his empire to the Indus River, but is forced by his generals to turn back -326 Alexander the Great d. in Babylon in -323 (b. -356); his empire partitioned among his generals A new Egyptian dynasty (-323) under Ptolemy Soter, one of Alexander's generals, lasting until death of Cleopatra (-30) Demosthenes commits suicide -322 (b. -384) Wars among Alexander's successors -321 Ptolemy Soter of Egypt invades Syria -320 Polysperchon, Antipater's successor, restores liberty to Grecian cities (-319) Chandragupta Maurya reconquers northern India from the Macedonians and founds the Mauryan dynasty -319 Olympias, mother of Alexander the Great, put to death by Cassander, son of Antipater -316 Cassander founds Salonika, rebuilds Thebes -316 *(contd)*	The Indian heroic epic "Mahabharata" being written (probably to A.D. 350) Ch'ü Yüan, earliest of the important Chin. poets, b. -343 (d. -277) Menander, Greek comedy author, b. -342 (d. -290) Earliest extant papyrus written in Greek, the "Persae" of Timotheus of Miletus -325 Theocritus, Greek bucolic poet, b. -320 (d. -250)	Heraclides, disciple of Plato, teaches heliocentric system c. -350 Shuang-tse, founder of Chin. monist religious philosophy, c. -350 The Parian Chronicle, an account of Greek history, engraved on marble (c. -350) Aristotle travels to Assos, Lesbos, and Pelia (c. -348) Plato d. -347 (b. -427) Aristotle becomes the teacher of Alexander the Great -343 Epicurus, Greek philosopher, b. -340 (d. -271) After the suicide of Plato's nephew Speusippus, Xenocrates of Chalcedon becomes the head of Athens Academy (-339 to -314) Isocrates, Athenian orator, d. -338 (b. -436) Zeno of Citium, Greek philosopher, founder of the Stoic school, b. -336 Aristotle returns to Athens and founds the Peripatetic school of philosophy -335 Aristotle d. -322 (b. -384) Alexandria center of Greek learning Museum and Library of Alexandria begun under Ptolemy Soter -307

D. VISUAL ARTS	E. MUSIC	F. SCIENCE, TECHNOLOGY, GROWTH	G. DAILY LIFE	
				-400 to -351 contd
Greek painter Pamphilus teaches that without mathematics and geometry no perfect art can exist (c. -350) The Greek theater of Epidaurus built c. -350 Corinthian columns appear in Greek architecture c. -350 Scopas, Greek sculptor, d. c. -340 (b. c. -420) Erection of choragic monument of Lysicrates of Athens -335 Apelles of Colophon, Greek painter, and Lysippus of Sicyon, Greek sculptor at the court of Alexander c. -330 Praxiteles, Greek sculptor, d. -330 (b. -400) Beginning of Mauryan culture in India Hellenistic period of Greek arts (-320 to -30) The Roman Censor Appius Claudius Caecus completes construction of Appian aqueduct and begins Appian Way -312	Aristotle lays the foundations of musical theory c. -340 Aristoxenus defines rhythm as tripartite: speech, melody, movement (c. -320)	Rain is measured in India Iron used as working material in China Praxagoras of Cos discovers the difference between arteries and veins c. -340 The Greek explorer Pytheas of Massilia (Marseilles) reaches Britain c. -330 Alexander orders his admiral, Nearchus, to explore the Indian Ocean, Persian Gulf, and Euphrates -325 Euclid: "Elements" (standard work on geometry) -323	The first Roman coins c. -338 Corinth becomes a trading center c. -338 Alexander the Great founds the Port of Alexandria -332 Jewish trading centers in Egypt and Cyrene	-350 to -301

	A. HISTORY, POLITICS	B. LITERATURE, THEATER	C. RELIGION, PHILOSOPHY, LEARNING
-350 to -301 contd	The Seleucids of Syria rule Palestine -314 Judea ruled by Antigonus I -312 End of civil wars in Alexander's empire: Macedonia goes to Cassander as regent, Thrace to Lysimachus, Egypt to Ptolemy Soter, and Asia to Antigonus -311 Demetrius Poliorcetes, king of Macedon, seizes Athens from Cassander -307 Carthaginians defeat Agathocles and besiege Syracuse -307 Antigonus I killed at the Battle of the Kings at Ipsus; Palestine reverts to Egyptian rule -301		
-300 to -251	Third Samnite War (-298 to -290): the Etruscans subjected to Rome -295; Romans under Lucius Papirius Cursor defeat Samnites at Aguilonia -293 Siege of Athens by Demetrius I -295 Romans defeated by the Senones a Gaulish tribe, at Arretium -289 Full equality between patricians and plebeians in Rome -287 Demetrius I of Macedon, deposed by army revolt, is replaced by Pyrrhus, king of Epirus, who is in turn replaced by Alexander's former general Lysimachus -287 Ptolemy Soter abdicates -285 and is succeeded by his son Ptolemy II Philadelphus (d. -247) Corsica captured by the Romans -283 War between Tarentum and Rome (-282 to -272) Pyrrhus, king of Epirus, lands in Italy to aid Tarentum, defeats Romans at Heraclea (-280) and at Asculum (-279), but does not know how to exploit his victories; defeated by the Romans at Beneventum, he leaves Italy -275 Antiochus I defeats the Gauls -275 End of history of Babylon; the Babylonians reestablished in the new city of Seleucia -275 After the defeat of Tarentum, Rome conquers central and southern Italy -272 Romans continue the Via Appia from Capua to Tarentum and Brundisium (c. -272) Athens taken by Antigonus II Gonatas -268 Calabria conquered by the Romans -266 The First Punic War (-264 to -241): Appius Claudius Pulcher defeats Hiero of Syracuse at Messana -264; the Roman fleet defeats Carthaginians at Ecnomus -256; Regulus, attacking Carthage, is captured by Xanthippus the Spartan -255; unsuccessful siege of Lilybaeum by Romans -250; Hamilcar Barca takes command of Carthaginian forces in Sicily -246; Hamilcar makes peace with Rome: end of First Punic War -241 Kingdom of Parthia founded by Arsaces -255 Antigonus II Gonatas liberates Athens -255	Rinthon of Tarentum, one of the founders of Roman comedy, -300 Apollonius of Rhodes, Greek poet, b. c. -293 (d. c. -215) Menander, master of the Greek New Comedy, d. -290 Philemon, Menander's rival as a New Comedy poet in Athens, d. -263	Roman plebeians admitted to the priesthood -300 Aristoxenus, Greek philosopher and musician, d. c. -300 Manetho, high priest of Egypt, writes a history of Egypt in Greek -275 Epicurus d. -271 (b. -340) Writing of "Septuagint," Greek version of Old Testament (c. -255)
-250 to -201	Invasion of Britain by La Tène, Iron-Age people (c. -250) Ptolemy III Euergetes, king of Egypt (-247 to -221) Hannibal, Carthaginian general, b. -246 (d. -182) Antiochus II Theos killed by his wife -246; succeeded by his son Seleucus II Callinicus Agis IV, king of Sparta, put to death -241 for attempting agrarian reform and trying to reintroduce the Lycurgan constitution Carthage begins conquest of Spain -238 Sardinia becomes part of Roman republic -238 Outbreak of war between Sparta and Achaean League -236 Marcus Portius Cato the Elder, Roman politician, b. -234 (d. -149) Publius Cornelius Scipio Africanus, Roman politician and *(contd)*	Plautus, Roman comedy author, b. c. -250 The comedies of Livius Andronicus first performed in Rome -240 Ennius, the poet, "father of Lat. literature," b. -239 (d. -170) Plautus: "Miles gloriosus," comedy -205 Gnaeus Naevius, Roman poet and comedy author, d. -201	Arcesilaus founds the Second Academy of Athens (c. -250) Asoka, the Indian emperor, erects columns 40 feet high inscribed with his laws (c. -250) Death of Sun-tsi (-233) marks the end of Chin. classical philosophy Quintus Fabius Pictor, the first Roman historian (c. -225)

D. VISUAL ARTS	E. MUSIC	F. SCIENCE, TECHNOLOGY, GROWTH	G. DAILY LIFE	
				-350 to -301 contd
Mexican sun temple Atetello at Teotihuacan -300 Completion of the Colossus of Rhodes c. -275; (destroyed by earthquake -224) Completion of lighthouse at Pharos, Alexandria (c. -275) Flowering of Iberian culture under Greek and Carthaginian influence		Euclid: "Optica" (c. -295) Diocles of Carystus, Greek physician, d. c. -293 Archimedes, Greek mathematician, b. -287 (d. -212) Eratosthenes of Cyrene, Greek scientist, b. c. -276 (d. -194) Apollonius of Perga, Greek mathematician, b. c. -265 (d. 170) First contact of the Romans with Greek medicine through prisoners of war (c. -265)	Ball games, dice playing, and games played on boards well known to Greeks and Romans First appearance of the Roman silver coin, denarius, -268 First public combats of gladiators in Rome -264 (see A.D. 325)	**-300 to -251**
Egyptian temple of sun god Horus at Edfu (c. -230)		Eratosthenes (c. -276 to -194) suggests that the earth moves around the sun and maps out the course of the Nile; he also makes close estimates of the earth's circumference	Parchment produced at Pergamum -250 The first Roman prison, Tullianum, erected -250 Introduction of leap year into Egyptian calender -239 Introduction of oil lamps in Greece (c. -230) Carthago Nova (Cartagena) founded by Hasdrubal (c. -228) Unification of all Chin. measures and weights -221 Construction of Flaminian Way from Rome to Rimini (c. -220) Great Wall of China (1,400 miles long) built to keep out invaders -215	**-250 to -201**

	A. HISTORY, POLITICS	B. LITERATURE, THEATER	C. RELIGION, PHILOSOPHY, LEARNING
-250 to -201 contd	general, b. -233 (d. -183) The first Roman ambassadors in Athens and Corinth -228 The Gauls defeated near Telamon in Etruria -225 Rome conquers northern Italy, including Mediolanum (Milan), in -222 Antigonus III Doson of Macedonia takes possession of Sparta -222 Ch'in dynasty in China (-221 to -206) Cleomenes, king of Sparta, flees to Egypt -221 (d. -220) Second Punic War (-219 to -201) Hannibal crosses the Alps (Little St. Bernard Pass), invades Italy from the north, takes Turin, and defeats Publius Cornelius Scipio at Ticinus River -218; defeats Romans at Lake Trasimene -217 Rome appoints Quintus Fabius Maximus dictator -217 Romans defeated at Cannae, with c. 50,000 killed -216 Philip V of Macedon makes alliance with Hannibal -216 Roman armies in Spain under Publius Cornelius and Gnaeus Cornelius Scipio -215; defeated -211 Romans under Marcus Claudius Marcellus conquer and sack Syracuse; Archimedes killed during fighting -212 "Hannibal ante portas!" The Carthaginians before Rome -211 After the defeat of his brother Hasdrubal on the Metaurus, Hannibal retires to southern Italy -207 Scipio Africanus decisively defeats Hannibal at Zama -202; end of Second Punic War -201 Antiochus III, ruler of Persia at the peak of his power -209 Shi Huang-ti, emperor of China since -221, d. -209 Liu Pang assumes the imperial title in China (-202)		
-200 to -151	Second Macedonian War (-200 to -197); Attica ravaged -200; Romans under Flamius defeat Philip V of Macedon at Cynoscephelae -197 Antiochus III of Syria takes Palestine from Egypt -198 Eumenes II, king of Pergamum (-197 to -159) Hannibal flees to Antiochus III of Syria -195 Cato the Elder becomes consul -195 Antiochus III, aided by Hannibal, lands in Greece -192 War between Sparta and Rome -192 Antiochus defeated by the Romans at Thermopylae (-191) and at Magnesia (-190) Hannibal defeated by Rhodian fleet at Eurymedon River -189 Insurrections in Upper Egypt owing to exorbitant taxes -189 Armenia independent from Seleucid rule -189 Scipio Africanus the Elder goes into voluntary exile -185; his adopted grandson is Scipio Africanus the Younger (-185 to -129) Shunga dynasty replaces Mauryan dynasty in India (-185 to -30) Scipio Africanus the Elder d. -183 (b. -233) Pisa and Parma in northern Italy become Roman colonies -183 Hannibal commits suicide in exile to avoid extradition by Rome -182 War between Rome and Macedon (-172 to -168); Roman army defeated by Perseus -172 Perseus defeated by Romans at Pydna -168; Macedon placed under Roman governor; beginning of Roman world domination Maccabean revolt against Antiochus IV -167	Third period of Chin. literature Terence, Roman dramatist, b. c. -195 (d. -159) Plautus: "Pseudolus," Lat. comedy -191 Plautus d. -184 (b. c. -250) Terence: "Andria," performed in Rome -167 Terence d. -159 (b. c. -195)	Inscription engraved on Rosetta Stone c. -200 (see 1799, 1821) Quintus Fabius Pictor: "Roman History" (in Greek) -198 Persecution of the Jews by Antiochus IV: desecration of the Temple at Jerusalem -168 Judas Maccabaeus rededicates Temple of Jerusalem after expelling the Syrians -165 The "Book of Daniel" (Old Testament) c. -165

D. VISUAL ARTS	E. MUSIC	F. SCIENCE, TECHNOLOGY, GROWTH	G. DAILY LIFE	
				-250 to -201 contd
		The use of gears leads to invention of ox-driven water wheel for irrigation (c. -200) Cato the Elder: "De agricultura" (c. -200) Hipparchus of Nicaea, who made important astronomical discoveries and invented trigonometry, b. c. -160 The first water clock (clepsydra) in Rome c. -159	Pons Aemilius, the first stone bridge in Rome, c. -179 The earliest known paved streets appear in Rome (c. -170) After the Battle of Pydna (-168) Macedonians sold as slaves in Rome; the prices vary between $50 and $75; prices for female slaves up to $1,000	**-200 to -151**

	A. HISTORY, POLITICS	B. LITERATURE, THEATER	C. RELIGION, PHILOSOPHY, LEARNING
-150 to -101	Cato the Elder d. –149 (b. –234) Third Punic War (–149 to –146): Roman forces destroy Corinth –147; Romans destroy Carthage: of 500,000 inhabitants only 50,000 remain alive; sold into slavery War between Sparta and Achaea –147 Greece comes under Roman control –147 The Roman Empire in –146 consists of seven provinces: Sicily, Sardinia and Corsica, the two Spains, Gallia Transalpina, Africa, and Macedonia Judas' successor Jonathan Maccabaeus assassinated –144; succeeded by Simon Maccabaeus (to –135), who expels Syrians from Jerusalem Asia Minor becomes eighth Roman province –133 Tiberius Gracchus, Roman reformer, murdered at instigation of the Senate –133 Scipio the Younger, destroyer of Carthage, d. –129 (b. –185) Gaius Gracchus, brother of Tiberius, elected tribune and plans wide reforms –123 Carthage rebuilt –123 Gaius Gracchus killed in a riot; his reforms abolished –121 Marcus Licinus Crassus, Roman politician, b. c. –115 (d. –53) Chin. army crosses Lop Nor desert, occupies Tarim basin, and imposes Chin. authority on local rulers (c. –115) The Cimbri, an ancient Ger. tribe, leave Jutland, which is devastated by storms, and reach the Roman province of Noricum (Carinthia) –113 War in Africa between Rome and Jugurtha, king of Numidia (–112 to –105); Marius, assisted by Sulla, defeats Jugurtha –105 Lucius Sergius Catilina, Roman politician, b. c. –108 (d. –62) Cicero, Roman politician and orator, b. –106 (d. –43) Cimbri and Teutones become allies and decide to invade Italy –103 Marius, having defeated the Teutones at Aquae Sextiae, defeats the Cimbri at Vercellae –101		Hu Shin produces Chin. dictionary of 10,000 characters –149 Rise of Pharisees and Sadducees in Palestine (c. –112) The first "Book of Maccabees" (in Hebrew)
-100 to -51	Gaius Julius Ceasar b. –100 (d. –44) Marius consul for the sixth time –100 Cato the Younger b. –95 (d. –46) Civil war in Rome: Marius driven out by Sulla –90 Roman army, led by Sulla, regains control of Italy –89 Risings against Roman rule at Athens –88 Marius d. –86 (b. –156) Marcus Junius Brutus, Roman politician, Cato's nephew and son-in-law, b. –85 (d. –42) Sulla defeats the younger Marius and is created dictator for life –82 Sulla voluntarily resigns his dictatorship –79 Sulla d. –78 (b. –138) Mithridates VI of Pontus renews war against Rome and is defeated by Lucullus –73 The Suevi, a Ger. tribe, cross the Upper Rhine under their King Ariovistus and invade Gaul –72 Revolt of slaves and gladiators under Spartacus, crushed by consuls Pompey and Crassus –71 Gaius Maecenas, Roman statesman, b. c. –70 (d. –8) Dynastic war in Palestine –69: Hyrcanus II deposed; rise of the House of Antipater Crete captured by the Romans –68 Defeated by Pompey, Mithridates VI commits suicide –63 Pompey enters Syria, completes conquest of Palestine (by –63), and makes it part of Roman province of Syria Gaius Octavius (Augustus), future Roman emperor, b. –63 (d. A.D. 14) *(contd)*	Cornelius Nepos, Roman author, b. c. –100 (d. c. –25) Catullus, Roman poet, b. –87 (d. –54) Sallust, Roman author and historian, b. –86 (d. –35) Oldest extant amphitheater erected at Pompeii –82 Virgil, Roman poet, b. –70 (d. –19) Horace, Roman poet, b. –65 (d. –8)	Titus Lucretius Carus, Roman poet and philosopher, b. c. –98 (d. –55) Alexander Polyhistor of Miletus writes a history of the Jews –82 Marcus Tullius Tiro, a former slave of Cicero, invents system of shorthand –63 Lucretius: "De rerum natura" (Epicurean doctrine of universe in poetic form) –60 Titus Livius (Livy), Roman historian, b. c. –59 (d. A.D. 17) Cicero: "De oratore" –55 Cicero: "De republica" –54 Caesar: "De bello Gallico," account of Gallic War –51

D. VISUAL ARTS	E. MUSIC	F. SCIENCE, TECHNOLOGY, GROWTH	G. DAILY LIFE	
The Venus of Milo, sculpture, c. –140 (see 1820)		Crates of Mallus forms his great globe of the world –140 The mathematician Heron founds the first College of Technology at Alexandria c. –105		**–150 to –101**
Erection of the Great Stupa, Sanchi, India (c. –100) Vitruvius: "De architectura" (on architecture and machines) –90		Asclepiades, Greek physician, practices nature healing in Rome –90	The first Chin. ships reach the east coast of India (c. –100) Lucullus imports the first cherry trees from Asia Minor to Rome (c. –79) Founding of Florence –62 Beginning of erection of new (Julian) forum, Rome, –54	**–100 to –51**

	A. HISTORY, POLITICS	B. LITERATURE, THEATER	C. RELIGION, PHILOSOPHY, LEARNING
-100 to -51 contd	Pompey captures Jerusalem -63 Catilina defeated and killed at Pistoria -62 Gaius Julius Caesar, nephew of Marius, wins his first victories in Spain -61 Caesar returns to Rome, is elected consul, and forms with Pompey and Crassus the first triumvirate -60 Roman colonies in Switzerland -60 Caesar in Gaul (-58 to -50) Northern Gaul conquered by Caesar; punitive expeditions sent to Britain -55 When Caesar invades Britain, Cassivellaunus, a powerful Belgic tribal leader in southern Britain, agrees to pay tribute to Rome -54 Crassus defeated and killed by Parthians at Carrhae -53 Pompey becomes consul in Rome -52 Gaul subdued by Caesar -51 Cleopatra VII, last queen of Egypt (to -31)		
-50 to -1	Rivalry between Caesar and Pompey for control of Rome (c. -50) Caesar crosses Rubicon to start civil war ("Alea jacta est") -49 Pompey defeated by Caesar at Pharsalia -48 Herod governor of Galilee -47 Pompey murdered in Egypt by order of Cleopatra -47 Africa made Roman province; Caesar returns to Rome (-46) Caesar, dictator in Rome, adopts his nephew Gaius Octavius as heir -45 Caesar murdered by conspirators led by Brutus and Cassius Longinus -44 Second triumvirate: Mark Antony, Marcus Aemilius Lepidus, and Gaius Octavius, now renamed Gaius Julius Caesar Octavianus (Octavian) Brutus and Cassius defeated by the triumvirs at Philippi -42; commit suicide Herod, at Rome, appointed king of Judaea -40 Mark Antony returns to Egypt -38 Dalmatia a Roman province -34 Battle of Actium; Mark Antony and Cleopatra defeated by Octavian, and commit suicide; Egypt becomes Roman province -31 Octavian retitled Augustus and becomes virtual emperor (-30 to A.D. 14) Roman army under Drusus and Tiberius penetrates Germania as far as the Elbe -9 Judaea annexed by Rome -6 Herod d.; Judaea divided among his sons -4	Ovid, Roman poet, b. -43 (d. A.D. 18) Horace, Roman poet, d. -8 (b. -65) Lucius Annaeus Seneca the Younger, Roman dramatist, statesman, and philosopher, b. -4 (d. A.D. 65) Ovid: "Ars Amatoria" (c. -2)	Library of Ptolemy I in Alexandria destroyed by fire -47 Caesar: "De bello civili" -47 Probable date of the birth of Jesus Christ at Bethlehem -4 (after adjustment of calendar; see -46)
1 to 50	Cymbeline, king of the Catuvellauni, recognized by Rome as "Rex Brittonum" (5—40) Judaea a Roman province (6) Roman army under Varus destroyed by the Cherusci under Arminius in Teutoburg Forest (9) Augustus d. 14; succeeded as emperor by Tiberius (—37) Later (Eastern) Han dynasty in China (22—220) Tiberius retires to Capri (26), leaving Rome in charge of Sejanus, prefect of the Praetorian Guard Tiberius d. 37; succeeded by Caligula (—42) Caligula assassinated by Praetorian Guard (42), succeeded by Claudius (—54) Roman invasion of Britain (43); British under Caractacus defeated at Medway Gothic kingdom set up on Lower Vistula (50)	Ovid: "Metamorphoses" (5); banished (9) to savage Tomis where his sweet nature overwhelmed the bitter townsmen; "Epistulae ex Ponto" (16); d. 18 (b. -43) Martial, Roman poet, b. 43 (d. 120)	Baptism of Jesus Christ (27) Probable date of crucifixion of Jesus Christ (30) One of the earliest Christian churches erected at Corinth (c. 40) St. Paul sets out on his missionary travels (45) Plutarch, Greek historian, b. 47 (d. 120)

D. VISUAL ARTS	E. MUSIC	F. SCIENCE, TECHNOLOGY, GROWTH	G. DAILY LIFE	
				-100 to -51 contd
The famous "Laocoon" marble sculpture -38 Building of the Pantheon at Rome begun -30 (completed A.D. 124)	The earliest form of the oboe known in Rome -50 The Chin. octave is subdivided into 60 notes -38		**Adoption of Julian calendar of 365.25 days; leap year introduced -46** The first recorded wrestling match in Japan -23 The Millearium aureum erected in the Via Sacra (names, and distances from Rome, of the chief towns in the Empire)	-50 to -1
			The first definite reference to diamonds (16) London founded (43) The Romans learn the use of soap from the Gauls (50)	1 to 50

	A. HISTORY, POLITICS	B. LITERATURE, THEATER	C. RELIGION, PHILOSOPHY, LEARNING
51 to 100	Claudius poisoned by his wife Agrippina (54); succeeded by her son Nero (–68) Ming-Ti, new emperor of China, introduces Buddhism (58) Nero has his mother Agrippina killed (59) Nero has his wife Octavia killed and marries Poppaea Sabina (62) Seneca commits suicide at Nero's orders (65) Nero commits suicide (68); succeeded by Galba (June 68–Jan. 69); Otho (Jan.–Apr. 69); Vitellius (Jan.–Dec. 69); Vespasian (Dec. 69–79) Revolt of the Jews against Rome: Jerusalem captured and destroyed (70) Titus emperor (79—81) Domitian emperor (81—96) Nerva emperor (96—98) Trajan emperor (98—116); under him the Roman Empire reaches its greatest geographical extent Colonia Nervia Glevensis (later Gloucester) founded (98)	Juvenal, Roman poet, b. 58 (d. 138)	St. Paul: "Letters to the Corinthians" (c. 58) Seneca resigns his position at Nero's court (62) First persecution of Christians (64) Gospel according to St. Mark (c. 65) St. Peter executed (67) St. Linus (—68) becomes second pope Flavius Josephus: "History of the Jewish War" (68) Gospels according to St. John and St. Matthew (85) Pope Clement I (88—97)
101 to 150	Emperor Hadrian (117—138) Hadrian visits Britain; Hadrian's Wall from Tyne to Solway (122—127) Jewish rising under Bar Kokhba (122—135) Antoninus Pius emperor (138—161)	Apuleius, Roman satirist, ("The Golden Ass"), b. 114 Roman theater built at Verulamium (St. Albans), England (140)	Tacitus: "Historiae" (c. 117) Earliest known Sanskrit inscriptions in India (150)
151 to 200	Marcus Aurelius emperor (161—180) Wars of the Marcomanni and Quadi (167—175) Marcus Aurelius d. 180; succeeded as emperor by his son Commodus (—192) Romans, defeated in Scotland, retire to Hadrian's Wall (180) Emperor Commodus murdered (192) Emperor Septimius Severus (193—211) Albinus proclaims himself emperor in Britain, but is killed in 197 in Battle of Lyons Afghanistan invaded by Huns (200—540)	Fourth period of Chin. literature (from 200)	Pope Victor I (189—199) Period of Neo-Platonism, last of Greek philosophies (c. 200) Formation of Neo-Hebrew language c. 200 The bishop of Rome gains his predominant position as pope c. 200
201 to 250	Emperor Septimius Severus visits Britain; d. at York (211); succeeded by his sons Caracalla (—217) and Geta, the latter being murdered by Caracalla "Civis Romanus sum!" Roman citizenship given to every freeborn subject in Empire (212) After the assassination of Caracalla (217) Heliogabalus becomes emperor (218—222) End of Han dynasty in China (220), followed by four centuries of division The Goths invade Asia Minor and Balkan Peninsula (220) Emperor Alexander Severus (222—235) After the end of the Andgra dynasty in the Deccan region, (225), the southern part of India breaks up into several kingdoms The Sassanids in Persia (Ctesiphon) (226) Emperor Alexander Severus murdered in army meeting (235); Maximinus emperor (—238) Emperor Maximinus assassinated by his troops (238); succeeded by Gordian I and II, Balbinus, Pupienus, and Gordian III (—244) Emperor Philip the Arabian (244—249) Emperor Decius (249—251)	Kalidasa: "Sakuntala," Sanskrit drama (220)	Pope Urban I (222—230) Origen (c. 185—254): "Hexapla" (the Old Testament in six Hebrew and Greek texts) Persecution of Christians increases; martyrs are being revered as saints (c. 250)

D. VISUAL ARTS	E. MUSIC	F. SCIENCE, TECHNOLOGY, GROWTH	G. DAILY LIFE	
Arch of Titus erected in Rome (81)				51 to 100
				101 to 150
The oldest Maya monuments (c. 164) Column of Marcus Aurelius, Rome (190) Period of carvings on Amaravati stupa, Madras (200)		Pausanias of Magnesia: "Periegesis," a guide through Greece and its history of art (10 vols.) c. 170 Ptolemy draws 26 maps of various countries (c. 170) Galen extracts plant juices for medicinal purposes (c. 190)	The great plague in the Roman Empire (164—180) Carthage, under Roman rule, becomes again world metropolis c. 200 Silkworms arrive from Korea in China, and subsequently in Japan (c. 200)	151 to 200
Building of the Baths of Caracalla in Rome (212—217)		Diophantus of Alexandria produces the first book on algebra (c. 250)	Rome celebrates its 1,000th anniversary in 248 (see -753)	201 to 250

	A. HISTORY, POLITICS	B. LITERATURE, THEATER	C. RELIGION, PHILOSOPHY, LEARNING
251 to 300	Emperor Gallus (251—253) Emperor Valerian (253—260) and his son Gallienus (260—268) Goths, divided into Visigoths and Ostrogoths, invade Black Sea area (257) Franks invade Spain (257); Alemanni and Suevi conquer Upper Italy, but are defeated at Milan (258) Emperor Claudius II (268—270) The Goths sack Athens, Sparta, and Corinth (268) Emperor Aurelian (270—275): "restitutor orbis" Marcomanni advance from Bohemia across the Danube (270) Aurelian defeats Marcomanni and Alemanni and rebuilds the walls of Rome (271) Aurelian overthrows kingdom of Palmyra (273) Emperor Marcus Aurelius Probus (276—282) Emperor Marcus Aurelius Carus (282—283) Emperor Diocletian (284—305) Partition of the Roman Empire into western and eastern empires (285) Carausius, Roman commander of Brit. fleet, proclaims himself independent Emperor of Britain (285) The Romans take Armenia from the Persians (297) Separate developments of the five German dukedoms: Saxons, Franks, Alemanni, Thuringians, and Goths (c. 300) Lombards move from the Lower Elbe southward c. 300 (arrive 568 in Italy)	Records of the earliest religious plays (c. 300)	Crucifixion of Mani (b. 215), the founder of the Manichaean sect in Persia (276) Christianity introduced in Armenia (c. 300) Growing Buddhist influence in China (c. 300) Bowling is considered part of religious ritual in Ger. monasteries (300)
301 to 350	In 305 Diocletian abdicates in the East, Maximian in the West: their empires go to Constantius Chlorus (—306) and Galerius (—308) Emperor Constantius Chlorus d. 306 (at York); succeeded by his son Constantine the Great (—337) Constantine reunites the two empires under Rome, and becomes sole emperor Chandragupta crowned first Gupta emperor of northern India (320) Seat of Roman Empire moved to Constantinople (331) Constantine the Great d. 337, being baptized on his deathbed; succeeded by his three sons Constantine II, Constantius II, and Constans Constantine II killed in Battle of Aquileia, fighting his brother Constans (340) Rome again splits into two empires, with Constans as Western and Constantius II as Eastern Emperor (340) Persians regain Armenia from Rome (350)	The actor Genesius dies a martyr's death during a performance in Rome (304)	The last persecution of Christians in Rome (303—311) Edict of Milan: Constantine establishes toleration of Christianity (313) Council of Nicaea decides against Arians in favor of Athanasius (325) Erection of first Church of the Nativity, Bethlehem (325; destroyed by fire, 529) Basilican Church of St. Peter's erected (330); pulled down in 1506 to make room for present cathedral The Jews improve their calendar by introducing different lengths of years (338) Christianity in Abyssinia (350)
351 to 400	Picts and Scots cross Hadrian's Wall and attack Britain (360) The Huns invade Europe (360) The Empire divided (364): Eastern half from Lower Danube to the Persian border under Valens; Western half from Caledonia to northwestern Africa under Valentinian I Picts and Scots driven out of Britain by Theodosius (370) The Huns invade Russia (376) Emperor Valens defeated and killed by Visigoths at Adrianople in Thrace (378) Emperor Theodosius I (379—395) resettles Visigoths in the empire (382) Roman legions begin to evacuate Britain (383) Emperor Magnus Maximus crosses Channel and conquers Gaul and Spain (383) Accession (392) of Theodosius the Great as Emperor of *(contd)*	Scrolls begin to be replaced by books (c. 360)	Emperor Julian the Apostate (—361) attempts to revive paganism in the Empire St. Ursus builds Ravenna Cathedral (c. 378)

D. VISUAL ARTS	E. MUSIC	F. SCIENCE, TECHNOLOGY, GROWTH	G. DAILY LIFE	
Construction of the amphitheater of Verona begins (290) The palace of Diocletian in Ragusa (Dubrovnik) begun (300)		The first form of a compass may have been used in China (271) Pappus of Alexandria describes five machines in use: cogwheel, lever, pulley, screw, wedge (c. 285)		**251 to 300**
	Foundation of Schola Cantorum for church song, Rome (350)		The oldest bridge over the Rhine, near Cologne (313) Teotihuacan, ancient Mexican city, mentioned 325 (—900) Constantine forbids public gladiatorial combats (see -264) Constantinople founded as new capital on site of old Greek colony of Byzantium (330) Fortifications built in London (350)	**301 to 350**
Lo-tsun, a Chin. monk, founds the Caves of the Thousand Buddhas in Kansu (360)	Hymn singing introduced (386) by Ambrose, Bishop of Milan, (d. 397; later canonized) The first "Hallelujah" hymns in the Christian Churches (390)		Theodosius forbids the Olympic Games	**351 to 400**

	A. HISTORY, POLITICS	B. LITERATURE, THEATER	C. RELIGION, PHILOSOPHY, LEARNING
351 to 400 contd	East and West (—395), the last ruler of a united Empire Theodosius d. 395; succeeded by Honorius and Arcadius who redivide the Empire Alaric, king of the Visigoths (—410) Alaric invades Greece (396) and plunders Athens and (398) the Balkans The first definite records of Jap. history (400)		
401 to 450	The Visigoths invade Italy in 401 (—403) Gunderic, king of the Vandals (406—428) Founding of Burgundian kingdom of Worms (406) Stilicho checks Ostrogothic invasion at Fiesole (406) Alaric captures and sacks Rome in 410; dies on his way to the south; buried in the bed of the Busento River near Cosenza Roman legions withdraw from Britain to protect Italy (410) The Visigoths conquer Vandal kingdom in Spain (416) Franks settle in parts of Gaul (418) Theodoric I, king of the Visigoths (418—451) Barbarians settled in Roman provinces (425): Vandals in southern Spain, Huns in Pannonia, Ostrogoths in Dalmatia, Visigoths and Suevi in Portugal and northern Spain Valentinian III (b. 419), Western Roman Emperor under the guardianship of his mother Galla Placidia (425) Gaiseric, king of the Vandals (428—477) Picts and Scots expelled from southern England by Saxons, Jutes, and Angles (429) Aetius, chief minister of Valentinian III, becomes the virtual ruler of Western Roman Empire (429—454) Gaiseric founds Vandal kingdom in northern Africa (429) Attila in 433 becomes ruler of the Huns (d. 453) The last Roman troops leave Britain (436) The Huns destroy Burgundian kingdom of Worms (436) The Alemanni settle in Alsace (443) Gaiseric takes last Roman possessions in northern Africa, and establishes absolute monarchy (443) Theodosius II d. 450; succeeded as Eastern Roman Emperor by Marcian (—457)		Pope Innocent I (401—417) St. Augustine: "The City of God" (written in 411 after the sack of Rome by Alaric) St. Patrick begins his mission to Ireland (432) Codex Theodosianus: summary of Roman law (439) Pope Leo I (440—461)
451 to 500	Attila d. 453 Theodoric II, king of the Visigoths (453—466) The Vandals sack Rome (455) Skandagupta, Emperor of India (455—467) Battle of Crayford: Britons defeated by Hengest, abandon Kent to Jutes (457) Leo I, Eastern Roman Emperor (457—474) Childeric I, king of the Salian Franks (457—481) Cologne captured by the Franks (460) Vandals destroy Roman fleet off Cartagena (460) Last Western Roman emperors (from 461): Severus (—465), Athemius (—467), Alybrius (—473), Glycerius (—474), Julius Nepos (—475), and Romulus Augustulus (—476) Theodoric II murdered (466) by his brother Euric, who succeeds him (—484) The Huns withdraw from Europe (470) Flowering of Maya city civilization in southern Mexico (c. 470) Theodoric the Great, king of the Ostrogoths (471—526) Zeno, Eastern Roman Emperor (474—491) End of the Western Roman Empire (476): the German Odoacer (433—493) captures and executes Orestes at Placentia, deposes Orestes' son, the derisively titled Emperor Romulus Augustulus, and is proclaimed king of Italy *(contd)*	The Christian Lat. poet Dracontius of Carthage writes his religious poem "De laudibus Dei," comprising 2,327 hexameters in three books (490) Codex Bezae, New Testament in Greek and Latin (500) Aristainetos describes vividly in a letter life in Alexandria (500) Johannes Stobaios from Macedonia issues an anthology of Greek literature (500)	The philosopher Proclus (c. 410—485), most important representative of the later Neo-Platonism, becomes head of the Platonic Academy at Athens (476) The first Shinto shrines appear in Japan (478) St. Benedict of Nursia, the patriarch of Western monasticism (480—543) Boëthius, Roman scholar, philosopher, and theologian, b. 480 (executed 524) Damascius, Greek Neo-Platonist philosopher, b. 480 Pope Simplicius d. 483; succeeded by Felix III (—492) The pope's excommunication of Patriarch Acacius of Constantinople leads to first schism between the Western and the Eastern Churches (484—519) Proclus, foremost Neo-Platonist, d. 485 (b. c. 410) Apollinaris Sidonius, Gallic prelate and author, d. 487 Eastern Roman Emperor Zeno destroys *(contd)*

D. VISUAL ARTS	E. MUSIC	F. SCIENCE, TECHNOLOGY, GROWTH	G. DAILY LIFE	
				351 to 400 contd
Building begins on Basilica of S. Maria Maggiore, Rome (432) Galla Placidia erects her famous Mausoleum at Ravenna (446)	Alternative singing between precentor and community at Roman Church services after Jewish pattern (450)	Beginnings of alchemy (c. 410) with the search for Philosopher's Stone and Elixir of Life as chief objects Founding of Constantinople University (425)	Nanking becomes once more the capital of northern China (420) The ancient town of Ys in Brittany submerged in great flood (440)	**401 to 450**
Cave temples at Yün-Kang, northern China, with figures of Buddha (c. 476) Kasyapa, the Parricide, builds his palace at Sigiriya, the Lion Rock, Ceylon (famous "cloud maidens" cave paintings) (477) Building of the Basilica of S. Stefano Rotondo, Rome, begun 483 Moshica culture of the Chimic Indians in Peru (agriculture, pottery, textiles) The first plans of the Vatican Palace in Rome (500) Transition from Basket-Maker period to Modified Basket-Maker period in N. America Basilica of Turmanin and Kalb-Luzch, Syria (500) Mississippi valley culture in N. America Pre-Inca culture in Tiahuanco, Peru	Boëthius: "De institutione musica" (500) In Peru, flutes, horns, tubas, and drums in use St. Romanos, called Melodos, writes his hymns for Christmas, Easter, and the Passion (c. 500)	Aryabhata, Hindu astronomer and mathematician and writer on powers and roots of numbers, b. 476	Venice founded by refugees from Attila's Huns (452) Lyons becomes the capital of Burgundy (461) Theodoric presents King Gundebald of Burgundy with a clepsydra, a chronometer that measures time by the flow of water (490) The Anglo-Saxons wear shirts, tunics, and coats (c. 500) Tamo brings tea from India to China (c. 500)	**451 to 500**

	A. HISTORY, POLITICS	B. LITERATURE, THEATER	C. RELIGION, PHILOSOPHY, LEARNING
451 to 500 contd	Gaiseric, king of the Vandals (428—477), sells eastern Sicily to Theodoric, king of the Visigoths (476) Founding of the kingdom of Sussex (477) Hunneric, king of the Vandals (477—484), son and successor of Gaiseric, fierce persecutor of the Catholics Basiliscus, Eastern Roman Emperor, deposes Zeno and is in turn deposed (477) Ch'i dynasty in southern China (479—502) Ex-Emperor Julius Nepos killed in Dalmatia (480) Childeric I, king of the Salian Franks, d. 481; succeeded by his 15-year-old son Clovis, who becomes the founder of the Merovingian power (d. 511) Justinian I, the Great, Byzantine Emperor (527—565), b. 483 Hunneric, king of the Vandals, d. 484; succeeded by his nephew Gunthamund (—496) The revolt of Vahan Mamikonian (481—484) secures religious and political freedom for Armenia Gupta empire in northern India overthrown by Epthalite invaders from beyond the Oxus River (c. 484) Alaric II, king of the Visigoths (484—507) Clovis defeats Syagrius, the last Roman governor of Gaul, near Soissons (486) Theodoric begins his conquest of Italy (487—493) Theodoric defeats Odoacer on the Isonzo River and again near Verona (489) The Saxons capture Pevensey, Sussex (491) Emperor Zeno d. 491; succeeded by Anastasius I (—518) Odoacer capitulates at Ravenna to the Ostrogoths (493) and is murdered by Theodoric; Theodoric founds the Ostrogoth kingdom of Italy, and marries a sister of Clovis Clovis I, king of the Franks, marries Burgundian princess Clothilda (493), who converts him to Christianity (496) The Ostrogoths in Malta (494—534) The kingdom of Wessex founded (495) Gunthamund, king of the Vandals, d. 496; succeeded by his brother Thrasamund (—523) Clovis defeats the Alemanni near Strasbourg (496) and is baptized by his friend St. Remigius (or Remy), Bishop of Rheims Thrasamund marries Theodoric's sister and obtains as dowry western Sicily (500) The Marcomanni, a German tribe in Bohemia, invade Bavaria (500); on their departure the Czechs settle in Bohemia The Lombards (Langobards) occupy the area north of the Danube (500) and expand, "seeking occasions for war" Brit. victory over the Saxons at Mount Badon, Dorset (500)		the school of the Nestorians at Edessa, and builds the Church of St. Simeon Stylites around the saint's pillar (489); Nestorians settle in Nisibis, Persia, in 498 Cassiodorus, Roman scholar, b. 490 (d. 583) Procopius, Byzantine historian, b. 490 (d. 562) The Armenian Church secedes from Byzantium and Rome (491) Pope Felix III d. 492; succeeded by Gelasius I (—496) Pope Gelasius I d. 496; succeeded by Anastasius II (—498) The Gelasian Missal, book of prayers, chants, and instructions for the celebration of Mass (496) Pope Anastasius II d. 498; succeeded by Symmachus (—514) The Synod of Rome issues a decree on papal elections (499) Neo-Platonic philosophical writings of the so-called Dionysius the Areopagite from Syria (500) Incense is introduced in Christian church service (500)
501			
502	Wu-Ti, Emperor of China (—549)	Narsai of Mealletha, Syrian poet, head of the Nestorian school in Nisibis, d.	
503			
504			

D. VISUAL ARTS	E. MUSIC	F. SCIENCE, TECHNOLOGY, GROWTH	G. DAILY LIFE	
				451 to 500 contd
				501
				502
				503
				504

	A. HISTORY, POLITICS	B. LITERATURE, THEATER	C. RELIGION, PHILOSOPHY, LEARNING
506			Lex Romana Visigothorum, law code of Alaric II
507	Alaric II killed by Clovis in the Battle of the Campus Vogladensis: Clovis annexes Visigoth kingdom of Toulouse Visigoth kingdom of Old Castile (—711)		Mayan altar with head of death god (Copan, Honduras)
508	Theodora, future wife of the Byzantine Emperor Justinian I, b. (d. 548)		
509			
510	Provence, southeastern part of France, goes to the Ital. Ostrogoths (—563)		
511	Clovis, king of the Franks since 481, d.; his realm is divided among his four sons Theodoric I (—534), Chlodomer (—524), Childebert I (—558), and Chlothar (—561), with courts at Soissons, Paris, Metz, and Orleans respectively		The convent of St. Césaire, Arles
512			
513			
514			Pope Symmachus d.; succeeded by Pope Hormisdas (—523)
515			
516	Sigismund, son of Gundobad, becomes king of Burgundy		

D. VISUAL ARTS	E. MUSIC	F. SCIENCE, TECHNOLOGY, GROWTH	G. DAILY LIFE	
				506
			Wooden coffins and wooden tools used in the burial places of the Alemanni	507
				508
				509
				510
				511
				512
				513
				514
				515
				516

	A. HISTORY, POLITICS	B. LITERATURE, THEATER	C. RELIGION, PHILOSOPHY, LEARNING
517	Emperor Wu-Ti becomes a Buddhist and introduces the new religion to central China		
518	Justin I (b. 450) becomes Byzantine Emperor (—527)		
519			End of the first schism (484): reconciliation of the Western and Eastern Churches
520			The great Lat. grammarian Priscian writes his "Institutiones grammaticae"
521			
522			
523	Thrasamund, king of the Vandals, d.; succeeded by Hilderic (—530)		Pope Hormisdas d.; succeeded by Pope John I (—526)
524	Sigismund, king of Burgundy, killed by Chlodomer, son of Clovis I; succeeded by Godomar		Boëthius, Roman scholar accused of high treason, imprisoned and executed; while in prison he writes "De consolatione philosophia" (b. 480)
525	Caleb of Abyssinia conquers the Yemen		Dionysius Exiguus (c. 500—560), Roman theologian and mathematician, in his "Easter Tables" wrongly dates the birth of Christ on Dec. 23 -753 years after the founding of Rome, which took place in -753 (see 735) Constance becomes bishop's see
526	Theodoric the Great, king of the Ostrogoths since 471, d.; his daughter Amalaswintha becomes regent of Italy (—534)		Pope John I d.; succeeded by Pope Felix IV (—530)
527	Justinian I, nephew of Justin I, becomes Byzantine Emperor (—565) Saxon kingdoms of Essex and Middlesex		
528			

D. VISUAL ARTS	E. MUSIC	F. SCIENCE, TECHNOLOGY, GROWTH	G. DAILY LIFE	
		Aryabhata (b. 476) compiles his manual of astronomy		517
				518
Chinese bronze sculpture: "Two Buddhas in Conversation" (T'ang period, archaic style)				519
				520
	Boëthius introduces Greek musical letter notation to the West			521
The oldest known pagoda from the Sung Yuen temple of Honan, China, a towerlike structure, derived from the stupa of ancient India				522
				523
				524
Arian Baptistery S. Maria in Cosmedin, Ravenna Buddhist caves at Ajanta with stone carvings		Cosmas Indicopleustes, explorer and geographer of Alexandria, travels up the Nile and writes his "Topographia Christiane"		525
Tomb of Theodoric, Ravenna				526
The Church of the Nativity, Bethlehem, being rebuilt (—565)		The first paddle-wheel boats with animal whim-drive		527
				528

	A. HISTORY, POLITICS	B. LITERATURE, THEATER	C. RELIGION, PHILOSOPHY, LEARNING
529	Ratisbon becomes the capital of Bavaria		Justinian closes the 1000-year-old School of Philosophy in Athens, an action directed against paganism rather than Greek philosophy; many professors go to Persia and Syria St. Benedict of Nursia (480—543) founds the Monastery of Monte Cassino and the Benedictine Order Justinian's Code of Civil Laws–the Codex Vetus–issued
530	Gelimer, nephew of Gunthamund and Thrasamund, establishes himself after the death of Hilderic as king of the Vandals (—534)		Pope Felix IV d.; succeeded by Pope Boniface II (—532)
531	Chosroes I becomes king of Persia (—579) and leads his country to new cultural and artistic heights Kingdom of Thuringia overthrown by Franks Byzantine general Belisarius (505—565), who defeated the Persians at Dara and was defeated by them, recalled to Constantinople		
532	The Franks overthrow the kingdom of Burgundy Belisarius saves the throne for Justinian by putting down the Nika revolt Constantinople destroyed during the Nika revolt, but soon rebuilt		Pope Boniface II d.
533	Belisarius overthrows Vandal kingdom and makes N. Africa a Byzantine province		Pope John II succeeds Pope Boniface II (d. 532)
534	Toledo becomes capital of the Visigoth kingdom of Spain (—711) Malta becomes a Byzantine province (—870)		Justinian replaces Codex Vetus by Codex Repeitae Praelectionis
535	Belisarius occupies Ostrogoth kingdom of Italy (—540)	Fortunatus Venantius, Christian-Lat. poet and bishop, b. (d. c. 600)	Pope John II d.; succeeded by Pope Agapetus I (—536)
536	After the destruction of the Ostrogoth kingdom Provence becomes part of the kingdom of the Franks Naples: part of the Byzantine Empire		Pope Agapetus I d.; succeeded by Pope Silverius (—537)
537	Arthur, king of the Britons, killed in the Battle of Camlan; semilegendary		Pope Silverius d.; succeeded by Pope Vigilius (—555)
538			

D. VISUAL ARTS	E. MUSIC	F. SCIENCE, TECHNOLOGY, GROWTH	G. DAILY LIFE	
				529
				530
				531
Building of St. Sophia Basilica, Constantinople, begun (—537)				532
				533
		Johannes Philoponus Grammaticus (c. 485—555) refutes the teachings of Proclus and other Neo-Platonists		534
Earliest Chin. roll paintings in Tun-hu-ang (landscapes) Christian basilica at Leptis Magna (N. Africa)				535
				536
St. Sophia Basilica, Constantinople, completed (begun 532)				537
				538

	A. HISTORY, POLITICS	B. LITERATURE, THEATER	C. RELIGION, PHILOSOPHY, LEARNING
539	War breaks out between Persia and the Byzantine Empire (—562)		
540	Totila the Ostrogoth ends Byzantine rule in Italy	The first Welsh poets: Taliesin, Aneirin, Llywarch Hên	Cassiodorus founds the great Monastery of Vivarium, near Squillace, where he writes his own works and directs the literary activities of his fellow monastics
541	Totila becomes, after the death of his uncle Hildebad, king of the Ostrogoths (—552)		
542			St. Gildas (c. 500—570) writes his "De excido et conquestu Britanniae," important source of early Brit. history
543			St. Benedict d. Justinian issues an edict condemning the writings of the early Greek theologian Origen (185—254)
544			
545			
546	Totila enters Rome Audoin founds the new Lombard dynasty and establishes his reign beyond the Save River		
547	King Ida accedes to the throne of Bernicia, the more northerly of the two Anglo-Saxon kingdoms Totila leaves Rome		
548	Theodora, Byzantine empress, d. (b. 508)		
549			

D. VISUAL ARTS	E. MUSIC	F. SCIENCE, TECHNOLOGY, GROWTH	G. DAILY LIFE	
				539
Tomb of Galla Placidia, Ravenna Lucius: crypt at Chur, Switzerland			Empress Theodora introduces long white dresses, purple cloaks, gold embroidery, tiaras, and pointed shoes	540
				541
Columned basilica with mosaics in Parenzo (Istria)			The plague in Constantinople, imported by rats from Egypt and Syria, soon spreads all over Europe	542
			Disastrous earthquakes shake the entire world	543
				544
				545
				546
Building of the Church of S. Vitale in Ravenna (double octagonal shape; mosaic portraits of Justinian and Theodora) Bamburgh Castle, built by Ida			The plague, medically described by Gildas, reaches Britain	547
				548
The church of S. Apollinare in Classe, near Ravenna, completed on site of the saint's grave (begun 535)			In the Neo-Persian Empire of the Sassanid dynasty (founded c. 224) music, dancing, chess, and hunting are cultivated	549

	A. HISTORY, POLITICS	B. LITERATURE, THEATER	C. RELIGION, PHILOSOPHY, LEARNING
550	Totila conquers Rome for the second time Westward migration of Turk. tribes (Avars) begins The kingdoms of Mercia, East Anglia, and Northumbria founded Slav tribes settle in Mecklenburg Poles settle in western, Ukrainians in eastern, Galicia Toltec kingdom in Mexico continues Teotihuacan civilization	Hesychios of Miletus compiles an encyclopedia of Greek authors Musaeus: "Hero and Leander," Greek epic poem Cûdraka: "Vasentasena," Indian drama Procopius: "De bellis" (description of Persian, Vandal, and Gothic wars)	Columban the Younger, Ir. missionary in France and Italy, b. (d. 615) Augsburg becomes bishop's see Wales converted to Christianity by St. David Church bells being used in France
551	Ostrogoth navy defeated by the Byzantines		
552	Totila, king of the Ostrogoths, killed at the Battle of Taginae, fighting against the Byzantines under Narses (c. 478—c. 573) Teias, last king of the Ostrogoths (—553)		Emperor Shotoko Taishi (—621), b.; introduces Buddhism into Japan; end of Jap. prehistory, beginning of Asuka period
553	Narses annexes Rome and Naples for Byzantine	Procopius: "Anecdota," true scandal about Justinian, Theodora, and Belisarius	Fifth Council of Constantinople (—555)
554	Narses, the eunuch general, appointed exarch, the highest military and civil authority in Italy		
555			Pope Vigilius d.
556			Pope Pelagius I
557			
558	Chlothar I, son of Clovis (see 511), reunites the kingdom of the Franks (—561)		
559	Belisarius repels an army of the Huns near Constantinople		
560	Ethelbert I, son of Eormenric, becomes king of Kent (—616)		Founding of the Abbey of Bangor, Caernarvonshire, Wales, by St. Deniol

D. VISUAL ARTS	E. MUSIC	F. SCIENCE, TECHNOLOGY, GROWTH	G. DAILY LIFE	
Mosaics at the Church of S. Apollinare in Classe with one of the first representations of the Last Supper The Golden Era of Byzantine art St. Servatius Church in Maastricht, Holland, begun (—1450) The crucifix develops as ornament			Draw looms used in Egypt for patterned silk weaving Beginnings of chess game in India	550
				551
Throne of Archbishop Maximian at Ravenna			Justinian sends missionaries to China and Ceylon to smuggle out silkworms; beginning of European silk industry	552
Crypt of St. Médard at Soissons			Silk industry becomes state monopoly in Byzantine Empire	553
				554
				555
				556
				557
				558
				559
				560

	A. HISTORY, POLITICS	B. LITERATURE, THEATER	C. RELIGION, PHILOSOPHY, LEARNING
561	Chlothar I, d., his kingdom being divided among his sons Charibert (—567), Guntram (—592), Sigebert (—575), and Chilperic (—584)		Pope Pelagius I d.; succeeded by Pope John III (—574)
562		Procopius, Byzantine historian, d. (b. 490)	
563			St. Columba (c. 521—597), Ir. abbot and missionary, establishing himself on the Isle of Iona, begins to convert the Picts and founds a monastery St. Sophia, Constantinople, consecrated
564			
565	Emperor Justinan I d. (b. 483); succeeded by his nephew Justin II (d. 578) The Lombards drive the Byzantines from northern Italy to the south, but leave them in Ravenna Audoin d. (see 546), after which his son and successor Alboin destroys, with the help of the Avars, the Gothic kingdom of the Gepidae on the lower Vistula		
566			
567	Leovigild, king of the Visigoths (—586), drives the Byzantines from western Spain Partition of the Frankish kingdom into Austrasia (Lorraine, Belgium, right bank of the Rhine), Neustria (France), and Burgundy		
568	Alboin founds a Lombard kingdom in northern and central Italy (—774)		
569			
570	Persians overthrow Abyssinian rule in the Yemen		Mohammed, founder of Islam, b. (d. 632) The Chin. monk Chi-Kai (531—597) interprets Buddhism as symbolic mysticism for the initiates
571			

D. VISUAL ARTS	E. MUSIC	F. SCIENCE, TECHNOLOGY, GROWTH	G. DAILY LIFE	
Basilica of San Juan Batista of Banos de Cerreto, Spain, consecrated				561
				562
				563
				564
				565
				566
				567
				568
				569
				570
				571

	A. HISTORY, POLITICS	B. LITERATURE, THEATER	C. RELIGION, PHILOSOPHY, LEARNING
572	War between Persia and the Byzantine Empire (—591)		
573	War between Chlothar's sons Chilperic and Sigebert		Abu Bekr, Mohammed's father-in-law and first Caliph of the Mohammedans, b. (d. 634)
574			Pope John III d.
575	The Slovenes move into Carniola		Pope Benedict I Buddhism firmly established in Japan
576	Sigibert, king of Austrasia, d., his widow Brunhild becoming regent of the kingdom (—613)		
577	The English of Wessex defeat the Welsh at Deorham		
578	Byzantine Emperor Justin II d; succeeded by Tiberius II (—582)		
579			Pope Benedict I d.; succeeded by Pope Pelagius II (—590)
580			
581	Accession of Yan Ch'ien to the throne of China and foundation of the Sui dynasty (—618)		
582	Emperor Tiberius II d.; succeeded by Maurice (—602)		

D. VISUAL ARTS	E. MUSIC	F. SCIENCE, TECHNOLOGY, GROWTH	G. DAILY LIFE	
				572
				573
				574
		Alexander of Tralles (c. 525—605): "De re medica"		575
				576
				577
				578
				579
				580
				581
				582

	A. HISTORY, POLITICS	B. LITERATURE, THEATER	C. RELIGION, PHILOSOPHY, LEARNING
583			Cassiodorus d. (b. c. 490); Roman historian, statesman, and monk, he wrote the "Chronica," the "Institutiones divinarum et saecularium litterarum," and, in his 93rd year, the "Ostographia"
584	Mercia, one of the kingdoms of Anglo-Saxon England, founded Authari, first king of the Lombards (—590) Chlothar II, son of Chilperic I, becomes king of Neustria (—628)		
585	Leovigild conquers the whole of Spain		
586	Recared, king of the Visigoths (—601)		The "Echmiadsin Evangliar," Byzantine-Armenian manuscript
587			The Visigoths in Spain are being converted to Christianity Foundation of the first Buddhist monastery in Japan
588			
589			Under King Authari and Queen Theodelinda, the Lombards are converted to Roman Catholicism
590	Authari, king of the Lombards, d.; succeeded by Agilulf (d. 615) Chosroes II ascends the throne of Persia and renews the war with the Byzantine Empire (—628)		Pope Pelagius II d.; succeeded by Pope Gregory I, the Great (—604) Lausanne, Switzerland, becomes bishop's see St. Gregory of Tours (c. 540—594) mentions in his writings church window-glass St. Columban leaves Ireland with 12 other monks and goes to Luxeuil in the Vosges
591			
592	Ethelfrith, king of Bernicia (—616)		
593			

D. VISUAL ARTS	E. MUSIC	F. SCIENCE, TECHNOLOGY, GROWTH	G. DAILY LIFE	
				583
				584
Building of the Horyuji temple in Nara, Japan				585
				586
				587
				588
				589
			The plague in Rome	590
				591
				592
Building of the Temple of Four Heavenly Kings (Shitenno-ji), Osaka, Japan, begins				593

	A. HISTORY, POLITICS	B. LITERATURE, THEATER	C. RELIGION, PHILOSOPHY, LEARNING
594			St. Gregory of Tours, author of the "Historiae Francorum," d. (b. c. 540)
595			
596			Pope Gregory dispatches St. Augustine of Canterbury as missionary to Britain
597			St. Augustine of Canterbury lands in Thanet, baptizes Ethelbert of Kent, and founds a Benedictine monastery in Canterbury
598			Probably the first English school, at Canterbury
599			
600	Tibet begins to develop into a unitary state Czechs and Slovaks settle in Bohemia and Moravia, Yugoslavs in Serbia The barbarian invasions halt in western Europe The Khazars form an empire between the lower Volga and the lower Don	Antara ibn Shaddad, one of the seven great pre-Mohammedan Arab poets, author of the "Divan," d. Fortunatus Venantius, Bishop of Poitiers, poet, and author of stories of saints, d. (b. 535) The lyric poetry of the T'ang dynasty helps to promote everyday Chin. language	Pope Gregory strives for the peaceful conversion of the Jews, introduces picture books for illiterates to replace the Bible, and writes a manual on the duties of the clergy Bishop Isidore of Seville (560—636) collects old Greek and Roman writings
601			The first York Minster (see 627)
602	Byzantine Emperor Maurice killed by Phocas, his successor (—610)		St. Augustine of Canterbury establishes the archiepiscopal see of Canterbury

D. VISUAL ARTS	E. MUSIC	F. SCIENCE, TECHNOLOGY, GROWTH	G. DAILY LIFE	
			End of the plague which began in 542 and halved the population of Europe	594
		First authenticated record of decimal reckoning in India		595
				596
				597
				598
				599
Beginning of the building of Arles Cathedral Development of the goldsmith's art in the Frankish-Merovingian era (jewelry) Coptic art in Egypt: a mixture of Egyptian, Greek, Byzantine, and Arab influences Flowering of architecture and sculpture in northern and southern India Classic Buddha figures in yoga postures in Bihar (northern India) Chin. and Korean artists and craftsmen settle in Japan	"Antiphonar," Pope Gregory's collection of church chants Pope Gregory founds the Schola Cantorum in Rome	Book printing in China	In Italy the monetary system is replaced by barter From India smallpox spreads via China and Asia Minor to southern Europe	600
				601
			Owing to disastrous floods the bed of the Yellow River (Huang Ho) in China has to be changed (further changes up to 1852)	602

	A. HISTORY, POLITICS	B. LITERATURE, THEATER	C. RELIGION, PHILOSOPHY, LEARNING
603	First mention of London		The Lombards converted to Roman Catholicism Founding of the bishopric of Rochester, England The first St. Paul's Church, London, and St. Andrew's Church, Rochester, built
604			Pope Gregory I, the Great, d.; succeeded by Pope Sabinian (—606) The Shotoko Taishi code in Japan demands veneration of Buddha, his priests and laws
605			
606	Founding of the last empire in northern India through a native ruler, Harsha of Thanesar (d. 647)		Fatima, daughter of Mohammed, b. (d. 632) Building of the St. Trophime Cathedral in Arles
607	The first Jap. ambassadors in China		Pope Boniface III d.
608	Pulakesin II Chalukya becomes ruler of the Deccan (—642)		Pope Boniface IV (—615), later canonized, as were so many of the early popes
609			The Pantheon in Rome consecrated as the Church of S. Maria Rotonda
610	Phocas, Emperor of the Eastern Roman Empire, deposed and killed; succeeded by Heraclius (—641), who inaugurates the dynasty of the Heraclians		Mohammed's vision on Mount Hira Sergius becomes patriarch of Constantinople (—638) First record of the use of episcopal rings
611			
612	Harsha of Thanesar (see 606) takes the title of Emperor of the Five Indies About this time Arnulf, counselor of Chlothar II, becomes Bishop of Metz; his wife enters a convent; his son marries the daughter of Chlothar's mayor of the palace, Pepin of Landen		Gallus, a disciple of Columban, founds the Monastery of St. Gallen, Switzerland
613	Northumbrians under Ethelfrit defeat Britons near Chester Austrasia and Burgundy united by Chlothar II		

D. VISUAL ARTS	E. MUSIC	F. SCIENCE, TECHNOLOGY, GROWTH	G. DAILY LIFE	
				603
			The first church bell in Rome	604
		Construction of the An-Chi bridge, Chou-Hsien, Hopei, China		605
			Examinations demanded for applicants to public offices in China	606
Completion of Horyuji temple and hospital in Japan by Emperor Yomei (oldest surviving wooden building in the world)				607
				608
	The crwth (crowd, chrotta), a Celtic string instrument, develops			609
				610
				611
				612
				613

	A. HISTORY, POLITICS	B. LITERATURE, THEATER	C. RELIGION, PHILOSOPHY, LEARNING
614	The Persians take Damascus and Jerusalem, and take as booty the Holy Cross (won back by the Byzantines in 628) The Edictum Chlotacharii defines the rights of king, nobles, and church		Columban founds the Monastery of Bobbio (northern Italy)
615	Agilulf, king of the Lombards, who introduced Christianity to his people, d. Anglians reach the Irish; massacre of the monks of Bangor		Pope Deusdedit or Adeodatus (—618) The earliest records of some of Mohammed's teachings Columban, the Ir. missionary, d.; originally of the Celtic rite, his foundations eventually became Benedictine
616	Persians overrun Egypt Kent passes to Wessex Adalwald becomes king of the Lombards (—626)		Benedictine nunnery and church in Folkestone
617			
618	Each of the three parts of the kingdom of the Franks, Austrasia, Neustria, and Burgundy, has a mayor (majordomus), who presides over the royal court–usually called mayor of the palace End of the Sui dynasty in China (see 581); from now on the T'ang dynasty rules the country (—907)		
619	The Persians in Egypt, Jerusalem, and Damascus and at the Hellespont		Pope Boniface V (—625)
620	The Isle of Man annexed by the kingdom of Northumbria The Northmen invade Ireland		
621			
622			The Hegira–Mohammed's flight from Mecca to Medina: year one in the Moslem calendar Monothelite controversy (—680)
623	Samo, a Frankish merchant from Sens, encountering Slav tribes in Carinthia, frees them from the Avars, and founds an empire Dagobert I, elder son of Chlothar II, becomes king of Austrasia; his adviser is Arnulf, Bishop of Metz; his mayor, Pepin of Landen (—639)		"Shaka Trinity," the famous altarpiece of the Kondo in Japan by Tori Pallava art: reliefs at Mamalhapuram Temple

D. VISUAL ARTS	E. MUSIC	F. SCIENCE, TECHNOLOGY, GROWTH	G. DAILY LIFE	
				614
Revival of stone sculpture and architecture in India through Harsavardhana and Mahendravarman I			"Burning water" (petroleum) used in Japan	615
				616
				617
				618
	Formation of orchestras of hundreds of players in China	The "Suan-Ching" ("Ten Classics"): scientific textbooks used for Chin. examinations (see 606)		619
Production of porcelain in China				620
				621
		"Originum sive etymologiarum libri XX," an encyclopedia on arts and sciences by Isidore of Seville		622
				623

	A. HISTORY, POLITICS	B. LITERATURE, THEATER	C. RELIGION, PHILOSOPHY, LEARNING
624			Mohammed married Aisha, the 10-year-old daughter of Abu Bekr
625	Double attack of the Avars and Persians on Constantinople repelled by Emperor Heraclius Narasimhavarman I, king of southern India of the Pallava dynasty (—645)		The Roman missionary Paulinus comes to Northumbria Mohammed begins to dictate the Koran Pope Boniface V d.; succeeded by Pope Honorius I (—638) Dagobert I founds the Abbey of St. Denis
626	Edwin of Northumbria founds Edinburgh and begins Christianizing his country		
627	The Persians decisively defeated by the Byzantines at Nineveh Kau-Tsu resigns his throne, his son T'ai-Tsung becoming Emperor of China (—649)		Mohammed's enemies from Mecca besiege Medina and slaughter 700 Jews Edwin of Northumbria replaces the first wooden York Minster with one of stone Pope Honorius I builds many new churches in Rome (—638)
628	Chosroes II, King of Persia (see 590), murdered by his son and successor Kavadh II		Emperor Heraclius wins back the Cross of Christ that the Persians carried off Mohammed captures Mecca and writes letters to all the rulers of the world, explaining the principles of the Moslem faith Founding of Lincoln Church
629	Heraclius recovers Jerusalem Chlothar II d.; Dagobert I succeeds to the whole Frankish kingdom (—638)		Hsüan Tsang, the Chin. Buddhist, travels to Cambodia to study Buddhism at its source Pope Honorius I sides with Emperor Heraclius in the Monothelite controversy, for which he is anathematized many years after his death
630	Olaf Tratelia, expelled from his native Sweden, founds a colony in Vermeland (Norway)		
631			
632	Mohammed d. (b. 570) Medina becomes the seat of the first Caliph, Abu Bekr, who succeeds his son-in-law Mohammed	Georgios Pisides: "The Hexameron," didactic poem on the creation of the world	Fatima, Mohammed's youngest daughter and mother of Hassan and Hussein, founder of the House of the Fatimids, d. (b. 606) Buddhism becomes state religion in Tibet Christianization of East Anglia
633	The Arabs attack Persia Oswald, king of Northumbria and Bernicia (—641) Spain becomes an elective kingdom of the Visigoths		Progress of Mohammedanism, the churches of Jerusalem, Antioch, and Alexandria being lost to Christian faith

D. VISUAL ARTS	E. MUSIC	F. SCIENCE, TECHNOLOGY, GROWTH	G. DAILY LIFE	
				624
Building of the Ch'ang-an Pagoda in China (—705) The first Ise shrine in Japan Gourdon gold chalice, France		Brahmagupta, the Indian mathematician, teaches at Ujjain		625
				626
		Upon capturing the Persian castle of Dastagerd, the armies of Heraclius find Indian sugar		627
				628
A set of Byzantine silver plates, depicting the life of King David, produced 610—629, found near Kyrenia in 1902				629
			Cotton supposed to have been introduced in Arab countries	630
				631
				632
				633

	A. HISTORY, POLITICS	B. LITERATURE, THEATER	C. RELIGION, PHILOSOPHY, LEARNING
634	Abu Bekr d. (b. 573); succeeded as caliph by Mohammed's adviser Omar I (—644), who conquers Syria, Persia, and Egypt and defeats Heraclius ("Holy War")	The legend of "Barlaam and Josaphat," written by the monk Johannes of Jerusalem	
635	Damascus becomes the capital of the caliphs (—750) The Mohammedans capture Gaza Emperor T'ai-Tsung receives Christian missionaries Harsha's invasion of the land of the Chalukyas repulsed		Christianization of Wessex
636	Rise of the feudal nobility in Japan Anglo-Saxon civilization advances with the introduction of Christianity In the Frankish empire the differentiation between the Fr. and Ger. languages appears Rothari, king of the Lombards (—652)		Churches built at Glastonbury, St. Albans, Winchester; castles at Conisborough, Castletown, etc. Persian fire worshipers settle in central India Southern Ir. Church submits to Roman Catholicism
637	Jerusalem conquered by the Arabs		
638	Persia appeals to China for help against Moslems Clovis II, king of Neustria and Burgundy (—657), succeeds Dagobert I		Pope Honorius I d.
639	The Arabs attack Armenia		
640		The Arabs find at Alexandria the famous library with 300,000 papyrus scrolls	Jacob of Edessa, theologian and historian, b. (d. 708) St. Aidan begins his missionary work in Northumbria Pope Severinus reigns for two months; succeeded by Pope John IV (—642) Syracuse Cathedral, integrating a Doric temple of c. –470, begun
641	Oswiu, king of Northumbria and Bernicia (—670) Emperor Heraclius d. (see 610) Constans II Pogonatus, Byzantine Emperor (—668) The Arabs under Omar destroy the Persian Empire; the caliphs rule the country till 1258; Islam replaces the religion of Zoroaster Chindaswinth, king of the Visigoths (—652)		The book-copying industry at Alexandria destroyed by the Arabs; end of Alexandrian school, the center of Western culture
642	Eastern Roman Empire is considerably weakened by the Arab conquest of Egypt, Mesopotamia, and Syria		Pope John IV d.; succeeded by Pope Theodore I (—649) Fredegar Scholasticus: "Historia Francorum"

D. VISUAL ARTS	E. MUSIC	F. SCIENCE, TECHNOLOGY, GROWTH	G. DAILY LIFE	
				634
The rock temple of Rathas at Mamalhapuram (southern India)				635
				636
Apse mosaics in the Church of S. Agnese, Rome				637
				638
				639
				640
Prime of Armenian architecture under Patriarch Nerses III			Founding of Fustat (Cairo)	641
Building of Amr Mosque in Cairo				642

	A. HISTORY, POLITICS	B. LITERATURE, THEATER	C. RELIGION, PHILOSOPHY, LEARNING
643	Moslems conquer Tripoli Grimoald, son of Pepin, becomes mayor of Austrasian court (—656)		
644	Chinese move into Korea King Rothari codifies the Lombard law		
645	The Taikwa reform completes the rebuilding of the central Jap. state, limiting powers of the nobility		
646	Byzantine fleet recaptures Alexandria		
647	Emperor Harsha's death breaks up his northern Indian empire		
648			
649	The Arabs conquer Cyprus		Pope Theodore I d.; succeeded by Pope Martin I (—655) Lateran Synod condemns Monothelitism
650	Hindu empire in Sumatra Croats and Serbs occupy Bosnia The Khazars conquer Great Bulgarian Empire in southern Russia	Amarasimka: "Amarakosha," Indian dictionary Bana: "Kadambari," Indian romantic novel	Wandering bishop Emmeram (d. 715) founds the Ratisbon Monastery Caliph Othman puts Mohammed's teachings (Koran) into 114 chapters (influenced by Jewish and Christian theology) Buddhist monk Bhartrihari writes 100 proverbs about love, life, and resignation The monk Shan-tao (612—681) fights Chi-kai's mystic Buddhism and popularizes Amida Buddhism
651	Yazgard III d., last of the Sassanid rulers in Persia		Benedictine abbey at Stavelot, Belgium
652	Aswan agreed upon with Nubians as southern limit of Arab expansion		

D. VISUAL ARTS	E. MUSIC	F. SCIENCE, TECHNOLOGY, GROWTH	G. DAILY LIFE	
Building of the Dome of the Rock, Jerusalem, begins				643
Ornaments on Swed. helmets show Odin, the principal god of Scandinavian mythology, on his eight-legged horse				644
Activity of Yen Li-pen (d. 673), the greatest of the artists of the T'ang period in China			The gold treasure of the Anglo-Saxon king Ethelhere (found 1939 in a ship grave at Sutton Hoo, Suffolk, England)	645
Early Nara period of Jap. art (—710)				646
				647
				648
				649
Development of the art of weaving in Byzantine empire Wooden Bodhisattva sculpture in the nunnery of Chuguji, Nara Tamamushi shrine with oil paintings from the life of Buddha in Nara Tomb of the Chin. Emperor T'ai Tsung (d. 649) Chin. artists use lamp-black ink for taking rubbings, which leads to introduction of wood blocks for printing Building of St. Martin's Church, Canterbury	Neumes, notation for groups of notes used in music (—1050)	Prime of the first surgical developments in India with bladder, peristalsis, and plastic operations	The caliphs introduce the first organized news service	650
Li Ssu-Hsün, Chin. painter, b. (d. 716)				651
				652

	A. HISTORY, POLITICS	B. LITERATURE, THEATER	C. RELIGION, PHILOSOPHY, LEARNING
654	Penda, heathen king of Mercia, overthrown and killed by Oswiu		
655	Moslem fleet destroys Byzantine fleet at Lycia		Founding of Benedictine monastery at Peterborough (see 870) Pope Martin I d.; succeeded by Pope Eugenius I (—657)
656	Caliph Othman murdered Chlothar III rules as sole king of the Franks (—660)		
657			Pope Eugenius I d.; succeeded by Pope Vitalian (—672) Whitby Monastery founded
658	Wulfhere, son of Penda (see 654), becomes king of Mercia (—675) Moawita sets up Omayyad dynasty at Damascus		
659			
660	The Omayyads become caliphs		
661	Caliph Ali, nephew of Mohammed, murdered		
662	Grimoald usurps Lombard Crown		
663	Childeric II, king of Austrasia(—673) Last visit to Rome by a Byzantine Emperor (Constans II)		
664			Synod of Whitby, England, adopts Roman Catholic faith, King Oswiu of Northumbria decides in favor of Roman ritual Founding of St. Peter's, York, boys' public school
665			

D. VISUAL ARTS	E. MUSIC	F. SCIENCE, TECHNOLOGY, GROWTH	G. DAILY LIFE	
				654
				655
				656
				657
				658
				659
Islamic buildings in Omayyad style (—750, in Spain till 1000)				660
Founding of Ripon Monastery				661
				662
				663
			Plague outbreak in Saxon England	664
				665

	A. HISTORY, POLITICS	B. LITERATURE, THEATER	C. RELIGION, PHILOSOPHY, LEARNING
668	Constantine IV, Byzantine Emperor (—685)		The Buddhist priest Gyogi of Korea, who united in Japan Buddhism and Shintoism, b. (d. 749)
669	Theodore of Tarsus, Archbishop of Canterbury (—690), organizes Anglo-Roman church		
670	The Arabs attack in N. Africa		Codification of the law of the Visigoths in Spain Building of Quairawan Tower in Tunis Cross of St. Osyth at Ely
671		Caedmon, the earliest Eng.-Christian poet, b.	The Chin. Buddhist monk I-Tsing travels to India and Malaya (—695)
672	Wamba, king of the Visigoths (—680)		The Venerable Bede, Eng. monk and historian, b. (d. 735; recently canonized) Pope Vitalian d.; succeeded by Pope Adeodatus II (—676)
673	The death of Childeric II leads to civil war and anarchy in Frankish kingdom		First synod of the Eng. Church (Hertford) Founding of Ely Abbey Boniface, the "Apostle of the Germans," b. (d. 754)
674	The Arabs arrive at the Indus River	Hassan ibn Thabit, Mohammed's court poet, d.	Monasteries founded at Wearmouth and Jarrow
675	Lombard kings rule in Farentum (Apulia) Bulgarians settle in districts south of the Danube and found the first (eastern) Bulgarian empire		Baptistery St. Jean, Poitiers
676			Pope Donus (—678)
677			
678			Pope Agatho (—681)
679	Caliph Yezid I (—683)		

D. VISUAL ARTS	E. MUSIC	F. SCIENCE, TECHNOLOGY, GROWTH	G. DAILY LIFE	
				668
				669
Li-Chao-tao, Chin. landscape painter and son of the painter Li-ssu-Hsün, b.				670
			"Greek Fire," a missile weapon of sulfur, rock salt, resin, and petroleum invented by Kallinikos of Byzantium, used against the Arabs at the siege of Constantinople (—678)	671
				672
				673
Glass windows in Eng. churches				674
				675
				676
				677
				678
				679

	A. HISTORY, POLITICS	B. LITERATURE, THEATER	C. RELIGION, PHILOSOPHY, LEARNING
680	Wamba, king of the Visigoths, becomes a monk Hussain, son of Ali, killed fighting aginst Yezid	Aldhelm, the first Anglo-Saxon writer in verse and prose	Sixth Council of Constantinople (—681) condemns the Monothelites
681			Gloucester Abbey founded
682			Pope Leo II (—683)
683	Caliph Moawiyah II (—684)		
684	Caliph Abdelmelik (—705)		Pope Benedict II (—685)
685	Battle of Nechtansmere: victory of the Picts prevents Northumbrians gaining control over Scotland Eastern Roman Emperor Justinian II Rhinotmetus (—695)		Founding of Winchester Cathedral Pope John V (—686) "Ravenna Cosmography," a catalog of all known countries, towns, and rivers
686			Sussex, the last heathen kingdom in England, converted to Christianity Pope Conon (—687)
687	Egica, king of the Visigoths (—701) Victory of Pepin the Younger at Testry unites the Frankish kingdom; Carolingians become hereditary mayors of the palace		Pope Sergius I (—701) St. Kilian, Bishop of Würzburg, executes St. Cuthbert, Bishop of Lindisfarne
688	Ine, king of Wessex, subdues Essex and part of Kent Charles Martel (the "Hammer"), b. (d. 741)		
689			
690	Wihtred, king of Kent (—725)		
691	Clovis III becomes king of all the Franks (—695)		

D. VISUAL ARTS	E. MUSIC	F. SCIENCE, TECHNOLOGY, GROWTH	G. DAILY LIFE	
				680
Eastern pagoda of Yakashi Temple, Nara; wooden, earthquake-proof building				681
				682
				683
				684
				685
				686
				687
				688
				689
				690
				691

	A. HISTORY, POLITICS	B. LITERATURE, THEATER	C. RELIGION, PHILOSOPHY, LEARNING
692			The Quinisext Council at Constantinople, not recognized by Rome, settles the Biblical canon of the Eastern Church
693	The Arabs defeat Justinian II at Sebastopolis, Cilicia		
694	Arabs overrun Armenia		
695	Justinian II deposed by Leontius (—698) Childebert III, king of all the Franks (—711)		Persecution of the Jews in Spain Law code of King Wihtred
696	Paoluccio Anafesto becomes the first doge of Venice		Willibrord (657—739), the "Apostle of the Frisians," appointed Bishop of Utrecht by Pepin
697	The Arabs destroy Carthage		Northern Ir. Church submits to Roman Catholicism
698	Emperor Leontius (see 695) deposed by Tiberius III (—705)	Wang Wei, the Chin. poet and painter, b. (d. 759)	St. Rupert founds the Monastery of St. Peter's in Salzburg, Austria
699			
700	Thuringia becomes part of the Frankish empire The family of the Agilolfings, hereditary dukes of Bavaria, makes Ratisbon their capital Arabs conquer Algiers–Christianity in N. Africa almost exterminated	Bharavabhuti, the great Indian dramatist, last important poet of the classical era Dandin: "The Ten Princes," Indian humorous novel Omar ibn Abi Rabi'a, Arab poet, flourishes (d. 719) Greek, instead of Latin, becomes the official language of the Eastern Roman Empire	The Psalms translated into Anglo-Saxon The Lindisfarne Gospels, illuminated monastic manuscripts Easter eggs come into use among Christians
701		Li Po, the great Chin. poet, b. (d. 762)	Codification of Jap. political law; the Mikado becomes the sole proprietor of all land (—1192) Pope John VI (—705)
702			

D. VISUAL ARTS	E. MUSIC	F. SCIENCE, TECHNOLOGY, GROWTH	G. DAILY LIFE	
				692
				693
				694
			First Arab coinage	695
				696
				697
		Willibrord of Utrecht discovers the island of Heligoland		698
				699
Pagoda of Tsu-en Temple at Sian, China Wu-Tao-tzu, Chin. painter, b. c. (d. c. 760) Stone church buildings instead of wooden ones in England Arab desert castle at Mshatta, Transjordan Korean art achieves important position between Chinese and Japanese Cave temple at Ellora, western India Jokhang Temple at Lhasa, Tibet		Water wheels for mill drive in use all over Europe	Tapestry weaving well established in Peru Development of large landed property after the migration of nations; peasants become tributary or subject to soccage service Population explosion in China, the first large urban developments	700
				701
				702

	A. HISTORY, POLITICS	B. LITERATURE, THEATER	C. RELIGION, PHILOSOPHY, LEARNING
705	Empress Wou-Hou succeeds to Chin. throne but is forced to abdicate Justinian II becomes once more Byzantine Emperor (—711) Caliph Walid I (—715)		Pope John VII (—707) Circular church at Marienberg near Würzburg, built by Duke Hetan II Wells Cathedral founded The Great Mosque, Damascus
706			
707			
708			Pope Sisinius (Jan.—Feb.) succeeded by Pope Constantine (—715), the last pope to visit the emperor in Constantinople Jacob of Edessa d. (b. 640)
709			Aldhelm, Bishop of Sherborne, d.
710	The Bulgarians advance toward Constantinople Nara, after Fujiwara, becomes the capital of Japan China refuses to help the Kashgarians against the Arabs The reign of Walid I becomes the most brilliant in the history of the caliphate Ine's wars with the Britons of Cornwall Roderic, the last king of the Visigoths in Spain		Buddhist monasteries in Japan become centers of civilization Justinian II, the first to kiss the pope's foot, confirms the privileges of the Roman see
711	Justinian II murdered by Philip Bardanes, who as Emperor Philippicus ascends Byzantine throne Arab Gen. Tarik defeats King Roderic at Xeres de la Frontera, and Spain, with the exception of Asturias, becomes an Arab state Dagobert III, king of all the Franks (—716)		Span. Jews, freed by the Arabs, begin their cultural development
712	Height of the Lombard kingdom in northern Italy; King Liutprand (d. 744) The Arabs occupy Samarkand and make it a center of Islamic culture; here they learn the art of making paper Seville conquered by Arabs Moslem state established in Sind (India) by Muhammad ibn Kasim	"Kojiki," the first history of Japan, compiled Tu-Fu, Chin. poet, b. (d. 770)	Pope Constantine opposes the emperor on the question of the Monothelite heresy
713	Ming Huang, Emperor of China (—756); his court becomes a center of art and learning Anastasius II, Byzantine Emperor (—715)		
714			Founding of the Benedictine Abbey of Reichenau, at Lake Constance

D. VISUAL ARTS	E. MUSIC	F. SCIENCE, TECHNOLOGY, GROWTH	G. DAILY LIFE	
				705
				706
				707
				708
				709
			Sugar planted in Egypt	710
				711
				712
Chang Hsüan, court painter of Emperor Ming Huang, b. (d. 742)				713
				714

	A. HISTORY, POLITICS	B. LITERATURE, THEATER	C. RELIGION, PHILOSOPHY, LEARNING
715	The Moslem empire extends from the Pyrenees to China, with Damascus as its capital Emperor Theodosius III (—717) Charles Martel becomes mayor of the Frankish court		Pope Gregory II (—731) Benedictine monk Winfrith, the future St. Boniface, begins his missionary work among the Germans
716	The Arabs conquer Lisbon Chilperic II, king of Neustria (716—720) and of all the Franks (719—720) Duke Lantfrid issues Lex Alemannorum		
717	Leo III, the Isaurian, seizes the throne of Byzantium from Theodosius III and remains emperor (—741) Caliph Omar II (—720) grants tax exemption to all believers		
718	Leo III defends Constantinople for 13 months against the Arabs and destroys their fleet Pelagius founds the kingdom of the Asturias, Spain		
719			
720	The Moslems settle in Sardinia; their army crosses the Pyrenees into France, seizing Narbonne Caliph Yezid II Theodoric IV, king of the Franks	Period of Tchhouen-Khi heroic Chin. drama	"Nikongi," chronology of Jap. history Paulus Diaconus, Lombard historian, b. (d. 797) Glastonbury Abbey rebuilt by King Ine
721			
722			
723			
724	Caliph Hisham (—743)		

D. VISUAL ARTS	E. MUSIC	F. SCIENCE, TECHNOLOGY, GROWTH	G. DAILY LIFE	
The earliest extant Islamic paintings				715
Li Ssu-Hsün, Chin. landscape painter, d. (b. 651)				716
"Buddha with the Gods of the Sun and the Moon," above-life-size bronze sculpture in Nara				717
				718
				719
Opposition to the use of images in Byzantine churches–the Iconoclasts–official policy of Leo III and Constantine V		Abu Masa Dshaffar, famous Arab chemist who supposedly invented sulfuric acid, nitric acid, aqua regia, and nitrate of silver		720
				721
				722
				723
				724

	A. HISTORY, POLITICS	B. LITERATURE, THEATER	C. RELIGION, PHILOSOPHY, LEARNING
725	Chin. capital Ch'ang-an is the largest city in the world; Constantinople, the second largest While the Arabs ravage southern France, Charles Martel crosses the Rhine and conquers Bavaria		St. Boniface fells the famous Donar oak tree near Fritzlar, Hesse, thus destroying the old Germanic heathen beliefs Flower of Buddhist civilization in China
726	Ine, king of Wessex, begins the tax called Peter's pence to support a college at Rome		Image-worship controversy between the Byzantine Emperor and the pope
727			
728			St. Hubert, Bishop of Liège
729			
730	The dukedom of the Alemanni becomes part of the Frankish empire Pope Gregory II excommunicates the Byzantine emperor		Venerable Bede: "Historia ecclesiastica gentis Anglorum"
731			Pope Gregory III (—741)
732	Charles Martel's victory over the Arabs in the Battle of Tours and Poitiers stems the tide of their westward advance		The Pope appoints the future St. Boniface metropolitan of Germany beyond the Rhine
733			
734			

D. VISUAL ARTS	E. MUSIC	F. SCIENCE, TECHNOLOGY, GROWTH	G. DAILY LIFE	
	The court orchestra of Emperor Ming-Huang of China represents the high musical culture of the T'and dynasty: no harmony or polyphony, five-note scale without semitones; flutes, guitars, bells, gongs, drums		Casa Grande, an Indian fort and large irrigation works in Arizona	725
				726
				727
				728
				729
				730
				731
				732
				733
The Hachibushu dry-lacquer statues at Nara				734

	A. HISTORY, POLITICS	B. LITERATURE, THEATER	C. RELIGION, PHILOSOPHY, LEARNING
735	Charles Martel conquers Burgundy		Venerable Bede, Eng. historian and theologian who introduced the counting of dates before the birth of Christ, d. (b. 672) Egbert becomes Archbishop of York Alcuin, who after the death of Bede becomes England's most famous historian, b.
736			Founding of Benedictine abbey at Hersfeld, Hesse
737	Childeric III becomes king of all the Franks (—751)		
738			
739	Pope Gregory III asks Charles Martel for help against Lombards, Greeks, and Arabs		St. Boniface founds the bishoprics of Passau, Ratisbon, and Salzburg
740			St. Leodegar Monastery founded in Switzerland The oldest Western "Crucifixion" at the S. Quirico chapel of S. Maria Antiqua, Rome
741	Constantine V Copronymus succeeds to the throne of Byzantium (—775) and renews the prohibition of image worship Charles Martel dying, his son Pepin the Short becomes mayor of the Frankish court		Pope Zacharias (—752)
742	Charlemagne, son of Pepin the Short, b. (d. 814)		
743			
744	Caliph Mervan II, last of the Omayyads Swabia becomes part of Frankish Empire		
745	The Emperor Constantine V defeats the Arabs (—751) Pepin the Short fights the growing political influence of Boniface		

D. VISUAL ARTS	E. MUSIC	F. SCIENCE, TECHNOLOGY, GROWTH	G. DAILY LIFE	
				735
				736
				737
				738
				739
			Earthquake in Asia Minor	740
				741
				742
				743
	Singing school established at the Monastery of Fulda			744
				745

	A. HISTORY, POLITICS	B. LITERATURE, THEATER	C. RELIGION, PHILOSOPHY, LEARNING
748	Arab fleet destroyed during an attack on Cyprus Tassilo, last independent duke of Bavaria (—788)		
749	Aistulf, king of the Lombards (—757)		Gogi, Korean-Jap. Buddhist priest, d. (b. 668)
750	The dukedom of Bavaria extends to Carniola The Abbasids wipe out the Omayyads and obtain the caliphate (Abu-al-Abbas rules till 754) A time of darkness, profligacy, and misery precedes the age of Charlemagne The succession to the Byzantine throne is generally determined by violence and treachery End of Merovingian line in France: Childeric III deposed, Pepin the Short chosen king (—768)	Abu Nuwas, Arab poet, b. (d. 811) Symmetry and regularity in Chin. lyric (the "Golden Age" of poetry) Old High German the prevalent language in Germany till 11th century Earliest records of the existence of Tamil language	"Kamandaki," Indian manual on the art of government Heidenheim Monastery founded John of Damascus, Christian theologian, d. (b. c. 700)
751	In the Battle of Samarkand China loses western Asian dominion to the Arabs Aistulf takes Ravenna from Byzantium Pope Zacharias acknowledges election of Pepin		The four sects of Islam: Sunnites, Hafenites, Shafites, and Malikites
752	Cuthred of Wessex defeats Ethelbald at Burford		Pope Stephen II (752) dies the same year, and is succeeded by Pope Stephen III (—757)
753			
754	Pope Stephen III journeys to Pepin to ask for protection from the Lombards; Pepin helps with a large army and helps in creating the Papal states The Emperor Constantine V begins dissolution of monasteries Al Mansur becomes Caliph (—775)		St. Boniface murdered (b. 673)
755	Caliphate of Córdoba (—1031) founded by Abd-al-Rahman War between the Byzantine Empire and the Bulgarians		
756	Al Mansur sends military aid to Hsüan Tsung to crush rebellion in China after the Emperor Ming Huang resigned Pepin reduces Lombardy to vassal state		
757	Offa, king of Mercia (—796) Desiderius, the last king of the Lombards (—774)		Pope Stephen III d.; succeeded by his brother Pope Paul I (—767); both later canonized

D. VISUAL ARTS	E. MUSIC	F. SCIENCE, TECHNOLOGY, GROWTH	G. DAILY LIFE	
			The first printed newspaper appears in Peking	748
"The Neighing Stallion," famous small Chin. fire-clay sculpture				749
Shore Temple, Mamalhapuram: classic era of Indian art Hôriuji, pagoda, Japan Pueblo period in southwestern part of N. America (—900) Prime of Chin. paintings at court of Emperor Ming Huang The "Healing Buddha," gilded, dry-lacquer sculpture	Gregorian church music in Germany, France, and England Wind organs, coming from Byzantium, replace water organs	Prime of medicine, astronomy, mathematics, optics, and chemistry in Arab Spain Pharmacology and medicine become two separate sciences Founding of Hanlin Academy for the encouragement of Chin. arts and sciences (till 20th century)	Kiev becomes well known as fortress and trading center The Chin. royal stables contain about 40,000 horses, serving mostly for the game of polo Founding of Granada St. Vitus' dance epidemics in Germany Beds become popular in France and Germany Hops as beer wort used for the first time in Bavaria	750
Han Kan, Chin. painter of horses Wooden "Gigaku" masks in Japan			Chin. paper makers, captured at Samarkand, teach paper manufacture to Arabs	751
				752
				753
				754
				755
After the death of the Jap. Emperor Shomu all his household effects, furniture, mirrors, paintings, and jewels are dedicated to Buddha				756
				757

	A. HISTORY, POLITICS	B. LITERATURE, THEATER	C. RELIGION, PHILOSOPHY, LEARNING
759	The Franks get Narbonne back from the Arabs (see 720)		
760	Founding of Turkish Empire by a Tartar tribe in Armenia	"The Book of Kells," Latin gospels written in Irish, now at Trinity College, Dublin "Manyoshu," Jap. anthology of c. 4,500 short poems	The rock-cut temple of Kailasanatha, Ellora, India, begun by Krishna I
761			
762		Li Po, Chin. poet, d. (b. 701)	
763	Caliph al-Mansur moves his capital from Damascus to Baghdad		Founding of Benedictine monastery at Lorsch, Hesse
764			Benedictine abbey of Ottobeuren, Bavaria, founded
765	Tibetan army invades China Frankish royal court at Aix-la-Chapelle		Kasuga shrine, Nara, founded
766			Ethelbert and Alcuin make York a center of learning
767			Pope Constantine II, antipope (—768)
768	Pepin the Short d.; his kingdom is ruled by his two sons Charles (Charlemagne) and Carloman (—771)		Pope Stephen IV (—772)
769			
770		Tu Fu, Chin. poet, friend of Li Po, d. (b. 712)	Einhard, Frankish court diplomat and scholar, b. (d. 840)

D. VISUAL ARTS	E. MUSIC	F. SCIENCE, TECHNOLOGY, GROWTH	G. DAILY LIFE	
Wang Wei, Chin. painter and poet, d. (b. 698) Founding of Töshödai-ji Temple, Nara				759
		Arabic numerals of Indian origin known in Baghdad		760
				761
				762
				763
				764
		Pictorial book printing known in Japan		765
				766
				767
				768
				769
				770

	A. HISTORY, POLITICS	B. LITERATURE, THEATER	C. RELIGION, PHILOSOPHY, LEARNING
771	Charles becomes, after the death of his brother Carloman, sole ruler of the Frankish kingdom (—814): Charlemagne (Charles the Great)		
772	Charlemagne subdues Saxony under Widukind and converts it to Christianity (—804); imposition of tithes for the support of clergy, churches, schools, and the poor		Pope Hadrian I (—795) appeals to Charlemagne for help against the Lombards
773	Charlemagne annexes Lombard kingdom (—774)	Liu Tsung Yüan, Chin. essayist and poet, b. (d. 819)	
774	Offa subdues Kent and Wessex Charlemagne confirms Pepin's donation of territory to the pope, and enlarges it in 781		
775	Leo IV, Byzantine Emperor (—780) Tibet subdues Himalayan countries and concludes a boundary agreement with China Byzantine victory over the Bulgarians at Lithosoria		Caliph Mahdi (—785) institutes an inquisition
776			
777	Charlemagne, after his victory over the Saxons, holds his first Diet		Tassilo of Bavaria builds the Benedictine Abbey of Kremsmünster
778	Charlemagne defeated by the Basques at Roncesvalles in the Pyrenees (subject of the "Song of Roland") Louis I, the Pious, future Holy Roman Emperor (814—840), b.		
779	Offa of Mercia, king of all England		
780	Empress Irene becomes the virtual ruler of the Byzantine Empire (—802), and restores image worship		
781			The Nestorians, settled in China since 645, develop missionary activities and build Christian monasteries The "Wessobrunn Prayer," earliest Ger. ecclesiastical verse

D. VISUAL ARTS	E. MUSIC	F. SCIENCE, TECHNOLOGY, GROWTH	G. DAILY LIFE	
				771
				772
				773
		Euclid's "Elements" translated into Arabic		774
				775
				776
				777
				778
The earliest extant prints in Japan			"Ch'a Ching," the first Chin. handbook of tea	779
				780
				781

	A. HISTORY, POLITICS	B. LITERATURE, THEATER	C. RELIGION, PHILOSOPHY, LEARNING
782	Charlemagne executes 4500 Saxon hostages at Verden, and issues the "Capitulatio de partibus Saxoniae"		Alcuin leaves monastery at York (see 735) to aid Charlemagne's revival of learning Godescalc: "Evangelistary," Ada-school manuscript (Aix-la-Chapelle)
783			
784		Hrabanus Maurus, Ger. poet and scholar, b. (d. 856)	
785			Saxon Duke Widukind baptized Cologne becomes an archbishopric
786	Cynewulf, king of the West Saxons (—757) d. Caliph Harun al-Rashid (—809)	Han-Yü, Chin. essayist and poet, b. (d. 824)	
787	First Dan. invasion of Britain Charlemagne annexes Lombard duchy of Beneventum		Seventh Council of Nicaea regulates image worship Offa creates archbishopric of Lichfield
788	Charlemagne deposes Tassilo of Bavaria and annexes his country The Slovenes settle in Carniola Idris establishes a Shiite kingdom in Morocco		
789	Constantine I, king of Scotland (—820)		
790			Offa founds St. Albans Abbey "Libri Carolini" on image worship Alcuin appointed principal of Frankish court school Golden period of Arabic learning during reign of Harun al-Rashid
791	The Byzantine Emperor Constantine imprisons his mother Irene for her cruelty		

D. VISUAL ARTS	E. MUSIC	F. SCIENCE, TECHNOLOGY, GROWTH	G. DAILY LIFE	
		Construction of Offa's Dyke against Welsh attacks on Mercia The great Arab scientist Jabir (b. 722) begins his chemical studies, as distinct from alchemy		782
				783
				784
Building of the Mosque of Cordoba begins (—990)				785
				786
				787
				788
				789
	Schools for church music established at Paris, Cologne, Soissons, and Metz, all under the supervision of the Schola Cantorum in Rome			790
				791

	A. HISTORY, POLITICS	B. LITERATURE, THEATER	C. RELIGION, PHILOSOPHY, LEARNING
792	Irene regains power Beginning of the Viking era in Britain Vikings attack the Eng. island monastery of Lindisfarne		Building of Fulda Cathedral begins
793	East Anglia annexed to Mercia by Offa		
794			Charlemagne condemns image worship at the Synod of Frankfurt
795	Revolts in Egypt Charlemagne forms the Spanish march Lothar I, eldest son of the future Emperor Louis I, the Pious, b. The Northmen land in Ireland	Cynewulf, Anglo-Saxon poet, author of "Elena," "Juliana," "Christ," and "Fates of the Apostles": all preserved in 10th-century manuscript	Pope Leo III (—816)
796	Offa, king of Mercia, d.; succeeded by Cenwulf (—821) After his victory over the Avars, Charlemagne's son Pepin founds the Avar march with an archbishopric at Salzburg		The monastery school at Tours becomes a university with Alcuin as its head
797	The Byzantine Empress Irene overthrows her son Constantine, blinds him, assumes sole power, and reportedly proposes to marry Charlemagne (the Greek Church canonized her)		Flowering of Korean civilization Paulus Diaconus, Lombard historian, d. (b. 720)
798	Cenwulf of Mercia subdues Kent		
799	Charlemagne conquers and destroys Adriatic port of Fiume		
800	Charlemagne crowned first Holy Roman Emperor by Pope Leo III at Rome, Dec. 25 (the new empire of the West, as opposed to the Byzantine or Eastern Roman Empire) Rajputs occupy Kana Uj in northern India, setting up a kingdom that extends from Bihar to the Sutlej River Invasion of Bohemia by the Franks Slav tribes migrate into districts around the Oder, the Havel, and the Spree Rivers and the Ore mountains Harun al-Rashid sends an embassy to the court of Charlemagne Northmen invade Germany	The "Hildebrandsleid," important Old High German poem Earliest records of Persian poetry and literature Development of miniscule handwriting at Charlemagne's scholastic institutions	Pope Leo III separates from the Eastern Empire and becomes supreme bishop of the West Charlemagne reforms the Church and adopts at the Synod of Aix-la-Chapelle the "Filioque"
801		Bragi, the oldest known Norw. poet	

D. VISUAL ARTS	E. MUSIC	F. SCIENCE, TECHNOLOGY, GROWTH	G. DAILY LIFE	
				792
			Founding of Heian (later Kyoto), Japan Tea tax introduced in China	793
			Jap. capital moved (—1867) from Nara to Heian (Kyoto) State-owned paper mills established in Baghdad	794
				795
Charlemagne builds the Palatine Chapel at Aix-la-Chapelle				796
			Horse-changing posts for royal messengers installed in France	797
				798
				799
Li Chen paints five portraits of saints (T'ang period) "Sitting Buddha," Jap. wooden sculpture, Heian period	Poems sung to music at Charlemagne's court	Irish travelers reach Iceland, and the Northmen discover the Faroe Islands The city of Machu Picchu in Peru (rediscovered, 1911)		800
			Charlemagne prohibits prostitution	801

	A. HISTORY, POLITICS	B. LITERATURE, THEATER	C. RELIGION, PHILOSOPHY, LEARNING
802	Nicephorus I becomes Byzantine Emperor (—810), dethroning Irene Egbert, formerly an Eng. refugee at the court of Charlemagne, establishes himself as king of Wessex (—839) The Vikings dominate Ireland		Germanic tribal laws codified by order of Charlemagne Founding of the Münster Monastery with St. Ludger as bishop (—809)
803	Bulgarians free themselves from Tatar dominance Byzantine Empire recognizes independence of Venice		End of archbishopric of Lichfield; Canterbury restored as metropolitan see
804	Charlemagne's last war against Saxons; his domain extends now to the Elbe The future Louis the German, king of the East Franks (843—876), b.		Alcuin d. (b. 735)
805		Gottschalk, Ger. theologian and poet, b. (d. 870)	
806	Monastery of Iona sacked by Northmen		Lex Frisionum for the Frisians occupying 350 miles of marshy coastland
807	War between the Franks and the Eastern Empire		
808			
809	Bulgarians conquer Sofia Caliph al-Amin (—813) succeeds Harun al-Rashid		
810	King Godfred of Denmark d. Krum, king of Bulgaria, defeats and kills the Emperor Nicephorus I Michael I Rangabe, Byzantine Emperor (—813)		The Welsh monk Nynniaw writes his "Historia Britonum" Johannes Scotus Erigena, Irish scholar in Paris, b. (d. 877)
811		Abu Nuwas, Arab poet, d. (b. 750)	
812			

D. VISUAL ARTS	E. MUSIC	F. SCIENCE, TECHNOLOGY, GROWTH	G. DAILY LIFE	
			First planting of rose trees in Europe	802
Mosaics in Church of St. Germain-des-Prés				803
			Magdeburg becomes important trade center at the Slav frontier	804
				805
				806
				807
			Fez becomes capital of Morocco	808
				809
Mosque of Mulai Idris at Fez		Persian scientist and mathematician Muhammed ibn Musa al Chwarazmi writes a book on equations and coins the term "algebra"		810
				811
				812

	A. HISTORY, POLITICS	B. LITERATURE, THEATER	C. RELIGION, PHILOSOPHY, LEARNING
813	Charlemagne crowns his son Louis the Pious at the diet of Aix-la-Chapelle Leo V, the Armenian, becomes Byzantine Emperor (—820) Caliph Mamun (—833): his reign considered the Augustan age of Arabian literature and science		Al-Kindi, Arabian philosopher, b (d. 870) The Synod of Mainz decrees four days public Christmas celebrations
814	Charlemagne d.; succeeded by his son Louis the Pious (—840)		
815	Egbert of Wessex defeats the Britons of Cornwall		
816			Pope Stephen V (—817) Abbot Gosbert founds the library at St. Gallen
817	Louis the Pious divides France among his sons: Lothar becomes coregent, Louis receives Bavaria, Pepin Aquitania		Pope Paschal I (—824) Pactum Hludovicianum confirms papal territory
818			
819		Liu Tsung-yüan, Chin. poet, d. (b. 773)	
820	Michael II, the Amorian, Byzantine Emperor (—829): end of Syrian, beginning of Phrygian, dynasty Dismemberment of Abbassid caliphate, founding of Taherite dynasty at Khurasan	"Heliand" epic	
821	Cenwulf of Mercia d.–end of Mercian supremacy in England		
822	Abd-al-Rahmam, Caliph of Córdoba (—852)		Hrabanus Maurus becomes Abbot of Fulda
823			

D. VISUAL ARTS	E. MUSIC	F. SCIENCE, TECHNOLOGY, GROWTH	G. DAILY LIFE	
		School of Astronomy at Baghdad		813
Building of Doge's Palace, Venice begun		Arabs take over Indian numerals, including zero, to multiply by ten	Retrogression of Western Empire in political and social importance begins after Charlemagne's death	814
				815
				816
				817
				818
				819
				820
				821
				822
				823

	A. HISTORY, POLITICS	B. LITERATURE, THEATER	C. RELIGION, PHILOSOPHY, LEARNING
824	Constitutio Romana confirms imperial control of Rome Egbert subdues and unites Eng. part-states		Pope Eugenius II (—827) Han Yü, Chin. Confucian poet who actively fought Buddhism, d. (b. 786)
825	Battle of Ellandum: Mercia defeated by Egbert The Saracens in Crete		Pavia becomes center of science and literature
826	The Arabs conquer Crete and plunder from there to the Greek islands King Harold of Denmark, baptized at Mainz, returns to his country with missionary monk Ansgar (801—865) who spreads Christianity in Scandinavia		
827	Arab conquest of Sicily and Sardinia begins		Pope Valentine rules for 40 days and is succeeded by Pope Gregory IV (—844)
828	Egbert of Wessex recognized as overlord of the "Seven Kingdoms of the Heptarchy"		Founding of St. Mark's, Venice
829	Theophilus, Byzantine Emperor (—842) King Louis the Pious invests his six-year-old son Charles (the Bald) with the dukedom of Swabia	"Annales Regni Francorum," the official chronology of Fr. history, concluded	
830	Prince Moimir founds the Great Moravian Empire, and rules it till 846	Louis the Pious destroys the collection of Ger. epics started by his father Charlemagne	Wilfrid rebuilds Hereford Cathedral in stone Caliph Mamun founds the Academy of Translations at Baghdad
831		Einhard: "Vita Caroli Magni" (written in his retirement)	Bishopric of Hamburg, founded by Ansgar, raised to an archbishopric in 832 Founding of Venetian Order of Chivalry St. Mark
832	Caliph Mamun invades Egypt Kenneth MacAlpin, king of Kintyre, of the Scots (839), and of the Picts (844)		Persecution of the image worshipers in the Eastern Empire
833	Caliph Motassim, the builder of Samarra, the new seat of government King Louis I defeated by his three sons at Colmar and deposed		
834	The Danes raid England King Louis I restored to his throne (see 833)		
835			

D. VISUAL ARTS	E. MUSIC	F. SCIENCE, TECHNOLOGY, GROWTH	G. DAILY LIFE	
				824
Japan imports Buddhist paintings of the T'ang era from China				825
				826
				827
		The "Astronomical System" of Ptolemy (d. c. 178) translated into Arabic as "Almagest"		828
				829
				830
				831
"Utrecht Psalter" written at Rheims, richly illustrated				832
				833
				834
				835

	A. HISTORY, POLITICS	B. LITERATURE, THEATER	C. RELIGION, PHILOSOPHY, LEARNING
837	New division of the Frankish Empire between King Louis the Pious and his son Lothar I War between Wessex and the Danes		
838	Arabs sack Marseilles and settle in southern Italy; in battle at Amorion, Asia Minor, they defeat the Byzantine army		
839	Ethelwulf, king of England (—858) Charles III, the Fat, youngest son of Louis the German and grandson of Charlemagne, future Frankish king and emperor, b.		
840	Louis I, the Pious, Frankish emperor d. (see 814); succeeded by Lothar I (—855) Moimir forms confederation of Slavs in Bohemia, Moravia, Slovakia, Hungary, and Transylvania		Paschasius Radbertus, Abbot of Corbey, father of the doctrine of transubstantiation Einhard, scholar of the court of Charlemagne, d. (b. 770)
841	Lothar I defeated by his two brothers Louis and Charles in the battle of Fontenoy The Northmen plunder Rouen and advance to Paris Halfdan of Norway subjects the nobles and founds the monarchy		
842	Caliph Wathik (—847) Michael III, the Drunkard, Byzantine Emperor (—867) Turkish mercenaries join Arab armies	The Oaths of Strasbourg begin separation of Fr. and Lat. languages	Image worship reestablished Walafried Strabo (808—849), Abbot of Reichenau, writes his "Glossa ordinaria" to the Bible
843	Treaty of Verdun, division of the Frankish empire: Lothar receives Italy and Lorraine and remains Emperor; France goes to Charles II, the Bald; Germany, to Louis I, the German Three Carolingian dynasties: German (—911), French (—987), Italian (—875)		
844	Kenneth, king of the Scots, defeats the Picts and becomes sole monarch		Pope Sergius II (—847)
845	Northmen destroy Hamburg and penetrate into Germany	Abu Tammâm: "Hamâsa," collection of Arabian legends, proverbs, and heroic stories	Vivian Bible, one of the earliest illustrated manuscripts, written in Tours Buddhist persecution in China Johannes Scotus Erigena appointed head of palace school of Charles the Bald Bremen becomes archbishopric in place of Hamburg
846	The Arabs sack Rome and damage the Vatican Venetian fleet destroyed by Arabs Moimir I, prince of Moravia, d. and is succeeded by Rostislav		
847	Caliph Mottawakkil (—860)		Pope Leo IV (—855)

D. VISUAL ARTS	E. MUSIC	F. SCIENCE, TECHNOLOGY, GROWTH	G. DAILY LIFE	
				837
				838
				839
			Dan. settlers found Dublin and Limerick	840
				841
				842
				843
				844
			Paper money in China leads to inflation and state bankruptcy	845
				846
				847

	A. HISTORY, POLITICS	B. LITERATURE, THEATER	C. RELIGION, PHILOSOPHY, LEARNING
848			Pope Leo IV builds Leonine Wall around the Vatican hill to protect it from attack
849	Alfred the Great b. (d. 899)		
850	Bulgarian Empire on the Volga, with capital Bolgary Rurik, a Northman, becomes ruler of Kiev; his compatriots begin, along the waterways of Russia, to trade with Constantinople and the Khazans Tibetan power collapses	"The Edda," mythological poem (discovered 1643) Photius (820—893), Patriarch of Constantinople; his "Bibliotheça" extracts from ancient lost books	Groups of Jews settle in Germany and begin to develop their own language: Yiddish
851	Dan. forces enter Thames estuary, land and march on Canterbury; they are defeated by Ethelwulf at Oakley		Johannes Scotus Erigena: "De divina praedestinatione"
852			Mahomet I, Caliph of Córdoba (—886)
853	War between Charles the Bald and Louis of Germany		Founding of Gandersheim Abbey and Essen Minster
854			
855	Lothar I, emperor since 840, divides his empire among his three sons: Louis II receives Italy with the imperial crown; Charles, Provence and southern Burgundy; Lothar II, Lorraine (Lotharingia–named after him)		Pope Benedict III (—858) King Ethelwulf of Wessex begins to raise Peter's pence and goes with his son Alfred on pilgrimage to Rome
856	End of Lombard reign in Tarento Ethelbald's rebellion against his father Ethelwulf		Hrabanus Maurus, Ger. poet and scholar, d. (b. 784)
857			

D. VISUAL ARTS	E. MUSIC	F. SCIENCE, TECHNOLOGY, GROWTH	G. DAILY LIFE	
				848
				849
Construction of the Acropolis of Zimbabwe, Rhodesia	Origin of the Church modes, leading c. 750 years later to major and minor scales	Founding of Salerno University Astrolabe perfected by the Arabs The Arabian goatherd Kaldi credited with the discovery of coffee		850
Canterbury Cathedral sacked by Danes (rebuilt c. 950)			Earthquake in Rome Crossbow comes into use in France	851
				852
Kudara Kuwanari, the first important Jap. painter, d.				853
				854
Fresco "Ascension of Christ" at lower Church of St. Clement, Rome	Earliest known attempts at polyphonic music			855
				856
Building of wooden Ko Fuang Temple at Shansi, China			First reports of ergotism epidemics in western Europe, caused by poisoned grain	857

	A. HISTORY, POLITICS	B. LITERATURE, THEATER	C. RELIGION, PHILOSOPHY, LEARNING
858	King Ethelwulf d.; succeeded by his son Ethelbert (—865) The two sons of the Emperor Buntoku wrestle for their father's throne, the victor Koreshito becoming ruler of Japan Vikings sack Algeciras, but are expelled by the Arabs		Johannes Scotus Erigena translates Dionysius the Areopagite into Latin Pope Nicholas I (—867)
859	Norse pirates enter the Mediterranean and sack the coast up to Asia Minor Ashot I founds Bagratide dynasty in Armenia		
860	Kenneth I MacAlpine d., the first king of united Scotland Gorm the Elder, after uniting Jutland and the Dan. isles, becomes king of Denmark		The False Decretals forged to defend the rights of diocesan bishops against their metropolitans and to claim early authority for papal supremacy
861	Paris, Toulouse, Cologne, Aix-la-Chapelle, and Worms sacked by the Northmen		"Codex aureus" at St. Emmeram, Ratisbon
862	Rurik, the first Russian grand prince, founds Novgorod		Servatus Lupus, Abbot of Ferrières, scholar, d. Rostislav, ruler of Moravia, asks the Byzantine Emperor Michael III to send missionaries to his country
863	Constantine II, son of Kenneth I, king of Scotland (—877)		Cyril and Methodius, the "Apostles of the Slavs," start their work in Moravia and invent a Slavic alphabet—the Cyrillic
864			Prince Boris I of Bulgaria accepts Christianity
865	The Russian Northmen attack Constantinople Ethelbert I, king of England, d.; succeeded by Ethelred (—871) The Danes occupy Northumbria		
866	The Danes establish a kingdom in York		
867	Basil I, Byzantine Emperor (—886), begins the Macedonian dynasty and the compilation of the Basilian code		Pope Hadrian II (—872)
868	Tulunid dynasty in Egypt (—935)	Otfrid von Wessenburg: "Diatessaron," Ger. epic poem	

D. VISUAL ARTS	E. MUSIC	F. SCIENCE, TECHNOLOGY, GROWTH	G. DAILY LIFE	
				858
				859
			Founding of Angkor Thom, city in Cambodia	860
		Iceland discovered by the Northmen		861
				862
				863
				864
				865
				866
				867
				868

	A. HISTORY, POLITICS	B. LITERATURE, THEATER	C. RELIGION, PHILOSOPHY, LEARNING
869	Malta captured by the Arabs		Eighth Council of Constantinople (—870) Jahiz, the great Arab scholar, d.
870	Partition of Lorraine agreed upon in the Treaty of Mersen between Charles the Bald and Louis II The Danes occupy East Anglia, kill its last king, St. Edmund, and destroy Peterborough Monastery	Gottschalk, the Ger. poet, d. (b. 805)	Al-Farabi, Arab philosopher, b. (d. 950) Al-Kindi, Arab philosopher and mathematician, d. (b. 813)
871	Alfred the Great, king of England (—899)		
872	Harold Haarfagr makes himself king of Norway		Pope John VIII (—882)
873			First church built on the site of Cologne Cathedral
874	The Northmen settle in Iceland Popular uprising against Chin. T'ang dynasty		
875	Charles the Bald crowned emperor		
876	Charles III, the Fat, becomes emperor (—887)		
877	Egypt annexes Damascus Louis II, the Stammerer, king of France (—879) Mercia partitioned between the English and Danes		Johannes Scotus Erigena, philosopher, d. (b. 810)
878	The Arabs conquer the whole of Sicily from Byzantium and make Palermo the capital King Alfred recaptures London from the Danes and defeats them at Edington: Treaty of Chippenham		
879	France partitioned: Louis III, king of the North, his brother Carloman, king of the South Nepal gains independence from Tibet Kingdom of the Arelate under Count Boso Rurik of Novgorod d.; succeeded by Oleg, who becomes prince of Kiev		The pope and the patriarch of Constantinople excommunicate each other Ibn Tulun, the oldest mosque in Cairo, built

D. VISUAL ARTS	E. MUSIC	F. SCIENCE, TECHNOLOGY, GROWTH	G. DAILY LIFE	
				869
	"Musica enchiriadis," a musical manuscript using Lat. letters for musical notation	Johannes Scotus Erigena compiles his encyclopedia on nature	Calibrated candles used in England for the first time to measure the time	870
				871
				872
		Honain ibn Iszhak, great Arab physician, d.		873
				874
				875
				876
			The Edict of Quierzy makes fiefs hereditary in France	877
		The Arab astronomer al-Battani begins his observations		878
				879

	A. HISTORY, POLITICS	B. LITERATURE, THEATER	C. RELIGION, PHILOSOPHY, LEARNING
880	The Emperor Basil reconquers Italy from the Arabs Treaty of Ribemont: Charles III cedes Lorraine to Louis II		Founding of Benedictine monastery, Monserrat, in Catalonia
881	Constantine II of Scotland, defeated and killed by the Danes, succeeded by King Eocha (—889) Louis III defeats Northmen at Saucourt Charles III crowned emperor Burgos built as fortress against Arabs	The "Ludwigslied," first Ger. ballad	
882			Pope Marinus I (—884)
883		Notker Balbulus (c. 840—912): "Gesta Caroli," epic poem on the deeds of Charlemagne	
884	The Emperor Charles III becomes king of France (—887) and once more unites the empire of Charlemagne		Pope Hadrian VI (—885)
885	Northmen besiege Paris Ashot I of Armenia assumes title of king		King Alfred translates Gregory's "Cura pastoralis" into English Pope Stephen VI (—891)
886	The Emperor Basil I d.; succeeded by Leo VI, the Wise King Alfred gives London and Eng. Mercia to his son-in-law Ethelred		
887	Charles III, deposed, is succeeded as emperor by Arnulf of Carinthia (—899), who fights the Slavs and Northmen Final separation of Germany and France		
888	Charles III d. Odo, count of Paris, becomes king of France (d. 898) Berengar of Friuli becomes king of Italy (—924) Abdallah, Caliph of Córdoba (—912) The Arabs occupy Garde-Freinet on the coast of Provence	Thjodolf's "Ynglinga-Tal" and Thorbjorn's "Haralds-mal," two Norw. poems	
889	Donald I, king of Scotland (—900)		Ibn Koteiba, Arab scholar and historian, d. (b. 828)
890	Alfred the Great establishes a regular militia and navy, extends the power of the king's courts, and institutes fairs and markets	"Taketori Monogatari" ("the story of a bamboo gatherer"), earliest Jap. narrative work "Cantilène de Ste-Eulalie," earliest Fr. poem	Reliquary of the tooth of John, Carolingian jewel

D. VISUAL ARTS	E. MUSIC	F. SCIENCE, TECHNOLOGY, GROWTH	G. DAILY LIFE	
				880
				881
				882
				883
				884
		Ibn Khordadhbeh: "The Book of the Roads and Countries"		885
				886
				887
				888
	Regino, Abbot of Prüm, writes his treatise on church music: "De harmonica institutione"			889
Kose no Kanaoka, Jap. painter at the court of Heian	Ratbert of St. Gallen, hymn writer and composer, d.			890

	A. HISTORY, POLITICS	B. LITERATURE, THEATER	C. RELIGION, PHILOSOPHY, LEARNING
891	Emperor Arnulf defeats Northmen at Louvain		Pope Formosus (—896) "Anglo-Saxon Chronicle" (—1154)
892			
893	Charles the Simple, king of France (—929) The Danes renew their attacks on England but are defeated		Asser, Bishop of Sherborne: "Life of Alfred the Great"
894	King Svatopluk of Moravia d. Gradual ending of the close political and cultural connection between Japan and China Emperor Arnulf marches to Italy		
895	Alfred defeats and captures Dan. fleet on the Lea River Expelled from southern Russia, the Magyars under Arpad settle in Hungary The Fujiwaras become the ruling family in Japan (—1192)		Earliest Hebrew manuscript of the Old Testament
896			Pope Stephen VII (—897)
897	War between the Bulgarians and the Saracens		Pope Romanus (—898)
898			Pope Theodore (dies in a few months) John of Tivoli, a non-Roman, becomes Pope John IX (—900)
899	Alfred the Great d. Edward the Elder, king of England (—924) Louis III, the Child, Ger. king (—911) Germany invaded by the Hungarians		
900	Beginning of the Christian reconquest of Spain under Alfonso III, the Great, of Castile Founding of the Bohemian fortress of Wrotizlav (later Breslau) The Mayas relinquish their settlements in the lowlands of Mexico and emigrate to the Yucatan peninsula The Czechs assert their authority over all Bohemian tribes Constantine III, king of Scotland (—942) England divided into shires, with county courts as the safeguard of the civil rights of the inhabitants Constantinople still the first city in the world, its commercial and cultural center	Farces make their first appearance The beginnings of the famous Arabian tales "A Thousand and One Nights" Sixth period of Chin. literature begins (—1900) The Jewish Book of Creation: "Sepher Yetzirah"	Pope Benedict IV (—903) Abû Tabari (838—923), the Arab scholar and compiler of Koran commentaries

D. VISUAL ARTS	E. MUSIC	F. SCIENCE, TECHNOLOGY, GROWTH	G. DAILY LIFE	
				891
				892
				893
				894
				895
				896
				897
				898
				899
Second Pueblo period in southwestern part of America produces houses built entirely above ground The monk Tutilo of St. Gallen, one of the great artistic personalities of his time (d. 909) Period of the Oseberg art (wood carvings, sleighs, carts, tools, implements) Islamic ornamentation (arabesques) develops from late Greek and Byzantine elements The time of the great Chin. landscape *(contd)*	Beginnings of part song in fourths, fifths, and octaves, not to be confused with polyphony (see 855) Development of the neumes in musical notation	The Arab physician Rhases mentions as infectious diseases: plague, consumption, smallpox, rabies–and describes them Founding of the medical school of Salerno Vikings have developed the art of shipbuilding Vikings discover Greenland Paper manufacturing at Cairo	Castles become the seats of the European nobility	900

	A. HISTORY, POLITICS	B. LITERATURE, THEATER	C. RELIGION, PHILOSOPHY, LEARNING
900 contd			
901	Edward the Elder takes the title "King of the Angles and Saxons" Emperor Louis III, the Blind, king of Lower Burgundy (—905) Beginning of Samanid rule in Persia		
902			
903			Pope Leo V, deposed in a month Pope Christopher, antipope (—904)
904	Salonika sacked by Moslem pirates Russians again attack Constantinople		With Pope Sergius III (—911) begins the era of pornocracy, the darkest period in the history of the papacy; his mistress Marozia becomes the mother of Pope John XI (931—936), the aunt of John XIII (965—972), and the grandmother of Benedict VI (973—974) Ibn Doreid (837—933): "Manual of Genealogy and Etymology"
905	The Tulunid dynasty of Egypt deposed County of Navarre made kingdom	"Kokinshu," the official imperial anthology of Jap. poetry of the preceding 150 years	
906			
907	The Magyars destroy the Moravian empire and undertake raids into Germany and Italy Epoch of the Five Dynasties in China (—960)		
908			
909	Rise of the Fatimid dynasty in Kairouan, N. Africa		

D. VISUAL ARTS	E. MUSIC	F. SCIENCE, TECHNOLOGY, GROWTH	G. DAILY LIFE	
painter Ching Hao (855—915) The Buddhist temples of Nara become the focal points of Jap. art Jaina rock temple of Ellora, India				900 contd
				901
Work begins on the Campanile of St. Mark's, Venice (collapses in 1902)				902
				903
				904
				905
				906
			Commercial treaties between Kiev and Constantinople	907
				908
				909

	A. HISTORY, POLITICS	B. LITERATURE, THEATER	C. RELIGION, PHILOSOPHY, LEARNING
910	The name of León given to the kingdom of Asturias The Byzantine emperor pays tributes to the Magyars Ethelred of Mercia d., and his brother-in-law Edward the Elder takes possession of London and Oxford		Founding of the Benedictine Abbey of Cluny
911	Treaty of St. Clair-sur-Epte establishes dukedom of Normandy, with Rouen as capital and Robert I (Rollo) as duke (—931) Lorraine transfers allegiance from Germany to France The Carolingians dying out, the empire becomes elective, with Conrad I as king		Pope Anastasius III (—913)
912	Constantine VII, Byzantine Emperor (d. 959) Valley of the Thames annexed by Wessex Abd-al-Rahman III of Córdoba, greatest of the Arab caliphs of Spain–zenith of Omayyad rule (d. 961)	Notker Balbulus, poet and hymn writer, d. (b. c. 840)	
913	Edward the Elder recaptures Essex from the Danes Symeon of Bulgaria invades Thrace and Macedonia but fails to take Constantinople		Pope Lando (—914); hereafter, no Pope assumes a name not used by a predecessor, thus, John XXIII, Gregory XII, Benedict XV, and so on
914			Pope John X (—928)
915	Egypt invaded from Tunisia by Fatimid armies Berengar of Italy crowned emperor	Mutanabi, Arab poet, b. (d. 965)	Abbey church of Cluny consecrated
916	Renewed Dan. attacks on Ireland Arabs expelled from central Italy		"Codex Babylonicus Petzopolitanus" Synod of Hohen-Altheim, a papal delegate presiding
917	Symeon I assumes the title "Czar of the Bulgarians and Greeks"		Bulgarian Church separates from Rome and Constantinople
918			
919	Henry, duke of Saxony, becomes Ger. king (—936) Romanus I Lecapenus, coregent with Constantine VII Byzantine Empire extended to Euphrates and Tigris		
920			

D. VISUAL ARTS	E. MUSIC	F. SCIENCE, TECHNOLOGY, GROWTH	G. DAILY LIFE	
				910
				911
				912
Ethelfleda, daughter of Alfred the Great, erects the great earthen mound of Warwick Castle				913
				914
				915
				916
				917
				918
				919
				920

	A. HISTORY, POLITICS	B. LITERATURE, THEATER	C. RELIGION, PHILOSOPHY, LEARNING
921			The Bohemians embrace Christianity
922	Robert, duke of Francia, antiking in France (—923)		
923	Robert defeated and killed at Soissons, succeeded as antiking by Rudolph II of Burgundy		
924	Symeon devastates Greece and again threatens Constantinople Edward the Elder d.		
925	King Henry I conquers Lorraine Athelstan becomes king of England (—940)	Ekkehard of St. Gallen writes the epic poem "Walter of Aquitaine" The dialogue of The Three Maries and the Angels is performed at many churches on Easter morning (beginnings of the Easter play)	
926	Athelstan drives Guthfrith out of Northumbria and annexes his realm; the kings of Wales, of Strathclyde, of the Picts and Scots, submit to him Hugh of Vienne, king of Italy (—945)		
927	Peter, Czar of Bulgaria (—968)		Odo, Abbot of Cluny, establishes his code of discipline for Benedictines
928	King Henry I conquers the Slav province of Brennabor (Brandenburg)		Pope Leo VI (—929)
929	Henry subdues Bohemia and the Slavs east of the Elbe River Founding of Meissen in Saxony Zurich mentioned After the death of Charles the Simple, Rudolph becomes sole ruler of France Wenceslas of Bohemia murdered by reactionaries led by his brother Boleslav I		Pope Stephen VIII (—931)
930			

D. VISUAL ARTS	E. MUSIC	F. SCIENCE, TECHNOLOGY, GROWTH	G. DAILY LIFE	
				921
				922
		Rhases, the great Arab physician, d.		923
"Concert at the Palace," Chin. picture showing contemporary costumes and musical instruments				924
				925
				926
				927
				928
		Al-Battani, famous Arab astronomer, d.		929
			Córdoba becomes the seat of Arab learning, science, commerce, and industry in Spain	930

	A. HISTORY, POLITICS	B. LITERATURE, THEATER	C. RELIGION, PHILOSOPHY, LEARNING
931	Ramiro II, king of León William Longsword, duke of Normandy (—942) Abd-al-Rahman takes Ceuta from the Berbers		Pope John XI (—936)
932			
933	King Henry defeats Hungarians at Merseburg King Harold I Haarfagr of Norway d.		
934	Eric Blodöxe, king of Norway; his cruelty leads to revolts Henry I acquires Schleswig marches		
935	Harold Bluetooth, first Christian king of Denmark (—986) Fernan Gonzales, count of Castile (—970) Wang Chien establishes central monarchy in China Algiers founded by Arabs	Roswitha of Gandersheim, Ger. nun and playwright, b. (d. c. 1000)	
936	King Henry I d.; succeeded by his son Otto I the Great (—973) Louis IV, king of France (—954) Dynasty of Hou-Chin in China (—947)		Pope Leo VII (—939)
937	Battle of Brunanburh: Athelstan defeats Danes, Scots, and Strathclyde Britons		
938	Khitans leave the Old Chin. capital on the Liaotung peninsula and establish new capital of Yenching, later called Peking Louis IV tries in vain to invade Lorraine Rebellions in Franconia and Bavaria against Otto I		Athelstan founds Milton Abbey, Dorset
939	The Arabs lose Madrid to the kingdom of León Revolts against imperial rule set off a period of civil war in Japan (—1185) Abd-al-Rahman defeated by Ramiro II in the Battle of Simancas	Firdausi, Persian poet, b. (d. 1020)	Pope Stephen IX (—942)
940	Edmund I, brother of Athelstan, becomes king of England		
941	Russian fleet attack on Constantinople repulsed The Danes in England make war on Edmund I Berengar refugee at the court of Otto I (—945)		

D. VISUAL ARTS	E. MUSIC	F. SCIENCE, TECHNOLOGY, GROWTH	G. DAILY LIFE	
				931
				932
				933
				934
				935
Beginning of the "Ottonian period" in architecture				936
				937
				938
				939
		Abü'l Wefa, Arab mathematician and astronomer, b. (d. 998)		940
				941

	A. HISTORY, POLITICS	B. LITERATURE, THEATER	C. RELIGION, PHILOSOPHY, LEARNING
942	Malcolm I, king of Scotland (—953) Richard the Fearless, duke of Normandy (—996)		Pope Marinus II (—946) Christianization of Hungary begins Oda, Archbishop of Canterbury (—958)
943			
944			
945	Cumberland and Westmorland annexed by Scots Louis IV taken prisoner by Hugo the Great, duke of France The Buyides rule over Baghdad (—1055) Romanus overthrown, the Emperor Constantine VII reigns alone Russia: Igor is succeeded by Sviatoslav Lothar III, king of Italy (—950)		
946	Edmund I, king of England, succeeded by Edred, his brother (—955) Otto I supports Louis IV and advances to Paris and Rouen	Tsuraguki, Jap. poet, d. (b. 884)	Pope Agapetus II (—955)
947			
948			Founding of the bishopric of Brandenburg
949			
950	Europe in the "Dark Ages" The Lapps enter Norway Bohemia becomes tributary to Otto I Ordono III, king of León Berengar and his son Adalbert crowned kings of Italy	Constantinus Cephalas: "Palatine Anthology"	"Book of the Prefect," on the guild organization of Constantinople
951	Otto I marries Adelheid, daughter of Rudolph II, king of Burgundy, the widow of Lothar, king of Italy–and becomes king of the Franks and Lombards		
952			

D. VISUAL ARTS	E. MUSIC	F. SCIENCE, TECHNOLOGY, GROWTH	G. DAILY LIFE	
Building of Augsburg Cathedral	The Arabs bring kettledrums and trumpets to Europe		Postal and news services in the caliph's empire have at their disposal approx. 1000 stations Manufactories of linens and woolens in Flanders	942
				943
				944
				945
				946
				947
				948
				949
				950
				951
				952

	A. HISTORY, POLITICS	B. LITERATURE, THEATER	C. RELIGION, PHILOSOPHY, LEARNING
953	Bruno I, Archbishop of Cologne and brother of Otto I, becomes ruler of his realm (—965) Duke Liudolf of Swabia rebels against his father Otto I and loses his dukedom Indulf, king of Scotland (—962)		
954	Expulsion of Eric Blodöxe, last Dan. king of York Lothar, son of Louis IV and nephew of Otto I becomes king of France (—986)		
955	Edwy, son of Edmund, becomes king of England (—959) Otto defeats the Magyars at the Lechfeld, near Augsburg, and the Slavs at the Battle of Recknitz		Pope John XII (—964) Russian Grand Duchess Olga christened at Constantinople Aelfric, Eng. Benedictine abbot and author, b. (d. 1020)
956	Edwy exiles St. Dunstan Sancho I, king of León (—966)		
957	Rebellion by Mercians and Northumbrians against Edwy		
958			
959	Edgar the Peaceful, king of England (—975) Romanus II, Byzantine Emperor (—963)	Roswitha of Gandersheim writes her Lat. comedies	Dunstan, Archbishop of Canterbury (—988) "Suidas," a Greek lexicon (meaning "Fortress")
960	Tai Tsoo, founder of the Sung dynasty, defeats the Tatars Mieczyslav I becomes the first ruler of Poland	Hi-Khio, the first Chin. plays with music	
961	The Byzantines reconquer Crete from the Arabs Hakam II, Caliph of Córdoba (—976)	"Eyvind Skaldaspillir": Hakonarmal, Norw. epic poem	Luitprand, Bishop of Cremona: "Antapodosis"
962	Otto I crowned Holy Roman Emperor Alptigin founds Turk. principality at Gharzni, Afghanistan		
963	Nicephorus II Phocas, Byzantine Emperor (—969) marries Theophano, his predecessor's widow, and defeats Arabs and Bulgarians		First monastic foundation at Mt. Athos, Greece

D. VISUAL ARTS	E. MUSIC	F. SCIENCE, TECHNOLOGY, GROWTH	G. DAILY LIFE	
				953
				954
				955
				956
				957
				958
				959
Building of Nayin Mosque, Persia Period of the great watercolor painters of the Sung era				960
Li Yü, Emperor of Nanking, founds Academy of Painting Rebuilding of St. Paul's, London, after a fire				961
			Founding of the Hospice of St. Bernard at St. Bernard's Pass, Switzerland	962
		"The Book of Fixed Stars" by Al Sûfi mentions nebula (see 1612)	First record of existence of a London bridge	963

	A. HISTORY, POLITICS	B. LITERATURE, THEATER	C. RELIGION, PHILOSOPHY, LEARNING
964	New Maya empire (—c. 1191) Nicephorus II Phocas conquers Cyprus from Arabs		Pope Benedict V (—965) Revival of monasticism in England after the Dan. wars
965	The English invade Celtic kingdom of Gwynedd	Lin Pu, Chin. poet, b. (d. 1026) Mutanabi, Arab poet, murdered	Pope John XIII (—972) Widukind of Corvey: "Saxon History" ("Res gestae saxonicae") St. Dunstan enforces celibacy for Eng. clerics
966	With Emperor Michinaga (d. 1027) the Jap. Fujiwara family reaches its zenith; he is the father of three empresses and grandfather of four emperors Ramiro III, king of León Otto I's third expedition to Italy against Byzantines in Apulia		Founding of Worcester Cathedral by St. Oswald The Poles under Mieczyslav I converted to Christianity
967	Cuilean, king of Scotland (—971) Otto II crowned emperor in Rome Boleslav II, duke of Bohemia (—999)		
968	Russians ravage eastern Bulgaria Janhar el-Kaid founds El-Kähira (Cairo): earlier settlements go back to 525 Byzantines take Antioch		Founding of Córdoba University Founding of archbishopric of Magdeburg
969	The Emperor Nicephorus murdered; succeeded by John I Tzimisces (—976) Fatimid caliphs of Tunisia rule Egypt		
970	Russians driven out of Balkans Sancho, king of Navarre (—1035)	"The Exeter Book": collection of Eng. poetry	
971	Tzimisces defeats Russians at Presthlava and Dorystolum Kenneth II, king of Scotland (—995)		
972	Eastern Slav tribes in Russia unified Otto II marries the Byzantine Princess Theophano N. Africa freed from Egypt		Founding of Cairo University Second church of Peterborough built Grand Prince Géza of Hungary converted to Christianity
973	Otto I, the founder of the Holy Roman Empire of the Ger. Nation d.; he is succeeded by his son Otto II (—983; already crowned in 967) King Edgar crowned at Bath		Pope Benedict VI (—974)
974			Pope Benedict VII (—983)

D. VISUAL ARTS	E. MUSIC	F. SCIENCE, TECHNOLOGY, GROWTH	G. DAILY LIFE	
			Working of silver and copper mines in the Harz Mountains, Germany	964
		Alhazen, Arab physicist, b. (d. 1038)		965
			Otto grants Bremen the authority to hold markets	966
				967
				968
Fatimid style in Syrian-Egyptian architecture (—1170)				969
St. Lawrence, Bradford-on-Avon, Saxon church of rare design Founding of El-Ahzar Mosque at Cairo		Abû'l Wefa, astronomer and mathematician at Baghdad		970
				971
				972
Revival of Deccan sculpture and architecture in India			Direct commercial relations between Egypt and Italy	973
			The earliest authenticated earthquake in Great Britain	974

	A. HISTORY, POLITICS	B. LITERATURE, THEATER	C. RELIGION, PHILOSOPHY, LEARNING
975	St. Edward the Martyr, king of England (—979) William, count of Arles, takes Garde-Freinet from Arabs		Bishoprics of Prague and Olomouc founded
976	Basil II Bulgaroktonos ("Slayer of the Bulgarians"), Byzantine Emperor (—1025) Samuel, Czar of Bulgaria (—1014) Henry the Quarrelsome of Bavaria defeated and dethroned by Otto II, Bavaria losing Carinthia and Verona Leopold I, first of the House of Babenberg, becomes margrave of Austria Hisham, Caliph of Córdoba: prime of Arab science, art, and philosophy		
977			
978	Mohammed ibn abi-Amir al-Mansur (Almanzor) becomes chief minister of the Omayyad caliphate, at Córdoba (d. 1002) Otto II at war with Lothair of France; sacking of Aix-la-Chapelle		Chin. encyclopedia of 1000 volumes begun, completed c. 984
979	King Edward of England murdered at Corfe Castle Ethelred II, the Unready, crowned at Kingston Louis V coregent in France Northmen in Ireland defeated by Malachi at Tara		
980	St. Vladimir becomes prince of Kiev (d. 1015) Renewal of Dan. raids on England: they attack Chester, Southampton, and Thanet End of the rule of the nobles in Rome		
981	Beginning of Bulgarian war Hugh Capet and Otto II sign agreement Hisham II of Córdoba makes León tributary		
982	Otto II defeated by the Saracens in southern Italy Viking raids on coasts of Dorset, Portland, and South Wales First Viking colonies established in Greenland by Eric the Red		
983	Otto II d. (b. 955); succeeded by his and Theophano's three-year-old son Otto III (—1002) Slav rebellion east of Elbe River against Ger. rule		Hall of Kuan Yin at Tu Lo Temple, Chisien, Hopei, China Pope Benedict VII d. (see 974)
984			Pope John XIV (—985)

D. VISUAL ARTS	E. MUSIC	F. SCIENCE, TECHNOLOGY, GROWTH	G. DAILY LIFE	
		The present arithmetical notation brought into Europe by the Arabs		**975**
Building of St. Mark's, Venice, begins				**976**
				977
				978
			Earliest mention of Billingsgate Wharf, London	**979**
Building of Mainz Cathedral begins Monastery church at Cluny	Organ with 400 pipes at Winchester Monastery, England "Antiphonarium Codex Montpellier," important musical manuscript			**980**
				981
				982
			Venice and Genoa carry on flourishing trade between Asia and Western Europe	**983**
				984

	A. HISTORY, POLITICS	B. LITERATURE, THEATER	C. RELIGION, PHILOSOPHY, LEARNING
985	Sweyn, king of Denmark and (from 995) of Sweden (d. 1014) Quarrel between Ethelred II and Witan begins		The chapter of Melk in Lower Austria established by Leopold I Pope John XV (—996)
986	Louis V, king of France (—987), last of the Carolingians Sabuktigin of Ghazni invades India, opposed by Jaipal ruler of Kangra		
987	Hugh Capet, founder of the Capetian line, king of France (d. 996)		
988	Vikings attack Devon and Somerset, and Irish Danes raid Wales		Vladimir of Kiev marries Anne, sister of the Emperor Basil II, and introduces the Eastern form of Christianity into his dominion
989			
990	Danzig becomes the capital of Slav duchy of Pomerania William V, duke of Aquitaine (—1029)		Poland submits to the Holy See Aelfric the Grammarian, Abbot of Eynsham: "Homilies"
991	At the Battle of Maldon Byrhtnoth of Essex is defeated by the Danes		
992	Treaty between Ethelred and the Normans Boleslav I, duke of Poland (—1025)		
993	Vikings ravage Yorkshire Olaf Tryggvesson, the first Christian king of Norway		First canonization of saints
994	Olof Skötkonung, king of Sweden, accepts Christianity Arabs destroy the Monastery of Monte Cassino Olaf of Norway and Sweyn of Denmark besiege London		
995	The Slavnici, last independent tribe of Bohemia, subdued by the Germans Constantine IV, king of Scotland (—997)		

D. VISUAL ARTS	E. MUSIC	F. SCIENCE, TECHNOLOGY, GROWTH	G. DAILY LIFE	
				985
			Rebuilding of Peking begins	986
				987
				988
				989
At the Nanking Academy the great landscape painter Tung Yüan and his pupil, the monk Chü-jan, teach	Development of systematic musical notation			990
				991
				992
Bernward, Bishop of Hildesheim, protector of the arts				993
				994
	Guido d'Arezzo, Ital. musical theorist and teacher, b. (d. c. 1050)			995

	A. HISTORY, POLITICS	B. LITERATURE, THEATER	C. RELIGION, PHILOSOPHY, LEARNING
996	Otto III crowned emperor by Gregory V, the first Ger. pope (—999) Hugh Capet d.; succeeded by his son Robert II (—1031) Richard II, the Good, duke of Normandy (—1026) Icelandic settlers arrive in Greenland Civil war in Rome		Pope Gregory V, a Saxon (—999)
997	Kenneth III, king of Scotland (—1005) Stephen I, the Saint, king of Hungary (—1038) Mahmud, son of Sabuktigin, Sultan of Ghazni (—1030)		Adalbert of Prague, missionary to Prussia, murdered
998	Isle of Wight attacked by Danes		Feast of All Souls celebrated for the first time in Cluny
999	The Poles conquer Silesia Last expedition of the Emperor Basil II against the Fatimid in Syria		Gerbert of Aurillac, mathematician, inventor, and philosopher, becomes Pope Sylvester II (—1003), the first French pope
1000	Bohemia and Moravia united King Olaf I of Norway killed in the Battle of Svolder; Norway becomes Danish Piasts rule in Poland (—1370) Venice rules over Dalmatian coast and Adriatic Sea King Rajaraja of the Chola dynasty conquers Ceylon Ethelred II ravages Cumberland and Anglesey King Stephen of Hungary receives from the pope the title of Apostolic Majesty Sancho III, the Great, of Navarre Emperor Otto III makes Rome his permanent residence	Roswitha of Gandersheim d. "Diary of a May-Fly," written by an anonymous Jap. lady "Beowulf," heroic poem written in Old English Sei Shonagan: Makurano Soshi ("The Pillow Book"), diary of a woman writer's thoughts and experiences in the Imperial Jap. court (—1015)	Archbishopric of Gniezno established Berengar of Tours, Fr. scholastic, b. (d. 1088) King Stephen of Hungary founds the Monastery of Gran Christianity reaches Iceland and Greenland Spiritual center of Judaism switches from Mesopotamia to Spain
1001			
1002	Otto III d. (b. 980); succeeded by his cousin Henry II, the Saint (—1024) Edward the Confessor, future king of England (1042—1066) Massacre of St. Brice's Day; Dan. settlers in England murdered by order of Ethelred II Basil II defeats Bulgarians at Vidin Almanzor d.: beginning of the fall of caliphate of Córdoba Muzaffar, Caliph of Córdoba (—1008)		
1003	War between Germany and Poland Sweyn lands with his army in England		Pope John XVII (—1004) Founding of Bamberg Cathedral under Henry II

D. VISUAL ARTS	E. MUSIC	F. SCIENCE, TECHNOLOGY, GROWTH	G. DAILY LIFE	
			Cane sugar arrives in Venice from Alexandria	996
Rebuilding of St. Martin, Tours				997
				998
				999
Tiahuanaco civilization extends all over Peru Artistic revival in Italy (fresco and mosaic paintings) Art, science, and commerce flourish in Ghazni Abbey of St. Hilaire, in Poitiers S. Pietro, Perugia Shiwa Temple at Prambanan, Java "Bridge of Ten Thousand Ages," Foochow, China Climax of Mayan civilization in Yucatan peninsula	Musical notation improved by Guido d'Arezzo	Leif Ericson, son of Eric the Red, is supposed to have discovered America (Nova Scotia) Indian mathematician Sridhara recognizes the importance of the zero Mention of several abortive attempts to fly or to float in air Arabs and Jews become court physicians in Germany	Widespread fear of the End of the World and the Last Judgment Danegeld–general tax in England Potatoes and corn planted in Peru The Frisians build dikes against floods and invasions Chinese perfect their invention of gunpowder, made up of charcoal, sulfur, and potassium nitrate Saxons settle at Bristol	1000
				1001
				1002
				1003

	A. HISTORY, POLITICS	B. LITERATURE, THEATER	C. RELIGION, PHILOSOPHY, LEARNING
1004	King Henry's first Ital. campaign: he defeats Ardoin and is crowned King of Lombardy at Pavia Henry's war against Boleslav (—1018) Arabs sack Pisa China becomes tributary to the Tungusic Khitans		Pope John XVIII (—1009)
1005	Malcolm II, King of Scotland (—1034)		
1006	Rudolph III of Burgundy appoints Henry II his heir Mohammedans settle in northwestern India Robert II of France allies himself with Henry II against Baldwin of Flanders		
1007	Ethelred II pays 30,000 pounds to the Danes to gain two years' freedom from attacks		
1008	Mahmud of Ghazni defeats Hindus at Peshawar		
1009	The Mohammedans sack the Holy Sepulcher in Jerusalem First Imperial Diet at Goslar		Bruno of Querfurt martyred by the Prussians Thietmar, Bishop of Merseburg: "Chronicle" (—1018) Pope Sergius IV (—1012)
1010	Robert II of France proclaims the "Peace of God"		Richer of St. Remy, author of "Historia Remensis ecclesiae"
1011	Ethelred invades South Wales, and the Danes take Canterbury		The "Handkerchief of St. Veronica" kept in a special altar in Rome
1012	Ethelred pays additional 48,000 pounds to the Danes		First persecution of heretics in Germany The "Decretum" of Bishop Burchard of Worms Pope Benedict VIII (—1024)
1013	The Danes masters of England; Ethelred flees to Normandy		
1014	On Henry's second Ital. campaign he is crowned emperor in Rome End of Norse rule in Ireland–battle at Clontarf Western part of Bulgaria to Byzantium; Basil II has Bulgarian army blinded Sweyn d.; succeeded by Canute: Ethelred returns		

D. VISUAL ARTS	E. MUSIC	F. SCIENCE, TECHNOLOGY, GROWTH	G. DAILY LIFE	
				1004
				1005
				1006
				1007
	Berno, Abbot of Reichenau (d. 1048), writes his books on musical theory			1008
		Ibn Junis, Arab astronomer, author of the "Hakimite Tables," d. (b. c. 950)		1009
				1010
				1011
Heinrich Cathedral, Bamberg Hakim Mosque, Cairo				1012
				1013
				1014

	A. HISTORY, POLITICS	B. LITERATURE, THEATER	C. RELIGION, PHILOSOPHY, LEARNING
1015	Wessex submits to Canute Arabs conquer Sardinia Jaroslav, Prince of Kiev (—1054) King Olaf II, the Saint, restores Norw. independence and Christianity		
1016	Ethelred II, the Unready, d. and Canute ascends Eng. throne Norman knights in southern Italy		
1017	Canute divides England into four earldoms		Eshin, Jap. Buddhist priest and theologian, d. (b. 942)
1018	End of war between Germany and Poland (see 1003) Union of southern and northern Scotland Byzantium regains Macedonia; Bulgarians submit Council of Oxford: Canute confirms laws of Edgar Sacred Indian city of Muttra pillaged by Mahmud of Ghazni		
1019			
1020	Jaroslav the Wise, Prince of Kiev (—1054), codifies Russ. law and builds cities, schools, and churches Pisa annexes Corsica Faroes, Shetlands, and Orkneys recognize Olaf Haraldsson as king Rebellion of Bernard II, Duke of Saxony	Firdausi, Persian poet, d. (b. 939)	Bamberg Cathedral consecrated by Pope Benedict VIII Aelfric, Eng. author and historian, d.
1021	Henry's third Ital. campaign Basil's campaign against Armenia	Wang-Anshi, Chin. poet, b. (d. 1086)	Gabirol (Solomon ben Yehuda ibn), Jewish-Span. philosopher, b. (d. 1070)
1022	The Emperor Henry II defeats the Greeks in southern Italy Eric the Saint, King of Sweden, d.		Synod of Pavia insists on celibacy of higher clergy Notker Teutonicus, monk of St. Gallen, translator of Boëthius, Aristotle, and the Psalter, d.
1023			
1024	Henry II d.; succeeded as Ger. king by Conrad II, the Salic (—1039), first of Franconian line Mahmud storms Somnath in Gujarat, India		Pope John XIX (—1032)

D. VISUAL ARTS	E. MUSIC	F. SCIENCE, TECHNOLOGY, GROWTH	G. DAILY LIFE	
Beginning of building of Strasbourg Cathedral	At Pomposa Monastery, near Ravenna, sight singing is introduced		First mention of Leipzig (Slav settlement) Municipal self-government at Benevento–first "communitas"	**1015**
St. Paul's, Worms				**1016**
				1017
Brihadisva Rasvamin Temple, Tangore, India				**1018**
				1019
The crypt of Chartres Cathedral Kuo Hsi, Chin. painter, b. (d. 1090)				**1020**
			St. Vitus' dance epidemics in Europe	**1021**
				1022
				1023
				1024

	A. HISTORY, POLITICS	B. LITERATURE, THEATER	C. RELIGION, PHILOSOPHY, LEARNING
1025	Boleslav I accepts title King of Poland Beginning of decline of Byzantine power Indecisive battle between Canute and Olaf at Holy River, Sweden		
1026	Canute goes on pilgrimage to Rome	Lin Pu, Chin. poet, d. (b. 965)	
1027	Robert the Devil, Duke of Normandy (d. 1035) Pope John XIX crowns Conrad II Holy Roman Emperor at Rome	Omar Khayyam, Persian poet and scientist, b. (d. 1123)	
1028	Canute conquers Norway Romanus III, Byzantine Emperor (—1034) Sancho of Navarre takes Castile		
1029			
1030	Battle of Stiklestad: Canute defeats and kills the former Norw. king, Olaf Haraldsson Jaroslav of Kiev founds Dorpat		
1031	Henry I, King of France (—1060) Pol.-Hung. frontier treaty The caliphate of Córdoba abolished		
1032	Rudolph III of Burgundy d., and Conrad unites Burgundy with the Empire		Pope Benedict IX (—1044) Canute completes restoration of Bury St. Edmunds
1033	The Germans and Russians defeat Mieczyslav II of Poland, which becomes fief of the Empire Castile becomes a separate kingdom		Anselm of Canterbury, philosopher, b. (d. 1109)
1034	Malcolm II of Scotland d.; succeeded by his grandson Duncan (—1040) Bratislav, Duke of Bohemia (—1055) Michael IV, the Paphlagonian, Byzantine Emperor (—1041)		
1035	Canute d., his kingdom being divided among his three sons: Harold is given England, Sweyn Norway, Hardicanute Denmark Ferdinand I of Castile		
1036			

D. VISUAL ARTS	E. MUSIC	F. SCIENCE, TECHNOLOGY, GROWTH	G. DAILY LIFE	
Takayoshi founds Tosa school of painting				1025
	Guido d'Arezzo introduces solmization in music (do, re, mi, fa, sol, la)			1026
				1027
				1028
				1029
			Vienna mentioned for the first time in documents (Wien)	1030
				1031
				1032
				1033
Beginning of building of Würzburg Cathedral				1034
				1035
				1036

	A. HISTORY, POLITICS	B. LITERATURE, THEATER	C. RELIGION, PHILOSOPHY, LEARNING
1037			Avicenna (Ibn Sina), Arab physician and philosopher, d. (b. 980)
1038	After the death of Stephen of Hungary, Abo usurps the throne, and Peter, the legal heir, flees to Germany		Founding of Order of Vallombrosa
1039	Conrad II d.; succeeded by Henry III (—1056) Prince Gruffydd of Gwynedd and Powys defeats the English		
1040	Duncan of Scotland murdered by Macbeth, who becomes king (—1057) Harold d., succeeded by Hardicanute (—1042) "Truce of God" proclaimed in Aquitaine		
1041	Siward murders Eardwulf and becomes sole ruler of Northumbria Battle of Montemaggiore; Lombards and Normans defeat Greeks Casimir I, Duke of Poland (—1058)		
1042	Hardicanute d.; succeeded by Ethelred's son Edward the Confessor (—1066) Magnus, King of Denmark (—1047) Constantine IX Monomachus, Byzantine Emperor (—1054) Rise of the Seljuk Turks		
1043			
1044			Pope Gregory VI (—1046), the papacy being sold by the deposed Pope Benedict IX
1045	The Cid (Rodrigo Diaz), Span. national hero, b. (d. 1099) King Peter returns to Hungary (see 1038) and does homage to Henry III		
1046	Henry III crowned emperor in Rome		Both popes dethroned; Synod of Rome elects Pope Clement II, a Saxon (—1047)

D. VISUAL ARTS	E. MUSIC	F. SCIENCE, TECHNOLOGY, GROWTH	G. DAILY LIFE	
			Conrad II issues the Constitutio de feudis, which makes fiefs of small holders hereditary in Italy	1037
		Alhazen, Arab physicist, d. (b. c. 965)		1038
				1039
		Petrocellus: "Practica," important medical work of the school of Salerno		1040
	Magister Franco, writer on music			1041
				1042
				1043
			Copenhagen first mentioned	1044
				1045
				1046

	A. HISTORY, POLITICS	B. LITERATURE, THEATER	C. RELIGION, PHILOSOPHY, LEARNING
1047	William of Normandy defeats rebellious nobles at Val-des-Dunes Sweyn Estrithson, King of Denmark (—1076) Harald Hardrada, King of Norway (—1066) Henry III reestablishes the duchies of Carinthia, Bavaria, and Swabia Andrew I, King of Hungary (—1060)		Pope Benedict IX (—1048)
1048		Ou Yang Hsiu (1007—1072), Chin. poet, writes stories of the T'ang dynasty	Pope Damascus II (—1049) Beruni, Arab historian, d. (b. 973)
1049			Pope Leo IX, a German (—1054; later canonized) Elias bar Shinaya, Syrian historian, d.
1050	Egypt collapses under military dictatorship Normans penetrate into England	"Vie de St. Alexis," Fr. biography "The Mabinogion," collection of Welsh tales	Ssu-ma-Kuang: "History of China from 500 B.C. to A.D. 1000" The oldest Russ. monasteries, in Kiev
1051			
1052	Pisa takes Sardinia from the Arabs Rebellion of Conrad, Duke of Bavaria Return of Earl Godwin (d. 1053)		
1053	The Norman Robert Guiscard (c. 1015—1085) conquers southern Italy and founds Norman empire there Danegeld abolished Henry IV, son of Henry III, elected and crowned Holy Roman Emperor Harold succeeds his father Godwin as Earl of Wessex		Adalbert of Bremen appointed papal vicar of northern Europe
1054	Macbeth defeated by Malcolm and Siward of Northumbria, at Dunsinane Jaroslav of Kiev d.; followed by decline of his empire Poland recaptures Silesia from Bohemia Henry I of France invades Normandy and is defeated at Mortemer		The papal chair remains empty for one year Cleavage between Roman and Eastern Churches becomes permanent
1055	Siward of Northumbria d.; succeeded by Tostig, son of Godwin Spitigniev II of Bohemia (—1061)		Pope Victor II, a Bavarian (—1057)

D. VISUAL ARTS	E. MUSIC	F. SCIENCE, TECHNOLOGY, GROWTH	G. DAILY LIFE	
				1047
				1048
Li Lung-mien, Chin. painter, b. (d. 1106)				1049
Jap. sculptor Jocho sets up his school Building of Exeter Cathedral and Winchester Cathedral begins Jain temples at Mount Abu, India Palazzo Reale, Palermo St. Sophia Cathedral in Novgorod The Ger. imperial crown is being made	Polyphonic singing replaces Gregorian chant "Sys willekommen heirre kerst," first Ger. Christmas carol Guido d'Arezzo d. (b. 995) The harp arrives in Europe Time values given to musical notes	Geographer Adam of Bremen believes the Baltic Sea to be an ocean open to the east Important astronomic instruments (astrolabes) arrive in Europe from Eastern countries	Earliest references to Nuremberg, Oslo, Delhi, and Timbuctu Eng. monks excel in embroidery	1050
				1051
Edward the Confessor begins building Westminster Abbey				1052
Hoodo pavilion, Japan				1053
			Expansion of commercial relations between Italy and Egypt	1054
				1055

	A. HISTORY, POLITICS	B. LITERATURE, THEATER	C. RELIGION, PHILOSOPHY, LEARNING
1056	Henry III d.; succeeded by Henry IV, till 1065 under the guardianship of Empress Agnes Gruffydd does homage to Harold of Wessex and Leofric of Mercia Michael VI, Eastern Emperor (—1057) Beginning of the democratic Pataria movement in Milan		
1057	Macbeth murdered by Malcolm; succeeded by his stepson Lulach Leofric of Mercia d.; succeeded by Alfgar Isaac Comnenus, Eastern Emperor (—1059)		Pope Stephen X (—1058) "Ostromic Gospel," written in Novgorod
1058	Malcolm slays Lulach and becomes King of Scotland (—1093) Battle of Varaville: William of Normandy defeats Geoffrey of Anjou Boleslav II, Duke of Poland (—1081)		Pope Benedict X (—1059)
1059	Philip I made coregent in France Treaty of Melfi: Robert Guiscard and Richard of Aversa, Prince of Capua, become papal vassals Constantine X, Eastern Emperor (—1067)		Pope Nicholas II (—1061) Papal decree establishing papal elections by cardinals only Al Gazali, Arab theologian, b. (d. 1111) Work begins on Bonn Cathedral
1060	Henry I of France d.; succeeded by Philip I (—1108) Bela I, King of Hungary (—1063)		
1061	Malcolm of Scotland invades Northumbria Normans conquer Messina		Pope Alexander II (—1073)
1062	Coup d'état of Kaiserswerth; Archbishop Anno II of Cologne seizes Henry IV		Berengar of Tours opposes doctrine of transubstantiation
1063	Harold and Tostig subdue Wales Victorious Ger. campaign against Hungary Alp Arslan, ruler of the Seljuks (—1072)		
1064	The Seljuks conquer Armenia Hungarians seize Belgrade from Byzantium	"Ezzolied" by Ger. crusaders	
1065	Sancho II, King of Castile (—1072) Henry IV comes of age		Consecration of Westminster Abbey

D. VISUAL ARTS	E. MUSIC	F. SCIENCE, TECHNOLOGY, GROWTH	G. DAILY LIFE	
Pagoda of Ko Fuang Temple at Shansi, China				1056
				1057
Parma Cathedral begun (—1074)				1058
				1059
"Christ as Ruler of the World," Byzantine mosaic, Daphni, Greece				1060
				1061
			Marrakesh founded	1062
Pisa Cathedral built (—1118)				1063
				1064
	Wilhelm von Hirsau, Ger. Benedictine monk, writes manuals on musical theory (d. 1091)			1065

	A. HISTORY, POLITICS	B. LITERATURE, THEATER	C. RELIGION, PHILOSOPHY, LEARNING
1066	Edward the Confessor d. Jan 5 and Harold II is crowned Jan. 6; he defeats invaders at Stamford Bridge Sept. 25; William of Normandy lands at Pevensey Sept. 28; Harold killed in Battle of Hastings Oct. 14; William I, the Conqueror, crowned Dec. 25	Norman invasion leads to loss of prestige for Eng. language	
1067	Boleslav II of Poland takes Kiev Romanus IV, Eastern Emperor (—1071)		
1068	She-tsung, Emperor of China (—1086): nationalization of agricultural production and distribution Nationalist risings in the north and west of England crushed by William I		
1069			
1070	Rising in Ely under Hereward Bavaria bestowed upon Welf IV by Henry IV		Gabirol (Solomon ben Yehuda ibn), first Jewish philosopher in Europe (Spain), d. (b. 1021) Amalfi merchants found in Jerusalem the Order of St. John
1071	Philip I defeated near Cassel by Robert of Flanders Normans conquer last Byzantine possessions in Italy Romanus IV defeated and captured by Seljuks at Manzikert Michael VII, Eastern Emperor (—1078)		
1072	Normans under Robert Guiscard conquer Palermo		Petrus Damiani, Cardinal Bishop of Ostia, d. (b. 1007)
1073			Pope Gregory VII, Hildebrand of Soana (—1085; later canonized) Reorganization of Eng. Church: York subordinated to Canterbury
1074	Peace of Gerstungen between Henry IV and the Saxons Robert Guiscard excommunicated by Gregory VII Geza I, King of Hungary (—1078)		Excommunication of married priests
1075	Syria and Palestine subdued by Seljuk leader Malik Shah		Dictatus papae on papal world dominance
1076	Gregory VII, challenged by Ger. bishops at the Synod of Worms, dethrones and excommunicates Henry IV Godfrey, Duke of Lower Lorraine, assassinated		

D. VISUAL ARTS	E. MUSIC	F. SCIENCE, TECHNOLOGY, GROWTH	G. DAILY LIFE	
Beginning of Norman (Romanesque) architecture Work begins at Fotheringay Castle, Northamptonshire			Appearance of comet, later called "Halley's Comet"	**1066**
Work begins on Bayeux tapestry Rebuilding of Monte Cassino Monastery William I founds Battle Abbey, Hastings				**1067**
"Shotoku Taishi Eden," oldest extant painting of Yamatoe style				**1068**
				1069
Building of York Cathedral begins				**1070**
		Constantine the African (c. 1020—1087) brings Greek medicine to Western world		**1071**
St. Etienne and La Trinité built in Caen				**1072**
Pueblo ruins at Mesa Verde, southwestern Colorado Alrava tesh vara Temple, Darasuram, India, begun				**1073**
				1074
Richmond Castle, Yorkshire St. James's Cathedral, Santiago de Compostela				**1075**
				1076

	A. HISTORY, POLITICS	B. LITERATURE, THEATER	C. RELIGION, PHILOSOPHY, LEARNING
1077	Henry IV goes as penitent to Canossa and is absolved by Gregory VII		First Eng. Cluniac monastery at Lewes
1078	Nicephorus III, Eastern Emperor (—1081)		Michael Psellos, Byzantine Platonist philosopher, d. (b. 1018)
1079	Frederick of Staufen marries a daughter of Henry IV and is made Duke of Swabia		Peter Abelard, Fr. theologian and philosopher, b. (d. 1142)
1080	Canute IV, the Saint, King of Denmark (—1086) Rudolf of Swabia d. Henry IV again deposed and excommunicated Armenian state established in Cilicia		Consecration of Otranto Cathedral
1081	Alexius I Comnenus, Eastern Emperor (—1118) Henry IV marches into Italy Robert Guiscard invades the Balkans		
1082			
1083	Henry IV storms Rome	Jehuda Halevy, Jewish poet and philosopher in Spain, b. (d. 1140)	
1084	Robert Guiscard frees Gregory VII, who was imprisoned by Henry IV at the Castel Sant'Angelo, Rome		
1085	Henry IV extends the "Peace of God" over his whole empire Toledo taken from the Arabs by Alfonso VI Vratislav, Duke of Bohemia, crowned king Robert Guiscard, d.		
1086	Almoravid dynasty revives Mohammedan rule in Spain Compilation of Domesday Book (survey of assessment for tax)		Pope Victor III (—1087) Bruno of Cologne founds Carthusian Order
1087	William the Conqueror, d.; succeeded by William II "Rufus" in England (—1100) and Robert in Normandy (—1106) Conrad, eldest son of Henry IV, crowned king of Ger.		

D. VISUAL ARTS	E. MUSIC	F. SCIENCE, TECHNOLOGY, GROWTH	G. DAILY LIFE	
St. Albans Abbey built (—1115)				1077
Building of Tower of London begins (—1300)				1078
			Founding of Newcastle	1079
		Toledan table of positions of stars		1080
Rebuilding of Mainz Cathedral			Commercial treaty between Venice and Byzantium	1081
				1082
				1083
				1084
				1085
				1086
St. Paul's, London, burns down and is rebuilt				1087

	A. HISTORY, POLITICS	B. LITERATURE, THEATER	C. RELIGION, PHILOSOPHY, LEARNING
1088	The Patzinak Turks settle between the Danube and the Balkans		Pope Urban II (—1099) Berengar of Tours, Fr. theologian, d. (b. 1000)
1089			Lanfranc, Archbishop of Canterbury, d., the see remaining vacant for four years
1090	Ingo I, King of Sweden (—1112)		
1091	Treaty of Caen between William II and Robert of Normandy		
1092	William II conquers Cumberland Vratislav II of Bohemia d. Seljuk Sultan Malik Shah d.; capital moved from Iconium to Smyrna		Ibn Ezra, Jewish Bible commentator, b. (d. 1167)
1093	Malcolm of Scotland killed during invasion of England; succeeded by his brother Donald Bane		Hugh le Gros founds Benedictine monastery, Chester
1094	The Cid takes Valencia from the Moors		
1095	Eric I, King of Denmark (—1103) The Hungarians conquer Croatia and Dalmatia		Pope Urban II consecrates the rebuilt abbey church of Cluny Council of Clermont: Pope Urban II proclaims First Crusade
1096	Start of the First Crusade (—1099) with Godfrey of Bouillon, Duke of Lorraine, and Tancred, nephew of Robert Guiscard		
1097	Edgar, son of Malcolm, becomes King of Scotland (—1107) The Crusaders defeat Turks at Dorylaeum, conquer Nicaea Henry IV returns from Italy to Germany		
1098	Louis VI made coregent of Philip I of France Orkneys, Hebrides, and Isle of Man seized by Magnus III of Norway Crusaders defeat Turks at Antioch		Monastery of Cîteaux, the first Cistercian house, founded by St. Robert

D. VISUAL ARTS	E. MUSIC	F. SCIENCE, TECHNOLOGY, GROWTH	G. DAILY LIFE	
Chung-Jen, Chin. painter and priest, paints with India ink on silk				1088
				1089
		The first water-driven mechanical clock constructed in Peking		1090
		Walcher of Malvern notes eclipse of the moon in Italy		1091
Building of Carlisle Castle begins				1092
				1093
St. Mark's, Venice completed (see 976)			The first record of gondolas in Venice	1094
				1095
Nave of Norwich Cathedral built (—1145)				1096
				1097
Rajarani Temple at Bhubanesvara, Orissa		Nicholas Prevost of Tours: "Antidotarum," a collection of 2650 medical prescriptions from Salerno		1098

	A. HISTORY, POLITICS	B. LITERATURE, THEATER	C. RELIGION, PHILOSOPHY, LEARNING
1099	Crusaders take Jerusalem; Godfrey, appointed Defender of the Holy Sepulcher, defeats Egyptians at Ascalon The Cid d. (b. 1045)		Pope Paschal II (—1118)
1100	William Rufus killed accidentally by Sir Walter Tyrel in the New Forest; succeeded by Henry I (—1135) Baldwin I, King of Jerusalem (—1118)	Jayadeva: "Gitagovinda," Indian love poem Wace, Anglo-Norman poet, b. (d. 1183) "Chanson de Roland," Fr. heroic poem "The play of the Wise and Silly Virgins" Krishnamisra: "Prahodha-Chandro-daya," Indian allegorical play	The dialect of the Ile-de-France becomes the prevailing idiom of France, and Middle English supersedes Old English
1101	Treaty of Alton: Robert of Normandy is bought off after invading England King Conrad d. Roger II, Count of Sicily (—1154) Minsk, capital of independent principality Accession of the Emperor Hai-tsung (d. 1135)	Su Tung-p'o, Chin. poet and painter, d. (b. 1036)	
1102	Boleslav III, Duke of Poland (—1138)		
1103	Magnus III of Norway invades Ireland and is killed Public Peace of Mainz for the Holy Roman Empire (—1107)		
1104	Acre taken by Crusaders		
1105	Henry IV is captured by his son and abdicates Colonization of eastern Germany begins		
1106	Henry IV d.; succeeded by Henry V, the last Salic emperor (—1125)		
1107	Edgar of Scotland d.; succeeded by his brother Alexander I (—1124)		
1108	Philip I of France d.; succeeded by Louis VI (—1137)		

D. VISUAL ARTS	E. MUSIC	F. SCIENCE, TECHNOLOGY, GROWTH	G. DAILY LIFE	
Notre-Dame-du-Port at Clermont-Ferrand				1099
Appearance of Gothic architecture St. Germain-des-Près, Paris Castle Chillon, near Geneva, Switzerland Erection of Baptistery, Florence	Beginnings of secular music Music school of St. Martial at Limoges develops polyphonic style	Decline of Islamic science begins	Sinchi Roca civilization in Peru Third Pueblo period in southwestern part of N. America Munich and Stettin mentioned in records Probable colonization of Polynesia from S. America (see 1947, Heyerdahl's Kon-tiki expedition)	1100
				1101
				1102
"Ying Tsao Ea Shih" (method of architecture published in China)				1103
				1104
Angoulême Cathedral erected				1105
				1106
				1107
				1108

	A. HISTORY, POLITICS	B. LITERATURE, THEATER	C. RELIGION, PHILOSOPHY, LEARNING
1109	Anglo-French war (—1113)		Anselm of Canterbury d. and the see is vacant for five years (a great theologian, he produced the "ontological proof" of the existence of God–naturally he was declared a Doctor of the Church in 1720)
1110		Earliest record of a miracle play, Dunstable, England	
1111	Henry V crowned emperor in Rome		Al-Gazali, Arab theologian, d. (b. 1059)
1112	Henry V excommunicated by the Synod of Vienne		
1113	Balearic Islands conquered by Pisa Vladimir II Monomakh, Grand Duke of Kiev (—1125)		"Leges Henrici" codified Order of Knights Hospitalers of St. John, Jerusalem, founded St. Bernard joins the Cistercian Order
1114			Founding of Chichester Cathedral
1115	Stephen II, King of Hungary (—1131) State of Chin established in northern China Florence becomes free republic		Founding of Clairvaux with St. Bernard as first abbot (—1153)
1116	The Aztecs leave the Mythical Aztlan		
1117			
1118	John II Comnenus, Byzantine Emperor (—1143)		Pope Gelasius II (—1119) Thomas à Becket of Canterbury b. (d. 1170)
1119	Charles the Good, Count of Flanders (—1127)		Pope Calixtus II, a Burgundian noble (—1124)

D. VISUAL ARTS	E. MUSIC	F. SCIENCE, TECHNOLOGY, GROWTH	G. DAILY LIFE	
				1109
				1110
				1111
				1112
Founding of St. Nicholas, Novgorod, one of the earliest onion-domed churches				1113
				1114
				1115
				1116
				1117
				1118
		Bologna University founded		1119

	A. HISTORY, POLITICS	B. LITERATURE, THEATER	C. RELIGION, PHILOSOPHY, LEARNING
1120	Peace between Henry I of England and Louis VI of France Disaster of the "White Ship": the only legitimate son of Henry I of England drowned off Harfleur		John of Salisbury, Eng. historian, b. (d. 1180) Full development of Scholastic philosophy
1121	The Ger. princes meet at Würzburg to work out a compromise between the pope and Emperor Henry V		The Synod of Soissons condemns Abelard's teachings on the Trinity
1122	The Byzantines exterminate Patzinak Turks Henry I creates earldom of Gloucester for his illegitimate son Robert of Caen Frederick I Barbarossa b.		Concordat of Worms settles investiture question
1123	The Byzantine Emperor John II defeats Serbs	Omar Khayyam, Persian poet and astronomer, d. (b. 1027)	First Lateran Council suppresses simony and marriage of priests
1124	Alexander I of Scotland d.; succeeded by David I (—1153) The Emperor John II defeats Hungarians		William of Malmesbury: "On the Antiquity of the Church of Glastonbury" (historical record) Pope Honorius II (—1130)
1125	Henry V d.; succeeded by Lothar of Saxony as king (—1137) Almohades conquer Morocco		Tarnenari: "O-Kagami," Jap. history (851—1036) Cosmas of Prague, author of "Chronica Bohemorum," d.
1126	The Eng. barons accept Matilda, widow of Emperor Henry V and daughter of Henry I of England, as successor to Henry I Lothar III makes his son-in-law Henry the Proud (Welf) Duke of Bavaria, and (from 1137) Duke of Saxony		Averroës, Arab scholar and philosopher, b.
1127		Guillaume de Poitou, one of the first troubadours, d. (b. 1070)	
1128	Empress Matilda marries Geoffrey Plantagenet of Anjou Alfonso I, King of Portugal (—1185)		Order of the Templars recognized by the pope Abbey of Holyrood founded by David I of Scotland
1129			

D. VISUAL ARTS	E. MUSIC	F. SCIENCE, TECHNOLOGY, GROWTH	G. DAILY LIFE	
			The Chinese may have invented playing cards	1120
				1121
Piacenza Cathedral				1122
			Founding of St. Bartholomew's hospital, London	1123
Rochester Cathedral completed			First Scottish coinage struck	1124
	Beginning of troubadour and trouvère music in France	Alexander Neckam: "De utensilibus" (earliest account of a mariner's compass)		1125
			Venetian commercial privileges in Byzantine Empire renewed	1126
				1127
				1128
				1129

	A. HISTORY, POLITICS	B. LITERATURE, THEATER	C. RELIGION, PHILOSOPHY, LEARNING
1130	Roger II crowned King of Sicily at Palermo		Pope Innocent II (—1143) Anacletus II, antipope (—1138); a distinguished scholar and diplomat, he is canonically more acceptable than Innocent II but fails to get secular backing because he is the son of a rich, converted Jew, founder of the influential Pierleani family
1131			
1132			
1133	Lothar III crowned emperor by Pope Innocent II		Diocese of Carlisle founded
1134	The Emperor Lothar III invests Albert the Bear with the Nordmark		
1135	King Conrad, Frederick of Swabia, the King of Denmark, and the Duke of Poland submit to Lothar III King Henry I of England d.; succeeded by his nephew Stephen of Boulogne (—1154), a grandson of William the Conqueror Foundation of the Italian line of the House of Este (—1803)		Moses Maimonides, Jewish religious philosopher, b. (d. 1204)
1136	Matilda asserts her right to the Eng. throne Lothar invades southern Italy, conquers Apulia	Abelard: "Historia calamitatum mearum," description of his love affair with Héloïse	
1137	Gruffydd, Prince of North Wales, d.; succeeded by Owain the Great (—1170) Louis VI of France d.; succeeded by Louis VII (—1180) The Emperor Lothar III d. Antioch becomes a vassal to Byzantium	The Provençal troubadour Marcabrun (d. 1150)	Creation of bishopric of Aberdeen
1138	Conrad III elected king (d. 1152), first of the Hohenstaufen line Boleslav III of Poland, having divided his realm among his five sons, d. David I of Scotland invades England on behalf of Matilda and is defeated at the Battle of the Standards		Pretended Messiah appears in France and Persia

D. VISUAL ARTS	E. MUSIC	F. SCIENCE, TECHNOLOGY, GROWTH	G. DAILY LIFE	
New Church of Sant' Ambrogio, Milan				1130
				1131
			Henry I of France grants charters of corporate towns protecting commerce and industry	1132
			St. Bartholomew's Fair, Smithfield, London (—1855)	1133
Western façade of Chartres Cathedral built (—1150)				1134
				1135
				1136
Mainz Cathedral completed Rochester Cathedral burns down and is rebuilt				1137
				1138

	A. HISTORY, POLITICS	B. LITERATURE, THEATER	C. RELIGION, PHILOSOPHY, LEARNING
1139	Matilda lands at Arundel: civil war in England Bavaria falls to Austria		Second Lateran Council ends schism "Decretum Gratiani," summary of Eng. ecclesiastical law
1140	Vladislav II of Bohemia (—1173)	Bertrand de Born, Eng. troubadour, b. (d. 1215) Jehuda Halevy, Jewish poet, d. (b. 1083)	Council of Sens condemns the heresies of Abelard
1141	Matilda proclaimed queen at Winchester Geza II, King of Hungary (—1161)	Nisami, Persian poet, b. (d. 1202)	
1142		Abelard, poet and theologian, d. (b. 1079)	
1143	Manuel I, Byzantine Emperor (—1180)		Pope Celestine II (—1144)
1144	Geoffrey of Anjou made Duke of Normandy The Seljuks take Edessa Republican regime established in Rome under Arnold of Brescia	Chrétien de Troyes, Fr. court poet, b. (d. 1190)	Pope Lucius II (—1145)
1145	Pope Eugene III (—1153) proclaims Second Crusade		
1146	Nureddin, Sultan of Syria (—1174)		
1147	Matilda leaves England Crusaders perish in Asia Minor: failure of the Second Crusade		Geoffrey of Monmouth: "Historia regum Britanniae"
1148			
1149			

D. VISUAL ARTS	E. MUSIC	C. RELIGION, PHILOSOPHY, LEARNING	G. DAILY LIFE	
				1139
				1140
				1141
				1142
		The Spanish Jew Benjamin of Tudela travels via Constantinople to India and returns via Egypt	Founding of Lübeck	1143
		Robert of Chester: "Liber de Compositione Alchemiae"		1144
			Bridge over the Danube at Ratisbon completed (begun 1135)	1145
		"Antidotarium Niclai," a treatise on drugs		1146
Lisbon Cathedral built			Moscow mentioned for the first time	1147
				1148
				1149

	A. HISTORY, POLITICS	B. LITERATURE, THEATER	C. RELIGION, PHILOSOPHY, LEARNING
1150	Albert the Bear inherits Brandenburg Eric the Saint, King of Sweden (—1160) Alauddin Husain, Sultan of Ghor, destroys the empire of Ghazni		Founding of Paris University The Black Book of Carmarthen, oldest Welsh manuscript
1151	Geoffrey Plantagenet of Anjou d.; succeeded by Henry, his son by Matilda of England End of Toltec Empire in Mexico		Simon Darschan: "Jalkut," Jewish commentaries to the Old Testament
1152	Conrad III d. and his nephew Frederick I Barbarossa becomes king (—1190) Louis VII divorces his queen, Eleanor, who marries Henry of Anjou, afterward King of England		
1153	David I of Scotland d.; succeeded by his grandson Malcolm IV (—1165)		Pope Anastasius IV (—1154) Bernard of Clairvaux d. (b. 1091)
1154	Stephen d.; Henry II, King of England (—1189); from now till 1485 the House of Plantagenet rules England Thomas à Becket becomes Henry's chancellor		Pope Hadrian IV, Nicholas Breakspear, the only Eng. pope (—1159)
1155	Pope Hadrian IV bestows Ireland on Henry II Arnold of Brescia hanged (see 1144) Henry II abolishes fiscal earldoms and restores royal demesne Genghis Khan, founder of Mongol empire, b.		Carmelite Order founded
1156	War of the Jap. clans Taira and Minamoto Austria made a duchy with special privileges Frederick Barbarossa marries Beatrice, heiress of Upper Burgundy		
1157	Eric of Sweden conquers Finland		
1158	Frederick Barbarossa makes Vladislav II King of Bohemia		
1159			The great Pope Alexander III (—1181)

D. VISUAL ARTS	E. MUSIC	F. SCIENCE, TECHNOLOGY, GROWTH	G. DAILY LIFE	
	Troubadour music in southern France becomes organized	Medical faculty at Bologna University	Arabs in Spain manufacture paper	1150
The Golden Age of Buddhist art in Burma Imperial castle at Nuremberg	Leoninus, Fr. composer in the "Ars antiqua" style New dance forms develop in Europe	"Civitas Hippocratica" founded by 20 Salerno physicians	The first fire and plague insurance (in Iceland) The game of chess arrives in England The Chinese use explosives in warfare	1151
	"Ladies' strophes," the earliest Ger. "Minnelieder"			1152
				1153
		Mohammed al-Idrisi: "Geography," published at Palermo		1154
				1155
				1156
	Kurenberg, the first famous Ger. minnesinger			1157
Construction of cathedral in Oxford			Munich becomes center of salt trade	1158
				1159

	A. HISTORY, POLITICS	B. LITERATURE, THEATER	C. RELIGION, PHILOSOPHY, LEARNING
1160	Normans expelled from North Africa	"Tristan et Iseult," Celtic epic by Beroul and Thomas "Jeu de St.-Nicolas" by Jean Bodel, performed on the saint's day at Arras "Ludus de Antichristo": Tegernsee, Bavaria Walter Map, Anglo-Lat. poet	
1161			Edward the Confessor canonized
1162	Frederick Barbarossa destroys Milan		Thomas à Becket elected Archbishop of Canterbury
1163	Quarrel starts between Henry II and Thomas à Becket	Hartmann von der Aue, Ger. poet, b. (d. 1215)	Notre Dame, Paris, built (—1235)
1164	Becket flees to France	Gautier d'Arras, Fr. court poet: "Eracle"	
1165	Malcolm IV d.; succeeded by his brother William the Lion (—1214) Byzantium allies with Venice against the Emperor Frederick I Barbarossa		Canonization of Charlemagne Dec. 29 (his sainthood fades in the 18th century when Pope Benedict XIV reduces him to a "blessed")
1166		"The Song of Canute," Eng. ballad by a monk of Ely	Assize of Clarendon orders erection of jails in all Eng. counties and boroughs
1167	Frederick Barbarossa crowned emperor		Oxford University founded Ibn Ezra, Jewish scholar and theologian, d. (b. 1092)
1168	Milan rebuilt Bogolubsky sacks Kiev and assumes title of Grand Prince		
1169			
1170	Although Henry II and Becket formally reconciled, Becket returns to Canterbury and is murdered by four Norman knights Albert the Bear d. Saladin of Damascus (—1193) subdues Egypt (—1171)	Chrétien de Troyes: "Lancelot," romance of courtly love	Pope Alexander III establishes rules for canonization of saints

D. VISUAL ARTS	E. MUSIC	F. SCIENCE, TECHNOLOGY, GROWTH	G. DAILY LIFE	
				1160
				1161
				1162
				1163
				1164
				1165
Saladin builds Cairo citadel				1166
				1167
				1168
				1169
			"Inquest of Sheriffs," financial inquiry, results in strengthening the Exchequer	1170

	A. HISTORY, POLITICS	B. LITERATURE, THEATER	C. RELIGION, PHILOSOPHY, LEARNING
1172	Queen Eleanor raises Aquitaine against Henry II Reconciliation between Henry II and the Pope The Venice Grand Council restricts the powers of the doges	Wace: "Roman de Rou," chronicle of Norman dukes Wolfram von Eschenbach, Ger. poet, b. (d. 1220) Walther von der Vogelweide, most famous of all Ger. minnesingers, b. (d. 1230)	
1173	Queen Eleanor imprisoned (—1185) Béla III, King of Hungary (—1196)		Canonization of Thomas à Becket Waldensian movement begins at Lyons
1174	The Emperor Frederick I buys Tuscany, Spoleto, Sardinia, and Corsica from Welf VI Henry II does penance at Canterbury for murder of Becket		
1175			
1176	The Emperor Frederick I defeated by the Lombard League at Legnano Saladin conquers Syria	First eisteddfod held at Cardigan Castle "Roman de Renard," the first version of the Reynard the Fox fables, written in French Walter Map organizes the Arthurian legends in their present form	Assize of Northampton extends use of Grand Jury
1177	Treaty of Ivry between Henry II and Louis VII Peace of Venice between Emperor Frederick I and Pope Alexander III		
1178	Emperor Frederick I Barbarossa crowned King of Burgundy	Snorri Sturluson, Icelandic poet and historian, b. (d. 1241)	
1179			
1180	Louis VII of France d.; succeeded by his son Philip II Augustus (—1223) Alexius II Comnenus, Byzantine Emperor (—1183)		Ranulf de Glanville reforms Eng. judicial system
1181			First Carthusian monastery in England at Witham Pope Lucius III (—1185)

D. VISUAL ARTS	E. MUSIC	F. SCIENCE, TECHNOLOGY, GROWTH	G. DAILY LIFE	
				1172
			First authenticated influenza epidemics	1173
Campanile of Pisa ("Leaning Tower") built			Earliest horse races in England	1174
				1175
				1176
			Founding of Belfast	1177
			The famous bridge at Avignon built (—1188) Richard Fitznigel: "Dialogus de Saccario," on the financial administration of England	1178
				1179
Benedetto Antelami, Ital. sculptor, flourishes			Glass windows appear in Eng. private houses First windmills with vertical sails in Europe	1180
				1181

	A. HISTORY, POLITICS	B. LITERATURE, THEATER	C. RELIGION, PHILOSOPHY, LEARNING
1182	Canute VI, King of Denmark (—1202)		St. Francis of Assisi b. (d. 1226) The Jews banished from France
1183	Peace of Constance: Lombard League recognized under imperial overlordship The Emperor Alexius II murdered; succeeded by Andronicus I (—1185) Saladin takes Aleppo		
1184	Diet of Mainz: the Emperor Frederick I's power at its height Cyprus frees itself from Byzantium Tamara, Queen of Georgia (—1212)	Saadi, popular Persian poet, b. (d. 1283)	
1185	Isaac II Angelus, Byzantine Emperor (—1195) Renewal of quarrel between the pope and the emperor Second Bulgarian Empire founded by the brothers Ivan and Peter Asen		Pope Urban III (—1187) Knights Templars established in London
1186	Henry VI, son of Frederick Barbarossa, marries Constance, heiress of Sicily, and assumes title of Caesar Beginning of Kamakura era in Japan (—1333)		
1187	Saladin defeats Christians at Hittin and takes Jerusalem Punjab conquered by Mohammed of Ghor		Pope Gregory VIII Pope Clement III (—1191)
1188			
1189	King Henry II of England d.; succeeded by Richard I, Coeur-de-Lion (—1199) Third Crusade (—1193)		Massacre of the Jews at the coronation of Richard I
1190	Frederick I Barbarossa drowned in River Saleph in Cilicia; succeeded by his son Henry VI (—1197)	Chrétien de Troyes, Fr. poet, d. (b. 1144)	Order of German Hospitalers founded (transformed in 1198 into Teutonic Order)
1191	Richard I conquers Cyprus and sells it to the Templars	The "Nibelungenlied" (—c. 1204)	Pope Celestine III (—1198)

D. VISUAL ARTS	E. MUSIC	F. SCIENCE, TECHNOLOGY, GROWTH	G. DAILY LIFE	
				1182
				1183
Consecration of Modena Cathedral (begun 1099)				1184
				1185
				1186
Completion of Verona Cathedral (begun 1139)				1187
				1188
			First silver florins minted at Florence Commercial treaty between Novgorod and Ger. merchants Henry Fitzailwin, first Mayor of London (—1212)	1189
				1190
Second era of Maya civilization in Central America			Tea arrives in Japan from China	1191

	A. HISTORY, POLITICS	B. LITERATURE, THEATER	C. RELIGION, PHILOSOPHY, LEARNING
1192	Richard I returns from the Crusade and is captured by Leopold, Duke of Austria Dukedom of Styria becomes part of the Babenberg realm of Austria		
1193	Richard is handed over to Henry VI and imprisoned Saladin d.	Benedict of Peterborough, Eng. historian ("Gesta Henrici II"), d.	Albertus Magnus, Ger. philosopher, b. (d. 1280)
1194	Richard I is released and crowned for the second time Henry VI conquers Sicily and is crowned King of Sicily	The "Elder Edda," collection of Scandinavian mythology	
1195	Alexius III, Byzantine Emperor (—1203)		The future St. Antony of Padua (a Portuguese) b. (d. 1231)
1196	Peter II, King of Aragon (—1213) Emeric I, King of Hungary (—1204)		
1197	Ottokar I, King of Bohemia (—1230) The Emperor Henry VI d.; succeeded (1198) by Otto IV (—1218)		
1198			Pope Innocent III (—1216) William of Newburgh: "Historia rerum Anglicarum"
1199	King Richard I, Coeur-de-Lion, killed at a siege in France; succeeded by King John (Lackland), the youngest son of Henry II and Eleanor of Aquitaine (—1216) Declaration of Speyer: Ger. princes confirm the right to elect a king		
1200	Peace of Le Goulet between England and France Llywelyn the Great siezes Anglesey	Robert de Borron: "Roman de Merlin" "Fabliaux," collection of Fr. farcical stories Hartmann von Aue: "Der arme Heinrich," Ger. epic poem	Chu-Hsi, Chin. philosopher, d. (b. 1130) Cambridge University founded Development of Jewish cabalistic philosophy in southern Europe Islam begins to replace Indian religions

D. VISUAL ARTS	E. MUSIC	F. SCIENCE, TECHNOLOGY, GROWTH	G. DAILY LIFE	
Rebuilding of Bamberg Cathedral begun (—1237)				1192
			Indigo and brazilwood imported from India to Britain for dyeing purposes	1193
Erection of present Chartres Cathedral (—1260)				1194
				1195
			Heidelberg mentioned in records	1196
Richard I builds Château Gaillard on the Seine				1197
				1198
Work begins on Siena Cathedral			Founding of Liverpool	1199
Early Gothic in England Duke Leopold VI of Austria builds the Burg (castle) in Vienna	"Faux bourdon" style in Eng. music Professional "bards" in Ireland Cymbals introduced as musical instrument "Carmina Burana," Ger. collection of Latin monastic songs (set to music by Carl Orff, 1937)	Ibn al-Baitar, Arab scientist, b. (d. 1248) Alcohol is being used for medical purposes	60,000 Ital. merchants live and work in Constantinople Paris develops into a modern capital Engagement rings come into fashion	1200

	A. HISTORY, POLITICS	B. LITERATURE, THEATER	C. RELIGION, PHILOSOPHY, LEARNING
1201	Thibaut IV, King of Navarre, Fr. poet, b. (d. 1253)	Renaud de Coucy, Fr. poet, d.	
1202	Fourth Crusade under Boniface of Montferrat: Venice takcs the lead in fighting Constantinople (—1204)		Decretal "Venerabilem" asserts superiority of papacy over empire First trial of a peer (King John of England as Duke of Normandy) in France
1203	Genghis Khan defeats his rival Ongkhan Mohammed of Ghor completes conquest of Upper India Arthur, Duke of Brittany, murdered by order of his uncle, King John of England	Wolfram von Eschenbach: "Parzival," Ger. epic poem	
1204	Crusaders take Constantinople and establish Latin Empire The Emperor Michael sets up independent Greek kingdom of Epirus		Moses Maimonides, Jewish philosopher, d. (b. 1135)
1205			
1206	Genghis Khan, chief prince of the Mongols (—1227) Declaration of sultanate of Delhi		
1207	St. Elizabeth, Hungarian princess, who in 1221 marries Louis IV of Thuringia, b. (d. 1231)	Reinmar the Old of Hagenau, minnesinger, d.	
1208	Philip of Swabia, Ger. King (from 1198) murdered by Otto of Wittelsbach Theodore Lascaris founds empire of Nicaea Pope Innocent III places England under interdict		
1209	King John invades Scotland and is excommunicated Otto IV crowned emperor in Rome		Francis of Assisi issues first rules of his brotherhood (the Franciscans)
1210	Otto IV excommunicated by Pope Innocent III	Gottfried von Strassburg: "Tristan und Isolde"	

D. VISUAL ARTS	E. MUSIC	F. SCIENCE, TECHNOLOGY, GROWTH	G. DAILY LIFE	
Façade of Notre Dame, Paris		Nasir ed-Din et-Tusi, Arab scholar, b. (d. 1274) Pass of St. Gotthard, Switzerland, opened		1201
		Leonardo Pisano Fibonacci (1180—1250): "Liber abaci" introduces Arabic numerals in Europe	The first court jesters at European courts	1202
		Siena University founded		1203
		Vicenza University founded	Founding of Amsterdam, Holland	1204
				1205
				1206
				1207
				1208
				1209
				1210

	A. HISTORY, POLITICS	B. LITERATURE, THEATER	C. RELIGION, PHILOSOPHY, LEARNING
1211	Alfonso II, King of Portugal (—1223) Genghis Khan invades China (—1215)		
1212	Venice conquers Crete Frederick II elected Ger. king and makes Bohemia hereditary kingdom Children's Crusade		
1213	James I of Aragon (—1276) King John of England submits to the Pope, making England and Ireland papal fiefs Council of St. Albans, precursor of Parliament		
1214	Frederick II invests the House of Wittelsbach with the Palatinate Peking captured by Genghis Khan Battle of Bouvines: Philip II of France defeats Otto IV and the English		
1215	Frederick II crowned at Aix-la-Chapelle King John seals Magna Carta at Runnymede	Hartmann von der Aue, Ger. poet, d. (b. 1163)	Fourth Lateran Council prohibits trial by ordeal Dominican Friars founded by the future St. Dominic, Span. priest
1216	King John d.; succeeded by Henry III (—1272) A Fr. force lands in England		Pope Honorius III (—1227)
1217	French, defeated at Lincoln and Sandwich, leave England Haakon IV, King of Norway (—1263) Crusade against sultanate of Egypt fails		
1218	Peace of Worcester between Henry III and Wales Otto IV d. Genghis Khan conquers Persia		
1219			
1220	Henry III crowned at Westminster Frederick II crowned emperor in Rome, his son Henry being elected Ger. king	Wolfram von Eschenbach, Ger. poet, d. (b. 1172)	Saxo Grammaticus, Dan. historian, d. (b. 1150)
1221		"Huon de Bordeaux," Fr. epic The form of the "sonnet" develops in Ital. poetry	

D. VISUAL ARTS	E. MUSIC	F. SCIENCE, TECHNOLOGY, GROWTH	G. DAILY LIFE	
				1211
Rheims Cathedral built (—1311)			Tiles replace thatched and wooden roofs of London houses	1212
			The limestone grotto of Adelsberg (Postojna) near Trieste discovered	1213
		Roger Bacon, the greatest scientist of his time, b. (d. 1294)		1214
				1215
				1216
		Salamanca University founded		1217
Amiens Cathedral burned (rebuilt 1220—1269)			Newgate Prison, London Danneborg, the oldest national flag in the world, adopted by Denmark	1218
				1219
Salisbury Cathedral begun (—1258) Brussels Cathedral begun Nicola Pisano, Ital. sculptor, b. (d. 1278)	Boys' Choir at the Kreuz-Kirche, Dresden, founded		The first giraffes are shown in Europe	1220
Building of Burgos Cathedral begins			Vienna becomes a city	1221

	A. HISTORY, POLITICS	B. LITERATURE, THEATER	C. RELIGION, PHILOSOPHY, LEARNING
1222			Council of Oxford establishes Apr. 23, St. George's Day, as national holiday in England
1223	Philip II Augustus of France d.; succeeded by Louis VIII (—1226) Mongols invade Russia, battle at Kalka River		
1224	Anglo-French war (—1227) Henry VII proclaims Public Peace ("Treuga Henrici") at Würzburg		Franciscan friars in England St. Berthold probable founder of the Carmelite Order
1225	Magna Carta reissued for third time in definitive form	Guillaume de Lorris: "Roman de la Rose," story of courtly wooing	
1226	Louis VIII d.; succeeded by Louis IX, the Saint (—1270; canonized, 1297)		Francis of Assisi d.
1227	Henry III declares himself of age Truce in Anglo-Fr. war Genghis Khan d.; his empire is divided among his three sons		Pope Gregory IX (—1241)
1228	Sixth Crusade, led by Emperor Frederick II		Francis of Assisi canonized
1229	Frederick II, crowned King of Jerusalem, signs treaty with the Sultan of Egypt Aragon conquers Balearic Islands		The Inquisition in Toulouse forbids Bible reading by all laymen
1230	Peace of San Germano between the emperor and pope, Frederick II being absolved from excommunication Wenceslas I, King of Bohemia (—1253)	Walther von der Vogelweide, Ger. poet and minnesinger, d. (b. c. 1172)	
1231			

D. VISUAL ARTS	E. MUSIC	F. SCIENCE, TECHNOLOGY, GROWTH	G. DAILY LIFE	
				1222
				1223
		Founding of Naples University Abdallah ur-Rüml (1179—1229): "Mu'jam ul-Buldân," Arab geographical encyclopedia		1224
	"Sumer is icumen in," probably earliest Eng. round		Cotton manufactured in Spain	1225
				1226
Building of Toledo Cathedral begins The Jap. potter Toshiro, who traveled for four years in China, returns home and starts porcelain manufacture in his country				1227
				1228
		Founding of Toulouse University		1229
			Leprosy imported to Europe by the Crusaders Founding of Berlin (on the site of former Slav settlements)	1230
				1231

	A. HISTORY, POLITICS	B. LITERATURE, THEATER	C. RELIGION, PHILOSOPHY, LEARNING
1232	Ezzelino de Romano, Lord of Verona (—1259) Muhammad I (—1272), founder of Nasrid dynasty in Granada		Antony of Padua (d. 1231) canonized
1233	Rebellion of Earl of Pembroke, aided by Welsh		The "Great Halleluyah"–penitential movement in northern Italy The pope entrusts the Dominicans with the Inquisition
1234			
1235	Rebellion of his son Henry VII suppressed by Frederick II; Henry imprisoned Mainz Public Peace, first imperial law in Ger. language		Elizabeth of Hungary (d. 1231) canonized
1236	Alexander Nevski, Grand Duke of Novgorod (—1263) The Arabs lose Córdoba to Castile	Neidhardt von Reuenthal, Bavarian minnesinger, d.	
1237	Frederick II defeats Lombard League at Cortenuova Mongols conquer Russia (—1240), take Moscow		
1238			
1239			
1240	Dafydd ap Llywelyn, Prince of Snowdon (—1246) Crusade of Richard of Cornwall and Simon de Montfort to Jaffa Border fixed between England and Scotland	Guido Guinizelli, Ital. poet establishes a school of poetry ("dolce stil nuovo")	
1241	Battle of Liegnitz, Silesia: Mongols defeat Germans, invade Poland and Hungary; the death of their ruler Ughetai forces them to withdraw from Europe		Pope Celestine IV (reigns for 17 days)
1242	Batu, grandson of, Genghis Khan, establishes his warriors–the "Golden Horde"–at Sarai, on the Lower Volga		
1243	Five-year truce between England and France		Pope Innocent IV (—1254)

D. VISUAL ARTS	E. MUSIC	F. SCIENCE, TECHNOLOGY, GROWTH	G. DAILY LIFE	
				1232
			Coal mined for the first time in Newcastle, England	1233
				1234
				1235
				1236
		Jordanus Nemorarius, Ger. scientist, d.		1237
	Adam de la Halle, Fr. composer of musical plays, b. (d. 1287)	Arnold of Villanova, Ital. physician and alchemist, b. (d. 1311)		1238
				1239
Cimabue, Florentine painter, b. (d. 1302)		Roger Bacon returns to England from Paris		1240
The Master of Naumburg: sculptures at Meissen, Mainz, and Naumburg (—1260)				1241
			First record of a ship convoy Kiel established as a town	1242
				1243

	A. HISTORY, POLITICS	B. LITERATURE, THEATER	C. RELIGION, PHILOSOPHY, LEARNING
1244	Egyptian Khwarazmi takes Jerusalem		
1245	Frederick II deposed by the Council of Lyons		Alexander of Hales, Eng. philosopher and theologian, d. (b. 1175)
1246	Frederick II seizes the vacant dukedom of Austria and Styria	Wernher der Gartenaere: "Meier Helmbrecht," earliest Ger. peasant romance	
1247			
1248	Lombards defeat Frederick II at Parma Genoese take Rhodes Seventh Crusade, led by Louis IX	Gonzalo de Berceo, earliest Span. poet, d. (b. 1180)	
1249	Louis IX lands in Egypt		University College, Oxford founded
1250	Frederick II d.; succeeded by Conrad IV (—1254) Valdeman I, King of Sweden (—1275) The Saracens capture Louis IX	Heinrich Frauenlob von Meissen, early mastersinger, b. (d. 1318) "Easter Play of Muri," beginnings of the Ger. drama	Establishment of four national colleges at Paris University
1251	Ottokar, Margrave of Moravia, son of King Wenceslas I, elected Duke of Austria Portugal seizes Algarve Kublai Khan becomes Governor of China, and in 1259 Mongol ruler (—1294)		
1252	Alfonso X, the Wise, of Castile (d. 1284) Founding of Ahom kingdom in Assam		The Inquisition begins to use instruments of torture
1253	Ottokar II, King of Bohemia (—1278)		

D. VISUAL ARTS	E. MUSIC	F. SCIENCE, TECHNOLOGY, GROWTH	G. DAILY LIFE	
			First "Dunmow Flitch" competition (England)	1244
Giovanni Pisano, Ital. sculptor, son of Nicola Pisano, b. (d. 1320) Choir and cloisters of Westminster Abbey, London, built (—1270)				1245
Erection of La Sainte-Chapelle, Paris (—1258)				1246
				1247
Present Cologne Cathedral begun Work begins on Alhambra, Granada		Ibn al-Baitar, writer on Arab pharmacology, d. (b. 1200)		1248
		Roger Bacon records the existence of explosives		1249
High Gothic period in Ger. art (—c. 1500) Building begins on St. Thomas Church, Leipzig Jaina Temple in Mount Abu Johannes Church in Thorn (Torun), northwest India Synagogues at Toledo and Worms	Beginnings of the choral Passion The "Portatio," a portable small organ Magister Perotinus, main representative of the Fr. "Ars antiqua"	Vincent of Beauvais (d. 1264): "Speculum naturale, historiale, doctrinale" (encyclopedia) Jordanus Rufus: "De medicina equorum" (veterinary manual)	Commercial and industrial boom in northern and central Italian cities Hats come into fashion Goose quill used for writing	1250
				1251
Completion of the Church of St. Francis, Assisi			Golden florins minted at Florence	1252
		William of Rubruque travels in Central Asia and reports his experiences (—1255)	Linen first manufactured in England	1253

	A. HISTORY, POLITICS	B. LITERATURE, THEATER	C. RELIGION, PHILOSOPHY, LEARNING
1254	Louis IX returns to France from Palestine Conrad IV d.		Pope Alexander IV (—1261) Court chaplain Robert de Sorbon founds the Paris School of Theology (to be called the Sorbonne)
1255	Henry III of England accepts Sicily for his son Edmund	Ulrich von Lichtenstein: "Frauendienst," poem about chivalry Thomas of Celano, author of "Dies irae," d.	
1256	"Hundred Years War" between Venice and Genoa		Founding of the Order of Augustine Hermits
1257	Llywelyn assumes the title Prince of Wales, and establishes (1259) peace between England and Wales Richard of Cornwall elected King of the Romans and crowned at Aix-la-Chapelle (he was soon "dispossessed")	Saadi, the Persian poet (b. 1184), who lived for 107 years: "The Fruit Garden"	
1258	Manfred, illegitimate son of Frederick II, crowned King of Sicily at Palermo Mongols take Baghdad and overthrow caliphate Establishment of House of Commons (Provisions of Oxford)		
1259			
1260	Florentine Ghibellines defeat Guelphs at Montaperti		Meister Eckhart, Ger. preacher and mystic, b. (d. 1327) The first flagellant movements in southern Germany and northern Italy Chartres Cathedral consecrated
1261	Ottokar II obtains Styria Michael VIII Palaeologus regains Constantinople		Pope Urban IV (—1264)
1262			
1263	Haakon of Norway defeated by the Scots at Largs, cedes Hebrides Alexander Nevski d.		Balliol College, Oxford, founded
1264			Thomas Aquinas (1225-1274): "Summa contra Gentiles" Roger Bacon: "De computo naturali" Merton College, Oxford, founded

D. VISUAL ARTS	E. MUSIC	F. SCIENCE, TECHNOLOGY, GROWTH	G. DAILY LIFE	
Chao Meng-fu, Chin. painter of the transitional era between the Sung and the Yüan dynasties, b. (d. 1322)		Marco Polo, Venetian traveler, b. (d. 1324)		1254
			Prague and Stockholm become towns	1255
				1256
				1257
				1258
				1259
Cimabue: "Madonna," for Trinità, Florence	The first mastersinger school (Mainz)	Henri de Mondeville, Fr. surgeon and anatomist, b. c. (d. 1320)		1260
		Thaddeus Florentinus teaches medicine at Bologna University		1261
	Adam de la Halle: "Le Jeu de la Feuillée," first Fr. "operette"			1262
				1263
				1264

	A. HISTORY, POLITICS	B. LITERATURE, THEATER	C. RELIGION, PHILOSOPHY, LEARNING
1265		Dante Alighieri b. (d. 1321)	Pope Clement IV (—1268)
1266	Manfred defeated and killed by Charles of Anjou at Benevento Balban, Sultan of Delhi (—1287)		Roger Bacon: "Opus maius"
1267	The Aztecs arrive in the Valley of Mexico		
1268			Three years' vacancy in the papacy (—1271)
1269	Ottokar acquires Carinthia and Carniola from Hungary		
1270	Louis IX d. on the Eighth Crusade, and is succeeded by Philip III (—1285) Stephen V of Hungary (—1272)	Tannhäuser, Ger. poet and minnesinger, d. (b. 1205)	
1271			Pope Gregory X (—1276) (later beatified)
1272	Henry III of England d.; succeeded by Edward I (—1307) Richard of Cornwall, King of the Romans, d.		
1273	Rudolf, Count of Hapsburg, elected king and crowned at Aix-la-Chapelle	Djelaleddin Rumi, Persian poet, founder of the Order of Dancing Dervishes, d.	Thomas Aquinas: "Summa theologica" ("Credo ut intelligam")
1274	Edward I crowned at Westminster Kublai Khan fails to conquer Japan		Thomas Aquinas d. (b. 1225)
1275			Moses de León, Jewish theologian, author of "Zohar," the fundamental work on Jewish mysticism

D. VISUAL ARTS	E. MUSIC	F. SCIENCE, TECHNOLOGY, GROWTH	G. DAILY LIFE	
	Franco of Cologne and Pierre de la Croix develop the musical form of the motet (musica mensurata)			1265
Giotto, Ital. painter, b. (d. 1337) Erection of Sanjüsangendö Temple, Kyoto, Japan				1266
			The guilds of goldsmiths and tailors of London fight each other in fierce street battles	1267
				1268
			The first toll roads in England	1269
	Giovanni da Cascia, Ital. composer, b.			1270
		Marco Polo journeys to China (—1295)		1271
				1272
				1273
		Nasir ed-Din, Arab scientist, d. (b. 1201)		1274
		Mondino di Luzzi, Ital. astronomer, b. (d. 1326) William of Saliceto: "Chirurgia," earliest record of human dissection	Marco Polo in the service of Kublai Khan (—1292)	1275

	A. HISTORY, POLITICS	B. LITERATURE, THEATER	C. RELIGION, PHILOSOPHY, LEARNING
1276	Ottokar, outlawed by Rudolf, submits to him and keeps Bohemia and Moravia		The year of the four popes: Pope Gregory X, Pope Innocent V, Pope Hadrian V, and Pope John XXI
1277			Roger Bacon imprisoned for heresy (—1292) Pope Nicholas III (—1280)
1278	Ottokar takes up arms and is defeated by Rudolf and killed at Dürnkrut, Marchfeld; succeeded by Wenceslas II (—1305)		Martin of Troppau, chronicler and historian, d.
1279			
1280	Eric II of Norway (—1299) Asen dynasty in Bulgaria extinguished, the country becoming subject to Serbs, Greeks, and Mongols Kublai Khan founds Yüan dynasty in China (—1368)	Rutebeuf: "Oeuvres," Fr. lyrical and satirical poems	Albertus Magnus, Ger. philosopher and scientist, d. (b. 1193)
1281			Pope Martin IV (—1285)
1282	The Sicilian Vespers: the massacre of the French in Sicily Rudolf invests his sons Albert and Rudolf with Austria, Styria, and Carniola	Juan Manuel, Span. poet, b. (d. 1348)	
1283	The Teutonic Order completes subjection of Prussia A false "Emperor Frederick II" appears in Germany		
1284	Genoa defeats Pisa, thus beginning Pisa's decline		
1285	Philip III d.; succeeded by Philip IV, the Fair (—1314)	The Ger. epic poem "Lohengrin," by an unknown author	Pope Honorius IV (—1287)
1286	Alexander III of Scotland d.; succeeded by his infant niece Margaret, "the Maid of Norway," under six guardians		Bar-Hebräus, Syrian lexicographer, d. (b. 1226)

D. VISUAL ARTS	E. MUSIC	F. SCIENCE, TECHNOLOGY, GROWTH	G. DAILY LIFE	
				1276
				1277
Building of St. Maria Novella, Florence			278 Jews hanged in London for clipping coin; Christians guilty of the same offense, fined Invention of the glass mirror	1278
				1279
			Rebellion of the textile workers of Flanders against their exploiters	1280
				1281
End of Sung Academy, China			Florence is the leading European city in commerce and finance	1282
Erection of Caernarvon Castle (—1323)				1283
Simone Martini, Ital. painter, b. (d. 1344)			The "Pied Piper of Hamelin" Sequins first coined in Venice Gianciotto Malatesta of Rimini, who in 1275 married Francesca, daughter of the Prince of Ravenna, kills her and his brother	1284
	Adam de la Halle: "Jeu de Robin et Marion"			1285
				1286

	A. HISTORY, POLITICS	B. LITERATURE, THEATER	C. RELIGION, PHILOSOPHY, LEARNING
1287	Rudolf proclaims Public Peace at the Diet of Würzburg Mongol invasion of Burma	Conrad of Würzburg, Ger. poet ("The Trojan War"), d.	
1288	Osman I (—1326), founder of Ottoman Empire		Pope Nicholas IV (—1292)
1289			
1290	Margaret of Scotland, who was supposed to marry Edward, son of King Edward I of England, d. Kaikobad, Sultan of Delhi, murdered; succeeded by Jalaluddin	Dante: "La Vita Nuova"	
1291	Rudolf I d. Everlasting League between Uri, Schwyz, and Unterwalden Mamelukes conquer Acre, ending Christian rule in the East End of the Crusades; Knights of St. John of Jerusalem settle in Cyprus		
1292	Scottish throne to John Baliol Adolf, Count of Nassau, elected Ger. King; crowned at Aix-la-Chapelle (—1298)		
1293			
1294	Hanseatic cities recognize Lübeck as their leading member Kublai Khan d.		Roger Bacon, Eng. philosopher and scientist, d. (b. 1214) Pope Celestine V (—1294; renounced the throne–later canonized) Pope Boniface VIII (—1303)
1295	Alliance between France and Scotland	"The Harrowing of Hell," early Eng. miracle play Jacob van Maertant, Dutch poet, d. (b. 1235)	
1296	John Baliol resigns Scot. crown to Edward I Frederick II, King of Sicily (—1337) Jalaluddin of Delhi murdered; succeeded by Alauddin Khilji Scot. coronation stone moved from Scone to Westminster John of Luxembourg, son of Henry VII, b.: King of Bohemia (1310—1346)		

D. VISUAL ARTS	E. MUSIC	F. SCIENCE, TECHNOLOGY, GROWTH	G. DAILY LIFE	
	Adam de la Halle d. (b. 1238)			1287
				1288
		Founding of Montpellier University	Block printing practiced in Ravenna	1289
	Philippe de Vitry, Fr. composer, b. (d. 1361)	Lisbon University founded	Invention of spectacles (see 1303)	1290
Erection of York Minster nave				1291
				1292
				1293
				1294
Cimabue: "Madonna with St. Francis" (at Assisi)		Marco Polo returns to Italy and, in 1298, begins to dictate his memoirs in a Genoese jail		1295
Building of Florence Cathedral begins under Arnolfo di Cambio				1296

	A. HISTORY, POLITICS	B. LITERATURE, THEATER	C. RELIGION, PHILOSOPHY, LEARNING
1297	Genoese defeat Venetians in sea battle at Curzola Scots defeat English at Stirling Bridge		
1298	Adolf of Nassau dethroned by the electors and killed in Battle of Göllheim; succeeded (—1308) as Ger. King by Albert I of Austria	Jacobus de Varagine, author of "The Golden Legend," d.	
1299	Treaties between Venice and the Turks, and France and Germany		
1300	Jubilee Year proclaimed ("Antiquorum habet fide") by Pope Boniface VIII Edward I invades Scotland Wenceslas II of Bohemia elected King of Poland	Guillaume de Machaut, Fr. poet and composer, b. (d. 1377) "Aucassin et Nicolette," famous Fr. love story Development of Chin. drama	Jean Buridan, Fr. scholar, b. c. (d. 1358)
1301	Andrew III of Hungary, last of the Arpads, d. Osman defeats Byzantines at Baphaion Edward I's son made Prince of Wales	Antonio Pucci, Ital. poet, b. (d. 1390)	
1302	Anglo-Scot. truce First meeting of Fr. States General	Dante exiled from Florence	Papal bull "Unam sanctam" pronounces highest papal claims to supremacy
1303			Pope Boniface VIII quarrels with Philip IV of France and dies a prisoner in the Vatican
1304		Petrarch (Francesco Petrarca), Ital. poet, b. (d. 1374)	
1305	Wenceslas II, King of Bohemia, Poland, and Hungary, d.		Pope Clement V (—1314)
1306	Robert Bruce crowned King of Scots and defeated by the English at Methuen and Dalry Wenceslas III, last of the Premyslids, d.–Albert invests his son Rudolf with Bohemia	Jacopone da Todi, author of "Stabat Mater," d. (b. 1230)	Philip IV expels the Jews from France
1307	Edward I d.; succeeded by Edward II (—1327) The legendary Rütli vow of the three Swiss cantons	Dante composes his "Divina Commedia" (—1321)	Archbishopric of Peking set up

D. VISUAL ARTS	E. MUSIC	F. SCIENCE, TECHNOLOGY, GROWTH	G. DAILY LIFE	
			Moas, giant giraffe birds of New Zealand, die out	1297
				1298
Building of Palazzo Vecchio, Florence (—1301)				1299
Giovanni Pisano: "Madonna," Prato Building of St. Mary the Virgin, Oxford (—1498)	The "Jongleurs," professional musical entertainers in France	In the Ger. cities apothecaries become popular Urine examination as means of diagnosis used in medicine	Temporary end of European slave trade Trade fairs at Bruges, Antwerp, Lyons, and Geneva	1300
Giovanni Pisano: pulpit in Pisa Cathedral (—1311)				1301
Cimabue d. (b. 1240)				1302
		Rome University founded Bernard of Gordon: first medical reference to spectacles		1303
	Rüdiger Manesse, collector of the minnesingers' songs, d. (Manessien Manuscript)			1304
Giotto: frescoes in S. Maria dell' Arena, Padua ("Life of Christ," "Last Judgment," etc.)			Edward I standardizes the yard and the acre	1305
		Pietro d'Abano (1250—1315) becomes professor of medicine at Padua University		1306
Completion of Lincoln Cathedral tower				1307

	A. HISTORY, POLITICS	B. LITERATURE, THEATER	C. RELIGION, PHILOSOPHY, LEARNING
1308	Coronation of Edward II Albert I murdered; Henry VII, Count of Luxembourg, is elected Ger. King.		Duns Scotus, Scot. theologian, d. (b. 1266)
1309			Clement V (a Frenchman) fixes papal residence at Avignon–beginning of the "Babylonian captivity," during which Rome is not the papal seat
1310	Council of Ten established in Venice Edward II is forced to appoint Lords Ordainers for better ruling of England		
1311			
1312	Treaty of Vienne: Lyons incorporated into France Henry VII of Luxembourg crowned emperor in Rome		
1313	Henry VII of Luxembourg d.	Giovanni Boccaccio, the Florentine novelist, b. (d. 1375) Hugo von Trimberg, Ger. poet, d. (b. 1230)	
1314	Philip IV of France d.; succeeded by his three sons Louis X (—1316), Philip V (—1322), and Charles IV (—1328) Double election of Frederick of Austria (d. 1330) and Louis of Bavaria (d. 1347) Battle of Bannockburn: Robert Bruce's Scots rout the English under Edward II		Jacques de Molay, Grand Master of the Templars, burned at the stake in Paris for alleged heresy Vacancy in the papal chair for more than two years
1315	Leopold of Austria defeated at Morgarten; Swiss League renewed		
1316	Edward Bruce crowned King of Ireland Muberak, last of the Khilji rulers of Delhi (—1320)		Pope John XXII (—1334)
1317	Salic Law, excluding women from succession to throne, adopted in France		
1318	Edward Bruce killed in Battle of Faughart, near Dundalk Truce between Swiss League and Hapsburgs	Heinrich Frauenlob von Meissen, Ger. mastersinger, d. (b. 1250)	

D. VISUAL ARTS	E. MUSIC	F. SCIENCE, TECHNOLOGY, GROWTH	G. DAILY LIFE	
			King Philip IV purchases the Hôtel des Nesle, in which he builds a tennis court, one of the earliest indoor courts in Paris	1308
Doge's Palace, Venice, built on site of earlier palaces (—1438)	Marchettus of Padua pleads for the introduction of counterpoint into musical composition	Founding of Orleans University		1309
				1310
				1311
		The Canary Islands rediscovered by Genoa		1312
		The Ger. Grey Friar Berthold Schwarz invents gunpowder		1313
Completion of (old) St. Paul's Cathedral, London				1314
			Lyons silk industry developed by Ital. immigrants	1315
				1316
				1317
				1318

	A. HISTORY, POLITICS	B. LITERATURE, THEATER	C. RELIGION, PHILOSOPHY, LEARNING
1320	Gharzi Khan, Sultan of Delhi (Tughlak dynasty) Peace of Paris between Flanders and France Vladislav I Lokietek (crowned in Cracow), King of Poland (—1333)	Hafiz, Persian poet, b. (d. 1389)	
1321		Dante Alighieri d. at Ravenna (b. 1265)	Monte Cassino becomes bishopric
1322	Battle of Mühldorf: Frederick of Austria defeated and taken prisoner by Louis of Bavaria		
1323			Thomas Aquinas canonized
1324			
1325	Louis of Bavaria accepts Frederick of Austria as coregent The Aztecs found their capital, Mexico-Tenochtitlan, which would become Mexico City	Development of No plays in Japan	
1326	Isabella, wife of Edward II, and her lover Roger Mortimer invade England and capture the king Osman I, ruler of Turkey, d.		
1327	Edward II, deposed by Parliament and murdered at Berkeley Castle, is succeeded by Edward III (—1377)		Meister Eckhart, Ger. mystic, d. (b. c. 1260)
1328	Charles IV, last of the direct line of the Capets, d.; succeeded by Philip VI of the House of Valois Louis IV of Bavaria crowned emperor in Rome, Jan. 17; declares Pope John XXII deposed for heresy Ivan I, Grand Duke of Russia (—1341), makes Moscow his capital		John Wyclif, Eng. Church reformer, b. c. (d. 1384)
1329	David II, King of Scots (—1371) Compact of Pavia: separation of Bavaria and the Palatinate		
1330	Frederick of Austria d.; in the Treaty of Hagenau, the Hapsburgs recognize Louis IV of Bavaria as emperor		Monastery of Ettal, Bavaria, founded

D. VISUAL ARTS	E. MUSIC	F. SCIENCE, TECHNOLOGY, GROWTH	G. DAILY LIFE	
Giovanni Pisano, Ital. sculptor, d. (b. 1245)		Henri de Mondeville, Fr. surgeon and anatomist at Montpellier University, d. (b. c. 1260)		**1320**
				1321
	The pope forbids the use of counterpoint in church music			**1322**
				1323
Burgos Cathedral consecrated		Marco Polo, Venetian traveler, d. (b. 1254)		**1324**
	Francesco Landino, Ital. composer and organist, b. c. (d. 1397) Organ pedals come into use "Tournai Mass," first polyphonic Mass still extant			**1325**
		Founding of Oriel College, Oxford, and Clare College, Cambridge		**1326**
			The great fire of Munich	**1327**
			Invention of the sawmill	**1328**
	Philippe de Vitry coins the name "Ars nova" for the new, strongly contrapuntal style of music			**1329**
	Paris Musicians' Guild, Ménétriers (—1773)			**1330**

	A. HISTORY, POLITICS	B. LITERATURE, THEATER	C. RELIGION, PHILOSOPHY, LEARNING
1331	Stephen IV Dushan, founder of Greater Serbia (—1355) Disputed Imperial succession in Japan leads to civil war against Hojo regents		
1332	Edward Baliol, crowned King of Scots, recognizes Edward III as overlord Lucerne joins Swiss League First record of Parliament divided into two houses		
1333	Casimir III of Poland (—1370) Yusuf I, Caliph of Granada (—1354): zenith of Arabic civilization in Granada		
1334			Pope Benedict XII (—1342)
1335	Louis IV invests the Hapsburgs with Carinthia		
1336			
1337	Edward III, claiming Fr. crown, assumes title King of France Beginning of the Hundred Years' War		Jean Froissart, Fr. chronicler, b. (d. 1410)
1338	The French burn Portsmouth Alliance of Coblenz between Louis IV and Edward III		
1339	Venice conquers Treviso; gains first mainland possession		
1340	English defeat French off Sluys; French occupy Guienne	Geoffrey Chaucer b. c. (d. 1400)	
1341		Petrarch crowned poet on the Capitol, Rome	
1342	Louis of Bavaria, son of Louis IV, marries Margaret of Tirol (the "Ugly Duchess") and acquires Tirol and Carinthia		Pope Clement VI (—1352)

D. VISUAL ARTS	E. MUSIC	F. SCIENCE, TECHNOLOGY, GROWTH	G. DAILY LIFE	
			First record of weaving in England (York)	1331
	Company of mastersingers formed at Toulouse		Bubonic plague originates in India	1332
				1333
Erection of the Palace of the Popes, Avignon (—1362) Giotto begins to build the campanile at Florence				1334
				1335
				1336
Giotto d. (b. 1266)		William Merlee of Oxford attempts first scientific weather forecasts		1337
		Founding of Pisa University		1338
		Founding of Grenoble University		1339
	Guillaume de Machaut, the greatest musician of his day (d. 1377)	Queen's College, Oxford, founded		1340
				1341
				1342

	A. HISTORY, POLITICS	B. LITERATURE, THEATER	C. RELIGION, PHILOSOPHY, LEARNING
1344	Philip VI invests his son Philip with the newly created dukedom of Orleans		
1345			
1346	The French defeated at Crécy		
1347	Calais surrenders to Edward III Cola di Rienzi, tribune of the people, rules Rome (Apr.—Dec.) Louis IV d.; Charles IV of Luxembourg succeeds him as emperor (—1378)		
1348	The "false Valdemar" gains rule of Brandenburg before being exposed as swindler (1350) Edward III founds the Order of the Garter	Boccaccio: "Decameron" (—1353)	
1349			Persecution of the Jews in Germany William of Ockham, Eng. philosopher, d. (b. 1290)
1350	Philip VI of France d.; succeeded by John II (d. 1364) Treaty of Bautzen: Charles IV cedes Brandenburg and Tirol to the Wittelsbachs Cola di Rienzi imprisoned in Prague	Li Hsing Tao: "The Chalk Circle," famous Chin. play	
1351	Zurich joins Swiss League Firoz Shah, Sultan of Delhi (—1388) Leopold III, Duke of Austria (—1386)	Jan de Weert of Ypres, Dutch poet Petrarch: "Epistle to Posterity" (autobiography)	
1352	Glarus and Zug join Swiss League (Bern follows in 1353) Rienzi extradited to Rome		Pope Innocent VI (—1362)
1353	Rupert I elector palatine (—1390)		Nicholas d'Autrecourt, Fr. philosopher, d.
1354	Rienzi murdered in Rome after another attempt to establish tyranny The Turks take Gallipoli		

D. VISUAL ARTS	E. MUSIC	F. SCIENCE, TECHNOLOGY, GROWTH	G. DAILY LIFE	
St. Vitus' Cathedral, Prague, begun by Matthew of Arras				1344
			Bankruptcy of the great Florentine banking houses of Bardi and Peruzzi	1345
				1346
			Black Death devastates Europe	1347
		Prague University founded by Charles IV Gonville and Caius College, Cambridge, founded,		1348
Andrea Pisano, Ital. sculptor, d. (b. 1290)			Black Death kills a third of population of England	1349
Cathedral at Palma, Majorca Completion of Bergamo Cathedral and Salisbury Cathedral Edward III of England begins to rebuild Windsor Castle	Cambrai, instead of Paris, becomes center of Fr. music Lute playing popular in Europe Mastersinger movement in Germany		Till Eulenspiegel, Ger. popular figure, d. The Shogun of Japan prohibits the drinking of tea	1350
			Tennis becomes an open-air game in England Between 1347 and 1351, approx. 75 million people die of the Black Death	1351
		Arab geographer Ibn Battuta explores Sahara desert	Corpus Christi College, Oxford, founded	1352
				1353
			The mechanical clock at Strasbourg Cathedral	1354

	A. HISTORY, POLITICS	B. LITERATURE, THEATER	C. RELIGION, PHILOSOPHY, LEARNING
1355	Scots defeat English at Nesbit Charles IV of Luxembourg crowned emperor at Rome Stephen Dushan of Serbia d. The Doge Marino Falieri executed in Venice		
1356	The Black Prince defeats French at Poitiers, John II and his son Philip being taken prisoners Charles IV issues "Golden Bull," settling election of Ger. kings.		
1357	Revolution in Paris against the Dauphin, led by Marcel and Robert le Coq	Hugo von Montfort, Ger. poet from Styria, b.	
1358	The Hapsburgs, twice defeated at Zurich, sign peace treaty with Swiss League		Jean Buridan, Fr. philosopher, d. (b. c. 1300)
1359	Treaty of London restores Fr. possessions once held by Henry II of England to Eng. crown		
1360	Treaty of Calais between Edward III and Philip of Burgundy		
1361			
1362	Dmitri IV Donskoi, Grand Duke of Moscow (—1389)	"Piers Plowman," poem in Middle English, ascribed to William Langland of Malvern	Pope Urban V (—1370)
1363	Rudolf IV of Austria obtains Tirol Timur the Lame (Tamerlaine) begins conquest of Asia		
1364	John II of France d.; succeeded by Charles V (—1380) Pact of succession between the Hapsburg and the Luxembourg dynasties signed at Brno (Moravia) Revolts in Crete against Venetian rule		
1365	Charles V crowned King of Burgundy at Arles Leopold III, Duke of Austria (—1386)		
1366	Adrianople made Turk. capital Eng. Parliament refuses to pay feudal dues to the pope	Petrarch: "Canzoniere"	

D. VISUAL ARTS	E. MUSIC	F. SCIENCE, TECHNOLOGY, GROWTH	G. DAILY LIFE	
St. Mary's Church, Nuremberg, begun	Jean de Muris, Fr. composer, d. (b. 1289)			1355
				1356
				1357
				1358
Work on the nave of St. Stephen's, Vienna, begins				1359
Ca d'Oro, Venice Alcazar of Seville (—1402)	Beginnings of the development of the clavichord and cembalo		The first francs coined in France	1360
	Philippe de Vitry, Fr. composer, d. (b. 1290)		Black Death reappears in England	1361
				1362
		Guy de Chauliac: "Chirurgia magna" (on surgery in the Middle Ages)		1363
	Guillaume de Machaut: "Mass for four voices," composed for the coronation of Charles V at Rheims		The Aztecs of Mexico build their capital, Tenochtitlan	1364
		Founding of Vienna University		1365
Meier Abdeli completes El Transito Synagogue at Toledo			The Fuggers come as weavers to Augsburg	1366

	A. HISTORY, POLITICS	B. LITERATURE, THEATER	C. RELIGION, PHILOSOPHY, LEARNING
1368	Mongol Yüan dynasty in China overthrown by national Ming dynasty (—1644) Timur ascends throne of Samarkand (—1405)		
1369	Venice repels Hungarian invasion	Chaucer: "The Book of the Duchesse"	Jan Hus b. c. (d. 1415)
1370	The Black Prince sacks Limoges Casimir III of Poland, last of the House of Piasts d.; Louis of Hungary elected king (d. 1382)		Pope Gregory XI (—1378)
1371	Robert II, King of Scots (—1390): accession of the House of Stewart English defeat Flemings at Bourgneuf		
1372	French defeat English, take Poitiers, Angoulême, and La Rochelle Owen-ap-Thomas, self-styled Prince of Wales, aided by French, captures Guernsey		Oxford becomes the spiritual center of England
1373	John of Gaunt invades France from Calais to Bordeaux Charles IV gains Brandenburg from the Wittelsbachs		
1374		Petrarch (Francesco Petrarca) d. (b. 1304)	
1375	Truce of Bruges between England and France The Mamelukes take Sis; end of Armenian independence	Boccaccio d. (b. 1313) John Barbour (1320—1395): "The Bruce" "Robin Hood" appears in Eng. popular literature	
1376	The Black Prince d. Wenceslas, son of Charles IV, crowned King of the Romans		
1377	Edward III d.; succeeded by his grandson Richard II (—1399)		Pope Gregory XI returns to Rome; end of the Church's "Babylonian Captivity"
1378	Renewal of Anglo-Fr. war Charles IV of Luxembourg d.; succeeded by Wenceslas IV (—1400)		The Great Schism begins (—1417): after the death of Pope Gregory XI, two popes elected; Urban VI at Rome, Clement VII at Avignon

D. VISUAL ARTS	E. MUSIC	F. SCIENCE, TECHNOLOGY, GROWTH	G. DAILY LIFE	
			Restoration of the Great Wall of China	1368
	John Dunstable, Eng. composer, b. (d. 1453)		Building of the Bastille, Paris	1369
Hubert van Eyck, Dutch painter, b. (d. 1426) Carthusian monks build the Charterhouse, London			Steel crossbow used as weapon of war	1370
Jacopo della Quercia, Ital. sculptor, b. (d. 1438)				1371
				1372
			Tunnage and poundage imposed on merchants in England	1373
Ni Tsan, Chin. painter and poet, d. (b. 1301)				1374
				1375
				1376
	Guillaume de Machaut, Fr. composer, d. (b. 1300) The musicians of the papal chapel, Avignon, return with the court; beginnings of Rome as the center of music		Playing cards displace dice in Germany	1377
Lorenzo Ghiberti, Ital. sculptor, b. (d. 1455)				1378

	A. HISTORY, POLITICS	B. LITERATURE, THEATER	C. RELIGION, PHILOSOPHY, LEARNING
1379	Treaty of Neuberg: Albert III and Leopold III divide Hapsburg territories between them		
1380	Charles V of France d.; succeeded by Charles VI, the Mad (—1422) Dmitri IV of Moscow defeats Mongols at Kulikov Timur begins his 35 successful campaigns to Persia, Georgia, Russia, Egypt, etc.		Catherine of Siena d. (canonized 1461) Thomas à Kempis, Ger. mystic, b. (d. 1471)
1381	Anglo-Fr. truce for six years Peasants' Revolt in England under Wat Tyler Venice wins the "Hundred Years War" against Genoa; flourishing of commerce, arts, and sciences	Chaucer: "House of Fame"	
1382	Leopold III of Austria acquires Trieste Turks capture Sofia		Wyclif expelled from Oxford, his doctrines being condemned by London synod
1383			
1384	Anglo-Scot. war renewed Jadviga, daughter of King Louis I (d. 1382), crowned "king" of Poland	Chaucer: "The Parlement of Foules"	John Wyclif d. (b. c. 1328)
1385	Anglo-Fr. war renewed	Alain Chartier, Fr. poet, b. (d. 1450) Chaucer: "Troilus and Cryseide"	
1386	Leopold III of Austria defeated and killed by the Swiss at Sempach Grand Prince Jagiello of Lithuania marries Jadviga and becomes Vladislav II, King of Poland (—1434)		
1387	Sigismund of Brandenburg, son of Charles IV, becomes King of Hungary (—1437) by marriage	Jean d'Arras: "L'Histoire de Lusignan" (Fr. prose romance) Chaucer: "Canterbury Tales" (—1400)	
1388	Scots defeat English in the Battle of Chevy Chase (Otterburn)	Leonardo Giustiniani, Ital. poet, b. (d. 1446)	
1389	William of Wykeham, Lord Chancellor of England Truce between England, Scotland, and France Bajazet I, Emir of the Turks (—1403)	Hafiz, Persian poet, d. (b. 1320)	Pope Boniface IX elected at Rome (—1404)
1390	Robert III, King of Scots (—1406) Byzantines lose last possessions in Asia Minor to Turks		Wyclif's writings reach Bohemia

D. VISUAL ARTS	E. MUSIC	F. SCIENCE, TECHNOLOGY, GROWTH	G. DAILY LIFE	
		William of Wykeham founds New College, Oxford		1379
				1380
				1381
				1382
				1383
			Incorporation of Fishmongers' Company, London	1384
	The first Fr. court ball at the wedding of Charles VI and Isabella of Bavaria			1385
Work begins on Milan Cathedral		Heidelberg University founded		1386
Fra Angelico, Ital. painter, b. (d. 1455)				1387
		Cologne University founded		1388
				1389
Jan van Eyck, Dutch painter, b. c. (d. 1441)				1390

	A. HISTORY, POLITICS	B. LITERATURE, THEATER	C. RELIGION, PHILOSOPHY, LEARNING
1392	Charles VI seized with madness; his brother Louis becomes Duke of Orleans Succession dispute in Japan: the Ashikagas become shoguns of Muromachi		
1393	Bajazet subdues Bulgaria King Wenceslas has St. John of Nepomuk murdered in Prague		
1394	Richard II starts on expedition to Ireland Wenceslas taken prisoner by his cousin, Jobst of Moravia		
1395	Ir. rulers do homage to Richard II, receive amnesty		
1396	Richard II of England marries Isabella of France at Calais; Anglo-Fr. truce extended to 28 years Bajazet defeats Christian army under Sigismund of Hungary at Nicopolis		Manuel Chrysoloras opens Greek classes in Florence: beginning of revival of Greek literature in Italy
1397	Duke of Gloucester murdered Union of Kalmar between Sweden, Denmark, and Norway		
1398	Timur conquers Delhi	Confrérie de la Passion at Paris performs religious plays (—1548)	Jan Hus lectures on theology at Prague University
1399	Richard II deposed: Henry of Lancaster, son of John of Gaunt, succeeds to the throne as Henry IV		
1400	Henry IV suppresses rebellion of the barons Richard II murdered Wenceslas IV deposed and succeeded by Rupert III of the Palatinate (—1410) Ascent of the Medici in Florence	Chaucer d. (b. c. 1340) Flourishing of the ecclesiastical drama in Italy Earliest known literature written in Cornish tongue	Jean Froissart: "Chronicles"
1401	Timur conquers Damascus and Baghdad		Nicholas of Cusa, Ger. philosopher, b. (d. 1464)
1402	Timur defeats Bajazet at Ankara and takes him prisoner		

D. VISUAL ARTS	E. MUSIC	F. SCIENCE, TECHNOLOGY, GROWTH	G. DAILY LIFE	
			Foreigners in England forbidden to retail goods	1392
The Gothic Town Hall of Thorn built				1393
				1394
				1395
Michelozzo di Bartolommeo, architect of the early Ital. Renaissance in Florence, b.		Johann Gutenberg, inventor of printing in Europe, b. c. (d. 1468)		1396
Pisanello (Antonio Pisano), Ital. painter, b. c. (d. 1450)	Francesco Landino, Ital. composer, d. (b. 1325)			1397
				1398
Luca della Robbia, Ital. sculptor, b. (d. 1482)	Guillaume Dufay, Dutch composer, b. (d. 1474)			1399
Development of Middle and Upper Mississippi phases of Mound-builders, N. America Rogier van der Weyden, Dutch painter, b. (d. 1464) Early Renaissance period (—1500) Alt-Neu Synagogue in Prague	Gilles Binchois, Dutch-Burgundian composer, b. (d. 1460) First mention of the dulcimer	Alchemy becomes more and more a field for swindlers		1400
Masaccio, Ital. painter, b. (d. 1428)			Klaus Störtebeker, the pirate, executed at Hamburg	1401
Seville Cathedral begun Work begins on Brussels Town Hall				1402

	A. HISTORY, POLITICS	B. LITERATURE, THEATER	C. RELIGION, PHILOSOPHY, LEARNING
1403	Henry IV subdues Northumberland Bajazet d.; succeeded (—1411) by his son Suleiman I		
1404		"Pi Pa Ki" (Story of the Lute), important Chin. play in its last version by Mao-Tseu	Pope Innocent VII (—1406)
1405	Timur d.; succeeded by Shah Rokh (—1447)	Eustache Deschamps, Fr. poet, d. (b. 1346)	
1406	Venice acquires Padua, and Florence subdues Pisa Robert II of Scotland d.; succeeded by James I, who is imprisoned in England		Pope Gregory XII (—1409; abdicated)
1407	Louis, Duke of Orleans, murdered by Burgundians; start of civil war in France		
1408			Cardinals of Rome and Avignon meet to end Great Schism
1409	Venice recovers Dalmatia		Council of Pisa: Pope Alexander V (—1410)
1410	King Rupert d.		Pope John XXIII, antipope (—1415) Hus and his followers excommunicated by the Archbishop of Prague Jean Froissart, Fr. poet and chronicler, d. (b. 1337)
1411	Sigismund, King of Hungary, son of Charles IV, elected Ger. King, and crowned emperor (—1437)		Pope John XXIII excommunicates Jan Hus
1412	Joan of Arc b. (d. 1431)		
1413	Henry IV d.; succeeded by his son Henry V (—1422)		The Disputation of Tortosa (Spain): Joseph Albo (1380—1444) defends the Jewish faith

D. VISUAL ARTS	E. MUSIC	F. SCIENCE, TECHNOLOGY, GROWTH	G. DAILY LIFE	
Lorenzo Ghiberti begins work on porches of Florence baptistery		Compilation of "Yung Lo Ta Tien," Chin. encyclopedia in 22,937 vols. (only three copies made)		1403
				1404
Erection of Bath Abbey (—1499)		Konrad Kyeser: "Bellifortis" (book of military technology)		1405
Fra Filippo Lippi, Ital. painter, b. c. (d. 1469) Mausoleum of Timur in Samarkand				1406
			Bethlehem Hospital, London (Bedlam), becomes an institution for the insane	1407
Donatello: "David," "St. John" (statues)				1408
		Leipzig University founded by Ger. refugees from Prague		1409
Dirk Bouts, Dutch painter, b. (d. 1475)				1410
London Guildhall built (—1426)		Founding of St. Andrews University, Edinburgh		1411
Filippo Brunelleschi:" "Rules of Perspective" Donatello: "St. Peter," "St. George," "St. Mark" (statues)				1412
				1413

	A. HISTORY, POLITICS	B. LITERATURE, THEATER	C. RELIGION, PHILOSOPHY, LEARNING
1414			The Council of Constance to settle "causa unionis, reformationis, fidei" Thomas à Kempis: "Imitatio Christi"
1415	Henry V takes Harfleur, and defeats the French at Agincourt		Pope John XXIII deposed Hus burned at the stake at Constance for heresy
1416			Jerome of Prague, a follower of Hus, burned for heresy
1417	Henry V takes Caen		Council of Constance deposes Pope Benedict XIII, who holds out as pretender-pope until his death Pope Martin V (—1431) elected in Rome: end of Great Schism
1418			
1419	Rouen capitulates to Henry V Henry allies with Philip II of Burgundy War between Empire and Bohemian Hussites (—1436) Ex-King Wenceslas d.; Sigismund obtains Bohemia		
1420	Treaty of Troyes; Henry V, recognized by Charles VI as heir apparent to the French throne, marries Catherine of France and enters Paris The Hussites defeat Sigismund at Vysehrad	Dafydd Nanmor, Welsh bard, b. (d. 1485)	Torquemada, the future Span. Grand Inquisitor, b. (d. 1498)
1421			
1422	Henry V of England d.; succeeded by nine-month-old Henry VI (—1461) Charles VI of France d.; succeeded by Charles VII (—1461) Blind Hussite general John Ziska of Trocnov (d. 1424) defeats the imperial army near Prague		
1423	James I of Scotland released by the English		
1424			

D. VISUAL ARTS	E. MUSIC	F. SCIENCE, TECHNOLOGY, GROWTH	G. DAILY LIFE	
			The Medici of Florence become bankers to the papacy (—1476)	1414
				1415
			Dutch fishermen the first to use drift nets	1416
				1417
				1418
Filippo Brunelleschi (1377—1446) designs the Foundling Hospital, Florence				1419
Erection of the Great Temple of the Dragon, Peking Brunelleschi: cupola of Florence Cathedral				1420
				1421
				1422
Doge's Palace, Venice, enlarged (—1438)		Georg Purbach, Aust. mathematician and astronomer, b. (d. 1461)		1423
				1424

	A. HISTORY, POLITICS	B. LITERATURE, THEATER	C. RELIGION, PHILOSOPHY, LEARNING
1425	John VIII, Byzantine Emperor (—1448) Struggles in Bohemia between Ziska's followers, the Utraquists, and the radical Taborites	Alain Chartier: "La Belle Dame sans merci," Fr. poem	
1426			
1427	Itzcoatl, King of the Aztecs, in Mexico, enlarges his empire		
1428	Treaty of Delft: peace between England and Flanders Joan of Arc leads Fr. armies against England Venetian condottiere Carmagnola conquers Brescia and Bergamo		
1429	Joan of Arc raises siege of Orleans; Charles VII crowned in Rheims Henry VI crowned at Westminster Philip of Burgundy creates the Order of the Golden Fleece		
1430	Joan of Arc captured by Burgundians at Compiègne	Modern English develops from Middle English Pérez de Guzmán (1376—1460), Span. author, flourished	
1431	Joan of Arc burned at the stake at Rouen Henry VI of England crowned King of France in Paris First Ger. peasant revolt at Worms	François Villon, Fr. poet, b. (d. after 1463)	Pope Eugene IV (—1447)
1432			
1433	Sigismund crowned Holy Roman Emperor		
1434	Vladislav III, King of Poland (—1444) Taborites defeated at Lipan, their ruler Prokops killed Cosimo de' Medici becomes ruler of Florence (—1464)		Revolt in Rome: Pope Eugene IV flees to Florence
1435	Peace of Arras between Charles VII and Philip of Burgundy Swed. Parliament (Riksdag) meets for the first time		

D. VISUAL ARTS	E. MUSIC	F. SCIENCE, TECHNOLOGY, GROWTH	G. DAILY LIFE	
				1425
Hubert van Eyck, Dutch painter, d. (b. 1370)	Holland becomes the center of European music	Louvain University founded		1426
		Lincoln College, Oxford, founded		1427
Giovanni Bellini, Venetian painter, b. (d. 1516) Masaccio, Ital. painter, d. (b. 1401)				1428
				1429
	Beginning of first Dutch school (Gilles Binchois, Guillaume Dufay) Jakob Obrecht (d. 1505) and Johannes Okegham b. (d. 1494)		"Mad Marjorie," the great cast-iron gun, introduced	1430
Andrea Mantegna, Ital. painter, b.		Universities of Caen and of Poitiers founded		1431
		Port. sailor Gonzalo Cabral discovers the Azores		1432
Donatello: "David," sculpture, Florence Hans Memling, Dutch painter, b. (d. 1494)			The double-eagle becomes the emblem of the Holy Roman emperors	1433
Florence Cathedral completed (begun 1420)		Joao Diaz, Port. explorer, rounds Cape Bojador		1434
Rogier van der Weyden: "Descent from the Cross" Michael Pacher, Bavarian painter and woodcarver, b. (d. 1498)				1435

	A. HISTORY, POLITICS	B. LITERATURE, THEATER	C. RELIGION, PHILOSOPHY, LEARNING
1436	Eng. troops withdraw from Paris Scots defeat English near Berwick Compact of Iglau ends Hussite Wars, Emperor Sigismund being acknowledged as King of Bohemia		
1437	James I murdered at Perth; succeeded by James II (—1460) Emperor Sigismund d., last of the House of Luxembourg; succeeded as king of Hungary, Bohemia, and (1438) Germany by his son-in-law, Albert V		
1438	Nine-years' truce between England and Scotland Pachacutec founds Inca rule in Peru		
1439	The heirs to the Fr. throne receive the title Conte du Dauphiné		
1440	Frederick of Styria and Carinthia elected Ger. King (—1493)		Platonic Academy, Florence, founded
1441			
1442			
1443	János Hunyady, the Hungarian national hero, defeats the Turks at Nish		
1444	Vladislav III of Poland and Hungary killed by the Turks at the Battle of Varna	Hans Rosenplut, one of the early mastersingers of Nuremberg	Leonardo Bruni, Ital. humanist, d. (b. 1369)
1445	Henry VI of England marries Margaret of Anjou		
1446	János Hunyady elected regent of Hungary	Leonardo Giustiniani, Ital. poet, d. (b. 1388)	

D. VISUAL ARTS	E. MUSIC	F. SCIENCE, TECHNOLOGY, GROWTH	G. DAILY LIFE	
Fra Angelico works at the San Marco Monastery, Florence Andrea del Verrocchio, Ital. painter and sculptor, b. (d. 1488)				**1436**
	John Dunstable develops counterpoint in musical composition	All Souls' College, Oxford, founded		**1437**
Jacopo della Quercia, Ital. sculptor, d. (b. 1371) Erection of the Jamma Musjid Mosque of Husain, Jaunpur				**1438**
				1439
				1440
Jan van Eyck, Dutch painter, d. (b. c. 1390) Luca Signorelli, Ital. painter, b. (d. 1523)		Eton College and King's College, Cambridge, founded Port. navigators find the first Negroes near Cape Blanc, western Africa, and start slave trade again		**1441**
				1442
			Eng. plague order on quarantine and cleansing	**1443**
Sandro Botticelli, Ital. painter, b. (d. 1510) Donato Bramante, Ital. architect, b. (d. 1514)		Cosimo de' Medici founds the Biblioteca Medicea Laurenziana, Florence		**1444**
		Port. navigator Diniz Diaz discovers Cape Verde	Copenhagen becomes Dan. capital	**1445**
Filippo Brunelleschi, Ital. architect, d. (b. 1377) Pietro Perugino, Ital. painter, b. (d. 1523) Building of King's College Chapel, Cambridge (—1515)				**1446**

	A. HISTORY, POLITICS	B. LITERATURE, THEATER	C. RELIGION, PHILOSOPHY, LEARNING
1447	Scanderbeg defeats Murad II, and gains independence for India, Persia, and Afghanistan		Pope Nicholas V (—1455), a renowned scholar
1448	Anglo-Scot. war renewed, Lancaster and York forming the two rival groups in England Knutson Bonde elected King Charles VIII of Sweden (—1470) Murad II defeats János Hunyady at Kossovo Constantine XI Palaeologus the last Byzantine Emperor (—1453)		
1449	English break truce with France, capture Fougères Lorenzo de' Medici (The Magnificent), future ruler of Florence, b. (d. 1492)		
1450	Francesco Sforza enters Milan and assumes title of duke (—1466) Jack Cade's rebellion in England The Incas subdue the Indians of Chimu in northern Peru	Alain Chartier, Fr. poet, d. (b. 1385) Vatican Library founded	Gutenberg prints the "Constance Mass Book"
1451	Mohammed II, Sultan of the Turks (—1481)		
1452	Borso, Marquis of Este, created Duke of Modena and Reggio by Frederick III Frederick III crowned emperor George of Podebrad elected Regent of Bohemia		Girolamo Savonarola, Ital. preacher, b. (d. 1498)
1453	Turks capture Constantinople and kill Emperor Constantine XI, end of East Roman (or Byzantine) Empire End of Hundred Years' War between England and France: England gives up all possessions except Calais		Turks convert St. Sophia Basilica, Constantinople, into a mosque
1454	Peace of Lodi between Venice and Milan Richard, Duke of York, named "Protector of England" during insanity of Henry VI; Edward, son of Henry, named Prince of Wales		
1455	Duke of York, excluded from Council, defeats royal forces at St. Albans, May, and becomes again "Protector": beginning of the Wars of the Roses		

D. VISUAL ARTS	E. MUSIC	F. SCIENCE, TECHNOLOGY, GROWTH	G. DAILY LIFE	
		Founding of Palermo University		1447
				1448
Domenico Ghirlandajo, Ital. painter, b. (d. 1494)				1449
Florence under the Medici becomes center of Renaissance and humanism Hieronymus Bosch, Dutch painter, b. (d. 1516) Pisanello, Ital. painter, d. (b. 1397) Veit Stoss, Pol.-Ger. sculptor, b. (d. 1533)	Josquin des Prés, Dutch composer, b. (d. 1521) Heinrich Isaak, Ger.-Dutch composer, b. (d. 1517)		Mocha in southwestern Arabia becomes main port for coffee export	1450
Stephen Lochner, Cologne painter, d. (b. 1405)		Christopher Columbus, the discoverer of America, b. (d. 1506) Amerigo Vespucci, Ital. navigator, b. (d. 1512) Glasgow University founded		1451
Ghiberti completes Gates of Paradise at Florence baptistery (work began 1425) Leonardo da Vinci, universal genius, b. (d. 1519)		Metal plates are used for printing		1452
	John Dunstable, Eng. composer, d. (b. 1369) Conrad Paumann, Ger. blind organist (1410—1473), publishes his "Fundamentum organisandi," a collection of organ pieces, songs, and dances	Gutenberg and his financier, Johannes Fust, print the 42-line (Mazarin) bible at Mainz (—1455)		1453
			Gutenberg produces Indulgences, bearing printed data	1454
Lorenzo Ghiberti d. (b. 1378) Fra Angelico d. (b. 1387) Erection of Palazzo Venezia, Rome		The Venetian navigator Cadamosto explores the Senegal River		1455

	A. HISTORY, POLITICS	B. LITERATURE, THEATER	C. RELIGION, PHILOSOPHY, LEARNING
1456	The trial of Joan of Arc annulled Turks conquer Athens János Hunyady d. after repelling the Turks at Belgrade	François Villon: "Le Petit Testament"	
1457	Ladislas V Posthumus, King of Hungary and Bohemia, d. (b. 1440); Frederick III inherits Upper and Lower Austria	Sebastian Brant, Ger. satirist, b. (d. 1521)	
1458	The Hussite leader, George of Podebrad, becomes King of Bohemia (—1471) Matthias Corvinus, son of János Hunyady, becomes King of Hungary (—1490)	Jacopo Sannazaro, Ital. poet, b. (d. 1530) Marques de Santillana, Span. poet, d. (b. 1389)	Aeneas Sylvius Piccolomini becomes Pope Pius II (—1464)
1459	Renewal of civil war in England		
1460	Richard of York defeats Henry VI at Northampton, but is defeated and killed by Queen Margaret at Wakefield James II of Scotland, killed at Roxburgh, succeeded by James III (—1488)		
1461	Edward, son of Richard of York, crowned Edward IV, King of England (—1483) Charles VII of France d.; succeeded by Louis XI (—1483) Scanderbeg (1403—1468) becomes Prince of Albania		
1462			
1463	Emperor Frederick III recognizes Matthias Corvinus of Hungary, who recognizes Hapsburg claims to succession The Turks conquer Bosnia	François Villon, saved from gallows, disappears (b. 1431)	Pico de Mirandola, Ital. humanist, b. (d. 1494)
1464	Peace between England and Scotland Cosimo de' Medici, ruler of Florence, d. (b. 1434)		Nicholas of Cusa, Ger. philosopher, d. (b. 1401) Pope Paul II (—1471)
1465			Erasmus of Rotterdam, European humanist, b. (d. 1536)
1466			

D. VISUAL ARTS	E. MUSIC	F. SCIENCE, TECHNOLOGY, GROWTH	G. DAILY LIFE	
Paolo Uccello (1397—1475): "The Battle of San Romano," painting				1456
Filippino Lippi, Filippo Lippi's son, Ital. painter, b. (d. 1504)				1457
The Turks sack the Acropolis				1458
	Paul Hofhaimer, Aust. composer and organist, b. (d. 1537)	Martin Behaim, Ger. geographer and navigator, b. (d. 1507)		1459
Completion of Winchester Cathedral Palazzo Pitti, Florence, begun				1460
Leonardo da Vinci becomes a pupil of Verrocchio				1461
				1462
Construction of Sultan Mohammed II's mosque, Constantinople			Monte di Pietà at Orvieto: money loaned at low interest to poor people	1463
			Louis XI establishes Fr. royal mail service	1464
Hans Holbein the Elder, Ger. painter, b. (d. 1524)	First printed music		Edward IV passes edict forbidding "hustling of stones" and other bowlinglike sports	1465
Donatello, Ital. sculptor, d. (b. 1386)		Johann Mentel prints first Ger. Bible (Strasbourg)		1466

	A. HISTORY, POLITICS	B. LITERATURE, THEATER	C. RELIGION, PHILOSOPHY, LEARNING
1467	Philip II of Burgundy d.; succeeded by Charles the Bold (—1477) The Turks conquer Herzegovina	The first ballad about the Swiss national hero William Tell	
1468			Bishopric of Vienna established
1469	Ferdinand of Aragon marries Isabella of Castile Lorenzo de' Medici, "the Magnificent," ruler of Florence (—1492)	Juan del Encina, the "father of the Span. drama," b. (d. 1529)	Niccolò Machiavelli, Ital. author and politician, b. (d. 1527)
1470		Bernard Dovizi da Bibbiena, Ital. poet and cardinal, b. (d. 1520) Gil Vicente, Port. poet and actor, b. (d. 1536) "Maître Pathelin," the first Fr. farce	Willibald Pirckheimer, Ger. humanist, b. (d. 1530)
1471	Edward IV, King of England, defeats and kills Richard, Earl of Warwick at Barnet, defeats Queen Margaret and kills Prince Edward at Tewkesbury, and enters London; Henry VI murdered in the Tower King George of Bohemia d.; succeeded by Vladislav II (—1490)		Pope Sixtus IV (—1484) Thomas à Kempis, Ger. mystic d. (b. 1380)
1472	Ivan III of Moscow marries Sophia Palaeologus, niece of the last Byzantine Emperor	Dante's "Divine Comedy" first printed at Foligno	
1473	Cyprus comes under Venetian rule Duke Albrecht Achilles declares indivisibility of electorates of Brandenburg		
1474	Isabella I, Queen of Aragon (—1504)	William Caxton prints (at Bruges) the first book in English	
1475	Cesare Borgia, son of future Pope Alexander VI, b. Bartolomeo Colleoni, Ital. condottiere, d. (b. 1400) Francisco Pizarro, Span. conquerer of Peru, b. (d. 1541)	Thomas Murner, Ger. satirist, b. (d. 1537)	
1476			

D. VISUAL ARTS	E. MUSIC	F. SCIENCE, TECHNOLOGY, GROWTH	G. DAILY LIFE	
			Scot. Parliament decrees that "fute-ball and golfe not to be used"	**1467**
		Johann Gutenberg d. (b. c. 1396)		**1468**
Fra Filippo Lippi, Ital. painter, d. (b. c. 1406)		Vasco da Gama, Port. navigator, b. (d. 1524)		**1469**
		Port. navigators discover Gold Coast, West Africa First Fr. printing press set up at the Sorbonne, Paris		**1470**
Albrecht Dürer, Ger. artist, b. (d. 1528)	Jakob Obrecht: "St. Matthew Passion" (on Latin text)			**1471**
Memling: "The Last Judgment" (altarpiece at Danzig)			Dan. navigator Deitrich Pining claims to have discovered Newfoundland	**1472**
		Nicolaus Copernicus, European astronomer, b. (d. 1543)	The Fuggers of Augsburg begin business dealings with the Hapsburgs	**1473**
	Guillaume Dufay, Dutch composer, d. (b. 1399)			**1474**
Michelangelo Buonarotti, Ital. sculptor, painter, and architect, b. (d. 1564)				**1475**
				1476

	A. HISTORY, POLITICS	B. LITERATURE, THEATER	C. RELIGION, PHILOSOPHY, LEARNING
1477	Maximilian, son of Emperor Frederick III, marries Mary of Burgundy, heiress of Charles the Bold–the Hapsburgs acquire the Netherlands	Caxton prints Chaucer's "Canterbury Tales"	
1478	Grand Prince Ivan III of Moscow subdues Novgorod Giuliano de' Medici, brother of Lorenzo de' Medici, murdered in Florence Cathedral		Thomas More, Eng. humanist and statesman, b. (d. 1535)
1479	Union of Aragon and Castile under Ferdinand the Catholic and Isabella; beginning of Span. state		
1480	Ivan III styles himself Czar of the Russians Ludovico Sforza, Regent of Milan (—1499)		Ferdinand and Isabella appoint inquisitors against heresy among converted Jews
1481	Bajazet II, Sultan of the Turks (—1512) Beginning of the Spanish Inquisition under the joint direction of state and church		
1482	Peace of Arras between Louis XI and Hapsburgs		
1483	Edward IV of England d.; succeeded by his son young Edward V Edward V and his brother disappear, probably murdered by their uncle, Richard of Gloucester, who claims the throne as Richard III (—1485) Louis XI of France d.; succeeded by Charles VIII (—1498) The Russians begin to explore Siberia		Martin Luther, Ger. Reformation leader, b. Nov. 10 (d. 1546)
1484		Luigi Pulci, Ital. poet, d. (b. 1432)	Pope Innocent VIII (—1492) Papal bull "Summis desiderantes" against witchcraft and sorcery Ulrich Zwingli, Swiss humanist and reformer, b. (d. 1531)
1485	Henry Tudor, Earl of Richmond defeats and kills Richard III at Bosworth; succeeds as Henry VII (—1509); starts Tudor dynasty Matthias Corvinus captures Vienna		Rudolf Agricola, humanist at Heidelberg University, d. (b. 1443)

D. VISUAL ARTS	E. MUSIC	F. SCIENCE, TECHNOLOGY, GROWTH	G. DAILY LIFE	
Botticelli: "Primavera" Michael Pacher: altar at St. Wolfgang, Austria (—1481) Veit Stoss: Carved altar at St. Mary's, Cracow, Poland (—1489) Tiziano Vecelli (Titian), Ital. artist, b. (d. 1576)				1477
				1478
		Copenhagen University founded	After the destruction of Arras, Brussels becomes the center of European tapestry industry	1479
Jean Fouquet, Fr. painter, d. (b. 1420) Palma Vecchio, Ital. painter, b. (d. 1528)		Ferdinand Magellan, Port. navigator, b. (d. 1521) The Ger. magician Georg Faust b., the prototype of Faust legend	Leonardo da Vinci invents parachute	1480
Botticelli, Ghirlandajo, Perugino, Pinturicchio, and Signorelli paint frescoes in the Sistine Chapel, Rome Verrocchio: statue of Bartholomeo Colleoni in Venice Baldassare Peruzzi, Ital. architect and painter, b. (d. 1536)				1481
Hugo van der Goes, Dutch painter, d. (b. 1440) Luca della Robbia, Florentine sculptor, d. (b. 1399)				1482
Raffaelo Santi (Raphael), Ital. painter, b. (d. 1520) Dosso Dossi, Ital. painter, b. (d. 1542) Dante's tomb at Ravenna		King John II of Portugal refuses to finance Columbus's voyage		1483
Botticelli: "Birth of Venus" Dürer: "Self-portrait"	Joannes de Tinctoris (1436—1511): "De inventione et usu musicae"	Port. navigator Diego Cam discovers mouth of the Congo River	Richard III reforms law, trade, and tax collection	1484
Sebastiano del Piombo, Ital. painter, b. (d. 1547)	Clement Janequin, Fr. composer, b. (d. 1559)		Establishment of Yeomen of the Guard in England	1485

	A. HISTORY, POLITICS	B. LITERATURE, THEATER	C. RELIGION, PHILOSOPHY, LEARNING
1486	Maximilian I elected Ger. King (d. 1519)	Antoine de la Sale: "Cent Nouvelles Nouvelles"	
1487	Rebellion of Lambert Simnel, defeated at Stoke-on-Trent Spaniards conquer Malaga from the Arabs		
1488	James III of Scotland murdered; succeeded by James IV (—1513) Revolt of Fl. towns against Maximilian		Ulrich von Hutten, Ger. humanist, b. (d. 1523)
1489	Hans Waldmann, Mayor of Zurich, executed as dictator Caterina Cornaro, Queen of Cyprus, forced to cede her kingdom to Venice Yasuf Adil Shah, a former slave, becomes ruler of Bijapur, India		Thomas Cranmer, Eng. reformer, b. (d. 1556)
1490	Matthias Corvinus of Hungary d.; Vladislav II of Bohemia elected to succeed him (—1516) Maximilian I acquires the Tirol	"Corpus Christi Play" of Eger, Bohemia Beginning of development of Span. drama	
1491	Five-year truce of Coldstream between England and Scotland Treaty of Pressburg: Vladislav II of Hungary and Bohemia acknowledges the Hapsburg right of succession The future King Henry VIII of England b. (d. 1547)		Ignatius Loyola, founder of Jesuit Order, b. (d. 1556)
1492	The Spanish conquer Granada and extinguish Moorish kingdom, consolidating monarchy of Ferdinand of Aragon and Isabella of Castile Charles VIII takes control of affairs in France Lorenzo de' Medici, "The Magnificent," d. (b. 1449); his son Piero becomes ruler of Florence Casimir IV, King of Poland, d. (b. 1447); succeeded in Poland by John Albert, in Lithuania by Alexander Henry VII of England invades France after French support Perkin Warbeck, Fl.-born impostor, as claimant to Eng. throne Peace of Etaples: France expels Warbeck and pays England an indemnity of £159,000 Albert, Duke of Bavaria, joins Swabian League and undertakes to uphold authority of Holy Roman Empire Bajazet II of Turkey, invading Hungary, defeats the Hungarians at the Save River Sikander II Lodi, Sultan of Delhi, annexes Bihar	Pietro Aretino, Ital. author and "journalist," b. (d. 1556) "La cárcel de amor" ("The Prison of Love") by Diego de San Pedro, one of the first Span. novels of courtly love Margaret of Navarre, author of the "Heptameron," b. (d. 1549)	Pope Innocent VIII d. (b. 1432) Roderigo Borgia (b. 1430) becomes Pope Alexander VI (d. 1503) Elio Antonio Nebrija: Latin-Spanish dictionary By order of the inquisitor-general, Torquemada, Span. Jews are given three months to accept Christianity or leave the country Johann Reuchlin, Ger. humanist, begins to study Hebrew Juan Louis Vives, Span. humanist, b. (d. 1540)

D. VISUAL ARTS	E. MUSIC	F. SCIENCE, TECHNOLOGY, GROWTH	G. DAILY LIFE	
Jacopo Sansovino, Ital. architect, b. (d. 1570) Andrea del Sarto, Florentine painter, b. (d. 1531)		The Portuguese discover Angola		**1486**
				1487
Andrea del Verrocchio, Ital. artist, d. (b.1436)			Construction of Henry VII's famous ship "Great Harry" The first dispensary (Apotheke) in Berlin	**1488**
Benedetto da Majano begins to build the Palazzo Strozzi in Florence			The symbols + (plus) and - (minus) come into use	**1489**
	First beginnings of ballet at Ital. courts	Leonardo da Vinci observes capillary action of liquids in small-bore tubes	The first orphanages in Italy and Holland	**1490**
		Copernicus studies at Cracow University		**1491**
Bramante (at 48) starts building choir and cupola of S. Maria della Grazie, Milan (—1498) Carlo Crivelli: "The Immaculate Conception" Leonardo da Vinci draws a flying machine Piero della Francesca d. (b. c. 1420)	"Opera," treatise on theory of music by Roman philosopher Boëthius (480—524), published in Venice Ludwig Senfl, Swiss-Ger. composer, b. (d. 1543) Antoine Busnois, Fr.-Fl. composer, d. (birth date unknown)	The first terrestrial globe constructed by Nuremberg geographer Martin Behaim (1459—1507) Ferdinand and Isabella of Spain finance the voyage of the Italian Christopher Columbus to the New World Columbus (at 41) sails from Palos, Spain, Aug. 3 (flagship "Santa Maria," 235 tons, 70 crew) Columbus discovers Watling Island in the Bahamas Oct. 12; Cuba Oct. 18; Haiti Dec. 6 The "Santa Maria" is wrecked off Haiti Dec. 25 Edward Wotton, Eng. naturalist, b. (d. 1555)	The profession of book publisher emerges, consisting of the three pursuits of type founder, printer, and bookseller	**1492**

	A. HISTORY, POLITICS	B. LITERATURE, THEATER	C. RELIGION, PHILOSOPHY, LEARNING
1493	Pope Alexander VI publishes bull "Inter cetera divina" dividing the New World between Spain and Portugal May 4 (revised June 28) Statute of Piotrkow grants Pol. aristocracy privileges at expense of burghers and peasants Frederick III d. (b. 1415); succeeded as Holy Roman Emperor by Maximilian I (1459—1519) The first Bundschuh (peasants' revolt) in Alsace and southwest Germany The Turks invade Dalmatia and Croatia Maximilian I invests Lodovico ("Il Moro") Sforza with the duchy of Milan Charles VIII of France prepares to invade Italy Jean de La Valette, Fr. general, b. (d. 1568) Maximilian I marries Bianca Maria Sforza Lucrezia Borgia (b. 1480), daughter of Pope Alexander VI, marries Giovanni Sforza (marriage annulled, 1497)	Anna Bijns, Fl. religious poetess, b. (d. 1575) The Nuremberg Chronicle, an illustrated world history from the Creation to the present, by Hartmann Schedel (1440—1514) published in Latin and German Agnolo Firenzuolo, Ital. poet, b. (d. 1543) Richard Pynson prints his first dated book: Henry Parker, "Dialogue of Dives and Pauper"	Pope Alexander VI appoints his son Cesare Borgia (b. 1475) a cardinal Jacques Lefèvre d'Etaples: "Paraphrasis in Aristotelis octo physicos libros" Olaus Petri, Swed. reformer, b. (d. 1552) François Bonivard ("The Prisoner of Chillon"), b. (d. 1570)
1494	Treaty of Tordesillas (June 7): Spain and Portugal divide New World between them Charles VIII begins invasion of Italy, enters Florence, deposes Piero de' Medici, and enters Rome; Pope Alexander VI takes refuge in Castel Sant' Angelo The future Francis I of France b. Henry VII of England sends Edward Poynings as deputy to Ireland to end support for Perkin Warbeck; Poynings' Laws make Ir. legislature dependent on England The future Suleiman "The Magnificent," Sultan of the Ottoman Empire (1520—1566), b. Maximilian I recognizes Perkin Warbeck as King of England Ferdinand I (Ferrante) of Naples, d. (b. 1423) Parliament of Drogheda marks subservience of Ireland to England	Matteo Maria Bogardo, Ital. poet and humanist, d. (b. 1434) Sebastian Brant: "Das Narrenschiff" (Eng. translation 1509: "The Ship of Fools") John Lydgate (1370—1450): "The Fall of Princes," published posth. François Rabelais, Fr. writer and humanist, b. (d. 1553) Hans Sachs, Ger. poet and mastersinger, b. (d. 1576) Walter Hylton (d. 1396), Eng. mystic: "Ladder of Perfection," published posth.	Giovanni Pico della Mirandola, Ital. humanist ("The Dignity of Men"), d. (b. 1463) Aemilius Paulus of Verona appointed historiographer royal to Charles VIII of France Johann Reuchlin: "De verbo mirifico," a study of cabalism Theocracy of Girolamo Savonarola in Florence David Beaton, Scot. cardinal, b. (d. 1546) Politian (Angelo Poliziano), Ital. humanist, d. (b. 1454) King's College, Aberdeen, founded
1495	Sir William Stanley, Lord Chamberlain to Henry VII, executed for complicity in Warbeck's conspiracy Charles VIII enters Naples, is crowned King of Naples, then retreats toward northern Italy Pope Alexander VI forms Holy League which aims at expelling Charles VIII from Italy; its forces defeated at Battle of Fornovo, the Holy League ends; Charles VIII returns to France The Imperial Diet opens in Worms, proclaims Perpetual Peace, sets up an Imperial Chamber and Court of Appeal, imposes common penny as general tax Perkin Warbeck, failing to land at Deal, Kent, decides to move to court of James IV of Scotland; received at Stirling Ferdinand II reconquers Naples, Fr. fleet is captured at Rapallo, Fr. army capitulates at Novara English Parliament frames new statute of treasons and an act against vagabonds and beggars Manuel the Fortunate (1469—1521) succeeds John II as King of Portugal Peace between France and the allies, with Lodovico Sforza as agent, foreshadows idea of balance of power in European politics	"Arcadia," Ital. pastoral romance by Jacopo Sannazzaro (1458—1530) Dutch morality play "Elckerlijk," by Peter Dorland van Diest, is the original of the Eng. "Everyman" About this time, Aldus Manutius begins his series of printed editions of the Greek classics (called Aldines). Almost the first printed edition ("editio princeps") is the five-vol. folio "Aristotle" (finished 1498), ed. by Aldus himself Mattea Mario Boiardo (d. 1494): "Orlando Innamorato," first Ital. romantic epic, published posth.	"De Proprietatibus Rerum," by Bartholomeus Angelicus, trans. by John de Trevisa Jews expelled from Portugal John Bale, Eng. reformer and writer, b. (d. 1563)

D. VISUAL ARTS	E. MUSIC	F. SCIENCE, TECHNOLOGY, GROWTH	G. DAILY LIFE	
Baccio Bandinelli, Ital. sculptor, b. (d. 1560) Barthel Bruyn, Ger. painter, b. (d. 1555) Tilman Riemenschneider, Ger. sculptor: "Madonna," Würzburg Cathedral	Maximilian I makes Paul Hofhaimer (1459—1537) court organist and Heinrich Isaak (1450—1517) court composer	Columbus returns to Palos; leaves Spain on second voyage (Sept. 25, 1493—June 11, 1496), during which he discovers Puerto Rico, Dominica, and Jamaica Paracelsus (born Theophrastus Bombastus von Hohenheim) Swiss physician and alchemist, b. (d. 1541)		**1493**
Sandro Botticelli: "Calumny" Correggio (Antonio Allegri), Ital. painter, b. (d. 1534) Da Vinci finishes his "Madonna of the Rocks" after 11 years Rosso Fiorentino (Jacopo di Rosso), Ital. painter, b. (d. 1541) Ghirlandajo (Domenico di Tomaso Bigordi), Ital. painter and decorator, d. (b. 1449) Hans Memling, Ger.-Fl. painter, d. (b. c. 1433) Ulm Minster finished (begun 1377) Lucas van Leyden, Dutch painter, b. (d. 1533) Pontormo (Jacopo Carucci), Ital. painter, b. (d. 1556) Moretto (Alessandro Bonvicino), Ital. portrait painter, b. (d. 1555)	Jean Mauburnus: "Rosetum exercitiarum spiritualium," the first systematic study of musical instruments Johannes Okeghem, Fl. composer, d. (b. 1430)	Luca di Pacioli: "Algebra," including a study of the problems of cubic equations	Goods lottery (Pots of Luck) introduced in Germany as popular amusement Grand Prince Ivan III of Moscow closes Hanseatic trading office in Novgorod	**1494**
Hieronymus Bosch: "The Garden of Worldly Delights" Da Vinci: "The Last Supper" (—1498) Albrecht Dürer opens his own studio at Nuremberg and travels to Italy Mantegna: "Holy Family with St. Elizabeth and the young St. John" Perugino: "The Entombment" Cosimo Tura, Ital. painter, d. (b. 1430)	Josquin des Prés (c. 1450—1521), Fl. composer, appointed organist and choirmaster at Cambrai Cathedral John Taverner, Eng. composer, b. (d. 1545)	Dry dock in Portsmouth, Eng. Pedro de Alvarado, Span. explorer, b. (d. 1541)	Syphilis epidemic spreads from beleaguered Naples all over Europe through Fr. soldiers	**1495**

	A. HISTORY, POLITICS	B. LITERATURE, THEATER	C. RELIGION, PHILOSOPHY, LEARNING
1496	James IV of Scotland invades Northumberland in support of Perkin Warbeck Teneriffe becomes Spanish Ferdinand II of Naples d.; succeeded as king by Frederick III (—1501) Philip the Handsome, Duke of Burgundy, son of Maximilian I, marries Juana, heiress of Spain	Juan del Encina: "Cancionero," Easter play Clément Marot, Fr. poet, b. (d. 1544) Johann Reuchlin: "Sergius," Lat. comedy	John Colet lectures at Oxford Jesus College, Cambridge, founded by John Alcock Marino Sanudo begins diary of Venetian life and politics (—1535); published at end of 19th century
1497	Rising in Cornwall; Lord Audley's rebellious army defeated by Henry VII at Blackheath Perkin Warbeck arrives in Cork from Scotland, finds no support, lands in Cornwall, and attempts to take Exeter with the rebels; captured by royalist troops at Taunton King Manuel of Portugal marries Infanta Isabella of Spain King John II of Denmark defeats Swed. army at Brunkeberg, enters Stockholm, and revives Scandinavian Union Lucrezia Borgia, divorced from Giovanni Sforza (see 1493), marries Alfonso of Naples John, the Infante of Spain, marries Margaret of Austria	John Heywood, Eng. dramatist, b. (d. 1580)	John Alcock: "The Hill of Perfection" Conradus Celtis (1459—1508) introduces humanism in Vienna Philipp Melanchthon, Ger. humanist and reformer, b. (d. 1560) Savonarola excommunicated for attempting to depose Pope Alexander VI
1498	Charles VIII of France d. (b. 1470); succeeded by his cousin, Louis XII, Duke of Orleans (1462—1515), also a Valois (see 1328) Perkin Warbeck makes public confession of his treason, and is imprisoned in Tower of London Infanta Isabella of Spain d. at birth of a prince (see 1497)	The comedies of Aristophanes published by Aldine Press, Venice (see 1495) "Mémoires" by Philippe de Commines (1445—1509), the "Fr. Macchiavelli" Johann Reuchlin: "Henno," Lat. comedy Hinrek van Alkmar: "Reinke de Vos," Dutch animal epic	Erasmus of Rotterdam teaches at Oxford Savonarola burned at the stake in Florence (b. 1452) Torquemada, inquisitor-general of Spain, d. (b. 1420)
1499	Louis XII of France marries Anne of Brittany, widow of Charles VIII, to keep duchy of Brittany for the Fr. Crown Partition of Milan: Lodovico Sforza flees to the Tirol; French take Milan; Louis XII enters the city War between Swabian League and Swiss cantons; ends with the Peace of Basel, the Swiss establishing their independence War between Turks and Venice; defeat of Venetian fleet at Sapienza; Lepanto surrenders to the Sultan Conspiracy of Perkin Warbeck to escape from Tower of London discovered; tried for treason, he is finally executed	Fernando de Rojas: "Celestina," one of first Span. comedies Sir Thomas Elyot, Eng. author and translator, b. (d. 1546) Sebastian Franck, Ger. religious author, b. (d. 1543) Willibald Pirckheimer (1470—1530): "Bellum Helveticum" (with his autobiography)	Marsilio Ficino, Ital. philosopher and scholar, d. (b. 1433) The Span. inquisitor-general, Francisco Jiménez de Cisneros (1436—1517), introduces forced mass conversions of Moors, thus causing great Moorish revolt in Granada University of Alcalá founded
1500	Lodovico Sforza (see 1499) recovers Milan from the French; two months later the town is reconquered; Sforza is captured and imprisoned in France (—1508) Future Emperor Charles V, son of Juana and Philip, b. (see 1496) Diet of Augsburg establishes Council of Regency for administering the Holy Roman Empire and divides Germany into six "circles" or regions Dom Miguel, heir to thrones of Spain and Portugal, d., leaving Juana and Philip heirs to Spain Pope Alexander VI proclaims a Year of Jubilee, and imposes a tithe for crusade against Turks Ferdinand of Aragon suppresses Moorish revolt in Granada Manuel of Portugal (see 1495, 1497, 1498) marries Maria, Infanta of Spain Alfonso of Naples, second husband of Lucrezia Borgia, murdered	Aldus of Venice (see 1495) founds academy for study of Greek classics and invents italics "Mariken van Nieumeghen," Dutch miracle play First edition of Ger. Schwank book, "Till Eulenspiegel," published in Lübeck Erasmus: "Adagia," collection of proverbs	University of Valencia founded

D. VISUAL ARTS	E. MUSIC	F. SCIENCE, TECHNOLOGY, GROWTH	G. DAILY LIFE	
Michelangelo's first stay in Rome (—1501) Perugino: "Madonna with the Saints of Perugia"	Franchino Gafori (1451—1522): "Practica Musica," treatise on composition	Henry VII commissions Venetian navigator John Cabot (1450—1498) and his son Sebastian (1476—1557) to discover new trade route to Asia Columbus returns from second voyage after 2 years, 8.5 months	Romano Pane, a monk who accompanied Columbus, first to describe the tobacco plant	**1496**
Benedetto da Maiano, Ital. architect, d. (b. 1442) Hans Holbein the Younger, Ger. painter, b. (d. 1543) Filippino Lippi: "Meeting of Joachim and Anne at the Golden Gate" Michelangelo: "Bacchus," sculpture	Henry Abyngdon, Eng. composer and organist, d. (b. 1418)	Cabots, father and son, reach the east coast of N. America Vasco da Gama rounds Cape of Good Hope Nov. 22, having left Lisbon on a voyage to India	Severe famine in Florence	**1497**
Da Vinci–numerous scientific and technical drawings Albrecht Dürer: "Self- portrait"; "Apocalypse"; "Knight, Death, and Devil" Michelangelo: "Pietà," sculpture, St. Peter's, Rome Michael Pacher, Bavarian painter and woodcarver, d. (b. 1435)		John Cabot, Ital. explorer, d. (b. 1450) Columbus, on third voyage, discovers Orinoco River Vasco da Gama discovers sea route to India, arrives on Malabar coast	The first Ger. pawnshop at Nuremberg	**1498**
Dürer: Oswald Krell, portrait Giorgione: "Portrait of a Young Man" First political cartoons (on the Fr.-Ital. war) appear Signorelli: frescoes at Orvieto Cathedral (—1504)	University of Oxford institutes degrees in music	Amerigo Vespucci and Alonso de Ojeda leave Spain on voyage of discovery to S. America	Antimony, produced in Hungary, exported to neighboring countries	**1499**
Antwerp Cathedral finished (begun 1352) Hieronymus Bosch: "Ship of Fools" Botticelli: "Mystic Nativity" Benvenuto Cellini, Florentine goldsmith and sculptor, b. (d. 1571) Diego de Siloe, Span. architect, b. (d. 1563) The turn of the century marks end of Early and beginning of High Renaissance Michelangelo: "Madonna and Child," Bruges	Ottavio de' Petrucci of Venice prints music with movable types Josquin des Prés at the court of Louis XII Hans Folz of Nuremberg (1450—1515) reforms songs of the Mastersingers; from now on worldly subjects admitted	Hieronymus Brunschwig: "Liber de arti distillandi," the first herbal medicine Pedro Alvarez Cabral (1468—1526) discovers Brazil, claiming it for Portugal Juan de la Cosa's map of the New World De Ojeda and Vespucci return from their voyage during which they discovered the mouth of the Amazon River Portuguese navigator Bartolomeo Diaz drowns near Cape of Good Hope (b. 1450) Vicente Yañez Pinzón lands on Brazilian coast at Cape Santo Agostinho Columbus arrested, put in irons, brought to Spain, and rehabilitated First commercial colleges founded in Venice	First black-lead pencils used in England First recorded Caesarean operation performed on a living woman by Swiss pig gelder Jakob Nufer First manufacture of faience (in Faenza) and majolica (in Majorca) First regular postal connection between Vienna *(contd)*	**1500**

	A. HISTORY, POLITICS	B. LITERATURE, THEATER	C. RELIGION, PHILOSOPHY, LEARNING
1500 contd			
1501	Moors in Granada resist Span. army; Ferdinand I declares Granada a Christian kingdom French enter Rome; the Pope declares Louis XII King of Naples Peace of Trent between France and Emperor Maximilian I; Fr. conquests in Upper Italy recognized Henry VII of England declines the pope's request to lead crusade against Turks; Turks take Durazzo from Venice Basel and Schaffhausen admitted as members of Swiss Confederation Ismail I (1487—1524), Sheikh of Ardabil, conquers Persia, founding Safavid dynasty (—1736) Ivan III of Moscow invades Lithuania Arthur, elder son of Henry VII, marries Catherine of Aragon	Conradus Celtis writes allegorical play, "Ludus Dianae"; discovers in Nuremberg manuscripts of plays by the nun Roswitha of Gandersheim, who lived c. 1000 Dream allegory, "The Palice of Honour," by Scot. poet and bishop Gawin Douglas (1475—1522)	Burning of books against the authority of the Church ordered by papal bull Erasmus: "Enchiridion militis christiani" Martin Luther (at 18) in Erfurt Giorgio Valla: "De expetendis fugiendis rebus"
1502	The Council of Regency (see 1500) loses its effectiveness; Archchancellor Berthold von Henneberg dismissed by command of Emperor Maximilian I Peasants' revolt in the bishopric of Speyer, Germany Arthur, elder son of Henry VII, d. (b. 1486)	Ambrogio Calepino: "Cornucopiae," a polyglot dictionary Conradus Celtis: "Amores," humanistic poem One of the first plays by Gil Vicente (1470—1536) given before the royal family of Portugal	Margaret, Countess of Richmond and Derby, mother of Henry VII, founds professorships of divinity at Oxford and Cambridge University of Wittenberg founded by Frederick, Elector of Saxony
1503	The Casa Contratacción (Colonial Office) founded in Madrid to deal with American affairs Venice abandons Lepanto and signs peace treaty with Turks Gonzalo de Córdoba defeats Fr. army, enters Naples, and completes Span. victory at Battle of the Garigliano War of Succession between Bavaria and the Palatinate breaks out Poland surrenders left bank of Dnieper River to Russia Zanzibar becomes Port. colony Lucrezia Borgia marries Duke of Ferrara Henry, Prince of Wales, betrothed to Catherine of Aragon James IV of Scotland marries Margaret Tudor, daughter of Henry VII	William Dunbar: "The Thrissil and the Rois," an allegorical prothalamium in honor of James IV of Scotland's marriage with Margaret Tudor Diego Hurtado de Mendoza, Span. poet, b. (d. 1575) Thomas Wyatt, Eng. poet, b. (d. 1542)	First Eng. translation of Thomas à Kempis's "Imitation of Christ" Pope Alexander VI d. (b. 1430) Francesco Todeschini-Piccolomini (b. 1439) elected Pope Pius III Giuliano della Rovere (b. 1443) elected Pope Julius II (—1513) William Warham (b. 1456) becomes last Archbishop of Canterbury of the Eng. pre-Reformation Church (—1532)

D. VISUAL ARTS	E. MUSIC	F. SCIENCE, TECHNOLOGY, GROWTH	G. DAILY LIFE	
			and Brussels Silver guilders introduced in Germany (remain in use in Austria till 1892) First annual horserace meetings at Chester	1500 contd
Dürer: "Life of the Virgin" Filippino Lippi: "St. Catherine" Michelangelo: "David," sculpture (—1504)		Swift development of book printing and typography; since 1445 more than 1,000 printing offices have produced approx. 35,000 books with approx. 10 million copies Geronimo Cardano, Ital. mathematician and astrologer, b. (d. 1576) Rodrigo de Bastides explores coast of Panama Leonhard Fuchs, "Father of Ger. Botany," b. (d. 1566) First voyage of Anglo-Port. Syndicate to N. America	Card games (since 1400) gain great popularity all over Europe Population of Dresden: 2,565 inhabitants	1501
Giovanni Bellini: "Baptism of Christ" Botticelli: "The Last Communion of St. Jerome" Church of St. Mary's at Danzig finished (begun 1400) Lucas Cranach: "Crucifixion," Vienna Gerard David: "St. John the Baptist," triptych in Bruges (—1507)	First Book of Masses by Josquin des Prés published by Ottaviano de Petrucci	Columbus sails, on his fourth and last voyage, to Honduras and Panama (—1504) Vasco da Gama founds Port. colony at Cochin, India Joao de Nova discovers St. Helena Vespucci, after his second voyage, concludes that S. America is an independent continent, not identical with India Second voyage of Anglo-Port. Syndicate, to Newfoundland Peter Henlein of Nuremberg (1480—1542) constructs the "Nuremberg Egg," the first watch		1502
Canterbury Cathedral finished (begun 1070) Da Vinci: "Mona Lisa" Dürer in Wittenberg Filippino Lippi: "Virgin and Saints" Matthias Grünewald: "The Mockery of Christ" Henry VII's chapel in Westminster Abbey begun (finished 1519) Francesco Mazzola (called Parmigianino), Ital. painter, b. (d. 1540)		Nicolaus Copernicus (at 30) made doctor of canon law at Ferrara Nostradamus, Fr. astrologer, b. (d. 1566)	Pocket handkerchief comes into use	1503

	A. HISTORY, POLITICS	B. LITERATURE, THEATER	C. RELIGION, PHILOSOPHY, LEARNING
1504	Treaty of Lyons: Louis XII cedes Naples to Ferdinand II of Aragon; Naples under Span. control (—1707) In the Bavarian War, Rupert, son of the Elector Palatine, defeated by Albert of Bavaria; hero of feuds is Götz von Berlichingen with the Iron Hand (see 1773: Goethe) Treaty of Blois: Charles (at 4), son of Philip and Juana, future Emperor Charles V, betrothed to Claude, infant daughter of Louis XII; engagement broken off, 1506 Isabella of Castile d.; Juana now heir to Castile Vasili III (b. 1479), "Sovereign of All-Russia" (d. 1533)	Nicholas Udall, Eng. dramatist, b. (d. 1556)	Bull by Pope Julius II establishes University of Santiago de Compostela in Spain
1505	Henry, Prince of Wales, denounces marriage contract with Catherine of Aragon (see 1503) Treaty of Salamanca: Ferdinand of Aragon undertakes to rule Castile jointly with his daughter Juana and her husband Philip Maximilian I begins reformation of Holy Roman Empire (he interprets it as universal Hapsburg monarchy)	Mikolaj Rej, Pol. poet, b. (d. 1569)	Christ's College, Cambridge, founded by Margaret, Countess of Richmond and Derby John Colet (1466—1519) made Dean of St. Paul's, London John Knox, leader of Scot. Reformation, b. (d. 1572) Martin Luther enters Augustinian monastery at Erfurt Jakob Wimpfeling (1450—1528): "Epitome rerum Germanicarum" (history of Germany based on original sources)
1506	Treaty of Windsor: Archduke Philip's sister Margaret of Austria betrothed to Henry VII's son, Henry, Prince of Wales (see 1503, 1505); Philip undertakes extradition of Yorkist pretender, Edmund, Earl of Suffolk Ferdinand II of Aragon (at 54) marries Germaine de Foix, niece of Louis XII of France Philip the Handsome d.; because of the insanity of his widow Juana, a Council of Regency is nominated under Cardinal Jiménez (see 1499) Edmund, Earl of Suffolk, imprisoned in Tower of London Sigismund I (1467—1548) ascends throne of Poland	Dunbar: "The Dance of the Sevin Deidly Synnis" Reuchlin: "Rudimenta linguae Hebraicae," grammar and dictionary	George Buchanan, Scot. humanist, b. (d. 1582) Activity of Johann Tetzel (1465—1519), the Dominican monk, as seller of indulgences in Germany University of Frankfurt an der Oder founded (transferred to Breslau, 1811) St. Francis Xavier, "The Apostle of the Indies," b. (d. 1552)
1507	Diet of Constance recognizes unity of Holy Roman Empire and founds Imperial Chamber Marriage treaty for the Archduke Charles (at seven) to marry Mary, daughter of Henry VII of England Margaret of Austria Regent of the Netherlands during minority of the Archduke Charles		Martin Luther ordained Polydore Vergil (1479—1555), Ital. humanist, appointed historiographer to Henry VII of England

D. VISUAL ARTS	E. MUSIC	F. SCIENCE, TECHNOLOGY, GROWTH	G. DAILY LIFE	
Lucas Cranach: "Rest on the Flight to Egypt" Dürer: "Nativity" Giorgione: "Madonna," Castelfranco Cathedral Filippino Lippi, Ital. painter, d. (b. 1457) Raphael: "Marriage of the Virgin"	Francesco di Bernardo Corteccia, Ital. organist and composer, b. (d. 1571)	Columbus returns from his last voyage Venice sends ambassadors to Sultan of Turkey, proposing construction of a Suez Canal	Henry VII places Eng. guilds and trade companies under supervision of the Crown Postal service between Vienna and Brussels (see 1500) extended to Madrid	**1504**
Dürer travels to Venice for the second time (traveling time: 14 days) Lorenzo Lotto: "The Maiden's Dream" Pope Julius II calls Michelangelo to Rome Raphael: "Madonna del Granduca"	Jacob Obrecht, Dutch composer, d. (b. 1430) Thomas Tallis, Eng. composer, b. (d. 1585)	Scipione del Ferro, Ital. mathematician (1465—1526), solves a form of cubic equation	Portuguese found factories on east coast of Africa	**1505**
Donato Bramante (1444—1514) begins to rebuild St. Peter's, Rome Lucas Cranach: "St. Catherine," altarpiece "Laocoön" group unearthed in Rome Andrea Mantegna, Ital. painter, d. (b. 1431) Raphael: "Madonna di Casa" Tilman Riemenschneider: altar at St. Jacob's, Rothenburg	Alexander Agricola, Fl. composer, d. (b. 1446)	Christopher Columbus d. (b. 1451)	Jakob Fugger, Augsburg merchant, imports spices from E. Indies to Europe by sea Niccolò Machiavelli (at 37) creates Florentine militia, first national army in Italy	**1506**
Gentile Bellini, Venetian painter, d. (b. 1429) Dürer: "Adam and Eve" Giorgione and Titian paint Fondaco dei Tedeschi, Venice Lorenzo Lotto: "Madonna with Child and Four Saints" Palazzo Strozzi in Florence finished (begun 1489) Pope Julius II proclaims indulgence for aiding rebuilding of St. Peter's, Rome	Balint Bakfark, Hungarian- Pol. composer and lutanist, b. (d. 1576)	Alvise Cadamosto: "La Prima Navigazione per l'Oceano alle terre de' Negri della Bassa Ethiopia," exploration of Gambia Martin Waldseemüller: "Cosmographiae introductio," proposes the New World be called "America" after Amerigo Vespucci (see 1499, 1500, 1502) Martin Behaim of Nuremberg, geographer and navigator, d. (b. 1459)	Cesare Borgia, son of Pope Alexander VI, the typical Renaissance "condottiere," model for Macchiavelli's "Principe," d. (b. 1474) Orlando Galla of Venice improves manufacture of glass mirrors	**1507**

	A. HISTORY, POLITICS	B. LITERATURE, THEATER	C. RELIGION, PHILOSOPHY, LEARNING
1508	Maximilian I assumes title of emperor without being crowned; Pope Julius II confirms the fact that the Ger. King from now on becomes automatically Holy Roman Emperor The League of Cambrai formed by Margaret of Austria, the Cardinal of Rouen, and Ferdinand of Aragon for purpose of despoiling Venice Lodovico Sforza ("Il Moro") of Milan d. (b. 1451)	Ludovico Ariosto: "Cassaria," Ital. comedy Conradus Celtis d. (b. 1459) "The Maying or Disport of Chaucer," first book printed in Scotland García Rodríguez de Montalvo: "Amadis de Gaula," revision of a 14th-century narrative of chivalry	Isaac Abrabanel, Jewish philosopher, theologian, and statesman, d. (b. 1437) Girolamo Aleandro (1480—1542), Ital. humanist (later cardinal) begins courses in Greek at University of Paris Guillaume Budé: "Annotationes in Pandectas" (interpretations of Roman Law) Luther, student at the University of Wittenberg
1509	Pope Julius II joins League of Cambrai and excommunicates Venetian Republic; France declares war on Venice; Venetians defeated at Agnadello Henry VII of England d. (b. 1457) Henry, Prince of Wales (at 18), succeeds his father as King Henry VIII of England and marries Catherine of Aragon, his brother's widow	Sebastian Brant's "Ship of Fools" (1494), trans. by Alexander Barclay, published in England "Fortunate and his Sons," Ger. book of "Schwank" stories, printed at Augsburg	Brasenose College, Oxford, and St. John's College, Cambridge, founded John Calvin, Swiss reformer, b. (d. 1564) Erasmus lectures at Cambridge (—1514); dedicates his "Praise of Folly" to Thomas More John Fisher: "The Seven Penitential Psalms" printed in London Persecution of Jews in Germany; the converted Jew, Johann Pfefferkorn, receives authority of Emperor Maximilian I to confiscate and destroy all Jewish books, especially the Talmud; the humanist Johann Reuchlin opposes the action
1510	Pope Julius II absolves Venice from excommunication Sir Richard Empson and Edmund Dudley, Eng. lawyers and ministers of Henry VII, beheaded by Henry VIII for their unpopular administration of crown revenues Portuguese acquire Goa	"Everyman," Eng. morality play based on Dutch morality "Elckerlijk" (see 1495)	Erasmus: "Institutio Christiani principis" Luther in Rome as delegate of his order (—1511) Sir Thomas More: "The Lyfe of Johan Picus Erle of Mirandula" (translation) John Colet founds St. Paul's School, London Johann Geiler von Kaisersberg, Ger. preacher and theologian, d. (b. 1445)
1511	Pope Julius II forms Holy League with Venice and Aragon to drive the French out of Italy Henry VIII joins Holy League and begins to reform Royal Navy	Johannes Secundus (Jan Nicolai Everaerts), Dutch New Latin poet, b. (d. 1536) Gil Vicente: "Auto de los cuatro tiempos," Span.-Port. religious play	Erasmus made professor of Greek at Cambridge

D. VISUAL ARTS	E. MUSIC	F. SCIENCE, TECHNOLOGY, GROWTH	G. DAILY LIFE	
Lorenzo Lotto: "Sacra conversazione" Michelangelo begins to paint ceiling of Sistine Chapel, Rome (—1512) Andrea Palladio, Ital. architect, b. (d. 1580) Baldassare Peruzzi (1481—1536) begins to build the Villa Farnesina, Rome (—1511) Raphael enters the service of Pope Julius II			Jakob Fugger, Augsburg merchant, created a hereditary knight of the Holy Roman Empire	**1508**
Simone de Cronaca, Ital. architect, d. (b. 1454) Andrea del Sarto: "Miracles of St. Philip" Dürer: "Little Passion" (—1511) Adam Krafft, Nuremberg sculptor, d. (b. 1460) Leone Leoni, Ital. goldsmith and sculptor, b. (d. 1590)		First attempts to restrict right to practice medicine to licensed and qualified doctors	Earthquake destroys Constantinople Jakob Fugger lends Emperor Maximilian I 170,000 ducats to finance war against Venice Beginnings of slave trade; Bartolomé de Las Casas, Roman Catholic bishop of Chiapas, proposes that each Span. settler should bring a certain number of Negro slaves to the New World	**1509**
Sandro Botticelli, Ital. painter, d. (b.1444) Sebastiano del Piombo: "Salome" Luis de Morales, Span. painter, b. (d. 1586) Bernard de Palissy, Fr. faience potter and writer, b. (d. 1589) Giorgione, Ital. painter, d. (b. 1478) Raphael: "Triumph of Galatea" Titian: "The Gypsy Madonna"	Louis Bourgeois, Fr. musician, b. (d. 1561)	Amer. east coast discovered up to Charleston Leonardo da Vinci designs horizontal water wheel (principle of the water turbine) Ambroise Paré, Fr. surgeon–one of the greatest of all times, b. (d. 1590)	Hamburg becomes Free City of the Holy Roman Empire	**1510**
Da Vinci: studies for the Trivulzio monument Dürer: "Adoration of the Trinity" Giorgio Vasari, Ital. painter, architect, and art historian, b. (d. 1574) Matthias Grünewald begins the Isenheim altar (finished 1515)	Arnolt Schlick: "Spiegel der Orgelmacher und Organisten," on organ building and playing	Portuguese discover Amboyna and conquer Malacca Diego de Velasquez de Cuellar occupies Cuba Michael Servetus, Span. theologian and physician, b. (executed at Geneva as heretic, 1553)		**1511**

	A. HISTORY, POLITICS	B. LITERATURE, THEATER	C. RELIGION, PHILOSOPHY, LEARNING
1512	French defeat Span. and papal forces at Ravenna with Pierre du Terrail, Chevalier de Bayard (1473—1524), "le chevalier sans peur et sans reproche" as hero of the battle German Diet assembles in Cologne and undertakes further imperial reorganization Selim I, Sultan of Turkey (—1520) War between Russia and Poland (—1522)	First use of word "masque" to denote a poetic drama Thomas Murner (1475—1537): "Die Narrenbeschwörung," Ger. satirical poem	Fifth Lateran Council (—1517): "Immortality of the Soul" pronounced dogma of the Church Martin Luther Doctor of Divinity Shi'ism state religion in Persia
1513	Christian II, King of Denmark and Norway (—1523) Edmund, Earl of Suffolk, executed (see 1506) James IV of Scotland d. (at 40) at Battle of Flodden against English; succeeded by his infant son James V (—1542), for whom his mother Margaret Tudor assumes regency Appenzell joins Swiss Confederation Peasants' revolts in Württemberg and Black Forest Treaty of Mechlin: Maximilian I, Henry VIII, the pope, and Ferdinand of Aragon agree to invade France	Bibbiena (Cardinal Bernardo Dovizi): "La Calandria," Ital. comedy Niccolò Machiavelli: "La Mandragola," Ital. comedy	Pope Julius II d. (b. 1443) Giovanni de' Medici (b. 1475) elected Pope Leo X (—1521)
1514	Anne of Brittany, Queen of France, d. Selim I, Sultan of Turkey, attacks Persia Margaret Tudor, Regent of Scotland, marries Archibald Douglas, Earl of Angus Anglo-Fr. truce: Louis XII marries Mary Tudor, sister of Henry VIII; Louis XII's daughter Claude marries Francis, Duke of Angoulême Albert of Brandenburg becomes Archbishop of Mainz in return for 30,000 ducats Peasants' revolt in Hungary led by George Dózsa Vasili III, ruler of Moscow, takes Smolensk	Lucas Fernández: "Farsas y églogas," plays "Septem horae canonicae," first book printed in Arabic type, published in Italy	Thomas Wolsey (1473—1530) made Archbishop of York
1515	Louis XII of France d.; his nephew, the Duke of Angoulême, succeeds him as Francis I (—1547) Anglo-Fr. peace treaty signed Treaty of Vienna between Emperor Maximilian I, Sigismund of Poland, and Vladislav of Hungary concerning mutual succession of Hapsburgs and Jagellons Battle of Marignano: Francis I conquers Milan Archduke Charles of Austria becomes governor of the Netherlands Scottish Parliament names Duke of Albany, nephew of James III, as Protector of Scotland; Margaret Tudor, Queen Regent, escapes to England Selim I, Sultan of Turkey, conquers eastern Anatolia and Kurdistan	The Lateran Council's decree, "De impressione librorum," forbids printing of books without permission of Roman Catholic authorities Teresa de Jesùs, mystical Span. poetess, b. (d. 1582) "Epistolae obscurorum virorum," satire of scholarship, written in dog-Latin by Mutianus Rufus, Ulrich von Hutten, and other Ger. humanists in support of Reuchlin Aldus Manutius, Ital. printer and publisher, d. (b. 1450) John Skelton (1460—1529): "Magnificence," Eng. morality play "Till Eulenspiegel" published by Johann Grieninger, Strasbourg (see 1500) Giovanni Giorgio Trissino: "Sofonisba," first play in blank verse	Filippo Neri, one of the outstanding figures of the Counter Reformation, b. (d. 1595) Thomas Wolsey appointed cardinal and Lord Chancellor of England

D. VISUAL ARTS	E. MUSIC	F. SCIENCE, TECHNOLOGY, GROWTH	G. DAILY LIFE	
Galeazzo Alessi, Ital. architect, b. (d. 1572) Hans Baldung-Grien: "Mystic Pietà" Andrea del Sarto: "The Annunciation" Michelangelo finishes work on Sistine Chapel (begun 1508) Raphael: "Julius II," portrait	Second Book of Masses by Josquin des Prés (see 1502) Erhart Deglin, music printer of Augsburg, publishes the "Liederbuch zu vier Stimmen"	Portuguese discover Celebes Copernicus: "Commentariolus," in which he states that the earth and the other planets turn around the sun Gerardus Mercator (Gerhard Kremer), Fl. geographer, b. (d. 1594) Amerigo Vespucci d. (b. 1451)	Ban on quacks in Augsburg Royal Navy builds double-deck ships with 70 guns, 1,000 tons Public resistance to trading monopolies in Germany founders on indebtedness of Emperor Maximilian I to Jakob Fugger	**1512**
Michelangelo: "Moses," part of the tomb of Julius II, begun Pope Leo X starts the sculpture gallery at the Vatican Raphael designs excavation of ancient Rome Tilman Riemenschneider finishes tomb of Emperor Henry II at Bamberg Cathedral	Domenico Ferrabosco, Ital. singer and composer, b. (d. 1574)	Port. expedition under Jorge Alvarez reaches Canton Vasco Nuñez de Balboa crosses Panama Isthmus and discovers Pacific Ocean, which he sights from Darien (Sep. 26) Juan Ponce de Leon discovers Florida		**1513**
Hieronymus Bosch: "The Garden of Worldly Desires" Donato Bramante, Ital. architect, d. (b. 1444) Salamanca Cathedral begun (—1733) Correggio discovers chiaroscuro Lucas Cranach: "Henry of Saxony," portrait Dürer: "Melancholia" Cornelis Floris, Dutch architect, b. (d. 1575) Titian: "The Tribute Money"	Gaspar van Weerbecke, Fl. composer, d. (b. 1440)	The Corporation of Trinity House founded in London to provide navigational help for Thames River Santiago, founded by Diego de Velásquez de Cuellar, becomes capital of Cuba Andreas Vesalius, Dutch physician, founder of modern anatomy, physician-in-ordinary to Charles V and Philip II, b. (d. 1564)	The first European (Port.) vessels in Chinese waters The House of Fugger secures right to sell papal indulgences in Germany Pineapples arrive in Europe	**1514**
Alonzo Sanchez Coello, Span. painter, b. (d. 1590) Correggio: "Madonna of St. Francis" Dürer: Marginal drawings in the prayer book of Emperor Maximilian I Matthias Grünewald finishes Isenheim altar (begun 1511) Hampton Court Palace, London (—1530) Raphael appointed architect-in-chief of St. Peter's, Rome Titian: "Flora"		Diaz de Solis reaches mouth of the Rio de la Plata	Anne of Cleves, fourth queen of Henry VIII, b. (d. 1557) First nationalized factories (weapons, tapestries) open in France	**1515**

	A. HISTORY, POLITICS	B. LITERATURE, THEATER	C. RELIGION, PHILOSOPHY, LEARNING
1516	Archduke Charles (at 16), later Emperor Charles V, succeeds as King of Spain on death of Ferdinand II Concordat of Bologna between Pope Leo X and Francis I; France secures internal independence in ecclesiastical appointments Selim I defeats Egyptian forces near Aleppo and annexes Syria Treaty of Freiburg: perpetual peace between France and the Swiss Future Queen Mary b., eldest child of Henry VIII	Ludovico Ariosto: "Orlando Furioso" Garcia de Resende: "Cancioneiro Geral," anthology of Port. and Span. poems Henry Howard, Earl of Surrey, Eng. poet, b. (d. 1547)	Erasmus publishes the New Testament with Greek and Lat. text Sir Anthony Fitzherbert: "La Grande Abridgement," a digest of important legal cases written in Old French Sir Thomas More: "Utopia" Corpus Christi College, Oxford, founded by Richard Fox
1517	Turks take Cairo; Arabia, after Mecca's surrender to Selim I, under Turk. suzerainty Archduke Charles arrives in Spain from Netherlands; on death of Cardinal Jímenez he makes his former tutor Guillaume de Chièvres chief minister of Spain and makes triumphal entry into Valladolid "Evil May Day" riots in London; 60 rioters hanged on Cardinal Wolsey's orders	Teofilo Folengo (1496—1544): "Opus maccaronicum," satirical Lat. poems on contemporary romantic epics Bartolomé de Torres Naharro: "Propalladia," collection of seven Span. comedies Hans Sachs of Nuremberg begins to write his farces Ulrich von Hutten crowned "King of Poets" by Emperor Maximilian I	End of Lateran Council Martin Luther, in protest against sale of indulgences, posts his 95 theses on door of Palast Church in Wittenberg (Oct. 31); beginning of Reformation in Germany Pope Leo X publishes bull for a five-year peace in Christendom Johann Reuchlin: "De arte cabbalistica" Collège des Trois Langues, Louvain, founded
1518	Francis, the Dauphin, b. (d. 1536) Peace of London between England, France, Emperor Maximilian I, the pope, and Spain devised by Cardinal Wolsey The Barbary States of Algiers and Tunis founded	Ariosto at the court of Ferrara arranges regular performances at the court theater	Martin Luther, summoned by Cardinal Cajetan to Diet of Augsburg, refuses to recant Melanchthon appointed professor of Greek at University of Wittenberg
1519	Emperor Maximilian I d. (b. 1459); his grandson, Charles I of Spain, becomes Holy Roman Emperor as Charles V (—1556) Henry, future King Henry II of France, b. (d. 1559) Lucrezia Borgia d. (b. 1480)		Erasmus: "Colloquia" The papal chamberlain Karl von Militz advises Martin Luther to write a letter of submission to Pope Leo X, which Luther promises to do In his Leipzig Disputation with Johann Eck, Luther questions the infallibility of papal decisions Ulrich Zwingli (1484—1531), preaching in Zurich, begins Swiss Reformation

D. VISUAL ARTS	E. MUSIC	F. SCIENCE, TECHNOLOGY, GROWTH	G. DAILY LIFE	
Giovanni Bellini, Ital. painter, d. (b. 1428) Hieronymus Bosch, Dutch painter, d. (b. 1450) Da Vinci invited by Francis I to France Michelangelo: "Moses" finished Raphael: "The Sistine Madonna" Titian: "The Assumption"	Cyprien de Rore, Fl. composer, b. (d. 1565) Josquin des Prés: Third Book of Masses Engraving of music on plates used for first time in Italy (see 1609)	Diaz de Solis, d., killed near the Rio de la Plata while searching on coast of Argentina for a passage to the Pacific Ocean Peter Martyr: "Decades," on the discoveries of the New World Konrad von Gesner, Ger.-Swiss naturalist and zoologist, b. (d. 1565)	Dyestuff indigo comes to Europe Franz von Taxis made postmaster-general of the Netherlands; imperial mail service is extended to Rome and Naples	**1516**
Fra Bartolommeo, Ital. painter, d. (b. 1472) Sebastiano del Piombo: "Raising of Lazarus" Andrea del Sarto: "Madonna of the Harpies" Quentin Massys: "Erasmus," portrait Raphael: "Lo Spasimo" Seville Cathedral finished (begun 1402)	Heinrich Isaak, Ger. composer, d. (b. 1450) Ludwig Senfl made court composer to Emperor Maximilian I in Isaak's place	Portuguese found a factory in Colombo, Ceylon, and reach Canton by sea	Coffee in Europe for the first time Archduke Charles grants monopoly of Negro slave trade to Fl. merchants	**1517**
Albrecht Altdorfer: "St. Florian," altarpiece Dürer: portraits of Emperor Maximilian I and Jakob Fugger Raphael: portrait of Pope Leo X with cardinals Tintoretto (born Jacopo Robusti), Ital. painter, b. (d. 1594)	Ihan Gero, Fl. composer, b. (d. 1583)	Juan de Grijalva explores coast of Yucatán; discovers Mexico Royal College of Physicians,-London, founded Adam Riese, Ger. mathematician (1492—1559), publishes his first book on practical arithmetic	License to import 4,000 African slaves to Span. American colonies granted to Lorens de Gominot E. Asian porcelain comes to Europe Spectacles for the shortsighted	**1518**
Da Vinci, universal genius of Ital. Renaissance, d. (b. 1452) Domenico Fancelli, Ital. sculptor, d. in Spain (b. 1469) Mannerism (—c. 1600) as artistic manifestation and as reaction to classic tendencies of the Renaissance begins to appear in Italy and later in the Netherlands St. George's Chapel, Windsor, finished (begun 1473) Michael Wolgemut, Ger. painter, teacher of Dürer, d. (b. 1434)		Hernando Cortes enters Tenochtitlan, capital of Mexico, and is received by Montezuma, the Aztec ruler Ferdinand Magellan (1480—1521), Port. navigator in the service of Spain, leaves Europe (Sept. 20) to circumnavigate the globe Domenico de Pineda explores Gulf of Mexico from Florida to Vera Cruz	Thomas Gresham, Eng. merchant, founder of the Royal Exchange, London, b. (d. 1579) Cortes brings Arabian horses from Spain to N. American continent	**1519**

	A. HISTORY, POLITICS	B. LITERATURE, THEATER	C. RELIGION, PHILOSOPHY, LEARNING
1520	Christian II of Denmark and Norway defeats Swedes at Lake Asunden and is crowned King of Sweden in Stockholm; four days later, in spite of his grant of an amnesty, he massacres Eric Vasa with leading Swed. bishops and nobles Emperor Charles V visits Henry VIII at Dover and Canterbury; England signs commercial treaty with French empire Sultan Selim I d.; succeeded as Sultan of Turkey by his son Suleiman I, the Magnificent (d. 1566) Charles V crowned Holy Roman Emperor at Aix-la-Chapelle	Cardinal Bibbiena (Bernardo Dovizi), Ital. comedy author, d. (b. 1470) Royal Library of France founded by King Francis at Fontainebleau	Beginning of the Anabaptist movement in Germany under Thomas Münzer (1489—1525) Pope Leo X excommunicates Luther (bull "Exsurge") and declares him a heretic; Luther publicly burns the bull
1521	Gustaf Eriksson, Gustavus Vasa (the future King Gustavus I of Sweden), leads Swed. resistance to Christian II and Dan. rule Charles V grants his brother Ferdinand certain Hapsburg possessions and rights in Austria; Ferdinand marries Anne of Hungary; Louis II of Hungary marries Mary of Austria Edward Stafford, Duke of Buckingham, potential claimant to the Eng. throne, executed by order of Henry VIII Sultan Suleiman I conquers Belgrade; begins to invade Hungary Hernando Cortes assumes control of Mexico after destruction of Aztec state King Manuel I of Portugal d.; his son, John III, the Pious (d. 1557), succeeds him	Sebastian Brant, Ger. satirist ("The Ship of Fools"), d. (b. 1457)	Pope Leo X confers title "Defender of the Faith" on King Henry VIII for his "Assertio septem sacramentorum," against Luther Ignatius Loyola begins to formulate his Exercitiae (see 1548) Luther, cross-examined before Diet of Worms by Cardinal Alexander, the papal nuncio, is banned from the Holy Roman Empire; imprisoned in the Wartburg, he begins his Ger. translation of the Bible Niccolò Machiavelli: "Dell' arte della guerra" Melanchthon: "Loci Communes," on the Lutheran dogma Pope Leo X d. (Dec.)
1522	Treaty of Brussels: Charles V grants his brother Ferdinand of Austria Hapsburg possessions in southwestern Germany and the Tirol Gustavus Vasa becomes Regent of Sweden Sultan Suleiman I takes Rhodes from the Knights of St. John (see 1530) Span. forces conquer Guatemala	Johann Pauli (1455—1530): "Schimpf und Ernst," collection of humorous Ger. stories and anecdotes Jacopo Sannazzaro: "De partu Virginis," religious poem fusing pagan and Christian myth	Adrian of Utrecht, Regent of Spain, elected Pope Adrian VI, the last non-Italian Pope (—1523) Alessandro Alessandri (1461—1523), Ital. scholar: "Dies Geniales," nonsequential encyclopedia Luther returns to Wittenberg, condemning fanatics and iconoclasts; finishes translation of the New Testament (Old Testament finished 1534); the Wittenberg printer, Hans Lufft, produces 100,000 copies in course of next 40 years Polyglot Bible (in Latin, Greek, Hebrew, and Aramaic) published by the University of Alcalá
1523	Dan. nobles depose Christian II, electing his uncle the Duke of Schleswig-Holstein King Frederick I of Denmark and Norway (—1533) Sir Thomas More elected Speaker of the House of Commons The Portuguese are expelled from their settlement in China Gustavus Vasa becomes King Gustavus I of Sweden (—1560)	Hans Sachs: "Die wittenbergische Nachtigall," an allegory in verse in honor of Luther John Skelton: "A Goodly Garland, or Chapelet of Laurell"	Pope Adrian VI d. Giulio de' Medici becomes Pope Clement VII (—1534) Part One of Jean Froissart's Chronicles, trans. by John Bourchier, Lord Berners (see 1400, 1525) Ulrich von Hutten d. (b. 1488)

D. VISUAL ARTS	E. MUSIC	F. SCIENCE, TECHNOLOGY, GROWTH	G. DAILY LIFE	
Hans Baldung-Grien: "Nativity" Pieter "Peasant" Brueghel the Elder, Dutch painter, b. (d. 1569) Lucas Cranach: "Luther," portrait Dürer travels in the Netherlands (—1521) Matthias Grünewald: "St. Erasmus and Maurice" Michelangelo: Medici Chapel, Florence Raphael d. (b. 1483)	Vincenzo Galilei, Ital. lutanist and composer, father of the great astronomer Galileo Galilei, b. (d. 1591)	Scipione del Ferro (1465—1526) solves cubic equations (see 1545) Magellan passes through the Straits of Magellan into Pacific Ocean and sails for the Philippines Paracelsus wanders through Europe Port. traders settle in China	Chocolate brought from Mexico to Spain Henry VIII orders building of bowling lanes in Whitehall	**1520**
Lorenzo Lotto: "Virgin and Child with Saints" Palma Vecchio: "Adoration"	Josquin des Prés, Dutch composer, d. (b. 1450)	Francisco de Gordillo explores the Amer. Atlantic coast up to S. Carolina Ferdinand Magellan killed in the Philippines by natives; his expedition continues under Juan Sebastiano del Cano	Manufacture of silk introduced to France	**1521**
Jean Cousin, Fr. painter, b. (d. 1594) Francesco Parmigianino: frescoes in Palma Cathedral Tilman Riemenschneider: tomb of Archbishop Lorenz in Würzburg Cathedral	Richard Edwards, Eng. composer and poet, b. (d. 1566)	Pascuel de Andagoya leads land expedition from Panama to discover Peru Francisco Montano ascends Mount Popocatepetl, Mexico Dürer designs a flying machine for use in war		**1522**
Adolf Daucher, Ger. sculptor, d. (b. 1460) Perugino (Pietro Vannucci), Ital. painter, d. (b. 1446) Luca Signorelli, Ital. painter, d. (b. 1441) Veit Stoss: altar of Maria at Bamberg Cathedral Titian: "Bacchus and Ariadne"	Hans Judenkünig of Vienna (d. 1526) publishes first manual of lute playing	Anthony Fitzherbert: "Book of Husbandry," first Eng. manual of agriculture Town of Jamaica founded by the Spanish	First marine-insurance policies issued at Florence	**1523**

	A. HISTORY, POLITICS	B. LITERATURE, THEATER	C. RELIGION, PHILOSOPHY, LEARNING
1524	The Chevalier de Bayard (b. 1473) mortally wounded in Italy; French driven out of Italy James V (1512—1542), King of Scotland Protestant princes of Germany meet at Ulm against Emperor Charles Peasants' revolt in southern Germany under leadership of Thomas Münzer, Florian Geyer, and Michael Gaismair Treaty of Malmö: Denmark confirms independence of Sweden under Gustavus I	Aretino expelled from Rome Luis Vaz de Camões, Port. poet, b. (d. 1580)	London printer Jan Wynkyn de Worde publishes a translation of the "Gesta Romanorum"; uses italic type for the first time in England in Robert Wakefield's "Oratio" Zwingli abolishes Catholic Mass in Zurich
1525	Germans and Spanish defeat French and Swiss at Pavia; King Francis I is taken prisoner; Charles V becomes master of Italy; first use of muskets by Span. infantry Grand Master Albert of the Teutonic Knights (1490—1568) transforms Prussia into secular duchy of Brandenburg with himself as duke Peasants' revolt in southern Germany suppressed; Thomas Münzer executed Peace signed between England and France Mogul Emperor Babar invades Punjab Seven-year truce signed between Sultan of Turkey and King of Hungary	Pietro Bembo: "Prose della volgar lingua," earliest example of popular Ital. writing, Latin being usual among men of letters Pierre de Ronsard, Fr. poet, b. (d. 1585) Louise Labé ("La Belle Cordière"), Fr. humanist poet, b. (d. 1566)	Matteo Bassi founds Capuchin Order Bourchier's translation of Part Two of Froissart's Chronicles (see 1523) Luther marries former nun Katherine von Bora (1499—1552) William Tyndale's translation of New Testament printed by Peter Schoeffer at Worms Cardinal Wolsey presents Hampton Court to King Henry VIII, and endows Cardinal College, Oxford (see 1546)
1526	Anglo-Scot. peace signed Charles V marries Isabella of Portugal Battle of Mohacs: Turks defeat Hungarians, killing Louis II of Hungary; Sultan Suleiman I takes Buda; Pressburg (Bratislava) is declared capital of Hungary; both John Zápolya and Ferdinand of Austria are crowned King of Hungary Babar founds Mogul dynasty in Delhi (—1761)	Francisco de Sáde Miranda founds Italianate school of literature in Portugal	The Anabaptists settle down as "Moravian Brothers" in Moravia (—1622) Hector Boece: "Historia gentis Scotorum" Persecution of Jews in Hungary Luther: German Mass
1527	Reorganization of the Hapsburg administration in Austria; Ferdinand is crowned King of Bohemia in Prague and is recognized as sole King of Hungary The Sack of Rome: imperial troops pillage the city, killing 4,000 inhabitants and looting art treasures; Pope Clement VII imprisoned in Castel Sant' Angelo; (referred to as "End of the Renaissance") Future King Philip II of Spain b. (d. 1598)	Baldassare Castiglione (1478—1529): "Il Cortegiano" ("The Courtier"), on courtly manners Niccolò Machiavelli, Ital. political theorist and historian, d. (b. 1469) Marco Girolamo Vida (1490—1560): "De arte poetica," on poetic theory	Reformation in Sweden First Protestant university founded at Marburg
1528	The weavers of Kent riot against Wolsey's policy to move Eng. staple town for wool from Antwerp to Calais At Bridewell Henry VIII explains to nobles and citizens of London his motives for seeking a divorce from Catherine of Aragon	Johannes Agricola (1494—1566): German proverbs Sebastian Franck: "The Vice of Drinking" Ulrich von Hutten: "Arminius" (posth.)	Alfonso de Valdés: "Diálogo de Mercurio y Carón," on current political questions Erasmus: "Ciceronianus," satire on Lat. scholarship Aust. Anabaptist Balthasar Hubmair burned at the stake in Vienna (b. 1485) Melanchthon suggests educational reforms in Germany Reformation begins in Scotland Wang Yang-ming, Chin. philosopher, d. (b. 1472)

D. VISUAL ARTS	E. MUSIC	F. SCIENCE, TECHNOLOGY, GROWTH	G. DAILY LIFE	
Lucas Cranach: "Judgment of Paris" Giovanni da Bologna, Ital. sculptor, b. (d. 1608) Dürer: "Willibald Pirckheimer," portrait Hans Holbein the Elder, Ger. painter, d. (b. 1465) Michelangelo: Biblioteca Laurenziana, Florence	Johann Walther (1496–1570) produces, in collaboration with Martin Luther, the hymnal "Geystlich Gesangk-Büchleyn"	Petrus Apianus of Ingolstadt (1501–1552): "Cosmographia," first textbook on theoretical geography Vasco da Gama, Port. navigator, d. (b. 1469) Giovanni da Verrazano discovers New York Bay and Hudson River Bartolomeo Eustacchio, Ital. anatomist, b. (d. 1574)	Turkeys from S. America eaten for first time at the Eng. court	**1524**
Lorenzo Lotto: "Portrait of a Young Man" Palma Vecchio: "Three Sisters" Titian: "Vanitas"	Giovanni Pierluigi da Palestrina, Ital. composer, b. (d. 1594)	Dürer compiles first Ger. manual on geometry	Hops introduced to England from Artois Juan Luis Vives: "De subventione pauperum," demanding state help for the poor Jakob Fugger of Augsburg d. (b. 1459)	**1525**
Dürer: "The Four Apostles" Hans Holbein the Younger visits England for the first time	Hans Judenkünig, Aust. lutanist and composer, d.	Port. vessels in New Guinea	Card game piquet first played	**1526**
Hans Holbein the Younger: "Thomas More and His Family" Parmigianino: "St. Jerome" Pellegrino Tebaldi, Ital. painter and architect, b. (d. 1597)	Fl. composer Adrian Willaert (1490–1562) made maestro di capella at St. Mark's, Venice	Sebastian Cabot builds fortifications of Santa Espirtu in Paraguay Paracelsus lectures on medicine at University of Basel		**1527**
Diego de Siloe: Granada Cathedral Paolo Veronese, Ital. painter, b. (d. 1588) Albrecht Dürer d. (b. 1471) Matthias Grünewald, Ger. painter, d. (b. 1465) Hans Holbein the Younger: "The Artist's Family" Palma Vecchio, Ital. painter, d. (b. 1480)	Martin Agricola (c. 1500–1556): "Eyn kurtz deudsche Musica" published	Paracelsus: "Die kleine Chirurgia," first manual of surgery	Severe outbreaks of the plague in England The Augsburg merchants Welser receive from Charles V the privilege of colonizing Venezuela	**1528**

	A. HISTORY, POLITICS	B. LITERATURE, THEATER	C. RELIGION, PHILOSOPHY, LEARNING
1529	Treaty of Cambrai between Francis I and Charles V ("Ladies' Peace"), joined by England Turks attack Austria, lay siege to Vienna, but are forced to raise it Cardinal Wolsey falls from power; Sir Thomas More made Lord Chancellor Second Diet of Speyer opens; the Lutheran minority protests against decisions of Catholic majority ("Protestants")	Antonio de Guevara: "El Relos de principes," on the education of Span. princes William Dunbar, Scot. poet, d. (b. 1460) John Skelton, Eng. dramatist, d. (b. 1460) Antonio Telesio: "Imber Aureus," Ital. mythological tragedy Women seen for first time on Ital. stages	King Francis I founds the College de France Luther and Zwingli hold their disputation on the Eucharist at Marburg
1530	Charles V crowned Holy Roman Emperor and King of Italy by Pope Clement VII at Bologna; last imperial coronation by a pope Ivan IV, The Terrible, of Russia b. (d. 1584) Cardinal Wolsey d. after having been arrested as a traitor Francis I marries Eleanor of Portugal, widow of Manuel I and sister of Charles V Knights of St. John reestablished in Malta by Charles V (see 1522) Mogul Emperor Babar d. (b. 1482)	Claude Garamond created "imprimeur du roi" by King Francis I Jan Kochanowsky, Pol. poet, b. (d. 1584) Jacopo Sannazaro, Ital. poet, d. (b. 1458)	The Confession of Augsburg, prepared by Melanchthon, is signed by the Protestant princes; they form the Schmalkaldic League against Emperor Charles V and his Catholic allies Melanchthon: "Apologia" Willibald Pirckheimer, Ger. humanist, d. (b. 1470)
1531	Henry VIII recognized as Supreme Head of the Church in England War in Switzerland between Protestant Zurich and Catholic cantons; Zwingli (b. 1484) killed at Battle of Kappel; forest cantons defeated	Clément Marot (1496—1544): "Adolescence Clémentine," Fr. poems	First complete edition of Aristotle's works published by Erasmus Sir Thomas Elyot: "The Boke named the Governour," on education for statesmen Inquisition in Portugal Beatus Rhenanus (1485—1547): "Rerum Germanicarum libri tres," a history of Germany University of Granàda founded Ulrich Zwingli, Swiss Protestant reformer, d. (b. 1484)
1532	Suleiman I invades Hungary; his attack on Carinthia and Croatia repelled Francisco Pizarro leads expedition from Panama to Peru Robert Dudley, Earl of Leicester, b. (d. 1588)	Chaucer's works published posth.; Robert Henryson's "The Testament of Cresseid" included among them in error François Rabelais (1494—1553): first book of "Pantagruel" published	Eng. clergy submit to Henry VIII Robert Estienne (Stephanus): "Thesaurus linguae Latinae," first Lat.-Eng. dictionary Machiavelli's "Il Principe" published posth. (written 1513) Reformation in France (John Calvin)
1533	Henry VIII secretly marries Anne Boleyn Thomas Cranmer becomes Archbishop of Canterbury: he declares marriage between Henry and Catherine of Aragon void and marriage with Anne Boleyn lawful; Anne crowned queen; Henry is excommunicated by pope William the Silent, Dutch leader, b. (d. 1584) The future Queen Elizabeth I b. (d. 1603), daughter of Henry VIII and Anne Boleyn Accession of Ivan IV of Russia (at three) Pizarro executes the Inca of Peru	Lodovico Ariosto, Ital. poet, d. (b. 1474) Michel de Montaigne, Fr. author, b. (d. 1592) John Heywood: "The Pardoner, the Frere, the Curate, and Neighbour Pratte," interlude	Isaak Luria, Jewish mystic, b. (d. 1572) Nicholas Udall: "Floures for Latine Speaking"

D. VISUAL ARTS	E. MUSIC	F. SCIENCE, TECHNOLOGY, GROWTH	G. DAILY LIFE	
Albrecht Altdorfer: "Battle of Alexander" Jean Clouet (1485—1541) becomes court painter to King Francis I Lorenzo Lotto: "Christ and the Woman taken in Adultery" Andrea Sansovino, Ital. sculptor, d. (b. 1467)	Bartolommeo Spontone, Ital. madrigal composer, b. (d. after 1586)	Ital. physician Giovanni Battista da Monte introduces in Padua clinical examinations of patients at the sickbed Bernardino de Sahagún starts his Franciscan mission in Mexico Michelangelo: fortifications of Florence	"Kunst- und recht Alchämei-Büchlein," a manual on alchemy published in Worms	**1529**
Correggio: "Adoration of the Shepherds" Juan de Herrera, Span. architect, b. (d. 1597) Titian: "Cardinal Ippolito de' Medici," portrait	Elias Nikolaus Ammerbach, Ger. organist and composer, b. (d. 1597) Andrea Amati, founder of Ital. family of violin makers, b. (d. 1578)	Georg Agricola: "De re metallica," first treatise on mineralogy Regnier Gemma Frisius suggests that longitude can be found by means of difference of times Peter Martyr: "Decades de orbe novo" (posth.), on the discoveries in the New World Portuguese colonize Brazil	The Antwerp exchange founded Criminal code and police regulations for the Holy Roman Empire General use of the spinning wheel in Europe Workman's bench comes into use	**1530**
Hans Burgkmair, Ger. painter, d. (b. 1473) Andrea del Sarto, Ital. painter, d. (b. 1486) Parmigianino: "Cupid Carving His Bow" Tilman Riemenschneider, Ger. sculptor, d. (b. 1460) Titian: "The Magdalen"	Guillaume Costeley, Fr. Scot. composer and organist, b. (d. 1606)	Nicolas Villegagnon discovers the site of Rio de Janeiro	The "great comet" (later Halley's) arouses a wave of superstition	**1531**
Lucas Cranach: "The Payment" Hans Holbein the Younger settles in England	Orlando di Lasso, Dutch composer, b. (d. 1594)	Ger. botanist Otto Brunfels (1488—1534): "Book of Herbs"	Sugar cane first cultivated in Brazil	**1532**
Hans Holbein the Younger: "The Ambassadors" Veit Stoss, Ger. woodcarver and sculptor, d. (b. 1450) Titian: "Charles V," portrait Lucas van Leyden, Dutch painter, d. (b. 1494)	First madrigals by Philippe Jacques Verdelot, Arcadelt, and others, printed in Rome Johannes Ott, Ger. printer: "121 neue Lieder, von Berümbten dieser Kunst gesetzt," published at Nuremberg	"Allerhand Farben and mancherley weyse Dünten zu bereyten," manual for the production of paints and inks, published in Augsburg	First lunatic asylums (without medical attention)	**1533**

	A. HISTORY, POLITICS	B. LITERATURE, THEATER	C. RELIGION, PHILOSOPHY, LEARNING
1534	"Communist state" of Anabaptists under leadership of John of Leiden at Münster, Westphalia Final rift between England and Rome	John Heywood: "A Play of Love," interlude François Rabelais: "Gargantua," Part Two of "Pantagruel"	Elizabeth Barton, "The Nun of Kent" (b. 1506), Eng. ecstatic opposed to matrimonial policy of Henry VIII, executed at Tyburn Confession of Basel drafted by Oswald Myconius Pope Clement VII d. (b. 1475) Cardinal Alessandro Farnese (1468—1549) elected Pope Paul III Jesuit Order founded by Ignatius Loyola (1491—1556) Luther completes translation of the Bible into German
1535	Eng. clergy abjure authority of the pope. Sir Thomas More, who refuses the oath of the king's supremacy, tried for treason and executed (canonized 1935) Münster capitulates to the Hessian army; Catholicism prevails again; Anabaptist leader John of Leiden tortured to death Charles V conquers Tunis and frees 20,000 Christian slaves		John Bourchier, Lord Berners, translates "The Golden Book" of Marcus Aurelius Study of canon law forbidden in Cambridge Order of the Ursulines founded by Angela Merici in Brescia Marino Sanudo's "Diarii" finished (begun 1496), source for the history and daily life of Venice Heinrich Cornelius Agrippa von Nettesheim, Ger. physician and philosopher, d. (b. 1486)
1536	Catherine of Aragon d. (b. 1485) Queen Anne Boleyn sent to the Tower of London and executed Henry VIII marries Jane Seymour, his third wife The Pilgrimage of Grace, a rising against the dissolution of monasteries, begins under Robert Aske of Doncaster Thomas Cromwell (1485—1540) made Lord Privy Seal Francis, the Dauphin , d. (b. 1518)	Johannes Secundus (Jan Everaerts), Dutch poet, d. (b. 1511) Gil Vicente, Port. actor and poet, d. (b. 1470)	Act of Parliament declares the authority of the pope void in England John Calvin: "Christianae religionis Institutio" Desiderius Erasmus, European humanist, d. (b. 1465) Luther's "Table Talks" Reginald Pole: "Pro ecclesiasticae unitatis defensione" Reformation in Denmark and Norway 376 religious houses dissolved in England by royal decree William Tyndale, Eng. reformer, burned at the stake (b. 1494)
1537	The Pilgrimage of Grace and similar risings are put down; Robert Aske is sentenced to death for treason and executed Queen Jane Seymour d. after birth of Prince Edward (later Edward VI)	Thomas Murner, Ger. satirist, d. (b. 1475)	First Catholic hymnal (Vete) Cicero: "Opera omnia," published in Venice (four vols.) Robert Recorde: "Introductions for to Lerne to Recken with the Pen"
1538	James V of Scotland marries Mary of Guise	Giovanni Battista Guarini, Ital. poet, b. (d. 1612) Marot: "Thirty Psalms of David," in French Paul Rebhun (1506—1540): "Hochzeitsspiel auf die Hochzeit zu Kana," early Ger. verse drama	Carlo Borromeo, future Archbishop of Milan, b. (d. 1584) Calvin, expelled from Geneva, settles in Strasbourg Destruction of relics and shrines in southern England (Thomas à Becket's shrine at Canterbury) Melanchthon: "Ethica doctrinae elementa"

D. VISUAL ARTS	E. MUSIC	F. SCIENCE, TECHNOLOGY, GROWTH	G. DAILY LIFE	
Correggio, Ital. painter, d. (b. 1494) After finishing tomb of the Medici, Michelangelo moves from Florence to Rome Regensburg Cathedral finished (begun 1275) Erection of St. Basil's, Moscow (—1561) Jacopo Sansovino (1486—1570), Ital. architect: St. Francesco della Vigna, Venice	Fernando Las Infantas, Span. composer and theologian, b. (d. after 1609)	Jacques Cartier (1491—1557), on his first voyage to N. America, sights coast of Labrador	Decree forbidding Eng. farmers to own more than 2,000 sheep	**1534**
Holbein: "King Henry VIII," portrait	Giaches de Wert, Dutch composer, b. (d. 1596)	Jacques Cartier's second voyage: St. Lawrence River, Quebec, Montreal	First diving bells (see 1778) Beginnings of the London Exchange Statute of Uses curbs power of Eng. landowners	**1535**
Holbein made court painter to Henry VIII Michelangelo paints "Last Judgment" on altar wall of Sistine Chapel (—1541) Baldassare Peruzzi, Ital. painter and architect, d. (b. 1481) Sansovino (Jacopo Tatti): St. Mark's Library, Venice	Heinrich Finck (1445—1527): "Schöne auserlesene Lieder," collection of songs published (posth.) First song book with lute accompaniment printed in Spain	Pedro de Mendoza founds Buenos Aires and sends expeditions in search of a route to Peru	India rubber mentioned for the first time	**1536**
Sansovino (Jacopo Tatti): façade of the Doge's Palazzo loggietta, Venice Sebastiano Serlio: "Trattato di Architettura," (six vols.) Titian: "King Francis I," portrait	First conservatories of music are founded; in Naples for boys, in Venice for girls Paul Hofhaimer, Aust. organist and composer, d. (b. 1459)	Niccolò Fontana, called "Tartaglia" (1500—1575), initiates the science of ballistics Paracelsus: "Grosse Astronomie," manual of astrology First map of Flanders by Gerardus Mercator (—1540)		**1537**
Albrecht Altdorfer, Ger. painter, d. (b. 1480) Palladio: Villa Godi, Lonedo Titian: "The Urbino Venus"		Bogotá founded by Gonzalo Jiménez de Quesada Mercator uses the name America for the first time, also N. America		**1538**

	A. HISTORY, POLITICS	B. LITERATURE, THEATER	C. RELIGION, PHILOSOPHY, LEARNING
1539	Marriage treaty signed at Hampton Court for Henry VIII to marry Anne of Cleves, his fourth wife Spain annexes Cuba	"Gentse Spelen," a collection of allegorical plays, performed at Ghent Marnix van St. Aldegonde, Dutch writer and statesman, b. (d. 1598)	Calvin: "Commentary on the Epistle to the Romans" Erasmus: "Proverbs or Adagies," trans. by Richard Taverner Melanchthon: "De officio principum"
1540	Henry VIII marries Anne of Cleves; marriage annulled by the convocation of Canterbury and York; Henry marries Catherine Howard, his fifth wife Treaty between Venice and Turkey signed at Constantinople Thomas Cromwell executed; Lord Treasurer Norfolk, uncle of Catherine Howard, becomes his successor Afghan rebel Sher Shah becomes Emperor of Delhi	Pierre de Bourdeille, Seigneur de Brantôme, Fr. author, b. (d. 1614) Sir David Lindsay: "Ane Satyre of the Thrie Estaits," morality play	Francesco Guicciardini, Ital. historian, d. (b. 1487) Order of the Jesuits confirmed by Pope Paul III Henry VIII founds regius professorships of Greek, Hebrew, divinity, civil law, and physics at Oxford and Cambridge Augustinus Steuchus: "De perenni philosophia"
1541	Henry VIII assumes titles of King of Ireland and Head of the Irish Church Suleiman I takes Buda and annexes Hungary (see 1686) Queen Catherine Howard sent to the Tower on suspicion of immoral conduct; her alleged paramours, Thomas Culpepper and Dereham, executed (see 1542)	Giambattista Cinzio Giraldi: "Orbeche," Ital. tragedy on classical lines	Calvin returns to Geneva John Knox (1505—1572) leads Calvinist Reformation in Scotland Loyola elected General of the Jesuits
1542	Queen Catherine Howard executed Lord John Russell made Lord Privy Seal Mary, Queen of Scots (b. Aug. 12), ascends the throne six days later, after death of her father James V; James Hamilton, Earl of Arran, Regent Akbar the Great, future Mogul Emperor, b. (d. 1605)	Sir Thomas Wyatt, Eng. poet, d. (b. 1503)	Pope Paul III establishes Inquisition in Rome Magdalen College, Cambridge, founded University of Pisa refounded by Cosimo I de' Medici
1543	Henry VIII marries Catherine Parr, his sixth queen, who survives him Philip of Spain marries Maria of Portugal	Thomas Deloney, Eng. author, b. (d. 1607)	Johann Eck, Ger. Catholic theologian, d. (b. 1483) Sebastian Franck, Ger. religious author, d. (b. 1499) Index librorum prohibitorum issued by Pope Paul III First Protestants burned at the stake by Span. Inquisition
1544	Act of hereditary settlement fixes Swed. succession in male line	Matteo Bandello: "Il Canzoniere," lyric poetry Clément Marot, Fr. poet, d. (b. 1496) Torquato Tasso, Ital. poet, b. (d. 1595)	Pope Paul III calls a general council for 1545 at Trent University of Königsberg founded

D. VISUAL ARTS	E. MUSIC	F. SCIENCE, TECHNOLOGY, GROWTH	G. DAILY LIFE	
Holbein: "Anne of Cleves," portrait Michelangelo replans the Capitol, Rome	Georg Forster (1514—1568): "Frische teutsche Liedlein," secular songs (—1556)	Hernando de Soto explores Florida Olaus Magnus: map of the world	First Christmas tree, at Strasbourg Cathedral A public lottery held in France	**1539**
François Clouet (1516—1572), son of Jean Clouet, becomes court painter to King Francis I Parmigianino (Francesco Mazzola), Ital. painter, d. (b. 1503) Titian: "A Young Englishman"	Orfeo Vecchi, Ital. composer, b. (d. before 1604)	G. L. de Cardenas discovers the Grand Canyon, Ariz. Ether produced from alcohol and sulfuric acid William Gilbert, Eng. naturalist, b. (d. 1603) Michael Servetus discovers pulmonary circulation of the blood	Antwerp becomes a most important commercial city	**1540**
Jean Clouet, Fr. painter, d. (b. 1481) El Greco (Dominico Theotocopuli), Span.-Greek painter, b. (d. 1614) Rosso Fiorentino, Ital. painter working at Fontainebleau, d. (b. 1494) Damian Forment, Span. sculptor, d. (b. 1480)	Wulfard Hellinck, Fl. composer d.	Coronado's expedition from New Mexico across Texas, Oklahoma, and eastern Kansas Hernando de Soto discovers Mississippi River Francisco de Orellana descends the Amazon River Paracelsus, Swiss physician, alchemist, and philosopher, d. (b. 1493)		**1541**
Dosso Dossi, Ital. painter, d. (b. 1483) Barend van Orley, Dutch painter, d. (b. 1490)	Jakob Meiland, Ger. composer, b. (d. 1577)	Antonio da Mota enters Japan as the first European Hernando de Soto, Span. explorer of southeastern United States, d. (b. 1492) Andreas Vesalius: "De fabrica corporis humani," modern anatomy St. Francis Xavier (canonized 1602) arrives at Goa as a Jesuit missionary	Heavy taxes on drinks in Bavaria	**1542**
Benvenuto Cellini: saltcellar for Francis I of France Hans Holbein the Younger, Ger. painter, d. (b. 1497) Titian: "Ecce Homo"	William Byrd, Eng. composer, b. (d. 1623) Ludwig Senfl, Ger. composer, d. (b. 1492)	Portuguese land in Japan and bring firearms Nicolaus Copernicus, Pol. astronomer, d. (b. 1473) Span. navigator and mechanician Blasco da Garay submits to Charles V the design for a steamboat		**1543**
Francesco Primaticcio, Ital. painter (1504—1570), works at Fontainebleau	Benedictus Ducis, Ger. composer, d.	Georg Agricola initiates the study of physical geology Luca Ghini publishes the first herbarium Sebastian Münster (1489—1552): "Cosmographia generalis" Michael Stifel (1487—1567): "Aritmetica integra"	St. Bartholomew's Hospital in London refounded Silver mines of Potosí, Peru, discovered	**1544**

	A. HISTORY, POLITICS	B. LITERATURE, THEATER	C. RELIGION, PHILOSOPHY, LEARNING
1545	Don John of Austria, natural son of Emperor Charles V, b. (d. 1578) Duke of Orleans, third son of King Francis I, d. (b. 1522) Truce of Adrianople between Charles V, Ferdinand of Austria, and Suleiman I	Antonio de Guevara, Span. author and historiographer to Charles V, d. (b. 1480) Perez de Hita, Span. poet, b. (d. 1619) John Heywood: "The Four P's," Eng. interlude Stage comedians create a new type of improvised theatrical entertainment in northern Italy	Sir Thomas Bodley, Eng. diplomat and founder of the Bodleian Library, Oxford, b. (d. 1613) Council of Trent meets to discuss Reformation and Counter Reformation (—1564) Konrad von Gesner: "Biblioteca universalis" (finished 1549)
1546	Civil war in Germany (Schmalkaldic War) between Emperor Charles V and the Schmalkaldic League (—1547) Eng. Navy Board founded Turks occupy Moldavia	Aretino: "Orazia," Ital. tragedy Hans Sachs: "Lisabetha," Ger. tragedy	Cardinal College, Oxford, refounded as Christ Church Etienne de La Boétie: "Le Discours de la servitude volontaire" Martin Luther d. (b. 1483) First Welsh book printed: "Yny Lhyvyr Mwnn"
1547	Conspiracy of Gianluigi Fiesco against Andrea Doria at Genoa Ivan IV (at 17) crowned Czar of Russia in Moscow Henry VIII of England d. (b. 1491); succeeded by his and Jane Seymour's son Edward VI (1537—1553) Francis I of France d. (b. 1494); succeeded by his son Henry II (1519—1559) Crown of Bohemia proclaimed hereditary in the House of Hapsburg	Mateo Alemán, Span. novelist, b. (d. 1615) Pietro Bembo, Ital. poet and cardinal, d. (b. 1470) Vittoria Colonna, Ital. poet and wife of famous condottiere Pescara, friend of Michelangelo, d. (b. 1490) Miguel de Cervantes Saavedra, Span. writer, b. (d. 1616) Henry Howard, Earl of Surrey, Eng. poet, executed for high treason (b. 1516) Giangiorgio Trissino: "L'Italia liberata dai Goti," epic poem	William Baldwin: "A Treatise of Morall Phylosophie" La chambre ardente created in France for the trial of heretics
1548	Sigismund I of Poland d.; succeeded by his son Sigismund II Augustus (d. 1571) Mary, Queen of Scots (at six), betrothed to the Dauphin, lands in France Gonzalo Pizarro, son of Francisco Pizarro, defeated at Battle of Xaquixaguane (Peru) by Pedro de la Gasca and executed Turks occupy Tabriz, Persia	John Bale: "Kynge Johan," first Eng. historical drama Hôtel de Bourgogne, first roofed theater, opened in Paris Royal edict forbids performance of "mystères" in Paris	Giordano Bruno, Ital. philosopher, b. (d. 1600) Ignatius Loyola: "Spiritual Exercises" published (written 1521) Francisco Suarez, Span. philosopher, b. (d. 1617) University of Messina founded Francis Xavier founds a Jesuit mission in Japan
1549	Ivan IV calls first national assembly in Russia	Friedrich Dedekind (1525—1598): "Grobianus," Ger. satire against the coarseness of the times Joachim du Bellay, leader of the poetic Pléiade group, states the program of Fr. classicism: "Défense et illustration de la langue française"	Only the new Book of Prayer may be used in England (from May 20) Consensus Tigurinus agreement between Calvin and Zwinglians on Holy Communion (Zurich) Melanchthon objects to the theories of Copernicus Pope Paul III d. Siegmund von Herberstein: "Rerum Moscovitarum commentarii," report on Russia

D. VISUAL ARTS	E. MUSIC	F. SCIENCE, TECHNOLOGY, GROWTH	G. DAILY LIFE	
Hans Baldung-Grien, Ger. painter, d. (b. 1480) Benvenuto Cellini writes his autobiography Lorenzo Lotto: "Apollo Sleeping" Palladio: Palazzo Thiene, Vicenza (—1550) Titian: "Pietro Aretino," portrait	John Taverner, Eng. composer, d. (b. 1495)	Geronimo Cardano (1501—1576) works out Scipione del Ferro's equations of the third and fourth degree (see 1520) Claude Garamond designs his antique typography	First European botanical garden in Padua	**1545**
Lucas Cranach: "Martin Luther," portrait Pierre Lescot (1510—1578) begins to build the Louvre, Paris Michelangelo designs the dome and undertakes the completion of St. Peter's, Rome Titian: group portrait of Pope Paul III and his nephews		Tycho Brahe, Dan. astronomer, b. (d. 1601) Ital. physician Girolamo Fracastoro (1478—1553) states his view on infections and epidemic diseases Andreas Libavius, Ger. alchemist, b. (d. 1616) Fl. geographer Gerardus Mercator (1512—1594) states that the earth has a magnetic pole First pharmacopoeia by Valerius Cordus Abortive efforts to find the legendary Dorado in Venezuela	Fortune of the Fuggers of Augsburg valued at four million guldens	**1546**
Sebastiano del Piombo, Ital. painter, d. (b. 1485)	Swiss musical theorist Henricus Glareanus (1488—1563) publishes his work on the 12 church modes, "Dodekachordon" Louis Bourgeois (1510—1561): Psalter	First predictions of the Fr. astrologer Nostradamus (1503—1566)	French instead of Latin declared the official language of the Fr. authorities Moscow destroyed by fire Poor rate levied in London	**1547**
Tintoretto: "St. Mark Rescuing a Slave" Titian: "Charles V on Horseback"	Tomás Luis de Victoria, Span. church composer, b. (d. 1611)	Sir Thomas Gresham founds seven professorships in London (University of London not founded until 1828)	Guinea pepper plant is grown in England Silver mines of Zaatecar, Mexico, mined by the Spanish	**1548**
Piero Ligorio: Villa d'Este, Tivoli Palladio: Basilica, Vicenza Sodoma (Giovanni Antonio Bazzi), Ital. painter, d. (b. 1478)	Adrian Willaert: "Fantasie e Ricercari," combining Dutch and Ital. musical styles	Thomé de Souza founds Sao Salvador	Court jesters (dwarfs, cripples) appear in Europe Jesuit missionaries in S. America	**1549**

	A. HISTORY, POLITICS	B. LITERATURE, THEATER	C. RELIGION, PHILOSOPHY, LEARNING
1550	Sir William Cecil made Eng. Secretary of State Spain at the peak of her political and economic power (till end of the century)	Pierre de Ronsard: "Odes" Olaus Petrie: "Tobia Commedia," earliest Swed. stage play Giovanni Francesco Straparola (1490—1557), Ital. author, publishes first European collection of fairy tales Nicholas Udall: "Ralph Roister Doister," earliest Eng. comedy	Thomas Cranmer: "A Defence of the Catholic Doctrine of the Sacrament" Cardinal Giovanni Maria del Monte (b. 1487) becomes Pope Julius III (d. 1555) Siegmund von Herberstein: "De natura fossilium"
1551	Turks fail to capture Malta but take Tripoli	More's "Utopia" trans. into English from the original Latin by Ralph Robinson	Jesuits found Collegio Romano in Rome as papal university Jews persecuted in Bavaria University of Lima founded
1552	Ivan IV of Russia begins conquest of Kazan and Astrakhan	Pierre de Ronsard: "Amours," Vol. 1 Etienne Jodelle: "Cléopâtre captive," first classical tragedy in French	Collegium Germanicum, Rome, founded by Jesuits Francesco López de Gómara, private secretary to Cortes, publishes his "Historia general de las Indias" (—1553) Second Prayer Book of Edward VI
1553	King Edward VI of England d. (b. 1537) Lady Jane Grey proclaimed Queen of England; deposed nine days later Mary I, daughter of Henry VIII and Catherine of Aragon, becomes Queen of England (—1558) Sultan Suleiman I makes peace with Persia	François Rabelais, Fr. author, d. (b. 1494) Hans Sachs: "Tristan und Isolde"	Domingo de Soto: "De justicia et jure" Sir Thomas More: "A Dialogue of Comfort Against Tribulation" (posth.) Thomas Wilson: "The Arte of Rhetorique"
1554	Lady Jane Grey executed Princess Elizabeth sent to the Tower for suspected participation in rebellion against Mary I Queen Mary I marries Philip of Spain, son of Emperor Charles V	Matteo Bandello: "Le Novelle," 214 short stories and tales John Lyly, Eng. novelist and dramatist, b. (d. 1606) Jörg Wickram: "Der Goldfaden," early Ger. novel	Catholic restoration in England Trinity College, Oxford, founded
1555	Peace of Augsburg: Lutheran states to enjoy equal rights with Catholic Charles V turns over government of Netherlands to his son Philip French colony founded on the Bay of Rio de Janeiro Jap. pirates besiege Nanking	An Aztec dictionary published Lewis Brecht: "Euripus," first Jesuit play, given in Vienna Pierre de Ronsard: "Hymnes" Jörg Wickram: "Das Rollwagenbüchlein," collection of farcical anecdotes	John Knox returns to Scotland from his exile in Geneva Pope Julius III d. Mar. 23 (b. 1487) Cardinal Marcello Cervino elected Pope Marcellus II (d. Apr. 30) Cardinal Giovanni Pietro Caraffa elected Pope Paul IV
1556	Charles V abdicates, assigning Spain to his son Philip II, and the Holy Roman Empire to his brother Ferdinand I, and retires into the monastery of Yuste Akbar the Great, Mogul Emperor of India (—1605)	Pietro Aretino, Ital. author and satirist, d. (b. 1492) Hans Sachs becomes leader of the Nuremberg Mastersingers Nicholas Udall, Eng. author and dramatist, d. (b. 1504)	Thomas Cranmer (b. 1489) burned at the stake; Cardinal Pole consecrated Archbishop of Canterbury Juan de Ávila: "Audi filia," ascetic Christian text Ignatius Loyola d. (b. 1491) Jesuit Order established in Prague

D. VISUAL ARTS	E. MUSIC	F. SCIENCE, TECHNOLOGY, GROWTH	G. DAILY LIFE	
Benvenuto Cellini: "Perseus," sculpture, Florence Beginnings of early Baroque Beginnings of Jap. "Ukiyoe" painting Lorenzo Lotto: "A Nobleman in His Study" Michelangelo: "Deposition from the Cross," painting Palladio: Palazzo Chiericati and Villa Rotunda, Vicenza Titian: portrait of his daughter Lavinia Giorgio Vasari: "Lives of the Artists"	Giulio Caccini, Ital. composer and singer, b. (d. 1618) John Marbeck: "The Booke of Common Praier noted," first musical setting of Eng. liturgy	G. D. Rhaeticus: trigonometric tables	Game of billiards played for the first time in Italy Sealing wax used for first time First written reference to game of cricket (creag) in young Edward VI's wardrobe accounts	**1550**
Titian: "Philip II," portrait	Giovanni Pierluigi da Palestrina made director of music at St. Peter's, Rome	Pierre Belon: "Histoire naturelle des estranges poissons" Konrad von Gesner: "Historia animalium," modern zoology	First licensing of alehouses and taverns in England and Wales	**1551**
Titian: "Self-portrait"	Johannes Cochlaeus, Ger. musical theorist, d. (b. 1479)	Bartolommeo Eustachio: "Tabulae anatomicae," Eustachian tube and valve	Christ's Hospital, London, founded by King Edward VI St. Andrew's Golf Club, Scotland, founded; Mary, Queen of Scots, probably first woman golfer	**1552**
Lucas Cranach the Elder, Ger. painter, d. (b. 1472) Palladio: Villa Pisana, Montagnana Titian: "Danaë" Veronese: ceiling for the Doge's Palace, Venice	Johann Eccard, Ger. composer, b. (d. 1611) Luca Marencio, Ital. composer, b. (d. 1599) The violin in its present form begins to develop	Richard Chancellor's expedition to Russia via Archangel Michael Servetus, author of "Christianismi restitutio" executed for heresy Hugh Willoughby discovers Novaya Zemlya, and dies while wintering on the Kola Peninsula	Pedro de Cieza de Leon describes the potato in his "Chronicle of Peru"	**1553**
Antonio Moro made court painter to Philip and Mary Titian: "Venus and Adonis"	Palestrina's first Book of Masses, dedicated to Pope Julius III	John Locke's voyage to Guinea Sir Walter Raleigh, Eng. explorer, author, and courtier, b. (d. 1618) Ulisse Aldrovandi (1522—1605): "Herbarium" (17 vols.)	State supervision for mines in Saxony	**1554**
Building of Gray's Inn Hall, London (—1560) Michelangelo: "Pietà," sculpture, Florence Tintoretto: "St. George and the Dragon"	Bartolomäus Gese, Ger. composer, b. (d. 1613)	Pierre Belon: "L'Histoire de la nature des oyseaux"	Tobacco brought for the first time to Spain from America	**1555**
Lorenzo Lotto, Ital. painter, d. (b. 1480) Carlo Maderna, Ital. architect, b. (d. 1629) Suleiman's Mosque in Constantinople finished (begun 1550)	Orlando di Lasso publishes his first book of motets	Georg Agricola: "De re metallica," a study of mineralogy (posth.)	Stationers' Company of London granted monopoly of printing in England	**1556**

	A. HISTORY, POLITICS	B. LITERATURE, THEATER	C. RELIGION, PHILOSOPHY, LEARNING
1557	John III, King of Portugal, d.; succeeded by his grandson Sebastian I (—1562) State bankruptcy in Spain and France	"The Sack-Full of Newes," first Eng. play to be censored	Gonville College, Cambridge, refounded as Gonville and Caius College Robert Recorde: "Whetstone of Wit," first Eng. treatise on algebra Repton School, Derbyshire, founded
1558	The English lose Calais Ferdinand I assumes the title of Holy Roman Emperor Mary, Queen of Scots, marries the Dauphin, future Francis II of France Ex-Emperor Charles V d. Queen Mary I of England d.; succeeded by Elizabeth I (—1603) Sir William Cecil appointed principal Secretary of State (see 1550)	Margaret of Navarre: "Heptameron," tales Robert Greene, Eng. author and dramatist, b. (d. 1592) Thomas Kyd, Eng. dramatist, b. (d. 1594) George Peele, Eng. dramatist, b. (d. 1598)	John Knox: "The First Blast of the Trumpet Against the Monstrous Regiment of Women" Julius Caesar Scaliger, Fr. scholar, d. (b. 1484) "Zohar," cabbalistic work of Jewish mysticism (13th century), printed University of Jena founded
1559	King Christian III of Denmark and Norway d.; succeeded by Frederick II (—1588) Coronation of Queen Elizabeth I King Henry II of France killed in a tournament; succeeded by his son Francis II, whose wife Mary, Queen of Scots, assumes title Queen of England Robert, Lord Dudley, becomes Elizabeth I's favorite Johann Tzerclaes, Count Tilly, future imperial general, b. (d. 1632) Margaret of Parma, sister of Philip II, Regent in the Netherlands (—1567)	Jorge de Montemayor: "La Diana," Span. pastoral romance Thomas Sackville: "Induction," introducing the new age of Elizabethan literature	Elizabethan Prayer Book Mattias Flacius: "Ecclesiastica historica" Pope Paul IV d. Giovanni Angelo de' Medici (1499—1565) elected Pope Pius IV University of Geneva founded
1560	Huguenot conspiracy at Amboise; liberty of worship promised in France King Francis II of France d.; succeeded by Charles IX with Catherine de' Medici, his mother, as regent Turk. galleys rout Span. fleet under the Duke of Medina off Tripoli	Pierre de Ronsard: "Les Discours," poems on the Wars of Religion Joachim du Bellay, Fr. author and poet, d. (b. 1522) Hsu Wei: "Ching P'Ing Mei," first classic Chin. novel	Church of Scotland founded Philipp Melanchthon, Ger. humanist, d. (b. 1497) Francesco Patrizi: "Della historia," on the philosophy of history Beginnings of Puritanism in England (—1660) Westminster School, London, founded
1561	Edict of Orleans suspends persecution of Huguenots Mary, Queen of Scots, denied passage through England on returning from France; she lands at Leith, Scotland Baltic states of the Order of the Teutonic Knights secularized	Luis de Góngora y Argote, Span. baroque poet, b. (d. 1627) William Baldwin: "A Marvellous History intituled Beware the Cat" Sir Thomas Hoby translates "Il Cortegiano" (1527) by Baldassare Castiglione Thomas Sackville and Thomas Norton: "Gorboduc, or Ferrex and Porrex," historical tragedy Julius Caesar Scaliger: "Poetics" (posth.)	Francis Bacon, Eng. philosopher and statesman, b. (d. 1626) First Calvinist refugees from Flanders settle in England Scot. Church ministers draw up the Confessions of Faith, mainly the work of John Knox Thomas Norton translates Calvin's "Institution of the Christian Religion" (1536)

D. VISUAL ARTS	E. MUSIC	F. SCIENCE, TECHNOLOGY, GROWTH	G. DAILY LIFE	
Accademia di San Luca, Rome Agostino Carracci, Ital. painter, b. (d. 1602)	Giovanni Gabrielli, Ital. composer, b. (d. 1612) Thomas Morley, Eng. composer and theorist, b. (d. 1603)	Thomas Tusser: "A Hundreth Good Pointes of Husbandrie"	Influenza epidemic all over Europe	**1557**
Brueghel: "Children's Games" Hon-ami Koetsu, Jap. artist, b. (d. 1637)	Gioseffo Zarlino (1517—1590): "Institutioni harmoniche," definitions of modern major and minor scales	Thomas Gresham suggests reform of Eng. currency ("Gresham's Law") Anthony Jenkinson travels to Bokhara	Hamburg Exchange founded Portuguese introduce Europeans to the habit of taking snuff	**1558**
Brueghel: "Proverbs" Kano Motonobu, Jap. court painter, d. (b. 1476) Titian: "Diana and Calliste"	Jachet da Mantova, Fr. composer, d.	Realdo Colombo describes position and posture of human embryo Adam Riese, Ger. mathematician, d. (b. 1492)		**1559**
Baccio Bandinelli, Ital. sculptor, d. (b. 1493) Annibale Carracci, Ital. painter, b. (d. 1609) Adriaen de Vries, Dutch sculptor, b. (d. 1627) Tintoretto: "Susannah and the Elders" The Uffizi at Florence founded	Orlando di Lasso made Court Kapellmeister in Munich	First scientific society founded at Naples by Giambattista della Porta	Madrid becomes capital of Spain Tobacco plant imported to Western Europe by Jean Nicot Visiting cards used for the first time by Ger. students in Italy	**1560**
Basilica of St. Basil, Moscow, finished (begun 1534) Alonso Berruguete, Span. painter and sculptor, pupil of Michelangelo, d. (b. 1480) Cornelis Floris: Antwerp Town Hall (—1572) Michelangelo: St. Maria degli Angeli, Rome Palladio: Convent of the Carità, Venice	Jacopo Peri, Ital. composer, b. (d. 1633)	Gabriele Fallopius: "Observationes anatomicae"	Ruy López develops in Spain the modern technique of chess playing Forerunners of hand grenades made for the first time Madrid declared capital of Spain by Philip II (see 1560) Merchant Taylors' School, London, founded St. Paul's Cathedral, London, badly damaged by fire Tulips from the Near East first come to Western Europe	**1561**

	A. HISTORY, POLITICS	B. LITERATURE, THEATER	C. RELIGION, PHILOSOPHY, LEARNING
1562	Shane O'Neill rebels in Ireland Emperor Ferdinand I signs eight-year truce with Suleiman I of Turkey Maximilian, son of Ferdinand I, becomes King of Bohemia Eng. troops occupy Le Havre Rajah of Jaipur submits to Akbar the Great Queen Elizabeth I dangerously ill from smallpox	Matteo Bandello, Ital. novelist and poet, d. (b. 1485) Lope Félix de Vega Carpio, Span. dramatist, b. (d. 1635) Rabelais: Book five of "Pantagruel" (posth.) Torquato Tasso: "Rinaldo," epic poem	Third session of Council of Trent convenes (—1563) 1,200 Fr. Huguenots slain at Massacre of Vassy; first War of Religion begins Eng. Articles of Religion of 1552 reduced to the Thirty-Nine Articles
1563	Peace of Amboise ends first War of Religion in France; the Huguenots are granted limited toleration Fr. army regains Le Havre Charles IX of France (at 13) is declared of age Maximilian II elected King of Hungary	First printing presses in Russia Blossoming of Span. mystic poetry: Teresa de Jesús (1515—1582); Luis de Granada (1515—1588); Juan de la Cruz (1542—1563); Luis de León (1527—1591)	John Foxe's "Book of Martyrs," first Eng. edition Council of Trent ends (begun 1545) Counter Reformation begins in Bavaria Term "Puritan" first used in England
1564	Peace of Troyes ends war between England and France Robert, Lord Dudley, made Earl of Leicester English Merchant Adventurers company granted new royal charter Ferdinand I, Holy Roman Emperor since 1556, d. (b. 1503); succeeded by his son Maximilian II (—1576) Catherine de' Medici presents her son Charles IX to his subjects on a three-month tour through France Ivan IV of Russia, in his struggle for power against the boyars, forced to withdraw from Moscow Spaniards occupy Philippines and build Manila	Christopher Marlowe b. (d. 1593) William Shakespeare b. Apr. 23 (d. 1616)	John Calvin d. (b. 1509) Council of Trent's "Professio Fidei" confirmed by Pope Pius IV Counter Reformation begins in Poland Index librorum prohibitorum published after receiving papal approval Philip Neri founds the Congregation of the Oratory in Rome Scots' Psalter
1565	Knights of St. John, under Jean de La Valette, defend Malta from the Turks (May to Sept.); with the arrival of Span. troops the Turks are obliged to abandon the siege Mary, Queen of Scots, marries Henry, Lord Darnley, her cousin	Pierre de Ronsard: "Elegies" Giambattista Cinzio Giraldi: "Ecatommiti," Ital. collection of moral and love tales Arthur Golding's translation of first four books of Ovid's "Metamorphoses" Torquato Tasso, court poet at Ferrara	Jacobus Anconcio: "Stratagemata Satanae," advocating religious toleration Thomas Cooper: "Thesaurus linguae Romanae et Britannicae" Pierre de la Place: "Histoire de nostre temps" Pope Pius IV d. (b. 1499)

D. VISUAL ARTS	E. MUSIC	F. SCIENCE, TECHNOLOGY, GROWTH	G. DAILY LIFE	
Pieter Brueghel: "Two Chained Monkeys" Hall of the Middle Temple, London, erected Tintoretto: "Christ at the Sea of Galilee" Paolo Veronese: "The Marriage at Cana"	Gasparo Bertolotti da Salò moves to Brescia to become first great Ital. violin maker John Bull, Eng. organist and composer, b. (d. 1628) Jan Sweelinck, Dutch organist and composer, b. (d. 1621) Adrian Willaert, Fl. composer, d. (b. 1490)	Famous Fr. surgeon Pierre Franco d.; he performed bladder and cataract operations	French attempt to colonize Florida John Hawkins makes his first journey to the New World: begins slave trade between Guinea and West Indies Milled coins introduced in England Plague in Paris	**1562**
Pieter Brueghel: "Tower of Babel" Giovanni da Bologna: Neptune fountain, Bologna (—1567) Diego de Siloe, Span. Gothic architect, d. (b. 1500) Juan de Herrera begins to build the Escorial for Philip II of Spain (—1586) John Shute: "First and Chief Grounds of Architecture"	William Byrd made organist at Lincoln Cathedral	Gerardus Mercator draws the first accurate map of Lorraine Ambroise Pare (1509—1590): "Cinq livres de chirurgie"	Eng. Parliament passes acts for relief of the poor and for regulating apprentices (repealed 1814) General outbreak of plague in Europe kills over 20,000 people in London	**1563**
Pieter Brueghel: "Christ Carrying the Cross" Pieter Brueghel the Younger, Fl. painter, b. (d. 1638) Philibert Delorme (1510—1560) begins work on the Tuileries, Paris Michelangelo d. (b. 1475) Jacopo Tintoretto: paintings for the Scuola di San Rocco (—1587)	One of Andrea Amati's first violins made Lodovico Grossi Viadana, Ital. composer, b. (d. 1627)	Bartolommeo Eustachio: "Opuscula anatomica" Galileo Galilei, great scientist, b. Feb. 15 (d. 1642) Andreas Vesalius, founder of modern anatomy, d. (b. 1514)	John Hawkins leaves on his second voyage to the New World Horse-drawn coach introduced in England from Holland	**1564**
Pieter Brueghel: "A Country Wedding" Giovanni da Bologna: "Samson" Palladio: S. Giorgio Maggiore, Venice Tintoretto: "Flight into Egypt"	Cyprien de Rore, Dutch composer, d. (b. 1516) Palestrina: "Missa Papae Marcelli"	Royal College of Physicians, London, empowered to carry out human dissections Bernardino Telesio (1508—1588): "De rerum natura," foreshadowing empirical methods of science Konrad von Gesner, Ger-Swiss naturalist and zoologist, d. (b. 1516)	Sir Thomas Gresham founds the Royal Exchange, London Pencils manufactured in England Sir John Hawkins introduces sweet potatoes and tobacco into England	**1565**

	A. HISTORY, POLITICS	B. LITERATURE, THEATER	C. RELIGION, PHILOSOPHY, LEARNING
1566	David Rizzio, confidential secretary of Mary, Queen of Scots, murdered in Holyrood House, Edinburgh The future James VI of Scotland b. (d. 1625), son of Mary and Darnley Suleiman I d.; succeeded by Selim II as Sultan of Turkey (—1574) Robert Devereux, Earl of Essex, b. (d. 1601) Calvinist riots in the Netherlands; Regent Margaret of Palma abolishes Inquisition Sigismund III, King of Poland (—1632) Turko-Hungarian war renewed in spite of truce of 1562	William Adlington translates "The Golden Ass" by Apuleius Earliest Eng. prose comedy: George Gascoigne's "The Supposes," based on Lodovico Ariosto's "Gli Suppositi" Louise Labé ("La Belle Cordière"), Fr. Renaissance poetess, d. William Painter's "Palace of Pleasure Beautified," translation of a collection of Ital. novellas	Jean Bodin: "Methodus ad facilem historiarum cognitionem," on the philosophy of history Heinrich Bullinger unites Calvinism with Zwinglianism in Second Helvetian Confession Cardinal Michaele Ghislieri becomes Pope Pius V (—1572)
1567	Lord Darnley murdered, possibly on Earl of Bothwell's orders Bothwell carries Mary, Queen of Scots, off to Dunbar Mary, Queen of Scots, marries Bothwell Ir. rebel Shane O'Neill assassinated Earl of Morton discovers Queen Mary's so-called Casket Letters Queen Mary forced to abdicate; makes her stepbrother, the Earl of Moray, regent Duke of Alba arrives as military governor in the Netherlands and begins reign of terror; arrests Counts Egmont and Hoorn; Margaret of Parma resigns regency Akbar the Great conquers Chitor In Japan Nobunaga deposes shogunate and centralizes government	Richard Burbage, Eng. actor, first player of many Shakespeare heroes, b. (d. 1619) Elizabeth I recognizes eisteddfod Bardic competitions held in Wales since 12th century Thomas Nashe, Eng. poet and dramatist, b. (d. 1601) George Turberville: "Epitaphs, Epigrams, Songs, Sonets"	Francesco Guicciardini: "Storia d'Italia" (posth.) Edward Hake translates Thomas à Kempis' "The Imitation of Christ" Maximilian II establishes monastery council to superintend clergy St. Francis de Sales, future Bishop of Geneva, b. (d. 1622) University of Helmstedt, Brunswick, founded
1568	Peace between Selim II and Maximilian II Mary, Queen of Scots, defeated at Langside by Moray; takes refuge in England Treaty of Longjumeau ends second War of Religion in France Counts Egmont and Hoorn pronounced guilty of high treason; beheaded in Brussels Swedes declare Eric XIV unfit to reign and proclaim John III king (—1592) York Conference into Queen Mary's conduct opens; reopens later at Westminster Don Carlos, son of Philip II of Spain, d. (b. 1545)	First modern eisteddfod for Welsh music and literature held at Caerwys First public theater presentation in Madrid	Maffeo Barberini, future Pope Urban VIII, b. (d. 1644) First translation of the Bible into Czech Archbishop Parker's "Bishops' Bible" Tommaso Campanella, Ital. philosopher, b. (d. 1639) English College founded at Douai by William Allen to train Jesuit missionaries for work in England Jesuit missionaries welcomed in Japan Pope Pius V issues revised Brevarium Romanun
1569	Sigismund II of Poland unites Poland with Lithuania: Union of Lublin Rebellion in northern England; sacking of Durham Cathedral Pope Pius V makes Cosimo de' Medici Grand Duke of Tuscany Don John of Austria suppresses Morisco rebellion in Granada	Alfonso de Ercilla y Zuñiga: "La Araucana," Span. epic on the conquest of Chile Giambattista Marini, Ital. baroque poet, b. (d. 1625) Mikolaj Rej, "Father of Pol. literature," d. (b. 1505)	Richard Tottel translates Henry de Bracton's "On the Laws and Customs of England"

D. VISUAL ARTS	E. MUSIC	F. SCIENCE, TECHNOLOGY, GROWTH	G. DAILY LIFE	
Pieter Brueghel: "St. John the Baptist"	Antonio de Cabezón, Span. composer, d. (b. 1500)	Nostradamus, Fr. astrologer, d. (b. 1503)	Diane de Poitiers, mistress of Henry II of France, d. (b. 1499) "Notizie Scritte," one of first newspapers, appears in Venice	**1566**
Pieter Brueghel: "Adoration of the Magi" Giovanni da Bologna: "Mercury," sculpture Titian: "Jacopo de Strada"	Waclaw of Szamotuli, Pol. composer, d. (b. 1533)	Hawkins' third journey to West Indies, accompanied by Francis Drake Alvaro Mendana de Neyra (1541—1595) discovers Solomon Islands in Pacific Ocean	Rio de Janeiro founded Rugby School founded by Laurence Sheriff Construction of S. Trinità Bridge in Florence Two million Indians die in S. America of typhoid fever	**1567**
Jan Brueghel ("Velvet Brueghel"), Dutch painter, b. (d. 1625) Pieter Brueghel: "The Faithlessness of the World" Juan Fernández de Navarrete made court painter to Philip II of Spain Robert Smythson works on Longleat House, Wiltshire (—1574) Giacomoda Vignola (1507—1573) begins building the Gesù Church in Rome	William Whytbroke, Eng. cleric and composer, d. (b. 1495)	Gerardus Mercator devises cylindrical projection for charts Costanzo Varolio studies the anatomy of the human brain	Alexander Nowell, Dean of St. Paul's, London, invents bottled beer The Company of London Bricklayers and Tylers incorporated	**1568**
Pieter Brueghel ("Peasant Brueghel"), d. (b. 1520) Hans Eworth (Fl. painter): "Queen Elizabeth Confounding Juno"	Thomas Caustun, Eng. composer, d.	Tycho Brahe begins at Augsburg construction of a 19-foot quadrant and a celestial globe, five feet in diameter Mercator: "Cosmographia," and map of the world for navigational use	40,000 inhabitants of Lisbon die in carbuncular fever epidemic Public lottery held in London to finance repairs to the port	**1569**

	A. HISTORY, POLITICS	B. LITERATURE, THEATER	C. RELIGION, PHILOSOPHY, LEARNING
1570	Earl of Moray assassinated; succeeded as Regent of Scotland by Earl of Lennox Peace of St. Germain-en-Laye ends third civil war in France; Huguenots gain amnesty Peace of Stettin: Denmark recognizes independence of Sweden Charles IX of France marries Elizabeth, a daughter of Maximilian II Imperial Diet meets at Speyer Japan opens port of Nagasaki to overseas trade Margaret of Valois betrothed to Henry of Navarre Philip II marries as his fourth wife Anne of Austria, another daughter of Maximilian II Turks sack Nicosia, Cyprus Turks declare war on Venice	John Barber: "The Brus," Scot. national epic poem on Robert Bruce (posth.) Lodovico Castelvetro (1505—1571) demands introduction of Aristotelian principles to contemporary drama Jean Antoine de Baïf founds Académie de Poésie et de Musique, Paris (see 1576) Thomas Dekker, Eng. dramatist, b. (d. 1632) Robert Henryson: "The Moral Fables of Aesop"	Roger Ascham: "The Scholemaster," manual on education Consensus of Sendomir: Calvinists, Lutherans, and Moravian Brothers of Poland ally against Jesuits Blaise de Monluc: "Commentaires" on Fr. politics Thomas Kirchmeyer: "The Polish Kingdom," trans. by Barnabe Googe Pope Pius V issues bull, "Regnans in Excelsis," excommunicating Elizabeth I "Missale Romanum" issued by Pius V
1571	Sir William Cecil created Lord Burghley Pope Pius V signs alliance with Spain and Venice to fight Turks Sigismund II of Poland d.; end of Jagellon dynasty Turks take Famagusta, Cyprus, and massacre its inhabitants Earl of Lennox, Regent of Scotland, killed; succeeded by Earl of Mar Reconciliation between Charles IX of France and Huguenots Don John of Austria defeats Turk. fleet off Lepanto Act of Parliament forbids export of wool from England and enforces subscription to the Thirty-Nine Articles among clergy Negotiations for marriage between Elizabeth I and Henry, Duke of Anjou (abandoned a year later)	Tirso de Molina, Span. dramatist, b. (d. 1648)	Bibliotheca Laurenziana in Florence opened to the public Hugh Latimer: "Frutefull Sermons" Francesco Patrizi: "Discussiones peripateticae," anti-Aristotelian arguments Harrow School founded by John Lyon Jesus College, Oxford, founded by Hugh Price
1572	Dutch War of Independence begins Duke of Norfolk tried for treason and executed Estates of Poland declare the monarchy elective Henry of Navarre marries Margaret of Valois, sister of Charles IX of France Earl of Northumberland executed for treason Massacre on St. Bartholomew's Day in Paris: 2,000 Huguenots murdered there, among them Gaspard de Coligny Earl of Mar, Regent of Scotland, d.; succeeded by Earl of Morton Lord Burghley made Lord High Treasurer (—1598) Eng. Parliament demands execution of Mary, Queen of Scots Fourth War of Religion begins in France	Guillaume de Salluste, Seigneur du Bartas (1544—1590): "Judith" Luis Vaz de Camöens: "Os Lusíados," Port. epic poem on voyages of Vasco da Gama Pierre de Ronsard: "La Franciade," epic poem on the kings of France John Donne, Eng. poet, b. (d. 1631) Ben Jonson, Eng. dramatist, b. (d. 1637) Aegidius Tschudi, Swiss historian, d. (b. 1505)	Annibale Caro: "Lettere Familiari," history of Tuscan literary language in Italy Jean de Serres: "Commentarii de statu religionis et reipublicae," survey of Fr. Wars of Religion Henri Estienne: "Thesaurus linguae Graecae" John Knox d. (b. 1505) Isaak Luria, Jewish mystic (cabalist), d. (b. 1533) Matthew Parker: "De antiquitate Britannicae ecclesiae" Pope Pius V d. (b. 1504); Cardinal Ugo Buoncompagni (b. 1502) elected Pope Gregory XIII (—1585)
1573	Peace of Constantinople ends war between Turks and Venice Michel de l'Hôpital, Chancellor of France, d. (b. 1505) Henry, Duke of Anjou, elected King of Poland; returns to France to succeed his brother Charles IX (1574) Fourth Fr. War of Religion ends; Huguenots granted an amnesty Spanish capture Haarlem after seven-month siege Duke of Alba leaves Brussels for Spain Sir Francis Walsingham made chief Secretary of State in England Wan-Li (1563—1620) begins reign as 13th emperor of the Ming dynasty in China	Johann Fischart: "Der Flöhatz," Ger. satiric poem on women Torquato Tasso: "Aminta," Ital. pastoral (published 1580)	Collegium Germanicum established in Rome François Hofman: "Francogallia," a treatise on election and deposition of kings Laurentius Petri, Lutheran Bishop of Upsala, author of the Swed. Church Order, d. (b. 1499)

D. VISUAL ARTS	E. MUSIC	F. SCIENCE, TECHNOLOGY, GROWTH	G. DAILY LIFE	
Nicholas Hilliard: "Queen Elizabeth I," portrait Palladio: "I quattro libri dell' architettura" Hans Reichelt, Ger. sculptor, b. (d. 1636) Jacopo Sansovino, Ital. architect, d. (b. 1486) Tintoretto: "Moses Striking the Rock"	Earliest known music festival to honor St. Cecilia, in Normandy Culminating point of vocal polyphonic a cappella style (Palestrina, Orlando di Lasso)	Bell foundry of Whitechapel, London, founded Abraham Ortelius (Antwerp): "Theatrum orbis terrarum," first modern atlas, with 53 maps	Guy Fawkes, Eng. conspirator (Gunpowder Plot), b. (executed 1605) Nuremberg postal services begin	**1570**
Benvenuto Cellini, Ital. goldsmith and sculptor, d. (b. 1500) Palladio: Loggia del Capitanio, Vicenza Titian: "Christ Crowned with Thorns" Giorgio Vasari, Ital. painter and art historian, d. (b. 1512) Veronese: paintings in San Sebastiano, Venice	Andrea Gabrieli: "Canzoni alla francese" Michael Praetorius, Ger. composer and author, b. (d. 1621)	Johann Kepler, Ger. astronomer, b. (d. 1630)	Incorporation of Blacksmiths' and of Joiners' Companies, London	**1571**
Galeazzo Alessi, Ital. architect, d. (b. 1512) François Clouet, Fr. painter, d. (b. 1522)	William Byrd and Thomas Tallis organists at the Chapel Royal "Il Re," one of earliest cellos by Andrea Amati of Cremona	"Artis auriferae quam chemium vocant," one of earliest books on alchemy, published in Basel Tycho Brahe discovers the "New Star" in the Milky Way Francis Drake attacks Span. harbors in America Daniel Sennert, Ger. scientist and physicist, b. (d. 1637) Society of Antiquaries founded in London	Pigeons carrying letters used by Dutch during Span. siege of Haarlem	**1572**
Michelangelo da Caravaggio, Ital. painter, b. (d. 1610) Inigo Jones, Eng. architect, b. (d. 1652) Work begun on Mexico City Cathedral (finished 1813) Paolo Veronese called before Inquisition tribunal in Rome	Orlando di Lasso: "Patrocinium musices"	Francis Drake sees Pacific Ocean for first time	First Ger. cane-sugar refinery at Augsburg	**1573**

	A. HISTORY, POLITICS	B. LITERATURE, THEATER	C. RELIGION, PHILOSOPHY, LEARNING
1574	Charles IX of France d.; succeeded by his brother Henry III, King of Poland Selim II, Sultan of Turkey, d.; succeeded by Murad III Spain loses Tunis to Turks Fifth Fr. War of Religion (—1576)	Richard Burbage receives license to open theater in London	First auto-da-fé in Mexico Jean Bodin: "Discours sur les causes de l'extrême cherté en France," on luxury Hubert Languet: "Vindiciae contra tyrannos," political theories of the Huguenots Justus Lipsius edits Tacitus' "The Annals," published by Plantin, Antwerp University of Berlin founded
1575	King Henry III of France crowned at Rheims Stephen Báthory of Transylvania becomes King of Poland (—1586) Mogul Emperor Akbar conquers Bengal Freedom from arrest granted by Eng. Parliament for its members and their servants Edmund Grindal becomes Archbishop of Canterbury (d. 1583) At conference in Breda Philip II refuses to grant concessions to Dutch rebels State bankruptcy in Spain	Giovanni Battista Basile, Ital. poet, b. (d. 1632) Diego Hurtado da Mendoza, Span. poet and statesman, d. (b. 1503) Johann Fischart: "Geschichtsklitterung," Ger. adaptation of Rabelais' "Gargantua" "Gammer Gurton's Needle," early Eng. farce, author unknown George Gascoigne: "The Posies" Tasso: "Gerusalemme liberata," epic poems about the Crusades Cyril Tourneur, Eng. dramatist, b. (d. 1626)	Jakob Böhme, Ger. mystic and theologian, b. (d. 1624) Archbishop Matthew Parker (1505—1575) leaves his collection of historical documents to Corpus Christi College, Cambridge Christopher Saxton: "Country Atlas of England and Wales" University of Leiden founded by William of Orange
1576	Philip II makes his half brother Don John of Austria Governor of the Netherlands Act of Federation between Holland and Zeeland signed in Delft Edict of Beaulieu tolerating Reformed religion in France Emperor Maximilian II d.; succeeded by his brother Rudolf II (1552—1612) Congress of Ghent discusses pacification of the Netherlands Spanish sack Antwerp	Richard Burbage obtains 21-year lease of land in Shoreditch, London, with permission to build a playhouse; "The Theatre" opens in Dec. Académie du Palais founded in Paris by Henry III, associated with Baïf's Académie of 1570 Johann Fischart: "Das glückhafft Schiff von Zürich," satirical report of journey from Zurich to Strasbourg George Gascoigne: "The Steele Glas," verse satire Hans Sachs, Ger. poet and dramatist, d. (b. 1494)	Jean Bodin: "La république," advocating constitutional monarchy League of Torgau, supporting opinions of the Lutherans, draws up Articles of Faith University of Warsaw, Poland, founded
1577	Henry of Navarre recognized head of Huguenot party Perpetual Edict to settle civil war in the Netherlands issued by Don John of Austria; rejected by William of Orange Sixth Fr. War of Religion breaks out Peace of Bergerac ends sixth War of Religion Don John of Austria deposed by States General; William of Orange enters Brussels Danzig surrender ends Pol. opposition to Stephen Báthory	Remy Belleau, Fr. poet, d. (b. 1527) Robert Burton, Eng. prose writer, b. (d. 1640) George Gascoigne, Eng. author, d. (b. 1525) London's second playhouse, "The Curtain," opens in Finsbury "Chronicles of England, Scotland, and Ireland," a history in 2 vols. published by Raphael Holinshed (d. c. 1580), (Holinshed Chronicles)	William Allot: "Thesaurus Bibliorum" Richard Eden: "History of Travel in East and West Indies" Lutheran Book of Concord, drafted by Jacob Andreae, Martin Chemnitz, and others Milan Cathedral consecrated by Cardinal Carlo Borromeo

D. VISUAL ARTS	E. MUSIC	F. SCIENCE, TECHNOLOGY, GROWTH	G. DAILY LIFE	
Longleat House, Wiltshire, finished (begun 1568) Tintoretto: "Paradiso," Doge's Palace, Venice	Domenico Maria Ferrabosco, Ital. singer and composer, d. (b. 1513)	Ulissi Aldovrandi: "Antidotarii Bononiensis epitome," a treatise on drugs Conrad Dasypodius builds the famous Strasbourg clock Bartolommeo Eustachio, Ital. anatomist, d. (b. 1524) Portuguese colonize Angola and found Sao Paulo		**1574**
Cornelis Floris, Dutch architect, d. (b. 1514) Guido Reni, Ital. painter, b. (d. 1642) Veronese: "Moses Saved from the Waters"	William Byrd and Thomas Tallis: "Cantiones sacrae," 34 motets Marco da Gagliano, Ital. composer, b..(d. 1642)	Tycho Brahe constructs an observatory at Uraniborg for Frederick II of Denmark George Turberville: "Book of Falconrie"	First European imitations of Chin. porcelain made in Venice and Florence Outbreaks of plague in Sicily, spreading through Italy up to Milan Population figures: Paris c. 300,000; London c. 180,000; Cologne c. 35,000	**1575**
Palladio: Il Redentore, church in Venice (—1577) Titian d. (b. 1477)	Tomás Luis de Victoria: "Liber primus," masses and canticles	Clusius publishes his treatise on flowers of Spain and Portugal; beginning of modern botany Martin Frobisher (1535—1594), Eng. navigator, discovers Frobisher Bay, Canada Robert Norman, English hydrographer, discovers magnetic "dip," or inclination François Viète introduces decimal fractions		**1576**
El Greco: "Assumption of the Virgin," altarpiece in San Domingo el Antiguo, Toledo Peter Paul Rubens, Fl. painter, b. (d. 1640) Tintoretto: "The Doge Alvise Mocenigo"	Mattheus Le Maistre, Walloon composer, d. (b. 1505)	Francis Drake embarks (Nov.) on voyage around the world via Cape Horn William Harrison: "Description of England" Johann Baptista van Helmont, Fl. physician and scientist, b. (d. 1644)	Beatrice Cenci, Ital. tragic heroine, b. (d. 1599)	**1577**

	A. HISTORY, POLITICS	B. LITERATURE, THEATER	C. RELIGION, PHILOSOPHY, LEARNING
1578	James VI takes over government of Scotland after Earl of Morton resigns regency Sebastian, King of Portugal, killed at Alcazar during invasion of Morocco Elizabeth I offers to mediate between Don John of Austria and the Dutch Don John d. (b. 1545); Alessandro Farnese, Duke of Parma, succeeds as Governor of the Netherlands Earl of Leicester secretly marries Viscountess Hereford John III of Sweden secretly converted to Catholicism Mohammed Khudabanda becomes Shah of Persia (—1587) Otomo Yoshishige, one of chief rulers of Japan, converted to Christianity	Guillaume de Salluste, Seigneur du Bartas: "La Semaine," religious epic on the Creation Pierre de Ronsard: "Sonnets pour Hélène," to Hélène de Surgères John Lyly: "Euphues, the Anatomy of Wit," complete edition 1617	Jacques Cujas: "Commentaries on Roman Law" Eng. College of Douai removed to Rheims
1579	Eng.-Dutch military alliance signed Signing of Union of Utrecht marks foundation of Dutch Republic Francis Drake proclaims sovereignty of England over New Albion, Calif. Duke Albert of Bavaria d.; succeeded by Duke William V (—1597)	Samuel Coster, Dutch dramatist, b. (d. 1665) John Fletcher, Eng. dramatist, b. (d. 1625) Stephen Gosson: "The Schools of Abuse," against the theater Thomas Lodge: "A Defense of Poetry, Music and Stage Plays," answer to Gosson Edmund Spenser: "The Shepheard's Calendar," 12 eclogues	Eng. College removed from Rheims to Rome Sir Thomas North translates Plutarch's "Lives" Paolo Paruta, official historian of Venice and disciple of Macchiavelli, begins his "Historia Vinetiana" St. John of the Cross: "Dark Night of the Soul"
1580	Seventh Fr. War of Religion breaks out Spanish invade Portugal under Duke of Alba Ivan IV, The Terrible, kills his son and heir with his own hands	Luis Vaz de Camöens, Port. poet, d. (b. 1524) Johann Fischart: "Das Jesuitenhütlein" attacks Jesuits Daniel Heinsius, Dutch poet, b. (d. 1655) Jan Kochanowski (1530—1584): "Threny," Pol. laments Thomas Middleton, Eng. dramatist, b. (d. 1627) Last performance of a miracle play in Coventry John Webster, Eng. dramatist, b. (d. 1625)	Jean Bodin: "Démonomanie des sorciers," against witchcraft Jesuits Edmund Campion and Robert Parsons land in England, begin Jesuit mission (July) François de la Noue: "24 Discours politiques et militaires," Huguenot point of view on Fr. Wars of Religion Michel de Montaigne (1533—1592): "Essais" John Stow: "The Chronicles of England" (—1592)
1581	Port. Cortes submits to Philip II of Spain Earl of Morton executed for complicity in Lord Darnley's murder (1567) Akbar conquers Afghanistan Stephen Báthory, King of Poland, invades Russia Russian conquest of Siberia (—1598)	Pieter Corneliszoon Hooft, Dutch poet, b. (d. 1647) George Peele: "The Arraignment of Paris," pastoral play	Edmund Campion, Eng. Jesuit, tried for treason and executed Pope Gregory XIII attempts to reconcile Roman Catholic and Russian Orthodox Churches James VI of Scotland signs Second Confession of Faith Richard Mulcaster: "Positions," treatise on education Lancelot Popelinière: "Premier Livre de l'idée de l'histoire accomplié," contemporary history

D. VISUAL ARTS	E. MUSIC	F. SCIENCE, TECHNOLOGY, GROWTH	G. DAILY LIFE	
Adam Elsheimer, Ger. landscape painter, b. (d. 1610)		Catacombs of Rome discovered	Faience pottery opened in Nevers by the Conrade brothers Levant Trading Company founded in London for trade with Turkey Work begun on Pont Neuf, oldest bridge over Seine River, Paris	**1578**
Giovanni da Bologna: "The Rape of the Sabines," sculpture El Greco: "L'Espolio" Palladio: Teatro Olimpico, Vicenza Frans Snyders, Dutch painter, b. (d. 1657)		Father Thomas Stephens, first Englishman to settle in India (Goa)	Eng. Eastland Company founded for trading with Scandinavia Port. merchants set up trading station in Bengal	**1579**
Frans Hals, Dutch painter, b. (d. 1666) Andrea Palladio, Ital. architect, d. (b. 1508) Robert Smythson: Wollaton Hall, near Nottingham (—1610)	Eng. folk tune "Greensleeves" mentioned for first time Jan Sweelinck made organist at Dude Kerk, Amsterdam	Francis Drake returns to England from voyage of circumnavigation	Venice imports coffee from Turkey to Italy Earthquake in London Ital. cooking predominant in Europe New buildings banned in London to restrict growth of city	**1580**
Caravaggio: "Martyrdom of St. Maurice" Domenichino (Domenico Zampieri), Ital. painter, b. (d. 1641) Bernardo Strozzi, Ital. baroque painter, b. (d. 1644)	Coroso: "Il Ballerino," treatise on dance technique "Ballet comique de la Reyne" by Balthazar de Beaujoyeux given at Fr. court Vincenzo Galilei: "Dialogo della musica antica e moderna" "Geuzenlied Boek," an anthology of Dutch songs, including national anthem "Wilhelmus van Nassauwe"	William Borough: "A Discourse on the Variation of the Compass or Magneticall Needle" Elizabeth I knights Francis Drake at Deptford Galileo Galilei discovers isochronous property of the pendulum	Eng. translation by George Pettie of Stafano Guazzo's "Civil Conversations," on courtesy and good behavior Sedan chairs in general use in England	**1581**

	A. HISTORY, POLITICS	B. LITERATURE, THEATER	C. RELIGION, PHILOSOPHY, LEARNING
1582	Peace of Jam-Zapolski: Russia loses access to Baltic and abandons Livonia and Estonia to Poland Attempt on life of William of Orange Raid of Ruthven: James VI kidnaped by Protestant nobles Gregorian Calendar adopted in Papal States, Spain, and Portugal (Oct.); France, the Netherlands, and Scandinavia (Dec.); England 1752 Nobunaga, ruler of Japan, assassinated Venetian Constitution amended: authority of Council of Ten restricted	Phineas Fletcher, Eng. poet, b. (d. 1650)	George Buchanan: "Rerum Scoticarum historiae" St. Teresa de Jesús, Span. mystic, d. (b. 1515) Jesuit mission founded in China Utrecht Library founded University of Edinburgh founded
1583	Duke of Anjou sacks Antwerp and retires from the Netherlands Albrecht von Wallenstein, military leader in Thirty Years' War, b. (d. 1634) Sommerville plot to assassinate Elizabeth I discovered; John Sommerville executed James VI of Scotland escapes from hands of Ruthven raiders after 10 months Throgmorton plot for Span. invasion of England discovered; Francis Throgmorton arrested and executed William of Orange accepts sovereignty of the northern Netherlands	Robert Ganier (1545—1590): "Les Juives," early Fr. tragicomedy Baptista Honwaerd: "Pegasides Pleyn Amorosity," Dutch didactic poem Queen's Company of Players formed in London by Sir Edmund Tilney	Edmund Grindal, Archbishop of Canterbury, d. (b. 1519); succeeded by John Whitgift Hugo Grotius, Dutch statesman and jurist, b. (d. 1645) Francesco Sansovino: "Del Governo et ammistrazione di diversi regni et republiche" Joseph Justus Scaliger: "Opus de emendatione temporum," foundation of modern chronology Sir Thomas Smith: "De republica Anglorum," on government machinery in England
1584	Ivan IV, The Terrible, d. (b. 1530); succeeded as Czar of Russia by his son Fyodor, who relinquishes most of his powers to his brother-in-law Boris Godunov Francis, Duke of Anjou, d. (b. 1554) William of Orange assassinated, at instigation of Philip II, by Balthazar Gérard	Francis Beaumont, Eng. dramatist, b. (d. 1616) Jan Kochanowski, Pol. poet, d. (b. 1530) John Lyly: "Alexander and Campaspe" produced at Blackfriars Theatre, London	Foundation of Accademia dei Scienze, Lettere ed Arti in Lucca Cardinal Carlo Borromeo, Archbishop of Milan, d. (b. 1538) Giordano Bruno: "Spaccio della bestia trionfante" Nicholas Sanders: "De origine ac progressu schismatis Anglicani" Reginald Scot: "The Discoverie of Witchcraft," attacking superstition Lucilio Vanini, Ital. philosopher, b. (d. 1619) John Cotton, religious controversialist in America, b. (d. 1652) Emmanuel College, Cambridge, founded by Sir Walter Mildmay Uppingham School founded
1585	Henry III of France and Elizabeth I of England decline sovereignty of the Netherlands; but Elizabeth takes the Netherlands under her protection Sir Francis Drake attacks Vigo and Santo Domingo on Elizabeth's orders Hideyoshi sets up dictatorship in Japan	Eng. actor Edward Alleyn (1566—1626) becomes head of Lord Chamberlain's Men and the Lord Admiral's Company Gerbrand Adriensz Bredero, Dutch poet, b. (d. 1618) Cervantes: "Galatea," pastoral romance Pierre de Ronsard, Fr. poet, d. (b. 1525) Battista Guarini: "Il Pastor fido," pastoral play, given at Turin Shakespeare leaves Stratford on Avon for London Teatro Olimpico, in Vicenza, opened	Pope Gregory XIII d.; Cardinal Felice Peretti becomes Pope Sixtus V (—1590) Jesuit University founded in Graz, Austria

D. VISUAL ARTS	E. MUSIC	F. SCIENCE, TECHNOLOGY, GROWTH	G. DAILY LIFE	
David Teniers the Elder, Dutch painter, b. (d. 1649)	Gregorio Allegri, Ital. tenor singer and composer, b. (d. 1652)	First Eng. colony in Newfoundland founded Richard Hakluyt (1552—1616): "Divers Voyages Touching the Discovery of America" Urbain Hémand investigates the anatomy of the teeth	Royal Navy gets graduated pay according to rank London's first waterworks founded; water wheels installed on London Bridge	**1582**
Gen. Toyotomi Hideyoshi (1536—1598) lays foundation of Osaka Castle	Girolamo Frescobaldi, Ital. organist and composer, b. (d. 1643) Orlando Gibbons, Eng. organist and composer, b. (d. 1625)	Eng. expeditions to Mesopotamia, India, and Persian Gulf led by merchants Ralph Fitch and John Eldred (—1591)	First known life insurance in England, on life of William Gibbons	**1583**
	Pietro Vinci, Ital. composer, d. (b. 1535)	Dutch trading post founded at Archangel, Russia Sir Walter Raleigh discovers and annexes Virginia	Banco di Rialto founded in Venice Oldest extant wave-swept lighthouse erected at Cordouan, at the mouth of the Gironde River	**1584**
Jean Lemercier, Fr. architect, b. (d. 1654) Veronese: "Apotheosis of Venice," Sala de Gran Consiglio, Venice	Heinrich Schütz, Ger. composer, b. (d. 1672) Thomas Tallis, Eng. composer, d. (b. 1505)	John Davis discovers Davis Strait between Canada and Greenland Simon Stevin formulates the law of equilibrium Lucas Janszoon Waghearen: "Spiegel der Zeevaart," a book of sailing directions Bartholomew Newsam constructs first Eng. traveling and standing clocks	Antwerp loses its importance as international port to Rotterdam and Amsterdam	**1585**

	A. HISTORY, POLITICS	B. LITERATURE, THEATER	C. RELIGION, PHILOSOPHY, LEARNING
1586	Sir Francis Walsingham unravels Babington Plot to murder Elizabeth I, proving involvement of Mary Queen of Scots in the plan Anthony Babington and fellow conspirators tried and executed for plot Mary, Queen of Scots, tried for treason at Fotheringay; sentence is pronounced against her; Elizabeth confirms it Abbas I becomes Shah of Persia (—1628) Stephen Báthory, King of Poland, d. (b. 1533) Mary, Queen of Scots, recognizes Philip II of Spain as her heir Pope Sixtus V promises financial aid to send Span. Armada against England	John Ford, Eng. dramatist, b. (d. 1640) Beginning of Kabuki theater, Japan Sir Philip Sidney, Eng. poet and soldier, d. (b. 1551) William Webbe: "Discourse of English Poetrie"	Caesar Baronius: "Annales ecclesiastici," history of the Roman Catholic Church Ludwig Pfyffer forms League of the Seven Swiss Catholic Cantons William Camden: "Britannia," guide to the counties of Britain Pope Sixtus V fixes number of cardinals at 70; issues bull, "Detestabilis," forbidding usury
1587	Mary, Queen of Scots, executed at Fotheringay (b. 1542) Sir Christopher Hatton (1540—1591) becomes Lord Chancellor A son of King John of Sweden succeeds Stephen Báthory as Sigismund III of Poland (—1632) Hideyoshi banishes Port. missionaries from Japan Pope Sixtus V proclaims Catholic crusade for invasion of England John Winthrop b. (d. 1649), first governor of Massachusetts Bay colony	First company of Eng. players in Germany Robert Greene: "Euphues, his Censure of Philautus," continuation of Lyly's "Euphues" of 1578 Marlowe: "Tamburlaine," blank verse drama Joost van den Vondel, Dutch dramatist, b. (d. 1679) "Volksbuch von Dr. Faust," first printed at Frankfurt; Eng. translation 1588	Antonio Agustino: "Dialogo de medallas y inscriciones," on numismatics (posth.) John Knox: "Hystory of the Reformation in Scotland" (posth.) "Rederijckkunst," Dutch manual on rhetoric Isaac Casaubon edits works of Strabo
1588	Frederick II of Denmark d.; succeeded by Christian IV (—1648) Duke of Medina Sidonia sails from Lisbon in command of "Invincible" Span. Armada; defeated by the English under Charles Howard Henry, Duke of Guise, and his brother Louis, Cardinal of Guise, assassinated by order of Henry III; another brother, the Duke of Mayenne, becomes leader of Catholic League	Robert Greene: "Pandosto, or Dorastus and Fawnia," romance Marlowe: "Doctor Faustus," tragedy Montaigne: "Essais," Vol. III	William Morgan's translation of the Bible into Welsh Jan Blahoslav's (1523—1571) Czech translation of New Testament incorporated in Kralice Bible Thomas Hobbes, Eng. philosopher, b. (d. 1679) Marin Mersenne, Fr. philosopher, b. (d. 1648) Thomas Stapleton: "Tres Thomae," controversial Roman Catholic tract Vatican Library opened in Rome
1589	Catherine de'Medici, Queen Mother of France, d. Henry III, King of France, last of the house of Valois, assassinated; on his deathbed he recognizes Henry, King of Navarre, as his successor, who, as Henry IV, is the first Burbon to become King of France Sir Francis Drake, with 150 ships and 18,000 men, fails to take Lisbon House of Commons first appoints a Standing Committee for Privileges	Robert Greene: "Menaphon," romance Thomas Nashe (1567—1601): "Anatomie of Absurdities," criticism of contemporary literature George Puttenham: "The Arte of English Poesie"	Amador Arrais: "Dialogues de Dom Frei Amador Arraiz," Port. conversations on moral and religious themes Boris Godunov asserts Moscow's religious independence of Constantinople Justus Lipsius: "Politicorum sive Civilis Doctrinae" Kiev Academy founded Sidney Sussex College, Cambridge, founded

D. VISUAL ARTS	E. MUSIC	F. SCIENCE, TECHNOLOGY, GROWTH	G. DAILY LIFE	
Luis de Morales, Span. painter, d. (b. 1510) El Greco: "Burial of Count Orgaz" Rebuilding of St. John Lateran, Rome	Johann Hermann Schein, Ger. composer, b. (d. 1630)	Thomas Cavendish leaves Plymouth on voyage of circumnavigation (returns 1588)	Corn severely short in England	**1586**
Cobham Hall, Kent, begun by Inigo Jones and completed by Adam brothers Osaka Castle, Japan, finished	Monteverdi: first book of madrigals Samuel Scheidt, Ger. organist and composer, b. (d. 1654) Zeminoth Israel publishes early collection of Jewish songs	Richard Hakluyt (1552—1616): "Notable History, Containing Four Voyages made by Certain French Captains Into Florida"	Construction of Rialto Bridge, Venice, by Antonio da Ponte (—1591)	**1587**
Annibale Carracci: frescoes in Magnani Palace, Bologna Domenico Fontana (1543—1607) works on completion of dome of St. Peter's, Rome (1585—1590) Paolo Veronese, Ital. painter, d. (b. 1528)	William Byrd: "Psalms, Sonets and Songs of Sadnes and Pietie" Nicholas Yonge: "Musica Transalpina," 57 madrigals published in London	Joachim Camerarius: "Hortus medicus"	Timothy Bright: "An Arte of Shorte, Swifte, and Secrete Writing by Character," manual of shorthand Eng. Guinea Company founded	**1588**
Caravaggio: "Bacchus" Bernard Palissy, Fr. Huguenot writer on art and pottery, d. (b. 1510)	Thoinot Arbeau (1519—1595): "Orchésographie," early treatise on dancing, with several dance tunes William Byrd: "Songes of Sundrie Natures"	Galileo Galilei becomes professor of mathematics at University of Pisa Richard Hakluyt: "The Principall Navigations and Discoveries of the English Nation"	Forks used for first time at Fr. court The Reverend William Lee (Cambridge) invents the stocking frame, first knitting machine	**1589**

	A. HISTORY, POLITICS	B. LITERATURE, THEATER	C. RELIGION, PHILOSOPHY, LEARNING
1590	Catholic League proclaims Cardinal de Bourbon King Charles X of France (Jan.); he dies (May) Sir Francis Walsingham, Eng. statesman, d. (b. 1530) Henry IV lays siege to Paris, causing famine there Shah Abbas I of Persia, abandoning Tabriz and Georgia, makes peace with Turkey Akbar of India conquers Orissa The Emperor of Morocco annexes Timbuctoo	Ital. Commedia dell' arte company, "I Accesi," begins activities Johann Fischart, Ger. author, d. (b. 1547) Robert Greene: "Mourning Garment" and "Never Too Late," pamphlets Thomas Lodge: "Rosalynde," pastoral romance Marlowe: "The Jew of Malta," tragedy George Peele: "Polyhymnia," verses for a tournament Shakespeare: "Henry VI," Parts 2 and 3 (—1591); the Shakespeare chronology in the following pages is taken from Sir Edmund Chamber's standard work "William Shakespeare" (1930), which, however, according to the Encyclopaedia Britannica, does not lay "claim to more than approximate accuracy" Battista Guarini: "Il Pastor fido," pastoral play, published Edmund Spenser: "The Faerie Queene," Books 1—3 Robert Wilson: "Three Lords and Three Ladies of London," morality play	Pope Sixtus V d.; Cardinal Giambattista Castagna succeeds him as Pope Urban VII and dies 12 days later Cardinal Niccolò Sfondrato becomes Pope Gregory XIV (—1591)
1591	Henry IV of France excommunicated by Pope Gregory XIV Dmitri, son of Ivan the Terrible, assassinated on instigation of Boris Godunov, regent under Czar Fyodor Christian I of Saxony d.; succeeded by his eight-year-old son Christian II (—1601)	Luis de León, Span. poet, d. (b. 1527) Robert Greene: "Philomela," romance Robert Herrick, Eng. poet, b. (d. 1674) "The Troublesome Reigne of King John of England," anonymous, attributed to Shakespeare John Lyly: "Endymion, the Man in The Moon," allegorical comedy Shakespeare: "Henry VI," Part 1 (—1592) Sir Philip Sidney: "Astrophel and Stella" (posth.) Edmund Spenser: "Complaints"	Giordano Bruno: "De immenso et innumerabilis seu de universo et mundis" Pope Gregory XIV d. (Oct.); Cardinal Antonio Facchinetti becomes Pope Innocent IX (—Dec.) John of the Cross (Juan de Yepez y Alvarez), Span. mystic, d. (b. 1542; canonized 1726) Trinity College, Dublin, founded by Elizabeth I
1592	John III of Sweden d.; succeeded by Sigismund III of Poland Akbar, Mogul Emperor, takes Sind Hideyoshi of Japan fails in invasion of Korea, as the country refuses passage of his troops to invade China Portuguese settle at Mombasa Emperor Rudolf II makes peace with Poland	Nicholas Ferrar, Eng. theologian and poet, b. (d. 1637) Robert Greene: "A Quip for an Upstart Courtier," pamphlet Robert Greene, Eng. dramatist and pamphleteer, d. (b. 1558) Philip Henslowe, London theatrical manager, writes his "Diary" (—1603) Thomas Kyd: "The Spanish Tragedy," play John Lyly: "Midas," play Thomas Nashe: "Pierce Pennilesse His Supplication to the Devil," satire Shakespeare mentioned as actor for the first time Shakespeare: "Richard III," "Comedy of Errors"	Cardinal Ippolito Aldobrandini elected Pope Clement VIII (—1605), succeeding Pope Innocent IX (d. Dec. 30, 1591) Johann Amos Comenius, Moravian educational reformer, b. (d. 1670) Michel de Montaigne, Fr. essayist, d. (b. 1533) Pierre Gassendi, Fr. philosopher, b. (d. 1655) Thomas Sanchez: "De sacramento matrimonii," on religious and legal aspects of marriage
1593	Rudolf II renews war against Turkey Henry IV becomes a Roman Catholic, hearing Mass at St. Denis: "Paris is well worth a mass"	Robert Henryson: "Testament of Cresseid," poem (posth.) George Herbert, Eng. poet, b. (d. 1633) Christopher Marlowe, Eng. dramatist, killed in tavern brawl (b. 1564) George Peele: "The Chronicle of Edward the First," play London theaters closed because of the plague Shakespeare: "Titus Andronicus," "The Taming of the Shrew" Izaak Walton, Eng. biographer and angler, b. (d. 1683)	Pierre Charron: "Les Trois Vérités," Fr. theological treatise

D. VISUAL ARTS	E. MUSIC	F. SCIENCE, TECHNOLOGY, GROWTH	G. DAILY LIFE	
Alonso Sanchez Coello, Span. painter, d. (b. 1515) Giovanni da Bologna: "Mercury" El Greco: "St. Jerome" Leone Leoni, Ital. goldsmith and sculptor, d. (b. 1509)	Emilio de' Cavalieri: "Il Satiro," pastoral fable	José de Acosta: "Historia natural y moral de las Indias" Drake, Hawkins, and Frobisher return from unsuccessful expedition to Span. coast Galileo: "De Motu," description of experiments on dropping of various bodies	Coal mining begins in the Ruhr First Eng. paper mill at Dartford	**1590**
Jusepe de Ribera (Lo Spagnoletto), Span. painter, b. (d. 1652) Guercino (Giovanni Francesco Barbieri), Ital. painter, b. (d. 1666)	Vincenzo Galilei, Ital. lutanist and composer, father of Galileo Galilei, d. (b. 1520)	James Lancaster leaves Plymouth on first voyage to E. Indies François Viète (1540—1603): "In Artem analyticam isagoge," on using letters for algebraic quantities	Skittle alleys, in use since end of 12th century, become popular in Germany	**1591**
Jacques Callot, Fr. painter, b. (d. 1635) Tintoretto: "The Last Supper"	Monteverdi: third book of madrigals Lodovico Zacconi: "Prattica di musica," original edition	Thomas Cavendish, Eng. navigator, d. (b. 1555) Juan de Fuca discovers British Columbia Galileo: "Della scienza mechanica," problems of raising weights Sir James Lancaster sails around Malay Peninsula Ruined Roman city of Pompeii discovered	Plague kills 15,000 people in London Windmills used in Holland to drive mechanical saws	**1592**
Guiseppe Archimboldo, Ital. painter, d. (b. 1530) El Greco: "The Crucifixion," "The Resurrection" Jacob Jordaëns, Dutch painter, b. (d. 1678) Nicolas Poussin, Fr. painter, b. (d. 1665)	Paolo Agostini, Ital. composer, b. (d. 1629)	First. Fr. botanical gardens established by University of Montpellier Giambattista della Porta: "De refractione, optices parte," with an account of binocular vision Anthony van Diemen, Dutch navigator, b. (d. 1645)	Purana Pul bridge built across Musí River, Hyderabad Sant' Ambrogio Bank founded in Milan	**1593**

	A. HISTORY, POLITICS	B. LITERATURE, THEATER	C. RELIGION, PHILOSOPHY, LEARNING
1594	Henry IV, having been crowned King of France at Chartres, enters Paris Gustavus Adolphus, future King Gustavus II of Sweden, b. (d. 1632) Akbar takes Kandahar Edict of St. Germain-en-Laye grants Huguenots freedom of worship Turks conquer Raab at Austro-Hungarian border	Diego Bernades: "Várias rimas ao Bom Jesus," Port. religious poems Robert Greene: "Friar Bacon and Friar Bungay," comedy (posth.) London theaters open again (May) John Lyly: "Mother Bombie," comedy Christopher Marlowe: "Edward the Second," tragedy (posth.) Thomas Nashe: "The Unfortunate Traveller," picaresque novel George Peele: "The Battle of Alcazar," play Shakespeare: "The Two Gentlemen of Verona," "Love's Labour's Lost," "Romeo and Juliet"	Giordano Bruno seized by the Vatican for supporting Copernican theory of the universe (see 1600) Richard Hooker: "Of the Laws of Ecclesiastical Polity," vols. 1—4 Piere Matthieu: "Histoire des derniers troubles de France" Gerardus Mercator (Kremer), Fl. geographer and mathematician, d. (b. 1512)
1595	Henry IV declares war on Spain Spanish land in Cornwall, burning Penzance and Mousehole Sigmund Báthory defeats Turks at Giurgevo Dutch begin to colonize E. Indies Sultan Murad III of Turkey d.; succeeded by Mohammed III (—1603) Peasant revolt in Upper Austria	Thomas Kyd, Eng. dramatist, d. (b. 1557) George Peele: "The Old Wives' Tale," comedy Shakespeare: "Richard II," "A Midsummer Night's Dream" Robert Southwell, Eng. Jesuit poet, hanged at Tyburn (b. 1561) Torquato Tasso, Ital. poet, d. (b. 1544) Sir Philip Sidney: "An Apologia for Poetrie" (posth.)	Pope Clement VIII absolves Henry IV, recognizing him as King of France Andrew Maunsell: "The Catalogue of English Printed Books" Philip Neri, Ital. mystic, d. (b. 1515)
1596	Decrees of Folembray end war of Catholic League in France Pacification of Ireland English sack Cadiz; Spanish take Calais Peace between Japan and China after Japanese fail to invade Korea Turks defeat Imperial army at Keresztes, northern Hungary	Blackfriars Theatre, London, opens Sir John Davies: "Orchestra," poem Sir John Harington: "The Metamorphosis of Ajax," satire Shakespeare: "King John," "The Merchant of Venice" Edmund Spenser: "The Faerie Queene," Books 4—6	Caesar Baronius: "Martyrologium Romanum" Jean Bodin, Fr. philosopher, d. (b. 1530) René Descartes, Fr. philosopher, b. (d. 1650) Gresham College, London, founded
1597	Second Span. Armada leaves for England; scattered by storms Sigmund Báthory cedes Transylvania to Emperor Rudolf II Hideyoshi of Japan resumes Korean campaign Philip II opens peace talks with Henry IV Re-Catholicization of Upper Austria effected by force William V, Duke of Bavaria, abdicates in favor of his son Maximilian I, then retires to a monastery (—1626)	Hernando de Herrera, Span. poet, d. (b. 1534) John Lyly: "The Woman in the Moone," play Thomas Nashe: "The Isle of Dogs," satirical comedy Martin Opitz, Ger. poet, b. (d. 1639) Shakespeare: "Henry IV," Parts 1 and 2 (—1598) Shakespeare buys New Place, Stratford on Avon Aldine Press, Venice, founded 1494, ceases after publication of 908 works Aldus Manutius the Younger d. (b. 1547)	Sir Francis Bacon: "Essays, Civil and Moral" Peter Canisius, Ger. Jesuit Counter Reformationist, d. (b. 1521; canonized, 1925) Jean de Serres: "Inventaire général de l'histoire de France" James VI of Scotland: "Demonologie," on witchcraft

D. VISUAL ARTS	E. MUSIC	F. SCIENCE, TECHNOLOGY, GROWTH	G. DAILY LIFE	
Caravaggio: "The Musical Party" Jean Cousin, Fr. painter, d. (b. 1522) Giovanni da Bologna: statues of Cosimo I de' Medici and Fernando de' Medici Tintoretto, Ital. painter, d. (b. 1518)	Elizabeth I sends a Thomas Dallam organ to Sultan of Turkey Orlando di Lasso, Fl. composer, d. (b. 1532) Giovanni Pierluigi da Palestrina, Ital. composer, d. (b. 1525) "Dafne," by Jacopo Peri (1561—1633), first opera	Eng. traveler Ralph Fitch returns from overland journey to India and Ceylon Martin Frobisher d. at recapture of Brest from Spanish (b. 1535) Galileo's Golden Rule	Eng. navigator James Lancaster breaks Port. trade monopoly in India	**1594**
Annibale Carracci: "Venus and Adonis"	John Wilson, Eng. singer and composer, b. (d. 1674)	Sir Francis Drake and Sir John Hawkins leave Plymouth on last voyage to Span. Main Sir John Hawkins, Eng. navigator, d. at sea near Puerto Rico (b. 1532) Andreas Libavius: "Opera omnia medico-chymica" Mercator's atlas published (posth.) Sir Walter Raleigh explores 300 miles up Orinoco River	Eng. army finally abandons bow as weapon of war First appearance of heels on shoes Warsaw, capital of Poland	**1595**
Caravaggio: "Basket of Fruit" Jan van Goyen, Dutch painter, b. (d. 1656)	Nicola Amati, the most eminent of all the Amati, b. (d. 1684) Lodovico Zacconi: "Prattica di musica," reprinted from original edition, Venice, 1592	Willem Barents discovers Spitzbergen and Barents Sea Sir Francis Drake d. (b. 1546) Galileo invents thermometer J. Kepler: "De admirabili proportione coelestium orbium" G. D. Rheticus (1514—1576): "Trigonometric Tables" (posth.) Ludolph van Ceulen's "Van den Circkel" gives ratio of the diameter to the circumference of a circle to twenty places	Tomatoes introduced in England First water closets, designed by Sir John Harington, courtier and author (1561—1612), installed at the Queen's Palace, Richmond	**1596**
Juan de Herrera, Span. architect, d. (b. 1530) El Greco: "St. Martin and the Beggar"	John Dowland: "First Booke of Songes" Thomas Morley: "A Plaine and Easie Introduction to Practicall Musick" Orazio Vecchi (1551—1605): "L'Amfiparnasso," Modena	Willem Barents, Dutch navigator, d. (b. 1547) Dutch found Batavia, Java	Eng. Act of Parliament prescribes sentences of transportation to colonies for convicted criminals Eng. merchants expelled from Holy Roman Empire in retaliation for treatment of the Hanseatic League in London First field hospitals and field dispensaries	**1597**

	A. HISTORY, POLITICS	B. LITERATURE, THEATER	C. RELIGION, PHILOSOPHY, LEARNING
1598	Fyodor I of Russia d.; Boris Godunov, seizing throne, formally elected Czar of Russia by national assembly After death of Duke Alfonso II, last of the House of Este (1597), Pope Clement VIII seizes duchy of Ferrara Treaty of Ponts de Cé ends civil war in France Steelyard, London headquarters of Hanseatic League, closed Peace of Vervins: Philip II resigns claim to Fr. crown; country united under Henry IV as single sovereign King Philip II of Spain d. (b. 1527); succeeded by Philip III (—1621) Dutch take Mauritius Hideyoshi of Japan d.; his successor, Ieyasu Tokugawa, restores shogunate, which endures until the revolution of 1867—68	Thomas Carew, Eng. poet, b. (d. 1639) Lope de Vega: "La Dragontea," fanciful account of Drake's adventures, in verse form Ben Jonson: "Every Man in His Humour" George Peele, Eng. dramatist, d. (b. 1558) Shakespeare: "Much Ado about Nothing," "Henry V" (—1599) Vincent Voiture, Fr. poet, b. (d. 1648)	Juan de Mariana: "De rege et regis institutione," on kingship Edict of Nantes grants Fr. Huguenots freedom of worship (revoked, 1685) John Florio: "A World of Wordes," Eng.-Ital. dictionary John Manwood: "Treatise on the Laws of the Forest" Philibert Mareschal: "Le Guide des arts et sciences" Francis Meres: "Palladis Tamia," anthology of quotations from 125 Eng. writers Sir Thomas Bodley (1545—1613) begins rebuilding of library at Oxford Philip van Marnix, Heer van Sainte-Adelgonde, Dutch religious author, d. (b. 1538)
1599	Earl of Essex, made Lord Lieutenant of Ireland, signs truce with Ir. rebel, Lord Tyrone; he is arrested on his return to England Oliver Cromwell, Eng. general and statesman, b. (d. 1658) Octavio Piccolomini, Aust. gen, b. (d. 1656) Agreement of Gera between branches of Hohenzollern family concerning mutual succession Duke of Sully, Fr. superintendent of finances, reforms taxation, economic policy, overseas trade, and agriculture Henry IV of France obtains divorce from Margaret of Valois Swedish Diet, deposing Sigismund III, proclaims Charles of Södermanland ruler as Charles IX	Mateo Alemán: "Guzmán de Alfarache," picaresque novel Building of the Globe Theatre, Southwark, London, where Shakespeare's plays are performed George Peele: "The Love of King David and Fair Bethsabe," play (posth.) Shakespeare: "Julius Caesar," "As You Like It," "Twelfth Night" (—1600) Edmund Spenser, Eng. poet, d. (b. 1552)	Fabio Chigi, future Pope Alexander VII, b. (d. 1667) James VI of Scotland: "Basilikon doron," on divine right of kings
1600	Maurice of Nassau defeats Archduke Albert's army at Nieuport Henry IV marries Maria de'Medici Future King Charles I of England b. (d. 1649) Earl of Essex, tried for misdemeanors in Ireland, loses offices at court Ieyasu, defeating his rivals at Sekigahara, sets himself up as unquestioned ruler in Japan; he moves capital from Kyoto to Yedo (Tokyo); Eng. navigator William Adams, first Englishman to visit Japan, becomes his adviser on shipbuilding	Thomas Dekker: "The Shoemaker's Holiday" Pedro Caldéron de la Barca, Span. dramatist, b. (d. 1681) Fortune Theatre, London, opened "William Kemp's Nine Daies Wonder" Thomas Nashe: "Summer's Last Will and Testament," satirical masque Shakespeare: "Hamlet," "The Merry Wives of Windsor" (—1601)	Giordano Bruno burned as heretic in Rome Persecution of Catholics in Sweden under Charles IX Scottish College founded in Rome

D. VISUAL ARTS	E. MUSIC	F. SCIENCE, TECHNOLOGY, GROWTH	G. DAILY LIFE	
Giovanni Lorenzo Bernini, Ital. sculptor, b. (d. 1680) Jan Brueghel: "Adoration of the Kings" El Greco: "Cardinal Don Fernando Niño de Guevara" François Mansart, Fr. architect, b. (d. 1666) Rubens a member of Antwerp painters' guild	Johann Crüger, Ger. composer, b. (d. 1662)	Francesco Cavalieri, Ital. scientist, b. (d. 1647) Reorganization of the University of Paris by Henry IV Carlo Ruini: "Dell' anatomia e dell' infirmità de cavallo, e suoi remedii," manual of veterinary science Fourth circumnavigation of world by Olivier van Noort Korean Admiral Visunsin invents iron-clad warship Tycho Brahe: "Astronomicae Instauratae Mechanica," account of his discoveries and description of his instruments		**1598**
Anthony Van Dyck, b. (d. 1641) Velázquez, Span. artist, b. (d. 1660)	Luca Marencio, Ital. composer, d. (b. 1553)	Ulissi Aldrovandi, Ital. naturalist (1522—1605), publishes his studies in ornithology	In Marseilles first chamber of commerce founded Outbreak of plague in Spain First postal rates fixed in Germany	**1599**
Caravaggio: "Doubting Thomas" Building of Royal Palace, Naples, begun Rubens in Italy (—1608)	Andrea Amati, Ital. violin maker, d. (b. 1530) Giulio Caccini: "Euridice," opera Sethus Calvisius (1556—1615) begins his "Exercitationes musicae duae," first history of music (finished 1611) Emilio de' Cavalieri's opera "La Rappresentazione di anima e di corpo" published Harps used in orchestras Thomas Morley: "First Book of Ayres" Jacopo Peri: "Euridice," opera Recorder (flute-à-bec) becomes popular in England	Tycho Brahe and Johann Kepler work together at Prague Eng. East India Company founded; initial capital, £70,000 William Gilbert: "De Magnete," treatise on magnetism and electricity Ger. Athanasius Kircher (1570—1629) invents magic lantern Caspar Lehmann, jewel cutter to Emperor Rudolf II, begins cut-glass process Dutch opticians invent the telescope	Amsterdam Bank founded Population figures (approx., in millions): France 16, Germany 14.5, Poland 11, Spain 8, Hapsburg dominions 5.5, England and Ireland 5.5, Holland 3 Wigs and dress trains become fashionable	**1600**

	A. HISTORY, POLITICS	B. LITERATURE, THEATER	C. RELIGION, PHILOSOPHY, LEARNING
1601	Earl of Essex leads revolt against Elizabeth I; is tried for treason and executed Archduke Albert of Austria besieges Ostend (—Sept. 1604) Michael, Prince of Moldavia, assassinated by Hungarians Future Louis XIII, son of Henry IV and Maria de' Medici, b. Elizabeth I, in her "Golden Speech" to Parliament, surveys achievements of her reign Abolition of monopolies in England Akbar annexes Khandest The "False Dmitri" (see 1591), claiming to be a son of Czar Ivan IV, appears in Poland, winning support for an invasion of Russia	Johann Michael Moscherosch, Ger. satirist, b. (d. 1669) Thomas Nashe, Eng. dramatist, d. (b. 1567) Bento Teixeira Pinto: "Prosopopeya," first Brazilian epic Shakespeare: "Troilus and Cressida" (—1602)	Pierre Charron: "De la sagesse," a system of Stoic philosophy University of Parma founded
1602	Span. army, after landing in Ireland (Sept. 1601), surrenders to English at Kinsala (Jan.) Jules Mazarin, future Fr. statesman and cardinal, b. in Italy (d. 1661) War between Persia and Turkey (—1627)	Thomas Campion: "Observations in the Art of English Poesie" Thomas Dekker: "Satiromastix," satirical comedy Lope de Vega: "La hermosura de angélica," epic poem Ben Jonson: "The Poetaster," comedy Sir David Lindsay: "Ane Pleasant Satyre of the Three Estaitis" (posth.) John Marston: "Antonio and Mellida," tragedy Shakespeare: "All's Well That Ends Well" (—1603)	Conrad Kircher: "A Concordance to the Septuagint" Emperor Rudolf II, continuing persecution of Protestants in Hapsburg lands, suppresses meetings of Moravian Brethren Ambrosian Library, Milan, founded (opened 1609) Bodleian Library, Oxford, opened
1603	Queen Elizabeth I of England d. (b. 1533); succeeded by her cousin James VI of Scotland as James I of England and Ireland (—1625) Amnesty in Ireland James I arrives in London Sir Walter Raleigh, arrested for suspected complicity in the "Main Plot," which sought de- thronement of James I, is tried for high treason and sentenced to imprisonment Coronation of James I Henry IV recalls Jesuits to France Mohammed III, Sultan of Turkey, d.; succeeded by Ahmad I (—1617) Revolts in Transylvania against Emperor Rudolf II Tokugawa family obtains shogunate in Japan and keeps it	Francisco Gómez de Quevedo: "La vida de buscón," picaresque novel Philip Henslowe, London theatrical manager, ends his "Diary" (begun 1592) Samuel Daniel: "A Defençe of Rhyme," in reply to Campion's "Art of English Poesie" (1602) "The Standard Grammar" by Nudozersky leads to development of modern Czech language	Johannes Althusias (1557—1638): "Politica methodice digesta," a grammar of politics Thomas Craig: "Jus feudale" Jan Gruter: "Inscriptiones antiquae totius orbis Romanorum" Richard Knolles: "General Historie of the Turkes" Roger Williams, religious controversialist in America, b. (d. 1683)

D. VISUAL ARTS	E. MUSIC	F. SCIENCE, TECHNOLOGY, GROWTH	G. DAILY LIFE	
Alonso Cano, Span. painter and architect, b. (d. 1667) Caravaggio: "Conversion of St. Paul" Simon de Vlieger, Dutch painter, b. (d. 1653)	Caccini's new vocal style: "Nuove musiche" Carlo Gesualdo, Prince of Venosa (1560—1613): "Madrigals," to lyrics by Torquato Tasso Thomas Morley: "Triumphs of Oriana"	Tycho Brahe d. (b. 1546) Pierre de Fermat, Fr. mathematician, b. (d. 1665) Kepler becomes astronomer and astrologer to Emperor Rudolf II John Lancaster leads first East India Company voyage from Torbay to Sumatra Jesuit missionary Matteo Ricci admitted to Peking Dutch navigator Olivier van Noort returns from circumnavigating the world (begun 1598), fourth time since Magellan's journey John Wheeler: "A Treatise of Commerce"	Postal agreement between Germany and France Gobelin family of dyers lend their factory in the Faubourg St. Marcel, Paris, to King Henry IV, who sets up 200 workmen from Flanders to make tapestries Many Ger. "Badestuben" (type of brothel) closed by authorities, owing to spread of venereal disease	**1601**
Agostino Carracci, Ital. painter, d. (b. 1557) Philippe de Champaigne, Fr. portrait painter, b. (d. 1674)	Francesco Cavalli, Ital. opera composer, b. (d. 1676) Hans Leo Hassler (1564—1612): "Lustgarten," collection of Ger. lieder	Thomas Blondeville: "Theoriques of the Planets" Tycho Brahe: "Astronomia Instauratae progymnasmata" gives plans of 777 fixed stars (posth., ed. by Johann Kepler) Richard Carew (1555—1620): "Survey of Cornwall" Vincenzio Cascarido, Ital. chemist, discovers barium sulfide Dutch East India Company founded with capital of £540,000 in Batavia, first modern public company Galileo investigates laws of gravitation and oscillation (—1604) William Lilly, Eng. astronomer, b. (d. 1681) Span. traders admitted to eastern Japan Otto von Guericke, Ger. scientist, b. (d. 1686) John Willis: "The Art of Stenographie"	Paris Charité founded	**1602**
Carlo Maderna builds the façade at St. Peter's, Rome (—1612) Palazzo Rospigliosi, Rome, erected by Flaminio Ponzio Aert van der Neer, Dutch painter, b. (d. 1677)	Jean-Baptiste Besard: "Thesaurus harmonicus," collection of lute music Monteverdi: "Fourth Book of Madrigals" Thomas Robinson: "School of Musicke"	Founding of Accademia dei Lincei, Rome Benedito de Goes, a lay Jesuit, sets out for India in search of Cathay Fabricio di Acquapendente discovers the valves in vein William Gilbert, Eng. scientist, d. (b. 1540)	Heavy outbreak of plague in England	**1603**

	A. HISTORY, POLITICS	B. LITERATURE, THEATER	C. RELIGION, PHILOSOPHY, LEARNING
1604	"False Dmitri," claimant to Russ. throne, defeated by Czar Boris Godunov First Parliament of James I meets Sigismund III of Sweden finally deposed, his uncle Charles IX assuming title of king Peace between England and Spain Spanish capture Ostend from Dutch after siege of 3.5 years Shah Abbas of Persia takes Tabriz from Turks England and France sign commercial treaty	Lope de Vega: "Comedias," 25 vols. published (—1647) John Marston: "The Malcontent," tragicomedy Shakespeare: "Measure for Measure" (—1605) Friedrich von Logau, Ger. author, b. (d. 1655)	Richard Bancroft, Bishop of London, elected Archbishop of Canterbury Robert Cawdrey: "A Table Alphabetical" Jacques August de Thou: "Historiae sui temporis," 11 vols. (—1614) University of Oxford and University of Cambridge granted privilege of Parliamentary representation (withdrawn 1948)
1605	Czar Boris Godunov d.; succeeded by his son Fyodor II; on entry of "False Dmitri" into Moscow Fyodor is assassinated, Dmitri being crowned Czar of Russia Jan Zamoyski, Pol. patriot, d. (b. 1541) Akbar, Mogul Emperor of India, d.; succeeded by his son Jahangir (—1627) Guy Fawkes arrested in cellars of Parliament, accused of trying to blow up House of Lords during James I's state opening of Parliament: The Gunpowder Plot Barbados, West Indies, claimed as Eng. colony Stephen Bocskai, Prince of Transylvania (—1613) Ieyasu retires; his son Hidetada succeeds him as ruler of Japan (—1623)	Cervantes: "Don Quixote," Part 1, published (Part 2, 1615) George Chapman: "All Fooles," comedy Samuel Daniel: "Philotas," tragedy Michael Drayton: "Poems" First permanent Ger. theater in Cassel Ben Jonson: "Sejanus," tragedy Thomas Randolph, Eng. poet, b. (d. 1635) Shakespeare: "King Lear," "Macbeth" (—1606)	Sir Francis Bacon: "The Advancement of Learning" Pope Clement VIII d. (b. 1535); Alessandro de' Medici elected Pope Leo XI (Apr.) Pope Leo XI d. (b. 1535); Camillo Borghese elected Pope Paul V (—1621) Justus Lipsius: "Monita et exempla politica," on organization of the state
1606	Guy Fawkes and fellow conspirators sentenced to death King James I's proclamation for a national flag "False Dmitri" assassinated by the boyar Vasili Shuisky; Shuisky is elected czar Peace treaty between Turks and Austrians signed at Zsitva-Torok	Pierre Corneille, Fr. dramatist, b. (d. 1684) William Davenant, Eng. poet, b. (d. 1668); once reputed natural son of Shakespeare Thomas Dekker: "The Seven Deadly Sinnes of London," pamphlet Madeleine de Scudéry, Fr. novelist, b. (d. 1701) Ben Jonson: "Volpone" John Lyly, Eng. dramatist, d. (b. 1554) John Marston: "The Parasitaster," comedy Shakespeare: "Antony and Cleopatra" (—1607)	Johann Arndt: "Wahres Christentum" Joseph Justus Scaliger: "Thesaurus temporum," chronology of ancient times
1607	Charles IX crowned King of Sweden "Flight of the Earls" from Ireland to Spain, fearing arrest for attempted insurrection Union of England and Scotland rejected by Eng. Parliament	George Chapman: "Bussy d'Amboise," tragedy Thomas Deloney, Eng. poet, d. (b. 1543) Honoré d'Urfé: "Astrée," Fr. pastoral romance Paul Gerhardt, Ger. poet, b. (d. 1676) Thomas Heywood: "A Woman Killed with Kindness," tragedy John Marston: "What You Will," comedy Shakespeare: "Coriolanus," "Timon of Athens" (—1608) Cyril Tourneur: "The Revenger's Tragedy"	Joseph Calasanza organizes in Rome the Brotherhood of Piarists (canonized, 1767) John Cowell: "The Interpreter," a law dictionary (see 1610)

D. VISUAL ARTS	E. MUSIC	F. SCIENCE, TECHNOLOGY, GROWTH	G. DAILY LIFE	
Caravaggio: "The Deposition," Vatican Karel van Mander (1548—1606): "Het Schilderboek," history of art	Heinrich Albert, Ger. composer, b. (d. 1651) Company of Musicians incorporated in London Orlando di Lasso: "Magnum opus musicum," 516 motets (posth.) Negri: "Inventioni di balli," on dance technique	Voyages of Eng. East India Company to Java, the Moluccas, and Agra Johann Rudolf Glauber, Ger. scientist, b. (d. 1668) King James I: "Counterblast to Tobacco" Johann Kepler: "Optics"	Tomsk founded by Russ. Cossacks	**1604**
Annibale Carracci: frescoes in the Palazzo Farnese, Rome	Giacomo Carissimi, Ital. composer, b. (d. 1674) Tomás Luis de Victoria: "Officium Defunctorum" John Dowland: "Lachrymae, or Seaven Teares in Seaven Passionate Pavans" Monteverdi: "Fifth Book of Madrigals"	Gaspard Bauhin (1560—1624): "Theatrum anatomicum," modern anatomy Santa Fé, New Mex., founded Ulissi Aldrovandi, Ital. naturalist, d. (b. 1535)	Incorporation of Butchers' and Shipwrights' Companies in London Eng. government farms all customs revenue to a London consortium of merchants for an annual rent (—1671) Newspaper Nieuwe Tijdenghen issued in Antwerp Biblioteca Anglica, first public library in Rome, founded by Angelo Rosca	**1605**
Adriaen Brouwer, Dutch painter, b. (d. 1638) Jan Davids de Heem, Dutch painter, b. (d. 1683) Rembrandt van Rijn, Dutch painter, b. (d. 1669)	First open-air opera in Rome	Galileo Galilei invents proportional compass Port. navigator Luis Vaez de Torres sails between New Guinea and Australia Virginia Company of London, granted royal charter, sends 120 colonists to Virginia	Extensive program of road building begun in France Founding of Society of Apothecaries and Grocers, and of Fruiterers' Company, in London	**1606**
Domenico Fontana, Ital. architect, d. (b. 1543) Hatfield House, Hertfordshire, England, built (—1611) by John Thorpe for Robert Cecil, Earl of Salisbury	William Byrd: "Gradualia" Claudio Monteverdi: "Orfeo," opera	Founding of Jamestown, Va., first Eng. settlement on American mainland John Norden, Eng. topographer (1548—1625): "The Surveyors' Dialogue," manual of surveying	Bank of Genoa fails after announcement of national bankruptcy in Spain	**1607**

	A. HISTORY, POLITICS	B. LITERATURE, THEATER	C. RELIGION, PHILOSOPHY, LEARNING
1608	O'Dogherty rebellion in Ireland collapses Protestant States of Rhineland form Protestant Union under Christian of Anhalt and Frederick IV of the Palatinate The Emperor Rudolf II cedes Austria, Hungary, and Moravia to his brother Matthias The future Emperor Ferdinand III b. (d. 1657) Second "False Dmitri" defeats Czar Vasili Shuisky, and advances toward Moscow Jesuit State of Paraguay established	George Chapman: "The Conspiracy and Tragedy of Charles, Duke of Byron, Marshal of France" Joseph Hall: "Characters of Virtues and Vices" The King's Men, a London actors' company, play at Blackfriars Theatre Thomas Middleton: "A Mad World, My Masters," satirical comedy John Milton, Eng. poet, b. (d. 1674) Thomas Sackville, Earl of Dorset, Eng. poet and statesman, d. (b. 1536) Shakespeare: "Pericles" (—1609) Richard West: "A Century of Epigrams"	St. Francis de Sales (1567—1622): "Introduction à la vie dévote" Alberico Gentili, Ital. jurist and philosopher, d. (b. 1552) Edward Grimestone: "A General History of the Netherlands" William Perkins: "A Discourse of the Damned Art of Witchecraft" (posth.)
1609	John William, last Duke of Jülich-Cleves, d.; quarrel about succession between Brandenberg and Neuburg Twelve years' truce between Spain and Holland	Beaumont and Fletcher: "The Knight of the Burning Pestle" Thomas Dekker: "The Guls Hornbooke," satire of contemporary London life Paul Fleming, Ger. poet, b. (d. 1640) Ben Jonson: "Epicoene, or The Silent Women," comedy Shakespeare: "Cymbeline" (—1610)	Bacon: "De sapienta veterum" Catholic League of Ger. princes formed at Munich against Protestant Union of May 1608 Garcilaso de la Vega: "History of the Conquest of Peru" (—1616) Congregation of Female Jesuits founded (dissolved by Pope Urban VIII) Hugo Grotius: "Mare Librum," advocating freedom of the sea The Emperor Rudolf II permits freedom of religion in Bohemia
1610	Thomas West made governor of Virginia Henry IV of France assassinated; succeeded by his son Louis XIII (at 9) (—1643) with Queen Maria de' Medici as Regent (—1617) Prince Henry, eldest son of King James I, created Prince of Wales Arabella Stuart, pretender to the Eng. throne, imprisoned for marrying William Seymour Czar Vasili Shuisky deposed; Russ. throne offered to Vladislav, son of Sigismund III of Poland James I prorogues Parliament; Parliament reassembles Elector Palatine Frederick IV d.; succeeded by his son Frederick V Skirmishes between Eng. and Dutch settlers in India	Academy of Poetry founded at Padua Perez de Hita: "The Civil Wars of Granada," Span. novel John Fletcher: "The Faithful Shepherdess," pastoral drama Ben Jonson: "The Alchemist," comedy Paul Scarron, Fr. man of letters, b. (d. 1660) Shakespeare: "A Winter's Tale" (—1611)	John Cowell's "Interpreter" (see 1607) burnt by the common hangman for enhancing authority of the crown St. Francis de Sales founds, with Mme. de Chantal, Order of the Visitation nuns Robert Persons, leader of Eng. Jesuits, d. (b. 1545) Nicholas and Dorothy Wadham found Wadham College, Oxford
1611	Dissolution of Parliament by James I War of Calmar declared by Denmark on Sweden (—1613) Archduke Matthias crowned King of Bohemia; the Emperor Rudolf II resigns Bohemian crown Arabella Stuart escapes from Tower of London; is recaptured Charles IX of Sweden d. Gustavus II (Gustavus Adolphus) elected King; makes Axel Oxenstierna Chancellor	George Chapman completes his translation of Homer's "Iliad" (begun 1598) Thomas Coryate: "Crudities," stories of his travels John Donne: "An Anatomy of the World," elegy Ben Jonson: "Catiline," tragedy Thomas Middleton: "The Roaring Girl," comedy Shakespeare: "The Tempest" (—1612) Cyril Tourneur: "The Atheist's Tragedie"	George Abbot made Archbishop of Canterbury (—1633) Authorized version of the Holy Bible–"King James Bible"–published William Laud elected president of St. John's College, Oxford Etienne Pasquier: "Les Recherches de la France" John Speed: "A History of Great Britain" University of Rome founded

D. VISUAL ARTS	E. MUSIC	F. SCIENCE, TECHNOLOGY, GROWTH	G. DAILY LIFE	
Giovanni da Bologna, Ital. sculptor, d. (b. 1524) Domenichino: "Scourging of St. Andrew" El Greco: "Golgatha," "Cardinal Taverna" Sir Walter Cope builds Holland House, Kensington, London (—1610)	Girolamo Frescobaldi (1583—1643) made organist at St. Peter's, Rome Monteverdi: "Lamento d'Arianna"	Dutch scientist Johann Lippershey invents the telescope Giovanni Alfonso Borelli, Ital. physiologist, b. (d. 1679) Samuel de Champlain founds a Fr. settlement at Quebec Galileo constructs astronomical telescope Captain John Smith: "A True Relation of Virginia" Evangelista Torricelli, Ital. physicist, b. (d. 1647)	First checks–"cash letters"–in use in Netherlands Royal Blackheath Golf Club, London, founded; still in existence	**1608**
Blue Mosque, Constantinople, built (—1616) Annibale Caracci, Ital. painter, d. (b. 1560) El Greco: "Brother Paravicino" Rubens: Self-portrait with his Wife, Isabella Brant	Orlando Gibbons: "Fantazies of Three Parts," first example of engraved music in England Thomas Ravenscroft: "Pammelia," collection of rounds and catches	Charles Butler: "De feminine monarchie, or a Treatise concerning Bees" Henry Hudson explores Delaware Bay and Hudson River Johann Kepler: "De motibus stellae Martis"	Founding of Bank of Amsterdam Founding of Charterhouse public school Regular newspapers at Strasbourg and Wolfenbüttel, Germany Tea from China shipped for first time to Europe by Dutch East India Company Tin-enameled ware made at Delft	**1609**
Michelangelo Caravaggio, Ital. painter, d. (b. 1579) Adriaen van Ostade, Dutch painter, b. (d. 1684) El Greco: "The Opening of the Fifth Seal" Adam Elsheimer, Ger. landscape painter, d. (b. 1578) Rubens: "Raising of the Cross" David Teniers the Younger, Dutch painter, b. (d. 1690)	Michael Praetorius (1571—1621): "Musae Sioniae," collection of 1,244 church hymns Lodovico Grossi da Viadana: "Symphonies"	Jean Beguin: "Tyrocinium chymicum," first textbook on chemistry Galileo observes Jupiter's satellites, naming them "sideria Medicea" Thomas Harriott discovers sunspots Henry Hudson sails through Hudson's Straits and discovers Hudson's Bay Nicolas Pieresc (1580—1637) discovers Orion nebula John Speed: "Theatrum of Great Britain," collection of maps Founding of Port. settlement at Cape Coast	Dutch East India Company introduces the term "share" The Stationers' Company begins to send a copy of every book printed in England to Bodleian Library, Oxford	**1610**
Erection of Masjid-i-Shah, the Royal Mosque at Isfahan, Persia Rubens: "Descent from the Cross" John Webb, Eng. architect, b. (d. 1672)	William Byrd, John Bull, and Orlando Gibbons: "Parthenia," collection of music for virginals Tomás Luis de Victoria, Span. composer, d. (b. 1548) Johannes Eccard, Ger. composer, d. (b. 1553) Thomas Ravenscroft: "Melismata," 21 madrigals and other pieces	Marco de Dominis (1566—1624) publishes scientific explanation of rainbow Henry Hudson, Eng. navigator, d.	Dutch merchants permitted to trade in Japan James I institutes the baronetage as a means of raising money	**1611**

	A. HISTORY, POLITICS	B. LITERATURE, THEATER	C. RELIGION, PHILOSOPHY, LEARNING
1612	The Emperor Rudolf II d.; succeeded by Matthias, King of Bohemia Earl of Salisbury d.; succeeded as secretary of state by Viscount Rochester Henry, Prince of Wales, d. (b. 1594) Treaty between the Dutch and the King of Kandy in Ceylon	Samuel Butler, Eng. satirist, b. (d. 1680) Thomas Deloney: "Thomas of Reading" (posth.) Michael Drayton: "Polyolbion," Part 1 Samuel Purchas: "Hakluytus Posthumus," travels Shakespeare: "Henry VIII" (—1613) John Webster: "The White Devil," tragedy	Accademia della Crusca publishes the Ital. "Vocabolario" Jakob Böhme: "Aurora, oder Morgenröte im Aufgant," mystical philosophy Last recorded burning of heretics in England Sir John Davies: "Discoverie of the True Causes Why Ireland Was Not Entirely Subdued" Roger Fenton (1565—1616): "Treatie of Usurie"
1613	Peace of Knärod ends Dan.-Swed. War of Calmar Elizabeth, daughter of James I, marries Frederick V of the Palatinate Protestant Union of Germany signs treaty of alliance with Holland Lady Frances Howard, divorced wife of Earl of Essex, marries Earl of Somerset, James I's favorite Francis Bacon becomes attorney general Eng. colonists in Virginia destroy Fr. settlement at Port Royal, Nova Scotia; prevent Fr. colonization of Maryland Michael Romanov, son of the patriarch of Moscow, elected Czar of Russia (—1645), thus founding the House of Romanov Turks invade Hungary	William Browne: "Britannia's Pastorals" Cervantes: "Novelas ejemplares" George Chapman: "The Revenge of Bussy D'Ambois," tragedy Richard Crashaw, Eng. poet, b. (d. 1650) François de La Rochefoucauld, Fr. author, b. (d. 1680) Lope de Vega: "Fuenteovejuna" Fire destroys Globe Theatre, Southwark, London Mathurin Regnier, Fr. satirist, d. (b. 1573)	Oliver de Serra (1539—1619): "The Causes of Wealth" Francisco Suarez: "Defensio catholicae fidei contra anglicanae sectae errores"
1614	James I's second Parliament—"The Addled Parliament"—meets and refuses to discuss finance; dissolved Maria, Queen Regent of France, summons the States General of France to counteract power of nobility (last meeting, 1789) Treaty of Xanten: Jülich-Cleves divided between Brandenburg and Neuburg Gustavus Adolphus II of Sweden captures Novgorod from Russians Virginian colonists prevent Fr. settlements in Maine and Nova Scotia	Pierre de Bourdeille, Seigneur de Brantôme, Fr. author, d. (b. 1540) Ben Jonson: "Bartholomew Fayre," comedy Sir Thomas Overbury: "Characters" John Webster: "The Duchess of Malfi"	Jean de Gondi, Cardinal de Retz, Fr. churchman, b. (d. 1679) Henry More, Eng. philosopher, b. (d. 1687) Sir Walter Raleigh: "The History of the World"
1615	Fr. States General dismissed with promises of reforms Marguérite de Valois d. (b. 1553) Peace of Tyrnau: the Emperor Matthias recognizes Bethlen Gabor as Prince of Transylvania; confirms treaty with Turks Lady Arabella Stuart d. in Tower of London Exchange of Bourbon and Hapsburg brides at Burgos: Louis XIII marries Anna of Austria, Philip of the Asturias marries Elizabeth of Bourbon Dutch seize the Moluccas from Portuguese Eng. fleet defeats Portuguese off coast of Bombay	Mateo Alemán, Span. novelist, d. (b. 1547) Cervantes: "Don Quixote," Part 2 George Chapman completes his translation of Homer's "Odyssey" (begun 1614) Samuel Coster: "Spel van de Rijcke Man," farce John Denham, Eng. poet, b. (d. 1669) George Ruggle (1575—1622): "Ignoramus," Cambridge University farce	William Camden: "Annales rerum Anglicarum," of the reign of Elizabeth I Theodore Agrippa d'Aubigné's "Histoire Universelle," a Huguenot-inspired survey from 1553 to 1602, officially burnt in Paris Jesuits count 13,112 members in 32 provinces

D. VISUAL ARTS	E. MUSIC	F. SCIENCE, TECHNOLOGY, GROWTH	G. DAILY LIFE	
Federico Barocci, Ital. painter, d. (b. 1528) El Greco: "Baptism of Christ" Louis le Vau, Fr. architect, b. (d. 1670) Pierre Mignard, Fr. painter, b. (d. 1695) Rubens: "The Conversion of St. Bavon"	Giovanni Gabrieli, Ital. composer, d. (b. 1557) Orlando Gibbons: "First Set of Madrigals and Motets" Andreas Hammerschmidt, Ger. composer, b. (d. 1675)	Simon Marius (1573—1624) rediscovers Andromeda nebula (see 963) Antonio Neri: "L'Arte vetraria," manual on glassmaking Bartholomew Pitiscus, Ger. mathematician, uses decimal point in his trigonometrical tables John Smith: "A Map of Virginia"	Earliest colonization of the Bermudas from Virginia Dutch use Manhattan as fur-trading center for first time Tobacco planted in Virginia	**1612**
Salomon de Brosse builds the Château Coulommiers Guido Reni: "Aurora," frescoes in Rome	Pietro Cerone: "El Malopeo y maestro," musical history and theory Monteverdi made maestro di cappella at St. Mark's, Venice	Samuel de Champlain explores Ottawa River to Alumette Island	Amsterdam Exchange built Belfast granted charter of incorporation Thomas Bodley, Eng. diplomat and scholar, d. (b. 1545), leaving bulk of his fortune to Bodleian Library, Oxford Copper coins come into use John Dennys: "The Secrets of Angling" Hugh Myddleton constructs "New River" cut, to bring water to London	**1613**
Domenichino (1581—1641): "Last Communion of St. Jerome" El Greco, Cretan-Span. painter, d. (b. 1541) Salzburg Cathedral built by Santino Salari (—1680) Robert Smythson, Eng. architect, d. (b. 1536)	Girolamo Frescobaldi: "Toccate di Cembalo" Marco da Gagliano: "Masses and Motets" Sir William Leighton: "Teares and Lamentacions of a Sorrowful Soule," 54 psalms	Adriaen Block explores Long Island Sound Danish East India Company founded University of Groningen, Holland, founded Cornelius Jacobsen Mey explores the Lower Delaware John Napier: "Mirifici logarithmorum canonis descriptio" Santorio Santorio (1561—1636): "De medicina statica," study of metabolism and perspiration	Bankruptcy of Augsburg banking house of Welser Founders' Company, London, incorporated Development of glass industry in England The North American Pocahontas, an Indian princess, marries John Rolfe; from their son descend many celebrated persons	**1614**
Giovanni Lorenzo Bernini: "Amalthea," sculpture, Palazzo Borghese, Rome Salomon de Brosse works on Palais de Luxembourg, Paris (—1624) Domenichino: "Scenes from the Life of St. Cecilia" Inigo Jones (1573—1652) becomes England's chief architect Salvator Rosa, Span. painter, b. (d. 1673) Rubens: "The Battle of the Amazons"	Adriano Banchieri (1567—1634) founds Accademia dei Filomusi in Bologna	Giambattista della Porta, Ital. scientist, d. (b. 1538) Antoine de Montchrétien (1576—1621): "Traité de l'économie politique," mercantilistic tendencies Galileo Galilei faces the Inquisition for first time	Ninon de Lenclos, Fr. courtesan, b. (d. 1705) Frankfurter Oberpostamts-Zeitung founded by Egenolph Emmel (appears —1866) Merchant Adventurers granted monopoly for export of Eng. cloth	**1615**

	A. HISTORY, POLITICS	B. LITERATURE, THEATER	C. RELIGION, PHILOSOPHY, LEARNING
1616	Earl of Worcester, a Catholic, made Lord Privy Seal, Sir Thomas Lake secretary of state Sir Walter Raleigh released from Tower to lead expedition to Guiana in search of El Dorado Richelieu becomes Minister of State for Foreign Affairs and War in France Ieyasu of Japan d.; succeeded by Hidetada, a militant enemy of Christianity James I begins to sell peerages to improve serious financial position Archduke Maximilian of Tirol and Archduke Albert, Governor of the Netherlands, renounce their claims to Imperial throne in favor of Ferdinand of Styria Tartars of Manchu invade China (—1620) War between Venice and Austria	Francis Beaumont d. (b. 1584) Miguel de Cervantes d. (b. 1547) Andreas Gryphius, Ger. dramatist, b. (d. 1664) Works of Ben Jonson, first folio edition of its kind, published Thomas Middleton: "The Witch," tragedy William Shakespeare d. (b. 1564)	Johann Valentin Andrea: "Chymische Hochzeit Christiani Rosenkreutz," beginning of formation of the Rosicrucians Paulus Bolduanus: "Bibliotheca philosophica" Catholic oppression intensified in Bohemia St. Francis de Sales: "Traité de l'amour de Dieu"
1617	James I makes his favorite, George Villiers, Earl of Buckingham (Jan.) and Duke of Buckingham (May, 1623) Peace of Stolbovo ends war between Russia and Sweden; Gustavus Adolphus recognizes Czar Michael, returns Novgorod, and obtains Karelia Francis Bacon made Lord Keeper James I revisits Scotland; meets Scot. Parliament	Théophile de Viau (1590—1626): "Pyramus et Thisbe," tragedy in verse James I makes Ben Jonson poet laureate Thomas Middleton and William Rowley: "A Fair Quarrel," comedy Martin Opitz fôunds the Fruchtbringende Gesellschaft, a literary society, at Weimar Christian Hofmann von Hofmannswaldau, Ger. poet, b. (d. 1679)	John Calvin's collected works published in Geneva (posth.) Duytsche Academie founded in Amsterdam by Samuel Coster Papal bull of Leo X: "Epistolae obscurorum virorum" Francisco Suarez, Span. philosopher, d. (b. 1548)
1618	Francis Bacon created Lord Chancellor Sir Robert Naunton made chief secretary of state Peace of Madrid ratified, ending war between Venice and Austria Prince Philip William of Orange d.; succeeded by his brother Maurice of Nassau Count Matthias von Thurn leads Bohemians to revolt against Catholic policy of the Regents in Prague Defenestration in Prague, when the Regents Jaroslav von Martinitz and William Slawata are thrown down from windows in Hradcany Palace by the rebels; beginning of Thirty Years' War (—1648) Ferdinand of Styria crowned King of Hungary Duke Albert of Prussia d.; his possessions pass to the Electorate of Brandenburg Sir Walter Raleigh returns to England and is executed Count Mansfeld occupies Pilsen for Protestant Union Poland signs two-year truce with Sweden, 14-years truce with Turkey Aurangzeb, later Mogul Emperor of Hindustan, b. (d. 1707) Imperial Army under Count Karl Bucquoi enters Bohemia to suppress rebels Richelieu ordered into exile at Avignon for intriguing with Queen Mother Maria de'Medici	Gerbrand Adriensz Bredero, Dutch dramatist, d. (b. 1585) Abraham Cowley, Eng. poet, b. (d. 1667) Marquise de Rambouillet (1588—1665) starts her literary salon in Paris Teatro Farnese opened at Parma John Fletcher: "The Humorous Lieutenant," comedy Richard Lovelace, Eng. poet, b. (d. 1658)	Robert Balfour: "Commentarii in organum logicum Aristotelis" John Stow and E. Howes: A "Summarie of Englyshe Chronicles"

D. VISUAL ARTS	E. MUSIC	F. SCIENCE, TECHNOLOGY, GROWTH	G. DAILY LIFE	
Frans Hals: "The Banquet of the Civic Guard of the Archers of St. George" Notre Dame Cathedral, Antwerp, finished (begun 1352) Inigo Jones: "Queen's House," Greenwich, London (—1618) Rubens: "The Lion Hunt"	Collegium Musicum founded at Prague Johann Jakob Froberger, Ger. organist and composer, b. (d. 1667)	William Baffin (1584—1622) discovers Baffin Bay while searching for a Northwest Passage First rounding of Cape Horn by Willem Schouter and Jacob Lemaire Galileo prohibited by Catholic Church from further scientific work Andreas Libavius, Ger. alchemist, d. (b. 1546) John Smith: "A Description of New England" Dutch astronomer and mathematician Willebrord Snellius (1591—1626) discovers the law of refraction	Gustavus Selenus (August von Braunschweig): "Chess, or the Game of Kings"	**1616**
Domenichino: "Diana's Hunt" Bartolomé Estéban Murillo, Span. painter, b. (d. 1682) Guido Reni: "The Deeds of Hercules" (—1621) Gerard Terborch, Dutch painter, b. (d. 1681) Anthony Van Dyck: "A Study of Four Negro Heads" Peter Lely, Dutch-Eng. painter, b. (d. 1680)	Biagio Marini: "Musical Events," sonata for solo violin J. H. Schein: "Banchetto musicale," first dance suite Heinrich Schütz made Kapellmeister of electoral chapel, Dresden (—1672)	Bernardino Baldi, Ital. mathematician, d. (b. 1533) Dutch buy Goree Island, off Cap Verde, from the natives John Napier, Scot. mathematician, d. (b. 1550) Sir Walter Raleigh leaves England on expedition to Guiana and reaches mouth of Orinoco River Willebrord Snellius establishes technique of trigonometrical triangulation for cartography	Pocahontas, North American Indian princess, d. (b. 1595) "Stuart collars" become a fashion for men and women	**1617**
Building of Aston Hall, Birmingham (—1635) Bernini: "Aeneas, Anchises, and Ascanius," sculpture Jacob Jordaens: "Adoration of the Shepherds" Van Dyck becomes member of the Antwerp guild of painters	Guilio Caccini, Ital. composer and singer, d. ("bel canto")	Martin Böhme: "Ein neu Buch von bewehrten Rosz-Arzteneyen," veterinary science Founding of Dutch West African Company Kepler: "Harmonices mundi," stating the third law of planetary motion Royal College of Physicians, London, issues "Pharmacopoeia Londinensis" Johann Jakob Scheuchzer: "Natural History of the Swiss Landscape"	James I: "Book of Sports," the Puritans object to playing of popular sports	**1618**

	A. HISTORY, POLITICS	B. LITERATURE, THEATER	C. RELIGION, PHILOSOPHY, LEARNING
1619	Maria de'Medici challenges power of her son Louis XIII of France; Louis recalls Richelieu from Avignon to prevent revolt, marches his army into Angers, and defeats Maria de'Medici's supporters; Treaty of Angoulême ends conflict The Emperor Matthias d.; Archduke Ferdinand, who assumes crown of Bohemia, is elected Holy Roman Emperor Count von Thurn leads an army of Bohemian patriots toward Vienna, then withdraws Bohemian Diet deposes Ferdinand, and elects Frederick V, Elector Palatine, son-in-law of James I of England, King of Bohemia; Frederick, "The Winter King," crowned in Prague Bethlen Gabor of Transylvania, after invading Hungary, allies himself with Count Thurn; he captures Pressburg, crosses the Danube, and retreats from Vienna First representative colonial assembly in America held at Jamestown, Va., under Governor Sir George Yeardley	Beaumont and Fletcher: "A King and No King," "The Maid's Tragedy" Richard Burbage, Eng. actor, d. (b. 1567) Samuel Daniel, Eng. poet, d. (b. 1552) Savinien Cyrano de Bergerac, Fr. poet, b. (d. 1655) Honorat Racan: "Les Bergeries," Fr. pastoral poem Philipp von Zesen, Ger. poet, b. (d. 1689) Georg Rudolf Weckherlin (1584—1653): "Oden und Gesänge," Ger. poems	Johann Valentin Andreae: "Christianopolis" Jakob Böhme: "On the Principles of Christianity" Hugo Grotius: "De veritate religionis Christianae" Pietro Sarpi: "Istoria del Concilio Tridentino" (Council of Trent), published in London Lucilió Vanini, Ital. Catholic philosopher, burned as a heretic (b. 1584) Dulwich College, London, founded by Edward Alleyn
1620	Revolt of Fr. nobles against Louis XIII; Richelieu makes peace, reconciling the Queen Mother to her son War between Sweden and Poland: Gustavus Adolphus occupies Livonia Massacre of Protestants in the Valtelline Agreement of Ulm between Ger. Catholic League and Protestant Union Eng. volunteers leave for service with Elector Palatine's army in Bohemia Lower Austria submits to the Emperor Ferdinand, who is free to attack Bohemia Pilgrim Fathers, leaving Plymouth, England, in "Mayflower" for N. America, land at New Plymouth, Mass., to found Plymouth Colony; Miles Standish is their most experienced leader Turks defeat Pol. army at Jassy Frederick William, the "Great Elector" (of Brandenburg), b. (d. 1688) Battle of the White Mountain near Prague: Catholic League under Count Tilly defeats army of King Frederick of Bohemia; Bohemian revolt against the Emperor Ferdinand suppressed; leading rebels executed; Protestant clergy expelled John Carver first governor of Plymouth Colony	Thomas Campion, Eng. poet and musician, d. (b. 1567) Miklós Zrinyi, Hungarian poet and national hero, b. (d. 1664)	Johann Heinrich Alsted: "Encyclopaedia septem tomis distincta" Francis Bacon: "Instauratio magna: novum organum scientiarum"
1621	Frederick V, Elector Palatine, placed under the ban of the Holy Roman Empire; war moves from Bohemia to the Palatinate Francis Bacon, charged in Parliament with corruption, is fined £40,000, imprisoned, and declared incapable of holding office; pardoned by the King Philip III of Spain d.; succeeded by his son Philip IV (—1665) John Williams, bishop of Lincoln, made Lord Keeper; Lionel Cranfield, Lord Treasurer Huguenot rebellion against Louis XIII Twelve years' truce between Holland and Spain (see 1609) ends; war resumed Sir Francis Wyatt arrives as new governor in Virginia with new regulations for the colony (council of state, elected assembly)	John Barclay (1582—1621): "Argenis," allegorical political novel Jean de la Fontaine, Fr. poet, b. (d. 1695) John Fletcher: "The Wild Goose Chase," comedy Fortune Theatre, London, burnt down	Cardinal Roberto Bellarmine, Jesuit leader of the Counter-Reformation, d. (b. 1562) Robert Burton (1577—1640): "The Anatomy of Melancholy" Pope Paul V d.; Alexander Ludovisi becomes Pope Gregory XV (—1623)

D. VISUAL ARTS	E. MUSIC	F. SCIENCE, TECHNOLOGY, GROWTH	G. DAILY LIFE	
Lodovico Carracci, Ital. painter, d. (b. 1555) Nicholas Hilliard, Eng. painter, miniaturist, d. (b. 1547) Inigo Jones: Banqueting House, Whitehall (—1622) Rubens: Portrait of his son Nicholas Velázquez: "Adoration of the Kings" Philips Wouwerman, Dutch painter, b. (d. 1688)	"Fitzwilliam Virginal Book" compiled by Francis Tregian; a treasury of early Eng. keyboard music Marco da Gagliano: "Medoro," Ital. opera Heinrich Schütz: "Psalms" Jan Pieterszoon Sweelinck: "Cantiones sacrae"	John Bainbridge: "An Astronomical Description of the Late Comet" Jan Pieters Coen, Dutch explorer (1587—1630), founds Batavia Jean Baptiste Colbert, Fr. economist, b. (d. 1683) William Harvey announces at St. Bartholomew's Hospital, London, his discovery of the circulation of the blood	Giro-Bank, Hamburg, founded to improve "desolate state of currency" First Negro slaves in N. America arrive in Virginia	**1619**
Bernini: "Neptune and Triton," sculpture Aelbert Cuyp, Dutch landscape painter, b. (d. 1691) Jacob Jordaens: "Passage to Antwerp" Rubens: "Chapeau de paille" George Seton: Winton House, E. Lothian, Scotland Van Dyck: "St. Sebastian" Velázquez: "The Water Seller of Seville"	Monteverdi: "Seventh Book of Madrigals" Michael Praetorius: "Syntagma musicum," musical encyclopedia	Cornelius Drebbel, Dutch scientist, discovers scarlet "Bow dye" Edmund Gunter: "Canon triangulorum," treatise on logarithms Uppsala University Library founded by Gustavus Adolphus	J. P. Bonet: "The Art to Teach Dumb People to Speak," Span. manual Currency inflation in Germany (—1623) Density of population in Germany per square mile: 35. At time of Julius Caesar approx. 6; c. 1900 approx. 160; 1950 approx. 280 Oliver Cromwell denounced because he participates in the "disreputable game of cricket"	**1620**
Bernini: "Rape of Proserpina," sculpture Van Dyck: "Rest on the Flight into Egypt"	Michael Praetorius, Ger. composer and musicologist, d. (b. 1571) Jan Pieterszoon Sweelinck, Dutch musician, d. (b. 1562)	English attempt to colonize Newfoundland and Nova Scotia John Carver, Pilgrim Father, first governor of Plymouth Colony, d. (b. 1576) Dutch West India Company chartered; later acquired N. American coast from Chesapeake Bay to Newfoundland Johann Kepler: "The Epitome of the Copernican Astronomer," banned by the Roman Catholic Church Thomas Munn (1571—1641): "A Discourse of Trade from England unto the East Indies" University of Strasbourg opened	"Corante, or newes from Italy, Germany, Hungarie, Spaine, and France," first periodical published with news issued in London (Sept. 24) Heidelberg University Library sacked by Count Tilly's troops Potatoes planted in Germany for first time	**1621**

	A. HISTORY, POLITICS	B. LITERATURE, THEATER	C. RELIGION, PHILOSOPHY, LEARNING
1622	Richelieu recalled by Louis XIII to the Council; created Cardinal Ferdinand II and Bethlen Gabor sign peace treaty Treaty of Montpellier ends rebellion of the Huguenots Mannheim surrenders to imperial army English capture Ormuz from Portuguese Sir Ferdinando Gorges (1566—1647), Eng. naval commander, and John Mason (1586—1637) obtain grant of lands in Maine, N. America James I dissolves Eng. Parliament Count Olivares (the "count duke") becomes chief minister of Spain (—1643) Count Tilly, defeated at battle of Wiesloch, defeats George Frederick of Baden at battle of Wimpfen, and Christian of Brunswick at battle of Höchst William Bradford (1589—1657) governor of Plymouth Colony thirty years	Philip Massinger and Thomas Dekker: "The Virgin Martyr," tragedy Molière (Jean-Baptiste Poquelin), Fr. dramatist, b. (d. 1673) Charles Sorel: "Francion," Fr. burlesque novel Alessandro Tassoni: "La Secchia rapita" (The Rape of the Bucket), mock-heroic poem Henry Vaughan, Eng. mystic and poet, b. (d. 1695)	Francis Bacon: "History of the Reign of Henry VII" Jacob Böhme: "De signatura rerum" Saint Francis de Sales d. (b. 1567) Pope Gregory XV canonizes Philip Neri and grants Piarists a constitution
1623	The Emperor Ferdinand II grants Maximilian, Duke of Bavaria, the Upper Palatinate Charles, Prince of Wales, travels to Madrid to secure betrothal to Span. princess; leaves at breakdown of talks Papal troops occupy the Valtelline Abbas I, Shah of Persia (1586—1629), conquers Baghdad Commercial treaty between Holland and Persia Sir Edward Conway made chief secretary of state (—1628) Dutch massacre Eng. colonists at Amboyna, Molucca Islands Gustavus Adolphus reforms central administration of Sweden Count Tilly defeats Christian of Brunswick at Stadtlohn; advances to Westphalia	Antonio Hurtado de Mendoza: "Querer por sólo querer," comedy Philip Massinger: "The Duke of Milan," tragedy Maciej Sarbiewski (1595—1640), the "Polish Horace," crowned laureate in Rome by the Pope The First Folio, "Mr. William Shakespeares Comedies, Histories and Tragedies Published According to the True Originall Copies" Tulsi Das, Hindu poet, d. (b. 1532)	William Drummond: "A Cypresse Grove," philosophical thoughts on death Pope Gregory XV d.; Maffeo Barberini becomes Pope Urban VIII (—1644) Blaise Pascal, Fr. philosopher and mathematician, b. (d. 1662)
1624	James I's last Parliament; monopolies declared illegal England declares war on Spain Lionel Cranfield, Lord Treasurer of England, impeached for bribery and neglect of duty, is suspended from office Jan Sobieski, future King of Poland, b. (d. 1696) Virginia becomes crown colony; Virginia Company dissolved; Sir Francis Wyatt made governor again Cardinal Richelieu made first minister of France (—1642) Anglo-Fr. treaty for Charles, Prince of Wales, to marry Henrietta Maria, daughter of Henry IV and Maria de'Medici	Saruwaka Kanzaburo opens first Jap. theater in Yedo Philip Massinger: "The Bondman," drama Thomas Middleton: "A Game of Chess," comedy, given at Globe Theatre nine times– first "long run" in theatrical history Martin Opitz: "Das Buch von der deutschen Poeterey"	Jakob Böhme, Ger. mystic, d. (b. 1575) Lord Herbert of Cherbury: "De veritate," foundation of theory of Eng. deism John Donne: "Devotions Upon Emergent Occasions" Arnold Geulincx, Dutch philosopher, b. (d. 1669) George Fox, founder of the Society of Friends, b. (d. 1691)
1625	James I of England (James VI of Scotland) d.; succeeded by Charles I of England and Scotland (—1649) Wallenstein made general of the imperial forces by the Emperor Ferdinand II; and created Duke of Friedland Charles I marries Henrietta Maria First Parliament of Charles I meets; adjourned to Oxford, because of plague in London Span. Gen. Ambrogio Spinola (1569—1630) takes Breda from Dutch after 11-month siege Tilly invades Lower Saxony Sir Thomas Coventry made lord keeper (—1640) French occupy the Antilles and Cayenne	Honorat de Bueil: "Les Bergeries," pastoral dialogues Ben Jonson: "The Staple of News," comedy Giambattista Marini (Marino), Ital. poet, d. (b. 1569) Thomas Middleton: "A Game of Chess," comedy, published Martin Opitz crowned poet laureate in Vienna Joost van den Vondel: "Palamedes," political drama Johann Jakob Christoph von *(contd)*	Francis Bacon: "Of Masques and Triumphs" Hugo Grotius: "De jure belli et pacis," on international law Order of Sisters of Mercy founded in Paris by Vincent de Paul

D. VISUAL ARTS	E. MUSIC	F. SCIENCE, TECHNOLOGY, GROWTH	G. DAILY LIFE	
Willem Kalf, Dutch painter, b. (d. 1693) Guido Reni: "Job" Rubens: "The Medici Cycle"–24 paintings on the life of Maria de'Medici–Luxembourg Palace, Paris		Bacon: "Historia naturalis et experimentalis" William Baffin, Eng. explorer, d. (b. 1584) Benedictine University of Salzburg founded Edmund Gunter discovers that the magnetic needle does not retain same declination in same place all the time	Camillo Baldo: "Treatise of How to Perceive from a Letter the Nature and Character of the Person Who Wrote It" Bruges-Dunkirk Canal finished Papal chancellery adopts Jan. 1 as beginning of the year–up to then, Mar. 25 Weekeley Newes issued in London for first time on May 23	**1622**
Bernini: "David," sculpture Inigo Jones: Queen's Chapel, St. James's Palace, Westminster, built (—1627) François Mansart: St. Marie de la Visitation, Paris Rembrandt becomes pupil of J. I. Swanenburg in Leiden Guido Reni: "Baptism of Christ" Van Dyck: "Cardinal Bentivoglio" Velázquez made court painter to Philip IV	William Byrd, Eng. composer, d. (b. 1543) Marc' Antonio Cesti, Ital. composer, b. (d. 1669)	Bibliotheca Palatina removed from Heidelberg to Rome Piet Hein, Dutch adventurer, captures Bahia from Spain New Netherlands in America formally organized as a province	First Eng. settlement in New Hampshire, by David Thomas at Little Harbor, near Rye Patents law in England, to protect inventors	**1623**
Bernini: "Apollo and Daphne," sculpture Guarino Guarini, Ital. architect and writer, b. (d. 1683) Frans Hals: "The Laughing Cavalier" Jacques Lemercier: Extension of the Louvre, Paris Nicolas Poussin: "Rape of the Sabine Women"	Marco da Gagliano (1575—1642): "La Regina Sant' Orsola," opera-oratorio Monteverdi: "Il Combattimento di Tancredi e Clorinda"	Henry Briggs: "Arithmetica logarithmica" Antonio de Andrade leaves Jesuit mission at Agra to explore the Himalayas and Tibet Pembroke College, Oxford, founded Captain John Smith: "A General Historie of Virginia, New England and the Summer Isles" Thomas Sydenham, Eng. physician, b. (d. 1689)	Dutch settle in New Amsterdam First Eng. settlement in eastern India Johannes Baptista van Helmont, Belg. scientist (1577—1644), coins the name "gas" for compressible fluid	**1624**
Jan Brueghel the Elder, "Velvet Brueghel," d. (b. 1568) Inigo Jones: Covent Garden Church, Westminster, London Daniel Mylens made court painter by Charles I Nicolas Poussin: "Parnassus" (—1629)	Orlando Gibbons, Eng. musician, d. (b. 1583) Famous peal of bells installed in the Gate of Salvation, Kremlin, Moscow Heinrich Schütz: "Cantiones sacrae"	Giovanni Domenico Cassini, Ital. astronomer, b. (d. 1712) Johann Rudolf Glauber (1604—1668) discovers Glauber's salt	Colonial Office established in London First Eng. settlement on Barbados, under Sir William Courteen First fire engines in England Hackney coaches appear in streets of London Tobacco tax and tobacco monopoly in England Introduction of full-bottomed wigs in Europe	**1625**

	A. HISTORY, POLITICS	B. LITERATURE, THEATER	C. RELIGION, PHILOSOPHY, LEARNING
1625 contd		Grimmelshausen, Ger. novelist, b. (d. 1676) John Webster, Eng. dramatist, d. (b. 1580)	
1626	Knighthoods for all Englishmen with property over £40 year, to help king's revenue Peace of La Rochelle between Huguenots and Fr. crown Second Parliament of Charles I meets Treaty of Monzon between France and Spain confirms independence of the Grisons Wallenstein defeats Mansfeld at Dessau and pursues his troops to Silesia and Hungary Richelieu suppresses Chalais conspiracy, concentrating all political power in France in his own hands Richard Cromwell, future Eng. protector, b. (d. 1712) Christina, future Queen of Sweden, b. (d. 1689) Duchy of Urbino bequeathed to the Pope by last of the Della Rovere family General Count Ernst von Mansfeld d. (b. 1580)	John Aubrey, Eng. author, b. (d. 1697) Honorat de Bueil: "Les plus beaux vers" First production of Shakespeare's "Hamlet" in Germany at Dresden Eng. author and traveler George Sandys (1578—1644) makes first translation of a classic in America: Ovid's "Metamorphoses"	Francis Bacon, Eng. philosopher and statesman, d. (b. 1561) John Donne: "Five Sermons" Joseph Hall: "Contemplations" Irish College in Rome founded William Roper: "The Life of Sir Thomas More" (posth.) Sir Henry Spelman: "Glossarium archeologicum"
1627	Huguenots rise again; George Villiers, Duke of Buckingham, sails from Portsmouth with a fleet to aid them in defense of La Rochelle; failing to relieve them, he retires Vincent II, Duke of Mantua, last of the Gonzagas, d.; Charles, Duke of Nevers, claims succession Korea becomes a tributary state of China Richelieu signs treaty with Spain Shah Jahan (1592—1666), succeeding his father Jahangir, becomes Great Mogul of India (—1658) Wallenstein conquers Silesia, Tilly Brunswick; imperial forces seize Mecklenburg and Jutland; Christian IV withdraws to Denmark	Luis de Góngora y Argote, Span. poet, d. (b. 1561) Francisco Gómez de Quevedo: "Los Sueños," burlesques of hell, judgment day, and the world Lope de Vega made theological doctor by the Pope Michael Drayton: "Nimphidia" Ivan Gundulic (1589—1638): "Osman," Croatian epic Thomas Middleton, Eng. dramatist, d. (b. 1580) Dorothy Osborne, Eng. author and traveler, b. (d. 1695) Charles Sorel: "Le Berger extravagant," satirical novel	Robert Boyle, Eng. philosopher and physicist, b. (d. 1691) Collegium de Propaganda Fide founded Gabriel Naude: "Avis pour dresser une bibliothèque," on librarianship Alessandro Tassoni: "Manifesto" attacks the House of Savoy
1628	Third Parliament of Charles I meets; Oliver Cromwell enters it as Member for Huntingdon Wallenstein obtains duchy of Mecklenburg and assumes title Admiral of the Baltic; begins siege of Stralsund Duke of Buckingham assassinated embarking at Portsmouth with another La Rochelle expedition Wallenstein's first reverse: siege of Stralsund is raised La Rochelle capitulates to Fr. crown Dutch occupy Java and the Moluccas Swed-Dan. treaty for defense of Stralsund; Gustavus Adolphus enters Thirty Years' War Richard Weston made Lord Treasurer (—1635), Sir Dudley Carleton, chief secretary of state (—1632)	John Bunyan, Eng. author, b. (d. 1688) Juan Ruiz de Alarcón: "La verdad sospechosa," Span. comedy François de Malherbe, court poet to Henry IV. d. (b. 1555) Charles Perrault, Fr. author, b. (d. 1703) Sir William Temple, Eng. author and diplomat, b. (d. 1699)	The Alexandrian Codex (5th century) presented to Charles I by patriarch of Constantinople Johann Amos Comenius: "Informatorium der Mutterschul," on primary education (—1631) Robert Cotton: "Life of King Henry III" René Descartes: "Règles pour la direction de l'esprit" William Laud (1573—1645) made bishop of London Ignatius Loyola canonized by Pope Gregory XV Henry Spelman: "Glossary of Law Terms"

D. VISUAL ARTS	E. MUSIC	F. SCIENCE, TECHNOLOGY, GROWTH	G. DAILY LIFE	
				1625 contd
Jacques Lemercier: Sorbonne, Paris François Mansart: Château de Balleroy Rubens: "Assumption of the Virgin," altarpiece at Antwerp Façade of St. Peter's, Rome, finished, consecrated by Pope Urban VIII Jan Steen, Dutch painter, b. (d. 1679) Van Dyck: "Marchesa Paola Adorno and Her Son"	Professorship of music founded at Oxford University by William Heather (1563—1627) Giovanni Legrenzi, Ital. composer, b. (d. 1690)	Fr. "Company for the Islands of America" incorporated Jardin des Plantes established in Paris Salem, Mass., settled by Roger Conant Santorio Santorio, Ital. physician, measures human temperature with the thermometer for the first time	A royal edict condemns anyone to death who kills his adversary in a duel in France First Fr. settlement on the Senegal River Peter Minuit (1580—1638), director- general of Dutch West India Company's settlement in N. America, buys (May) the entire Island of Manhattan from native Indian chiefs for merchandise valued at 60 guilders (about $24); historians have questioned the size of the fee Dutch colony of New Amsterdam founded on Hudson River	1626
Adriaen de Vries, Dutch sculptor, d. (b. 1560) Frans Hals: "The Merry Drinker" Claude Lorrain arrives in Rome Rembrandt: "The Money- Changer" Rubens: "Mystic Marriage of St. Catherine"	Heinrich Schütz: "Dafne," first Ger. opera, libretto by Martin Opitz, given at Torgau Lodovico Viadana, Ital. composer, d. (b. 1564)	Francis Bacon: "New Atlantis," plans for a national museum of science and art (posth.) Charles I grants charter to the Guiana Company Johann Kepler compiles the Rudolphine Tables, giving places of 1,005 fixed stars	"Company of New France," Canada, incorporated by Richelieu Swedish South Sea Company founded	1627
Braemar Castle, Aberdeenshire, built by Earl of Mar Frans Hals: "Gypsy Woman" Nicolas Poussin: "Martyrdom of St. Erasmus" Andrea Spezza: Waldstein Palace, Prague Taj Mahal, Agra, built (—1650) Jacob van Ruisdael, Dutch painter, b. (d. 1682) Velázquez: "Christ on the Cross"	John Bull, Eng. composer, d. (b. 1562) Robert Cambert, Fr. composer, b. (d. 1677) Marco da Gagliano: "Flora," opera Heinrich Schütz becomes Monteverdi's pupil at Venice	William Harvey: "Exercitatio anatomica de motu cordis et sanguinis," on the circulation of blood (see 1619) Eng. adventurers acquire Nevis, one of the Leeward Islands John Ray, Eng. naturalist, b. (d. 1705) First harbor with sluices being constructed at Le Havre		1628

	A. HISTORY, POLITICS	B. LITERATURE, THEATER	C. RELIGION, PHILOSOPHY, LEARNING
1629	Charles I dissolves Parliament (Mar.); it does not meet again till Apr. 1640 Edict of restitution of church property in Germany, secularized since Peace of Augsburg (1555) Peace of Susa ends war between England and France Peace of Lübeck: Christian IV undertakes not to intervene in imperial affairs Wallenstein made Duke of Mecklenburg Peace of Alais ends Huguenot revolt Truce of Altmark signed between Sweden and Poland Bethlen Gabor of Transylvania d. Commercial treaty signed between Russia and France	Pedro Calderón de la Barca: "La dama duende," comedy Pierre Corneille: "Mélite," comedy John Ford: "The Lover's Melancholy," romantic play Philip Massinger: "The Roman Actor," tragedy	Lancelot Andrewes' "XCVI Sermons" Thomas Hobbes translates "The Peloponnesian War" by Thucydides
1630	John Winthrop, Eng. Puritan leader (1587—1649), sails with Plymouth Company's expedition (Apr.); arrives in Massachusetts with 1,000 settlers; founds Boston (Sept.); becomes first governor of the state; 16,000 more settlers follow (—1642) The future King Charles II b. (d. 1685) Gustavus Adolphus of Sweden marches his army into Germany The Emperor Ferdinand II dismisses Wallenstein; Tilly is the new commander Treaty of Madrid ends Anglo-Fr. war "Day of Dupes" in France: Richelieu overthrows conspiracy of Maria de' Medici, the Queen Mother	Andres Christensen Arrabo initiates modern Dan. literature with his religious poem "Hexaëmeron" Corneille: "Clitandre," tragicomedy Tirso de Molina: "El burlador de Sevilla y convidado de piedra," first of Don Juan plays Philip Massinger: "The Renegado," tragicomedy Thomas Middleton: "A Chaste Mayde in Cheapside," comedy	Congregation of the Eng. Ladies founded in Munich Sir John Hayward: "The Life and Raigne of King Edward VI"
1631	Ger. Protestant princes hold a convention at Neu Brandenburg, and decide to form alliance with Gustavus Adolphus Tilly destroys Swed. garrison at Neu Brandenburg, sacks Magdeburg, burns Halle, and invades Saxony Gustavus Adolphus sacks Frankfort-on-Oder, signs treaty of alliance with John George, Elector of Saxony, defeats Tilly at battle of Breitenfeld, and occupies Würzburg and Mainz Pope Urban VIII annexes Urbino Wallenstein reappointed Commander-in-Chief Maria de'Medici exiled to Brussels, joining forces with her son Gaston, Duke of Orleans, to bring about Richelieu's fall	Thomas Dekker: "Match Mee in London," tragicomedy John Donne, Eng. poet, d. (b. 1572) Michael Drayton, Eng. poet, d. (b. 1563) John Dryden, Eng. dramatist, b. (d. 1700) Thomas Heywood: "The Fair Maid of the West," comedy Ben Jonson: "The Devil is an Asse," comedy	Friedrich Spee von Langenfeld: "Cautio criminalis," against witch-hunting
1632	Gustavus Adolphus takes Nuremberg and defeats Tilly at the Lech; Tilly mortally wounded; Gustavus enters Munich, attacks Wallenstein at Nuremberg, defeats Wallenstein at battle of Lützen, and is killed in action Charles I issues charter for the colony Maryland (named in honor of Queen Henrietta Maria), under control of Lord Baltimore Queen Christina (b. 1626), daughter of Gustavus Adolphus, ascends throne of Sweden; five regents, headed by Chancellor Axel Oxenstierna, govern country (—1644) Portuguese driven out of Bengal Sigismund III, King of Poland, d.; succeeded by Vladislav IV (—1648) Sir Francis Windebank made chief Secretary of State in England	Giovanni Battista Basile, Ital. poet and writer of fairy tales, d. (b. 1575) Thomas Dekker, Eng. dramatist, d. (b. 1570) Philip Massinger: "The City Madam," comedy Second Shakespeare Folio published	Antonio Bosio: "Roma sotterranea," report on excavation of catacombs in Rome John Davies: "Welsh Dictionary" John Locke, Eng. philosopher, b. (d. 1704) John Selden: "Mare Clausum," on England's sovereignty of the sea Baruch Spinoza, Dutch philosopher, b. (d. 1677) Johann Angelus *(contd)*

D. VISUAL ARTS	E. MUSIC	F. SCIENCE, TECHNOLOGY, GROWTH	G. DAILY LIFE	
Bernini takes over direction of uncompleted work at St. Peter's, Rome Pieter de Hooch, Dutch painter, b. (d. 1683) Peter Paul Rubens knighted by Charles I Van Dyck: "Rinaldo and Armida" Velázquez: "The Drunkards" Francisco de Zurbarán: "St. Bonaventura"	Heinrich Schütz: "Sinfoniae sacrae"	Dutch mathematician Albert Gerard (1595—1632) uses brackets and other abbreviations in mathematics Christian Huygens, Dutch mathematician and scientist, b. (d. 1695) John Parkinson (1567—1650): "Paradisi in sole Paradisus terrestris," on flowers Edwin Sandys, Governor of Virginia, d. (b. 1561)	Royal charter granted to Guild of Spectacle Makers, London Shah Jahan, the Great Mogul, orders the making of the Peacock Throne Colony of Massachusetts founded	**1629**
Caius Gabriel Cibber, Eng. sculptor, b. (d. 1700) Frans Hals: "Daniel van Aken Playing the Violin" Jusepe Ribera: "Archimedes" Rubens: "Blessings of Peace" Michael Willmann, Ger. painter, b. (d. 1706) Beginning of the High Baroque period in Italy (—c.1680)	Girolamo Frescobaldi: "Arie musicale" Johann Hermann Schein, Ger. composer, d. (b. 1586)	Francis Higginson: "New England's Plantation," on living conditions in America Johann Kepler, Ger. astronomer, d. (b. 1571)	Pirates of all nationalities, called "buccaneers," settle in Tortuga, off northwest coast of Hispaniola Eng. poet Sir John Suckling invents, according to John Aubrey's "Brief Lives," the card game cribbage Beginning of public advertising, in Paris Fr. philanthropist Théophraste Renaudot (1586—1653) founds in Paris the Bureau d'adresse, a labor-exchange charity organization and intelligence office	**1630**
Jacques Lemercier: Château Richelieu Baldassare Longhena begins work on church of S. Maria della Salute, Venice Rembrandt: Portrait of his mother Velázquez: "Infanta Maria, Queen of Hungary"	Philipp Dulichius, Ger. composer, d. (b. 1562)	Dutch West India Company founds settlement at the Delaware River Eng. mathematician William Oughtred proposes symbol "X" for multiplication	T. Renaudot founds the "Gazette" in Paris; from 1752 on, "Gazette de France" London Clockmakers' Company incorporated Eng. settlement of Leeward Islands begins at St. Kitts Earthquake in Naples; eruption of Vesuvius	**1631**
Luca Giordano, Ital. painter, b. (d. 1705) Nicolaes Maes, Dutch painter, b. (d. 1693) Rembrandt: "The Anatomy Lesson of Dr. Nicolaas Tulp" Van Dyck made court painter to Charles I Jan Vermeer, Dutch painter, b. (d. 1675) Christopher Wren, Eng. architect, b. (d. 1723)	Jean Baptiste Lully, Fr.-Ital. composer, b. (d. 1687) Monteverdi takes holy orders	Galileo: "Dialogho sopra i due massimi sistemi del mondo" published; finished 1630: on terrestrial double motion Leiden University Observatory founded Antony van Leeuwenhoek, Dutch zoologist, b. (d. 1723)	First coffee shop opens in London Eng. settlers in Antigua and Montserrat Russian fur trade center established in Yakutsk, Siberia	**1632**

	A. HISTORY, POLITICS	B. LITERATURE, THEATER	C. RELIGION, PHILOSOPHY, LEARNING
1632 contd			Werdenhagen: "Introductio universalis in omnes republicas," on comparative politics
1633	Wallenstein invades Silesia, defeats Swed. army under Bernhard, Duke of Saxe-Weimar, at Steinau, and goes into winter quarters in Bohemia Charles I crowned King of Scotland in Edinburgh The future King James II of England, b. (d. 1701) The Emperor Ferdinand II begins to suspect Wallenstein of treachery Charles I revives forest eyre to raise money by fines Fr. army occupies Lorraine (—1659) Edward Winslow (1595—1655), Governor of Plymouth Colony	Abraham Cowley: "Poetical Blossoms" John Donne: "Poems" (posth.) John Ford: "'Tis Pity She's a Whore," tragedy George Herbert, Eng. poet, d. (b. 1593) Christopher Marlowe: "The Jew of Malta," tragedy (posth.) Philip Massinger: "A New Way to Pay Old Debts," comedy Outbreak of plague in Bavaria leads to passion play vow in Oberammergau (see 1634) Samuel Pepys, Eng. diarist, b. (d. 1703)	Galileo forced by the Inquisition to abjure the theories of Copernicus First Baptist church formed at Southwark, London Edmund Spenser: "A View of the Present State of Ireland" (posth.) John Cotton becomes a religious leader in Boston
1634	The Emperor Ferdinand II for second time deprives Wallenstein of his command, declaring him a traitor; Matthias Gallas (1584—1647) made Commander-in-Chief; Wallenstein assassinated Swed. army defeated at battle of Nördlingen; Württemberg and Franconia reconquered by imperial forces Island of Curaçao captured by Dutch forces Treaty of Polianovska: King Vladislav of Poland renounces claim to Russia	George Chapman, Eng. author, d. (b. 1559) Corneille: "La Veuve" and "La Suivante," comedies Marie-Madeleine de La Fayette, Fr. novelist, b. (d. 1693) John Fletcher: "Two Noble Kinsmen," tragedy (posth.) John Ford: "Perkin Warbeck," historical drama Jean Mairet: "Sophonisbe," first classical Fr. tragedy, based on the three unities John Marston, Eng. dramatist, d. (b. 1576) Milton: "Comus," masque The Oberammergau Passion Play given for first time; re-enacted every 10 years	Méric Casaubon (1599—1671): "The Meditations of the Roman Emperor Marcus Aurelius" Anne Hutchinson (1591—1643), religious controversialist, migrates to Massachusetts
1635	Franco-Swed. treaty of alliance signed by Richelieu and Oxtenstierna Peace of Prague signed between the Emperor Ferdinand II and the Elector John George of Saxony; Thirty Years' War now becomes a conflict between France and Sweden against the House of Hapsburg Treaty of Stuhmsdorf: 20-year truce between Sweden and Poland Treaty of St. Germain-en-Laye agrees on regular Fr. subsidies to the army of Bernhard of Saxe-Weimar Colonization of Connecticut begins: Eng. settlers led by John Winthrop the Younger, in Fort Saybrook; Windsor founded by religious refugees from Dorchester, Mass. Council of New England dissolved Dutch occupy Formosa, English Virgin Islands, French Martinique	Calderón writes "La Vida es sueño"; becomes head of Royal Theater, Madrid Corneille: "Medée," tragedy George Etherege, Eng. dramatist, b. (d. 1691) Thomas Heywood: "Hierarchie of Blessed Angels" Vitzentsos Kornaros, Cretan poet, writes "The Sacrifice of Abraham," first mystery drama in modern Greek Philippe Quinault, Eng. dramatist, b. (d. 1688) Thomas Randolph, Eng. poet, d. (b. 1605) Alessandro Tassoni, Ital. poet, d. (b. 1565) Daniel Caspar von Lohenstein, Ger. poet, b. (d. 1683)	Giulio Alenio, Ital. Jesuit, publishes first life of Christ in Chinese Cornelius Jansen: "Mars gallus," against Richelieu

D. VISUAL ARTS	E. MUSIC	F. SCIENCE, TECHNOLOGY, GROWTH	G. DAILY LIFE	
				1632 contd
Jacques Callot: "Les Grandes Misères de la guerre" Rebuilding of Kiyomizuderi (pavilion) of Seisuji, near Kyoto, Japan Rembrandt: "Saskia" Jacob van Campen and Pieter Post: "Mauritshuis, The Hague Willem van de Velde the Younger, Dutch painter, b. (d. 1707) Van Dyck: "Charles I"	Jacopo Peri, Ital. composer and inventor of the recitative, d. (b. 1561)	Eng. trading post established in Bengal	Dutch settle in Connecticut Trial of the Lancashire witches Reform of Eng. postal service by Thomas Witherings The Royal Scots, oldest regular regiment in Brit. Army, established Wind sawmill erected near the Strand, London	**1633**
Rembrandt: "Artemisia" Zurbarán: "The Siege of Cadiz"	Adam Krieger, Ger. composer, b. (d. 1666)	Jean Nicolet lands on Green Bay; explores Wisconsin Founding of University of Utrecht	Covent Garden Market, London, opened Eng. settlement at Cochin, Malabar	**1634**
Jacques Callot, Fr. painter, d. (b. 1592) Philippe de Champaigne: "Portrait of Richelieu" François Mansart: Château Blois Nicolas Poussin: "Kingdom of Flora" Rembrandt: "Self-Portrait with Saskia" Velázquez: "Surrender of Breda" Zurbarán: "St. Veronica's Kerchief"	Frescobaldi: "Fiori musicali di toccate," which influences J. S. Bach	Académie Française founded by Richelieu Budapest University established Eng. High and Latin School, Boston, Mass., oldest secondary school in N. America, founded Robert Hooke, Eng. physician, b. (d. 1703)	Marquise de Maintenon, consort of Louis XIV, b. (d. 1703) Speed limit on hackney coaches in London: 3 m.p.h. First inland postal service in Britain between London and Edinburgh Sale of tobacco in France restricted to apothecaries, only on doctors' prescriptions	**1635**

	A. HISTORY, POLITICS	B. LITERATURE, THEATER	C. RELIGION, PHILOSOPHY, LEARNING
1636	Battle of Wittstock; Swed. troops defeat Saxons Aust. troops retire from Burgundy The Emperor Ferdinand II has his son, Archduke Ferdinand, elected Ferdinand III, King of the Romans Manchus proclaim the Ch'ing Dynasty at Mukden Dutch settle in Ceylon Bishop John Juxon made Lord Treasurer of England Prince Octavio Piccolomini invades France; is repulsed	Corneille: "Le Cid" Italian Fedeli Company performs Commedia dell'arte at the Fr. court Philip Massinger: "The Great Duke of Florence," comedy	Welsh Puritan Roger Williams (1603—1683) banished from Massachusetts; establishes Providence, R.I.; proclaims complete religious freedom Joseph Glanvill, Eng. philosopher, b. (d. 1680) Peter Heylyn: "The History of the Sabbath" George Sandys: "A Paraphrase Upon the Psalmes"
1637	Ferdinand II d.; succeeded as Holy Roman Emperor by his son Ferdinand III (—1657) Bogislav XIV, last Duke of Pomerania, d. William Prynne, Puritan parliamentarian (1600—1669) condemned, with Henry Burton and John Bastwick, for seditious writing, to be pilloried and mutilated Dutch under Frederick Henry of Orange recapture Breda Destruction of Pequod Fort, Conn.	Calderón: "El magico prodigioso," religious drama Jean Desmarets de Saint-Sorlin: "Les Visionnaires," comedy Ben Jonson, Eng. poet and dramatist, d. (b. 1572) "Jonsonus Viribus, or The Memory of Ben Jonson Revived by the Friends of the Muses," ed. by Brian Duppa Martin Le Roy: "Polyxandre," romance John Milton: "Lycidas," elegy James Shirley: "A Lady of Pleasure," comedy	Extermination of Christianity in Japan; prohibition of foreign books; European contacts prohibited Thomas Hobbes: "A Briefe of the Art of Rhetorique," based on Aristotle Introduction of new liturgy into Scotland causes riots
1638	Bernhard of Saxe-Weimar takes Freiburg, defeats Duke of Lorraine at Sennheim, and conquers Breisach The future Louis XIV b. (d. 1715) Elector of Brandenburg moves his capital to Königsberg Franco-Swed. alliance renewed for three years Murad IV of Turkey recovers Baghdad from Persia	John Ford: "The Ladies Trial" Lars Johansson, Swed. poet, b. (d. 1674) Niccolò Sabbatini: "Practica di fabbricare scene e machine ne'teatri" Schouwburg Theater opens in Amsterdam Joost van den Vondel: "Gijsbrecht van Amstel," historical drama	William Chillingworth: "The Religion of Protestants a Safe Way to Salvation" Cornelius Jansen, Dutch theologian, father of "Jansenism," d. (b. 1585) Nicolas Malebranche, Fr. philosopher, b. (d. 1715) Scot. Covenant drawn up and signed; Charles I abandons liturgy and canons in Scotland
1639	The Grisons' leader Georg (Jürg) Jenatsch assassinated; the Valtelline returned to the Grisons under Peace of Milan Swed. army before Prague First Bishops' War in Scotland; Scots charged by Charles I with seeking to overthrow royal power; Covenanters take Edinburgh, Dumbarton, and Stirling; Charles joins army at York, dares no attack, and signs Pacification of Berwick to end war; episcopacy abolished in Scotland Bernhard of Saxe-Weimar d. (b. 1604) Jules Mazarin (1602—1661) enters Richelieu's service Russ. Cossacks advance over Urals to Pacific, to Okhotsk	Juan Ruiz de Alarcón, Span. dramatist, d. (b. 1581) Thomas Carew, Eng. poet, d. (b. 1598) William Cartwright: "The Royal Slave," drama Corneille: "Cinna," tragedy Drury Lane Theatre, London, receives its first patent Martin Opitz, Ger. poet, d. (b. 1597) Philip Massinger: "The Unnatural Combat" Racine, Fr. dramatist, b. (d. 1699)	Académie Française compiles dictionary of the Fr. language (—1694) Increase Mather, Amer. clergyman, b. (d. 1723)

D. VISUAL ARTS	E. MUSIC	F. SCIENCE, TECHNOLOGY, GROWTH	G. DAILY LIFE	
Rembrandt: "Portrait of an 83-year-old Woman" Van Dyck: "Charles I on Horseback" Velázquez: "Prince Baltasar Carlos as a Hunter"	Fr. theorist Marin Mersenne (1588—1648) publishes his most important work, "Harmonie Universelle," with full descriptions of all contemporary musical instruments Schütz: "Kleine geistliche Concerten," collection of motets	Harvard College (so called from 1639 in tribute to John Harvard, who endowed it by a legacy) founded at Newe Towne, Cambridge, Mass., with Nathaniel Eaton as first president	Tea appears for first time in Paris	**1636**
Frans Hals: "Hille Bobbe" Rembrandt: "Raphael Leaving Tobias" Ribera: "Pietà" Van Dyck: "Children of Charles I"	Dietrich Buxtehude, Dan. composer, b. (d. 1707) Teatro San Cassiano, first public opera house, opens in Venice, sponsored by the Trón family	René Descartes: "Géométrie" Dutch expel Portuguese from Gold Coast Eng. emigration to America restricted by royal proclamation Eng. traders established in Canton Fr. traders settle at St. Louis, at mouth of the Senegal River Daniel Sennert, Ger. scientist who formulated the conception "Atom," d. (b. 1572) Jan Swammerdam, Dutch naturalist, b. (d. 1680)	Commercial collapse of Dutch tulip trade	**1637**
Pieter Brueghel the Younger, Fl. painter, "Hell Brueghel," d. (b. 1564) Adriaen Brouwer, Dutch painter, d. (b. 1606) Meindert Hobbema, Dutch painter, b. (d. 1709) Nicolas Poussin: "Et in Arcadia ego" Rubens: "The Three Graces" Van Dyck: "Lords John and Bernard Stuart"	Monteverdi: "Eighth Book of Madrigals"	Galileo: "Discorsi e Dimonstrazioni Matematiche" Anne Hutchinson, leader of the New England Antinomians, is banished from Boston, Massachussetts, and sets up a community in Rhode Island	New Haven, Conn., founded Soldier-student becomes a common type in Germany Swedes settle on Delaware River (New Sweden) Torture abolished in England	**1638**
Louis Le Nau: Hôtel Lambert, Paris Rembrandt: portrait of his mother Rubens: "Judgment of Paris" Zurbarán: "St. Francis in Meditation"	Marco Marazzoli and Vergilio Mazzochi: "Chi soffre, speri," first comic opera Monteverdi's opera, "Adone," given at Teatro San Cassiano, Venice	Gérard Désargues (1593—1662) publishes his book on modern geometry William Gascoigne invents micrometer Sir Ferdinando Gorges (1566—1647), founder of the colony of Maine, receives charter Jeremiah Horrocks observes the transit of Venus, which he had predicted Quinine increasingly used for medicinal purposes	English settle at Madras First printing press in N. America, at Cambridge, Mass.	**1639**

	A. HISTORY, POLITICS	B. LITERATURE, THEATER	C. RELIGION, PHILOSOPHY, LEARNING
1640	French finish occupation of Alsace Short Parliament (Apr.—May) and Long Parliament (Nov.—1653) in England Swedes withdraw from Bohemia Second Bishops' War: Scots cross Tweed into England; the king leaves London for York, relieves Newcastle, and is defeated at Newburn-on-Tyne; agrees by Treaty of Ripon to pay Scots army £860 per day until settlement is reached Portugal becomes independent under John IV of Braganza Elector George William of Brandenburg d.; succeeded by the "Great Elector" Frederick William (—1688) Sultan Murad IV of Turkey d.; succeeded by Sultan Ibrahim (—1649)	Aphra Behn, Eng. novelist and dramatist, b. (d. 1689) Richard Brome: "The Antipodes," comedy Thomas Carew: "Poems" Corneille: "Polyeucte," tragedy Paul Fleming, Ger. poet, d. (b. 1609) John Ford, Eng. dramatist, d. (b. 1586) Philip Massinger, Eng. dramatist, d. (b. 1583) Joost van den Vondel: "Joseph in Egypt," religious drama William Wycherley, Eng. dramatist, b. (d. 1716)	Uriel Acosta, Dutch-Jewish philosopher, commits suicide Francisco Gómez de Quevedo: "Providencia de Dios" John Donne: "Eighty Sermons" (posth.) John Eliot: Bay Psalm Book, oldest surviving book printed in America Cornelius Jansen: "Augustinus," treatise against Jesuit doctrines (posth.) John Milton: "Of Reformation Touching Church Discipline in England" Izaak Walton: "The Life of Donne"
1641	Thomas Wentworth, Earl of Strafford, the king's chief adviser, beheaded Massacre of the Ulster Protestants; Catholic rebellion in Ireland Comte de Soissons' conspiracy against King Louis XIII fails Imperial army defeated at Wolfenbüttel	Corneille: "La Mort de Pompée," tragedy Luis Vélez de Guevara: "El diablo cojuelo," picaresque novel Madeleine de Scudéry: "Ibraham, ou L'Illustre Bassa," novel John Evelyn writes his "Diary" (—1706) Ben Jonson: "Timber, or Discoveries" (posth.)	René Descartes: "Méditations métaphysiques" William Habington: "Observations Upon Historie" General Court of Massachusetts Bay Company codifies 100 laws Mazarin made cardinal George Wither: "Hallelujah, or Britain's Second Remembrances," collection of hymns
1642	Charles I marches to Westminster to arrest five members of the Commons; attempt fails; he flees with his family to Hampton Court; Queen Henrietta Maria leaves England for Holland Imperial army defeated at Kempten, Schweidnitz, and Breitenfeld Eng. Civil War begins with raising of royal standard at Nottingham; Earl of Essex commands Parliamentary forces; indecisive battle at Edgehill; Cavaliers, the king's supporters, take Marlborough; his opponents, the Roundheads, take Winchester Inflation in Spain Cardinal Richelieu d. (b. 1585); succeeded as first minister by the Ital.-born Cardinal Mazarin Sir William Berkeley (1606—1677), Governor of Virginia	Corneille: "Le Menteur," comedy All theaters in England closed by order of the Puritans (—1660) Christian Weise, Ger. dramatist, b. (d. 1708)	Johann Amos Comenius: "A Reformation of Schooles," trans. by Samuel Hartlib Thomas Fuller: "The Holy State and the Profane State" Thomas Hobbes: "De cive" James Howell: "Instruction for Foreign Travel" Thomas Lechford: "Plain Dealing, or Newes from New England," political survey Pope Urban VIII issues bull "Universa per Orbem," reducing annual feast days to 32; at instigation of Jesuits he also condemns Jansen's "Augustinus"
1643	Eng. Civil War: Cavaliers lose Bradford, are defeated by Cromwell at Grantham, take Bristol, are beaten in Battle of Newbury; Roundheads victorious at Leeds, Reading, Wakefield, Gainsborough, Gloucester Unsuccessful peace talks between the two parties at Oxford Louis XIII of France d.; succeeded by his five-year-old son Louis XIV (—1715) Anne of Austria, the Queen Mother, invested with supreme power, confirms Mazarin as first minister Confederation of New England formed by Connecticut, New Haven, Plymouth, and Massachusetts Bay Colony Imperial envoys open peace conference at Münster and Osnabrück *(contd)*	Molière founds "Illustre Théâtre" in Paris ("Théâtre de la Comédie Française" from 1689)	Sir Richard Baker: "A Chronicle of the Kings of England" François Eudes de Mézeray: "Histoire de France" John Milton: "The Doctrine and Discipline of Divorce" William Prynne: "The Soveraigne Power of Parliaments and Kingdomes" Roger Williams: "Key into the Language of America"

D. VISUAL ARTS	E. MUSIC	F. SCIENCE, TECHNOLOGY, GROWTH	G. DAILY LIFE	
Nicolas Poussin: "The Inspiration of the Poet" Rembrandt: "Self-Portrait" Peter Paul Rubens d. (b. 1577) Adriaen van Ostade: "The Barrel Organ Player"	John Bull, Eng. composer, d. (b. 1585)	Abo University, Finland, founded Coke made from coal for first time James Howell: "Dodona's Grove, or The Vocall Forrest," manual of dendrology John Parkinson: "Theatrum botanicum," a herbal	Eng. settlers found Fort St. George in Bengal First European café opens in Venice Eight postal lines running in England	**1640**
Frans Hals: "The Governors of St. Elizabeth Hospital" Claude Lorraine: "Embarkation of St. Ursula" Nicolas Poussin: "The Seven Sacraments" Rembrandt: "Manoah" David Teniers: "Country Fair" Van Dyck: "Prince William of Orange" Anthony Van Dyck d. (b. 1599)	John Barnard: "First Booke of Selected Church Musick" Monteverdi: "Il Ritorno d'Ulisse in patria," opera	Arsenic prescribed for medicinal purposes for first time Henry Dunster (1612—1659) becomes president of Harvard College	Cotton goods begin to be manufactured in Manchester "Diurnal Occurrences," a weekly periodical issued in London French settle in Michigan Rise of Swed. iron industry Théophraste Renaudot publishes his plan for free medical treatment of needy in Paris; three years later faculty of medicine forbids him to practice	**1641**
Mansart: Maisons Lafitte, near Paris Rembrandt: "The Night Watch" Guido Reni, Ital. painter, d. (b. 1575)	Marco da Gagliano, Ital. composer, d. (b. 1575) Monteverdi: "L'Incoronazione di Poppea," given at Europe's second public opera house, Teatro di Santi Giovanni e Paolo, Venice	Galileo Galilei d. (b. 1564) Isaac Newton, Eng. mathematician and natural philosopher, b. (d. 1727) Portuguese cede the Gold Coast to the Dutch Abel Tasman (1603—1659) discovers Tasmania and New Zealand University of Ancona founded	Income and property tax introduced in England Loire—Seine canal finished (begun 1604) Montreal, Canada, founded	**1642**
Adriaen van Ostade: "Slaughtered Pig" Velázquez: "Venus and Cupid"	Girolamo Frescobaldi, Ital. composer, d. (b. 1583) Claudio Monteverdi, Ital. composer, d. (b. 1567) Cavalli: "Egisto," opera	Ital. physicist Evangelista Torricelli (1608—1647) invents the barometer	"Christiania Almanack," first Norw. printed book, appears Coffee drinking becomes popular in Paris Parcel post established in France First subscription loan in Austria	**1643**

	A. HISTORY, POLITICS	B. LITERATURE, THEATER	C. RELIGION, PHILOSOPHY, LEARNING
1643 contd	Austro-Bavarian army defeats French at Duttlingen Cavalier newssheet "Mercurius Aulicus" published at Oxford every Sunday; Roundhead counterpart "Mercurius Britanicus" appears in London Span. Minister of State, Olivares (1587–1645), loses his office		
1644	Eng. Civil War: in Battle of Nantwich, Royalists defeated, as at Copredy Bridge and Marston Moor; Queen Henrietta Maria flees to France; York surrenders to Roundheads; Parliamentarian army surrenders to King Charles I at Fowey; indecisive second battle at Newbury Fr. occupation of the Rhineland Queen Christina begins her actual reign in Sweden Connecticut unites with colony at Saybrook, Providence with Newport, Portsmouth with Rhode Island Ming dynasty in China ends, Manchu dynasty in power (–1912) William Penn, Eng. Quaker and colonizer, b. (d. 1718)	Calderón: "El alcalde de Zalamea" Corneille: "Rodogune," tragedy Pegnitzischer Blumenorden, Ger. poetical society founded at Nuremberg Abraham a Sancta Clara, Viennese preacher and satirist, b. (d. 1709)	René Descartes: "Principia philosophicae" ("Cogito, ergo sum") Henry Hammond: "A Practical Catechism" Sir Henry Manwayring: "The Seaman's Dictionary" John Milton: "Areopagitica," for the freedom of the press Samuel Rutherford: "Lex rex," on the elective nature of the monarchy Pope Urban VIII d.; Giovanni Battista Pamfili becomes Pope Innocent X (–1655) Roger Williams: "Queries of Highest Consideration," separation of Church and State
1645	Eng. Civil War: peace talks at Uxbridge fail, and armistice ends; Oliver Cromwell, Lt.-Gen. of New Model Army, defeats Royalists at Naseby and Langport; the Royalists also lose Carlisle, Bristol, Winchester, Basingstoke Michael I, Czar of Russia, d.; succeeded by Alexis I (–1676) Dutch occupy St. Helena Peace talks open between Holy Roman Empire and France at Münster and Osnabrück (see 1643) Turk.-Venetian war over Crete (–1669)	Calderón: "El gran teatro del mundo" Corneille: "Théodore, vierge et martyre," tragedy Vitzentzos Kornaros: "Rotokritos," Cretan epic poem John Milton: "L'Allegro," "Il Penseroso" Paul Scarron: "Jodolet," comedy	Sir Kenelm Digby: "A Treatise on Bodies and of Man's Soul" Hugo Grotius, Dutch jurist and statesman, d. (b. 1583) Lord Herbert of Cherbury: "De causis errorum" Dalai Lama's residence being built in Lhasa, Tibet
1646	Swedes take Prague; they invade Bavaria with the French Eng. Civil War ends with surrender of Oxford to Roundheads; Parliamentary commissioners present Charles I with the Newcastle Propositions, demanding religious reforms and surrender of control of armed forces for 20 years; the king tries to escape, but his plan fails English occupy Bahamas The "Great Elector" of Brandenburg marries Louise, daughter of Frederick Henry of Orange	Jean Rotrou: "Le Véritable Saint Genest," religious drama James Shirley: "Poems" John Suckling: "Fragmenta aurea" Henry Vaughan: "Poems"	Gottfried Wilhelm von Leibniz, Ger. philosopher, b. (d. 1716) Jeremy Taylor: "A Discourse Concerning Prayer"

D. VISUAL ARTS	E. MUSIC	F. SCIENCE, TECHNOLOGY, GROWTH	G. DAILY LIFE	
				1643 contd
Bernini: Cornaro Chapel, S. Maria della Vittoria, Rome, including "Ecstasy of St. Teresa," sculpture Last age of fine Chin. porcelain Jacques Lemercier: Val- de-Grâce Church, Paris Rembrandt: "Woman Taken in Adultery" Ribera: "St. Paul the Hermit" Bernardo Strozzi, Ital. painter, d. (b. 1581) Teniers: "Kitchen of the Archduke Leopold Wilhelm"	Antonio Stradivari, Ital. violin maker, b. (d. 1737) Heinrich Ignaz Franz von Biber, Ger. composer, b. (d. 1704)	Dutch settlement in Mauritius Tasman charters parts of northern and western Australia (New Holland)		**1644**
Jacob Jordaens: "Wife of Candaules" Rembrandt: "The Rabbi" Teniers: "Tavern Scene" Jacob van Campen: Niewe Kerk, Haarlem Velázquez: "King Philip IV on a Boar Hunt"	Lully made violinist at Fr. court Mazarin calls a Venetian opera company to Paris "La Finta Pazza" by Francesco Paolo Sacrati given as possibly first opera in Paris Heinrich Schütz: "Die sieben Worte Christi am Kreuz," oratorio	Capuchin monks sail up Congo River Preliminary meetings of London scientists which will eventually lead to foundation of Royal Society (see 1662) University of Palermo founded	"Ordinarie Post-Tidende" begins to appear in Stockholm	**1645**
Jules Hardouin-Mansart, grandnephew and pupil of Jules Mansart, b. (d. 1708) Godfrey Kneller, Ger.-Eng. portrait painter, b. (d. 1723) Murillo: "The Angel's Kitchen" Rembrandt: "Adoration of the Shepherds" Jan van Goyen: "Village Church in the Sand Dunes"	Johann Stobaeus, Ger. composer, d. (b. 1580) Johann Theile, Ger. singer and composer, b. (d. 1724)	Ger. mathematician Athanasius Kircher (1601—1680) constructs first projection lantern (laterna magica)	First lime trees planted between Royal Palace and Zoological Gardens, Berlin: beginning of "Unter den Linden"	**1646**

	A. HISTORY, POLITICS	B. LITERATURE, THEATER	C. RELIGION, PHILOSOPHY, LEARNING
1647	Treaty of Ulm: Electors of Bavaria and Cologne undertake to remain neutral till end of war, but intervene again in favor of Emperor Ferdinand III Elector of Mainz and Landgrave of Hesse withdraw from the war Eng. Civil War: Commons votes to disband most of the army; Charles I taken prisoner; army marches into London; the king escapes, is recaptured, and is imprisoned at Carisbrooke Castle; he agrees to abolish episcopacy and restore Presbyterianism Masaniello revolts against the Spanish in Naples; Masaniello assassinated Frederick Henry of Orange d.; succeeded by his son William II of Orange (—1650) Revolt against Czar Alexis I in Moscow	Francis Beaumont and John Fletcher: "Comedies and Tragedies," collection of 24 hitherto unpublished plays Abraham Cowley: "The Mistress, or Several Copies of Love Verses" Pieter Corneliszoon Hooft, Dutch poet, d. (b. 1581) Henry More: "Philosophical Poems" Jean Rotrou: "Venceslas," political drama	Pierre Bayle, Fr. philosopher, b. (d. 1706) Calvinists acknowledged by Lutherans as coreligionists Thomas May: "History of the Long Parliament" Dismissal of Anglican professors at Oxford University
1648	Eng. Civil War: Cromwell demands end of allegiance to the king; Parliamentary "Declaration" on Charles I's misdeeds; Scots begin Second Civil War, and are defeated at Preston; the king offers some concessions to Parliament, which are rejected; Parliament votes to bring Charles I to trial King Christian IV of Denmark d.; succeeded by Frederick III (—1670) Naples restored to Span. rule Outbreak of the Fronde in France Peace of Westphalia ends Thirty Years' War; is condemned by Pope Innocent X (bull "Zelo Domus Dei") John II Casimir succeeds his brother Vladislav IV as King of Poland	Tirso de Molina, Span. dramatist, d. (b. 1571) Madeleine de Scudéry: "Artamène, ou Le Grand Cyrus" Paul Scarron: "Le Roman comique"	George Fox (1624—1691) founds the Society of Friends (Quakers) John Lilburne: "The Foundation of Freedom" "The Book of the General Lawes and Libertyes of Massachusetts" John Stearne: "Confirmation and Discovery of Witchcraft" Sabbatai Zevi (1626—1676), self-proclaimed Messiah, founds a Jewish sect
1649	War of the Fronde begins in France; the Court leaves Paris Trial of Charles I opens (Jan. 19) Charles I beheaded (Jan. 30); Prince of Wales, in exile at The Hague, takes title Charles II and is proclaimed king by the Scots in Edinburgh Treaty of Ruel ends first Fronde; Court returns after treaty has been signed England declared a Commonwealth Cromwell invades Ireland, sacking Drogheda and Wexford Outbreak of second Fronde Holy Roman Empire establishes standing army in Austria Sultan Ibrahim deposed and murdered; succeeded by his son Mohammed IV (—1687)	William Drummond of Hawthornden, Scot. author, d. (b. 1585) Andreas Gryphius: "Carolus Stuardus," Ger. tragedy about Charles I Richard Lovelace: "Lucasta" Friedrich Spee von Langenfeld: "Trutz Nachtigall," religious poems (posth.)	Maryland Assembly passes act of toleration, professing belief in the Holy Trinity René Descartes: "Les Passions de l'âme" In Great Britain, English becomes language of all legal documents in place of Latin John Lilburne: "An Agreement for the Free People of England" John Milton: "The Tenure of Kings and Magistrates," defense of Charles I's execution
1650	Mazarin allies himself with leaders of first Fronde, imprisoning leaders of second Fronde Cromwell forms permanent economic council Marquis of Montrose, Scot. Royalist general, executed (b. 1612) Charles II lands in Scotland Treaty of Nuremberg between the Holy Roman Emperor and Sweden amplifies Peace of Westphalia Dutch and English agree about respective frontiers of their N. Amer. colonies John Churchill, future Duke of Marlborough, b. (d. 1722)	Corneille: "Andromède," tragedy Phineas Fletcher, Eng. poet, d. (b. 1582) Andreas Gryphius: "Horribilicribrifax," satirical comedy about state of affairs in Germany after the war (published 1663) Beginning of modern development of Jap. "No" drama Joost van den Vondel: "Manual of Dutch Poetry"	Richard Baxter: "The Saints' Everlasting Rest" René Descartes d. (b. 1596) Matthew Hale: "Analysis of the Civil Law" Thomas Hobbes: "The Elements of Law, Moral and Political" Gilles Ménage: "Dictionnaire étymologique" (new edition, 1670) James Ussher: "Annales Veteris et Novi Testamenti" (giving beginning of world as 4004 B.C.)

D. VISUAL ARTS	E. MUSIC	F. SCIENCE, TECHNOLOGY, GROWTH	G. DAILY LIFE	
Dresden Academy of Arts founded Peter Lely: "The Young Children of Charles I" Claude Lorrain: "The Mill" Adriaen van Ostade: "Peasant Family in an Interior" Rembrandt: "Susannah and the Two Old Men"	Pelham Humfrey, Eng. composer, b. (d. 1674)	Francesco Cavalieri, Ital. astronomer and mathematician, d. (b. 1598) Johann Hevel: "Selenographia," on the lunar surface Evangelista Torricelli, Ital. physicist, d. (b. 1608)	First newspaper advertisement (for the book "The Divine Right of Church Government") appears in "Perfect Occurences of Every Daie Journall in Parliament" (Apr.) Yellow fever in Barbados	**1647**
Claude Lorrain: "Embarcation of the Queen of Sheba" Rembrandt: "The Pilgrims at Emmaus" Ribera: "The Holy Family with St. Catherine" Jacob van Campen: Amsterdam Town Hall (—1655)	Aria and recitative become two distinct unities in opera John Blow, Eng. musician, b. (d. 1708) Heinrich Schütz: "Musicalia ad chorum sacrum" Johann Stadlmayr, Ger. composer, d. (b. 1560)	University of Bamberg founded J. R. Glauber obtains hydrochloric acid Marin Mersenne, Fr. philosopher and naturalist, d. (b. 1588) John Wilkins: "Mathematical Magic"	Population of Germany has sunk from 17 million in 1618 to eight million owing to war, famine, and plague In Murano, near Venice, mirrors and chandeliers are manufactured	**1648**
David Teniers the Elder, Dutch painter, d. (b. 1582) Gerard Terborch: "Philip IV of Spain," portrait Velázquez: "Pope Innocent X," portrait	Cavalli: "Giasone," opera Giuseppe Torelli, Ital. composer, b. (d. 1708)	Dutch physician Isbrand de Diemerbrock publishes his study of the plague, "De peste" Puritan exiles from Virginia settle in Providence, Md. First Brit. navy frigate, "Constant Warwick," constructed	Free enterprise in England receives state support According to official inventories, King Charles I had stud of 139 horses with 37 brood mares	**1649**
Bernini: Palazzo di Montecitorio Leonardo de Figueroa, Span. architect, b. (d. 1730) Murillo: "The Holy Family with the Little Bird" Poussin: "Self-Portrait" Jan van Goyen: "View of Dordrecht"	Beginning of modern harmony; development of modulation Athanasius Kircher: "Musurgia universalis," theory The overture as musical form emerges in two types, Italian and French	Harvard College granted charter Christoph Scheiner, Ger. astronomer, Jesuit, and opponent of Galileo, d. (b. 1575)	Opening of first coffee house in England, at Oxford First fiacres in Paris Leather upholstery being used for furniture World population estimated at 500 million; in 1850: 1.1 billion; 1950: 2.4 billion George Fox (see 1648) says: "I bid them tremble at the word of the Lord," whence "Quakers" for his followers Beginning of extermination of N. Amer. Indian Tea first drunk in England Sir Richard Weston (1591—1652), Eng. agriculturalist, advocates cultivation of turnips	**1650**

	A. HISTORY, POLITICS	B. LITERATURE, THEATER	C. RELIGION, PHILOSOPHY, LEARNING
1651	Charles II crowned King of Scots; flees to France after his defeat by Cromwell at Worcester Parlement votes for release of Condé, Fronde leader; Mazarin forced to leave Paris; the queen forced to ally herself with the Fronde against him Treaty between Czar Alexis I and the Cossacks King Louis XIV attains majority Eng. Navigation Act, directed against the Dutch, gives Eng. ships monopoly of foreign trade Yetuna, new shogun of Japan (—1680), overcomes two rebellions in Edo	William Cartwright: "Comedies, Tragicomedies, with Other Poems" John Cleveland: "Poems" First public "Comedy-house" in Vienna Sir William Davenant: "Gondibert," romantic epic poem Calderón becomes a priest	John Donne: "Essays in Divinity" (posth.) Thomas Hobbes: "Leviathan," defense of absolute monarchy Jeremy Taylor: "Rule and Exercises of Holy Dying"
1652	Eng. Parliament passes Act of Pardon and Oblivion to reconcile Royalists English defeat Dutch at Battle of the Downs off Folkestone before they declare war Provisional Fronde government set up in Paris Louis XIV reestablishes lawful government, recalling Mazarin Maine is joined to Massachusetts Bay Colony Governor William Stone of Maryland deprived of office by Cromwell's commissioners	Corneille: "Nicomède," tragedy Johann Lauremberg "Veer Schertz-Gedichte," comic poems in Low German Thomas Otway, Eng. dramatist, b. (d. 1685) Nahum Tate, Eng. poet laureate, b. (d. 1715)	Jean-Louis Guez de Balzac: "Socrate Chrétien," religious dialogues John Donne: "Paradoxes, Problems" (posth.) Hayashi Shunsai (1618—1680): "O-Dai- Ichi-Ran," a history of Japan Gerrard Winstanley: "The Law of Freedom in a Platform"
1653	Ferdinand IV becomes King of the Romans (—1654) End of Fronde The "Great Elector" abolishes the estates; establishes a standing army Oliver Cromwell becomes Lord Protector English defeat Dutch off Portland, North Foreland, and Texel Peasants' revolt in Bern under Nikolaus Leuenberg	Chetham's Library, Manchester, founded; named after rich manufacturer Humfrey Chetham (1580—1653) Molière: "L'Etourdi," comedy	James Naylor (1618—1660), Eng. Quaker, recognized by some as the new Messiah Blaise Pascal joins the Jansenists at Port-Royal "The London Polyglot Bible," (in 10 languages), ed. by Brian Walton (—1657)
1654	Treaty of Westminster ends Anglo-Dutch war; Dutch recognize Navigation Act Treaty of Commerce between England and Sweden Queen Christina of Sweden abdicates on becoming a Roman Catholic; succeeded by her cousin Charles X (—1660) Coronation of Louis XIV at Rheims Axel Oxenstierna, Swed. statesman, d. (b. 1575) First Eng. Protectorate Parliament meets War between Russia and Poland; Czar Alexis takes Smolensk Portuguese finally drive Dutch out of Brazil	Augustin Moreto y Cabaña (1618—1669): "El desdén con el desdén" ("Donna Diana"), Span. comedy George Chapman: "Revenge for Honour," tragedy Savinien Cyrano de Bergerac: "Le Pedant joué," comedy Madeleine de Scudéry: "Clélie," "histoire romaine" Molière: "Le Dépit amoureux," comedy Joost van den Vondel: "Lucifer," drama John Webster: "Appius and Virginia," tragedy	Johann Amos Comenius publishes in Nuremberg first picture book for children, "Orbis sensualium pictus" John Milton: "Defensio secunda"

D. VISUAL ARTS	E. MUSIC	F. SCIENCE, TECHNOLOGY, GROWTH	G. DAILY LIFE	
Balthasar Permoser, Ger. sculptor, b. (d. 1732) Paulus Potter: "Landscape with Cows" Rembrandt: "Girl with a Broom" Teniers: "Village Feast"	Heinrich Albert, Ger. composer, d. (b. 1604) The young King Louis XIV of France appears as a dancer in a court ballet	Dutch settle at Cape of Good Hope Mazarin's library closed by order of the Parlement Ital. astronomer Giovanni Riccioli introduces in his map of the moon many of the modern names of lunar features	Nell Gwyn, Eng. actress, b. (d. 1687) Division of publisher and printer begins in book trade	**1651**
Carel Fabritius: "View of Delft" Inigo Jones, Eng. architect, d. (b. 1573) Adriaen van Ostade: "Cottage Dancers" Rembrandt: "Portrait of Hendrickje"	John Hilton: "Catch As Catch Can," collection of catches, rounds, and canons The minuet comes into fashion at Fr. court First opera house in Vienna	Imperial Ger. Academy of Naturalists founded at Schweinfurt (moved to Halle in 1878) Casper Thomeson Bartholin, Dan. anatomist, b. (d. 1738) Ger. scientist Otto von Guericke (1602—1686) invents the air pump	First London coffee house opened in St. Michael's Alley, Cornhill William Byrd I, Virginia planter, b. (d. 1704)	**1652**
Francesco Borromini: S. Agnese in Agone, Rome Simon de Vlieger, Dutch painter of seascapes, d. (b. 1601) Peter Lely: "Oliver Cromwell" Jacob van Ruisdael: "Schloss Bentheim" Gerard Terborch: "The Dispatch" Jan van Goyen: "View of the Rhine"	Arcangelo Corelli, Ital. composer, b. (d. 1713) Matthew Locke's music for James Shirley's masque, "Cupid and Death" Lully made director of "les petits-violins du roi" Johann Pachelbel, Ger. composer and organist, b. (d. 1706)	Théophraste Renaudot, Fr. physician and philanthropist, d. (b. 1568) "Armamentarium chirurgicum," work of Ger. surgeon Johann Schultes (1595—1645) on surgical instruments and procedures (posth.) Izaak Walton: "The Compleat Angler" (—1676)	First letter boxes in Paris	**1653**
Pieter de Hooch: "Delft after the Explosion" Carel Fabritius: "The Linnet" Jean Lemercier, Fr. architect, d. (b. 1585) Rembrandt: "Portrait of Jan Six" John Webb (1611—1672): Lamport Hall, Northamptonshire, England	Samuel Scheidt, Ger. composer and organist, d. (b. 1587)	Jacques Bernoulli, Swiss mathematician, b. (d. 1705) Blaise Pascal and Pierre de Fermat state the theory of probability	Entailor, fee tail, after Span. model, introduced in Germany; signifies an interest in land, bound up inalienably forever in the grantee and his direct descendants	**1654**

	A. HISTORY, POLITICS	B. LITERATURE, THEATER	C. RELIGION, PHILOSOPHY, LEARNING
1655	Cromwell dissolves Parliament and divides England into 11 districts, each with a major-general as governor; prohibits Anglican services English capture Jamaica Charles X of Sweden invades Poland and the "Great Elector" invades Prussia: outbreak of first Northern War; Swed. army takes Warsaw and Cracow	John Cotgrave: "The English Treasury of Literature and Language" Savinien Cyrano de Bergerac, Fr. poet, d. (b. 1619) Daniel Heinsius, Dutch author, d. (b. 1580) James Shirley: "The Gentleman of Venice," tragicomedy William Strode: "The Floating Island," political drama	Pierre Borel: "Trésor des recherches et antiquités Gauloises" Oliver Cromwell readmits Jews into England William Drummond: "A History of the Five Jameses" (posth.) Thomas Fuller: "Church History of Britain" Pierre Gassendi, Fr. philosopher and scientist, d. (b. 1592) Thomas Hobbes: "Elementorum philosophiae" Pope Innocent X d.; Fabio Chigi (b. 1599) becomes Pope Alexander VII (—1667) Thomas Stanley: "A History of Philosophy" (vol. 1; 2, 1656; 3, 1660; 4, 1662; collected, 1687) Christian Thomasius, Ger. philosopher, b. (d. 1728)
1656	Treaty of Königsberg and Alliance of Marienberg between Sweden and Brandenburg Second Protectorate Parliament (—June 1657) Swedes cede Prussia to the "Great Elector" Dutch take Colombo from Portuguese King John IV of Portugal d.; succeeded by his son Alfonso VI Albanian Mohammed Kiuprili becomes grand vizier to Sultan Mohammed IV of Turkey	Jean Chapelain: "La Pucelle d'Orléans," poem Abraham Cowley: "Poems" John Ford: "The Sun's Darling," masque (posth.)	Manasseh ben Israel: "Vindiciae Judaeorum," reply to attacks on Cromwell's readmission of Jews John Bunyan: "Some Gospel Truths Opened" Marchamont Needham (1620—1678): "The Excellency of a Free State" Blaise Pascal: "Lettres provinciales," against Jesuits Spinoza excommunicated
1657	Emperor Ferdinand III d.; his son Leopold I succeeds him (—1705) Oliver Cromwell rejects offer of title "king" Creation of new House of Lords increases Cromwell's power The future King Frederick I of Prussia b. (d. 1713) Denmark attacks Charles X of Sweden, already involved in wars with Russia, Poland, and Austria Treaty of Bromberg: Brandenburg allied with Poland against Sweden	Bernard de Fontenelle, Fr. author, b. (d. 1757) John Dennis, Eng. dramatist and critic, b. (d. 1734) Andreas Gryphius: "Herr Peter Squentz," comedy based on Shakespeare's "A Midsummer Night's Dream" François Hédelin: "Practique du théâtre" Thomas Middleton: "No Wit Like a Woman," comedy Angelus Silesius: "Sinn- und Schlussreime" (—1674), with additions called "Der Cherubinische Wandersmann," all being mystical writings Savinien Cyrano de Bergerac: "Les Etats et empires de la lune," pretended trip to the moon (posth.)	Richard Baxter: "A Call to the Unconverted" Johann Amos Comenius: "Opera didactice omnia" Le Sieur Saunier: "L'encyclopédie des beaux esprits," believed to be first reference book with "encyclopédie" in title

D. VISUAL ARTS	E. MUSIC	F. SCIENCE, TECHNOLOGY, GROWTH	G. DAILY LIFE	
Jordaens: "Presentation in the Temple" Rembrandt: "Woman Bathing in a Stream"	Sigmund Gottlieb Staden, Ger. composer and organist, d. (b. 1607)	Chin. scientist and naturalist Ch'en yüan-lung publishes "Ko-chih-ching-yüan," on new inventions	First regular newspaper in Berlin	**1655**
Academy of Painting in Rome founded Bernini: Piazza of St. Peter's, Rome André Le Nôtre designs the gardens at Vaux-le-Viscomte (—1661) Rembrandt declared bankrupt; his possessions are put up for sale Jan van Goyen, Dutch painter, d. (b. 1596) Velázquez: "Las Meninas," family of Philip IV Vermeer: "The Procuress" Johann Bernhard Fischer von Erlach, Aust. architect, b. (d. 1723)	Opening of first London opera house "The Siege of Rhodes," opera with music by Matthew Locke and others, given at Rutland House, London	Edmund Halley, Eng. astronomer, b. (d. 1742) Thomas Wharton (1614—1673) describes anatomy of glands	Regiment of grenadier guards formed Hôpital général, Paris, opens, combining hospital, poorhouse, and factory	**1656**
Rembrandt: Portrait of his son Titus Frans Snyders, Dutch painter, d. (b. 1579) Velázquez: "Las Hilanderas" ("The Spinners")	Michel de Lalande, Fr. composer and organist, b. (d. 1726) Adam Krieger: "Deutsche Lieder"	Accademia del Cimento founded in Florence by Vincenzo Viviani (1622—1705) Dutch scientist Christiann Huygens (1629—1695) designs first pendulum for clocks	Manasseh ben Israel, Jewish leader, d. (b. 1604) Drinking chocolate introduced in London First stockings and fountain pens manufactured in Paris	**1657**

	A. HISTORY, POLITICS	B. LITERATURE, THEATER	C. RELIGION, PHILOSOPHY, LEARNING
1658	Cromwell dissolves Parliament Treaty of Roskilde between Sweden and Denmark ends first war Aurangzeb (1618—1707) imprisons his father, Shah Jahan, and succeeds him as Mogul Emperor Charles X begins Second Northern War; siege of Copenhagen Oliver Cromwell d. (b. 1599); succeeded as Lord Protector by his son Richard (—1659) Leopold I elected Holy Roman Emperor (—1705) Formation of Rhenish League under Fr. protectorate	John Dryden: "Heroic Stanzas," on Cromwell's death Richard Lovelace, Eng. poet, d. (b. 1618) Philip Massinger: "The City Madam," comedy William Rowley: "The Witch of Edmonton," tragicomedy Georg Stiernhielm: "Hercules," Swed. epic poem	Sir William Dugdale: "History of St. Paul's Cathedral" James Harrington: "The Prerogative of Popular Government" Edward Phillips: "A New World of Words" Société des missions étrangères founded in Paris
1659	Derby petition for permanent settlement of the constitutional crisis between army and Parliament Richard Cromwell resigns Peace of the Pyrenees between France and Spain The "Great Elector" drives Swedes out of Prussia	Corneille: "Oedipe," tragedy John Day: "The Blind Beggar of Bethnal Green," drama Molière: "Les Précieuses ridicules," comedy Joost van den Vondel: "Jephta," tragedy	Henry More: "The Immortality of the Soul" William Somner: "Dictionarium Saxonico-Latino-Anglicum"
1660	Charles X of Sweden d.; succeeded by Charles XI (—1697) Virginia proclaims Charles II king; restores Governor William Berkeley Parliament invites Charles II to return to England Peace of Oliva signed, ending war between Austria, Poland, Sweden, and Brandenburg, and recognizing the "Great Elector's" sovereignty in E. Prussia The future Eng. King George I b. (d. 1727) Charles II enters London Peace of Copenhagen ends war between Sweden and Denmark Louis XIV of France marries Maria Teresa, Infanta of Spain George Rákoczy II, Prince of Transylvania, dies in battle against Turks; Emperor Leopold I sends army to check Turk. advance Dan. crown becomes hereditary Long Parliament dissolves itself	Actresses on Ger. and Eng. stages Jacob Cats, Dutch poet, d. (b. 1577) Corneille: "La Toison d'or," tragedy John Dryden: "Astraea Redux" Patents granted for reopening of London theaters (see 1642) Molière: "Sganarelle" Samuel Pepys begins his "Diary" (Jan. 1) (—1669) Paul Scarron, Fr. author, d. (b. 1610)	James Harrington: "Political Discourses" James Howell: "Lexicon Tetraglotten," Eng.-Fr.-Ital.-Span. dictionary
1661	Cardinal Mazarin d.; Louis XIV begins his personal rule Philip, Duke of Orleans, marries Henrietta, sister of Charles II Coronation of Charles II Peace of Kardis between Russia and Sweden ends Northern War "Cavalier Parliament" meets (—1678) Charles II receives Tangier, Bombay, and £300,000 from Portugal as dowry of Catherine of Braganza (see 1662) Jean Baptiste Colbert (1619—1683) becomes Fr. Minister of Finance (—1683); Fr. revenue shows deficit of 22 million francs Famine in India; no rain since 1659 Mohammed Kiuprili, Grand Vizier of Turkey, d.; succeeded by his son Ahmed Kiuprili (—1676)	Sir William Davenant, poet and dramatist (1606—1668), opens Lincoln's Inn Theatre, London (first to have a proscenium arch) with "Hamlet" Daniel Defoe, Eng. author, b. (d. 1731) Molière: "L'Ecole des maris" and "Les Fâcheux"	John Eliot (1604—1690) translates the Bible into Algonquin (first Amer. Bible edition) Joseph Glanvill: "The Vanity of Dogmatizing"

D. VISUAL ARTS	E. MUSIC	F. SCIENCE, TECHNOLOGY, GROWTH	G. DAILY LIFE	
Bernini: church at Castel Gandolfo (—1661) Pieter de Hooch: "Courtyard of a House in Delft" Peter Lely: "The Family of the Earl of Carnarvon" Adriaen van de Velde: "Farm with a Dead Tree"	Johann Caspar von Kerll (1627—1693): "Applausi Festivi," opera, Munich	Fr. physician Sylvius de la Boé (1614—1672) becomes professor of medicine in Leiden J. R. Glauber: "De natura salium" Jan Swammerdam (1637—1680) first observes red blood corpuscles Robert Hooke (1635—1703), naturalist and philosopher, invents the balance spring for watches	Eng. physician Sir Thomas Browne (1605—1682) advocates cremation Swed. financier Johann Palmstruck devises first bank note, issued by the Swed. state bank	**1658**
Velázquez: "Infante Philip Prosper," "Infanta Maria Teresa" Vermeer: "Young Girl with Flute"	Henry Purcell, Eng. composer, b. (d. 1695) Alessandro Scarlatti, Ital. composer, b. (d. 1725)	Pierre Esprit Radisson and Médart Chouart de Grosellier reach Minnesota, southwest of Lake Superior Eng. physician Thomas Willis (1621—1675) describes first typhoid fever	Prussian State Library, Berlin, founded	**1659**
Palace of Potsdam built (—1682) Jan Steen: "Poultry Yard" Velázquez d. (b. 1599) Vermeer: "The Cook" Zurbarán: "The Young Virgin"	Cavalli: "Serse," opera for the marriage of Louis XIV Johann Joseph Fux, Aust. composer and music theorist, b. (d. 1741)	Dutch peasants (Boers) settle in S. Africa Royal African Company founded	Famous "Café Procope" opens in Paris Friedrich Staedtler founds pencil factory in Nuremberg Water closets arrive from France in England	**1660**
Peter Lely made court painter to Charles II Louis Le Vau: Galerie d'Apollon, Louvre, Paris Rembrandt: "The Syndics of the Cloth Hall" Jacob van Ruisdael: "Landscape with Watermill" Jan Steen: "Easy Come, Easy Go"	Académie Royale de Danse founded by Louis XIV Matthew Locke (1603—1677) made court composer to Charles II Edward Lowe: "Short Direction for the Performance of Cathedral Services," to revive organ accompaniment, suppressed during Commonwealth	Robert Boyle (1627—1691): "The Skeptical Chymist," with definition of chemical elements Christian Huyghens invents the manometer for ascertaining elastic force of gases	John Evelyn (1620—1706): "Fumifugium, or The Inconvenience of the Air and Smoke of London Dissipated," an early attack on air pollution Kongelige Bibliothek, Copenhagen, founded Georg Praetorius: "Ludicrum chiromanticum," treatise on palmistry	**1661**

	A. HISTORY, POLITICS	B. LITERATURE, THEATER	C. RELIGION, PHILOSOPHY, LEARNING
1662	Elizabeth of Bohemia, "the Winter Queen," d. (b. 1596) Connecticut granted a liberal charter The future Mary II, Queen of England, wife of William III, b. Charles II marries Catherine of Braganza, daughter of King John IV of Portugal (see 1661) Charles II sells Dunkirk to France for £400,000 Shun Chih, first Manchu Emperor of China, d.; succeeded by his son K'ang-hsi (at eight) (—1722)	Samuel Butler: "Hudibras," Part 1 Marie Madeleine de La Fayette: "La Princesse de Montpensier," novel Molière: "L'Ecole des femmes," comedy First edition of "Poor Robin's Almanac" Michael Wigglesworth: "The Day of Doom"	Act of Uniformity gives assent to revised Eng. prayer book Thomas Fuller: "The Worthies of England," biographical reference work (posth.) Blaise Pascal, Fr. philosopher, d. (b. 1623)
1663	Charles II grants charters to Royal African Company and to eight proprietors of N. Carolina and Rhode Island Turks declare War on Holy Roman Empire, invade Transylvania and Hungary, overrun the fortress of Nové Zamky, Slovakia Prince Eugene of Savoy b. (d. 1736) Colbert forms N. Amer. colony of New France into a province with Quebec as capital	Colbert founds Académie des Inscriptions et Belles Lettres in Paris Samuel Butler: "Hudibras," Part 2 Abraham Cowley: "The Cutter of Coleman Street," comedy Sir William Davenant: "The Siege of Rhodes" The Theatre Royal, Drury Lane, London, opens Third Folio of Shakespeare's works	Robert Boyle: "Concerning the Usefulness of Experimental Philosophy" Lord Herbert of Cherbury: "De religione gentilium" (posth.) Writings of Descartes put on the Index Leibniz: "De principiis individui" Pascal: "L'Equilibre des liqueurs" (posth.) Cotton Mather, Massachusetts writer and witch hunter, b. (d. 1728)
1664	Alliance between France and Brandenburg Truce of Vasvar, after Austrians defeat Turks at St. Gotthard on Raab River British annex New Netherlands from Connecticut to Delaware and rename New Amsterdam (which had surrendered under Peter Stuyvesant) New York Fort Orange surrenders to Britain and is renamed Albany Union of Connecticut and New Haven Swed. colonies on Gold Coast sold to Dutch	Dryden: "The Rival Ladies," tragicomedy Sir George Etherege: "The Comical Revenge, or Love in a Tub," comedy Andreas Gryphius, Ger. dramatist, d. (b. 1616) Molière: "Le Tartuffe" Matthew Prior, Eng. poet, b. (d. 1721) Racine: "La Thébaïde" Miklós Zrinyi, Hungarian poet and patriot, d. (b. 1620)	Conventicle Act, against Nonconformists, forbids meetings of more than five people John Evelyn: "Sylva" The Trappist Order founded at La Trappe, Normandy, by Armand de Rancé
1665	Anne, future Queen of Great Britain, b. (d. 1714) Allied British and Portuguese defeat Span. army at Montes Claros and Villa Viciosa, securing independence of Portugal Philip IV of Spain d.; succeeded by his son Charles II (—1700) Absolutism introduced into Denmark by Lex Regia Eng. law and administration introduced into New York	Samuel Coster, Dutch dramatist, d. (b. 1579) Pierre de Brantôme (1540—1614): "Les Dames galantes" (posth.) Richard Head: "The English Rogue," picaresque novel "Journal des Savants," first literary periodical, started in Paris Jean de La Fontaine: "Contes et Nouvelles en verse" (—1674) La Rochefoucauld: "Maximes" Molière: "Don Juan," tragicomedy Racine: "Alexandre le Grand"	John Bunyan: "The Holy City" "Codex Theodosianus," ed. by Jacques Godefroy John Eliot: "Communion of Churches," privately printed at Harvard, Mass. Five-Mile Act puts restrictions on Nonconformist ministers "Philosophical Transactions," first scientific journal in England Izaak Walton: "The Life of Richard Hooker"

D. VISUAL ARTS	E. MUSIC	F. SCIENCE, TECHNOLOGY, GROWTH	G. DAILY LIFE	
André Le Nôtre designs park and gardens of Versailles Louis XIV begins to build palace of Versailles; he makes Charles Lebrun (1619—1690) his chief artistic adviser Mattheus Daniel Pöppelmann, Ger. architect, b. (d. 1736)	Cavalli: "Ercole amante," Ital. ballet opera (given in Paris)	Founding of the Academia Leopoldina in Vienna The Royal Society receives charter from Charles II	Last silver pennies minted in London	**1662**
Bernini: Scala Regia, Vatican, Rome Pieter de Hooch: "At the Linen Closet" Building of Castle Nymphenburg, near Munich (—1728) Poussin: "The Four Seasons" Adriaen van de Velde: "Cattle near a Building"	Marc' Antonio Cesti: "La Dori," Ital. opera James Clifford (1622—1698): "The Divine Services and Anthems," first collection of words of anthems published in London Lully: "Le Ballet des arts"	Guericke constructs a frictional electrical machine John Newton (1622—1678) discovers the binomial theorem Dan. physician Nicolaus Steno (1638—1687) teaches, "The heart is a muscle"	"Europäische Zeitung" published in Copenhagen First gold guinea pieces coined in England Hearth tax in England Journalist Roger L'Estrange (1616—1704) becomes licenser of the Eng. press Turnpike tolls introduced in England Robert ("King") Carter, powerful Virginia planter, b. (d. 1732); ancestor of six presidents of the U.S.	**1663**
Pieter de Hooch: "Young Woman Weighing Gold" Poussin: "Apollo and Daphne" Andreas Schlüter, Ger. architect, b. (d. 1714) Jan Steen: "The Christening Feast" John Vanbrugh, Eng. architect and dramatist, b. (d. 1726) Vermeer: "The Lacemaker" Christopher Wren: Sheldonian Theatre, Oxford (—1669) Francisco de Zurbarán, Span. painter, d. (b. 1598)	French horn becomes an orchestral instrument Heinrich Schütz: "Christmas Oratorio," Dresden	Thomas Willis: "Cerebri anatome," on the nervous system	Fr. furniture prevails in European palaces and castles "Compagnie des Indes Occidentales" formed to control Fr. trade in Canada, S. America, W. Africa, and W. Indies Introduction of large periwig style First Royal Marine Regiment	**1664**
Bernini finishes high altar, St. Peter's, Rome (begun 1656) Murillo: "Rest on the Flight into Egypt" (—1670) Nicolas Poussin d. (b. 1593) Rembrandt: "The Jewish Bride" Adriaen van Ostade: "The Physician in His Study" Vermeer: "The Artist's Studio"	Giuseppe Aldrovandini, Ital. composer, b. (d. 1707) Heinrich Schütz: "Johannes Passion"	Giovanni Cassini determines rotations of Jupiter, Mars, and Venus Peter Chamberlen (1601—1683), court physician to Charles II, invents midwifery forceps Pierre de Fermat, Fr. mathematician, d. (b. 1601) Francis Grimaldi: "Physico-mathesis de lumine" (posth.) explains diffraction of light Robert Hooke: "Micrographia," on the microscope University of Kiel founded Colony of New Jersey founded Isaac Newton experiments on gravitation; invents differential calculus	First modern census taken in Quebec Caleb Cheeshateaumuck, first N. Amer. Indian to take an A.B. degree at Harvard First issue of the "London Gazette" The Prince Archbishop of Münster sells 7,000 of his subjects as soldiers The Great Plague of London begins (July—Oct.), killing 68,596 First known turf race in New York	**1665**

	A. HISTORY, POLITICS	B. LITERATURE, THEATER	C. RELIGION, PHILOSOPHY, LEARNING
1666	France and the Dutch declare war on England; Dutch sign treaty of alliance with the "Great Elector" Quadruple alliance between Holland, Brandenburg, Brunswick, and Denmark to secure safety of Holland Treaty of Cleves between Brandenburg and Neuburg for partition of Jülich-Cleves Eng. privateers take Tobago French capture Antigua, Montserrat, and St. Christopher Hungarian noblemen revolt against Emperor Leopold I	Collection of Lat. plays–"Ludi theatrales sacri"–by Aust. Jesuit dramatist Jakob Bidermann (1578–1639), published (posth.) Dryden: "Annus Mirabilis" Molière: "Le Misanthrope"	First Armenian Bible printed John Bunyan: "Grace Abounding to the Chief of Sinners" Leibniz: "De arte combinatoria" "Raskol" (Great Schism) breaks out in Russ. Church John Tillotson: "The Rule of Faith"
1667	Truce of Andrusovo ends 13-year war between Russia and Poland; Kiev ceded to Russia Secret treaty between Louis XIV and Charles II against Spain War of Devolution begins as Fr. troops invade Netherlands Shah Abbas II of Persia d. (b. 1642); succeeded by his son Suleiman (—1694) Alfonso VI of Portugal banished to the Azores by his brother Pedro, the regent Anne of Austria, mother of Louis XIV, d. (b. 1602) Peace of Breda between the Dutch, France, and England	John Arbuthnot, Eng. satirist, b. (d. 1745) Abraham Cowley, Eng. dramatist, d. (b. 1618) Milton: "Paradise Lost" (—1674) Racine: "Andromaque" Jonathan Swift, Eng. author, b. (d. 1745) George Wither, Eng. poet, d. (b. 1588)	Pope Alexander VII d.; Giulio Rospigliosi becomes Pope Clement IX (—1670) Fr. jurist Guillaume Lamoignon (1617—1677) compiles the Code Louis Leibniz: "Nova methodus discendique juris" Samuel Pufendorf: "De statu republicae Germanicae," attack on the Hapsburgs
1668	Alliance of the Hague signed by English and Dutch Treaty of Lisbon: Spain recognizes independence of Portugal Brit. East India Company obtains control of Bombay Peace of Aix-la-Chapelle ends War of Devolution between France and Spain John II Casimir, King of Poland since 1648, abdicates Government of Maine passes to Massachusetts Treaty between Louis XIV and Leopold I concerning future partition of Span. realms	Aphra Behn: "Oroonoko," novel Sir William Davenant, Eng. poet and dramatist, d. (b. 1606) Dryden: "Sir Martin Mar-All," comedy Sir George Etherege: "She Wou'd If She Cou'd," comedy La Fontaine: "Fables choisies mises en vers" Alain René Lesage, Fr. dramatist and novelist, b. (d. 1747) Molière: "L'Avare," "Amphitryon," "George Dandin" Racine: "Les Plaideurs"	Joseph Glanvill: "Plus ultra, or Progress of Knowledge since Aristotle" Henry More: "Divine Dialogues" William Penn: "Sandy Foundation Shaken," questions the doctrine of the Trinity Giovanni Battista Vico, Ital. philosopher, b. (d. 1744)
1669	Michael Wisniowiecki, a Lithuanian, elected King of Poland (—1673) John Locke's constitution for Carolina approved; S. Carolina founded Venetians lose Crete, their last colonial possession, to the Turks Aurangzeb bans Hindu religion in India Last meeting of the Hanseatic League	Sir John Denham, Eng. poet, d. (b. 1615) Dryden: "The Wild Gallant," comedy Molière: "Monsieur de Pourceaugnac" Johann Michael Moscherosch, Ger. satirist, d. (b. 1601) Last entry in Samuel Pepys' "Diary" (May 31) (begun 1660) Racine: "Britannicus," tragedy Johann Jakob Christoph von Grimmelshausen: "Simplicius Simplicissimus," Ger. novel of adventure and spiritual quest	Pope Clement IX d. (see 1670) Arnold Geulincx, Dutch philosopher, d. (b. 1624) William Penn: "No Cross, No Crown" Abraham a Sancta Clara made court preacher in Vienna

D. VISUAL ARTS	E. MUSIC	F. SCIENCE, TECHNOLOGY, GROWTH	G. DAILY LIFE	
Frans Hals, Dutch painter, d. (b. 1580) François Mansart, Fr. architect, d. (b. 1598)	Marc' Antonio Cesti made court Kapellmeister in Vienna Adam Krieger, Ger. composer, d. (b. 1634) Heinrich Schütz: "Historia des Leidens und Sterbens unsers Herrens Jesu Christi" Antonio Stradivari (1644—1737) labels his first violin	Isaac Newton measures the moon's orbit Puritans from Connecticut settle in Newark, N.J.	First Cheddar cheese Great Fire of London, Sept. 2–6 Gobelin workshops established in Paris by Colbert Cricket Club founded at St. Alban's, Hertfordshire, England	**1666**
Gabriel Boffrand, Fr. architect, b. (d. 1754) Francesco Borromini, Ital. sculptor and architect, d. (b. 1599) Alonso Cano, Span. painter and architect, d. (b. 1601) Gabriel Metsu, Dutch painter, d. (b. 1629) Mexico Cathedral finished (begun 1573)	Johann Jakob Froberger, Ger. composer, d. (b. 1616) Carlo Pallavicino (1630—1688) becomes court Kapellmeister in Dresden	"Abrégé chronologique" by Fr. historian F. E. de Mézeray (1610—1683) National Observatory, Paris, founded Thomas Sprat: "Early History of the Royal Society"	Jean Baptiste Colbert founds the Manufacture Royale des Meubles de la Couronne Feltmakers' Company, London, incorporated Fr. army uses hand grenades	**1667**
Rembrandt: "Return of the Prodigal Son" Gabriel van de Velde: "Golfers on the Ice" Johann Lukas von Hildebrandt, Aust. architect, b. (d. 1745) Philips Wouwerman, Dutch painter, d. (b. 1619)	Dietrich Buxtehude becomes organist of St. Mary's, Lübeck François Couperin, Fr. composer, b. (d. 1733) Thomas Tomkins (1572—1656): "Musica Deo sacra" (posth.)	Sir Josiah Child (1630—1699): "Brief Observations Concerning Trade and the Interest of Money" Johann Rudolf Glauber, Ger. scientist, d. (b. 1604) Robert Hooke: "Discourse on Earthquakes" Isaac Newton constructs reflecting telescope First accurate description of red corpuscles by Antony van Leeuwenhoek	Oder—Spree Canal finished (begun 1661)	**1668**
Le Vau begins remodeling Versailles Rembrandt d. (b. 1606) Vermeer: "Girl at the Spinet"	Royal patent for founding Académie Royale des Opéras granted to Pierre Perrin (1620—1675) Marc' Antonio Cesti, Ital. composer, d. (b. 1623) Matthew Locke: "The Treasury of Musick"	Edmund Castell: "Lexicon Heptaglotton" Ital. anatomist Marcello Malpighi (1628—1694) studies the life and activity of silkworms Phosphorus prepared for first time by alchemist Hennig Brand of Hamburg Nicolaus Steno (1638—1687) begins the modern study of geology Jan Swammerdam: "History of the Insects"	Outbreak of cholera in China Earliest Fr. trading station in India	**1669**

	A. HISTORY, POLITICS	B. LITERATURE, THEATER	C. RELIGION, PHILOSOPHY, LEARNING
1670	Defensive alliance between France and Bavaria Augustus II, future Elector of Saxony and King of Poland, b. (d. 1733) Treaty of Dover between England and France France occupies Lorraine Frederick III, King of Denmark, d.; succeeded by Christian V (—1699) Rebellion of Ukrainian Cossacks crushed by Jan Sobieski William of Orange made Cap.-Gen. of United Provinces	William Congreve, Eng. dramatist, b. (d. 1729) Corneille: "Tite et Bérénice," tragedy Dryden: "The Conquest of Granada," heroic play Molière: "Le Bourgeois Gentilhomme," ballet-comedy Racine: "Bérénice," tragedy John Dryden appointed historiographer royal and poet laureate First Ital. "commedia dell'arte" companies appear in Germany	Cardinal Emilio Altieri (b. 1590) becomes Pope Clement X (—1676) Johann Amos Comenius, Czech school reformer, d. (b. 1592) John Milton: "The Historie of Britain" Pascal: "Pensées" (posth.) John Ray: "A Collection of English Proverbs" Spinoza: "Tractatus theologico-politicus"
1671	Turks declare war on Poland Stenka Razin, leader of Cossack and peasant rebellion in Don and Volga region, executed Former buccaneer Sir Henry Morgan (1635—1688) made deputy governor of Jamaica by Charles II Philip of Orleans, brother of Louis XIV, marries Princess Liselotte, heiress to the Palatinate	Aphra Behn: "The Forced Marriage," drama Colley Cibber, Eng. actor and dramatist, b. (d. 1757) Marquise de Sévigné (1626—1696) begins writing her famous letters on Fr. court life to her daughter, Mme. de Grignan (published 1726) Milton: "Paradise Regained," "Samson Agonistes" Molière: "Les Fourberies de Scapin," comedy	First Bible edition in Arabic, printed in Rome John Bunyan: "A Confession of My Faith" 3rd Earl of Shaftesbury, Eng. philosopher, b. (d. 1713) Stephen Skinner: "Etymologicon linguae anglicanae"
1672	Stop of Eng. exchequer; cash payments suspended for 12 months Declaration of Indulgence issued by Charles II; withdrawn, 1673 Britain declares war on the Dutch; indecisive naval battle at Southwold Bay Czar Peter the Great b. (d. 1725) France declares war on the Dutch; Fr. army crosses Rhine; Dutch sluices opened to save Amsterdam; Louis XIV rejects Dutch peace offer; William of Orange made Cap.-Gen. of United Provinces	Joseph Addison, Eng. poet and essayist, b. (d. 1719) Clarendon Press, official printers of Oxford University, founded Molière: "Les Femmes savantes" Racine: "Bajazet," tragedy Richard Steele, Ir. journalist and essayist, b. (d. 1729) Georg Stiernhielm, Swed. poet, d. (b. 1598) George Villiers, 2nd Duke of Buckingham: "The Rehearsal," burlesque on Dryden's "Conquest of Granada" William Wycherley: "Love in a Wood," comedy	Elias Ashmole: "Institutions, Laws, Ceremonies of the Order of the Garter" William Cave: "Primitive Christianity" Confessions of faith of the Greek Orthodox Church revived by the Synod of Jerusalem William Temple: "Observations upon the United Provinces of the Netherlands"
1673	Test Act excludes Roman Catholics from office in England After preliminary peace between Brandenburg and France the "Great Elector" promises, in Treaty of Vossen, not to support any enemies of Louis XIV Emperor Leopold I declares war on France King Michael of Poland d.; the next day Pol. army under Jan Sobieski defeats Turks at Khorzim Founding of Fort Frontenac, Robert de La Salle its commander Fr. expedition against Ceylon	Aphra Behn: "The Dutch Lover," comedy Dryden: "Marriage à la mode," comedy Molière d., shortly after presentation of his "Malade imaginaire" (b. 1622) Racine: "Mithridate" Thomas Shadwell: "Epsom Wells," comedy William Wycherley: "The Gentleman Dancing Master," comedy Robert Clavel: "Catalogue of All the Books Printed in England Since the Dreadful Fire of London in 1666"	Archpriest Petrovich Avvakum (1620—1682) writes his "Zhitie" (Life), first Russ. autobiography

D. VISUAL ARTS	E. MUSIC	F. SCIENCE, TECHNOLOGY, GROWTH	G. DAILY LIFE	
Louis Le Vau, Fr. architect, d. (b. 1612) Jacob van Ruisdael: "Haarlem" Vermeer: "The Pearl Necklace"	John Blow (1648—1708) organist of Westminster Abbey (—1680)	Paul Amman: "Medicina critica" Ital. scientist Giovanni Borelli (1608—1679) attempts to use artificial wings for flying Eng. settlement in Charles Town (Charleston), S. C. Eng. physician Thomas Willis (1621—1675) describes for first time typical symptoms of diabetes	Hudson's Bay Company incorporated by royal charter to trade in region of N. America draining into Hudson Bay Louis XIV's Minister of War, the Marquis de Louvois (1641—1691), introduces uniforms and paper cartridges in Fr. army First minute hands on watches Tobacco monopoly in Austria	**1670**
Lionel Bruant: Hôtel des Invalides, Paris (—1675) Adriaen van Ostade: "Travelers Resting" Christopher Wren: The Monument (—1677) to commemorate the Great Fire of London in 1666	Paris Opéra opened with Robert Cambert's opera "Pomone" Francesco (son of Antonio) Stradivari, Ital. violin maker, b. (d. 1743)	William Carter: "England's Interest by Trade Asserted" Leibniz defines nature and existence of the ether	Eng. Crown resumes direct control of customs system, farmed since 1605 Founding of the Fr. Senegal Company Rob Roy, Scot. highwayman, b. (d. 1734)	**1671**
Fulham Pottery, London, founded by John Dwight Kao-ts'en: "Autumn Landscape," famous Chin. India-ink picture John Webb, Eng. architect, d. (b. 1611) Christopher Wren: St. Stephen's, Walbrook, London	First public concert at Whitefriars, London, given by violinist John Banister (1630—1679) Heinrich Schütz, Ger. composer, d. (b. 1585)	Root ipecacuanha introduced for medicinal purposes in Europe Flexible hose for use in fighting fires, constructed by Jan van der Heyde and his son John Josselyn: "New England's Rarities Discovered," on local flora and fauna Environments of Chicago, north of Missouri River, explored by Fr. missionary Jacques Marquette	"Mercure galant," a journal for light reading, begun by Jean Donneau de Vizé in Paris Charter granted to the Royal African Company	**1672**
Salvator Rosa, Span. painter, d. (b. 1615) Willem van de Velde: "Three Ships in a Gale" Adriaen van Ostade: "The Violin Player" Christopher Wren knighted	Buxtehude begins at Lübeck his famous "Abendmusiken" concerts Matthew Locke: "The Present Practice of Music Vindicated" Lully: "Cadmus et Hermione," opera, first given in Paris	University of Innsbruck founded Fr. explorers Jacques Marquette and Louis Joliet reach headwaters of Mississippi River and descend to Arkansas Stalactic grotto of Antiparos (Aegean Sea) discovered	Financier Richard Hoare (1648—1718) founds Hoare's Bank, London Mitsui family's trading and banking house in Japan founded	**1673**

	A. HISTORY, POLITICS	B. LITERATURE, THEATER	C. RELIGION, PHILOSOPHY, LEARNING
1674	Treaty of Westminster recognizes inhabitants of New York and New Sweden as Brit. subjects Jan Sobieski elected as Jan III, King of Poland (—1696) Fr. troops devastate the Palatinate Sivaji Bhonsla (1627—1680) declares himself independent of the Mogul Emperor Aurangzeb; founds Mahratta state and is crowned at Raigarh Office of Stadholder of the United Provinces becomes hereditary in the House of Orange	Giovanni Battista Basile: "Il Pentamerone," tales Nicolas Boileau: "L'Art poétique" Jean Chapelain, Fr. poet, d. (b. 1585) Prosper Jolyot de Crébillon, Fr. dramatist, b. (d. 1762) Lars Johansson, Swed. poet, d. (b. 1638) Milton: "Paradise Lost," 2nd edition John Milton d. (b. 1608) Racine: "Iphigénie en Aulide" Theatre Royal, Drury Lane, London, rebuilt after the fire and reopened Thomas Traherne, Eng. poet, d. (b. 1638)	Anthony à Wood: "Historia et antiquitates universitatis Oxoniensis" Nicolas Malebranche: "De la recherche de la vérité" Louis Moreri: "Le Grand Dictionnaire historique," first encyclopedic reference work on history Isaac Watts, Eng. hymn writer, b. (d. 1748)
1675	Alliance between France and Poland The "Great Elector" defeats Swed. army decisively at Fehrbellin War between Sweden and Denmark Charles II of England receives 500,000 crowns from Louis XIV and is able to prorogue Eng. Parliament for 15 months King Charles II of Spain attains majority	Poems of Basho (pseudonym of Matsuo Munefusa) (1644—1694) help popularize Jap. haiku poetry William Wycherley: "The Country Wife," comedy	Sir William Dugdale: "The Baronage of England" Jacques Savary (1622—1690): "Le Parfait Négociant" Philipp Jacob Spener: "Pia desideria" Spinoza finishes his "Ethics" (begun 1662) Thomas Traherne: "Christian Ethics" (posth.)
1676	Czar Alexis of Russia d.; succeeded by his son Feodor III (—1682) Robert Walpole, Eng. statesman, b. (d. 1745) Ahmed Kiuprili d.; succeeded as Grand Vizier of Turkey by his brother-in-law Kara Mustafa Dan. army defeated by Swedes at Battle of Lunden "Declaration of the People of Virginia" by Nathaniel Bacon (1642—1676) gains support for rebellion against authorities Francis II Rákóczy, future claimant of Transylvania, b. (d. 1732) Prince Leopold I of Anhalt-Dessau ("Der alte Dessauer"), organizer of Prussian army, b. (d. 1747) Settlement of boundary between Eastern and Western New Jersey	Dryden: "Aureng-Zebe," drama Sir George Etherege: "A Man of Mode," comedy Thomas Otway: "Don Carlos," tragedy Johann Jakob Christoph von Grimmelshausen, Ger. author, d. (b. 1625)	Pope Clement X d.; Benedetto Odescalchi becomes Pope Innocent XI (—1689) Paul Gerhardt, Ger. hymn writer, d. (b. 1607) Benjamin Thompson: "New England's Crisis" Roger Williams: "George Fox Digg'd Out of His Burrowes," anti-Quaker tract
1677	Duke of Orleans defeats Dutch at Cassel Combined Dutch-Dan. fleet defeats Swedes at Oland William III of Orange marries Princess Mary, daughter of the Duke of York The "Great Elector" takes Stettin and, later, Rügen Massachusetts buys part of Maine from heirs of Sir Ferdinando Gorges	Racine: "Phèdre," tragedy Angelus Silesius, Ger. mystic and poet, d. (b. 1624) William Wycherley: "The Plain Dealer," comedy	William Cave: "History of Martyrdoms" Johann Jacob Hofmann: "Lexicon Universale," on science and arts John Houghton: "England's Great Happiness, or A Dialogue between Content and Complaint" Increase Mather (1639—1723): "The Troubles That Have Happened in New England" Spinoza, Dutch-Jewish philosopher, d. (b. 1632)

D. VISUAL ARTS	E. MUSIC	F. SCIENCE, TECHNOLOGY, GROWTH	G. DAILY LIFE	
Philippe de Champaigne, Fr. painter, d. (b. 1602) Godfrey Kneller (1646—1723), Ger. portrait painter, arrives in England Murillo: "St. Francis"	Giacomo Carissimi, Ital. composer, d. (b. 1605) Reinhard Keiser, Ger. opera composer, b. (d. 1739) Lully: "Alceste," opera Paris	John Mayow: "Tractatus quinque medico-physici," on the nature of combustion Thomas Willis: "Pharmaceutice rationalis"	Richard ("Beau") Nash, Eng. dandy, b. (d. 1762) William Byrd II, rich Virginia planter and builder of Westover, b. (d. 1744)	**1674**
Jacob van Ruisdael: "Jewish Cemetery" Jan Vermeer of Delft, Dutch painter, d. (b. 1632) Sir Christopher Wren begins rebuilding St. Paul's Cathedral, London (—1710)	Andreas Hammerschmidt, Ger. church composer, d. (b. 1612) Matthew Locke: incidental music to Thomas Shadwell's "Psyche" Antonio Vivaldi, Ital. composer, b. (d. 1741)	Greenwich Observatory established under John Flamsteed (1646—1719) Leibniz invents differential and integral calculus Isaac Newton: "Opticks" Ger. astronomer Olaus Romer discovers the finite velocity of light	Paris becomes center of European culture, with approx. 0.5 million inhabitants (in 1800 approx. 650,000; in 1926 approx. 2.8 million)	**1675**
Godfrey Kneller: "Mr. Banks" Murillo: "Madonna purissima" Sir Christopher Wren: Trinity College Library, Cambridge (—1684)	Francesco Cavalli, Ital. opera composer, d. (b. 1602) Thomas Mace (1613—1709): "Musick's Monument"	Thomas Sydenham: "Observationes medicae"	Influenza epidemic in England "Le Grand Vatel," famous chef, commits suicide because a dinner that his master, the Prince de Condé, gives in honor of Louis XIV does not come up to the king's expectations Legal protection of Sabbath observance in England	**1676**
Pieter de Hooch: "Musical Party in a Courtyard" Wenceslaus Hollar, Anglo-Czech engraver, d. (b. 1607) Godfrey Kneller: "Mr. Vernon" Aert van der Neer, Dutch landscape painter, d. (b. 1603)	Robert Cambert, Fr. opera composer, d. (b. 1628) Lully: "Isis," opera	Isaac Barrow, Eng. mathematician, d. (b. 1630)	Ice cream becomes popular as dessert in Paris	**1677**

	A. HISTORY, POLITICS	B. LITERATURE, THEATER	C. RELIGION, PHILOSOPHY, LEARNING
1678	The future Emperor Joseph I b. (d. 1711) Peace of Nijmegen between France and the Dutch "Popish Plot" in England revealed; trials of many leading Roman Catholics Peace of Nijmegen between France and Spain The "Great Elector" takes Stralsund from the Swedes Roman Catholics in England excluded from both Houses of Parliament Fr. army captures Ghent and Ypres Hungarian rebellion against Hapsburgs under Emeric Tökölyi Outbreak of war between Russia and Sweden	Samuel Butler: "Hudibras," Part 3 Corneille: "Le Comte d'Essex," tragedy Marie Madeleine de La Fayette: "La Princesse de Clèves," novel Jean de La Fontaine: "Fables choisies, mises en vers" Dryden: "All for Love," tragedy George Farquhar, Ir. dramatist, b. (d. 1707) Andrew Marvell, Eng. poet, d. (b. 1621)	John Bunyan: "The Pilgrim's Progress," Part 1 Ralph Cudworth: "The True Intellectual System of the Universe"
1679	Peace of Nijmegen between Louis XIV and Leopold I Habeas Corpus Amendment Act in England Peace of St. Germain-en-Laye between Sweden and Brandenburg King Charles II of Spain marries Marie Louise of Orleans New Hampshire separated as special province from Massachusetts Peace Treaty of Lund between Denmark and Sweden Hapsburg influence reestablished in Madrid by the Queen Mother, Marie of Austria	Beaumont and Fletcher–50 of their plays published posth. Dryden and Nathaniel Lee "Oedipus," tragedy P'u-Sungling: "Liao Chai," collection of Chin. short stories Joost van den Vondel, Dutch author, d. (b. 1587) Christian Hofmann von Hofmannswaldau, Ger. poet, d. (b. 1617)	Gilbert Burnet: "History of the Reformation of the Church of England," Vol. 1 Thomas Hobbes, Eng. philosopher, d. (b. 1588) Sir William Petty: "A Treatise on Taxes and Contributions" Abraham a Sancta Clara: "Merk's Wien!," sermons against corruption of morals in Vienna Elias Ashmole (1617—1692) founds Ashmolean Museum at Oxford
1680	Absolutism in Sweden under King Charles XI Fr. colonial empire, reaching from Quebec to mouth of Mississippi River, is organized Maximilian II Emanuel becomes Elector of Bavaria (—1726) Tsunayoshi becomes Shogun of Japan	Samuel Butler, Eng. satirist, d. (b. 1612) Comédie Française formed by merging Théâtre Guénégaud Paris, with Théâtre de'Hôtel de Bourgogne Thomas Otway: "The Orphan," tragedy François de La Rochefoucauld, Fr. moralist, d. (b. 1613)	Robert Filmer: "Patriarche, or The Natural Power of Kings" César-Pierre Richelet: "Dictionnaire François" Sir William Temple: "An Essay on Government"
1681	Defensive alliances between Brandenburg and France and between Brandenburg and Sweden Royal Charter for Pennsylvania European Congress meets at Frankfurt	Calderón d. (b. 1600) Dryden: "Absalom and Achitophel," satirical poem, Part 1	Jacques-Bénigne Bossuet: "Discours sur l'histoire universelle" Jean Mabillon: "De re diplomatica" (—1704), study of historical documents as foundation of historical criticism James Dalrymple of Stair: "Institutions of the Law of Scotland"

D. VISUAL ARTS	E. MUSIC	F. SCIENCE, TECHNOLOGY, GROWTH	G. DAILY LIFE	
Jacob Jordaens, Dutch painter, d. (b. 1593) Murillo: "The Immaculate Conception," once belonging to Marshal Soult (Murillo used the same theme for 30 paintings)	Thomas Britton, Eng. patron of music (1644—1714), introduces weekly concerts in Clerkenwell, London (—1714) First Ger. opera house opens in Hamburg	Ital. mathematician Giovanni Ceva (1648—1734) states the geometrical theorem on the nature of concurrency Christiaan Huygens records (in his "Traité de la lumière," published 1690) his discovery of the polarization of light Robert de La Salle explores the Great Lakes (—1679) Thomas Thatcher: "A Brief Rule in Small Pocks or Measles," first medical treatise published in America	First chyrsanthemums arrive in Holland from Japan Import of all Fr. goods to England prohibited (—1685)	**1678**
Charles Lebrun decorates the Galérie des Glaces at Versailles (—1684) Jan Steen, Dutch painter, d. (b. 1626)	Lully: "Bellérophon," opera Alessandro Scarlatti's first opera, "Gli Equivoci nell' amore," Rome	Edmund Halley: "Catalogus stellarum australium" Fr. Jesuit Louis Hannepin discovers Niagara Falls	Colbert issues order that all Fr. merchants be examined in bookkeeping and commercial law Edict against dueling in France First Ger. coffeehouse in Hamburg Ger. chemist Johann Kunckel von Löwenstern (1630—1703) becomes director of glass works in Potsdam	**1679**
Gian Lorenzo Bernini, Ital. architect, d. (b. 1598) Jules Hardouin-Mansart: Chapel des Invalides, Paris (—1719) Emperor K'ang-Hsi founds factories for development of art industries in China Sir Peter Lely, Eng. painter, d. (b. 1617) Sir Christopher Wren: St. Clement Danes, London	First ballets arrive in Germany from France Henry Purcell made organist of Westminster Abbey Sadler's Wells at Islington, London, begins musical entertainments Stradivari makes his earliest known cello	First Brandenburgian expedition to W. Africa Jan Swammerdam, Dutch naturalist, d. (b. 1637)	Dodo, flightless bird of the Raphidae family, extinct Penny post established in London by merchant William Dockwra	**1680**
Gerard Terborch, Dutch painter, d. (b. 1617) Sir Christopher Wren: Tom Tower, Christ Church, Oxford	Female professional dancers appear for first time at the Paris Opéra Georg Philipp Telemann, Ger. composer, b. (d. 1767)	Academy of Sciences, Moscow, founded Canal du Midi, joining Bay of Biscay to the Mediterranean, finished (begun 1664) Wren elected president of the Royal Society	Founding of the Chelsea Hospital, London, for wounded and discharged soldiers First checks in England	**1681**

	A. HISTORY, POLITICS	B. LITERATURE, THEATER	C. RELIGION, PHILOSOPHY, LEARNING
1682	La Salle claims Louisiana territory for France and takes possession of Mississippi Valley The future King Charles XII of Sweden b. Czar Feodor III of Russia d.; his sister Sophia becomes Regent for her infant brothers, Ivan and Peter (—1689) Great Charter of Pennsylvania Emeric Tökölyi proclaimed King of Hungary by Turks	Dryden: "Absalom and Achitophel," Part 2 Thomas D'Urfey edits "Wit and Mirth," anthology Thomas Otway: "Venice Preserv'd," tragedy	Pierre Bayle: "Thoughts on the Comet of 1680," against superstitions on comets John Bunyan: "The Holy War" François Eudes de Mézeray: "De l'origine des Français" 58,000 Fr. Huguenots forced to conversion Sir George MacKenzie founds Advocates' Library, Edinburgh, later to become Scot. National Library Sir William Petty: "Essay Concerning Multiplications of Mankind"
1683	Pol.-Aust. alliance against Turks Rye House Plot to assassinate Charles II discovered Turks begin siege of Vienna (July) Colbert d. (b. 1619) King Jan Sobieski of Poland and Charles, Duke of Lorraine, raise siege of Vienna (Sept.) The future King George II of England b. (d. 1760) Spain declares war on France Alfonso VI, King of Portugal, d.; succeeded by his brother Peter II (—1707) Dutch traders admitted to Canton League of The Hague: the Emperor Leopold I and Charles II of Spain join Dutch-Swed. alliance against France Manchus conquer Formosa (in Chin. possession —1895) Peace treaty between William Penn and N. American Indians	Edmonde Boursault: "Le Mercure galand," satirical comedy Elijah Fenton, Eng. poet, b. (d. 1730) Izaak Walton, Eng. author, d. (b. 1593)	Matthew Hale: "A Discourse Touching Provision for the Poor" William Penn: "A General Description of Pennsylvania" Sir William Petty: "The Growth of the City of London"
1684	Louis XIV, after death of Queen Maria Theresa, marries Mme. de Maintenon The Emperor, Poland and Venice conclude Holy League of Linz against Turks Bermudas become crown colony Court at chancery in England annuls charter of Massachusetts The "Great Elector" offers Fr. Huguenots refuge in Brandenburg	"Nouvelles de la République des Lettres," literary review, published by Pierre Bayle in Rotterdam John Bunyan: "The Pilgrim's Progress," Part 2 Corneille d. (b. 1606) Alexander Olivier Esquemeling: "History of the Buccaneers of America" Takemoto Gidayu begins puppet theater "Joruri" in Tokyo Ludvig Holberg, Dan. dramatist, b. (d. 1754) Giovanni Paolo Marana (1672—1692): "L'Espion du grand seigneur," spy story	93 Jewish families expelled from Bordeaux Increase Mather: "Remarkable Providences"
1685	Charles II of England d.; succeeded by his brother James II (—1688) Charles, the Elector Palatinate, d; electorate claimed by Louis XIV for his sister-in-law Liselotte Duke of Monmouth's rebellion: Monmouth defeated at Sedgemoor and beheaded; Judge George Jeffreys (1648—1689) conducts "Bloody Assizes" against Monmouth's followers The future Emperor Charles VI b. (d. 1740) All Chin. ports opened to foreign trade	Dryden: "Albion and Albanius," libretto to opera by Lewis Grabu John Gay, author of "The Beggar's Opera," b. (d. 1732) Thomas Otway, Eng. dramatist, d. (b. 1652) Fourth Folio of Shakespeare's works	George Berkeley, Ir. philosopher, b. (d. 1753) César de Rochefort: "Dictionnaire général et curieux" Louis XIV revokes Edict of Nantes (1598), exiles thousands of Fr. Protestants Increase Mather president of Harvard College (—1701)

D. VISUAL ARTS	E. MUSIC	F. SCIENCE, TECHNOLOGY, GROWTH	G. DAILY LIFE	
Claude Lorraine, Fr. painter, d. (b. 1600) Murillo, Span. painter, d. (b. 1617) Jacob van Ruisdael, Dutch painter, d. (b. 1628)	Lully: "Persée," opera	Jean Picard, Fr. astronomer, d. (b. 1620)	"Acta eruditorum," first learned periodical appears (in Latin) in Leipzig (—1776) Versailles becomes royal residence (—1789) Weaving mill with 100 looms established in Amsterdam	**1682**
Pieter de Hooch, Dutch painter, d. (b. 1629) Guarino Guarini, Ital. architect, d. (b. 1624) Godfrey Kneller: "Sir Charles Cotterell" Charles Lebrun made director of the Académie royale Sir Christopher Wren: St. James's, Piccadilly, London	Henry Purcell made court composer to Charles II Jean Philippe Rameau, Fr. composer, b. (d. 1764)	Eng. navigator William Dampier (1652—1715) begins voyage round the world René-Antoine Ferchault de Réaumur, Fr. scientist, b. (d. 1757) Newton explains mathematical theory on tides under gravitational attraction of sun, moon, and earth Roger Williams, Rhode Island colonist, d. (b. 1603)	First Ger. immigrants in N. America First coffeehouses in Vienna Wild boars become extinct in Great Britain	**1683**
Sir Godfrey Kneller: "Duchess of Portsmouth" Adriaen van Ostade d. (b. 1610) Jean Antoine Watteau, Fr. painter, b. (d. 1721)	Nicolo Amati d. (b. 1596)	Giovanni Cassini: "Les Éléments de l'astronomie vérifiés" Ger. explorer Engelbert Kämpfer travels to Persian Gulf, Java, and Japan	First attempts in London to light the streets Siamese embassy arrives at court of Louis XIV at Versailles	**1684**
Kneller: "Philip, Earl of Leicester" Dominikus Zimmermann, Ger. architect, b. (d. 1766)	J. S. Bach, Ger. composer, b. (d. 1750) George Frederick Handel, Ger.-Eng. composer, b. (d. 1759) Domenico Scarlatti, Ital. composer, b. (d. 1757)	David Abercromby: "De pulsis variatione" First Fr. settlers in Texas	Construction of the Pont Royal, Paris Fr. Huguenots begin silk manufacture in Great Britain	**1685**

	A. HISTORY, POLITICS	B. LITERATURE, THEATER	C. RELIGION, PHILOSOPHY, LEARNING
1686	Federation of New England formed by James II in order to remodel Brit. colonies in N. America League of Augsburg against Louis XIV Charles, Duke of Lorraine, takes Buda from Turks, who held it for 145 years Russia declares war on Turkey French annex Madagascar Roman Catholics readmitted to Eng. army	"Shusse Kagekiyo," famous Jap. puppet play by Chikamatsu Monzaemon, given in Tokyo Allan Ramsay, Scot. poet, b. (d. 1758) First Swed. theater opens in Stockholm	Ger. pietist and educator August Hermann Francke (1663—1727) begins at Leipzig his Collegium Philobiblicum for the study of the Bible
1687	James II issues Declaration of Indulgence for liberty of conscience Papal nuncio received by James II Battle of Mohacs: defeat of Turks under Suleiman Pasha Parthenon and Propylaea at the Acropolis, Athens, badly damaged by Venetian bombardment Hungarian diet of Pressburg recognizes the crown as hereditary possession of the male line of Hapsburgs Sultan Mohammed IV of Turkey deposed; succeeded by Suleiman III Arguin, Guinea, established as colony by Brandenburg	Dryden: "The Hind and the Panther," allegorical poem Gerard Langbaine: "A New Catalogue of English Plays" William Winstanley: "Lives of the English Poets"	Fénelon: "Traité de l'éducation des filles" Samuel von Pufendorf: "The Relation of Religious Liberty to Civilian Life" John Wallis: "Institutio logicae"
1688	Frederick William, the "Great Elector," d.; succeeded by his son Frederick III Transylvania becomes province under King of Hungary Seven Eng. lords invite William of Orange to England (the "Glorious Revolution," June 6); he accepts invitation, lands at Torbay, enters London (Dec.) The future King Frederick William I of Prussia b. (d. 1740) Imperial forces occupy Belgrade War between France and the Empire: Louis XIV invades Palatinate and takes Heidelberg King James II escapes to France (d. at Versailles, 1701)	John Bunyan, Eng. author, d. Pierre de Marivaux, Fr. dramatist, b. (d. 1763) Alexander Pope, Eng. poet, b. (d. 1744) Philippe Quinault, Fr. dramatist, d. (b. 1635) Thomas Shadwell: "The Squire of Alsatia," comedy	Jacques-Bénigne Boussuet: "Histoires des variations des églises protestantes" Hermann Busenmann d. (b. 1600), author of "Medulla theologiae moralis," one of most important handbooks of Jesuit moral theology ("The end justifies the means") Ralph Cudworth, Eng. philosopher, d. (b. 1617) Emanuel Swedenborg, Swed. mystic and philosopher, b. (d. 1772)
1689	Parliament confirms abdication of James II Declaration of Rights in England, William and Mary proclaimed King and Queen for life (also in Scotland), crowned Ex-Queen Christina of Sweden d. (b. 1626) Louis XIV declares war on Great Britain Massacre of Fr. settlers at Lachine, near Montreal, Canada, by Iroquois Indians (July) Peter the Great becomes Czar of Russia Louis de Frontenac (1620—1698) appointed Governor of Canada French burn Baden-Baden Ger. diet declares war on France Natal becomes Dutch colony William and Mary recognize old charters of the English colonies	Aphra Behn, Eng. author, d. (b. 1640) Racine: "Esther," tragedy Samuel Richardson, Eng. novelist, b. (d. 1761) Anselm von Ziegler (1663—1696): "Die asiatische Banise," Ger. novel	Pope Innocent XI d.; Pietro Ottoboni becomes Pope Alexander VIII (—1691) John, Lord Somers: "A Brief History of the Succession to the Crown of England" Baron de Montesquieu, Fr. political philosopher, b. (d. 1755) William Sherlock: "A Practical Discourse Concerning Death"

D. VISUAL ARTS	E. MUSIC	F. SCIENCE, TECHNOLOGY, GROWTH	G. DAILY LIFE	
Cosmas Damian Asam, Ger. painter and architect, b. (d. 1739) Jules Hardouin-Mansart: Notre Dame, Versailles Jean Baptiste Oudry, Fr. painter, b. (d. 1755)	Lully: "Armide et Renaud," opera (Paris) Nicola Porpora, Ital. composer, b. (d. 1766)	Gabriel Daniel Fahrenheit, Ger. physicist, b. (d. 1736) First Fr. settlers in Arkansas Halley draws first meteorological map Jean Le Clerc: "Bibliothèque universelle et historique," 25 vols. (—1693) Otto von Guericke, Ger. physicist, d. (b. 1602) Francis Willughby (1635—1672): "Historia piscium" (posth.)	Maison St. Cyr founded by Louis XIV and Mme. de Maintenon as convent school for daughters of poor gentlefolk	**1686**
Leonardo de Figueroa: Hospital de Venerables Sacerdotes, Seville Kneller: "The Chinese Convent" Balthasar Neumann, Ger. architect, b. (d. 1739)	Lully d. (b. 1632)	Isaac Newton: "Philosophiae naturalis principia mathematica" (—1727) Sir Hans Sloane, Eng. naturalist and physician (1660—1753), begins his botanical collection on a visit to Jamaica University of Bologna founded	Nell Gwyn, actress and Charles II's mistress, d. (b. 1651)	**1687**
30th and last volume of Matthäus Merian's "Topographia Germanicae" (with over 2,000 illustrations) published posth. (begun 1642) Joachim Sandrart, Ger. art historian and painter, d. (b. 1606)	Domenico Zipoli, Ital. composer and organist, b. (d. 1726)	Joseph Nicolas Delisle, Fr. astronomer, b. (d. 1768)	Joseph de la Vega: "Confusion de confusiones," description of transactions on Amsterdam Exchange London underwriters begin meeting regularly at Lloyd's Coffee House Plate glass being cast for first time Smyrna destroyed by earthquake	**1688**
Kilian Ignaz Dientzenhofer, Bohemian architect, b. (d. 1751) Meindert Hobbema: "Avenue at Middleharnis"	Henry Purcell: "Dido and Aeneas," opera	Fr. explorer Baron de La Hontan visits Great Salt Lake, Utah Thomas Sydenham, Eng. physician, d. (b. 1624)	William III establishes Devonport Naval Dockyards Heidelberg Castle destroyed by the French First modern trade fair held in Leiden, Holland	**1689**

	A. HISTORY, POLITICS	B. LITERATURE, THEATER	C. RELIGION, PHILOSOPHY, LEARNING
1690	Joseph I elected King of the Romans Act of Grace passed in England Spain joins Great Alliance against France William III leaves for Ireland, defeats his father-in-law (James II) at Battle of the Boyne; fails to take Limerick; returns to England Turks reconquer Belgrade	Dryden: "Amphitryon," comedy Nathaniel Lee: "The Massacre of Paris," tragedy	John Locke: "An Essay Concerning Human Understanding" Sir William Petty: "Political Arithmetics"
1691	Turks defeated at Szcelankemen; Mustafa Kiuprili killed in action Massachusetts absorbs Plymouth Colony, and is given new charter Hapsburgs recognized as rulers of Transylvania New East India Company formed in London Sultan Suleiman III of Turkey d.; succeeded by Ahmad II (—1695) Treaty of Limerick ends Ir. rebellion	Sir George Etherege, Eng. dramatist, d. (b. 1635) Racine: "Athalie"	Pope Alexander VIII d.; Antonio Pignatelli becomes Pope Innocent XII (—1700) Robert Boyle, Eng. philosopher and physicist, d. (b. 1627) Christian Faith Society for West Indies founded in London Claude Fleury: "Histoire ecclésiastique," 20 vols. (finished 1720) Kaspar Stieler: "Teutsche Sprachschatz" Henry Wharton· "Anglia sacra" Anthony à Wood: "Athenae Oxonienses"
1692	Massacre of Clan Macdonald at Glencoe Destruction of Fr. Navy by English at La Hogue ends attempted Fr. invasion of England Imperial troops capture Grosswardein from Turks William III defeated at Steinkirk Duke Ernst August of Hanover becomes 9th Elector of the Holy Roman Empire	William Congreve: "Incognita," novel Florent Carton Dancourt: "Les Bourgeoises à la mode," comedy Carlo Fragoni, Ital. poet, b. (d. 1768) Thomas Shadwell, Eng. dramatist, d. (b. 1642) Nahum Tate made poet laureate	Joseph Butler, Eng. philosopher, b. (d. 1752) Edict of Toleration for Christians in China
1693	French sack Heidelberg for second time (see 1688) Battle of Lagos: French defeat Eng. merchant fleet Carolina divided into N. and S. Carolina Louis XIV begins his peace policy, reconciliation with the Vatican National Debt begins in England Robert Dinwiddie, Governor of Virginia, b. (d. 1770)	Congreve: "The Old Bachelor," comedy Marie-Madeleine, Comtesse de La Fayette, Fr. novelist, d. (b. 1634) La Fontaine: "Fables," Vol. 3 George Lillo, Eng. dramatist, b. (d. 1739)	Edmund Halley: "The Degrees of Mortality of Mankind" Secret society, Knights of the Apocalypse, founded in Italy to defend the church against the antichrist Leibniz: "Codex Juris gentium diplomaticus" (—1700) John Locke: "Thoughts Concerning Education," on learning foreign languages Cotton Mather: "Wonders of the Invisible World" William Penn: "An Essay on the Present and Future Peace of Europe"

D. VISUAL ARTS	E. MUSIC	F. SCIENCE, TECHNOLOGY, GROWTH	G. DAILY LIFE	
Hobbema: "The Mill" Nicolas Lancret, Fr. painter, b. (d. 1745) Charles Lebrun, Fr. architect, d. (b. 1619) David Teniers the Younger, Dutch painter, d. (b. 1610)	Giovanni Legrenzi, Ital. opera composer, d. (b. 1626) Purcell: "The Prophetess, or The History of Dioclesian" (Dorset Gardens Theatre, London)	Calcutta founded by Eng. colonial administrator Job Charnock Huyghens publishes his theory of the undulation of light Fr. engineer Denis Papin (1647—1714) devises pump with piston, raised by steam	Academia dell' arcadia founded in Rome "Athenian Gazette," first Eng. periodical to answer readers' letters Calico printing introduced to Great Britain from France England's population: approx. 5 million (1600: 2.5 million)	**1690**
Aelbert Cuyp, Dutch painter, d. (b. 1620) Leonardo de Figueroa: Magdalene Church, Seville (—1709) Peter Scheemakers, Fl. sculptor, b. (d. 1770)	Purcell: "King Arthur, or The British Worthy," opera; libretto by John Dryden Andreas Werckmeister (1645—1706): "Musikalische Temperatur"	Leibniz: "Protagaea," on geology	First directory of addresses published in Paris	**1691**
Egid Quirin Asam, Ger. sculptor and architect, b. (d. 1750) Johann Michael Fischer, Ger. architect, b. (d. 1766)	Purcell: "The Fairy Queen" Giuseppe Tartini, Ital. composer and violinist, b. (d. 1770)	William and Mary College, Va., founded	Johann Konrad Amman (1669—1730): "Der redende Stumme," manual of language for deaf-mutes The Bank, later becomes banking house of Coutts and Co., opened in Strand, London Earthquake in Jamaica Queen Mary II founds Greenwich Hospital for wounded sailors and pensioners	**1692**
G. R. Donner, Aust. sculptor, b. (d. 1741) Willem Kalf, Dutch painter, d. (b. 1622) Kneller: "Dr. Burnet" Nicolaes Maes, Dutch painter, d. (b. 1632)	Alessandro Scarlatti: "Teodora," opera	Kingston, Jamaica, founded		**1693**

	A. HISTORY, POLITICS	B. LITERATURE, THEATER	C. RELIGION, PHILOSOPHY, LEARNING
1694	Founding of the Bank of England Eng. fleet bombards Dieppe, Le Havre, and Dunkirk Triennial Bill providing for new Parliamentary election every third year Queen Mary II of England, wife of William III, d. Augustus the Strong, Elector of Saxony (—1733) Hussain becomes Shah of Persia (—1721)	Congreve: "The Double Dealer," comedy	Dictionnaire de l'Académie française, first edition, 2 vols. Francis Hutcheson, Scot. philosopher, b. (d. 1746) Voltaire, Fr. writer and philosopher, b. (d. 1778)
1695	Ahmad II, Sultan of Turkey, d.; succeeded by Mustafa II (—1703) William III takes Namur in Sept. after serving with his army in Holland since May End of government press censorship in England Russo-Turk. War: Peter the Great returns to Moscow, having failed to take Azov	Congreve: "Love for Love" Johann Christian Günther, Ger. poet, b. (d. 1723) Nikolaes Heinsius: "Den Vermakelijkten Avonturier," Dutch picaresque novel La Fontaine d. (b. 1621) Henry Vaughan, Eng. poet, d. (b. 1622)	John Locke: "The Reasonableness of Christianity"
1696	New coinage in England carried out by John Locke and Isaac Newton William III campaigning in Holland against French Jan Sobieski, Jan III of Poland, d. Peter the Great takes Asov from Turks Russia conquers Kamchatka Eng. Habeas Corpus Act suspended	Colley Cibber: "Love's Last Shift," comedy Mme. de Sévigné d. (b. 1626) Jean-François Regnard: "Le Joueur," comedy Christian Reuter: "Schelmuffsky," Ger. adventure novel Thomas Southerne: "Oroonoko," tragedy	Nicolas Antonio: "Bibliotheca Hispana vetus," Span. bibliography Alphonsus di Liguori, Ital. Catholic philosopher, b. (d. 1787; canonized 1839; Doctor of the Church 1871) William Nicolson: "The English Historical Library," 3 vols. (—1699)
1697	Peter the Great, calling himself Peter Michailoff, sets out on a year-and-a-half journey to Prussia, Holland, England and Vienna to study European ways of life Charles XI, King of Sweden d.; succeeded by Charles XII (—1718) Augustus, Elector of Saxony, converted to Roman Catholicism, elected King of Poland in succession to Jan III Prince Eugene defeats Turks at Zenta In Treaty of Ryswick: France recognizes William III as King of England, Princess Anne as heir presumptive Renewal of Bank of England charter (—1711) China conquers western Mongolia French under André de Brue attempt to colonize West Africa	Congreve: "The Mourning Bride," tragedy Friederike Caroline Neuber ("Die Neuberin"), Ger. actress and theater manager, b. (d. 1760) Charles Perrault: "Contes de ma mère l'Oye," collection of fairy tales Antoine François Prévost, Fr. novelist, b. (d. 1763) Richard Savage, Eng. author, b. (d. 1743) Sir John Vanbrugh: "The Relapse, or Virtue in Danger," comedy John Aubrey, Eng. biographer, d. (b. 1626)	Pierre Bayle: "Dictionnaire historique et critique," 2 vols. William Wotton: "Reflections on Ancient and Modern Learning"

D. VISUAL ARTS	E. MUSIC	F. SCIENCE, TECHNOLOGY, GROWTH	G. DAILY LIFE	
Kneller: "Hampton Court Beauties" John Michael Rysbrack, Fl. sculptor, b. (d. 1770) Johann Bernhard Fischer von Erlach begins building Castle Schönbrunn (finished by Nikolas Pacassi) Sir Christopher Wren: Greenwich Hospital	Purcell writes the incidental music for Dryden's "Love Triumphant," and "Te Deum" for St. Cecilia's Day	"De sexu plantarum epistola" by Ger. botanist Rudolf Camerarius (1665—1721) University of Halle founded	Salt tax doubled in England	**1694**
Melchior d'Hondecoeter, Dutch painter, d. (b. 1636) Pierre Mignard, Fr. painter, d. (b. 1612) Louis François Roubiliac, Fr. sculptor, b. (d. 1762) Wren designs Morden College, Blackheath, London	Maurice Greene, Eng. organist and composer, b. (d. 1755) Purcell: "The Indian Queen" Henry Purcell d. (b. 1659)	Fr. scientist Guillaume Amontons invents pendant barometer University of Berlin founded Christian Huygens, Dutch mathematician and scientist, d. (b. 1629) Eng. botanist Nehemiah Grew isolates magnesium sulfate, "Epsom salts," from North Downs springs John Woodward: "Essay Toward a Natural History of the Earth and Terrestrial Bodies"	Royal Bank of Scotland founded Window tax in England (—1851)	**1695**
Kunstakademie, Berlin, founded Giovanni Battista Tiepolo, Ital. painter, b. (d. 1770)	Johann Kuhnau (1660—1722): "Frische Clavier-Früchte, oder sieben Suonaten," the sonata as a piece in several contrasting movements	John Bellers: "Proposals for Raising a College of Industry," on the education of children Eng. naturalist John Ray (1627—1705) describes for first time the aromatic herb peppermint Building of Fort William, Calcutta	Board of Trade and Plantations founded in England Strike of hatter journeymen in England "Lloyd's News," a thrice-weekly newspaper published by London coffeehouse keeper Edward Lloyd Peter the Great sends 50 young Russians to England, Holland, and Venice to study shipbuilding and fortifications First Eng. property insurance company founded	**1696**
Antonio ("Canaletto") Canale, Ital. painter, b. (d. 1768) William Hogarth, Eng. painter, b. (d. 1764) Last remains of Maya civilization destroyed by Spanish in Yucatan	John Blow's anthem, "I Was Glad When They Said," written for and given at opening of Wren's Choir of St. Paul's Cathedral, London Johann Joachim Quantz, Ger. flautist and composer, b. (d. 1773)	Daniel Defoe: "An Essay Upon Projects," recommending income tax Fr. mathematician Abraham Demoivre (1667—1754) elected Fellow Royal Society	Sedan chair a popular means of transportation Court of Versailles becomes model for European courts Whitehall Palace, London, burnt down	**1697**

	A. HISTORY, POLITICS	B. LITERATURE, THEATER	C. RELIGION, PHILOSOPHY, LEARNING
1698	Rebellion of Czar Peter's praetorian guard (Streltzy) in Moscow; leaders executed Elector Ernest August of Hanover d.; his eldest son George Louis, future King George I of England, becomes electoral prince Leopold of Anhalt-Dessau introduces goose-stepping and iron ramrods in Prussian army	Marie Champmeslé, Fr. actress, d. (b. 1642) Gerard Langbaine and Charles Gildon: "The Lives and Characters of the English Dramatick Poets"	Johann Jakob Bodmer, Swiss-Ger. writer and historian, b. (d. 1783) Society for Promoting Christian Knowledge (SPCK) founded by London divine and philanthropist Dr. Thomas Bray (1656—1730) Bibliotheca Casanatense founded in Rome by Cardinal Casanatense Algernon Sidney: "Discourses Concerning Government" (posth.)
1699	Peace of Karlowitz signed by Austria, Russia, Poland, and Venice with Turkey Denmark and Russia sign mutual defense pact Treaty of Preobrazhenskoe signed by Denmark, Russia, Poland, and Saxony for partition of Swed. empire Christian V King of Denmark, d.; succeeded by Frederick IV (—1730)	Robert Blair, Scot. poet, b. (d. 1746) Dryden: "Fables, Ancient and Modern" George Farquhar: "Love and a Bottle," comedy Fénelon: "Télémaque" Racine d. (b. 1639)	Richard Bentley: "Dissertation Upon the Epistles of Phalaris" Gilbert Burnet: "Exposition of the Thirty-nine Articles"
1700	Great Northern War begins with Saxon invasion of Livonia Duke of Gloucester, only surviving child of Princess Anne, d.; succession to Eng. throne passes to the Electress Sophia of Hanover, mother of the electoral prince, the future George I King Charles II of Spain d.; end of the Spanish Hapsburgs; Philip V, grandson of Louis XIV, heir to throne Crown treaty between the Emperor Leopold I and Elector Frederick III, of Brandenburg, who is recognized as Frederick I, "King in Prussia" Charles XII of Sweden defeats Peter the Great at Narva	Armande Béjart, Fr. actress, d. (b. 1645) Congreve: "The Way of the World," comedy George Farquhar: "The Constant Couple, or A Trip to the Jubilee," comedy Johann Christoph Gottsched, Ger. author and critic, b. (d. 1766) Development of the Kabuki Theater in Japan	Thomas Hyde: "Historia religionis veterum Persarum" Pope Innocent XII d.; Gian Francesco Albani becomes Pope Clement XI (—1721) Earl of Bellomont as governor establishes a reading room that in 1754 becomes the New York Society Library
1701	Elector Frederick III of Brandenburg crowns himself King Frederick I of Prussia War of Spanish Succession begins (—1714) Act of Settlement provides for Protestant succession in England of House of Hanover Charles XII of Sweden invades Courland and Poland Prince Eugene defeats French at Carpi and Chiara James II of England d.; Louis XIV recognizes the "Old Pretender," James Edward, son of James II, as King James III	Daniel Defoe: "The True-Born Englishman," satire George Farquhar: "Sir Harry Wildair," comedy Sir Charles Sedley, Eng. author, d. (b. 1640) Sir Richard Steele: "The Funeral, or Grief à la Mode," comedy	Jeremy Collier: "The Great Historical, Geographical, Genealogical, and Political Dictionary," 2 vols. Arai Hakuseki (1675—1725): "Hankampu," History of the feudal lords (Daimyo) of Japan Benjamin Whichcote: "Several Discourses; Moral and Religious Aphorisms" Father Francisco Ximénes translates sacred national book of the Quiché Indians of Guatemala, "Popul Vah" (—1721)
1702	William III d.; succeeded by Queen Anne (—1714) Duke of Marlborough becomes Capt.-Gen. of Eng. armed forces; takes Venlo, Ruremonde, and Liège Charles XII takes Warsaw, Cracow Rebellion of Protestant peasants, "Camisards," in Cévennes	George Farquhar: "The Twin Rivals," comedy Earliest form of Eng. pantomime given at Drury Lane, London Yokai Yagu, Jap. poet, b. (d. 1783) Edward Busshe: "The Art of English Poetry"	Earl of Clarendon: "The History of the Rebellion and Civil Wars in England," eyewitness accounts (posth.) Daniel Defoe: "The Shortest Way with Dissenters" Cotton Mather: "Magnalia Christi Americana," ecclesiastical history of New England Armenian priest Mekhitar of Sebaste (1676—1749) founds in Constantinople Order of the Mekhitarists, Roman Catholic Armenian monks

D. VISUAL ARTS	E. MUSIC	F. SCIENCE, TECHNOLOGY, GROWTH	G. DAILY LIFE	
Jules Hardouin-Mansart: Place Vendôme, Paris Andreas Schlüter: Royal Palace, Berlin (—1706)	Metastasio, famous opera librettist, b. (d. 1782) Giovanni Battista Sammartini, Ital. organist and composer, b. (d. 1755)	Henry Baker, Eng. naturalist, b. (d. 1774) The General Society (New East India Trading Company) founded in London	Paper manufacturing begins in N. America Tax on beards in Russia Mrs. White's Chocolate House opens in London, soon to become headquarters of Tory Party Henry Winstanley (1644—1703) begins building Eddystone Lighthouse (—1700)	**1698**
Jean Chardin, Fr. painter, b. (d. 1779) Georg Wenzeslaus von Knobelsdorff, Ger. architect, b. (d. 1753)	Raoul Anger Feuillet: "Choréographie," manual on dance notation Johann Adolf Hasse, Ger. composer, b. (d. 1783)	William Dampier explores northwest coast of Australia Pierre Lemoyne founds first European settlement in Louisiana, at Fort Maurepas	Billingsgate, London, becomes a market Peter the Great decrees that New Year in Russia will begin on Jan. 1 instead of Sept. 1	**1699**
L. S. Adam, Fr. sculptor, b. (d. 1759) Approx. beginning of late baroque period (—c. 1715) Kneller: "Matthew Prior" Palace of Forty Pillars (Ispahan) redesigned Bartolomeo Rastrelli, Ital. architect, b. (d. 1771)	William Croft: Incidental music to "Courtship à la mode" Joseph Sauveur measures and explains vibrations of musical tones	Berlin Academy of Science founded, Leibniz elected president Fr. chemist J. P. de Tournefort (1656—1708) discovers ammonium chloride	The commode becomes a popular piece of furniture Population figures (approx.): France 19 million, England and Scotland 7.5 million, Hapsburg dominions 7.5 million, Spain 6 million Samuel Sewall (1652—1730): "The Selling of Joseph," first Amer. protest against slavery Unmarried women taxed in Berlin Andalusian, Francisco Romero, becomes first famous Span. bull fighter	**1700**
Hyacinthe Rigaud: "Louis XIV"	Music publisher Henry Playford (1657—1709) establishes a series of weekly concerts at Oxford	University of Venice founded Yale Collegiate School founded at Saybrook, Conn.; and Yale College, New Haven, Conn. Antoine de la Mothe Cadillac (1656—1730) founds settlement at Detroit to control Illinois trade	Royal charters to weavers in Axminster and Wilton for making carpets "Captain" William Kidd hanged for piracy (b. 1645)	**1701**
Jap. painter Ogota Korin (1661—1716) unites the two imperial schools of Jap. painting–Kano and Yamato Fischer von Erlach finishes Church of the Holy Trinity, Salzburg (begun 1694) Jean Antoine Watteau arrives in Paris	N. A. de Le Bègue, Fr. organist and composer, d. (b. 1630)	Fr. settlement in Alabama Jesuit College (University) founded in Breslau	Asiento Guinea Company founded for slave trade between Africa and Amercia "The Daily Courant," first daily newspaper issued in London "Moskovskya Viedomosti" (Moscow Gazette) published Many Ger. towns lit by oil Serfdom abolished in Denmark Queen Anne of England gives royal approval to horseracing, originates sweepstakes idea–racing for cash awards	**1702**

	A. HISTORY, POLITICS	B. LITERATURE, THEATER	C. RELIGION, PHILOSOPHY, LEARNING
1703	Delaware separates from Pennsylvania and becomes colony Swed. victory over Russians at Rultusk Marlborough takes Bonn; Prince Eugene campaigns in southern Germany Marie Leszczynska, future Queen Consort of Louis XV of France, b. (d. 1768) Archduke Charles proclaimed King of Spain in Madrid Methuen Treaty between England and Portugal	Samuel Pepys, Eng. diarist, d. (b. 1633) Charles Perrault, Fr. author, d. (b. 1628) Richard Steele: "The Lying Lover," comedy John Adair: "Description of the Sea Coasts and Islands off Scotland"	"Universal, Historical, Geographical, Chronological and Classical Dictionary," first A-Z treatment in England John Wesley, founder of Methodism, b. (d. 1791) Jonathan Edwards, Amer. theologian, revivalist, and president of the future Princeton University, b. (d. 1758)
1704	Augustus II of Poland deposed; Stanislas Leszczynski elected King Stanislas I (—1709) French and Indians massacre inhabitants of Deerfield, Conn. Marlborough marches toward Danube, meets Prince Eugene near Mandelsheim; they approach Ulm, defeat French and Bavarians at Blenheim English take Gibraltar Peter the Great takes Dorpat, Narva	George Farquhar: "The Stage Coach," comedy Jean-François Regnard: "Les Folies amoureuses," comedy of manners Jonathan Swift: "A Tale of a Tub" William Wycherley: "Miscellany Poems"	"Dictionnaire de Trévoux," of terms used in arts and sciences, published by the Jesuits at Trévoux John Locke, Eng. philosopher, d. (b. 1632) "Memorie del Generale Principe di Montecuccoli" by Raimondo Montecuccoli (1609—1680) published (posth.) Voltaire enters Jesuit college (—1710)
1705	The Emperor Leopold I d.; succeeded by his eldest son, Joseph I (—1711) Rebellion in Astrakhan against Czar Peter's westernization in Russia Eng. Navy takes Barcelona	Colley Cibber: "The Careless Husband," comedy His Majesty's Theatre opens in London Sir Richard Steele: "The Tender Husband," comedy Sir John Vanbrugh: "The Confederacy," comedy	Thomas Birch, Eng. historian, b. (d. 1766) Samuel Clarke: "The Being and Attributes of God" Christian Thomasius (1655—1728): "Fundamenta juris naturalis et gentium"
1706	Benjamin Franklin, Amer. statesman, b. (d. 1790) Charles XII of Sweden defeats Russians and Saxons at Franstadt Marlborough conquers Span. Netherlands Prince Eugene defeats French at Turin Charleston, S.C., successfully defended against French and Spanish Peace of Altrandstadt: Augustus renounces Pol. throne, recognizes King Stanislas I	Daniel Defoe: "The Apparition of One Mrs. Veal" John Evelyn, Eng. diarist, d. (b. 1620) George Farquhar: "The Recruiting Officer," comedy Sir John Vanbrugh: "The Mistake," comedy Isaac Watts: "Horae Lyricae"	Matthew Tindal: "Rights of the Christian Church"

D. VISUAL ARTS	E. MUSIC	F. SCIENCE, TECHNOLOGY, GROWTH	G. DAILY LIFE	
François Boucher, Fr. painter, b. (d. 1770) Work begun on Buckingham Palace, London	Nicolas de Grigny, Fr. composer, d. (b. 1671)	Isaac Newton elected President of the Royal Society	Eddystone Lighthouse destroyed by storm Peter the Great lays foundations of St. Petersburg	**1703**
Maurice Quentin de Latour, Fr. painter, b. (d. 1788) John Wood the Elder, Eng. architect, b. (d. 1754)	J. S. Bach writes his first cantata, "Denn Du wirst meine Seele" Jeremiah Clarke becomes organist at Chapel Royal Handel: "St. John Passion" H. I. F. von Biber, Ger. composer and violinist, d. (b. 1644)	John Harris: "Lexicon technicum," encyclopedia of the sciences Isaac Newton: "Optics," defense of the emission theory of light	Daniel Defoe, in prison, begins his weekly newspaper "The Review" (—1713) Sir Roger L'Estrange, Eng. journalist, d. (b. 1616) Beau Nash becomes master of ceremonies at Bath "Boston News-Letter," first newspaper in America to survive, issued weekly Earliest subscription library in Berlin "Vossische Zeitung," Berlin (—1933) The Darley Arabian, greatest racehorse of its time, arrives in England from Aleppo	**1704**
Ange-Jacques Gabriel: Ecole Militaire, Paris Luca Giordano, Ital. painter, d. (b. 1632)	Young J. S. Bach walks 200 miles to Lübeck to hear the Abendmusiken, directed by Buxtehude Farinelli (Carlo Broschi), great Ital. castrato singer, b. (d. 1782) Handel: "Almira," opera (given at Hamburg)	Jacques Bernoulli, Swiss mathematician, d. (b. 1654) Edmund Halley correctly predicts the return in 1758 of the comet seen in 1682 John Ray, Eng. naturalist, d. (b. 1628) Royal Observatory, Berlin, founded	Ninon de Lenclos, Fr. courtesan, d. (b. 1615)	**1705**
Filippo Juvara: Church of La Superba, Turin Johann Joachim Kändler, Ger. sculptor and porcelain designer, b. (d. 1775) Michael Willmann, Ger. painter, d. (b. 1630)	Johann Pachelbel, Ger. organist and composer, d. (b. 1653)	Giovanni Morgagni: "Adversaria anatomica" Olous Römer's catalogue of astronomical observations	Second Eddystone Lighthouse begun First evening paper, "The Evening Post," issued in London Eng. inventor Henry Mill constructs carriage springs The Sun Fire Office founded in London Dick Turpin, Eng. highwayman, b. (d. 1739)	**1706**

	A. HISTORY, POLITICS	B. LITERATURE, THEATER	C. RELIGION, PHILOSOPHY, LEARNING
1707	King Peter II of Portugal d.; succeeded by John V (—1750) Union between England and Scotland under name Great Britain "Perpetual Alliance" signed between Prussia and Sweden Aurangzeb, Mogul Emperor of Hindustan, d. (b. 1618); succeeded by Bahadur Shah Charles XII and Stanislas I come to understanding with Cossack hetman Ivan Stepanovich Mazeppa (1644—1709) concerning the Ukraine	Farquhar: "The Beaux' Stratagem," comedy George Farquhar, Eng. dramatist, d. (b. 1678) Henry Fielding, Eng. author, b. (d. 1754) Carlo Goldoni, Venetian dramatist, b. (d. 1793) Alain René Lesage: "Le Diable boiteux"	Edward Lhuyd (1660—1709): "Archeologica Britannica," on Celtic language Jean Mabillon, Fr. Benedictine scholar, d. (b. 1632) Isaac Watts: "Hymns and Spiritual Songs"
1708	"Old Pretender" arrives at Firth of Forth; returns four days later to France Marlborough and Eugene defeat French at Oudenarde British capture Minorca and Sardinia British East India Company and New East India Company merged Charles XII invades the Ukraine Peter the Great divides Russia into eight government districts to ease administration	Petter Dass, Norw. poet, d. (b. 1648) Lavinia Fenton, Eng. actress, later Duchess of Bolton, b. (d. 1760) First Ger. theater opens in Vienna Jean-François Regnard: "Le Légataire universal," comedy Christian Weise, Ger. dramatist, d. (b. 1642)	Jeremy Collier: "The Ecclesiastical History of Great Britain" (—1714) Bernard de Montfaucon: "Paleographia Graeca" Professorship of poetry founded at Oxford University
1709	Peace negotiations at The Hague Peter the Great defeats Charles XII at Battle of Poltava Marlborough ("The Butcher") and Prince Eugene take Tournai, defeat French at Malplaquet, and conquer Mons Elizabeth Petrovna, daughter of Peter the Great, Czarina (1741—1762), b. Ienobe becomes Shogun in Japan 14,000 inhabitants of the Palatinate emigrate to N. America (c. 100,000 Germans will follow during next 100 years, and 5 million during 1800s)	Alain René Lesage: "Turcaret, ou Le financier," comedy of manners Alexander Pope: "Pastorals" First issue of Steele's and Addison's: "The Tatler" Samuel Johnson, Eng. author, b. (d. 1784)	Julien Offray de Lamettrie, Fr. philosopher and biologist, b. (d. 1751) Abraham a Sancta Clara, Viennese preacher and satirist, d. (b. 1644) John Strype: "Annals of the Reformation" (—1714)
1710	First budget in Russia British conquer Port Royal (Annapolis) in Acadia Future Louis XV, King of France, b. (d. 1774) Mauritius, formerly part of Dutch East Indies, becomes French	Thomas Betterton, Eng. actor and dramatist, d. (b. 1635) William Congreve's collected works published (3 vols.) Marie de Camargo, Fr. ballet dancer, b. (d. 1770) "The Examiner," literary periodical, issued for first time First appearance of comedy character of Hanswurst in suburban theaters of Vienna	George Berkeley: "A Treatise Concerning the Principles of Human Knowledge" William King (1663—1712): "An Historical Account of the Heathen Gods and Heroes" Leibniz: "Théodicée" ("God created the best of all possible worlds") Cotton Mather: "Essays to Do Good" Thomas Reid, Scot. philosopher, b. (d. 1796)

D. VISUAL ARTS	E. MUSIC	F. SCIENCE, TECHNOLOGY, GROWTH	G. DAILY LIFE	
Fischer von Erlach finishes Kollegien-Kirche in Salzburg (begun 1696)	Dietrich Buxtehude, Dan. composer, d. (b. 1637) Handel in Venice; meeting with Domenico Scarlatti Great Ger. organ builder Gottfried Silbermann (1683—1753) builds first organ at Frauenstein, Saxony	British land in Acadia, E. Canada Leonhard Euler, Swiss mathematician, b. (d. 1783) Sir John Floyer (1649—1734) introduces counting of rate of pulse beats Fr. engineer Denis Papin invents high-pressure boiler Carl von Linné (Linnaeus), Swed. botanist, b. (d. 1778) E. W. von Tschirnhans, assisted by alchemist J. F. Böttger, discovers in Dresden secret of "hard" porcelain similar to that of China	Billiards introduced in Berlin coffeehouses Last eruption of Mount Fujiyama Cricket mentioned in Chamberlayne's "State of England" among people's recreations	**1707**
Pompeo Batoni, Ital. painter, b. (d. 1787) Jules Hardouin-Mansart, Fr. architect, d. (b. 1646)	John Blow, Eng. composer, d. (b. 1648) Handel in Rome and Naples	Hermann Boerhaave: "Institutiones medicae," theory of inflammation Albrecht von Haller, Swiss scientist and poet, b. (d. 1777)	New figures of Gog and Magog at London Guildhall to replace earlier ones destroyed in Great Fire	**1708**
Johann Michael Feichtmayr, Ger. sculptor, b. (d. 1772) Meindert Hobbema, Dutch painter, d. (b. 1638)	"Malbrouk s'en va-t-en guerre" ("For he's a jolly good fellow") becomes increasingly popular after battle of Malplaquet–but it's doubtful whether "Malbrouk" refers to the Duke of Marlborough Invention of the pianoforte; the great Ital. harpsichord maker Bartolomeo Cristofori (1655—1731) makes 4 "gravicembali col piano e forte" Franz Xaver Richter, Ger. composer, b. (d. 1789)	George Berkeley: "New Theory of Vision"	Jap. magnolias introduced into England Ital. Johann Maria Farina (1685—1766) produces in Cologne his eau-de-cologne Postage rates in England regulated by mileage First Russ. prisoners sent to Siberia First Copyright Act in Britain	**1709**
Gabriel Boffrand: Hôtel Amelot, Paris Wren: Marlborough House, Westminster, London	Thomas Augustine Arne, Eng. composer, b. (d. 1778) Wilhelm Friedemann Bach, eldest son of Johann Sebastian, b. (d. 1784) William Boyce, Eng. composer, b. (d. 1779) Handel becomes Kapellmeister to the elector prince, George of Hanover; on a visit to London he completes in 14 days score of "Rinaldo," given at Queen's Theatre Giovanni Battista Pergolesi, Ital. composer, b. (d. 1736)	Eng. South Sea Company founded Ger. cleric and explorer Theodor Krump publishes account of his travels in Abyssinia (1700—1702) Jakob Christoph Le Blon (1667—1741), Ger. engraver, invents three-color printing	The Berlin Charité (Hospital) founded Porcelain factory at Meissen, Saxony, founded	**1710**

	A. HISTORY, POLITICS	B. LITERATURE, THEATER	C. RELIGION, PHILOSOPHY, LEARNING
1711	War between Russia and Turkey The Dauphin d.; within one year his heir, the Duke of Burgundy, the Duchess, and their eldest son also die Joseph I d.; is ultimately succeeded by his brother Charles VI, father of Maria Theresa Peace of Szathmar: Charles VI guarantees Hungarian constitution Rio de Janeiro captured by French Tuscarora War in N. Carolina: Indians massacre 200 settlers Duke of Marlborough dismissed as Commander-in-Chief	Kitty Clive, Eng. actress, b. (d. 1785) Prosper Jolyot de Crébillon: "Rhadamiste et Zénobie," tragedy "The Spectator" begun by Addison and Steele Jonathan Swift: "The Conduct of the Allies" Alexander Pope: "Essay on Criticism"	Francis Atterbury: "Representation of the State of Religion" Berlin Academy started, with Leibniz as president Anthony Ashley Cooper (3rd Earl of Shaftesbury): "Characteristics of Men, Manners, Opinions, and Times" (3 vols.) David Hume, Scot. philosopher and historian, b. (d. 1776) Thomas Maddox: "The History and Antiquities of the Exchequer" William Whiston: "Primitive Christianity Revived"
1712	Future Frederick the Great, King of Prussia, b. (d. 1786) Peace congress opens at Utrecht Treaty of Aarau ends Swiss war Antoine Crozat (1655—1738) granted possession of Lousiana for 15 years Peter the Great marries his mistress Catharina Alexajovna Henry St. John (1678—1751) created Lord Bolingbroke War of Succession between Shah Bahadur's four sons in India	William King, Eng. author, d. (b. 1663) Alexander Pope: "The Rape of the Lock" Christian Reuter, Ger. poet, b. (d. 1765) Jonathan Swift: "A Proposal for Correcting the English Language"	Académie des sciences, belles lettres et arts, Bordeaux, founded Biblioteca nacional, Madrid, founded Jean-Jacques Rousseau, Fr. philosopher and writer, b. (d. 1778)
1713	King Frederick I of Prussia d.; succeeded by Frederick William I (—1740) Spain agrees at Utrecht to cede Gibraltar and Minorca to Great Britain Peace of Utrecht signed Swedes capitulate at Oldenburg Peace of Adrianople between Turkey and Russia Pragmatic Sanction issued by the Emperor Charles VI states female right of succession in Hapsburg domains Charles XII of Sweden taken prisoner by Turks at Bender, Moldavia An infant, Ietsugu, becomes Shogun of Japan	Joseph Addison: "Cato," classical tragedy Alison Cockburn, Scot. poet, b. (d. 1794) Alexander Pope: "Ode on St. Cecilia's Day" Scriblerus Club founded in London by Swift, Pope, Congreve, and others Laurence Sterne, Eng. novelist, b. (d. 1768)	Arthur Collier: "Clavis Universalis, or A New Inquiry After Truth" Denis Diderot, Fr. philosopher, b. (d. 1784) Fénelon: "Traité de l'existence et des attributs de Dieu" Abbé Saint Pierre: "Projet pour la paix perpétuelle" Clarendon Building erected at Oxford
1714	Peace of Rastatt between France and the Holy Roman Empire Battle of Storkyro establishes Russ. domination of Finland Queen Anne of England d.; succeeded by George Louis, Elector of Hanover, as King George I (—1727) Peace of Baden: France keeps Strasbourg and Alsace Philip V of Spain marries Elizabeth Farnese King George I lands in England; Marlborough reinstated Charles XII of Sweden ends his Turk. captivity; arrives at Stralsund Tripoli becomes independent of Turkey	John Gay: "The Shepherd's Week," pastoral Nicholas Rowe's Stage Edition of Shakespeare (9 vols.)	Gottfried Arnold: "Unpartheyische Kirchen- und Ketzer-Historie" (3 vols.) Ger. jurist Justus Böhmer (1674—1749) publishes his "Jus ecclesiasticum Protestantium" Leibniz: "Monadologie" Worcester College, Oxford, founded

D. VISUAL ARTS	E. MUSIC	F. SCIENCE, TECHNOLOGY, GROWTH	G. DAILY LIFE	
Arthur Devis, Eng. painter, b. (d. 1787) Christoph Dientzenhofer works on St. Nikolas, Prague (finished by his son, 1732) Dresden Zwinger, built by M. D. Pöppelmann (—1722) London Academy of Arts established under Geoffrey Kneller	Clarinet for first time in an orchestra (in J. A. Hasse's opera "Croesus") Handel: "Rinaldo," opera Eng. trumpeter John Shore (1662—1752) said to have invented tuning fork	M. W. Lemonossov, Russ. chemist, b. (d. 1766) Encounter between Peter the Great and Leibniz	Queen Anne establishes Ascot races	1711
Thomas Archer: St. Paul's, Deptford, near London (—1730) Gabriel Boffrand: Hôtel de Montmorency, Paris Pierre Simon Fournier, Fr. printer and engraver, b. (d. 1768) Francesco Guardi, Ital. painter, b. (d. 1793) John James: St. George's, Hanover Square, London (—1725) John Christopher Smith, Ger. engraver, b. (d. 1795)	Arcangelo Corelli: "12 Concerti grossi" Handel: "Il Pastor fido," opera, (London)	Giovanni Dominico Cassini, Ital. astronomer, d. (b. 1625) Cotton Mather (1663—1728), Amer. clergyman, begins his "Curiosa Americana" (—1724) Denis Papin, Fr. physicist, d. (b. 1647)	Last execution for witchcraft in England Newspaper Stamp Act in England St. Petersburg, capital of Russia (—1922) Slave revolts in New York	1712
Boffrand: Hôtel de Seigneley, Paris Alexandre François Desportes (1661—1743): "Spaniels with Dead Game" Building of Prince Eugene's Palais Belvedere, Vienna, begun Allan Ramsay, Scot. painter, b. (d. 1784) Jacques Germain Soufflot, Fr. architect, b. (d. 1780) Span. Royal Academy, Madrid, founded Johann Lukas von Hildebrandt (1668—1746): Palais Kinsky, Vienna Watteau: "L'Indifférent"	Arcangelo Corelli, Ital. composer, d. (b. 1653) Handel: "Utrecht Te Deum" School of Dance established at Paris Opéra	Board of Longitude in England Roger Cotes (1682—1716), Eng. mathematician, revises Newton's "Principia"	Francis Child, Eng. banker, d. (b. 1642) Pigtails introduced in Prussian Army	1713
Thomas Archer: St. John's, Smith Square, London (—1728) Boffrand: Hôtel de Torcy, Paris James Gibbs: St. Mary-le-Strand, London (—1717) Jean Baptiste Pigalle, Fr. sculptor, b. (d. 1785) Andreas Schlüter, Ger. architect, d. (b. 1664) Richard Wilson, Eng. painter, b. (d. 1782)	Karl Philipp Emanuel Bach, Bach's second son, b. (d. 1788) Christoph Willibald Gluck, Ger. composer, b. (d. 1787)	Fr. surgeon Dominique Anel invents fine-pointed syringe for surgical purposes D. G. Fahrenheit constructs mercury thermometer with temperature scale	Witch trials abolished in Prussia	1714

	A. HISTORY, POLITICS	B. LITERATURE, THEATER	C. RELIGION, PHILOSOPHY, LEARNING
1715	First Parliament of George I opens Rising of Indian tribes in S. Carolina Louis XIV of France d.; succeeded by his great-grandson (at 5) Louis XV (—1774) under regency of the Duc d'Orleans Jacobite rebellion ("The Fifteen") in Scotland under Earl of Mar; Jacobites defeated at Sheriffmuir and Preston; "Pretender" James III arrives from France at Peterhead Mir Abdullah becomes ruler in Kandahar	Christian Gellert, Ger. author, b. (d. 1769) Gian Vincenzo Gravina: "Della tragedia" Lesage: "Gil Blas de Santillane" (—1735) Matthew Prior: "Solomon, or The Vanity of the World," didactic poem Ir. actor James Quin (1693—1760) appears for first time at Drury Lane, London, as Bajazet in Nicholas Rowe's "Tamerlane" Nicholas Rowe: "Lady Jane Grey," drama Nahum Tate, poet, d. (b. 1652) Ewald Christian von Kleist, Ger. poet, b. (d. 1759)	Etienne Bonnot de Condillac, Fr. philosopher, b. (d. 1780) Claude Adrien Helvétius, Fr. philosopher, b. (d. 1771) Isaac Watts: "Divine Songs for Children"
1716	James III, the "Old Pretender," leaves Great Britain, lands in France The Emperor Charles VI declares war on Turkey Treaty of Westminster between England and the Emperor Prince Eugene defeats Turks at Peterwardein; Temesvar, last Turk. possession in Hungary, falls Peter the Great visits Europe for second time Yoshimune becomes Shogun of Japan	Jean-Jacques Barthélemy, Fr. author, b. (d. 1795) "Fénix Renascida," anthology of Port. poetry, edited by da Silva First company of Eng. actors appears in America, at Williamsburg, Va. John Gay: "Trivia" Thomas Gray, Eng. poet, b. (d. 1771) Hakuseki: "Ori-Taku-Shiba," Jap. autobiography William Wycherley, Eng. dramatist, d. (b. 1640)	Christian religious teaching prohibited in China Gottfried Wilhelm von Leibniz, Ger. philosopher, d. (b. 1646)
1717	James III, the "Old Pretender," forced to leave France Future Empress Maria Theresa of Austria b. (d. 1780) Peter the Great in Paris Prince Eugene defeats Turks at Belgrade Separate Afghan state under Abdalis of Herat Mongols occupy Lhasa	David Garrick, Eng. actor, b. (d. 1779) Great Fr. actress Adrienne Lecouvreur (1692—1730) appears for first time at the Comédie française, Paris, in "Electre" by Prosper Jolyot de Crébillon Horace Walpole, Eng. statesman and man of letters, b. (d. 1797)	Armenian Mekhitarist monks settle on the island of San Lazzaro, Venice Cardinal de Retz (1614—1679): "Mémoires," period of the Fronde (posth.)
1718	Peter the Great has his son and heir, Alexis, murdered Peace of Passarowitz ends war between the Empire and Turkey Quadruple Alliance signed by France, the Empire, England, and Holland Charles XII of Sweden killed at Fredriksten during an expedition against Norway England declares war on Spain	Colley Cibber: "The Non-Juror," comedy P. A. Motteux, Fr. dramatist, d. (b. 1660) Nicholas Rowe, Eng. poet and dramatist, d. (b. 1674) Voltaire imprisoned in the Bastille, writes "Edipe," tragedy	Accademia dei Scienze, Lettere, ed Arti founded at Palermo Maria Gaetana Agnesi, Ital. mathematician and philosopher, b. (d. 1799) Philibert-Joseph Le Roux: "Dictionnaire comique, satyrique, critique, burlesque, libre, et proverbial" London Society of Antiquaries founded

D. VISUAL ARTS	E. MUSIC	F. SCIENCE, TECHNOLOGY, GROWTH	G. DAILY LIFE	
Ital. Jesuit missionary Giuseppe Castiglione (1688—1766) arrives in China, influences Chin. painting Early beginnings of rococo G. B. Tiepolo: "Sacrifice of Isaac"	Vaudevilles, popular musical comedies, appear in Paris	Brit. mathematician Brook Taylor (1685—1731) invents the calculus of finite differences	A prize for annual rowing race of Thames watermen, "Doggett's Coat and Badge," founded by Thomas Doggett Eng. painter and architect William Kent (1686—1748) "frees the Eng. garden from formality" First Liverpool dock built	**1715**
Lancelot "Capability" Brown, Eng. landscape designer, b. (d. 1783) Étienne Maurice Falconet, Fr. sculptor, b. (d. 1791) Fischer von Erlach builds the Karlkirche, Vienna (—1739) Watteau: "La Leçon d'amour"	Couperin: "L'Art de toucher le clavecin"	Scot. economist John Law (1671—1729) establishes the Banque générale in France	Diario di Roma, first Ital. newspaper, published "The Historical Register" published (—1738) Mineral waters discovered in Cheltenham, England Royal Regiment of Artillery founded	**1716**
Burlington House, London, remodeled by Colin Campbell Watteau: "Embarkation for the Isle of Cythera"	J. S. Bach: "Orgelbüchlein," 46 chorales for organ Handel's "Water Music" first given on the Thames Johann Stamitz, Bohemian composer, violinist, and conductor, b. (d. 1757) "The Loves of Mars and Venus," ballet, given at Drury Lane, London, by John Weaver (1673—1760)	Jean le Rond d'Alembert, Fr. mathematician and chemist, b. (d. 1783) John Law's Mississippi Company holds monopoly of trade with Louisiana Inoculation against smallpox introduced in England by Lady Mary Wortley Montagu (1690—1762)	Mother Grand Lodge of Freemasons established in London Value of golden guinea fixed at 21 shillings School attendance in Prussia made compulsory	**1717**
Suzuki Harunobu, Jap. painter, b. (d. 1770) Kneller: "Duke of Norfolk" Watteau: "Parc Fête"	Handel succeeds John Christopher Pepusch as Kapellmeister to the Duke of Chandos Johann Gottfried Müthel, Ger. composer and organist, b. (d. 1788)	Fr. scientist Etienne Geoffroy (1672—1731) presents tables of affinities to the Académie Eng. inventor Sir Thomas Lombe (1685—1739) patents machine which makes thrown silk William Penn, Amer. colonist, d. (b. 1644) Collegiate School of America transferred to new site in New Haven, and renamed Yale University *(contd)*	First bank notes in England "The Leeds Mercury" published Porcelain manufactured for first time in Vienna	**1718**

	A. HISTORY, POLITICS	B. LITERATURE, THEATER	C. RELIGION, PHILOSOPHY, LEARNING
1718 contd			
1719	France declares war on Spain Liechtenstein becomes independent principality Peace of Stockholm between Sweden and Hanover Ireland declared inseparable from England Mohammed Shah, grandson of Bahadur Shah, becomes the Great Mogul (—1748)	Daniel Defoe: "Robinson Crusoe" Thomas D'Urfey (1653—1723): "Wit and Mirth, or Pills to Purge Melancholy" Johann Wilhelm Gleim, Ger. poet, b. (d. 1803) Ludvig Holberg: "Pedar Paars," comic Dan. heroic poem Joseph Addison, Eng. essayist, d. (b. 1672)	Jesuits expelled from Russia
1720	Treaty of Stockholm between Sweden and Prussia Ulrica, Queen of Sweden, abdicates; succeeded by her husband Frederick, Prince of Hesse-Cassel (—1751) Treaty of Fredericksborg between Sweden and Denmark "South Sea Bubble," Eng. speculation craze, bursts Prince Charles Edward Stuart, the "Young Pretender," b. (d. 1788) Failure of John Law's Mississippi Company leads to French national bankruptcy William Burnet, Governor of New York, extends trade with the Indians Pragmatic Sanction recognized by estates of Upper and Lower Austria Spain occupies Texas (—1722) Tibet becomes Chin. protectorate	Defoe: "Memoires of a Cavalier" Samuel Foote, Eng. dramatist and actor, b. (d. 1777) John Gay: "Collected Poems" Old Haymarket Theatre opens in London First serialization of novels in newspapers	Arthur Collins: "Baronetage of England" Bernard de Montfaucon: "L'Antiquité expliquée" (—1724) Vico: "De uno universo juris principis"
1721	John Aislabie (1670—1742), Chancellor of the Exchequer, sent to Tower of London for fraud ("South Sea Bubble"); Robert Walpole made Chancellor (—1742), and soon restores public credit Peter I proclaimed Emperor of All the Russias China suppresses Formosa revolt	William Collins, Eng. poet, b. (d. 1759) Pierre de Marivaux: "Arlequin poli par l'amour," comedy Montesquieu: "Lettres persanes," novel in letters Matthew Prior, Eng. poet, d. (b. 1664) Tobias Smollett, Eng. novelist, b. (d. 1771)	Nathaniel Bailey: "An Universal Etymologycal English Dictionary" (—1731) Michele Angelo Conti elected Pope Innocent XIII (—1724) in succession to Pope Clement XI Johann Theodor Jablonski of Danzig publishes his "Allgemeines Lexikon," first short encyclopedia

D. VISUAL ARTS	E. MUSIC	F. SCIENCE, TECHNOLOGY, GROWTH	G. DAILY LIFE	
		Founding of New Orleans by Mississippi Company		**1718 contd**
Jan Weenix, Dutch painter, d. (b. 1640)	Dimitrie Cantemir (1673—1723), Rum. musician, writes first book on Turk. music, "Tratat de musica Turcéasea" Handel director of Royal Academy of Music, London Leopold Mozart b. (d. 1787)	John Flamsteed, Eng. astronomer, d. (b. 1646)	"The American Mercury" published in Philadelphia Oldest Eng. barracks erected in Berwick-upon-Tweed "The Boston Gazette" founded by William Brooker Mme. de Maintenon, wife of Louis XIV, d. (b. 1638) Oriental Company founded in Vienna to trade in the East Westminster Hospital, London, founded First cricket match: "Londoners" v. "Kentish Men" James Figg (1695—1734), first boxing champion of England, keeps title 15 years	**1719**
Bernardo Canaletto, Ital. painter, b. (d. 1780) James Gibbs: Octagon, Orleans House, Twickenham, Middlesex (—1725) Nicholas Hawksmoor builds St. George's, Bloomsbury, London (—1730) G. B. Tiepolo: "Martyrdom of St. Bartholomew"	Handel: Harpsichord Suite, No. 5 (with the "Harmonious Blacksmith")	Charles Bonnet, Swiss entomologist, b. (d. 1793)	Palatinate court moved from Heidelberg to Mannheim First collective settlement in Vermont, New England Wallpaper becomes fashionable in England First yacht club established at Cork Harbor, Ireland	**1720**
Grinling Gibbons, Eng. sculptor, d. (b. 1648) Jean Antoine Watteau d. (b. 1684)	J. S. Bach: "The Brandenburg Concertos" Barberina Campanini, Ital. dancer, b. (d. 1799) Handel: "Acis and Galatea," serenata Georg Philipp Telemann arrives in Hamburg as director of music	Elihu Yale, Amer. administrator, d. (b. 1648)	Mme. de Pompadour b. (d. 1764) Emigration problems in Prussia Regular postal service between London and New England Swiss immigrants introduced rifles into America	**1721**

	A. HISTORY, POLITICS	B. LITERATURE, THEATER	C. RELIGION, PHILOSOPHY, LEARNING
1722	John Churchill, Duke of Marlborough, d. (b. 1650) Hungary rejects Pragmatic Sanction Mir Mahmud conquers Afghanistan and becomes Shah Samuel Adams, Amer. Revolutionary statesman, b. (d. 1803) Aust. East India Company founded With Shih Tsung the Yung Cheng dynasty accedes in China	Daniel Defoe: "Moll Flanders" Dan. dramatist Ludvig Holberg begins his theater in Copenhagen Richard Steele: "The Conscious Lovers," comedy John Burgoyne, Eng. general and dramatist, b. (d. 1792)	Herrnhut founded as Moravian settlement in Saxony by Count Zinzendorf
1723	Louis XV attains majority Treaty of Charlottenburg between England and Prussia; grandson of George I to marry Prussian princess; Prince Frederick to marry the daughter of the Prince of Wales Prussia establishes a ministry of war, finance, and domains	Johann Christian Günther, Ger. poet, d. (b. 1695) John Thurmond: "Harlequin Dr. Faustus" given as pantomime at Drury Lane, London Voltaire: "La Henriade," history	"T'u Shu Chi Ch'eng," Chin. encyclopedia (—1736) Lodovico Antonio Muratori: "Rerum italicarum scriptores," collection of medieval historical material, 28 vols. (—1751)
1724	Philip V of Spain abdicates; his successor Luis I d.; Philip King again Mahmud of Afghanistan becomes insane Czar Peter the Great crowns his wife, Catherine, Czarina Austrian Netherlands agree to Pragmatic Sanction	Daniel Defoe: "Roxana" Friedrich Gottlieb Klopstock, Ger. poet, b. (d. 1803) Longman's, the oldest Eng. publishing house still extant, founded	Franz Aepinus, Ger. philosopher, b. (d. 1802) Nöel Alexandre, Fr. historian, d. (b. 1639) Pope Innocent III d.; Pierro Francesco Orsini becomes Pope Benedict XIII (—1730) Immanuel Kant, Ger. philosopher, b. (d. 1804) John Oldmixon: "A Critical History of England" Professorships of modern history and languages founded at Oxford and Cambridge
1725	Peter the Great of Russia d.; succeeded by his wife Catherine (—1727) Treaty of Vienna guarantees the Pragmatic Sanction Louis XV of France marries Maria Leszczynska of Poland Ashraf, Shah of Afghanistan, succeedes Mahmud in Persia	Letters of Mme. de Sévigné (1626—1696) published (posth.) Allan Ramsay: "The Gentle Shepherd," dramatic pastoral James Thompson (1700—1748): "The Seasons," poem in blank verse Alexander Pope: "The Odyssey" of Homer translated	Francis Hutcheson: "An Inquiry into the Original of Our Ideas of Beauty and Virtue"

D. VISUAL ARTS	E. MUSIC	F. SCIENCE, TECHNOLOGY, GROWTH	G. DAILY LIFE	
Christoph Dientzenhofer, Ger. architect, d. (b. 1655) James Gibbs builds St. Martin-in-the-Fields, London (—1726) Johann Heinrich Tischbein, Ger painter, b. (d. 1789)	J. S. Bach: "Das wohltemperierte Klavier," Vol. I Johann Mattheson: "Critica Musica," on musical criticism Rameau: "Traité de l'harmonie"	Ger. chemist Friedrich Hoffmann (1660—1742) discovers that the base of alum is an individual substance R. A. Ferchault de Réaumur: "L'Art de convertir le fer forgé en acier," on steel making	Brit. Parliament forbids journalists to report debates London bookseller Thomas Guy dedicates £300,000 for founding Guy's Hospital Flora MacDonald, Scot. heroine, b. (d. 1790) Fr. painter Hyacinthe Rigaud (1659—1743) publishes his handbook on traveling, "Grand Tour" Workhouse Test Act for care of poor	**1722**
Pedro de Ribiere: Toledo Bridge Sir Godfrey Kneller, Ger.-Eng. painter, d. (b. 1646) Joshua Reynolds, Eng. painter, b. (d. 1792) Fischer von Erlach, Aust. architect, d. (b. 1656) Sir Christopher Wren, Eng. architect, d. (b. 1632)	J. S. Bach: "St. John Passion" Bach appointed Thomascantor in Leipzig, after Telemann refuses post Handel: "Ottone," opera (London)	M. A. Capeller: "Prodromus Crystallographiae" Antony van Leeuwenhoek, Dutch scientist, d. (b. 1632)	Johann Bernhard Basedow, Ger. pedagogue, b. (d. 1790) Duty on tea reduced by Sir Robert Walpole	**1723**
Leonardo de Figueroa: West entrance, St. Telmo Palace, Seville, Spain James Gibbs: Fellows' Building, King's College, Cambridge (—1749) George Stubbs, Eng. painter, b. (d. 1806) Prince Eugene's Belvedere in Vienna finished by J. L. von Hildebrandt	Couperin: "Le Parnasse, ou L'Apothéose de Corelli" Handel: "Giulio Cesare," opera (London) Three Choirs Festival founded for Gloucester, Hereford, and Worcester	Hermann Boerhaave: "Elemente chemicae" Daniel Defoe: "A Tour Through the Whole Island of Great Britain" (—1727)	Gin drinking becomes popular in Great Britain Charles Johnson: "General History of the Robberies and Murders of the Most Notorious Pyrates" Paris Bourse opens Jack Sheppard, Eng. highwayman, executed (b. 1702)	**1724**
Antonio Canaletto: "Four Views of Venice" Jean Baptiste Greuze, Fr. painter, b. (d. 1805) Spanish Steps, Rome, finished (begun 1721)	Bach: "Notenbuch" for Anna Magdalena Bach J. J. Fux (1660—1741): "Gradus ad Parnassum," treatise on counterpoint Handel: "Rodelinde," opera (London) First public concert (Concerts spirituels) given in Paris by A D. Philidor Prague opera house (Ständetheater) founded Alessandro Scarlatti, Ital. composer, d. (b. 1659)	Guillaume Delisle (1675—1725): "Map of Europe" St. Petersburg Academy of Science founded by Catherine I	Casanova, Ital. adventurer and author, b. (d. 1798) George I revives Military Order of the Bath "The New York Gazette" issued James Otis, Amer. patriot, b. (d. 1783)	**1725**

	A. HISTORY, POLITICS	B. LITERATURE, THEATER	C. RELIGION, PHILOSOPHY, LEARNING
1726	Cardinal André Fleury (1653—1743) Chief Minister in France Alliance between Empire and Russia against Turkey In Treaty of Wusterhausen Prussia guarantees Pragmatic Sanction	Jeremy Collier, Eng. author, d. (b. 1650) Daniel Defoe: "The Four Voyages of Captain George Roberts" Louis Florence d'Epinay, Fr. author, b. (d. 1783) Jonathan Swift: "Gulliver's Travels" John Vanbrugh, Eng. dramatist and architect, d. (b. 1664) Voltaire, banished from France, flees to England (—1729)	St. John of the Cross canonized Johann Lorenz von Mosheim: "Institutiones historiae ecclesiasticae"
1727	Span. siege of Gibraltar; war between England and Spain Catherine, Russ. Czarina, d.; Peter II, grandson of Peter the Great, becomes Czar of Russia (—1730) George I of England d.; succeeded by his son George II (—1760) Amur frontier between Russia and China rectified England first uses Hessian mercenaries	Hester Chapone, Eng. writer, b. (d. 1791) Philippe Destouches: "Le Philosophe marie," comedy John Gay: "Fables," Vol. 1 Moses Hayyim Luzzatto: "Migda Oz," allegorical drama in Hebrew	American Philosophical Society founded in Philadelphia John Balguy: "The Foundation of Moral Goodness" Francesco Scipione Maffei: "Istoria diplomatica" Ezra Stiles, U.S. scholar, president of Yale, and diarist, b. (d. 1795)
1728	Spain raises siege of Gibraltar after 14 months Congress of Soissons (—1729) Treaty of Berlin between the Emperor Charles VI and Frederick William of Prussia Horatio Gates, Amer. Revolutionary general, b. (d. 1806)	Henry Fielding: "Love in Several Masques," comedy Oliver Goldsmith, Anglo-Ir. man of letters, b. (d. 1774) Alexander Pope: "The Dunciad" (Books 1—3) Allan Ramsay: "Poems" Richard Savage: "The Bastard" Thomas Warton, Eng. poet laureate, b. (d. 1790)	Ephraim Chambers: "Cyclopaedia, or An Universal Dictionary of Arts and Sciences" (2 vols.) Francis Hutcheson: "An Essay on the Nature and Conduct of the Passions and the Affections" William Law: "A Serious Call to Devout and Holy Life" Jonathan Swift: "A Short View of the State of Ireland"
1729	Future Czarina of Russia, Catherine the Great, b. at Stettin (d. 1796) Treaty of Seville between France, Spain, and England Portugal loses Mombasa to the Arabs Founding of Baltimore N. and S. Carolina become crown colonies Corsica becomes independent of Genoa (—1732)	Edmund Burke, Brit. author and statesman, b. (d. 1797) William Congreve, Eng. dramatist, d. (b. 1670) Henry Fielding: "The Author's Farce" (Haymarket Theatre, London) John Gay: "Polly," ballad opera Gotthold Ephraim Lessing, Ger. author, b. (d. 1781) Clara Reve, Eng. novelist, b. (d. 1807) Albrecht von Haller: "Die Alpen," Swiss pastoral poem Richard Steele, Eng. author, d. (b. 1672)	Moses Mendelssohn, Ger.-Jewish philosopher, b. (d. 1786) Thomas Sherlock: "A Tryal of the Witnesses of the Resurrection of Jesus"

D. VISUAL ARTS	E. MUSIC	F. SCIENCE, TECHNOLOGY, GROWTH	G. DAILY LIFE	
Colin Campbell: Compton Place, Eastbourne, Sussex Daniel Chodowiecki, Ger. painter, b. (d. 1801) G. B. Tiepolo: Frescoes in the palace, Udine (—1728)	Charles Burney, Eng. music historian, b. (d. 1814) Handel becomes Brit. subject La Camargo, Fr. ballerina (1710—1770), makes debut at Paris Opéra Rameau: "Nouveau système de musique théorique"	Stephen Hales (1671—1761) measures blood pressure John Harrison, Eng. clockmaker (1693—1776), invents gridiron pendulum James Hutton, Eng. geologist, b. (d. 1797)	"Lloyd's List" issued in London twice weekly First circulating library established by Allan Ramsay in Edinburgh General George Wade builds 250 miles of military roads in Scot. Highlands (—1737)	**1726**
Francesco Bertolozzi, Ital. artist, b. (d. 1815) Giovanni Battista Cipriani, Ital. artist, b. (d. 1785) Thomas Gainsborough, Eng. painter, b. (d. 1788) Hildebrandt: Mirabell Palace, Salzburg (begun 1721) William Kent: "The Designs of Inigo Jones" John Michael Rysbrack: "George I"	Francesco Gasparini, Ital. composer, d. (b. 1668)	Daniel Defoe: "The Complete English Tradesman" Stephen Hales: "Vegetable Staticks" or "Statical Essays," on nutrition of plants and plant physiology Isaac Newton d. (b. 1642)	Coffee first planted in Brazil First marriage advertisement in a newspaper (Manchester, England) "Miscellanies," satirical periodical issued by Pope, Swift, and Dr. Arbuthnot Quakers demand abolition of slavery Racing Calendar published for first time (records of horse races run previous year)	**1727**
Robert Adam, Scot. architect, b. (d. 1792) Chardin: "The Rain" James Gibbs: "Book of Architecture" Anton Raphael Mengs, Ger. artist, b. (d. 1779)	John Gay: "Beggar's Opera" Nicola Piccini, Ital. composer, b. (d. 1800)	Dutch explorer Vitus Behring (1681—1741) discovers Behring Strait James Bradley (1692—1762) discovers aberration of light of fixed stars William Byrd: "History of the Dividing Line," between Britain and the Amer. colonies James Cook, Eng. navigator and explorer, b. (d. 1779) P. Fauchard: "Le Chirurgien dentiste, ou Traité des dents"	Madrid Lodge of Freemasons founded; soon suppressed by Inquisition	**1728**
Desportes: "Still Life with Oysters" J. F. de Troy: "Rape of the Sabines" John Wood builds Queen's Square, Bath, England (—1736)	J. S. Bach: "St. Matthew Passion"	Academia de buenas letras, Barcelona, founded Eng. scientist Stephen Gray discovers that some bodies are conductors and some nonconductors of electricity Newton's "Principia" translated into English by Andrew Motte	The Emperor Yung Cheng prohibits opium smoking in China Benjamin and James Franklin publish "The Pennsylvania Gazette" (—1765)	**1729**

	A. HISTORY, POLITICS	B. LITERATURE, THEATER	C. RELIGION, PHILOSOPHY, LEARNING
1730	Czar Peter of Russia d.; succeeded by Anne, daughter of Czar Ivan V (—1740) Crown Prince Frederick of Prussia imprisoned by his father Sultan Ahmad XII of Turkey deposed; succeeded by Mahmoud I (—1754) Frederick IV of Denmark d.; succeeded by Christian VI (—1746) Ashraf. Shah of Persia, murdered Friedrich Wilhelm von Steuben. Ger. general in Amer. Revolutionary war, b. (d. 1794)	Elijah Fenton, Eng. poet, d. (b. 1683) Henry Fielding: "Rape Upon Rape," comedy Pierre Carlet de Chamblain de Marivaux: "Le Jeu de l'amour et du hasard," comedy Anne Oldfield, Eng. actress, d. (b. 1683)	Pope Benedict XIII d.; Cardinal Lorenzo Corsini becomes Pope Clement XII (—1740) Matthew Tindal: "Christianity as Old as the Creation" John and Charles Wesley found Methodist sect at Oxford Martin Wright: "Introduction to the Law of Tenures," on Eng. land law
1731	Treaty of Vienna between England, Holland, Spain, and the Holy Roman Emperor Russia, Prussia, and the emperor agree to oppose Stanislas I in Poland French fortify Crown Point on Lake Champlain Charles Lee, Eng.-born Amer. Revolutionary general, noted for his criticism of Washington, b. (d. 1782)	Charles Churchill, Eng. poet, b. (d. 1764) William Cowper, Eng. poet, b. (d. 1800) Daniel Defoe d. (b. 1661) Ramón de la Cruz, Span. dramatist, b. (d. 1794) George Lillo: "The London Merchant," drama Marivaux: "La Vie de Marianne" (—1741) Abbé Prévost: "Manon Lescaut" Katharina Elisabeth Textor, Goethe's mother, b. (d. 1808) Girolamo Tiraboschi, Ital. author, b. (d. 1794)	Ralph Cudworth: "Treatise Concerning Eternal and Immutable Morality" Mass expulsion of Protestants from Salzburg Voltaire: "Histoire de Charles XII"
1732	Emperor Charles VI gets recognition of the Pragmatic Sanction George Washington b. Feb. 22 (d. 1799) King Frederick William I of Prussia settles 12,000 Salzburg Protestants in E. Prussia Genoa regains Corsica James Oglethorpe (1696—1785) obtains charter to establish colony in Georgia (see 1733) Stanislas II Poniatowski, last independent King of Poland, b. (d. 1798) Warren Hastings, Eng. Gov.-Gen. of India, b. (d. 1818)	Pierre-Augustin Caron de Beaumarchais, Fr. dramatist, b. (d. 1799) Julie de Lepinasse, Fr. author, b. (d. 1776) Philippe Néricault (Destouches): "Le Glorieux," comedy John Gay, Eng. dramatist, d. (b. 1685) A London theatrical company performs for the first time in New York (Pearl Steet)	Conrad Beissel founds Seventh Day Baptists (Ephrata Community) in Germantown, Pa. George Berkeley: "The Minute Philosopher" The Moravian Brethren start missionary work J. J. Moser: "Foundations of International Law"
1733	Augustus II of Poland and Saxony d. (b. 1670) Santa Cruz (West Indies) comes under Dan. control War of Polish Succession begins France declares war against Emperor Charles VI Conscription introduced in Prussia James Oglethorpe founds Savannah, Ga.	Christoph Friedrich Nicolai, Ger. author, b. (d. 1811) Christoph Martin Wieland, Ger. author, b. (d. 1813)	Alexander Pope: "Essay on Man" Corporation for the Propagation of the Gospel in New England founded Voltaire: "Lettres sur les Anglais"

D. VISUAL ARTS	E. MUSIC	F. SCIENCE, TECHNOLOGY, GROWTH	G. DAILY LIFE	
Boucher returns from Rome to Paris Canaletto: "Scuola di San Rocco" Leonardo de Figueroa, Span. architect, d. (b. 1650) Hogarth: "Before and After" Rococo in its fullest form Josiah Wedgwood, Eng. pottery manufacturer, b. (d. 1795) Augustin Pajou, Fr. sculptor, b. (d. 1809)	J. A. Hasse: "Artaserse," Ger. opera in Ital. style	James Bruce, Scot. explorer, b. (d. 1794) Réaumur constructs alcohol thermometer with graduated scale Zinc-smelting first practiced in England	"The Daily Advertiser" issued in London (—1807) Edinburgh Royal Infirmary founded Freemason Lodge in Philadelphia "Grub Street Journal" appears (—1737) Reduction of slavery in China under the Emperor Yung Cheng Four-course system of husbandry started in Norfolk by Viscount ("Turnip") Townshend (1674—1738)	**1730**
Hogarth: "The Harlot's Progress" Nicolas Lancret: "La Camargo" Building of State House, Philadelphia, designed by Andrew Hamilton (—1751); later named Independence Hall	Lodovico Giustini: "Sonate da Cimbalo di piano e forte," probably first compositions for modern piano J. A. Hasse becomes Kapellmeister at the Dresden Opera, his wife Faustina Bordoni its prima donna Public concerts held at Boston, Mass., and Charleston, S.C.	Dr. John Arbuthnot: "An Essay Concerning the Nature of Ailments," advocates dieting Erasmus Darwin, Eng. scientist and poet, b. (d. 1802) Eng. mathematician John Hadley (1682—1744) invents quadrant for use at sea	10 Downing Street, Westminster, London residence of Brit. prime ministers, built Eng. factory workers not allowed to emigrate to America Benjamin Franklin founds a subscription library, Philadelphia	**1731**
Chardin: "Kitchen Table with Shoulder of Mutton" Jean Honoré Fragonard, Fr. painter, b. (d. 1806) Balthasar Permoser, Ger. sculptor, d. (b. 1651) Nicola Salvi: Fontana di Trevi, Rome	Academie of Ancient Music founded in London Covent Garden Opera House, London, opened Franz Joseph Haydn, Aust. composer, b. (d. 1809) J. G. Walther: Musik-Lexikon, first of its kind	Hermann Boerhaave: "Elements of Chemistry" Jacques Necker, Swiss economist, b. (d. 1804)	Benjamin Franklin: "Poor Richard's Almanack" issued (—1757) Ger. bookseller Johann Heinrich Zedler (1706—1760) publishes his "Grosses, vollständiges Universal-Lexikon," 64 vols. (—1750) Ninepins played for first time in New York	**1732**
Okyo, Jap. painter, b. (d. 1795) Fr. painter J. B. Oudry (1686—1755) appointed director of the Beauvais tapestry factory Johann Zoffany, Ger.-Eng. painter, b. (d. 1810)	J. S. Bach: short version of the Mass in B minor (see 1738) Couperin d. (b. 1668) Pergolesi: "La Serva padrona," opera buffa, Naples–once called the oldest opera in the standard repertoire Rameau: "Hippolyte et Aricie," opera, Paris	John Kay patents his flying shuttle loom Franz Anton Mesmer, Aust. physician, b. (d. 1815)	First Ger. Freemason lodge in Hamburg (—1933) Lat. language abolished in Eng. courts Molasses Act prohibits Amer. trade with Fr. West Indies "The New York Weekly Journal" first issued The Serpentine, Hyde Park, London, laid out "Czar Kolokol," great bell of Moscow, weighing 193 tons, cast	**1733**

	A. HISTORY, POLITICS	B. LITERATURE, THEATER	C. RELIGION, PHILOSOPHY, LEARNING
1734	War breaks out between Turkey and Persia Prince of Orange-Nassau marries Marie Anne, daughter of George II Russians occupy Danzig Anglo-Russ. trade agreement Robert Morris, U.S. financier and statesman, b. (d. 1806)	John Dennis, Eng. dramatist, d. (b. 1657) François Goyot de Pitaval (1673—1743): "Causes célèbres et intéressantes" Charles Johnson: "The Lives and Adventures of the Most Famous Highwaymen"	Mme. de Lambert, in her "Avis d'une Mère à sa Fille," recommends university education for women University of Göttingen founded by King George II The Koran translated into English by George Sale Emanuel Swedenborg (1688—1772): "Prodromus philosophiae"
1735	End of Turko-Persian war John Adams, 2nd President of the U.S., b. (d. 1826) William Pitt elected Member of Parliament for Old Sarum Paul Revere, Amer. patriot, b. (d. 1818)	P. C. Nivelle de La Chaussée (1692—1754): "Le Préjugé à la Mode," "comédie larmoyante" Marivaux: "Le Paysan parvenu" First 4 vols. of "Swift's Collected Works" published in Dublin (—1772, 20 vols.)	The Bible translated into Lithuanian Thomas Hearne, Eng. historian, d. (b. 1678) John Wesley writes his "Journals" (—1790) Arthur Collins: "Peerage of England" (begun 1709)
1736	Stanislas I abdicates as King of Poland Maria Theresa marries Francis, Duke of Lorraine Ger. adventurer Theodor von Neuhof (1694—1756) elected King of Corsica Prince Eugene d. (b. 1663) Porteous riots in Edinburgh Chi-en Lung becomes Emperor of China (—1796) Nadir Shah, of Persia (—1747) War between Russia and Turkey (—1739) Patrick Henry, Amer. Revolutionary leader, b. (d. 1799)	James Macpherson, Scot. poet, b. (d. 1796)	Joseph Butler: "Analogy of Religion" Charles Augustin de Coulomb, Fr. philosopher, b. (d. 1806) Eng. statutes against witchcraft repealed Pope Clement XII condemns Freemasonry William Warburton: "The Alliance between Church and State"
1737	William Byrd founds Richmond, Va. Last of the Medici, the Grand Duke of Tuscany, d.; Francis, Duke of Lorraine, husband of Maria Theresa, receives Tuscany; Stanislas of Poland acquires Lorraine Quarrel between George II and his son Frederick, Prince of Wales Count Alexei Grigorievich Orlov, Russ. nobleman, officer, and naval commander, b. (d. 1808) Queen Caroline, wife of George II, d.	Frances Abington, Eng. actress, b. (d. 1815) Licensing Act restricts number of London theaters, and all plays before public performance to be subjected to censorship of Lord Chamberlain Matthew Green: "The Spleen," poem Dr. Samuel Johnson and David Garrick leave Lichfield for London Thomas Paine, Anglo-Amer. author, b. (d. 1809) Ignacio de Luzán Claramunt de Suelves y Gurrea: "Poética," laying down classic rules in Span. literary composition	Alexander Cruden: "Concordance of the Holy Scripture" Vincent de Paul (1576—1660) canonized by Pope Clement XII Edward Gibbon, Eng. historian, b. (d. 1794) Lady Mary Wortley Montagu: "The Nonsense of Common Sense" J. J. Moser: "German Law" William Oldys: "The British Librarian" John Wesley: "Psalms and Hymns," published in Charleston

D. VISUAL ARTS	E. MUSIC	F. SCIENCE, TECHNOLOGY, GROWTH	G. DAILY LIFE	
Boucher: illustrations for Molière edition William Kent: Treasury, Whitehall, London George Romney, Eng. painter, b. (d. 1802) James Thornhill, Eng. painter, d. (b. 1676)	Handel: 6 concerti grossi, Op. 3	8,000 Salzburg Protestants settle in Georgia	"The Boston Weekly Post-Boy" issued First horse race in America at Charleston Neck, S.C. Jack Broughton (1704—1789) wins Eng. boxing championship from James Figg	**1734**
Thomas Banks, Eng. sculptor, b. (d. 1805) Hogarth: "The Rake's Progress"	Johann Christian Bach, Bach's youngest son, b. (d. 1782) Handel: "Alcina," opera (Covent Garden, London) Imperial ballet school at St. Petersburg Rameau: "Les Indes galantes," ballet opera Ballad opera "Flora," first musical theater in America, at Charleston, S.C.	Linnaeus: "Systema naturae" Fr. scientist Benoît de Maillet (1656—1738): "Telliamed," evolutionary hypothesis	"The Boston Evening Post" issued Fr. settlement at Vincennes, Ind. Sale of spirits prohibited in Georgia (—1742) Royal Burgess Golfing Society, Edinburgh, founded John Peter Zenger (1697—1746), Ger.-born printer and publisher of the New York "Weekly Journal," acquitted of seditious libel in landmark trial for freedom of the press	**1735**
Jean-Jacques de Boissieu, Fr. painter, b. (d. 1810) Anton Graff, Ger. portrait painter, b. (d. 1813) Hogarth: "The Good Samaritan" Mattheus Daniel Pöppelmann, Ger. architect, d. (b. 1662)	Handel: "Alexander's Feast," London, Covent Garden Pergolesi: "Stabat Mater" Pergolesi d. (b. 1710)	Claudius Aymand (1660—1740) performs first successful operation for appendicitis Fr. expedition to Lapland under Anders Celsius, sponsored by the Académie Française Leonhard Euler begins study of analytical mechanics Gabriel Daniel Fahrenheit, Ger. physicist, d. (b. 1686) Manufacture of glass begins in Venice at Murano Joseph Louis Lagrange, Fr. mathematician, b. (d. 1813) James Watt, Scot. inventor, b. (d. 1819)	Hard rubber caoutchouc ("India rubber") comes to England	**1736**
Boucher: designs for Beauvais tapestries Chardin: "The Draughtsman" James Gibbs builds Radcliffe Camera, Oxford (—1749) Joseph Nollekens, Eng. sculptor, b. (d. 1823) Roubiliac: "Handel"	William Boys conducts Three Choirs Festivals (—1745) Handel: "Berenice," opera, Covent Garden, London Rameau: "Castor et Pollux," opera Antonio Stradivari d. (b. 1644)	Luigi Galvani, Ital. physiologist, b. (d. 1798) René de Réaumur: "History of the Insects"	Charles Carroll, rich Amer. politician, b. (d. 1832)	**1737**

	A. HISTORY, POLITICS	B. LITERATURE, THEATER	C. RELIGION, PHILOSOPHY, LEARNING
1738	Brit. troops sent to Georgia to settle border dispute with Spain Turks take Orsova; Imperial troops driven back to Belgrade The future King George III b. (d. 1820) Jean H. L. Orry, controller-general of Fr. finances, devises the "corvée," a system of forced labor to construct roads	Samuel Johnson: "London," epic poem Alexis Piron: "La Métromanie," Fr. comedy Jonathan Swift: "A Complete Collection of Genteel and Ingenious Conversations" Olof von Dalin: "The Envious Man," Swed. tragedy John Wolcot (Peter Pindar), Eng. author, b. (d. 1819)	Papal bull "In eminenti" against Freemasonry Lodovico Antonio Muratori: "Antiquites Italicae" (—1742) Voltaire introduces ideas of Isaac Newton to France John Wesley's evangelical conversion; George Whitefield follows him to Georgia as "Leader of the Great Awakening"
1739	As Turks approach Belgrade, Emperor Charles VI signs peace treaty Sack of Delhi by Persians under Nadir Shah New Granada parted from Peru Prince Potemkin, Russ. statesman, b. (d. 1791) George Clinton, twice Vice President of the U.S., b. (d. 1812)	Jonathan Swift: "Verses on the Death of Doctor Swift"	Crown Prince Frederick of Prussia: "Anti-Machiavell," against Machiavelli's philosophy of monarchy David Hume: "A Treatise of Human Nature" Moravian Church founded in America by Bishop A. G. Spengenberg (1704—1792)
1740	Frederick William I of Prussia d.; succeeded by his son Frederick II, the Great (—1786) Charles VI d.; succeeded by his daughter Maria Theresa (—1780) Anne, daughter of Peter the Great, d.; succeeded by Czar Ivan VI (—1741) Frederick the Great of Prussia begins First Silesian War against Maria Theresa	Carl Michael Bellmann, Swed. poet, b. (d. 1795) James Boswell, Scot. author, b. (d. 1795) Colley Cibber: "An Apology for the Life of Mr. Colley Cibber, Comedian" Louis de Rouvroy, Duc de Saint-Simon: "Mémoires" (—1752) Samuel Richardson: "Pamela, or Virtue Rewarded"	Ephraim Chambers, Eng. lexicographer, d. (b. 1660) Pope Clement XII d.; succeeded by Cardinal Prospero Lambertini as Pope Benedict XIV (—1758) William Stukeley: "Stonehenge"
1741	Future Emperor Joseph II b. (d. 1790) Maria Theresa accepts crown of Hungary Frederick the Great conquers Silesia, captures Brieg, Neisse, Glatz, and Olmütz England mediates between Prussia and Austria Prague occupied by French, Bavarian, and Saxon troops Czar Ivan VI deposed and imprisoned; Elizabeth, daughter of Peter the Great, becomes czarina (—1762)	Thomas Betterton: "A History of the English Stage" Founding of Burgtheater, Vienna Pierre A. F. Choderlos de Laclos, Fr. novelist, b. (d. 1803) Robert Dodsley: "The Blind Beggar of Bethnal Green," drama David Garrick's debut in London as "Richard III" (Goodman's Fields) Samuel Richardson: "Familiar Letters" First Ger. Shakespeare translation printed ("Julius Caesar," by C. W. von Borck) Voltaire: "Mahomet," tragedy	Jonathan Edwards: "Sinners in the Hands of an Angry God," sermon delivered at Enfield, Mass. David Hume: "Essays, Moral and Political"

D. VISUAL ARTS	E. MUSIC	F. SCIENCE, TECHNOLOGY, GROWTH	G. DAILY LIFE	
Chardin: "La Gouvernante" Claude Michel (Clodion), Fr. sculptor, b. (d. 1814) Roubiliac: "Alexander Pope" G. B. Sacchetti begins work on Royal Palace, Madrid Benjamin West, Amer. painter, b. (d. 1820) John Singleton Copley, Amer.-Brit. portrait painter, b. (d. 1815)	J. S. Bach: Mass in B minor, full version	Daniel Bernoulli: "Hydrodynamica," pressure and velocity of fluids William Herschel, Eng. astronomer, b. (d. 1822) Joseph Guillotin, Fr. physician, inventor of guillotine, b. (d. 1814) Excavation of Herculaneum begun	First cuckoo clocks in Black Forest district Joseph Süss Oppenheimer (Jew Süss), financial adviser to Duke Karl Alexander of Württemberg, hanged (b. 1698)	**1738**
C. D. Asam, Ger. architect, d. (b. 1686) Chardin: "Saying Grace" George Dance: Mansion House, London (—1752)	Handel: oratorios "Saul" and "Israel in Egypt" first given (King's Theatre, London) Johann Mattheson: "Der vollkommene Kapellmeister," treatise on conducting Rameau: "Dardanus," opera Karl Ditters von Dittersdorf, Aust. composer, b. (d. 1799)	J. F. Gronovius: "Flora Virginica" Amer. astronomer John Winthrop IV (1714—1779) publishes his "Notes on Sunspots"	First camellias arrive in Europe from Far East Foundling Hospital established in London Peacock Throne of Shah Jahan taken to Persia Dick Turpin, Eng. highwayman, d. (b. 1706)	**1739**
Boucher: "Morning Toilet" Canaletto: "Return of the Bucintoro" Hogarth: "Captain Coram" Jean Antoine Houdon, Fr. sculptor, b. (d. 1828) Johann Kupetzky, Aust. Bohemian portrait painter, d. (b. 1667)	Thomas Augustine Arne: "Alfred," masque containing "Rule Britannia" (London) Haydn enters the court chapel, Vienna, as a choirboy Domenico Scarlatti in London and Dublin J. A. Scheibe (1708—1776): "Der critische Musicus," against Bach Ger. organ builder John Snetzler establishes himself in England	George Anson (1697—1762) sets out on voyage around the world (Sept.—June 1744) Louis Castel: "Optique des couleurs" Eng. inventor Benjamin Huntsman improves "crucible" process for smelting steel University of Pennsylvania founded Berlin Academy of Science founded by Frederick the Great	Frederick the Great introduces freedom of press and freedom of worship in Prussia Smallpox epidemic in Berlin	**1740**
Boucher: "Autumn" Henry Fuseli, Swiss-Eng. painter, b. (d. 1825) Angelica Kauffmann, Swiss painter, b. (d. 1807) Bartolomeo Rastrelli: Summer Palace, St. Petersburg Jacques Germain Soufflot: Hôtel-Dieu, Lyons Charles Willson Peale, portraitist of Washington, b. (d. 1827)	Johann Joseph Fux, Aust. musician, d. (b. 1660) Gluck: "Artaserse," his first opera, Milan André Grétry, Fr. composer, b. (d. 1813) Handel: "The Messiah," oratorio composed in 18 days Giovanni Paisiello, Ital. composer, b. (d. 1816) Johann Joachim Quantz becomes court composer to Frederick the Great Rameau: "Pièces de clavecin en concert" published Antonio Vivaldi, Ital. composer, d. (b. 1675)	Victor Behring, after discovering Alaska and Aleutian Islands, dies of hunger and cold (b. 1681) Russ. navigator Alexei Cherikov lands in California	Botanical Garden, Uppsala, founded by Linnaeus "The General Magazine" founded in Philadelphia by Benjamin Franklin Highway Act in England to improve roads Royal Military Academy, Woolwich, England, opened	**1741**

	A. HISTORY, POLITICS	B. LITERATURE, THEATER	C. RELIGION, PHILOSOPHY, LEARNING
1742	Charles Albert, Elector of Bavaria, elected and crowned emperor as Charles VII (d. 1745) Prussians evacuate Olmütz; defeat Austrians at Chotusitz Peace of Berlin ends First Silesian War Nathanael Greene, Amer. Revolutionary general, b. (d. 1786) Gebhard von Blücher, Prussian general, b. (d. 1819)	Crébillon fils: "La Sopha," Fr. novel Henry Fielding: "Joseph Andrews" Georg Christoph Lichtenberg, Ger. critic and aphorist, b. (d. 1799) William Somerville, Eng. poet, d. (b. 1675)	John Campbell: Lives of the Admirals" Etienne Fourmont: "Grammatica Sinaica" Charles Viner: "Legal Encyclopaedia," 23 vols. (—1753)
1743	Maria Theresa crowned at Prague Thomas Jefferson, third U.S. President, b. (d. 1826) Jean Paul Marat, Fr. revolutionist, b. (d. 1793) French defeated by English at Dettingen Alliance between Austria and Saxony Turko-Persian war continues	Johannes Ewald, Dan. poet, b. (d. 1781) Henry Fielding: "Jonathan Wild the Great" Richard Savage, Eng. author, d. (b. 1697) Voltaire: "Mérope," drama	Pogroms in Russia
1744	Josiah Quincey, Amer. patriot, b. (d. 1775) France declares war on England and on Maria Theresa Peter, heir to the Russian throne, marries Princess Catherine (born Sophia) of Anhalt-Zerbst Second Silesian War begins; Frederick the Great takes Prague but is driven back to Saxony Robert Clive arrives in Madras as clerk with East India Company Adolphus Frederick, heir to Swed. throne, marries Princess Ulrica, daughter of Frederick the Great of Prussia Fr. troops occupy Annapolis, Nova Scotia, but withdraw Elbridge Gerry, U.S. statesman, b. (d. 1814)	Alexander Pope, Eng. poet, d. (b. 1688) Johann Gottfried von Herder, Ger. author, b. (d. 1803) Samuel Johnson: "Life of Mr. Richard Savage"	George Berkeley: "A Chain of Philosophical Reflexions and Inquiries" Benjamin Franklin edits Cicero's "Cato Major" in Philadelphia Lodovico Antonio Muratori: "Annali d'Italia" (—1749) Ruling Arab family Sa-Udi adopts teachings of Abd-al-Wahhab (1703—1792), becomes Wahhabi Giovanni Battista Vico, Ital. jurist and philosopher, d. (b. 1668)
1745	Emperor Charles VII d.; Francis, husband of Maria Theresa, elected Holy Roman Emperor (—1765), first of the Lorraine-Tuscany line French, under the Maréchal de Saxe, defeat English at Fontenoy; take Aust. Netherlands England, after undertaking to subsidize Maria Theresa and to provide her with troops, withdraws Prussian victory at Hohenfriedberg British take Louisburg, Canada Charles Edward Stuart, the "Young Pretender," lands on Eriskay Island, Scotland, defeats Eng. army at Prestonpans, advances south toward Derby, is forced to retreat Timothy Pickering, U.S. statesman, b. (d. 1829) Peace of Dresden: Prussia recognizes Pragmatic Sanction but retains Silesia Ishege becomes Shogun of Japan	Jonathan Swift: "Directions to Servants in General" Jonathan Swift d. (b. 1667) James Thomson: "Tancred and Sigismunda," tragedy Samuel Johnson: "Observations on the Tragedy of Macbeth"	Philip Doddridge: "The Rise and Progress of Religion in the Soul" John Jay, first Chief Justice of the United States, b. (d. 1829) Oliver Ellsworth, U.S. jurist, b. (d. 1807)

D. VISUAL ARTS	E. MUSIC	F. SCIENCE, TECHNOLOGY, GROWTH	G. DAILY LIFE	
Boucher: "Bath of Diana" Hogarth: "The Graham Children" William Kent: Horse Guards, Whitehall, London J. B. Oudry: "The Gardens of Arcueil"	Karl Heinrich Graun (1704—1759) introduces Ital. opera in Berlin Handel's "Messiah" first performed in Dublin	Swiss astronomer Anders Celsius (1701—1744) invents centigrade thermometer Edmund Halley, Eng. astronomer, d. (b. 1656) Colin Maclaurin: "Treatise on Fluxions" Karl Wilhelm Scheele, Ger. chemist, b. (d. 1786)	Construction of canal linking Elbe and Havel Cotton factories established in Birmingham and Northampton	**1742**
Thomas Archer, Eng. architect, d. (b. 1668) Hogarth: "Marriage à la Mode"	Luigi Boccherini, Ital. composer, b. (d. 1805) Handel: "Samson," Covent Garden, London	Francis Dana, Amer. jurist, b. (d. 1811) Fr. geographer Jean d'Anville (1697—1782): "Map of Italy" University of Erlangen, Germany, founded Fr. explorers reach Rocky Mountains Antoine Laurent Lavoisier, Fr. chemist, b. (d. 1794) John Lowell, Amer. jurist, b. (d. 1802) First settlement in S. Dakota	Cagliostro, Ital. adventurer, b. (d. 1795) Mme. Du Barry, mistress of Louis XV, b. (executed 1793) East India yarns imported into Lancashire for manufacture of finer goods	**1743**
J. M. Rysbrack: "Dr. Radcliffe of Oxford," sculpture	J. S. Bach: "Das wohltemperierte Klavier," Part 2 Gluck· "Iphigénie en Aulide," opera (Paris) "God Save the Queen" published in "Thesaurus Musicus" Madrigal Society, London, founded	Sir George Anson returns from voyage around the world Jean d'Alembert: "Traité de l'équilibre et du mouvement des fluides" Jean-Baptiste Monet de Lamarck, Fr. naturalist, b. (d. 1829)	Eruption of Mount Cotopaxi, S. America First recorded cricket match: Kent versus All England	**1744**
Hogarth: "Self-Portrait" Henry Holland, Eng. architect, b. (d. 1806) Oudry: "Still Life with Pheasants" Tiepolo: "Antony and Cleopatra," frescoes for Labia Palace, Venice Johann Lukas von Hildebrandt, Aust. architect, d. (b. 1668)	"The Campbells are Coming," Scot. national song, published Charles Dibdin, Eng. singer and composer, b. (d. 1814) Johann Stamitz (1717—1757) becomes court Kapellmeister in Mannheim	Charles Bonnet: "Traité d'insectologie" Gerard van Swieton (1700—1772), founder of Viennese School of Medicine, becomes court physician to Maria Theresa Alessandro Volta, Ital. physicist, b. (d. 1827) Ewald Jurgen von Kleist invents the capacitor ("Leyden jar"), a fundamental electrical circuit element New royal charter for Yale College, Conn. Benjamin Rush, U.S. physician, b. (d. 1813)	Middlesex Hospital, London, founded Earliest Oddfellows Lodge in England The quadrille becomes a fashionable dance in France	**1745**

	A. HISTORY, POLITICS	B. LITERATURE, THEATER	C. RELIGION, PHILOSOPHY, LEARNING
1746	Charles Edward Stuart, the "Young Pretender", wins a victory at Falkirk, but is defeated finally at Culloden; with help of Flora MacDonald he escapes to France William Pitt, paymaster-general for the Brit. forces Alliance between Russia and Austria against Prussia Philip V of Spain d.; succeeded by Ferdinand VI (—1759) Christian VI of Denmark d.; succeeded by Frederick V (—1766) Fr. victory at Raucoux; Austria loses the Netherlands	Gellert: "Fabeln und Erzählungen"	Denis Diderot (1713—1784): "Pensées philosophiques" Jonathan Edwards: "A Treatise Concerning Religious Affections" Frances Hutcheson, Scot. philosopher, d. (b. 1694)
1747	William IV of Orange-Nassau becomes hereditary stadholder of the seven provinces of the Netherlands (—1751) Prusso-Swed. alliance for mutual defense Nadir Shah murdered; Ahmed Shah becomes King of Afghanistan (—1773) John Paul Jones, Amer. Revolutionary naval officer, b. (d. 1792)	Gottfried August Bürger, Ger. author, b. (d. 1794) Charles Collé: "La Vérité dans le vin," comedy of manners David Garrick: "Miss in her Teens, or The Medley of Lovers," comedy Christian Gellert: "Die kranke Frau," comedy Thomas Gray: "Ode on Eton College" Alain René Lesage, Fr. author, d. (b. 1668) Voltaire: "Zadig," philosophical tale Samuel Johnson: "Plan of a Dictionary of the English Language"	Biblioteca Nazionale founded in Florence, Italy Biographia Britannica (—1766) Benjamin Franklin: "Plain Truth" National Library founded in Warsaw Gilbert West: "Observations on the Resurrection"
1748	Russ. troops march through Bohemia toward the Rhine Peace of Aix-la-Chapelle; general recognition of Pragmatic Sanction and of Francis I as Holy Roman Emperor Shah Rukh, grandson of Nadir Shah, ruler of Persia	Marie-Thérèse Geoffrin opens salon as meeting place for Parisian men of letters Carlo Goldoni: "The Liar," Venetian comedy Carlo Gozzi: "Turandot" Klopstock: "Der Messias" (—1773) Samuel Richardson: "Clarissa, or The History of a Young Lady" Tobias Smollett: "The Adventures of Roderick Random"	Archibald Bower: "History of the Popes," 7 vols. (—1766) David Hume: "Philosophical Essays Concerning Human Understanding" (—1753) Peter Whalley: "An Inquiry Into the Learning of Shakespeare"
1749	Comte de Mirabeau, Fr. revolutionist, b. (d. 1791) Consolidation Act of Brit. navy (reorganization of the service) First settlement of Ohio Company Establishment of Halifax, Nova Scotia, as fortress	Vittorio Alfieri, Ital. dramatist, b. (d. 1803) William Chetwood: "A General History of the Stage" Henry Fielding: "The History of Tom Jones, a Foundling" Johann Wolfgang Goethe, the greatest Ger. writer, b. (d. 1832) Samuel Johnson: "Irene," tragedy	Denis Diderot: "Lettre sur les aveugles à l'usage de ceux qui voient" David Hartley: "Observations on Man"

D. VISUAL ARTS	E. MUSIC	F. SCIENCE, TECHNOLOGY, GROWTH	G. DAILY LIFE	
Boucher: "The Milliners" Antonio Canaletto in England (—1755) Francisco de Goya, Span. painter, b. (d. 1828) Joshua Reynolds: "The Eliot Family"		Jean-Etienne Guettard draws first geological map of France College of New Jersey founded; becomes Princeton University, 1896 Johann Heinrich Pestalozzi, Swiss educator, b. (d. 1827)	Wearing of tartans prohibited in Great Britain (—1782)	**1746**
G. W. von Knobelsdorff completes Sanssouci Palace, Potsdam	J. S. Bach: "Das musikalische Opfer" Handel: "Judas Maccabaeus," oratorio, Covent Garden, London Rousseau: "Les Muses galantes," opera	Ger. chemist A. S. Marggraf (1709—1782) discovers sugar in beetroot Eng. military engineer Benjamin Robins speaks to Royal Society on physics of a spinning projectile	Carriage tax in England	**1747**
Jacques Louis David, Fr. painter, b. (d. 1825) Thomas Gainsborough: "Cornard Wood" Hogarth: "Calais Gate"	Bach: "Die Kunst der Fuge" (—1750) Holywell Music Room, Oxford, opened (still in use)	Joseph Bramah, Eng. engineer, b. (d. 1814) Leonhard Euler: "Analysis Infinitorum," on pure analytical mathematics Eng. physician John Fothergill (1712—1780) describes diphtheria Thomas Lowndes (1692—1748) founds chair of astronomy at Cambridge	Abolition of hereditary jurisdiction in Scotland Platinum arrives in Europe from S. America Subscription library opened in Charleston, S.C. Court of King's Bench rules that "cricket is a legal sport"	**1748**
Gainsborough: "Mr. and Mrs. Robert Andrews" Peter Harrison: Redwood Library, Newport, R.I. (—1758) J. B. Pigalle: "Mme de Pompadour," sculpture Bartolomeo Rastrelli: Great Palace, Tsarskoe Selo, Russia (—1756)	Domenico Cimarosa, Ital. composer, b. (d. 1801) Handel: "Music for the Royal Fireworks" Georg "Abbé" Vogler, Ger. music teacher, b. (d. 1814)	Georgia becomes Crown Colony Pierre Simon, Marquis de Laplace, Fr. mathematician, b. (d. 1827) François Philidor: "Analyse des échecs," a study of chess, written by the famous composer Philadelphia Academy founded; becomes University of Pennsylvania, 1791	Dan. newspaper "Berlingske Tidende" appears Port. Giacobbo Rodriguez Pereire invents sign language for deaf-mutes	**1749**

	A. HISTORY, POLITICS	B. LITERATURE, THEATER	C. RELIGION, PHILOSOPHY, LEARNING
1750	Anglo-Fr. discussions on boundary between Canada and Nova Scotia Karl August von Hardenberg, Prussian statesman, b. (d. 1822) John V of Portugal d.; succeeded by José I (—1777) Span.-Port. treaty on S. America Henry Knox, Amer. Revolutionary leader, b. (d. 1806) Thomas Pinckney, U.S. diplomat, b. (d. 1828)	Goldoni: "The Café," comedy Thomas Gray: "Elegy Written in a Country Church Yard" Aaron Hill, Eng. dramatist, d. (b. 1685) Samuel Johnson begins "The Rambler" (—1752) First playhouse opens in New York	"Dictionnaire de l'art de vérifier les dates des faits historiques," ed. by the Benedictine monks of St.-Maur King Frederick the Great: "Oeuvres du Philosophe de Sanssouci" Baal Shem (1699—1760) founds Jewish sect of Chassidim in Carpathian mountain region
1751	Prince of Wales d. Frederick II of Sweden d.; succeeded by his brother-in-law Adolphus Frederick (—1771) England joins Austro-Russ. alliance of June 1746 against Prussia William IV of Holland d.; his widow, Anne, daughter of George II of England, becomes regent China invades Tibet James Madison, fourth President of the U.S., b. (d. 1836) Henry Dearborn, U.S. Secretary of War, b. (d. 1829) Benjamin Stoddert, first U.S. Secretary of the Navy, b. (d. 1813) Maria Luisa Teresa, future Queen of Spain, b. (d. 1819) Joseph Habersham, future U.S. Postmaster-General, b. (d. 1815)	Lessing becomes literary critic of the "Vossische Zeitung," Berlin Robert Paltock: "The Life and Adventures of Peter Wilkins, a Cornish Man" Richard Brinsley Sheridan, Ir. dramatist, b. (d. 1816) Tobias Smollett: "The Adventures of Peregrine Pickle" Johann Heinrich Voss, Ger. poet, b. (d. 1826)	Fr. "Encyclopédie" published (—1772) David Hume: "Enquiry concerning the Principles of Morals" Powers of Port. Inquisition curtailed by government Linnaeus: "Philosophia Botanica" Prussian Minister of Justice, Heinrich von Cocceji: "Code Fredéric"
1752	Treaty of Aranjuez between Spain and the Holy Roman Empire Great Britain adopts Gregorian calendar on Sept. 14, 1752 (Sept. 3—13 omitted)	Fanny Burney (Mme. D'Arblay), Eng. novelist and diarist, b. (d. 1840) Thomas Chatterton, Eng. poet, b. (d. 1770) Henry Fielding: "Amelia" Charlotte Lennox: "The Female Quixote" Philip Freneau, "poet of the American Revolution," b. (d. 1832)	Jonathan Edwards: "Misrepresentations Corrected and Truth Vindicated" David Hume: "Political Discourses" William Law: "The Way to Divine Knowledge" Timothy Dwight, U.S. educator, b. (d. 1817)
1753	Fr. troops from Canada seize Ohio Valley Frederick the Great fights Austro-Russ. agreement (see 1746) James McHenry, U.S. Secretary of War (1796—1800), b. (d. 1816) Edmund Randolph, U.S. statesman, b. (d. 1813)	Goldoni: "La Locandiera," comedy Samuel Richardson: "Sir Charles Grandison" Tobias Smollett: "Ferdinand Count Fathom"	George Berkeley, Ir. philosopher, d. (b. 1685) Robert Lowth: "De sacra poesi Hebraeorum" Eng. Act of Parliament permits naturalization of Jews

D. VISUAL ARTS	E. MUSIC	F. SCIENCE, TECHNOLOGY, GROWTH	G. DAILY LIFE	
Lancelot ("Capability") Brown designs gardens of Warwick Castle François de Cuvilliés, a dwarf, court architect to the Elector of Bavaria, builds Residenztheater, Munich Neoclassicism, as reaction against baroque and rococo, spreading over Europe	J. S. Bach d. (b. 1685) Johann Breitkopf, Leipzig music publisher, uses movable type for printing music Pergolesi: "La Serva padrona," opera buffa, first performed in London Antonio Salieri, Ital. composer, b. (d. 1825) "The Beggar's Opera" given for first time in New York	Fr. astronomer Nicolas de Lacaille (1713—1762) leads expedition to Cape of Good Hope to determine solar and lunar parallax Johann Tobias Mayer: "Map of the Moon" Eng. engineer William Watson (1715—1787) analyzes platinum	Hambledon Cricket Club, Hampshire, England, founded Eng. Jockey Club founded in London Population of Europe: approx. 140 million First Westminster Bridge, London, finished	**1750**
Boucher: "Toilet of Venus" Ralph Earle, Amer. painter, b. (d. 1801) Hogarth: "Four Stages of Cruelty" Thomas Sheraton, Eng. cabinetmaker, b. (d. 1806) Tiepolo paints ceiling of the Würzburg Residenz	Francesco Geminiani: "The Art of Playing on the Violin" Handel: "Jephta," oratorio The minuet becomes Europe's fashionable dance "War of the Operas" (La Guerre des Bouffons) divides Paris into pro-Italian and pro-French music lovers	Ecole supérieure de guerre, Paris, founded Göttinger wissenschaftliche Akademie founded Gaetano Filangieri, Ital. jurist b. (d. 1788)	British calendar altered by Act of Parliament: Jan. 1 henceforth to be beginning of New Year "Halifax Gazette," first Eng. newspaper in Canada, appears First mental asylums in London	**1751**
John Nash, Eng. architect, b. (d. 1835)	Muzio Clementi, Ital. composer, b. (d. 1832) Charles Avison (1710—1770): "Essay on Musical Expression" Sébastien Erard, Fr. manufacturer of pianofortes, b. (d. 1831) Rousseau: "Le devin du village" (Fontainebleau)	Benjamin Franklin invents the lightning conductor Luke Hansard, Eng. printer, b. (d. 1828)	Manchester Royal Infirmary founded	**1752**
Hogarth's essay: "The Analysis of Beauty" Pigalle: tomb of the Maréchal de Saxe, Strasbourg (—1776) Joshua Reynolds: "Commodore Keppel" Kitagawa Utamaro, Jap. painter, b. (d. 1806)	Johann Schenk, Aust. composer, b. (d. 1836) Gottfried Silbermann, Ger. organ builder, d. (b. 1683) Giovanni Viotti, Ital. violinist and composer, b. (d. 1824)	British Museum, London, granted royal foundation charter Linnaeus: "Species Plantorum" Benjamin Thompson, Count Rumford, physicist and adventurer, b. (d. 1814)	Jockey Club establishes permanent racetrack at Newmarket Jean Baptiste Kléber, Fr. general, b. (d. 1800) Land Tax two shillings in the pound in England and Wales Brit. Marriage Act forbids weddings by unauthorized persons Vienna Stock Exchange founded	**1753**

	A. HISTORY, POLITICS	B. LITERATURE, THEATER	C. RELIGION, PHILOSOPHY, LEARNING
1754	Talleyrand, Fr. statesman, b. (d. 1838) Anglo-Fr. war in N. America; discussion on boundaries The future King Louis XVI b. (d. 1793)	Thomas Bowdler, Eng. Shakespeare editor, b. (d. 1825) George Crabbe, Eng. poet, b. (d. 1832) Crébillon père: "Le Triumvirat," tragedy Henry Fielding, Eng. novelist, d. (b. 1707) Salomon Gessner: "Daphnis" Ludvig Holberg, Dan. dramatist, d. (b. 1684) Joel Barlow, U.S. poet and diplomat, b. (d. 1812)	Jonathan Edwards: "Inquiry into Freedom of the Will" David Hume: "History of Great Britain," vol. 1 Rousseau: "L'Inégalité par les hommes: discours" John Woolman: "Some Considerations on the Keeping of Negroes"
1755	Pasquale de Paoli (1725—1807) elected general in Corsica, leader of revolt against Genoa Landgrave of Hesse sells mercenaries to England for defense of Hanover P. F. N. Barras, Fr. politician, b. (d. 1829) Brit. army defeated by French near Fort Duquesne (modern Pittsburgh) End of Anglo-Aust. alliance Marie Antoinette b. (d. 1793) The future King Louis XVIII b. (d. 1824) Gerhard von Scharnhorst, Prussian general, b. (d. 1813) Alexander Hamilton, Amer. Revolutionary, lawyer, and statesman, b. (killed in duel with Aaron Burr, 1804)	Philibert Louis Debucourt, Fr. poet, b. (d. 1832) Sarah Kemble (Mrs. Siddons), Eng. actress, b. (d. 1831) Elizabeth Lebrun, Fr. poet, b. (d. 1842) Lessing: "Miss Sara Sampson," domestic tragedy Jean-Georges Noverre (1727—1810), Fr. choreographer, becomes ballet master at Drury Lane, London Voltaire: "La Pucelle d'Orléans" Samuel Johnson: "Dictionary of the English Language" (—1773)	Benjamin Franklin: "Observations Concerning the Increase of Mankind, Peopling of countries" Francis Hutcheson: "A System of Moral Philosophy" Immanuel Kant's doctoral thesis: "The True Measure of Forces" Montesquieu, Fr. political philosopher, d. (b. 1689) J. J. Winckelmann: "Gedanken über die Nachahmung der griechischen Werke" John Marshall, future Chief Justice of the United States (1801—1835), b. (d. 1835)
1756	Anglo-Prussian Treaty of Westminster Britain declares war on France Six leading Quakers resign from Pennsylvania Assembly 120 Brit. soldiers imprisoned and die in India ("Black Hole of Calcutta") French drive Britain from Great Lakes in N. America Outbreak of Seven Years War: Battle of Lobosik, Bohemia; Saxon army capitulates to Frederick the Great at Pirna Robert Clive sets out from Calcutta against Nawab of Bengal and relieves Eng. fugitives at Fulta Aaron Burr, U.S. statesman and adventurer, b. (d. 1836) Henry ("Light-Horse Harry") Lee, Amer. Revolutionary soldier and statesman, b. (d. 1818)	Robert and James Dodsley: "Theatrical Records" William Mason: "Odes" Russ. Royal Court Theater founded at St. Petersburg Voltaire: "Désastre de Lisbonne"	Thomas Birch (1705—1766): "History of the Royal Society of London" (—1757) Edmund Burke: "Origin of Our Ideas of the Sublime and Beautiful" Alban Butler: "Lives of the Saints," vol. 1 Arthur Collins: "The Peerage of England" finished (begun 1709) Mirabeau: "Ami des hommes ou traité de la population" Voltaire finishes his "Siècle de Louis XIV" (begun 1735)
1757	Clive retakes Calcutta J. F. Damiens attempts to assassinate Louis XV; is executed Frederick the Great defeats Austrians at Prague, and is defeated by them at Kolin; defeats them again at Rossbach and Leuthen Lafayette, Fr. politician, b. (d. 1834) Karl vom Stein, Prussian statesman, b. Robert Smith, U.S. statesman, b. (d. 1842)	Karl August, Grand Duke of Saxe-Weimar, Goethe's patron, b. (d. 1828) William Blake, Eng. poet and artist, b. (d. 1827) Swiss poet J. J. Bodmer (1698—1782) edits "Das Nibelungenlied" Bernard le Bovier de Fontenelle, Fr. author, d. (b. 1657) John Dyer: "The Fleece," poem Gellert: "Geistliche Oden und Lieder" John Home: "Douglas," tragedy John Philip Kemble, Eng. actor, *(contd)*	Denis Diderot: "Entretiens sur le fils natural" Richard Price: "Review of the Principal Questions in Morals"

D. VISUAL ARTS	E. MUSIC	F. SCIENCE, TECHNOLOGY, GROWTH	G. DAILY LIFE	
Gabriel Boffrand, Fr. architect, d. (b. 1667) Boucher: "Judgment of Paris," series, for Mme. de Pompadour Thomas Chippendale: "The Gentleman and Cabinetmaker's Directory" Hogarth: "The Election" Rastrelli: Winter Palace, St. Petersburg Society for the Encouragement of Arts and Manufactures founded in England	Vicente Martín y Soler, Span. composer, b. (d. 1806)	Scot. chemist Joseph Black (1728—1799) discovers carbonic acid gas Anton Büsching: "Erdbeschreibung," geography (—1761) King's College, New York, founded; becomes Columbia University, 1784 First female M.D. (University of Halle, Germany)	First iron-rolling mill at Fareham, Hampshire, England St. Andrews Royal and Ancient Golf Club, Scotland, founded	**1754**
Boucher: "La Noble Pastorale" (Beauvais tapestry designs) Gainsborough: "Milkmaid and Woodcutter" Gilbert Stuart, Washington portraitist, b. (d. 1828)	Egidio Romoaldo Duni: "Ninette à la cour" ("opéra-comique")	Joseph Black: "Experiments upon Magnesia, Quicklime, and other Alkaline Substances" Ital. chemist Sebastian Menghini studies action of camphor on animals University of Moscow founded Aloung P'Houra founds Rangoon, Burma	Lisbon earthquake kills 30,000 people	**1755**
Henry Raeburn, Scot. painter, b. (d. 1823) Reynolds: "Admiral Holbourne and His Son" Thomas Rowlandson, Eng. caricaturist, b. (d. 1827) George Stubbs, Eng. painter (1724—1806), works on the anatomy of the horse	Wolfgang Amadeus Mozart, Aust. composer, b. Jan. 2 (d. 1791) Leopold Mozart: "Versuch einer gründlichen Violinschule"	Cotton velvets first made at Bolton, Lancashire, England John Smeaton (1724—1792) builds tower on Eddystone Lighthouse	Casanova escapes from Piombi in Venice First chocolate factory in Germany Porcelain factory founded at Sèvres	**1756**
Antonio Canova, Ital. sculptor, b. (d. 1822) Gainsborough: "The Artist's Daughter with a Cat" James Gillray, Eng. caricaturist, b. (d. 1815) Daniel Gran, Aust. painter, d. (b. 1694) Greuze: "La Paresseuse Italienne" Soufflot: St. Geneviève, Paris; later the "Panthéon"	Niccolò Pasquali, Ital. violinist and composer d. ("Thoroughbass Made Easy") Ignaz Pleyel, Fr.- Aust. composer and pianoforte maker, b. (d. 1831) First public concert in Philadelphia Domenico Scarlatti, Ital. composer, *(contd)*	René-Antoine Ferchault de Réaumur, Fr. scientist, d. (b. 1683)	Royal Library, London, transferred to British Museum "The London Chronicle" appears	**1757**

	A. HISTORY, POLITICS	B. LITERATURE, THEATER	C. RELIGION, PHILOSOPHY, LEARNING
1757 contd		(d. 1823)	
1758	E. Prussia occupied by Russia James Monroe, fifth President of the U.S., b. (d. 1831) Maximilien de Robespierre, Fr. revolutionist, b. (d. 1794) Prussian blockade of Olmütz British take Louisburg Battle of Zorndorf between Prussians and Russians (undecided) Horatio Nelson, Brit. admiral, b. (d. 1805) Austrians besiege Neisse; defeat Frederick the Great at Hochkirch George Washington and John Forbes take Fort Duquesne, later renamed Pittsburgh China occupies eastern Turkestan Dutch capitulate at Chinsura; Clive becomes Governor of Bengal André Masséna, Fr. marshal, b. (d. 1817)	Diderot: "Le Père de famille," drama Salomon Gessner: "Der Tod Abels," Ger. Biblical play Samuel Johnson: "The Idler," weekly periodical (—1760) Jonathan Swift: "The History of the Four Last Years of the Queen"	Pope Benedict XIV d.; succeeded by Carlo della Torre Rezzonico as Pope Clement XIII (—1769) Emerich de Vattel: "Le Droit des gens" Claude Adrien Helvétius: "De l'esprit" Serjeant's Inn (London Court) formed Noah Webster, Amer. lexicographer, b. (d. 1843)
1759	William Pitt the Younger, Brit. statesman, b. (d. 1806) King Ferdinand VI of Spain d.; succeeded by Charles III Aust. General Laudon defeats Frederick the Great at Kunersdorf British gain Quebec from French; Louis Joseph Montcalm (b. 1712) and James Wolfe (b. 1727), Fr. and Eng. generals, killed in action Georges Jacques Danton, Fr. revolutionist, b. (d. 1794)	Robert Burns, Scot. poet, b. (d. 1796) William Collins, Eng. poet, d. (b. 1721) Thomas Godfrey: "The Prince of Parthia," tragedy A. W. Iffland, Ger. actor, b. (d. 1814) Samuel Johnson: "Rasselas," moral tale Lessing: "Philotas," tragedy Schiller, Ger. poet and dramatist, b. (d. 1805) Voltaire: "Candide," philosophical novel Thomas Wilkes: "A General View of the Stage"	Thomas Cooper, Amer. philosopher, b. (d. 1840) Alexander Gerard: "An Essay on Taste" Oliver Goldsmith: "An Enquiry Into the Present State of Polite Learning in Europe" Expulsion of Jesuits from Portugal Adam Smith: "Theory of Moral Sentiments"
1760	Robert Clive leaves India Camille Desmoulins, Fr. revolutionist, b. (d. 1794) Prussian army defeated at Landshut; Austrians take Glatz; are defeated at Liegnitz and Torgau Russians occupy and burn Berlin King George II of England d.; succeeded by his grandson George III (—1820) Dutch explorer Jakobus Coetsee advances beyond Orange River, S. Africa Oliver Wolcott, future U.S. Secretary of the Treasury, b. (d. 1833)	Claude Joseph Rouget de Lisle, Fr. poet, b. (d. 1836) Lavinia Fenton, Eng. actress, d. (b. 1708); she made her theatrical fame in 2 years (by 1728), and died Duchess of Bolton Oliver Goldsmith: "Citizen of the World" Johann Peter Hebel, Ger. author, b. (d. 1826) James Macpherson ("Ossian"): "Fragments of Ancient Poetry, Collected in the Highlands," famous literary fraud Friederike Caroline Neuber, Ger. actress, d. (b. 1697) Laurence Sterne: "Tristram Shandy," vols. 1 and 2 Peg Woffington, Eng. actress, d. (b. 1714)	Claude Henri de Saint-Simon, Fr. political writer, b. (d. 1825)

D. VISUAL ARTS	E. MUSIC	F. SCIENCE, TECHNOLOGY, GROWTH	G. DAILY LIFE	
	d. (b. 1685) Johann Stamitz, Ger. composer, d. (b. 1717)			**1757 contd**
John and Robert Adam: Harewood House (—1771) Boucher: "The Mill at Charenton" John Hoppner, Eng. painter, b. (d. 1810) Allan Ramsay: "Dr. William Hunter" J. H. von Dannecker, Ger. sculptor, b. (d. 1841)	First Eng. manual on guitar playing published Karl Friedrich Zelter, Ger. composer, friend of Goethe, b. (d. 1832)	Ribbing machine for manufacture of hose invented by Jedediah Strutt (1726—1797)	Bridgwater Canal between Liverpool and Leeds begun (—1761)	**1758**
William Chambers: "Treatise on Civil Architecture" J. B. Greuze: "The Bookseller Babuti" Peter Harrison: synagogue at Newport, R.I. (—1763) Hogarth: "Sigismonda" Reynolds: "The 7th Earl of Lauderdale"	Handel d. (b. 1685) Haydn: Symphony No. 1 in D major	Franz Aepinus: "Testamen theoriae electricitatis et magnetesmi" Bavarian Academy of Science founded	The "Annual Register" issued for first time, ed. by Robert Dodsley and Edmund Burke Eugene Aram, Eng. scholar and murderer, executed (b. 1704) British Museum opened (at Montagu House —1823) "The Public Ledger," London daily paper, appears William Wilberforce, Eng. philanthropist, b. (d. 1833)	**1759**
First exhibition of contemporary art at Royal Society of Arts, London Gainsborough: "Mrs. Philip Thicknesse" Peter Harrison: "Christ Church, Cambridge, Mass. Katsushika Hokusai, Jap. painter, b. (d. 1849) Angelica Kauffmann: "Music and Painting" Joshua Reynolds: "Georgiana"	William Boyce (1710—1779): collection of cathedral music (—1778) Luigi Cherubini, Ital. composer, b. (d. 1842) Haydn: Symphonies 2 to 5 Noverre, ballet master at Stuttgart, publishes his "Letter on Dancing and Ballets"	First Brit. school for deaf and dumb opened by Thomas Braidwood, Edinburgh Josiah Wedgwood founds pottery works at Etruria, Staffordshire, England	Botanical Gardens in Kew, London, opened Thomas Clarkson, Eng. antislavery agitator, b. (d. 1846) Portsmouth dockyard destroyed by fire First silk hats from Florence Marie ("Madame") Tussaud b. (d. 1850) Rules of whist laid down by Edmund Hoyle (1672—1769)	**1760**

	A. HISTORY, POLITICS	B. LITERATURE, THEATER	C. RELIGION, PHILOSOPHY, LEARNING
1761	Ieharu, the new Shogun of Japan Austrians take Schweidnitz Albert Gallatin, U.S. statesman and diplomat, b. (d. 1849) Samuel Dexter, U.S. lawyer, b. (d. 1816)	Charles Churchill: "The Rosciad" George Colman: "The Jealous Wife," comedy Goldoni: "Una delle ultime sere di Carnevale," comedy Samuel Richardson, Eng. novelist, d. (b. 1689) Rousseau: "Julie, or La Nouvelle Héloïse" (—1765) Benjamin Victor: "History of the Theatres of London and Dublin" August Friedrich Ferdinand von Kotzebue, Ger. dramatist, b. (d. 1819)	Henry Home: "An Introduction to the Art of Thinking" Collected works of Voltaire, trans. by Smollett and others, appear in England (—1774)
1762	Czarina Elizabeth of Russia d.; succeeded by Peter III, who dies by assassination; succeeded by Catherine II (—1796) British capture Martinique, Grenada, Havana, and Manila Treaty of Hamburg between Sweden and Prussia Russo-Prussian alliance against Austria signed Truce between Prussia, Saxony, and the Holy Roman Empire First Brit. settlement at Maugerville, New Brunswick	Crébillon père, Fr. dramatist, d. (b. 1674) André de Chénier, Fr. poet, b. (d. 1794) Diderot: "Le Neveu de Rameau" William Falconer: "The Shipwreck" Goldoni: "Le Baruffe chiozzotte," Venetian comedy Tobias Smollett: "Sir Lancelot Greaves" Wieland translated 17 Shakespeare plays into German (—1766) Edward Young: "Resignation," poetry Robert Lowth: "Introduction to English Grammar" William Cobbett, Eng. reformer and journalist, b. (d. 1835)	George Campbell: "Dissertation on Miracles" Johann Gottlieb Fichte, Ger. philosopher, b. (d. 1814) John Parkhurst: "Hebrew and English Lexicon" Rousseau: "Du Contrat social, ou principes du droit politique" Sorbonne Library, Paris, opened
1763	Peace of Paris ends Seven Years' War Rising of Indians near Detroit spreads toward east King Augustus III of Poland d. Brit. proclamation provides government for Quebec, Florida, and Grenada Indian adventurer Hyder Ali (1722—1782) conquers Kanara, Mysore Jean Baptiste Jules Bernadotte, later Charles XIV of Sweden, b. (d. 1844) Joseph Fouché, future Fr. Minister of Police, b. (d. 1820)	Boswell meets Johnson for the first time Xavier de Maistre, Fr. author, b. (d. 1852) Giuseppe Parini: "Il Mattino," first section of the four-part poem "Il Giorno" Jean Paul Friedrich Richter (pseudonym, Jean Paul), Ger. author, b. (d. 1825)	Voltaire: "Treatise on Tolerance"
1764	Amendment of Brit. Sugar Act to tax Amer. colonies Stanislas Poniatowski elected King of Poland Sir Hector Munro defeats Nawab of Dudh at Buxar, Bengal Hyder Ali usurps throne of Mysore Confiscation of Church lands in Russia Deposed Czar Ivan VI murdered in prison Jesuits suppressed in France Edward Livingston, U.S. statesman, b. (d. 1836) William Pinkney, U.S. legislator, b. (d. 1822) Return J. Meigs, U.S. legislator, b. (d. 1823)	The Literary Club founded in London by Dr. Johnson, with Burke, Gibbon, Goldsmith, Reynolds, etc. Literary salons founded in Paris by Mme. Necker and Mlle. de Lespinasse	Adam Anderson: "The Origins of Commerce" Cesare Beccaria-Bonesana: "On Crimes and Punishments" Charles Bonnet: "Contemplation de la nature" Brown University, Providence, R.I., founded Voltaire: "Philosophical Dictionary" J. J. Winckelmann: "History of Ancient Art"

D. VISUAL ARTS	E. MUSIC	F. SCIENCE, TECHNOLOGY, GROWTH	G. DAILY LIFE	
Boucher: "Girl and Birdcatcher" Peter Harrison: Brick Market, Newport, R.I. (—1772) Anton Raphael Mengs plans the Villa Albani, Rome	Thomas Augustine Arne: "Judith," oratorio, London Johann Ludwig Dussek, Bohemian composer, b. (d. 1812) Gluck: "Don Juan," ballet, Vienna Haydn appointed Kapellmeister to Prince Paul Esterházy	Leopold Avenbrugger: "Inventum novum," to recognize chest diseases by percussion Dan. expedition to explore Arabia under Castens Niebuhr (1733—1815) John Dollond, Eng. optician, d. (b. 1706) Russ. scientist and poet Mikhail V. Lomonosov (1711—1765) discovers the atmosphere of Venus B. G. Morgagni: "On the Causes of Diseases," beginning of pathological anatomy Johann Peter Süssmilch initiates study of statistics First Fr. veterinary school founded at Lyons	Bridgwater Canal finished (see 1758) Society of Arts, London, opens first exhibition of agricultural machines	**1761**
Stuart and Revett: "Classical Antiquities of Athens," vol. I, inspires neoclassical movement Pierre Fontaine, Fr. sculptor, b. (d. 1853) Petit Trianon built by Louis XV for Mme. DuBarry Louis François Roubiliac, Fr. sculptor, d. (b. 1695) George Stubbs: "Mares and Foals" Tiepolo: frescoes in Royal Palace, Madrid	Thomas Augustine Arne: "Artaxerxes," opera, Covent Garden, London Benjamin Franklin improves the harmonica, turning it into a practical musical instrument Gluck: "Orpheus and Euridice," opera, Vienna Mozart (at six) tours Europe as musical prodigy St. Cecilia Society active in Charleston, S.C. (—1912)	At Carron ironworks in Stirlingshire, Scotland, cast iron converted for first time into malleable iron	Beau Nash, Eng. dandy and master of ceremonies at Bath, d. (b. 1674)	**1762**
Francesco Guardi: "Election of the Doge of Venice" La Madeleine, Paris, finished George Morland, Eng. painter, b. (d. 1804)	Adalbert Gyrowetz, Bohemian composer, b. (d. 1850) Etienne Méhul, Fr. composer, b. (d. 1817)	Frederick the Great establishes village schools in Prussia Ger. botanist J. G. Kölreuter (1733—1806): fertilization experiments on plants by animal carriers of pollen	First issue of "Almanach de Gotha" First Chambers of Commerce in New York and New Jersey Earliest use of ponies in pits "St. James' Chronicle" published in London	**1763**
Robert Adam: Kenwood House, Middlesex, England William Hogarth d. (b. 1697) Jean Antoine Houdon: "St. Bruno," sculpture Charles Percier, Fr. architect, b. (d. 1838) Johann Gottfried Schadow, Ger. sculptor, b. (d. 1850)	J. C. Bach gives popular recitals in London Haydn: Symphony No. 22 in E-flat ("The Philosopher") Mozart (at eight) writes his first symphony Rameau, Fr. composer, d. (b. 1683)	First permanent settlement at St. Louis James Watt (1736—1819) invents condenser, first step toward steam engine	Mme. de Pompadour d. (b. 1721) London introduces practice of numbering houses	**1764**

	A. HISTORY, POLITICS	B. LITERATURE, THEATER	C. RELIGION, PHILOSOPHY, LEARNING
1765	Brit. Parliament passes Stamp Act for taxing Amer. colonies; Virginia Assembly challenges right of Great Britain to the tax; at Stamp Act Congress in New York delegates from nine colonies draw up a declaration of rights and liberties Emperor Francis I, Maria Theresa's husband, d.; their son Joseph II succeeds as Holy Roman Emperor, becomes coregent with his mother Brit. government acquires fiscal rights in Isle of Man Robert Clive's first administrative reforms in Bengal On death of the Dauphin, his son Louis Augustus becomes heir to the Fr. throne (future Louis XVI)	Thomas Chatterton forges the "Rowley" poems Thomas Percy and William Shenstone: "Reliques of Ancient English Poetry," collection of ballads M. J. Sedaine (1719—1797): "Philosophe sans le savoir," Fr. social drama Horace Walpole: "The Castle of Otranto," so-called Gothic novel	C. F. Nicolai (1733—1811) begins to edit the "Allgemeine deutsche Bibliothek" in Berlin, for popular philosophy A. R. J. Turgot: "Refléxions sur la formation et la distribution des richesses"
1766	Stanislas Leszczynski d.; Duchy of Lorraine incorporated in France Repeal of Stamp Act, but Declaratory Act states Britain's right to tax Amer. colonies Pitt created Earl of Chatham, forms a ministry Nizam Ali of Hyderabad cedes Northern Circars, Madras, to Great Britain Frederick V of Denmark d.; succeeded by the mad Christian VII Mason-Dixon Line, drawn by two Eng. surveyors, Charles Mason and Jeremiah Dixon (—1768), marks boundary between Pennsylvania and Maryland, later separating free and slave regions	Oliver Goldsmith: "The Vicar of Wakefield," novel Theatre Royal, Bristol, opens, oldest Brit. theater still in use Dan.-Ger. diplomat and author Heinrich Wilhelm von Gerstenberg formulates in his "Briefe über die Merkwürdigkeiten der Literatur" the principles of "Sturm und Drang" Wieland: "The Story of Agathon," Ger. psychological novel	Czarina Catherine the Great grants freedom of worship in Russia Adam Ferguson: "Essay on the History of Civil Society" Lessing: "Laokoon," against Winckelmann's theories
1767	Andrew Jackson, seventh President of the U.S., b. (d. 1845) Taxes on imports of tea, glass, paper, and dyestuffs in Amer. colonies; nonimportation agreement at public protest meeting in Boston John Quincy Adams, sixth President of the U.S., b. (d. 1848) Invasion of Siam by Burmese Andreas Hofer, popular Tirolean hero in Napoleonic Wars, b. (d. 1810) Chaos in India; Robert Clive leaves the country Joachim Murat, Fr. general, brother-in-law of Napoleon I, b. (d. 1815) First Mysore War (—1769) New York Assembly suspended for refusing to support quartering of troops Gideon Granger, U.S. Postmaster-General for considerable period, b. (d. 1822)	Michael Bruce: "Elegy Written in Spring" Oliver Goldsmith: "The Good Natur'd Man," comedy Lessing: "Minna von Barnhelm," comedy Rousseau settles in England, receives pension from George III August Wilhelm von Schlegel, Ger. author, b. (d. 1845) Laurence Sterne completes "Tristram Shandy" (begun 1759)	Jesuits expelled from Spain, Parma, and the Two Sicilies Moses Mendelssohn: "Phaedon, or The Immortality of Soul" Wilhelm von Humboldt, Ger. humanist, b. (d. 1835) J. J. Winckelmann: "Monumenti antichi inediti" (—1768)
1768	Secretary of State for Colonies appointed in Britain Massachusetts Assembly dissolved for refusing to assist collection of taxes Boston citizens refuse to quarter Brit. troops Austria renounces all claims to Silesia Frederick the Great completes his political testament Ali Bey, leader of the Mamelukes, Sultan of Egypt (—1773) France buys Corsica from Genoa Gurkhas conquer Nepal Smith Thompson, U.S. jurist, b. (d. 1843)	François de Chateaubriand, Fr. author, b. (d. 1848) Thomas Gray: "Poems" M. J. Sedaine: "La Gageure imprévue," play Laurence Sterne d., having finished his "Sentimental Journey" (b. 1713) Zacharias Werner, Ger. religious poet, b. (d. 1823)	Abraham Booth: "Reign of Grace" Joseph Priestley: "Essay on the First Principles of Government" Friedrich Schleiermacher, Ger. theologian, b. (d. 1834) Swedenborg: "Delitiae sapientiae" Johann Joachim Winckelmann d., murdered by a casual male acquaintance (b. 1717)

D. VISUAL ARTS	E. MUSIC	F. SCIENCE, TECHNOLOGY, GROWTH	G. DAILY LIFE	
Boucher court painter at Versailles Fragonard: "Corésus et Callirhoé" A. J. Gabriel: Place de la Concorde, Paris Greuze: "La Bonne Mère"	Thomas Attwood, Eng. composer and organist, b. (d. 1838) Daniel Steibelt, Ger. composer and pianist, b. (d. 1823)	Spallanzani suggests preserving by means of hermetic sealing	Potato becomes most popular European foodstuff Bank of Prussia founded by Frederick the Great Lord Nelson's future flagship H.M.S. "Victory" launched	**1765**
Diderot: "Essai sur la Peinture" E. M. Falconet: "Monument to Peter the Great," St. Petersburg (—1779) Johann Michael Fischer, Ger. church architect, d. (b. 1692) Fragonard: "The Swing"	Haydn: Great Mass in E-flat (No. 4 with organ)	Henry Cavendish (1731—1810) discovers hydrogen less dense than air John Dalton, founder of chemical atom theory, b. (d. 1844) Louis de Bougainville (1729—1811) sets out on voyage to Pacific on which he discovers Tahiti, the Solomon Islands, and New Guinea T. R. Malthus, Eng. political economist, b. (d. 1834)	Famine in Bengal First paved sidewalk laid in Westminster, London Tobacco monopoly in Prussia	**1766**
Jean Baptiste Isabey, Fr. painter, b. (d. 1855) Allan Ramsay made court painter to George III	Gluck: "Alceste," Burgtheater, Vienna Rousseau: "Dictionnaire de musique" Georg Philipp Telemann, Ger. composer, d. (b. 1681); Karl Philipp Emanuel Bach becomes his successor as director of church music in Hamburg	Olaf Bergman of Uppsala (1735—1784) examines the "chemical affinities" Astronomer Royal, Nevill Maskelyne (1732—1811), issues "Nautical Almanac" Maria Theresa and Joseph II introduce educational reforms in Austria Joseph Priestley (1733—1804): "The History and Present State of Electricity"	Electrical machine with glass pane becomes a fashionable toy	**1767**
Antonio Canaletto, Ital. painter, d. (b. 1697) Joseph Anton Koch, Ger. painter, b. (d. 1839) Founding of the Royal Academy, London, with Joshua Reynolds as president	Jomelli: "Fetonte," opera, Stuttgart Mozart's first produced opera "Bastien and Bastienne" given in Vienna	James Boswell: "Account of Corsica" James Cook (1728—1779) sails (late May) on first circumnavigation; returns June 1771 New criminal code, on humanist principles, introduced in Austria Jean Baptiste Fourier, Fr. mathematician and physicist, b. (d. 1830) Ger. naturalist P. S. Pallas (1741—1811) travels through Russia to Chin. frontier to observe transit of Venus	First of the weekly numbers of the "Encyclopaedia Britannica" published; 100 are planned Work begun on Forth—Clyde Canal (—1790)	**1768**

	A. HISTORY, POLITICS	B. LITERATURE, THEATER	C. RELIGION, PHILOSOPHY, LEARNING
1769	Austria occupies Lwow and Zips region of Poland Mme. Du Barry becomes mistress to Louis XV Privy council in London decides to retain tea duty in Amer. colonies Arthur Wellesley, future Duke of Wellington, b. (d. 1852) Virginian Assembly dissolved after protesting against colonial treason trials held in Westminster Frederick II and Joseph II meet at Neisse, Silesia, to discuss partition of Poland The future Emperor Napoleon I b. in Corsica (d. 1821) Russ. troops occupy Moldavia, enter Bucharest Nicolas Soult, Duke of Dalmatia, Fr. marshal, b. (d. 1851) De Witt Clinton, U.S. statesman, b. (d. 1828) Michel Ney, Fr. marshal, b. (executed for treason in 1815)	Ernst Moritz Arndt, Ger. poet, b. (d. 1860) Fr. dramatist Jean-François Ducis (1733—1816) produces Shakespeare's "Hamlet" in Paris Christian Gellert, Ger. poet, d. (b. 1715)	Charles Bonnet: "Palingénésie philosophique" Pope Clement XIII d.; Lorenzo Ganganelli becomes Pope Clement XIV (—1774) Egidio Forcellini (1688—1768): "Totius Latinitatis Lexicon" (posth.) Johann Gottfried von Herder: "Kritische Wälder" "Letters of Junius," published: anonymous attacks on men in public life, exposing corruption, written probably by Sir Philip Francis William Robertson (1721—1793): "History of Charles V"
1770	"Boston Massacre," a brawl between civilians and troops Brit. Parliament repeals duties on paper, glass, and dyestuffs in Amer. colonies, retaining tea duty Dauphin of France marries Marie Antoinette, daughter of Empress Maria Theresa of Austria F. J. Struensee, favorite of Dan. Queen Caroline Matilde, becomes supreme minister Mahlon Dickerson, U.S. legislator and Secretary of the Navy, b. (d. 1853)	Thomas Chatterton, Eng. poet, d. (b. 1752) Johannes Ewald: "Rolf Krage," first Dan. tragedy Oliver Goldsmith: "The Deserted Village," poem Friedrich Hölderlin, Ger. poet, b. (d. 1843) William Wordsworth, Eng. poet, b. (d. 1850)	Edmund Burke: "Thoughts on the Cause of the Present Discontents" Georg Wilhelm Friedrich Hegel, Ger. philosopher, b. (d. 1831) Kant (made professor of philosophy at Königsberg University): "De mundi sensibilie et intelligibilis forma et principiis" Printers and publishers of "Letters of Junius" tried for seditious libel
1771	Russia and Prussia agree about partition of Poland Russia completes conquest of the Crimea Adolphus Frederick of Sweden d.; succeeded by Gustavus III Damascus seized by troops of Ali Bey	Matthias Claudius publishes his poems and essays in "Wandsbecker Bote" Thomas Gray, Eng. poet, d. (b. 1716) Klopstock: "Odes" Walter Scott, Scot. novelist, b. (d. 1832) Tobias Smollett, Eng. novelist, d. (b. 1721) Wieland: "Der neue Amadis," poem Charles Brockden Brown, the first professional U.S. writer, b. (d. 1810)	Encyclopaedia Britannica, first edition John William Fletcher (1729—1785): "Five Checks to Antinomianism" Claude Adrien Helvétius, Fr. antireligious philosopher, d. (b. 1715) Robert Owen, Eng. social reformer, b. (d. 1858) William Robertson (1721—1793): "History of America" Sydney Smith, Eng. author and divine, b. (d. 1845)
1772	Boston Assembly demands rights of colonies, threatens secession Royal Marriage Act in Britain to prevent undesirable royal marriages Clive defends in the Commons his administration in India; Warren Hastings made Governor of Bengal Struensee, Dan. dictator, arrested and beheaded First Partition of Poland Samuel Adams (1722—1803) forms Committees of Correspondence in Massachusetts for action against Great Britain William H. Crawford, U.S. statesman, b. (d. 1834) Caesar A. Rodney, future U.S. Attorney-General and diplomat, b. (d. 1824) William Wirt, future U.S. Attorney-General, b. (d. 1834)	György Bessenyei (1747—1811): "The Tragedy of Agis," Hungarian drama Samuel Taylor Coleridge, Eng. poet and philosopher, b. (d. 1834) Choderlos de Laclos: "Les Liaisons dangereuses," novel The Göttinger Hainbund, society of young patriotic Ger. poets, formed Sandór Kisfaludi, Hungarian poet, b. (d. 1801) Lessing: "Emilia Galotti," tragedy Novalis (Friedrich von *(contd)*	Herder: "On the Origin of Speech," on comparative philology Inquisition abolished in France "Letters of Junius" end Mirabeau: "Essai sur le despotisme" Friedrich von Schlegel, Ger. scholar and poet, b. (d. 1829) Swedenborg d. (b. 1688) F. S. Sullivan, Ir. jurist (1719—1776): "Lectures On the Feudal Law and the Constitution and Laws of England"

D. VISUAL ARTS	E. MUSIC	F. SCIENCE, TECHNOLOGY, GROWTH	G. DAILY LIFE	
Adam brothers: Adelphi, London Fragonard: "The Study" Thomas Lawrence, Eng. painter, b. (d. 1830) Joshua Reynolds knighted	Bonifacio Asioli, Ital. music scholar and composer, b. (d. 1832) Joseph Elsner, Ger.-Pol. composer, Chopin's teacher, b. (d. 1854)	N. J. Cugnot constructs first steam road carriage G. L. Cuvier, Fr. biologist and geologist, b. (d. 1832) First lightning conductors on high buildings Alexander von Humboldt, Ger. naturalist, b. (d. 1859)	Old Blackfriars Bridge, London, built (destroyed 1860) "The Morning Chronicle" issued in London Johann Friedrich Oberlin (1740—1826) opens first crêche at Steintal, Alsace	**1769**
François Boucher, Fr. painter, d. (b. 1703) Gainsborough: "The Blue Boy" François Gérard, Fr. painter, b. (d. 1837) Suzuki Harunobu, Jap. painter, d. (b. 1718) Bertel Thorvaldsen, Dan. sculptor, b. (d. 1844) Giovanni Battista Tiepolo, Ital. painter, d. (b 1696)	Ludwig van Beethoven, Ger. composer, b. (d. 1827) Gluck: "Paride ed Elena," opera, Vienna Handel's "Messiah" first performed in New York Haydn: "La Pescatrice," opera buffa Giuseppe Tartini, Ital. composer and violinist, d. (b. 1692)	Scot. explorer James Bruce (1730—1794) discovers source of the Blue Nile James Cook discovers Botany Bay, Australia Elementary school education reformed in Austria Eng. "quack" John Hill (1716—1775) introduces method of obtaining specimens for microscopic study Leonhard Euler: "Introduction to Algebra"	Civil liberties, international free trade, textile machines, and steam power lead in England to an industrial revolution which slowly spreads all over the world "The Massachusetts Spy" begins publication An opal of nearly 3000 carats found in Hungary First public restaurant opens in Paris Visiting cards introduced in England	**1770**
Houdon: "Diderot" Bartolomeo Rastrelli, Ital. architect in Russia, d. (b. 1700) Horace Walpole: "Anecdotes of Painting" Benjamin West: "The Death of Wolfe"	Haydn: "Sun" quartets (nos. 25—30) Piccini: "Le Finte Gemelle," Rome	Luigi Galvani discovers electrical nature of nervous impulse The Smeatonian Club for engineers founded in London, named after John Smeaton (1724—1792)	Sir Richard Arkwright (1732—1792) produces first spinning mill in England The Assembly Room, Bath, England, opened New York Hospital founded Richard Price: "Appeal to the Public on the National Debt"	**1771**
Johann Michael Feuchtmayr, Ger. sculptor, d. (b. 1709)	Flight and Kelly, London firm of organ builders, produces first barrel organs First Ger. performance of Handel's "Messiah" Haydn: six symphonies, Op. 20 Mozart: "Lucio Silla," opera, Milan	James Bruce traces the Blue Nile to its confluence with the White Nile Leonhard Euler: "Lettres à une princesse d'Allemagne," on mechanics, optics, acoustics, and astronomy Daniel Rutherford and Joseph Priestley independently discover nitrogen James Cook leaves England on second voyage (—1775)	The Bromberg Canal, linking the Oder and the Vistula, is begun First carriage traffic across Brenner Pass Judge William Murray (1705—1793) decides in the Somerset case that a slave is free on landing in England	**1772**

	A. HISTORY, POLITICS	B. LITERATURE, THEATER	C. RELIGION, PHILOSOPHY, LEARNING
1772 contd		Hardenberg), Ger. poet, b. (d. 1801) Manuel José Quintana, Span. poet, b. (d. 1857)	
1773	Virginia House of Burgesses appoints Provincial Committee of Correspondence Brit. East India Company Regulating Act Prince Klemens von Metternich, Aust. statesman, b. (d. 1859) Denmark cedes duchy of Oldenburg to Russia Boston Tea Party: protest against tea duty William Henry Harrison, ninth President of the U.S., b. (d. 1841) Peter B. Porter, U.S. political and military leader, b. (d. 1844)	Gottfried August Bürger: "Lenore," famous Ger. ballad Goethe: "Götz von Berlichingen," drama; "Urfaust," first version of "Faust" Oliver Goldsmith: "She Stoops To Conquer," comedy Herder: "Von deutscher Art und Kunst," manifesto of "Sturm und Drang" movement Klopstock finishes his "Messiah" (begun 1748) Swed. national theater established in Stockholm Ludwig Tieck, Ger. poet, b. (d. 1853)	Pope Clement XIV dissolves Jesuit Order John Erskine: "Institutes of the Law in Scotland" Joseph II expels Jesuits from the Empire
1774	Brit. House of Commons refuses Massachusetts petition to remove Thomas Hutchinson as governor-general Coercive acts against Massachusetts include closing of port of Boston Quebec Act, to secure Canada's loyalty to Great Britain, establishes Roman Catholicism in Canada Louis XV, King of France, d.; succeeded by his grandson Louis XVI Virginia House of Burgesses decides to call Continental Congress; it meets at Philadelphia with representatives of all colonies except Georgia Suffolk Convention resolves to disregard coercive acts Nonimportation of Brit. goods to Amer. colonies, decided upon by Continental Congress, comes into force Daniel P. Tompkins, twice Vice President of the U.S., b. (d. 1825) Accession of Abdul Hamid I as Sultan of Turkey Austria occupies Bukovina Robert Clive, ex-Governor of Bengal, d. (b. 1725)	Lord Chesterfield: "Letters to His Son," on how a gentleman should behave Goethe: "The Sorrows of Werther," novel Oliver Goldsmith d. (b. 1728) Robert Southey, Eng. author, b. (d. 1843) Wieland: "The Story of the Abderites," satirical novel	Edmund Burke: "On American Taxation" John Campbell: "A Political Survey of Great Britain" John Cartwright: "American Independence, The Glory and Interest of Great Britain" Pope Clement XIV d. (Sept.) Jesuits expelled from Poland Anne Lee (1736—1784) of Massachusetts settles in New York to begin a spiritualist revival François Quesnay, founder of physiocratic school of political economy, d. (b. 1694)
1775	Peasants' revolts in Bohemia against servitude American Revolution (—1783): Paul Revere's ride from Charleston to Lexington; defeat of British at Lexington; Americans conquer Fort Ticonderoga, N.Y., and Crown Point; Second Continental Congress assembles at Philadelphia; George Washington made commander-in-chief of Amer. forces; Brit. victory at Bunker Hill; Amer. war aims stated in Philadelphia; Benedict Arnold's attack on Quebec fails England hires 29,000 Ger. mercenaries for war in N. America James Barbour, U.S. statesman, b. (d. 1842) Lucien Bonaparte, future Prince of Canino, reputedly the most gifted of the Bonapartes, b. (d. 1840)	Vittorio Alfieri: "Cleopatra," Ital. tragedy Jane Austen, Eng. novelist, b. (d. 1817) Beaumarchais: "The Barber of Seville," comedy Goethe settles in Weimar Samuel Johnson: "A Journey to the Western Islands of Scotland" Charles Lamb, Eng. essayist, b. (d. 1834) Sheridan: "The Rivals" Sarah Siddons appears for first time at Drury Lane, London	Cardinal Gianangelo Braschi elected in Feb. as Pope Pius VI (—1799) after a long conclave Edmund Burke: "Speech on Conciliation with America" Anselm Feuerbach, Ger. jurist, b. (d. 1833) Justus Moser: "Patriotische Phantasien," plea for one organic Germany

D. VISUAL ARTS	E. MUSIC	F. SCIENCE, TECHNOLOGY, GROWTH	G. DAILY LIFE	
				1772 contd
Hubert François Gravelot, Fr. painter and caricaturist, d. (b. 1699) Sir Joshua Reynolds: "The Graces Decorating Hymen"	Charles Burney: "The Present State of Music in Germany, the Netherlands, and the United Provinces" The waltz becomes fashionable in Vienna	First cast-iron bridge built at Coalbrookdale, Shropshire (—1792)	Philadelphia Museum founded	**1773**
Caspar David Friedrich, Ger. landscape painter, b. (d. 1840) Gainsborough: "Lord Kilmorey"	Gluck: "Iphigénie en Aulide," Paris	Astronomisches Jahrbuch begun in Berlin by J. E. Bode J. G. Gahn isolates manganese K. W. Scheele discovers chlorine and baryta John Wilkinson's boring mill to facilitate manufacture of cylinders for steam engine Aust. physician F. A. Mesmer (1733—1815) uses hypnosis for health purposes	Rules of cricket first drawn up Swiss educator Johann Heinrich Pestalozzi (1746—1827) founds school for orphaned and neglected children in Zurich to enable them to lead productive lives	**1774**
Chardin: "Self-Portrait" Houdon: "Gluck," sculpture Sir Joshua Reynolds: "Miss Bowles" George Romney becomes fashionable in London as portrait painter J. M. W. Turner, Eng. painter, b. (d. 1851)	K. P. E. Bach: "Die Israeliten in der Wüste," oratorio François-Adrien Boieldieu, Fr. opera composer, b. (d. 1834) Mozart: "La Finta Giardiniera," opera buffa, Salzburg	André Ampère, Fr. physicist, b. (d. 1836) James Cook returns from second voyage Digitalis used for first time as a diuretic in dropsy by William Withering of Birmingham, England J. C. Fabricius: "Systema entomologiae," classification of insects Pierre-Simon Girard invents water turbine Joseph Priestley discovers hydrochloric and sulfuric acids Louis St. Martin: "Des Erreurs et de la vérité" James Watt perfects his invention of the steam engine	First Brit. banks' clearing-house established in Lombard Street, London Bromberg Canal finished (begun 1772) First Thames Regatta	**1775**

	A. HISTORY, POLITICS	B. LITERATURE, THEATER	C. RELIGION, PHILOSOPHY, LEARNING
1776	Amer. Congress resolves suppression of authority of Brit. Crown; Washington forces British to abandon Boston; Amer. troops forced out of Canada; Virginia Convention instructs its delegates to Congress to propose independence; Virginia publishes its Bill of Rights; Congress carries Declaration of Independence; William Howe, commander-in-chief of Brit. army in America, takes New York and Rhode Island; Benedict Arnold defeated at Lake Champlain; Congress retires to Baltimore; Fort Lee surrenders to British; Washington retreats to Pennsylvania and defeats Hessian troops at Trenton Treaty of Copenhagen between Russia and Denmark Jacques Necker made Minister of Finance in France The future Queen Louise of Prussia b. (d. 1810) Unification of Port. administration in S. America, with Rio de Janeiro as capital Potemkin (1739—1791), favorite of Czarina Catherine II, organizes Russ. Black Sea fleet	Alfieri: "Antigone" The Burgtheater, Vienna, becomes National Theater Goethe: "Stella," tragedy E. T. A. Hoffmann, Ger. author and composer, b. (d. 1822) ("Tales of Hoffmann") J. M. R. Lenz: "Die Soldaten," drama F. M. von Klinger: "Sturm und Drang," drama which gave the movement its name, "storm and stress"	John Cartwright: "Take your Choice," on parliamentary reform Edward Gibbon: "Decline and Fall of the Roman Empire" (—1788) David Hume, Scot. philosopher and historian, d. (b. 1711) Richard Price: "Observations on Civil Liberty and the Justice and Policy of the War with America" Adam Smith: "An Inquiry into the Nature and Causes of the Wealth of Nations"
1777	American Revolution: British defeated at Princeton, N.J., and Bennington, Vt.; Lafayette's Fr. volunteers arrive in America; Amer. forces defeated at the Brandywine, Pa., and Germantown, Pa.; British secure control of Delaware; Gen. Burgoyne loses two battles at Bemis Heights, N.Y., and capitulates to Americans at Saratoga, N.Y.; the Ger. General von Steuben arrives to become inspector-general of Amer. forces Future Czar Alexander I of Russia b. (d. 1825) Spain and Portugal settle disputes concerning their S. American colonies	Court and National Theater, Mannheim, founded Friedrich de la Motte-Fouqué, Ger. romantic poet, b. (d. 1843) R. B. Sheridan: "The School for Scandal," comedy Heinrich von Kleist, Ger. poet, b. (d. 1811)	James Anderson: "Nature of the Corn Laws" Henry Hallam, Eng. historian, b. (d. 1859) John Howard: "The State of the Prisons of England and Wales" Lessing pleads for toleration in religious and political matters ("Ernst und Falk") Joseph Priestley: "Disquisition Relating to Matter and Spirit" Roger B. Taney, future Chief Justice of the U.S. Supreme Court, b. (d. 1864)
1778	American Revolution: Amer. colonies sign treaties with France and Holland; reject Brit. peace offer; Washington defeats British at Monmouth, N.J.; Fr. fleet arrives off Delaware; British capture Savannah, Ga. William Pitt the Elder, Earl of Chatham, d. (b. 1708) Indian massacres at Wyoming, Pa., and Cherry Valley, N.Y. War of Bavarian Succession (—May 1779) Warren Hastings takes Chandernagore, Bengal Henry Peter Brougham, Baron Brougham and Vaux, Scot. statesman, b. (d. 1868)	Clemens Brentano, Ger. poet, b. (d. 1842) Fanny Burney: "Evelina," novel Ugo Foscolo, Ital. author, b. (d. 1827) William Hazlitt, Eng. author, b. (d. 1830) Herder publishes his collection of folk songs (—1779) Voltaire: "Irène" James Kirke Paulding, U.S. writer and Secretary of the Navy, b. (d. 1860)	G. L. L. Buffon: "Epoques de la Nature" Humphry Davy, Eng. chemist, b. (d.1829) J. A. Deluc: "Lettres physiques et morals sur les montagnes" Rousseau d. (b. 1712) Voltaire d. (b. 1694)
1779	British attack Fr. Senegal, W. Africa, gain Goree British surrender to Americans at Vincennes Peace of Teschen ends War of Bavarian Succession Fr. forces take St. Vincent and Grenada, West Indies Spain declares war on Britain; siege of Gibraltar (—1783) U.S. Congress dispatches force into Wyoming Valley against Indians (see 1778) Brit. war against Mahrattas in India (—1782) Stephen Decatur, U.S. naval hero ("My country, right or wrong"), b. (d. 1820)	David Garrick, Eng. actor, d. (b. 1717) Samuel Johnson: "Lives of the Poets" (—1781) Lessing: "Nathan der Weise," verse drama Thomas Moore, Ir. lyric poet, b. (d. 1852) Adam Gottlieb Oehlenschläger, Dan. poet, b. (d. 1850) Sheridan: "The Critic," farce Wieland: "Oberon," romantic poem	David Hume: "Dialogues of Natural Religion" (posth.) Friedrich Karl von Savigny, Ger. jurist, b. (d. 1861)

D. VISUAL ARTS	E. MUSIC	F. SCIENCE, TECHNOLOGY, GROWTH	G. DAILY LIFE	
Sir William Chambers builds Somerset House, London (—1786) John Constable, Eng. painter, b. (d. 1837) Fragonard: "The Washerwoman" Pigalle: "Voltaire," sculpture	Charles Burney: "History of Music" (—1789) "Concerts of Ancient Music," London (—1848) Mozart: Serenade in D major, K. 250 ("Haffner")	Cook's third voyage to the Pacific	U.S. Congress institutes a national lottery Col. Anthony St. Leger establishes his St. Leger horse race at Doncaster Military ski competitions in Norway	**1776**
Gainsborough: "The Watering Place" Greuze: "La Cruche cassée" Francesca Guardi: "Santa Maria della Salute," Venice Christian Daniel Rauch, Ger. sculptor, b. (d. 1857) Philipp Otto Runge, Ger. painter, b. (d. 1810)	Gluck: "Armide," Paris Haydn: Symphony No. 63 in C major ("La Roxolane")	Amer. engineer David Bushnell (1750—1824) invents torpedo C. A. Coulomb (1736—1806) invents torsion balance Karl Gauss, Ger. mathematician and astronomer, b. (d. 1855) Lavoisier proves that air consists mainly of oxygen and nitrogen Albrecht von Haller, Swiss scientist and poet, d. (b. 1708)	Julie ("Mme.") Récamier, Chateaubriand's friend, Napoleon's opponent, b. (d. 1849) Stars and Stripes adopted as Continental Congress flag Cooperative workshop for tailors at Birmingham	**1777**
Giambattista Piranesi, Ital. etcher and architect, d. (b. 1720)	Thomas Augustine Arne, Eng. composer, d. (b. 1710) Beethoven (at eight) presented by his father as six-year-old infant prodigy La Scala, Milan, opened Mozart: "Les Petits Riens," ballet, Paris	James Cook discovers Hawaii Franz Mesmer, Viennese doctor, practices "mesmerism" in Paris Smeaton experiments with improved diving bell (see 1535)	Act of Congress prohibits import of slaves into the U.S. Joseph Bramah from Yorkshire (1748—1814) constructs improved water closet (see 1596)	**1778**
Canova: "Daedalus and Icarus," sculpture Jean Baptiste Siméon Chardin, Fr. painter, d. (b. 1699) Thomas Chippendale, Eng. master cabinetmaker, d. (b. 1719) James Gillray's first cartoons appear Houdon: "Molière," sculpture Anton Raphael Mengs, Ger. painter and critic, d. (b. 1728)	J. C. Bach: "Amadis de Gaule," opera, Paris Gluck: "Iphigénie en Tauride," Paris	Jöns Jakob Berzelius, Swed. chemist, b. (d. 1848) James Cook murdered b. (1728) James Rennel: "Bengal Atlas" Spallanzani proves that semen is necessary for fertilization Joel R. Poinsett, U.S. diplomat, b. (d. 1851); poinsettia named after him	First children's clinic, London The Derby established at Epsom racetrack, Surrey, England, by 12th Earl of Derby (first winner "Diomed," owned by Sir Charles Bunbury) Pope Pius VI begins draining Pontine Marshes First "velocipedes" appear in Paris First running of The Oaks (horse racing)	**1779**

	A. HISTORY, POLITICS	B. LITERATURE, THEATER	C. RELIGION, PHILOSOPHY, LEARNING
1780	Henry Grattan (1746—1820) demands Home Rule for Ireland House of Commons affirms principle of periodic scrutiny of Civil List American Revolution: Charleston, S.C., surrenders to British; Fr. troops arrive at Newport, R.I.; Americans defeated at Camden; Brit. army defeated at King's Mountain, N.C.; Benedict Arnold's plot to surrender West Point is revealed Gordon riots in London ("No Popery") Serfdom abolished in Bohemia and Hungary Empress Maria Theresa d.; succeeded by her son Joseph II (—1790) Outbreak of Second Mysore War (—1784) Rebellion in Peru against Span. rule Pitt the Younger enters Parliament John Forsyth, U.S. Secretary of State to Jackson and Van Buren, b. (d. 1841)	Matthias Claudius: "Lieder für das Volk" Frederick the Great: "De la littérature allemande" John Wilson Croker, Brit. Tory leader, founder of Athenaeum Club, b. (d. 1857)	Catholic population of England: 70,000 Etienne Bonnot de Condillac, Fr. philosopher, d. (b. 1715) Gaetano Filangieri: "Science of Legislation"
1781	American Revolution: British defeated at Cowpens, N.C., and Eutaw, N.C., Americans at Guilford, Conn.; end of all land operations with the Brit. capitulation at Yorktown and evacuation of Charleston and Savannah Dutch settlement at Negapatam, Madras, captured by British Warren Hastings deposes Rajah of Benares, plunders treasure of the Nabob of Oudh	Gotthold Ephraim Lessing, Ger. dramatist and critic, d. (b. 1729) Rousseau: "Confessions" Schiller: "Die Räuber," drama Adelbert von Chamisso, Ger poet, b. (d. 1838)	Clarendon Press, Oxford, established Franciscan monks settle at Los Angeles Joseph II grants patent of religious tolerance and freedom of press in Austria Kant: "Critique of Pure Reason," fundamental work of modern philosophy Moses Mendelssohn: "On the Civil Amelioration of the Condition of the Jews" Pestalozzi states in his social novel, "Leonard and Gertrude," his educational aims
1782	Spanish capture Minorca from British American Revolution: Thomas Grenville sent from London to Paris to open peace talks with Benjamin Franklin; preliminaries accepted by Great Britain and America Treaty of Salbai ends Mahratta war Spain completes conquest of Florida Brit. Admiral Howe (1726—1799) relieves Gibraltar Tippoo Sahib succeeds Hyder Ali in Mysore Rama I founds new dynasty in Siam, makes Bangkok his capital John C. Calhoun, U.S. proslavery statesman, b. (d. 1850) Lewis Cass, U.S. political leader who opened up the Middle West, b. (d. 1866) John Branch, U.S. political leader, b. (d. 1863)	Fanny Burney: "Cecilia," novel William Cowper: "Poems" H. F. R. de Lamennais, Fr. author, b. (d. 1854) Herder: "The Spirit of Hebrew Poetry"	Friedrich Fröbel, Ger. pedagogue, b. (d. 1852) Pope Pius VI in Vienna fails to persuade Joseph II to rescind program of tolerance Joseph Priestley: "A History of the Corruptions of Christianity" Royal Irish Academy, Dublin, founded Dugald Stewart: "Elements of the Philosophy of the Human Mind" Girolamo Tiraboschi: "History of Italian Literature"
1783	American Revolution: Britain and America proclamations for cessation of arms; Peace of Versailles: Great Britain recognizes independence of the U.S. Joseph II enforces Ger. language in Bohemia Simón Bolívar, Lat.-Amer. soldier-statesman, b. (d. 1830) William Pitt forms ministry (—1801) Famine in Japan Potemkin conquers the Crimea for Russia	William Blake: poetical sketches George Crabbe: "The Village," Suffolk poem (see 1945 "Peter Grimes") Washington Irving, Amer. author, b. (d. 1859) Schiller: "Fiesco" Stendhal (Marie Henri Beyle), Fr. novelist, b. (d. 1842) Yokai Yagu, Jap. poet, d. (b. 1702)	Johann Jakob Bodmer, Swiss philologist, d. (b. 1698) William Herschel: "Motion of the Solar System in Space" Kant: "Prolegomena to Any Possible Metaphysics" Moses Mendelssohn: "Jerusalem," plea for freedom of conscience Charles Simeon (1759—1836) begins evangelical movement at Cambridge

D. VISUAL ARTS	E. MUSIC	F. SCIENCE, TECHNOLOGY, GROWTH	G. DAILY LIFE	
Bernardo Canaletto (Bellotto), Ital. painter, d. (b. 1720) J. S. Copley: "Death of Chatham" J. A. D. Ingres, Fr. painter, b. (d. 1867) Sir Joshua Reynolds: "Mary Robinson as Perdita" Jacques Germain Soufflot, Fr. architect, d. (b. 1713)	Span. dance "bolero" invented by dancer Sebastiano Carezo Sébastien Erard (Paris) makes first modern pianoforte Haydn: "Toy" Symphony Giovanni Paisiello: "Il Barbiere di Siviglia," St. Petersburg Karl Ditters von Dittersdorf: "Job," oratorio	Circular saw invented by Gervinus Felice Fontana produces water gas American Academy of Sciences founded at Boston Scheller constructs first fountain pen	"The British Gazette" and "Sunday Monitor," first Sunday newspapers, appear in London (Mar. 26) Richard Rush, U.S. lawyer and financier, b. (d. 1859)	**1780**
David: "Belisarius" Karl Friedrich Schinkel, Ger. architect, b. (d. 1841)	Haydn: "Russian" String Quartets (37—42) Johann Adam Hiller (1728—1804) establishes the Gewandhaus Concerts at Leipzig Mozart: "Idomeneo, re di Creta," opera, Munich	Bernhard Bolzano, Aust. mathematician, b. (d. 1848) Herschel discovers the planet Uranus George Stephenson, Eng. inventor, b. (d. 1848) Composition of mineral tungsten discovered by K. W. Scheele	Peter Beckford (1740—1811): "Thoughts on Hunting" First Building Society established in Birmingham Serfdom abolished in Aust. dominions Construction of Siberian highway begun	**1781**
Canova: monument to Pope Clement XIV Guardi: "Fetes for the Grand Duke Paul of Russia," Venetian painting Richard Wilson, Eng. painter, d. (b. 1714)	Daniel Auber, Fr. composer, b. (d. 1871) J. C. Bach d. (b. 1735) John Field, Eng. composer, b. (d. 1837) Mozart: "Die Entführung aus dem Serail" ("The Abduction from the Seraglio"), opera, Vienna Nicolò Paganini, Ital. composer and violinist, b. (d. 1840)	Montgolfier brothers construct air balloon James Watt invents double-acting rotary steam engine	Bank of North America established in Philadelphia Josiah Wedgwood develops pyrometer for checking temperature in pottery furnace	**1782**
J. L. David: "Grief of Andromache" Peter von Cornelius, Ger. painter, b. (d. 1867)	Beethoven's first works printed John Broadwood (1732—1812), Eng. pianoforte maker, patents his piano pedals Mozart: Mass in C minor	Copper cylinder for calico printing by Henry Bell Jouffroy d'Abbans sails a paddle-wheel steamboat on the Saône River Jean le Rond d'Alembert, Fr. mathematician and encyclopedist, d. (b. 1717) Horace de Saussure (1740—1799) invents hair hygrometer Leonhard Euler, Swiss mathematician, d. (b. 1707) Montgolfier brothers ascend in fire balloon at Annonay	Bank of Ireland founded Civil marriage and divorce in Aust. dominions Society of the Cincinnati, elite Amer. Revolutionary group, founded	**1783**

	A. HISTORY, POLITICS	B. LITERATURE, THEATER	C. RELIGION, PHILOSOPHY, LEARNING
1784	Treaty of Constantinople: Turkey agrees to Russ. annexation of the Crimea Brit. peace treaty with Tippoo Sahib of Mysore Thomas Jefferson's land ordinance passed Joseph II abrogates constitution in Hungary, suppressing feudal rights Pitt's India Act; East India Company under government control Lord Palmerston, Brit. statesman, b. (d. 1865)	Beaumarchais: "The Marriage of Figaro," comedy Ludwig Devrient, Ger. actor, b. (d. 1832) Leigh Hunt, Eng. author, b. (d. 1859) Schiller: "Kabale und Liebe," drama Samuel Johnson d. (b. 1709) Phillis Wheatly, Amer. Negro poet, d. (b. 1753)	First Anglican bishop for the colonies Bengal Asiatic Society (study of Sanskrit) founded by William Jones Bernardin de Saint-Pierre: "Etudes de la nature" Herder: "Ideas Toward a Philosophy of History" (—1791) Kant: "Notion of a Universal History in a Cosmopolitan Sense" William Mitford: "History of Greece" (—1810) John Wesley's Deed of Declaration, the charter of Wesleyan Methodism
1785	Warren Hastings resigns as Governor-General of India, returns to England Der Fürstenbund (League of German Princes) formed by Frederick the Great against Joseph II Diamond Necklace Affair in Versailles: Marie Antoinette discredited, Cardinal de Rohan arrested Commercial Treaty signed between Prussia and the U.S. Russians settle in Aleutian Isles, N. Pacific John McLean, U.S. jurist, b. (d. 1861) Oliver Hazard Perry, U.S. naval hero, b. (d. 1819)	William Cowper: "John Gilpin" Thomas de Quincey, Eng. author, b. (d. 1859) Jakob Grimm, Ger. author and folklorist, b. (d. 1863) Alessandro Manzoni, Ital. poet and novelist, b. (d. 1873) Thomas Love Peacock, Eng. author, b. (d. 1866) The Reverend James Wilmot of Warwickshire identifies Francis Bacon, Viscount St. Albans (1561—1626), as author of Shakespeare's plays	Educational reforms in Germany by Johann Heinrich Campe (1746—1818) Kant: "Groundwork of the Metaphysic of Ethics" James Madison's Religious Freedom Act abolishes religious tests in Virginia William Paley: "Principles of Moral and Political Philosophy"
1786	Lord Cornwallis made Governor-General of India Annapolis convention under Madison and Hamilton Rajah of Kedah cedes Penang to Great Britain Frederick the Great d.; succeeded by his nephew Frederick William II (—1797) Rebellion of Daniel Shays in Massachusetts Louis I, King of Bavaria, b. (d. 1868) Nicholas Biddle, U.S. financier, b. (d. 1844) Louis McLane, U.S. statesman and diplomat, b. (d. 1857)	Berlin Court Theater opens Ludwig Börne, Ger. author, b. (d. 1837) John Bourgoyne: "The Heiress," play Bürger: "Gedichte" Robert Burns: "Poems chiefly in the Scottish dialect," beginning a Burns vogue Goethe's Italian journey (—1788) Wilhelm Grimm, Ger. author and folklorist, b. (d. 1859) Musäus: "Volksmärchen der Deutschen," Ger. fairy tales	Moses Mendelssohn, Ger.-Jewish philosopher, d. (b. 1729) Mennonites from Central Europe settle in Canada
1787	Aust. Netherlands declared province of Hapsburg monarchy Catherine II visits the Crimea, sees in passing Potemkin's artificial villages New York Assembly imposes duties on foreign goods; Philadelphia convention meets to frame a constitution; the Constitution of the U.S. signed; Federal U.S. government established; Pennsylvania admitted to statehood Parlement of Paris demands summoning of States-General; King Louis XVI declares that they will be summoned July 1792 Turkey declares war on Russia *(contd)*	Beaumarchais: "Tarare," comedy Jacques-Henri Bernardin de Saint-Pierre: "Paul et Virginie," Fr. idyll Goethe: "Iphigenie auf Tauris" Johann Heinse: "Ardinghello und die glückseligen Inseln," Ger. novel Edmund Kean, Ir. actor, b. (d. 1833) Mary Russell Mitford, Eng. author, b. (d. 1855) Schiller: "Don Carlos" *(contd)*	John Adams: "A Defence of the Constitution of Government of the U.S.A." Jeremy Bentham: "Defence of Usury" Imperial Russian Dictionary with 285 words in 200 languages (initiated by Catherine II) James Madison: "The Vices of the Political System of the United States"

D. VISUAL ARTS	E. MUSIC	F. SCIENCE, TECHNOLOGY, GROWTH	G. DAILY LIFE	
Brighton Pavilion (for the Prince Regent) built (—1827), in part by John Nash Goya: "Don Manuel de Zuniga" Leo von Klenze, Ger. architect, b. (d. 1864) Reynolds: "Mrs. Siddons as The Tragic Muse" First political cartoons by Thomas Rowlandson (1756—1827)	Wilhelm Friedemann Bach d. (b. 1710) André Grétry: "Richard Coeur de Lion," opera, Paris Salieri: "Les Danaïdes," opera, Paris Louis Spohr, Ger. composer, b. (d. 1859)	Swiss inventor Aimé Argand (1755—1803) designs oil burner Eng. mathematician George Atwood accurately determines acceleration of a free-falling body Joseph Bramah (1748—1814) constructs first patent lock Eng. ironmaster Henry Cort (1740—1800) introduces puddling process for manufacture of wrought iron Goethe discovers human intermaxillary bone Scot. millwright Andrew Meikle (1719—1811) invents threshing machine First balloon ascent in England, by Vincent Lunardi	First school for the blind in Paris "The Boston Sentinel" appears Serfdom abolished in Denmark	**1784**
Emerald Buddha Chapel, Bangkok J. L. David: "The Oath of the Horatii" Houdon, in America: sculpture of George Washington Reynolds: "The Infant Hercules" David Wilkie, Scot. painter, b. (d. 1841)	Baldassare Galuppi, Ital. composer, d. (b. 1706) Mozart: six "Haydn" String Quartets	C. L. Berthollet invents chemical bleaching Salsano: seismograph for measuring earthquakes James Watt and Matthew Boulton install a steam engine with rotary motion in a cotton-spinning factory at Papplewick, Nottinghamshire Blanchard and Jeffries cross Eng. Channel in a balloon	"Daily Universal Register" (becomes "The Times" 1788) begun by John Walter	**1785**
Goya: "The Seasons," designs for tapestries B. R. Haydon, Eng. painter, b. (d. 1846) George Hepplewhite, Eng. master cabinetmaker, d. (b. 1726) Hoppner: "A Lady" Sir Joshua Reynolds: "The Duchess of Devonshire"	Ditters von Dittersdorf: "Doctor und Apotheker," comic opera, Vienna Mozart: "The Marriage of Figaro," Vienna Carl Maria von Weber, Ger. composer, b. (d. 1826)	Georges Buffon: "Histoire naturelle des oiseaux" John Franklin, Eng. navigator and naturalist, b. (d. 1847) William Herschel: "Catalogue of Nebulae" M. H. Klaproth, Ger. chemist (1743—1817), discovers uranium Amer. inventor Ezekiel Reed makes nail-making machine K. W. Scheele, Swed. chemist, d. (b. 1742) Balmat and Paccard first climb Mont Blanc Amer. inventor James Rumsey designs first mechanically driven boat	Earliest attempts at internal gas lighting in Germany and England Charleston, S.C., Golf Club (America) founded	**1786**
Pompeo Batoni, Ital. painter, d. (b. 1708) Sir Joshua Reynolds: "Lady Heathfield" Tischbein: "Goethe on the Ruins in the Roman Campagna"	Luigi Boccherini made court composer in Berlin Gluck d. (b. 1714) Mozart: "Don Giovanni," Prague	Ernst Chladni (1756—1827) experiments with sound patterns on vibrating plates Amer. inventor John Fitch (1743—1798) launches a steamboat on Delaware River Lavoisier: "Méthode de nomenclature chimique" Horace de Saussure reaches summit of Mont Blanc, takes weather observations	Dollar currency introduced in the U.S. (see 1792) Eng. settlement founded for freed slaves in Sierra Leone M.C.C. (Marylebone Cricket Club) founded; moves to Lord's cricket ground	**1787**

	A. HISTORY, POLITICS	B. LITERATURE, THEATER	C. RELIGION, PHILOSOPHY, LEARNING
1787 contd	Samuel L. Southard, U.S. Secretary of the Navy, b. (d. 1842) John J. Crittenden, U.S. Attorney-General and legislator, b. (d. 1863)	John S. Miles, U.S. editor and legislator, b. (d. 1856)	
1788	Parlement of Paris presents list of grievances; Louis XVI decides to call States-General for May 1789 and recalls Jacques Necker as Minister of Finance Charles Edward Stuart, the "Young Pretender," d. (b. 1720) Austria declares war on Turkey Brit. parliamentary motion for abolition of slave trade U.S. constitution, ratified by New Hampshire, the ninth state, comes into force New York declared federal capital of the U.S. George III's first attack of mental illness; regency crisis in England Trial of Warren Hastings for maladministration in India (—1795)	Lord Byron, Eng. poet, b. (d. 1824) Goethe: "Egmont," tragedy Friendship between Goethe and Schiller Friedrich Rückert, Ger. author, b. (d. 1866) Joseph von Eichendorff, Ger. romantic poet, b. (d. 1857)	Georg Johann Hamann, Ger. religious philosopher, d. (b. 1730) Kant: "Critique of Practical Reason," the "Categorical Imperative" John Lemprière: "Classical Dictionary" Hannah More: "Thoughts on the Importance of the Manners of the Great to General Society" Arthur Schopenhauer, Ger. philosopher, b. (d. 1860) John C. Spencer, U.S. lawyer, b. (d. 1855)
1789	King George III of England recovers First U.S. Congress meets in New York; George Washington inaugurated as President of the U.S.; John Adams Vice President, Thomas Jefferson Secretary of State, Alexander Hamilton Secretary of the Treasury; the U.S. declare themselves an economic and customs union The French Revolution: States-General meet at Versailles; Third Estate declares itself the National Assembly, decides not to depart until a constitution is drawn up; Mirabeau emerges as a national figure; the three Estates unite; the king dismisses Necker; Paris mob storms the Bastille; Lafayette becomes commander of National Guard; abolition of Fr. feudal system; Declaration of the Rights of Man; the king and court move from Versailles to Paris; Fr. royalists begin to emigrate; National Assembly decides on nationalization of church property, forbids any member to accept office under Louis XVI; issue of assignats (paper money) in France Austrians take Belgrade Aust. Netherlands declare independence as Belgium Abdul Hamid I d.; succeeded as Sultan of Turkey by his nephew Selim III (d. 1807) Levi Woodbury, U.S. statesman and jurist, b. (d. 1851) Amos Kendall, U.S. politician, influential in Jackson's "Kitchen Cabinet," b. (d. 1859) Thomas Ewing, U.S. Secretary of the Treasury and of the Interior, b. (d. 1871)	William Blake: "Songs of Innocence" James Fenimore Cooper, Amer. author, b. (d. 1851) Goethe: "Torquato Tasso," tragedy Kàlidàsa: "Sakuntala," trans. into English by William Jones	Jeremy Bentham (1748—1832): "Introduction to the Principles of Morals and Legislation" P. H. D. Holbach, Fr. philosopher, d. (b. 1723) E. J. Sieyès: "Qu'est-ce que le Tiers Etat?"
1790	William Pitt refuses to recognize Belg. independence Joseph of Austria d., succeeded by his brother Leopold II (—1792) U.S. Funding Bill introduced by Alexander Hamilton Poland cedes Thorn and Danzig to Prussia Reichenbach Conference between Austria and Prussia Brit. alliance with the Nizam of Hyderabad Festival of Champ de Mars, Paris; Louis XVI accepts the constitution Austrians in Brussels, suppress Belg. revolution Benjamin Franklin d. (b. 1706) Third Mysore War (—1792) Philadelphia becomes federal capital of the U.S.	Robert Burns: "Tam O'Shanter" Royal Literary Fund initiated by David Williams (1738—1816) Alphonse de Lamartine, Fr. author, b. (d. 1869)	J. B. Basedow, Ger. pedagogue, d. (b. 1723) Edmund Burke: "Reflections on the Revolution in France" André de Chénier: "Avis au peuple français" Jews in France are granted civil liberties Kant: "Kritik der Urteilskraft," philosophy The first Roman Catholic bishop consecrated in America: John Carroll of Baltimore *(contd)*

D. VISUAL ARTS	E. MUSIC	F. SCIENCE, TECHNOLOGY, GROWTH	G. DAILY LIFE	
				1787 contd
Brandenburger Tor, Berlin, built by C. G. Langhaus (—1791) David: "Love of Paris and Helena" Maurice Quentin de Latour, Fr. painter, d. (b. 1704) Thomas Gainsborough, Eng. painter, d. (b. 1727)	K. P. E. Bach d. (b. 1714) Mozart: The three "great" symphonies: E-flat, G minor, "Jupiter"	James Hutton: "New Theory of the Earth" Marquis Pierre Simon de Laplace: "Laws of the Planetary System"	Bread riots in France First Ger. cigar factory opened in Hamburg First hortensia and fuchsia imported to Europe from Peru M.C.C. codifies laws of cricket "The Times," London (see 1785)	**1788**
François Gérard: "Joseph and His Brothers" Johann Friedrich Overbeck, Ger. painter, b. (d. 1869)	Charles Burney: "History of Music" finished Grétry: "Raoul Barbe-Bleue," opera, Paris Friedrich Silcher, Ger. composer, b. (d. 1860)	Aloisio Galvani's experiments on muscular contraction of dead frogs Antoine Jussieu: "Genera plantarum," modern classification of plants Friedrich List, Ger. political economist, b. (d. 1846) University of Pennsylvania (founded 1749 as Philadelphia Academy) Louis Daguerre, Fr. pioneer of photography, b. (d. 1851)	Mutineers of H.M.S. "Bounty" settle on Pitcairn Islands, E. Pacific Chrysanthemums introduced from the Orient to Britain First steam-driven cotton factory in Manchester "Eclipse," one of the most famous racehorses, unbeaten through its career, d. "Journal des débats" founded in Paris Tammany founded as benevolent institution, but shortly after becomes political	**1789**
Charles Nicolas Cochin, Fr. artist, d. (b. 1715) Théodore Géricault, Fr. artist, b. (d. 1824) Guardi: "Gondola on the Lagoon," Venetian painting	Mozart: "Così fan tutte," opera, Vienna First musical competition in America	James Bruce: "Travels to Discover the Sources of the Nile, 1768—1773" Building of Firth-Clyde and Oxford-Birmingham canals begins Goethe: "Versuch, die Metamorphose der Pflanzen zu erklären" Lavoisier: "Table of Thirty-One Chemical Elements" First patent law in U.S. Eng. naval officer, George *(contd)*	First steam-powered rolling mill built in England Alexander Raditcheff: "Journey from St. Petersburg to Moscow," a plea for the emancipation of serfs Washington, D.C., founded	**1790**

	A. HISTORY, POLITICS	B. LITERATURE, THEATER	C. RELIGION, PHILOSOPHY, LEARNING
1790 contd			Adam Smith, Scot. political economist, d. (b.1723) First session of the Supreme Court of the U.S.
1791	Mirabeau elected president of Fr. Assembly; d. (b. 1749) Louis XVI, trying to leave France with his family, is caught at Varennes and returned to Paris Massacre of the Champ de Mars, Paris Fr. National Assembly dissolves Vermont becomes a state of the U.S. The first ten amendments to U.S. Constitution (Bill of Rights) ratified Canada Constitutional Act divides the country into two provinces, Upper and Lower Canada Negro slaves revolt in Fr. Santo Domingo Odessa founded	M. J. de Chénier (1764—1811): "Henry VIII" and "Jean Calas," two plays produced in Paris with F. J. Talma Goethe is named director of the Weimar Court Theater (—1817) Franz Grillparzer, Aust. dramatist, b. (d. 1872) Theodor Körner, Ger. poet, b. (d. 1813) Christian Schubart, Ger. poet and musician, d. (b. 1739) Eugène Scribe, Fr. dramatist and librettist, b. (d. 1861)	Boswell: "Life of Johnson" Michael Faraday, Eng. natural philosopher and physicist, b. (d. 1867) Herder: "Ideen zur Philosophie der Geschichte der Menschheit" Thomas Paine: "The Rights of Man," Part I (in defense of the French Revolution) Philippe Pinel: "Traité médico-philosophique sur l'aliénation mentale" John Wesley, founder of the Methodist movement, d. (b. 1703)
1792	Peace of Jassy ends war between Russia and Turkey Leopold II of Austria d.; succeeded as Holy Roman Emperor by his son Francis II (—1806) The Girondists form ministry in France; the mob invades Tuileries; the revolutionary Commune established; Legislative Assembly suspended; the royal family imprisoned; the Fr. Republic proclaimed Sept. 22; the revolutionary calendar comes into force; Jacobins under Danton seize power; trial of Louis XVI; the first guillotine in Paris Gustavus III assassinated in Stockholm Opera House; succeeded as King of Sweden by Gustavus IV (—1809) France declares war on Austria, Prussia, and Sardinia; Prussian and Aust. invaders are stopped at Battle of Valmy; Fr. troops cross Rhine, take Brussels, and conquer Aust. Netherlands Kentucky becomes a state of the U.S. Denmark is the first nation to abolish the slave trade Two political parties formed in U.S.: the Republican under Thomas Jefferson and the Federalist under Alexander Hamilton and John Adams	John Keble, Eng. poet, b. (d. 1866) Frederick Marryat, Eng. novelist, b. (d. 1848) Percy Bysshe Shelley, Eng. poet, b. (d. 1822)	Baptist Missionary Society founded in London J. B. Cloots: "La République universelle" Fichte: "Versuch einer Kritik aller Offenbarung" Thomas Paine: "Rights of Man," Part 2 Mary Wollstonecraft: "Vindication of the Rights of Women"
1793	Louis XVI executed Committee of Public Safety established in France with Danton as its head Reign of Terror begins Marat murdered by Charlotte Corday Robespierre and St. Just join Committee of Public Safety Roman Catholicism banned in France Queen Marie Antoinette executed Philippe Egalité, Duke of Orleans, executed Napoleon takes Toulon First Coalition against France formed Holy Roman Empire declares war on France U.S. proclaims its neutrality Fr. troops driven out of Germany Second Partition of Poland	John Clare, Eng. poet, b. (d. 1864) Goldoni, Venetian dramatist, d. (b. 1707) Marquis de Sade (1740—1814): "La philosophie dans le boudoir," Fr. novel	Charles Bonnet, Fr. philosopher, d. (b. 1720) J. B. Cloots: "Base constitutionelle de la république du genre humain" Compulsory public education in France from the age of six M. J. Condorcet: "Esquisse d'un tableau historique des progrès de l'esprit humain" "The Feast of Reason" in St. Eustache Church, Paris William Godwin: "The Inquiry concerning Political Justice" Kant: "Religion innerhalb der Grenzen der blossen Vernunft" ("Religion Within the Limits of Mere Reason")

D. VISUAL ARTS	E. MUSIC	F. SCIENCE, TECHNOLOGY, GROWTH	G. DAILY LIFE	
		Vancouver, (1758—1798) explores northwest coast of America		1790 contd
Karl Langhans: Brandenburg Gate, Berlin George Morland: "The Stable," Eng. painting Augustin Pajou (1730—1809): "Psyche Abandoned," sculpture	Cherubini: "Lodoiska," opera, Paris Carl Czerny, Aust. composer, b. (d. 1857) Haydn: "Surprise" Symphony Giacomo Meyerbeer, Ger. composer, b. (d. 1864) First performance of Mozart's "Magic Flute," Vienna Mozart d. (b. 1756) The waltz becomes fashionable in England	Samuel F. B. Morse, Amer. inventor, b. (d. 1872) William Bartram (1739—1823): "Travels through North and South Carolina..."	John Sinclair: "The Statistical Account of Scotland" Bank of North America founded The "Observer" founded in London Prince Potemkin, favorite of Empress Catherine II, d. (b. 1739) Wilberforce's motion for abolition of slave trade carried through Parliament London School of Veterinary Surgery founded First general strike, Hamburg The "English Stud Book" published for the first time	1791
Ir.-Amer. architect James Hoban (1762—1831) begins the White House, Washington Joshua Reynolds, Eng. painter, d. (b. 1723) Robert Adam, Scot. architect, d. (b. 1728)	Beethoven becomes Haydn's pupil in Vienna Domenico Cimarosa: "Il matrimonio segreto," comic opera, Vienna Rossini, Ital. composer, b. (d. 1868) C. J. Rouget de Lisle: "La Marseillaise"	World's first chemical society founded, Philadelphia Fr. engineer Claude Chappe invents mechanical semaphore signal Arthur Young: "Travels in France"	Illuminating gas used in England for the first time Libel Act passed in Britain Dollar coinage minted in U.S. David Mendoza (1763—1836), an Eng. Jew, the first scientific boxer, becomes champion	1792
Canova: "Cupid and Psyche," sculpture Building of the Capitol, Washington, D.C., designed by William Thornton, begins David: "The Murder of Marat," Fr. painting Francesco Guardi, Venetian painter, d. (b. 1712) The Louvre, Paris, becomes national art gallery Ferdinand Waldmüller, Aust. painter, b. (d. 1865)	Paganini (at 11) makes his debut as violin virtuoso, Genoa	Kermadec Islands, northeast of New Zealand, discovered N. I. Lobachevsky, Russ. mathematician, b. (d. 1856) Sir Alexander Mackenzie (1764—1820) the first to cross Canada from coast to coast Eli Whitney (1765—1825) invents the cotton gin	Board of Agriculture established in Britain U.S. law compels escaped slaves to return to their owners	1793

	A. HISTORY, POLITICS	B. LITERATURE, THEATER	C. RELIGION, PHILOSOPHY, LEARNING
1794	Danton and Desmoulins executed; followed by mass executions "Feast of the Supreme Being" in Paris The Commune of Paris abolished Robespierre and St. Just executed Jacobin Club closed Rising of Pol. patriots under T. A. Kosciusko suppressed by Russians Habeas Corpus Act suspended in Britain (—1804) "Whiskey Insurrection" in Pennsylvania 11th Amendment to U.S. Constitution Agha Mohammed founds the Kajar dynasty in Persia Friedrich Wilhelm von Steuben, Prussian general, d. (b. 1730) U.S. Navy established	William Blake: "Songs of Experience" André de Chénier executed (b. 1762) Ramón de la Cruz, Span. dramatist, d. (b. 1731) Drury Lane Theatre, London, reopened Goethe: "Reinecke Fuchs," satirical poem Xavier de Maistre: "Voyage autour de ma chambre" Jean Paul: "Hesperus"	Condorcet, Fr. philosopher and mathematician, d. (b. 1743) Erasmus Darwin: "Zoonomia, or the Laws of Organic Life" Fichte: "Grundlagen der gesamten Wissenschaftslehre" Edward Gibbon, Eng. historian, d. (b. 1737) Thomas Paine: "The Age of Reason"
1795	Bread riots and White Terror in Paris Third Fr. Constitution enacted, vesting power in the Directory Napoleon appointed commander-in-chief, Italy Secret treaty between Austria and Russia for Third Partition of Poland; joined by Prussia Third Partition of Poland King Stanislas II abdicates The Dutch surrender Ceylon to the British Warren Hastings acquitted of high treason Luxembourg capitulates to France French occupy Mannheim and Belgium; Austria signs armistice with French Brit. forces occupy Cape of Good Hope Treaty of San Lorenzo between U.S. and Spain settles boundary with Florida and gives U.S. right to navigate the Mississippi Frederick William IV of Prussia b. (d. 1861)	Carl Michael Bellmann, Swed. poet, d. (b. 1740) James Boswell d. (b. 1740) Goethe: "Wilhelm Meisters Lehrjahre," John Keats, Eng. poet, b. (d. 1821) Robert Southey: "Poems" J. H. Voss: "Luise," epic idyll	Thomas Arnold, Eng. educator, b. (d. 1842) Thomas Carlyle, Scot. historian, b. (d. 1881) Freedom of worship in France Kant: "Zum ewigen Frieden" Leopold von Ranke, Ger. historian, b. (d. 1886) Augustin Thierry, Fr. historian, b. (d. 1856)
1796	Napoleon marries Josephine de Beauharnais; assumes command in Italy; defeats Austrians at Lodi; enters Milan; establishes Lombard Republic and Cispadane Republic and defeats Austrians at Arcol Francois Babeuf (1760—1797): plot to restore Constitution of 1793 fails General Jean Moreau crosses the Rhine General J. B. Jourdan invades Germany, is defeated at Amberg and Würzburg, and resigns his command Tennessee becomes a state of the U.S. George Washington, refusing to accept a third term, delivers Farewell Address John Adams defeats Thomas Jefferson in U.S. presidential election; Jefferson elected vice-president British capture Elba Spain declares war on Britain Empress Catherine II of Russia d.; succeeded by her son Paul I (—1801) Agha Mohammed of Persia seizes Khurasan in Khuzistan, and makes Teheran his capital Kau-Tsung, great Manchu Emperor of China, d. (b. 1736); succeeded by Kia-King (—1820) W. H. Prescott, U.S. historian, b. (d.1859)	Fanny Burney: "Camilla" Robert Burns d. (b. 1759) August Wilhelm Iffland (1759—1814) becomes director of the Berlin National Theater Karl Immermann, Ger. author, b. (d. 1840) Thomas Morton: "The Way to Get Married," comedy Jean Paul: "Siebenkäs" August von Platen, Ger. poet, b. (d. 1835) L. Tieck: "William Lowell" (novel of "Weltschmerz") Wordsworth: "The Borderers," tragedy	Louis de Bonald: "Théorie du pouvoir politique et religieux" Jean Jacques Cambacérès: "Projet de code civil" (used later as basis of the Code Napoléon) Fichte: "Grundlage des Naturrechts" Joseph de Maistre: "Considérations sur la France" Thomas Reid, Scot. "common sense" philosopher, d. (b. 1710) Richard Watson: "An Apology for the Bible"

D. VISUAL ARTS	E. MUSIC	F. SCIENCE, TECHNOLOGY, GROWTH	G. DAILY LIFE	
Julius Schnorr von Carolsfeld, Ger. painter, b. (d. 1872) Goya: "Procession of the Flagellants," Span. paintings John Trumbull (1756—1843): "The Declaration of Independence," Amer. painting	"Auld Lang Syne" (Burns, 1781) published "Tammany, or The Indian Chief," one of the earliest Amer. operas, music by James Hewitt (1770—1827), performed in New York	Antoine Laurent Lavoisier, Fr. chemist, executed (b. 1743) Adrien Legendre: "Eléments de géométrie" First telegraph, Paris—Lille	Slavery abolished in Fr. colonies Ecole Normale founded in Paris Ecole Polytechnique, the world's first technical college, opens in Paris	**1794**
Charles Barry, Eng. architect, b. (d. 1860) A. J. Carstens: "Night with Her Children," Dan. painting Goya: "The Duchess of Alba," portrait Okyo, Jap. painter, d. (b. 1733) Sir John Soane (1753—1837) begins building the Bank of England, London (—1827)	Pedro Albéniz, Span. composer, b. (d. 1855) Beethoven: three piano trios, Op. 1 Haydn completes the 12 London symphonies Heinrich Marschner, Ger. composer, b. (d. 1861) Paris Conservatoire de Musique founded	Joseph Bramah invents hydraulic press Institut National, Paris, to replace the abolished academies Mungo Park (1777—1806) explores the course of the Niger River	François Appert designs preserving jar for foods Rowland Hill, Eng. inventor of penny postage, b. (d. 1879) First horse-drawn railroad in England Metric system adopted in France Speenhamland Act for poor relief in Britain: wages supplemented by dole Josiah Wedgwood, Eng. porcelain manufacturer, d. (b. 1730)	**1795**
John Bacon (1740—1799): Dr. Johnson memorial at St. Paul's Cathedral, London Jean Baptiste Camille Corot, Fr. painter, b. (d. 1875) Goya: "Los Caprichos" Edward Savage (1761—1817): "The Washington Family," Amer. paintings	"The Archers of Switzerland," a William Tell opera by Benjamin Carr (1740—1799), produced in New York Karl Loewe, Ger. composer, b. (d. 1869)	G. L. C. Cuvier founds the science of comparative zoology C. W. Hufeland: "Macrobiotics, or The Art to Prolong One's Life" Eng. physician Edward Jenner (1749—1823) introduces vaccination against smallpox J. T. Lowitz (1757—1804) prepares pure ethyl alcohol	First edition Brockhaus Konversations Lexikon appears in Leipzig Population of China: 275 million (460 million in 1960) Edict of Peking forbids import of opium into China Freedom of press in France Royal Technical College, Glasgow, founded	**1796**

	A. HISTORY, POLITICS	B. LITERATURE, THEATER	C. RELIGION, PHILOSOPHY, LEARNING
1797	Napoleon defeats Austrians at Rivoli; seizes Mantua and advances through the Tirol to Vienna Preliminary peace treaty between Austria and France signed at Leoben Napoleon proclaims Venetian Constitution, founds the Ligurian Republic in Genoa, and unites Cisalpine with Cispadane Republic Peace of Campo Formio between France and Austria Napoleon, appointed to command forces for invasion of England, arrives in Paris Talleyrand becomes Fr. Foreign Minister Paul Barras prevents royalist reaction in coup d'état of 18 Fructidor (Sept. 4) Final treaty of Polish partition Nelson and Jervis defeat Span. fleet at Cape St. Vincent; naval mutiny at Spithead John Adams inaugurated President of U.S. Marquis Wellesley (1760—1842) appointed Governor-General of India Frederick William II d.; succeeded as King of Prussia by his son Frederick William III (—1840), the husband of Queen Louise The future Ger. Emperor William I b. (d. 1888) Fath Ali, Shah of Persia (—1832) Edmund Burke, Brit. statesman, d. (b. 1729)	Samuel Taylor Coleridge: "Kubla Khan" (published 1816) Annette von Droste-Hülshoff, Ger. novelist, b. (d. 1848) Ugo Foscolo (1778—1827): "Tieste," tragedy Goethe: "Hermann und Dorothea," pastoral poem Jeremias Gotthelf, Swiss author, b. (d. 1854) Heinrich Heine, Ger. poet. b. (d. 1856) Friedrich Hölderlin: "Hyperion" Ann Radcliffe: "The Italian" August Wilhelm von Schlegel begins his Shakespeare translation	Chateaubriand: "Essai historique, politique, et moral sur les révolutions" Kant: "Metaphysik der Sitten" Adolphe Thiers, Fr. historian and statesman, b. (d. 1877) Schelling: "Ideen zu einer Philosophie der Natur" Wackenroder and Tieck: "Outpourings of a Monk," romantic religious essays William Wilberforce: "Practical View of the Religious System"
1798	French capture Rome; proclaim Roman Republic; Pope Pius VI leaves the city for Valence The Lemanic Republic proclaimed in Geneva The Helvetian Republic proclaimed in Bern France annexes left bank of Rhine Fr. expedition to Egypt Malta seized by French Alexandria occupied by French Battle of the Pyramids makes Napoleon master of Egypt Horatio Nelson destroys Fr. fleet in Abukir Bay Fr. force lands in Ireland but fails to invade the country King Ferdinand IV of Naples declares war on France and enters Rome French recapture the city and overrun Kingdom of Naples Treaty of Hyderabad between Britain and the Nizam The last King of Poland, Augustus Stanislas II d. (b. 1732) (see 1795)	Willibald Alexis, Ger. novelist, b. (d. 1871) Charles Brockden Brown: "Wieland, or the Transformation" Ugo Foscolo: "The Last Letters of Jacopo Ortis" Kotzebue: "The Stranger," Drury Lane Theatre, London (an adaptation of Kotzebue's play "Menschenhass und Reue," 1789) Giacomo Leopardi, Ital. author, b. (d. 1837) Adam Mickiewicz, Pol. poet, b. (d. 1855) Wordsworth and Coleridge: "Lyrical Ballads"	Auguste Comte, Fr. philosopher, b. (d. 1857) Jules Michelet, Fr. historian, b. (d. 1874) T. R. Malthus: "Essay on the Principle of Population"
1799	Napoleon advances into Syria; organizes Parthenopean Republic in Piedmont; begins siege of Acre, which he abandons two months later; defeats the Turks at Abukir; leaves Egypt, lands at Fréjus, overthrows the Directory, appoints Talleyrand Foreign Minister, and becomes Consul Austria declares war on France; defeats Fr. army at Stockach, Magnano, and Zurich; is defeated at Bergen-op-Zoom Fr. defeat at Cassano ends Cisalpine Republic; Russians enter Turin Britain joins Russo-Turk. alliance Kingdom of Mysore divided between Britain and Hyderabad Joseph Fouché (1763—1820) appointed Fr. Minister of Police George Washington d. (b. 1732)	Honoré de Balzac, Fr. novelist, b. (d. 1850) Beaumarchais d. (b. 1732) Georg Christoph Lichtenberg, Ger. author, d. (b. 1742) Novalis: "Heinrich von Ofterdingen" Aleksandr Sergeyevich Pushkin, Russ. poet, b. (d. 1837) Schiller: "Wallenstein," trilogy Schlegel: "Lucinde"	Church Missionary Society founded in London Fichte: "System der Sittenlehre" Herder: "Metakritik" (attacks Kant ana Fichte) Pope Pius VI d. (b. 1717) J. F. Saint-Lambert: "Principe des moeurs chez toutes les nations, ou Catéchisme universal" Schlegel: "Geschichte der Poesie der Griechen und Römer" Schleiermacher: "Reden über die Religion" Universities of Cologne and Mainz closed

D. VISUAL ARTS	E. MUSIC	F. SCIENCE, TECHNOLOGY, GROWTH	G. DAILY LIFE	
Ando Hiroshige, Jap. painter, b. (d. 1858) Thorvaldsen settles in Rome Turner: "Millbank, Moon Light," Eng. painting	Cherubini: "Medée," opera, Paris Gaetano Donizetti, Ital. composer, b. (d. 1848) Franz Schubert, Aust. composer, b. (d. 1828) Haydn: "Emperor" Quartet	Thomas Bewick: "British Birds" (—1804) J. L. Lagrange: "Théorie des fonctions analytiques" Henry Maudslay invents carriage lathe Ger. astronomer H. W. M. Olbers (1758—1840) publishes his method of calculating the orbits of comets Nicolas de Saussure: "Recherches chimiques sur la végétation" Fr. chemist L. N. Vauquelin (1763—1829) discovers chromium	England begins to export iron First copper pennies minted in England and first one-pound notes issued John MacArthur (1767—1834) introduces Merino sheep to Australia	**1797**
		Ger. inventor Aloys Senefelder invents lithography	Casanova, Ital. adventurer, d. (b. 1725) Johann Cotta publishes "Allgemeine Zeitung" (Leipzig) Income tax of 10 per cent of all incomes over £200 introduced in Britain as wartime measure Ir. emigration to Canada begins	**1798**
J. L. David: "Rape of the Sabine Women," Fr. painting Ferdinand Delacroix, Fr. painter, b. (d. 1863)	Beethoven: Symphony No. 1 in C major (—1800) Barberina Campanini, Ital. dancer, d. (b. 1721) Karl Ditters von Dittersdorf, Aust. composer, d. (b. 1739) Haydn: "The Creation," oratorio, Vienna	Egyptian Institute founded at Cairo Mungo Park: "Travels in the Interior of Africa"	Pestalozzi's school in Burgdorf, Switzerland, opened Rosetta Stone (now at the British Museum, London) found near Rosetta, Egypt, makes the deciphering of hieroglyphics possible Russ. government grants the monopoly of trade in Alaska to the Russia-American Company In Siberia a perfectly preserved mammoth is found	**1799**

	A. HISTORY, POLITICS	B. LITERATURE, THEATER	C. RELIGION, PHILOSOPHY, LEARNING
1800	Napoleon establishes himself as First Consul in the Tuileries; Fr. army defeats Turks at Heliopolis and advances on Cairo; defeats Austrians at Biberach, Höchstädt, and Hohenlinden and advances on Vienna Napoleon's army crosses the Great St. Bernard Pass, defeats Austrians at Marengo, and conquers Italy British capture Malta U.S. federal offices are moved from Philadelphia to Washington, D.C., the new capital city: free inhabitants 2,464, slaves 623 Thomas Jefferson wins U.S. presidential election A plot to assassinate Napoleon discovered in Paris Helmuth von Moltke, Prussian general, b. (d. 1891)	William Cowper, Eng. poet, d. (b. 1731) Maria Edgeworth: "Castle Rackrent," Gothic novel Thomas Morton: "Speed the Plough," comedy in which, for the first time, a reference to the character Mrs. Grundy appears Jean Paul: "Titan," Ger. novel Schiller: "Maria Stuart" Mme. de Staël: "On Literature"	Napoleon appoints committee of jurists to draw up Civil Code Cardinal Barnaba Chiaramonti elected Pope Pius VII (—1823) Fichte: "Der geschlossene Handelsstaat" Arnold Heeren: "European Political Systems" Thomas Babington Macaulay, Eng. historian, b. (d. 1859) Schelling: "System des transzendentalen Idealismus" Church of United Brethren in Christ founded in the U.S.
1801	Act of Union of Great Britain and Ireland comes into force Peace of Lunéville between Austria and France marks the actual end of the Holy Roman Empire Thomas Jefferson inaugurated President of U.S. at Washington Czar Paul I assassinated; succeeded by Alexander I (—1825) Nelson defeats the Danes off Copenhagen Prussians march into Hanover English enter Cairo; Fr. troops leave Egypt, which the Turks recover	Chateaubriand: "Atala," novel C. D. Grabbe, Ger. dramatist, b. (d. 1836) Kotzebue: "Die deutschen Kleinstädter," comedy Johann Nestroy, Aust. dramatist and comedian, b. (d. 1862) Novalis (Friedrich von Hardenberg), Ger. poet, d. (b. 1772) Schiller: "Die Jungfrau von Orleans," Leipzig Robert Southey: "Thalaba the Destroyer," poem	K. F. Gauss: "Disquisitiones arithmeticae" Hegel and Schelling publish the "Critical Journal of Philosophy" John Henry Cardinal Newman, Eng. theologian, b. (d. 1890)
1802	Napoleon becomes President of Italian (formerly Cisalpine) Republic; creates Order of Legion of Honor; becomes First Consul for life; annexes Piedmont, Parma, and Piacenza Peace of Amiens between Britain and France France suppresses Negro rebellion in Santo Domingo led by Toussaint-L'Ouverture Lajos Kossuth, Hungarian freedom fighter, b. (d. 1894)	Alexandre Dumas père, Fr. novelist, b. (d. 1870) Wilhelm Hauff, Ger. author, b. (d. 1827) Victor Hugo, Fr. poet, b. (d. 1885) Nikolaus Lenau, Aust. poet, b. (d. 1850) Sir Walter Scott: "Minstrelsy of the Scottish Border" Mme. de Staël: "Delphine," novel	Jeremy Bentham: "Civil and Penal Legislation" G. F. Grotefend (1775—1853) deciphers Babylonian cuneiform Schelling: "Bruno" Daniel Webster: "The Rights of Neutral Nations in Time of War"

D. VISUAL ARTS	E. MUSIC	F. SCIENCE, TECHNOLOGY, GROWTH	G. DAILY LIFE	
David: "Mme. Récamier," portrait Goya: "Portrait of a Woman"	Boieldieu: "Le Calife de Bagdad," opera, Paris Cherubini: "Les Deux Journées" ("The Water Carrier"), opera, Paris Nicola Piccini, Ital. composer, Gluck's rival in Paris, d. (b. 1728)	Humphry Davy: "Researches, Chemical and Philosophical, Concerning Nitrous Oxide" Ger. physician F. J. Gall (1758—1828) founds practice of phrenology William Herschel discovers existence of infrared solar rays Royal College of Surgeons, London, founded Richard Trevithick constructs light-pressure steam engine Alessandro Volta produces electricity from cell: first battery of zinc and copper plates Eli Whitney makes muskets with interchangeable parts	Grossglockner, in the Aust. Alps, first successfully scaled Letter post introduced in Berlin Ottawa founded Robert Owen (1771—1858) takes over New Lanark mills and starts social reforms Paris counts c. 550,000 inhabitants (2,800,000 in 1931); New York c. 60,000 (7,400,000 in 1931) Bill Richmond (1763—1829), a former Negro slave, becomes one of the first popular boxers	**1800**
Daniel Chodowiecki, Ger. painter, d. (b. 1726) David: "Napoléon au Grand Saint-Bernard," painting Goya: "The Two Majas" Joseph Paxton, Eng. architect, b. (d. 1865)	Beethoven: "Die Geschöpfe des Prometheus," ballet, Vienna Vincenzo Bellini, Ital. opera composer, b. (d. 1835) Haydn: "The Seasons," oratorio, completed Joseph Lanner, Viennese waltz composer, b. (d. 1843) Albert Lortzing, Ger. opera composer, b. (d. 1851)	M. F. X. Bichat (1771—1802): "Anatomie générale" Amer. civil engineer Robert Fulton (1765—1815) produces the first submarine "Nautilus" (Brest) J. J. Lalande catalogues 47,390 stars	Bank of France founded European population statistics: Italy 17.2 million; Spain 10.5 million; Britain 10.4 million; London 864,000; Paris 547,000; Vienna 231,000; Berlin 183,000 First iron trolley tracks, Croydon-Wandsworth, England The Union Jack becomes official flag of the United Kingdom of Great Britan and Ireland Victoria Regia ("Queen of the Night") discovered in Amazon Territory	**1801**
Canova: "Napoleon Bonaparte," sculpture Period of the Classicist Empire style Gérard: "Madame Récamier," portrait George Romney d. (b. 1734) Ludwig von Schwanthaler, Bavarian sculptor, b. (d. 1848)	Beethoven: Symphony No. 2 in D major, Op. 36 J. N. Forkel (1749—1818): "Life of Johann Sebastian Bach"	John Dalton (1766—1844) introduces atomic theory into chemistry Erasmus Darwin, Eng. scientist, d. (b. 1731) William Herschel discovers binary stars Ger. naturalist Gottfried Treviranus (1776—1837) coins the term "biology" Englishmen John Truter and William Somerville explore in Bechuanaland	"Peerage" published in London by John Debrett (1753—1822), followed in 1808 by "Baronetage" The Duke of Richmond introduces horse racing at Goodwood "Health and Morals of Apprentices" Act in Britain (protection of labor in factories) Alexander von Humboldt almost succeeds in climbing Mount Chimborao in Ecuador West India Docks, London, built	**1802**

	A. HISTORY, POLITICS	B. LITERATURE, THEATER	C. RELIGION, PHILOSOPHY, LEARNING
1803	Swiss cantons regain independence (Act of Mediation) Ohio becomes a state of the U.S. U.S. buys large tract of land from Gulf of Mexico to northwest, including Louisiana and New Orleans, from France (Louisiana Purchase) Renewal of war between France and Britain French complete occupation of Hanover Robert Emmet, leader of Ir. July rebellion, executed Second Mahratta War against Sindhia of Gwalior who (defeated by Arthur Wellesley, later 1st Duke of Wellington, at Assaye) submits to the British	Vittorio Alfieri, Ital. author. d. (b. 1749) Edward George Bulwer-Lytton, Eng. novelist, b. (d. 1873) J. W. Gleim, Ger. poet, d. (b. 1719) F. Klopstock, Ger. poet, d. (b. 1724) Prosper Mérimée, Fr. author, b. (d. 1870) Jane Porter: "Thaddeus of Warsaw," historical novel Schiller: "Die Braut von Messina," tragedy	Greek patriot Adamantios Coräes (1748—1833) publishes his "Present Conditions of Civilization in Greece" Ralph Waldo Emerson, Amer. philosopher, b. (d. 1882) Joseph Lancaster: "Improvements in Education as it Respects the Industrious Classes" Herder, Ger. philosopher, d. (b. 1744)
1804	The Duc d'Enghien executed for a plot against Napoleon Napoleon, proclaimed emperor by Senate and Tribunate, is crowned in the presence of Pope Pius VII in Paris War breaks out between East India Company and Holkar of Indore; ends with defeat of Holkar's army Francis II assumes the title of Emperor of Austria as Francis I (—1835) 12th Amendment added to the U.S. Constitution Spain declares war on Britain Napoleonic general Jean Bernadotte (1763—1840) becomes Marshal of France Alexander Hamilton, former U.S. Secretary of the Treasury, killed in a duel with Aaron Burr (b. 1755) Benjamin Disraeli, Eng. statesman, b. (d. 1881)	C. A. Sainte-Beuve, Fr. critic and historian, b. (d. 1869) Nathaniel Hawthorne, Amer. author, b. (d. 1864) Eduard Mörike, Ger. poet, b. (d. 1875) George Sand (Amantine Dupine-Dudevant), Fr. author, b. (d. 1876) Schiller: "Wilhelm Tell," Weimar	British and Foreign Bible Society founded in London Code Napoléon promulgated Thomas Brown: "Inquiry into the Relation of Cause and Effect" Ludwig Feuerbach, Ger. philosopher, b. (d. 1872) Immanuel Kant d. (b. 1724)
1805	Arthur Wellesley, later 1st Duke of Wellington, resigns in India Thomas Jefferson begins his second term as Pres. of U.S. Treaty of St. Petersburg by Britain and Russia against France, joined by Austria Napoleon crowned as King of Italy in Milan Cathedral Giuseppe Mazzini, Ital. patriot and revolutionary, b. (d. 1872) Battle of Austerlitz: Napoleon's victory over Austro-Russ. forces Peace of Pressburg between Austria and France: Austria gives up the Tirol and all her Ital. possessions; Bavaria and Württemburg become kingdoms; Baden becomes a grand duchy Establishment of modern Egypt; Mehemet Ali proclaimed Pasha Break between Brit. and U.S. over trade with the W.I. Victory of Trafalgar: Admiral Lord Horatio Nelson's defeat of the Franco-Spanish fleets at Cape Trafalgar; dies after hearing of his victory (b. 1758)	Hans Christian Andersen, Dan. poet, b. (d. 1875) Chateaubriand: "René," romantic novel Schiller d. (b. 1759) Walter Scott: "The Lay of the Last Minstrel" Robert Southey: "Madoc" Adalbert Stifter, Aust. novelist, b. (d. 1868) Alexis de Tocqueville, Fr. author, b. (d. 1859)	Hosea Ballou: "A Treatise on Atonement" Lord Liverpool: "Treatise on the Coins of the Realm"
1806	British occupy Cape of Good Hope William Pitt the Younger d. (b. 1759) Charles James Fox d. (b. 1749) Joseph Bonaparte named King of Naples Louis Bonaparte named King of Holland Britain blockades Fr. coast Prussia declares war on France Following his victories at Jena and Auerstädt Napoleon enters Berlin Napoleon's Berlin Decree begins "Continental System" (closing Continental ports to Brit. vessels) Fr. army under Murat enters Warsaw Confederation of Rhine founded Official end of Holy Roman Empire Peace of Posen: Saxony is made a kingdom The Burr plot in the U.S.	Arnim and Brentano: "Des Knaben Wunderhorn" (collection of Ger. folk songs) Elizabeth Barrett Browning, Eng. poetess, b. (d. 1861) Goethe marries Christiane Vulpius (1765—1816) Kleist: "Der zerbrochene Krug," village comedy Heinrich Laube, Ger. dramatist, b. (d. 1884) Jane and Ann Taylor: "Rhymes for the Nursery"	J. C. Adelung: "Mithridates, a History of Languages and Dialects" Fichte: "Bericht über die Wissenschaftslehre" Institut de France created by combining Académie Française with other academies James Madison: "An Examination of the British Doctrine which Subjects to Capture a Neutral Trade not Open in Time of Peace" John Stuart Mill, Eng. *(contd)*

D. VISUAL ARTS	E. MUSIC	F. SCIENCE, TECHNOLOGY, GROWTH	G. DAILY LIFE	
A. G. Decamps, Fr. painter, b. (d. 1860) Henry Raeburn: "The Macnab," portrait Gottfried Semper, Ger. architect, b. (d. 1879) Turner: "Calais Pier," exhibited Benjamin West: "Christ Healing the Sick," painting	Adolphe Adam, Fr. composer, b. (d. 1856) Beethoven: Sonata for violin and piano, Op. 47 ("Kreutzer") Hector Berlioz, Fr. composer, b. (d. 1869) Franz Xaver Süssmayer, Aust. composer, who completed Mozart's "Requiem," d. (b. 1766)	Claude Berthollet: "Essai de statique chimique" J. J. Berzelius discovers cerium Lazare Carnot (1753—1823): "Principes fondamentaux de l'équilibre et du mouvement" Robert Fulton propels a boat by steam power Lamarck: "Recherches sur l'organisation des corps vivants" Henry Shrapnel (1761—1842), Eng. inventor, invents shell	Building of Caledonian Canal begins Technical College, Prague, founded	**1803**
George Morland, Eng. painter, d. (b. 1763) Moritz von Schwind, Ger. painter, b. (d. 1871) English Water Colour Society founded	Beethoven: Symphony No. 3 in E-flat major, Op. 55 ("Eroica") M. I. Glinka, Russ. composer, b. (d. 1867) Johann Strauss, Viennese waltz composer, b. (d. 1849)	Thomas Bewick completes his "History of British Birds" Joseph Priestley, Eng. chemist, d. (b. 1733) Eng. scientist W. H. Wollaston (1766—1828) finds palladium in platinum	The first dahlias in England Hobart, Tasmania, founded	**1804**
Goya: "Doña Isabel Cobos de Procal," portrait Philipp Otto Runge: "The Morning," painting Turner: "Shipwreck," painting	Beethoven: "Fidelio," opera, Vienna Luigi Boccherini, Ital. composer, d. (b. 1743) Paganini begins to tour Europe as violin virtuoso	Rockets, originally constructed by Sir William Congreve, are reintroduced as weapons into the Brit. army William R. Hamilton, Ir. mathematician, b. (d. 1865) Mungo Park undertakes his second expedition to the Niger River F. W. A. Sartürner (1783—1841) isolates morphine	Napoleon abandons Fr. revolutionary calendar Pestalozzi school at Yverdun, Switzerland Total state expenditure of Great Britain: £62.8 million	**1805**
Brera Gallery, Milan, opens Claude Clodion begins the Arc de Triomphe, Paris (—1836) Fragonard d. (b. 1732) Thorvaldsen: "Hebe," sculpture Kitagawa Utamaro, Jap. portrait painter, d. (b. 1753) David Wilkie: "Village Politicians," painting	Beethoven: Symphony No. 4 in B-flat major, Op. 60, and Violin Concerto, Op. 61 Rossini's first opera, "Demetrio a Polibio," produced, Rome	Humphry Davy discovers electrolytic method for preparation of potassium and soda P. A. Latreille: "Genera Crustaceorum et Insectorum"	Sir Francis Beaufort (1774—1857) designs scale (from 0 to 12) to indicate wind strength Brit. cotton industry employs 90,000 factory workers and 184,000 handloom weavers Beginning of building of Dartmoor Prison, England First Gentlemen vs. Players cricket *(contd)*	**1806**

	A. HISTORY, POLITICS	B. LITERATURE, THEATER	C. RELIGION, PHILOSOPHY, LEARNING
1806 contd			philosopher, b. (d. 1873) Napoleon establishes a consistorial organization for Jews in France
1807	Indecisive battle of Eylau between French and Russo-Prussian armies Fr. victory at Friedland Treaty of Tilsit between Napoleon, the czar, and the King of Prussia Jerome Bonaparte becomes King of Westphalia Napoleon ensures dictatorship by suppressing Tribunate Sultan Selim III of Turkey deposed and succeeded by Mustafa IV The Chesapeake Incident between U.S. and Britain U.S. Embargo Act against Britain and France Giuseppe Garibaldi, Ital. patriot, b. (d. 1882) Baron vom Stein becomes Prussian Prime Minister and emancipates serfs France invades Portugal; dethroned Port. royal family flees to Brazil	Mme. de Staël: "Corinne" Lord Byron: "Hours of Idleness" Ugo Foscolo: "Carme sui sepolcri" Charles and Mary Lamb: "Tales from Shakespeare" Henry Wadsworth Longfellow, U.S. poet, b. (d. 1882) F. T. Vischer, Ger. poet and philosopher, b. (d. 1887) Wordsworth: "Ode on Intimations of Immortality"	U.S. Evangelical Association, founded by Jacob Albright, holds its first convention Commercial Law Code introduced in France Hegel: "Phänomenologie des Geistes" Gottlieb Hufeland: "New Foundations of Political Economy"
1808	U.S. prohibits importation of slaves from Africa Fr. army occupies Rome, invades Spain, and takes Barcelona and Madrid; Joseph Bonaparte becomes King of Spain; Joachim Murat, in his stead, King of Naples Erfurt Congress Rebellion in Madrid: King Joseph flees; Napoleon takes city The future Napoleon III (Charles Louis Napoleon Bonaparte) b. (d. 1873) Municipal Councils introduced in Prussia	Chateaubriand: "Les Aventures du dernier Abencérage" (published 1826) Goethe: "Faust," part I Kleist: "Das Kätchen von Heilbronn" Oehlenschläger (1779—1850): "Hakon Jarl," Dan. tragedy Théâtre St. Philippe, New Orleans, opened Walter Scott: "Marmion," story in verse	John Dalton: "New System of Chemical Philosophy" (—1827) K. F. Eichhorn: "Geschichte des deutschen Rechts" J. F. Fries: "New Critique of Reason" Napoleon abolishes the Inquisition in Spain and Italy Schlegel: "Von der Sprache und Weisheit der Inder"
1809	Treaty of Dardanelles between Britain and Turkey War between France and Austria Fr. army takes Vienna, is defeated at Aspern, and defeats Austrians at Wagram Peace of Schönbrunn Austria joins Continental System William Gladstone, Brit. statesman, b. (d. 1898) James Madison becomes 4th President of the U.S. King Gustavus IV of Sweden deposed; succeeded by Charles XIII (—1818) Marshal Jean Bernadotte elected Crown Prince of Sweden Treaty of friendship between Britain and the Sikhs at Amritsar Arthur Wellesley defeats French at Oporto and Talavera and is created Duke of Wellington; his brother Marquis Wellesley, appointed Foreign Secretary Napoleon annexes Papal States Pope Pius VII taken prisoner Metternich named chief minister of Austria Napoleon divorces Josephine French lose Martinique and Cayenne to British Abraham Lincoln, 16th President of the U.S., b. (d. 1865) Ecuador gains independence from Spain	Thomas Campbell: "Gertrude of Wyoming" Chateaubriand: "Les Martyrs" Edward Fitzgerald, Eng. poet, b. (d. 1883) Goethe: "Die Wahlverwandtschaften" ("The Elective Affinities"), novel Nikolai Gogol, Russ. author, b. (d. 1852) Washington Irving: "Rip van Winkle" Ivan Kriloff: "Fables" (—1811) Hannah More: "Coelebs in Search of a Wife," novel Edgar Allan Poe, Amer. author, b. (d. 1849) Schlegel: "Lectures on Dramatic Art and Literature" Alfred, Lord Tennyson. Eng. poet, b. (d. 1892)	Charles Darwin, Eng. naturalist, b. (d. 1882) Thomas Paine, Anglo-Amer. author, d. (b. 1737) David Ricardo: "The High Price of Bullion, Proof of the Depreciation of Bank Notes" All property of Teutonic Order confiscated

D. VISUAL ARTS	E. MUSIC	F. SCIENCE, TECHNOLOGY, GROWTH	G. DAILY LIFE	
			match Population of Germany, 27 million (in 1930, 65 million)	**1806 contd**
Canova: "Paolina Bonaparte as Reclining Venus," sculpture David: "Coronation of Napoleon," painting, completed Jean Auguste Dominique Ingres (1780—1867) begins his most famous painting, "La Source" (finished 1858), Louvre Angelica Kauffmann, Swiss painter, d. (b. 1741) John Opie, Eng. painter, d. (b. 1761) Turner: "Sun Rising in a Mist," painting	Beethoven: "Leonora Overture" No. 3 Etienne Nicolas Méhul: "Joseph," opera, Paris J.G. Pleyel founds his pianoforte factory in Paris Spontini: "La Vestale," opera, Paris Thomas Moore's "Irish Melodies," with music by John Stevenson (—1834)	Charles Bell: "System of Comparative Surgery" Robert Fulton's paddle steamer "Clermont" navigates on Hudson River Alexander von Humboldt and Bonpland: "Voyage aux régions équinoxiales du nouveau continent, 1799—1804," on Span. America, first of 30 vols. published	Horse racing: first Ascot Gold Cup England prohibits slave trade Sierra Leone and Gambia become Brit. Crown Colonies Street lighting by gas in London	**1807**
Honoré Daumier, Fr. painter, b. (d. 1879) Kaspar Friedrich: "The Cross on the Mountains," painting Goya: "Execution of the Citizens of Madrid," painting Ingres: "La Grande Baigneuse," painting Karl Spitzweg, Ger. genre painter, b. (d. 1885)	Beethoven: Symphonies No. 5, Op. 67, and No. 6 ("Pastoral"), Op. 68	Ships' iron anchor-chains patented by Captain S. Brown, R.N. J. L. Gay-Lussac: "The Combination of Gases" The source of the Ganges River discovered	Disappearance of fashion of pigtails in men's hair Goethe and Napoleon meet at Erfurt Extensive excavations begin at Pompeii (—1815) Henry Crabb Robinson, the first war correspondent, sent by "The Times of London" to Spain to report on the Peninsular War	**1808**
Constable: "Malvern Hill," painting Kaspar Friedrich: "Mönch am Meer," painting Raeburn: "Mrs. Spiers," painting	Beethoven: Piano Concerto No. 5 in E-flat major, Op. 73 ("The Emperor") Joseph Haydn d. (b. 1732) Felix Mendelssohn, Ger. composer, b. (d. 1847) Spontini: "Fernand Cortez," opera, Paris	Friedrich Wilhelm University, Berlin, founded; Fichte appointed rector K. F. Gauss: "Theoria motus corporum coelestium" Lamarck: "Système des animaux sans vertèbres" William Maclure (1763—1840): "Observations on the Geology of the U.S." S. T. von Sömmering (1755—1830), Ger. physiologist, invents water voltameter telegraph	Louis Braille, Fr. inventor of reading system for the blind, b. (d. 1852) Construction of Bristol Harbor The Two Thousand Guineas established at Newmarket Races Elizabeth Seton founds Sisters of Charity of St. Joseph in U.S.	**1809**

	A. HISTORY, POLITICS	B. LITERATURE, THEATER	C. RELIGION, PHILOSOPHY, LEARNING
1810	The year of Napoleon's zenith: he marries Archduchess Marie Louise of Austria; by Decree of Rambouillet orders sale of seized U.S. ships; annexes Holland; issues Decree of Fontainebleau (confiscation of Brit. goods); and annexes Hanover, Bremen, Hamburg, Lauenburg, and Lübeck Venezuela breaks away from Spain Simón Bolívar emerges as major figure in S. American politics Revolts in New Granada, Rio de la Plata, and Mexico British seize Guadaloupe, last Fr. colony in West Indies Camillo, Count Cavour, Ital. statesman, b. (d. 1861) Queen Louise of Prussia d. (b. 1776) Andreas Hofer, Aust. freedom fighter against Napoleon, executed at Mantua (b. 1767)	Charles de Montalembert, Fr. author, b. (d. 1870) Alfred de Musset, Fr. poet, b. (d. 1857) Scott: "The Lady of the Lake" Mme. de Staël: "De l'Allemagne"	Lazare Carnot: "De la défense des places fortes" The Cumberland Presbytery of Kentucky, U.S., excluded from Presbyterian Church Société des Amis formed in Geneva by Protestant revivalists Joseph de Maistre (1754—1821): "Essay on the Generation of Political Constitutions"
1811	Napoleon annexes Oldenburg George III of England insane; Prince of Wales becomes Prince Regent Russians seize Belgrade Austria bankrupt Massacre of the Mamelukes at Cairo Napoleon's son, Napoléon François-Joseph Charles, King of Rome, Duke of Reichstadt, b. (d. 1832) Duke of Wellington's victories at Fuentes de Oñoro and Albuera Paraguay independent of Spain British occupy Java William Henry Harrison, later President of U.S., defeats Indians under Tecumseh at Tippecanoe, Indiana	Jane Austen: "Sense and Sensibility" Harriet Beecher Stowe, Amer. author, b. (d. 1896) Friedrich de la Motte-Fouqué: "Undine" Théophile Gautier, Fr. author, b. (d. 1872) Goethe: "Aus meinem Leben: Dichtung und Wahrheit" Karl Gutzkow, Ger. dramatist, b. (d. 1878) Heinrich von Kleist d. (b. 1777) W. M. Thackeray, Eng. novelist, b. (d. 1863)	K. A. Böttiger: "Kunstmythologie" Civil Code introduced in Austria "Great Schism" of Welsh Protestants; two thirds leave Anglican Church Barthold G. Niebuhr: "Roman History" (—1832) J. P. A. Récusat: "Essai sur la langue et la littérature" University of Christiania, Oslo, founded National University of Nicaragua founded
1812	Prussia agrees to allow Fr. troops free passage in case of war with Russia Generals Gneisenau and Scharnhorst resign Napoleon, crossing Niemen River, enters Russia June 24; crosses Viliya River, defeats Russians at Smolensk and Borodino, and enters Moscow; he begins to retreat from Moscow Oct. 19, across the Berezina; leaves Joachim Murat in command and sets out for Paris where he arrives Dec. 18 (out of his army of 550,000 only 20,000 survive the Russian campaign) Conspiracy of General Claude François Malet (b. 1754) against Napoleon during the emperor's absence in Russia; attempt to end war and install Louis XVIII fails; Malet executed Louisiana becomes a state of the U.S. Brit. Prime Minister Spencer Perceval assassinated in the House of Commons U.S. declares war on Britain Duke of Wellington enters Madrid U.S. presidential election, James Madison defeats De Witt Clinton	Robert Browning, poet, b. (d. 1889) The Brothers Grimm: "Fairy Tales" Lord Byron: "Childe Harold's Pilgrimage" (—1818) Charles Dickens, Eng. novelist, b. (d. 1870) Present Drury Lane Theatre, London, erected I. A. Goncharov, Russ. novelist, b. (d. 1891) John Nichols (1745—1826): "Literary Anecdotes of the 18th Century" (—1815) Samuel Smiles, Scot. author, b. (d. 1904) Zygmunt Krasinski, Pol. romantic author, b. (d. 1859) Joseph Ignatius Kraszewski, Pol. novelist, b. (d. 1887)	Baptist Union of Great Britain formed H. F. Genesius: "Hebrew and Chaldaic Dictionary" Hegel: "Die objektive Logik" Jews in Prussia emancipated (Hardenberg reforms) W. M. Leake: "Greece" Hamilton College, Clinton N.Y., founded

D. VISUAL ARTS	E. MUSIC	F. SCIENCE, TECHNOLOGY, GROWTH	G. DAILY LIFE	
J. J. de Boissieu, Fr. painter, d. (b. 1736) Goya: "Los Desastres de la Guerra," engravings (—1813) John Hoppner, Eng. painter, d. (b. 1759) The "Nazarenes" founded by J. F. Overbeck to revive Ger. religious art Philipp Otto Runge, Ger. painter, d. (b. 1777)	Beethoven: Music to Goethe's "Egmont, Vienna Frédéric Chopin, Pol. composer, b. (d. 1849) Otto Nicolai, Ger. composer b. (d. 1849) Rossini: "La Cambiale di Matrimonio," opera, Venice San Carlo Opera House, Naples, built (—1812) Robert Schumann, Ger. composer, b. (d. 1856)	Gall and Spurzheim: "Anatomie et physiologie du système nerveux" Samuel Hahnemann, in his "Organon of Therapeutics," founds homeopathy François Appert (c. 1750—1840) develops techniques for canning food Henry Cavendish, Eng. scientist, d. (b. 1731)	First public billiards rooms in England at the Piazza, Covent Garden, London Durham miners' strike The Krupp works open at Essen, Germany Sale of tobacco in France is made a government monopoly U.S. population: 7,239,881 Phineas T. Barnum, Amer. showman, b. (d. 1891)	**1810**
Jules Dupré, Fr. painter, b. (d. 1889) Ingres: "Jupiter and Thetis," painting Thomas Lawrence: portrait of Benjamin West John Nash begins design of Regent Street, London John Rennie begins the building of Waterloo Bridge, London (—1817) Thorvaldsen: "Procession of Alexander the Great," sculpture	Franz Liszt, Hungarian composer, b. (d. 1886) Prague Conservatoire is opened C. M. von Weber: "Abu Hassan," opera, Munich	Amadeo Avogadro (1776—1856), Ital. chemist: hypothesis of the molecular composition of gases Sir Charles Bell (1774—1842): "New Idea of the Anatomy of the Brain" Robert Bunsen, Ger. chemist, b. (d. 1899) S. O. Poisson: "Traité de Mécanique" (—1833)	Ludwig Berblinger, a tailor of Ulm, Germany, fails in his attempts to fly French Press Agency, later to become Agence Havas, founded Hampden Clubs for extending the franchise formed in England "Luddites" destroy industrial machines in North England Johann Rudolf Meyer, a Swiss mountaineer, climbs the Jungfrau	**1811**
Elgin Marbles brought to England Goya: "Portrait of the Duke of Wellington" Théodore Rousseau, Fr. landscape painter, b. (d. 1867) F. A. Tischbein, Ger. painter, b. (d. 1851)	Beethoven: Symphonies No. 7 (Op. 92) and No. 8 (Op. 93) Encounter between Beethoven and Goethe at Teplitz Friedrich von Flotow, Ger. opera composer, b. (d. 1883) Founding of Gesellschaft der Musikfreunde, Vienna	The "Comet" (25 tons), Henry Bell's steamship, operates on the Clyde River, Scotland Swiss explorer J. L. Burckhardt (1784—1817) discovers the Great Temple of Abu Simbel Georges Cuvier: "Recherches sur les ossements fossiles de quadrupèdes" Humphry Davy: "Elements of Chemical Philosophy" Philippe Girard invents machine for spinning flax Laplace: "Théorie analytique"	Alfred Krupp, Ger. arms manufacturer, b. (d. 1887) Red River Settlement, Manitoba, Canada, founded Royal Yacht Squadron formed Gas, Light and Coke Company, London, developed by F. A. Winsor	**1812**

	A. HISTORY, POLITICS	B. LITERATURE, THEATER	C. RELIGION, PHILOSOPHY, LEARNING
1813	Prussia declares war on France; combined Russo—Prussian forces enter Dresden; Napoleon's victory at Lützen Austria declares war on France The French defeated by Blücher at Wahlstatt on the Katzbach; defeat the allied army at Dresden The "Battle of the Nations" at Leipzig; Napoleon defeated French expelled from Holland; return of William of Orange Prussian army under Blücher crosses the Rhine The Americans capture York (Toronto) and Fort St. George H.M.S. Shannon captures U.S. frigate Chesapeake Detroit reoccupied by U.S. U.S. forces defeated at Chrysler's Farm near Montreal; burn Newark (Niagara-on-the-Lake); Brit. forces take Fort Niagara and burn Buffalo Wellington defeats French at Vitoria, seizes San Sebastian, and enters France Simón Bolívar becomes dictator of Venezuela Mexico declares itself independent	Jane Austen: "Pride and Prejudice" Georg Büchner, Ger. dramatist ("Wozzek"), b. (d. 1837) Byron: "The Giaour" Adelbert von Chamisso: "Peter Schlemihl" Friedrich Hebbel, Ger. dramatist, b. (d. 1863) Theodor Körner, Ger. poet, d. (b. 1791) Otto Ludwig, Ger. dramatist, b. (d. 1865) Manzoni: "Inni sacri" Shelley: "Queen Mab" Robert Southey: "Life of Nelson" C. M. Wieland, Ger. author, d. (b. 1733)	J. F. Herbart: "Introduction to Philosophy" Sören Kierkegaard, Dan. philosopher, b. (d. 1855) Methodist Missionary Society founded Robert Owen: "A New View of Society" Schopenhauer: "Über die vierfache Wurzel des Satzes vom zureichenden Grunde," thesis Colby College, Maine, founded
1814	Murat deserts Napoleon and joins Allies Allied armies defeat French at La Rothière, Bar-sur-Aube, and Laon, and enter Paris Mar. 30 Napoleon abdicates and is banished to Elba Apr. 11 Louis XVIII enters Paris and takes up the throne as his hereditary right Congress of Vienna opens Christian Frederick of Denmark elected King of Norway U.S. forces defeat the British at Chippewa Brit. force burns Washington, D.C. Brit. flotilla captured on Lake Champlain Treaty of Ghent ends Brit.-Amer. war Dec. 24 Cape Province becomes Brit. colony Hanover proclaimed a kingdom Lord Hastings, Governor-General of India, declares war on the Gurkhas (Nepal)	Jane Austen: "Mansfield Park" Byron: "The Corsair" E. T. A. Hoffmann: "Phantasiestücke in Callots Manier" (4 vol. of "Hoffmann's Tales"—1815) A. W. Iffland, Ger. actor and dramatist, d. (b. 1759) Edmund Kean's debut (as Shylock) at Drury Lane Theatre, London Mikhail Yurievich Lermontov, Russ. poet, b. (d. 1841) Scott: "Waverley" Wordsworth: "The Excursion"	First Anglican bishop in India (Calcutta) Chateaubriand: "De Buonaparte et les Bourbons" Johann Fichte, Ger. philosopher, d. (b. 1762) John Lothrop Motley, Amer. historian, b. (d. 1877) Pope Pius VII returns to Rome and restores the Inquisition Savigny: "The Claim of Our Age on Legislation"
1815	Americans defeat British at Battle of New Orleans before news of Treaty of Ghent arrives in America Napoleon leaves Elba and lands in France; Louis XVIII flees; the "Hundred Days" begin Austria, Britain, Prussia, and Russia form new alliance; Napoleon issues liberal constitution "Le Champ de Mai" Congress of Vienna closes Wellington and Blücher defeat Napoleon at Waterloo, June 18 Napoleon abdicates for the second time; Louis XVIII returns to Paris, Napoleon banished to St. Helena; Second Peace of Paris Michel Ney executed for aiding Napoleon at Waterloo Corn Law passed in Britain Otto von Bismarck, Ger. statesman, b. (d. 1898) Swiss Federal Pact ratified: the Confederation now consists of 22 contiguous cantons Joachim Murat, King of Naples (b. 1767), executed after attempt to regain Naples Brazil declares itself an independent empire (from 1816 on under Dom John)	Pierre Béranger: "Chansons I' Byron: "Hebrew Melodies" Matthias Claudius, Ger. poet, d. (b. 1740) Emanuel Geibel, Ger. poet, b. (d. 1884) E. T. A. Hoffmann: "Die Elixiere des Teufels," novel J. S. Knowles: "Caius Gracchus," tragedy Scott: "Guy Mannering" Anthony Trollope, Eng. novelist, b. (d. 1882) Wordsworth: "White Doe of Rhylstone"	Protestant Baseler Missionsgesellschaft (Basel Missionary Society) founded T. R. Malthus: "An Inquiry into the Nature and Progress of Rent" David Ricardo: "The Influence of a Low Price of Corn on the Profits of Stock" Savigny: "History of Roman Law in the Middle Ages" Dugald Stewart: "Progress of Metaphysical, Ethical, and Political Philosophy"

D. VISUAL ARTS	E. MUSIC	F. SCIENCE, TECHNOLOGY, GROWTH	G. DAILY LIFE	
David Cox: "Treatise on Landscape Painting and Effect in Water Colours" Anton Graff, Ger. portrait painter, d. (b. 1736) Turner: "Frosty Morning," painting	André Grétry, Fr. composer, d. (b. 1741) London Philharmonic Society founded Rossini: "L'Italiana in Algeri," opera, Venice Giuseppe Verdi, Ital. operatic composer, b. (d. 1901) Richard Wagner, Ger. composer, b. (d. 1883)	Joseph Lagrange, Fr. mathematician, d. (b. 1736) David Livingstone, Scot. explorer, b. (d. 1873) Founding of McGill University, Montreal	Grand Freemason Lodge founded Last gold guinea coins issued in England Indian trade monopoly of East India Company abolished Yorkshireman Thomas Lord moves White Conduit Club to St. John's Wood, London The waltz conquers the European ballrooms	**1813**
Dulwich Gallery, London, opened Goya: "The Second of May 1808" and "The Third of May 1808," paintings Ingres: "L'Odalisque," painting Thomas Lawrence: "The Congress of Vienna," painting Jean François Millet, Fr. painter, b. (d. 1875)	Beethoven: "Fidelio," final version, Vienna John Field: "Nocturnes" J. N. Maelzel invents the metronome in Vienna Schubert's great lied production begins (till 1828 c. 700 songs) Francis Scott Key writes poem, "Defense of Fort McHenry," later set to music of "Anacreon in Heaven" to become U.S. national anthem ("The Star-Spangled Banner")	Berzelius: "Theory of Chemical Proportions and the Chemical Action of Electricity" M. J. B. Orfila: "Toxicologie générale" At Killingworth Colliery, near Newcastle, George Stephenson constructs the first practical steam locomotive	Mikhail Bakunin, Russ. anarchist, b. (d. 1876) The London "Times" printed by steam-operated press M. C. C., London, move to Lord's Cricket Ground Eng. Statute of Apprentices (1563) repealed St. Margaret's, Westminster, London, is the first district to be illuminated by gas	**1814**
The Biedermeier style arrives (—1848) Canova: "The Three Graces," sculpture John Singleton Copley, Amer. painter, d. (b. 1738) Goya: "Tauromaquia," etchings Adolf Menzel, Ger. painter, b. (d. 1905) Nash rebuilds Brighton Pavilion in pseudooriental style (—1823) Turner: "Crossing the Brook," painting	Robert Franz, Ger. composer, b. (d. 1892) Halfdan Kjerulf, Norw. composer, b. (d. 1868) Robert Volkmann, Ger. composer, b. (d. 1883)	Humphry Davy invents miner's safety lamp Augustin Fresnel: research on the diffraction of light Lamarck: "Histoire naturelle des animaux" (—1822) Franz Mesmer, Viennese physician, d. (b. 1733) L. J. Prout: hypothesis on relation between specific gravity and atomic weight	Apothecaries Act forbids unqualified doctors to practice in Britain Brit. income tax ended (resumed 1842) Economic postwar crisis in England Brit. road surveyor John Macadam constructs roads of crushed stone Allan Robertson, first of the great golfers, b. (d. 1858) Eruption of Sumbawa Volcano in Indonesia–more than 50,000 dead Technological College, Vienna, founded The first steam warship: U.S.S. Fulton (38 tons)	**1815**

	A. HISTORY, POLITICS	B. LITERATURE, THEATER	C. RELIGION, PHILOSOPHY, LEARNING
1816	Maria I, Queen of Portugal, d.; succeeded by her son, Dom John VI (—1826) The Grand Duke of Saxe-Weimar grants first Ger. constitution Argentina declared independent Prince Metternich opens Diet of Ger. Confederation at Frankfurt Indiana becomes a state of the U.S. Java restored to the Netherlands	Jane Austen: "Emma" Charlotte Brontë, Eng. novelist, b. (d. 1855) Byron: "The Siege of Corinth" Samuel Taylor Coleridge: "Kubla Khan" (written 1797) Gustav Freytag, Ger. author, b. (d. 1895) Leigh Hunt: "The Story of Rimini" Leopardi: "Appressamento alla Morte" Shelley: "Alastor" Sheridan, Ir. dramatist, d. (b. 1751)	American Bible Society founded Count Gobineau, Fr. author and historian, b. (d. 1882) Nikolai Karamzin: "History of the Russian Empire"
1817	Attempt on the life of Prince Regent after opening of Parliament James Monroe (1758—1831) inaugurated as fifth President of the U.S. (—1825) "March of the Blanketeers" from Manchester to London halted at Stockport Wartburg Festival of revolutionary Ger. students Simón Bolívar establishes independent government of Venezuela Partial autonomy granted to Serbs by Turk. government Mississippi becomes a state of the U.S.	Jane Austen, Eng. novelist, d. (b. 1775) Byron: "Manfred" Franz Grillparzer: "Die Ahnfrau," tragedy William Hazlitt: "Characters in Shakespeare's Plays" Thomas Moore: "Lalla Rookh" Mme. de Staël, Fr. novelist, d. (b. 1766) Theodor Storm, Ger. author, b. (d. 1888) Henry David Thoreau, Amer. author, b. (d. 1862)	August Böckh: "The Public Economy of Athens" William Cobbett: "Paper against Gold, the History and Mystery of the Bank of England" Lutheran and Reformed Churches in Prussia form Evangelical Union Hegel: "Encyclopedia of the Philosophical Sciences" H. F. R. de Lamennais: "Essai sur l'indifférence en matière de religion" Juan Llorente, a former secretary of the Inquisition, publishes his "History of the Inquisition in Spain" Joseph de Maistre: "Du Pape" Theodor Mommsen, Ger. historian, b. (d. 1903) David Ricardo: "Principles of Political Economy and Taxation"
1818	The dominions of the Holkar of Indore, the Rajput States, and Poona come under Brit. control Act suspending Habeas Corpus is repealed Charles XIII of Sweden d.; succeeded by Jean Bernadotte as Charles XIV Chile proclaims its independence Bavarian constitution proclaimed; followed by constitution in Baden Internal customs in Prussia abolished Allies evacuate their troops from France Border between Canada and U.S. agreed upon (49th parallel) Illinois becomes a state of the U.S.	Jane Austen: "Northanger Abbey" and "Persuasion" (posth.) Byron: "Don Juan" (—1823) Grillparzer: "Sappho," drama Hazlitt: "Lectures on the Eng. Poets" Keats: "Endymion" T. L. Peacock: "Nightmare Abbey" Walter Scott: "Heart of Midlothian" and "Rob Roy" Mary Wollstonecraft Shelley: "Frankenstein" Ivan Turgenev, Russ. author, b. (d. 1883)	Bonn University founded Josef Dobrovsky: "History of the Czech Language" James Anthony Froude, Eng. historian, b. (d. 1894) Henry Hallam: "The View of the State of Europe during the Middle Ages" Hegel succeeds Fichte (d. 1814) as professor of philosophy at Berlin Karl Marx, Ger. political philosopher and socialist, b. (d. 1883) Schlegel appointed professor of Indian languages at Bonn

D. VISUAL ARTS	E. MUSIC	F. SCIENCE, TECHNOLOGY, GROWTH	G. DAILY LIFE	
The Elgin Marbles are bought for the British Museum, London Goya: "The Duke of Osuna," painting Leo von Klenze builds the Munich Glyptothek (—1830)	Viscount Fitzwilliam d. (b. 1745): leaves the Fitzwilliam Virginal Book of 17th Century Music to Cambridge Rossini: "Barbiere di Siviglia," Rome Spohr: "Faust," opera, Prague, conducted by C. M. von Weber	Sir David Brewster (1781—1868) invents kaleidoscope R. T. Laënnec (1781—1826) invents stethoscope E. W. Siemens, Ger. electrical engineer and industrialist, b. (d. 1892)	Blackwood's Magazine founded, Edinburgh William Cobbett's: "Political Register," the first cheap periodical, published Eng. economic crisis causes large-scale emigration to Canada and U.S. Ger. educator Friedrich Fröbel (1782—1852) moves his first educational community from Griesheim to Keilhau, Thuringia Protective tariff in U.S.	**1816**
Constable: "Flatford Mill," painting Charles Daubigny, Fr. painter, b. (d. 1878) John Leech, Eng. caricaturist, b. (d. 1864) Braccia Nuova begins building Vatican Museum, Rome (—1821) G. F. Watts, Eng. painter, b. (d. 1904)	Clementi: "Gradus ad Parnassum," studies for piano Rossini: "La Gazza," Milan, and "Cenerentola," Rome	Berzelius discovers selenium and lithium Karl Ritter: "Geographie in ihrer Beziehung zu Natur und Geschichte"	Riots in Derbyshire, England, against low wages U.S. begins construction of Erie Canal between Buffalo and Albany (—1825) "The Scotsman" founded in Edinburgh Opening of Waterloo Bridge, London (replaced 1945)	**1817**
Jakob Burckhardt, Swiss art historian, b. (d. 1897) Edwin Landseer: "Fighting Dogs," painting Prado Museum, Madrid, founded	Donizetti: "Enrico, Conte di Borgogna," opera, Venice Charles Gounod, Fr. composer, b. (d. 1893) Franz Xaver Huber (1787—1863), an Aust. schoolteacher, writes to words of the young curate, Joseph Mohr, the most famous of all Christmas carols: "Stille Nacht, heilige Nacht" Rossini: "Mosè in Egitto," opera, Naples	F. W. Bessel: "Fundamenta Astronomiae," catalog of 3,222 stars Berzelius publishes molecular weights of 2,000 chemical compounds Jeremiah Chubb invents detector lock J. F. Encke discovers orbit of Encke's comet Cadmium discovered by Stromeyer and Hermann	Brit. Order of St. Michael and St. George instituted by the Prince Regent F. W. Raiffeisen, Ger. economist (cooperative saving banks), b. (d. 1888) First professional horse racing in U.S. "Savannah" becomes the first steamship to cross the Atlantic (26 days)	**1818**

	A. HISTORY, POLITICS	B. LITERATURE, THEATER	C. RELIGION, PHILOSOPHY, LEARNING
1819	Brit. settlement established in Singapore by East India Company Florida purchased by U.S. from Spain The future Queen Victoria b. (d. 1901) "Peterloo" Massacre in Manchester, England The future Prince Consort Albert b. (d. 1861) Constitutions for Württemberg and Hanover Alabama becomes a state of the U.S. Simón Bolívar becomes President of Colombia	Byron: "Mazeppa" George Eliot (Mary Ann Evans), Eng. novelist, b. (d. 1880) Theodor Fontane, Ger. novelist, b. (d. 1898) Goethe: "West-östlicher Diwan" Julia Ward Howe, Amer. author, b. (d. 1910) Victor Hugo: "Odes" Keats: "Hyperion" (published 1856) Gottfried Keller, Swiss novelist, b. (d. 1890) August Friedrich Ferdinand von Kotzebue, Ger. playwright (b. 1761), assassinated as Russ. agent at Mannheim James Russell Lowell, Amer. author, b. (d. 1891) K. F. Schinkel builds the Schauspielhaus, Berlin (—1822) Shelley: "The Cenci" Walt Whitman, Amer. poet, b. (d. 1892)	Jakob Grimm: "German Grammar" Georg Hermes: "Philosophical Introduction to Christian Theology" Schopenhauer: "Die Welt als Wille und Vorstellung" Jean Sismondi: "Nouveaux principes d'economie politique" Horace Wilson: "Sanskrit-English Dictionary"
1820	Revolution in Spain–King Ferdinand VII forced to restore Constitution of 1812 King George III of England d., succeeded by Prince Regent as George IV (—1830) Caroline, wife of George IV demands recognition as queen; the king wishes to dissolve marriage, but popular sympathy for her demands ends inquiry into her conduct Assassination of the Duc de Berry, heir presumptive to Fr. throne; his son, the Comte de Chambord, b. (d. 1883) Cato Street murder conspiracy against Brit. cabinet ministers discovered; leaders executed "Missouri Compromise"–Maine enters Union as free state, and Missouri as slave state (in 1821) U.S. Land Law fixes land price at a minimum of $1.25 per acre Final Act of Vienna Congress passed Revolution in Portugal, demand for constitution Conference at Troppau (Silesia), to discourage revolutionary tendencies in Europe, adjourned; to reopen at Laibach (Jan. 1821)	Washington Irving: "The Sketch Book of Geoffrey Crayon, Gent." Edmund Kean appears as Richard III in New York Keats: "Ode to a Nightingale" Alphonse de Lamartine: "Méditations poétiques" Pushkin: "Ruslan and Ludmila," poem Scott: "Ivanhoe" Shelley: "Prometheus Unbound"	Thomas Brown: "Lectures on the Philosophy of the Human Mind" Friedrich Engels, Ger. socialist, b. (d. 1895) Thomas Erskine: "Internal Evidence for the Truth of Revealed Religion" J. J. von Görres: "Germany and the Revolution" Jesuits driven out of Rome T. R. Malthus: "Principles of Political Economy" Herbert Spencer, Eng. philosopher, b. (d. 1903)
1821	Congress of Laibach opens; Austria agrees to send troops to Naples to suppress revolt Brit. Parliament grants Queen Caroline an annuity of £50,000 James Monroe begins second term as President of the U.S. Revolution in Piedmont; Victor Emmanuel abdicates, names his brother Charles Felix successor; the intervening Aust. army victorious at Novara Reign of Terror begins between Greeks and Turks Napoleon d. (b. 1769) Simón Bolívar defeats Span. army at Carabobo, and ensures independence of Venezuela Coronation of George IV Death of Queen Caroline Missouri becomes a state of the U.S. Peru proclaimed independent from Spain, followed by Guatemala, Mexico, Panama, and Santo Domingo	Charles Baudelaire, Fr. poet, b. (d. 1867) James Fenimore Cooper: "The Spy" Feodor Dostoevsky, Russ. novelist, b. (d. 1881) Gustave Flaubert, Fr. novelist, b. (d. 1880) Goethe: "Wilhelm Meisters Wanderjahre" William Hazlitt: "Table Talk" (—1822) Heinrich Heine: "Poems" John Keats d. (b. 1795) Joseph de Maistre, Fr. author, d. (b. 1754) Manzoni: "Il Cinque Maggio" Thomas de Quincey: "Confessions of an English Opium Eater" Scott: "Kenilworth" Shelley: "Adonais"	Ecole des Chartes founded in Paris for historical studies Concordat between Vatican and Prussia Mary Baker Eddy, founder of Christian Science, b. (d. 1910) George Grote: "Statement of the Question of Parliamentary Reform" Hegel: "Grundlinien der Philosophie des Rechts" James Mill: "Elements of Political Economy" Saint-Simon: "Du Système industriel" Champollion deciphers Egyptian hieroglyphics using Rosetta Stone

D. VISUAL ARTS	E. MUSIC	F. SCIENCE, TECHNOLOGY, GROWTH	G. DAILY LIFE	
Gustave Courbet, Fr. painter, b. (d. 1877) Théodore Géricault: "The Raft of the Medusa," painting John Ruskin, Eng. art critic, b. (d. 1900) Thorvaldsen: "Christ and the Twelve Apostles," sculpture (—1838) Turner: "Childe Harold's Pilgrimage," painting	Beethoven deaf Jacques Offenbach, Fr. composer, b. (d. 1880) Clara Wiek-Schumann, Ger. pianist, b. (d. 1896)	Mitscherlich discovers isomorphism David Napier constructs the flat- bed cylinder press for printing Dan. physicist Hans C. Oersted (1777—1851) discovers electromagnetism James Watt, Scot. inventor, d. (b. 1736)	Opening of Burlington Arcade, Piccadilly, London Mehemet Ali presents Cleopatra's Needle to Britain (see 1475 B.C. and 1878) Freedom of the press in France Maximum 12-hour working day for juveniles in England	**1819**
William Blake: illustrations to the Book of Job Constable: "Harwich Lighthouse," painting Sir John Tenniel, Eng. illustrator, b. (d. 1914) Thorvaldsen: "The Lion of Lucerne," sculpture (see 1821) Discovery of the Venus de Milo	Henri Vieuxtemps, Fr. violinist and composer, b. (d. 1881)	André Ampère: "Laws of the Electrodynamic Action"	"Ballown," a kind of soccer, played for the first time in the U.S. Brit. emigration to Cape Colony Joseph Fouché, Fr. Minister of Police, d. (b. 1763) Florence Nightingale, Eng. nurse, b. (d. 1910) Rich deposits of platinum are discovered in the Russ. Urals Regent's Canal, London Washington Colonization Society founds Liberia for repatriation of Negroes Susan B. Anthony, Amer. suffragette leader, b.	**1820**
Constable: "Hay Wain," painting Using the model by Thorvaldsen, the Swiss sculptor Lucas Ahorn finishes the Lucerne Lion Monument	Weber: "Der Freischütz," opera, Berlin	Faraday discovers fundamentals of electromagnetic rotation Hermann von Helmholtz, Ger. physicist, b. (d. 1894) T. J. Seebeck discovers thermoelectricity Rudolf Virchow, Ger. surgeon, b. (d. 1902) Sir Charles Wheatstone (1802—1875) demonstrates sound reproduction	London Co-operative Society founded "Manchester Guardian" founded by J. E. Taylor (weekly, from 1855 daily) Population of European countries (in millions) France: 30.4; Great Britain: 20.8; Italy: 18.0; Austria: 12.0; Germany: 26.0 Population of the U.S.: 9.6 million	**1821**

	A. HISTORY, POLITICS	B. LITERATURE, THEATER	C. RELIGION, PHILOSOPHY, LEARNING
1822	Greeks adopt liberal republican constitution and proclaim independence Turk. fleet captures island of Chios and massacres inhabitants; as reprisal Greeks set fire to Turk. admiral's vessel Turks invade Greece Ulysses S. Grant, Amer. general and president, b. (d. 1885) Augustin de Iturbide elected Emperor of Mexico (see 1823) British Foreign Secretary Lord Castlereagh commits suicide at the age of 52 Brazil becomes independent of Portugal Congress of Verona opens to discuss European problems Bottle riots in Dublin, viceroy attacked by Orangemen	Edmond de Goncourt, Fr. author, b. (d. 1896) Grillparzer: "The Golden Fleece," dramatic trilogy E. T. A. Hoffmann d. (b. 1776) Washington Irving: "Bracebridge Hall" Charles Nodier (1780—1844): "Trilby," novel Pushkin: "Eugene Onegin" (—1832) Shelley d. (b. 1792) Stendhal: "De l'amour" Alfred de Vigny: "Poèmes"	H. T. Colebrooke founds Royal Asiatic Society (study of Eastern languages) Jean B. J. Fourier (1768—1830): "Théorie analytique de la chaleur" ("Analytical Theory of Heat") J. V. Poncelet: "Traité des propriétés projectives des figures," on projective geometry
1823	Mexico becomes republic Iturbide forced to abdicate Guatemala, San Salvador, Nicaragua, Honduras, and Costa Rica form Confederation of United Provinces of Central America Switzerland refuses to give asylum to political refugees The Monroe Doctrine closes Amer. continent to colonial settlements by European powers	James Fenimore Cooper: "The Pioneers," first of the "Leather- Stocking" novels Lamartine: "Nouvelles méditations poétiques" Alexander Ostrovski, Russ. dramatist, b. (d. 1886) Alexander Petöfi, Hungarian poet, b. (d. 1849) Charlotte M. Yonge, Brit. authoress b. (d. 1901)	Oxford Union Society founded Pope Pius VII d.; succeeded by Pope Leo XII (Annibale de la Genga) Ernest Renan, Fr. historian, b. (d. 1892) Saint-Simon: "Catéchisme des industriels" Louis Thiers: "Histoire de la Révolution Française" (—1827)
1824	Simón Bolívar proclaimed Emperor of Peru First Burmese War British take Rangoon Frontier treaty signed between Russia and U.S. Egyptians capture Crete Turks seize island of Ipsara from Greeks but are defeated at Mitylene U.S. House of Representatives elects John Quincy Adams as president when none of the four candidates wins a majority in the national election	Lord Byron, d. (b. 1788) at Missolonghi, in Turko-Greek war Alexandre Dumas fils, Fr. author, b. (d. 1895) W. S. Landor: "Imaginary Conversations" (—1837) Leopardi: "Canzoni" and "Versi" Mary Mitford: "Our Village" (—1832) Scott: "Redgauntlet"	August Böckh (ed.): "Corpus Inscriptionum Graecum" (—1859) Carlo Botta: "History of Italy, 1789—1814" Leopold von Ranke: "History of the Latin and Teutonic People, 1494—1535" Sunday School Union formed in U.S.
1825	Ferdinand IV of Naples d., succeeded by Francis I Anglo-Russ. Treaty over Brit. territory in northwestern N. America John Quincy Adams (1767—1848) inaugurated as sixth President of the U.S. Fr. law compensates the aristocrats for losses in Revolution Bolivia becomes independent of Peru, Uruguay of Brazil Portugal recognizes Brazilian independence Paul Kruger, S. African statesman, b. (d. 1904) Maximilian I, King of Bavaria, d.; succeeded by his son Louis I (—1848) Czar Alexander I d.; succeeded by Nicholas I Decembrist revolt in Russia crushed	William Hazlitt: "The Spirit of the Age, or Contemporary Portraits" Manzoni: "I Promessi Sposi," ("The Betrothed") Conrad Ferdinand Meyer, Swiss author, b. (d. 1898) Jean Paul (pseud. of Johann Paul Friedrich Richter), Ger. author, d. (b. 1763) "The Diaries of Samuel Pepys" (1633—1703) published Pushkin: "Boris Godunov" Esaias Tegnér: "Frithjofs Saga," Swed. epic poem	Fr. law makes sacrilege a capital offense Comte de Saint-Simon, Fr. socialist, d. (b. 1760) Augustin Thierry: "Histoire de la Conquête de l'Angleterre par les Normands"

D. VISUAL ARTS	E. MUSIC	F. SCIENCE, TECHNOLOGY, GROWTH	G. DAILY LIFE	
Antonio Canova Ital. sculptor, d. (b. 1757) Delacroix: "Dante and Virgil Crossing the Styx," painting John Martin: "Destruction of Herculaneum," painting	César Franck, Belg. composer, b. (d. 1890) Franz Liszt (at 11) makes his debut as pianist in Vienna Royal Academy of Music, London, founded Schubert: Symphony No. 8 in B minor ("The Unfinished")	Daguerre and Bouton invent the diorama, paintings illuminated in dark room to give illusion of reality A. J. Fresnel perfects lenses for lighthouses Sir William Herschel, Eng. astronomer, d. (b. 1738) Gregor Mendel, Aust. founder of the science of genetics, b. (d. 1884) Louis Pasteur, Fr. microbiologist, b. (d. 1895) Heinrich Schliemann, Ger. archeologist, b. (d. 1890)	Streets of Boston, Mass., lit by gas "Sunday Times," London, founded World's first iron railroad bridge built by Stephenson for Stockton- Darlington line	**1822**
Louis Lebas begins building of Notre Dame-de-la-Lorette, Paris P. P. Prudhon, Fr. painter, d. (b. 1758) Sir Henry Raeburn, Scot. portrait painter, d. (b. 1756) Sir Robert Smirke designs British Museum, London (—1847) Ferdinand Waldmüller: portrait of Beethoven	Beethoven finishes the "Missa Solemnis," Op. 123 "Clari, or the Maid of Milan," opera, London, by Henry R. Bishop (1786—1855), contains the song "Home Sweet Home" Sébastien Erard constructs a grand piano with double escapement Schubert: music to "Rosamunde," Vienna Weber: "Euryanthe," opera, Vienna	Charles Babbage's early attempts to construct a calculating machine Faraday succeeds in liquefying chlorine Charles Macintosh invents waterproof fabric Mechanics' Institute founded in London and Glasgow Walter Oudney, on an expedition from Tripoli, discovers Lake Chad in Central Africa Brit. medical journal "The Lancet" first issued	First Cologne Carnival festivities Death penalty for over 100 crimes abolished in Britain "Forget-me-not," the first illustrated Brit. annual, appears George IV presents the library of George III to British Museum Founding of Royal Thames Yacht Club Rugby Football originates at Rugby School, England	**1823**
Delacroix: "Les Massacres de Chios," painting John Flaxman: "Pastoral Apollo," sculpture National Gallery, London, founded Théodore Géricault, Fr. painter, d. (b. 1790) Ingres: "Vow of Louis XIII," painting Joseph Israels, Dutch painter, b. (d. 1911) J. F. Overbeck: "Christ's entry into Jerusalem," painting	Beethoven: Symphony No. 9 in D major ("Choral"), Op. 127, Vienna Anton Bruckner, Aust. composer, b. (d. 1896) Peter von Cornelius, Ger. composer, b. (d. 1874) Bedrich Smetana, Czech composer, b. (d. 1884)	Portland Cement developed by Joseph Aspdin (1779—1855) Eric Canal finished Nicolas Carnot: "Puissance motrice du feu" (on thermodynamics) J. L. Prévost and J. B. Dumas prove that the sperm is essential to fertilization William Thomson, Lord Kelvin, Eng. scientist, b. (d. 1907)	Founding of Athenaeum Club, London Beginning of Ger. emigration to Brazil Combinations Law of 1799—1800 repealed; Brit. workers are allowed to unionize "Le Globe," Paris, begins publication R.S.P.C.A. founded in London	**1824**
Constable: "Leaping Horse," painting Jacques Louis David, Fr. painter, d. (b. 1748) Samuel Morse: "Portrait of Lafayette," painting John Nash: Buckingham Palace	Beethoven's Symphony No. 9 first performed in England Boieldieu: "La Dame blanche," opera, Paris Antonio Salieri, Ital.-Viennese opera composer, d. (b. 1750) Johann Strauss, the "Waltz King," b. (d. 1899)	Jean Martin Charcot, Fr. psychiatrist, b. (d. 1893) Faraday succeeds in isolating benzene Sir Goldsworthy Gurney (1798—1875) invents oxygen-hydrogen limelight Hungarian Academy of Sciences founded in Budapest Opening of Stockton-Darlington railroad–the first line to carry passengers	A Baseball Club organized at Rochester, New York Horse-drawn buses in London Ferdinand Lasalle, Ger. socialist, b. (d. 1864) Tea roses from China introduced in Europe Expansion of Trade Union movement in Britain	**1825**

	A. HISTORY, POLITICS	B. LITERATURE, THEATER	C. RELIGION, PHILOSOPHY, LEARNING
1826	Treaty of Yandabu ends Burmese War John VI, King of Portugal, d.; succeeded by Peter IV (Dom Pedro of Brazil, who promulgates liberal constitution), who abdicates Port. throne in favor of his daughter, Maria II Russ. ultimatum to Turkey over Serbia Pan American Congress in Panama Thomas Jefferson d. (b. 1743) Russia declares war on Persia A commercial treaty between Prussia and Mecklenburg-Schwerin begins the idea of the Zollverein Dost Mohammed becomes Amir of Kabul (—1863)	James Fenimore Cooper: "The Last of the Mohicans" Benjamin Disraeli: "Vivian Grey" Johann Peter Hebel, Ger. author, d. (b. 1760) Heine: "Reisebilder I" Josef Viktor von Scheffel, Ger. poet, b. (d. 1886) Scott: "Woodstock" Alfred de Vigny: "Cinq-Mars," historical novel Johann H. Voss, Ger. poet, d. (b. 1751)	Wilhelm Liebknecht, Ger. socialist, b. (d. 1900) Ngüan Ngüan (1764—1849) edits the writings of Confucius
1827	Peru secedes from Colombia Russia, France, and Britain urge Turkey to end war with Greece; their note is rejected by the sultan Count Kapodistrias elected President of Greece Turks enter Athens By the Treaty of London the Allies agree to force a truce on the sultan Battle of Navarino: Turk. and Egyptian fleets destroyed Sultan Mohammed II rejects right of Allies to mediate in war Russia defeats Persia and takes Erivan (Armenia) Dom Miguel of Port., betrothed to his niece, Maria II, made regent	Charles de Coster, Belg. poet, b. (d. 1879) Ugo Foscolo, Ital. author, d. (b. 1778) Wilhelm Hauff, Ger. poet, d. (b. 1802) Heine: "Buch der Lieder" Victor Hugo: "Cromwell," novel Leopardi: "Operette morali"	John Darby founds the Plymouth Brethren Henry Hallam: "The Constitutional History of England" John Keble: "The Christian Year"
1828	The Duke of Wellington (1769—1852) becomes Prime Minister of Great Britain Alexander Ypsilanti, Greek politician, d. (b. 1792) Henry Peter Brougham (1778—1868) delivers the longest recorded speech (six hours) in the House of Commons De Witt Clinton, U.S. political leader, d. (b. 1769) Maria II deposed, Dom Miguel proclaimed King of Port Russia declares war on Turkey "Tariff of Abominations" passed by U.S. Congress, curtailing imports Karl August, Grand Duke of Saxe-Weimar, friend of Goethe, d. (b. 1757) Mehemet Ali agrees to Britain's demand to quit Greece Uruguay (since 1821 part of Brazil) becomes independent republic following Treaty of Rio de Janeiro U.S. presidential election; Andrew Jackson defeats John Quincy Adams Liberal revolt in Mexico, Vicente Guerrero (1783—1831) becomes president	Edmond About, Fr. author and journalist, b. (d. 1885) James Fenimore Cooper: "The Red Rover" Alexandre Dumas père (1802—1870): "Les Trois Mousquetaires" Henrik Ibsen, Norw. dramatist, b. (d. 1906) Washington Irving: "History of the Life and Voyage of Christopher Columbus" Bulwer-Lytton: "Pelham," novel George Meredith, Eng. novelist, b. (d. 1909) Margaret Oliphant, Scot. novelist, b. (d. 1897) Francisque Sarcey, Fr. drama critic, b. (d. 1899) Scott: "Tales of a Grandfather" and "The Fair Maid of Perth" Count Leo Nikolayevich Tolstoi, Russ. novelist, b. (d. 1910) Jules Verne, Fr. author of Utopian novels, b. (d. 1905)	Thomas Arnold (1795—1842) appointed headmaster of Rugby School Brit. Test and Corporation Acts repealed; Catholics and Nonconformists may hold public office Friedrich Albert Lange, Ger. philosopher and sociologist, b. (d. 1875) Ger. scholar K. O. Müller (1797—1840) publishes his treatise on Etruscan antiquities Sir W. F. Napier begins his "History of the War in the Peninsula" (—1840) Dugald Stewart, Scot. philosopher, d. (b. 1753) Hippolyte Adolphe Taine, Fr. thinker and historian, b. (d. 1893) University College, London, founded in 1826, opened "American Dictionary of the English Language," by Noah Webster (1758—1843), published

D. VISUAL ARTS	E. MUSIC	F. SCIENCE, TECHNOLOGY, GROWTH	G. DAILY LIFE	
Gustave Moreau, Fr. painter, b. (d. 1898) U.S. Academy of Design founded	Mendelssohn: Overture to "A Midsummer Night's Dream," Op. 21 Weber: "Oberon," opera, London Carl Maria von Weber, Ger. composer, d. (b. 1786)	André Ampère: "Electrodynamics" N. J. Lobachevsky develops his system of non-Euclidean geometry Munich University founded University College, London, founded Galvanometer invented by Leopoldo Nobili Otto Unverdorben (1806—1873) obtains aniline from indigo	Unter den Linden, Berlin, lit by gas Stamford Raffles founds Royal Zoological Society, London First railroad tunnel, on Liverpool-Manchester line, in England	**1826**
William Blake, Eng. artist and poet, d. (b. 1757) Arnold Böcklin, Swiss painter, b. (d. 1901) Constable: "The Cornfield," painting William Holman Hunt, Eng. painter, b. (d. 1910) Nash designs Carlton House Terrace, Westminster, London	Beethoven d. (b. 1770) Bellini: "Il Pirate," opera, Milan Schubert: "Die Winterreise," song cycle to words by Wilhelm Müller	J. J. Audubon (1785—1851): "Birds of North America" Karl von Baer: "Epistola de Ova Mammalium et Hominis Generis" Eng. physician Richard Bright describes Bright's disease Marquis Pierre Simon de Laplace, Fr. mathematician and astronomer, d. (b. 1749) Joseph Lister, Eng. surgeon, b. (d. 1912) Joseph Niepce produces photographs on a metal plate George S. Ohm (1787—1854) formulates Ohm's Law, defining electrical current potential and resistance Aust. engineer Joseph Ressel (1793—1857) invents ship's screw propeller James Simpson constructs sand filter for purification of London's water supply Alessandro Volta, Ital. physicist, d. (b. 1745) Friedrich Wöhler obtains metallic aluminum from clay	Karl Baedeker begins publishing his travel guides "Evening Standard," London, appears J. H. Pestalozzi, Swiss educator, d. (b. 1746) Sulfur friction matches introduced by John Walker	**1827**
Richard P. Bonington, Eng. romantic painter, d. (b. 1802) Delacroix: 19 "Faust" lithographs Francisco José de Goya y Lucientes, Span. painter and engraver, d. (b. 1746) Jean Antoine Houdon, Fr. sculptor, d. (b. 1740) Dante Gabriel Rossetti, Eng. Pre-Raphaelite poet and painter, b. (d. 1882) Alfred Stevens, Belg. painter, b. (d. 1906) Gilbert Stuart, Amer. painter, d. (b. 1755)	Auber: "La Muette de Portici," Paris Opéra Marschner: "Der Vampire," Leipzig Rossini: "Le Comte Ory," Paris Opéra Franz Schubert, Aust. composer, d. (b. 1797)	Norw. mathematician Niels Henrik Abel (1802—1829) begins study of elliptic functions Sir John Burdon-Sanderson, Eng. physiologist, b. (d. 1905) Charles Carroll of Carrollton, the richest American of his time, inaugurates construction of the Baltimore and Ohio, first railroad built in U.S. for the transportation of passengers and freight Ferdinand Julius Cohn, Ger. botanist, b. (d. 1898) Theodore De Vinne, Amer. printer and typographer, b. (d. 1914) John Franklin publishes an account of his Arctic explorations (1825—1827) Franz Joseph Gall, Ger. physician, founder of phrenology, d. (b. 1758) The "Promethean match," a glass bead containing acid, patented by Samuel Jones of London Cap and ring spinning machines invented (respectively) by Amer. engineers Charles Danforth and John Thorp Balfour Stewart, Scot. physicist (spectrum analysis), b. (d. 1887) Sir Joseph Swan, Eng. chemist and electrician (invented carbon filament), b. (d. 1914) Friedrich Wöhler's (1800—1882) synthesis of urea begins organic chemistry William Hyde Wollaston, Eng. scientist who discovered palladium and rhodium, invented camera lucida, and discovered Frauenhofer lines and ultraviolet rays, d. (b. 1766)	London weekly "Athenaeum" issued Ger. publisher Karl Baedeker (1801—1859) publishes his guide book "The Rhine from Mainz to Cologne" Jean Henri Dunant, Swiss humanitarian, founder (1864) of the Red Cross, b. (d. 1910) Ger. youth Kaspar Hauser (1812—1833), central figure of the celebrated mystery, brought before the authorities of Nuremberg "The Spectator," London weekly periodical, founded Working Men's Party founded in New York	**1828**

	A. HISTORY, POLITICS	B. LITERATURE, THEATER	C. RELIGION, PHILOSOPHY, LEARNING
1829	Carl Schurz, Ger.-Amer. statesman and soldier, b. (d. 1906) Andrew Jackson (1767—1845) inaugurated as seventh President of the U.S. In a message to Congress President Jackson attacks the Second Bank of the U.S., controlled by Nicholas Biddle (1786—1844) New Act of Parliament establishes an effective police force in London Peace of Adrianople ends Russo-Turk. war; Turkey acknowledges independence of Greece Slavery abolished in Mexico Eng. economist Thomas Attwood (1783—1856) founds the Birmingham Political Union to demand parliamentary reform President Guerrero of Mexico overthrown by General Anastasio Bustamante Ir. political leader Daniel O'Connell (1775—1847), M.P., commences agitation for repeal of Act of Union Venezuela withdraws from Gran Colombia to begin its independent existence Ferdinand VII of Spain marries his fourth wife, Maria Christina of Naples	Balzac: "Les Chouans" Bestseller: Washington Irving's "The Conquest of Granada" Goethe's novel "Wilhelm Meisters Wanderjahre" (second version) Aleksandr Sergeyevich Griboyedov, Russ. playwright, d. (b. 1795) Victor Hugo: "Marion Delorme," drama, and "Le Dernier Jour d'un Condamné," novel Joseph Jefferson, Amer. actor, b. (d. 1905) Lamartine (1790—1869) elected to the Académie Française Bulwer-Lytton: "Devereux," novel E. A. Poe: "Al Araaf, Tamerlane, and Other Poems" Tommaso Salvini, Ital. actor, b. (d. 1916) Friedrich von Schlegel, Ger. poet and critic, d. (b. 1772) Scott: "Anne of Geierstein" Tennyson: "Timbuctoo" Henry Timrod, Amer. poet ("Laureate of the Confederacy"), b. (d. 1867) Charles Dudley Warner, Amer. essayist and novelist, b. (d. 1900)	Edward White Benson, Archbishop of Canterbury, b. (d. 1896) Catholic Emancipation Act allows Roman Catholics in Great Britain to sit in Parliament and to hold almost any public office Samuel Rawson Gardiner, Eng. historian, b. (d. 1902) John Jay, U.S. jurist, first Chief Justice of the U.S. Supreme Court, d. (b. 1745) Pope Leo XII d. (b. 1760) Cardinal Francisco Castiglione (b. 1761) elected Pope Pius VIII Mark Rutherford (pen name of William Hale White), Eng. philosopher, b. (d. 1913) Walker's Appeal, Amer. pamphlet against slavery, by David Walker (1785—1830)
1830	In a debate with Robert Y. Hayne, Daniel Webster negates States' Rights doctrine James G. Blaine, Amer. statesman, b. (d. 1893) 3rd Marquis of Salisbury, Brit. statesman, b. (d. 1903) Antonio José de Sucre, S. American liberator, d. (b. 1795) France captures Algeria Revolution in Paris William IV (1765—1837), third son of George III, becomes King of Great Britain and Ireland Charles X (1757—1836), King of France since 1824, abdicates Louis Philippe (1773—1850), King of the French, "the Citizen King" (—1848) Francis Joseph I, Emperor of Austria from 1848, King of Hungary from 1867, b. (d. 1916) Disturbances in Brussels after a performance of Auber's "La Muette de Portici" Porfirio Diaz, Mexican soldier and statesman, b. (d. 1915) Talleyrand (1754—1838) becomes Louis Philippe's ambassador to London Ecuador secedes from Gran Colombia and becomes an independent republic *(contd)*	Honoré de Balzac (1799—1850) states his intention to group together approx. 40 novels; beginnings of "La Comédie humaine" Bestseller: G. P. R. James' "Richelieu" T. E. Brown, Manx poet, b. (d. 1897) Emily Dickinson, Amer. poet, b. (d. 1886) Comtesse de Genlis, prolific Fr. writer, d. (b. 1746) Jules de Goncourt, Fr. novelist and diarist, b. (d. 1870) William Hazlitt, Eng. writer and critic, d. (b. 1778) Paul Hamilton Hayne, Amer. poet and man of letters, b. (d. 1886) Paul Heyse, Ger. writer, Nobel Prize for Literature 1910, b. (d. 1914) Victor Hugo: "Hernani" Lamartine: "Harmonies poétiques et religieuses" Frédéric Mistral, Provençal poet, Nobel Prize for Literature 1904, b. (d. 1914) *(contd)*	Jeremy Bentham: "Constitutional Code for all Nations" William Cobbett: "Rural Rides" Numa Fustel de Coulanges, Fr. historian, b. (d. 1889) Sir Clements R. Markham, Eng. geographer, b. (d. 1916) The religious society of Mormons or Latter-day Saints, founded by Joseph Smith and his friends at Fayette, N.Y. Jean Jacques Elisée Reclus, Fr. geographer, b. (d. 1905) *(contd)*

D. VISUAL ARTS	E. MUSIC	F. SCIENCE, TECHNOLOGY, GROWTH	G. DAILY LIFE	
"Tivoli" by Karl Blechen (1798—1840), beginning of landscape realism in Ger. painting Delacroix: "Sardanapalus," Louvre Anselm Feuerbach, Ger. painter, b. (d. 1880) John Everett Millais, Eng. painter, b. (d. 1896) Johann Heinrich Wilhelm Tischbein, Ger. romantic painter, d. (b. 1751) Turner: "Ulysses Deriding Polyphemus," painting, National Gallery, London	Bach's St. Matthew Passion rediscovered and revived by Felix Mendelssohn at the Berlin Singakademie, 100 years after its first performance in Leipzig (Good Friday, 1729) Bellini: "La Straniera," Milan Chopin's debut in Vienna Louis Gottschalk, Amer. pianist and composer, b. (d. 1869) Rossini: "Guillaume Tell," Paris Opéra Anton Rubinstein, Russ. pianist and composer, b. (d. 1894) The concertina patented by Sir Charles Wheatstone (1802—1875)	Moritz Benedikt Cantor, Ger. mathematician, b. (d. 1920) L. J. M. Daguerre (1789—1851) forms a partnership with J. N. Niepce (1765—1833) for the development of their photographic inventions Sir Humphry Davy, Eng. chemist, d. (b. 1778) The Delaware and Hudson's gravity railroad opens (constructed with locomotive operation in view) J. W. Dobereiner (1780—1849): classification of similar elements Josef Dobrovsky, Czech philologist, d. (b. 1753) J. N. von Drayse invents the breechloading needle gun Amer. physicist John Henry (1797—1878) constructs an early version of the electromagnetic motor Ger. naturalist Alexander von Humboldt (1769—1859) travels to the Chinese border Hydropathy, the system of treating diseases by water, developed by Silesian farmer Vincenz Priessnitz (1801—1851) Friedrich August von Kekulé, Ger. chemist, b. (d. 1896) Jean Baptiste Monet de Lamarck, Fr. naturalist, d. (b. 1744) Silas Weir Mitchell, Amer. physician, b. (d. 1914) Franz Ressel, inventor of the screw-propeller for steamships, attains speed of six knots with his speedboat "Civetta" at Trieste James Smithson, Brit. chemist, d. (b. 1765); bequeaths £100,000 to found Smithsonian Institution, Washington, D.C. George Stephenson's (1781—1848) engine "The Rocket" wins a prize of £500 in the Rainhill trials	William Booth, founder of the Salvation Army, b. (d. 1912) The first cooperative stores in America (Philadelphia and New York) The omnibuses designed by George Shillibaer become part of London public transport First Oxford-Cambridge boat race takes place at Henley; Oxford wins Fr. printer Claude Genoux invents papier-mâché matrix Centralized Metropolitan Police Force installed in London Suttee, the Indian custom of immolating a widow along with her dead husband, abolished in Brit. India Roger Charles Tichborne, the true heir to the Tichborne estates, b. (d. 1854) (see 1874) The first U.S. patent on a typewriter granted to William B. Burt of Detroit ("Typographer") The Royal Zoological Society takes over the menagerie at the Tower of London: origin of the London Zoo at Regent's Park	**1829**
Albert Bierstadt, Amer. landscape painter, b. (d. 1902) Jean Baptiste Camille Corot: "Chartres Cathedral," painting Honoré Daumier (1808—1879) begins his association with Charles Philipson and his journals ("La Caricature," later "Le Charivari") Delacroix: "Liberty Guiding the People," Louvre Sir Thomas Lawrence, Eng. *(contd)*	Auber: "Fra Diavolo," Paris, Opéra-Comique Bellini: "I Capuleti ed i Montecchi," Venice Hans von Bülow, Ger. pianist and conductor, first husband of Cosima Wagner, b. (d. 1894) Donizetti: "Anna Bolena," Milan Karl Goldmark, Austro-Hungarian composer, b. (d. 1915) "Jim Crow," an early Amer. popular song, sung by Thomas "Daddy" *(contd)*	Scot. botanist Robert Brown (1773—1858) discovers the cell nucleus in plants Exportation of nitrates begins from Chile (300 tons; in 1900, 1.5 million tons) Discussion between the two Fr. naturalists Georges Cuvier and E. Gouvion Saint-Hilaire on the latter's theory of unity of plan in organic composition Jean Baptiste Fourier, Fr. mathematician and physicist, d. (b. 1768) Ger. botanist Johann Friedrich Hessel proves that crystals can have 37 different kinds of symmetry Liverpool-Manchester railroad formally opened Scot. geologist Charles Lyell (1795—1875) divides the geological system into three groups which he names eocene, miocene, and pliocene James Perry obtains a patent for his steel slit pen François Marie Raoult, Fr. chemist, b. (d. 1901) Ger. naturalist and industrialist Karl von Reichenbach (1788—1869) discovers paraffin Founding of Royal Geographic Society, London Carriage road across St. Gotthard (Switzerland) *(contd)*	Ladies' skirts grow shorter; sleeves become enormous; hats extremely large, ornamented with flowers and ribbons Belva Lockwood, Amer. lawyer, first woman to practice before Supreme Court and to be nominated for presidency, b. (d. 1917) Stiff collars become part of men's dress 26 steam cars in the streets of London	**1830**

	A. HISTORY, POLITICS	B. LITERATURE, THEATER	C. RELIGION, PHILOSOPHY, LEARNING
1830 contd	Ludwig Yorck von Wartenburg, Prussian general during the Napoleonic Wars, d. (b. 1759) Chester A. Arthur, the 21st President of the U.S., b. (d. 1886) Peter II, last of the Vladikas dynasty, statesman, warrior, and poet, ascends the throne of Montenegro (d. 1851) Charles, 2nd Earl Grey (1764—1845) becomes Prime Minister of Great Britain (—1834) Military insurrection in Warsaw against Russian rule Serbia a fully autonomous state with Milos Obrenovic as "Supreme Chief" Simón Bolívar, Lat.-Amer. soldier-statesman, d. (b. 1783) Mysore added to Britain's possessions in India Red Jacket, Amer. Indian leader, d. (b. 1758)	Christina Rossetti, Eng. poet, daughter of Gabriele Rossetti, b. (d. 1894) Alexander Smith, Scot. poet ("Dreamthorp"), b. (d. 1867) The fictional letters of Major Jack Downing by the Amer. humorist Seba Smith (1792—1868) begin to appear Stendhal: "Le Rouge et le Noir" Tennyson: "Poems, Chiefly Lyrical"	Pope Pius VIII d.
1831	Polish Diet declares independence of Poland; Russians defeat Pol. forces at Ostroleka; revolt collapses Leo Count von Caprivi, Ger. statesman, Chancellor 1890—1894, b. (d. 1899) Charles Albert, King of Sardinia-Piedmont, till abdication 1849 Prince Leopold of Saxe-Coburg (1790—1865) elected Leopold I, King of the Belgians Separation of Belgium from the Netherlands Baron H. F. K. vom und zum Stein, Ger. statesman, d. (b. 1757) James Monroe, fifth President of the U.S., d. (b. 1758) Viscount Goschen, Brit. politician, b. (d. 1907) Southampton insurrection: Virginia slave revolt led by Negro Nat Turner (1800—1831); 55 Whites die August Neithardt von Gneisenau, Prussian Field Marshal during the Napoleonic Wars, d. (b. 1757) Ioannes A. Kapodistrias, Greek statesman, d. (b. 1776) Henry Labouchere, Eng. politician and wit, b. (d. 1912) Karl von Clausewitz, Prussian general and military historian, d. (b. 1780) James Abram Garfield, 20th President of the U.S., b. (assassinated 1881) Former President John Quincy Adams becomes U.S. representative from Massachusetts Syria, since 1516 part of the Ottoman Empire, conquered by the Egyptians The Grand Duchy of Luxembourg, part of the Netherlands since the Congress of Vienna, divided into two parts, the larger of which goes to Belgium Wretched conditions of the working classes in Lyons, *(contd)*	Balzac: "La Peau de chagrin" C. S. Calverley, Eng. poet, b. (d. 1884) Disraeli: "The Young Duke," second novel Ignatius Donnelly, Amer. author, pro-Bacon versus Shakespeare, b. (d. 1901) Victor Hugo: "Notre Dame de Paris" Helen Hunt Jackson, Amer. poet and novelist ("Ramona," 1884), b. (d. 1885) Friedrich Maximilian von Klinger, whose drama "Sturm und Drang" gave its name to the Ger. literary movement, d. (b. 1752) Giacomo Leopardi (1798—1837): "Canti," collection of poems Nikolai Semenovich Leskov, Russ. novelist, b. (d. 1895) Thomas L.Peacock (1785—1866): "Crotchet Castle," satirical novel Edgar Allen Poe: "Poems" Wilhelm Raabe, Ger. novelist, b. (d. 1910) Victorien Sardou, Fr. dramatist, b. (d. 1908) Sarah Siddons, Eng. tragic actress, d. (b. 1755) John Trumbull, Amer. poet and lawyer, leader of the "Hartford Wits," *(contd)*	Helena Petrovna Blavatsky, founder of the Theosophical Society, b. (d. 1891) Cardinal Mauro Capellari (1765—1846) elected Pope Gregory XVI F. W. Farrar, Anglican cleric, who wrote a bestselling "Life of Christ," became Dean of Westminster, and was involved in sordid financial affairs, b. (d. 1903) Daniel Coit Gilman, Amer. educator, first president of Johns Hopkins University and the Carnegie Institution, b. (d. 1908) Frederic Harrison, Eng. jurist, positivist leader, b. (d. 1923) Friedrich Hegel, Ger. philosopher, d. (b. 1770) William Miller (1782—1849), leader of the Second Adventists in America, begins his preachings Barthold Georg Niebuhr, Ger. historian ("History of Rome"), d. (b. 1776) *(contd)*

D. VISUAL ARTS	E. MUSIC	F. SCIENCE, TECHNOLOGY, GROWTH	G. DAILY LIFE	
portrait painter, d. (b. 1769) Lord Leighton, Eng. painter and sculptor, b. (d. 1896) End of the Nazarene Brotherhood, an antiacademic society of Ger. painters in Rome (Overbeck, Schnorr von Carolsfeld, etc.) Camille Pissarro, Fr. impressionist painter, b. (d. 1903) John Quincy Adams Ward, Amer. sculptor, b. (d. 1910) Alfred Waterhouse, Eng. architect, among the first to use structural ironwork, b. (d. 1905)	Rice Teodor Leschetitzky, Pol.-Viennese pianist and piano teacher, b. (d. 1915) Eduard Reményi, Hungarian violinist, toured Germany with Brahms 1852—53, b. (d. 1898)	finished (begun 1820) Samuel Thomas von Sömmering, Ger. anatomist, d. (b. 1755) Fr. tailor Barthélemy Thimmonier devises a machine for utilitarian stitching (beginning of the sewing machine) Sir Charles W. Thomson, Scot. naturalist ("The Voyage of the Challenger"), b. (d. 1882)		**1830 contd**
Reinhold Begas, Ger. sculptor, b. (d. 1911) Delacroix: "Le 28 Juillet 1830," painting Constantin Meunier, Belg. painter and sculptor, b. (d. 1905)	Bellini: "La Sonnambula," Milan, Teatro Carcano, and "Norma," Milan, La Scala Chopin arrives in Paris Hérold: "Zampa," Paris, Opéra-Comique Joseph Joachim, Hungarian violinist, founder (1869) of the Joachim Quartet, b. (d. 1907) Meyerbeer: "Robert le Diable," Paris Opéra Ignaz Pleyel, Fr.-Aust. composer and pianoforte maker, d. (b. 1757)	Heinrich de Barry, Ger. botanist (fungus research), b. (d. 1888) Chloroform simultaneously invented by Samuel Guthrie (Amer.) and Justus von Liebig (Ger.) Philip Howard Colomb, Brit. naval officer who devised signaling system, b. (d. 1899) Charles Darwin (1809—1882) sails as naturalist on a surveying expedition in "H.M.S. Beagle" to S. America, New Zealand, and Australia (—1836) Michael Faraday (1791—1867) carries out a series of experiments demonstrating the discovery of electromagnetic induction James Clerk Maxwell, Scot. chemist who theorized (1873) that light and electromagnetism have identical source, b. (d. 1879) Sir James Clark Ross determines position of magnetic North Pole Edward J. Routh, Brit. mathematician, b. (d. 1907) Charles Sauria of France develops method of making matches easy to ignite	The great cholera pandemic, which began in India in 1826, spreads from Russia into Central Europe, reaching Scotland in 1832 Joseph Cowan, Eng. liberal orator, b. (d. 1900) Ger. emigration to America c. 15,000 (in 1841, c. 43,000) William Lloyd Garrison (1805—1879) begins publishing the abolitionist periodical "The Liberator," in Boston E. L. Godkin, Amer. journalist, founder of "The Nation," b. (d. 1902) Baron Moritz von Hirsch, Ger.-Jewish banker and philanthropist, b. (d. 1896) John Bell Hood, Confederate general in Civil War, b. (d. 1879) Légion Etrangère (Fr. Foreign Legion) formed to help control Fr. colonial possessions in Africa London Bridge opened The first horse-drawn buses appear in New York Population of Great Britain, 13.9 million; America, 12.8 million George M. Pullman, Amer. inventor, designer of railroad *(contd)*	**1831**

	A. HISTORY, POLITICS	B. LITERATURE, THEATER	C. RELIGION, PHILOSOPHY, LEARNING
1831 contd	France, lead to uprisings Lord John Russell introduces Reform Bill that abolishes all "nomination" boroughs Mass demonstrations in Swiss cities lead to introduction of more liberal legislation, expansion of franchise, and the principle of popular sovereignty Emperor Pedro I of Brazil (1798—1834) abdicates; succeeded by Pedro II (b. 1825), his son (—1889)	d. (b. 1750)	William Roscoe, Eng. historian, d. (b. 1753) Isaiah Thomas, Amer. printer who printed the first Eng. Bible in U.S., d. (b. 1749) U.S. copyright law amended: 28 years, renewable for 14 years Justin Winsor, Amer. historian ("Narrative and Critical History of America"), b. (d. 1897) William Aldis Wright, Eng. Biblical and Shakespearean scholar, b. (d. 1914)
1832	Mehemet Ali (1769—1849), Viceroy of Egypt, defeats the Turks in Syria Mass demonstrations at Hambach, Germany, in favor of the liberal and national cause The First Reform Act to enfranchise the upper-middle classes passed by the House of Lords; number of voters increased from 500,000 to 1,000,000 Friedrich von Gentz, Aust. statesman and political writer, d. (b. 1764) The Duke of Reichstadt, son of Napoleon, d. (b. 1811) Earl Roberts, Brit. Field Marshal, b. (d. 1914) Andrew Jackson, nominated by the newly styled "Democratic Party," reelected President of the U.S., defeating Henry Clay W. E. Gladstone (1809—1898) enters Eng. politics as Conservative M.P. for Newark John Caldwell Calhoun (1782—1850), Vice-President in the Jackson administration, resigns Giuseppe Mazzini (1805—1872), Ital. patriot, founds the organization "Giovine Italia" (Italian Youth) with the aim of achieving national independence The word "socialism" comes into use in English and French Britain occupies Falkland Islands	Louisa May Alcott, Amer. author of children's books ("Little Women"), b. (d. 1888) Horatio Alger, Amer. author of novels for boys, b. (d. 1899) Sir Edwin Arnold, Eng. poet ("The Light of Asia"), b. (d. 1904) Balzac: "Le Colonel Chabert" Björnstjerne Björnson, Norw. poet and dramatist, Nobel Prize for Literature 1903, b. (d. 1910) Bulwer-Lytton: "Eugene Aram," bestseller Wilhelm Busch, Ger. painter and poet, b. (d. 1908) Lewis Carroll (Charles Lutwidge Dodgson), author of "Alice in Wonderland," b. (d. 1898) George Crabbe, Eng. poet, d. (b. 1754) Casimir Delavigne: "Louis XI," drama Ludwig Devrient, most celebrated Ger. actor of his time, d. (b. 1784) Disraeli: "Contarini Fleming," autobiographical novel José Echegaray, Span. dramatist, shared (with F. Mistral) Nobel Prize for Literature 1904, b. (d. 1916) Goethe: "Faust," part II (posth.) Philip Freneau, "Poet of the American Revolution," d. (b. 1752) Johann Wolfgang von Goethe, the greatest Ger. poet, d. (b. 1749) Leigh Hunt: "Poetical Works" Washington Irving: "The Alhambra," a series of tales and sketches of the Moors and Spaniards John P. Kennedy (1795—1870): "Swallow Barn," sketches of Southern plantation life Nikolaus Lenau: "Gedichte" Silvio Pellico (1788—1854): "Le Mie prigioni" Aleksandr Sergeyevich Pushkin: "Eugene Onegin," completed after eight years of work Sir Walter Scott, Scot. poet and novelist, d. (b. 1771) Tennyson: "Lady of Shalott" Theodore Watts-Dunton, Eng. poet and critic, friend of A. C. Swinburne, b. (d. 1914)	Hubert Howe Bancroft, Amer. historian of the Amer. West, b. (d. 1918) Jeremy Bentham, Eng. utilitarian philosopher and economist, d. (b. 1748) Jean Champollion, Fr. archeologist who found clue to Egyptian writing in Rosetta Stone, d. (b. 1790) Thomas Fowler, Eng. educator and writer on logic, b. (d. 1907) Karl C. F. Krause, Ger. philosopher, formulated "All-in-God" pantheism, d. (b. 1781) Final volume of B. G. Niebuhr's epoch-making "Roman History" published Wilhelm Wundt, Ger. philosopher and psychologist, b. (d. 1920) Zurich University founded Rasmus Rask, Dan. philologist, one of the founders of the science of comparative linguistics, d. (b. 1787) Sir Leslie Stephen, Eng. philosopher, first editor of "Dictionary of National Biography," b. (d. 1904) Herbert Vaughan, Eng. Roman Catholic prelate, cardinal (1893), builder of Westminster Cathedral, b. (d. 1903) Andrew White, Amer. educator, president of Cornell University 1868—1885, ambassador to Russia and Germany, b. (d. 1918)

D. VISUAL ARTS	E. MUSIC	F. SCIENCE, TECHNOLOGY, GROWTH	G. DAILY LIFE	
			cars, b. (d. 1897) John McAllister Schofield, Amer. general, b. (d. 1906) Samuel Francis Smith (1809—1895), probably then a student at Andover, Mass., writes the words "My Country, 'Tis of Thee" to the tune of "America"; until 1931 one of the national anthems of the U.S. Heinrich von Stephan, Ger. statesman, chief promoter of the First International Postal Union, b. (d. 1897) William Whiteley, founder of London's first department store (1866), b. (murdered by a blackmailer, 1907)	**1831 contd**
Constable: "Waterloo Bridge from Whitehall Stairs," Royal Academy, London P. L. Debucourt, Fr. painter and cartoonist, d. (b. 1755) Gustave Doré, Fr. painter and book illustrator, b. (d. 1883) Ando Hiroshige (1797—1858), great master of Jap. color prints (Ukiyoe) publishes his series "Fifty-three stages of the Tokaido" Edouard Manet, Fr. impressionist painter, b. (d. 1883) Sir William Orchardson, Scot. painter, b. (d. 1910)	Berlioz: "Symphonie Fantastique," Op. 14 revised version, Paris Muzio Clementi, Ital. composer and pianist ("Gradus ad Parnassum"), d. (b. 1752) Leopold Damrosch, Ger.-Amer. conductor, b. (d. 1885) Donizetti: "L'Elisir d'Amore," Milan, Teatro della Canobbiana Manuel García, Span. tenor composer and singing teacher, father of three famous singers: María Malibran, Michelle Viardot, and Manuel García, Jr., d. (b. 1775) Ferdinand Hérold: "Le Pré aux clercs," Paris Karl Friedrich Zelter, Ger. composer and conductor, Goethe's friend and musical adviser, d. (b. 1758)	Nicolas Carnot, Fr. physicist, pioneered in the Second Law of Thermodynamics, d. (b. 1796) Sir William Crookes, Eng. physicist and chemist, b. (d. 1919) Baron Georges Cuvier, Fr. naturalist, founder of comparative anatomy, d. (b. 1769) Faraday proposes pictorial representation of electric and magnetic lines of force The first French railroad line, from St. Etienne to Andrézieux (opened 1828), begins to carry passengers Manufacture of friction matches well established in Europe Isaac Israel Hayes, Amer. Arctic explorer, b. (d. 1881) Hungarian mathematician János Bolyai (1802—1860) publishes his system of non-Euclidean geometry Rodolphe Koenig, Fr.-Ger. physicist and acoustician, b. (d. 1901) Nils A. E. Nordenskjöld, Swed. explorer of Spitzbergen and Greenland, Northeast Passage, b. (d. 1901) Reichenbach discovers creosote in wood tar Antonio Scarpa, Ital. anatomist (aural researches), d. (b. 1747) J. K. Spurzheim, Ger. physician, founder (with Franz Gall) of phrenology, d. (b. 1776) Armin Vámbéry, Hungarian writer and traveler (real name Hermann Bamberger), some feats doubted, b. (d. 1913)	New England Anti-Slavery Society founded in Boston Charles Carroll of Carrollton, last surviving signer of Declaration of Independence, d. (b. 1737) Moncure D. Conway, Amer. abolitionist and journalist, b. (d. 1907) First horse-drawn trolleys in New York	**1832**

	A. HISTORY, POLITICS	B. LITERATURE, THEATER	C. RELIGION, PHILOSOPHY, LEARNING
1833	Charles G. Gordon ("Chinese Gordon"), Brit. soldier, b. (d. 1885 at the fall of Khartoum) Prince Otto (1815—1867), second son of King Louis I of Bavaria, arrives in Nauplia to occupy the newly erected throne of Greece as King Otto (—1862) John Randolph of Roanoke, Virginia planter, U.S. senator and representative, flamboyant orator, d. (b. 1773) Benjamin Harrison, 23rd President of the U.S., b. (d. 1901) William IV grants Hanover a new liberal constitution Isabella II (1830—1904) proclaimed Queen of Spain, with her mother Maria Christina as regent General Antonio López de Santa Anna becomes President of Mexico; country threatened by civil war Beginning of Whig Party in America Mehemet Ali is given Egypt and Syria; founds the dynasty that rules Egypt until 1952 President Jackson moves against the Bank of U.S. (withdrawal of all governmental deposits) All German states join the Zollverein (customs union)	Pedro Antonio de Alarcón, Span. novelist, b. (d. 1891) Balzac: "Eugénie Grandet" Bestseller: Davy Crockett's autobiography Edwin Booth, Anglo-Amer. actor, b. (d. 1893) Robert Browning: "Pauline" Charles Dickens: "Sketches by Boz," published in "Monthly Magazine" (from 1835 in "Evening Chronicle") Joseph von Eichendorff: "The Wooers" ("Die Freier"), romantic comedy (first performance in 1849) Edmund C. Erdman, Amer. poet, b. (d. 1908) Adam Lindsay Gordon, Australian poet, b. (d. 1870) Edmund Kean, one of England's greatest actors, d. (b. 1787) Lamb: "Last Essays of Elia" Longfellow: "Outre-Mer" Sir Lewis Morris, Welsh poet, "The Epic of Hades," b. (d. 1907) Johann Nestroy: "Lumpaziva gabundus," farce George Sand: "Lélia" The great Ger. Shakespeare translation (begun in 1794) by A. W. von Schlegel in collaboration with Ludwig and Dorothea Tieck and W. von Baudissin completed	Franz Bopp: "Vergleichende Grammatik" Charles Bradlaugh, Eng. reformer and free-thought leader, b. (d. 1891) Wilhelm Dilthey, Ger. Kantian philosopher, b. (d. 1911) Henry Fawcett, Eng. economist and statesman, b. (d. 1884) Anselm Feuerbach, Ger. jurist and criminal law reformer, d. (b. 1775) H. H. Furness, Amer. scholar who began "Variorum Shakespeare," b. (d. 1912) Robert G. Ingersoll, Amer. lawyer and agnostic, b. (d. 1899) Adrien Legendre, Fr. mathematician, d. (b. 1752) Hannah More, Eng. religious writer, d. (b. 1745) Edward Bouverie Pusey (1800—1882) begins his association with the Oxford Movement
1834	The Ger. Zollverein (customs union) begins to operate Lord Grenville, Brit. statesman, d. (b. 1754) Grand National Consolidated Trades Union, led by Robert Owen, formed Jan.; collapses Oct. Lord Palmerston, Brit. Foreign Secretary, contrives Quadruple Alliance with France, Spain, and Portugal General Lafayette, Fr. soldier and statesman, hero of the Amer. Revolution, d. (b. 1757) Spanish Inquisition, begun during 13th century, finally suppressed Viscount Melbourne (1764—1845) becomes Prime Minister of Great Britain in July; followed in Dec. by Sir Robert Peel (1786—1850) South Australia Act allows establishment of colony there Maria II (1819—1853) ascends throne of Portugal William IV, disapproving of Melbourne's Ir. church policy, dismisses ministry Monopoly of the China trade by the East India Company abolished; friction between China and Britain Sixth Kaffir War (—1835); severe clashes between Bantu people and White settlers on eastern frontier of Cape Colony Dutch farmers of the Cape Colony begin to settle in the country north of Orange River Daniel O'Connell's motion to repeal Union with Great Britain defeated 523 to 38 Carlist Wars begin in Spain President Jackson censured by Senate for removing deposits from the Bank of the U.S. (see 1833) Abraham Lincoln (at 25) enters politics as assemblyman in the Illinois legislature	Balzac: "Le Père Goriot" George Bancroft (1800-1891): "History of the United States" appears (first vol.; second in 1837; third in 1840) Bestseller: Victor Hugo, "The Hunchback of Notre Dame" William Blackwood, Eng. writer, d. (b. 1776) Edward Bulwer-Lytton (1803—1873): "The Last Days of Pompeii," novel Samuel Taylor Coleridge, Eng. poet and literary critic, d. (b. 1772) Felix Dahn, Ger. novelist and historian, b. (d. 1912) Disraeli: "The Infernal Marriage" Leigh Hunt: "London Journal" Charles Lamb, Eng. essayist, d. (b. 1775) Frederick Marryat: "Peter Simple" The last of Thomas Moore's "Irish Melodies" (begun in 1808) appear William Morris, Eng. poet and artist, b. (d. 1896) Alfred de Musset: "Lorenzaccio" Pushkin: "The Queen of Spades," short story J. H. Shorthouse, Eng. novelist, b. (d. 1903) Frank R. Stockton, Amer. fiction writer, b. (d. 1902) Artemus Ward, pen name of Charles Farrar Browne, Amer. humorous writer, b. (d. 1867)	Lord Acton, Eng. historian, founder of the "Cambridge Modern History," b. (d. 1902) Charles W. Eliot, Amer. educator, president of Harvard University, b. (d. 1926) James Cardinal Gibbons, Roman Catholic prelate, Archbishop of Baltimore, b. (d. 1921) Ernst Haeckel, Ger. philosopher and zoologist, b. (d. 1919) Leopold von Ranke: "Die römischen Päpste" ("The Roman Popes") Friedrich D. E. Schleiermacher, Ger. theologian and philosopher, d. (b. 1768) Sir John Seeley, Eng. historian, b. (d. 1895) Charles H. Spurgeon, Eng. Baptist preacher, b. (d. 1892) Heinrich von Treitschke, Ger. historian, b. (d. 1896) William Wirt, Amer. jurist, Attorney-General of the U.S., d. (b. 1772) Thomas Robert Malthus, Eng. economist, d. (b. 1766)

D. VISUAL ARTS	E. MUSIC	F. SCIENCE, TECHNOLOGY, GROWTH	G. DAILY LIFE	
Edward Burne-Jones, Eng. painter and designer, b. (d. 1898) Raffaello Morghen, Ital. engraver, d. (b. 1758) Felician Rops, Belg. painter and engraver, b. (d. 1898) First Venetian pictures by Turner at Royal Academy, London	Johannes Brahms, Ger. composer, b. (d. 1897) Chopin: Twelve Etudes, Op. 10 Heinrich Marschner: "Hans Heiling," romantic opera, Berlin Mendelssohn: "Italian Symphony," Op. 90, London	K. F. Gauss and Wilhelm E. Weber devise the electromagnetic telegraph which functions over a distance of 9,000 feet "The Handbook of Human Physiology" by Johannes Peter Müller (1801—1858) completed 1840 Henry E. Roscoe, Eng. chemist, b. (d. 1915) Richard Trevithick, Eng. engineer and inventor who built first steam-powered vehicle to carry passengers (1801), d. (b. 1771) Wheatstone bridge, for the comparison of electric resistances, inductances, and capacitances, devised by S. H. Christie; used for the first time in 1847 by Sir Charles Wheatstone	Brit. Factory Act provides a system for factory inspection Scot. explorer Alexander Burnes (1805—1841) crosses Hindu Kush mountain range in Central Asia Charity bazaars become popular in England Daniel Douglas-Home, Scot. medium, b. (d. 1886) Ger. economist Friedrich List (1789—1846) advocates extension of Ger. railroad system "New York Sun," the first successful penny daily, founded Alfred Nobel, Swed. chemist and engineer, donor of the Nobel Prize Fund, b. (d. 1896) Olympic Club of Philadelphia organizes two "Town Ball" teams Sir John Ross (1777—1856) returns from his second Arctic expedition (discovery of magnetic North Pole) Canadian S.S. "Royal William" crosses the Atlantic in 25 days Abolition of slavery in Brit. Empire General Trades Union in New York (—1837)	**1833**
Rudolph Ackermann, Anglo-Ger. lithographer, d. (b. 1764) F. A. Bartholdi, Fr. sculptor (Statue of Liberty, New York Harbor), b. (d. 1904) Edgar Dégas, Fr. impressionist painter, b. (d. 1917) George du Maurier, Fr.-Eng. artist and novelist, b. (d. 1896) The Munich Glyptothek (sculpture gallery), earliest of all special museum buildings, designed by Leo von Klenze (1784—1864) finished (begun in 1816) Ingres: "Martyrdom of Saint Symphorian," painting, Autun Cathedral Aloys Senefelder, Ger. inventor of lithography, d. (b. 1771) Thomas Stothard, Eng. illustrator and painter, d. (b. 1755) James Abbot McNeill *(contd)*	Adolphe Adam: "Le Chalet," Paris John Barnett: "The Mountain Sylph," opera, London Berlioz: "Harold en Italie," symphony based on Byron's "Childe Harold," Op. 16, Paris François-Adrien Boieldieu, Fr. opera composer, d. (b. 1775) Aleksandr Porfyrevich Borodin, Russ. composer, b. (d. 1887) Fanny Elssler (1810—1884), Aust. ballerina, makes her sensational debut at the Paris Opéra ("La Tempête") Konradin Kreutzer: "Das Nachtlager in Granada" ("The Night Camp at Granada"), *(contd)*	François Arago: "Astronomie populaire" Eng. mathematician Charles Babbage (1792—1871) invents the principle of the "analytical engine" (modern computer) Christian Leopold von Buch (1774—1853) publishes his "Theory of Volcanism" Faraday: "Law of Electrolysis" Samuel P. Langley, Amer. airplane pioneer, b. (d. 1906) The Amer. inventor Cyrus Hall McCormick (1809—1884) patents his reaping machine Dmitri Ivanovich Mendeleyev, Russ. chemist, b. (d. 1907) Ger. chemist F. F. Runge (1795—1853) discovers phenol, or carbolic acid Swiss mathematician Jakob Steiner (1796—1863), one of the founders of modern synthetic geometry, appointed professor at Berlin University Sir Charles Wheatstone (1802—1875) uses revolving mirror to measure the speed of electric discharge in a conductor	The Castle Garden Boat Club Association, first Amer. organization of amateur rowing clubs, formed in New York Robin Carver: "Book of Sports" (Boston, Mass.), the first Amer. book on baseball Chauncey M. Depew, Amer. lawyer and wit, b. (d. 1928) Disastrous fire in the Brit. Houses of Parliament Bavarian civil servant Franz Xaver Gabelsberger (1789—1849) publishes his system of Ger. shorthand Two-wheeled, one-horse Hansom cabs, designed by J. A. Hansom, introduced in London Walter Hunt of New York constructs one of the first sewing machines (vibrating arm with curved needle) Lloyd's Register of Shipping (published since 1764) placed under control of Lloyd's Register Society Arthur Orton, the false claimant to the Tichborne estates, b. (d. 1898) (see 1874) Poor Law Amendment Act decrees that no able-bodied man in Great Britain shall receive assistance unless he enters a workhouse University of Brussels founded	**1834**

	A. HISTORY, POLITICS	B. LITERATURE, THEATER	C. RELIGION, PHILOSOPHY, LEARNING
1834 contd			
1835	Francis II, the last Holy Roman Emperor (1792—1806), Emperor of Austria as Francis I, d. (b. 1768) Ferdinand I (1793—1875), eldest son of Francis II, becomes Emperor of Austria (abdicates in 1848) Christian Gunther von Bernstorff, Prussian statesman, d. (b. 1769) Henri Brisson, Fr. statesman, b. (d. 1912) Prince Matsukata, Jap. statesman, b. (d. 1924) Richard Olney, Amer. statesman, b. (d. 1917) Fitzhugh Lee, Amer. general in Span.-Amer. War, b. (d. 1905) The Municipal Corporation Act revolutionizes borough government in England Marquis Inouye, Jap. statesman, b. (d. 1915) Tomas Estrada Palma, first President of Cuba, b. (d. 1908) Riaz Pasha, Egyptian statesman, b. (d. 1911) Sir George S. White, Brit. Field Marshal in Boer War (defender of Ladysmith), b. (d. 1912) Second Seminole War (till 1842) Texas declares its right to secede from Mexico	Hans Christian Andersen publishes the first four of his 168 tales for children Alfred Austin, Brit. poet laureate, b. (d. 1913) Bestseller: William Wordsworth, "Poems" Robert Browning: "Paracelsus" Bulwer-Lytton: "Rienzi," novel Samuel Butler, Eng. novelist and critic, b. (d. 1902) William Cobbett, Eng. man of letters, d. (b. 1762) Emile Gaboriau, Fr. writer of detective fiction, b. (d. 1873) Mrs. Felicia Hemans, Eng. poet, d. (b. 1793) James Hogg, Scot. poet (the "Ettrick Shepherd"), d. (b. 1770) Wilhelm von Humboldt, Ger. man of letters and diplomat, d. (b. 1767) William Henry Ireland, forger of "Shakespearean" plays ("Vortigern"), d. (b. 1793) J. P. Kennedy: "Horse Shoe Robinson," novel of the Revolutionary War Charles Mathews, Eng. comedian, d. (b. 1776) Adah Isaacs Menken, Amer. poet and actress, b. (d. 1868) Leopold von Sacher-Masoch, Ger. novelist and eccentric ("Masochism"), b. (d. 1895) William Gilmore Simms (1806—1870): "The Yemassee," novel of the Indians Mark Twain (Samuel Langhorne Clemens), Amer. novelist and humorist, b. (d. 1910) An edict of the Ger. Federal Diet bans the books of Heine, Börne, Gutzkow, and other "Young Germany" writers Giosuè Carducci, Ital. poet, 1906 Nobel Prize, b. (d. 1907)	Lyman Abbott, Amer. preacher, b. (d. 1922) Phillips Brooks, Amer. Episcopal bishop, b. (d. 1893) Edward Caird, Scot. philosopher, master of Balliol College, Oxford, b. (d. 1908) F. G. Dahlmann (1785—1860), Ger. historian, publishes his fundamental treatise, "Politics, traced back to the elements and extents of the given conditions" Charles G. Finney, Amer. evangelist (1792—1875): "Lectures on Revivals of Religion" Sir Archibald Geikie, Scot. geologist, b. (d. 1924) William T. Harris, Amer. philosopher, editor of "Webster's New International Dictionary," b. (d. 1909) Viktor Hensen, Ger. physiologist ("Hensen cells" in the ear), b. (d. 1924) W. S. Jevons, Eng. economist and logician, b. (d. 1882) John Marshall, Amer. jurist, Chief Justice of Supreme Court, d. (b. 1755) Simon Newcomb, Amer. astronomer, b. (d. 1909) Giovanni Schiaparelli, Ital. astronomer, b. (d. 1910) W. W. Skeat, Eng. philologist, b. (d. 1912) David Friedrich Strauss (1808—1874), Ger. theologian: "The Life of Jesus"
1836	Davy Crockett, Amer. frontiersman and politician, killed at the Alamo (b. 1786) Texas wins independence from Mexico and becomes a republic with General Sam Houston as first president Joseph G. Cannon, Amer. politician, b. (d. 1926) Edward Livingston, Amer. statesman, d. (b. 1764) The People's Charter initiates the first national working-class movement in Great Britain; Chartism demands universal suffrage and vote by ballot Arkansas admitted to the Union *(contd)*	T. B. Aldrich, Amer. author ("Story of a Bad Boy"), b. (d. 1907) Sir Walter Besant, Eng. novelist, b. (d. 1901) Bestseller: Frederick Marryat, "Mr. Midshipman Easy" Sir Francis Burnand, Eng. dramatist and editor of "Punch," b. (d. 1917) Carlyle: "Sartor Resartus" Dickens: "Pickwick Papers," serialized 1837 J. P. Eckermann (1792—1854), Ger. writer, begins publication of his "Conversations with Goethe" W. S. Gilbert, Eng. librettist and satirist, b. (d. 1911) *(contd)*	Ralph Waldo Emerson (1803—1882): "Nature," published in Boston Joseph von Görres (1778—1848), the Ger. Catholic writer, begins his monumental work "Christian Mysticism" (—1842) James Mill, Scot. historian and philosopher, d. (b. 1773) Ramakrishna, Hindu saint and teacher, b. (d. 1886) Schopenhauer: "Über den Willen in der Natur" *(contd)*

D. VISUAL ARTS	E. MUSIC	F. SCIENCE, TECHNOLOGY, GROWTH	G. DAILY LIFE	
Whistler, Anglo-Amer. painter, b. (d. 1903) Eng. architect William Wilkins (1778—1839) begins building the National Gallery, London	romantic opera, Vienna Sir Charles Santley, Eng. baritone, b. (d. 1922)			**1834 contd**
The expression "L'Art pour l'Art" (Art for Art's sake), coined by Fr. philosopher Victor Cousin (1792—1867), comes into general use Constable: "The Valley Farm," Tate Gallery, London Corot: "Hagar in the Desert," Salon, Paris Franz Defregger, Aust. genre painter, b. (d. 1921) John La Farge, Amer. painter, b. (d. 1910) Baron A. J. Gros, Fr. historical painter, d. (b. 1771)	Vincenzo Bellini, Ital. composer, d. (b. 1801) César Cui, Russ. composer, one of the "Great Five," b. (d. 1918) Donizetti: "Lucia di Lammermoor," opera, Naples, Teatro San Carlo Halévy: "La Juive," Paris, Opéra Camille Saint-Saëns, Fr. composer, b. (d. 1921) Theodore Thomas, Ger.-Amer. conductor, b. (d. 1905) Henri Wieniawski, Pol. violinist and composer, b. (d. 1880)	Paul du Chaillu, Fr. explorer in Africa, b. (d. 1903) Halley's Comet reappears The first efforts to propel railroad vehicles by electric batteries; first successful application of electric traction 1879	U.S. showman Phineas Taylor Barnum (1810—1891) begins his career with the exhibition of Joyce Heth, a Black woman, alleged to be George Washington's nurse and over 160 years old James Gordon Bennet (1795—1872) publishes the first number of his four-page penny paper, "N.Y. Herald" Andrew Carnegie, Amer. industrialist, b. (d. 1919) Charles Chubb patents burglar-proof safe (see 1818) Samuel Colt (1814—1865) takes out Eng. patent for his single-barreled pistol and rifle Marshall Field, Amer. merchant and publisher, b. (d. 1906) First Ger. railroad line opens between Nuremberg and Furth Hetty Green, "the richest woman in the world," a notorious miser, b. (d. 1916) Melbourne, Australia, founded 1,098 miles of railroad in use in America "Lacock Abbey, Wiltshire," the earliest negative photograph, taken in England by Wm. Henry Fox Talbot (1800—1877)	**1835**
Lawrence Alma-Tadema, Dutch-Eng. painter, b. (d. 1912) Corot: "Diana Surprised by Actaeon," Paris, Salon Henri Fantin-Latour, Fr. painter, b. (d. 1904) Winslow Homer, Amer. painter, b. (d. 1910) Franz von Lenbach, Ger. portrait painter, b. (d. 1904) Homer D. Martin, Amer. *(contd)*	Adolphe Adam: "Le Postillon de long jumeau," Paris, Opéra-Comique Leo Delibes, Fr. composer, b. (d. 1891) Glinka: "A Life for the Tzar," first Russ. opera, St. Petersburg Maria Malibran, Fr.-Span. soprano, d. (b. 1808) Mendelssohn: "St. Paul," oratorio, Düsseldorf *(contd)*	A. M. Ampère, Fr. physicist, d. (b. 1775) Ernst von Bergmann, Ger. surgeon, b. (d. 1907) John Frederic Daniell (1790—1845) develops a voltaic cell which effectively prevents polarization Edmond Davey discovers and identifies acetylene Swed.-Amer. inventor John Ericsson (1803—1889) patents screw propeller *(contd)*	Adelaide, South Australia, founded The first cricket match, North versus South, played in London Jay Gould, Amer. financier, b. (d. 1892) "The Lancers" becomes the fashionable dance throughout Europe Amer. patent for the manufacture of white phosphorus matches granted to A. D. Phillips Betsy Ross, reputed maker of the first Amer. flag (June 1776), d. (b. 1752)	**1836**

	A. HISTORY, POLITICS	B. LITERATURE, THEATER	C. RELIGION, PHILOSOPHY, LEARNING
1836 contd	James Madison, fourth President of the U.S., d. (b. 1751) Joseph Chamberlain, Brit. statesman, b. (d. 1914) Sir Henry Campbell-Bannerman, Brit. Liberal statesman, b. (d. 1908) Aaron Burr, Amer. vice president and intriguer, d. (b. 1756) Charles Louis Napoleon Bonaparte (1808—1873) tries to bring about a revolt of the garrison at Strasbourg and is banished to America Boer farmers launch "The Great Trek" (systematic emigration across the Orange River) away from Brit. rule; founding of Natal, Transvaal, and Orange Free State	William Godwin, Eng. novelist and philosopher, d. (b. 1756) Gogol: "The Government Inspector," comedy Bret Harte, Amer. novelist, b. (d. 1902) Orpheus C. Kerr (R. H. Newell), Amer. humorist, b. (d. 1901) Alfred de Musset: "Confession d'un enfant du siècle," autobiographical novel Fritz Reuter, the Plattdeutsch novelist (1810—1874), condemned to death for high treason; the sentence commuted to imprisonment for 30 years in a Prussian fortress C. J. Rouget de Lisle, Fr. soldier and poet who wrote lyrics and music of "La Marseillaise" (1792), d. (b. 1760)	("On the Will in Nature") Roger B. Taney (1777-1864) becomes fifth Chief Justice of U.S. Supreme Court
1837	William IV, King of Great Britain, d. (b. 1765); his death terminates personal union between Great Britain and Hanover Michigan becomes a state of the U.S. Mazzini arrives in London as an exile Martin Van Buren (1782—1862) inaugurated as eighth President of the U.S. Grover Cleveland, twice President of the U.S., b. (d. 1908) Count Taisuke Itagaki, Jap. liberal statesman, b. (d. 1919) Friedrich von Holstein, Ger. statesman, b. (d. 1909) Georges Boulanger, Fr. soldier and popular hero, b. (suicide 1891) Victoria (1819—1901) becomes Queen of Great Britain Sadi Carnot, fourth President of the Fr. Republic, b. (assassinated 1894) Benjamin Disraeli delivers his maiden speech in the House of Commons U.S.S. "Caroline" is set on fire and sunk by Canadian troops while transporting supplies to Canadian insurgents across Niagara River Ernst Augustus (1771—1851), successor to William IV as King of Hanover, cancels constitution of 1833 and dismisses seven professors of Göttingen University who protest against his action Constitutional revolts in Lower and Upper Canada Sitting Bull, Amer.-Indian chief, b. (killed 1890) Osman Pasha, Turk. general and statesman, b. (d. 1901)	Balzac: "Illusions perdues" Best seller: Nathaniel Hawthorne, "Twice-told Tales" Ludwig Börne, Ger. political writer and satirist, d. (b. 1786) Mary Elizabeth Braddon, Eng. bestselling novelist, b. (d. 1915) Edward Eggleston, Amer. writer ("The Hoosier Schoolmaster"), b. (d. 1902) Georg Ebers, Ger. novelist and Egyptologist, b. (d. 1898) William Dean Howells, Amer. novelist and critic, b. (d. 1920) Lamartine: "Chute d'un ange," epic poem Giacomo Leopardi, Ital. poet, d. (b. 1798) William H.Prescott (1796—1859): "The History of the Reign of Isabella and Ferdinand" Aleksandr Sergeyevich Pushkin, mortally wounded in a duel, d. (b. 1799) Algernon Charles Swinburne, Eng. poet, b. (d. 1909) Sir Charles Wyndham, Eng. actor and theatrical manager, b. (d. 1919)	Founding of the University of Athens Bernhard Bolzano (1781—1848): "Wissenschaftslehre" ("The Philosophy of Logic") Thomas Carlyle: "The French Revolution" Henry T. Colebrooke, Eng. Sanskrit scholar, d. (b. 1765) Friedrich Fröbel (1782—1852), Ger. educational reformer, opens his first kindergarten in the village of Blankenburg, Thuringia J. R. Green, Eng. historian, b. (d. 1883) Mount Holyoke Female Seminary opens, Mary Mason Lyon (1797—1849) founder and principal Horace Mann (1796—1859) begins educational reforms in Massachusetts Dwight L. Moody, Amer. evangelist, b. (d. 1899) Sir James Murray, Scot. philologist, editor of the Oxford English Dictionary, b. (d. 1915) Amer. Presbyterians split into the "old" and "new" school

D. VISUAL ARTS	E. MUSIC	F. SCIENCE, TECHNOLOGY, GROWTH	G. DAILY LIFE	
landscape painter, b. (d. 1877) Sir Edward Poynter, Eng. painter, b. (d. 1919) James Tissot, Fr. painter, b. (d. 1902) Carle Vernet, Fr. painter, d. (b. 1758)	Meyerbeer: "Les Huguenots," Paris, Opéra Richard Wagner marries Minna Planer in Magdeburg	which is tried (1837) on the London-built S.S. "Francis B. Ogden" Asa Gray: "Elements of Botany," first botanical textbook Sir Norman Lockyer, Eng. astronomer, b. (d. 1920) Patent Arms Manufacturing Company of Paterson, N.Y., formed to manufacture and sell revolvers and rifles J. L. McAdam, Brit. engineer, originator of crushed-stone (macadam) roads, d. (b. 1756) Pepsin, the powerful ferment in gastric juice, recognized by the Ger. physiologist Theodor Schwann (1810—1882) George A. Schweinfurth, Ger. traveler in Africa (discovered pygmies), b. (d. 1925) Ger. botanist K. F. Schimper (1803—1867) begins researches into the pleistocene epoch		**1836 contd**
John Constable, Eng. landscape painter, d. (b. 1776) Carolus-Duran (C.A.E. Durand), Fr. portraitist, b. (d. 1917) Baron François Gérard, Fr. portrait painter, d. (b. 1770) Alphonse Legros, Fr.-Eng. painter and etcher, b. (d. 1911) Hans von Marées, Ger. painter, b. (d. 1887)	Auber: "Le Domino noir," Paris, Opéra-Comique Mily Balakirev, Russ. composer, founder of the "Great Five" group, b. (d. 1910) Berlioz: "Grande Messe des Morts," Op. 5, Paris Théodore Dubois, Fr. composer and organist, b. (d. 1924) John Field, Eng. pianist and composer, d. (b. 1782) Johann Nepomuk Hummel, Austro-Hungarian composer and pianist, d. (b. 1778) J. F. Lesueur, Fr. composer, d. (b. 1760) Lortzing: "Zar und Zimmermann" ("Czar and Carpenter"), Leipzig Cosima, daughter of Franz Liszt, second wife of Richard Wagner, b. (d. 1930) Emile Waldteufel, Fr. waltz and dance composer, b. (d. 1915) Nicola Zingarelli, Ital. composer, choirmaster of St. Peters, Rome, d. (b. 1752)	Ger. industrialist August Borsig (1804—1854) opens his iron foundry and engine-building factory in Berlin John Burroughs, Amer. naturalist, b. (d. 1921) Wheatstone and W. F. Cooke patent electric telegraph Wilhelm Kuhne, Ger. physiologist, b. (d. 1900) Samuel Morse (1791—1872) exhibits his electric telegraph at the College of the City of New York Fr. mathematician Siméon D. Poisson (1781—1840) publishes his fundamental study, "Recherches sur la probabilité des jugements" Johannes Diderik van der Waals, Dutch physicist, 1910 Nobel Prize, b. (d. 1923)	The first boat race, sponsored by the Castle Garden Boat Club Association, held at Poughkeepsie, N.Y. First Canadian railroad England introduces official birth registration Mrs. Fitzherbert, morganatic wife of King George IV, d. (b. 1756) Gag Law, aimed at suppressing debate on slavery, passed by U.S. Congress Alonzo Mark Hanna, Amer. financier and president maker (McKinley), b. (d. 1904) E. P. Lovejoy, editor of abolitionist paper, murdered by mob in Alton, Ill. J. Pierpont Morgan, Amer. financier and banker, b. (d. 1913) Financial and economic panic in America (inflated land values, wildcat banking, paper speculation) Eng. teacher Isaac Pitman (1813—1897) publishes his manual "Stenographic Soundhand" Records of the 11-mile 220-yard Crick Run Race at Rugby School, Warwickshire, England, begun	**1837**

A. HISTORY, POLITICS — B. LITERATURE, THEATER — C. RELIGION, PHILOSOPHY, LEARNING

1838

A. HISTORY, POLITICS

Osceola, Indian leader in Second Seminole War, d. (b. 1804)
Léon Gambetta, Fr. statesman, b. (d. 1882)
Talleyrand, Fr. statesman, d. (b. 1754)
Queen Victoria's coronation
Battle of Blood River, Natal: Boers defeat Zulus
First Brit.-Afghan War (—1842)
Anti-Corn Law League established in Manchester by Richard Cobden and his friends
John Rodgers, ranking Amer. naval officer in war of 1812, d. (b. 1773)
Valeriano Weyler, Span. soldier and statesman, b. (d. 1930)
Sir Evelyn Wood, first Brit. Sirdar of Egyptian army, b. (d. 1919)

B. LITERATURE, THEATER

Elizabeth Barrett Browning (1806—1861): "The Seraphim and Other Poems"
Bulwer-Lytton: "The Lady of Lyons," London, Covent Garden
Adelbert von Chamisso, Ger. romantic poet, d. (b. 1781)
Augustin Daly, Amer. playwright and theatrical manager, b. (d. 1899)
Bestsellers: Dickens, "Oliver Twist" and "Nicholas Nickleby"
Victor Hugo: "Ruy Blas," verse play
Henry Irving, Eng. actor, b. (d. 1905)
P. A. M. de Villiers de L'Isle-Adam, Fr. man of letters, b. (d. 1889)
J. P. Kennedy: "Rob of the Bowl," novel of colonial Maryland
Rachel's debut at the Théâtre Français, Paris, in Corneille's "Horace"
E. P. Roe, Amer. bestselling novelist, b. (d. 1888)
Ger. writer and philosopher Gustav Schwab (1792—1850) publishes his collection, "Die schönsten Sagen des klassischen Altertums"
Horace E. Scudder, Amer. man of letters, editor of "The Atlantic Monthly," b. (d. 1902)
Thomas Creevey, Eng. diarist and gossip, d. (b. 1768)

C. RELIGION, PHILOSOPHY, LEARNING

Henry Adams, Amer. historian, b. (d. 1918)
Nathaniel Bowditch, Amer. mathematician and astronomer, author of "The New American Practical Navigator," d. (b. 1773)
Viscount Bryce, Brit. historian and diplomat, b. (d. 1922)
Fr. philosopher Auguste Comte (1798—1857) gives the basic social science of sociology its name
Montagu Corry, Lord Rowton, Eng. philanthropist, Disraeli's aide, b. (d. 1903)
W. E. H. Lecky, Ir. historian, b. (d. 1903)
Thomas R. Lounsbury, Amer. scholar and educator, b. (d. 1915)
Ernst Mach, Aust. physicist and philosopher, b. (d. 1916)
J. A. Möhler, Ger. historian of religion, d. (b. 1796)
Baron de Sacy, Fr. orientalist, d. (b. 1758)
Henry Sidgwick, Eng. philosopher, founder of Society for Psychical Research, b. (d. 1900)
Sir George Otto Trevelyan, Eng. historian and statesman, b. (d. 1928)

1839

A. HISTORY, POLITICS

Uruguay declares war against Argentina
Marchese Antonio de Rudini, Ital. statesman, b. (d. 1908)
Treaty of London settles the dispute between the Dutch and their former Belg. subjects
Outbreak of First Opium War between Britain and China (—1842)
Eugen Richter, Ger. liberal politician, Bismarck's most vehement opponent, b. (d. 1906)
Frederick IV, King of Denmark, d.; succeeded by his nephew Christian VIII (—1848)
The independent republic of Natal founded by the Boers
Abdul Mejid (1823—1861) becomes Sultan of Turkey
Ranjit Singh, Indian ruler, founder of Sikh kingdom, d. (b. 1780)
Stephen Van Rensselaer, Amer. politician and soldier, d. (b. 1764)
Pascual Cervera, Span. naval commander in Span.-Amer. War, b. (d. 1908)

B. LITERATURE, THEATER

Ludwig Anzengruber, Aust. playwright, b. (d. 1889)
Bestseller: Jared Sparks, "Life of Washington"
John Galt, Scot. novelist, d. (b. 1779)
James A. Herne, Amer. playwright and actor, b. (d. 1901)
Longfellow: "Hyperion" and "Voices of the Night"
William De Morgan, Eng. novelist, b. (d. 1917)
Ouida (Louise de la Ramée), Eng. novelist, b. (d. 1908)
Walter Pater, Eng. critic and essayist, b. (d. 1894)
Poe: "The Fall of the House of Usher"
W. M. Praed, Eng. poet of light and satirical verse, d. (b. 1802)
James Smith, joint author with his brother Horatio (1779—1849) of "Rejected Addresses," d. (b. 1775)
R. F. Armand Sully-Prudhomme, Fr. poet, 1901 Nobel Prize, b. (d. 1907)
Stendhal: "La Chartreuse de Parme"

C. RELIGION, PHILOSOPHY, LEARNING

Ger. philologist Franz Bopp (1791—1867) identifies Celtic as part of the Indo-European language family
Joseph Fesch, Fr. cardinal, half uncle of Napoleon I, d. (b. 1763)
Henry George, Amer. economist, b. (d. 1897)
August Kundt, Ger. physicist, b. (d. 1894)
Ludwig Mond, Ger.-Eng. chemist and industrialist, founded Mond Nickel Company, b. (d. 1909)
Gaston Paris, Fr. philologist, b. (d. 1903)
Charles S. Peirce, Amer. philosopher ("Pragmatism"), b. (d. 1914)
Thomas B. Reed, Amer. legislator, b. (d. 1902)
William Smith, Eng. geologist, d. (b. 1769)
Amer. traveler John Lloyd Stephens (1805—1852) discovers and examines (with Frederick Catherwood) the antiquities of the ancient Maya culture in Central America

D. VISUAL ARTS	E. MUSIC	F. SCIENCE, TECHNOLOGY, GROWTH	G. DAILY LIFE	
Jules Dalou, Fr. sculptor, b. (d. 1902) London National Gallery opened Anton Mauve, Dutch painter, b. (d. 1888) Charles Percier, Fr. architect under Napoleon, creator of the Empire style in decoration, d. (b. 1764) Henry Hobson Richardson, Amer. architect, b. (d. 1886) Bertel Thorvaldsen (1770—1844) completes his colossal series "Christ and the Twelve Apostles" for the Frauenkirche in Copenhagen (commissioned in 1819)	Berlioz: "Benvenuto Cellini," opera, Paris, Opéra Georges Bizet, Fr. composer, b. (d. 1875) Max Bruch, Ger. composer, b. (d. 1920) Chopin's liaison with George Sand begins (—1847) Jenny Lind makes debut in Stockholm (in Weber's "Der Freischütz")	Cleveland Abbe, Amer. meteorologist, b. (d. 1916) Fourth and last volume of series by John James Audubon (1785—1851): "The Birds of America" Ger. astronomer F. W. Bessel (1784—1846) makes the first definite parallax measurement for a fixed star William Clark, Amer. explorer (from upper Mississippi to Pacific), d. (b. 1770) Fr. economist A. A. Cournot (1801—1877): "Researches into the Mathematical Principles of the Theory of Wealth" The Daguerre-Niepce method of photography presented by the physicist François Arago to the Académie des Sciences and the Académie des Beaux Arts, Paris Pierre Dulong, Fr. chemist and physicist, d. (b. 1785) Alpheus Hyatt, Amer. naturalist and paleontologist, b. (d. 1902) John Muir, Scot.-Amer. naturalist, b. (d. 1914) Sir William H. Perkin, Eng. chemist, b. (d. 1907) John Stevens, Amer. inventor, pioneer in steam navigation, d. (b. 1749) Count Ferdinand von Zeppelin, Ger. airship designer, b. (d. 1917)	703-ton steamer "Sirius" sails with 100 passengers from London to New York; within a few hours of her arrival, the 1,440-ton steamer "Great Western" arrives after a crossing of 15 days from Bristol Octavia Hill, Eng. housing reformer, b. (d. 1912) Navy statistics: Great Britain has 90 ships of the line, Russia 50, France 49, America 15 "The New York Herald" is the first U.S. newspaper to employ European correspondents The first traveling post office, running between Birmingham and Liverpool, England John Wanamaker, Amer. department store innovator, b. (d. 1922) Victoria Woodhull, Amer. feminist, b. (d. 1927)	**1838**
Sir William Beechey, Eng. portrait painter, d. (b. 1753) Paul Cézanne, Fr. painter, b. (d. 1906) Joseph Anton Koch, Ger. landscape painter, d. (b. 1768) Alfred Sisley, Fr. impressionist painter, b. (d. 1899) Karl Spitzweg (1808—1885): "The Poor Poet" ("Der arme Poet"), one of the most famous genre paintings Hans Thoma, Ger. landscape painter, b. (d. 1924)	A. Carlos Gomez, Brazilian composer, b. (d. 1896) Modest Petrovich Moussorgsky, Russ. composer, b. (d. 1881) John K. Paine, Amer. musicologist and music teacher, b. (d. 1906) James Rider Randall, Amer. song writer ("Maryland, My Maryland"), b. (d. 1908) Mendelssohn conducts the first performance of Franz Schubert's Symphony in C major ("The Great"), composed in 1828, Leipzig, *(contd)*	Two Brit. ships, the "Erebus" and the "Terror," set out on their Antarctic voyage commanded by James C. Ross and F. R. M. Crozier François Garnier, Fr. explorer in China, b. (d. 1873) Charles Goodyear (1800—1860), Amer. inventor, makes possible the commercial use of rubber by his discovery of the process of "vulcanization" Moritz Jacobi of St. Petersburg, Russia, announces his process of electrotyping: making duplicate plates for relief printing Metallic element lanthanum discovered by Carl Gustav Mosander (1797—1858) N. M. Przhevalski, Russ. explorer in Central Asia, b. (d. 1888) Ger.-Swiss chemist Christian F. Schönbein (1799—1868) discovers and names ozone Theodor Schwann (1810—1882): cell-growth theory Swiss physicist Carl August Steinheil (1801—1870) builds the first electric clock	Amer. army officer Abner Doubleday lays out first baseball field and conducts first baseball game ever played (Cooperstown, Otsego County, N.Y.) First bicycle constructed by Scot. inventor Kirkpatrick Macmillan (1810—1878) Fr. political leader Louis Blanc (1811—1882) publishes his famous essay "L'Organisation du Travail" ("to each according to his needs, from each according to his abilities") Detroit Boat Club, oldest survivor of the early Amer. rowing clubs, formed George Cadbury, Eng. chocolate manufacturer and social reformer, b. (d. 1922) Samuel Cunard (1787—1865) starts, with his partners, the British and North-American Royal Mail Steam Packet Company (later known as Cunard Line) First Grand National run at Aintree, England Prussia restricts juvenile labor to a maximum of 10 hours a day Lowell Institute, Boston, founded by John Lowell, Jr., to provide free lectures by eminent scholars John D. Rockefeller, Amer. industrialist, b. (d. 1937) Lady Hester Stanhope, Eng. eccentric who settled among the Druses of Lebanon, *(contd)*	**1839**

	A. HISTORY, POLITICS	B. LITERATURE, THEATER	C. RELIGION, PHILOSOPHY, LEARNING
1839 contd			
1840	Queen Victoria of Great Britain marries Prince Albert of Saxe-Coburg-Gotha August Bebel, cofounder of the Ger. Social Democratic Party, b. (d. 1913) Frederick William III, King of Prussia since 1797, d. (b. 1770) Frederick William IV (b. 1795) succeeds to the throne of Prussia (d. 1861) Carlotta, wife of Emperor Maximilian of Mexico, b. (d. 1927) London Conference on Turko-Egyptian conflict signs the Protocol des Droits; straits closed to warships of all powers, Black Sea to Russ. warships Lower and Upper Canada united by Act of Parliament New conspiracy of Louis Napoleon Bonaparte followed by his imprisonment at the fortress of Ham (—1846) José Francia, dictator of Paraguay, d. (b. 1766) Alexandre Macdonald, Duc de Taranto, Napoleonic marshal, d. (b. 1765) William II (1792—1849) ascends the throne of the Netherlands after abdication of his father William I Afghan forces surrender to Brit. Army; end of Afghan War The ashes of Napoleon I deposited at the Invalides, Paris Lord Durham, the first Governor-General of Canada, d. (b. 1792) Édouard Vaillant, Fr. socialist politician, member of the Commune, b. (d. 1915) William T. Sampson, Amer. naval commander in Span.-Amer. War, b. (d. 1902) Sir W. S. Smith, Eng. admiral in Napoleonic wars, d. (b. 1755)	Bestseller: James Fenimore Cooper, "The Pathfinder" Wilfred S. Blunt, Eng. poet and traveler, b. (d. 1922) Rhoda Broughton, Eng. novelist, b. (d. 1920) Robert Browning: "Sordello" Fanny Burney, Eng. novelist ("Evelina"), d. (b. 1752) Alphonse Daudet, Fr. novelist, b. (d. 1897) Austin Dobson, Eng. man of letters, b. (d. 1921) Thomas Hardy, Eng. novelist and poet, b. (d. 1928) Friedrich Hebbel (1813—1863): "Judith," tragedy, Berlin L. J. Lemercier, Fr. dramatist, d. (b. 1771) Lermontov: "The Demon," poem, and "Geroï Nashevo Vremeni" ("A Hero of Our Times"), novel Manzoni republishes his romantic novel "I Promessi Sposi" ("The Betrothed") in a revised form in Tuscan dialect Prosper Mérimée: "Colomba," Corsican short story Helena Modjeska, Pol.-Amer. actress, b. (d. 1909) Fritz Reuter, Ger. poet, political prisoner since 1833, set free by general amnesty John Addington Symonds, Eng. poet and essayist, b. (d. 1893) Giovanni Verga, Ital. novelist ("Cavalleria Rusticana"), b. (d. 1922) Emile Zola, Fr. novelist, b. (d. 1902)	Sir Robert Ball, Ir. astronomer, b. (d. 1913) J. F. Blumenbach, Ger. botanist and originator of physical anthropology, d. (b. 1752) F. W. Kohlrausch, Ger. physicist, b. (d. 1910) London Library opened H. W. M. Olbers, Ger. astronomer, d. (b. 1758) Fr. socialist writer Pierre Joseph Proudhon (1809—1865) asks in the treátise of the same name the question "Qu'est-ce que la propriété?." answering it: "La propriété, c'est le vol" ("Property is theft") John C. Ridpath, Amer. popularizer of history and general knowledge, b. (d. 1900) Ira D. Sankey, Amer. evangelist, b. (d. 1908)

D. VISUAL ARTS	E. MUSIC	F. SCIENCE, TECHNOLOGY, GROWTH	G. DAILY LIFE	
	Gewandhaus		d. (b. 1776) W. H. Fox Talbot (1800-1877) claims that he obtained successes with his photographic experiments before Daguerre and communicates the results to the Royal Society George D. Weed's antislavery pamphlet, "Slavery As It Is" E. P. Weston, Amer. marathon walker, who at 70 walks from New York to San Francisco (3,895 miles), b. (d. 1928) Frances E. Willard, Amer. temperance worker and reformer, b. (d. 1898)	**1839 contd**
Sir Charles Barry begins the building of the Houses of Parliament in London (completed 1860) Delacroix: "Entry of the Crusaders into Constantinople," Louvre, Paris Caspar David Friedrich, Ger. romantic painter, d. (b. 1774) Hans Makart, Aust. painter, b. (d. 1884) Claude Monet, Fr. painter, b. (d. 1926) Alexander Nasmyth, Scot. landscape painter, d. (b. 1758) Thomas Nast, Amer. cartoonist, b. (d. 1902) Nelson's Column erected in Trafalgar Square, London (designed by William Railton, statue by E. H. Bailey) Pierre Auguste Renoir, Fr. impressionist painter, b. (d. 1919) Auguste Rodin, Fr. sculptor, b. (d. 1917)	Fr. instrument maker A. F. Debain (1809—1877) constructs the first harmonium (orgue expressif), patented in 1842 Donizetti: "La Fille du Régiment," Paris, Opéra-Comique Fanny Elssler, the Viennese dancer, tours the U.S. (—1842) Franz Xaver Haberl, Ger. musical scholar, b. (d. 1910) Nicolo Paganini, Ital. violinist and composer, d. (b. 1782) Robert Schumann marries Clara Wieck Peter Ilich Tchaikovsky, Russ. composer, b. (d. 1893) The Swabian merchant Max Schneckenburger (1819—1849) writes at the time of a Fr. invasion threat the poem "Wacht am Rhein" ("Watch on the Rhine"); set to music 14 years later by the conductor Carl Wilhelm (1815—1873) to become Germany's most popular patriotic song in the days of the Franco-Prussian war (1870—71)	Swiss naturalist Louis Agassiz (1807—1873) publishes his "Etudes sur les Glaciers," on the movements and effects of glaciers Ger. physician Karl A. von Basedow (1799—1854) describes exophthalmic toxic goiters (Basedow's or Graves' disease) Emin Pasha (Eduard Schnitzer), Ger. explorer in Africa, b. (d. 1892) Edward Whymper, Eng. mountaineer, first to gain top of Chimborazo (1880), b. (d. 1911) Liebig discovers the fundamentals of artificial fertilizer Sir Hiram Maxim, Anglo-Amer. inventor (Maxim gun), b. (d. 1916)	Beau Brummell (George Bryan Brummell), Eng. man of fashion and wit, d. (b. 1778) Blue Riband for the fastest crossing of the Atlantic awarded to S.S. "Britannia" Father Damien (J. de Veuster), who gave life to caring for lepers in Molokai, Hawaii, b. (d. 1889) During the following decade Connecticut, Massachusetts, and Pennsylvania pass laws limiting the hours of employment of minors in textile factories Botanical Gardens at Kew, London, opened Transportation of criminals from England to New South Wales comes to end The game of ninepins reaches peak of favor in America Penny postage established in Great Britain 2,816 miles of railroad in operation in U.S.; 1,331 in England Washington Temperance Society formed	**1840**

	A. HISTORY, POLITICS	B. LITERATURE, THEATER	C. RELIGION, PHILOSOPHY, LEARNING
1841	Bertrand Barère de Vieuzac, Fr. Revolutionary leader, d. (b. 1755) Lord Fisher, the future Brit. admiral, b. (d. 1920) Britain's sovereignty proclaimed over Hong Kong Luigi Luzzatti, Ital. statesman, b. (d. 1927) John X. Merriman, Eng.-born S. African statesman, b. (d. 1926) William Henry Harrison, ninth President of the U.S., dies one month after his inauguration (b. 1773) John Tyler (1790—1862), vice president, succeeds William H. Harrison to become tenth President of the U.S. General Baldomero Espartero becomes Regent of Spain Prince Ito Hirobumi, Jap. statesman and one of the creators of modern Japan, b. (d. 1909) Georges Clemenceau, Fr. statesman, b. (d. 1929) Edward, eldest son of Queen Victoria, future King Edward VII, b. (d. 1910) U.S.S. "Creole," carrying slaves from Virginia to Louisiana, is seized by the slaves and sails into Nassau where they become free Sir Wilfred Laurier, Canadian statesman, b. (d. 1919) New Zealand becomes Brit. colony Tyler's cabinet resigns; Daniel Webster remains Secretary of State Lord Melbourne (Whig) resigns as Brit. Prime Minister; succeeded by Sir Robert Peel (Tory) Lajos Kossuth (1802—1894) becomes Hungarian nationalist leader Turkey's sovereignty guaranteed by the five Great Powers	William Black, Scot. novelist, b. (d. 1898) Robert Browning: "Pippa Passes," play in verse Robert Buchanan, Brit. poet, b. (d. 1901) James Fenimore Cooper: "The Deerslayer," the opening of the Leather-Stocking Tales Benoît Coquelin, Fr. actor-manager (the first "Cyrano"), b. (d. 1909) Bestseller: Dickens, "The Old Curiosity Shop" Juliana Horatia Ewing, Eng. writer of children's books, b. (d. 1885) Jeremias Gotthelf (1797—1854): "Uli der Knecht" ("Uli the Farmhand"), Swiss folk tale Edward Rowland Hill, Amer. poet and essayist, b. (d. 1887) Theodore Hock, Brit. humorist and novelist, d. (b. 1788) W. H. Hudson, Eng. writer ("Green Mansions"), and naturalist, b. (d. 1922) Victor Hugo elected to the Académie Française Mikhail Yurievich Lermontov, Russ. poet and novelist, d. (b. 1814) James Russell Lowell (1819—1891): "A Year's Life," first vol. of poems Frederick Marryat: "Masterman Ready," adventure novel Catulle Mendès, Fr. poet, novelist, and playwright, b. (d. 1909) Jean Mounet-Sully, Fr. tragic actor, b. (d. 1916) Poe: "The Murders in the Rue Morgue," his first detective story, appears in "Graham's Magazine" The London humorous periodical "Punch" begins to appear Charles Sealsfield (K. A. Postl), Aust. writer (1793—1864): "Das Kajütenbuch" ("The Cabin Book"), an adventure novel with a Texan background Clement Scott, Brit. drama critic, b. (d. 1904) Joseph Blanco White, Brit. poet and theologian, d. (b. 1775)	Carlyle: "On Heroes, Hero-Worship and the Heroic in History" T. K. Cheyne, Eng. Biblical scholar, b. (d. 1915) Emerson: "Essays, First Series" Ludwig Feuerbach: "Das Wesen des Christentums" ("The Essence of Christianity") Johann Friedrich Herbart, Ger. philosopher and educator, d. (b. 1776) Oliver Wendell Holmes Jr., Amer. jurist, Justice of the U.S. Supreme Court, b. (d. 1935) H. E. von Holst, Ger.-born Amer. historian, b. (d. 1904) Sir Richard C. Jebb, Scot. classical scholar, b. (d. 1905) Lester F. Ward, Amer. sociologist, b. (d. 1913)
1842	Count C. A. Pozzo di Borgo, Corsican-born Russ. diplomat, d. (b. 1764) Count E. A. D. de Las Cases, Napoleon's companion on St. Helena, d. (b. 1766) Webster-Ashburton Treaty between Great Britain and the U.S. defines Canadian frontier Treaty of Nanking ends Opium War between Britain and China and confirms cession of Hong Kong to Great Britain Riots and strikes in the industrial areas in the north of England Marquis Wellesley, Brit. statesman, Governor of India, d. (b. 1760) Bernardo O'Higgins, liberator of Chile, d. (b. 1778) Giovanni Giolitti, Ital. statesman, b. (d. 1928) Orange Free State set up by the Boers	John Banim, Ir. poet and playwright, d. (b. 1798) Publication of Balzac's "La Comédie humaine" begins Bestseller: Eugene Sue, "The Mysteries of Paris" Ambrose Bierce, Amer. writer, b. (d. 1914) George Brandes, Dan. critic and scholar, b. (d. 1927) Clemens Brentano, Ger. poet and novelist, d. (b. 1778) Bulwer-Lytton: "Zanoni" Fanny Burney: "Diary and Letters" (posth.) Lady (Maria Dundas) Callcott, Brit. author, d. (b. 1785) François Coppée, Fr. poet and writer, b. (d. 1908) Allan Cunningham, Scot. poet, d. (b. 1784) Charles Dickens: "American Notes" José de Espronceda, Span. poet, d. (b. 1810) First part of Gogol's novel "Dead Souls" published George Washington Harris (1814—1869), a forerunner of Mark Twain, begins to publish his humorous tales in the New York periodical "Spirit of the Times" Bronson Howard, Amer. playwright, b. (d. 1908) Amer. author Washington Irving appointed U.S. ambassador to Spain Sidney Lanier, Amer. poet, b. (d. 1881) Longfellow: "Poems of Slavery" *(contd)*	Thomas Arnold, Eng. educator, headmaster of Rugby, d. (b. 1795) John Fiske, Amer. historian, b. (d. 1901) Eduard von Hartmann, Ger. philosopher, b. (d. 1906) Henry M. Hyndman, Brit. socialist reformer, b. (d. 1921) William James, Amer. philosopher and psychologist, b. (d. 1910) Prince Peter Kropotkin, Russ. anarchist and social philosopher, b. (d. 1921) Ernest Lavisse, Fr. historian, b. (d. 1922) Macaulay: "Lays of Ancient Rome" *(contd)*

D. VISUAL ARTS	E. MUSIC	F. SCIENCE, TECHNOLOGY, GROWTH	G. DAILY LIFE	
Sir Francis Chantrey, Eng. sculptor (Chantrey Bequest), d. (b. 1781) Berthe Morisot, Fr. painter, b. (d. 1905) Karl Friedrich Schinkel, Ger. architect, d. (b. 1781) Otto Wagner, Aust. architect, founder of modern reinforced concrete architecture, b. (d. 1918) Paul Wallot, codesigner (with Friedrich von Thiersch) of the Berlin Reichstag, b. (d. 1912) Sir David Wilkie, Scot. genre painter, d. (b. 1785)	Emmanuel Chabrier, Fr. composer, b. (d. 1894) T. J. Dibdin, Eng. prolific musician and dramatist, d. (b. 1771) Anton Dvorák, Czech composer, b. (d. 1904) Felipe Pedrell, Span. composer and musicologist, b. (d. 1922) Rossini: "Stabat Mater," Paris, Salle Herz Adolphe Sax (1814—1894), Belg. instrument maker invents the saxophone (patented 1846) Schumann: Symphony No. 1 in B-flat major, Op. 38 ("The Spring"), Leipzig Giovanni Sgambati, Ital. pianist and composer, b. (d. 1914)	Bessel deduces a value 1/299 for the ellipticity of the earth Scot. surgeon James Braid (1795—1860) discovers hypnosis Austin de Candolle, Swiss botanist, d. (b. 1778) C. J. Fritzsche shows that by treating indigo with potassium hydroxide it yields an oil (aniline) Emil Theodor Kocher, Swiss surgeon, 1909 Nobel Prize, b. (d. 1917) Swiss embryologist Rudolf Albert von Kölliker (1817—1905) describes the spermatozoa and contributes important evidence supporting the neuron doctrine Ger. economist Friedrich List (1789—1846) publishes his principal work, "The National System of Political Economy" Viennese mathematician Joseph Petzval (1807—1891) produces a photographic portrait lens with a speed of f/3.6 Sir Henry M. Stanley (John Rowlands), Eng. journalist and explorer in Africa, b. (d. 1904) Johann Eugenius Bülow Warming, Dan. botanist, b. (d. 1924) Eng. mechanical engineer Sir Joseph Whitworth (1803—1887) proposes standard screw threads	Barnum opens the "American Museum," an exhibition of freaks, curios, etc., in New York City First issue of George Bradshaw's Railway Guide Eng. travel agent Thomas Cook (1808—1892) arranges his first excursion to a temperance meeting at Loughborough, Leicestershire Sir Astley Cooper, Eng. surgeon, discoverer of method of treating aneurysm, d. (b. 1768) Amer. boxer Tom Hyer becomes first recognized champion Population statistics: Great Britain 18.5 million; America 17 million; Ireland 8 million "The New York Tribune" begins to appear The first university degrees granted to women in America	**1841**
John S. Cotman, Eng. landscape painter, d. (b. 1782) Vasili Vereshchagin, Russ. painter, b. (d. 1901) Marie Anne Elisabeth Vigée-Lebrun, Fr. portrait painter, d. (b. 1755)	Arrigo Boito, Ital. composer and librettist, b. (d. 1918) Luigi Cherubini, Ital. composer, d. (b. 1760) Glinka: "Russlan and Ludmilla," St. Petersburg Joseph Hopkinson, Amer. lawyer who wrote "Hail Columbia," d. (b. 1770) Lortzing: "Der Wildschütz" ("The Poacher"), Leipzig Jules Massenet, Fr. composer, b. (d. 1912) Meyerbeer-general musical director of the Royal Opera House, Berlin Karl Millöcker, Aust. operetta composer, b. (d. 1899) New York Philharmonic *(contd)*	Sir Charles Bell, Scot. anatomist, d. (b. 1774) Sir James Dewar, Scot. chemist, b. (d. 1923) Aust. physicist C. J. Doppler (1803—1853) publishes a paper "On the Colored Light of the Binary Stars" (Doppler effect) Camille Flammarion, Fr. astronomer, b. (d. 1925) Emil Hansen, Dan. microbiologist, b. (d. 1909) Joseph Henry's discovery of the oscillatory character of electrical discharge Amer. physician Crawford W. Long (1815—1878) uses ether to produce surgical anesthesia Amer. naval officer Matthew F. Maury (1806—1873) begins his researches in oceanography Ger. physicist Julius Robert von Mayer (1814—1878) publishes his paper "On the Forces of the Inanimate Nature" (beginnings of thermodynamics) Pierre Joseph Pelletier, Fr. chemist and codiscoverer of strychnine and quinine, d. (b. 1788) John William Strutt, Baron Rayleigh, Eng. physicist, 1904 Nobel Prize, b. (d. 1919) *(contd)*	Grace Darling, Eng. heroine, savior of nine persons in shipwreck, d. (b. 1815) Charity Davis, longest-lived Amer. woman, b. (d. 1961, aged 119 years 160 days) The polka, a lively dance of Czech origin, comes into fashion Boston and Albany connected by railroad Queen Victoria makes her first railroad journey, Windsor to Paddington, London	**1842**

	A. HISTORY, POLITICS	B. LITERATURE, THEATER	C. RELIGION, PHILOSOPHY, LEARNING
1842 contd		Samuel Lover: "Handy Andy" Steele Mackaye, Amer. actor, playwright, and producer, b. (d. 1894) William Maginn, Ir. man of letters, d. (b. 1793) Stéphane Mallarmé, Fr. poet, b. (d. 1898) Karl May, popular Ger. author of boy's stories, b. (d. 1912) "Einen Jux will er sich machen" ("He Wants to Have a Lark"), a Viennese farce by Johann Nestroy (1801—1862) first performed; used by Thornton Wilder as basis for his comedy "The Matchmaker" (1956) Poe: "The Masque of the Red Death" Antero de Quental, Port. poet, b. (d. 1891) Eugène Scribe: "Le Verre d'eau" ("A Glass of Water") Stendhal, Fr. novelist and essayist, d. (b. 1783) Samuel Woodworth, Amer. author, d. (b. 1784)	Alfred Marshall, Eng. economist, b. (d. 1924) Martin Tupper (1810—1889): "Proverbial Philosophy," second series George C. Robertson, Scot. philosopher, b. (d. 1892) Jean Simonde de Sismondi, Swiss historian, d. (b. 1773) Albert Sorel, Fr. historian, b. (d. 1906)
1843	William McKinley, 25th President of the U.S., b. (d. 1901) Teofilo Braga, first interim President of Portugal, poet and scholar, b. (d. 1924) Military revolt in Spain drives General Espartero from power: Isabella II (b. 1830) declared of age and Queen of Spain Maori revolts against Britain in New Zealand Sir Charles Dilke, Eng. politician, b. (d. 1911) Serbian Skupstina summons Prince Alexander Karageorgevich to the throne Daniel Webster retires as Secretary of State Andrew Johnson (1808—1875) elected to Congress Jefferson Davis (1808—1889), future Confederate leader, enters politics as delegate to Democratic State Convention in Jackson, Ala.	W. H. Ainsworth: "Windsor Castle," novel Robert Browning: "A Blot in the Scutcheon" Bulwer-Lytton: "The Last of the Barons" Carmen Sylva (Princess Elizabeth of Wied), future Queen of Rumania and writer, b. (d. 1916) Casimir Delavigne, Fr. poet and dramatist, d. (b. 1793) Dickens: "Martin Chuzzlewit" and "A Christmas Carol" C. M. Doughty, Eng. author, b. (d. 1926) Edward Dowden, Ir. critic, b. (d. 1913) D. D. Emmett (1815—1904) produces the first minstrel show Friedrich de la Motte-Fouqué, Ger. romantic author, d. (b. 1777) Friedrich Hölderlin, Ger. poet, d. (b. 1770) Thomas Hood: "Song of the Shirt" (in "Punch") R. H. Horne: "Orion" Henry James, Anglo-Amer. novelist, b. (d. 1916) William H. Prescott: "History of the Conquest of Mexico" Peter Rosegger, Aust. writer and poet, b. (d. 1918) Robert Southey, Eng. poet laureate, d. (b. 1774) Bertha von Suttner, Aust. writer and pacifist, 1905 Nobel Peace Prize, b. (d. 1914) Tennyson: "Morte d'Arthur," "Locksley Hall" William Wordsworth appointed Eng. poet laureate	Richard Avenarius, Ger. philosopher, b. (d. 1896) George Borrow: "The Bible in Spain" Richard Carlile, Eng. reformer, d. (b. 1790) Thomas Carlyle: "Past and Present" Mandell Creighton, Anglican Bishop of London ("History of the Papacy"), b. (d. 1901) Liddell and Scott: "Greek-English Lexicon" John Stuart Mill (1806—1873): "Logic" Noah Webster, Amer. lexicographer, d. (b. 1758) James Ward, Eng. philosopher and psychologist, b. (d. 1925)
1844	Sir Hudson Lowe, Napoleon's jailer at St. Helena, d. (b. 1769) J. B. Drouet d'Erlon, Fr. marshal, hero of the war in Algiers, d. (b. 1765) Charles XIV, King of Sweden and Norway since 1818, d. (b. 1763 as Jean Bernadotte); his son succeeds to the throne as Oscar I (—1859) Sanford B. Dole, Amer. pioneer in Hawaii, b. (d. 1926) Jacques Laffitte, Fr. financier and statesman, d. (b. 1767) Joseph Bonaparte, brother of Napoleon, d. (b. 1768) *(contd)*	Sarah Bernhardt, Fr. actress, b. (d. 1923) Bestseller: Dumas père, "Le Comte de Monte Cristo" Robert Bridges, Eng. poet laureate, b. (d. 1930) Elizabeth Barrett Browning: "Poems" George W. Cable, U.S. novelist, b. (d. 1925) Thomas Campbell, Brit. poet, d. (b. 1777) Richard D'Oyly Carte, Eng. theatrical manager for Gilbert and Sullivan, b. (d. 1901) Henry Francis Cary, Eng. translator of Dante, d. (b. 1772) Dickens: "The Chimes" Disraeli: "Coningsby," novel Anatole France (pseudonym for Jacques Anatole Thibault), Fr. novelist, 1921 Nobel Prize, b. (d. 1924) Friedrich Hebbel: "Maria Magdalena" Heinrich Heine: "Neue Gedichte" Gerard Manley Hopkins, Eng. poet, b. (d. 1889) *(contd)*	Anthony Comstock, U.S. reformer (Society for the Suppression of Vice), b. (d. 1915) Emerson: "Essays," second series Bishop Nikolai F. S. Grundtvig (1783—1872), Dan. poet and educator, founds the first institute for adult education G. Stanley Hall, U.S. psychologist, b. (d. 1924) J. S. Mill: "Essays on Some Unsettled Questions of Political Economy" *(contd)*

D. VISUAL ARTS	E. MUSIC	F. SCIENCE, TECHNOLOGY, GROWTH	G. DAILY LIFE	
	Society founded by violinist Ureli C. Hill and other Amer. professional musicians Sir Arthur Sullivan, Eng. composer, b. (d. 1900) Wagner: "Rienzi," Dresden	Gustaf Retzius, Swed. anatomist, b. (d. 1919)		**1842 contd**
Washington Allston, U.S. painter and writer, d. (b. 1779) John Ruskin (1819—1900): "Modern Painters," vol. 1 (—1860, 5 vols.) John Trumbull, U.S. painter, d. (b. 1756) Anton von Werner, Ger. painter of patriotic subjects, b. (d. 1915)	M. W. Balfe: "The Bohemian Girl," London, Drury Lane Donizetti: "Don Pasquale," Paris, Théâtre Italien Edward Grieg, Norw. composer, b. (d. 1907) Mendelssohn: music to Shakespeare's "A Midsummer Night's Dream" performed for the first time, Potsdam; overture, 1826 Christine Nilsson, Swed. coloratura soprano, b. (d. 1921) Adelina Patti, Span.-born Amer. soprano, b. (d. 1919) Hans Richter, Ger. conductor, b. (d. 1916) Schumann: "Das Paradies und die Peri" ("Paradise and the Peri"), secular oratorio, Leipzig Wagner: "Der fliegende Holländer" ("The Flying Dutchman"), Dresden	Brit. Archaeological Association and Royal Archaeological Institute of Great Britain and Ireland founded T. C. Chamberlin, U.S. geologist, b. (d. 1928) Sir David Ferrier, Scot. neurologist, b. (d. 1928) John C. Frémont crosses Rocky Mountains to California Samuel C. S. Hahnemann, founder of homeopathy, d. (b. 1755) Oliver Wendell Holmes: "The Contagiousness of Puerperal Fever" Alexander von Humboldt: "Asie centrale" (2 vols) Eng. physicist James Prescott Joule (1818-1889) determines the amount of work required to produce a unit of heat (mechanical equivalent of heat) Robert Koch, Ger. bacteriologist, 1905 Nobel Prize for Medicine, b. (d. 1910) Metallic element erbium discovered by C. G. Mosander The Thames Tunnel between Rotherhithe and Wapping, London, built by M. I. Brunel (1769—1849)	Slave population of Cuba estimated at 436,000 Amer. social reformer Dorothea Dix (1802—1887) reveals in a report to the Massachusetts legislature the shocking conditions in prisons and asylums London weekly financial paper "The Economist" founded by Sir James Wilson Guy's Hospital Football Club founded in London S.S. "Great Britain," first propeller-driven ship to cross the Atlantic, launched at Bristol docks Congress grants S. F. B. Morse $30,000 to build first telegraph line (Washington—Baltimore) World's first night club, "Le Bal des Anglais," opens in Paris Sequoya, Cherokee Indian leader, created Cherokee alphabet, d. (b. c. 1770) The conjoined Siamese twins Chang and Eng Bunker (1811—1874) marry the Misses Sarah and Adelaide Yates Beginning of skiing as sport (Tromso, Norway)	**1843**
Charles Bulfinch, U.S. architect, d. (b. 1763) Thomas Eakins, U.S. painter, b. (d. 1916) Moses Ezekiel, U.S. sculptor and musician, b. (d. 1917) Sir Luke Fildes, Eng. portrait painter, b. (d. 1927) Wilhelm Leibl, Ger. painter, b. (d. 1900) *(contd)*	Berlioz: "Traité de l'instrumentation et d'orchestration modernes" H. M. Berton, Fr. composer, d. (b. 1767) Flotow: "Alessandro Stradella," Hamburg Mendelssohn: Violin Concerto in E minor, Op. 64 Nikolai Andreyevich Rimsky-Korsakov, Russ. composer, b. (d. 1908) Pablo de Sarasate y Navascues, Span. violin virtuoso and composer, b. (d. 1908) *(contd)*	Hermann Günther Grassmann (1809—1877): Die Ausdehnungslehre (Calculus of extension) Francis Baily, Eng. astronomer, d. (b. 1774) Ludwig Boltzmann, Aust. physicist, b. (d. 1906) John Dalton, Eng. chemist and physicist, d. (b. 1766) G. W. De Long, Amer. Arctic explorer, b. (d. 1881) Camillo Golgi, Ital. physician, 1906 Nobel Prize for Medicine (with Ramon y Cahal), b. (d. 1926) *(contd)*	First public bath and wash houses opened in Liverpool, England William Beckford, Eng. eccentric, d. (b. 1759) Rochdale Society of Equitable Pioneers founded (beginning of modern cooperative movement) Ger. humorous weekly paper "Fliegende Blätter," Munich Karl Hagenbeck, Ger. animal trainer and circus director, founder of Hamburg zoo, b. (d. 1913) Wood-pulp paper invented by Friedrich Gottlob Keller (1816—1895) *(contd)*	**1844**

	A. HISTORY, POLITICS	B. LITERATURE, THEATER	C. RELIGION, PHILOSOPHY, LEARNING
1844 contd	Treaty of Tangier ends Fr. war in Morocco James Knox Polk (1795—1849) elected 11th President of the U.S. Military revolts in Mexico; José Joaquín de Herrera head of the military administration Karl Marx meets Friedrich Engels in Paris Revolts of the weavers in Silesia China and the U.S. sign first treaty of peace, amity, and commerce Texas annexation plan rejected by U.S. Senate Daniel O'Connell (1778—1847) found guilty of political conspiracy against Brit. rule in Ireland Attempt on the life of Frederick William IV, King of Prussia Catherine Breshkovsky ("Grandmother of the Russian Revolution"), b. (d. 1934)	Ivan Andreyevich Krylov, "the Russ. La Fontaine," d. (b. 1768) Andrew Lang, Scot. writer, b. (d. 1912) Charles Lever (1806—1872): "Tom Burke of Ours" Detlev von Liliencron, Ger. poet, b. (d. 1909) James Russell Lowell: "Poems" John Boyle O'Reilly," Ir.-Amer. poet, b. (d. 1890) A. W. O'Shaughnessy, Eng. poet, b. (d. 1881) Coventry Patmore: "Poems" John Sterling, Brit. poet, d. (b. 1806) W. M. Thackeray: "Barry Lyndon" Paul Verlaine, Fr. lyric poet, b. (d. 1896)	Friedrich Nietzsche, Ger. philosopher, b. (d. 1900) Edmund Rice, Ir. founder of the Christian Brothers, d. (b. 1762) Alois Riehl, Aust. Kantian philosopher, b. (d. 1924) A. P. Stanley: "Life and Correspondence of Thomas Arnold"
1845	Elihu Root, Amer. statesman, b. (d. 1937) Texas and Florida become states of the U.S. James K. Polk inaugurated as 11th President of the U.S. Maori rising against Brit. rule in New Zealand New Span. constitution Andrew Jackson d. (b. 1767) The future King Louis II of Bavaria b. (d. 1886) Anglo-Sikh War begins Swiss Sonderbund for the protection of Catholic cantons formed	Balzac: "Les Paysans" (completed 1855) Disraeli: "Sybil, or The Two Nations" Dumas père: "Vingt ans après" ("Twenty Years After," sequel to "The Three Musketeers") Henrik Hertz: "King René's Daughter," romantic play Prosper Mérimée: "Carmen" Poe: "The Raven and Other Poems" August Wilhelm von Schlegel d. (b. 1767) Carl Spitteler, Swiss author, 1919 Nobel Prize, b. (d. 1924) Henrik Wergeland, Norw. author, d. (b. 1808)	Thomas Carlyle: "Oliver Cromwell's Letters and Speeches" Friedrich Engels: "The Condition of the Working Class in England," published in Leipzig Sir Austen H. Layard (1817—1894) begins excavations in Nineveh John Henry Newman (1801—1890) becomes a Catholic Max Stirner (1806—1856): "Der Einzige und sein Eigentum," egocentric anarchistic philosophy
1846	East India Company's forces defeat Sikhs at Aliwal and Sobraon Treaty of Lahore ends First Sikh War Revolts break out in Poland Aust. and Russ. troops enter Cracow; Austria annexes Cracow Negotiations between U.S. and Mexico for purchase of New Mexico fail in Apr.; Amer. troops move into disputed area, defeat Mexicans at Palo Alto; formal declaration of war by U.S. follows; U.S. forces move into Santa Fe and U.S. annexes New Mexico in Aug. Louis Napoleon escapes from the fortress of Ham to London Iowa becomes a state of the U.S. Nikola Pasic, Serbian statesman, b. (d. 1926)	Hans Christian Andersen: "Fairy Tale of My Life," autobiography Balzac: "La Cousine Bette" Edmondo De Amicis, Ital. novelist, b. (d. 1908) Dostoevsky: "Poor Folk" Maurus Jókai: "Weekdays," novel Gottfried Keller: "Gedichte" Edward Lear (1812—1888): "Book of Nonsense" Longfellow: "The Belfry of Bruges" Herman Melville: "Typee" George Sand: "La Mare au diable" Henryk Sienkiewicz, Pol. novelist, 1905 Nobel Prize for Literature, b. (d. 1916)	Evangelical Alliance founded, London Rudolf Eucken, Ger. philosopher, 1908 Nobel Prize for Literature, b. (d. 1926) Pope Gregory XVI d; succeeded by Cardinal Mastai-Ferretti as Pope Pius IX (—1878) Friedrich T. Vischer: "Aesthetics" (—1857) Theodor Waitz: "Foundation of Psychology" William Whewell: "Elements of Morality" Brigham Young leads the Mormons from Nauvoo City, Ill., to the Great Salt Lake, Utah (—1847)

D. VISUAL ARTS	E. MUSIC	F. SCIENCE, TECHNOLOGY, GROWTH	G. DAILY LIFE	
Mihály von Munkácsy, Hungarian painter, b. (d. 1900) Ilya Efimovich Repin, Russ. historical painter, b. (d. 1930) Henri Rousseau, called "Le Douanier," Fr. primitive painter, b. (d. 1910) E. L. Sambourne, Eng. cartoonist ("Punch"), b. (d. 1910) Albert Bertel Thorvaldsen, Dan. sculptor, d. (b. 1770) Turner: "Rain, Steam, and Speed," painting, Tate Gallery, London	Verdi: "Ernani," Venice	K. F. Kielmeyer, Ger. naturalist ("Fundamental Biogenetic Law"), d. (b. 1765) A. W. Kinglake: "Eothen" S. F. B. Morse's telegraph used for the first time between Baltimore and Washington Eduard Strasburger, Ger. botanist, b. (d. 1912)	Gustaf Pasch of Sweden proposes safer matches by placing some combustion ingredients on striking surface Brit. railroad mileage (26 in 1828) reaches 2,236 Fr. missionaries Evariste R. Huc and Joseph Gabet begin journey from China to Tibet (arriving at Lhasa 1846) Young Men's Christian Association (YMCA) founded in England by George Williams (1821—1905)	**1844 contd**
Wilhelm von Bode, Ger. art historian, b. (d. 1929) First artistic photo portraits by David Octavius Hill (1802—1870) J. T. Huvé completes Madeleine Church, Paris Ingres: portrait of the Countess Haussonville Adolf Oberländer, Ger. caricaturist, b. (d. 1923) The Portland Vase, a famous Grecian urn maliciously destroyed, completely restored	Gabriel Fauré, Fr. composer, b. (d. 1924) "Leonora," Amer. opera by W. H. Fry (1813—1864) produced at Philadelphia Lortzing: "Undine," opera, Magdeburg Wagner: "Tannhäuser," Dresden Charles Marie Widor, Fr. composer and organist, b. (d. 1937)	Sir William G. Armstrong (1810—1900) patents hydraulic crane Amer. inventor E. B. Bigelow (1814—1879) constructs power loom for manufacturing carpets Arthur Cayley (1821—1895): "Theory of Linear Transformations" First submarine cable laid across English Channel Fr. inventor Joshua Heilman (1796—1848) patents machine for combing cotton and wool Humboldt: "Cosmos" (—1862 five vols.) Ger. chemist Adolf Kolbe (1818—1884) synthesizes acetic acid Charles Laveran, Fr. physician, 1907 Nobel Prize for Medicine. b. (d. 1922) Brit. engineer William M'Naught develops compound steam engine Ilya Ilich Mechnikov, Russ. physiologist, 1908 Nobel Prize for Medicine, b. (d. 1916)	Knickerbocker Baseball Club codifies rules of baseball U.S. Naval Academy, Annapolis, Md., opened Oxford-Cambridge boat race transferred from Henley-on-Thames to Putney	**1845**
The Propylaea, Munich, built by Franz Klenze (—1862) Millet: "Oedipus Unbound," painting G. F. Watts: "Paolo and Francesca," painting	Berlioz: "Damnation de Faust," dramatic cantata, Paris, Opéra-Comique Electric arc lighting at the Opéra, Paris Lortzing: "Der Waffenschmied," opera, Vienna Mendelssohn: "Elijah," oratorio, Birmingham	F. W. Bessel, Ger. astronomer, d. (b. 1784) Amer. inventor John Deere constructs plow with steel moldboard F. G. J. Henle: "Manual of Rational Pathology" (—1852) Sewing machine patented by Elias Howe, improved 1851 by I. M. Singer Friedrich List, Ger. economist, d. (b. 1789) Ger. botanist H. von Mohl (1805—1872) identifies protoplasm Amer. dentist W. T. Morton (1819—1868) uses ether as anesthetic Ital. chemist Ascanio Sobrero (1811—1870) prepares nitroglycerine	"Daily News," the first cheap Eng. newspaper, appears; Charles Dickens editor First painted Christmas card designed by John C. Horseley (1817—1903) Famine in Ireland caused by failure of potato crop Smithsonian Institution, Washington, founded Optical factory of Carl Zeiss (1816—1888) founded in Jena	**1846**

	A. HISTORY, POLITICS	B. LITERATURE, THEATER	C. RELIGION, PHILOSOPHY, LEARNING
1847	Liberia proclaimed independent republic U.S. forces capture Mexico City Paul von Hindenburg, future President of German Weimar Republic, b. (d. 1934) Sonderbund War in Switzerland; Catholic cantons refuse to dissolve union	Charlotte Brontë: "Jane Eyre" Emily Brontë: "Wuthering Heights" Heinrich Hoffmann (1809—1904), a Frankfurt physician, publishes his "Struwwelpeter" Marryat: "The Children of the New Forest" W. H. Prescott: "History of the Conquest of Peru" George Sand: "Le Péché de M. Antoine" Thackeray: "Vanity Fair" (—1848)	Amer. preacher Henry Ward Beecher (1813—1887) minister at Plymouth Congregational Church, Brooklyn Louis Blanc: "History of the Revolution" (—1862) Karl Marx attacks Proudhon's "Philosophy of Poverty" in "The Poverty of Philosophy" The Mormons found Salt Lake City Leopold von Ranke: "Neun Bücher preussischer Geschichte" (—1848)
1848	King Christian VIII of Denmark d.; succeeded by Frederick III (—1863) Treaty of Guadalupe Hidalgo ends Mexican-U.S. war in Feb.; ratified in Oct.; U.S. gets Texas, New Mexico, California, Utah, Nevada, Arizona, and parts of Colorado and Wyoming from Mexico in return for large indemnity Revolt in Paris; Louis Philippe abdicates; National Assembly meets; worker uprising in Paris; the "June Days"; Louis Napoleon elected President of Fr. Republic in Dec. Revolution in Vienna; Metternich resigns Revolutions in Venice, Berlin, Milan (cinque Giornate), and Parma Second Sikh War begins Sardinia declares war on Austria and wins Battles of Goito and Pastrengo; Austrians victorious at Vicenza and (under Radetzky) at Custozza; armistice signed at Vigevano; Sardinian troops forced to leave Venice Second rising in Vienna; Emperor Ferdinand I flees to Innsbruck Pan-Slav congress in Prague leads to Czech revolts which are suppressed by Aust. troops under Windischgrätz Lajos Kossuth proclaimed president of Committee for National Defence of Hungary Third revolution in Vienna; the emperor abdicates in favor of his nephew who becomes Emperor Francis Joseph I (—1916) Nasr-ed-Din becomes Shah of Persia (—1896) Switzerland, by its new constitution, becomes a federal union Ibrahim, Viceroy of Egypt, d.; succeeded by Abbas (—1854) Revolt in Rome; Count Rossi, the papal premier, assassinated; Pius IX flees to Gaeta Wisconsin becomes a state of the U.S. Arthur James Balfour, Brit. statesman, b. (d. 1930) First U.S. women's rights convention meets in Seneca Falls, New York	Emile Augier (1820—1889): "L'Aventurière," play Chateaubriand: "Mémoires d'outre-tombe" Annette von Droste-Hülshoff, Ger. poet, d. (b. 1797) Dumas fils: "La Dame aux Camélias," novel (see 1852) Elizabeth Gaskell: "Mary Barton" J. R. Lowell: "The Biglow Papers" Frederick Marryat, Eng. novelist, d. (b. 1792) Henri Murger: "Scènes de la vie de Bohème" Ellen Terry, Eng. actress, b. (d. 1928)	Hans Delbrück, Ger. historian, b. (d. 1929) Jakob Grimm: "History of the German Language" Macaulay: "History of England" (—1861) "Communist Manifesto" issued by Marx and Engels J. S. Mill: "Principles of Political Economy" Spiritualism becomes popular in U.S.

D. VISUAL ARTS	E. MUSIC	F. SCIENCE, TECHNOLOGY, GROWTH	G. DAILY LIFE	
Adolf von Hildebrand, Ger. sculptor, b. (d. 1921) Max Liebermann, Ger. impressionist painter, b. (d. 1935)	Friedrich von Flotow: "Martha," opera, Vienna Mendelssohn d. (b. 1809) Verdi: "Macbeth," opera, Florence	George Boole (1815—1864): "Mathematical Analysis of Logic" Thomas Alva Edison, Amer. inventor, b. (d. 1931) Evaporated milk made for the first time First Swiss railroad between Zurich and Baden opens Alexander Graham Bell, Scot.-born Amer. inventor, b. (d. 1922) Helmholtz: "On the Conservation of Energy" Justus von Liebig produces meat extract I. T. Semmelweis (1818—1865), Hungarian physician, discovers connection between childbed fever and puerperal infection	Brit. Factory Act restricts the working day for women and children between 13 and 18 to 10 hours First Roman Catholic working men's club, Cologne, Germany Millicent Garrett Fawcett, Brit, suffragist, b. (d, 1929) Founding of Hamburg-America Line Founding of electrical firm of Siemens and Halske	**1847**
Paul Gauguin, Fr. painter, b. (d. 1903) Millais: "Ophelia," painting Millet: "The Winnower," painting Fritz von Uhde, painter, b. (d. 1911) Holman Hunt, Millais, and D. G. Rossetti found the Pre-Raphaelite Brotherhood	Donizetti d. (b. 1797) Sir Hubert Parry, Eng. composer, b. (d. 1918)	Jöns Jakob Berzelius, Swed. chemist, d. (b. 1779) Böttger: first safety matches First appendectomy by Hancock	Serfdom abolished in Austria Bismarck founds the "Neue Preussische Zeitung," Marx the "Neue Rheinische Zeitung" First Public Health Act in Britain First settlers arrive in New Zealand (Dunedin) W. G. Grace, Eng. cricketer, b. (d. 1915) New York News Agency founded by Hale and Burnett (from 1856, Associated Press) Sebastian Kneipp (1821—1897) introduces cold-water cures at Worrishofen, Germany Otto Lilienthal, Ger. aviation pioneer, b. (d. 1896) Belle Starr, Amer. outlaw, b, (d. 1889) Gold discoveries in California lead to first gold rush	**1848**

	A. HISTORY, POLITICS	B. LITERATURE, THEATER	C. RELIGION, PHILOSOPHY, LEARNING
1849	British defeat Sikhs at Chillianwalla and Gujarat; force them to surrender at Rawalpindi Rome proclaimed a republic under Giuseppe Mazzini Disraeli leader of the Conservative Party Aust. victory at Novara Charles Albert of Sardinia abdicates in favor of his son Victor Emmanuel II Peace of Milan ends war Venice submits to Austria Zachary Taylor (1784—1850) inaugurated as 12th President of the U.S. Ger. National Assembly passes constitution; elects King Frederick William IV of Prussia "Emperor of the Germans"; he refuses to accept Britain annexes Punjab by treaty with the Maharajah of Lahore Hungarian Diet proclaims independence; Kossuth governor-president Revolts in Dresden and Baden French enter Rome and restore Pope Pius IX Hungary capitulates to Austria at Vilagos	Matthew Arnold: "The Strayed Reveller" Dickens: "David Copperfield" Dostoevsky sentenced to death; sentence commuted to penal servitude in Siberia (—1858) Charles Kingsley: "Alton Locke" Edgar Allan Poe, Amer. poet, d. (b. 1809) Scribe: "Adrienne Lecouvreur," drama August Strindberg, Swed. poet, b. (d. 1912)	J. M. Kemble: "History of the Saxons in England" Ellen Key, Swed. author and pedagogue, b. (d. 1926) "Who's Who" begins publication
1850	Henry Clay's compromise slavery resolutions laid before U.S. Senate Liberal constitution in Prussia (—1918) Outbreak of Anglo-Kaffir War (—1853) Tomás Garrigue Masaryk, first Czechoslovak president, b. (d. 1937) Horatio Herbert Kitchener, Brit. general, b. (d. 1916) Prussia and Denmark sign Peace of Berlin on Schleswig-Holstein U.S. President Zachary Taylor d.; Millard Fillmore (1800—1874) becomes 13th president California becomes a state of the U.S. Louis Philippe, King of France (1830—1848), d. (b. 1773) Camillo Cavour (1810—1861) becomes minister in Piedmont Taiping rebellion in China; Hung Hiu-tsuen proclaims himself emperor, attacks Peking, and takes Nanking and Shanghai Austro-Hungarian customs union formed	Balzac d. (b. 1799) E. B. Browning: "Sonnets from the Portuguese" Emerson: "Representative Men" Hawthorne: "The Scarlet Letter" Alexander Herzen: "From Another Shore," essays Ibsen: "Cataline" Nikolaus Lenau, Aust. poet, d. (b. 1802) Pierre Loti, Fr. novelist, b. (d. 1923) Otto Ludwig: "Der Erbförster," play Guy de Maupassant, Fr. writer, b. (d. 1893) Robert L. Stevenson, Scot. author, b. (d. 1894) Turgenev: "A Month in the Country," play William Wordsworth d. (b. 1770); succeeded as poet laureate by Alfred, Lord Tennyson	Church council to manage Protestant churches in Prussia Public Libraries Act in Britain Schopenhauer: "Parerga und Paralipomena" Herbert Spencer: "Social Statics," beginnings of sociology
1851	Prussia recognizes German Confederation and concludes commercial treaty with Hanover Cuba declares its independence Victoria, Australia, proclaimed separate colony Beginning of Basuto War (—1853) Ferdinand Foch, later Fr. marshal, b. (d. 1929) Coup d'état of Louis Napoleon; plebiscite in France favors new constitution Danilo II converts Montenegro into a secular principality	James Fenimore Cooper, Amer. novelist, d. (b. 1789) Hawthorne: "The House of Seven Gables" Heinrich Heine: "Romanzero" Gottfried Keller: "Der grüne Heinrich," novel Longfellow: "The Golden Legend" Herman Melville: "Moby Dick" Mrs. Humphry Ward, Eng. novelist, b. (d. 1920) Ruskin: "The Stones of Venice" (—1853)	Vincenzo Gioberti: "Il Rinnovamento civile d'Italia"

D. VISUAL ARTS	E. MUSIC	F. SCIENCE, TECHNOLOGY, GROWTH	G. DAILY LIFE	
Courbet: "After Dinner at Ornans," painting Delacroix paints ceiling of Salon d'Apollon at Louvre Katsushika Hokusai, Jap. painter, d. (b. 1760) John Ruskin: "The Seven Lamps of Architecture"	Chopin d. (b. 1810) Liszt: "Tasso," symphonic poem, Weimar Meyerbeer: "Le Prophète," Paris Otto Nicolai: "The Merry Wives of Windsor," opera, Vienna Nicolai d. (b. 1810) Schumann: music to Byron's "Manfred" Johann Strauss I d. (b. 1804) Richard Wagner takes part in Dresden revolt and is forced to flee to Zurich	Fr. physicist Armand Fizeau (1819—1896) measures speed of light Eng. chemist Edward Frankland (1825—1899) isolates amyl David Livingstone crosses Kalahari Desert and discovers Lake Ngami	Bedford College for Women, London, founded Amelia Bloomer (1818—1884) begins Amer. women's dress reform Cape Colony forbids landing of convicts Petropavlosk founded in Siberia Julie ("Madame") Récamier d. (b. 1777) W. T. Stead, Eng. journalist, b. (d. 1912)	**1849**
Corot: "Une Matinée" Courbet: "The Stone Breakers," painting Goya: "Proverbios," engravings (posth.) Menzel: "Round Table at Sansouci," painting Millais: "Christ in the House of His Parents," painting Millet: "The Sower," painting Era of the Neo-Gothic architectural style Joseph Paxton builds Crystal Palace, London J. G. Schadow, Ger. sculptor, d. (b. 1764)	Foundation of Bach-Gesellschaft to publish the complete works of J. S. Bach (—1900, 46 vols.) George F. Bristow: "Rip Van Winkle," Amer. opera, New York Jenny Lind, the "Swed. Nightingale," tours America under the management of P. T. Barnum Schumann: "Genoveva," Leipzig Wagner: "Lohengrin," Weimar	Claude Bernard demonstrates glycogenic function of the liver R. W. Bunsen (1811-1899) produces gas burner Ger. physicist Rudolf Clausius (1822—1888) formulates second law of thermodynamics, and kinetic theory of gases Hermann von Helmholtz establishes speed of nervous impulse Stephenson's cast-iron railroad bridge at Newcastle, England, opened Pafnuti L. Chebyshev: "On Primary Numbers"	Old-age insurance in France Population of U.S., 23 million (3.2 million Black slaves) Royal Meteorological Society founded School of Mines, London (later to become College of Science and Technology) established University of Sydney, Australia, established	**1850**
Corot: "La Danse des Nymphes," painting William Cubitt builds King's Cross Station, London Tenniel's cartoons appear in "Punch" J. M. W. Turner, Eng. painter, d. (b. 1775) Thomas Walter, designer of the present dome and House and Senate wings, appointed architect of U.S. Capitol (—1865) Leslie Ward ("Spy"), Eng. cartoonist, b. (d. 1922)	Gounod: "Sappho," opera, Paris Vincent d'Indy, Fr. composer, b. (d. 1931) Albert Lortzing, Ger. composer, d. (b. 1801) Verdi: "Rigoletto," Venice	Cast-iron frame building constructed by Amer. James Bogardus (1800—1874) Louis Daguerre, one of the fathers of photography, d. (b. 1789) Helmholtz's ophthalmoscope Franz Neumann: law of electromagnetic induction H. D. Ruhmkorff (1803—1877) invents high tension induction coil Isaac Singer devises the continuous stitch sewing machine William Thomson, later Lord Kelvin, begins papers on the laws of conservation and dissipation of energy	The schooner "America" wins race around Isle of Wight and brings the America's Cup to the U.S. Mary Carpenter: "Reformatory Schools... for Juvenile Offenders" First double-decker bus introduced Gold found in Victoria, New South Wales, Australia Knickerbocker Baseball Team beats Washington at Red House Grounds, New York "The New York Times" appears (Sept.) Maine and Illinois begin to enforce prohibition against liquor Population statistics (in millions): China, 430; Germany, 34: France, 33; Great Britain, 20.8; U.S. 23	**1851**

	A. HISTORY, POLITICS	B. LITERATURE, THEATER	C. RELIGION, PHILOSOPHY, LEARNING
1852	Joseph Jacques Césaire Joffre, Fr. marshal, b. (d. 1931) South African Republic (Transvaal) established New Fr. constitution gives president monarchical powers; Louis Napoleon has Orléans family banished from France; plebiscite in support of revival of empire; two weeks later the president proclaims himself Emperor Napoleon III; reign of the Second Empire (—Sept. 1870) Outbreak of Second Burmese War; Brit. forces annex Pegu New constitution for New Zealand Herbert Henry Asquith, Brit. Prime Minister, b. (d. 1928) The Duke of Wellington d. (b. 1769) Franklin Pierce elected 14th President of the U.S.	Paul Bourget, Fr. author, b. (d. 1935) Sir Edward Creasy (1812—1878): "Fifteen Decisive Battles of the World" Charles Dickens: "Bleak House" Dumas fils: "La Dame aux Camélias," play (see 1848) Théophile Gautier: "Emaux et Camées" Gogol d. (b. 1809) Hebbel: "Agnes Bernauer," Ger. play George Augustus Moore, Ir. novelist, b. (d. 1933) Charles Reade: "Masks and Faces" Harriet Beecher Stowe: "Uncle Tom's Cabin" Thackeray: "History of Henry Esmond" Turgenev: "A Sportsman's Sketches"	The Convocation of the Church of England revived Léopold Delisle (1826—1920) begins at the Bibliothèque Impériale, Paris, the study of modern paleography Kuno Fischer: "History of Modern Philosophy" (—1893, 10 vols.) First Plenary Council of Amer. Roman Catholics held in Baltimore Ranke: "History of France" (principally in the 16th and 17th centuries) (—1861, 5 vols.) Hans Vaihinger, Ger. philosopher, b. (d. 1933)
1853	Napoleon III marries Eugénie de Montijo (1826—1920) Franklin Pierce inaugurated as 14th President of the U.S. Oldenburg and Hanover join Zollverein (customs union) Turks reject Russ. ultimatum; Czar Nicholas I orders occupation of Danubian principalities; they are invaded; Austria endeavors to solve conflict; Turkey declares war on Russia; Crimean War begins (—1856); the Russians destroy Turk. fleet off Sinope Peace between Britain and Burma Cecil John Rhodes, Brit. adventurer and statesman, b. (d. 1902) Maria II of Portugal d.; succeeded by her son Pedro V (—1861) Britain annexes Mahratta State of Nagpur	Matthew Arnold: "The Scholar-Gipsy" Charlotte Brontë: "Villette" Hall Caine, Eng. novelist, b. (d. 1931) Gustav Freytag: "Die Journalisten," Ger. comedy Elizabeth Gaskell: "Ruth" and "Cranford" Nathaniel Hawthorne: "Tanglewood Tales" Charles Kingsley: "Hypatia" Ludwig Tieck, Ger. poet, d. (b. 1773) Herbert Beerbohm Tree, Eng. actor, b. (d. 1917) C. M. Yonge: "The Heir of Redclyffe"	Johann Herzog: "Encyclopedia of Protestant Theology" (—1868) Mommsen: "History of Rome" (—1856) Hippolyte Taine: "Essai sur les fables de La Fontaine"
1854	Convention of Bloemfontein; British leave territory north of Orange River Britain and France conclude alliance with Turkey and declare war on Russia; unopposed landing of the Allies in Crimea; siege of Sebastopol begins; Allied victories at Balaklava and Inkerman Commodore M. C. Perry negotiates first Amer.-Jap. treaty Francis Joseph I, Emperor of Austria, marries the Bavarian Princess Elizabeth U.S. Senate ratifies Gadsden Purchase for acquisition of parts of southern New Mexico and Arizona "War for Bleeding Kansas" between free and slave states Elgin Treaty between Britain and U.S. on Canadian trade Turkey agrees to Aust. occupation of Danubian principalities till end of the war *(contd)*	Angier and Sandeau: "Le Gendre de M. Poirier," Fr. social play Jeremias Gotthelf, Swiss author, d. (b. 1797) F. D. Guerazzi: "Beatrice Cenci" Charles Kingsley: "Westward Ho!" De Nerval: "Les Filles du Feu" Coventry Patmore: "Angel in the House" Arthur Rimbaud, Fr. poet, b. (d. 1891) Josef Viktor von Scheffel: "Der Trompeter von Säckingen," immensely popular Ger. verse romance Tennyson: "The Charge of the Light Brigade" (poem celebrating the Battle of Balaklava) Thackeray: "The Rose and the Ring" Thoreau: "Walden, or Life in the Woods"	George Boole: "An Investigation of the Laws of Thought, on Which Are Founded the Mathematical Theories of Logic and Probabilities" Jewish seminary established at Breslau Juvenile Offenders Act in Great Britain Henri Poincaré, Fr. mathematician and philosopher, b. (d. 1912) Pope Pius IX declares the dogma of the Immaculate Conception of the Blessed Virgin Mary to be an article of faith

D. VISUAL ARTS	E. MUSIC	F. SCIENCE, TECHNOLOGY, GROWTH	G. DAILY LIFE	
F. M. Brown: "Christ Washing Peter's Feet," painting William Holman Hunt: "The Light of the World" John E. Millais: "Ophelia" Paddington Station, London, designed by Brunel and Wyatt	Robert Schumann: "Manfred," first performed at Weimar Sir Charles Villiers Stanford, Ir. composer and conductor b. (d. 1924)	Antoine Henri Becquerel, Fr. physicist, 1903 Nobel Prize, b. (d. 1908) C. F. Gerhardt: "New Theory of Organic Compounds" J. H. van't Hoff, Dutch physicist, 1901 Nobel Prize, b. (d. 1911) David Livingstone explores Zambezi (—1856) Dutch army surgeon Mathysen impregnates bandages with plaster Albert Michelson, Amer. physicist, b. (d. 1931) William Ramsay, Eng. chemist, b. (d. 1916) Herbert Spencer: "The Development Hypothesis" (first use of the word "evolution") James Sylvester: "Calculus of Forms"	The U.S. imports sparrows from Germany as defense against caterpillars First Congress of Co-operative Societies meets in London Niagara Falls suspension bridge Saltwater aquarium in London Formation of United All-English Cricket Eleven Wells Fargo and Co. founded	**1852**
Rebuilding of Balmoral Castle, Aberdeenshire, Scotland, begun under direction of P. C. Albert (—1855) Georges Haussmann begins reconstruction of Paris–Boulevards, Bois de Boulogne Carl Larsson, Swed. painter, b. (d. 1919) Vincent Van Gogh, Dutch painter, b. (d. 1890)	Henry Steinway (Heinrich E. Steinweg, 1797—1871) and his three sons begin the New York firm of piano manufacturers Verdi: "Il Trovatore," Rome, and "La Traviata," Venice Wagner completes the text of his tetralogy "Der Ring des Nibelungen" (music —1847)	Samuel Colt revolutionizes the manufacture of small arms Melbourne University founded Alexander Wood uses hypodermic syringe for subcutaneous injections	The Ger. family magazine "Die Gartenlaube" founded in Leipzig First International Statistical Congress held in Brussels First railroad through the Alps (Vienna—Trieste) Queen Victoria allows chloroform to be administered to her during the birth of her seventh child, thus ensuring its place as an anesthetic in Britain Telegraph system established in India Vaccination against smallpox is made compulsory in Britain Wellingtonia gigantea, the largest tree in the world, discovered in California	**1853**
Karl Begas, Ger. painter, d. (b. 1794) Courbet: "Bonjour, Monsieur Courbet," painting William Frith: "Ramsgate Sands" Millet: "The Reaper" Waldmüller: "Vienna Woods Landscape"	Berlioz: "The Infant Christ," Christmas oratorio, Paris Engelbert Humperdinck, Ger. composer, b. (d. 1921) Liszt: "Les Préludes," symphonic poem Schumann attempts suicide	S.S. "Brandon," the first ship with compound expansion engines George Eastman, Amer. photography pioneer, b. (d. 1932) Christian Ehrenberg: "Microgeology" Paul Ehrlich, Ger. biochemist, b. (d. 1915) Manuel Garcia, singing teacher, invents laryngoscope Ger. watchmaker Heinrich Goebel invents first form of electric light bulb Georg Riemann: "On the Hypotheses Forming the Foundation of Geometry" University College, Dublin, founded	"Le Figaro," Paris, begins publication The first street-poster pillars erected in Berlin by Ernst Litfass Northcote-Trevelyan report leads to Brit. Civil Service Commission Turin-Genoa railroad opened Working Men's College, London, founded by F. D. Maurice	**1854**

	A. HISTORY, POLITICS	B. LITERATURE, THEATER	C. RELIGION, PHILOSOPHY, LEARNING
1854 contd	Republican Party formed in the U.S. Abbas I, Viceroy of Egypt assassinated; succeeded by Mohammed Said (—1863) Ostend Manifesto advises U.S. to annex Cuba		
1855	Czar Nicholas I of Russia d.; succeeded by Alexander II (—1881) Britain and Afghanistan join against Persia in Treaty of Peshawar Taiping Rebellion ends Russians capitulate at Sebastopol; Allies enter town	Charlotte Brontë d. (b. 1816) Robert Browning: "Men and Women," poems Dickens: "Little Dorrit" (—1857) Dumas fils: "Le Demi-monde" Gustav Freytag: "Soll und Haben," novel Ludwig Ganghofer, Ger. popular novelist, b. (d. 1920) Longfellow: "The Song of Hiawatha" Marie Corelli (Mary Mackay), Eng. novelist, b. (d. 1924) Adam B. Mickiewicz d. (b. 1798) Arthur Wing Pinero, Eng. dramatist, b. (d. 1934) W. H. Prescott: "The History of the Reign of Philip II" (—1858) Tennyson: "Maud," and other poems Anthony Trollope: "The Warden" Turgenev: "Rudin" Walt Whitman: "Leaves of Grass"	Alexander Bain: "Senses and Intellects" Johann Droysen: "History of Prussian Policy" (—1886) Auguste Gratry: "Connaissance de Dieu" Sören Kierkegaard, Dan. philosopher, d. (b. 1813) Henry Milman: "History of Latin Christianity" Pierre Le Play: "Les Ouvriers européens" (on working-class incomes) Herbert Spencer: "Principles of Psychology"
1856	Queen Victoria institutes the Victoria Cross Britain annexes Oudh, India, and establishes Natal as a Crown Colony Reform edict in Turk. Empire; peace conference in Paris recognizes integrity of Turkey Fr. Prince Imperial, son of Napoleon III, b. (d. 1879) Massacre of Potawatomie Creek, Kansas– slavers murdered by free-staters Aust. amnesty for Hungarian rebels of 1848—49 Anglo-Chin. war begins; Brit. fleet bombards Canton Persia occupies Herat–outbreak of Brit.-Persian war James Buchanan wins U.S. presidential election Fr.-Span. frontier defined South African Republic (Transvaal) organized under Marthinius Pretorius Woodrow Wilson, future President of the U.S., b. (d. 1924) Britain grants self-government to Tasmania Emperor Francis Joseph visits Lombardy and Venice and appoints his brother Archduke Maximilian governor of the provinces	Edmond About: "Le Roi des montagnes" Flaubert: "Madame Bovary" (—1857) H. Rider Haggard, Eng. novelist, b. (d. 1925) Heinrich Heine d. (b. 1797) Victor Hugo: "Les Contemplations," poems Ibsen: "The Banquet at Solhaug," Norw. play Gottfried Keller: "Die Leute von Seldwyla," short stories Mörike: "Mozart auf der Reise nach Prag," short story Charles Reade: "It Is Never Too Late to Mend" George Bernard Shaw, Anglo-Ir. writer and dramatist, 1925 Nobel Prize, b. (d. 1950) Oscar Wilde, Anglo-Ir. author, b. (d. 1900)	J. A. Froude: "History of England from the Fall of Wolsey to the Defeat of the Armada" (—1870) Theodor Goldstücker: "Sanskrit Dictionary" Rudolf Lotze: "Mikrokosmos" (—1864) J. R. Motley: "Rise of the Dutch Republic" Hippolyte Taine: "Les Philosophes classiques du XIXe siècle en France" Augustin Thierry, Fr. historian, d. (b. 1795) Alexis de Tocqueville: "L'Ancien régime et la révolution"
1857	Peace of Paris ends Anglo-Persian war; shah recognizes independence of Afghanistan James Buchanan inaugurated as 15th President of the U.S. Indian Mutiny against Brit. rule; siege of Delhi begins; Delhi captured; British enter Cawnpore Royal Navy destroys Chin. fleet; relief of Lucknow; Britain and France take Canton Garibaldi forms Ital. National Association for unification of the country William H. Taft, future President of the U.S., b. (d. 1930) Irish Republican Brotherhood (Fenians) founded *(contd)*	George Borrow: "Romany Rye" Charles Baudelaire: "Les Fleurs du mal" Björnstjerne Björnson: "Synnöve Solbakken" Joseph Conrad (Korzeniowski), Anglo-Pol. novelist, b. (d. 1924) Joseph von Eichendorff, Ger. poet, d. (b. 1788) George Eliot: "Scenes from Clerical Life" Thomas Hughes: "Tom Brown's Schooldays" Dinah Mulock: "John Halifax, Gentleman" Alfred de Musset, Fr. poet, d. (b. 1810) Hendrik von Pontoppidan, Dan. author, 1917 Nobel Prize, b. (d. 1943) Adalbert Stifter: "Nachsommer," Aust. novel *(contd)*	Henry T. Buckle: "History of Civilization in England" (—1861) Auguste Comte, Fr. philosopher, d. (b. 1798) Sir Charles T. Newton (1816—1894) discovers remains of the Mausoleum of Halicarnassus Ernest Renan: "Etudes d'histoire religieuse"

D. VISUAL ARTS	E. MUSIC	F. SCIENCE, TECHNOLOGY, GROWTH	G. DAILY LIFE	
				1854 contd
Jakob Burckhardt: "Cicerone," art history Courbet: "Pavillon du Réalisme" at Paris World Fair J. B. Isabey, Fr. painter, d. (b. 1767)	Berlioz: "Te Deum," Paris (written 1849) Verdi: "Les Vêpres Siciliennes," opera, Paris Wagner conducts a series of orchestral concerts in London	George Audemars takes out first patent for production of rayon Sir Richard Burton: "Pilgrimage to Mecca," travel book Professorship of technology created at Edinburgh University David E. Hughes (1831—1900) invents printing telegraph Aust. engineer Franz Köller develops tungsten steel R. S. Lawrence of Vermont, U.S., constructs turret lathe Livingstone discovers Victoria Falls of Zambezi River Percival Lowell, Amer. astronomer, b. (d. 1916) Matthew Maury: "Physical Geography of the Sea"	First iron Cunard steamer crosses Atlantic (in nine and a half days) Founding of "The Daily Telegraph," London Ferdinand de Lesseps (1805—1894) granted concession by France to construct Suez Canal Electric telegraph between London and Balaklava London sewers modernized after outbreak of cholera Florence Nightingale (1820—1910) introduces hygienic standards into military hospitals during Crimean War Paris World Fair	**1855**
Hendrik Petrus Berlage, Dutch architect, b. (d. 1934) Heinrich von Ferstel begins the Votivkirche, Vienna (—1879) Jean A. D Ingres: "La Source," painting	Karl Bechstein founds his piano factory Alexander Dargomijsky: "Russalka," opera, St. Petersburg Maillart: "Les Dragons de Villars," opera, Paris Robert Schumann d. (b. 1810) Christian Sinding, Norw. composer, b. (d. 1941)	Sir Henry Bessemer (1813—1898) introduces converter in his process for making steel Pure cocaine extract from cocoa beans Sigmund Freud, Aust. neurologist, founder of psychoanalysis, b. (d. 1939) Hermann von Helmholtz: "Manual of Physiological Optics" (—1866) Nikolai I. Lobachevsky, Russ. mathematician, d. (b. 1793) Robert E. Peary, Amer. explorer, b. (d. 1920) William H. Perkin prepares first aniline dye Ger. botanist Nathaniel Pringsheim (1823—1894) observes sperm entering ovum in plants Sir William Siemens (1823—1883) makes ductile steel for boiler plating	Baseball: Chicago Unions organized Black Forest railroad with 40 tunnels opened First Australian interstate cricket match: Victoria versus New South Wales Keir Hardie, Brit. socialist leader, b. (d. 1915) Longest bare-knuckle boxing fight in history: James Kelly versus Jack Smith, Melbourne, Australia, 186 rounds lasting 6 hours 15 minutes Neanderthal skull found in Feldhofer Cave near Düsseldorf Frederick W. Taylor, Amer. inventor and pioneer in scientific industrial management techniques, b. (d. 1915) "Big Ben," 13.5 ton bell at Brit. Houses of Parliament, cast at Whitechapel Bell Foundry (named after Sir Benjamin Hall, Director of Public Works)	**1856**
Max Klinger, Ger. sculptor, b. (d. 1920) Millet: "The Gleaners," painting National Portrait Gallery, London, opened Christian D. Rauch, Ger. sculptor, d. (b. 1777) Victoria and Albert Museum, *(contd)*	Hans von Bülow marries Cosima Liszt Edward Elgar, Eng. composer, b. (d. 1934) Mikhail I. Glinka, Russ. composer, d. (b. 1803) Charles Hallé founds the Hallé Concerts in Manchester Wilhelm Kienzl, Aust. composer, *(contd)*	Emile Coué, Fr. psychologist, b. (d. 1926) Heinrich Hertz, Ger. physicist, b. (d. 1894) Julius Wagner von Jauregg, Aust. neurologist and psychiatrist, 1927 Nobel Prize, b. (d. 1940) Pasteur proves that fermentation is caused by living organisms Ronald Ross, Eng. physician, specialist in tropical diseases, 1902 Nobel Prize, b. (d. 1932)	Alpine Club, London, founded "Atlantic Monthly" founded Robert Baden-Powell, Brit. general, founder of the Boy Scout movement, b. (d. 1941) Financial and economic crisis throughout Europe, caused by speculation in U.S. railroad shares Matrimonial Causes Act in Britain North German Lloyd founded (transatlantic steamship company) American civil engineer E. G. Otis installs first safety elevator Science Museum, South Kensington, *(contd)*	**1857**

	A. HISTORY, POLITICS	B. LITERATURE, THEATER	C. RELIGION, PHILOSOPHY, LEARNING
1857 contd	in New York Czar Alexander II begins the emancipation of serfs in Russia	Hermann Sudermann, Ger. dramatist, b. (d. 1928) Thackeray: "The Virginians" Anthony Trollope: "Barchester Towers"	
1858	Felice Orsini's attempt to assassinate Napoleon III Lord Derby (Conservative) becomes Brit. Prime Minister Minnesota becomes a state of the U.S. Treaty of Tientsin ends Anglo-Chin. war British proclaim peace in India Powers of East India Company transferred to Brit. Crown Andrew Bonar Law, Brit. statesman, b. (d. 1923) Prince William of Prussia declared regent for the insane King Frederick William IV Alexander Karageorgevich deposed by Serbian Diet; Milos Obrenovic declared king Theodore Roosevelt, 26th President of the U.S., b. (d. 1919)	Sir Frank Benson, Eng. actor-manager, b. (d. 1939) Wilhelm Busch: "Max und Moritz" Octave Feuillet: "Roman d'un jeune homme pauvre" Oliver Wendell Holmes (1809—1894): "The Autocrat of the Breakfast Table" Joseph Kainz, Ger. actor, b. (d. 1910) Selma Lagerlöf, Swed. novelist, 1909 Nobel Prize, b. (d. 1940) William Morris: "The Defence of Guinevere," poems	The Blessed Virgin Mary reputed to have appeared to Bernadette Soubirous (1844—1879) at Lourdes, France Henry Carey: "Principles of Social Science" Thomas Carlyle: "Frederick the Great" (—1865) Amer. Catholic priest Isaac Hecker (1819—1888) founds the Paulist Fathers Lionel de Rothschild becomes first Jewish member of Brit. Parliament Philip Schaff: "History of the Christian Church" (—1892)
1859	Treaty of Alliance between Sardinia and France Oregon becomes a state of the U.S. Austria sends ultimatum to Sardinia and begins invasion in Apr.; France declares war on Austria in May; Aust. forces defeated at Magenta and Solferino in June; Franco-Aust. armistice followed by peace of Villafranca, which is later formalized by Treaty of Zurich King Ferdinand of the Two Sicilies d.; succeeded by Francis II Lord Derby resigns; Lord Palmerston (Liberal) becomes Brit. Prime Minister Prince Metternich d. (b. 1773) King Oscar I of Sweden d.; succeeded by Charles XV (—1872) Ger. National Association formed; aimed at uniting Germany under Prussia Jean Léon Jaurès, Fr. socialist politician, b. (d. 1914) Albert von Roon, new Prussian War Minister, reforms Prussian army Queensland separated from New South Wales with Brisbane as capital Bismarck becomes Prussian ambassador to St. Petersburg The future Ger. Emperor William II b. (d. 1941)	Pedro Alarcón: "Diary of a Witness of the War in Africa" Dickens: "A Tale of Two Cities" Arthur Conan Doyle, Eng. novelist and detective-story writer, b. (d. 1930) Eleonora Duse, Ital. actress, b. (d. 1924) George Eliot: "Adam Bede" Edward Fitzgerald: "Rubáiyát of Omar Khayyám" Ivan Goncharov: "Oblomov" Knut Hamsun, Swed. novelist, 1920 Nobel Prize, b. (d. 1952) Verner von Heidenstam, Swed. poet, 1916 Nobel Prize, b. (d. 1940) A. E. Housman, Eng. poet, b. (d. 1936) Victor Hugo: "La Légende des siècles" (—1883) Leigh Hunt, Eng. author, d. (b. 1784) Washington Irving, Amer. author, d. (b. 1783) Jerome K. Jerome, Eng. author, b. (d. 1927) Thomas de Quincey, Eng. author, d. (b. 1785) George Sand: "Elle et lui" Tennyson: "Idylls of the King"	Henri Bergson, Fr. philosopher, b. (d. 1941) Charles Darwin: "On the Origin of Species by Natural Selection" John Dewey, Amer. philosopher, b. (d. 1952) Alexander von Humboldt, Ger. astronomer and explorer, d. (b. 1769) Edmund Husserl, Aust. philosopher, b. (d. 1938) Ferdinand Lassalle: "The Italian War and the Mission of Prussia" Thomas B. Macaulay, Eng. historian, d. (b. 1800) Karl Marx: "Critique of Political Economy" J. S. Mill: "Essay on Liberty" W. H. Prescott, Amer. historian, d. (b. 1796) Ranke: "History of England in the 16th and 17th Centuries" (—1868) Ernest Renan: "Essais de morale et de critique" L. F. K. Tischendorf (1815—1874) discovers Codex Sinaiticus Pasquale Villari: "Life of Savonarola"

D. VISUAL ARTS	E. MUSIC	F. SCIENCE, TECHNOLOGY, GROWTH	G. DAILY LIFE	
London, opened ("Museum of Ornamental Art" till 1899)	b. (d. 1941) Liszt: "Eine Faust-Symphonie," Weimar		London, founded Transatlantic cable laid (—1866)	**1857 contd**
Charles Barry designs the third Covent Garden Opera House, London Lovis Corinth, Ger. painter, b. (d. 1925) William P. Frith: "Derby Day," painting Ando Hiroshige, Jap. painter, d. (b. 1797) Menzel: "Bon soir, Messieurs" (painting of Frederick the Great and his circle in Lissa) Rebuilding of the Ringstrasse in Vienna begins Giovanni Segantini, Ital. painter, b. (d. 1899) Heinrich Zille, Berlin cartoonist, b. (d. 1929)	Peter von Cornelius: "Der Barbier von Bagdad," opera, Weimar Ruggiero Leoncavallo, Ital. opera composer, b. (d. 1919) New York Symphony Orchestra gives its first public concert Offenbach: "Orphée aux enfers," operetta, Paris Giacomo Puccini, Ital. opera composer, b. (d. 1924)	Richard Burton and John Speke discover Lake Tanganyika and Lake Victoria Nyanza Rudolf Diesel, Ger. automotive engineer, b. (d. 1913) T. H. Huxley: "The Theory of the Vertebrate Skulls" Joseph Lister (1827—1912) studies coagulation of blood Max Planck, Ger. physicist, b. (d. 1947) William Thomson, later Lord Kelvin, invents mirror galvanometer	First meeting of General Medical Council, London Suez Canal Company formed National Association of Baseball Players organized in America Ottawa becomes capital of Canada Robert Owen, Eng. social reformer, d. (b. 1771) South Foreland lighthouse lit by electricity S.S. "Great Eastern" is launched–largest ship of her time (displacement, 27,000 tons) Beatrice Webb (née Potter), Eng. socialist writer and politician, b. (d. 1943)	**1858**
Corot: "Macbeth," painting Cass Gilbert, Amer. architect, b. (d. 1934) Millet: "The Angelus" Georges Seurat, Fr. painter, b. (d. 1891) Whistler: "At the Piano," painting	Daniel Decatur Emmett (1815—1904) composes "Dixie" Gounod: "Faust," opera, Paris Adelina Patti's New York debut in Donizetti's "Lucia di Lammermoor" Louis Spohr, Ger. composer, d. (b. 1784) Verdi: "Un Ballo in Maschera," opera, Rome	Anthropological Society, Paris, founded Svante Arrhenius, Swed. scientist, 1903 Nobel Prize, b. (d. 1927) Bunsen and Kirchhoff begin experiments with spectrum analysis (—1861) Pierre Curie, Fr. physicist, b. (d. 1906) First oil well drilled at Titusville, Pa. R. L. G. Planté: first practical storage battery Steamroller invented H. J. S. Smith: "Report on the Theory of Numbers" (—1865)	Baseball Club of Washington, D.C., organized Fr. tightrope walker Charles Blondin crosses Niagara Falls on tightrope George Lansbury, Brit. Labour politician, b. (d. 1940) Founding of Port Said, Egypt Samuel Smiles (1812—1904): "Self-Help," manual on how to succeed in life Work on Suez Canal begun under de Lesseps' direction (—1869)	**1859**

	A. HISTORY, POLITICS	B. LITERATURE, THEATER	C. RELIGION, PHILOSOPHY, LEARNING
1860	Plebiscites in Tuscany, Emilia, Romagna, Parma, and Modena favor union with Sardinia Treaty of Turin cedes Nice and Savoy to France; first Ital. Parliament convenes at Turin Garibaldi and his 1,000 redshirts ("i Mille") sail from Genoa; reach Marsala; take Palermo and Naples Victor Emmanuel II, King of Sardinia, invades Papal States and defeats papal troops Garibaldi proclaims Victor Emmanuel II King of Italy Second Maori War begins (—1870) Founding of Vladivostok Anglo-Fr. troops defeat Chinese at Pa-li-Chau; Treaty of Peking Abraham Lincoln elected 16th President of the U.S.; S. Carolina secedes from the Union in protest Raymond Poincaré, Fr. statesman, b. (d. 1934)	J. M. Barrie, Scot. dramatist, b. (d. 1937) Dion Boucicault: "The Colleen Bawn," domestic drama, London Wilkie Collins: "The Woman in White" George Eliot: "The Mill on the Floss" Salvatore di Giacoma, Ital. poet, b. (d. 1934) Eugène Labiche: "Le Voyage de M. Perrichon" Multatuli (E. D. Dekker): "Max Havelaar," Dutch novel Mori Ogai, Jap. poet, translator of "Faust," b. (d. 1922) Alexander Ostrovski: "The Storm," Russ. drama Friedrich Spielhagen: "Problematische Naturen," Ger. novel A. C. Swinburne: "The Queen Mother," drama "The Cornhill Magazine" founded, W. M. Thackeray editor Anton Chekhov, Russ. author, b. (d. 1904)	Eng. Church Union founded J. S. Mill: "Considerations on Representative Government" Charles de Montalembert: "Les Moines d'Occident" J. L. Motley: "The History of the United Netherlands" (—1868) Russ. Orthodox Church establishes monastery in Jerusalem Arthur Schopenhauer d. (b. 1788)
1861	Frederick William IV of Prussia d.; succeeded by William I (—1888) Kansas becomes a state of the U.S. Washington Peace Convention tries to preserve Union, but Congress of Montgomery forms Confederate States of America with S. Carolina, Georgia, Alabama, Mississippi, Florida, and Louisiana; Abraham Lincoln inaugurated as 16th President of the U.S.; Confederates take Fort Sumter, Charleston, Apr. 12–outbreak of Civil War; Lincoln calls for militia to suppress Confederacy; Confederate victory at Bull Run; Union forces later capture Forts Clark and Hatteras The King of Naples surrenders to Garibaldi at Gaeta; Italy proclaimed a kingdom by Parliament, with Victor Emmanuel II as king Count Cavour d. (b. 1810) Warsaw Massacre–troops fire at demonstrators against Russ. rule Emancipation of Russ. serfs Sultan Abdul Mejid of Turkey d.; succeeded by his brother Abdul Aziz Pedro V of Portugal d.; succeeded by Louis I Prince Consort Albert d. (b. 1819)	Elizabeth Barrett Browning d. (b. 1806) Dickens: "Great Expectations" Dostoevsky: "The House of the Dead" George Eliot: "Silas Marner" Oliver Wendell Holmes: "Elsie Venner" Henri Murger, Fr. novelist, d. (b. 1823) Rabindranath Tagore, Indian philosopher and poet, b. (d. 1941) Charles Reade: "The Cloister and the Hearth" Eugène Scribe, Fr. dramatist, d. (b. 1791) Mrs. Henry Wood: "East Lynne"	Vladimir Dahl: "Dictionary of the Living Russian Tongue" (—1866) Ferdinand Lassalle: "System of Assigned Rights" Friedrich Karl von Savigny, Ger. jurist, d. (b. 1779) Herbert Spencer: "Education: Moral, Intellectual, Physical" Arthur P. Stanley: "Lectures on the History of the Eastern Church" Rudolf Steiner, founder Anthroposophical Society, b. (d. 1925) Alfred North Whitehead, Eng. mathematician and philosopher, b. (d. 1947)
1862	Union Forces capture Fort Henry, Roanoke Island, Fort Donelson, Jacksonville, and New Orleans; they are defeated at second Battle of Bull Run and Fredericksburg; Sept. 22–"Emancipation Proclamation"– effective Jan. 1, 1863, all slaves held in rebelling territory declared free Monaco sells Menton and Roquebrune to France Bismarck becomes Prussian Prime Minister King Otto I of Greece resigns after military revolt Edward Grey, Brit. statesman, b. (d. 1933) Aristide Briand, Fr. statesman, b. (d. 1932)	Ivan Turgenev: "Fathers and Sons" Sarah Bernhardt's debut at the Comédie Française in Racine's "Iphigénie en Aulide" Flaubert: "Salammbô" Victor Hugo: "Les Misérables" Artemus Ward (C. F. Browne): "His Book" Friedrich Hebbel: "Die Nibelungen," dramatic trilogy Henry David Thoreau, Amer. author, d. (b. 1817) Maurice Barrès, Fr. author, b. (d. 1923) Maurice Maeterlinck, Fr.-Belg. poet, 1911 Nobel Prize, b. (d. 1949) Gerhart Hauptmann, Ger. dramatist, b. (d. 1946) *(contd)*	James Bryce: "The Holy Roman Empire" George Rawlinson: "The Five Great Monarchies of the Ancient Eastern World" (—1867) Herbert Spencer: "First Principles"

D. VISUAL ARTS	E. MUSIC	F. SCIENCE, TECHNOLOGY, GROWTH	G. DAILY LIFE	
Jakob Burckhardt: "The Civilization of the Renaissance in Italy" A. G. Decamps, Fr. painter, d. (b. 1803) Degas: "Spartan Boys and Girls Exercising" W. Holman Hunt: "Finding of the Saviour in the Temple" Manet: "Spanish Guitar Player," painting Philip Wilson Steer, Eng. artist, b. (d. 1942)	Gustav Mahler, Ger. composer, b. (d. 1911) Ignace Paderewski, Pol. pianist and statesman, b. (d. 1941) Franz von Suppé: "Das Pensionat," the first of all Viennese operettas First modern Welsh Eisteddfod Hugo Wolf, Aust. composer, b. (d. 1903)	Bunsen and Kirchhoff discover the elements cesium and rubidium G. T. Fechner: "Elements of Psychophysics" Lenoir constructs first practical internal-combustion engine Frederick Walton invents cork linoleum	Baseball becomes popular in New York and Boston; first recorded game in San Francisco "The Catholic Times" published During the last decade 424,000 people emigrated from Britain and 914,000 from Ireland to U.S. Food and Drugs Act enacted in Britain John C. Heenan (American) and Tom Sayers (British) fight a championship bout; fight ended by crowd breaking into the ring Brit. Open Golf Championship started; first champion, W. Park Christopher L. Sholes, Amer. inventor, devises primitive form of typewriter Beginning of skiing as competitive sport First horse-drawn tram	**1860**
Corot: "Orphée, Le Repos" Charles Garnier designs the Opéra, Paris (—1875) Aristide Maillol, Fr. sculptor, b. (d. 1944) Sandringham House built in Norfolk as country residence for Queen Victoria (—1870)	Heinrich Marschner, Ger. opera composer, d. (b. 1795) Nellie Melba, Australian operatic soprano, b. (d. 1931) Royal Academy of Music, London, founded "Tannhäuser," a scandal in Paris	Archaeopteryx: skeleton of link between reptile and bird discovered at Solnhofen, Germany; now at the British Museum, London William Crookes discovers thallium Frederick G. Hopkins, Eng. chemist, 1929 Nobel Prize for Medicine, b. (d. 1947) T. S. Mort (Sydney) builds first machine-chilled cold storage unit Fridtjof Nansen, Norw. Arctic explorer, b. (d. 1930) Pasteur: germ theory of fermentation Semmelweis: "Childbed Fever"	Mrs. Beeton (1836—1865): "Book of Household Management" Daily weather forecasts are begun in Britain Maximilian Harden, Ger. publicist, b. (d. 1927) First horse-drawn trams appear in London Krupp begins arms production in Essen, Germany Queen Victoria creates the Order of the Star of India U.S. introduces passport system Population figures (in millions): Russia, 76; U.S., 32; Great Britain, 23; Italy, 25	**1861**
Albert Memorial, London, designed by Gilbert Scott Manet: "Lola de Valence," painting Manet: "La Musique aux Tuileries" Moritz von Schwind: "The Honeymoon" Ingres: "Bain Turque"	Berlioz: "Béatrice et Bénédict," opera, Baden-Baden Claude Debussy, Fr. composer, b. (d. 1918) Frederick Delius, Eng. composer, b. (d. 1934) Edward German, Eng. composer, b. (d. 1936) Ludwig Köchel (1800—1877): "Catalogue of Mozart's Works" *(contd)*	W. H. Bragg, Eng. physicist, 1915 Nobel Prize, b. (d. 1942) Lion Foucault (1819—1868) successfully measures the speed of light R. J. Gatling (1818—1903) constructs 10-barrel gun bearing his name Helmholtz: "The Doctrine of the Sensations of Tones" Johann von Lamont discovers earth currents Pnilipp Lenard, Ger. physicist, 1905 Nobel Prize, b. (d. 1947) Ger. botanist Julius Sachs (1832—1897) demonstrates that starch is produced by *(contd)*	Swiss humanist Jean Henri Dunant (1828—1910) proposes in his book "Souvenir de Solferino" the foundation of an international voluntary relief organization–the Red Cross Eng. cricket team tours Australia for first time International Exhibition, London	**1862**

	A. HISTORY, POLITICS	B. LITERATURE, THEATER	C. RELIGION, PHILOSOPHY, LEARNING
1862 contd		Edith Wharton, Amer. author, b. (d. 1937) Johann Nestroy, Aust. dramatist, d. (b. 1801) Arthur Schnitzler, Aust. poet, b. (d. 1931) Ludwig Uhland, Ger. poet, d. (b. 1787)	
1863	Arizona and Idaho organized as U.S. territories; West Virginia becomes a state of the U.S. Lincoln issues Emancipation Proclamation Jan. 1 Confederate victory at Chancellorsville, Va.; defeats at Gettysburg, Pa., and Vicksburg, Miss.; surrender at Fort Hudson; further defeat at Chattanooga, Tenn.; victory at Chickamauga, Ga.; Lincoln's "Gettysburg Address" at the dedication of military cemetery Mohammed Said, Khedive of Egypt, d.; succeeded by Ismail (d. 1879) William, Prince of Denmark, becomes George I, King of Greece (—1919) Civil War breaks out in Afghanistan after the death of Dost Mohammed Schleswig incorporated into Denmark Frederick VII, King of Denmark, d.; succeeded by Christian IX Saxon and Hanoverian troops enter Holstein Austen Chamberlain, Brit. statesman, b. (d. 1937) David Lloyd George, Brit. statesman, b. (d. 1945) French capture Mexico City and proclaim Archduke Maximilian of Austria emperor	Gabriele D'Annunzio, Ital. poet, b. (d. 1938) Hermann Bahr, Aust. author, b. (d. 1934) Richard Dehmel, Ger. poet, b. (d. 1920) Gautier: "Le Capitaine Fracasse" Jakob Grimm, Ger. writer and philologist, d. (b. 1785) Edward Everett Hale: "Man without a Country" Friedrich Hebbel, Ger. dramatist, d. (b. 1813) Anthony Hope, Eng. novelist, b. (d. 1933) Charles Kingsley: "The Water Babies" Henry Wadsworth Longfellow: "Tales of a Wayside Inn," Part I, verse narrative Arthur Quiller-Couch, Eng. novelist and critic, b. (d. 1944) Constantin Stanislavsky, Russ. theatrical producer, b. (d. 1938) W. M. Thackeray, Eng. novelist, d. (b. 1811) Alfred de Vigny, Fr. poet, d. (b. 1797)	S. R. Gardiner: "History of England ... 1603—1642" (—1882) T. H. Huxley: "Evidence as to Man's Place in Nature" A. W. Kinglake: "The Invasion of the Crimea" (—1887) Charles Lyell: "The Antiquity of Man" J. S. Mill: "Utilitarianism" Ernest Renan: "Vie de Jésus" Werner Sombart, Ger. sociologist and economist b. (d. 1941) University of Massachusetts, Amherst, founded as Massachusetts Agricultural College
1864	Austria and Prussia send ultimatum to Denmark; troops enter Schleswig; Dan. forces defeated at Düppel; Denmark invaded; London conference tries in vain to solve Schleswig-Holstein question, but in Peace of Vienna Denmark cedes Schleswig, Holstein, and Lauenburg to Austria and Prussia Archduke Maximilian of Austria accepts Mexican crown, and he and his wife, Carlotta, are made Emperor and Empress of Mexico (—1867) Gen. Ulysses S. Grant succeeds Gen. Halleck as Commander-in-Chief of Union armies Gen. Sherman marches his army from Chattanooga, Tenn., through Georgia; defeats Confederate army at Atlanta, and occupies Savannah Abraham Lincoln re-elected President of the U.S. Massacre of the Cheyenne and Arapahoe Indians at Sand Creek, Colo. Italy renounces its claims to Rome; Florence is made the capital (—1870) in place of Turin Territory of Montana organized in U.S.; Nevada becomes a state Eleutherios Venizelos, Greek statesman, b. (d. 1936) King Maximilian II of Bavaria d.; succeeded by Louis II First International Workingmen's Association founded by Karl Marx, London and New York Confederate agents set Barnum Museum and Astor House afire in attempt to burn New York City	Deutsche Shakespeare-Gesellschaft founded at Weimar Dickens: "Our Mutual Friend" Jules de Goncourt: "Renée Mauperin" Nathaniel Hawthorne, Amer. novelist, d. (b. 1804) Henrik Ibsen: "The Crown Pretenders" Erik A. Karlfeldt, Swed. author, 1931 Nobel Prize, b. (d. 1931) Walter Savage Landor, Eng. author, d. (b. 1775) Wilhelm Raabe: "Der Hungerpastor," Ger. novel Tolstoi: "War and Peace" (—1869) Anthony Trollope: "The Small House at Allington" Frank Wedekind, Ger. dramatist, b. (d. 1918) Israel Zangwill, Eng. novelist and Zionist, b. (d. 1926)	Cesare Lombroso (1836—1909): "Genius and Madness" Cardinal Newman: "Apologia pro Vita Sua" Syllabus Errorum issued by Pope Pius IX: condemns Liberalism, Socialism, and Rationalism

D. VISUAL ARTS	E. MUSIC	F. SCIENCE, TECHNOLOGY, GROWTH	G. DAILY LIFE	
	Verdi: "La Forza del Destino," opera, St. Petersburg	photosynthesis		1862 contd
Ferdinand Victor Eugène Delacroix, Fr. painter, d. (b. 1799) Gustave Doré: "Don Quichotte," illustrations Manet: "Déjeuner sur l'herbe" and "Olympia," paintings Edvard Munch, Norw. painter, b. (d. 1944) Lucien Pissarro, Fr. painter, b. (d. 1944) Dante Gabriel Rossetti: "Beata Beatrix," painting The "Salon des Refusés" in Paris Whistler: "Little White Girl," painting	Berlioz: "Les Troyens," opera, Paris Bizet: "Les Pêcheurs de perles," opera, Paris Pietro Mascagni, Ital. composer, b. (d. 1945) Felix von Weingartner, Aust. composer and conductor, b. (d. 1942)	Billroth: "Die allgemeine chirurgische Pathologie und Therapie" Ebenezer Butterick develops first paper dress patterns Henry Ford, Amer. automobile manufacturer, b. (d. 1947) Sir Francis Galton (1822-1911): "Meteorographica or Methods of Mapping the Weather" Thomas Graham (1805—1869) invents process for separating gases by atmolysis National Academy of Sciences founded Washington, D.C. Henry Clifton Sorby (1826—1908) discovers microstructure of steel leading to development of science of metallurgy John Speke and James Grant descend Nile to Gondokoro, where they meet Sir Samuel White Baker on his way upriver Open-hearth steel furnace developed by Martin brothers in France based on Siemens process First railroad in New Zealand opens between Christchurch and Ferrymead	Football Association founded, London Grand Prix de Paris first run at Longchamp Beginning of construction of London Underground railroad (see 1884) William Randolph Hearst, Amer. newspaper publisher, b. (d. 1951) Fr. photographer A. F. Nadar makes ascent in his balloon "Le Géant" Edward, Prince of Wales, marries Princess Alexandra of Denmark Henry Royce, Eng. automotive engineer and industrialist, b. (d. 1933) U.S. Congress establishes free city mail delivery Travelers Insurance Company founded in Hartford, Conn. Roller skating introduced to America First stolen base in baseball by Eddie Cuthbert of Philadelphia Keystones against Brooklyn Atlantics Joe Coburn wins Amer. boxing championship from Mike McCoole in 63-round match, Charleston, Md.	1863
Leo von Klenze, Ger. architect, d. (b. 1784) John Leech, Eng. cartoonist, d. (b. 1817) Henri Toulouse-Lautrec, Fr. painter, b. (d. 1901)	Eugen D'Albert, Scot.-born Ger. composer and pianist, b. (d. 1932) Bruckner: Symphony No. 0 ("Die Nullte"), revised 1869 Stephen Foster, Amer. songwriter, d. (b. 1826) Giacomo Meyerbeer, Ger. composer, d. (b. 1791) Offenbach: "La Belle Hélène," operetta, Paris Richard Strauss, Ger. composer, b. (d. 1949)	Sir Samuel White Baker discovers Lake Albert Joseph Bertrand: "Treatise on Differential and Integral Calculus" (—1870) Walther Nernst, Ger. physicist and chemist, 1920 Nobel Prize, b. (d. 1941) Louis Pasteur invents pasteurization (for wine) Wilhelm Wien, Ger. physicist, 1911 Nobel Prize, b. (d. 1928)	First salmon cannery in U.S. at Washington, Calif. Geneva Convention establishes the neutrality of battlefield medical facilities Octavia Hill begins London tenement-dwelling reforms Knights of Pythias founded, Washington, D.C. Ferdinand Lasalle, Ger. socialist leader, d. (b. 1825) "Neue Freie Presse" founded in Vienna Ital. archaeologist, Giovanni B. de Rossi publishes the results of his exploration of Roman catacombs "In God We Trust" first appears on U.S. coins Travers Stakes established at first racetrack in Saratoga, N.Y. Admiral Farragut, attacking Confederate forces in Mobile Bay, Ala., says, "Damn the torpedoes! Full speed ahead!"	1864

	A. HISTORY, POLITICS	B. LITERATURE, THEATER	C. RELIGION, PHILOSOPHY, LEARNING
1865	Union fleet takes Charleston; Richmond, Va., surrenders to Grant; Jefferson Davis appoints Gen. Robert E. Lee General-in-Chief of Confederate Army; Confederate States of America formally surrender at Appomattox Apr. 9 Abraham Lincoln assassinated Apr. 14; succeeded as president by Andrew Johnson Jefferson Davis, President of Confederacy, captured and imprisoned U.S. Civil War ends May 26 (surrender of last Confederate army at Shreveport, La.) Bismarck and Napoleon III meet in Biarritz Lord Palmerston d. (b. 1784); succeeded as Brit. Prime Minister by Lord John Russell King Leopold I of Belgium d.; succeeded by his son Leopold II (—1909) Thirteenth Amendment to U.S. Constitution abolishes slavery Wellington becomes capital of New Zealand Warren G. Harding, b. (d. 1923), President of U.S. 1921—1923 King George V of Great Britain, b. (d. 1936) Erich Ludendorff, Ger. general and politician, b. (d. 1937) Outbreak of war (—1866) between Boers of Orange Free State and Basutos	Matthew Arnold: "Essays in Criticism" Josh Billings: "Sayings" David Belasco (aged 12): "Jim Black, or The Regulator's Revenge," drama Mrs. Patrick Campbell (Beatrice Tanner), Eng. actress, b. (d. 1940) Lewis Carroll (C. L. Dodgson, 1832—1898): "Alice's Adventures in Wonderland" Mary Mapes Dodge: "Hans Brinker, or The Silver Skates," children's story Elizabeth Gaskell, Eng. novelist, d. (b. 1810) Rudyard Kipling, Eng. author, b. (d. 1936) Dimitri Merezhkovsky, Russ. author, b. (d. 1942) Cardinal Newman: "Dream of Gerontius," poem later set to music by Edward Elgar, 1900 Ouida (Louise de la Ramée, 1840—1908): "Strathmore," novel Adalbert Stifter: "Witiko" A. C. Swinburne: "Atalanta in Calydon" Mark Twain: "The Celebrated Jumping Frog of Calaveras County," short story Paul Verlaine: "Poèmes saturniens" Walt Whitman: "Drum Taps" William Butler Yeats, Irish poet, 1923 Nobel Prize, b. (d. 1939)	Henri Baudrillart: "La Liberté du travail" W. S. Jevons: "The Coal Question" W. E. H. Lecky: "A History of the Rise and Influence of Rationalism in Europe" J. S. Mill: "Auguste Comte and Positivism" Ger. mathematician Julius Plücker (1801—1868) invents line geometry Pierre Joseph Proudhon, Fr. political philosopher, d. (b. 1809) J. R. Seeley: "Ecce Homo" Purdue University, Cornell University, University of Maine, and University of Kentucky founded
1866	Alexander Cuza, Prince of Rumania, dethroned; succeeded by Karl, Prince of Hohenzollern, as King Carol I (—1914) Prussan-Ital. alliance against Austria; Prussian troops annex the duchy of Holstein; secret treaty between Austria and France concerning Fr. neutrality; end of Ger. Confederation; Prussia invades Saxony, Hanover, and Hesse; Italy declares war on Austria; Italians defeated at Custozza; Prussian victory at Langensalza against Hanover, and at Sadowa (Königgrätz) against Austria; Ital. fleet destroyed by Austrians at Lissa; preliminary peace treaty between Prussia and Austria at Nikolsburg followed by armistice and confirmed by Peace of Prague; Prussia annexes Hanover, Hesse, Nassau, and Frankfurt (as agreed in Peace of Prague); Treaty of Vienna ends Austro-Ital. war; Venetian plebiscite endorses union with Italy; peace between Prussia and Saxony; Schleswig-Holstein incorporated into Prussia Ismail, Khedive of Egypt, granted rights of primogeniture by the Sultan of Turkey Revolts in Crete against Turk. rule *(contd)*	Charles Baudelaire: "Les Epaves" Jacinto Benavente, Span. dramatist, 1922 Nobel Prize, b. (d. 1954) Alphonse Daudet: "Lettres de mon moulin" Dostoevsky: "Crime and Punishment" Robert Hamerling: "Ahasver in Rom," novel Ibsen: "Brand" Henry Irving makes his London debut Kingsley: "Hereward the Wake," historical novel Thomas Love Peacock, Eng. novelist, d. (b. 1785) Romain Rolland, Fr. author, 1915 Nobel Prize, b. (d. 1944) Marie Tempest, Eng. actress, b. (d. 1942) H. G. Wells, Eng. author, b. (d. 1946)	Benedetto Croce, Ital. philosopher, b. (d. 1952) Nathan Söderblom, Archbishop of Uppsala, b. (d. 1931) Pierre Larousse: "Grand dictionnaire universel du XIX siècle" (—1876) Friedrich Lange: "History of Materialism" American Evangelical Alliance founded

D. VISUAL ARTS	E. MUSIC	F. SCIENCE, TECHNOLOGY, GROWTH	G. DAILY LIFE	
Doré: illustrations to the Bible Winslow Homer: "Prisoners from the Front," paintings George Innes: "Peace and Plenty," landscape painting Joseph Paxton, Eng. architect, d. (b. 1801) Hippolyte Taine: "La Philosophie de l'art" (—1869) Ferdinand Waldmüller, Aust. painter, d. (b. 1793) Yale University opens first Department of Fine Arts in U.S.	Paul Dukas, Fr. composer, b. (d. 1935) Alexander Glazunov, Russ. composer, b. (d. 1936) Meyerbeer: "L'Africaine," posth. opera, Paris Schubert: "Unfinished Symphony" (see 1822) first performed, Vienna Jean Sibelius, Finn. composer, b. (d. 1957) Suppé: "Die schöne Galathee," operetta, Vienna Wagner: "Tristan und Isolde," Munich	Atlantic cable finally completed William R. Hamilton, Ir. mathematician d. (b. 1805) John Wesley Hyatt invents composition billiard ball, replacing ivory Ger. chemist F. A. Kekulé (1829—1896) explains the structure of aromatic compounds through his benzene ring theory Joseph Lister initiates antiseptic surgery by using carbolic acid on a compound wound Thaddeus Lowe (1832—1913) invents ice machine Massachusetts Institute of Technology founded Clerk Maxwell: "Treatise on Electricity and Magnetism" Gregor Mendel enunciates his Law of Heredity First oil pipeline (six miles) in Pennsylvania, U.S. Pasteur succeeds in curing silkworm disease, saving the French silk industry Ivan M. Sechenov (1829—1905): "Reflexes of the Brain," on physiological basis of psychic processes	Baseball Convention, representing 91 baseball clubs, held in New York; at the same time professionalism appears Nottingham pawnbroker William Booth (1829—1912) moves to London to organize the Christian Revival Association, renamed (1878) The Salvation Army First carpet sweeper comes into use Debut of W. G. Grace as cricketer in Gentlemen vs. Players Ku Klux Klan founded, Pulaski, Tenn. London Metropolitan Fire Service established Eng. barrister John Macgregor pioneers canoeing as a sport James Miller McKim founds "The Nation" The first railroad sleeping cars, designed by George M. Pullman, appear in U.S. The Queensberry Rules governing boxing are first outlined "San Francisco Examiner" and "San Francisco Chronicle" founded First train holdup at North Bend, Ohio Union stockyards open at Chicago 1700 die in explosion of "Sultana" on Mississippi River Edward Whymper climbs the Matterhorn First woman, Maria Mitchell, appointed as professor of astronomy, Vassar College	**1865**
Degas begins to paint his ballet scenes Roger Fry, Eng. artist and art critic, b. (d. 1934) Vassili Kandinsky, Russ. painter, b. (d. 1944) Monet: "Camille," painting	Ferruccio Busoni, Ital. pianist and composer, b. (d. 1924) Offenbach: "La Vie Parisienne," operetta, Paris Smetana: "Prodaná Nevěstá" (The Bartered Bride), opera, Prague Ambroise Thomas: "Mignon," opera, Paris	Aeronautical Society of Great Britain founded Ernst Haeckel: "General Morphology" (fundamental law of biogenetics) T. H. Morgan, Amer. scientist, 1933 Nobel Prize, b. (d. 1945) Charles Nicolle, Fr. bacteriologist, 1928 Nobel Prize, b. (d. 1936) Alfred Nobel invents dynamite Alfred Werner, Swiss chemist, 1913 Nobel Prize, b. (d. 1919) Eng. engineer Robert Whitehead (1823—1905) invents underwater torpedo	Dr. T. J. Barnardo (1845—1905) opens his first home for destitute children at Stepney, London "Black Friday" on London Stock Exchange Tom Morris of St. Andrews (1850—1875) wins his first professional golf championship	**1866**

	A. HISTORY, POLITICS	B. LITERATURE, THEATER	C. RELIGION, PHILOSOPHY, LEARNING
1866 contd	James Ramsay MacDonald, Brit. statesman, b. (d. 1937) Sun Yat-sen, Chin. statesman, b. (d. 1927)		
1867	Fenian outrages in Ireland and in Manchester Austro-Hungarian dual monarchy created by "Ausgleich" ("compromise"); Francis Joseph I crowned King of Hungary at Budapest; new Aust. constitution accepts dual system Nebraska becomes a state of the U.S. Napoleon III withdraws his support from Maximilian in Mexico; Fr. troops leave the country; Maximilian executed British North America Act establishes Dominion of Canada Russia sells Alaska to U.S. for $7,200,000 N. Ger. Confederation founded Brit. Parliamentary Reform Act Ferdinand Bebel–first socialist member of N. Ger. Reichstag Garibaldi begins "The March on Rome," is defeated by Fr. and papal troops at Mentana, and taken prisoner Princess Mary of Teck, the future queen consort of George V of Great Britain, b. (d. 1953) Stanley Baldwin, Brit. statesman, b. (d. 1947) Walther Rathenau, Ger. statesman, b. (assassinated 1922) Joseph Pilsudski, Pol. soldier and statesman, b. (d. 1935)	G. W. Russell ("A.E."), Ir. poet, b. (d. 1935) Arnold Bennett, Eng. author, b. (d. 1931) Luigi Pirandello, Ital. dramatist, 1934 Nobel Prize, b. (d. 1936) John Galsworthy, Eng. author, b. (d. 1933) Charles Pierre Baudelaire d. (b. 1821) Reclams Universal Bibliothek, first of all paperback series, founded at Leipzig (first number, Goethe's "Faust I") Natsume Soseki, Jap. novelist, b. (d. 1916) Ludwig Thoma, Ger. author, b. (d. 1921) Charles de Coster: "La Légende de Thyl Ulenspiegel" Oliver Wendell Holmes: "The Guardian Angel" Ouida: "Under Two Flags" Trollope: "The Last Chronicle of Barset" Turgenev: "Smoke" Zola: "Thérèse Raquin" Ibsen: "Peer Gynt" Mark Twain: "The Jumping Frog" Wladislau Reymont, Pol. novelist, 1924 Nobel Prize, b. (d. 1925)	Walter Bagehot: "The English Constitution" E. A. Freeman: "History of the Norman Conquest" (—1876) Marx: "Das Kapital," vol. I Pope Pius IX, on the 18th centenary of St. Peter and St. Paul, announces his intention to hold an ecumenical council
1868	Brit. armed expedition dispatched to Ethiopia; Magdala captured Shogun Kekei of Japan abdicates; shogunate abolished; Meiji dynasty restored U.S. President Johnson impeached for violating Tenure-of-Office Act but acquitted by Senate Disraeli becomes Brit. Prime Minister (resigns same year) Prussia confiscates territory of King of Hanover Russians occupy Samarkand King Michael III of Serbia assassinated; succeeded by Milan IV (—1889) Revolution in Spain; Queen Isabella II is deposed and flees to France Ulysses S. Grant elected President of the U.S. William E. Gladstone becomes Brit. Prime Minister (—1874) Nicolaus von Horthy, Hungarian admiral and politician, b. (d. 1957) 14th Amendment to U.S. Constitution protects individual's rights against infringement by state governments, denies government office to certain Civil War rebels, and repudiates Confederate war debts	L. M. Alcott: "Little Women" Georg Brandes: "Aesthetic Studies" Robert Browning: "The Ring and the Book" Wilkie Collins: "The Moonstone," one of the first detective stories Dostoevsky: "The Idiot" Stefan George, Ger. poet, b. (d. 1933) Maxim Gorki, Russ. author, b. (d. 1936) Edmond Rostand, Fr. dramatist, b. (d. 1918) Adalbert Stifter, Aust. novelist, d. (b. 1805)	Bakunin founds Alliance internationale de la démocratie sociale Aust. schools freed from Church control Charles Darwin: "The Variation of Animals and Plants under Domestication" Ernst Haeckel: "Natural History of Creation" A. H. Stephens: "A Constitutional View of the War between the States"

D. VISUAL ARTS	E. MUSIC	F. SCIENCE, TECHNOLOGY, GROWTH	G. DAILY LIFE	
				1866 contd
Cézanne: "Rape," painting Peter von Cornelius, Ger. painter, d. (b. 1783) Jean Dominique Ingres, Fr. painter, d. (b. 1780) Käthe Kollwitz, Ger. artist, b. (d. 1945) Millais: "Boyhood of Raleigh" Emil Nolde, Ger. painter, b. (d. 1956) Paris World's Fair introduces Jap. art to the West Théodore Rousseau, Fr. painter, d. (b. 1812)	Bizet: "La Jolie Fille de Perth," opera, Paris Gounod: "Roméo et Juliette," opera, Paris Offenbach: "La Grande-duchesse de Gérolstein, operetta, Paris Johann Strauss II: The "Blue Danube," waltz A. S. Sullivan: "Cox and Box," comic opera Arturo Toscanini, Ital. conductor, b. (d. 1957) Verdi: "Don Carlos," Paris	Marie (Sklodowska) Curie, Pol.-Fr. scientist, Nobel Prizes, 1903 and 1911, b. (d. 1934) Michael Faraday, Eng. chemist and physicist, d. (b. 1791) Livingstone explores Congo Pierre Michaux begins to manufacture bicycles Joseph F. Monier (1823—1906) patents a reinforced concrete process Railroad completed through Brenner Pass Discovery of S. African diamond field Brit. scientist William Thomson, later Lord Kelvin, (1824—1907), invents syphon recorder	Prussia buys mail service from the Thurn und Taxis family "The Queensberry Rules," by John Graham Chambers of the London Amateur Athletic Club Gold discovered in Wyoming	**1867**
Degas: "L'Orchestre," painting Development of Fr. impressionist style Hans Makart: "The Plague in Florence" Renoir: "The Skaters," painting George Street designs the Law Courts, London (—1882)	Granville Bantock, Eng. composer, b. (d. 1946) Brahms: "Ein deutsches Requiem," Op. 45 Moussorgsky begins work on "Boris Godunov" (—1874) Rossini d. (b. 1792) Max von Schillings, Ger. composer and conductor, b. (d. 1933) Wagner: "Die Meistersinger von Nürnberg," Munich Tchaikovsky: Symphony No. 1	Skeleton of Cro-Magnon man from Upper Paleolithic age (first homo sapiens in Europe, successor of Neanderthal man) found in France by Louis Lartet Fritz Haber, Ger. chemist, 1918 Nobel Prize, b. (d. 1934) Robert A. Millikan, U.S. physicist, 1923 Nobel Prize, b. (d. 1953) T. W. Richards, U.S. chemist, 1914 Nobel Prize, b. (d. 1928) R. F. Scott, Eng. Antarctic explorer, b. (d. 1912)	Meat-packing factory of P. D. Armour opens in Chicago The game of badminton devised at the Duke of Beaufort's residence, Badminton Hall, Gloucestershire Earliest recorded bicycle race (over two kilometers) at the Parc de St. Cloud, Paris The first professional U.S. Baseball Club, The Cincinnati Red Stockings, founded Cincinnati Red Stockings introduce uniforms J. L. Garvin, Eng. journalist, b. (d. 1947) Harold Harmsworth, Lord Rothermere, Eng. newspaper proprietor, b. (d. 1940) First regular Trades Union Congress held at Manchester, England Whitaker's Almanack appears in England	**1868**

	A. HISTORY, POLITICS	B. LITERATURE, THEATER	C. RELIGION, PHILOSOPHY, LEARNING
1869	Following a Turk. ultimatum, Greece agrees to leave Crete Gen. Grant inaugurated as 18th President of the U.S. Parliamentary system reintroduced in France U.S. National Prohibition Party formed in Chicago Red River Rebellion in Canada Opening of Suez Canal by Empress Eugénie Neville Chamberlain, Brit. politician, b. (d. 1940) Mahatma Gandhi, Indian nationalist leader, b. (d. 1948)	R. D. Blackmore: "Lorna Doone" Flaubert: "L'Education sentimentale" André Gide, Fr. author, b. (d. 1951) W. S. Gilbert: "Bab Ballads" Ludovic Halévy: "Froufrou" Bret Harte: "The Outcasts of Poker Flat" Victor Hugo: "L'Homme qui rit" Alphonse de Lamartine, Fr. author, d. (b. 1790) Stephen Leacock, Canadian humorist, b. (d. 1944) Charles Augustin Sainte-Beuve d. (b. 1804) Mark Twain: "The Innocents Abroad" Verlaine: "Fêtes Galantes"	Matthew Arnold: "Culture and Anarchy" Walter Bagehot: "Physics and Politics, etc." Eduard Hartmann: "The Philosophy of the Unconscious" W. E. H. Lecky: "A History of European Morals from Augustus to Charlemagne" J. S. Mill: "On The Subjection of Women" Meeting of the First Vatican Council–Cardinal Manning advocates a definition of papal infallibility
1870	Baden decides to join N. Ger. Confederation End of Red River Rebellion; Manitoba becomes Canadian province Isabella of Spain abdicates in favor of Alfonso XII Prince Leopold of Hohenzollern accepts Span. throne but is forced to withdraw by the head of the House of Hohenzollern, King William I, following Fr. protests Bismarck's "Ems Telegram" Franco-Prussian War: France declares war on Prussia and is defeated at Weissenburg, Worth, Mars-la-Tour, Gravelotte, and finally Napoleon III capitulates at Sedan Revolt in Paris and proclamation of the Third Republic; siege of Paris by Prussians begins; Metz and Strasbourg surrender Western Australia granted representative government Italians enter Rome and name it their capital city Nikolai Lenin, Russ. Communist leader, b. (d. 1924) Jan Smuts, S. African soldier and statesman, b. (d. 1950)	Karl Anzengruber: "Der Pfarrer von Kirchfeld" Aust. play depicting peasant life Ivan Bunin, Russ. poet, 1933 Nobel Prize, b. (d. 1953) Charles Dickens d. (b.1812) Disraeli: "Lothair" Alexandre Dumas père d. (b. 1802) Jules de Goncourt, Fr. author, d. (b. 1830) Ivan Goncharov: "The Precipice," Russ. novel Harry Lauder, Scot. music-hall star, b. (d. 1950) Marie Lloyd, Eng. music-hall star, b. (d. 1922) Prosper Mérimée, Fr. author, d. (b. 1803) Charles de Montalembert, Fr. author, d. (b. 1810) Jules Verne: "Twenty Thousand Leagues Under the Sea"	Alfred Adler, Aust. psychiatrist, b. (d. 1937) Keble College, Oxford, founded Heinrich Schliemann begins to excavate Troy First Vatican Council promulgates the dogma of papal infallibilty
1871	William I, King of Prussia, proclaimed Ger. Emperor at Versailles; Paris capitulates; France signs armistice; Fr. National Assembly meets at Bordeaux; preliminary peace between Germany and France is followed by Peace of Frankfurt, by which France cedes Alsace-Lorraine to Germany and pays indemnity of five billion francs The Commune in Paris rules for two months L. A. Thiers elected Fr. President Treaty of Washington settles existing difficulties between Britain and U.S. Italian Law of Guarantees allows the pope possession of Vatican Brit. Act of Parliament legalizes labor unions British Columbia joins Dominion of Canada "Kulturkampf" against Catholic Church in Prussia Basutoland becomes part of Cape Colony; Britain annexes diamond fields of Kimberley Friedrich Ebert, Ger. Social Democratic leader, b. (d. 1925) Rasputin, Russ. monk, b. (d. 1916)	Willibald Alexis, Ger. novelist, d. (b. 1798) Lewis Carroll: "Through the Looking Glass" Stephen Crane, Amer. author, b. (d. 1900) Theodore Dreiser, Amer. novelist, b. (d. 1945) George Eliot: "Middlemarch" Heinrich Mann, Ger. novelist, b. (d. 1950) Christian Morgenstern, Ger. poet, b. (d. 1914) Ostrovsky: "The Forest," Russ. play Marcel Proust, Fr. novelist, b. (d. 1922) Paul Valéry, Fr. poet, b. (d. 1945) Zola: "Les Rougon-Macquart," series of novels (—1893)	First congress of Old Catholics meets in Munich Charles Darwin: "The Descent of Man" Jehovah's Witnesses founded Mommsen: "Roman Constitutional Law" (—1876) John Ruskin: "Fors Clavigera" (—1887) Adolph Wagner: "The Social Question"

D. VISUAL ARTS	E. MUSIC	F. SCIENCE, TECHNOLOGY, GROWTH	G. DAILY LIFE	
Edwin Lutyens, Brit. architect. b. (d. 1944) Manet: "The Execution of Emperor Maximilian of Mexico" Henri Matisse, Fr. painter, b. (d. 1954) Manet: "The Balcony," painting Hans Poelzig, Ger. architect, b. (d. 1936) Frank Lloyd Wright, Amer. architect, b. (d. 1959)	Berlioz d. (b. 1803) Sidney Jones, Eng. composer, b. (d. 1946) Karl Loewe, Ger. composer d. (b. 1796) Hans Pfitzner, Ger. musician and director, b. (d. 1949) Siegfried Wagner, Ger. composer, b. (d. 1930) R. Wagner: "Rheingold," opera, Munich Henry J. Wood, Eng. conductor, b. (d. 1944)	Francis Galton: "Hereditary Genius," pioneering treatise on eugenics J. W. Hyatt (1837—1920) invents celluloid Mendeleyev formulates his periodic law for the classification of the elements Gustav Nachtigal (1834—1888) explores the Sudan and the Sahara	Brit. debtors' prisons are abolished Cincinnati Red Stockings become first salaried baseball team The famous clipper ship "Cutty Sark" is launched Girton College, Cambridge, founded First Nihilist Congress meets at Basel, Switzerland First postcards introduced in Austria Princeton and Rutgers originate intercollegiate football at New Brunswick, N. J. Skoda works, Pilsen, Bohemia, open	**1869**
Ernst Barlach, Ger. sculptor, b. (d. 1938) Corot: "La perle," painting Fantin-Latour: "Un Atelier à Batignolles," painting	Delibes: "Coppélia," ballet, Paris Founding of Société Nationale de Musique, France Tchaikovsky: Fantasy-overture "Romeo and Juliet," Moscow Wagner marries Cosima von Bülow, daughter of Franz Liszt Wagner: "Die Walküre," Munich	T. H. Huxley: "Theory of Biogenesis" Adolf Nordenskjöld explores the interior of Greenland	"Dictionary of American Biography" is issued for the first time W. G. Grace and his brothers found the Gloucester Cricket Club Robert E. Lee, Amer. Confederate general, d. (b. 1807) Rosa Luxemburg, Ger. socialist leader, b. (murdered 1919) John D. Rockefeller (1839—1937) founds Standard Oil Company	**1870**
Lyonel Feininger, Amer. painter, b. (d. 1956) Rossetti: "The Dream of Dante" Georges Rouault, Fr. painter, b. (d. 1958) Moritz von Schwind, Ger. painter, d. (b. 1804)	Albert Hall, London, opened "L'Internationale" ("Debout, les damnés de la Terre!") written and composed by Pottier and Degeyter, two Fr. workers Saint-Saëns: "Le Rouet d'Omphale," symphonic poem, Op. 31 Verdi: "Aïda," Cairo	Simon Ingersoll (U.S.) invents pneumatic rock drill Mount Cenis Tunnel opened G. A. Hansen discovers leprosy bacillus Ernest Rutherford, Eng. scientist, 1908 Nobel Prize, b. (d. 1937)	Bank Holidays introduced in England and Wales P. T. Barnum opens his circus, "The Greatest Show on Earth," in Brooklyn, N.Y. F.A. Cup established The Great Fire in Chicago National Association of Professional Baseball Players founded in New York (dissolved 1876) Stanley meets Livingstone at Ujiji Population figures (in millions): Germany 41; U.S. 39; France 36; Japan 33; Great Britain 26; Ireland 5.4; Italy 26.8 S.S. "Oceanic," White Star Line, launched–first of the large modern luxury liners	**1871**

	A. HISTORY, POLITICS	B. LITERATURE, THEATER	C. RELIGION, PHILOSOPHY, LEARNING
1872	Civil war in Spain–Carlists are defeated and Don Carlos escapes to France T. F. Burgers elected President of Transvaal Republic Ballot Act in Britain, voting by secret ballot Three-Emperors League established in Berlin; alliance between Germany, Russia, and Austria-Hungary Grant reelected President of U.S. (in spite of public scandals during his administration) Compulsory military service introduced in Japan U.S. General Amnesty Act pardons most ex-Confederates Leon Blum, Fr. statesman, b. (d. 1950) Calvin Coolidge, future President of U.S., b. (d. 1933) Giuseppe Mazzini, Ital. patriot and nationalist, d. (b. 1805)	Max Beerbohm, Eng. essayist, b. (d. 1956) Samuel Butler: "Erewhon, or Over the Range" Alphonse Daudet: "Aventures prodigieuses de Tartarin de Tarascon" Sergei Diaghilev, Russ. ballet impresario, b. (d. 1929) Eleonora Duse's debut at 14 in Verona as Juliet Théophile Gautier, Fr. author, d. (b. 1811) Franz Grillparzer, Aust. dramatist, d. (b. 1791) Thomas Hardy: "Under the Greenwood Tree" Turgenev: "A Month in the Country" Jules Verne: "Around the World in 80 Days"	Jesuits expelled from Germany D. F. Strauss: "The Old Faith and the New" Bertrand Russell, Eng. philosopher, b. (d. 1970) Ludwig Feuerbach, Ger. philosopher, d. (b. 1804) Ludwig Klages, Ger. philosopher, b. (d. 1956)
1873	Napoleon III, at Chiselhurst, England, d. (b. 1808) Republic proclaimed in Spain Thiers falls and MacMahon is elected Fr. President Financial panic in Vienna (May) and New York (Sept.) Abolition of slave markets and exports in Zanzibar Germans evacuate France Famine in Bengal	Henri Barbusse, Fr. novelist, b. (d. 1935) Edward Bulwer-Lytton, Eng. author, d. (b. 1803) Ford Madox Ford, Eng. author, b. (d. 1939) Paul Heyse: "Kinder der Welt" Alessandro Manzoni, Ital. author, d. (b. 1785) Gerald du Maurier, Brit. actor-manager, b. (d. 1934) J. S. Mill: "Autobiography" Max Reinhardt, Ger. theatrical producer, b. (d. 1943) Rimbaud: "Une Saison en enfer" Tolstoi: "Anna Karenina" (—1875)	John Stuart Mill, Eng. philosopher, d. (b. 1806) Walter Pater: "Studies in the History of the Renaissance" Herbert Spencer: "The Study of Sociology" Hippolyte Taine: "Les Origines de la France contemporaine"
1874	End of Ashanti war Disraeli becomes prime minister (—1880) Political disturbances in Arkansas Swiss Constitution revised Prince of Wales (the future King Edward VII) visits France Britain annexes Fiji Islands Alfonso XII, son of Queen Isabella, proclaimed King of Spain (—1885) Herbert Hoover, U.S. statesman and President, b. (d. 1964) Chaim Weizmann, first President of Israel, b. (d. 1952) Winston Churchill, Brit. statesman, b. (d. 1965)	Alarcón: "The Three-cornered Hat" G. K. Chesterton, Eng. author, b. (d. 1936) Flaubert: "La Tentation de Saint Antoine" Robert Frost, Amer. poet, b. (d. 1963) Thomas Hardy: "Far from the Madding Crowd" Hugo von Hofmannsthal, Aust. poet, b. (d. 1929) Victor Hugo: "Ninety-Three" W. Somerset Maugham, Eng. author, b. (d. 1965) Leopold von Sacher-Masoch (1835—1895): "Die Messalinen Wiens," "masochist" novel Gertrude Stein, Amer. poet, b. (d. 1946) Verlaine: "Romances sans paroles"	Ernst Cassirer, Ger. philosopher, b. (d. 1945) Ernst Haeckel: "Anthopogenie" Henry Sidgwick: "Methods of Ethics"

D. VISUAL ARTS	E. MUSIC	F. SCIENCE, TECHNOLOGY, GROWTH	G. DAILY LIFE	
Böcklin: "Battle of the Centaurs," painting Cézanne and Pissarro at Auvers-sur-Oise Whistler: "The Artist's Mother"	Bizet: incidental music to Daudet's "L'Arlésienne" Alexandre Lecocq: "La Fille de Mme. Angot," Brussels Alexander Scriabin, Russ. composer, b. (d. 1915)	Billroth makes first resection of esophagus Louis Blériot, aviation pioneer, b. (d. 1936) Edison perfects the "duplex" telegraph Brooklyn Bridge opened William Thomson, later Lord Kelvin, invents a machine by which ships can take accurate soundings while at sea Amer. engineer George Westinghouse (1846—1916) perfects automatic railroad air brake	Bakunin expelled from the First International at the Hague conference First international soccer game, England versus Scotland C. P. Scott becomes editor of the "Manchester Guardian" (—1929) Building of St. Gotthard Tunnel begins (—1881) First U.S. ski club founded at Berlin, N. H.	**1872**
Cézanne: "The Straw Hat," painting Corot: "Souvenir d'Italie" Olaf Gulbransson, Ger.-Norw. artist, b. (d. 1958) Manet: "Le bon Bock" Senaper designs the new Burgtheater, Vienna	Bruckner: Symphony No. 2, Vienna Clara Butt, Eng. singer, b. (d. 1936) Carl Rosa Opera Company founded in England Enrico Caruso, Ital. opera singer, b. (d. 1921) Feodor Chaliapin, Russ. singer, b. (d. 1938) Delibes: "Le Roi l'a Dit," opera, Paris Max Reger, Ger. composer, b. (d. 1916) Sergei Rachmaninoff, Russ. composer and pianist, b. (d. 1943) Rimsky-Korsakov: "Ivan the Terrible," opera, St. Petersburg Tchaikovsky: Symphony No. 2, Moscow	Jean Charcot: "Leçons sur les maladies du système nerveux" James Clerk Maxwell: "Electricity and Magnetism" Color photographs first developed Hans von Euler-Chelpin, Swed. chemist, 1929 Nobel Prize, b. (d. 1964) Leo Frobenius, Ger. ethnologist, founder of the doctrine of culture stages, b. (d. 1938) Justus von Liebig, Ger. chemist, d. (b. 1803) Aust. explorers Payer and Weyprecht discover Franz Josef Land, islands in the Arctic Ocean Gunsmith firm of E. Remington and Sons begins to produce typewriters Wilhelm Wundt: "Physiological Psychology"	American Football clubs adopt uniform rules The cities of Buda and Pest are united to form the capital of Hungary Initiation of modern cricket county championship Germany adopts the mark as its unit of currency Building of Severn Tunnel (England) begins (—1886) Vienna World Exibition Major W. C. Wingfield (Britain) introduces the modern game of lawn tennis at a garden party, under the name Sphairistike	**1873**
First impressionist exhibition, Paris (the term "impressionism" derived from name of Monet's painting, "Impression: Sunrise") Max Liebermann: "Women Plucking Geese," painting Renoir: "La Loge"	Brahms: "Hungarian Dances" Peter Cornelius, Ger. composer, d. (b. 1824) Hermann Götz: "Der Widerspenstigen Zähmung," opera, Mannheim Gustav Holst, Eng. composer, b. (d. 1934) Moussorgsky "Boris Godunov," St. Petersburg Paris Opéra completed (—1863) Arnold Schönberg, Ger. composer, b. (d. 1951) Smetana: "Ma Vlast" ("My Fatherland"), cycle of symphonic poems Johann Strauss II: "Die Fledermaus," operetta, Vienna Verdi: "Requiem," Milan	Carl Bosch, Ger. chemist and industrialist, 1931 Nobel Prize, b. (d. 1940) Guglielmo Marconi, Ital. physicist, b. (d. 1937) Excavation of Olympia (underwritten by Ger. government) begins (—1880) Ernest Shackleton, Brit. explorer, b. (d. 1922) Billroth discovers streptococci and staphylococci A. T. Still (1828—1917) founds osteopathy (Kansas) H. Solomon (U.S.), introduces pressure-cooking methods for canning foods	Union Générale des Postes established in Berne, Switzerland Society for the Prevention of Cruelty to Children founded in New York by E. T. Gerry Civil marriage is made compulsory in Germany The Tichborne claimant, Arthur Orton, found guilty of perjury First Amer. zoo established in Philadelphia Miss Mary E. Outerbridge (U.S.), while vacationing in Bermuda, watches Eng. officers play tennis and introduces the game to America	**1874**

	A. HISTORY, POLITICS	B. LITERATURE, THEATER	C. RELIGION, PHILOSOPHY, LEARNING
1875	Kwang Hsu becomes Emperor of China (—1898) Risings in Bosnia and Herzegovina against Turk. rule; sultan promises reforms to meet the rebels' demands Prince of Wales visits India Public Health Act is passed in Britain Rebellion in Cuba Britain buys 176,602 Suez Canal shares from Khedive of Egypt	Hans Christian Andersen, Dan. author, d. (b. 1805) John Buchan, Lord Tweedsmuir, Scot. novelist, b. (d. 1940) Grazia Deledda, Ital. author, 1927 Nobel Prize, b. (d. 1936) Charles Kingsley, Eng. author, d. (b. 1819) Thomas Mann, Ger. novelist, 1929 Nobel Prize, b. (d. 1955) Eduard Mörike, Ger. poet, d. (b. 1804) Alfred Polgar, Aust. essayist and critic, b. (d. 1955) Gabrielle Réjane (1857—1920) makes debut at the Théâtre Vaudeville, Paris Rainer Maria Rilke, Aust. poet, b. (d. 1926) Mark Twain: "The Adventures of Tom Sawyer"	Theosophical Society founded by Helena Blavatsky in New York Mary Baker Eddy: "Science and Health" C. G. Jung, Swiss psychiatrist and philosopher, b. (d. 1961) Emile Laveleye: "Le Protestantisme et le Catholicisme" Religious orders abolished in Prussia
1876	Korea becomes an independent nation Ethiopians defeat Egyptian forces at Gura Massacre of Bulgarians by Turk. troops Sultan Abdul Aziz deposed in May; his successor, Murad V, deposed in Aug. and succeeded by Abdul Hamid II (—1909) Serbia declares war on Turkey Montenegro declares war on Turkey Colorado becomes a state of the U.S. Disraeli made Earl of Beaconsfield Presidential election in U.S.: Tilden (Democrat), 184 electoral votes; Hayes (Republican), 165; 20 votes still in dispute (see 1877) New Ottoman constitution proclaimed Hilarión Daza–President of Bolivia Konrad Adenauer, Ger. statesman, b. (d. 1967)	Felix Dahn: "Ein Kampf um Rom," Ger. historical novel Henry James: "Roderick Hudson" Else Lasker-Schüler, Ger. poet, b. (d. 1945) Jack London, Amer. novelist, b. (d. 1916) Mallarmé: "L'Après-Midi d'un faune" C. F. Meyer: "Jürg Jenatsch," Swiss historical novel George Sand, Fr. writer, d. (b. 1804)	F. H. Bradley: "Ethical Studies" Lombroso: "The Criminal" G. M. Trevelyan, Eng. historian, b. (d. 1962) Eugenio Pacelli (Pope Pius XII), b. (d. 1958)
1877	Queen Victoria proclaimed Empress of India Presidential election in U.S. (see 1876): electoral commission decides in favor of Hayes (Republican) Rutherford B. Hayes inaugurated as 19th President of the U.S. Russia declares war on Turkey and invades Rumania; Russians cross Danube and storm Kars; Russians take Plevna, Bulgaria; Bismarck declines to intervene; Serbia declares war on Turkey First Kaffir War Satsuma revolt in Japan suppressed Porfirio Diaz–President of Mexico (—1911)	Gobineau: "Renaissance," historical scenes Harley Granville-Barker, Eng. theatrical producer, b. (d. 1946) Hermann Hesse, Ger. author, 1946 Nobel Prize, b. (d. 1962) Ibsen: "The Pillars of Society" Henry James: "The American" Zola: "L'Assommoir"	Patent Protection Law enacted in Germany Louis Lucien Rochet, Swiss theologian, founds the "Blue Cross" to fight alcoholism J. C. F. Zöllner: "Treatise of Spiritualism"

D. VISUAL ARTS	E. MUSIC	F. SCIENCE, TECHNOLOGY, GROWTH	G. DAILY LIFE	
Corot, Fr. painter, d. (b. 1796) The "Hermes" of Praxiteles found at Olympia, Greece Menzel: "The Steel Mill," painting J. F. Millet, Fr. painter, d. (b. 1814) Monet: "Boating at Argenteuil," painting	Bizet: "Carmen," Paris Georges Bizet, Fr. composer, d. (b. 1838) Ignaz Brüll: "Das goldene Kreuz," opera, Berlin Samuel Coleridge-Taylor, Eng. composer, b. (d. 1912) "Trial by Jury"–the first Gilbert and Sullivan operetta Karl Goldmark: "Die Königin von Saba," opera, Vienna Maurice Ravel, Fr. composer, b. (d. 1937) Tchaikovsky: Piano Concerto No. 1, Op. 23, Boston	P. E. Lecoq discovers the element gallium London Medical School for Women founded Heinrich Schliemann: "Troy and Its Remains" Albert Schweitzer, philosopher, medical missionary, and musician, b. (d. 1965)	Japanese courts of law are reformed London's main sewerage system is completed First roller-skating rink opens in London First swim across English Channel, by Captain Matthew Webb, from Dover to Cap Griz Nez, 21 hours 45 minutes (Aug. 24—25) Strength of European armies: Russia 3,360,000; Germany 2,800,000; France 412,000; Great Britain 113,000	**1875**
Paula Modersohn-Becker, Ger. painter, b. (d. 1907) Renoir: "Le Moulin de la Galette," painting	Bayreuth Festspielhaus opens with first complete performance of Wagner's "Ring des Nibelungen" Brahms: Symphony No. 1, Op. 68 Pablo Casals, Span. cellist, b. (d. 1973) Léo Delibes: "Sylvia," ballet, Paris Manuel de Falla, Span. composer, b. (d. 1946) Ponchielli: "La Gioconda," opera, Milan Wagner: "Siegfried," opera, Bayreuth Bruno Walter, Ger. conductor, b. (d. 1962) Ermanno Wolf-Ferrari, Ital.-Ger. composer, b. (d. 1948)	Alexander Graham Bell invents the telephone Johns Hopkins University, Baltimore, opens Robert Koch discovers anthrax bacillus J. J. R. Macleod, Canadian physiologist, discoverer of insulin, 1923 Nobel Prize, b. (d. 1935) Heinrich Schliemann excavates Mycenae	Mikhail Bakunin, Russ. socialist, politician, and writer, d. (b. 1814) Deutsche Reichsbank opens First Chin. railroad is completed First tennis tournament in U.S. (Nehant) U.S. National Baseball League founded Nickel ore found in New Caledonia Reformatory for juvenile offenders founded at Elmira, N.Y., by Z. R. Brockway World Exhibition at Philadelphia	**1876**
Gustave Courbet, Fr. painter, d. (b. 1819) Raoul Dufy, Fr. painter, b. (d. 1953) Winslow Homer: "The Cotton Pickers" Alfred Kubin, Aust.-Bohemian artist, b. (d. 1959) Manet: "Nana," painting Building of the Rijksmuseum, Amsterdam Rodin: "The Age of Bronze," sculpture Third impressionist exhibition, Paris	Brahms: Symphony No. 2, Op. 75 Ernst von Dohnányi, Hungarian pianist and composer, b. (d. 1960) Publication of complete edition of Mozart's works begins (—1904) Camille Saint-Saëns: "Samson et Delila," opera, Weimar Tchaikovsky: "Francesca da Rimini," symphonic poem	F. W. Aston, Eng. physicist, 1922 Nobel Prize, b. (d. 1945) Charles Barkla, Eng. physicist, 1917 Nobel Prize, b. (d. 1944) Cailletet (French) and Pictet (Swiss) independently liquefy oxygen Edison invents phonograph Robert Koch develops a technique whereby bacteria can be stained and identified Lord Rayleigh (John W. Strutt): "Treatise on Sound" Ital. astronomer Giovanni V. Schiaparelli (1835—1910) observes Mars' canals	All-England Lawn Tennis championship first played at Wimbledon, London (Spencer Grove, champion) Famine in Bengal First public telephones (U.S.) Frozen meat shipped from Argentina to Europe for the first time André Maginot, Fr. statesman and politician, b. (d. 1932)	**1877**

	A. HISTORY, POLITICS	B. LITERATURE, THEATER	C. RELIGION, PHILOSOPHY, LEARNING
1878	Victor Emmanuel II, King of Italy, d.; succeeded by his son Humbert I (—1900) Turks capitulate at Shipka Pass and appeal to Russia for armistice; Russians take Adrianople; Brit. fleet arrives at sultan's request in Constantinople ("Jingoist" war fever in Britain); Turk.-Russ. armistice signed Greece declares war on Turkey; preliminary treaty of San Stefano between Russia and Turkey; Anglo-Turk. agreement to check Russ. advance in Asia Minor; Berlin Congress to discuss Eastern Question ends with Treaty of Berlin Attempt to assassinate Emperor William I of Germany Anti-Socialist Law enacted in Germany Beginning of Irredentist agitation in Italy to obtain Trieste and South Tirol from Austria Gustav Stresemann, Ger. statesman, b. (d. 1929)	Theodor Fontane: "Vor dem Sturm," Ger. novel Karl Gutzkow, Ger. dramatist, d. (b. 1811) Thomas Hardy: "The Return of the Native" Georg Kaiser, Ger. dramatist, b. (d. 1945) John Masefield, Eng. poet, b. (d. 1967) Carl Sandburg, Amer. poet, b. (d. 1967) Upton Sinclair, Amer. author and reformer, b. (d. 1968) René Sully-Prudhomme: "La Justice" Swinburne: "Poems and Ballads" Ellen Terry joins Irving's Company at the Lyceum Theatre, London	Martin Buber, Aust.-Jewish philosopher, b. (d. 1965) W. E. H. Lecky: "History of England in the Eighteenth Century" (—1890) Charles Pierce (1839—1914): "How to Make Our Ideas Clear" (Philosophy of Pragmatism) Pope Pius IX d. (b. 1792); Cardinal Count Pecci succeeds as Leo XIII (—1903) George Romanes: "A Candid Examination of Theism" Ger. historian Heinrich Treitschke begins racial anti-Semite movement, and Berlin court preacher Adolf Stoecker founds Christlich-Soziale Arbeiterpartei
1879	Brit. Zulu War: Zulus massacre Brit. soldiers in Isandhlwana, British capture Cetewayo Fr. Prince Imperial, son of Napoleon III, killed in action Peace signed with Zulu chiefs Alexander of Battenberg elected Prince Alexander I of Bulgaria Treaty of Gandamak: Britain occupies Khyber Pass; Brit. legation in Kabul massacred Ismail, Khedive of Egypt, deposed; succeeded by Tewfik (—1892) Alsace-Lorraine is declared an integral part of Germany Fr. Panama Canal Co. organized under Ferdinand de Lesseps Joseph Stalin, Russ. Communist dictator, b. (d. 1953) Leon Trotsky, Russ. Communist leader, b. (d. 1940)	Charles de Coster, Belg. author, d. (b. 1827) E. M. Forster, Eng. novelist, b. (d. 1970) Ibsen: "A Doll's House" Henry James: "Daisy Miller" Meredith: "The Egoist" R. L. Stevenson: "Travels with a Donkey" Strindberg: "The Red Room" Juan Valera: "Doña Luz" F. T. Vischer: "Auch einer," Ger. humorous novel	Anti-Jesuit Laws introduced in France St. Thomas Aquinas proclaimed a Doctor of the Roman Catholic Church A. J. Balfour: "Defence of Philosophic Doubt" William Beveridge, Brit. economist, b. (d. 1963) Mary Baker Eddy becomes pastor of Church of Christ, Scientist, Boston Henry George: "Progress and Poverty" Robert Giffen: "Essay on Finance" Herbert Spencer: "Principles of Ethics" (—1893) Treitschke: "History of Germany in the XIXth Century" (—1895)
1880	Lord Beaconsfield (Disraeli) resigns as Brit. Prime Minister; succeeded by W. E. Gladstone Cape Parliament rejects scheme for S. African federation France annexes Tahiti Transvaal declares itself independent of Britain; the Boers under Kruger declare a republic Pacific War: Chile against Bolivia and Peru (—1884) The future Queen Wilhelmina of Holland b. (d. 1962) J. A. Garfield elected President of the U.S.	Disraeli: "Endymion" Dostoevsky: "The Brothers Karamazov" Gustave Flaubert d. (b. 1821) George Eliot (Mary Ann Evans), Eng. novelist, d. (b. 1819) J. C. Harris: "Uncle Remus" Jens Jacobson: "Nils Lyhne" Longfellow: "Ultima Thule" Pierre Loti: "Le Mariage de Loti" Maupassant: "Contes" Lytton Strachey, Eng. author, b. (d. 1932) Lew Wallace: "Ben Hur" Zola: "Nana"	Walter Bagehot: "Economic Studies" (posth.) John Clairde: "Philosophy of Religion" Helen Keller, Amer. deaf and blind educator, b. (d. 1968) Oswald Spengler, Ger. philosopher, b. (d. 1936)

D. VISUAL ARTS	E. MUSIC	F. SCIENCE, TECHNOLOGY, GROWTH	G. DAILY LIFE	
Charles Daubigny, Fr. painter, d. (b. 1817) Garnier designs the Casino at Monte Carlo William Morris: "The Decorative Arts" A. J. Munnings, Eng. painter, b. (d. 1959) Cleopatra's Needle, originally erected in Heliopolis, is removed from Alexandria to London (see 1475 B.C. and A.D. 1819) Libel action Whistler vs. Ruskin (over Ruskin's essay "Nocturne in Black and Gold: a Falling Rocket")	A. W. Ambros: "Geschichte der Musik" (1862—) Rutland Boughton, Eng. composer, b. (d. 1963) Gilbert and Sullivan: "H.M.S. Pinafore" George Grove begins "Dictionary of Music and Musicians" (—1889)	David Hughes invents the microphone First use of iodoform as an antiseptic Mannlicher produces repeater rifle A. A. Pope manufactures first bicycles in America John B. Watson, Amer. psychologist, b. (d. 1958)	Karl Benz, Ger. engineer, builds motorized tricycle with top speed of seven miles per hour Bicycle Touring Club founded in England C.I.D., New Scotland Yard, established in London Deutscher Fussballverein, Hanover, founded Electric street lighting is introduced in London First European crematorium established at Gotha, Germany Fur farming begun in Canada Paris World Exhibition Salvation Army (see 1865) becomes known under its new name	**1878**
Bastien-Lepage: "Portrait of Sarah Bernhardt" Honoré Daumier, Fr. painter, d. (b. 1808) Paul Klee, Swiss painter, b. (d. 1940) Renoir: "Mme. Charpentier and Her Children," painting Rodin: "John the Baptist," sculpture	Millöcker: "Gräfin Dubarry," operetta Vienna Suppé: "Boccaccio," operetta, Vienna Tchaikovsky: "Eugen Onegin," opera, Moscow	First electric tram exhibited by E. W. Siemens at Berlin Trade Exhibition Albert Einstein, Ger. physicist, 1921 Nobel Prize, b. (d. 1955) Fahlberg and Remser discover saccharin J. C. Maxwell, Eng. physicist, b. (d. 1931) The element scandium discovered by L. F. Nilson Collapse of Tay Bridge, Scotland London's first telephone exchange established	Australian frozen meat on sale in London Lord Beaverbrook, Brit.-Canadian newspaper proprietor and statesman, b. (d. 1964) Brit. churchman W. L. Blackley (1836—1902) proposes a scheme for old-age pensions The public granted unrestricted admission to the British Museum First large-scale skiing contest at Huseby Hill, Oslo, Norway	**1879**
Cézanne: "Château de Medan" Cologne Cathedral completed (begun 1248) André Derain, Fr. painter, b. (d. 1954) Jacob Epstein, Anglo-Amer. sculptor, b. (d. 1959) Franz Marc, Ger. painter, b. (d. 1916) Pissarro: "The Outer Boulevards," painting Renoir: "Place Clichy" Rodin: "The Thinker," sculpture	Ernest Bloch, Swiss-Amer. composer, b. (d. 1959) Gilbert and Sullivan: "The Pirates of Penzance" London Guildhall School of Music founded Jacques Offenbach, Fr. composer, d. (b. 1819) Philipp Spitta (1841—1894): "Johann Sebastian Bach," biography	T. A. Edison and J. W. Swan independently devise the first practical electric lights Laveran discovers the malarial parasite Owens College, Manchester, becomes a university Pasteur discovers a chicken cholera vaccine James Wimshurst: electrostatic generator	The game of Bingo is developed from the Ital. lotto game of tumbula (Tombola) Captain C. C. Boycott, land agent in Mayo, Ireland, is "boycotted" for refusing to accept rents fixed by his tenants Carnegie develops first large steel furnace New York streets are first lit by electricity First Test Match between England and Australia in England Canned fruits and meats first appear in stores Douglas MacArthur, Amer. general, b. (d. 1964) Parcel post introduced in England Railroad mileage in operation: U.S. 87,800; Great Britain 17,900; France 16,400; Russia 12,200 Skis used in mountaineering in Norway World Exhibition takes place in Melbourne	**1880**

	A. HISTORY, POLITICS	B. LITERATURE, THEATER	C. RELIGION, PHILOSOPHY, LEARNING
1881	Transvaal Boers repulse British at Laing's Nek and defeat them at Majuba Hill; in the Treaty of Pretoria Britain recognizes independent Transvaal Republic James A. Garfield inaugurated as 20th President of the U.S.; he is shot and killed in Sept.; succeeded by Vice President Chester Arthur (—1885) Lord Beaconsfield (Disraeli) d. (b. 1804) The Bey of Tunis accepts Fr. protectorate Austro-Serbian treaty of alliance C. S. Parnell imprisoned Léon Gambetta–Fr. Prime Minister Political parties founded in Japan Kemal Ataturk, Turk. statesman, b. (d. 1938) Ernest Bevin, Brit. socialist politician, b. (d. 1951)	Dostoevsky d. (b. 1821) Ethel M. Dell, Eng. novelist, b. (d. 1939) P. G. Wodehouse, Eng. author, b. (d. 1975) Asta Nielsen, Swed. film star, b. (d. 1972) The first of all cabarets, "Chat Noir," Paris, founded by Rodolphe Salis Anton Wildgans, Aust. poet, b. (d. 1932) Stefan Zweig, Aust. author, b. (d. 1942) Flaubert: "Bouvard et Pécuchet" Anatole France: "Le Crime de Sylvestre Bonnard" Henry James: "Portrait of a Lady" Maupassant: "La Maison Tellier" R. L. Stevenson: "Virginibus Puerisque" D'Oyly Carte builds the Savoy Theatre, London (lit by electricity) Alexander Moissi, Ger. writer, b. (d. 1935)	Edward Tylor: "Anthropology" Persecution of Jews in Russia Thomas Carlyle, Eng. historian, d. (b. 1795) Ranke: "Weltgeschichte," 16 vols. (—1888) Vatican archives opened to scholars
1882	Prince Milan Obrenovich of Serbia proclaims himself king Kilmainham agreement between Parnell and the Brit. government; Fenians murder Lord Frederick Cavendish and T. H. Burke in Phoenix Park, Dublin; terrorist massacres in Maamtrasne U.S. bans Chin. immigrants for 10 years Triple Alliance between Italy, Austria, and Germany Three-mile limit for territorial waters agreed upon at Hague Convention The British occupy Cairo Franklin D. Roosevelt, U.S. President from 1933 to 1945, b. (d. 1945) Eamon de Valera, Ir. statesman, b. (d. 1975)	R. L. Stevenson: "Treasure Island" Becque: "Les Corbeaux" Ibsen: "An Enemy of the People" Virginia Woolf, Eng. novelist, b. (d. 1941) James Joyce, Ir. novelist, b. (d. 1941) H. W. Longfellow, Amer. author, d. (b. 1807) John Drinkwater, Eng. dramatist, b. (d. 1937) Anthony Trollope, Eng. novelist, d. (b. 1815) Jean Giraudoux, Fr. author, b. (d. 1944) Sigrid Undset, Norw. novelist, b. (d. 1949) F. Anstey: "Vice Versa" George Bernard Shaw: "Cashel Byron's Profession" Sardou: "Fédora"	Bakunin: "God and the State" (posth.) Charles Darwin d. (b. 1809) Ralph Waldo Emerson, Amer. philosopher, d. (b. 1803) Besant: "All Sorts and Conditions of Men" Nietzsche: "Die fröhliche Wissenschaft" Leslie Stephen: "Science of Ethics" Jacques Maritain, Fr. philosopher, b. (d. 1972)
1883	Reform of U.S. Civil Service begins (—1901) Paul Kruger–President of South African Republic The French gain control of Tunis Comte de Chambord, the last male Bourbon, d. (b. 1820) Clement Attlee, Brit. socialist politician, b. (d. 1967) Benito Mussolini, Ital. Fascist dictator, b. (d. 1945) Pierre Laval, Fr. politician, b. (d. 1945) Britain decides to evacuate Sudan Sojourner Truth, Amer. reformer, d. (b. 1797?)	Compton Mackenzie, Eng. author, b. (d. 1972) Edward Fitzgerald, Eng. poet, d. (b. 1809) Ivan Turgenev, Russ. novelist, d. (b. 1818) Franz Kafka, Aust. novelist, b. (d. 1924) Olive Schreiner: "The Story of an African Farm" Björnson: "Beyond Human Endurance" Maupassant: "Une Vie" Renan: "Souvenirs d'enfance et de jeunesse" Verhaeren: "Les Flamandes" Zola: "Au bonheur des dames"	Lester Ward: "Dynamic Sociology" J. R. Seeley: "The Expansion of England" F. H. Bradley: "The Principles of Logic" Nietzsche: "Thus Spake Zarathustra" Karl Marx d. (b. 1818) John Maynard Keynes, Eng. economist, b. (d. 1946) Fabian Society founded in London

D. VISUAL ARTS	E. MUSIC	F. SCIENCE, TECHNOLOGY, GROWTH	G. DAILY LIFE	
Pablo Picasso b. (d. 1973) Böcklin: "Die Toteninsel," painting Max Pechstein, Ger. painter, b. (d. 1955) Max Liebermann: "Alt-Männer-Heim," painting Monet: "Sunshine and Snow," painting	Béla Bartók, Hungarian composer, b. (d. 1945) Brahms: "Academic Festival Overture," Op. 80, Breslau Moussorgsky d. (b. 1835) Offenbach: "Les Contes d'Hoffmann," posth. opera, Paris	Alexander Fleming, Eng. physician and scientist, b. (d. 1955) Canadian Pacific Railway Company founded Natural History Museum, South Kensington, London, opened University College, Liverpool, founded Tuskegee Institute founded by Booker T. Washington	Freedom of press established in France Flogging abolished in Brit. Army and Navy Federation of Organized Trades and Labor Unions of the U.S. and Canada formed First U.S. Lawn Tennis Championship (R. D. Sears, champion —1888) St. Gotthard Tunnel completed (begun 1872) City Populations (in millions): London 3.3; Paris 2.2; New York 1.2; Berlin 1.1; Vienna 1.0; Tokyo 0.8; St. Petersburg 0.6	**1881**
Georges Braque, Fr. painter, b. (d. 1963) Cézanne: "Self-portrait" Eric Gill, Eng. artist, b. (d. 1940) Samuel Goldwyn, Hollywood film producer, b. (d. 1974) Manet: "Bar aux Folies-Bergère," painting D. G. Rossetti d. (b. 1828)	Igor Stravinsky, Russ. composer, b. (d. 1971) Millöcker: "Der Bettelstudent," operetta, Vienna Tchaikovsky: "1812 Overture" Gounod: "The Redemption," oratorio, Birmingham Rimsky-Korsakov: "The Snow Maiden," opera, St. Petersburg Gilbert and Sullivan: "Iolanthe," London Wagner: "Parsifal," Bayreuth Berlin Philharmonic Orchestra founded Debussy: "Le Printemps," orchestral suite	Viennese physician Joseph Breuer uses hypnosis to treat hysteria (beginnings of psychoanalysis) Edison designs first hydroelectric plant, Appleton, Wis. Eng. engineer Hiram S. Maxim patents recoil-operated machine gun	World Exhibition in Moscow Queen Victoria gives Epping Forest to the nation Amer. Baseball Association founded London Chamber of Commerce established Charles University, Prague, divided into Ger. and Czech institutions Bank of Japan founded First issue of "Berliner Tageblatt" John L. Sullivan (1858—1918) defeats Paddy Ryan to win heavyweight boxing crown (—1892) J. B. Hobbs, Brit. cricketer, b. (d. 1964)	**1882**
Walter Gropius, Ger.-Amer. architect, b. (d. 1969) Gustave Doré, Fr. artist, d. (b. 1832) Edouard Manet, Fr. artist, d. (b. 1833) Maurice Utrillo, Fr. painter, b. (d. 1955) Cézanne: "Rocky Landscape," painting Renoir: "Umbrellas"	Chabrier: "España," rhapsody Metropolitan Opera House, New York, opened Royal College of Music, London, founded Delibes: "Lakmé," opera, Paris Richard Wagner, Ger. opera composer, d. (b. 1813) Friedrich von Flotow, Ger. composer, d. (b. 1812) Anton von Webern, Aust. composer, b. (d. 1945)	Eng. scientist Sir Joseph Swan (1828—1914) produces a synthetic fiber Brit. scientist William Thomson, later Lord Kelvin (1824—1907): "On the Size of Atoms" Robert Koch describes a method of preventive inoculation against anthrax	Bismarck introduces sickness insurance in Germany Northern Pacific Railroad line completed The first skyscraper built in Chicago, 10 stories Orient Express–Paris-Istanbul–makes its first run U.S. frontiersman W. F. Cody ("Buffalo Bill"), 1846—1917, organizes his "Wild West Show" World Exhibition opens in Amsterdam Brooklyn Bridge, New York, opened to traffic	**1883**

	A. HISTORY, POLITICS	B. LITERATURE, THEATER	C. RELIGION, PHILOSOPHY, LEARNING
1884	Gen. C. G. Gordon reaches Khartoum; Mahdi refuses to negotiate and occupies Omdurman London Convention on Transvaal Germans occupy South-West Africa Fr. law excludes members of former dynasties from presidency Grover Cleveland elected U.S. President Berlin Conference of 14 nations on African affairs Harry S. Truman, U.S. President (1945—1953), b. (d. 1972) Eduard Benes, Czech statesman, b. (d. 1948)	Damon Runyon, Amer. author, b. (d. 1946) J. E. Flecker, Eng. poet and dramatist, b. (d. 1915) Georges Duhamel, Fr. novelist, b. (d. 1966) D'Annunzio: "Il Libro delle Vergini" Jean Moréas: "Les Syrtes," poems Mark Twain: "Huckleberry Finn" Verlaine: "Jadis et Naguère" Daudet: "Sappho," novel Ibsen: "The Wild Duck" Sean O'Casey, Ir. author, b. (d. 1964) Emanuel Geibel, Ger. author, d. (b. 1815) Heinrich Laube, Ger. dramatist, d. (b. 1806) Sienkiewicz: "With Fire and Sword," Pol. historical novel	Divorce reestablished in France Kropotkin: "Paroles d'un revolte" Herbert Spencer: "The Man versus the State" Oxford English Dictionary begins publication (—1928) G. B. Shaw becomes a member of the Fabian Society
1885	The Mahdi takes Khartoum; Gen. Gordon killed in the fighting; British evacuate Sudan; death of Mahdi The Congo becomes a personal possession of King Leopold II of Belgium Germany annexes Tanganyika and Zanzibar Grover Cleveland inaugurated as 22nd President of the U.S. Great Britain establishes protectorate over N. Bechuanaland, Niger River region, and S. New Guinea; occupies Port Hamilton, Korea Ulysses S. Grant, Amer. soldier and president, d. (b. 1822) King Alfonso XII of Spain d.; Queen Maria Christina becomes regent	Paul Bourget: "Cruelle Enigme" Richard Burton: "The Arabian Nights" (—1888) Maupassant: "Bel Ami" George Meredith: "Diana of the Crossways" George Moore: "A Mummer's Wife" Walter Pater: "Marius the Epicurean" Tolstoi: "The Power of Darkness" Zola: "Germinal" Becque: "La Parisienne" Victor Hugo d. (b. 1802) D. H. Lawrence, Eng. novelist, b. (d. 1930) Ezra Pound, Amer. poet, b. (d. 1972) Sinclair Lewis, Amer. novelist, 1930 Nobel Prize, b. (d. 1951) H. Rider Haggard: "King Solomon's Mines," adventure novel	Henry Maine: "Popular Government" Karl Marx: "Das Kapital," vol. 2 (posth.) The Mormons split into polygamous and monogamous sections Albert Sorel: "Europe and the French Revolution" (—1904) Tolstoi: "My Religion"
1886	Gen. Georges Boulanger becomes Fr. War Minister Brit. Prime Minister W. E. Gladstone introduces bill for Home Rule in Ireland The future King Alfonso XIII of Spain b.– posthumous son of Alfonso XII Bonaparte and Orléans families banished from France King Ludwig II of Bavaria d. (b. 1845); succeeded by the insane Otto I; his uncle Luitpold becomes regent Alexander of Bulgaria abdicates after coup d'état; Stefan Stambulov becomes regent David Ben-Gurion, Israeli statesman, b. (d. 1973) First Indian National Congress meets	Henry James: "The Bostonians" Pierre Loti: "Pêcheur d'Islande" Nietzsche: "Jenseits von Gut und Böse" Rimbaud: "Les Illuminations" R. L. Stevenson: "Dr. Jekyll and Mr. Hyde" August Strindberg: "The Son of a Servant" Ibsen: "Rosmersholm" Alexander Ostrovski, Russ. dramatist, d. (b. 1823) Josef Viktor von Scheffel, Ger. poet, d. (b. 1826) Frances Hodgson Burnett: "Little Lord Fauntleroy" Marie Corelli: "A Romance of Two Worlds"	Leopold von Ranke, Ger. historian, d. (b. 1795) Ramakrishna, Hindu mystic, d. (b. 1836) Andrew Carnegie: "Triumphant Democracy" Karl Marx: "Das Kapital," published in English Richard von Krafft-Ebing: "Psychopathia Sexualis" Adolf von Harnack: "History of Dogma" Auguste Fournier: "Napoleon I" (3 vols.)

D. VISUAL ARTS	E. MUSIC	F. SCIENCE, TECHNOLOGY, GROWTH	G. DAILY LIFE	
Seurat: "Une Baignade, Asnières," painting Burne-Jones: "King Cophetua and the Beggar Maid" Rodin: "The Burghers of Calais," sculpture (—1895) Hans Makart, Aust. painter, d. (b. 1840) Amedeo Modigliani, Ital. painter, b. (d. 1920) Sacconi: monument to King Victor Emmanuel II in Rome (—1911)	Brahms: Symphony No. 3 in F major, Op. 90 Bruckner: Symphony No. 7, Leipzig César Franck: "Les Djinns," symphonic poem Massenet: "Manon," opera, Paris C. V. Stanford: "Savonarola," opera, Hamburg Gustav Mahler: "Lieder eines fahrenden Gesellen" Viktor Nessler: "Der Trompeter von Säckingen," opera, Leipzig	Friedrich Bergius, Ger. chemist, 1931 Nobel Prize, b. (d. 1940) Auguste Piccard, Swiss physicist, b. (d. 1952) Ilya Mechnikov: "Theory of Phagocytes" Ger. physician Arthur Nicolaier (1862—1934) discovers tetanus bacillus Sir Charles Parsons invents first practical steam turbine engine Eng. physicist Sir Oliver Lodge discovers electrical precipitation	"Le Matin," Paris, issued First deep tube (underground railroad), London Gold discovered in the Transvaal, rise of Johannesburg	**1884**
Carl Spitzweg, Ger. painter, d. (b. 1808) Van Gogh: "The Potato Eaters" Cézanne: "Mont Sainte-Victoire" (—1887)	Brahms: Symphony No. 4 in E minor, Op. 98 César Franck: "Symphonic Variations" Gilbert and Sullivan: "The Mikado," London Alban Berg, Aust. composer, b. (d. 1935) Anna Pavlova, Russ. ballet dancer, b. (d. 1931) Strauss: "The Gypsy Baron," operetta, Vienna	Karl Auer von Welsbach invents the incandescent gas mantle Niels Bohr, Dan. physicist, b. (d. 1962) Pasteur devises a rabies vaccine to cure hydrophobia Sir Francis Galton proves the individuality of fingerprints Karl Benz builds single-cylinder engine for motor car George Eastman manufactures coated photographic paper	Cape railroad reaches Kimberley First Leipzig Fair First Eng. electrical tram car in Blackpool John M. Fox of Philadelphia learns about golf on a trip to Scotland and introduces the game to America (Foxburg, Pa.)	**1885**
J. S. Sargent: "Carnation, Lily, Lily, Rose," painting Seurat: "Sunday Afternoon on the Grande Jatte," painting Eighth and last Impressionist Exhibition, Paris Statue of Liberty dedicated Oskar Kokoschka, Aust. painter, b. (d. 1980) Max Klinger: "Beethoven," sculpture Rodin: "The Kiss," sculpture Millais: "Bubbles" Ferdinand Hodler: "Meditation," painting	Franz Liszt, Hungarian composer, d. (b. 1811) Wilhelm Furtwängler, Ger. conductor, b. (d. 1954) Charles Mustel of Paris invents the celesta	The element germanium discovered by Ger. chemist Clemens Winkler Fr. chemist Henri Moissan produces fluorine Aminopyrine and acitanelide discovered Ernst von Bergmann uses steam to sterilize surgical instruments Charles M. Hall (Amer.) and P. L. T. Héroult (Fr.) independently produce aluminum by electrolysis Hydroelectric installations are begun at Niagara Falls Pasteur Institute, Paris, founded	American Federation of Labor founded Canadian Pacific Railway completed Severn Tunnel opened Brit. School of Archaeology opens at Athens Ty Cobb, Amer. baseball player, b. (d. 1961) Amateur Golf Championship first played Eng. Lawn Tennis Association founded	**1886**

	A. HISTORY, POLITICS	B. LITERATURE, THEATER	C. RELIGION, PHILOSOPHY, LEARNING
1887	First Colonial Conference opens in London Queen Victoria celebrates her Golden Jubilee Prince Ferdinand of Saxe-Coburg elected King of Bulgaria (—1918) Gen. Boulanger fails in a coup d'état in Paris Union Indo-Chinoise organized by France Chiang Kai-shek, Chin. general and statesman, b. (d. 1975)	F. T. Vischer, Ger. author, d. (b. 1807) Hall Caine: "The Deemster," novel Sir Arthur Conan Doyle: "A Study in Scarlet," the first Sherlock Holmes story Strindberg: "The Father," drama Thomas Hardy: "The Woodlanders" Conrad Ferdinand Meyer: "The Temptation of Pescara" Hermann Sudermann: "Frau Sorge" Sardou: "La Tosca," play Antoine founds the Théâtre Libre in Paris	Sir Thomas More (1478—1535) beatified by Pope Leo XIII (canonized 1935) I. Donnelly: "The Great Cryptogram, Francis Bacon's Cypher in the So-called Shakespeare Play"
1888	Lobengula, King of Matabele, accepts Brit. protection and grants Cecil Rhodes mining rights Ger. Emperor William I dies (Mar.); succeeded by his son Frederick III, who dies (June) and is succeeded by his son William II, the "Kaiser" (—1918) Sarawak accepts status of Brit. protectorate Gen. Boulanger is retired from Fr. army and elected to Fr. Chamber of Deputies Suez Canal convention Benjamin Harrison elected President of the U.S.	Maurice Barrès: "Sous l'oeil des barbares" Edward Bellamy: "Looking Backwards, 2000—1887" Kipling: "Plain Tales from the Hills" Maupassant: "Pierre et Jean" Quiller-Couch: "Astonishing History of Troy Town" Mark Rutherford: "The Revolution in Tanner's Lane" Verlaine: "Amour" Zola: "La Terre" A. W. Pinero: "Sweet Lavender," play Matthew Arnold, Eng. author, d. (b. 1822) Maurice Chevalier, Fr. revue star, b. (d. 1972) Katherine Mansfield, New Zealand-born Brit. author, b. (d. 1923) T. S. Eliot, Anglo-Amer. poet, 1948 Nobel Prize, b. (d. 1965) Eugene O'Neill, Amer. dramatist, b. (d. 1953) Theodor Storm, Ger. novelist, d. (b. 1817) Oscar Wilde: "The Happy Prince, and Other Tales" Georges Courteline: "Le Train de 8h47," farce Theodor Fontane: "Irrungen, Wirrungen," novel	James Bryce: "The American Commonwealth" Bernard Bosanquet: "Logic, or the Morphology of Knowledge" G. J. Romanes: "Mental Evolution in Man" James Martineau: "The Study of Religion"
1889	The Aust. Crown Prince, Archduke Rudolf, commits suicide at his hunting lodge at Mayerling N. Dakota, S. Dakota, Montana, and Washington become states of the U.S.; Oklahoma is opened to non-Indian settlement Benjamin Harrison inaugurated as 23rd President of the U.S. Gen. Boulanger flees from France Milan Obrenovich abdicates from Serbian throne in favor of his son Adolf Hitler, Nazi dictator, b. (d. 1945) London Dock Strike Cecil Rhodes' Brit. South Africa Company granted royal charter Pedro II abdicates; Brazil proclaimed a republic Johannes IV, Emperor of Abyssinia, d.; succeeded by Menelik II (—1913)	J. M. Barrie: "A Window in Thrums" Björnson: "In God's Way" André Gide begins writing his Journal (—1949) Gerhart Hauptmann: "Vor Sonnenaufgang," Ger. social drama Jerome K. Jerome: "Three Men in a Boat" Maurice Maeterlinck: "Serres chaudes" W. B. Yeats: "The Wanderings of Oisin" Charles Chaplin, Eng.-born film actor, b. (d. 1977) Jean Cocteau, Fr. author, b. (d. 1963) George S. Kaufman, Amer. dramatist, b. (d. 1961) Robert Browning d. (b. 1812) Bertha von Suttner: "Die Waffen nieder," Aust. war novel Mark Twain: "A Connecticut Yankee in King Arthur's Court" R. L. Stevenson: "The Master of Ballantrae" Anatole France: "Thaïs" Hermann Sudermann: "Die Ehre," novel	Henri Bergson: "Essai sur les données immédiates de la conscience" T. H. Huxley: "Agnosticism" Martin Heidegger, Ger. philosopher, b. (d. 1969)

D. VISUAL ARTS	E. MUSIC	F. SCIENCE, TECHNOLOGY, GROWTH	G. DAILY LIFE	
Alexander Archipenko, Russ. sculptor, b. (d. 1964) Marc Chagall, Russ. painter who worked in the U.S. and France, b. (d. 1985) Le Corbusier (C. E. Jeaneret), Swiss architect, b. (d. 1965) Van Gogh: "Moulin de la Galette"	Aleksandr Borodin, Russ. composer, d. (b. 1834) Sir John Stainer: "The Crucifixion," oratorio Chabrier: "Le Roi malgré lui," opera, Paris Richard Strauss: "Aus Italien," tone poems, Munich Verdi: "Otello," opera, Milan Gilbert and Sullivan: "Ruddigore," London Ignace Paderewski gives his first recital in Vienna Bruckner: "Te Deum"	Joseph Lockyer: "The Chemistry of the Sun" Phenacetin, an analgesic drug, discovered Emil Berliner improves the phonograph's sound quality Julian Huxley, Eng. biologist and philosopher, b. (d. 1975) Erwin Schrödinger, Aust. physicist, 1933 Nobel Prize, b. (d. 1961) Edison and Swan combine to produce Ediswan electrical lamps H. W. Goodwin invents celluloid film	L. L. Zamenhof (1859—1917) devises "Esperanto" Alfred Krupp, Ger. industrialist, d. (b. 1812) Brit. Field Marshal Viscount Montgomery of Alamein b. (d. 1976)	**1887**
James Ensor: "The Entrance of Christ into Brussels," painting Van Gogh: "The Yellow Chair" Toulouse-Lautrec: "Place Clichy"	Irving Berlin, Amer. composer, b. (d. 1989) Gilbert and Sullivan: "The Yeomen of the Guard," London Tchaikovsky: Symphony No. 5, St. Petersburg Rimsky-Korsakov: "Sheherazade," Op. 35, symphonic suite, St. Petersburg Gustav Mahler becomes musical director of the Budapest opera	Nikola A. Tesla constructs electric motor (manufactured by George Westinghouse) George Eastman perfects "Kodak" box camera J. B. Dunlop invents pneumatic tire Heinrich Hertz and Oliver Lodge independently identify radio waves as belonging to same family as light waves	Football League founded Lawn Tennis Association founded T. E. Lawrence, "Lawrence of Arabia," b. (d. 1935) "Jack the Ripper" murders six women in London Cecil Rhodes amalgamates Kimberley diamond companies Aeronautical Exhibition in Vienna "The Financial Times," London, first published First of all beauty contests held in Spa, Belgium Fridtjof Nansen leads an exploring party across Greenland on snowshoes Jim Thorpe, one of the greatest all-around athletes of all time, b. (d. 1953)	**1888**
Van Gogh: "Landscape with Cypress Tree," painting Alexander Gustave Eiffel (1832—1923) designs the 1,056-ft.-high Eiffel Tower for the Paris World Exhibition Paul Nash, Eng. painter, b. (d. 1946)	César Franck: Symphony in D major Richard Strauss: "Don Juan," symphonic poem, Weimar Gilbert and Sullivan: "The Gondoliers," London	Catholic University, Washington, D.C., opens G. V. Schiaparelli discovers synchronous rotations of planets Mercury and Venus Frederick Abel invents cordite E. P. Hubble, Amer. astronomer, b. (d. 1953) Von Mehring and Minkowski prove that the pancreas secretes insulin, preventing diabetes	London County Council formed Barnum and Bailey's Circus at Olympia, London Fr. Panama Canal Company bankrupt The first May Day celebration, Paris Punch card system created by H. Hollerith	**1889**

	A. HISTORY, POLITICS	B. LITERATURE, THEATER	C. RELIGION, PHILOSOPHY, LEARNING
1890	Bismarck dismissed by William II Swiss government introduces social insurance Britain exchanges Heligoland with Germany for Zanzibar and Pemba Idaho and Wyoming become states of the U.S. Cecil Rhodes–Premier of Cape Colony First general election in Japan William II and Alexander III meet at Narva Ger. Social Democrats adopt Marxist program at Erfurt Congress Accession of Queen Wilhelmina; Luxembourg separated from the Netherlands V. M. Molotov, Russ. statesman, b. (d. 1986) Dwight D. Eisenhower, Amer. general and president, b. (d. 1969) Charles de Gaulle, Fr. soldier and statesman, b. (d. 1970)	Knut Hamsun: "Hunger" Tolstoi: "The Kreutzer Sonata" Ibsen: "Hedda Gabler" Karel Capek, Czech author, b. (d. 1938) Gottfried Keller, Swiss novelist, d. (b. 1819) A. P. Herbert, Eng. writer, b. (d. 1971) Walter Hasenclever, Ger. dramatist, b. (d. 1940) Franz Werfel, Aust. author, b. (d. 1945) Hall Caine: "The Bondman," novel First moving-picture (film) shows appear in New York Wilde: "The Picture of Dorian Gray"	Heinrich Schliemann, Ger. archaeologist, d. (b. 1822) Cardinal Newman d. (b. 1801) Alfred Marshall: "Principles of Economics" William Booth: "In Darkest England and the Way Out" J. G. Frazer: "The Golden Bough" (—1914) William James: "The Principles of Psychology"
1891	Triple Alliance–Germany, Austria, Italy–renewed for 12 years William II visits London Franco-Russ. entente Gen. Boulanger commits suicide (b. 1837) Young Turk Movement, hoping to secure liberal reforms, is formed in Geneva	Maurice Barrès: "Le Jardin de Bérénice" James Barrie: "The Little Minister" Conan Doyle: "The Adventures of Sherlock Holmes," published in "Strand" magazine Thomas Hardy: "Tess of the D'Urbervilles" Frank Wedekind: "Frühlings Erwachen," Ger. play Kipling: "The Light That Failed" Sardou: "Thermidor" J. T. Grein founds Independent Theatre Society, London James Russell Lowell, Amer. author, d. (b. 1819) Herman Melville, Amer. novelist, d. (b. 1819) Ilya Ehrenburg, Russ. author, b. (d. 1967) Selma Lagerlöf: "Gösta Berling" Shaw: "Quintessence of Ibsenism" Arthur Rimbaud, Fr. poet, d. (b. 1854)	Goldwin Smith: "The Canadian Question" R. W. Church: "History of the Oxford Movement" (posth.) "Rerum novarum," papal encyclical on the condition of the working classes
1892	Tewfik, Khedive of Egypt, d.; succeeded by Abbas II (—1918) Giolitti becomes Premier of Italy; Prince Ito, Premier of Japan Gladstone becomes Prime Minister of Great Britain; Witte is named Russ. Minister of Finance Britain and Germany agree on Cameroons Grover Cleveland elected U.S. President Pan-Slav Conference held at Cracow Tito, Yugoslav statesman, b. (d. 1980) Haile Selassie, future Ethiopian Emperor, b. (d. 1975) Keir Hardie becomes first Labour member of Parliament	Pearl S. Buck, Amer. novelist, 1938 Nobel Prize, b. (d. 1973) Knut Hamsun: "Mysteries," novel Gerhart Hauptmann: "Die Weber," Ger. social drama Bernard Shaw: "Mrs. Warren's Profession" Kipling: "Barrack-Room Ballads" Israel Zangwill: "Children of the Ghetto" Zola: "La Débâcle" Maeterlinck: "Pelléas et Mélisande," drama Oscar Wilde: "Lady Windermere's Fan" Ibsen: "The Master Builder" Eng. music-hall star Lottie Collins sings "Ta-ra-ra boom-de-ay" Walt Whitman d. (b. 1819) Alfred Lord Tennyson d. (b. 1809)	Ernest Renan, Fr. historian, d. (b. 1823) Emile Faguet: "Politiques et moralistes du dix-neuvième siècle" G. J. Romanes: "Darwin and after Darwin"

D. VISUAL ARTS	E. MUSIC	F. SCIENCE, TECHNOLOGY, GROWTH	G. DAILY LIFE	
Cézanne: "The Cardplayers," painting Frederick Leighton: "The Bath of Psyche" Vincent Van Gogh d. (b. 1853) Giovanni Segantini: "Plowing in the Engadine"	César Franck d. (b. 1822) Bruckner: Symphonies No. 3 and 4, last versions Richard Strauss: "Tod und Verklärung" Borodin: "Prince Igor," opera, St. Petersburg (posth.) Pietro Mascagni: "Cavalleria Rusticana," opera, Rome Tchaikovsky: "Queen of Spades," opera, St. Petersburg	T. G. Curtius produces azoimide from organic sources Anthony Fokker, Dutch aircraft designer who worked in Germany and (after 1922) the U.S., b. (d. 1939) Rubber gloves are used for the first time in surgery, Johns Hopkins Hospital, Baltimore Emil von Behring announces the discovery of antitoxins	Global influenza epidemics Daughters of the American Revolution founded in Washington First Eng. electrical power station, Deptford Forth Bridge opened The first entirely steel-framed building erected in Chicago Charles Forepaugh, Amer. circus proprietor, d. (b. 1831)	**1890**
Gauguin settles in Tahiti Van Gogh exhibits at the Salon des Indépendents Henri Toulouse-Lautrec produces his first music hall posters Georges Seurat, Fr. painter, d. (b. 1859) David Low, New Zealand-born Brit. caricaturist, b. (d. 1963)	Léo Delibes, Fr. composer, d. (b. 1836) Sir Arthur Bliss, Eng. composer, b. (d. 1975) Gustav Mahler: Symphony No. 1 Sergei Prokofiev, Russ. composer, b. (d. 1953) Karl Zeller: "Der Vogelhändler," Viennese operetta Rachmaninoff finishes the first version of his Piano Concerto No. 1 (revised 1917)	Frederick Banting, Canadian physician, 1923 Nobel Prize, b. (d. 1941) Samuel P. Langley: "Experiments in Aerodynamics" Beginnings of wireless telegraphy Trans-Siberian railroad construction begins (—1917)	All-Deutschland Verband (Pan-Germany League) founded In the libel action Gordon-Cummings v. Lycett, concerning cheating at cards, the Prince of Wales, as a witness, admits he played baccarat for high stakes Widespread famine in Russia Earthquake in Japan kills as many as 10,000 people In Java Dutch anthropologist Eugène Dubois discovers Pithecanthropus erectus (Java Man) W. L. Judson (U.S.) invents clothing zipper (not in practical use until 1919)	**1891**
Monet begins his series of pictures on the Rouen Cathedral (—1895) Toulouse-Lautrec: "At the Moulin Rouge," painting	Bruckner: Symphony No. 8, Vienna Leoncavallo: "I Pagliacci," opera, Milan Tchaikovsky: "The Nutcracker," ballet, St. Petersburg Dvorák becomes director of New York National Conservatory of Music	C. F. Cross and E. J. Bevan discover viscose (manufacture of rayon) Diesel patents his internal-combustion engine First automatic telephone switchboard introduced Louis de Broglie, Belg. physicist, 1929 Nobel Prize, b. (d. 1987) A. H. Compton, U.S. physicist, b. (d. 1962) E. W. Siemens d. (b. 1816)	Iron and steel workers strike in U.S. Cape—Johannesburg railroad completed First cans of pineapples "Gentleman Jim" Corbett defeats John L. Sullivan to win heavyweight boxing title	**1892**

	A. HISTORY, POLITICS	B. LITERATURE, THEATER	C. RELIGION, PHILOSOPHY, LEARNING
1893	Independent Labour Party formed at conference in Bradford, England, under Keir Hardie Hawaii proclaimed a republic; annexed by treaty to U.S. in Feb.; in Mar. treaty withdrawn Franco-Russ. alliance signed Trial over Panama Canal corruption in Paris Natal granted self-government Revolt against Brit. South Africa Company in Matabele; crushed by Starr Jameson; occupation of Bulawayo Second Irish Home Rule Bill passed by Commons but rejected by Lords Swaziland annexed by Transvaal France acquires protectorate over Laos Hermann Goering, Nazi leader, b. (d. 1946)	Anatole France: "La Rôtisserie de la Reine Pédauque" Mark Rutherford: "Catherine Furze" Courteline: "Boubouroche" Pinero: "The Second Mrs. Tanqueray" Wilde: "A Woman of No Importance" Hippolyte Taine, Fr. author, d. (b. 1828) Maupassant d. (b. 1850) Ernst Toller, Ger. dramatist, b. (d. 1939) Max Halbe: "Jugend," Ger. play Gerhart Hauptmann: "Der Biberpelz" Arthur Schnitzler: "Anatol," Viennese one-act plays Sardou: "Madame Sans-Gêne," Fr. comedy Sudermann: "Die Heimat" (Eng. title "Magda")	F. H. Bradley: "Appearance and Reality" W. T. Stead: "If Christ Came to Chicago"
1894	Starr Jameson completes occupation of Matabeleland Ger.-Russ. commercial treaty Harold Macmillan, Brit. statesman, b. (d. 1986) Uganda becomes a Brit. protectorate Nikita Khrushchev, Russ. statesman, b. (d. 1971) M. F. Sadi Carnot assassinated by an Ital. anarchist (b. 1837) Jap. troops in Seoul; Korea and Japan declare war on China and defeat Chinese at Port Arthur Fr. army Capt. Alfred Dreyfus arrested on treason charge; convicted "in camera" and deported to Devil's Island, French Guiana Prince Hohenlohe becomes Ger. Chancellor Czar Alexander III d.; succeeded by his son Nicholas II (—1917) Lajos Kossuth, Hungarian patriot, d. (b. 1802)	Aldous Huxley, Eng. author, b. (d. 1963) Oliver Wendell Holmes, Amer. author, d. (b. 1809) Robert Louis Stevenson d. (b. 1850) James Thurber, Amer. author, b. (d. 1961) J. B. Priestley, Eng. author, b. (d. 1984) Knut Hamsun: "Pan" Gerhart Hauptmann: "Hanneles Himmelfahrt," play George du Maurier: "Trilby," novel G. and W. Grossmith: "Diary of a Nobody" Anthony Hope: "The Prisoner of Zenda" Kipling: "The Jungle Book" George Moore: "Esther Waters" S. B. Weyman: "Under the Red Robe" Zola: "Trilogy of the Three Cities" (—1898) Bernard Shaw" "Arms and the Man" Edison opens his Kinetoscope Parlor, New York	Benjamin Kidd: "Social Revolution" Sidney and Beatrice Webb: "History of Trade Unionism" Pollock and Maitland: "History of English Law Before the Time of Edward I"
1895	Chinese defeated by Japanese at Wei-hai-Wei; end of Chin.-Jap. war; Formosa and Port Arthur ceded to Japan but returned to China in exchange for indemnity; Queen of Korea assassinated with Jap. help Brit. South Africa Company territory south of Zambezi becomes Rhodesia Stefan Stambulov, Bulgarian Premier, assassinated Armenians massacred in Turkey; Sultan Abdul Hamid II promises reforms in Turkey Italians defeated by Abyssinians at Amba Alagi Starr Jameson's raid into Transvaal Cuba fights Spain for its independence The future King George VI of Great Britain b. (d. 1952) Frederick Douglass, Amer. abolitionist, reformer and orator, d. (b. 1817)	Oscar Hammerstein, Amer. librettist, b. (d. 1960) Lewis Mumford, Amer. author, b. (d. 1990) First public film show in Paris, at the Hôtel Scribe Hilaire Belloc: "Verses and Sonnets" Joseph Conrad: "Almayer's Folly" Sienkiewicz: "Quo Vadis" Henry James: "The Middle Years," autobiography George Moore: "The Celibates" H. G. Wells: "The Time Machine" W. B. Yeats: "Poems"	Thomas Masaryk: "The Czech Question" Karl Marx: "Das Kapital," vol. 3 (posth.) London School of Economics and Political Science founded Cardinal Vaughan lays foundation stone of Westminster Cathedral T. H. Huxley, Eng. scientist, d. (b. 1825)

D. VISUAL ARTS	E. MUSIC	F. SCIENCE, TECHNOLOGY, GROWTH	G. DAILY LIFE	
"Art Nouveau" appears in Europe George Grosz, Ger. painter, b. (d. 1959)	Cole Porter, Amer. songwriter, b. (d. 1964) Tchaikovsky d. (b. 1840) Charles Gounod d. (b. 1818) Dvorák: Symphony No. 5., Op. 95 ("From the New World") Sibelius: "Karelia Suite," Op. 10 Tchaikovsky: Symphony No. 6 ("Pathetique"), Op. 74 Engelbert Humperdinck: "Hänsel und Gretel," opera, Weimar Puccini: "Manon Lescaut," opera, Turin Verdi: "Falstaff," opera, Milan	Karl Benz constructs his four-wheel car J. M. Charcot, Fr. psychiatrist, d. (b. 1825) Henry Ford builds his first car Marietta Blau, Aust. mathematician and atomic physicist, b. (d. 1970)	Imperial Institute, South Kensington, London, founded Manchester Ship Canal completed Fridtjof Nansen begins his unsuccessful expedition to the North Pole (—1896) Corinth Canal, Greece, opened World Exhibition in Chicago Longest recorded boxing fight, Apr. 6—7 in New Orleans, U.S.; Andy Bowen versus Jack Burk, 110 rounds in 7 hours, 4 minutes Lady Margaret Scott wins first Brit. golf championship	**1893**
Aubrey Beardsley: drawings to Oscar Wilde's "Salome" Matthew Corbett: "Morning Glory," painting Gustave Caillebotte's collection of impressionist paintings rejected by the Musée Luxembourg, Paris Degas: "Femme à sa toilette," painting	Sibelius: "Finlandia" Debussy: "L'Après-midi d'un faune" Massenet: "Thaïs," opera, Paris Richard Strauss: "Guntram," opera, Weimar Anton Rubinstein, Russ. composer and pianist, d. (b. 1829)	Hermann von Helmholtz d. (b. 1821) Swed. explorer Sven Hedin travels in Tibet Louis Lumière (1862—1948) invents the cinematograph Yersin and Kitasato independently discover the plague bacillus Berliner uses a horizontal gramophone disc instead of a cylinder as a record for sound reproduction Lord Rayleigh and William Ramsay discover argon Flagstaff Observatory erected, Arizona, U.S.	New York Jockey Club founded Death duties (inheritance tax) introduced in Britain Baron de Coubertin founds committee to organize modern Olympic Games	**1894**
Art Nouveau style predominates "Revolt of the Weavers," three prints by Käthe Kollwitz (—1898)	Tchaikovsky: "Swan Lake," ballet, St. Petersburg, (first complete performance) Mahler: Symphony No. 2 Richard Strauss: "Till Eulenspiegel's Merry Pranks," symphonic poem, Cologne Robert Newman arranges the first Promenade Concerts at Queen's Hall, London; conductor: Henry J. Wood Paul Hindemith Ger. composer, b. (d. 1963) Wilhelm Kienzl: "Der Evangelimann," opera, Berlin	Wilhelm Röntgen discovers x-rays Marconi invents radio telegraphy Sigmund Freud: "Studien über Hysterie" Louis Pasteur d. (b. 1822) Auguste and Louis Lumière invent a motion-picture camera Konstantin Isiolkovski formulates the principle of rocket reaction propulsion C. von Linde constructs a machine for the liquefaction of air	King C. Gillette invents the safety razor Babe Ruth, baseball great, b. (d. 1948) Friedrich Engels, Ger. socialist, d. (b. 1820) Jack Dempsey, U.S. boxing champion, b. (d. 1983) Peter Latham (Great Britain) becomes world lawn tennis champion Kiel Canal, Germany, opened Oscar Wilde's unsuccessful libel action against Marquis of Queensberry Amer. Bowling Congress formed to govern the game First professional football game played in U.S. at Latrobe, Pa. First U.S. Open Golf Championship held	**1895**

	A. HISTORY, POLITICS	B. LITERATURE THEATER	C. RELIGION, PHILOSOPHY, LEARNING
1896	Starr Jameson surrenders at Doornkop; Kaiser William II sends "Kruger telegram"; Cecil Rhodes resigns premiership; military alliance between Transvaal and Orange Free State; Matabele revolt in Rhodesia put down by Baden-Powell Utah becomes a state of the U.S. Italy defeated by Abyssinians at Adowa; Italy sues for peace and withdraws its protectorate from Abyssinia New evidence for the innocence of Alfred Dreyfus suppressed in France Nasr-ed-Din, Shah of Persia, assassinated France annexes Madagascar Further massacres of Armenians in Constantinople Kitchener begins his campaign against the Mahdi in Sudan Russia and China sign Manchuria Convention Czar Nicholas II visits Paris and London William McKinley elected 25th President of the U.S.	Verlaine d. (b. 1844) John Dos Passos, Amer. novelist, b. (d. 1970) Harriet Beecher Stowe, Amer. novelist, d. (b. 1811) Edmond de Goncourt, Fr. author, d. (b. 1822) William Morris, Eng. poet and artist, d. (b. 1834) Pierre Louys: "Aphrodite," Fr. novel R. M. Rilke: "Larenopfer," poems Chekhov: "The Sea Gull," Russ. drama	Heinrich von Treitschke, Ger. historian, d. (b. 1834) Henri Bergson: "Matière et mémoire" Five annual Nobel Prizes established for those who during the preceding year shall have conferred the greatest benefits on mankind in the fields of physics, physiology and medicine, chemistry, literature, and peace Theodor Herzl: "Der Judenstaat," foundation of Zionism
1897	Crete proclaims union with Greece; Turkey declares war on Greece and is defeated in Thessaly; armistice, followed by Peace of Constantinople William McKinley inaugurated as President of the U.S. King of Korea proclaims himself emperor Mathieu Dreyfus discovers that the document on which his brother, Alfred, was convicted was actually written by Major M. C. Esterhazy Germany occupies Kiao-chow, North China Russia occupies Port Arthur Anthony Eden (Lord Avon), Brit. statesman, b. (d. 1977) Aneurin Bevan, Brit. Labour politician, b. (d. 1960)	Alphonse Daudet, Fr. novelist, d. (b. 1840) Joseph Conrad: "The Nigger of the Narcissus" John Galsworthy: "From the Four Winds" Stefan George: "Das Jahr der Seele" Kipling: "Captains Courageous" Strindberg: "Inferno" H. G. Wells: "The Invisible Man" Edmond Rostand: "Cyrano de Bergerac" Shaw: "Candida"	Sidney and Beatrice Webb: "Industrial Democracy" Havelock Ellis: "Studies in the Psychology of Sex" (—1928)
1898	Major Esterhazy acquitted in Dreyfus forgery trial; Zola publishes open letter to Fr. President, "J'accuse," and is imprisoned; Col. Henry admits forgery of a document in Dreyfus case Paul Kruger reelected President of Transvaal Russia obtains lease of Port Arthur, China; Britain, the lease of Kowloon Kitchener wins battles at Atbara River and Omdurman, and reaches Fashoda U.S. declares war on Spain over Cuba: Americans destroy Span. fleet at Manila; Treaty of Paris between U.S. and Spain; Spain cedes Cuba, Puerto Rico, Guam, and the Philippines for $20 million Bismarck d. (b. 1815) Gladstone d. (b. 1809) Empress Elizabeth of Austria murdered by Ital. anarchist in *(contd)*	Lewis Carroll, author of "Alice in Wonderland," d. (b. 1832) Stéphane Mallarmé d. (b. 1842) Bertolt Brecht, Ger. writer, b. (d. 1956) Theodor Fontane, Ger. novelist, d. (b. 1819) Knut Hamsun: "Victoria" Ernest Hemingway, Amer. writer, b. (d. 1961) Anthony Hope: "Rupert of Hentzau" Thomas Hardy: "Wessex Poems" J. K. Huysmans: "La Cathédrale" Henry James: "The Turn of the Screw" H. G. Wells: "The War of the Worlds" Oscar Wilde: "The Ballad of Reading Gaol" Shaw: "Caesar and Cleopatra"	Bismarck: "Reflections and Memoirs"

D. VISUAL ARTS	E. MUSIC	F. SCIENCE, TECHNOLOGY, GROWTH	G. DAILY LIFE	
Frederick Leighton: "Clytie," painting National Portrait Gallery, London, moved from Bethnal Green to Westminster The Cartoonist Phil May joins "Punch" John E. Millais, Eng. painter, d. (b. 1829) "Die Jugend" and "Simplicissimus," two important Ger. art magazines, appear in Munich	Anton Bruckner d. (b. 1824) Sidney Jones: "The Geisha," operetta, London Clara Wiek-Schumann, Ger. pianist, d. (b. 1819) Edward MacDowell: "Indian Suite," on N. Amer. Indian folk tunes Richard Strauss: "Also Sprach Zarathustra," symphonic poem, Frankfurt Puccini: "La Bohème," opera, Turin Hugo Wolf: "Der Corregidor," opera, Mannheim Giordano: "Andrea Chenier," opera, Milan The last of the Gilbert and Sullivan comic operettas, "The Grand Duke," London	William Ramsay discovers helium Ernest Rutherford: magnetic detection of electrical waves Niagara Falls hydroelectric plant opens Alfred Nobel d. (b. 1833) Fr. physicist A. H. Becquerel discovers radioactivity First Eng. all-steel building, West Hartlepool	Alfred Harmsworth issues the London "Daily Mail" First modern Olympics held in Athens "Persimmon," owned by the Prince of Wales, wins the Derby First Alpine ski school founded at Lilienfeld, Austria Royal Victorian Order founded Beginning of Klondike gold rush, Bonanza Creek, Canada	**1896**
Jakob Burckhardt, Swiss art historian, d. (b. 1818) Matisse: "Dinner Table," painting Rodin: "Victor Hugo," sculpture "Katzenjammer Kids," first Amer. comic strip, begun by Rudolph Dirks Henri "Le Douanier" Rousseau (1844—1910): "Sleeping Gypsy," painting Sir Henry Tate donates Tate Gallery, London, to the Brit. people Max Klinger: "Christ in Olympus," painting Pissarro: "Boulevard des Italiens"	Johannes Brahms d. (b. 1833) Erich Wolfgang Korngold, Aust. composer, b. (d. 1957) Gustav Mahler becomes conductor of the Vienna Opera Vincent d'Indy: "Fervaal," opera, Brussels	Ronald Ross discovers malaria bacillus William Thomson (Lord Kelvin) studies cathode rays Julius Hann: "Handbook of Climatology" J. J. Thomson discovers electron	Severe famine in India World Exhibition at Brussels Founding of Royal Automobile Club, London The Sultan of Zanzibar abolishes slavery Zionist Congress in Basel, Switzerland, under Theodor Herzl and Max Nordau Queen Victoria's Diamond Jubilee	**1897**
Félicien Rops, Belg. painter, d. (b. 1833) The Mackintosh School of Art in Glasgow	Paul Robeson, Negro bass singer, b. (d. 1976) Toscanini appears at La Scala, Milan	Ramsay discovers the inert atmospheric gases xenon, crypton, and neon The Jap. bacteriologist Shiga discovers dysentery bacillus Pierre and Marie Curie discover radium and polonium Ger. Count Ferdinand von Zeppelin builds his airship	Photographs first taken utilizing artificial light Paris Métro opened Gene Tunney, Amer. boxing champion, b. (d. 1978)	**1898**

	A. HISTORY, POLITICS	B. LITERATURE, THEATER	C. RELIGION, PHILOSOPHY, LEARNING
1898 contd	Geneva Emperor William II of Germany visits Palestine and Syria "The Boxers," an antiforeign, anti-Western organization formed in China		
1899	Anglo-Egyptian Sudan Convention Philippines demand independence from U.S. Johannesburg Uitlanders complain to Queen Victoria against Boers Bloemfontein Conference on Transvaal; Paul Kruger's ultimatum provokes Boer War between Britain and the Boers; Boers defeated at Glencoe; Boer Gen. Piet Joubert wins Battle of Nicholson's Nek and takes Ladysmith, Natal; the British are defeated at Stormberg, Magersfontein, and Colenso (The "Black Week"); Canadian and Australian volunteers land in S. Africa First Peace Conference at The Hague Fr. "cour de cassation" annuls Dreyfus judgment and orders retrial; Dreyfus pardoned by presidential decree Emperor William II visits England Germany secures Baghdad Railroad contract	Erich Kästner, Ger. author, b. (d. 1974) Charles Laughton, Eng. actor, b. (d. 1962) Noel Coward, Eng. author, dramatist, composer, and actor, b. (d. 1973) Federico García Lorca, Span. author, b. (d. 1936) Karl Kraus begins to publish his "Fackel" in Vienna Hofmannsthal: "Der Tor und der Tod," verse drama Arthur Schnitzler: "Reigen" Pinero: "Trelawny of the Wells" Ibsen: "When We Dead Awaken" Stefan George: "Der Teppich des Lebens," Ger. poems André Gide: "Le Prométhée mal enchaîne" Kipling: "Stalky and Co." Tolstoi: "Resurrection" Oscar Wilde: "The Importance of Being Earnest"	H. S. Chamberlain: "The Foundations of the Nineteenth Century" John Dewey: "School and Society" Ernst Haeckel: "Die Welträtsel" Alexander Bain: "The Realization of the Possible" James Ward: "Naturalism and Agnosticism" Pope Leo XIII's bull "Testem Benevolentiae" condemns the "Americanism" of Isaac Thomas Hecker
1900	Roberts named Brit. commander-in-chief in S. Africa, Kitchener his chief of staff; relief of Ladysmith in Feb.; British capture Bloemfontein in Mar.; relief of Mafeking in May; British annex Orange Free State and Transvaal, take Pretoria and Johannesburg Ramsay MacDonald appointed secretary of Brit. Labour Party Boxer risings in China against Europeans King Umberto I of Italy murdered by anarchist; succeeded by his son Victor Emmanuel III (—1946) The Commonwealth of Australia created Bernhard von Bülow is named Ger. Chancellor William McKinley, 25th President of the U.S., reelected	Colette: "Claudine à l'école" (first "Claudine" novel) Joseph Conrad: "Lord Jim" Maxim Gorki: "Three People" Edmond Rostand: "L'Aiglon" Tolstoi: "The Living Corpse" Theodore Dreiser: "Sister Carrie" Anton Chekhov: "Uncle Vanya" Stephen Crane, Amer. author, d. (b. 1871) Oscar Wilde d. (b. 1856) J. C. Heer: "König der Bernina," Swiss novel Ignazio Silone, Ital. author, b. (d. 1978) Thomas Wolfe, Amer. author, b. (d. 1938)	Nietzsche d. (b. 1844) Ellen Key: "Century of the Child" Shintoism reinstated in Japan against Buddhist influence Leslie Stephen: "The English Utilitarians" Henri Bergson: "Le Rire" Sigmund Freud: "The Interpretation of Dreams" Bertrand Russell: "A Critical Exposition of the Philosophy of Leibniz" Wilhelm Wundt: "Comparative Psychology"

D. VISUAL ARTS	E. MUSIC	F. SCIENCE, TECHNOLOGY, GROWTH	G. DAILY LIFE	
				1898 contd
Giovanni Segantini, Ital. painter, d. (b. 1858) Alfred Sisley, Fr. painter, d. (b. 1839)	Elgar: "Enigma Variations" Sibelius: Symphony No. 1 in E minor Bruckner: Symphony No. 5 (posth.) Francis Poulenc, Fr. composer, b. (d. 1963) Johann Strauss d. (b. 1825) Karl Millöcker, Viennese operetta composer, d. (b. 1842) Richard Strauss: "Ein Heldenleben," symphonic poem, Frankfurt	Rutherford discovers alpha and beta rays in radioactive atoms Pringsheim and Lummer undertake important radiation studies First magnetic recording of sound	London borough councils established	**1899**
Wallace Collection, London, opened John Ruskin, Eng. art historian, d. (b. 1819) Picasso: "Le Moulin de la Galette," painting Gauguin: "Noa Noa," report on his travels through Tahiti Lawrence Alma-Tadema: "Vain Courtship" Cézanne: "Still Life with Onions" Renoir: "Nude in the Sun" Sargent: "The Sitwell Family" Toulouse-Lautrec: "La Modiste" Film: "Cinderella," directed by Georges Méliès	Ernst Krenek, Aust. composer, b. Sir Arthur Sullivan d. (b. 1842) Kurt Weill, Ger. composer, b. (d. 1950) Samuel Coleridge-Taylor: "Hiawatha" Gustave Charpentier: "Louise," opera, Paris Elgar: "Dream of Gerontius," oratorio, Birmingham Puccini: "Tosca," opera, Rome Aaron Copland, Amer. composer, b. (d. 1990)	F. E. Dorn discovers radon Max Planck formulates quantum theory The first Browning revolvers manufactured Amer. scientist R. A. Fessenden transmits human speech via radio waves First trial flight of Zeppelin Arthur Evans's excavations in Crete: discovery of Minoan culture (—1908)	Ger. Civil Law Code comes in force George Cadbury founds Bourneville Village trust "Daily Express," London, appears The Cake Walk becomes the most fashionable dance D. F. Davis presents international lawn tennis cup bearing his name World Exhibition in Paris Ray C. Ewry, U.S., wins eight Olympic gold medals (—1908) W. G. Grace ends his cricket career–54,000 runs in his lifetime William Muldoon proclaimed first professional wrestling champion	**1900**

	A. HISTORY, POLITICS	B. LITERATURE, THEATER	C. RELIGION, PHILOSOPHY, LEARNING
1901	Edmund Barton inaugurated as first Prime Minister of the Commonwealth of Australia Queen Victoria d.; succeeded by her son Edward VII The Boers begin organized guerrilla warfare; negotiations between Kitchener and Botha at Middleburg on amnesty of Cape rebels Cuba Convention makes the country a U.S. protectorate W. H. Taft becomes Governor-General of the Philippines Negotiations for Anglo-Jap. alliance in London Peace of Peking ends Boxer uprising U.S. President William McKinley assassinated by anarchist; succeeded by Theodore Roosevelt Prince Ito of Japan in St. Petersburg seeking concessions in Korea; negotiations end without agreement Negotiations for Anglo-Ger. alliance end without agreement Treaty on building of Panama Canal under U.S. supervision Social Revolutionary Party founded in Russia Nobel Peace Prize: Henri Dunant (Swiss) and Frédéric Passy (French)	Samuel Butler: "Erewhon Revisited" Hall Caine: "The Eternal City" Kipling: "Kim" Selma Lagerlöf: "Jerusalem" Maeterlinck: "The Life of the Bees" Thomas Mann: "Buddenbrooks" Strindberg: "Dance of Death" André Malraux, Fr. author, b. (d. 1976) Louis Couperus: "Babel," Dutch novel Wilhelm Meyer-Förster: "Alt-Heidelberg," Ger. play Charles Louis Philippe: "Bubu de Montparnasse," Fr. novel Frank Wedekind: "Der Marquis von Keith" Stefan Zweig: "Silberne Saiten," poems Cabaret "Überbretti" founded in Berlin J. M. Barrie: "Quality Street," play Frank Norris: "The Octopus," Amer. novel	B. S. Rowntree: "Poverty; a Study of Town Life" James Bryce: "Studies in History and Jurisprudence" Rudolf Steiner founds anthroposophy Rabindranath Tagore founds his Santiniketan school (Bengal)
1902	Anglo-Jap. treaty recognizes the independence of China and Korea Coal strike in U.S., May—Oct. National bankruptcy declared in Portugal Treaty of Vereeniging ends Boer War; Orange Free State becomes Brit. Crown Colony Triple Alliance between Germany, Austria, and Italy renewed for another six years U.S. acquires perpetual control over Panama Canal Colonial Conference meets in London Arthur Balfour becomes Brit. Prime Minister First meeting of Committee of Imperial Defence, London Cecil Rhodes d. (b. 1853) Leon Trotsky escapes from a Siberian prison and settles in London Elizabeth Cady Stanton, Amer. suffragette leader, d. (b. 1815)	Hilaire Belloc: "The Path to Rome" Joseph Conrad: "Youth" A. Conan Doyle: "The Hound of the Baskervilles" André Gide: "The Immoralist" Kipling: "Just-so Stories" Maxim Gorki: "Lower Depths," novel John Masefield: "Salt Water Ballads" D'Annunzio: "Francesca da Rimini" J. M. Barrie: "The Admirable Crichton" Chekhov: "Three Sisters" "The Times Literary Supplement" issued, London John Steinbeck, Amer. novelist, b. (d. 1968) Samuel Butler, Eng. author, d. (b. 1835) Emile Zola d. (b. 1840) Nobel Prize for Literature: Theodor Mommsen Arnold Bennett: "Anna of the Five Towns," novel Maeterlinck: "Monna Vanna," verse drama Merezhkovski: "Leonardo da Vinci," biographic novel A. E. W. Mason: "The Four Feathers" Beatrix Potter: "Peter Rabbit," children's stories	J. A. Hobson: "Imperialism" William James: "The Varieties of Religious Experience" Paul Hoensbroich: "The Papacy in Its Social and Cultural Influence" Benedetto Croce: "Philosophy of the Spirit" Pauli and Herbig: "Corpus inscriptionum etruscarum" (1893—) Werner Sombart: "Modern Capitalism"

D. VISUAL ARTS	E. MUSIC	F. SCIENCE, TECHNOLOGY, GROWTH	G. DAILY LIFE	
Gauguin: "The Gold in Their Bodies," painting Edvard Munch: "Girls on the Bridge" Arnold Böcklin, Swiss painter, d. (b. 1827) Walt Disney, film producer, b. (d. 1966) Henri Toulouse-Lautrec d. (b. 1864) Feradin and Holder: "Spring," painting Max Liebermann: "Self-Portrait" Picasso's Blue Period (—1905) The Siegesallee in Berlin: 32 marble statues of members of the House of Hohenzollern Film: "The Little Doctor" (English)	Richard Strauss: "Feuersnot," opera, Dresden Stanford: "Much Ado about Nothing," opera, London Dvorák: "Rusalka," opera, Prague Elgar: "Cockaigne," overture, Op. 40 Ravel: "Jeux d'eau" Rachmaninoff: Piano Concerto No. 2 Bruckner: Symphony No. 6 (posth.) Verdi d. (b. 1813) Edmund Rubbra, Eng. composer, b. (d. 1986) Werner Egk, Ger. composer, b. (d. 1983) Tenor Leo Slezak joins the Vienna Opera Ragtime jazz develops in U.S. Wigmore Hall, London, opened	Following a "century of steam," the "century of electricity" begins Max Planck: "Laws of Radiation" The hormone adrenalin first isolated Marconi transmits telegraphic radio messages from Cornwall to Newfoundland First motor-driven bicycles Nobel Prizes: physics, Wilhelm Roentgen; medicine, E. von Behring Enrico Fermi, Ital. physicist, 1938 Nobel Prize, b. (d. 1954) Wilhelm Maybach, technical director at the Daimler works, constructs the first Mercedes car W. H. Nernst postulates the "third law of thermodynamics"	Mombasa—Lake Victoria railway completed J. P. Morgan organizes U.S. Steel Corporation Trans-Siberian Railroad reaches Port Arthur Fifth Zionist Congress begins Jewish National Fund Oil drilling begins in Persia Boxing recognized as a legal sport in England First Brit. submarine launched First Amer. Bowling Club tournament held in Chicago	**1901**
Gauguin: "Riders by the Sea" Monet: "Waterloo Bridge" J. S. Sargent: "Lord Ribblesdale" Rodin: "Romeo and Juliet" Olaf Gulbransson becomes political cartoonist for the "Simplicissimus" Slevogt: portrait of the singer Francesco d'Andrade as Don Giovanni Film: "Salomé" (Oskar Messter) Max Klinger: "Nietzsche," sculpture	Elgar composes the first of his "Pomp and Circumstance" marches (—1930) Debussy: "Pelléas et Mélisande," opera, Paris Edward German: "Merrie England," operetta, London Frederick Delius: "Appalachia" William Walton, Eng. composer, b. (d. 1983) Leo Blech: "Das War Ich," comic opera, Dresden Lehár: "Der Rastelbinder," operetta, Vienna Massenet: "Le Jongleur de Notre Dame," opera, Monte Carlo Sibelius: Symphony No. 2 Enrico Caruso makes his first phonograph recording	Oliver Heaviside, Eng. physicist, states the existence of an atmospheric layer which aids the conduction of radio waves Amer. neurological surgeon H. W. Cushing begins study of pituitary body Bayliss and Starling discover the hormone secretin Fr. physician Charles Richet discovers anaphylaxis (abnormal sensitivity to a serum treatment) Valdemar Poulsen (U.S.) invents the arc generator J. M. Bacon becomes the first man to cross the Irish Channel in a balloon Nobel Prize for Medicine: Sir Ronald Ross Adolf Miethe invents panchromatic plate Rudolph Virchow, Ger. physician, d. (b. 1821)	Aswan Dam opened Casualties in Boer War: 5,774 British and 4,000 Boers killed King Edward VII establishes Order of Merit (limited to 24 Brit. subjects at any one time) Anglo-Amer. "Pilgrims" Association founded Metropolitan Water Board, London, established Martinique volcanic fire destroys the town of St. Pierre	**1902**

	A. HISTORY, POLITICS	B. LITERATURE, THEATER	C. RELIGION, PHILOSOPHY, LEARNING
1903	British complete conquest of Northern Nigeria King Edward VII visits Paris; Fr. President Loubet visits London–the "Entente Cordiale" established King Alexander I of Serbia and Queen Draga murdered; Peter Karageorgevich accedes to the throne as Peter I (—1921) Alaskan frontier is settled At its London Congress the Russ. Social Democratic Party splits into Mensheviks (led by Plechanoff) and Bolsheviks (led by Lenin and Trotsky) Coronation durbar for Edward VI, King-Emperor, at Delhi	Evelyn Waugh, Eng. novelist, b. (d. 1966) Samuel Butler: "The Way of All Flesh" (posth.) Hofmannsthal: "Electra" Henry James: "The Ambassadors" Shaw: "Man and Superman" Nobel Prize for Literature: Björnsterne Björnson (Norw.) Gerhart Hauptmann: "Rose Bernd," Ger. drama Theodor Herzl: "Alt-Neuland," Zionist novel Jack London: "The Call of the Wild," novel Strindberg: "Queen Christina," historical play	Theodor Mommsen, Ger. historian, d. (b. 1817) Herbert Spencer, Eng. philosopher, d. (b. 1820) G. E. Moore: "Principia Ethica" Pope Leo XIII d.; succeeded by Cardinal Guiseppe Sarto, Pope Pius X (—1914) Johannes Haller: "The Papacy and Church Reform" Wilhelm Bölsche: "Das Liebesleben in der Natur" Anti-Jewish pogroms in Russia Henri Poincaré: "Science and Hypothesis" Otto Weininger: "Sex and Character" (the Viennese author commits suicide at the age of 23)
1904	Russo-Japanese War breaks out in Feb.; Japanese besiege Port Arthur and occupy Seoul; Russ. Minister of the Interior, Viacheslav Plehve, assassinated; Russ. fleet partially destroyed off Port Arthur; Russians defeated at Liaoyang, China, in Oct. Rafael Reyes becomes dictator of Colombia Hereros and Hottentots revolt in Ger. South-West Africa (—1908) Treaty between Bolivia and Chile Theodore Roosevelt wins U.S. presidential election Nikola Pasic, nationalist anti-Austrian, becomes Serbian Prime Minister	Leslie Stephen, Eng. author, d. (b. 1832) Anton Chekhov d. (b. 1860) Christopher Isherwood, Eng. author, b. (d. 1986) Graham Greene, Eng. novelist, b. (d. 1991) Marlene Dietrich, Ger.-born actress, b. G. K. Chesterton: "The Napoleon of Notting Hill" Joseph Conrad: "Nostromo" W. H. Hudson: "Green Mansions" Jack London: "The Sea-Wolf" Romain Rolland: "Jean-Christophe" (—1912) James Barrie: "Peter Pan" Anton Chekhov: "The Cherry Orchard" Thomas Hardy: "The Dynasts" J. M. Synge: "Riders to the Sea" Abbey Theatre, Dublin, founded Max Halbe: "Der Strom," Ger. play Hermann Hesse: "Peter Camenzind," novel O. Henry: "Cabbages and Kings," short stories Frank Wedekind: "Die Büchse der Pandora," Ger. play Henry James: "The Golden Bowl"	L. T. Hobhouse: "Democracy and Reaction" Church and state separated in France Elizabeth Förster-Nietzsche: "Das Leben Friedrich Nietzsches" Lafcadio Hearn (1850—1904): "Japan: an Attempt at Interpretation" Hermann Oncken: "Lassalle," biography Freud: "The Psychopathology of Everyday Life" Max Weber: "The Protestant Ethic and the Birth of Capitalism"

D. VISUAL ARTS	E. MUSIC	F. SCIENCE, TECHNOLOGY, GROWTH	G. DAILY LIFE	
James Whistler, Anglo-Amer. painter, d. (b. 1834) John Piper, Eng. artist, b. Paul Gauguin, Fr. painter, d. (b. 1848) Camille Pissarro, Fr. painter, d. (b. 1830) P. W. Steer: "Richmond Castle," painting Alma-Tadema: "Silver-favorites" Building of Liverpool Cathedral, designed by G. G. Scott, begins Joseph Israels: "Jewish Wedding" Gustav Klimt: "Philosophy, Medicine and Jurisprudence," painted ceiling at Vienna University Film: "The Great Train Robbery" (longest film to date: 12 minutes)	Delius: "Sea Drift" Bruckner: Symphony No. 9, Vienna (posth.) Oscar Hammerstein builds the Manhattan Opera House, New York Hugo Wolf d. (b. 1860) Lennox Berkeley, Eng. composer, b. (d. 1989) Edmund Eysler: "Bruder Straubinger," operetta, Vienna Boris Blacher, Ger. composer, b. (d. 1975) Juan Manén: "Giovanna di Napoli," Span. opera Ermanno Wolf-Ferrari: "Le Donne curiose," opera, Munich D'Albert: "Tiefland," opera, Prague Elgar: "The Apostles," oratorio, Birmingham First recording of an opera: Verdi's "Ernani"	Agnes Clerke: "Problems in Astrophysics" J. J. Thomson: "The Conduction of Electricity through Gases" Orville and Wilbur Wright successfully fly a powered airplane R. A. Zsigmondy invents the ultramicroscope Nobel Prizes: H. Becquerel, M. Sklodowska-Curie, P. Curie (physics); S. Arrhenius (chemistry) Universities of Liverpool and Manchester founded Wilhelm Einthoven invents the electrocardiograph	Motor-car regulations in Britain set a 20 mile-per-hour speed limit Emmeline Pankhurst founds National Women's Social and Political Union Royal Naval College, Dartmouth, established First motor taxis appear in London Deutsches Museum, Munich, opened Albert I, Prince of Monaco, founds International Peace Institute Ger. Hans Meyer climbs and explores Chimborazo (Ecuador) Henry Ford, with capital of $100,000, founds the Ford Motor Company J. P. Morgan founds the International Mercantile Marine Company Sixth Zionist Congress declines offer for Jewish settlement in E. Africa First coast-to-coast crossing of the Amer. continent by car: 65 days Richard Steiff designs first teddy bears (named after President Theodore Roosevelt) First Tour de France (bicycle race) The first post-season baseball series	**1903**
Max Beerbohm: "Poets Corner," drawings of Eng. authors Picasso: "The Two Sisters," painting Henri Rousseau: "The Wedding" Salvador Dali, Span. painter, b. (d. 1989) Henri Fantin-Latour, Fr. painter, d. (b. 1836) Films: "Le Barbier de Seville" and "Le Damnation de Faust" (Fr.)	G. M. Balanchine and Anton Dolin, choreographers, b. (both d. 1983) Anton Dvorák d. (b. 1841) Delius: "Koanga," opera, Elberfeld Puccini: "Madame Butterfly," opera, Milan Richard Strauss: "Sinfonia Domestica," New York Luigi Dallapiccola, Ital. composer, b. (d. 1975) First radio transmission of music at Graz, Austria London Symphony Orchestra gives its first concert Victor Herbert: "Mlle. Modiste," operetta, New York Leos Janácek: "Jenufa," opera, Brno	Rutherford and Soddy postulate general theory of radioactivity J. P. L. Elster devises first practical photoelectric cell The first ultraviolet lamps W. C. Gorgas eradicates yellow fever in Panama Canal Zone Work begins on the Panama Canal Rolls-Royce Company founded Nobel Prize: J. W. Rayleigh (physics), William Ramsay (chemistry) Marie Curie: "Recherches sur les substances radioactives" First telegraphic transmission of photographs; Arthur Korn, Munich to Nuremberg Sir John Fleming uses thermionic tube to generate radio waves F. S. Kipping discovers silicones First railroad tunnel *(contd)*	World Series between Giants and Boston called off as result of dispute with John McGraw "Elwood," F. Prior up, wins Kentucky Derby Amer. Walter J. Travis wins Brit. amateur golf championship; U.S. amateur won by H Chandler Egan; U.S. open won by Will Anderson 10-hour work day established in France Paris Conference on white slave trade Drink Licensing Laws in Britain Broadway subway opened in New York World Exhibition and (first Amer.) Olympics at St. Louis New York policeman arrests woman for smoking cigarette in public Ger. industrialist Carl Duisberg creates I. G. Farben Company Carl Lindström Company founded in Berlin for the production of phonographs and phonograph records Deaf and blind Helen Keller is graduated from Radcliffe College First trenches used in Russo-Japanese war First Vanderbilt Cup auto race won by Mercedes National Ski Association of America formed at Ishpeming, Mich. Jean Jaurès issues socialist newspaper "L'Humanité," Paris U.S. Lawn Tennis Men's Singles won by Holcombe Ward; Women's Singles by May G. Sutton Steerage rates for immigrants to U.S. cut to $10 by foreign lines	**1904**

	A. HISTORY, POLITICS	B. LITERATURE, THEATER	C. RELIGION, PHILOSOPHY, LEARNING
1904 contd			
1905	Port Arthur surrenders to Japanese; demonstration in St. Petersburg brutally crushed by police ("Bloody Sunday"); Russ. defeats at Mukden and in Tsushima Straits; William II of Germany and Nicholas II of Russia sign Treaty of Bjorko for mutual help in Europe; Imperial Duma (Russ. Parliament) created; Treaty of Portsmouth (mediated by U.S. President Theodore Roosevelt) ends war; general strike in Russia; the first workers' soviet formed in St. Petersburg; sailors mutiny on the battleship "Potemkin"; the czar's "October Manifesto" establishes reforms Louis Botha and his "Het Volk" Party demand responsible government in Transvaal and are dissatisfied with the new constitution Greeks in Crete revolt against Turks The Tangier crisis precipitated by the Kaiser's visit Norw. Parliament decides on separation from Sweden; Prince Charles of Denmark elected King Haakon VII of Norway Anglo-Jap. alliance renewed for 10 years Provinces of Alberta and Saskatchewan formed in Canada Sinn Fein Party founded in Dublin Theodore Roosevelt inaugurated as president for second term Henry Campbell-Bannerman (Liberal) becomes Prime Minister of Britain Sun Yat-sen founds a union of secret societies to expel the Manchus from China William Haywood and others found the International Workers of the World ("Wobblies")	Henry Irving, Eng. actor, d. (b. 1838) C. P. Snow, Eng. novelist, b. (d. 1980) Tristan Bernard: "Triplepatte," Fr. comedy Strindberg: "Historical Miniatures" H. G. Wells: "Kipps" Edith Wharton: "House of Mirth" Oscar Wilde: "De Profundis" (posth.) Nobel Prize for Literature: Henryk Sienkiewicz (Pol.) Richard Beer-Hofmann: "Der Graf von Charolais," Ger. verse drama Hermann Hesse: "Unterm Rad," novel Heinrich Mann: "Professor Unrat" ("The Blue Angel"), novel F. T. Marinetti: "Futurist Manifesto" Christian Morgenstern: "Galgenlieder," Ger. poems Rilke: "Das Stundenbuch," Ger. poems Jules Verne, Fr. author, d. (b. 1828) Lew Wallace, Amer. novelist, d. (b. 1827) E. M. Forster: "Where Angels Fear to Tread" Baroness Orczy: "The Scarlet Pimpernel" Bernard Shaw: "Major Barbara"; "Mrs. Warren's Profession" opens in New York; police censor closes it after one performance Belasco produces "The Girl of the Golden West," Pittsburgh; later made into opera by Puccini	Lenin: "Two Tactics" Wilhelm Dilthey: "Experience and Poetry" George Santayana: "The Life of Reason"
1906	Algeciras Conference gives France and Spain control of Morocco Armand Fallières elected President of France Reform Laws promulgated in Russia; first meeting of Duma in May; Duma dissolved in July Joao Franco becomes Prime Minister of Spain; Giovanni Giolitti of Italy; Peter Stolypin of Russia Alfred Dreyfus rehabilitated Edward VII of England and William II of Germany meet Self-government granted to the Transvaal and Orange River colonies All India Moslem League founded by Aga Khan In his magazine, "Die Zukunft," Maximilian Harden attacks Emperor William and his corrupt court camarilla Carl Schurz, Ger.-Amer. statesman, d. (b. 1829) Young Turks committee moves from Geneva to Salonika U.S. troops occupy Cuba (—1909) after reconciliation following Liberal revolt fails Brit. ultimatum forces Turkey to cede Sinai Peninsula to Egypt President Theodore Roosevelt, on first trip outside U.S. by a president in office, visits Canal Zone	George M. Cohan produces "Forty-five Minutes from Broadway," New York Nazimova in "Hedda Gabler," Amer. debut Samuel Beckett, Ir.-Fr. dramatist, b. (d. 1989) Algernon Blackwood: "The Empty House" Ruth St. Denis introduces modern dancing John Galsworthy: "The Man of Property" "Everyman's Library" begun in London Paul Claudel: "Partage de midi" Pinero: "His House in Order" P. L. Dunbar, Amer. Negro poet, d. (b. 1872) Karl Gjellerup: "The Pilgrim Kamanita," Dan. novel O. Henry: "The Four Million" Gerhart Hauptmann: "Und Pippa tanzt," Ger. fairy-tale play Henrik Ibsen, Norw. dramatist, d. (b. 1828) André Antoine takes over management of Odéon Theater, Paris Edgar Wallace: "The Four Just Men" John Galsworthy: "The Silver Box" Upton Sinclair: "The Jungle" Bernard Shaw: "Caesar and Cleopatra," "Arms and the Man," "Man and Superman," and "John Bull's Other Island" open in New York	Albert Sorel, Fr. historian, d. (b. 1842) Winston S. Churchill: "Life of Lord Randolph Churchill," biography "The English Hymnal," ed. by Percy Dearmer and R. Vaughan Williams Eduard von Hartmann, Ger. philosopher, d. (b. 1842) The Jesuit general, Franz X. Wernz (1842—1914), reforms the order's plan for studies L. T. Hobhouse: "Mind in Evolution" Albert Schweitzer: *(contd)*

D. VISUAL ARTS	E. MUSIC	F. SCIENCE, TECHNOLOGY, GROWTH	G. DAILY LIFE	
		under North (Hudson) River between Manhattan and New Jersey		**1904 contd**
Cézanne: "Les Grandes Baigneuses," painting "Les Fauves" christened by Louis Vauxcelles Picasso arrives in Paris and begins his "Pink Period" (—1906) Henri Rousseau: "Jungle with a Lion" J. S. Sargent: "The Marlborough Family" W. Holman Hunt: "Pre-Raphaelitism" Adolf Menzel, Ger. painter, d. (b. 1815) Films: the first regular cinema established (Pittsburgh, Pa.), the first films feature comedian Max Linder (1883—1925), Fr. "Potemkin" film by Nonguet Jacob Epstein (1880—1959), Amer. sculptor, settles in London Matisse: "Luxe, calme et volupté"	Serge Lifar, Russ. choreographer, b. (d. 1986) Michael Tippett, Eng. composer, b. Debussy: "La Mer," Paris Franz Lehár: "The Merry Widow," operetta, Vienna Richard Strauss: "Salomé," opera, Dresden "Zenobia" by L. A. Coerne becomes the first Amer. opera to be produced in Europe (Bremen) Albert Schweitzer: "J. S. Bach" Sir Thomas Beecham makes debut as conductor in London Victor Herbert: "The Red Mill," operetta, New York	Albert Einstein formulates Special Theory of Relativity; establishes law of mass-energy equivalence; creates Brownian theory of motion; and formulates the photon theory of light Sigmund Freud: "Three Contributions to the Theory of Sex" Nobel Prize for Medicine awarded to Robert Koch Rayon yarn manufactured commercially through viscose process	Ty Cobb begins major league baseball career with the Detroit Tigers London Automobile Association founded Austin Motor Company formed, England First motor buses in London; opening of Piccadilly and Bakerloo underground (subway) lines The first neon light signs appear World boxing champion James Jeffries (U.S.) retires undefeated The Cullinan diamond, the largest (over 3,000 carats) found to that date Mount Wilson observatory completed in California Rotary Club founded U.S. Lawn Tennis Men's Singles won by Beals C. Wright; Women's Singles by Elisabeth H. Moore New York (NL) beats Philadelphia (AL) 4—1 in second World Series	**1905**
André Derain: "Port of London" Georges Rouault: "At the Mirror" Aristide Maillol: "Chained Action," sculpture Paul Cézanne d. (b. 1839) Walter Sickert: "The Lady in the Gondola" Greta Garbo, Swed.-born film actress, b. (d. 1990)	Massenet: "Ariane," opera, Paris Ethel Smyth: "The Wreckers," opera, Leipzig Mozart Festival in Salzburg Dmitri Shostakovich, Russ. composer, b. (d. 1975) Ermanno Wolf-Ferrari: "I quattro rusteghi" ("The School for Fathers"), comic opera, Munich Max von Schillings: "Moloch," opera, Dresden Elgar: "The Kingdom," oratorio, Birmingham Geraldine Farrar makes Amer. debut	Fridtjof Nansen et. al.: "Norwegian North Pole Expedition 1893—1896" (6 vols.) Patents Act and Merchant Shipping Act both adopted in Britain J. J. Thomson awarded Nobel Prize for Physics Harden discovers cases of catalysis among enzymes Pierre Curie, Fr. physicist, d. (b. 1859) Clemens von Pirquet introduces the term allergy to medicine Norw. explorer Roald Amundsen traverses Northwest Passage and determines position of magnetic North Pole U.S. Pure Food and Drugs Act China and Britain agree to reduction of opium production "Typhoid Mary," carrier of typhoid, found and *(contd)*	City populations (in millions): London, 4.5; New York, 4; Paris, 2.7; Berlin, 2; Tokyo, 1.9; Vienna, 1.3 Army strengths (in millions): Russia, 13; Germany, 7.9; Austria-Hungary, 7.4; France, 4.8; Italy, 3 Night-shift work for women internationally forbidden Revelations of conditions in Chicago stockyard contained in Upton Sinclair's novel "The Jungle" lead to the U.S. Pure Food and Drugs Act Beginning of Zuider Zee drainage scheme 12.5 mile-long Simplon Tunnel between Italy and Switzerland opened H.M.S. "Dreadnought" launched–displacement 17,900 tons; speed 21 knots Fr. Grand Prix motorcar race first run The case of the cobbler Wilhelm Voigt (The "Captain of Koepenick") in Berlin San Francisco earthquake kills 700; $400 million property loss U.S. Lawn Tennis Men's Singles won by William J. Clothier; Women's singles by Helen Homans Chicago (AL) beats Chicago (NL) 4—2 to win World Series	**1906**

	A. HISTORY, POLITICS	B. LITERATURE, THEATER	C. RELIGION, PHILOSOPHY, LEARNING
1906 contd			"The Quest of the Historical Jesus"
1907	Universal direct suffrage instituted in Austria Second Russ. Duma meets in Mar.; is dissolved in Aug.; Third Duma is organized in Nov. (—1912) English and French agree on Siamese independence Edward VII in Rome, Paris, and Marienbad, where he meets Russ. Foreign Minister Izvolski The "open door" agreement on China between France and Japan President Theodore Roosevelt bars Japanese from immigrating to U.S. Peace Conference at the Hague Emperor of Korea abdicates; Japan granted protectorate over Korea William II of Germany and Nicholas II of Russia meet at Swinemünde Oklahoma becomes 46th state of the U.S. Oscar II, King of Sweden, d.; succeeded by his son Gustavus V (—1950) Lenin leaves Russia and founds the newspaper "The Proletarian" Stalin captures 375,000 rubles from a transport of the State Bank in Tiflis Shah of Persia d.; succeeded by his son Mohammed Ali (—1909) Sun Yat-sen announces the program of his Chinese Democratic Republic Rasputin gains influence at the court of Czar Nicholas II Dutch complete occupation of Sumatra with defeat of Achinese tribe New Zealand becomes a dominion within the Brit. Empire Panic of 1907 causes run on banks, stopped by J. P. Morgan's importation of $100 million in gold from Europe	W. H. Auden, Eng. poet, b. (d. 1973) J. K. Huysmans, Fr. novelist, d. (b. 1848) Sully Prudhomme, Fr. author, d. (b. 1839) Alberto Moravia, Ital. novelist, b. (d. 1990) Christopher Fry, Eng. poet, b. Joseph Conrad: "The Secret Agent" Maxim Gorki: "Mother" Nobel Prize for Literature: Rudyard Kipling Hans Bethge: "Die chinesische Flöte," Ger. translations of Chin. poetry Giosué Carducci, Ital. poet, d. (b. 1835) Romain Rolland: "The Life of Beethoven" Strindberg: "The Ghost Sonata," drama Jacinto Benavente: "Los intereses credos," Span. comedy "Cambridge History of English Literature " (—1927)	Henri Bergson: "L'Evolution créatrice" William James: "Pragmatism" Papal encyclical "Pascendi gregis" condemns modernism United Methodist Church established in Britain Alfred Adler: "Study of Organ Inferiority and Its Psychical Compensation"
1908	Abdul Hafid proclaimed Sultan of Morocco; defeats his enemy Abdul Aziz at Marrakesh Aehrenthal, the Aust. Foreign Minister, and Izvolski, the Russ. Foreign Minister, agree in Sept. on Austria's occupation of Bosnia and Herzegovina, which takes place in Oct. King Carlos I of Portugal and the crown prince both assassinated at Lisbon; Manuel II becomes king (—1910) H. H. Asquith becomes Brit. Prime Minister, David Lloyd George Chancellor of the Exchequer Edward VII and Nicholas II meet at Reval Young Turks revolt at Resina, Macedonia; the new Ottoman Parliament, with a large Young Turk majority, meets Leopold II transfers the Congo (his private possession since 1885) to Belgium Ferdinand I of Bulgaria assumes the title czar and declares his country's independence Crete proclaims union with Greece Union of South Africa established "The Daily Telegraph"'s famous William II interview William Howard Taft elected U.S. President Russ. Foreign Minister Izvolski confers in London Lyndon B. Johnson, future President of the U.S., b. (d. 1973) *(contd)*	Simone de Beauvoir, Fr. author, b. (d. 1986) "Ouida," Eng. novelist, d. (b. 1839) Ian Fleming, Eng. author, b. (d. 1964) Isadora Duncan becomes popular interpreter of dance The Tiller Girls appear on the London stage for the first time Arnold Bennett: "The Old Wives' Tale," novel G. K. Chesterton: "The Man Who Was Thursday" Colette: "La Retraite sentimentale" E. M. Forster: "A Room with a View" Anatole France: "L'Ile des pingouins" Kenneth Grahame: "The Wind in the Willows" Laurids Bruun: "Van Zanten's Happy Time," Dan. novel Holger Drachmann, Dan. poet, d. (b. 1846) Lucy M. Montgomery: "Anne of Green Gables" Mary Roberts Rinehart: "The Circular Staircase" Jules Romains: "La Vie unanime," Fr. poems Schnitzler: "Der Weg ins Freie," Viennese *(contd)*	F. Meinecke: "Cosmopolitanism and the National State" G. Sorel: "Reflections on Violence" Graham Wallas: "Human Nature in Politics" Karl Liebknecht: "Militarism and Antimilitarism"

D. VISUAL ARTS	E. MUSIC	F. SCIENCE, TECHNOLOGY, GROWTH	G. DAILY LIFE	
		incarcerated First radio program of voice and music broadcast in U.S. by R. A. Fessenden		**1906 contd**
First Cubist exhibition in Paris Derain: "Blackfriars Bridge, London," painting Picasso: "Demoiselles d'Avignon" Henri Rousseau: "The Snake Charmer" Basil Spence, Brit. architect, b. (d. 1976) Chagall: "Peasant Women" Edvard Munch: "Portrait of Walter Rathenau" Films: titles replace commentator; "Skating" (with Max Linder) is screened; slow-motion effect invented by August Musger Augustus Saint-Gaudens d. (b. 1848)	Joseph Joachim, Ger. violinist, d. (b. 1831) Edvard Grieg d. (b. 1843) Delius: "A Village Romeo and Juliet," opera, Berlin Paul Cukas: "Ariane et Barbe bleue," opera, Paris Oskar Straus: "A Waltz Dream," operetta, Vienna Leo Fall: "The Dollar Princess," operetta, Vienna Franz Lehàr: "The Merry Widow," New York Gustav Mahler: Symphony No. 8 in E-flat major ("The Symphony of a Thousand") The first "Ziegfeld Follies," staged in New York	Ivan Pavlov studies conditioned reflexes Amer. pathologist Ross Harrison develops tissue culture techniques Emil Fischer: "Researches on the Chemistry of Proteins" Anschütz and Schuler improve the gyrocompass Louis Lumière develops a process for color photography using a three-color screen Dmitri Mendeleyev, Russ. chemist, d. (b. 1834) Ernst von Bergmann, Ger. surgeon, d. (b. 1836) Nobel Prize for Physics: A. A. Michelson	Baden-Powell founds Boy Scout movement Immigration to U.S. restricted by law Henry Deterding forms Royal Dutch Shell Company S. S. "Lusitania" and "Mauretania" launched (each 31,000 tons); "Lusitania" breaks transatlantic record, steaming from Queenstown (Cobh), Ireland, to New York in 5 days, 45 min. Crown Princess Louise of Sachsen, divorced on grounds of adultery (1903), marries Ital. violinist Enrico Toselli Carl Hagenbeck (1844—1913) opens his modern zoo in Hamburg-Stellingen Highest ever break in billiards: Tom Reece plays 499.135 in 85 hours 49 minutes Chicago (NL) defeats Detroit (AL) 4—0 to win World Series Second Sunday in May established in Philadelphia as Mother's Day First daily comic strip, "Mr. Mutt" (later, "Mutt and Jeff"), by Bud Fisher, begins in "San Francisco Chronicle"	**1907**
Marc Chagall: "Nu Rouge" Maurice de Vlaminck: "The Red Trees" Augustus John: "The Lord Mayor of Liverpool" Monet: "The Ducal Palace, Venice" Maurice Utrillo begins his "White Period" (—1912) Jacob Epstein: "Figures" for the Brit. Medical Association Building, The Strand, London, cause general indignation Robert Henri, John Sloan, George Luks, William Glackens, George Bellows, Everett Shinn establish "Ashcan School" with realistic portrayals of life The first steel and glass building: A. E. G. Turbine factory, Berlin, by Peter Behrens Wilhelm Busch, Ger. painter *(contd)*	Béla Bartók: String Quartet No. 1. Elgar: Symphony No. 1 in A-flat, Op. 55 Rimsky-Korsakov d. (b. 1844) Herbert von Karajan, Aust. conductor, b. (d. 1989) 11-year-old E. W. Korngold writes his first stage work, the ballet "The Snowman" (produced 1910) Oliver Messiaen, Fr. composer, b. Sarasate, Span. violinist, d. (b. 1844) Oskar Straus: "The Chocolate Soldier," operetta, Vienna Leo Fall: "The Girl in the Train," operetta, Vienna	Vivian Fuchs, Eng. explorer, b. Henri Becquerel, Fr. physicist, d. (b. 1852) Hermann Minkowski formulates a four-dimensional geometry Fritz Haber synthesizes ammonia Nobel Prizes: chemistry, Rutherford; medicine, Mechnikov and Ehrlich Sven Hedin explores Persia and Tibet H. Kamerlingh Onnes liquefies helium Bakelite invented by L. H. Baekeland, U.S.	Earthquake in southern Calabria and Sicily: 150,000 killed London hosts the Olympic Games; Americans win 15 firsts out of 28 in track and field Donald Bradman, Australian cricketer, b. Jack Johnson becomes first black world heavyweight boxing champion Port of London Authority established Lord Northcliffe buys "The Times," London Zeppelin disaster near Echterdingen General Motors Corporation formed Cairo University opened New baseball regulation rules spitball illegal Fountain pens become popular Wilbur Wright flies 30 miles in 40 minutes The Ford Motor Company produces the first Model "T"– 15 million eventually sold W. H. Saven of Princeton, N.J., becomes the first American to play cricket for Gentlemen of England *(contd)*	**1908**

	A. HISTORY, POLITICS	B. LITERATURE, THEATER	C. RELIGION, PHILOSOPHY, LEARNING
1908 contd	Tzu-Hsi, Dowager Empress of China, d. (b. 1834) Dutch establish rule in Bali Grover Cleveland, U.S. President, d. (b. 1837)	novel Gertrude Stein: "Three Lives"	
1909	Turkey and Serbia recognize Aust. annexation of Bosnia and Herzegovina W. H. Taft inaugurated as 27th President of the U.S. (—1913) Sultan Abdul Hamid II deposed by Young Turks; succeeded by his brother Mohammed V (—1918) Bethmann-Hollweg becomes Ger. Chancellor; Aristide Briand, Fr. Premier; Sonnion, Ital. Prime Minister Mohammed Ali, Shah of Persia, deposed; succeeded by Sultan Ahmed Shah (aged 12) Anglo-Ger. discussions on control of Baghdad Railroad King Leopold II of the Belgians d. (b. 1835); succeeded by Albert I (—1934) Civil War in Honduras (—1911) State visits of Edward VII to Berlin and Rome Juliana, the future Queen of the Netherlands, b.	Stephen Spender, Eng. poet, b. A. C. Swinburne, Eng. poet, d. (b. 1837) George Meredith, Eng. novelist, d. (b. 1828) Maeterlinck: "L'Oiseau bleu," fairy- tale play J. M. Synge: "Deirdre of the Sorrows" Apollinaire: "L'Enchanteur pourrissant" H. G. Wells: "Tono-Bungay" Detlev von Liliencron, Ger. poet, d. (b. 1844) Thomas Mann: "Königliche Hoheit," novel Jakob Wassermann: "Casper Hauser," novel Ezra Pound: "Exultations" Ferenc Molnár: "Liliom," play	Lenin: "Materialism and Empiric Criticism" William Beveridge: "A Problem for Industry" William James: "A Pluralistic Universe" Sigmund Freud lectures in the U.S. on psychoanalysis Jewish world population: Russia, 5,200,000; Austria-Hungary, 2,000,000; U.S., 1,700,000; Germany, 600,000; Turkey, 400,000; Great Britain, 200,000; France, 100,000 Eduard Suess: "The Face of the Earth" (1885--) G. M. Trevelyan: "Garibaldi and the Thousand"
1910	Egyptian Premier Butros Ghali assassinated Louis Botha and James Hertzog found South African Party; Star Jameson founds Unionist Party; Union of South Africa becomes a dominion within the Brit. Empire with Botha as premier Revolt in Albania King Edward VII d.; succeeded by George V (—1936) Japan annexes Korea Montenegro proclaimed kingdom under Nicholas I Revolution in Portugal; King Manuel II flees to England; Portugal becomes a republic Venizelos named Premier of Greece U.S. Congress passes Mann Act: prohibits transportation of women across state lines for immoral purposes China abolishes slavery W. E. B. DuBois founds National Association for the Advancement of Colored People (NAACP) in U.S. Start of the Mexican revolution	Arnold Bennett: "Clayhanger" Paul Claudel: "Cinq grandes odes" E. M. Forster: "Howard's End" Charles Pierre Péguy: "Le Mystère de la charité de Jeanne d'Arc," Fr. drama H. G. Wells: "The History of Mr. Polly" Mark Twain d. (b. 1835) Jean Anouilh, Fr. dramatist, b. (d. 1987) Leo Tolstoi d. (b. 1828) Karl May: "Winnetou," Ger. novel for boys Wilhelm Raabe, Ger. novelist, d. (b. 1831) Frank Wedekind: "Schloss Wetterstein," Ger. play Josef Kainz, Ger. actor, d. (b. 1858) John Galsworthy: "Justice," drama Björnstjerne Björnson, Norw. poet, d. (b. 1832) Karin Michaelis: "The Dangerous Age," Dan. novel	William James, Amer. psychologist and philosopher, d. (b. 1842) Mary Baker Eddy, founder of Christian Science, d. (b. 1821) Sir Edward Durning-Lawrence: "Bacon in Shakespeare" Irving Fisher: "National Vitality" Sir Norman Angell: "The Great Illusion" (on the futility of war) Julia Ward Howe, Amer. suffragist, d. (b. 1819)

D. VISUAL ARTS	E. MUSIC	F. SCIENCE, TECHNOLOGY, GROWTH	G. DAILY LIFE	
and poet, d. (b. 1832) Kokoschka: portrait of the Viennese tailor Ebenstein Matisse coins the term "Cubism" Film: "The Last Days of Pompeii," by Arturo Ambrosio			Chicago (NL) beats Detroit (AL) 4—1 to win World Series	**1908 contd**
Bellows: "Both Members of This Club" Matisse: "The Dance" Sir William Orpen: "Homage to Manet" Frank Lloyd Wright: Robie House, Chicago Picasso: "Harlequin" Films: "Carmen" (Fr.); the first newsreels; D. W. Griffith features Mary Pickford, the first film star Cinematograph Licensing Act in Britain Vassily Kandinsky's first abstract paintings Frederick Remington, d. (b. 1861) Charles McKim d. (b. 1847)	Robert Helpmann, Brit.-Australian ballet dancer and choreographer, b. (d. 1986) Delius: "A Mass of Life" Richard Strauss: "Elektra," opera, Dresden Rimsky-Korsakov: "The Golden Cockerel" (posth.) Gustav Mahler: Symphony No. 9 R. Vaughan Williams: "Fantasia on a Theme of Tallis" Sergei Diaghilev presents his "Ballet Russe" for the first time in Paris Arnold Schönberg: "Three Piano Pieces," Op. 11 Wolf-Ferrari: "Il Segreto di Susanna," comic opera, Munich Franz Lehár: "The Count of Luxembourg," operetta, Vienna	Paul Ehrlich prepares Salvarsan for cure of syphilis (Ehrlich-Hata 606) T. H. Morgan begins researches in genetics Louis Blériot crosses Eng. Channel from Calais to Dover in 37 minutes in airplane Eng. aviator Henri Farman completes first 100-mile flight U.S. explorer Robert E. Peary reaches the North Pole; Dr. Frederick Cook fails to prove he preceded Peary by one year Nobel Prizes: physics, Marconi; chemistry, Ostwald Rockefeller Sanitary Commission established (beginnings of Rockefeller Foundation) First commercial manufacture of Bakelite marks beginning of Plastic Age	Women admitted to Ger. universities Anglo-Persian Oil Company formed Girl Guides established in Britain King Edward VII's horse "Minoru" wins the Derby First permanent waves are given by London hairdressers First six-day bicycle race held in Berlin Amer. businessman H. G. Selfridge (1857—1947) opens his department store in London's Oxford Street	**1909**
Fernand Léger: "Nues dans le forêt" Amedeo Modigliani: "The Cellist" Roger Fry arranges Post-Impressionist Exhibition in London (Cézanne, van Gogh, Matisse) William Holman Hunt, Eng. artist, d. (b. 1827) Henri ("Douanier") Rousseau, Fr. painter, d. (b. 1844) Works by Gaston Lachaise, John Marin, Joseph Stella, Abraham Walkowitz, Max Weber, William Zorach, and others exhibited by Alfred Stieglitz's 291 Gallery in New York Frank Lloyd Wright becomes well known and influential in Europe for his domestic architecture Films: "A Child of the Ghetto" (Amer.); "Messaline" (Fr.); "Lucrezia Borgia" (Ital.); *(contd)*	Elgar: Concerto for Violin in B minor, Op. 61, London Puccini: "La Fanciulla del West" ("The Girl of the Golden West"), opera, New York R. Vaughan Williams: "Sea Symphony" Stravinsky: "The Firebird," ballet, Paris Thomas Beecham's first opera season at Covent Garden, London Alban Berg: "String Quartet," Op. 3 Busoni: "Fantasia Contrapuntistica" for orchestra Jean Gilbert: "Die keusche Susanne," operetta Massenet: "Don Quichotte," opera, Monte Carlo The S. Amer. tango gains immense popularity in *(contd)*	Marie Curie: "Treatise on Radiography" Arthur Evans completes the excavation of Cnossus, Crete Prince Albert I of Monaco founds Institute for Oceanography Murray and Hjort undertake the first deep-sea research expedition Robert Koch, Ger. physician and bacteriologist, d. (b. 1843) J. J. Thomson's work on deflection of "positive rays" in magnetic field Halley's comet observed	Florence Nightingale d. (b. 1820) 122,000 telephones in use in Great Britain U.S. Postal Savings program established The Eng. wife poisoner, H. H. Crippen, executed First labour exchanges open in Britain Manhattan Bridge, N.Y., completed (begun 1901) Jean Henri Dunant, founder of the Red Cross, d. (b. 1828) Farman flies 463 km. (approx. 300 miles) in 8.25 hours Carnegie Endowment for International Peace established The "week-end" becomes popular in the U.S. Barney Oldfield drives a Benz at 133 m.p.h. at Daytona Beach, Fla. *(contd)*	**1910**

	A. HISTORY, POLITICS	B. LITERATURE, THEATER	C. RELIGION, PHILOSOPHY, LEARNING
1910 contd			
1911	Ramsay MacDonald elected chairman of the British Labour Party U.S.-Jap. and Anglo-Jap. commercial treaties signed Armistice ends Mexican Civil War Lloyd George introduces National Health Insurance Bill in Paliament Coronation of King George V and durbar in Delhi, India Joseph Caillaux named Premier of France Arrival of Ger. gunboat "Panther" in Agadir creates international crisis Liberal constitution promulgated in Portugal The Kaiser's Hamburg speech asserts Germany's "Place in the Sun" Peter Stolypin, the Russ. Premier, assassinated Beginning of Turk.-Ital. war: Ital. fleet bombards Tripoli coast–first use of aircraft for offensive measures; Italy annexes Tripoli and Cyrenaica and decisively defeats Turks Revolution in Central China; Chin. Republic proclaimed; pigtails abolished; calendar reformed; Manchu dynasty falls (in power since 1644); Sun Yat-sen elected president; appoints Chiang Kai-shek his military adviser Winston S. Churchill appointed First Lord of the Admiralty Karl von Stürgkh named Aust. Prime Minister (—1916) Gen. Joseph Joffre becomes Chief of Fr. General Staff	Max Beerbohm: "Zuleika Dobson" Rupert Brooke: "Poems" Theodore Dreiser: "Jennie Gerhardt" Hugo von Hofmannsthal: "Jedermann" D. H. Lawrence: "The White Peacock" Katherine Mansfield: "In a German Pension" Saki: "The Chronicles of Clovis" Hugh Walpole: "Mr. Perrin and Mr. Traill" H. G. Wells: "The New Machiavelli" Edith Wharton: "Ethan Frome" W. S. Gilbert, Sullivan's librettist, d. (b. 1836) Nobel Prize for Literature: Maeterlinck Carl Sternheim: "Die Hose," Ger. satirical comedy G. K. Chesterton: "The Innocence of Father Brown" Ezra Pound: "Canzoni"	Cambridge Medieval History appears (—1936) Hans Vaihinger: "The Philosophy of As If" J. M. Thompson: "Miracles in the New Testament" Friedrich Fundolf: "Shakespeare und der deutsche Geist" Wilhelm Dilthey, Ger. philosopher, d. (b. 1833) Frank William Taussig (1859—1940): "Principles of Economics"
1912	Raimond Poincaré becomes Fr. Premier Arizona and New Mexico become states of the U.S. Brit. coal strike, London dock strike, and transport workers' strike Turkey closes Dardanelles to shipping Tewfik Pasha becomes Grand Vizier of Persia Montenegro declares war on Turkey; Bulgaria and Serbia mobilize their armies; Turkey asks Powers for intervention in Balkan war; armistice between Bulgaria, Serbia, Montenegro, and Turkey Treaty of Lausanne signed between Italy and France Woodrow Wilson wins U.S. presidential election Nobel Peace Prize: Elihu Root (U.S.) Ger.-Aust.-Ital. alliance renewed King Frederick VIII of Denmark d.; succeeded by Christian X (—1947) Lenin establishes connection with Stalin and takes over editorship of "Pravda" Textile workers strike in Lawrence, Mass., showing power of I.W.W. Sun Yat-sen founds Kuomintang (Chinese National Party) Emperor Mutsuhito of Japan d.; succeeded by Yoshihito (—1926) Raoul Wallenberg, Swedish diplomat, b. (d. c. 1947)	E. M. Dell: "The Way of an Eagle" Gerhart Hauptmann: "Atlantis," Ger. novel Pierre Loti: "Le Pélérin d'Angkor" Compton Mackenzie: "Carnival" Rabindranath Tagore: "Gitanjali," poems August Strindberg, Swed. dramatist, d. (b. 1849) Paul Claudel: "L'Annonce faite à Marie" Nobel Prize for Literature: Gerhart Hauptmann Felix Dahn, Ger. novelist, d. (b. 1834) Eugene Ionesco, Fr.-Rumanian dramatist, b. Somerset Maugham: "The Land of Promise," Eng. social drama Karl May, Ger. author of adventure novels, d. (b. 1842) Arthur Schnitzler: "Professor Bernhardi," Viennese play John M. Synge: "Playboy of the Western World," drama Edmund C. Bentley: "Trent's Last Case," crime novel "Poetry: A Magazine of Verse" founded in Chicago Amy Lowell: "A Dome of Many-Colored Glass," collection of poems	Alfred Adler: "The Nervous Character" (individual psychology and psychotherapy) C. G. Jung: "The Theory of Psychoanalysis" Paul Häberlin: "Science and Philosophy" (2 vols.) F. Oppenheimer: "The Social Problem and Socialism" E. Maunde Thompson: "Introduction to Latin and Greek Paleography" Church of Scotland: revised "Prayer Book"

D. VISUAL ARTS	E. MUSIC	F. SCIENCE, TECHNOLOGY, GROWTH	G. DAILY LIFE	
"Hamlet" (Dan.); "Peter the Great" (Russ.) Robert Delaunay (1885—1941): "Eiffel Tower," painting Oskar Kokoschka: "Portrait of the Duchess of Rohan-Montesquieu" Winslow Homer d. (b. 1836) John La Farge d. (b. 1835)	Europe and the U.S. Franz Lehár: "Gypsy Love," operetta, Vienna Victor Herbert: "Naughty Marietta," Amer. operetta, New York		Father's Day first celebrated in Spokane, Wash. Jack Johnson, heavyweight titleholder, defeats Jim Jeffries, who has been persuaded to come out of retirement Philadelphia (AL) defeats Chicago (NL) 4—1 to win World Series	**1910 contd**
Renoir: "Gabrielle with a Rose" Georges Braque: "Man with a Guitar" Matisse: "Red Studio" Leonardo da Vinci's "Mona Lisa" stolen from the Louvre, Paris (found in Italy, 1913) Jacob Epstein: tomb of Oscar Wilde, Paris Joseph Israels, Dutch painter, d. (b. 1824) Paul Klee: "Self-Portrait" Films: "Anna Karenina" (Russ.); "Spartacus" and "Pinocchio" (Ital.); "Nick Carter" (Fr.); "Enoch Arden" (Amer., with D. W. Griffiths); "The Abyss" (Dan., with Asta Nielsen)	Gustav Mahler d. (b. 1860) Edward Elgar: Symphony No. 2 in E-flat, Op. 63 Mahler: "Das Lied von der Erde," Munich (posth.) Richard Strauss: "Der Rosenkavalier," opera, Dresden Wolf-Ferrari: "I guoielli della Madonna," opera, Berlin Arnold Schönberg: "Manual of Harmony" Irving Berlin: "Alexander's Ragtime Band" Lehár: "Eva," opera, Vienna Ravel: "L'Heure espagnole," opera, Paris Stravinsky: "Petrouchka," ballet, Paris Richard Wagner: "Mein Leben," autobiography (posth.) Émile Jaques-Dalcroze founds his institute for the teaching of eurhythmics at Hellerau, Germany	Roald Amundsen reaches the South Pole Nobel Prize for Chemistry: Marie Curie Jacobus Henricus van't Hoff, Dutch scientist, d. (b. 1852) Rutherford formulates his theory of atomic structure Charles F. Kettering (U.S.) develops the first practical electric self-starter for automobiles	Gordon-Bennett International Aviation Cup given for the first time British Official Secrets Act becomes law First flight Munich—Berlin reaches record height of 12,800 ft. Aug. 9: temperature in London reaches unprecedented 100 degrees Fahrenheit Robert T. Jones of Atlanta, Ga., the great Amer. golfer, wins his first title, the Junior Championship of Atlanta, at the age of nine Philadelphia (AL) defeats New York (NL) 4—2 to win World Series	**1911**
Marc Chagall: "The Cattle Dealer" Picasso: "The Violin" Franz Marc: "Tower of Blue Horses" Modigliani: "Stone Head," sculpture "Peter Pan" statue by George Frampton erected in Kensington Gardens, London Lovis Corinth: "The Actor Rittner as Florian Geyer" Duncan Grant: "The Lemon Gatherers" Films: "Quo Vadis" (Ital.); "War and Peace" (Russ.); "Dance of Death" (Dan.); "Queen Elizabeth" (Fr., with Sarah Bernhardt) London has 400 cinemas; in the U.S. approx. 5,000,000 people visit cinemas daily	Jules Massenet, Fr. composer, d. (b. 1842) Samuel Coleridge-Taylor, Eng. composer, d. (b. 1875) Ravel: "Daphnis and Chloe," ballet, Paris Delius: "On Hearing the First Cuckoo in Spring" Schönberg: "Pierrot Lunaire," song cycle, Berlin Richard Strauss: "Ariadne auf Naxos," opera, Stuttgart Franz Schreker: "Der ferne Klang," opera, Frankfurt Leopold Stokowski named conductor of the Philadelphia Symphony Orchestra Rudolf Friml: "The Firefly," operetta, New York	Pol. chemist Kasimir Funk coins the term "vitamine" Edwin Bradenberger invents a process for manufacturing cellophane R. F. Scott ("Scott of the Antarctic") reaches South Pole Joseph, Lord Lister, Eng. surgeon, d. (b. 1827) V. Stefansson and R. Anderson explore Arctic Canada (—1909) Wilson's cloud-chamber photographs lead to the detection of protons and electrons Debye propounds theory of specific heat of solids Viktor F. Hess discovers *(contd)*	Royal Flying Corps established in Britain (later R.A.F.) G.P.O. takes over Brit. telephone systems S.S. "Titanic" sinks on her maiden voyage after colliding with an iceberg; 1,513 drowned Remains of Piltdown Man "found" near Lewes, England; believed to be 50,000 years old (proved to be a hoax in 1953) Olympic Games held in Stockholm Germany claims to have 30,000 millionaires F. W. Woolworth Company founded First successful parachute jump International Lawn Tennis Federation formed Jim Thorpe is the outstanding sportsman at the Stockholm Olympic Games, but when it is discovered that he played semi-professional baseball in 1911, his gold medals and trophies are taken from him, and his records erased from the books *(contd)*	**1912**

	A. HISTORY, POLITICS	B. LITERATURE, THEATER	C. RELIGION, PHILOSOPHY, LEARNING
1912 contd			
1913	Raymond Poincaré elected President of France; visits England Aristide Briand becomes Fr. Premier Suffragette demonstrations in London; Mrs. Pankhurst sentenced for inciting persons to place explosive in Lloyd George's house Federal income tax introduced in the U.S. through the 16th Amendment Woodrow Wilson inaugurated as 28th President of the U.S. King George I of Greece assassinated; succeeded by Constantine I Balkan War: Bulgarians take Adrianople and Turkey signs armistice; London Peace Treaty between Turkey and the Balkan states signed; outbreak of Second Balkan war; Bulgarian attacks on Serbia and Greece; Russia declares war on Bulgaria; the Turks recapture Adrianople; armistice signed at Bucharest; Bulgarian-Turk. treaty on frontier in Thrace; Serbia invades Albania; peace treaty between Greece and Turkey Yüan Shih-kai elected President of Chin. Republic Mahatma Gandhi, leader of Indian Passive Resistance Movement, arrested The "Zabern affair" in Alsace-Lorraine endangers relations between France and Germany U.S. Federal Reserve System established Richard Nixon, 37th President of the U.S., b. August Bebel, leader of Ger. Social Democrats, d.; succeeded by Friedrich Ebert Menelik II, Emperor of Abyssinia, d.; succeeded by Lij Yasu (–1916) Harriet Tubman, Amer. abolitionist and reformer, d. (b. 1821)	Willa Cather: "O Pioneers!" D. H. Lawrence: "Sons and Lovers" Thomas Mann: "Death in Venice" Marcel Proust: "Du côté de chez Swann," first part of "A la recherche du temps perdu" (—1927) Edith Wharton: "The Custom of the Country" Luigi Pirandello: "Se non così" Shaw: "Pygmalion," first performed in Vienna Angus Wilson, Eng. novelist, b. Albert Camus, Fr. author, b. (d. 1960) Maxim Gorki: "My Childhood" Berhard Kellermann: "Der Tunnel," Ger. bestseller Jack London: "John Barleycorn," novel Robert Frost: "A Boy's Will," poems Nobel Prize for Literature: Rabindranath Tagore Irene and Vernon Castle, dancers, make debut in New York in "The Sunshine Girl" Eleanor H. Porter: "Pollyanna"	Miguel de Unamuno: "Del Sentimiento Trágico de la Vida" Jaspers: "Allgemeine Psychopathologie" W. C. Mitchell: "Business Cycles" "Goetheanum" founded in Dornach, Switzerland (anthroposophy) Edmund Husserl: "Phenomenology" Sigmund Freud: "Totem and Taboo" Russell and Whitehead: "Principia Mathematica" (from 1900)
1914	Northern and Southern Nigeria united The Calmette-Caillaux affair in France; Mme. Caillaux kills Gaston Calmette Gen. Zamon becomes President of Haiti Peace treaty between Serbia and Turkey World War I: Archduke Francis Ferdinand, heir to the Aust. throne, and his wife assassinated in Sarajevo June 28; Austro-Hungarian ultimatum to Serbia July 23 and declaration of war July 28; Jean Jaurès, pacifist and socialist, murdered in Paris; Germany declares war on Russia and France and invades Belgium; Britain declares war on Germany; Austria declares war on Russia; Serbia and Montenegro declare war on Germany; Brit. troops land in France; France declares war on Austria; Britain declares war on Austria; Austria declares war on Belgium; Russia declares war on Turkey; France and Britain declare war on Turkey; Russians invade E. Prussia; Germans occupy Liège; the Ger. warships "Breslau" and "Goeben" escape through Dardanelles; Germans in Brussels; Battles of Manur and Mons; Germans occupy Lille; Russians defeated at Tannenberg; Germans occupy Rheims; Battle of Marne, Sept. 9—15; Germans retreat; Russians defeated in Battle of Masurian Lakes; Hindenburg appointed Ger. commander in the east; Russians invade Hungary; Germans in Antwerp; First Battle of Ypres; Austrians take Belgrade and are driven out again; *(contd)*	Georg Trakl, Aust. poet, d. (b. 1887) Francis Brett Young: "Deep Sea" Joseph Conrad: "Chance" James Joyce: "Dubliners" Joyce Kilmer: "Trees" George Moore: "Hail and Farewell" Frédéric Mistral, Fr. poet, d. (b. 1830) Theodore Dreiser: "The Titan" Robert Frost: "North of Boston" André Gide: "Les Caves du Vatican" Paul Heyse, Ger. author, d. (b. 1830) Christian Morgenstern, Ger. poet, d. (b. 1871) Elmer Rice: "On Trial," first drama to use device of flashback Anton Wildgans: "Armut," Aust. drama Bertha von Suttner, Aust. novelist, d. (b. 1843) Paul Bourget: "Le Démon de midi" E. R. Burroughs: "Tarzan of the Apes" Tennessee Williams, Amer. dramatist, b. (d. 1983) Booth Tarkington: "Penrod" Vachel Lindsay: "The Congo and Other Poems"	Pope Pius X d.; succeeded by Cardinal della Chiesa as Pope Benedict XV (—1922) Edwin Cannan: "Wealth" Bertrand Russell: "Our Knowledge of the External World" Austin Dobson: "Eighteenth-Century Studies" Magnus Hirschfeld: "Homosexuality of Man and Wife"

D. VISUAL ARTS	E. MUSIC	F. SCIENCE, TECHNOLOGY, GROWTH	G. DAILY LIFE	
		cosmic radiation Paul Ehrlich introduces acriflavine as antiseptic Nobel Prize for Medicine: Dr. Alexis Carrel	Boston (AL) defeats New York (NL) 4—3 to win World Series	**1912 contd**
"Armory Show" introduces Postimpressionism and cubism to New York Walter Sickert: "Ennui" Stanley Spencer: "Self-portrait" J. S. Sargent: "Portrait of Henry James" Apollinaire: "The Cubist Painters" Woolworth Building, New York, designed by Cass Gilbert, opens Grand Central Terminal opens in New York Films: "The Vampire" (Amer.); "The Squaw Man" (Amer., with Cecil B. De Mille); "Der Student von Prag" (Ger.); the first Paramount and the first Charlie Chaplin movies	De Falla: "Vida Breve," opera, Nice Scriabin: "Prometheus," symphonic poem, Moscow Stravinsky: "Le Sacre du Printemps," ballet, Paris Debussy: "Jeux," ballet, Paris Benjamin Britten, Eng. composer, b. (d. 1976) Bruno Walter becomes director at the Munich Opera (—1922) Elgar: "Falstaff," symphonic poem, London Jack Judge, an Eng. music-hall comedian, writes the song "Tipperary" Victor Herbert: "Sweethearts," operetta, New York	J. J. Thomson: "Rays of Positive Electricity and Their Application to Chemical Analysis" H. Geiger introduces the first successful electrical device capable of counting individual alpha rays Niels Bohr formulates his theory of atomic structure Frederick Soddy coins the term "isotope" Diphtheria immunity test discovered by Béla Schick Composition of chlorophyll discovered by Richard Willstätter Vitamin A isolated by biochemist McCollum at Yale Univesity Robert Lieben, Aust. physicist, d. (b. 1878) H. N. Russell formulates theory of stellar evolution Friedrich Bergius converts coal dust into oil Max Bodenstein formulates his concept of chemical chain reaction Rene Lorin states the basic ideas of jet propulsion Chemical element protactinium discovered	Ivar Kreuger founds Swedish Match Company "Imperator," Ger. turbine liner, begins service: 52,100 tons Albert Schweitzer opens his hospital in Lambaréné, French Congo Zippers (in use since 1891) become popular Sidney and Beatrice Webb found the "New Statesman," London The foxtrot comes into fashion J. Pierpont Morgan d. (b. 1837) Henry Ford pioneers new assemblyline techniques in his car factory The first woman magistrate is sworn in in England Walter Hagen appears on the U.S. golf scene John D. Rockefeller founds Rockefeller Institute with initial grant of $100 million U.S. team wins Davis Cup tennis trophy 3—2 Philadelphia (AL) defeats New York (NL) 4—1 to win World Series Grand Central Terminal, New York City, completed	**1913**
Augustus John: "George Bernard Shaw" Matisse: "The Red Studio" Braque: "Music" Henry Bacon designs Lincoln memorial, Washington, D.C. John Tenniel, Eng. cartoonist, d. (b. 1820) Films: Charlie Chaplin in "Making a Living," and (with Marie Dressler) in "Tillie's Punctured Romance," produced by Mack Sennett (Amer.); "The Golem" (Ger.); "The Destruction of Carthage" (Ital.); "The Little Angel" (Dan.) *(contd)*	Irving Berlin: "Watch Your Step," New York Rutland Boughton: "The Immortal Hour," opera, Glastonbury Vaughan Williams: "A London Symphony" Paul Graener: "Don Juans letztes Abenteuer," opera, Leipzig Richard Heuberger, Aust. composer, d. (b. 1850) Richard Strauss: "Josephs Legende," ballet, Paris Stravinsky: "Le Rossignol," opera, Paris Ital. tenor Beniamino Gigli (1890—1957) makes debut American Society of Composers, *(contd)*	J. H. Jeans: "Radiation and the Quantum Theory" Fertilization through peat discovered by Bottomley C. D. Broad: "Perception, Physics, and Reality" The American Robert H. Goddard begins his rocketry experiments The American E. C. Kendall prepares pure thyroxin for treatment of thyroid deficiencies John B. Watson: "Behavior; an Introduction to Comparative Psychology" Nobel Prize for Chemistry: Theodore W. Richards U.S. Court decides patent suit on airplanes in favor of Wright brothers against Glenn Curtiss Dr. Alexis Carrel performs first successful heart surgery on dog Cape Cod Canal opened between Cape Cod and Buzzard's Bay	Bank of England authorized by government to issue money in excess of statutory limit Pierre Balmain, Paris fashion designer, b. (d. 1982) Name of St. Petersburg changed to Petrograd (—1924) Panama Canal opened E. H. Shackleton leads Antarctic expedition (—1917) Jack Dempsey starts fighting under the name "Kid Blackey" U.S. Federal Trade Commission established to police business practices in interstate commerce Almost 10.5 million immigrants entered U.S. from southern and eastern Europe in period 1905—1914 Yale Bowl opened, seating 80,000 Walter Hagen wins U.S. Golf Association Open Australia wins Davis Cup tennis championship from U.S. Boston (NL) defeats Philadelphia (AL) 4—0 to win World Series	**1914**

	A. HISTORY, POLITICS	B. LITERATURE, THEATER	C. RELIGION, PHILOSOPHY, LEARNING
1914 contd	Germans take Lodz in Poland Gandhi returns to India and supports government Party of U.S. Marines land at Tampico, Mexico, for supplies and are detained; upon release 1.5 hours later, Admiral Mayo demands 21-gun salute to American flag; refused by President Huerta; President Wilson sends U.S. fleet to Tampico; U.S. Marines occupy Vera Cruz; Huerta resigns, ending incident		
1915	World War I: Ger. airship bombs E. Anglian ports; cruiser "Blücher" is sunk at Dogger Bank; first Ger. submarine attack, Le Havre; Germans take Memel; Ger. blockade of England begins; Russians take Przemysl, Galicia; Second Battle of Ypres; Anglo-Fr. landings at Gallipoli; Italy declares war on Austria-Hungary and Turkey; Germans sink "Lusitania"; first Zeppelin attack on London; Mesopotamia surrenders to Britain; First Battle of the Isonzo; Second Battle of Isonzo; Germans in Warsaw and Brest-Litovsk; Czar Nicholas II takes over command of Russ. army; Allied troops at Salonika; execution of Edith Cavell in Brussels; Third and Fourth Battles of the Isonzo; Joseph Joffre becomes Fr. Commander-in-Chief; Douglas Haig becomes Brit. Commander-in-Chief in France; Britain's merchant shipping losses during the year: over 1,000,000 tons Erich Muenter, Ger. instructor at Cornell University, plants bomb that destroys U.S. Senate reception room (July 2), then shoots J. Pierpont Morgan, Jr. (July 3); commits suicide July 6 U.S. recognizes government of President Venustiano Carranza of Mexico	Van Wyck Brooks: "America's Coming of Age" John Buchan: "The Thirty-Nine Steps" Paul Claudel: "Corona" Joseph Conrad: "Victory" D. H. Lawrence: "The Rainbow" W. Somerset Maugham: "Of Human Bondage" Ezra Pound: "Cathay," poems James Elroy Flecker, Brit. poet, d. (b. 1884) Rupert Brooke, Eng. poet, d. (b. 1887) Saul Bellow, Amer. novelist, b. Arthur Miller, Amer. dramatist, b. Nobel Prize for Literature: Romain Rolland Hermann Hesse: "Knulp," novel Edgar Lee Masters: "A Spoon River Anthology" Robert Frost: "A Boy's Will" and "North of Boston," published in U.S. Washington Square Players (reorganized as the Theater Guild, 1919), Neighborhood Playhouse, and Provincetown Players established	Wlodimierz Halka von Ledóchowski (1866—1942) becomes General of the Jesuits Booker T. Washington, Amer. educator, founder of Tuskegee Institute, d. (b. 1856)
1916	World War I: First Zeppelin raid on Paris; Brit. Military Service Act in force; Battle of Verdun: Germany declares war on Portugal, Fifth Battle of the Isonzo; Allied attack on Zeebrugge; Roger Casement lands in Ireland, is arrested and executed; Sinn Fein Easter Rebellion in Dublin; Anzacs arrive in France; Battle of Jutland; H.M.S. "Hampshire" sunk with Lord Kitchener on board; beginning of Allied Somme defensive; Sixth Battle of the Isonzo; Italy declares war on Germany; Hindenburg appointed Chief of Ger. General Staff; Seventh Battle of the Isonzo; British first use tanks on Western Front; Eighth Battle of the Isonzo; Count Carl Sturgkh, Aust. Premier, assassinated; Ninth Battle of the Isonzo; Emperor Francis Joseph of Austria d. (b. 1830); succeeded by his grandnephew Charles I (—1918); Hussein proclaimed King of the Arabs; Beatty appointed Commander-in-Chief of Brit. navy, Jellicoe First Sea Lord; Lloyd George becomes Brit. Prime Minister; Briand becomes Fr. War Minister; Germany sends peace note to Allies; Wilson sends peace note to all belligerents; Gen. Joffre named Marshal of France; Brit. merchant shipping *(contd)*	Vicente Blasco Ibánez: "The Four Horsemen of the Apocalypse," Span. novel John Buchan: "Greenmantle" D'Annunzio: "La Leda Senza Gigno" (—1918) James Joyce: "Portrait of the Artist as a Young Man" George Moore: "The Brook Kerith" Leonid Andreyev: "He Who Gets Slapped" Harold Brighouse: "Hobson's Choice" Eugene O'Neill: "Bound East for Cardiff" Henry James d. (b. 1843) Henri Barbusse: "Under Fire," war novel Max Brod: "Tycho Brahe's Weg zu Gott," Ger. novel José Echegaray, Span. dramatist, d. (b. 1832) Friedrich Gundolf: "Goethe" Jack London, Amer. novelist, d. (b. 1876) Henryk Sienkiewicz, Pol. novelist, d. (b. 1846) Natsume Soseki, Jap. novelist, d. (b. 1867) "The Bing Boys Are Here," London wartime revue with George Robey *(contd)*	G. Lowes Dickinson: "The European Anarchy" Lionel Curtis: "The Commonwealth of Nations" Martin Buber: "The Spirit of Judaism" Ernst Mach, Aust. physicist, d. (b. 1838) Vilfredo Pareto: "Mind and Society" John Dewey: "Democracy and Education"

D. VISUAL ARTS	E. MUSIC	F. SCIENCE, TECHNOLOGY, GROWTH	G. DAILY LIFE	
August Macke, Ger. painter, d. (b. 1887)	Authors, and Publishers (ASCAP) founded Sviatoslav Richter, Russ. pianist, b.			**1914 contd**
Raoul Dufy: "Hommage à Mozart," painting Chagall: "The Birthday" Marcel Duchamp: the first Dada-style paintings Films: "Birth of a Nation" (D. W. Griffith); "Carmen" (Cecil B. De Mille); "The Lamb" (Douglas Fairbanks); "The Fire" (Ital.)	Alexander Scriabin, Russ. composer, d. (b. 1872) Humphrey Searle, Eng. composer, b. (d. 1982) Max Reger: "Mozart Variations," Op. 32 The remains of Rouget de Lisle, the composer of "La Marseillaise," brought to the Invalides, Paris Kalman: "Die Czardasfürstin," operetta, Vienna Max von Schillings: "Mona Lisa," opera, Stuttgart Emil Waldteufel, Fr. waltz composer, d. (b. 1837) Classic New Orleans Jazz in bloom Richard Strauss: "Eine Alpensinfonie," Berlin Ivor Novello writes the war song "Keep the Home Fires Burning"	Albert Einstein postulates his General Theory of Relativity Brit. chemist James Kendall isolates dysentery bacillus Hugo Junkers constructs the first fighter airplane Nobel Prize for Physics: W. H. and W. L. Bragg (father and son) Nobel prize for Chemistry: R. Willstätter Paul Ehrlich, Ger. bacteriologist, d. (b. 1854) Henry Ford develops a farm tractor Georg Cantor: "Contributions to the Founding of a Theory of Transfinite Numbers" First transcontinental telephone call between Alexander Graham Bell in New York and Dr. Thomas A. Watson in San Francisco Wireless service established between U.S. and Japan Ford produces one millionth car Archibald Thorburn: "British Birds"	James Keir Hardie, Eng. socialist politician, d. (b. 1856) W. G. Grace, Eng. cricketer, d. (b. 1848); his career spanned period 1864—1908, during which he scored 54,896 runs, 2,876 wickets Tetanus epidemics in the trenches U.S. Coast Guard established by Congress The largest railroad station in Europe completed in Leipzig, Germany Lord Beaverbrook buys the London "Daily Express" Frederick Winslow Taylor, industrial relations pioneer, d. (b. 1856) Margaret Sanger jailed for writing "Family Limitation," first book on birth control President Wilson marries Mrs. Edith Galt Motorized taxis appear Jess Willard defeats Jack Johnson to win heavyweight boxing crown Boston (AL) defeats Philadelphia (NL) 4—1 to win World Series Automobile speed record of 102.6 m.p.h. set at Sheepshead Bay, N.Y., by Gil Anderson driving a Stutz	**1915**
Dadaist cult in Zurich; its main representatives are Tristan Tzara and Hans Arp Franz Marc, Ger. painter, d. (b. 1880) John Marin, Amer. artist (1870—1953), becomes popular Matisse: "The Three Sisters" Frank Lloyd Wright designs the Imperial Hotel, Tokyo Films: "Intolerance" *(contd)*	E. W. Korngold: "Violanta," opera, Munich Ethel Smythe: "The Boatswain's Mate," opera, London Jazz sweeps U.S. Yehudi Menuhin, Amer.-born violinist, b. D'Albert: "Die toten Augen," opera, Dresden Max Reger d. (b. 1873) Felix von Weingartner: "Dame Kobold," opera, Darmstadt Schubert-Berté: "Das Dreimäderlhaus" ("Lilac Time"), operetta, Vienna Leo Fall: "Die Rose von Stambul," operetta, Vienna Granados: "Goyescas," opera, New York De Falla: "Noches en los jardines de España," *(contd)*	Sir Arthur Eddington investigates the physical properties of stars Sympathectomy for relief of angina pectoris performed for first time by Ionescu Blood for transfusion is refrigerated Percival Lowell, Amer. astronomer, d. (b. 1855) Ilya Mechnikov, Russ. scientist, d. (b. 1845) William Ramsay, Eng. chemist, d. (b. 1852) New valence theory stated by G. N. Lewis Theory of shell shock suggested by F. W. Mott Paul Langevin (Fr.) constructs an underwater ultrasonic *(contd)*	Women's International Bowling Congress established in America Len Hutton, Eng. cricketer, b. (d. 1990) Harold Wilson, Brit. statesman, b. Edward Heath, Brit. statesman, b. National Savings movement founded in Britain Food rationed in Germany "Summertime" (daylight-saving time) introduced in Britain The Russ. monk Rasputin d. (b. 1871) Foundation of Federation of Brit. Industries Bobby Jones makes his debut in U.S. golf National Park Service established under U.S. Department of the Interior Margaret Sanger joins in opening first birth control clinic Prohibition gains ground as 24 states vote against alcoholic beverages U.S. Golf Association Amateur and Open championships both won by Charles *(contd)*	**1916**

	A. HISTORY, POLITICS	B. LITERATURE, THEATER	C. RELIGION, PHILOSOPHY, LEARNING
1916 contd	losses during the year: 1,500,000 tons; gas masks and steel helmets introduced in Ger. army T. E. Lawrence ("Lawrence of Arabia") appointed Brit. political and liaison officer to Faisal's army Woodrow Wilson reelected President of U.S., barely defeating Charles Evans Hughes Francisco "Pancho" Villa, Mexican revolutionary general, crosses border with guerrillas and raids Columbus. N. Mex., killing 17 Americans; Brig.-Gen. John J. Pershing pursues Villa with 6,000 troops but cannot find him; withdraws (1917) after differences are settled by arbitration U.S. purchases Dan. West Indies (Virgin Islands) for $25 million U.S. troops land in Santo Domingo, Dominican Republic, to settle internal strife; not withdrawn until 1924 Louis Brandeis named to U.S. Supreme Court by President Wilson Law establishing eight-hour work day for railroad workers prevents nation-wide strike German saboteurs blow up munitions arsenal on Black Tom Island, N.J.: $22 million loss	Alan Seeger, Amer. poet, d. (b. 1888) Carl Sandburg: "Chicago Poems" Edwin Arlington Robinson: "The Man Against the Sky" Theodore Dreiser: "The Genius," suppressed by New York censors Edna Ferber: "Our Mrs. McChesney," drama starring Ethel Barrymore Zoë Akins: "Magical City," one-act drama	
1917	World War I: Bread rationed in Britain; Ger. withdrawal on Western Front; February Revolution in Russia; the czar abdicates Mar. 16; Poincaré receives peace offer from Emperor Charles of Austria (Sixtus Letter); U.S. and Cuba declare war on Germany; Pétain becomes Chief of Fr. General Staff; Isonzo battle rages on; Pétain Fr. Commander-in-Chief; Albanian independence proclaimed; King Constantine I of Greece abdicates in favor of his son Alexander I (—1920); Brit. royal family renounces Ger. names and titles; Gen. Pershing arrives in Paris to head Amer. forces; Russ. Black Sea fleet mutinies at Sebastopol; General Allenby takes over Brit. Palestine command; fuel and food controls in U.S.; first U.S. division arrives in France; air attacks on England; Kerensky Russ. Premier; beginning of Passchendaele battle; China declares war on Germany and Austria; peace note of Pope Benedict XV; Ger. aircraft attack London; Ital. army routed at Caporetto; Balfour Declaration on Palestine; October Revolution in Petrograd Nov. 7 (old style calendar Oct. 26); Lenin appointed Chief Commissar, Trotsky Commissar for Foreign Affairs; Clemenceau Premier of France; first tank battle takes place at Cambrai; Ger.-Russ. armistice signed at Brest-Litovsk; Finnish Republic proclaimed; U.S. declares war on Hungary and Austria; Turks surrender Jerusalem; Brit. merchant shipping losses during the year: approx. four million tons John Fitzgerald Kennedy, future President of the U.S., b. (assassinated 1963) Starvation year in Germany The Allies execute dancer Mata Hari as a spy U.S. government purchases Dutch West Indies Literacy requirements for U.S. citizenship passed over Wilson's veto Woodrow Wilson inaugurated to second term as President of U.S.	Norman Douglas: "South Wind" T. S. Eliot: "Prufrock and Other Observations" Leon Feuchtwanger: "Jud Süss" Knut Hamsun: "Growth of the Soil" Henry James: "The Middle Years" (posth.) Paul Valéry: "La Jeune Parque" James Barrie: "Dear Brutus" Herbert Beerbohm-Tree, Brit. actor manager, d. (b. 1853) Upton Sinclair: "King Coal" Unamuno: "Abel Sánchez," Span. novel Siegfried Sassoon: "The Old Huntsman," poems Alec Waugh: "The Loom of Youth," novel on public-school life Hugo von Hofmannsthal, Richard Strauss, and Max Reinhardt initiate the Salzburg Festival Laura E. Richards, Maude Howe Elliott: "Julia Ward Howe," wins first Pulitzer Prize for biography J. J. Jusserand: "With Americans of Past and Present Days," wins first Pulitzer Prize for history Edwin Arlington Robinson: "Merlin" Amy Lowell: "Tendencies in Modern American Poetry" Hamlin Garland: "A Son of the Middle Border" Sinclair Lewis: "The Job: An American Novel"; "The Innocents" Sarah Bernhardt, 72, begins last tour of America	Hermann Fernau: "The Coming Democracy" C. G. Jung: "Psychology of the Unconscious"

D. VISUAL ARTS	E. MUSIC	F. SCIENCE, TECHNOLOGY, GROWTH	G. DAILY LIFE	
(D. W. Griffith); "Civilization" (Thomas Ince); "The Pawn Shop" (Chaplin, satire); "Resurrection" (Ital.); "Homunkulus" (five parts, Ger.) Odilon Redon d. (b. 1840) Thomas Eakins d. (b. 1844)	symphonic impressions, Madrid Frederic Norton: "Chu- Chin-Chow," musical, London	source for submarine detection	Evans, Jr. First Rose Bowl football game between Washington State College and Brown University won by Washington, 14—0 Professional Golf Association (PGA) formed Boston (AL) defeats Brooklyn (NL) 4—1 to win World Series	**1916 contd**
Picasso designs surrealist sets and costumes for Satie's ballet "Parade' Modigliani: "Crouching Female Nude" Pierre Bonnard: "Nude at the Fireplace" J. S. Sargent: "Portrait of John D. Rockefeller" Degas d. (b. 1834) Rodin d. (b. 1840) Albert P. Ryder d. (b. 1847) C. D. Carrà and Giorgio de Chirico found the school of Ital. "metaphysical painting" George Grosz: "The Face of the Ruling Class," Ger. lithographs Films: "The Little Princess" (with Mary Pickford); "Mater dolorose" (Fr.); "U.F.A." (Universum Film, Berlin) becomes foremost Ger. production firm; Chaplin's yearly salary reaches one million dollars	Hans Pfitzner: "Palestrina," opera, Munich Prokofiev: "Classical Symphony," Op. 25 Ottorino Respighi: "Fontane di Roma," four symphonic poems Busoni: "Turandot" and "Harlequin" (two one-act operas, Zurich) Chicago becomes the world's jazz center Sigmund Romberg: "May-time," operetta, New York George M. Cohan writes American war song "Over There" Bartók: "The Wooden Prince," ballet, Budapest Original Dixieland Jass Band opens at Reisenweber's Restaurant, New York First jazz recordings made by same musicians Fr. composers Auric, Durey, Honegger, Milhaud, Poulenc, and Tailleferre form group eventually known as "Les Six"	Ferdinand, Count Zeppelin, d. (b. 1838) Sigmund Freud: "Introduction to Psychoanalysis" Emil Behring, Ger. physician and bacteriologist, d. (b. 1854) Wagner von Jauregg (Aust.) treats syphilitic paralysis by injecting malaria 100-in. reflecting telescope installed at Mount Wilson, Calif.	Quebec railroad bridge 1,800 ft. long, completed Imperial War Museum, London, founded (opened 1936) Trans-Siberian Railroad completed (begun 1891) "Buffalo Bill" (W. F. Cody), d. (b. 1846) Bobbed hair as ladies' hair fashion sweeps Britain and the U.S. Companion of Honour and Order of the British Empire decorations established Four women arrested for picketing White House in behalf of women's suffrage sentenced to six months in jail U.S. Senate rejects President Wilson's suffrage bill I.W.W. demonstrations against war result in raids on their offices First baseball game played in Polo Grounds on a Sunday, between New York Giants and Cincinnati Reds results in arrests of managers John McGraw (Giants) and Christy Mathewson (Reds) for violating New York blue law Chicago (AL) defeats New York (NL) 4—2 to win World Series	**1917**

	A. HISTORY, POLITICS	B. LITERATURE, THEATER	C. RELIGION, PHILOSOPHY, LEARNING

1918

A. HISTORY, POLITICS

World War I: Woodrow Wilson propounds Fourteen Points for world peace; Russ. constituent assembly in Petrograd dissolved by Bolsheviks; meat and butter rationed in London; peace treaty of Brest-Litovsk between Russia and Central Powers; transfer of Soviet government to Moscow; Gen. Foch takes over united command on Western Front; 1,388 planes of the Ger. Luftwaffe assembled for attack; Brit. R.A.F. replaces R.F.C.; Rumania signs peace treaty with Central Powers; Ger. offensive on Western Front; Germans bomb Paris; Pittsburgh Agreement between Czechs and Slovaks; Second Battle of the Marne; Japanese advance into Siberia; Allied offensive on Western Front opens; attempted assassination of Lenin in Moscow; Hsu-Shih-Chang President of Chinese Republic; collapse of Turk. resistance in Palestine; Ger. Chancellor Count Hertling resigns; Prince Max of Baden Ger. Chancellor; Germany and Austria agree to President Wilson's demand that they should retreat to their own territory before the armistice is signed; Germany suspends submarine warfare; Ludendorff dismissed; Czechoslovakia proclaimed independent republic; Hungarian Premier Count Tisza assassinated; Allies sign armistice with Austria-Hungary Nov. 3; Ger. fleet mutinies at Kiel; Allied conference at Versailles agrees on peace terms for Germany; Ger. republic proclaimed by Philipp Scheidemann; Armistice signed between Allies and Germany Nov. 11; Ger. fleet surrenders

Mexico nationalizes her oilfields

Brit. government abandons Home Rule for Ireland

Sultan Mohammad VI of Turkey ascends throne

Ex-Czar Nicholas II and family executed

King Ferdinand of Bulgaria abdicates in favor of his son Boris

U.S. Congressional elections–Republican majority of 43

Pol. republic proclaimed

Revolution in Berlin; William II abdicates

Austria becomes a republic

Charles I renounces all participation in Aust. affairs of state

T. G. Masaryk elected President of Czechoslovakia

Jozef Pilsudski vested with dictatorial powers in Poland and elected chief of state

Eugenio Pacelli (later Pius XII) named papal nuncio to the Weimar Republic

Montenegro united with Serbia

Iceland becomes sovereign state

Serbo-Croatian-Slovene Kingdom of Yugoslavia proclaimed

Gen. Mannerheim, Regent of Finland

Brit. general election–coalition majority of 262

Woodrow Wilson arrives in Paris for peace conference

Poles occupy Posen

Ger. revolutionary Communist Workers' Party (KPD) founded in Berlin by Karl Liebknecht and Rosa Luxemburg

Women over 30 get the vote in Britain

John Redmond, Ir. leader, d. (b. 1856)

Lavr Kornilov, Russ. Cossack leader, d. (b. 1870)

Georgi Plekhanov, Russ. politician, d. (b. 1857)

(contd)

B. LITERATURE, THEATER

George Alexander, London actor-manager, d. (b. 1858)

Arnold Bennett: "The Pretty Lady"

Aleksander Aleksandrovich Blok: "Dvenadtsat" ("The Twelve"), Russ. revolutionary poem

Rupert Brooke: "Collected Poems" (posth.), ed. by Edward Marsh

Willa Cather: "My Antonia"

Arthur Dinter: "Die Sünde wider das Blut" ("The Sin against Blood"), early Nazi novel

Anatole France: "Le Petit Pierre"

Leonhard Frank: "Der Mensch ist Gut" ("Man is Good"), collection of Ger. pacifist short stories

Gerhart Hauptmann: "The Heretic of Soana"

Gerard Manley Hopkins: "Poems" (posth.), ed. by R. Bridges

Laurence Housman: "The Sheepfold"

Richard Huelsenbeck starts the political and literary Dada movement in Germany

James Joyce: "Exiles," drama

Georg Kaiser: "Brand im Opernhaus" ("Fire at the Opera"), Hamburg

Alfred Kerr: "Die Welt im Drama" ("The World of Drama"), 5 vols. of Ger. theatrical criticism

Selma Lagerlöf: "Bannlyst," Swed. novel

Thomas Mann: "Betrachtungen eines Unpolitischen" ("Reflections of a Non-Political Man"), essays

Pinero: "The Freaks, an Idyll of Suburbia," London

Ladislaw Stanislaw Reymont: "The Insurrection," Pol. novel

Peter Rosegger, Aust. (Styrian) poet and novelist, d. (b. 1843)

Edmond Rostand, Fr. dramatist, d. (b. 1868)

Arthur Schnitzler: "Casanovas Heimfahrt" ("Casanova's Return"), short story

Lytton Strachey: "Eminent Victorians"

W. H. Hudson: "Far Away and Long Ago"

Aldous Huxley: "The Defeat of Youth"

D. H. Lawrence: "New Poems"

Eduard Stucken: "Die weissen Götter" ("The White Gods"), trilogy of novels on the fall of the Aztecs

Theater Guild of New York founded by Lawrence Langner

Miguel de Unamuno: "Essais" (7th vol. since 1916)

Frank Wedekind, Ger. dramatist, d. (b. 1864)

H. G. Wells: "Joan and Peter"

Rebecca West: "The Return of the Soldier"

Wyndham Lewis: "Tarr"

Amy Lowell: "Can Grande's Castle"

Wilfred Owen, Eng. poet, d. (b. 1873)

Guillaume Apollinaire, Fr. poet and essayist, d. (b. 1880)

André Maurois: "Les Silences du Colonel Bramble"

H. L. Mencken: "In Defense of Women"

Luigi Pirandello: "Così è, se vi pare"

Henry Adams, Amer. man of letters, d. (b. 1838)

Joyce Kilmer, Amer. poet ("Trees"), d. (b. 1886)

Vernon Castle, dance partner of Irene Castle, d. (b. 1887)

Best seller: V. Blasco-Ibáñez, "The Four Horsemen of the Apocalypse"

Booth Tarkington: "The Magnificent Ambersons" (Pulitzer Prize)

U.S. Post Office burns installments of James Joyce's "Ulysses," published in the "Little Review"

W. Smith and F. Bacon: "Lightnin'," drama, opens

(contd)

C. RELIGION, PHILOSOPHY, LEARNING

Gustav Cassel (1866—1945): "Theory of Social Economy"

Charles Horton Cooley (1864—1929), pioneer in the development of Amer. sociology, publishes "Social Process"

Georges Duhamel (1884—1966): "Civilization" (antiwar essays)

Controversies over the new psychology of Sigmund Freud and C. G. Jung

Billy Graham, Amer. evangelist, b.

Romano Guardini, Ger. Catholic philosopher: "The Spirit of Liturgy"

Harold Höffding (1843—1931), Dan. philosopher: "Opleuelse og Tydning" on humor as vital consciousness

Ellen Key (1849—1926), Swed. essayist and educationalist: "Women in the World War"

Second Moscow University founded (first in 1755)

Joséphin Péladan, Fr. novelist and philosopher, d. (b. 1858)

Bertrand Russell: "Mysticism and Logic"

Moritz Schlick (1822—1936): "Allgemeine Erkenntnislehre" (General Epistemology)

Oswald Spengler: "Untergang des Abendlandes" ("Decline of the West") (—1922)

A. E. Newton: "The Amenities of Book-Collecting"

Georg Simmel, Ger. philosopher and sociologist, d. (b. 1858)

Alexander Liapunov,

(contd)

1918

D. VISUAL ARTS

Films: "Ma the Mummy" and "Carmen" (Lubitsch); "A Dog's Life" and "Shoulder Arms!" (Chaplin); "The Tenth Symphony" (Abel Gance)
Juan Gris (1887—1927): "Scottish Girl," cubist painting
Ferdinand Hodler, Swiss painter and sculptor, d. (b. 1853)
Paul Klee (1879—1940): "Gartenplan," abstract painting
Oskar Kokoschka: "Friends" and "Saxonian Landscape," expressionist paintings
Fernand Léger (1881—1955): "Engine Rooms," glorification of modern machinery
David Low's cartoons appear in "The Star," London
Amedeo Modigliani (1884—1920): "Act," linear style painting
Edvard Munch (1863—1944): "Bathing Man"
Paul Nash (1889—1946): "We Are Making a New World"
A. Ozenfant and Le Corbusier publish their manifesto on "Purism," "After Cubism"
Henri Matisse: "Odalisques"
Robert Delauney: portrait of Igor Stravinsky
W. Kandinsky becomes a member of the arts section of the Commissariat for Popular Culture
Joan Miró first exhibits his works

E. MUSIC

Eugene D'Albert: "Der Stier von Olivera," opera, Leipzig
Béla Bartók: "Bluebeard's Castle," opera, Budapest
Irving Berlin: "Yip Yip Yaphank," New York
Leonard Bernstein, Amer. composer and conductor, b. (d. 1990)
Arrigo Boito, Ital. composer and librettist, d. (b. 1842)
Claude Debussy, Fr. impressionist composer, d. (b. 1862)
Gottfried von Einem, Aust. composer, b.
Rudolf Friml: "Sometime," New York
Jerome Kern: "Rock-a-Bye Baby," New York
Hubert Parry, Eng. composer, d. (b. 1848)
Hans Pfitzner: "Sonata for Violin and Piano in E minor," Op. 27
Giacomo Puccini: "Il Trittico"
Erik Satie: "Socrate"
Franz Schreker: "Die Gezeichneten," opera, Frankfurt
Karl Straube (1873–1950), Ger. organist, appointed cantor of St. Thomas School, Leipzig
Igor Stravinsky: "Histoire du soldat" ("The Soldier's Story"), Lausanne
New York Philharmonic Society bans compositions by living Ger. composers
A. S. Taneiev, Russ. composer, d. (b. 1850)
Paris Opéra, despite daily bombardment, opens with Gounod's "Faust"
César Cui, Russ. composer, b. (b. 1835)
Karl Muck, Ger. conductor of Boston Symphony Orchestra, arrested as enemy alien
Mrs. Elizabeth Sprague Coolidge gives the first of her music festivals, Pittsfield, Mass. (Tanglewood)
Liza Lehmann, Eng. singer and songwriter, d. (b. 1862)

F. SCIENCE, TECHNOLOGY, GROWTH

Georg F. L. P. Cantor, Ger. mathematician, d. (b. 1845)
Sir Arthur Stanley Eddington (1882—1944): "Gravitation and the Principle of Relativity"
Nobel Prize for Chemistry: Fritz Haber (1868—1934), Ger. physical chemist, for the direct synthesis of ammonia from nitrogen and hydrogen
Leonard Woolley begins Babylonian excavations
Nobel Prize for Physics: Max Planck (1858—1947), Ger. physicist, for introducing the quantum theory
Ludwig Prandtl (1875—1953), Ger. physicist, develops wing theory (flow over airplane wings of finite span)
Harlow Shapley, Amer. astronomer, discovers the true dimensions of the Milky Way
Vilhjálmur Stefánsson (1879—1962), Canadian Arctic explorer, returns from his five-year voyage of discovery north of the Arctic Circle
Mount Wilson telescope completed near Pasadena, Calif.
Karl Peters, Ger. African explorer, founder of Ger. E. Africa, d. (b. 1856)

G. DAILY LIFE

Regular airmail service established between New York City and Washington; first airmail postage
Daylight saving time introduced in America
Eight-hour day established by law in Germany
Food shortage in Britain leads to the establishment of national food kitchens and rationing
U.S. boxing champion Abraham Hollandersky ("Abe the Newsboy") retires after having fought 1,309 fights during his 14-year career
Hong Kong Jockey Club racetrack grandstand collapses, 600 die
World-wide influenza epidemic strikes; by 1920 nearly 22 million are dead
Knute Rockne (1888—1931) named head football coach at the University of Notre Dame
John L. Sullivan, world heavyweight boxing champion, d. (b. 1858)
Statistics– War casualties: approx. 8.5 million killed, 21 million wounded, 7.5 million prisoners and missing; total shipping losses, 15 million tons (9 million of them British); mobilized forces: 63 million; total gross cost of World War I (according to E. R. A. Seligman of Columbia University) during the fiscal years of combat: $232,058 million (net cost $210,935 million); daily war expenditure average for all belligerents: $164.5 million; U.S. pays $179 million in war pensions to 646,000 pensioners
Total population of the U.S.A.: 103.5 million
H. H. Bancroft, Amer. collector of Western material, d. (b. 1832)
Missouri last state to ratify compulsory school attendance law
R. Lindley Murray wins U.S. Lawn Tennis Men's Singles championship
Molla Bjurstedt wins U.S. Lawn Tennis Women's Singles championship
Jack Dempsey, Amer. heavyweight boxing champion, knocks out Carl Morris in 14 seconds
"Exterminator" wins Kentucky Derby
Boston (AL) defeats Chicago (NL) to win World Series
First Chicago—New York airmail delivered: flying time 10 hrs. 5 min.

	A. HISTORY, POLITICS	B. LITERATURE, THEATER	C. RELIGION, PHILOSOPHY, LEARNING
1918 contd	Eugene V. Debs, Amer. socialist and presidential candidate, sentenced to 10 years in prison for violating espionage and sedition law (commuted in 1921) Gamal Abdel Nasser, later President of the United Arab Republic, b. (d. 1970)	in New York to long run Stars and Stripes, U.S. Army newspaper, starts publication Henry Adams: "The Education of Henry Adams" (Pulitzer Prize)	Russ. mathematician, d. (b. 1857) Randolph Bourne, Amer. philosopher, d. (b. 1886) United Lutheran Church established (U.S.)
1919	Herbert Hoover named director-general of international organization for European relief Spartacist revolt in Berlin Theodore Roosevelt, 26th President of the U.S., d. (b. 1858) Karl Liebknecht, Ger. left-wing socialist (b. 1871), murdered by counterrevolutionary Ger. Freikorps officers together with Rosa Luxemburg, socialist leader (b. 1870) Prohibition amendment (18th) to U.S. Constitution ratified Jan. 16 Ignace Paderewski–Premier of Poland Peace Conference opens at Versailles President Wilson presides over first League of Nations meeting in Paris Friedrich Ebert–President of Ger. Republic Sir Wilfred Laurier, first French- Canadian Prime Minister of Canada, d. (b. 1841) Amanullah becomes Amir of Afghanistan Kurt Eisner, Bavarian Premier, assassinated (b. 1867) Benito Mussolini founds Fasci del Combattimento Third International founded at Moscow Canadian Grand Trunk Pacific Railway declared bankrupt Socialist Karl Renner becomes Chancellor of Austria Soviet government formed by Béla Kun in Budapest Hapsburg dynasty exiled from Austria Eamon de Valera becomes President of the Sinn Fein Red Army enters Crimea New Ger. constitution (drawn up by democratic politician Hugo Preuss) promulgated at Weimar Ger. delegates arrive at Peace Conference General Strike in Winnipeg, Canada War between Brit., Indian, and Afghan forces War between Finland and U.S.S.R. Red Army takes Ufa; beginning of White defeat Gustav Bauer follows Scheidemann as Ger. Chancellor Ger. fleet scuttled at Scapa Flow Ger. peace treaty signed at Versailles Edward Carson demands repeal of Home Rule in Ireland Peace celebrations in Britain Race riots in Chicago Béla Kun regime in Hungary overthrown Mackenzie King becomes Canadian Liberal leader Prince of Wales tours Canada and the U.S. Louis Botha, S. African general and statesman, d. (b. 1862) Jan Christian Smuts succeeds Botha as Prime Minister of the Union of South Africa (—1924) Allied peace treaty with Austria signed at St. Germain With an unofficial Ital. army, Gabriele D'Annunzio seizes Fiume (Rijeka) from Yugoslavia Amer. steel strike till Jan. 1920 Brit. troops withdraw from Murmansk New York dock workers go out on strike George Curzon succeeds A. J. Balfour as Brit. Foreign Secretary International Labor Conference in Washington endorses eight-hour workday First two-minutes' silence in Britain on anniversary of Armistice Day U.S. Senate's resolution on Article X of League of Nations Covenant *(contd)*	Sherwood Anderson: "Winesburg, Ohio," volume of interrelated short stories James B. Cabell: "Jurgen" Joseph Conrad: "The Arrow of Gold" John Drinkwater: "Abraham Lincoln," London André Gide: "La Symphonie pastorale" Thomas Hardy: "Collected Poems" Hermann Hesse: "Demian," Ger. novel about adolescence W. R. Inge: "Outspoken Essays," first series Ring Lardner: "Own your Own Home," short stories Hugh Lofting: the first of the "Dr. Doolittle" stories W. S. Maugham: "The Moon and Sixpence," "Caesar's Wife," "Home and Beauty" H. L. Mencken: "The American Language" Max Reinhardt opens the Grosses Schauspielhaus, Berlin, with the "Oresteia" by Aeschylus Upton Sinclair: "Jimmy Higgins" Nobel Prize for Literature: Carl Spitteler, Swiss novelist Aleksandr Taïrov: "The Unchained Theater," Russ. stage expressionism Hugh Walpole: "The Secret City" War memoirs by Tirpitz, Ludendorff, Lord Fisher, Field Marshal French, Admiral Jellicoe, and General Falkenhayn appear Franz Werfel: "Der Gerichtstag" ("The Day of Judgment"), Ger. expressionist drama Israel Zangwill: "Jimmy the Carrier" Leonid Andreyev, Russ. novelist and dramatist, d. (b. 1871) W. W. Campbell, Canadian poet, d. (b. 1861) Karl Gjellerup, Dan. writer, d. (b. 1857) Ella Wheeler Wilcox, Amer. popular poet, d. (b. 1855) Rabindranath Tagore: "The Home and the World" Carl Sandburg: "Corn Huskers" (Pulitzer Prize) Andrew Ady, Hungarian poet, d. (b. 1877)	Karl Barth: "Der Römerbrief" ("The Epistle to the Romans"), beginning of Protestant dialectical theology Henri Bergson: "L'Energie spirituelle" Ernst Cassirer: "The Problem of Knowledge: Philosophy, Science, and History since Hegel" Church Assembly established by Brit. Parliament Havelock Ellis: "The Philosophy of Conflict" Irving Fisher: "Stabilizing the Dollar in Purchasing Power" Ernst Haeckel, Ger. zoologist and philosopher, d. (b. 1834) Johan Huizinga: "The Waning of the Middle Ages" Karl Jaspers: "Psychologie der Weltanschauungen" J. M. Keynes: "The Economic Consequences of the Peace" Count Hermann von Keyserling: "Reisetagebuch eines Philosophen" ("Travel Diary of a Philosopher") Vilfredo Pareto: "Trattato di sociologia generale" Church and State separated in Germany Rudolf Steiner: "The Essential Points of the Social Question," anthroposophical sociology Sigrid Undset: "A Woman's Point of View," against sexual licentiousness New universities in Hamburg, Posen, Bratislava, and Cologne John Broadus Watson: "Psychology from the Standpoint of a Behaviorist" William Cunningham, Brit. economist, d. (b. 1849) Sir John Pentland Mahaffy, Ir. educator, scholar, and wit, d. (b. 1839) Francis Haverfield, Eng. historian, d. (b. 1860)

D. VISUAL ARTS	E. MUSIC	F. SCIENCE, TECHNOLOGY, GROWTH	G. DAILY LIFE	
				1918 contd

1919

D. VISUAL ARTS

Ernst Barlach: "Moses," sculpture in wood

Bauhaus, founded and built by Walter Gropius in Weimar, Germany, revolutionizes teaching of painting, sculpture, architecture, and industrial arts

Films: "Madame Dubarry" and "J'Accuse!" (Abel Gance); "Half-Caste" (Fritz Lang); "The Devil's Passkey" (Stroheim)

William Gilbert Gaul, Amer. painter of Civil War scenes, d. (b. 1855)

Vassily Kandinsky: "Dreamy Improvisation" and "Arabian Cemetery"

Paul Klee: "Dream Birds"

Carl Larsson, Swed. painter, d. (b. 1853)

Fernand Léger: "Follow the Arrow"

Max Liebermann: "Samson and Delilah"

Edwin Lutyens design for the Cenotaph, Whitehall, London

Amedeo Modigliani: "La Marchesa Casati"

Claude Monet: "Nymphéas," late impressionist painting

Edvard Munch: "The Murder," Norw. expressionist painting

Pablo Picasso: "Pierrot et Harlequin," sets for Diaghilev's production of "The Three-Cornered Hat"

Ger. architect Hans Poelzig (1869—1936) carries out the conversion of the Grosses Schauspielhaus, Berlin

Pierre Auguste Renoir, Fr. impressionist painter, d. (b. 1840)

Henry Clay Frick, Amer. industrialist and art collector, d. (b. 1849)

William Michael Rossetti, last of the Pre- Raphaelite brotherhood, d. (b. 1829)

Sir Edward Poynter, Eng. painter, d. (b. 1836)

Hans Arp and Max Ernst

(contd)

E. MUSIC

Eugene D'Albert: "Revolutionshochzeit," opera, Leipzig

Adolf Busch (1891—1952), Ger. violinist, starts the Busch String Quartet

Edward Elgar: Concerto in E minor for Cello, London

Manuel de Falla: "The Three-Cornered Hat," ballet, London

Margot Fonteyn, Eng. ballerina, b. (d. 1991)

Jazz arrives in Europe

Fritz Kreisler: "Apple Blossoms," New York

Ruggiero Leoncavallo, Ital. composer, d. (b. 1858)

André Messager: "Monsieur Beaucaire," operetta, Birmingham

Adelina Patti, operatic soprano, d. (b. 1843)

Hugo Riemann, Ger. musicologist, d. (b. 1849)

Othmar Schoeck: "Don Ranudo," opera, Zurich

Oskar Straus: "Der letzte Walzer" ("The Last Waltz"), operetta

Richard Strauss: "Die Frau ohne Schatten" ("The Woman without a Shadow"), Vienna

Harry Tierney: "Irene," New York

Horatio V. Parker, Amer. composer, d. (b. 1863)

Xavier Leroux, Fr. opera composer, d. (b. 1863)

Edgar Varèse conducts the New York New Symphony Orchestra's first concert of modern music

A. D. Juilliard d. (b. 1836) leaving 20 million dollars to endow Juilliard School of Music, New York

Los Angeles Symphony Orchestra gives its first concert

C. T. Griffes (1884—1920): "The Pleasure Dome of Kubla Khan," Boston Symphony Orchestra, conductor, Pierre Monteux

F. SCIENCE, TECHNOLOGY, GROWTH

Eng. scientist F. W. Aston builds mass- spectrograph and establishes the phenomena of isotopy

Jakob Bjerknes discovers that cyclones originate as waves in the sloping frontal surfaces which separate different air masses

William Crookes, Eng. physicist, d. (b. 1832)

Observations of the total eclipse of the sun bear out Albert Einstein's theory of relativity

Emil Fischer, Ger. chemist, d. (b. 1852)

Robert H. Goddard (1882—1945), "father of Amer. rocketry": "A Method of Reaching Extreme Altitudes"

Thomas H. Morgan: "The Physical Basis of Heredity"

John William Strutt, Baron Rayleigh, Eng. physicist, d. (b. 1842)

Rutherford demonstrates that the atom is not the final building-block of the universe

Ernest Shackleton (1874—1922): "South," an account of his 1914—1917 expedition to the Antarctic

First experiments with shortwave radio (under 100 metres)

Ross and Keith Smith fly from London to Australia in 135 hours

Arnold Sommerfeld: "Atombau und Spektrallinien," standard work on the theory of spectroscopy

Nobel Prize for Physics: Johannes Stark (1874—1957), Ger. physicist, for his discovery that spectral lines are distorted in an electrical field

In collaboration with Massolle and Engl, Hans Vogt experiments on a new sound film system

Alfred Werner, Swiss chemist, d. (b. 1866)

Roland Eötvös, Hungarian physicist, d. (b. 1848)

Sir William Osler, Canadian professor of medicine in Canada, the U.S., and Oxford, England, d. (b. 1849)

(contd)

G. DAILY LIFE

J. W. Alcock and A. Whitten Brown make first nonstop flight across the Atlantic from Newfoundland to Ireland in 16 hours 27 minutes

Austria abolishes the death penalty

Andrew Carnegie, U.S. industrialist, d. (b. 1835)

Jack Dempsey (b. 1895), U.S. heavyweight boxer, takes the world championship from Jess Willard

Rose Bowl Football championship match held; Great Lake upsets Mare Island

Suzanne Lenglen (1899—1938), Fr. tennis player, begins to dominate Wimbledon Lawn Tennis Championships (—1923)

Radio Corporation of America founded

Railroad lines operated in America total 265,000 miles

Babe Ruth hits a 587-foot home run in a Boston Red Sox versus New York Giants game at Tampa, Fla.

Jim Thorpe (1888—1953), the great Amer. all-around athlete, finishes his six-year major-league baseball career with the Boston Braves; plays in 60 games; hits .327

Belgian war damage estimated at $7,600,000,000

Frank W. Woolworth, founder of the five-and-ten-cent stores, d. (b. 1852)

The "Black Sox" bribery scandal rocks baseball

American Legion formed

Sir Barton is first horse to win triple crown: Kentucky Derby, Preakness, and Belmont Stakes; J. Loftus jockey in all three

Cincinnati (NL) defeats Chicago (AL) in World Series

Juan Belmonte, Span. matador, kills 200 bulls in 109 corridas

(contd)

	A. HISTORY, POLITICS	B. LITERATURE, THEATER	C. RELIGION, PHILOSOPHY, LEARNING
1919 contd	Red Army takes Omsk Lady Astor, first Brit. woman Member of Parliament to take her seat, elected Amer. delegates leave Peace Conference Red Army captures Kharkov U.S. House of Representatives moves to curtail immigration Nobel Peace Prize: U.S. President Woodrow Wilson Count Taisuke Itagaki, Jap. statesman, d. (b. 1837) Aleksandr Izvolski, Russ. statesman, d. (b. 1856) Hugo Haase, Ger. socialist leader, assassinated (b. 1863) William P. Schreiner, S. African statesman, d. (b. 1857) Sir Evelyn Wood, Brit. field marshal, d. (b. 1838) Fighting begins between French and Syrians at Baalbek, Syria Under the Treaty of Neuilly Bulgaria cedes territories to Rumania Hungarian Red troops invade Czechoslovakia but are forced to withdraw F. S. Nitti succeeds V. E. Orlando as Ital. Prime Minister Anti-Bolshevik army of Admiral A. V. Kolchak is defeated in the Urals General A. I. Denikin effectively battles against Soviet forces		
1920	In Paris the League of Nations comes into being U.S. Senate votes against joining the League of Nations Paul Deschanel becomes President of France Clemenceau resigns; Millerand takes over as Premier of France Red Army captures Odessa Bainbridge Colby succeeds Robert Lansing as U.S. Secretary of State Nicolaus von Horthy (1868—1957) is named Regent of Hungary Emir Feisal becomes king of an independent Syria Wolfgang Kapp stages short-lived monarchist coup d'état in Berlin Conference of San Remo deals with the question of Ger. reparations; Britain receives Palestine Mandate Conscription abolished in Britain President Caranza of Mexico assassinated; succeeded by Adolfo de la Huerta Allies and Hungary sign Treaty of Trianon Republican convention nominates Warren G. Harding for the presidency with Calvin Coolidge as his running mate The Hague selected as seat of International Court of Justice Democratic convention nominates James M. Cox for the presidency with Franklin D. Roosevelt as his running mate John, Lord Fisher, Brit. admiral, d. (b. 1841) Eugénie, Empress of the French, consort of Napoleon III, d. (b. 1826) Treaty of St. Germain comes into force The Little Entente (Czechoslavakia, Yugoslavia, Rumania) formed 19th Amendment gives Amer. women the vote Alexandre Millerand elected Fr. Premier U.S. and China sign tariff treaty King Alexander of Greece d. (b. 1893) League of Nations headquarters moved to Geneva Warren G. Harding (1865—1923) elected 29th President of the U.S. New Austrian constitution comes into force Treaty of Rapallo signed *(contd)*	Sherwood Anderson: "Poor White," novel Max Beerbohm: "Seven Men" Arnolt Bronnen: "Vatermord," Ger. expressionist drama Van Wyck Brooks: "The Ordeal of Mark Twain" Agatha Christie: "The Mysterious Affair at Styles" Colette: "Chéri" F. Wills Crofts: "The Cask," one of the first modern detective stories Richard Dehmel, Ger. poet, d. (b. 1863) F. Scott Fitzgerald: "This Side of Paradise" Zona Gale: "Miss Lulu Bett," novel John Galsworthy: "In Chancery" and "The Skin Game" Ludwig Ganghofer, popular Ger. novelist, d. (b. 1855) Nobel Prize for Literature: Knut Hamsun Jaroslav Hasek: "The Adventures of the Good Soldier Schwejk" (—1923) William Dean Howells, Amer. novelist, d. (b. 1837) Franz Kafka: "A Country Doctor" Rhoda Broughton, Eng. novelist, d. (b. 1840) Georg Kaiser: "Gas," Ger. expressionist drama Karl Kraus: "Die letzten Tage der Menschheit" ("The Last Days of Mankind"), tragedy Sinclair Lewis: "Main Street" Vachel Lindsay: "The Golden Whales of California," poems Emil Ludwig: "Goethe" Katherine Mansfield: "Bliss" Vsevolod E. Meyerhold (1874—1942) opens his own theater in Moscow A. A. Milne: "Mr. Pym Passes By" Eugene O'Neill: "The Emperor Jones" and "Beyond the Horizon" (Pulitzer Prize for drama) E. Phillips Oppenheim: "The Great *(contd)*	Alfred Adler: "The Practice and Theory of Individual Psychology" Samuel Alexander: "Space, Time and Deity," Eng. metaphysical realism Joan of Arc (1412—1431) canonized by Pope Benedict XV C. G. Jung: "Psychological Types" Count Hermann von Keyserling opens the "School of Wisdom" at Darmstadt Jacques Maritain: "Art et Scolastique" Bertrand Russell: "The Practice and Theory of Bolshevism" George Santayana: "Character and Opinion in the United States" Nathan Söderblom: "Introduction to the History of Religion" New universities established in Honolulu and Rio de Janeiro Max Weber, Ger. *(contd)*

D. VISUAL ARTS	E. MUSIC	F. SCIENCE, TECHNOLOGY, GROWTH	G. DAILY LIFE	
execute their Fatagaga collages Wilhelm Lehmbruck, Ger. sculptor, d. (b. 1881)		Simon Schwendener, Swiss botanist, d. (b. 1829) Sir Edmund Percival Hillary, New Zealand mountaineer and explorer, b.	Development of mechanical rabbit by Oliver Smith, of California, marks origin of modern greyhound racing	**1919 contd**
Charles Burchfield: "February Thaw," Amer. romanticism Visitors to the exhibition of Dadaist Art in Cologne are allowed to smash paintings Lyonel Feininger (1871—1956): "Church," Amer. cubism Films: "The Cabinet of Dr. Caligari"; "The Golem"; "Pollyanna" (with Mary Pickford); "Cesare Borgia" (Guazzoni); Marcel Duchamp makes his first abstract movie Juan Gris (1887—1927): "Book and Newspaper," Span. cubism Max Klinger, Ger. painter and sculptor, d. (b. 1857) Max Liebermann (1847—1935) elected President of the Prussian Academy of Arts Henri Matisse (1869—1954): "L'Odalisque" *(contd)*	Max Bruch, Ger. composer, d. (b. 1838) Christmas Radio Concert from Königswusterhausen, Germany Beniamino Gigli makes his debut at the Metropolitan Opera, New York Vincent d'Indy: "The Legend of St. Christopher," Paris Opéra Jerome Kern: "Sally," New York Erich Wolfgang Korngold: "Die tote Stadt" ("The Dead City"), Hamburg Franz Lehár: "Die blaue Mazur" ("The Blue Mazurka"), Vienna Maurice Ravel: "La Valse" Oskar Straus: "Der Letzte Walzer" ("The Last Waltz"), Berlin Igor Stravinsky: "Pulcinella" and "Le Chant du rossignol," ballets, Paris Opéra Paul Whiteman tours Europe with his band Reginald De Koven, Amer. composer, d. (b. 1859) Charles Tomlinson Griffes, Amer. composer, *(contd)*	Sir William Abney, Brit. photographic chemist, d. (b. 1843) Amer. surgeon Harvey Cushing (1869—1939) develops new techniques in brain surgery Arthur Stanley Eddington (1882—1944): "Space, Time, and Gravitation" Aust. meteorologist Heinrich von Ficker recognizes the importance of the stratosphere in meteorological phenomena Ger. engineer Anton Flettner invents the rotor ship, originally intended to propel ships with metal sails William C. Gorgas, Amer. surgeon notable for controlling yellow fever, d. (b. 1854) Nobel Prize for Physics: Edouard Guillaume (1861—1938) for discoveries of anomalies in nickel-steel alloys Nobel Prize for Medicine: August Krogh (1874—1949) for the discovery of the capillary regulation of the conveyance of blood to the muscles Sir Norman Lockyer, Eng. astronomer, d. (b. 1836) Nobel Prize for Chemistry: Walther Nernst (1864—1941) for his formulation of the heat theorem Robert Edwin Peary, Amer. Arctic explorer, d. (b. 1856) *(contd)*	Ethelda M. Bleibtrey, Amer. swimming champion, three-time winner at the Antwerp Olympics Mexican Alfredo Codona, the great aerialist, becomes the first man ever to perfect a triple somersault In Britain, 3,747 divorces granted Earthquake in Kansu province, China, claims 200,000 victims Amer. Professional Football Association formed Marconi opens first public broadcasting station in Britain at Writtle Olympic Games, after eight-year hiatus, held at Antwerp: 24 sports, 154 events, 2,606 participants, 29 nations; U.S. wins most events (debut of Finn. runner, Paavo Nurmi) Pasadena Rose Bowl–Harvard defeats Oregon 7—6; New Year's Day tradition continues uninterrupted until 1942 "Sugar" Ray Robinson, the only boxer to win a world title five times (1951 twice, 1955, 1957, 1958), b. "Babe" Ruth (1895—1948), sold by the Boston Red Sox to the New York Yankees for $125,000 Statistics–coal production: U.S., 645 million tons; Britain, 229 million tons; Germany, 107 million tons; petroleum production: U.S., 443 million barrels; Mexico, 163 million barrels; Russia, 25 million barrels; motor vehicles licensed: U.S., 8,890,000; Britain, 663,000; World population: 1,811,000,000; New York population, 5,620,000; Los Angeles, 576,000 Hugo Stinnes (1870—1924), Ger. industrialist, begins his attempt to organize a colossal trust William T. Tilden (1893—1953) (U.S.) *(contd)*	**1920**

	A. HISTORY, POLITICS	B. LITERATURE, THEATER	C. RELIGION, PHILOSOPHY, LEARNING
1920 contd	Danzig declared a free city End of Russian Civil War Convention of Nicaragua, Honduras, and Costa Rica Jesse Collings, Brit. politician, d. (b. 1831) Alvaro Obregón elected President of Mexico King Constantine of Greece returns to Athens as a result of plebiscite Government of Ireland Act passed by Brit. Parliament: Northern and Southern Ireland each to have own Parliament Otto Meissner (1880—1953) head of the office of the Ger. President (—1945) Adolf Hitler announces his 25-point program at the Hofbräuhaus, Munich Gandhi (1869—1948) emerges as India's leader in its struggle for independence Royal Institute of International Affairs founded in London Nicola Sacco and Bartolomeo Vanzetti arrested and indicted for murder of two men in South Braintree, Mass.	Impersonation" Benito Pérez Galdós, Span. novelist, d. (b. 1843) Ezra Pound: "Instigations," essays Jules Romains: "Donogoo-Tonka" Carl Sandburg: "Smoke and Steel" Upton Sinclair: "100%, the Story of a Patriot" Sigrid Undset: "Kristin Lavransdatter," vol. 1 Paul Valéry: "Le Cimetière marin" John Reed, Amer. Communist author ("Ten Days That Shook the World") and journalist, d. (b. 1887) Olive Schreiner, S. African novelist, d. (b. 1855) Charles Vildrac: "Le Paquebot Tenacity" Mrs. Humphry Ward, Eng. novelist, d. (b. 1851) H. G. Wells: "Outline of History" Edith Wharton: "The Age of Innocence," novel (Pulitzer Prize 1921) Stefan Zweig: "Romain Rolland, an Appreciation" Aleksander Blok, Russ. poet, d. (b. 1880)	sociologist, d. (b. 1864) Alfred North Whitehead: "The Concept of Nature" Wilhelm Wundt, Ger. psychologist, d. (b. 1832) William Sanday, Eng. theologian, d. (b. 1843)
1921	Theobald von Bethmann-Hollweg, Ger. statesman, d. (b. 1856) First Indian Parliament meets Paris conference of Allies fixes Ger. reparation payments Winston S. Churchill becomes Colonial Secretary Reza Khan (1878—1944) carries out a coup d'état in Teheran Warren G. Harding inaugurated as 29th President of the U.S. Eduardo Dato, Span. Prime Minister, assassinated Anglo-Soviet trade agreement Upper Silesian plebiscite–63 per cent vote for incorporation in Germany Ex-Emperor Charles's first coup to regain throne of Hungary fails Reparation Commission fixes Germany's liability at $33,250 million Capital punishment abolished in Sweden Brit. Legion founded Walter Rathenau appointed Ger. Minister for Reconstruction Hitler's storm troopers (SA) begin to terrorize political opponents London Imperial Conference Faisal I (1885—1933) becomes King of Iraq Ger. finance minister Matthias Erzberger assassinated Revolution in Lisbon; António Machado Santos, founder of the republic, murdered Ex-Emperor Charles fails in his second attempt to regain the throne of Hungary Takashi Hara, Premier of Japan, assassinated Washington Conference on disarmament Jap. Crown Prince Hirohito (b. 1901) named prince regent; his father retires because of mental illness Rapid fall of Ger. mark: beginning of inflation Britain and Ireland sign peace treaty Mackenzie King (1874—1950) elected Prime Minister of Canada *(contd)*	Sherwood Anderson: "The Triumph of the Egg" Johan Bojer: "Der Sidste Viking," Norw. novel Karel and Josef Capek: "The Life of the Insects" Marc Connelly and George S. Kaufman: "Dulcy," comedy Grazia Deledda: "Il segreto dell' uomo solitario" ("The Secret") Austin Dobson, Eng. poet, d. (b. 1840) John Dos Passos: "Three Soldiers" Friedrich Dúrrenmatt, Swiss dramatist and novelist, b. (d. 1990) Nobel Prize for Literature: Anatole France John Galsworthy: "A Family Man" Gaiety Theatre, Manchester, first Brit. repertory theater (founded in 1907), closes due to lack of support Hugo von Hofmannsthal: "Der Schwierige" ("The Difficult One") Aldous Huxley: "Chrome Yellow" D. H. Lawrence: "Women in Love" Gabriel Marcel: "La Coeur des autres" W. Somerset Maugham: "The Circle," drama George Moore: "Héloïse and Abélard" Eugene O'Neill: "Anna Christie" Luigi Pirandello: "Sei personaggi in cerca d'autore" ("Six Characters in Search of an Author") Ezra Pound: "Poems 1918—1921" "Der Querschnitt" ("The Cross-Cut"), Ger. intellectual periodical, appears Jean Sarment: "Le Pêcheur d'ombres" Bernard Shaw: "Heartbreak House" Lytton Strachey: "Queen Victoria" Ivan Vazov, Bulgarian poet, d. (b. 1850) Virginia Woolf: "Monday or Tuesday" *(contd)*	Charles Baudouin: "Suggestion and Autosuggestion" (presentation of the method of Coué) James Bryce: "Modern Democracies" Prince Peter Kropotkin, Russ. scientist and anarchist, d. (b. 1842) J. M. E. McTaggart: "The Nature of Existence" (Eng. neo-Hegelianism) Maurice Maeterlinck: "Le Grand Secret" Gilbert Murray: "The Problem of Foreign Policy" Hermann Rorschach: "Psychodiagnostic" Bertrand Russell: "The Analysis of Mind" Albert Schweitzer: "On the Edge of the Primeval Forest" E. Stern-Rubarth: "Propaganda as a Political Weapon" Joseph Weissenberg (1855—1941), Berlin "Health Apostle," at the height of his fame Ludwig Wittgenstein: "Logico-Philosophicus" John Burroughs, Amer. naturalist, d. (b. 1837) Max Verworn, Ger. physiologist, d. (b. 1863) *(contd)*

D. VISUAL ARTS	E. MUSIC	F. SCIENCE, TECHNOLOGY, GROWTH	G. DAILY LIFE	
Amedeo Modigliani, Ital. painter, d. (b. 1884) William Nicholson (1872—1949): "Sunflowers," Eng. postimpressionism Stanley Spencer: "Christ carrying the Cross" Anders Zorn, Swed. impressionist painter, d. (b. 1860) Briton Riviere, Eng. painter, d. (b. 1840) Abbot Thayer, Amer. painter, d. (b. 1849) Sir William B. Richmond, Eng. painter, d. (b. 1842) Fernand Léger: "The Tug Boat"	d. (b. 1884) Maud Powell, Amer. violinist, d. (b. 1868) Henry Hadley: "Cleopatra's Night," Amer. opera, New York Metropolitan Opera Ralph Vaughan Williams: "London Symphony," final version Camille Saint-Saëns Festival held in Athens Gustav Holst: "The Planets," first complete performance given in London	Wilhelm Pfeffer, Ger. botanist, d. (b. 1845) Raschig-process utilizes hydrogen chloride in the chlorination of benzene Swiss psychiatrist Herman Rorschach (1884—1922) devises the "inkblot" test Hermann Staudinger (1881—1965) shows that small molecules polymerize by chemical interaction (plastics) Retired Amer. army officer John T. Thompson patents his submachine gun (Tommy gun) Ger. astronomer Max Wolf (1863—1932) shows the true structure of the Milky Way for the first time (early application of photography to the discovery of asteroids)	wins Wimbledon Lawn Tennis Championships, dominates world tennis till 1925 Site of original baseball field at Cooperstown, N.Y., dedicated as permanent memorial Westinghouse Company opens first Amer. broadcasting station in Pittsburgh, Pa. "Time and Tide" begins to appear Unemployment insurance introduced in Great Britain and Austria The sport of water skiing pioneered on Lake Annecy, Haute Savoie, France Jacob Schiff, Amer. financier and philanthropist, d. (b. 1847) Result of U.S. census of 1920: population 117,823,165 Bomb explosion in Wall Street kills 35, wounds 130 "Man O'War," U.S. thoroughbred, retired to stud after winning 20 of his 21 races, including Belmont and Preakness First airmail flight from New York to San Francisco 18th Amendment to U.S. Constitution goes into effect: Prohibition throughout U.S.	**1920 contd**
Georges Braque: "Still Life with Guitar" Carlo Carrà (1881—1966): "Stone-pine at the Sea," Ital. futurism Franz Defregger, Aust. genre painter, d. (b. 1835) Max Ernst: "The Elephant Celebes," surrealism Films: "Dream Street" (D. W. Griffith); "Anna Boleyn" (Lubitsch); "The Weary Death" (Fritz Lang); "The Kid" (Chaplin) Adolf von Hildebrand, Ger. sculptor, d. (b. 1847) Paul Klee: "The Fish" Oskar Kokoschka: "Music," expressionist painting Fernand Léger: "Three Women" Frans Masereel: "Passion of a Man" (series of woodcuts) William Friese-Greene, Eng. film *(contd)*	Irving Berlin, first of the "Music Box Revues," New York Enrico Caruso, Ital. operatic tenor, d. (b. 1873) Paul Hindemith: "Mörder, Hoffnung der Frauen" and "Das Nusch-Nuschi," one- act operas, Stuttgart Arthur Honegger: "Le Roi David" Engelbert Humperdinck, Ger. composer, d. (b. 1854) Leos Janácek: "Katya Kabynova," opera, Brno Eduard Künnecke: "Der Vetter aus Dingsda" ("The Cousin from Nowhere"), Berlin Brit. Musicians' Union founded in London Hans Pfitzner: "Von deutscher Seele," Op. 28, romantic cantata Sergei Prokofiev: "The Love for Three Oranges," opera, Chicago *(contd)*	Friedrich Bergius (1884—1949) successfully hydrogenates coal to oil J. N. Bronsted and G. von Hevesy successfully separate isotopes Albert Calmette and Camille Guérin develop the B-C-G tuberculosis vaccine Chromosome theory of heredity postulated by Amer. biologist Thomas Hunt Morgan (1866—1945) Edgar Dacqué (1878—1945) initiates phylogenetically oriented paleontology Friedrich Dessauer advocates medium voltage x-ray therapy Nobel Prize for Physics: Albert Einstein for his discovery of the photoelectric effect Northern approaches of Mount Everest explored by Brit. team under C. K. Howard-Bury William Speirs Bruce, Scot. Arctic explorer, d. (b. 1867) John Dunlop, Scot. inventor of pneumatic rubber tire, d. (b. 1840) Germanin, for the treatment of sleeping sickness, discovered by Dressel, Kothe, and Roehl Felix d'Hérelle (1873—1949) discovers bacteriophages National Institute for Industrial Psychology founded in London Ernst Kretschmer (1888—1964): "Physique and Character" U.S. physical chemist Irving *(contd)*	Australia wins the Ashes (cricket) First radio broadcast of a baseball game made by Graham McNamee from the Polo Grounds in New York Swiss physician M. O. Bircher-Benner (1867—1939) recommends the intake of more uncooked foods in his book, "The Fundaments of Our Nutrition" British Broadcasting Company founded Cuban chess player José Raoul Capablanca wins world championship from Emanuel Lasker, who has held the title since 1894 Country estate of Chequers presented to Great Britain by Lord Lee; becomes official country residence of the prime minister The old game of table tennis revived Radio station KDKA in Pittsburgh transmits the first regular radio programs in the U.S. Sir Ernest Cassel, Anglo-Ger. financier and philanthropist, d. (b. 1852) Sir Gordon Richards, jockey, rides his first winner; by the time of his retirement in 1954 he has won 4,870 races out of 21,834 mounts Sacco and Vanzetti found guilty of murder Statistics–population: U.S.S.R. 136 million, U.S. 107 million, Japan 78 million, Germany 60 million, Great Britain 42.5 million; divorces in Germany 39,000 (18,000 in 1913); gasoline production in U.S. 472 million barrels; books published in Britain 7,319 (14,399 in 1928); illegitimate births: Germany 173,000, Chile 55,000, Italy 49,000, France 65,000 Unknown Soldier interred at Arlington *(contd)*	**1921**

	A. HISTORY, POLITICS	B. LITERATURE, THEATER	C. RELIGION, PHILOSOPHY, LEARNING
1921 contd	Lord Reading (1860—1935) appointed Viceroy of India, succeeding Lord Chelmsford Eduard Benes (1884—1948) elected Prime Minister of Czechoslovakia Nobel Peace Prize: Hjalmar Branting and Christian Lange Prince Philip zu Eulenburg-Hertefeld, William II's friend and adviser, d. (b. 1847) Philander C. Knox, Amer. politician, d. (b. 1853) King Peter I of Serbia d. (b. 1844) H. M. Hyndman, Eng. socialist politician, d. (b. 1842) James Cardinal Gibbons, Amer. prelate, d. (b. 1834) A. H. Bruce, 6th Baron Balfour of Burleigh, Scot. statesman, d. (b. 1849) Sir John S. Cowans, Quartermaster-General of Brit. army in World War I, d. (b. 1862) H. S. Giffard, 1st Earl of Halsbury, Brit. statesman, d. (b. 1823) Charles Evans Hughes named U.S. Secretary of State Andrew Mellon named Secretary of the Treasury Former President William Howard Taft named Chief Justice of the Supreme Court Boies Penrose, senator from Pennsylvania, political boss, d. (b. 1860) President Harding commutes Eugene Debs' 10-year sentence	J. G. Huneker, Amer. man of letters, d. (b. 1860) V. G. Korolenko, Russ. novelist, d. (b. 1853) Emilia Pardo Bazán, Span. novelist, d. (b. 1851) Edgar Saltus, Amer. man of letters, d. (b. 1855) Harriet E. Spofford, Amer. poet and novelist, d. (b. 1835) Sir John Hare, Eng. actor and producer, d. (b. 1844) William Archer: "The Green Goddess," drama Walter de la Mare: "Memoirs of a Midget" Arthur Waley: "The No Plays of Japan" Best seller: "Scaramouche," by Rafael Sabatini Ed Wynn: "The Perfect Fool"	Barrett Wendell, Amer. scholar, Harvard educator, d. (b. 1855) William Warde Fowler, Eng. historian of ancient Rome, d. (b. 1847)
1922	Raymond Poincaré succeeds Aristide Briand as Prime Minister of France Walter Rathenau named Ger. Foreign Minister Cardinal Achille Ratti elected Pope Pius XI to succeed Pope Benedict XV U.S.-Jap. naval agreement signed Britain recognizes Kingdom of Egypt under Fuad I Gandhi sentenced to six years imprisonment for civil disobedience Ex-Emperor Charles of Austria d. (b. 1887) Conference of Genoa Treaty of Rapallo signed between Germany and the U.S.S.R. Germany cedes Upper Silesia to Poland Ignaz Seipel (1876—1932) Federal Chancellor of Austria Walter Rathenau assassinated by Ger. nationalist fanatics League of Nations council approves mandates for Palestine and Egypt Arab Congress at Nablus rejects Brit. mandate for Palestine Protectionist tariff established in the U.S. King Constantine of Greece abdicates; George II succeeds him till 1924 and again 1935—1947 Geneva Protocol: Austria denounces Anschluss Unemployed Glasgow workers undertake hunger march to London A. Bonar Law (Conservative) becomes Prime Minister of Britain; succeeds David Lloyd George (Liberal) Friedrich Ebert reelected Ger. President Mussolini's March on Rome Mussolini forms Fascist government *(contd)*	Kingsley Amis, Eng. author, b. Henri Bataille, Fr. dramatist, d. (b. 1872) J. J. Bernard: "Martine" Bertolt Brecht: "Baal" and "Trommeln in der Nacht" ("Drums at Night") John Buchan: "Huntingtower" Willa Cather: "One of Ours," 1923 Pulitzer Prize novel T. S. Eliot: "The Waste Land" F. Scott Fitzgerald: "Tales of the Jazz Age" and "The Beautiful and the Damned" John Galsworthy: "The Forsyte Saga" (parts of it appearing since 1906) Roger Martin du Gard: "Les Thibaults" (—1940) Maxim Gorki: "My Universities," autobiography Hermann Hesse: "Siddhartha" Hugo von Hofmannsthal: "Das grosse Salzburger Welttheater," mystery play Johannes V. Jensen: "Den lange Rejse," ("The Long Journey"), Dan. novel trilogy James Joyce: "Ulysses," published in Paris; U.S. Post Office burns 500 copies upon arrival in U.S. D. H. Lawrence: "Aaron's Rod" Sinclair Lewis: "Babbitt" Katherine Mansfield: "The Garden Party" Victor Margueritte: "La Garçonne" François Mauriac: "Le Baiser au lépreux" André Maurois: "Les discours du docteur O'Grady" A. A. Milne: "The Dover Road" Anne Nichols: "Abie's Irish Rose," New York plays 2,327 performances. closing in 1927 *(contd)*	Diedrich Bischoff: "The Religion of the Freemasons" James, Viscount Bryce, Brit. scholar, d. (b. 1838) Rudolf Carnap: "The Space," logical positivism John Dewey: "Human Nature and Conduct" A. V. Dicey, Eng. jurist, d. (b. 1835) Etienne Gilson: "Le Thomisme" Herbert Hoover: "American Individualism" C. E. Montague: "Disenchantment" Ferdinand Tönnies: "Kritik der Öffentlichen Meinung" ("Critique of Public Opinion") Lord Carnarvon and Howard Carter discover the tomb of Tutankhamen Max Weber: *(contd)*

D. VISUAL ARTS	E. MUSIC	F. SCIENCE, TECHNOLOGY, GROWTH	G. DAILY LIFE	
pioneer, d. (b. 1855) Edvard Munch: "The Kiss" Pablo Picasso: "Three Musicians" The Duke of Westminster sells Gainsborough's "Blue Boy" and Reynold's "Portrait of Mrs. Siddons" for £200,000 to Amer. collector Collis Huntington	Sigmund Romberg: "Blossom Time" (based on the Viennese operetta "Das Dreimäderlhaus") (the life and music of Franz Schubert), New York Camille Saint-Saëns, Fr. composer, d. (b. 1835) The remodeled Teatro alla Scala opens under the leadership of Arturo Toscanini Christine Nilsson, Swed. soprano, d. (b. 1843) Gervase Elwes, Eng. concert tenor, accidentally killed (b. 1866) "Die Walküre" becomes the first Wagnerian opera to be staged at the Paris Opéra since before the war Déodat de Sévérac, Fr. composer, d. (b. 1873) Igor Stravinsky: "Symphony for Wind Instruments," London Festival of Contemporary Music at Donaueschingen	Langmuir (1881—1957) formulates theories of atomic structure and absorption Hermann J. Oberth, one of the founders of modern astronautics, writes his dissertation "The Rocket into Interplanetary Space" As a preliminary to splitting the atom, Rutherford and Chadwick disintegrate all the elements except carbon, oxygen, lithium, and beryllium Indian physicist Meghmed N. Saha (1893—1956) develops the thermal ionization equation and applies it to the interpretation of stellar spectra Nobel Prize for Chemistry: Frederick Soddy for his studies of the occurrence and nature of isotopes Otto Stern and W. Gerlach show that a beam of atomic silver is split into two distinct beams on passing through a nonhomogeneous magnetic field Nicolai E. Zhukovski (mathematical theory of the circulation hypothesis in aerodynamics), d. (b. 1847)	National Cemetery Ku Klux Klan activities become violent throughout southern U.S., destroying property and branding and whipping blacks and those who sympathize U.S. tennis team retains Davis Cup, defeating Japanese 5—0 U.S. Lawn Tennis Association Men's Singles won by William T. Tilden II; Women's Singles by Mrs. Molla Bjurstedt Mallory Rose Bowl football game won by California over Ohio State, 6—0 Jack Dempsey defeats Georges Carpentier by fourth-round knockout in championship heavyweight boxing match New York (NL) defeats New York (AL) 5—3 to win World Series; Radio station WJZ, Newark, N.J., broadcasts first description of play-by-play action by Graham McNamee	**1921 contd**
Max Beckmann: "Before the Bell," expressionism Max Beerbohm: "Rossetti and His Circle," drawings Clive Bell: "Since Cézanne," art criticism Marc Chagall leaves Russia for Paris L.C.C. County Hall, London, completed Films: "Dr. Mabuse the Gambler" (Fritz Lang); "The Loves of Pharaoh" (Lubitsch); "Grandma's Boy" (Harold Lloyd); "Nosferatu" (F. W. Murnau); "Nanook of the North" (Flaherty); "The Orphans *(contd)*	Louis Armstrong, arriving in Chicago from New Orleans, joins Joe "King" Oliver's band Arnold Bax: Symphony No. 1 Irving Berlin: "April Showers" Arthur Bliss: "A Color Symphony" Fritz Busch (1890—1951) appointed general musical director of the State Opera at Dresden Alfred Einstein (editor): Riemann's "Musiklexikon" (10th edition) Wilhelm Furtwängler (1886—1954) conducts the Gewandhaus concerts at Leipzig Paul Hindemith: "Sancta Susanna," one-act opera, Frankfurt International Society for Contemporary Music (I.S.C.M.) formed at Salzburg following the "Young Viennese" composers' concert Arthur Nikisch, Hungarian conductor, d. (b. 1855) *(contd)*	Aniakchak, one of the world's greatest volcanos, discovered on the Alaskan coast Nobel Prize for Chemistry: Francis Aston for work with mass spectrography Alexander Graham Bell, Amer. inventor and physicist, d. (b. 1847) P. M. S. Blackett experiments with transmutation of elements Nobel Prize for Chemistry: Niels Bohr for his investigations into atomic structure and radiation W. W. Coblentz obtains accurate measurements of the relative thermal intensities of star images Eng, Massolle, and Vogt develop a sound film system, Tri-Ergon, but are not able to carry it through Evans and Bishop discover antisterility Vitamin E Henry Ford: "My Life and Work" John Harwood invents a self-winding wristwatch (patented 1924) John Moresby, Eng. explorer in Australia, d. (b. 1830) During his student days in London Czech chemist Jaroslav Hegrovsky (b. 1890) *(contd)*	The Austin Seven popularizes motoring B.B.C. 2LO begins to broadcast Stockmarket "boom" starts in America after depression Amer. cocktail becomes popular in Europe International Union for Cultural Cooperation founded in Vienna Remarkable gliding flights (up to three hours in the air) accomplished in Germany; first experimental congress for gliding held in France New Ku Klux Klan, assuming the name of the post-Civil War organization, gains political power in the U.S. Marie Lloyd, Eng. music hall artist and singer, d. (b. 1870) Mercedes-Daimler cars dominate racing Nansen Passports used as travel documents for stateless persons Emily Post: "Etiquette" George Cadbury, Eng. chocolate manufacturer and social reformer, d. (b. 1839) Federal Narcotics Control Board established by President Harding U.S. government revenues $4,919 million, expenditures $4,068 million Lord Rothermere (1868—1940) inherits the London "Daily Mail" *(contd)*	**1922**

	A. HISTORY, POLITICS	B. LITERATURE, THEATER	C. RELIGION, PHILOSOPHY, LEARNING
1922 contd	Mustapha Kemal proclaims Turkey a republic U.S. Congressional election reduces Republican majority General elections in Britain–Conservatives, 344 seats; Labour, 138; Liberals, 117 Wilhelm Cuno named Ger. Chancellor President Pilsudski of Poland resigns Irish Free State officially proclaimed Australian elections–Nationalists, 27 seats, Labour, 29; Country Party, 14 Soviet states form U.S.S.R. Marcelo Torcuato de Alvear (1868—1942) named President of the Argentine Nobel Peace Prize: Fridjof Nansen Erskine Childers, Ir. politician and writer, executed (b. 1870) Christiaan De Wet, Boer general and politician, d. (b. 1854) Sir Henry Wilson, Brit. field marshal and politician, assassinated (b. 1864)	Mori Ogai, one of the creators of modern Jap. literature, d. (b. 1860) "Nouvelles littéraires" founded in Paris Eugene O'Neill: "The Hairy Ape," drama P.E.N. Club founded in London by Mrs. Dawson Scott Luigi Pirandello: "Enrico IV" ("Henry IV") Marcel Proust, Fr. novelist, d. (b. 1871) R. M. Rilke: "Sonette au Orpheus" Edwin Arlington Robinson: "Collected Poems," Pulitzer Prize for Poetry Romain Rolland: "Annette et Sylvie" Stanislavsky goes on a tour of Europe with the Moscow Arts Theater (—1924) Booth Tarkington: "Alice Adams," Pulitzer Prize for novel Eugene Vakhtangov's first Habima production, "The Dybbuk," by Solomon Ansky Paul Valéry: "Charmes," poems Hugh Walpole: "The Cathedral" Rebecca West: "The Judge" Virginia Woolf: "Jacob's Room" Stefan Zweig: "Amok" Wilfred Scawen Blunt, Eng. poet, d. (b. 1840) T. S. Eliot founds the literary journal "The Criterion" Mr. and Mrs. Dewitt Wallace found "Reader's Digest" Maurice Baring: "The Puppet Show of Memory" James Elroy Flecker: "Hassan" David Garnett: "Lady into Fox" A. E. Housman: "Last Poems" Eugene O'Neill: "Anna Christie," Pulitzer Prize for drama Edith Sitwell: "Façade"	"Methodology of the Social Sciences" Sir William Christie, Eng. astronomer, d. (b. 1845) Sir John Edwin Sandys, Eng. classical scholar, d. (b. 1844) Pope Benedict XV d.; succeeded by Pope Pius XI (—1939)
1923	Alexander I succeeds his father, Peter I, as King of Yugoslavia Centers of Tokyo and Yokohama destroyed by earthquake, 120,000 dead Miguel Primo de Rivera assumes dictatorship in Spain Lord John Morley, Eng. Liberal statesman, d. (b. 1838) Germany abandons passive resistance Teapot Dome oil scandal hearings in Washington, D.C. Abyssinia admitted to League of Nations Value of Ger. mark drops to rate of four million to one U.S. dollar Ankara replaces Istanbul as capital of Turkey A. Bonar Law, the first Brit. Prime Minister of colonial (Canadian) origin, d. (b. 1858) Hitler's coup d'état (the "Beer Hall Putsch") in Munich fails Wilhelm Marx succeeds Stresemann as Ger. Chancellor Brit. general elections: Conservatives, 258 seats; Labour, 191; Liberals, 158 King George II deposed by Greek army Count Richard N. Condenhove-Kalergi founds Pan-Europa movement Crown Prince William returns to Germany from *(contd)*	François Mauriac: "Genitrix" Edna St. Vincent Millay: "The Ballad of the Harp-Weaver; A Few Figs from Thistles," 1922 Pulitzer Prize for poetry Ferenc Molnar: "The Swan," comedy, stars Eva LeGallienne and Basil Rathbone Elmer Rice: "The Adding Machine" Jules Romains: "Knock; ou Le Triomphe de la médicine" Felis Salten: "Bambi" Dorothy L. Sayers: "Whose Body?" Italo Suevo: "La conscienza di Zeno" Felix Timmermans: "The Parson of the Flowering Vineyard" Sutton Vane: "Outward Bound," London Franz Werfel: "Verdi," novel P. G. Wodehouse: "The Inimitable Jeeves" Nobel Prize for Literature: William Butler Yeats Louis Couperus, Dutch novelist, d. (b. 1863) e. e. cummings: "The Enormous Room," novel Charles Hawes, Amer. writer, d. (b. 1889) Maurice Hewlett, Eng. author, d. (b. 1861) Emerson Hough, Amer. writer, d. (b. 1857) Raymond Radiguet, Fr. poet, d. (b. 1903) Vincent Youmans: "No! No! Nanette," musical comedy Iwan Gilkin, Belg. poet, d. (b. 1858) Morris Rosenfeld, Russo-Amer. poet, d. (b. 1862) Kate Douglas Wiggin, Amer. writer ("Mrs. Wiggs of the *(contd)*	Martin Buber: "I and Thou" Cambridge Ancient History (ed. by J. B. Bury) begins to appear Sigmund Freud: "Das Ich und das Es" ("The Ego and the Id") Lutheran World Congress convened at Eisenach, Germany Salvador de Madariaga: "The Genius of Spain" Alfred Marshall: "Money, Credit and Commerce" Fritz Mauthner: *(contd)*

D. VISUAL ARTS	E. MUSIC	F. SCIENCE, TECHNOLOGY, GROWTH	G. DAILY LIFE	
of the Storm" (D. W. Griffith); "Last of the Mohicans" (Tourneur); "Glorius Adventure" (Stuart Blackton) Paul Klee: "The Twittering Machine" David Low: "Lloyd George and Co.," political cartoons John Marin: "Sunset," Amer. expressionism Joan Miró: "The Farm" P. W. Steer: "Mrs. Raynes," Eng. impressionism Robert Delaunay paints some of his most celebrated portraits (Aragon, Breton, etc.) Vassily Kandinsky elected professor at the Bauhaus, Weimar André Masson experiments with cubism Sir Leslie Ward (pseudonym "Spy"), Eng. cartoonist, d. (b. 1851)	Felipe Pedrell, Span. composer, d. (b. 1841) Carl Nielsen: Symphony No. 5 Ottorino Respighi: "Concerto Gregoriano," for violin and orchestra Igor Stravinsky: "Mavra," comic opera, Paris Opéra Ralph Vaughan Williams: "Pastoral Symphony," No. 3, London Rutland Barrington, Eng. singer and actor, d. (b. 1853) Lillian Russell, Amer. singer and actress, d. (b. 1861) Luigi Denza, Ital. composer ("Funiculi Funicula"), d. (b. 1846) The Benedictines of Solesmes, revivers of the authentic Gregorian chants, return to their abbey after 21 years of exile on the Isle of Wight Sir Charles Santley, Eng. concert baritone, d. (b. 1834)	investigates the electrode potential of aluminum (beginning of polarography) Nobel Prize for Medicine: A. V. Hill and O. Meyerhof for physiochemical muscle examinations W. H. Hudson, Eng. naturalist, d. (b. 1841) Insulin, prepared by Canadian physicians Banting, Best, and Macleod, is first administered to diabetic patients Alphonse Laveran, Fr. physician and pathologist, d. (b. 1845) Amer. zoologist T. H. Morgan experiments with the heredity mechanisms of fruit flies Sir Patrick Manson, Brit. pioneer in malaria research, d. (b. 1844) Dr. Alexis Carrel discovers white corpuscles Ernest Shackleton, Eng. Antarctic explorer, d. (b. 1874)	from his brother Lord Northcliffe (A. C. W. Harmsworth) (1865—1922) Hannes Schneider (1890—1955), Aust. skiing champion, opens ski school at St. Anton am Arlberg Victor Silvester (Brit.) becomes world dancing champion Statistics–Brit. cotton exports: 4,313 million yards; Brit. linens exports: 77 million yards; Brit. silk exports: 5 million yards; Brit. trade union membership: 5.6 million; marriages in the U.S.: 1,126,000; divorces in the U.S.: 148,000 Dr. Marie Stopes holds meetings in Queen's Hall, London, advocating birth control Joyce Wethered wins the first of her four golf championships King George V opens new concrete tennis stadium seating 15,000 at Wimbledon "Classic style" prevails in women's fashions Governor of Georgia appoints first woman, Mrs. W. H. Felton, as U.S. Senator to fill vacancy left by death of Thomas E. Watson; term is one day U.S. Golf Association Amateur championship won by Jess W. Sweetzer; Open won by Gene Sarazen W. T. Tilden, II and W. M. Johnston win singles and Tilden and V. Richards lose doubles but win Davis Cup California University and Washington and Jefferson College in scoreless tie at Rose Bowl football game New York (NL) defeats New York (AL) 4—0 to win World Series	**1922 contd**
Max Beckmann: "The Trapeze," Ger. expressionism Marc Chagall: "Love Idyll" End of Dada movement Raoul Dufy: "On the Banks of the River Marne" Films: "Fridericus Rex" (Gebühr); "The Old Law" (E. A. Dupont); "Robin Hood" (Douglas Fairbanks); "Why Worry" (Harold Lloyd); "The Pilgrim" (Chaplin); "Don Juan and Faust" (L'Herbier); "Gösta Berling" (Maritz Stiller) Royal Fine Arts Commission *(contd)*	Béla Bartók: "Dance Suite" "Bix" Beiderbecke organizes jazz band in Chicago Ernest Bloch: "Quintet for strings and pianoforte" Maria Callas, Greek-Ital. opera singer, b. (d. 1977) Leo Fall: "Madame Pompadour," Vienna Manuel de Falla: "Master Peter's Puppet Show" George Gershwin: "Rhapsody in Blue" Jean Gilbert: "Katya the Dancer," operetta Alois Hába begins teaching at the Prague Conservatory Gustav Holst: "The Perfect Fool," opera, London Honegger: "Pacific 231" Jazz: Joseph "King" Oliver and "Jelly Roll" Morton record New *(contd)*	E. N. da C. Andrade: "The Structure of the Atom" L. A. Bauer analyzes the earth's magnetic field Theory of acids and bases postulated by J. N. Brönsted Span. inventor Juan de la Cierva develops the basic principle of the Autogiro U.S. physicist A. H. Compton (1892—1962) discovers that x-rays change in wavelength when scattered by matter Emile Coué arrives in America for speaking tour Dutch physicist P. J. W. Debye extends the Arrhenius theory of ionization of salt in solution to the crystalline solid state Lee de Forest demonstrates process for sound motion pictures Gustave Eiffel, Fr. engineer, *(contd)*	Aeroflot, largest airline in the world, founded in the U.S.S.R. Baseball–Philadelphia Athletics lose 20 games in a row First birth-control clinic opens in New York Albert Chevalier, Eng. music hall star, d. (b. 1861) First Eng. F.A. Cup Final played at Wembley Stadium, London (won by Bolton Wanderers) Gregorian Calendar introduced in the U.S.S.R. William M. Johnston wins the men's singles at Wimbledon John Maynard Keynes: "A Tract on Monetary Reform" Ger. aircraft designer Willy Messerschmitt (b. 1898) establishes his aircraft factory Henry Morgenthau: "All in a Lifetime," autobiography Mother's Day, begun in America in 1907, first celebrated in Europe Nevada and Montana become the first Amer. states to introduce old-age pensions Paavo Nurmi runs one mile in 4 minutes, *(contd)*	**1923**

	A. HISTORY, POLITICS	B. LITERATURE, THEATER	C. RELIGION, PHILOSOPHY, LEARNING
1923 contd	exile in the Netherlands Chaim Weizmann named President of Zionist World Organization Stojan Protic, a founder and first Prime Minister of Yugoslavia, d. (b. 1857) Alexander Stambolisky, Premier of Bulgaria, d. (b. 1879) Yakub Khan Amir of Afghanistan, d. Charles D. Sigsbee, U.S. naval officer, d. (b. 1845) Pancho Villa, Mexican national hero, d. (b. 1878) Théophile Delcassé, Fr. statesman, d. (b. 1852) Tri-state conclave of Ku Klux Klan held in Kokomo, Ind.; 200,000 members attend U.S. Senate decides on recalling occupation forces from Rhineland Germany declares policy of passive resistance Max Nordau, Jewish writer and Zionist politician, d. (b. 1849) Fr. army occupies Darmstadt, Karlsruhe, and Mannheim Brit. Prime Minister Bonar Law resigns; Stanley Baldwin forms new government with Neville Chamberlain as Chancellor of the Exchequer Transjordan becomes independent under Amir Abdullah New York Prohibition Enforcement Act repealed by Governor Alfred E. Smith London dock strike Non-Fascist parties dissolved in Italy Ahmed Zogu (1895—1961) emerges as Albania's strong man U.S. President W. G. Harding d. (b. 1865); succeeded by Vice President Calvin Coolidge Gustav Stresemann elected Ger. Chancellor Mustapha Kemal elected President of Turkey Martial law established in Oklahoma to protect people and property from attacks by Ku Klux Klan	Cabbage Patch"), d. (b. 1856) Maurice Barrès, Fr. writer and politician, d. (b. 1862) Philip Barry: "You and I," drama Arnold Bennett: "Riceyman Steps" Sarah Bernhardt, Fr. actress, d. (b. 1844) Karel Capek: "R.U.R.," Czech science fiction drama Willa Cather: "A Lost Lady" Agatha Christie: "The Murder on the Links" Colette: "Le Blé en herbe" Joseph Conrad: "The Rover" E. E. Cummings: "Tulips and Chimneys" Owen Davis: "Icebound," Pulitzer Prize for drama Olav Duun: "Juvifolke," last volume of Norw. family saga, appears Robert Frost: "New Hampshire" Knut Hamsun: "The Last Chapter" Charles Hawtrey, Eng. actor- manager, d. (b. 1858) Fannie Hurst: "Humoresque," drama, stars Laurette Taylor D. H. Lawrence: "The Ladybird" Pierre Loti, Fr. novelist, d. (b. 1850) Katherine Mansfield, Eng. novelist, d. (b. 1888)	"Atheism and Its History in the Western World" José Ortega y Gasset: "El Tema de nuestro tiempo" Romain Rolland: "Mahatma Gandhi" Albert Schweitzer: "Philosophy of Civilization" Nathan Söderblom: "Christian Fellowship" Ernst Troeltsch, Ger. theologian, d. (b. 1865) Sidney and Beatrice Webb: "The Decay of Capitalist Civilization" Bernard Bosanquet, Eng. Hegelian philosopher, d. (b. 1848) Oscar Browning, Eng. historian, d. (b. 1837) Frederic Harrison, Eng. positivist philosopher, d. (b. 1831) William Roscoe Thayer, Amer. historian, d. (b. 1859)
1924	Venizelos becomes Prime Minister of Greece Lenin, founder of the U.S.S.R., d. (b. 1870) Stanley Baldwin resigns; Ramsay MacDonald forms first Labour government in Britain Britain recognizes U.S.S.R. Woodrow Wilson, 28th President of the U.S., d. (b. 1856) Edwin Denby, U.S. Navy Secretary, forced to resign (Teapot Dome oil leases) Ahmed, Shah of Persia, dethroned; Reza Khan appointed regent Greece proclaimed republic Hitler sentenced to five years imprisonment; released after eight months First elections in Italy under Fascist methods; 65 per cent favor Mussolini *(contd)*	Maxwell Anderson and Laurence Stallings: "What Price Glory?" Michael Arlen: "The Green Hat" Marc Connelly and George S. Kaufman: "Beggar on Horseback" Joseph Conrad, Eng.-Pol. novelist, d. (b. 1857) Marie Corelli, Eng. novelist, d. (b. 1855) Noel Coward: "The Vortex," London Eleonora Duse, Ital. actress, d. (b. 1859) Svend Fleuron: "Af en Vikings Saga," Dan. novel E. M. Forster: "A Passage to India" Anatole France, Fr. poet and novelist, d. (b. 1844) *(contd)*	Ancient Monuments Society founded in London Irving Babbitt: "Democracy and Leadership" Karl Barth: "The Word of God and the Word of Man" (dialectic Protestant theology) F. H. Bradley, Eng. philosopher, d. (b. 1846) Eng. orientalist E. A. W. Budge (1857—1934) *(contd)*

1923 contd

D. VISUAL ARTS

formed in Britain to advise on public buildings and memorials

Raymond Hood: Chicago Tribune Building

Augustus John: "Thomas Hardy"

Vassily Kandinsky: "Circles in the Circle"

Paul Nash: "The Coast," Eng. expressionism

Pablo Picasso: "Lady with Blue Veil," neoclassicism; "Women," surrealism; "Melancholy," expressionism

Stanley Spencer: "The Resurrection" (—1927)

Maurice Utrillo: "Ivry Town Hall," impressionism

Maurice de Vlaminck: "Village in Northern France"

Josquin Sorella Bastida, Span. painter, d.

Le Corbusier: "Towards a New Architecture"

E. MUSIC

Orleans-style jazz

Ernst Krenek: "Der Sprung über den Schatten," comic opera, Frankfurt

Robert Mayer founds Children's Concerts in London

Francis Poulenc: "Les Biches" ("The House Party"), ballet

Maurice Ravel: "L'Enfant et les sortilèges," opera, Monte Carlo

Ottorino Respighi: "Belfagor," comic opera, Milan

E. N. von Reznicek: "Holofernes," Berlin

Albert Roussel: "Padmâvati," opera-ballet, Paris Opéra

Othmar Schoeck: "Elegie," song cycle

Jean Sibelius: Symphony No. 6 in D minor, Op. 104

Igor Stravinsky: "Les Noces," Paris

Siegfried Wagner: "Der Schmied von Marienburg," opera

Vincent Youmans: "Wild- flower," New York

Popular songs: "Yes, We Have No Bananas"; "Barney Google"; "Tea for Two" and "I Want to be Happy" (both from "No! No! Nanette"); "Just a Kiss in the Dark"

Paul Hindemith: "Das Marienleben," song cycle

F. SCIENCE, TECHNOLOGY, GROWTH

d. (b. 1832)

Hevesy and Coster discover the element hafnium

U.S. astronomer Edwin P. Hubble (1889—1953) discovers a distance-indicating cepheid variable star in the Andromeda nebula

Brit. scientist Frederick Lindemann, Lord Cherwell, investigates the size of meteors and the temperature of the upper atmosphere

Nobel Prize for Physics: R. A. Millikan (U.S.) for his work on the elementary electric charge and the photoelectric effect

The U.S.S.R. establishes its first polar station

Nobel Prize for Chemistry: Fritz Pregl (Aust.) for his discovery of a method of microanalysis for organic substances

Wilhelm Conrad Röntgen, Ger. physicist, d. (b. 1845)

Ross Institute of Tropical Medicine, London, founded

Swed. chemist Theodor Svedberg develops the ultracentrifuge

John B. Tytus invents continuous hot- strip rolling of steel

J. Diderik van der Waals, Dutch physicist, d. (b. 1837)

5th Earl of Carnarvon, the discoverer of Tutankhamen's tomb, d. (b. 1860)

Sir James Dewar, Scot. chemist and physicist, d. (b. 1842)

Charles P. Steinmetz, Amer. electrical engineer, d. (b. 1865)

G. DAILY LIFE

10.4 seconds

Polo–Meadowbrook (U.S.) beats the Brit. Army team in the International Tournament

"London Radio Times" begins to appear (circulation by mid-century 9 million)

Briton Hadden and Henry R. Luce found the weekly newsmagazine "Time"

The first crossing of the Channel from France to England achieved by the swimmer Enrique Tiriboschi (Argentina) in 16 hours 33 minutes

Registered Trade Union membership: Germany, 9,193,000; U.S.S.R., 4,556,000; Great Britain, 4,369,000; U.S., 3,600,000

Sir Frederick Treves, Eng. physician (Brit. Red Cross Society), d. (b. 1853)

Col. Jacob Schick patents electric razor

U.S. tennis team defeats Australia to win Davis Cup

U.S. Lawn Tennis Association Men's Singles won by W. T. Tilden, II; Women's Singles by Helen N. Wills

U.S.Golf Association Amateur won by Max R. Marston; Open won by Bobby Jones

Southern California defeats Penn State to win Rose Bowl football game 14—3

Jack Dempsey retains heavyweight boxing championship against Luis Firpo: 11 knockdowns, including one in which Firpo knocks Dempsey out of the ring

New York (AL) defeats New York (NL) 4—2 to win World Series

1924

D. VISUAL ARTS

Die Blauen Vier (The Blue Four), a group of expressionist painters–Feininger, Jawlensky, Kandinsky, and Klee

Georges Braque: "Sugar Bowl," Fr. expressionist painting

Marc Chagall: "Daughter Ida at the Window"

Ital. cubist painter

(contd)

E. MUSIC

Paul Bekker: "Wagner, the Life in His Work"

Alban Berg: "Chamber Concerto" (written for the 50th birthday of Arnold Schönberg)

Ferruccio Busoni, Ital. pianist and composer, d. (b. 1866)

Gabriel Fauré, Fr. composer, d. (b. 1845)

(contd)

F. SCIENCE, TECHNOLOGY, GROWTH

R. C. Andrews discovers skulls and skeletons of Mesozoic dinosaurs in the Gobi Desert

Eng. physicist E. V. Appleton (1892—1965) demonstrates that radio waves of a sufficiently short wavelength will penetrate the Heaviside layer

F. M. Bailey, H. T. Morsehead, and F. K. Ward find the source of the Brahmaputra-Tsangpo River in Tibet

Fr. physicist Louis, Prince de Broglie (1892—1960), publishes his study concerning wave

(contd)

G. DAILY LIFE

"All Blacks," New Zealand rugby football team, make undefeated tour of Britain

Brit. Imperial Airways begins operations

World Chess League founded at The Hague

Brit. Empire Exhibition held at Wembley

Ford Motor Company produces 10 millionth car

Auguste Forel: "Why we should avoid alcohol"

Ger. mass murderer Fritz Haarmann (26 victims) sentenced to death

(contd)

1924 contd

A. HISTORY, POLITICS

Pan-American Treaty signed to prevent conflicts between nations
U.S. bill limits immigrants, excludes all Japanese
Attempt on the life of Aust. Chancellor Ignaz Seipel
Giacomo Matteotti, leader of Ital. socialists, murdered by Fascist Quadristi
Republican convention, Cleveland, Ohio, nominates Calvin Coolidge for U.S. presidency; Charles Dawes for vice presidency
Gaston Doumerque elected President of France; Edouard Herriot becomes premier
Democratic convention, New York City, nominates J. W. Davis for presidency, W. J. Bryan for vice presidency
J. B. M. Hertzog (1866—1942), S. African anti-Brit. statesman, becomes Prime Minister of the Union
London Conference approves Dawes Report which removes Ger. reparations from the sphere of political controversy
The new reichsmark introduced
London Foreign Office publishes Zinoviev letter in which the Third International allegedly instructs Britons to provoke revolution
Conservatives win Brit. General Election with 413 seats; Labour, 150; Liberals, 40
Calvin Coolidge wins U.S. presidential election
Stanley Baldwin elected Brit. Prime Minister; Winston Churchill, having switched from the Liberals to the Conservatives, is named Chancellor of the Exchequer
Albanian Republic founded
Stalin, Zinoviev, and Kamenev ally against Trotsky
Henry Cabot Lodge, Amer. legislator, d. (b. 1850)
Marquis Matsukata, Jap. statesman, d. (b. 1835)
Robert Nivelle, Fr. field marshal in World War I, d. (b. 1856)
J. Edgar Hoover (1875—1972) is appointed director of the Bureau of Investigation (renamed Federal Bureau of Investigation in 1935) (—1972)

B. LITERATURE, THEATER

Robert Frost: "A Poem with Notes and Grace Notes," Pulitzer Prize
John Galsworthy: "The White Monkey"
André Gide: "Si le grain ne meurt"
Sidney Howard: "They Knew What They Wanted," Pulitzer Prize for drama (1925)
Franz Kafka, Ger. writer, d. (b. 1883)
Georg Kaiser: "Kolportage," Ger. expressionist comedy
Margaret Kennedy: "The Constant Nymph"
E. E. Kisch: "Der rasende Reporter," collection of Continental newspaper reports
Klabund: "The Chalk Circle"
Ring Lardner: "How to Write Short Stories," a collection of short stories
Thomas Mann: "Der Zauberberg" ("The Magic Mountain")
E. F. T. Marinetti: "Futurism and Fascism"
John Masefield: "Sard Harker," novel
George Jean Nathan founds "The American Mercury," magazine
Sean O'Casey: "Juno and the Paycock"
Eugene O'Neill: "All God's Chillun Got Wings," drama, stars Paul Robeson; "Desire under the Elms," drama
Paul Raynal: "Le Tombeau sous l'Arc de Triomphe"
Max Reinhardt opens the New Theater in der Josefstadt, Vienna
Arthur Schnitzler: "Fräulein Else"
Alexander Serafimovic: "The Iron Flood," Russ. novel
Bernard Shaw: "Back to Methuselah" and "St. Joan"
K. S. Stanislavsky: "My Life in Art"
Tsukiji Little Theater opens in Tokyo; beginning of modern theater movement in Japan
Mark Twain: "Autobiography" (posth.)
Paul Valéry: "Eupalinos or the Architect"
Mary Webb: "Precious Bane"
Franz Werfel: "Juarez und Maximilian," drama
Sabine Baring-Gould, Eng. poet and hymn writer ("Onward Christian Soldiers"), d. (b. 1834)
John R. Coryell, Amer. popular novelist (Nick Carter), d. (b. 1848)
Valery Bryusov, Russ. poet, d. (b. 1873)
Carl Spitteler, Swiss author, Nobel Prize for Literature 1918, d. (b. 1845)
Frances Hodgson Burnett, Anglo-Amer. author ("Little Lord Fauntleroy"), d. (b. 1849)
Bestseller: P. G. Wodehouse, "Jeeves"

C. RELIGION, PHILOSOPHY, LEARNING

edits Baraalam and Yearsef
J. R. Commons: "Legal Foundations of Capitalism"
Sigmund Freud: "Collected Writings" (12 vols. —1939)
Gandhi fasts for 21 days in protest against the political and religious feuds of the Hindus and Moslems in India
Ellen Key: "The All Conqueror"
Paul Natorp, Ger. Neo-Kantian philosopher, d. (b. 1854)
Alois Riehl, Aust. Neo-Kantian philosopher, d. (b. 1844)
Albert Schweitzer: "Memoirs of Childhood and Youth"
Maffeo Pantaleoni, Ital. economist, d. (b. 1857)
Basil L. Gildersleeve, Amer. classical scholar, d. (b. 1831)

D. VISUAL ARTS

Giorgio de Chirico arrives in Paris
Films: "The Last Laugh" (Jannings); "The Nibelungs" (Fritz Lang); "America" (D. W. Griffith); "The Ten Commandments" (C. B. De Mille); "The Thief of Bagdad" (Douglas Fairbanks); "Nana" (Renoir); "The City that Never Sleeps" (James Cruze); "The Navigator" (Buster Keaton); "Entracte" (René Clair); "Le Ballet Mécanique" (Fernand Léger)
Juan Gris lectures at the Sorbonne, Paris, on "Possibilités de la Peinture"
Gwen John: "The Convalescent"
Oskar Kokoschka: "Venice," expressionist paintings
Edwin Lutyens, architect, designs Britannic House, Finsbury, London
The Wilhelm-Marx-Haus in Düsseldorf, built 1922—1924, one of the first Ger. skyscrapers
Joan Miro: "Catalan Landscape," surrealism
Pablo Picasso's abstract period
Hans Thoma, Ger. painter, d. (b. 1839)
Léon Bakst, Russ. painter and decorative artist, d. (b. 1866)
Emile Claus, Fl. impressionist painter, d. (b. 1849)
Lewis Mumford: "Sticks and Stones," social history of architecture
Maurice Prendergast d. (b. 1859)
Louis Sullivan d. (b. 1856)

E. MUSIC

Rudolf Friml: "Rose Marie," New York
George Gershwin: "Lady Be Good," New York
Victor Herbert, Ir.-Amer. composer, d. (b. 1859)
Leos Janácek: "The Cunning Little Vixen," opera, Brno
Emmerich Kálmán: "Countess Maritza," Vienna
Sergei Koussevitzky appointed chief conductor of the Boston Symphony Orchestra (—1949)
Giacomo Puccini, Ital. composer, d. (b. 1858)
Ottorino Respighi: "Pini di Roma," symphonic poem
Sigmund Romberg: "The Student Prince," New York
Arnold Schönberg: "Erwartung," monodrama, Prague, and "Die glückliche Hand," Vienna
Jean Sibelius: Symphony No. 7 in C major, Op. 105
Sir Charles V. Stanford, Ir. composer, d. (b. 1852)
Richard Strauss: "Intermezzo," opera, Dresden, "Schlagobers," ballet, Vienna
Igor Stravinsky: piano concerto

F. SCIENCE, TECHNOLOGY, GROWTH

theory of matter
Henry Draper Catalogue (spectra of 225,000 stars, published Harvard Observatory since 1918)
Ger. airship pioneer Hugo Eckener (1868—1952) flies his Z-R-3 across the Atlantic to Lakehurst, N. Y.
Eng. astronomer Arthur Eddington discovers that the luminosity of a star is approximately related to its mass
Nobel Prize for Medicine: Willem Einthoven for pioneering work in electrocardiography
Ger. engineer Anton Flettner, inventor of the rotor ship, constructs his three-masted, 960-ton schooner "Buckau"
Granville S. Hall, U.S. psychologist, d. (b. 1844)
Karl Haushofer (1869—1946): "Geopolitics of the Pacific Ocean"
Patent application for iconoscope (T.V.) filed by Russ.-Amer. inventor V. K. Zworikin
Insecticides used for the first time
W. P. Köppen and A. Wegener: "The Climates of Primeval Geological Periods"
Alfred Marshall, Eng. economist, d. (b. 1842)
Clifford Holland, Amer. civil engineer (Holland Tunnel, N.Y.), d. (b. 1883)
World Power Conference held at Wembley, London
Dan. polar exlorer Knud Rasmussen (1879—1933) completes the longest dog-sledge journey ever made across the N. Amer. Arctic; reaches Point Barrow on May 23
Central Office for the Examination of Rocket Problems founded in Moscow
Nobel Prize for Physics: Karl M. G. Siegbahn for his work in x-ray spectroscopy
Sir Archibald Geikie, Scot. geologist, d. (b. 1835)
Jacques Loeb, Ger.-Amer. physiologist, d. (b. 1859)
Georg H. Quincke, Ger. physicist, d. (b. 1834)
Wilhelm Roux, Ger. anatomist, d. (b. 1850)
Eugen Warming, Dan. botanist, d. (b. 1841)
Sir William Bayliss, Eng. physiologist, d. (b. 1860)

G. DAILY LIFE

by decapitation
Walter Hagen (U.S.) wins Brit. Open Golf championship for the second time
Mah-Jong–world craze
Notre Dame upsets Army at the Polo Grounds, N.Y.; the "Four Horsemen"–Layden, Stuhldreher, Miller, and Crowley–star
The Paris Olympic Games dominated by Finn Paavo Nurmi; 24 sports, 137 events, 3,092 participants, 44 nations; U.S. wins 12 gold medals, Nurmi four
Rocky Marciano, Amer. boxer, b. (d. 1969)
Statistics–coal production: U.S. 485 million tons; Great Britain 267 million tons; France 7 million tons; steel production: U.S. 45 million tons; Germany 9 million tons; Great Britain 8 million tons; strikes: U.S. 10 million days lost; Great Britain 8 million days lost; fire losses in U.S.: $548 million (in 1900, $161 million)
The first Winter Olympics held at Chamonix: 8 sports, 16 events, 293 participants, 16 nations
Samuel Gompers, Amer. labor unionist, president of the American Federation of Labor, d. (b. 1850)
Fédération Internationale des Echecs founded
U.S. Lawn Tennis Association Men's Singles won by W. T. Tilden, II; Women's Singles by Helen N. Wills
W. T. Tilden, V. Richards, and W. M. Johnston, Amer. tennis team, defeat Australia to win Davis Cup
U.S. Golf Association Amateur won by Bobby Jones; Open won by Cyril Walker
Notre Dame, under coaching of Knute Rockne, wins nine out of nine football games
University of Washington and Navy tie (14—14) in Rose Bowl football game
Nathan Leopold and Richard Loeb are sentenced to life imprisonment for kidnap-slaying of 12-year-old Bobby Franks; Loeb is murdered by another convict in 1936; Leopold is paroled in 1958 and dies in 1971
"Exterminator" ("Old Bones"), winner of 1918 Kentucky Derby and of many other cup races, put out to pasture
Will Rogers, U.S. comedian, at height of his career
2.5 million radios in use in U.S.

	A. HISTORY, POLITICS	B. LITERATURE, THEATER	C. RELIGION, PHILOSOPHY, LEARNING

1925

A. HISTORY, POLITICS

Christiania, Norw. capital, renamed Oslo
Mrs. Nellie Tayloe Ross of Wyoming becomes the first woman governor in America
F. B. Kellogg appointed U.S. Secretary of State
Hans Luther named Ger. Chancellor
Friedrich Ebert, Ger. President, d. (b. 1871)
Sun Yat-sen, Chin. statesman, d. (b. 1866)
Lord Curzon, Brit. statesman, d. (b. 1859)
Japan introduces general suffrage for men
Paul Painlevé elected Premier of France
Abd-el-Krim revolt begins in Morocco–Pétain Fr. Commander-in-Chief
Hindenburg elected President of Germany
Cyprus becomes a Brit. Crown Colony
Coup d'état in Athens; Theodore Pangalos becomes premier
Unemployment Insurance Act enacted in Britain
Surendranath Banerjea, Indian nationalist leader, d. (b. 1848)
Norway annexes Spitsbergen
Locarno Conference
Reza Khan ascends Persian throne
Queen Alexandra of Great Britain d. (b. 1844)
Brit. troops evacuate Cologne
K. J. Voroshilov named Minister of War in U.S.S.R.
Nobel Peace Prize: Austen Chamberlain (Great Britain) and C. G. Dawes (U.S.)
Hitler reorganizes Nazi Party (27,000 members) and publishes vol. 1 of "Mein Kampf"
Brit. Dominions Office established
Dopolavore, a Fascist recreation organization, introduced in Italy
Hjalmar Branting, Swed. socialist leader, d. (b. 1860)
William Jennings Bryan, Amer. Democratic politician, d. (b. 1860)
Mikhail Frunze, Russ. revolutionary army commander, d. (b. 1885)
Charles Lanrezac, Fr. general in World War I, d. (b. 1852)
Nelson A. Miles, Amer. army commander in Civil War, d. (b. 1839)
Robert M. La Follette, Amer. politician, d. (b. 1856)
René Viviani, Fr. statesman, d. (b. 1863)
Franz Conrad von Hötzendorf, Aust. field marshal in World War I, d. (b. 1852)
Sir George Goldie, Eng. colonial administrator, d. (b. 1846)

B. LITERATURE, THEATER

Johanna van Ammers-Küller: "The Rebel Generation," Dutch novel
Ivan Bunin: "Mitya's Love," Russ. novel
Willa Cather: "The Professor's House," Amer. novel
Noel Coward: "Hay Fever," London
e. e. cummings: "XLI Poems"
Warwick Deeping: "Sorrell and Son"
Maurice Dekobra: "La Madone des sleepings"
John Dos Passos: "Manhattan Transfer"
Theodore Dreiser: "An American Tragedy"
Ashley Dukes: "The Man with a Load of Mischief," London
John Erskine: "The Private Life of Helen of Troy," best seller
Edna Ferber: "So Big," Pulitzer Prize novel
F. Scott Fitzgerald: "The Great Gatsby"
Fyodor V. Gladkov: "Cement"
Maxim Gorki: "Delo Antamonovich"
H. Rider Haggard, Eng. novelist, d. (b. 1856)
Ernest Hemingway: "In Our Time," short stories
Aldous Huxley: "Those Barren Leaves," novel
Franz Kafka: "The Trial" (posth.)
George Kelly: "Craig's Wife," Pulitzer Prize for drama
Selma Lagerlöf: "Charlotte Löwensköld"
Sinclair Lewis: "Arrowsmith," Pulitzer Prize
Emil Ludwig: "Napoleon"
Heinrich Mann: "The Head," Ger. novel
Somerset Maugham: "The Painted Veil"
Alfred Neumann: "The Patriot," drama
"The New Yorker" (magazine) begins to appear
Martha Ostenso: "Wild Geese"
Teuvo Pakaala, Finn. novelist, d. (b. 1862)
C. F. Ramuz: "L'Amour du monde," novel
Wladislaw Reymont, Pol. novelist, d. (b. 1867)
E. A. Robinson: "Dionysus in Doubt," poems; Pulitzer Prize for poetry: "The Man Who Died Twice"
Gertrude Stein: "The Making of Americans"
Jules Supervielle: "Gravitations," poems
Teatro d'Arte in Rome (Pirandello)
James Lane Allen, Amer. novelist, d. (b. 1849)
George W. Cable, Amer. author, d. (b. 1844)
Amy Lowell, Amer. poet and critic, d. (b. 1874)
Edith M. Thomas, Amer. poet, d. (b. 1854)

C. RELIGION, PHILOSOPHY, LEARNING

Lord Beaverbrook: "Politicians and the Press"
Hilaire Belloc: "History of England" (four vols. —1931)
United Church of Canada founded
Etienne Gilson: "Saint Thomas Aquinas," Neo-Scholastic philosophy
Lord Grey: "Twenty-five Years, 1892—1916," political memoirs
H. Hardtman: "Psychology and the Church"
Hebrew University founded in Jerusalem
Harold Laski: "Grammar of Politics"
Alain Locke: "The New Negro"
London Bible Society distributes 10.5 million bibles in 566 languages
Lutheran World Conference held in Oslo
H. de Man: "The Psychology of Socialism"
Geza Róheim: "Australian Totemism"
The Jesuits count 18,718 members in 32 provinces
Rudolf Steiner, founder of anthroposophy, d. (b. 1861)
James Ward, Eng. philosopher, d. (b. 1843)
Sir Paul Vinogradoff, Russ. jurist and historian of England, d. (b. 1854)
Trinity College, N.C., changes its name to Duke University after grant of $40 million from James B. Duke, tobacco magnate

D. VISUAL ARTS

Marc Chagall: "The Drinking Green Pig"
Lovis Corinth, Ger. painter, d. (b. 1858)
Lyonel Feininger: "Tower," Amer. expressionist painting
Films: "Battleship Potemkin" (Eisenstein); "The Gold Rush" (Chaplin); "The Freshman" (Harold Lloyd); "Lady Windermere's Fan" (Lubitsch); "The Big Parade" (King Vidor); "The Joyless Street" (G. W. Pabst, Garbo); "The Ghost of the Moulin Rouge" (René Clair)
Alfred Gilbert: the Shaftesbury Memorial (Eros), Piccadilly Circus, London
Duncan Grant: "Nymph and Satyr"
Walter Gropius moves the Bauhaus to Dessau from Weimar
Oskar Kokoschka: "Tower Bridge," painting
Pablo Picasso: "Three Dancers"
George Rouault: "The Apprentice"
John Singer Sargent, Anglo-Amer. painter, d. (b. 1856)
Sir Hamo Thornycroft, Eng. sculptor, d. (b. 1850)
George Bellows d. (b. 1887)

E. MUSIC

Arnold Bax: Symphony No. 2
Alban Berg: "Wozzeck," Berlin
Ferruccio Busoni: "Doctor Faust," opera, Dresden (posth.)
Aaron Copland: Symphony for Organ and Orchestra
Leo Fall, Aust. operetta composer, d. (b. 1873)
Rudolf Friml: "The Vagabond King," New York
Jazz, Chicago style, arrives in Europe
James Weldon Johnson: "The Book of American Negro Spirituals"
Franz Lehár: "Paganini," operetta, Vienna
Dame Nellie Melba: "Memories and Melodies," autobiography
Moritz Moszkowski, Ger.-Pol. pianist and composer, d. (b. 1854)
Carl Nielsen: "Sinfonia semplice," Symphony No. 6
Jean de Reszke, Pol.-Fr. composer, d. (b. 1850)
Erik Satie, Fr. composer, d. (b. 1886)
Dmitri Shostakovich: Symphony No. 1
Popular song: "Show Me the Way to go Home"
First Guggenheim Fellowship is awarded to Aaron Copland
Pierre Boulez, Fr. conductor, b.

F. SCIENCE, TECHNOLOGY, GROWTH

Scot. inventor John Logie Baird (1888—1946) transmits recognizable human features by television
Ger. industrial chemist Carl Bosch (1874—1940) invents process for preparing hydrogen on manufacturing scale
Explorers Lincoln Ellsworth and Roald Amundsen reach latitude 87 degrees 44 minutes N in two amphibious phases
The (Franz) Fischer and (Hans) Tropsch synthesis leads to industrial development of synthetic oil
Nobel Prize for Physics: James Franck and Gustav Hertz for their discovery of the laws governing the impact of an electron upon an atom
Heisenberg, Bohr, and Jordan develop quantum mechanics for atoms
Felix Klein, Ger. mathematician, d. (b. 1849)
First Leica camera built by Oskar Barnack
U.S. physicist R. A. Millikan (1868—1953) discovers the presence of cosmic rays in the upper atmosphere
Aust. physicist Wolfgang Pauli (1900—1958) introduces his exclusion principle which helps to explain atomic structure statistically
First International Congress of Radiologists held in London
Professor A. O. Rankine predicts in a lecture "Hearing by Light" the possibility of talking motion pictures in the not distant future
Walter and Ida Noddack discover the very rare metallic element rhenium (atomic number 75)
Solar eclipse in New York is first in 300 years
The theory of Uhlenbeck and Goudsmit shows how the spinning electron accounts for the Pauli formalism
Theory of gene-centers postulated by Russ. botanist N. I. Vavilov (1887—1943)
Sir Thomas Thorpe, Eng. chemist, d. (b. 1845)
Fr.-Russ. surgeon Serge Voronoff, working in the field of induced rejuvenation, combines animal and human experimentation
August von Wassermann, Ger. bacteriologist, d. (b. 1866)
Nobel Prize for Chemistry: Richard Zsigmondy, for elucidation of the heterogenous nature of colloidal solutions
John T. Scopes, schoolteacher, goes on trial for violating Tennessee law that prohibits teaching of the theory of evolution; defended by
(contd)

G. DAILY LIFE

A copy of the Bible cost the equivalent of approximately $2,000 in the 14th century; in 1455 (Gutenberg), $500; in the 17th century, $100; by 1925, $3
Walter Camp, U.S. athlete and "Father of Football," d. (b. 1859)
Malcolm Campbell increases land speed record to 150.86 mph
The Charleston becomes the fashionable dance
The Chrysler Corporation founded by Walter P. Chrysler (1875—1940)
Crossword puzzles become fashionable
Female fashions feature straight dresses without waistline; skirts above the knees; "cloche" hats
Ford Motor Company's Ger. subsidiary begins operations
Alfred Jochim wins Amateur Athletic Union all-rounder (repeated every year till 1930)
New Madison Square Garden, New York City, opened
International convention inveighs against illegal narcotics trade
Grantland Rice's selection of All-American teams begins in "Collier's Weekly"
Peter Sellers, Eng. comedian, b. (d. 1980)
Statistics–railroad mileage: U.S. 261,000; Great Britain 29,000; U.S.S.R. 26,000; 40,000 blind people in Germany, 4,000 of them blinded in the war; 88,000 Catholic missionaries in 66,400 stations, 30,000 Protestant missionaries in 4,596 stations
State of Tennessee forbids sex education in schools
Tornado in south central states of the U.S. kills 689 people
Harold S. Vanderbilt (U.S.) devises contract bridge while on a Caribbean voyage (auction bridge introduced in 1904)
1,654,000 radio sets in Great Britain
First Viscount Leverhulme, Eng. soap manufacturer (Lever Bros. Ltd.), d. (b. 1851)
U.S. Golf Association Amateur championship won by Bobby Jones; U.S. Open won by Willie Macfarlane
W. T. Tilden, II, wins U.S. Lawn Tennis Association Men's Singles championship; Women's Singles won by Helen N. Wills
Notre Dame defeats Stanford, 27—10, in Rose Bowl football game
W. T. Tilden, II, and W. M. Johnston win singles and R. N. Williams and V. Richards win doubles to retain Davis Cup for U.S. against France
Pittsburgh (NL) defeats Washington (AL) to win World Series
Alexander Alekhine, blindfolded, plays 28 simultaneous games of chess

1925 contd

1926

A. HISTORY, POLITICS

Ibn Saud becomes King of Saudi Arabia
Tension between Italy and Germany over South Tirol
Fascist youth organizations "Ballilla" in Italy and "Hitlerjugend" in Germany founded
Queen Elizabeth II of Great Britain b.
General strike called in Britain
Jósef Pilsudski (1867—1935) stages his coup d'état in Poland
Republic of Lebanon proclaimed
End of Abd-el-Krim's Riff war
McNary-Haugen bill calling for a tariff on agricultural products defeated in U.S. Senate
Poincaré elected Premier of France (—1929)-National Union Ministry
Germany admitted to League of Nations
Ignaz Seipel elected Aust. Chancellor
Dr. Joseph Goebbels named Nazi Gauleiter of Berlin
Ger. ministers take office in Czechoslovak government
Trotsky and Zinoviev expelled from Moscow
Italy and Albania sign Treaty of Tirana
Hirohito succeeds his father Yoshihito as Emperor of Japan
Nobel Peace Prize: Briand and Stresemann
Lord Halifax named Viceroy of India (—1931)
Joseph G. ("Uncle Joe") Cannon, Amer. politician, d. (b. 1836)
Felix Dzerzhinsky, Russ. Soviet politician, d. (b. 1877)
Alton B. Parker, Amer. Democratic politician, d. (b. 1852)
Eugene V. Debs, Amer. socialist, d. (b. 1855)
John X. Merriman, S. African statesman, d. (b. 1841)

B. LITERATURE, THEATER

Georges Bernanos: "Sous le soleil de Satan"
Book-of-the-Month Club founded
Louis Bromfield: "Early Autumn"
Karel Capek: "Letters from England"
Nobel Prize for Literature: Grazia Deledda
Concha Espina: "Altar mayor"
William Faulkner: "Soldier's Pay"
John Galsworthy: "The Silver Spoon"
André Gide: "Les Faux Monnayeurs"
Paul Green: "In Abraham's Bosom," Provincetown
Ernest Hemingway: "The Sun Also Rises"
Sidney Howard: "The Silver Cord," drama
Franz Kafka: "The Castle" (posth.)
D. H. Lawrence: "The Plumed Serpent"
T. E. Lawrence: "The Seven Pillars of Wisdom"
Sinclair Lewis turns down $1,000 Pulitzer Prize for "Arrowsmith"
Amy Lowell: "What's O'Clock," Pulitzer Prize for poetry
Emil Ludwig: "Bismarck" and "Wilhelm II"
Maurice Maeterlinck: "The Life of the Termites"
W. Somerset Maugham: "The Casuarina Tree" and "The Constant Wife"
A. A. Milne: "Winnie the Pooh"
Henri de Montherlant: "Les Bestiaires"
Alfred Neumann: "Der Teufel"
Sean O'Casey: "The Plough and the Stars," London
Eugene O'Neill: "The Great God Brown"
Rainer Maria Rilke, Ger. poet, d. (b. 1875)
B. Traven: "Das Totenschiff"
Edgar Wallace: "The Ringer"
H. G. Wells: "The World of William Clissold"
Thornton Wilder: "The Cabala"
Israel Zangwill, Eng. novelist, d. (b. 1864)
Ronald Firbank, Eng. writer, d. (b. 1886)
W. L. George, Eng. novelist ("The City of Light"), d.
Jean Richepin, Fr. writer, d. (b. 1849)
George Sterling, Amer. poet, d. (b. 1869)
Arthur Walkley, Eng. dramatic critic, d. (b. 1855)
Bestseller: "Sorrell and Son," by Warwick Deeping

C. RELIGION, PHILOSOPHY, LEARNING

Rudolf Eucken, Ger. philosopher, d. (b. 1846)
Elley Key, Swed. educationalist, d. (b. 1849)
J. M. Keynes: "The End of Laissez-Faire"
Emil Kraepelin, Ger. psychiatrist, d. (b. 1856)
Kenneth Lindsay: "Social Progress and Educational Waste"
Ger. stigmatic Therese Neumann (1898—1962) in the Bavarian village of Konnersreuth
Reading University, England, founded
M. Rostovzeff: "Social and Economic History of the Roman Empire"
R. H. Tawney: "Religion and the Rise of Capitalism"
G. M. Trevelyan: "History of England"
Paul Valéry: "Propos sur l'intelligence"
Sir Erskine Holland, Eng. jurist, d. (b. 1835)
Ernest Belfort Bax, Eng. philosopher, d. (b. 1854)
Cardinal Joseph Mercier, Belg. philosopher, d. (b. 1851)
Charles W. Eliot, Amer. educator, president of Harvard University, d. (b. 1834)
Sarah Lawrence College founded in Bronxville, N.Y.

D. VISUAL ARTS	E. MUSIC	F. SCIENCE, TECHNOLOGY, GROWTH	G. DAILY LIFE	
		Clarence Darrow (prosecutor, William Jennings Bryan); Scopes is convicted, then acquitted on technicality		**1925 contd**
Marc Chagall: "Lover's Bouquet" Jacob Epstein: "The Visitation" Films: "Metropolis" (Fritz Lang); "Faust" (Murnau); "Mother" (Pudovkin); "Ben Hur" (Niblo); "Don Juan" (John Barrymore) Augustus John: "Lady Morrell," portrait Oskar Kokoschka: "Terrace in Richmond" Ernst Lubitsch leaves Berlin for Hollywood Claude Monet, Fr. painter, d. (b. 1840) Henry Moore: "Draped Reclining Figure" Edvard Munch: "The Red House" J. S. Sargent, Memorial Exhibition, Royal Academy, London Stanley Spencer, murals for Burghclere Chapel, Hampshire (—1934) Rudolph Valentino, after finishing the picture "The Son of the Sheik," d. (b. 1895) Mary Cassatt, Amer. impressionist painter, d. (b. 1845) Joseph Pennell, Amer. etcher, d. (b. 1857)	Eugene D'Albert: "The Golem," opera, Frankfurt George Antheil: "Ballet Mécanique" Béla Bartók: "The Miraculous Mandarin," ballet, Cologne Alban Berg: "Lyric Suite" Duke Ellington's first records appear Hans Werner Henze b. Paul Hindemith: "Cardillac," opera, Dresden Arthur Honegger: "Judith," opera, Monte Carlo Emmerich Kálmán: "Die Zirkusprinzessin," Vienna Zoltán Kodály: "Háry János," Budapest Ernst Krenek: "Orpheus und Eurydike," opera, Cassel "Jelly Roll" Morton's first recordings of jazz appear Giacomo Puccini: "Turandot," La Scala, Milan (posth.) Sigmund Romberg: "The Desert Song," New York The first edition Richard Strauss-Hugo von Hofmannsthal correspondence published Siegfried Wagner: "The Angel of Peace," opera, Karlsruhe William Walton: Suite No. 1, "Façade" Kurt Weill: "The Protagonist," opera, Dresden Franz Kneisel, Amer.-Rum. violinist (Kneisel string quartet), d. (b. 1865) *(contd)*	Amundsen, Ellsworth, and Nobile fly over North Pole to Alaska in airship "Norge" Richard E. Byrd and Floyd Bennett fly from Spitsbergen to North Pole and back Brit. General Electricity Board established John Dryer, Dan. astronomer, d. "Electrola," new electric recording technique, developed Nobel Prize for Medicine: Johannes Fibiger for cancer research Robert H. Goddard (U.S.) fires the first liquid fuel rocket Werner Heisenberg further develops the quantum theory B. C. P. Jansen and W. F. Donath isolate vitamin B in pure form James Jeans formulates a new stellar theory Kodak produces the first 16mm movie film Thomas H. Morgan (U.S.): "The Theory of the Gene" W. P. Murphy and George Minot treat pernicious anemia with liver extract Nobel Prize for Physics: Jean Baptiste Perrin for his discovery of the equilibrium of sedimentation Photomaton constructed by Russ. inventor Anatole Josepho Scott Polar Research Institute opened in Cambridge, England Hermann Staudinger (1881—1965) explores macromolecular chemistry U.S. biochemist James B. Sumner (1887—1955) observes urease, an enzyme essential to the nitrogen cycle Nobel Prize for Chemistry: Theodor Svedberg for work on disperse systems Gertrude Bell, Eng. traveler and archaeologist, d. (b. 1868) Luther Burbank, Amer. horticulturist, d. (b. 1849) Camillo Golgi, Ital. physician, Nobel Prize for Medicine 1906, d. (b. 1844) James F. Kemp, Amer. geologist, d. (b. 1859) William Bateson, Eng. biologist, d. (b. 1861) Heinke Kamerlingh-Onnes, Dutch physicist, Nobel Prize 1913, d. (b. 1853) Sir William Tilden, Eng. chemist, d. (b. 1842) George Washington Bridge planned to span Hudson River between Fort Lee, N. J., and Fort Washington in Manhattan *(contd)*	Alan Cobham flies from Croydon, England, to Capetown and back to investigate the feasibility of long-distance air routes Emile Coué, Fr. psychotherapist ("Day by day, in every way, I am getting better and better"), d. (b. 1857) Deutsche Lufthansa airline founded Gertrude Ederle (U.S.) becomes the first woman to swim the Eng. Channel; record time, 14 hours 34 minutes Brit. Imperial Chemical Industries (I.C.I.) formed H. L. Mencken: "Notes on Democracy" Permanent wave invented by Antonio Buzzacchino Statistics–population (in millions): U.S.S.R. 148, U.S. 115, Japan 85, Germany 64, Britain 45; petroleum production in U.S. 771 million barrels; Brit. merchant fleet: 12 million tons; Freemasons: 4.2 million in 28,000 lodges; religious orders in Germany: 559 male with 10,000 members, 6,600 female with 74,000 members August Thyssen, Ger. industrialist, d. (b. 1842) Gene Tunney wins heavyweight boxing championship from Jack Dempsey Reforms in Turkey include the abolition of polygamy, modernization of female attire, prohibition of fez, and (1928) adoption of Lat. alphabet H. Vierkotter swims the Channel in 12 hours, 40 minutes Edward W. Scripps, Amer. newspaper publisher, d. (b. 1854) Cushioned cork-center baseball introduced Tennis–Suzanne Lenglen (Fr.) defeats Helen Wills (U.S.) in "The Match of the Century"–the only time they meet U.S. Golf Association Amateur championship won by George Von Elm, defeating Bobby Jones; Open won by Bobby Jones Alabama defeats Washington 20—19 in Rose Bowl football game W. T. Tilden, II, loses singles to Lacoste of France, but U.S. retains Davis Cup for seventh year *(contd)*	**1926**

A. HISTORY, POLITICS | B. LITERATURE, THEATER | C. RELIGION, PHILOSOPHY, LEARNING

1926 contd

1927

A. HISTORY, POLITICS

Inter-Allied military control of Germany ends
Economic conference in Geneva attended by 52 nations
Parliament House in Canberra, Australia, opened
"Black Friday" in Germany–the economic system collapses
Masaryk reelected President of Czechoslovakia
Socialists riot in Vienna; general strike takes place following acquittal of Nazis for political murder
Gottfried Feder publishes "The Program of the N.S.D.A.P." (Hitler's Nazi Party)
F. B. Kellogg, U.S. Secretary of State, suggests pact for renunciation of war
Trotsky expelled from Communist Party
Ion Bratianu, Rum. statesman, d. (b. 1864)
Carlotta, former Empress of Mexico, d. (b. 1840)
John Dillon, Ir. nationalist leader, d. (b. 1851)
Ferdinand I, King of Rumania, d. (b. 1851)
Lyman J. Gage, Amer. politician, d. (b. 1836)
Leonid B. Krassin, Russ. Soviet politician, d. (b. 1870)
5th Marquis of Lansdowne, Eng. statesman, Governor General of Canada, Viceroy of India, d. (b. 1845)
Kevin O'Higgins, Ir. politician, assassinated (b. 1892)
Sergei Sazonov, Russ. czarist statesman, d. (b. 1861)
Zaghlul Pasha, Egyptian statesman, d. (b. 1860)
Janis Cakste, first President of Latvia, d. (b. 1859)

B. LITERATURE, THEATER

Nobel Prize for Literature: Henri Bergson (Fr.)
Georg Brandes, Dan. literary critic, d. (b. 1842)
Louis Bromfield: "Early Autumn," Pulitzer Prize for novel
Cambridge History of English Literature completed (begun 1907; 15 vols.)
Willa Cather: "Death Comes for the Archbishop"
Jean Cocteau: "Orphée" and "Oedipe-Roi"
Olav Duun: "Olsoy-gutane," Norw. novel
John Erskine: "Adam and Eve"
A. A. Fadeyev: "Razgrom," Russ. novel
Jean Giraudoux: "Eglantine," novel
Knut Hamsun: "Vagabonds"
Maximilian Harden, Ger. political writer, d. (b. 1861)
Ernest Hemingway: "Men without Women," short stories
Hermann Hesse: "Steppenwolf"
Jerome K. Jerome, Eng. novelist and dramatist, d. (b. 1859)
Franz Kafka: "Amerika," fragment of a novel (posth.)
E. A. Robinson: "Tristram," Pulitzer Prize for poetry (1928)
Mazo de la Roche: "Jalna"
Sinclair Lewis: "Elmer Gantry"
François Mauriac: "Thérèse Desqueyroux," novel
Henri Michaux: "Qui je fus," poems
Marcel Proust: "A la recherche du temps perdu" (posth.)
Robert E. Sherwood: "The Road to Rome"
Upton Sinclair: "Oil!"
B. Traven: "The Treasure of the Sierra Madre"
Georg von der Vring: "Soldier Suhren"
Best seller: Thornton Wilder, "The Bridge of San Luis Rey," Pulitzer Prize (1928)
Henry Williamson: "Tarka the Otter"
Virginia Woolf: "To the Lighthouse"
Arnold Zweig: "Der Streit um den Sergeanten Grischa," Ger. war novel
Stefan Zweig: "Sternstunden der Menschheit," essays
Mikhail Artzybashev, Russ. author, d. (b. 1878)
William Le Queux, Eng. novelist (mystery fiction), d. (b. 1864)
Matilda Serao, Ital. psychological novelist, d. (b. 1856)
Arnold Daly, Amer. actor and producer, d. (b. 1875)
W. B. Yeats: "The Tower"
Paul Claudel: "Christophe Colomb"

C. RELIGION, PHILOSOPHY, LEARNING

Léon Brunschvicg (1869—1944): "The Progress of Knowledge in the Western Philosophy" (Fr. rationalism)
John Dewey: "The Public and Its Problems"
Sigmund Freud: "The Future of an Illusion"
Adolf von Harnack: "The Origin of Christian Theology and the Canonical Dogma"
Martin Heidegger: "Sein und Zeit" (existentialist philosophy)
Lucien Lévy-Bruhl: "The Primitives and the Supernatural"
Bertrand Russell: "The Analysis of Matter"
Luigi Luzzatti, Ital. economist and statesman, d. (b. 1841)
Benjamin Purnell, Amer. religious leader, founder of "The House of David," Benton Harbor, Mich., d. (b. 1861)
Edward B. Titchener, Amer. psychologist, d. (b. 1867)
Charles D. Walcott, Amer. geologist and paleontologist, d. (b. 1850)
D. G. Hogarth, Eng. archaeologist, d. (b. 1862)
Walter Leaf, Eng. Homeric scholar and banker, d. (b. 1852)
Houston Stewart Chamberlain, Wagner's son-in-law, Eng.-born Ger. philosopher of Aryanism, d. (b. 1855)

D. VISUAL ARTS	E. MUSIC	F. SCIENCE, TECHNOLOGY, GROWTH	G. DAILY LIFE	
	Popular songs: "One Alone" and "Desert Song" from "The Desert Song"; "Blue Room"; "When Day Is Done"; "I Found a Million-Dollar Baby in the Five-and-Ten-Cent Store"; "Bye, Bye, Blackbird"		St. Louis (NL) defeats New York (AL) 4—3 to win World Series Harry Houdini, Amer. escapologist, d. (b. 1874)	**1926 contd**
Georges Braque: "Glass and Fruit," Fr. expressionism Edward Burra: "Terrace," Eng. expressionism Marc Chagall: "Fables of La Fontaine," 100 etchings (published 1952) Charles Demuth: "Egyptian Impression," Amer. cubism Jacob Epstein: "Madonna and Child" Films: "The Jazz Singer" (Jolson), the first talkie; "Flesh and the Devil" (Garbo); "King of Kings" (C. B. De Mille); "Berlin" (Ruttmann); "Underworld" (Sternberg); "Wedding March" (von Stroheim) George Grosz: "Portrait of the Poet Max Hermann-Neisse" Edward Hopper: "Manhattan Bridge," Amer. modern Oskar Kokoschka: "Courmayeur 1927" Le Corbusier, architect, designs Maison de Monzies (Garches) Henri Matisse: "Figures with Ornamental Background" Louis Fuertes, Amer. naturalist illustrator, d. (b. 1874) Rex Whistler: *(contd)*	Franco Alfano: "Madonna Imperia," opera, Turin Bach: "The Art of the Fugue," orchestral arrangement by Wolfgang Graeser (1906—1928) Aaron Copland: premiere of "Concerto for Piano and Orchestra," Boston Symphony Orchestra George Gershwin: "Funny Face," New York Alois Hába develops his theory of quarter-tone harmony Arthur Honegger: music to Abel Gance's film "Napoleon" Jerome Kern and Oscar Hammerstein II: "Show Boat," New York Erich Wolfgang Korngold: "Das Wunder der Heliane," opera, Hamburg Ernst Krenek: "Jonny spielt auf," Leipzig Franz Lehár: "The Tsarevich," Berlin Darius Milhaud: "Le Pauvre Matelot," Paris, Opéra-Comique Richard Rodgers and Lorenz Hart: "A Connecticut Yankee," New York Emil Mollenhauer, Amer. violinist and conductor, d. (b. 1855) Albert Roussel: Piano concerto in G major Feodor Chaliapin: "Pages from my Life," autobiography Dmitri Shostakovich: Symphony No. 2 Igor Stravinsky: "Oedipus Rex," Paris Lev Theremin invents the earliest electronic musical instrument Harry Tierney: "Rio Rita," New York Kurt Weill: "Royal Palace," Berlin; "Aufstieg und Fall der Stadt Mahagonny," Baden-Baden Jaromir Weinberger: "Schwanda the Bagpipe Player," Prague Ermanno Wolf-Ferrari: "Sly," La Scala, Milan *(contd)*	Svante Arrhenius, Swed. chemist, d. (b. 1859) Nobel Prize for Physics: A. H. Compton (U.S.) for the discovery of wavelength change in diffused x-rays, and C. T. R. Wilson (Scot.) for discovery of technique of making charged particle tracks visible Albert W. Hall adds improvements to fluorescent lamps W. Heitler researches the wave mechanics of valence Siegfried Junjhans perfects a process for continuous casting of nonferrous metal Hudson Maxim, Amer. inventor, d. (b. 1853) Thomas H. Morgan: "Experimental Embryology" C. K. Ogden founds the London Orthological Institute I. P. Pavlov: "Conditioned Reflexes" Nobel Prize for Medicine: Wagner von Jauregg (Aust.) for treatment of dementia paralytica with malaria inoculation George Whipple conducts his experiments on pernicious anemia and tuberculosis Ernest H. Starling, Eng. physiologist (secretin), d. (b. 1866) Nobel Prize for Chemistry: Heinrich Wieland (Ger.) for researches into the constitution of bile acids Nobel Prize for Physics: Charles Wilson (Brit.) for making visible the paths of electrically charged particles by vapor condensation Sir Harry H. Johnston, Brit. explorer (Mt. Kilimanjaro), d. (b. 1858) Charles A. Lindbergh (b. 1902) flies monoplane, "Spirit of St. Louis," *(contd)*	Alexander Alekhine (1892—1946) becomes world chess champion (—1935) Josephine Baker, Parisian star Brit. Broadcasting Corporation takes over from Brit. Broadcasting Company First Exhibition for Space Flights, Moscow Great Moffat Tunnel through Rocky Mountains opened Harlem Globetrotters basketball team organized by Abe Saperstein Sonja Henie (Norw.) ice-skating champion (—1936) Industrial Health and Safety Centre, London, opened Airplanes first used to "dust" crops with insecticide (forest trees in Canada) Jockey Johnny Longden (U.S.) begins career (5,232 wins up to 1953) Great flood disaster in Lower Mississippi Valley Babe Ruth hits 60 home runs for the New York Yankees Sacco and Vanzetti executed Slow fox trot fashionable dance Vickers-Armstrong Ltd. (machine, shipbuilding, and armament industries) formed in London Johnny Weissmuller swims 100 yards in 51 seconds Deepest well in the world (8,000 feet) sunk in Orange County, Calif. White City Grounds, London, taken over by Greyhound Racing Association Helen Wills wins Ladies Lawn Tennis Championship at Wimbledon Henry E. Huntington, Amer. railroad executive and collector (Huntington Library, San Marino, Calif.), d. (b. 1850) Lizzie Borden, central figure in unsolved Fall River, Mass., murder mystery, d. (b. 1860) Isadora Duncan, Amer. dancer, d. (b. 1878) U.S. Lawn Tennis Association Men's Singles championship won by René Lacoste (Fr.); Women's Singles by Helen N. Wills U.S. Golf Association Amateur championship won by Bobby Jones; Open by Tommy Armour Ruth Snyder and Judd Gray convicted of murder of Albert *(contd)*	**1927**

	A. HISTORY, POLITICS	B. LITERATURE, THEATER	C. RELIGION, PHILOSOPHY, LEARNING
1927 contd			

1928

A. HISTORY, POLITICS

Douglas, Earl Haig, Brit. field marshal d. (b. 1861)
H. H. Asquith, Earl of Oxford and Asquith, Prime Minister of Great Britain (1908—1916), d. (b. 1852)
Gen. Antonio Carmona becomes President of Portugal
Women's suffrage in Britain reduced from age of 30 to 21
Socialist Party nominates Norman Thomas for U.S. presidency
Workers' Party nominates William Z. Foster for U.S. presidency
Italy signs 20-year treaty of friendship with Ethiopia
Kellogg-Briand Pact, outlawing war, signed in Paris by 65 states
Albania proclaimed kingdom; Zog I elected king
Beginning of first Five-Year Plan in U.S.S.R.
Chiang Kai-shek elected President of China
Herbert Hoover, Republican, elected U.S. President with 444 electoral votes; Democratic candidate Al Smith gets 87 votes
Owen D. Young Committee appointed to examine reparations question
Chauncey M. Depew, U.S. politician, lawyer, and wit, d. (b. 1834)
Giovanni Giolitti, Ital. statesman, d. (b. 1842)
Robert Lansing, U.S. statesman, d. (b. 1864)
Prince Lichnowsky, Ger. diplomat, ambassador to Great Britain (1912—1914), d. (b. 1860)
Alvaro Obregón, President of Mexico, assassinated (b. 1880)
William O'Brien, Ir. nationalist leader, d. (b. 1852)
Stefan Radic, Croat politician, assassinated (b. 1871)
Rushdi Pasha, Egyptian statesman, d. (b. 1871)
Satyendra Sinha, Indian statesman, d. (b. 1864)
Baron Piotr Wrangel, Russ. anti-Bolshevik general, d. (b. 1878)

B. LITERATURE, THEATER

Philip Barry: "Holiday," comedy
Stephen Vincent Benét: "John Brown's Body," novel in verse, Pulitzer Prize for poetry (1929)
Colette: "La Naissance du jour"
John Van Druten: "Young Woodley," London
"The New English Dictionary" completed (10 vols. since 1888)
John Galsworthy: "Swan Song"
Federico García Lorca: "Mariana Pineda"
Jean Giraudoux: "Siegfried"
Moscow Habima Theater makes triumphant tour of Palestine
Margaret Radclyffe Hall: "The Well of Loneliness"
Thomas Hardy, Eng. poet and novelist, d. (b. 1840)
Ben Hecht and Charles MacArthur: "The Front Page," drama
Aldous Huxley: "Point Counterpoint"
Christopher Isherwood: "All the Conspirators"
Panait Istrati: "Mes départs"
Klabund, Ger. poet, d. (b. 1890)
Selma Lagerlöf: "Anna Svärd"
D. H. Lawrence: "Lady Chatterley's Lover"
Sinclair Lewis: "The Man Who Knew Coolidge"
Holbrook Blinn, Amer. actor, d. (b. 1872)
Avery Hopwood, Amer. dramatist, d. (b. 1882)
François Mauriac: "Vie de Racine"
André Maurois: "Climats"
Edna St. Vincent Millay "Buck in the Snow"
Sean O'Casey: "The Silver Tassie"
Eugene O'Neill: "Strange Interlude," Pulitzer Prize for drama; "Marco Millions"; "Lazarus Laughed"
Carl Sandburg: "Good Morning, America"
Dorothy L. Sayers: "Lord Peter Views the Body"
M. A. Sholokhov: "And Quiet Flows the Don" (4 vols. —1940)
Upton Sinclair: "Boston"
Hermann Sudermann, Ger. dramatist, d. (b. 1857)
Ellen Terry, Eng. actress, d. (b. 1848)
Nobel Prize for Literature: Sigrid Undset (Norw.)
Edgar Wallace: "The Squeaker"
Evelyn Waugh: "Decline and Fall"
Virginia Woolf: "Orlando"
Vicente Blasco-Ibáñez, Span. novelist, d. (b. 1867)
C. E. Montague, Eng. journalist and drama critic, d. (b. 1867)

C. RELIGION, PHILOSOPHY, LEARNING

Rudolf Carnap: "The Logical Structure of the World" (Neo-Positivism)
Emile Chartier: "Le Citoyen contre les pouvoirs"
Ecumenical Missionary Conference held in Jerusalem
A. S. Eddington: "The Nature of the Physical World"
A new edition of the "Encyclopaedia Judaica" begins to appear (—1934)
C. G. Jung: "Relationships between the Ego and the Unconscious"
Emil Ludwig: "Christ"
Salvador de Madariaga: "Ingleses, franceses, españoles"
Benito Mussolini: "My Autobiography"
Vernon L. Parrington: "Main Currents in American Thought," Pulitzer Prize for history
Ludwig Pastor (1854—1928): "History of the Popes" (begun in 1886)
Pope Pius XI's encyclical: "Mortalium animus"
Max Scheler, Ger. philosopher, d. (b. 1874)
George Bernard Shaw: "The Intelligent Woman's Guide to Socialism and Capitalism"
Theodor Hendrik van der Velde: "The Perfect Marriage"
Viscount Haldane, Brit. philosopher and statesman, d. (b. 1856)
Augusta Stetson, Amer. Christian Science leader, d. (b. 1842)
William G. Hale, Amer. classical scholar, d. (b. 1849)
Sir George Otto Trevelyan, Eng. historian, d. (b. 1838)
Talcott Williams, Amer. journalist (first director of the Columbia School of Journalism), d. (b. 1849)

D. VISUAL ARTS	E. MUSIC	F. SCIENCE, TECHNOLOGY, GROWTH	G. DAILY LIFE	
frescoes in the Tate Gallery restaurant, London Heinrich Zille: "The Great Zille-Album," scenes from daily life in Berlin Sir Sid Colvin, Eng. art critic, d. (b. 1845) Academy of Motion Picture Arts and Sciences founded	Vincent Youmans: "Hit the Deck" Popular songs: "Ol' Man River" from "Show Boat"; "My Heart Stood Still"; "My Blue Heaven"; "Let a Smile Be Your Umbrella"; "Blue Skies"	nonstop from New York to Paris in 33.5 hours 15 millionth Model "T" Ford produced "Iron Lung" developed by P. Drinker and L. A. Shaw Holland Tunnel opens as first vehicular tunnel linking New York and New Jersey	Snyder, her husband; electrocuted at Sing Sing in 1928 Alabama ties Stanford in Rose Bowl football game France wins Davis Cup (tennis) New York AL defeats Pittsburgh (NL) 4—0 to win World Series	**1927 contd**
Congrès Internationaux d'Architecture Moderne founded in Geneva Max Beckmann: "Black Lilies" Georges Braque: "Still Life with Jug," Fr. cubism Marc Chagall: "Wedding" Films: The first Mickey Mouse films (Disney); "The Circus" (Chaplin); "October" (Eisenstein); "Italian Straw Hat" (Clair); "The Passion of Joan of Arc" (Dreyer); "Thérèse Raquin" (Feyder); "Storm over Asia" (Pudovkin); "The Woman on the Moon" (Lang) Kenwood House, Middlesex (holding Lord Iveagh's art collection), opened to the public Hugo Lederer: "Runners," bronze sculpture Henri Matisse: "Seated Odalisque" Edvard Munch: "Girl on Sofa," Norw. expressionist painting Georgia O'Keeffe: "Nightwave," Amer. abstract painting Amédée Ozenfant: "L'art" ("Purism") Shakespeare Memorial Theatre, Stratford-upon-Avon, designed by Elisabeth Scott Arthur B. Davies, Amer. painter, d. (b. 1862) Richard E. Outcault, Amer. cartoonist ("Buster Brown" comic strip), d. (b. 1863) John Sloan: "Sixth *(contd)*	Eugene D'Albert: "The Black Orchid," opera, Leipzig Marion Bauer: "Lament on African Themes," for strings George Gershwin: "An American in Paris," New York Arthur Honegger: "Rugby," movement symphonie Leos Janácek, Czech composer, d. (b. 1854) Franz Lehár: "Frederika," operetta, Berlin Francesco Malipiero: "Filomela e l'Infatuato," opera, Prague Maurice Ravel: "Bolero" Sigmund Romberg: "New Moon," New York Karlheinz Stockhausen, Ger. composer, b. Richard Strauss: "Die Aegyptische Helena," opera, Dresden Igor Stravinsky: "Apollo Musagetes," ballet Toscanini named conductor of the New York Philharmonic Symphony Orchestra (—1936) Kurt Weill: "Die Dreigroschenoper," Berlin Henry F. B. Gilbert, Amer. composer (ballet "The Dance in Place Congo"), d. (b. 1868) Popular songs: "Bill"; "Am I Blue?"; "Crazy Rhythm"; "Makin' Whoopee"; *(contd)*	Roald Amundsen, Norw. explorer, d. (b. 1872) while attempting to rescue Ital. explorer Nobile whose airship has crashed in the Arctic J. L. Baird demonstrates color T.V. Franz Boas: "Anthropology and Modern Life," confutes Fascist theory of "master race" P. A. M. Dirac replaces the conventional single second-order wave equation with four simultaneous first-order equations Alexander Fleming (1881—1954) discovers penicillin H. Geiger and W. Muller construct the "Geiger counter" Hendrik Antoon Lorentz, Dutch physicist, d. (b. 1853) Nobel Prize for Medicine: Charles Nicolle (Fr.) for his work on typhus F. A. Paneth (1887—1958) founds radio chemistry Indian physicist C. V. Raman discovers the Raman effect: a change in wavelength of light that is scattered by molecules Nobel Prize for Physics: Sir Owen Richardson (Brit.) for the discovery of the "Richardson effect" Serge Veronoff: "The Conquest of Life" (on rejuvenation by transplanting glands) Brit. inventor and aviator Frank C. Whittle, trained at R.A.F. College, Cranwell, and qualifying as a pilot, is posted to No. 111 Fighter Squadron Wilhelm Wien, Ger. physicist, d. (b. 1864) Nobel Prize for Chemistry: Adolf Windaus (Ger.) for his work on the constitution of sterins and their connection with vitamins Otto Nordenskjöld, Swed. geologist and explorer, d. (b. 1869) Sir Henry Wickham, Eng. explorer, d. (b. 1846) John Coulter, Amer. botanist, d. (b. 1851) Johannes Fibiger, Dan. pathologist, *(contd)*	Brazil's economy collapses owing to over-production of coffee Joe Davis (Chesterfield) wins Brit. Professional Billiards Championship Female fashion–Garçonne style (after the novel "La Garçonne," by Victor Margueritte) A machine for boning and cleaning kippers makes its initial run at Fleetwood, England Köhl, Fitzmaurice, and Huenefeld become the first to fly the Atlantic from east to west: 6,750 km. in 35.5 hours Olympic Games in Amsterdam–22 sports, 120 events, 3,015 participants; Nurmi wins his sixth gold medal; 19-year-old Canadian schoolboy Percy Williams wins the sprints; women participate for the first time; Sonja Henie (Norw.) ice-skating champion (till 1936–three times Olympic, 10 times world champion) Emmeline Pankhurst, Eng. suffragist, d. (b. 1858) Statistics–1,776 Esperanto groups throughout the world; Al Jolson's song "Sonny Boy" sells 12 million records in four weeks; gold production: South Africa, $214 million; U.S., $44 million; Russia, $44 million; Canada, $39 million Teleprinters and teletypewriters come into restricted use in U.S., Britain, and Germany Abnormally high tide causes River Thames to overflow and burst its banks George W. Goethals, Amer. chief engineer on Panama Canal Commission, d. (b. 1858) Gene Tunney retires; Jack Sharkey becomes world heavyweight boxing champion First scheduled television broadcasts by WGY, Schenectady, N.Y. Amelia Earhart is first woman to fly across the Atlantic U.S. Lawn Tennis Association *(contd)*	**1928**

	A. HISTORY, POLITICS	B. LITERATURE, THEATER	C. RELIGION, PHILOSOPHY, LEARNING
1928 contd			
1929	Dictatorship is established in Yugoslavia under King Alexander I; constitution suppressed Inter-Amer. Treaty of Arbitration signed in Washington Trotsky expelled from the U.S.S.R. Lateran Treaty establishes independent Vatican City Ferdinand Foch, Marshal of France, d. (b. 1851) Herbert C. Hoover inaugurated as 31st President of the U.S. Brit. General Election: Labour 287 seats, Conservatives 261, Liberals 59 Ramsay MacDonald forms Labour Government in Britain; Arthur Henderson named Foreign Secretary Kellogg-Briand Pact comes into force Pope Pius XI leaves Vatican for the first time Aristide Briand elected Premier of France Arabs attack Jews in Palestine following disputes over Jewish use of the Wailing Wall Gustav Stresemann, Ger. statesman, d. (b. 1878) Name of Serbo-Croat-Slovene Kingdom changed to Yugoslavia Australian Labour Party wins elections Georges Clemenceau, Fr. statesman, d. (b. 1841) Round Table Conference between Viceroy and Indian leaders on dominion status Nobel Peace Prize: Frank B. Kellogg (U.S.) Hitler appoints Himmler "Reichsführer S.S." Jewish Agency becomes representative of all Zionist and non-Zionist Jews Count Gyula Andrassy, Hungarian statesman, d. (b. 1860) Myron Herrick, Amer. politician and diplomat, d. (b. 1854) 5th Earl of Rosebery, Brit. statesman who won his three wishes: he married the richest heiress in England, won the Derby (three times), and became prime minister, d. (b. 1847) Baron Tanaka, Jap. statesman and soldier, d. (b. 1863) Albert B. Fall, Secretary of the Interior under Coolidge, convicted of accepting $100,000 bribe from Edward L. Dohemy in Teapot Dome scandal; he is sentenced to one year's imprisonment and to $100,000 fine	Vicki Baum: "Grand Hotel" Robert Bridges: "The Testament of Beauty" Jean Cocteau: "Les Enfants terribles" Alfred Döblin: "Berlin Alexanderplatz" William Faulkner: "Sartoris" and "The Sound and the Fury," first of series in Yoknapatawpha County André Gide: "L'Ecole des femmes" (trilogy —1936) Jean Giono: "Un de Beaumugnes" Jean Giraudoux: "Amphitryon 38" Robert Graves: "Goodbye to All That" Julian Green: "Léviathan" Ernest Hemingway: "A Farewell to Arms" Audrey Hepburn, Eng. actress, b. Hugo von Hofmannsthal, Aust. poet, d. (b. 1874) Arno Holz, Ger. author, d. (b. 1863) Richard Hughes: "A High Wind in Jamaica" Mazo de la Roche: "Whiteoaks of Jalna" Sinclair Lewis: "Dodsworth" Vachel Lindsay: "Every Soul is a Circus," poems Nobel Prize for Literature: Thomas Mann (Ger.) Charles Morgan: "Portrait in a Mirror" Axel Munthe: "The Story of San Michele," best seller John Osborne, Eng. dramatist, b. Julia Peterkin: "Scarlet Sister Mary," Pulitzer Prize novel John Cowper Powys: "Wolf Solent" J. B. Priestley: "The Good Companions" Erich Maria Remarque: "All Quiet on the Western Front," best seller Elmer Rice: "Street Scene," Pulitzer Prize for drama Antoine de Saint-Exupéry: "Courrier Sud Shaw: "The Apple Cart," London R. C. Sherriff: "Journey's End," London Aleksei N. Tolstoi: "Peter the Great" (3 vols. —1945) Edmund Wilson: "I Thought of Daisy" Salvatore Quasimodo: "Acque e Terre" Thomas Wolfe: "Look Homeward, Angel" Virginia Woolf: "A Room of One's Own," essays Stefan Zweig: "Joseph Fouché" Katherine Lee Bates, Amer. author ("America the Beautiful"), d. (b. 1859) Bliss Carman, Canadian poet, d. (b. 1861) Edward Carpenter, Eng. writer, d. (b. 1844) Henry Arthur Jones, Eng. dramatist, d. (b. 1851) Brander Matthews, Amer. educator and author, d. (b. 1851) Flora Annie Steel, Eng. novelist, d. (b. 1847)	The Presbyterian Churches in Scotland unite to form the Church of Scotland John Dewey: "The Quest for Certainty" Martin Heidegger: "What is Philosophy?" Walter Lippmann: "Preface to Morals" Lutheran World Conference held in Copenhagen José Ortega y Gasset: "La Rebelión de las masas" Eugenio Pacelli (future Pope Pius XII) created a cardinal Erich Przywara: "Kierkegaard's Secret" Bertrand Russell: "Marriage and Morals" The "Vienna Circle" (logical positivism, operationism, behaviorism) formed by Carnap, Hahn, Neurath, Schlick, et al. A. N. Whitehead: "The Function of Reason" Thorstein Veblen, Amer. social scientist, d. (b. 1857) Katherine Tingley, Amer. theosophist leader, d. (b. 1847) Sir William Dawkins, Brit. geologist and archaeologist, d. (b. 1838) Harrison Dyar, Amer. entomologist, d. (b. 1866) Rodolfo Lanciani, Ital. archaeologist, d. (b. 1846)

D. VISUAL ARTS	E. MUSIC	F. SCIENCE, TECHNOLOGY, GROWTH	G. DAILY LIFE	
Avenue and Third Street," Ashcan school Warner Bros. releases "The Lights of New York," longest sound film to date Juan Gris d. (b. 1887)	"You're the Cream in My Coffee"; "Button Up Your Overcoat"	1926 Nobel Prize for Medicine, d. (b. 1867) Finn Malgran, Swed. metereologist, d. Hideyo Noguchi, Jap. bacteriologist, d. (b. 1876) Theodore Richards, Amer. chemist, d. (b. 1868) First color motion pictures exhibited by George Eastman in Rochester, N.Y. "New York Times" installs "moving" electric sign around Times Building	Men's Singles championship won by H. Cochet (Fr.); Women's Singles by Helen N. Wills U.S. Golf Association Amateur championship won by Bobby Jones; Open by Johnny Farrell Stanford defeats Pittsburgh 7—6 in Rose Bowl football game New York (AL) defeats St. Louis (NL) 4—0 to win World Series	**1928 contd**
Wilhelm von Bode, Ger. art expert, d. (b. 1845) Marc Chagall: "Love Idyll" Salvador Dali joins surrealist group Jacob Epstein: "Night and Day," sculpture (London Transport Building) Lyonel Feininger; "Sailing Boats," cubist painting Films: "The Love Parade" (Lubitsch); "Blackmail" (Hitchcock); "Hallelujah!" (Vidor); "Broadway Melody" (first of the great revue films); "Turksib" (Turin); "General Line" (Eisenstein); "Pandora's Box" (Pabst); the first musical Mickey Mouse films (Disney); revolutionary changes: "talkies" kill silent films Paul Klee: "Fool in a Trance" Le Corbusier: "The City of Tomorrow" Museum of Modern Art opens in New York with exhibition of works by Cézanne, Gauguin, Seurat, and Van Gogh Paul Nash: "March" Georgia O'Keeffe: "Black Flower and Blue Larkspur" Pablo Picasso: *(contd)*	George Antheil: "Transatlantic," opera Ralph Benatzky: "White Horse Inn," Berlin Aaron Copland: "Symphonic Ode" Noël Coward: "Bitter Sweet" operetta, London Sergei P. Diaghilev, Russ. ballet impressario, d. (b. 1872) George Gershwin: "Show Girl" Eugene Goossens: "Judith," opera, London Paul Hindemith: "Neues vom Tage," opera, Berlin Ernst Krenek: "Diary of a Journey through the Austrian Alps," song cycle, Op. 62 Constant Lambert: "Rio Grande" Franz Lehár: "The Land of Smiles," operetta, Berlin André Messager, Fr. composer, d. (b. 1853) Oxford History of Music begins to appear Walter Piston, Suite No. 1 Hermann Scherchen: "Handbook of Conducting" William Walton: *(contd)*	Matthews uses an ultrasensitive galvanometer to trace a single impulse in a single nerve fiber Nobel Prize for Physics: Prince Louis de Broglie (Fr.) for discovering the wave nature of electrons Cascade Tunnel, the longest railroad tunnel in N. America, finished (begun —1926) Dan. biochemist Henrik Dam discovers vitamin K E. A. Doisy (U.S.) and A. F. Butenandt (Ger.) almost simultaneously isolate estrone, one of the hormones responsible for sexual function in females Nobel Prize for Medicine: Christiaan Eijkman (Dutch) for the discovery of antineuritic vitamin B1 Einstein: "Unified Field Theory" 14th edition of the "Encyclopaedia Britannica" appears James Jeans: "The Universe Around Us" W. A. Morrison introduces quartz-crystal clocks for precise timekeeping U.S. Army monoplane completes 150 hours in flight, refueling in the air Emil Berliner, Ger.-Amer. inventor (loose-contact telephone transmitter or microphone, d. (b. 1851) Baron Auer von Welsbach, Aust. chemist, inventor of gaslight mantle and appliances, d. (b. 1858) Joseph Goldberger, Amer. physician (pellagra), d. (b. 1874) Richard Zsigmondy, Ger. chemist, 1925 Nobel Prize for Chemistry, d. (b. 1865) Construction begins on Empire *(contd)*	The term "apartheid" used for the first time Roger Bannister, Brit. athlete, b. "Black Friday" in New York; U.S. Stock Exchange collapses on Oct. 28; world economic crisis begins; U.S. securities lose $26 billion in value Margaret Bondfield becomes first Brit. woman Privy Councillor Donald G. Bradman, Australian cricketer, achieves world's record score 452 not out U.S. aviator Richard E. Byrd (1888—1957) and three companions fly over the South Pole The Bell Laboratories in the U.S. experiment with color television Amer. manufacturers begin to make aluminum furniture (especially chairs) Kodak introduces 16mm color movie film Stirling Moss, Brit. racing car champion, b. Railroad record: non-stop from Buenos Aires to Cipoletti (775 mi.) in 20 hours, 37 minutes Gen. Hans von Seeckt: "A Soldier's Thoughts" Rollin Kirby wins third Pulitzer Prize for cartoons (also 1922 and 1925) Statistics–percentage of world-wide industrial production: U.S. 34.4, Great Britain 10.4, Germany 10.3, U.S.S.R. 9.9, France 5.0, Japan 4.0, Italy 2.5; Brit. defense forces' spending: navy £55.8 million, army £40.5 million, air force £16.9 million New Tilbury Dock, London, opened Tootal's (St. Helens, England) develops first crease-resisting cotton fabric "Graf Zeppelin" airship flies around the world (21,255 miles) in 20 days, 4 hours, 14 minutes St. Valentine's Day Massacre: six notorious Chicago gangsters machine-gunned to death by a rival gang Millicent Fawcett, Eng. woman suffrage leader, d. (b. 1847) Melville Stone, Amer. newspaper man, founder of the Chicago "Daily News," the first daily penny paper in Chicago, d. (b. 1848) Aletta Jacobs, Dutch suffragist leader, first woman physician to practice in Holland, established (1882) first known birth control clinic, d. (b. 1849) Lily Langtry, Eng. actress ("The Jersey Lily"), d. (b. 1854) Edward Payson Weston, Amer. professional *(contd)*	**1929**

	A. HISTORY, POLITICS	B. LITERATURE, THEATER	C. RELIGION, PHILOSOPHY, LEARNING
1929 contd			

1930

A. History, Politics

Nazi politician Wilhelm Frick becomes a government minister in Thuringia
Austria and Italy sign a treaty of friendship
W. H. Taft, former U.S. President and Chief Justice of the Supreme Court, d. (b. 1857)
Miguel Primo de Rivera, Span. statesman, d. (b. 1870)
A. J. Balfour, Brit. statesman, d. (b. 1848)
Name of Constantinople changed to Istanbul
Heinrich Brüning forms right-wing coalition government in Germany
Reuben J. Clark's Memorandum of 1928 on Monroe Doctrine published
Edward L. Doheny is acquitted of bribing A. F. Fall in Teapot Dome scandal
Ras Tafari becomes Emperor Haile Selassie of Ethiopia
Britain, U.S., Japan, France, and Italy sign treaty on naval disarmament
Dunning tariff in Canada gives preferential treatment to Britain
Crown Prince Carol becomes King of Rumania
President Hoover approves Smoot-Hawley high tariff
Charles Evans Hughes is appointed Chief Justice of U.S. Supreme Court
Last Allied troops leave Rhineland
Litvinov named U.S.S.R. Foreign Minister
Catholic-Fascist Heimwehr units established in Austria under Prince von Starhemberg
Pilsudski forms right-wing government in Poland
Revolution in Argentina: José Uriburu becomes president
In the Ger. elections Nazis gain 107 seats from the center parties
Following a revolution in Brazil Getúlio Vargas becomes the new president
Passfield White Paper on Palestine suggests that Jewish immigration be halted
Japanese Premier Hamaguchi assassinated
Last Allied troops leave the Saar
Nobel Peace Prize: Swed. Lutheran Archbishop Nathan Söderblom (1866–1931)
Friedrich von Bernhardi, Ger. general, d. (b. 1849)
(contd)

B. Literature, Theater

Lascelles Abercrombie: "The Sale of St. Thomas"
Conrad Aiken: "Selected Poems," Pulitzer Prize for poetry
Maxwell Anderson: "Elizabeth the Queen"
W. H. Auden: "Poems"
Philip Barry: "Hotel Universe," Amer. drama
Boston bans all works by Leon Trotsky
Ivan Bunin: "The Life of Arsenev"
Paul Claudel: "Le Soulier de satin"
Marc Connelly: "Green Pastures," Pulitzer Prize drama
Noel Coward: "Private Lives," London
Hart Crane: "The Bridge"
Maurice Dekobra: "Tigres parfumés"
Earl Derr Biggers: "Charlie Chan Carries On"
Arthur Conan Doyle, Eng. novelist, d. (b. 1859)
T. S. Eliot: "Ash Wednesday"
William Faulkner: "As I Lay Dying"
Bruno Frank: "Sturm im Wasserglas" ("Storm in a Teacup")
Robert Frost: "Collected Poems"
Jean Giono: "Naissance de L'Odyssée"
Dashiell Hammett: "The Maltese Falcon"
Joseph Hergesheimer: "The Party Dress"
John Hersey: "42nd Parallel"
D. H. Lawrence, Eng. novelist, d. (b. 1885)
Oliver La Farge: "Laughing Boy," Pulitzer Prize novel
Nobel Prize for Literature: Sinclair Lewis, "Babbitt"
V. V. Majakovski, Russ. poet, d. (b. 1893)
W. Somerset Maugham: "The Breadwinner," London, and "Cakes and Ale"
Robert Musil: "Der Mann ohne Eigenschaften" (–1943)
Katherine Anne Porter: "Flowering Judas"
John Cowper Powys: "In Defence of Sensuality," essays
J. B. Priestley: "Angel Pavement"
Robert E. Sherwood: "Waterloo Bridge," tragedy
Sigrid Undset: "The Burning Bush"
Hugh Walpole: "The Herries Chronicle" (–1933)
Evelyn Waugh: "Vile Bodies"
Melville D. Post, Amer. detective story writer, d. (b. 1871)
Edward W. Bok, Amer. writer and journalist, d. (b. 1863)
(contd)

C. Religion, Philosophy, Learning

Alfred Adler: "Technik der Individualpsychologie" ("The Inferiority complex")
E. K. Chambers: "William Shakespeare"
Albert Einstein: "About Zionism"
Sigmund Freud: "Civilization and Its Discontents"
Adolf von Harnack, Ger. theologian, d. (b. 1851)
C. S. Johnson: "The Negro in American Civilization"
J. M. Keynes: "Treatise on Money"
Harold Laski: "Liberty in the Modern State"
F. R. Leavis: "Mass Civilization and Minority Culture"
Maurice Maeterlinck: "La Vie des fourmis"
Cardinal Eugenio Pacelli, later Pope Pius XII, named Vatican Secretary of State
Alfred Rosenberg: "The Myth of the 20th Century," Nazi philosophy
Albert Schweitzer: "The Mysticism of Paul the Apostle"
G. M. Trevelyan: "England under Queen Anne" (–1932)
Leon Trotsky: "Autobiography"
Christine Ladd-Franklin, Amer. psychologist and logician, d. (b. 1847)
Arthur MacDonnell, Brit. Sanskrit scholar, d. (b. 1854)

D. VISUAL ARTS	E. MUSIC	F. SCIENCE, TECHNOLOGY, GROWTH	G. DAILY LIFE	
"Woman in Armchair" St. Vitus' Cathedral, Prague, completed (begun in 1344) Stanley Spencer: "Country Girl" Second Surrealist Manifesto Grant Wood: "Woman With Plants" Heinrich Zille, Ger. cartoonist, d. (b. 1858) T. A. Dorgan, Amer. cartoonist, d. (b. 1877) Robert Henri, Amer. painter, d. (b. 1865)	Viola Concerto Lilli Lehmann, Ger. soprano, d. (b. 1848) Cole Porter: "Fifty Million Frenchmen" Popular songs: "Stardust"; "Tiptoe Through the Tulips"; "Singin' in the Rain"; "Moanin' Low"	State Building in New York City (—1931) Lt. James Doolittle pilots airplane solely using instruments Astronomer Edward Hubble measures large red shifts in the spectra of extragalactic nebulae	pedestrian, d. (b. 1839) U.S. Lawn Tennis Association Men's Singles championship won by W. T. Tilden, II; Women's Singles by Helen N. Wills U.S. Golf Association Amateur championship won by H. R. Johnston; Open won by Bobby Jones Georgia Tech. wins Rose Bowl football game from California 8—7 Philadelphia (AL) wins World Series defeating Chicago (NL) 4—1	**1929 contd**
Max Beckmann: "Self-Portrait with Saxophone," expressionism Films: "Blue Angel," (Marlene Dietrich); "All Quiet on the Western Front," Academy Award (Milestone); "Abraham Lincoln" (D. W. Griffith); "Anna Christie" (Greta Garbo); "Sous les Toits de Paris" (Cocteau); "Murder" (Hitchcock); "The Big House" (Wallace Beery); "Hell's Angels" (Howard Hughes) Chaim Gross: "Offspring," sculpture George Grosz: "Cold Buffet" R. Hood designs Daily News Building, New York Henri Matisse: "Tiaré" Ilya Repin, Russ. historical painter, d. (b. 1844) Van Doesburg first uses the term "l'art concrète" Edward Wadsworth: "Composition," Eng. abstract cubism Thomas Whittemore begins with cleaning up of the Byzantine mosaics at the Hagia Sophia in Istanbul *(contd)*	Paul Abraham: "Victoria and Her Hussar," Leipzig Béla Bartók: "Cantata Profana" BBC Symphony Orchestra formed with Sir Adrian Boult as musical director Ralph Benatzky: "Meine Schwester und ich," Berlin Emmy Destinn, Czech soprano singer, d. (b. 1878) Paul Hindemith: Concerto for viola and chamber orchestra, Op. 48 Arthur Honegger: "Les Aventures du Roi Pausole," opera, Paris Leos Janácek: "From the House of the Dead," opera, Brno (posth.) Zoltán Kodály: "Marosszék Dances" Ernst Krenek: "Das Leben des Orest," opera, Leipzig Arnold Schönberg: "Von Heute auf Morgen," opera, Frankfurt Igor Stravinsky: "Symphony of Psalms" Jacques Thibaud forms the famous trio with Casals and Cortot (—1935) The Trautonium, an electronic instrument invented by Friedrich Trautwein, Berlin Cosima Wagner, Wagner's second wife, d. (b. 1837) *(contd)*	Using x-rays, P. J. W. Debye investigates molecular structure A. S. Eddington attempts to unify general relativity and the quantum theory Nobel Prize in Chemistry: Hans Fischer (Ger.) for his chlorophyll research and synthesis of hemin Eric Haarmann (1882—1945): "Theory of Oscillation" Nobel Prize for Medicine: Karl Landsteiner (U.S.) for the grouping of human blood U.S. physicist Ernest O. Lawrence (1901—1958) pioneers development of cyclotron U.S. biochemist J. H. Northrop makes pepsin and trypsin in crystallized form Planet Pluto discovered by C. W. Tombaugh, Lowell Observatory Nobel Prize for Physics: Sir C. Raman (Indian) for his work on light diffusion J. Walter Reppe (Ger.) makes artificial fabrics from acetylene base B. V. Schmidt, Estonian optical instrument maker, builds the first coma-free 14-inch Schmidt mirror *(contd)*	Viktor Barna (Hungarian) wins world table tennis championship (again 1932—1935) Donald Bradman scores 334 runs for Australia in Leeds Test Match Contract bridge gains in popularity as a card game Comic strips grow in popularity in the U.S. ("Blondie" series) The clown Grock (Adrian Wettach) publishes a book of memoirs, "I Like to Live" Amy Johnson flies solo from London to Australia in 19.5 days France begins building the Maginot Line Magnitogorsk founded under the first U.S.S.R. Five-Year Plan in the southern Urals, with coke ovens, blast furnaces, open-hearth furnaces, blooming and rolling mills, tin-plating shops, etc. Fridtjof Nansen, Norw. explorer and humanitarian, d. (b. 1861) Photoflash bulb comes into use Picture telegraphy service begins between Britain and Germany Pilgrim Trust: E. S. Harkness, Amer. railroad magnate, places £2 million in the hands of Prime Minister Baldwin "for the benefit of Britain" Karl Schäfer (Aust.) ice-skating champion (—1936) Max Schmeling-Jack Sharkey fight held in New York City (gate $750,000; 80,000 attend) F. E. Smith, Lord Birkenhead, Brit. statesman and lawyer, d. (b. 1872) Statistics–U.S. population 122 million (118 million in 1920, 76 million in 1900); production of an industrial worker per working hour: U.S. 80 cwt. (50 in 1900, 130 in 1950); weekly movie visitors: all over the world 250 million, 115 million of them in U.S. Technocracy, the absolute domination of technology, becomes a talked-of phenomenon Turksib, the railroad line connecting Turkestan and Siberia, opened Youth Hostels Association founded in Great *(contd)*	**1930**

	A. HISTORY, POLITICS	B. LITERATURE, THEATER	C. RELIGION, PHILOSOPHY, LEARNING
1930 contd	Tasker H. Bliss, Amer. soldier, Chief of Staff, U.S. Army 1917, d. (b. 1853) Alfred von Tirpitz, Ger. naval commander World War I, d. (b. 1849) Owen J. Roberts is appointed to U.S. Supreme Court Congress creates Veterans Administration Federal Bureau of Narcotics is organized	William Bolitho, Brit. man of letters, d. (b. 1890) Robert S. Bridges, Eng. poet, poet laureate, d. (b. 1844) Bestseller: "Cimarron," by Edna Ferber Mary E. Wilkins Freeman, Amer. writer, d. (b. 1852) William J. Locke, Eng. novelist, d. (b. 1863) Georges de Porto-Riche, Fr. dramatist, d. (b. 1849) Romer Wilson, Anglo-Amer. novelist, d. (b. 1891)	
1931	Joseph Joffre, Marshal of France, d. (b. 1852) Pierre Laval, elected Premier of France Oswald Mosley leaves Brit. Labour Party to form new party along Fascist lines King Alfonso XIII leaves Spain and goes into exile U.S. Senate passes Veterans Compensation Act over President Hoover's veto Collapse of Aust. Credit-Anstalt leads to financial crisis in Central Europe Paul Doumer elected President of France Pope Pius XI: "Quadrigesimo anno," encyclical on the new social order U.S. President Hoover suggests a one-year moratorium for reparations and war debts Bankruptcy of Ger. Danatbank leads to closure of all Ger. banks Brit. naval force at Invergordon mutinies over pay cuts Heimwehr coup d'état in Austria fails (Britain) abandons gold standard; pound sterling falls from \$4.86 to \$3.49 Dwight W. Morrow, Amer. politician, diplomat, and banker, d. (b. 1873) Ger. millionaire Hugenberg undertakes to support the 800,000-strong Nazi Party; Kirdorf, Thyssen, and Schroder follow his example Brit. General Election: National Government 558 seats, Opposition 56 Ramsay MacDonald forms second National Government Statute of Westminister defines dominion status National Coffee Department in Brazil begins official destruction of surplus stocks Nobel Peace Prize: Jane Addams (U.S.) and Nicholas Murray Butler (U.S.) Ida B. Wells, Amer. journalist and civil rights leader, d. (b. 1862)	Frederick Lewis Allen: "Only Yesterday" Jacques Bainville: "Napoléon" David Belasco d. (b. 1833) Arnold Bennett, Eng. author, d. (b. 1867) Georges Bernanos: "La Grande Peur des bien-pensants" James Bridie: "The Anatomist," London John Buchan: "The Blanket of the Dark" Pearl S. Buck: "The Good Earth" (best seller) Hall Caine, Eng. novelist, d. (b. 1853) Noel Coward: "Cavalcade," London Theodore Dreiser: "Tragic America" William Faulkner: "Sanctuary" Robert Frost: "Collected Poems," Pulitzer Prize Jean Giono: "Le Grand Troupeau" Kristmann Gudmundsson: "Den bla kyst," Icelandic novel Habima Theater settles permanently in Tel Aviv Frank Harris, Brit.-Amer. author and biographer, d. (b. 1856) Hsü Chi-mo, Chin. poet, d. (b. 1896) Henry James: "Charles W. Eliot," Pulitzer Prize biography Eugene O'Neill: "Mourning Becomes Electra" Alja Rachmanova: "Students, Love, Tcheka, and Death," Russ. novel E. M. Remarque: "The Road Back" Elmer Rice: "Counsellor-at-Law," drama Joseph Roth: "Radetzky March," Aust. novel Victoria Sackville-West: "All Passion Spent" Arthur Schnitzler, Aust. writer, d. (b. 1862) Robert Sherwood: "Reunion in Vienna" Dodie Smith: "Autumn Crocus," London Lytton Strachey: "Portraits in Miniature" Carl Zuckmayer: "Der Hauptmann von Köpenick" Melvil Dewey, Amer. librarian who originated decimal system for classifying books, d. (b. 1851) Vachel Lindsay, Amer. poet, d. (b. 1879) Lincoln Steffens: "Autobiography" Katherine Tynan, Ir. poet and novelist, d. (b. 1861) Juan Zorrila, Uruguayan poet, d. (b. 1857) Tyrone Power III, Amer. actor, father of film-star Tyrone Power, d. (b. 1869)	Norman Angell and Harold Wright: "Can Governments Cure Unemployment?" John Dewey: "Philosophy and Civilization" Emile Meyerson: "The Way of Thinking" Otto Neurath: "Empirical Sociology" Max Planck: "Positivism and the Real Outside World" Albert Schweitzer: "My Life and Thoughts" Oswald Spengler: "Mankind and Technology" Paul Valéry: "Regards sur le monde actuel" Gustave Le Bon, Fr. physician and sociologist, d. (b. 1841) Jehovah's Witnesses formed from International Bible Students Association George F. Moore, Amer. theologian, d. (b. 1851)

D. VISUAL ARTS	E. MUSIC	F. SCIENCE, TECHNOLOGY, GROWTH	G. DAILY LIFE	
Grant Wood: "American Gothic" Frank McKinney Hubbard, Amer. cartoonist, d. (b. 1868) Edward V. Valentine, Amer. sculptor, d. (b. 1838)	Siegfried Wagner, Wagner's son, d. (b. 1869) Kurt Weill; "Der Jasager," students' opera Leopold Auer, Hungarian violinist and teacher, d. (b. 1845) Popular songs: "Georgia on My Mind"; "I Got Rhythm"; "Three Little Words"; "Time on My Hands"; "Walkin' My Baby Back Home"; "Body and Soul"	telescope at the Hamburg Observatory S. African microbiologist Max Theiler develops a yellow fever vaccine Glenn Curtiss, Amer. inventor and aviator, d. (b. 1878) Elmer A. Sperry, Amer. electrical engineer and inventor, d. (b. 1860) Leonard Woolley: "Digging Up the Past"	Britain "Deadwood Dick" (Richard W. Clarke), Eng.-born Amer. frontiersman, d. (b. 1845) Max Schmeling (Ger.) named world heavyweight boxing champion Bobby Jones' "Grand Slam," winning all four world golf titles–Brit. Open, U.S. Amateur, Brit. Amateur, and U.S. Open "Gallant Fox" wins Preakness and Belmont Stakes and Kentucky Derby; Earle Sande jockeys all three Pittsburgh wins Rose Bowl football game against California, 47—14 Philadelphia (AL) wins World Series, 4—2, against St. Louis (NL)	**1930 contd**
Max Beckmann: "Still Life with Studio Window" Pierre Bonnard: "The Breakfast Room" Constantin Brancusi: "Mlle. Pognany," sculpture Marc Chagall: "The Trick-Riders" Salvador Dali: "Persistence of Memory" Otto Dix: "Girls" A. Drury: statue of Sir Joshua Reynolds, Burlington House, London Jacob Epstein: "Genesis" Lyonel Feininger: "Market Church' Films: "City Lights" (Chaplin); "Congress Dances" (Lilian Harvey); "La Million" (Clair); "Girls in Uniform" (Sagan); "Front Page" (Milestone); "Kameradschaft" (Pabst); "Emil and the Detectives" (Lamprecht); "Frankenstein" (Karloff); "Flowers and Trees" (Disney's first color film); Clark Gable (1901—1960) begins his Hollywood career E. Hopper: "Route 6, Eastham" *(contd)*	George Dyson: "The Canterbury Pilgrims, oratorio Edward Elgar: "Nursery Suite" George Gershwin, George S. Kaufman, and Morrie Ryskind: "Of Thee I Sing," New York, Pulitzer Prize Alois Hába: "Matka" ("The Mother"), opera, Munich Paul Hindemith: "Das Unaufhörliche," oratorio Vincent d'Indy, Fr. composer, d. (b. 1851) Francesco Malipiero: "Torneo Notturno," Munich Dame Nellie Melba, Australian soprano, d. (b. 1861) Carl Nielsen, Dan. composer, d. (b. 1865) Anna Pavlova, Russ. dancer, d. (b. 1885) Hans Pfitzner: "Das Herz," opera, Berlin and Munich William Grant Still: "Afro-American Symphony" Edgar Varèse: "Ionisation" (for two groups of percussion) William Walton: "Belshazzar's Feast," oratorio Egon Wellesz: "Die Bachantinnen," opera, Vienna Ermanno Wolf-Ferrari: "La Vedova scaltra," comic opera, Rome Eugène Ysaye, Belg. violinist, d. (b. 1858) "Star-Spangled Banner," words by Francis Scott *(contd)*	Nobel Prize for Chemistry: Friedrich Bergius (Ger.) and Carl Bosch for their invention and development of chemical high-pressure methods U.S. physicist P. W. Bridgman (1882—1961) conducts research on materials at pressures up to 100,000 atmospheres Sir David Bruce, Australian physician, d. (b. 1855) Brit. physicist J. D. Cockcroft develops high-voltage apparatus for atomic transmutations Thomas Alva Edison, Amer. inventor, d. (b. 1847) Swiss chemist Paul Karrer isolates vitamin A J. G. Lansky discovers radio interference from Milky Way Amer. physicist E. O. Lawrence invents the cyclotron A. A. Michelson, Amer. physicist, d. (b. 1852) Julius A. Nieuwland devises a process for producing neoprene, a synthetic rubber Nobel Prize for Medicine: Otto Warburg (Ger.) for his researches on enzymes Australian explorer G. H. Wilkins (1888—1958) captains "Nautilus" submarine, navigating it under the Arctic Ocean to latitude 82 degrees, 15 minutes Aristides Agramonte, Cuban bacteriologist, d. (b. 1869) Edward G. Acheson, Amer. inventor, assistant to Thomas A. Edison, d. (b. 1856) *(contd)*	Benguella-Katanga, the first trans-African railroad line completed Alphonse ("Scarface") Capone, gangster with reputed $20 million annual income, is jailed for income tax evasion Mrs. Hattie T. Caraway (Democrat, Arkansas) becomes the first woman to be elected to the U.S. Senate Christopher Chataway, Brit. athlete, b. International Colonial Exhibition held in Paris King George V accepts the 2,000,000th Brit. telephone for use at Buckingham Palace Sir Thomas Lipton, Brit. tea merchant and sportsman, d. (b. 1850) The northern face of the Matterhorn climbed for the first time by Franz and Toni Schmid New York "World" suspends publication "The New Statesman" (London) is amalgamated with the "Nation" and "Athenaeum" (editor: Kingsley Martin) Dr. William Rose (ed.): "An Outline of Modern Knowledge" Spicer-Dufay process of natural color photography Starr Faithfull's mysterious death, shore at Long Beach, N.Y. Statistics–population (in millions): China 410, India 338, U.S.S.R. 168, U.S. 122, Japan 75, Germany 64, Great Britain 46; unemployed: Germany 5.66 million, U.S. 4—5 million, Bata, the Czech shoe factory, produces 75,000 pairs of shoes daily; world film production: 1,000 films (2,500,000 miles in length); world car production: 36 million Mortimer L. Schiff, Amer. banker and philanthropist, d. (b. 1877) Knute Rockne, Amer. football player and coach, d. (b. 1888) Nathan Straus, Amer. merchant, founder of Macy's, d. (b. 1848) U.S. Lawn Tennis Association Men's Singles championship won by H. Ellsworth Viner, Jr.; Women's Singles *(contd)*	**1931**

	A. HISTORY, POLITICS	B. LITERATURE, THEATER	C. RELIGION, PHILOSOPHY, LEARNING
1931 contd			
1932	Indian Congress declared illegal; Gandhi arrested Stimson Doctrine protests against Jap. aggression in Manchuria; U.S. declares it will not recognize gains made by armed force In U.S.S.R. the second Five-Year Plan begins André Tardieu, elected Prime Minister of France U.S. Federal Reserve System reorganized Aristide Briand, Fr. statesman, d. (b. 1862) Eamon de Valera elected President of Ireland Presidential elections in Germany: Hindenburg 18 million votes, Hitler 11 million, Communists 5 million; Hindenburg elected in second election Albert Lebrun named President of France Franz von Papen named Ger. Chancellor Oliviera Salazar elected Premier of Portugal Ger. Reichstag elections: Nazis 230 seats, Socialists 133, Center 97, Communists 89 Hitler refuses Hindenburg's offer to become Vice Chancellor Julius Gömbös, anti-Semitic Nationalist, forms government in Hungary Franklin D. Roosevelt wins U.S. presidential election in Democratic landslide; 472 electoral votes over Herbert Hoover's 59 Gen. Kurt von Schleicher is named Ger. Chancellor following von Papen's resignation Famine in U.S.S.R. Aust.-born Hitler receives Ger. citizenship and Frick appoints him Regierungsrat in Brunswick Ibn Saud renames his kingdom Saudi Arabia Jean Jules Jusserand, Fr. diplomat, ambassador to the U.S., d. (b. 1855) Eduard Bernstein, Ger. Social Democratic politician, d. (b. 1850) In May and June, 17,000 ex-servicemen arrive in Washington, D.C., to urge passage of law permitting cashing of their bonus certificates; bill defeated by Senate; government offers expenses for return home, but troops led by Gen. *(contd)*	Sherwood Anderson: "Beyond Desire" Jean Anouilh: "Le Bal des voleurs" W. H. Auden: "The Orators," poems Philip Barry: "The Animal Kingdom" Bertolt Brecht: "St. Joan of the Slaughter Houses" James Bridie: "Jonah and the Whale" Erskine Caldwell: "Tobacco Road" Louis-Ferdinand Céline: "Voyage au bout de la nuit" John Dos Passos: "1919" Hans Fallada: "Little Man, What Now?" Ger. social novel James T. Farrell: "Young Lonigan" William Faulkner: "Light in August" Rose Franken: "Another Language" Nobel Prize for Literature: John Galsworthy Jean Giono: "Jean le Bleu" The centenary of Goethe's death is celebrated throughout the world Louis Golding: "Magnolia Street" Julian Green: "Epaves" Graham Greene: "Stamboul Train" Dashiell Hammett: "The Thin Man" Gerhart Hauptmann: "Before Sunset," drama Ernest Hemingway: "Death in the Afternoon" Sidney Howard: "The Late Christopher Bean" Aldous Huxley: "Brave New World" Rosamond Lehmann: "Invitation to the Waltz" Rose Macauley: "They Were Defeated" W. Somerset Maugham: "The Narrow Corner" and "For Services Rendered" François Mauriac: "Le Noeud de vipères" André Maurois: "Le Cercle de famille" Henri Michaux: "Un Barbare en Asie" Charles Morgan: "The Fountain" Boris Pasternak: "Second Birth," poem Walter B. Pitkin: "Life Begins at Forty" J. B. Priestley: "Dangerous Corner," London Shakespeare Memorial Theatre opened in Stratford-upon-Avon F. E. Sillanpää: "A Man's Way," Finn. novel Upton Sinclair: "American Outpost" Lytton Strachey, Eng. author, d. (b. 1880) Felix Timmermans: "Franciscus" René Bazin, Fr. novelist, d. (b. 1853) Gamaliel Bradford, Amer. author, d. (b. 1862) Sigrid Undset: "Ida Elisabeth," Norw. novel Edgar Wallace, Eng. novelist, d. (b. 1875) Anton Wildgans, Aust. poet, d. (b. 1881) *(contd)*	Irving Babbitt: "On Being Creative" Karl Barth: "Christian Dogmatics" Henri Bergson: "Les Deux Sources de la morale et de la Religion" V. F. Calverton: "The Liberation of American Literature" The Folger Library opens in Washington Etienne Gilson: "The Spirit of Mediaeval Philosophy," Fr. Neo-Thomism Karl Jaspers: "Philosophie," existentialism Wyndham Lewis: "Doom of Youth" The Methodist Churches in England reunify John Strachey: "The Coming Struggle for Power" Sidney and Beatrice Webb visit the U.S.S.R.; their book of impressions, "Soviet Communism," published 1935 John B. McMaster, Amer. historian, d. (b. 1852) Salomon Reinack, Fr. archaeologist and historian of religion, d. (b. 1858) Charles W. Chesnutt, Amer. Negro educator and lawyer, d. (b. 1858) Will Durant begins "Story of Civilization" Bennington College opens in Vermont; Teachers College opens in New York City as adjunct to Columbia University

D. VISUAL ARTS	E. MUSIC	F. SCIENCE, TECHNOLOGY, GROWTH	G. DAILY LIFE	
Paul Klee: "The Ghost Vanishes" Henri Matisse: "The Dance," murals at the Barnes Foundation, Merion, Pa. Paul Nash: "Cinetic," Eng. abstract painting Building of Rockefeller Center, New York, begins (—1947) Empire State Building is completed, New York	Key, music from "Anacreon in Heaven," officially becomes U.S. national anthem Popular songs: "Minnie the Moocher"; "Mood Indigo"; "Goodnight, Sweetheart"; "When the Moon Comes Over the Mountain"	Francis Dercum, Amer. neurologist, d. (b. 1856) Clyde Pangborn and Hugh Herndon fly nonstop from Sabishiro, Japan, to Wenatchee, Washington, in 41 hours George Washington Bridge, New Jersey—New York, completed Harold C. Urey (U.S.) discovers heavy hydrogen (deuterium)	by Mrs. Helen Wills Moody U.S. Golf Association Amateur won by Francis Ouimet; Open by Billie Burke Alabama defeats Washington State to win Rose Bowl football game 24—0 "Twenty Grand," C. Kurtsinger up, wins Belmont Stakes and Kentucky Derby St. Louis (NL) wins World Series, defeating Philadelphia (AL) 4—3	**1931 contd**
Max Beckmann: "Seven Triptychs" (—1950) Broadcasting House, London, designed by Meyer and Hand Burra: "The Café," Eng. expressionism Alexander Calder exhibits "stabiles" and "mobiles" (sculptures moved by air currents) Films: "The Blue Light" (Riefenstahl); "M" (Lang); "A nous la liberté" (Clair); "A Farewell to Arms" (Gary Cooper); "Grand Hotel," Academy Award (Garbo); "Shanghai Express" (Dietrich); "Sign of the Cross" (De Mille); Johnny Weissmuller appears in his first "Tarzan" film; Shirley Temple's (b. 1928) first film, "Red-Haired Alibi"; "Fugitive from a Chain Gang" (Le Roy) Eric Gill: "Prospero and Ariel," sculpture for Broadcasting House, London Max Liebermann: "Professor Sauerbruch" Edwin Lutyens designs Metropolitan Cathedral, Liverpool *(contd)*	Eugen D'Albert, Ger. composer and pianist, d. (b. 1864) Samuel Barber: "Overture to School for Scandal" Arnold Bax: Symphony No. 5 in C-sharp minor Sir Thomas Beecham founds the London Philharmonic Orchestra Benjamin Britten: "Sinfonietta" for chamber orchestra, Op. 1 Ferde Grofé: "The Grand Canyon Suite" Cole Porter: "The Gay Divorcée," New York Sergei Prokofiev: Piano Concerto No. 5 in G major, Op. 55 Maurice Ravel: Piano Concerto in G major Arnold Schönberg finishes the first two acts of his opera "Moses and Aaron" (act three resumed in 1951) Franz Schreker: "Der Schmied von Gent," opera, Berlin John Philip Sousa, *(contd)*	Nobel Prize for Medicine: E. D. Adrian and C. Sherrington for their discovery regarding the functions of the neurons C. D. Anderson discovers positron W. H. Carothers (U.S.) (1896—1937) synthesizes polyamide (nylon in 1936) James Chadwick discovers the neutron The Cordoba catalogue (since 1892) mentions 613,993 stars on the southern firmament Nobel Prize for Physics: Werner Heisenberg (Ger.) for the creation of the matrix theory of quantum mechanics Karl Jansky (1905—1950) establishes a foundation for the development of radio astronomy Richard Kuhn (1900—1967) investigates riboflavin Edwin Land invents a synthetic light polarizer Nobel Prize for Chemistry: Irving Langmuir (U.S.) for discoveries in surface chemistry Fritz Mietzsch (1896—1958) and Josef Klarer (1898—1953): sulfonamide Wilhelm Ostwald, Ger. chemist, d. (b. 1853) Auguste Piccard (1884—1962) reaches a height of 17.5 miles in his stratosphere balloon Ronald Ross, Eng. bacteriologist, d. (b. 1857) Balloon tire produced for *(contd)*	Basic English proposed as a prospective international language BBC (London) takes over responsibility for developing television from the Baird company Amelia Earhart is first woman to fly solo across the Atlantic: Newfoundland to Londonderry, Ireland, in 13.5 hours George Eastman, U.S. inventor and manufacturer of photographic materials (Kodak), d. (b. 1854) Imperial Airways serves 22 countries, flies 1,722,000 miles, and carries 34,000 passengers and 6.3 million letters Japan begins its conquest of world markets by undercutting prices Expression "New Deal," used in Roosevelt's speech accepting the Democratic nomination for president Ivar Kreuger, the Swed. "match king," commits suicide (b. 1880); the Kreuger concern collapses The Lambeth Bridge, London, and the Harbour Bridge, Sydney, open The Lindbergh baby is kidnapped André Maginot, the sponsor of the Maginot Line, d. (b. 1877) Olympic Games at Los Angeles–23 sports, 124 events, 1,408 participants from 37 nations; Winter Games in U.S. for the first time (Lake Placid, N.Y.); strong U.S. comeback (Eddie Tolan, William Carr, Ben Eastman, George Sailing, William Miller, Edward Gordon, Lee Sexton, John Anderson, James Bausch) Thomas Hampson (Eng.) establishes world record in 800-meter run Fascist government in Italy begins drainage of the Pontine Marshes southeast of Rome (—1934) Statistics–unemployed in U.S., 13.7 million; in Great Britain, 2.8 million; world-wide, approx. 30 million; trade union membership in Great Britain, 4.44 million; 127 sound films made during the year (8 in 1929) Baseball player Evar Swanson (Columbus, Ohio) circles the bases in the record time of 13.3 seconds Brit. actor Tom Walls wins Derby with "April the Fifth" (100—6) *(contd)*	**1932**

	A. HISTORY, POLITICS	B. LITERATURE, THEATER	C. RELIGION, PHILOSOPHY, LEARNING
1932 contd	Douglas MacArthur finally drive out last 2,000 Reconstruction Finance Corporation, established by Congress to lend money for rebuilding of U.S. economy, provides $1.5 billion by year's end First unemployment insurance law enacted in Wisconsin	Eugène Brieux, Fr. dramatist, d. (b. 1858) Hart Crane, Amer. poet, d. (b. 1899) G. Lowes Dickinson, Eng. man of letters, d. (b. 1862) Kenneth Grahame, Eng. author ("The Wind in the Willows"), d. (b. 1859) Lady Gregory, Ir. poet and playwright, d. (b. 1852) Harold MacGrath, Amer. writer of escapist fiction, d. (b. 1871) Harold Monro, Eng. poet and critic, d. (b. 1879) Sir Gilbert Parker, Canadian novelist, d. (b. 1860) Minnie Maddern Fiske, Amer. actress, d. (b. 1866) Florenz Ziegfeld, Amer. theatrical producer, d. (b. 1869) James Oppenheim, Amer. poet and novelist, d. (b. 1882)	
1933	Calvin Coolidge, 30th President of the U.S., d. (b. 1872) U.S. Congress votes independence for Philippines Adolf Hitler appointed Ger. Chancellor Edouard Daladier becomes Premier of France 20th Amendment to U.S. Constitution: presidential inauguration on Jan. 20 First U.S. aircraft carrier, "Ranger," is launched The Reichstag fire in Berlin F. D. Roosevelt inaugurated as 32nd President of the U.S. Frances Perkins, appointed Secretary of Labor by President Roosevelt, becomes first woman cabinet member Hermann Goering named Prussian Prime Minister Amer. banks closed Mar. 6—Mar. 9 by presidential order Chancellor Dollfuss suspends parliamentary government in Austria U.S. Congress grants President Roosevelt wide powers Goebbels named Hitler's Minister of Propaganda Japan withdraws from League of Nations Hitler granted dictatorial powers (Enabling Law) The first concentration camps erected by the Nazis in Germany; by 1945 8 to 10 million prisoners have been interned and at least half of them killed *(contd)*	"Ulysses," by James Joyce, is allowed into the U.S. after court ruling All books by non-Nazi and Jewish authors are burned in Germany Hervey Allen: "Anthony Adverse" James Bridie: "A Sleeping Clergyman," London Nobel Prize for Literature: Ivan Bunin (Russ.) Erskine Caldwell: "God's Little Acre" Colette: "La Chatte" Gordon Daviot: "Richard of Bordeaux," London Georges Duhamel: "La Chronique des Pasquiers," T. S. Eliot: "The Use of Poetry and the Use of Criticism" John Galsworthy, Eng. novelist and dramatist, d. (b. 1867) Federico García Lorca: "The Blood Wedding" Stefan George, Ger. poet, d. (b. 1868) Trygve Gulbranssen: "Beyond Sing the Woods," Norw. novel Knut Hamsun: "The Road Leads On," Norw. novel Merton Hodge: "The Wind and the Rain," London Anthony Hope, Eng. novelist, d. (b. 1863) Hanns Johst: "Schlageter," Nazi drama Margaret Kennedy: "Escape Me Never," London Sidney Kingsley: "Men in White," Pulitzer Prize drama (1934) Mazo de la Roche: "The Master of Jalna" Jack Kirkland: "Tobacco Road," based on Erskine Caldwell's novel, opens to long run in New York Sinclair Lewis: "Ann Vickers" André Malraux: "La Condition humaine" Thomas Mann: "Joseph and His Brethren" (—1943) John Masefield: "The Bird of Dawning" François Mauriac: "Le Mystère Frontenac" André Maurois: "Edouard VII et son temps" George Augustus Moore, Ir. novelist, d. (b. 1852) *(contd)*	E. W. Barnes: "Scientific Theory and Religion" Winston S. Churchill: "Marlborough, his Life and Times" (—1938) W. Dubislaw: "Nature Philosophy," logical empiricism Ger. Evangelical Church, amalgamation of all Protestant Churches in Germany, established Cardinal von Faulhaber (Munich): "Judaism–Christendom–Germanism," anti-Nazi treatise R. Guardini: "Man and his Faith," Catholic religious philosophy Granville Hicks: "The Great Tradition" C. G. Jung: "Modern Man in Search of a Soul" W. Reich: "Character Analysis," Freudian theories Franklin D. Roosevelt: "Looking Forward" Nathan Söderblom: "The Living God," 1931 Gifford Lectures C. J. Jung: "Psychology and Religion" Leon Trotsky: "History of the Russian Revoltion" Hans Vaihinger, Ger. philosopher, d. (b. 1852) The Warburg Institute transferred from Hamburg to London (incorporated into London University 1944) A. N. Whitehead: "Adventures of Ideas" Irving Babbitt, Amer. scholar and educator, d. (b. 1865) Frederick Starr, Amer. anthropologist, d. (b. 1858) A. H. Sayce, Eng. philologist and Assyriologist, d. (b. 1846)

D. VISUAL ARTS	E. MUSIC	F. SCIENCE, TECHNOLOGY, GROWTH	G. DAILY LIFE	
W. Nicholson: "Black Swans," Eng. expressionism Pablo Picasso: "Head of a Woman," sculpture Ben Shahn: "Sacco and Vanzetti" Max Slevogt, Ger. painter, d. (b. 1868) Grant Wood: "Daughters of the American Revolution"	the Amer. "March King," d. (b. 1854) Johanna Gadski, Ger.-Amer. soprano, d. (b. 1872) Popular songs: "Brother, Can You Spare a Dime?"; "I'm Getting Sentimental Over You"; "Night and Day"; "Let's Have Another Cup of Coffee"; "April in Paris"	farm tractors Vitamin D discovered Sir Patrick Geddes, Scot. biologist, d. (b. 1854) Graham Lusk, Amer. physiologist, d. (b. 1866) Alberto Santos-Dumont, Brazilian airship pioneer, d. (b. 1873) Work begins on San Francisco—Oakland Bay Bridge (Golden Gate Bridge)	Zuider Zee (Holland) drainage project completed William Wrigley, Jr., Amer. industrialist, founder of the chewing-gum firm, d. (b. 1861) William J. Burns, Amer. detective, d. (b. 1861) Julius Rosenwald, Amer. merchant (Sears, Roebuck) and philanthropist, d. (b. 1862) U.S. Golf Association Amateur Championship won by C. R. Somerville; Open by Gene Sarazen U.S. Lawn Tennis Association Men's Singles Championship won by H. Ellsworth Vines, Jr.; Women's Singles by Helen Hull Jacobs "Burgoo King," wins Preakness Stakes and Kentucky Derby Southern California wins Rose Bowl football game against Tulane, 21—12 Jack Sharkey (U.S.) defeats Max Schmeling (Ger.) to capture world heavyweight boxing crown New York (AL) wins World Series against Chicago (NL) 4—0 Gustav Cassel: "The Crisis of the World's Money System"	**1932 contd**
Art in Germany being "gleichgeschaltet"; all modernism suppressed in favor of superficial realism Films: "Queen Christina" (Garbo); "The Testament of Dr. Mabuse" (Lang); "Hitlerjunge Quex" (Nazi propaganda); "Dinner at Eight" (George Cukor); "King Kong" (Schroedsack and Cooper); "14th July" (Clair); "Dr. Jekyll and Mr. Hyde" (Mamoulian); "Cavalcade," Academy Award (Noel Coward) Giacometti: "The Palace at Four a.m.," sculpture W. Holden designs the Senate House, London University Kandinsky and Klee leave Germany for France and Switzerland respectively Henri Matisse: "The Dance," Fr. expressionism Palace of the League of Nations in Geneva, *(contd)*	George Balanchine and Lincoln Kirstein found the School of American Ballet The Busch brothers–Fritz, the conductor, and Adolf, the violinist–leave Germany Aaron Copland: "The Short Symphony" Roy Harris: Symphony No. 1 Arthur Honegger: "La Belle de Moudon," Vaudeville Jerome Kern: "Roberta," New York Paul von Klenau: "Michael Kohlhaas," opera Selma Kurz, Aust. soprano singer, d. (b. 1875) Sergei Prokofiev, who left Russia in 1918, returns to the U.S.S.R. Max von Schillings, Ger. composer, d. (b. 1868) Richard Strauss: "Arabella," Dresden Bruno Walter leaves Berlin for Vienna Vladimir de Pachmann, Russ. pianist, d. (b. 1848) *(contd)*	Anderson and Millikan, while analyzing cosmic rays, discover positrons (positive electrons) Ludwig von Bertalanffy: "Theoretical Biology" Albert Calmette, Fr. bacteriologist, d. (b. 1863) Nobel Prize for Physics: Paul Dirac (Brit.) and Erwin Schrödinger (Aust.) for the discovery of new forms of atomic energy Philo Farnsworth develops electronic television Ger. scientific research is considerably hampered and weakened by new Nazi regulations De Haas researches low temperature phenomena Marconiphone Company manufactures an all-metal radio tube Nobel Prize for Physics: Thomas Hunt Morgan (U.S.) for his discovery of the heredity transmission functions of chromosomes Tadeusz Reichstein synthesizes pure vitamin C The theory that Neanderthal Man is in the line of descent of *(contd)*	Approx. 60,000 artists (authors, actors, painters, musicians) emigrate from Germany (—1939) First baseball all-star game played Annie Besant, Brit. social reformer, d. (b. 1847) Heywood Broun founds American Newspaper Guild R. E. Byrd, begins his second South Pole expedition (—1935) Sir Malcolm Campbell (knighted in 1931) achieves automobile speed record of 272.46 mph Edward Chamberlin: "Theory of Monopolistic Competition" Germany adopts a Four-Year Plan, claiming it will abolish unemployment Eugen Hadamovsky: "Radio as Means of Political Leadership" (Nazi theory) Brit. airplanes fly over Mount Everest National Playing Fields Association founded in London Henry Royce, Brit. car designer, d. (b. 1863) Starvation in U.S.S.R. reaches disastrous proportions Statistics– world film production: U.S., 547; Great Britain, 169; France, 158; Germany (1932), 127; U.S.S.R., 44; average winter temperature at Spitsbergen demonstrates notable warming in the Arctic region: 1900—1915–17.6 degrees C 1931—1935–8.6 degrees C Horatio W. Bottomley, Eng. newspaper editor and proprietor, d. (b. 1860) U.S. Golf Association Amateur won by George T. Dunlap, Jr.; Open by Johnny Goodman U.S. Lawn Tennis Association Men's Singles won by Frederick J. Perry (Eng.); Women's Singles by Helen Hull Jacobs Southern California wins Rose Bowl football game against Pittsburgh 35—0 Primo Carnera (Ital.) knocks out Jack Sharkey to win heavyweight boxing crown *(contd)*	**1933**

	A. HISTORY, POLITICS	B. LITERATURE, THEATER	C. RELIGION, PHILOSOPHY, LEARNING

1933 contd

A. History, Politics

Boycott of Jews begins in Germany
U.S. goes off gold standard (Apr. 19)
Ger. labor unions suppressed
U.S. Congress passes Agricultural Adjustment and Federal Emergency Relief Acts
Tennessee Valley Authority created in U.S.
U.S. Securities Act passed to protect investors by providing information on new securities issues
Chicago World's Fair (A Century of Progress International Exposition) opens
Nazis win Danzig elections
U.S. National Industrial Recovery Act and Farm Credit Act made law
Public Works Administration (PWA) created in U.S.
Nazi Party in Austria dissolved
Political parties, other than Nazi, suppressed in Germany
Assyrian Christians massacred in Iraq
Edward Grey, Lord Grey of Fallodon, Brit. statesman, d. (b. 1862)
92 per cent of Ger. electorate vote for the Nazis
U.S. recognizes U.S.S.R. and resumes trade
21st Amendment to U.S. Constitution repeals prohibition
Stavisky scandal (fraudulent transactions in high places) in France
Nobel Peace Prize: Norman Angell (Brit.)
Konrad Henlein organizes Nazi Party in Czechoslovakia; Vidkun Quisling in Norway
Cordell Hull (1871—1955) named U.S. Secretary of State (—1944) and Sumner Welles Undersecretary
Nikolai Yudenich, White Russ. general, d. (b. 1862)
Fiorello H. La Guardia is elected Mayor of New York City, defeating Tammany Hall

B. Literature, Theater

Allan Nevins: "Grover Cleveland," Pulitzer Prize biography
Eugene O'Neill: "Ah, Wilderness," comedy, stars George M. Cohan (New York production) and Will Rogers (San Francisco production)
George Orwell: "Down and Out in Paris and London"
Elmer Rice: "We, the People"
Kenneth Roberts: "Rabble in Arms"
Romain Rolland: "L'Ame enchantée" (since 1922)
Bernard Shaw: "On the Rocks," London
Gertrude Stein: "The Autobiography of Alice B. Toklas"
H. G. Wells: "The Shape of Things to Come"
Franz Werfel: "The Forty Days of Musa Dagh"
Virginia Woolf: "Flush"
Earl Derr Biggers, Amer. writer ("Charlie Chan"), d. (b. 1884)
Stella Benson, Eng. poet and novelist, d. (b. 1892)
Ring Lardner, Amer. humorist and short-story writer, d. (b. 1885)
George Saintsbury, Eng. critic and journalist, d. (b. 1845)
Louis Joseph Vance, Amer. novelist, d. (b. 1879)
Best seller: "Lost Horizon," by James Hilton

1934

A. History, Politics

Henry Morgenthau, Jr., named U.S. Secretary of the Treasury
U.S. Gold Reserve Act authorizes the president to revalue the dollar
U.S. Federal Farm Mortgage Corporation organized
A revolution in Austria overturns the Social Democrats
General strike staged in France
Civil Works Emergency Relief Act passed in U.S.
Leopold III becomes King of the Belgians following the death of his father, King Albert I
Brit. Road Traffic Act introduces driving tests
Gandhi suspends civil disobedience campaign in India
Oswald Mosley addresses Fascist mass meetings in Britain
U.S. Congress grants F. D. Roosevelt the power to conclude agreements for reducing tariffs
Hitler and Mussolini meet in Venice
Hitler promotes blood bath in Germany–Schleicher, Röhm, Strasser, and many others assassinated
Aust. Chancellor Engelbert Dollfuss assassinated by Nazis
Kurt von Schuschnigg appointed Aust. Chancellor, Starhemberg Vice Chancellor
Paul von Hindenburg Ger. President, d. (b. 1847)
Ger. plebiscite votes for Hitler as Führer
U.S.S.R. admitted to League of Nations
King Alexander of Yugoslavia and Fr. Foreign Minister Louis Barthou assassinated in Marseilles
Raymond Poincaré, Fr. statesman, d. (b. 1860)
Prince Paul named Regent of Yugoslavia
Ger. Labor Front founded
Depressed areas bill introduced in Britain
Winston Churchill warns Brit. Parliament of Ger. air menace
Stalin's close collaborator, Serge Kirov, assassinated in Leningrad; purge of Communist Party begins
(contd)

B. Literature, Theater

Jean Anouilh: "La Sauvage"
Louis Aragon: "Les Cloches de Bâle"
Hermann Bahr, Aust. author, d. (b. 1863)
Best sellers: "Good-Bye Mr. Chips," James Hilton; "While Rome Burns," Alexander Woollcott
John Buchan: "The Three Fishers"
Pearl S. Buck: "The Mother"
Agatha Christie: "Murder in Three Acts"
Jean Cocteau: "La Machine infernale"
F. Scott Fitzgerald: "Tender Is the Night"
Jean Giono: "Le Chant du monde"
Jean Giraudoux: "Combat avec l'ange"
Robert Graves: "I, Claudius" and "Claudius the God"
Julian Green: "Le Visionnaire"
Graham Greene: "It's a Battlefield"
Gerhart Hauptmann: "Hamlet in Wittenberg," play
Louis Jouvet (1887—1951) takes over the management of the Théâtre de l'Athène in Paris
John Knittel: "Via Mala"
Halper Leivick: "Die Gehule Comedys," Yiddish-Amer. poems
Sinclair Lewis: "Work of Art"
Gerald du Maurier, Eng. actor-manager, d. (b. 1873)
André Maurois: "L'Instinct du bonheur"
Sean O'Casey: "Within the Gates"
John O'Hara: "Appointment in Samarra"
Eugene O'Neill: "Days Without End"
Sir Arthur Wing Pinero, Eng. dramatist, d. (b. 1855)
(contd)

C. Religion, Philosophy, Learning

Ruth Benedict: "Patterns of Culture"
Martin Buber: "Tales of Angels, Ghosts, and Demons"
Karl Bühler: "Theory of Language"
R. Carnap: "Logical Syntax of Language"
Lionel Curtis: "Civitas Dei" (—1937)
Albert Einstein: "My Philosophy"
Pietro Gasparri, Ital. cardinal and canonist, d. (b. 1852)
Lazar Goldschmidt finishes the 12th and last vol. of his Ger. translation of the Babylonian Talmud (begun in 1893)
J. E. Neale; "Queen
(contd)

D. VISUAL ARTS | E. MUSIC | F. SCIENCE, TECHNOLOGY, GROWTH | G. DAILY LIFE

1933 contd

D. Visual Arts

completed (begun in 1929)
Edward W. Kemble, Amer. illustrator and cartoonist, d. (b. 1861)
George B. Luks d. (b. 1867)
Popular films: "Little Women," starring Katharine Hepburn, and "She Done Him Wrong," starring Mae West
Louis Comfort Tiffany d. (b. 1848)

E. Music

Andreas Dippel, Ger.-Amer. operatic tenor, codirector of the Metropolitan Opera, New York, d. (b. 1866)
Popular songs: "Smoke Gets in Your Eyes"; "Stormy Weather"; "Easter Parade"; "Who's Afraid of the Big, Bad Wolf?"; "Boulevard of Broken Dreams"

F. Science, Technology, Growth

Homo sapiens is rejected following the discovery of the Steinheim skull
Vitamin B2 (riboflavin) recognized by R. Kuhn, Szent-Gyorgyi, and Wagner von Jauregg
Knud Rasmussen, Dan. explorer and ethnologist, d. (b. 1879)

G. Daily Life

New York (NL) wins World Series against Washington (AL) 4—1

1934

D. Visual Arts

H. P. Berlage, Dutch architect, d. (b. 1856)
Salvador Dali: "William Tell," surrealism
John Dewey: "Art as Experience"
Films: "The Lost Patrol" (John Ford); "It Happened One Night," Academy Award (Capra); "Design for Living" (Lubitsch); "The Last Millionaire" (Clair); "Le Grand jeu" (Feyder); "Of Human Bondage" (Leslie Howard); "The Thin Man" (Van Dyke); "Man of Aran" (Flaherty); "The Private Life of Henry VIII" (Korda)
Roger Fry, Eng. painter and art critic, d. (b. 1866)
John Piper: "Rye Harbor"
Stanley Spencer: "The Angel"
Wornum, Royal Institute of Brit. Architects Building, London
John Collier, Eng. portrait painter, d. (b. 1884)
Harrison Fisher, Amer. illustrator ("The American Girl"), d. (b. 1877)
(contd)

E. Music

Benjamin Britten; "Fantasy Quartet" for oboe, violin, viola, and cello Op. 2; composed in 1932, first performed at the Florence Festival of the International Society for Contemporary Music
John Christie founds Glyndebourne operatic festival
Noel Coward: "Conversation Piece," operetta, London
Frederick Delius, Eng. composer, d. (b. 1862)
Edward Elgar, Eng. composer, d. (b. 1857)
Paul Hindemith: "Mathis der Maler," symphony
Gustav Holst, Eng. composer, d. (b. 1874)
Arthur Honegger: "Sémiramis," ballet, Paris
Franz Lehár: "Giuditta," operetta, Vienna
Cole Porter: "Anything Goes," New York
Franz Schreker, Aust. composer, d. (b. 1878)
Otakar Sevcík, Czech violinist, d. (b. 1852)
Philip Hale, Amer. music critic, d. (b. 1854)
Dmitri Shostakovich: "Lady
(contd)

F. Science, Technology, Growth

Adolph Butenandt isolates the first crystalline male hormone, androsterone
A refrigeration process for meat cargoes is devised
Marie Curie, Pol.-Fr. scientist, d. (b. 1867)
Enrico Fermi suggests that neutrons and protons are the same fundamental particles in two different quantum states
Alexander Fleming: "Recent Advances in Vaccine and Serum Therapy"
Fritz Haber, Ger. physical chemist, d. (b. 1868)
Nobel Prize for Medicine: G. R. Minot (U.S.), W. P. Murphy (U.S.), and G. H. Whipple (U.S.) for their work on liver therapy to overcome anemia
The first Nanga Parbat (Pakistan) expedition fails to reach the summit
Phthalocyanine dyes are prepared
U.S. physicist Isidor Isaac Rabi begins his work on the atomic and molecular beam magnetic resonance method for observing spectra in the radio-frequency range
(contd)

G. Daily Life

Max Baer wins world heavyweight boxing title
W. Beebe descends 3,028 feet into the ocean off Bermuda
Evangeline Booth, daughter of the Salvation Army's founder, elected General of the Salvation Army (—1939)
British Iron and Steel Federation established
Henry Cotton (Brit.) wins Open championship at Sandwich, thus ending Amer. golfers' dominance
Gordonstoun School founded
The Grossglockner Alpine Road (Austria) opened to traffic
Otto H. Kahn, Amer. banker and philanthropist, d. (b. 1867)
Sophia Loren, Ital. film star, b.
Joe Louis wins his first fight against Jack Kracken (Chicago)
(contd)

	A. HISTORY, POLITICS	B. LITERATURE, THEATER	C. RELIGION, PHILOSOPHY, LEARNING
1934 contd	Japan renounces Washington treaties of 1922 and 1930	Nobel Prize for Literature: Luigi Pirandello (Ital.) Ezra Pound: "ABC of Reading" J. B. Priestley: "English Journey" Elmer Rice: "Judgment Day" Joachim Ringelnatz, Ger. poet, d. (b. 1883) William Saroyan: "The Daring Young Man on the Flying Trapeze" Upton Sinclair: "The Book of Love" First Soviet Writers' Congress held in Moscow under Maxim Gorki	Elizabeth" Harold Nicolson: "Curzon: the Last Phase" R. Niebuhr: "Moral Man and Immoral Society" "Oxford History of England," ed. by G. N. Clark. appears Max Picard: "The Flight from God," Swiss Christian theology Bertrand Russell: "Freedom and Organization 1814—1914" William Temple: "Nature, Man and God" Arnold Toynbee: "A Study of History" (—1954)
1935	Mustafa Kemal, President of Turkey, adopts name of Kemal Atatürk Anglo-Indian trade pact signed Germany–the Saarland is incorporated into Germany following a plebiscite; Nazis repudiate Versailles Treaty and reintroduce compulsory military service; Stresa Conference; Anglo-Ger. Naval Agreement; Nuremberg Laws against Jews Show trials take place in Russia The U.S.S.R. concludes treaties with France, Czechoslovakia, the U.S., and Turkey Silver Jubilee Celebrations held in Britain Laval elected Fr. Premier Stanley Baldwin forms National Government in Britain Mussolini rejects Anthony Eden's concessions over Abyssinia and invades Abyssinia; League Council declares Italy aggressor and imposes sanctions Anti-Hapsburg laws abolished in Austria President Roosevelt signs U.S. Social Security Act Huey Long assassinated by Dr. Carl Weiss in Louisiana Capitol Building Wealth Tax Act passed in U.S. King George II returns to Greece Schuschnigg and Starhemberg stage their anti-Heimwehr coup d'état in Vienna Milan Hodza becomes Premier of Czechoslovakia Chiang Kai-shek named President of Chin. executive Hoare-Laval plan on Abyssinia published; Samuel Hoare resigns; Eden appointed Brit. Foreign Secretary T. G. Masaryk resigns as President of Czechoslovakia and is succeeded by Eduard Benes Nobel Peace Prize: Anti-Nazi Ger. author Carl von Ossietzky Josef Pilsudski, Pol. general and statesman, d. (b. 1867) Rama VIII, Ananda Mahidon, becomes King of Siam (assassinated 1946) *(contd)*	Zoë Akins: "The Old Maid," Pulitzer Prize drama London publisher Victor Gollancz founds Left Book Club Auden and Isherwood: "The Dog beneath the Skin" Ivy Compton-Burnett: "A House and Its Head" Cyril Connolly: "The Rock Pool" Clarence Day: "Life with Father" Walter de la Mare: "Poems 1919—1934" André Malraux: "Le Temps du mépris" T. S. Eliot: "Murder in the Cathedral" James T. Farrell: "Studs Lonigan" Clifford Odets: "Waiting for Lefty"; "Paradise Lost"; "Till the Day I Die" Robert E. Sherwood: "The Petrified Forest" Emlyn Williams: "Night Must Fall" Françoise Sagan, Fr. novelist, b. G. W. Russell ("A.E"), Ir. poet, d. (b. 1867) Henri Barbusse, Fr. author, d. (b. 1873) A. J. Cronin: "The Stars Look Down" Jean Giraudoux: "La Guerre de Troie n'aura pas lieu" Sinclair Lewis: "It Can't Happen Here" Kurt Tucholsky, Ger. author, d. (b. 1890) Thomas Wolfe: "Of Time and the River" Alexander Moissi, Ger. actor, d. (b. 1881) Graham Greene: "England Made Me" George Santayana: "The Last Puritan" John Steinbeck: "Tortilla Flat" Paul Bourget, Fr. author, d. (b. 1852)	Sidney and Beatrice Webb: "Soviet Communism: A New Civilization?" R. H. Hodgkin: "History of the Anglo-Saxons" J. B. S. Haldane: "Philosophy of a Biologist" Karl Jaspers: "Suffering and Existence" Karl Barth: "Credo"

D. VISUAL ARTS	E. MUSIC	F. SCIENCE, TECHNOLOGY, GROWTH	G. DAILY LIFE	
Cass Gilbert, Amer. architect (Woolworth Building, New York), d. (b. 1859)	Macbeth of Mzensk," opera, Moscow Igor Stravinsky: "Persephone," ballet-mime, Paris Virgil Thomson (on book by Gertrude Stein): "Four Saints in Three Acts," opera, Hartford, Conn. Rachmaninoff: "Rhapsody on a Theme of Paganini" Popular songs: "Blue Moon"; "The Continental"; "Stars Fell on Alabama"; "All through the Night"	(−1937) Nobel Prize for Chemistry: Harold Urey (U.S.) for his discovery of heavy hydrogen	S. S. "Normandie" (Fr.) launched; the largest ship afloat till "Queen Elizabeth" Osoaviakhim, U.S.S.R. balloon, ascends 13 miles into stratosphere Dionne quintuplets b. (Callendar, Ontario) "Morro Castle" burns and sinks off Asbury Park, N.J.; 130 die S.S. "Queen Mary" launched F.B.I. shoots John Dillinger, "Public Enemy No. 1" Statistics– world wide scheduled air service: route mileage, 223,100 (in 1920–9,700); miles flown, 103,432,000 (in 1920–2,969,000) Wavelength of European broadcasting stations altered to conform with recommendations of Lucerne Committee	**1934 contd**
Max Liebermann d. (b. 1847) Salvador Dali: "Giraffe on Fire" Russell Flint: "Majura the Strong" Stanley Spencer: "Workmen in the House" Exhibition of Chin. art at Burlington House, London Jacob Epstein: "Ecce Homo" Paul Signac, Fr. painter, d. (b. 1863) Films: "Anna Karenina" (Garbo); "David Copperfield" (David Selznick); "Mutiny on the Bounty," Academy Award (Clark Gable, Charles Laughton); "Becky Sharp" (Mamoulian); "Pasteur" (Paul Muni); "Toni" (Renoir); "The 39 Steps" (Hitchcock); "The Informer" (John Ford, Victor McLaglen) Gaston Lachaise d. (b. 1882) Childe Hassam d. (b. 1859)	Paul Dukas, Fr. composer, d. (b. 1865) Alban Berg, Aust. composer, d. (b. 1885) Electric Hammond organs become popular in the U.S. Gershwin: "Porgy and Bess," opera, New York Jazz becomes "Swing" Stravinsky: "Chroniques de ma vie," autobiography Popular songs: "Begin the Beguine"; "The Music Goes 'Round and 'Round"; "I Got Plenty o' Nuthin'"; "It Ain't Necessarily So"; "Just One of Those Things"	Radar equipment to detect aircraft built by Robert Watson Watt Ger. chemist Gerhard Domagk announces the discovery of Prontosil, the first sulfa drug for treating streptococcal infections Oil pipelines between Iraq, Haifa, and Tripolis opened The longest bridge in the world opened over the lower Zambesi Nobel Prize for Chemistry: Frédéric and Irène Joliot-Curie for the synthesis of new radioactive elements Ivan Mitshurin, Russ. naturalist, d. (b. 1855) Hugo De Vries, Dutch botanist, d. (b.1848) James Henry Breasted, Amer. Egyptologist and historian, d. (b. 1865)	Brit. Council founded Bank of Canada established Malcolm Campbell drives "Bluebird" at 276.8 mph (Daytona Beach, Fla.) S.S. "Normandie" crosses Atlantic in 107 hours, 33 minutes The U.S. Professional Golfers' Association hosts 34 tournaments with total prize money of $135,000 Rumba becomes the fashionable dance Moscow subway opened Max Euwe (Dutch) defeats Alekhine (Russ.-Fr.) for world chess title Alcoholics Anonymous organized in New York City CIO (Congress of Industrial Organizations) organized by John L. Lewis U.S. Golf Association Amateur championship won by W. Lawson Little, Jr.; Open by Sam Parks, Jr. "Omaha," W. Saunders up, wins Belmont and Preakness Stakes and Kentucky Derby James J. Braddock outpoints Max Baer to win world heavyweight boxing crown Detroit (AL) beats Chicago (NL) 4—2 to win World Series	**1935**

	A. HISTORY, POLITICS	B. LITERATURE, THEATER	C. RELIGION, PHILOSOPHY, LEARNING
1935 contd	Croix de Feu (Fascist organization) founded in France Ger. Luftwaffe formed Persia changes its name to Iran Oliver Wendell Holmes, Amer. jurist, d. (b. 1841)		
1936	King George V of England d.; succeeded by his son Edward VIII Fr. Premier Laval is replaced by Albert Sarraut in Jan.; Sarraut is succeeded by Léon Blum in June Koki Hirota named Premier of Japan German troops occupy Rhineland; elections in Germany give Hitler 99 per cent of the vote; Four-Year Plan inaugurated Italy, Austria, and Hungary sign Rome Pact Britain, France, and the U.S. sign the London Naval Convention King Fuad of Egypt d.; succeeded by his son Farouk (—1952) Arab High Committee formed to combat Jewish claims Abyssinian War ends and Italy annexes the country; King Victor Emmanuel proclaimed Emperor of Abyssinia Schuschnigg, the Aust. Chancellor, becomes leader of the Fatherland Front Count Ciano, Mussolini's son-in-law, appointed Ital. Foreign Minister Austro-Ger. convention acknowledges Aust. independence Spanish Civil War begins in July; Junta de Defensa Nacional set up in Burgos; Franco captures Badajoz; Franco appointed Chief of State by the insurgents in Oct.; siege of Madrid begins; Span. government moves to Valencia Chiang Kai-shek enters Canton France devalues franc; Italy devalues lira Oswald Mosley leads anti-Jewish march to Whitechapel, London, and is driven out Gossip begins in London about King Edward VIII's relationship with Mrs. Wallis Simpson Mussolini and Hitler proclaim Rome—Berlin Axis F. D. Roosevelt reelected President of the U.S. by landslide Anti-Comintern Pact signed by Germany and Japan King Edward VIII abdicates and is succeeded by his brother George VI Dec. 11; Edward is named Duke of Windsor Chiang Kai-shek declares war on Japan Trotsky exiled from Russia; settles in Mexico Germany begins building the Siegfried Line	Maxwell Anderson: "High Tor" W. H. Auden: "On the Island" Maurice Baring: "Have You Anything to Declare?" Georges Bernanos: "The Diary of a Country Priest" Dorothea Brande: "Wake Up and Live!" Dale Carnegie: "How to Win Friends and Influence People" Walter D. Edmonds: "Drums Along the Mohawk" John Gunther: "Inside Europe" F. Scott Fitzgerald: "The Crack-Up" Aldous Huxley: "Eyeless in Gaza" Margaret Mitchell: "Gone With the Wind," Pulitzer Prize novel Montherlant: "Les Jeunes filles" (—1939) Charles Morgan: "Sparkenbroke" Dylan Thomas: "Twenty-Five Poems" Allen Lane founds Penguin Books Terence Rattigan: "French without Tears" Armand Salacrou: "L'Inconnue d'Arras" Irwin Shaw: "Bury the Dead" Robert E. Sherwood: "Idiot's Delight," Pulitzer Prize drama Rudyard Kipling d. (b. 1865) A. E. Housman, Eng. poet, d. (b. 1859) G. K. Chesterton, Eng. author, d. (b. 1874) Maxim Gorki, Russ. author, d. (b. 1868) Luigi Pirandello, Ital. dramatist, d. (b. 1867) Winifred Holtby: "South Riding" (posth.) Kaufman and Hart: "You Can't Take It With You," Amer. comedy, Pulitzer Prize 1937 Jean Anouilh: "Voyageur sans bagage," Fr. play John Knittel: "El Hakim," novel Nobel Prize for Literature: Eugene O'Neill Grazia Deledda, Ital. novelist, d. (b. 1875) Federico García Lorca, Span. dramatist, d. (b. 1899) Miguel de Unamuno, Span. author, d. (b. 1864) Robert P. Tristram Coffin: "Strange Holiness," Pulitzer Prize poetry Robert Frost: "A Further Range," Pulitzer Prize poetry (1937) Tristan Tzara: "L'Homme approximatif"	Lancelot Hogben: "Mathematics for the Million" J. M. Keynes: "General Theory of Employment, Interest, and Money" John Strachey: "The Theory and Practice of Socialism" H. A. L. Fisher: "England and Europe" A. J. Ayer: "Language, Truth and Logic" Sigmund Freud: "Autobiography" Oswald Generer, Ger. philosopher, d. (b. 1880) Beatrice Webb: "My Apprenticeship"

D. VISUAL ARTS	E. MUSIC	F. SCIENCE, TECHNOLOGY, GROWTH	G. DAILY LIFE	
				1935 contd
Laura Knight: "Ballet" Mondriaan: "Composition in Red and Blue" Gropius and Fry design film studios in Denham, Buckinghamshire, Eng. Amer. painter Lyonel Feininger returns from Ger. home to New York Hans Poelzig, Ger. architect, d. (b. 1869) Nazi exhibition of "Degenerate Art" Films: "Modern Times" (Chaplin); "Things to Come" (Menzies); "Mr. Deeds Goes to Town" (Capra); "Fury" (Fritz Lang); "San Francisco" (Gable, Tracy); "The Ghost Goes West" (René Clair); "Intermezzo" (Ingrid Bergman); "The Great Ziegfeld," Academy Award	Richard Strauss: "Die Schweigsame Frau" opera, Dresden Constant Lambert: "Summer's Last Will and Testament" Ottorino Respighi, Ital. composer, d. (b. 1879) Popular songs: "It's De-Lovely"; "Whiffenpoof Song"; "I'm an Old Cowhand (from the Rio Grande)"; "Is It True What They Say about Dixie?"; "I Can't Get Started with You"; "Pennies from Heaven" Richard Rodgers and Lorenz Hart: "On Your Toes" Samuel Barber: Symphony No. 1, Rome	Ivan Pavlov, Russ. physiologist, d. (b. 1849) Ger. diesel-electric vessel "Wupperthal" is launched Philipp Fauth: "Our Moon" William Mitchell, Amer. pioneer in military aircraft design, d. (b. 1879) Boulder (Hoover) Dam on Colorado River in Nevada and Arizona is completed, creating Lake Mead, largest reservoir in the world Nobel Prize for Physics: Carl David Anderson (U.S.) for his work on the positron and Victor Francis Hess (Aust.) for work on cosmic radiation Dr. Alexis Carrel develops artificial heart Dirigible "Hindenburg" lands at Lakehurst, N. J., after transatlantic flight	Ford Foundation established London University moves into its new home in Bloomsbury Mrs. Amy Mollison flies from England to Cape Town in 3 days, 6 hours 25 minutes J. A. Mollison flies from Newfoundland to London in 13 hours 17 minutes Jean Batten flies solo from England to New Zealand in 11 days and 56 minutes Olympic Games held in Berlin–Jesse Owens wins four gold medals Len Hutton emerges as England's leading cricket player Max Schmeling (Ger.) defeats Joe Louis (U.S.) in 12 rounds Louis Blériot, Fr. flier, d. (b. 1872) BBC London inaugurates television service "Queen Mary," 81,235 tons, wins Blue Riband by crossing Atlantic in 3 days, 23 hours 57 minutes Population figures in millions: China, 422; India, 360; U.S.S.R., 173; U.S., 127; Japan, 89; Germany, 70; Great Britain, 47; France, 44 Henry Luce begins publication of "Life" magazine U.S. Lawn Tennis Association Men's Singles won by Frederick J. Perry, Women's by Alice Marble "Bold Venture" wins Preakness Stakes and Kentucky Derby U.S. Golf Association Amateur won by John W. Fischer; Open by Tony Manero Baseball Hall of Fame is founded at Cooperstown, N.Y. Stanford wins Rose Bowl football game from Southern Methodist, 7—0 New York (AL) wins World Series, 4—2, over New York (NL) Bruno Richard Hauptman convicted of kidnaping and killing Lindbergh baby Floods sweep Johnstown, Pa.	1936

1937

A. HISTORY, POLITICS

Poland refuses to sign agreement to return Danzig to Germany
Amnesty declared for illegal Aust. Nazis
Moscow show trial against Karl Radek and other political leaders takes place; purge of U.S.S.R. generals; Marshal Tukhachevsky executed
George VI crowned King of Great Britain; broadcast of ceremonies is first worldwide program heard in the U.S.
Spanish rebels take Malaga, destroy Guernica, and Gijón; Span. government moves to Barcelona; Franco begins naval blockade; government troops open offensive at Teruel
All-India Congress Party wins elections
Mussolini visits Libya and Berlin
Austen Chamberlain, Brit. statesman, d. (b. 1863)
Italy and Yugoslavia sign Belgrade Pact
Schuschnigg and Mussolini meet in Venice
F. D. Roosevelt signs U.S. Neutrality Act
Imperial Conference held in London
Stanley Baldwin retires; Neville Chamberlain becomes Prime Minister of Britain
Prince Konoye named Jap. Premier; aggressive Jap. war policy begins
Léon Blum resigns; Camille Chautemps becomes Fr. Premier
Elihu Root, U.S. political figure, d. (b. 1845)
Japanese seize Peking, Tientsin, Shanghai, Nanking, and Hangchow; Chiang Kai-shek unites with Communists, led by Mao Tse-tung and Chou En-lai; Chin. government makes Chungking its capital
Royal Commission on Palestine recommends the establishment of Arab and Jewish states
Britain signs naval agreements with Germany and the U.S.S.R.
President Roosevelt appoints Hugo Black to Supreme Court (—1971)
Bakr Sidqi, dictator of Iraq, assassinated
Germany guarantees inviolability of Belgium
Wall Street stock market decline signals serious economic recession in the U.S.
U.S. Supreme Court rules in favor of minimum wage law for women
U.S. government statistics show that one half-million Americans were involved in sitdown strikes between Sept. 1936 and May 1937
Riots in Sudeten area of Czechoslovakia; Sudeten Germans leave Czech Parliament
Italy joins Anti-Comintern Pact
Lord Halifax visits Hitler; beginning of policy of appeasement
Italy withdraws from League of Nations
Jap. planes sink U.S. gunboat "Panay" in Chin. waters
Aden becomes Brit. Crown Colony
Strike against Republic Steel, Chicago–4 killed, 84 hurt
Tomás Garrigue Masaryk, first president of Czechoslovakia d. (b. 1850)

B. LITERATURE, THEATER

Auden and Isherwood: "The Ascent of F.6"
Van Wyck Brooks: "The Flowering of New England," Pulitzer Prize history
John Dos Passos: "U.S.A."
Ernest Hemingway: "To Have and Have Not"
Malraux: "L'Espoir"
John P. Marquand: "The Late George Apley," Pulitzer Prize novel (1938)
Allan Nevins: "Hamilton Fish," Pulitzer Prize biography
Clifford Odets: "Golden Boy"
George Orwell: "The Road to Wigan Pier"
Sartre: "La Nausée"
John Steinbeck: "Of Mice and Men"
Giraudoux: "Elektre"
Laurence Housman: "Victoria Regina"
J. B. Priestley: "Time and the Conways"
Vanessa Redgrave, Eng. actress, b.
John Drinkwater, Eng. dramatist, d. (b. 1882)
J. M. Barrie, Scot. dramatist, d. (b. 1860)
Edith Wharton, Amer. author, d. (b. 1862)
Kenneth Roberts: "Northwest Passage"
Adele Sandrock, Ger. actress, d. (b. 1864)
A. J. Cronin: "The Citadel"
Compton Mackenzie: "The Four Winds of Love"

C. RELIGION, PHILOSOPHY, LEARNING

Walter Lippmann: "The Good Society"
Seebohm Rowntree: "The Human Needs of Labor"
Aldous Huxley: "Ends and Means"
Martin Niemöller, Protestant parson of Berlin-Dahlem, interned in a concentration camp by Hitler (—1945)
Karen Horney: "The Neurotic Personality of Our Time"

1937

D. VISUAL ARTS

Picasso: "Guernica," mural for Paris World Exhibition
Paul Mellon endows National Gallery, Washington, D.C.
Jacob Epstein: "Consummatum Est," sculpture
Klee: "Revolution of the Viaducts," surrealistic painting
Joan Miró: "Still Life with Old Shoe"
Albert Speer becomes Hitler's chief architect
Films: "Snow White and the Seven Dwarfs" (Disney); "Elephant Boy" (Sabu); "Un Carnet de Bal" (Duvivier); "Dead End" (William Wyler); "La Grande Illusion" (Jean Renoir); "Camille" (Garbo); "Life of Emile Zola," Academy Award (Muni)
Georges Braque: "Woman with a Mandolin"

E. MUSIC

Stravinsky: "Jeu des cartes," ballet, New York
Shostakovich: Symphony No. 5, Op. 47
Jaromir Weinberger: "Wallenstein," opera, Vienna
Maurice Ravel d. (b. 1875)
Richard Rodgers and Lorenz Hart (music), George S. Kaufman and Moss Hart (book): "I'd Rather Be Right"
Rodgers and Hart: "Babes in Arms," musical comedy, New York
Harold Rome: "Pins and Needles," revue, New York (1,108 consecutive performances)
Paul von Klenau: "Rembrandt van Rijn," opera, Berlin
George Gershwin d. (b. 1898)
Carl Orff: "Carmina Burana"
Albert Roussel, Fr. composer, d. (b. 1869)
Israel Philharmonic Orchestra founded in Tel-Aviv by Bronislaw Hubermann
Popular songs: "Bei Mir Bist Du Schön"; "The Lady Is a Tramp"; "Whistle While You Work"; "A Foggy Day in London Town"; "The Dipsy Doodle"; "Harbor Lights"; "It's Nice Work If You Can Get It"; "I've Got My Love to Keep Me Warm"

F. SCIENCE, TECHNOLOGY, GROWTH

Lord Ernest Rutherford d. (b. 1871)
Marconi d. (b. 1874)
Insulin used to control diabetes
Crystalline vitamin A and vitamin K concentrates are first obtained
Wallace H. Carothers patents nylon (for the du Pont Company)
The first jet engine built by Frank Whittle
Marietta Blau (Vienna) uses a photographic plate to examine cosmic radiation
Nobel Prize for Physics: Clinton Joseph Davisson (U.S.) and Sir George Paget Thomson (Eng.)
President Roosevelt dedicates Bonneville Dam on the Columbia River in Oregon

G. DAILY LIFE

Matrimonial Causes Bill facilitates divorce proceedings in England
Amelia Earhart lost on Pacific flight
A.R.P. introduced in England
Lincoln Tunnel provides second major vehicular tunnel between New York and New Jersey
Lord Nuffield founds Nuffield College, Oxford
Disaster of dirigible "Hindenburg" at Lakehurst described in first transcontinental radio broadcast
Fr. armament factories Schneider-Creuzot nationalized
Golden Gate Bridge, San Francisco, opens
Erich Ludendorff, Ger. general, d. (b. 1865)
John D. Rockefeller d. (b. 1839)
Alekhine (U.S.S.R.-Fr.) regains world chess title from Euwe (Dutch) (—1946)
E. A. Filene, Boston merchant, d. (b. 1860)
Andrew Mellon, industrialist, financier, and philanthropist, d. (b. 1855)
London bus strike
Duke of Windsor marries Mrs. Wallis Simpson
London "Daily Telegraph" and "Morning Post" merge
Joe Louis wins world heavyweight boxing title, defeating James J. Braddock (–1948)
Billy Butlin opens the first commercial holiday camp in Britain
"War Admiral," C. Kurtsinger up, wins Belmont and Preakness Stakes and Kentucky Derby
U.S. tennis team wins Davis Cup from England
U.S. Lawn Tennis Association Men's Singles won by Don Budge; Women's Singles by Anita Lizana (Chile)
U.S. Golf Association Amateur championship won by Johnny Goodman; Open won by Ralph Guldahl
Pittsburgh wins Rose Bowl football game, 21—0, against Washington
New York (AL) wins World Series, 4—1, defeating New York (NL)

	A. HISTORY, POLITICS	B. LITERATURE, THEATER	C. RELIGION, PHILOSOPHY, LEARNING
1938	Japanese enter Tsingtao, install Chin. puppet government in Nanking, withdraw from League, and take Canton and Hankow Hitler appoints himself War Minister, Ribbentrop Foreign Minister; meets Schuschnigg at Berchtesgaden and marches into Austria; Mussolini and Hitler meet in Rome; pogroms in Germany Sudeten Germans in Czechoslovakia demand autonomy–first Czechoslovak crisis–Runciman visits Prague and reports in favor of Nazi claims; Germany mobilizes; France calls up reservists; Chamberlain meets Hitler at Berchtesgaden and Godesberg; Hodza resigns from Czech cabinet; Munich conference takes place in Sept.; Germany occupies Sudetenland Oct. 10 Franco recaptures Teruel, takes Vinaroz, and begins offensive in Catalonia Eden resigns in protest against Chamberlain's policy; Winston Churchill leads country's outcry; Duff Cooper resigns as First Lord of the Admiralty; President Benes resigns; Slovakia and Ruthenia granted autonomy; Hungary annexes southern Slovakia; Emil Hacha installed as puppet President of Czechoslovakia U.S.S.R. show trials condemn Bukharin, Rykov, and Jagoda Martin Dies (Democrat, Texas) becomes chairman of newly formed House Un-American Activities Committee (HUAC) of U.S. House of Representatives King George VI visits Paris Anti-Jewish legislation enacted in Italy Kemal Atatürk d. (b. 1881); succeeded by Ismet Inönü as President of Turkey Keitel, Guderian, and Halder become the new leaders of the Ger. army Benjamin Cardozo, U.S. Supreme Court justice, d. (b. 1870) President Roosevelt sends appeal to Hitler and Mussolini to settle European problems amicably U.S. Supreme Court rules that University of Missouri Law School must admit Negroes because of lack of other facilities in the area President Roosevelt appoints Stanley F. Reed to the Supreme Court (—1957) President Roosevelt recalls Amer. ambassador to Germany; Germany recalls her ambassador to the U.S.	Stuart Chase: "The Tyranny of Words" Cyril Connolly: "Enemies of Promise" Daphne du Maurier: "Rebecca" William Faulkner: "The Unvanquished" Rachel Field: "All This, and Heaven, Too" Graham Greene: "Brighton Rock" Christopher Isherwood: "Goodbye to Berlin" Philip Barry: "Here Come the Clowns" Marjorie Kinnan Rawlings: "The Yearling," Pulitzer Prize novel (1939) Robert Sherwood: "Abe Lincoln in Illinois," Pulitzer Prize drama (1939) Thornton Wilder: "Our Town," Pulitzer Prize drama Emlyn Williams: "The Corn Is Green" Richard Wright: "Uncle Tom's Children" Gabriele D'Annunzio d. (b. 1863) Constantin Stanislavsky d. (b. 1863) Karel Capek, Czech author, d. (b. 1890) Owen Wister d. (b. 1860) Thomas Wolfe, Amer. novelist, d. (b. 1900) Nobel Prize for Literature: Pearl S. Buck (U.S.) Louis Bromfield: "The Rains Came" Bernanos: "Les Grands Cimetières sous la lune" Orson Welles's radio production of H. G. Wells's "War of the Worlds" causes considerable panic Sinclair Lewis: "The Prodigal Parents" Robert Benchley: "After 1903–What?" Ernest Hemingway: "The Fifth Column" Robinson Jeffers: "Selected Poetry" John Gould Fletcher: "Selected Poems," Pulitzer Prize (1939) Archibald MacLeish: "Land of the Free," poetry collection	David Lloyd George: "The Truth About the Peace Treaty" Johan Huizinga: "Homo Ludens" Lewis Mumford: "The Culture of Cities" Edwyn Bewan: "Symbolism and Belief" Edmund Husserl, Aust. philosopher, d. (b. 1859) John Dewey: "Logic: The Theory of Inquiry"; "Experience and Education" Alfred North Whitehead: "Modes of Thought" George Santayana:" "The Realm of Truth"
1939	Roosevelt asks Congress for $552 million for defense and demands assurances from Hitler and Mussolini that they will not attack 31 named states Chamberlain and Halifax visit Rome Walther Funk replaces Dr. Schacht as President of Ger. Reichsbank Germany occupies Bohemia and Moravia, places Slovakia under "protection," annexes Memel, renounces nonaggression pact with Poland and naval agreement with England, and concludes both 10-year alliance with Italy and nonaggression pact with U.S.S.R. Japanese occupy Hainan and blockade Brit. concession at Tientsin; U.S. renounces Jap. trade agreement of 1911 Britain and France recognize Franco's government; U.S. recognition follows; Span. Civil War ends; Spain joins Anti-Comintern Pact and leaves League of Nations Italy invades Albania Hungary quits League of Nations Conscription adopted in Britain Molotov succeeds Litvinov as U.S.S.R. Commissar for Foreign Affairs King George VI and Queen Elizabeth visit the U.S. England and Poland sign a treaty of mutual assistance *(contd)*	Russel Crouse and Howard Lindsay: "Life with Father" Robert Graves: "The Long Week-End" John Gunther: "Inside Asia" Adolf Hitler: "Mein Kampf" (complete Eng. translation) James Joyce: "Finnegans Wake" Richard Llewellyn: "How Green Was My Valley" Thomas Mann: "Lotte in Weimer" John Steinbeck: "The Grapes of Wrath," Pulitzer Prize novel (1940) Jan Struther: "Mrs. Miniver" T. S. Eliot: "The Family Reunion" William Saroyan: "The Time of Your Life," Pulitzer Prize drama (1940) George S. Kaufman and Moss Hart: "The Man Who Came to Dinner" W. B. Yeats, Ir. poet, d. (b. 1865) Ernst Toller, Ger. dramatist, d. (b. 1893) Heywood Broun, U.S. journalist, d. (b. 1888) Ford Madox Ford, Eng. author, d. (b. 1873) *(contd)*	Karl Haushofer: "German Cultural Policy in the Indo-Pacific Area" Pope Pius XI d.; Cardinal Eugenio Pacelli elected Pope Pius XII (—1958) E. H. Carr: "The Twenty Years' Crisis" Serge Chakotin: "The Rape of the Masses" John Dewey: "Freedom and Culture" Arthur Eddington: "The Philosophy of Physical Science" Charles Sherrington: "Man and His Nature" *(contd)*

D. VISUAL ARTS	E. MUSIC	F. SCIENCE, TECHNOLOGY, GROWTH	G. DAILY LIFE	
Raoul Dufy: "Regatta" Frank Lloyd Wright builds Taliesin West, Phoenix, Ariz. Walter Gropius and Marcel Breuer design Haggerty House, Cohasset, Mass. The Cloisters, endowed by Rockefeller, is built in upper Manhattan as a branch of the Metropolitan Museum to house medieval art Ernst Barlach, Ger. sculptor and poet, d. (b. 1870) Oskar Kokoschka leaves Germany and settles in England Films: "Pygmalion" (Leslie Howard); "Le Quai des Brumes" (Jean Gabin); "Alexander Nevski" (Eisenstein); "The Lady Vanishes" (Hitchcock); "Bank Holiday" (Carol Reed); "You Can't Take It with You," Academy Award William Glackens d. (b. 1870)	Feodor Chaliapin d. (b. 1873) Honegger: "Jeanne d'Arc au bûcher," stage-oratorio, Basel Béla Bartók: Violin Concerto Benny Goodman's band brings new style to jazz music Gian Carlo Menotti: "Amelia Goes to the Ball," Metropolitan Opera, New York Richard Strauss: "Daphne," opera, Munich Harvard University grants an honorary doctorate to Negro singer Marian Anderson Werner Egk: "Peer Gynt," opera, Berlin Kurt Weill: "Knickerbocker Holiday," musical comedy, New York Walter Piston: Symphony No. 1; "The Incredible Flutist," ballet score Popular songs: "Flat Foot Floogie with a Floy Floy"; "September Song"; "A Tisket, A Tasket"; "Jeepers Creepers"; "Falling in Love with Love"; "You Must Have Been a Beautiful Baby"	Franz Boas: "General Anthropology" Albert Einstein and Leopold Infeld: "The Evolution of Physics" Perlon invented Lajos Biró (Hungary) invents ballpoint pen Lancelot Hogben: "Science for the Citizen" Grote Reber receives short waves from Milky Way Karter, Salomon, and Fritzsche chemically identify vitamin E Isolation of pyridoxine (vitamin B6)	Women's Voluntary Services founded in Britain by Lady Reading Bartlett Dam, Ariz., completed (286 feet high) Clarence Darrow, U.S. lawyer, d. (b. 1857) Gas masks are issued to Brit. civilians during the Munich crisis 40-hour work week established in the U.S. Lambeth Walk becomes fashionable dance 20,000 TV sets are in service in New York City Howard Hughes flies around the world in 3 days, 19 hours 17 minutes S.S. "Queen Elizabeth" launched Edward Hulton starts "Picture Post" (London) Len Hutton scores 364 runs against Australia at Oval Test Match, London John Warde jumps after spending almost 12 hours on the ledge of the 17th floor of the Gotham Hotel, New York Don Budge, U.S. tennis player, accomplishes Grand Slam, winning all four major championships 32,000 people die in auto accidents in the U.S. U.S. Golf Association Amateur championship, Willie Turnesa; Open, Ralph Guldahl U.S. Lawn Tennis Association Men's Singles championship, Don Budge; Women's Singles, Alice Marble U.S. tennis team defeats Australia to retain Davis Cup Eddie Arcaro rides his first Kentucky Derby winner, "Lawrin" California wins Rose Bowl football game, 13—0, against Alabama New York (AL) wins World Series against Chicago (NL), 4—0 350 theaters in Germany and approx. 12,000 periodicals	**1938**
Laura Knight: "Golden Girl" Picasso: "Night Fishing at Antibes" Stanley Spencer: "Christ in the Wilderness" (—1953) Graham Sutherland: "Entrance to a Lane" "Grandma Moses" (Anna M. Robertson) becomes famous in the U.S. Jacob Epstein: "Adam," marble sculpture Lyonel Feininger: "San Francisco" Kandinsky: "Neighborhood" Henry Moore: "Reclining Figure," sculpture Utrillo: "La Tour Saint Jacques" *(contd)*	Rodgers and Hart: "The Boys from Syracuse" Aaron Copland: "Billy the Kid," ballet, New York Myra Hess organizes National Gallery lunchtime concerts in London War songs in England: "Roll out the Barrel" (of Czech origin); "Hang Out the Washing on the Siegfried Line"; "The Last Time I Saw Paris"; in Germany: "Wir fahren gegen England"; "Bomben auf England"; "Lili Marlene" Carl Orff: "Der Mond," fairy tale opera Ivor Novello: "The Dancing Years," operetta, *(contd)*	Hahn and Strassman obtain barium isotopes by bombarding uranium with neutrons Joliot-Curie demonstrates possibility of splitting the atom Paul Muller synthesizes DDT Polyethylene invented Sigmund Freud d. (b. 1856) Igor Sikorsky (Russ.-Amer.) constructs first helicopter *(contd)*	BOAC founded Malcolm Campbell establishes his water-speed record of 368.85 mph Pan-American Airways begins regularly scheduled commercial flights between the U.S. and Europe on "Dixie Clipper" Frank Buchman re-forms Oxford Group as Moral Re-Armament Baseball game is first televised in U.S. Earthquake in Anatolia, Turkey, claims 45,000 victims Anglo-Saxon burial ship is excavated at Sutton Hoo, Suffolk Balloons used as barriers against aircraft attacks in Britain Radar stations are used in Britain to give early warning of approaching enemy aircraft Nylon stockings first appear "Johnstown," J. Stout up, wins Belmont Stakes and Kentucky Derby Australia wins Davis Cup from U.S. U.S. Lawn Tennis Men's Singles won by Bobby Riggs; Women's by Alice Marble *(contd)*	**1939**

	A. HISTORY, POLITICS	B. LITERATURE, THEATER	C. RELIGION, PHILOSOPHY, LEARNING
1939 contd	Women and children are first evacuated from London Charles Schwab, U.S. industrialist, d. (b. 1862) World War II: Germany invades Poland and annexes Danzig Sept. 1; Britain and France declare war on Germany Sept. 3; Roosevelt declares U.S. neutral; Winston Churchill becomes First Lord of the Admiralty; Germans sink the "Athenia" off Ireland; Smuts becomes Premier of S. Africa; Germans overrun western Poland and reach Brest-Litovsk and Warsaw; U.S.S.R. invades Poland from the east; Brit. Expeditionary Force (158,000 men) sent to France; Britain and France reject Hitler's peace feelers; H.M.S. "Royal Oak" sunk; U.S.S.R. invades Finland and is expelled from the League; Battle of the River Plate; Hans Frank named Nazi Governor-General of Poland, Ernst Udet General of the Luftwaffe, von Papen ambassador to Turkey After 1938 recession, U.S. economy begins to recover and, by autumn, is booming from orders of European countries for arms and war equipment U.S. Supreme Court rules sitdown strikes are illegal Coal strike by United Mine Workers demonstrates power of John L. Lewis President Roosevelt appoints William O. Douglas and Felix Frankfurter (—1962) to the Supreme Court	Ethel M. Dell, Eng. novelist, d. (b. 1881) F. R. Benson, Eng. actor-manager, d. (b. 1858) Anna Seghers: "The Seventh Cross" Eric Ambler: "The Mask of Dimitrios" C. S. Forester: "Captain Horatio Hornblower" André Gide: "Journal 1885—1939" Saint-Exupéry: "Terre des hommes" Carl Van Doren: "Benjamin Franklin," Pulitzer Prize biography	Havelock Ellis, Eng. psychologist, d. (b. 1859) H. W. Briggs (U.S.): "The Law of Nations" Methodist Church, rent by schisms of 1830 and 1844, reunited José Ortega y Gasset: "On Love"
1940	World War II: Bacon, butter and sugar rationed in Britain; Finland signs peace treaty with the U.S.S.R. after being attacked; Germany invades Norway and Denmark; Chamberlain resigns and Churchill becomes Brit. Prime Minister; Home Guard formed in Britain; Germany invades Holland, Belgium, and Luxembourg; Churchill's "blood, toil, tears, and sweat" speech; Dutch army surrenders; Belgium capitulates; Brit. forces (340,000) evacuated from Dunkirk May 29—June 3; Italy declares war on France and Britain; Germans enter Paris June 14; Churchill offers France union with Britain; but Marshal Pétain, the new head of Fr. government, concludes armistice with Germany; Royal Navy sinks Fr. fleet in Oran; RAF begins night bombing of Germany; 90 Ger. bombers first shot down over Britain; Czechoslovak National Committee in London recognized as provisional government; Britain signs agreements with Pol. government and Free French under de Gaulle; the Battle of Britain in Aug.; Japan, Germany, and Italy sign military and economic pact; Congress passes Selective Service Act to mobilize U.S. military; 180 Ger. planes shot down Aug. 15; the London "Blitz" (all night raids) begins; U.S. destroyers sold to Britain; Hitler and Mussolini meet at Brenner Pass; heavy raids on London (Sept., Oct., Nov.); Britain re-opens Burma Road; Germany intensifies U-boat warfare; Molotov visits Berlin; Eighth Army under Wavell opens offensive in North Africa; air raid on Manchester; Eden named Brit. Foreign Secretary Trotsky assassinated in Mexico on Stalin's orders (b. 1879) Neville Chamberlain d. (b. 1869) Hitler names Hermann Goering "Reichs-Marschall" and successor-designate Brit. Fascist leader Oswald Mosley imprisoned under Defence Regulations F. D. Roosevelt re-elected President of the U.S. for third term, defeating Wendell Willkie John L. Lewis, anti-Roosevelt labor leader, resigns as head of CIO after election *(contd)*	Mortimer Adler: "How to Read a Book" Graham Greene: "The Power and the Glory" Ernest Hemingway: "For Whom the Bell Tolls" Eugene O'Neill: "Long Day's Journey into Night" (produced 1956) Kenneth Roberts: "Oliver Wiswell" Upton Sinclair: "World's End," first of the Lanny Budd novels Richard Wright: "Native Son" Eric Ambler: "Journey into Fear" Arthur Bryant: "English Saga" Raymond Chandler: "Farewell, My Lovely" Lillian Hellman: "Watch on the Rhine" Arthur Koestler: "Darkness at Noon" Charles Morgan: "The Voyage" Emlyn Williams: "The Corn Is Green" Robert Ardrey: "Thunder Rock" John Buchan (Lord Tweedsmuir), Scot. author, d. (b. 1875) F. Scott Fitzgerald, U.S. author, d. (b. 1896) Hamlin Garland, U.S. author, d. (b. 1860) Selma Lagerlöf d. (b. 1858) Mrs. Patrick Campbell, Eng. actress, d. (b. 1865) Walther Hasenclever, Ger. dramatist, d. (b. 1890) Nathanael West (Nathan Wallenstein Weinstein), U.S. author, d. (b. 1903) Thomas Wolfe: "You Can't Go Home Again" (posth.) Carl Sandburg: "Abraham Lincoln: The War Years," Pulitzer Prize history Mark Van Doren: "Collected Poems," Pulitzer Prize Elliott Nugent and James Thurber: "The *(contd)*	J. M. Keynes: "How to Pay for the War" A. J. Ayer: "The Foundations of Empirical Knowledge" C. G. Jung: "The Interpretation of Personality" George Santayana: "The Realms of Being" (since 1927) H. A. L. Fisher, Eng. historian, d. (b. 1865) Edmund Wilson: "To the Finland Station" Emma Goldman, U.S. anarchist, d. (b. 1869) Lillian D. Wald, U.S. social worker, d. (b. 1867) Bertrand Russell, Eng. philosopher and mathematician, is appointed to William James lectureship at Harvard University despite his rejection by City College of New York

D. VISUAL ARTS	E. MUSIC	F. SCIENCE, TECHNOLOGY, GROWTH	G. DAILY LIFE	
Frank Lloyd Wright's design for the Johnson Wax Company building becomes a reality Films: "Ninotchka" (Garbo); "Gone With the Wind," Academy Award (Selznick); "Good-Bye, Mr. Chips" (Robert Donat); "The Wizard of Oz" (Garland); "Stagecoach" (John Ford) Douglas Fairbanks, Amer. actor, d. (b. 1883)	London Cole Porter: "Du Barry Was a Lady," musical comedy, New York Popular songs: "God Bless America"; "Three Little Fishes"; "Over the Rainbow"; "Beer Barrel Polka"; "I'll Never Smile Again"	Nobel Prize for Physics: Ernest O. Lawrence (U.S.) for development of cyclotron Philip Levine and Rufus Stetson (both U.S.) discover Rh factor in human blood Edwin H. Armstrong (U.S.) invents frequency modulation (FM)	U.S. Golf Association Amateur championship won by Marrin Ward; Open by Byron Nelson Southern California wins Rose Bowl football game, 7—3, from Duke New York (AL) defeats Cincinnati (NL) to win World Series, 4—0	**1939 contd**
Max Beckmann: "Circus Caravan" Kandinsky: "Sky Blue" Matisse: "The Rumanian Blouse" John Piper: "St. Mary le Port, Bristol" Rex Whistler: "Miss Laura Ridly" Frank Lloyd Wright: Southern College, Lakeland, Fla. David Low's anti-Hitler cartoons The Lascaux caves discovered in France; prehistoric wall paintings, approx. 20,000 B.C. Eric Gill, Eng. artist, d. (b. 1882) Films: "Grapes of Wrath" (John Ford); "The Great Dictator" (Chaplin); "Rebecca," Academy Award (Hitchcock); "Gaslight" (Thorold Dickinson); "Fantasia" (Disney); "Jud Süss" (Ger. anti-Jewish propaganda film with Werner Krauss) Edouard Vuillard d. (b. 1868) Paul Klee d. (b. 1879) Edmund Duffy wins third Pulitzer Prize for cartoons (also 1931 and 1934)	Irving Berlin: "Louisiana Purchase" Stravinsky: Symphony in C European composers who have moved from Europe to the U.S. include: Schönberg, Stravinsky, Bartók, Hindemith, Krenek, Milhaud, Martinu, Weill, Toch, Kálmán, Benatzky, Abraham, Stolz, and Oskar Straus Rodgers and Hart: "Pal Joey" Duke Ellington becomes known as composer and jazz pianist Popular songs: "You Are My Sunshine"; "How High the Moon"; "The Last Time I Saw Paris"; "When You Wish upon a Star"; "It's a Big, Wide, Wonderful World"; "Oh, Johnny"; "South of the Border"; "Blueberry Hill"; "Woodpecker Song"	Brit. Scientific Advisory Committee appointed Giant cyclotron built at the University of California for producing mesotrons from atomic nuclei Howard Florey develops penicillin as a practical antibiotic Carl Bosch, Ger. chemist and industrialist, d. (b. 1874) Julius Wagner von Jauregg, Aust. psychiatrist, d. (b. 1857) New combustion chamber for jet engines designed Cavity magnetron invented First electron microscope demonstrated by Radio Corporation of America, Camden, N.J. Edwin McMillan and Philip Abelson (both U.S.) discover neptunium, first transuranic element (atomic number 93) First successful helicopter flight in U.S. by Vought-Sikorsky Corporation	George Cross instituted by King George VI Lord Rothermere d. (b. 1868) Jack Dempsey retires from the ring Statistics–U.S. Gross National Product 100.6 (up 10% from 1939); population of U.S. 132 million (7.3% increase since 1930– smallest increase since statistics were begun, in 1790), including 0.5 million immigrants, mostly European refugees; Alien Registration Act shows presence in U.S. of 5 million aliens; average life expectancy in U.S. 64 (from 49 in 1900); 30 million U.S. homes have radios U.S. Lawn Tennis Association Men's Singles won by W. Donald McNeill; Women's Singles won by Alice Marble U.S. Golf Association Amateur championship won by R. D. Chapman; Open by W. Lawson Little, Jr. "Bimelech," F. A. Smith up, wins Belmont and Preakness Stakes Southern California defeats Tennessee to win the Rose Bowl football game 14—0 World Series won by Cincinnati (NL) against Detroit (AL), 4—3 "Galloping Gertie," suspension bridge over the Narrows of Puget Sound, Tacoma, Wash., breaks up in wind and drops almost 200 feet	**1940**

	A. HISTORY, POLITICS	B. LITERATURE, THEATER	C. RELIGION, PHILOSOPHY, LEARNING
1940 contd	William T. Borah, U.S. Senator and vigorous isolationist, d. (b. 1865) President Roosevelt appoints Frank Murphy to Supreme Court (—1949)	Male Animal" Robert E. Sherwood: "There Shall Be No Night," Pulitzer Prize play (1941)	
1941	World War II General Wavell occupies Benghazi; British invade Abyssinia; Lend-Lease bill signed in U.S.; Ger. air raids on London resumed; pro-Nazi Prince Paul, regent of Yugoslavia, deposed; Ger. U-boat attacks intensified; Ger. counter-offensive in North Africa opens; Benghazi evacuated; blitz on Coventry; Rommel attacks Tobruk; Stalin undisputed head of Soviet government; Hitler's deputy, Rufolf Hess, lands in Scotland; Germans invade Crete; HMS "Hood" sunk; "Bismarck" sunk; U.S. freezes German and Italian assets in the U.S.; Germans invade Russia, capture Minsk, Smolensk, Tallinn, and enter Ukraine; Churchill and Roosevelt meet and sign Atlantic Charter; Germans advance to outskirts of Leningrad and continue towards Moscow; they take Kiev, Orel, Odessa, and Kharkov; Russ. government evacuated to Kuibyshev, but Stalin stays in Moscow; RAF bombs Nuremberg; HMS "Ark Royal" sunk; British begin attack in western desert; Marshal Timoshenko launches Russ. counter-offensive; Joseph C. Grew, U.S. ambassador to Japan, warns President Roosevelt of possibility of Jap. attack; Anthony Eden visits Moscow; Japanese bomb Pearl Harbor Dec. 7; U.S. and Britain declare war on Japan Dec. 8; Japanese sink HMS "Prince of Wales" and HMS "Repulse"; Japanese invade Philippines; Germany and Italy declare war on U.S.; U.S. declares war on Germany and Italy; Rommel retreats in North Africa; Churchill visits Washington and Ottawa; British gain control of Cyrenaica; Hong Kong surrenders to Japanese U.S. Office of Price Administration (OPA) established to regulate prices with Leon Henderson as its head; OPA freezes price of steel; rubber rationing instituted U.S. Savings Bonds and Stamps go on sale President Roosevelt appoints James F. Byrnes (—1942) and Robert H. Jackson (—1954) to the Supreme Court Louis D. Brandeis, U.S. jurist, d. (b. 1856)	Louis Aragon: "Le Crève-coeur" Ilya Ehrenburg: "The Fall of Paris" F. Scott Fitzgerald: "The Last Tycoon" Franz Werfel: "Das Lied der Bernadette" Bertolt Brecht: "Mutter Courage und ihre Kinder" Noel Coward: "Blithe Spirit" Rose Franken: "Claudia" Erwin Piscator founds Studio Theater, New York BBC Brains' Trust first broadcast James Joyce d. (b. 1882) Sherwood Anderson, Amer. author, d. (b. 1876) Virginia Woolf, Eng. novelist, d. (b. 1882) Rabindranath Tagore d. (b. 1861) A. J. Cronin: "The Keys of the Kingdom" Joseph E. Davies: "Mission to Moscow" Winston Churchill: "Blood, Sweat, and Tears" J. P. Marquand: "H. M. Pulham, Esquire" William L. Shirer: "Berlin Diary" Upton Sinclair: "Between Two Worlds"	John Masefield: "The Nine Days Wonder" (on Dunkirk) Benedetto Croce: "History as the Story of Liberty" Étienne Gilson: "God and Philosophy" Reinhold Niebuhr: "The Nature and Destiny of Man" (—1943) Henri Bergson d. (b. 1859) Rudolf Bultmann: "New Testament and Mythology"
1942	World War II The 26 Allies pledge not to make separate peace treaties with the enemies; the term United Nations achieves world-wide prominence (see 1945); Japanese invade Dutch East Indies, take Kuala Lumpur, invade Burma; Rommel launches new offensive; Quisling becomes Premier of Norway; the Japanese capture Singapore, Java, and Rangoon; Churchill reconstructs his ministry; British raid St. Nazaire and bomb Lübeck, and Cologne; U.S. government transfers more than 100,000 Niseis (Japanese-Americans) from West Coast to inland camps; Japanese occupy Bataan, force march ("Bataan Death March") of American and Philippine prisoners in which many die; Tokyo bombed by Major General Jimmy Doolittle; Americans win Battle of the Coral Sea; Japanese in Mandalay and Corregidor; Czech patriots assassinate Gestapo leader Heydrich and in retaliation Nazis burn the village of Lidice in Bohemia; Americans defeat Japanese at Midway; Rommel takes Tobruk; FBI captures eight Ger. saboteurs who landed in Florida and New York; Germans counter-attack near Kharkov and take *(contd)*	William Rose Benét: "The Dust Which is God," Pulitzer Prize poetry Ellen Glasgow: "In This Our Life," Pulitzer Prize novel Albert Camus: "L'Étranger" T. S. Eliot: "Four Quartets" William Faulkner: "Go Down, Moses" Elliot Paul: "The Last Time I Saw Paris" John Steinbeck: "The Moon Is Down" William L. White: "They Were Expendable" Jean Anouilh: "Antigone" Terence Rattigan: "Flare Path" Tommy Handley's ITMA the most popular BBC feature Marie Tempest, Eng. actress, d. (b. 1866) Sartre: "Les Mouches" Klaus Mann: "Turning Point," autobiography Upton Sinclair: "Dragon's Teeth" Thornton Wilder: "The Skin of Our *(contd)*	William Beveridge: "Report on Social Security" E. H. Carr: "Conditions of Peace" L. B. Namier: "Conflicts: Studies in Contemporary History" James Burnham: "The Managerial Revolution" G. M. Trevelyan: "English Social History" R. G. Collingwood: "The New Leviathan" Erich Fromm: "The Fear of Freedom" Reichenbach: *(contd)*

D. VISUAL ARTS	E. MUSIC	F. SCIENCE, TECHNOLOGY, GROWTH	G. DAILY LIFE	
				1940 contd
Edward Hopper: "Nighthawks" Stuart Davis: "New York Under Gaslight" Fernand Léger: "Divers against Yellow Background" Paul Nash: "Bombers over Berlin" Henry Moore's drawings of refugees in London air raid shelters Feliks Topolski executes his drawings of Brit. armed forces Stanley Spencer: "Shipbuilding in the Clyde" National Gallery of Art, Washington, D.C., opens Films: "The Two-Faced Woman" (Garbo's last film); "Citizen Kane" (Orson Welles); "Kipps" (Carol Reed); "The Big Store" (Marx Brothers); "The 49th Parallel" (Leslie Howard); "Ohm Krüger" (anti-Brit. Nazi propaganda film); "Suspicion" (Hitchcock) "How Green Was My Valley" (John Ford), Academy Award Robert Delaunay d. (b. 1885)	Roy Harris: "Folk Song Symphony," Boston Michael Tippett: "A Child of Our Time" William Walton: "Scapino," overture Benjamin Britten: Violin Concerto Paderewski d. (b. 1860) Shostakovich: Symphony No. 7 (written during the siege of Leningrad) Wilhelm Kienzl, Aust. composer, d. (b. 1857) Christian Sinding, Norw. composer, d. (b. 1856) Popular songs: "Bewitched, Bothered, and Bewildered"; "Deep in the Heart of Texas"; "I Don't Want to Set the World On Fire"; "Chattanooga Choo-Choo"; "I Got It Bad and That Ain't Good"	Donald Bailey invents the portable military bridge Hans Haas begins underwater photography "Manhattan Project" of intensive atomic research begins Whinfield and Dickson invent dacron Ferry Command aircraft crosses Atlantic from the West in 8 hours 23 minutes Walther Nernst, Ger. physicist and chemist, d. (b. 1864) Edwin McMillan and Glenn T. Seaborg (both U.S.) discover plutonium (atomic number 94) Construction of Gatun Locks, Panama Canal, begins Grand Coulee Dam, Washington, starts operation Rainbow Bridge over Niagara Falls, N.Y., opens	Air Training Corps established in Britain "Mosquito" fighter aircraft in use Brit. A.R.P. (Air Raid Precaution) reorganized as Civil Defence "Utility" clothing and furniture are encouraged in Britain, clothes rationing starts Amer. Bowling Congress Hall of Fame established Joe DiMaggio hits safely in 56 consecutive games, establishes a major league record Lord Baden-Powell d. (b. 1857) Amy Johnson, Eng. aviatrix, d. (b. 1904) Emperor William II of Germany d. (b. 1859) U.S. Supreme Court upholds Federal Wage and Hour Law restricting work of 16- and 18-year-olds and setting minimum wage for businesses engaged in interstate commerce Jeannette Rankin, U.S. Representative, casts sole dissenting vote in Congress against declaration of war on Japan after Pearl Harbor attack U.S. (Lawn Tennis) Association Amateur championship won by Bobby Riggs; Women's by Mrs. Sarah Palfrey Cooke U.S. Golf Association Amateur won by Marvin Ward; Open by Craig Wood "Whirlaway," Eddie Arcaro up, wins Belmont and Preakness Stakes and Kentucky Derby Lou Gehrig, baseball player, d. (b. 1903) Monument over Time Capsule, to be opened in 6939, sealed at site of 1939 New York World's Fair, is dedicated New York (AL) wins World Series from Brooklyn (NL), 4—1	**1941**
Pierre Bonnard: "L'Oiseau bleu" John Piper: "Windsor Castle" Graham Sutherland: "Red Landscape" Walter Richard Sickert d. (b. 1860) Grant Wood d. (b. 1892) Philip Wilson Steer d. (b. 1860) Braque: "Patience," cubist painting Films: "Bambi" (Disney); "Mrs. Miniver" (Greer Garson); "To Be or Not To Be" (Lubitsch); "Holiday Inn" (Bing Crosby); "The Evening Visitors" (Carné) *(contd)*	Ernest Bacon: "A Tree on the Plain," opera, Converse College Benjamin Britten: "Sinfonia da Requiem" Aaron Copland: "Rodeo," New York Gian Carlo Menotti: "The Island God," opera, New York Michel Fokine, Russ. choreographer, d. (b. 1880) Richard Strauss: "Capriccio," opera, Munich Randall Thompson: "Solomon and Balkis," opera, radio première Felix von Weingartner, Aust. conductor and *(contd)*	Enrico Fermi (U.S.) splits the atom The first electronic brain or automatic computer developed in the U.S. Magnetic recording tape invented Franz Boas, Ger.-Amer. ethnologist, d. (b. 1858) William Henry Bragg, Eng. physicist, d. (b. 1862) A. C. Hartley invents device for clearing fog from airfields (FIDO) Max Muller of Junkers *(contd)*	Malta awarded the George Cross Gilbert Murray founds Oxfam "Stars and Stripes," a daily paper for U.S. forces in Europe, appears Warmerdam (U.S.) establishes pole vault record (3.77 meters) First all-star bowling tournament held in U.S. Wartime "National Loaf" introduced in Britain Mildenhall Treasure, a hoard of Roman silverware is discovered in Suffolk 487 die in fire at Coconut Grove nightclub, Boston, most from asphyxiation when trapped by exit doors that open inward Sugar rationing begins in U.S.; OPA freezes rents; gasoline rationing; Elmer Davis is appointed director of newly formed Office of War Information (OWI); coffee rationing U.S. Supreme Court rules Nevada divorces valid in U.S. *(contd)*	**1942**

	A. HISTORY, POLITICS	B. LITERATURE, THEATER	C. RELIGION, PHILOSOPHY, LEARNING
1942 contd	Sebastopol; Second Front demonstrations in London; Americans in Guadalcanal; Germans sink HMS "Eagle" and HMS "Manchester"; Alexander Commander-in-Chief, Middle East, Montgomery Commander of Eighth Army; Germans reach Stalingrad; battle of El Alamein begins; 400,000 Amer. troops land in French North Africa; Rommel, in full retreat, loses Tobruk and Benghazi; Fr. navy scuttled in Toulon; Brit. and Indian troops advance in Burma; Germans work on V-2 rocket; Albert Speer named Ger. armament minister; the murder of millions of Jews in the Nazi gas chambers begins; Gandhi demands independence for India and is arrested; MacArthur appointed Commander-in-Chief, Far East; Admiral Darlan assassinated	Teeth," Pulitzer Prize drama (1943) Stefan Zweig, Ger. author, d. (b. 1881) James Gould Cozzens: "The Just and the Unjust" Lloyd C. Douglas: "The Robe" Sidney Kingsley: "The Patriot," drama Marion Hargrove: "See Here, Private Hargrove" Maxwell Anderson: "Eve of St. Mark" George M. Cohan d. (b. 1878) John Barrymore d. (b. 1882)	"Philosophic Foundations of Quantum Mechanics" C. S. Lewis: "The Screwtape Letters" Kenneth Walker: "The Diagnosis of Man" William Flinders Petrie, Brit. archaeologist, d. (b. 1853)
1943	World War II Germany withdraws from the Caucasus; Casablanca Conference between Churchill and Roosevelt; Japanese driven from Guadalcanal: new Ger. air attacks on London; Brit. Eighth Army reaches Tripoli; Russians destroy Ger. army southwest of Stalingrad; General Paulus surrenders at Stalingrad; Russians recapture Rostov and Kharkov; Hitler orders "scorched earth" policy; Allied armies in North Africa are placed under Eisenhower's command; RAF raid on Berlin; 22-ship Japanese convoy sunk in Battle of the Bismarck Sea by U.S. planes; Brit. and U.S. armies in Africa link up; Rommel retreats; massacre in Warsaw ghetto; Allies take Tunis and Bizerte; Ger. army surrenders in Tunisia; RAF bombs Ruhr dams; U.S. forces land in New Guinea; U.S. recaptures Aleutians; Allies land in Sicily July 10, and soon occupy Palermo; Mussolini dismissed; Marshal Badoglio takes over in Italy; Quebec conference between Churchill, Roosevelt and Mackenzie King; Ploesti oil fields in Rumania bombed by U.S.; U.S. troops enter Messina; Allies land in Salerno Bay and invade Italy; Eisenhower announces Italy's unconditional surrender Sept. 8; Russians cross Dnieper north of Kiev; take Smolensk; Amer. Fifth Army takes Naples; Italy declares war on Germany; Russians take Kiev; Mosley released from prison; Gen. and Mme. Chiang Kai-shek meet with Roosevelt and Churchill in Cairo and agree to liberate Korea after Jap. defeat; U.S. forces regain islands in Pacific; Churchill, Stalin, and Roosevelt hold Teheran conference; U.S.S.R.-Czechoslovak treaty for postwar cooperation; students Hans and Sophie Scholl distribute anti-Nazi pamphlets in Munich and are caught and executed; Allied "round- the-clock" bombing of Germany begins; Pol. General Wladyslaw Sikorski d. (b. 1881) President Roosevelt appoints Wiley B. Rutledge to the Supreme Court (—1949)	Henry Green: "Caught" Romain Rolland: "Péguy" James Bridie: "Mr. Bolfry" Noel Coward: "This Happy Breed" W. W. Jacobs, Eng. author, d. (b. 1863) Nigel Balchin: "The Small Back Room" Thomas Mann: "Joseph and His Brethren," tetralogy 1933 Max Reinhardt d. (b. 1873) Ernie Pyle: "Here Is Your War" Wendell Willkie: "One World" Betty Smith: "A Tree Grows in Brooklyn" Richard Tregaskis: "Guadalcanal Diary" James Thurber: "Men, Women and Dogs" Franz Werfel and S. N. Behrman: "Jacobowsky and the Colonel" John Van Druten: "The Voice of the Turtle" Upton Sinclair: "Dragon's Teeth," Pulitzer Prize novel Robert Frost: "A Witness Tree," Pulitzer Prize Ira Wolfert: "Battle for the Solomons" Robert L. Scott, Jr.: "God Is My Co-Pilot" Ted Lawson: "Thirty Seconds Over Tokyo" William Saroyan: "The Human Comedy" Martha Graham dances in "Deaths and Entrances" Stephen Vincent Benét d. (b. 1898)	D. W. Brogan: "The American Political Scene" Harold Laski: "Reflections on the Revolution of Our Time" A. D. Lindsay: "The Modern Democratic State" Walter Lippmann: "U.S. Foreign Policy" Keynes announces his plan for an international currency union J. M. Thompson: "The French Revolution" Sartre: "L'Être et le Néant" C. E. Raven: "Science, Religion and the Future" Beatrice Webb, Lady Passfield, d. (b. 1858) U.S. Supreme Court rules that children need not salute flag in schools if it is against their religion, in case brought by Jehovah's Witnesses (reverses 1940 decision)

D. VISUAL ARTS	E. MUSIC	F. SCIENCE, TECHNOLOGY, GROWTH	G. DAILY LIFE	
Carole Lombard killed in plane crash (b. 1909)	composer, d. (b. 1863) Irving Berlin: "White Christmas" Popular songs: "I Left My Heart at the Stage Door Canteen"; "White Christmas"; "The White Cliffs of Dover"; "Sleepy Lagoon"; "Praise the Lord and Pass the Ammunition"; "Be Careful, It's My Heart"; "Paper Doll"; "That Old Black Magic"	develops successful turbo-prop engine Bell Aircraft tests first U.S. jetplane Henry J. Kaiser, industrialist, develops techniques for building 10,000-ton Liberty Ships in four days	U.S. Lawn Tennis Association Men's Singles champion is F. R. Schroeder, Jr.; Women's is Pauline M. Betz Oregon State defeats Duke to win Rose Bowl football game 20—16 Joe Louis knocks out Buddy Baer to retain world heavyweight boxing crown	**1942 contd**
Thomas Hart Benton: "July Hay" Mondriaan: "Broadway Boogie-Woogie" Henry Moore: "Madonna and Child," Northampton Beckmann: "Odysseus and Calypso," expressionist painting Kokoschka: "Portrait of Ivan Maisky," Soviet ambassador in London Jackson Pollock's first one-man show Chagall: "The Juggler" Grant Wood and John Steuart Curry are active as are Yves Tanguy and Fernand Léger Films: "Jane Eyre" (Orson Welles); "Münchhausen" (Hans Albers); "Shadow of a Doubt" (Hitchcock); "Stalingrad" (Varlenow); "Children Look at You" (de Sica); "Desert Victory" (Roy Boulting): "Casablanca," Academy Award Chaim Soutine d. (b. 1894) Marsden Hartley d. (b. 1877)	Aaron Copland: "A Lincoln Portrait" and "Piano Sonata" Rachmaninoff d. (b. 1873) William Schuman: "Secular Cantata No. 2, A Free Song," Pulitzer Prize (first for music) Ralph Vaughan Williams: Symphony No. 5 in D Rodgers and Hammerstein: "Oklahoma!," musical play, New York (reached 2,248 consecutive performances), special Pulitzer Prize (1944) Kurt Weill: "One Touch of Venus," musical comedy, New York Max von Schillings, Ger. composer and conductor, d. (b. 1868) Francis Poulenc: "Les Animaux modèlés," ballet Schönberg: "Ode to Napoleon" Paul Creston: "First Symphony" Lorenz Hart d. (b. 1895) Popular songs: "Mairzy Doats"; "Oh, What a Beautiful Mornin'"; "People Will Say We're in Love"; "I'll Be Seeing You (in All the Old, Familiar Places)"; "Comin' in on a Wing and a Prayer"; "A Lovely Way to Spend an Evening"	Penicillin successfully used in the treatment of chronic diseases Waksman and Schatz discover streptomycin 1300-mile-long "Big Inch" oil pipeline, from Texas to Pennsylvania, begins operation Nobel Prize for Medicine and Physiology; Henrik Dam (Dan.) and E. A. Doisy (U.S.) for discovery and analysis of vitamin K Nobel Prize for Physics; Otto Stern (U.S.) for experiments and discoveries in molecular beam theory and proton movement Nikola Tesla d. (b. 1856) George Washington Carver, agronomist, d. (b. 1864) Institute, d. (b. 1864)	Henry Kaiser's first "Liberty" ships are launched Charlie Chaplin marries Oona O'Neill Nuffield Foundation formed Famine strikes Bengal President Roosevelt freezes wages, salaries, and prices to forestall inflation Infantile paralysis epidemic kills almost 1200 in U.S., cripples thousands more Shoe rationing begins in U.S., followed by rationing of meat, cheese, fats, and all canned foods U.S. War Labor Board orders coal mines to be taken over by the government when 0.5 million miners strike Pay-as-you-go income tax system instituted in U.S. Race riots break out in several major U.S. cities whose labor population has been bolstered by influx of southern Blacks Zoot suit (with reet pleat) becomes popular attire among hepcats in U.S. Lindy hop yields to jitterbugging in U.S. U.S. Lawn Tennis Association Men's Singles won by Lt. (j.g.) J. R. Hunt; Women's by Pauline M. Betz "Count Fleet," Johnny Longden up, wins Belmont and Preakness Stakes and Kentucky Derby In hockey, Detroit defeats Boston, 2—0, to win Stanley Cup Rose Bowl football game is won by Georgia New York (AL) defeats St. Louis (NL) to win World Series 4—1	**1943**

	A. HISTORY, POLITICS	B. LITERATURE, THEATER	C. RELIGION, PHILOSOPHY, LEARNING
1944	World War II Amer. Fifth Army launches attack east of Cassino; Allied landings at Nettuno and Anzio; Leningrad relieved; Monte Cassino monastery bombed; U.S. troops complete conquest of Solomon and Marshall Islands; heavy air raids on London; Russ. offensives in the Ukraine and Crimea; 800 Flying Fortresses drop 2,000 tons of bombs on Berlin; Sebastopol liberated; Monte Cassino and Rome in Allied hands June 4; Victor Emmanuel III names Crown Prince Umberto Lt.-Gen. of the realm, but retains the title King D-Day: landings in Normandy June 6 (over 700 ships and 4,000 landing craft involved, oil pipeline laid in Channel bed, Mulberry Harbor assembled off Normandy); first flying-bomb (V-1) dropped on London; Allies take Orvieto and Cherbourg; southern Japan bombed by U.S.; U.S. troops take Saigon; Russians capture 100,000 Germans at Minsk; Ger. officers attempt to assassinate Hitler: Premier Tojo of Japan and his Cabinet resign; Russians at Brest-Litovsk; Warsaw uprising; Americans capture Guam from Japanese; Brit. Eighth Army takes Florence; Dumbarton Oaks conference in Washington, D.C., discussion on UN; de Gaulle enters Paris Aug. 25; Brussels liberated; first V-2 rockets on Britain; Churchill and Roosevelt meet in Quebec; Americans cross Ger. frontier near Trier; Brit. airborne forces land at Eindhoven and Arnhem but have to withdraw; Churchill in Moscow; U.S. troops land in Philippines; Russians and Yugoslavs enter Belgrade; Red Army occupies Hungary; end of Horthy's dictatorship (from 1920); Battle of Leyte Gulf ends in heavy losses for Japanese; Roosevelt elected for a fourth term as President of the U.S., Harry S. Truman is Vice President; "Battle of the Bulge" (Ardennes) begins; North Burma cleared of Japanese; Budapest surrounded by Russians; Pétain imprisoned at fortress of Belfort; France regains Lorraine; Vietnam declares herself independent of France under Ho Chi Minh: Victor Emmanuel III yields his royal prerogatives to his son Umberto; Count Ciano, Fascist Foreign Minister, executed on orders of his father-in-law, Mussolini; Rommel commits suicide (b. 1891) Al Smith d. (b. 1873)	Stephen Vincent Benét: "Western Star," Pulitzer Prize Poetry H. E. Bates: "Fair Stood the Wind for France" Catherine Drinker Bowen: "Yankee from Olympus" Ivy Compton-Burnett: "Elders and Betters" T. S. Eliot: "Four Quartets" John Hersey: "A Bell for Adano," Pulitzer Prize novel (1945) Aldous Huxley: "Time Must Have a Stop" Rosamond Lehmann: "The Ballad and the Source" W. Somerset Maugham: "The Razor's Edge" Alberto Moravia: "Agostino" Ernie Pyle: "Brave Men" Terence Rattigan: "Love in Idleness" Sartre: "No Exit" Lillian Smith: "Strange Fruit" Irving Stone: "Immortal Wife" John Van Druten: "I Remember Mama" Van Wyck Brooks: "The World of Washington Irving" Kathleen Winsor: "Forever Amber" Tennessee Williams: "The Glass Menagerie" Arthur Quiller-Couch ("Q"), Eng. author, d. (b. 1863) Romain Rolland d. (b. 1866) Joyce Cary: "The Horse's Mouth" Camus: "Caligula" Jean Giraudoux: "The Mad Woman of Chaillot" Jean Giraudoux d. (b. 1882) Antoine de Saint-Exupéry, Fr. poet, d. (b. 1900) Stefan Zweig: "The World of Yesterday," autobiography (posth.) Mazo de La Roche: "The Building of Jalna" George Ade d. (b. 1866)	Norman Bentwich: "Judea Lives Again" William Beveridge: "Full Employment in a Free Society" John Hilton: "Rich Man, Poor Man" Julian Huxley: "On Living in a Revolution" Sumner Welles: "The Time for Decision" Lewis Mumford: "The Condition of Man" Sister Aimee Semple McPherson, U.S. fundamentalist preacher, d. (b. 1890)
1945	World War II: Brit. offensive begins in Burma; Russ. offensive in Silesia; Russians take Warsaw, Cracow, Tilsit, and reach Oder River; Yalta Conference between Churchill, Roosevelt, and Stalin; Americans enter Manila; Budapest falls; Brit. troops reach the Rhine; U.S. air raids on Tokyo, Cologne, and Danzig; Okinawa captured; Brit. Second Army crosses Rhine; the last of 1,050 Ger. V-2 rockets fall on Britain; Franklin D. Roosevelt d. (b. 1882) and is succeeded as President of the U.S. by Vice-President Harry S. Truman; Russians reach Berlin; Bologna falls; U.S. and U.S.S.R. troops meet at Torgau; San Francisco conference; Eden, Molotov, Smuts, and Stettinius sign United Nations Charter June 26 to take effect Oct. 24; League of Nations holds final meeting in Geneva and turns over assets to UN; Bremen, Genoa, Verona, and Venice taken; the Allies cross the Elbe; Mussolini killed by Ital. partisans; Hitler commits suicide Apr. 30; Ger. army on Ital. front surrenders; Berlin surrenders to Russians May 2 and Germany capitulates May 7; "V.E. Day" ends war in Europe May 8 Allied Control Commission divides Germany into four *(contd)*	Robert Benchley, Amer. humorist, d. (b. 1889) Mary Chase: "Harvey" (Pulitzer Prize) Henry Green: "Loving" Carlo Levi: "Christ Stopped at Eboli" Sinclair Lewis: "Cass Timberlane" George Orwell: "Animal Farm" Evelyn Waugh: "Brideshead Revisited" Paul Valéry d. (b. 1871) Theodore Dreiser d. (b. 1871) Georg Kaiser, Ger. dramatist, d. (b. 1878) Franz Werfel, Aust. novelist, d. (b. 1890) John Betjeman: "New Bats in Old Belfries," poems Nancy Mitford: "The Pursuit of Love" Ernie Pyle, Amer. war correspondent, d. (b. 1900) Osbert Sitwell: "Left Hand, Right Hand," autobiography James Thurber: "The Thurber Carnival" Sartre: "Les Chemins de la liberté" Hermann Hesse: "Das Glasperlenspiel," *(contd)*	D. W. Brogan: "The Free State" L. G. Curtis: "World War: Its Cause and Cure" Lord Moran: "The Anatomy of Courage" Shintoism abolished in Japan Martin Buber: "For the Sake of Heaven" William L. Sperry: "Religion in America" C. J. Webb: "Religious Experience" Ernst Cassirer, Ger. philosopher, d. (b. 1874) W. S. Melsome: "The Bacon-Shakespeare *(contd)*

D. VISUAL ARTS	E. MUSIC	F. SCIENCE, TECHNOLOGY, GROWTH	G. DAILY LIFE	
Feininger: "Steamboat on the Yukon" Vasili Kandinsky, Russ. painter, d. (b. 1866) Aristide Maillol, Fr. painter, d. (b. 1861) Matisse: "The White Dress" Piet Mondriaan, Dutch painter, d. (b. 1872) "Art Concrète" Exhibition at Basle (Arp, Kandinsky, Klee, Mondriaan, Henry Moore) Picasso: "The Tomato Plant" Braque: "The Slice of Pumpkin" Rouault: "Homo Homini Lupus" Rivera: "The Rug Weaver" Charles Dana Gibson, Amer. illustrator, creator of "Gibson Girl," d. (b. 1868) Lucien Pissarro d. (b. 1863) Edwin L. Lutyens, Eng. architect, d. (b. 1869) Edvard Munch, Norw. painter, d. (b. 1863) Films: "Henry V" (Olivier); "Les Enfants du Paradis" (Carné); "Lifeboat" (Hitchcock); "Zola" (Russian); "It Happened Tomorrow" (René Clair); "Going My Way," Academy Award	Bartók: Violin Concerto Aaron Copland: "Appalachian Spring," Pulitzer Prize for music (1945), danced by Martha Graham, Washington, D.C. Shostakovich: Symphony No. 8 Oxford University establishes a faculty of music Ethel Smyth, Eng. composer, d. (b. 1858) Henry J. Wood, Eng. conductor, d. (b. 1869) Leonard Bernstein: "On the Town," musical comedy, New York Paul Graener, Ger. composer, d. (b. 1872) Richard Strauss: "Die Liebe der Danae," opera, rehearsed in Salzburg but canceled when Nazis close theaters Prokofiev: "War and Peace," opera, Moscow Walter Piston: 2nd Symphony, Washington, D.C. Popular songs: "Don't Fence Me In"; "Rum and Coca-Cola"; "Swinging on a Star"; "Sentimental Journey"; "Accentuate the Positive"	Uranium pile built at Clinton, Tenn. New cyclotron completed at Washington Quinine synthesized	Ministry of National Insurance established in Britain "Blackout" restrictions relaxed in Britain First nonstop flight from London to Canada William Allen White, U.S. journalist, d. (b. 1868) Cost of living in U.S. rises almost 30% "Pensive," C. McCreary up, wins Preakness Stakes and Kentucky Derby Southern California wins Rose Bowl football game, 29—0, against Washington More than 165 killed and 175 injured in Hartford, Conn., Ringling Bros., Barnum & Bailey Circus fire St. Louis (AL) wins World Series, 4—2, against St. Louis (NL) Kenesaw Mountain Landis, baseball commissioner, d. (b. 1866)	**1944**
Stanley Spencer continues his series "Resurrection" Henry Moore: "Family Group" Stuart Davis: "For Internal Use Only," Amer. abstract painting Käthe Kollwitz, Ger. artist, d. (b. 1867) Max Weber: "Brass-band," Amer. expressionist painting The trial of Hans van Meegeren, the Dutch painter who forged great paintings Jacob Epstein: "Lucifer," sculpture Frank Lloyd Wright: design for Guggenheim Museum, New York Films: "Rome, Open City" (Rossellini); "Brief Encounter" (Noel Coward, David Lean); "The Lost Weekend" (Billy Wilder); "The Way to the Stars" (Asquith); "The Last *(contd)*	Richard Strauss: "Metamorphosen" Benjamin Britten: "Peter Grimes," opera, London Béla Bartók d. (b. 1881) Zoltán Kodály: "Missa Brevis" Prokofiev: "Cinderella," ballet, Moscow Pietro Mascagni, Ital. operatic composer, d. (b. 1863) Anton von Webern, Aust. composer, d. (b. 1883) Rodgers and Hammerstein: "Carousel," musical comedy, New York	Lajos Jánossy (Hungarian) explores cosmic radiation Vitamin A synthesized Nobel Prize for Medicine: Fleming, Florey, and Chain (Great Britain) for discovery of penicillin First atomic bomb detonated near Alamogordo, N. Mex., July 16 Arthur Korn, Ger. physicist, d. (b. 1870) *(contd)*	"Black Markets" for food, clothing, and cigarettes develop throughout Europe Family allowances introduced in Britain Women's suffrage becomes law in France "Bebop" comes into fashion Boxer of the Year: Rocky Graziano Frank A. Parker, Amer. army sergeant, wins U.S. Lawn Tennis Men's Singles championship Mrs. Sarah Palfrey Cooke, Amer., wins U.S. Lawn Tennis Women's Singles championship Heirs of Jacob Ruppert and Edward G. Barrow sell New York Yankees, baseball club, to syndicate controlled by Lawrence McPhail, Del Webb, and Dan Topping for estimated $2.8 million *(contd)*	**1945**

	A. HISTORY, POLITICS	B. LITERATURE, THEATER	C. RELIGION, PHILOSOPHY, LEARNING
1945 contd	Spain excluded from UN Three-power occupation of Berlin takes effect Churchill (later Attlee), Truman, and Stalin confer at Potsdam General election in Britain brings Labour landslide; Attlee becomes prime minister U.S. drops atomic bombs on Hiroshima Aug. 6 and Nagasaki Aug. 9 Japan surrenders; end of World War II, Aug. 14; war dead estimated at 35 million plus 10 million in Nazi concentration camps Pétain sentenced to death (sentence later commuted to life imprisonment) Independent republic of Vietnam formed with Ho Chi Minh as president Quisling sentenced to death in Norway Laval sentenced to death in France Fighting between Nationalists and Communists in north China; U.S. Gen. George Marshall tries to mediate Arab League founded to oppose creation of Jewish state De Gaulle elected president of Fr. provisional government Nuremberg trials of Nazi war criminals begin Nobel Peace Prize: Amer. Secretary of State Cordell Hull Federal People's Republic of Yugoslavia proclaimed; Tito chief of state Karl Renner elected President of Austria David Lloyd George d. (b. 1863) George S. Patton, Amer. general, killed in automobile accident (b. 1885) International Bank for Reconstruction and Development (the UN "World Bank") founded with authorized share capital of $27,000 million Raoul Wallenberg disappears in Budapest	novel Karl Shapiro: "V-Letter and Other Poems" (Pulitzer Prize) Nobel Prize for Literature: Gabriela Mistral (1889—1957), Chilean poet	Anatomy"
1946	Truce declared in Chinese Civil War UN General Assembly holds its first session in London, Jan. 7; Trygve Lie (Norw.) elected Secretary-General; New York is declared permanent UN headquarters Albania, Hungary, Transjordan, and Bulgaria become independent states De Gaulle resigns Presidency and is succeeded by Bidault; Léon Blum forms Socialist government Juan Perón elected President of Argentina Churchill gives his "Iron Curtain" speech at Fulton, Mo. Britain and France evacuate Lebanon East Ger. Social Democrats merge with Communists Victor Emmanuel III abdicates as King of Italy and is succeeded by his son, Umberto II; Ital. referendum in favor of republic; Umberto II leaves the country; de Gasperi becomes head of state Klement Gottwald becomes Premier of Czechoslovakia President Truman creates Atomic Energy Commission Peace Conference of 21 nations held in Paris Verdict of Nuremberg Tribunal: Ribbentrop, Goering, and 10 other Nazis sentenced to death; Hess and Funk life imprisonment; Schacht and von Papen acquitted; Goering commits suicide on the evening before his execution Power in Japan transferred from the Emperor to an elected assembly Dimitrov becomes premier of Bulgaria UN Atomic Energy Commission approves U.S. plan for control Sarawak ceded to Brit. Crown by the Rajah, Sir Charles Brooke John D. Rockefeller, Jr., donates $8.5 million to UN for site *(contd)*	Maxwell Anderson: "Joan of Lorraine" Simone de Beauvoir: "Tous les hommes sont mortels" Lillian Hellman: "Another Part of the Forest" Dylan Thomas: "Deaths and Entrances" Robert Penn Warren: "All the King's Men," Pulitzer Prize novel (1947) Jean Cocteau: "L'Aigle a deux têtes" Arthur Miller: "All My Sons" Eugene O'Neill: "The Iceman Cometh" Terence Rattigan: "The Winslow Boy" Sartre: "Morts sans sépulture" Gerhart Hauptmann d. (b. 1862) Gertrude Stein d. (b. 1874) Damon Runyon d. (b. 1884) Nobel Prize for Literature: Hermann Hesse Theodor Plievier: "Stalingrad," novel E. M. Remarque: "Arc de Triomphe" Booth Tarkington d. (b. 1864) Carl Zuckmayer: "The Devil's General," play John Hersey: "Hiroshima" Sean O'Casey: "Red Roses for Me" Edmund Wilson: "Memoirs of Hecate County" Benjamin Spock, M.D.: "Baby and Child Care" Frank Yerby: "The Foxes of Harrow"	Etienne Mantoux: "The Carthaginian Peace" Aldous Huxley: "The Perennial Philosophy" Pope Pius XII creates 32 new cardinals Count Hermann Keyserling, Ger. philosopher, d. (b. 1880) Francis Xavier Cabrini (1850—1917) canonized

D. VISUAL ARTS	E. MUSIC	F. SCIENCE, TECHNOLOGY, GROWTH	G. DAILY LIFE	
Chance" (Swiss, Lindtberg); "Ivan the Terrible" (Eisenstein); "The Man from the South" (Renoir)		Atomic Research Centre established at Harwell, England	Eddie Arcaro rides "Pavot" to victory in Belmont Stakes and "Hoop Jr." to win Kentucky Derby (his third winner) Empire State Building struck at 78-79 floors, July 28, by B-25 bomber Detroit (AL) defeats Chicago (NL) in World Series Branch Rickey, Walter O'Malley, and John L. Smith acquire controlling interest in Brooklyn Dodgers	**1945 contd**
Graham Sutherland: "Head of Thorns" Picasso founds the pottery at Vallauris Fernand Léger: "Composition with Branch" Chagall: "Cow with Umbrella" Paul Nash, Eng. artist, d. (b. 1889) Buckminster Fuller designs Dymaxion House Saul Steinberg: "All in Line," Amer. cartoons Films: "The Best Years of Our Lives" (William Wyler); "Die Mörder sind unter Uns" (Wolfgang Staudte); "Paisà" (Rossellini); "Gilda" (Charles Vidor); "La Belle et la Bête" (Cocteau); "Notorious" (Hitchcock); "Great Expectations" (David Lean) W. C. Fields d. (b. 1880) *(contd)*	Benjamin Britten: "The Rape of Lucretia," opera, Glyndebourne Gian Carlo Menotti: "The Medium" Frederick Ashton: "Symphonic Variations," ballet (César Franck, composer), London Balanchine: "Nightshadow," ballet (Bellini, composer), New York Salzburg Festival reopens Granville Bantock, Eng. composer, d. (b. 1868) Manuel de Falla, Span. composer, d. (b. 1876) Heinrich Kaminsky, Ger. composer, d. (b. 1886) Paul Lincke, Ger. popular composer, d. (b. 1866) Boris Blacher: "Die Flut," chamber opera Irving Berlin: "Annie *(contd)*	Appleton discovers that sun spots emit radio waves Isotope Carbon-13 discovered Pilotless rocket missile constructed by Fairey Aviation Company Electronic brain built at Pennsylvania University Xerography process invented by Chester Carlson John Logie Baird, Brit. T.V. inventor, d. (b. 1888) South Pole expedition of R. E. Byrd (—1947) U.S. Navy first tests an atomic bomb at Bikini James J. Walker d. (b. 1881) Nobel Prize for Medicine and Physiology: Hermann Joseph *(contd)*	John Maynard Keynes d. (b. 1883) Women ensured the right to vote in Italy New Bodleian Library, Oxford Brit. Arts Council inaugurated Joe Louis successfully defends his world heavyweight boxing title for the 23rd time Australia, with Donald Bradman as Captain, retains Ashes in MCC tour Shortest recorded boxing fight in history: Couture wins against Walton with one punch in 10.5 seconds London Airport opened (new terminal 1955) Hans de Meiss-Teuffen sails solo from Spain to U.S. in 58 days Mikhail Botvinnik, U.S.S.R., after Alekhine's death, considered the world's finest chess player World Population (in millions): China, 455; India, 311; U.S.S.R., 194; U.S., 140; Japan, 73; West Germany, 48; Italy, 47; Britain, 46; Brazil, 45; France, 40 Jack Johnson, U.S. boxer, d. (b. 1878) A. Alekhine d. (b. 1892) "Assault," W. Mehrtens up, wins Belmont and Preakness Stakes and Kentucky Derby U.S. Lawn Tennis Association Men's Singles won by John A. Kramer; Women's by Pauline M. Betz U.S. Golf Association Amateur championship won by Ted Bishop; Open by Lloyd Mangrum Davis Cup tennis trophy won by U.S. team against Australia *(contd)*	**1946**

	A. HISTORY, POLITICS	B. LITERATURE, THEATER	C. RELIGION, PHILOSOPHY, LEARNING
1946 contd	of permanent headquarters in New York City Harlan Fiske Stone d. (b. 1872) Sidney Hillman, U.S. labor leader, d. (b. 1887) Harry Hopkins, U.S. Presidential adviser, d. (b. 1890)		
1947	Brit. coal industry nationalized General George Marshall appointed U.S. Secretary of State; calls for European Recovery Program (Marshall Plan) Vincent Auriol elected President of France U.S. withdraws as mediator in China Brit. proposal to divide Palestine rejected by Arabs and Jews; question referred to UN which announces plan for partition Peace treaties signed in Paris Ex-President Tiso of Slovakia executed Burma proclaimed independent republic India is proclaimed independent and partitioned into India and Pakistan Cominform established at Warsaw conference Belgium, Netherlands, and Luxembourg ratify Benelux customs union Princess Elizabeth, heir to the Eng. throne, marries Philip Mountbatten, Duke of Edinburgh Stanley Baldwin d. (b. 1867) King Michael of Rumania abdicates Over President Truman's veto U.S. Congress passes Taft-Hartley Act restricting rights of labor unions Florello H. La Guardia d. (b. 1882)	Thomas Armstrong: "King Cotton" Nigel Balchin: "Lord I Was Afraid" Albert Camus: "The Plague" Willa Cather d. (b. 1873) Julian Green: "Si j'étais vous" Jean Anouilh: "L'Invitation au château" William Douglas-Home: "The Chiltern Hundreds" J. B. Priestley: "The Linden Tree" Tennesseé Williams: "A Streetcar Named Desire," Pulitzer Prize for drama (1948) James Agate, Eng. critic, d. (b. 1877) "The Diary of Anne Frank" published H. E. Bates: "The Purple Plain" John Gunther: "Inside U.S.A." Compton Mackenzie: "Whisky Galore" Sinclair Lewis: "Kingsblood Royal" Robert Lowell: "Lord Weary's Castle," Pulitzer Prize poetry Thomas Mann: "Doktor Faustus" Hans Fallada, Ger. novelist, d. (b. 1893) Ricarda Huch, Ger. author, d. (b. 1864) Nobel Prize for Literature: André Gide Michael Sadlier: "Fanny by Gaslight" Mickey Spillane: "I, the Jury" John Steinbeck: "The Wayward Bus"	L. S. Amery; "Thoughts on the Constitution" G. D. H. Cole: "The Intelligent Man's Guide to the Post-War World" McCallum and Readman: "The British General Election of 1945," analysis The Dead Sea Scrolls, dating from approx. 22 B.C. to A.D. 100, are discovered in Wadi Qumran H. W. Garrod: "Scholarship, Its Meaning and Value" H. R. Trevor-Roper: "The Last Days of Hitler" E. F. Carritt: "Ethical and Political Thinking" Guido Ruggiero: "Existentialism" Michael Polanyi: "Science, Faith and Society" Sidney Webb, Lord Passfield, d. (b. 1859) Karl Jaspers: "The Question of Guilt" Max Dessoir, Ger. philosopher, d. (b. 1867) Theodor Heuss: "Deutsche Gestalten" A. N. Whitehead, Eng. mathematician and philosopher, d. (b. 1861) Nicholas Murray Butler d. (b. 1862)

D. VISUAL ARTS	E. MUSIC	F. SCIENCE, TECHNOLOGY, GROWTH	G. DAILY LIFE	
Joseph Stella d. (b. 1877) Alfred Stieglitz d. (b. 1864)	Get Your Gun," musical comedy, New York Alan Jay Lerner and Frederick Loewe: "Brigadoon" Popular songs: "How Are Things in Gloccamorra?"; "Tenderly"; "South America, Take It Away"; "Zip-a-dee-doo-dah"; "Come Rain or Come Shine"; "The Gypsy"; "Ole Buttermilk Sky"; "Shoo-Fly Pie and Apple Pan Dowdy"; "Doin' What Comes Nacherly"	Muller (U.S.) for his study of mutations under the influence of x-ray radiation Nobel Prize for Chemistry: James B. Summer (U.S.) shared with John Northrop and Wendell M. Stanley (both U.S.) for their work on enzymes Nobel Prize for Physics: Percy W. Bridgman for his work in high-pressure physics	Alabama wins Rose Bowl football game, 34—14, against Southern California St. Louis, after defeating Brooklyn in run off for NL pennant, goes on to win World Series 4—3 by defeating Boston (AL)	**1946 contd**
Maurice de Vlaminck: "A Bunch of Flowers" Henry Moore: "Three Standing Figures" Giacometti: "The Pointing Man," sculpture Le Corbusier: Unité d'Habitation, Marseilles Pierre Bonnard, Fr. painter, d. (b. 1867) Marino Marini: "Riders," sculpture Kokoschka: "Das Matterhorn" Matisse: "Young English Girl" Films: "Monsieur Verdoux" (Chaplin); "Vivere in pace" (Luigi Zampe); "Black Narcissus" (Michael Powell); "Gentleman's Agreement," Academy Award	Benjamin Britten: "Albert Herring," opera, Glyndebourne Pablo Casals vows not to play in public as long as Franco is in power Alfredo Casella, Ital. composer, d. (b. 1883) Walter Felsenstein, Ger. opera producer, becomes head of Komische Oper, Berlin Bronislaw Hubermann, Pol. violinist, d. (b. 1882) Maria Callas makes her debut in Ponchielli's "Gioconda" at Verona Gottfried von Einem: "Dantons Tod," opera, Salzburg Carl Orff: "Die Bernauerin," opera, Stuttgart E. Y. Harburg: "Finian's Rainbow," musical play, New York Popular songs: "Papa, Won't You Dance With Me?"; "Almost Like Being in Love"; "I'll Dance at Your Wedding" Gian Carlo Menotti: "The Medium" and "The Telephone," operas, New York John Powell: "Symphony in A," Detroit	British establish their first atomic pile at Harwell Advisory Committee on Scientific Policy set up in Britain P. M. S. Blackett advances the theory that "all massive rotating bodies are magnetic" U.S. airplane first flies at supersonic speeds Ettore Bugatti, Ital. racing car designer, d. (b. 1882) Max Planck d. (b. 1858) Thor Heyerdahl sails on a raft from Peru to Polynesia in 101 days to prove prehistoric immigration Bell laboratories scientists invent the transistor	Amer. aviator Odom flies around the world in 73 hours 5 minutes Brit. racing driver John Cobb establishes a world ground speed record of 394.196 miles per hour Henry Ford, leaving a fortune of $625 million, d. (b. 1863) Henry Gordon Selfridge d. (b. 1857) "Flying Saucers" reported in the U.S. Most severe winter in Britain since 1894 Approx. Black Market prices in Berlin: 20 Amer. cigarettes, 150 RM; 1 lb. coffee, 550 RM; 6 eggs, 150 RM; 6 boxes of matches, 60 RM From the Nippur excavations (1888—1900), Francis Steele reconstructs the laws of Hammurabi (18th century B.C.) The "New Look" dominates female fashion Jackie Robinson becomes first Black to sign a contract with a major baseball club Blizzard in New York, Dec. 17, almost 28 inches More than one million war veterans enroll in colleges under U.S. "G.I. Bill of Rights" Al Capone, U.S. gangster, d. (b. 1899) U.S. Lawn Tennis Association Men's Singles championship won by J. A. Kramer; Women's by A. Louise Brough U.S. wins Davis Cup tennis matches, defeating Australia U.S. Golf Association Amateur championship won by R. H. Riegel; Open by Lew Worsham Illinois wins Rose Bowl football game, 45—14, over U.C.L.A. New York (AL) wins World Series, 4—3, over Brooklyn (NL)	**1947**

	A. HISTORY, POLITICS	B. LITERATURE, THEATER	C. RELIGION, PHILOSOPHY, LEARNING
1948	Gandhi assassinated (b. 1869) Communist coup d'état in Czechoslovakia Feb. 25; Klement Gottwald elected President Chiang Kai-shek reelected President of China by Nanking Assembly U.S. Congress passes Marshall Plan (Economic Cooperation) Act, $17 billion in aid for Europe Churchill chairs Hague Congress for European unity Month-long strike by soft coal miners in U.S.; injunction prevents nationwide rail strike; first escalator clause basing wage increases on cost-of-living index in General Motors-United Auto Workers contract The Jewish state comes into existence, Weizmann President, Ben-Gurion Premier U.S.S.R. stops road and rail traffic between Berlin and the West; airlift begins (—Sept. 1949) Brit. Citizenship Act grants Brit. passports to all Commonwealth citizens Eduard Benes d. (b. 1884) Queen Wilhelmina of the Netherlands abdicates and is succeeded by her daughter, Juliana Count Folke Bernadotte, UN mediator in Palestine, assassinated by Jewish terrorists Harry S. Truman elected President of the U.S. Attlee appoints Linskey tribunal to investigate charges of corruption against Brit. ministers and officials Ernst Reuter, Social-Democrat, elected Mayor of Berlin John J. Pershing, U.S. general, d. (b. 1860) Jan Masaryk, Czech statesman, d. (b. 1886) Charles Evans Hughes, U.S. jurist, d. (b. 1862)	Giovanni Guareschi: "The Little World of Don Camillo" Harold Acton: "Memoirs of an Aesthete" W. H. Auden: "Age of Anxiety," Pulitzer Prize poetry Bernard de Voto: "Across the Wide Missouri," Pulitzer Prize history T. S. Eliot: "Notes Towards the Definition of Culture" Graham Greene: "The Heart of the Matter" Aldous Huxley: "Ape and Essence" Norman Mailer: "The Naked and the Dead" James A. Michener: "Tales of the South Pacific," Pulitzer Prize novel Howard Spring: "There Is No Armour" Terence Rattigan: "The Browning Version" Nobel Prize for Literature: T. S. Eliot Lawrence Durrell: "On Seeming to Presume," poems Alfred Kerr, Ger. critic, d. (b. 1867) Egon Erwin Kisch, Ger.-Czech author and journalist, d. (b. 1885) Emil Ludwig, Ger. author and biographer, d. (b. 1881) Thornton Wilder: "The Ides of March" 135 million paperback books sold during the year in the U.S. Alan Paton: "Cry, the Beloved Country," South African novel Irwin Shaw: "The Young Lions" Nevil Shute: "No Highway," novel Evelyn Waugh: "The Loved One" Tennessee Williams: "Summer and Smoke" Sartre: "Les Mains sales," play Jean Cocteau: "Les Parents terribles" Dwight D. Eisenhower: "Crusade in Europe" Thomas Merton: "Seven Storey Mountain" Lloyd C. Douglas: "The Big Fisherman"	Churchill: "The Gathering Storm" Arthur Keith: "A New Theory of Human Evolution" L. B. Namier: "Diplomatic Prelude 1938—1939" "The White House Papers of Harry L. Hopkins" published World Jewish Congress meets in Montreux Malraux: "Psychologie de l'Art" Nikolai Aleksandrovich Berdyaev, Russ. Christian socialist, d. (b. 1874) Martin Buber: "Moses" W. R. Inge: "Mysticism in Religion" World Council of Churches organized in Amsterdam Harold Laski: "The American Democracy" Charles A. Beard, U.S. historian and educator, d. (b. 1874)
1949	Dean Acheson appointed U.S. Secretary of State President Harry S. Truman inaugurated President of the U.S. Tientsin falls to the Communists; Chiang Kai-shek resigns as President of China; Communist army resumes offensive against Nationalist troops; Chiang Kai-shek removes forces to Formosa; Communist People's Republic proclaimed under Mao Tse-tung, with Chou En-lai as Premier Vishinsky replaces Molotov as U.S.S.R. Foreign Minister North Atlantic Treaty signed in Washington Republic of Eire proclaimed in Dublin; Britain recognizes Eire's independence U.S. Foreign Assistance Bill grants $5.43 billion to Europe Statute of Council of Europe is established with Strasbourg as its headquarters Israel admitted to UN; capital moved from Tel Aviv to Jerusalem Berlin blockade officially lifted Ger. Federal Republic comes into being with Bonn as capital Transjordan re-named the Hashemite Kingdom of *(contd)*	Nelson Algren: "The Man with the Golden Arm," novel H. E. Bates: "The Jacaranda Tree," novel Joyce Cary: "A Fearful Joy," novel James Gould Cozzens: "Guard of Honor," Pulitzer Prize novel Nancy Mitford: "Love in a Cold Climate," novel Charles Morgan: "The River Line," novel George Orwell: "Nineteen Eighty-Four," novel T. S. Eliot: "The Cocktail Party" Arthur Miller: "Death of a Salesman," Pulitzer Prize drama John O'Hara: "A Rage to Live," novel Brecht forms the Berliner Ensemble Tommy Handley, Brit. comedian, d. (b. 1894) Tom Lea: "The Brave Bulls," novel Axel Munthe d. (b. 1857) Maurice Maeterlinck d. (b. 1862) Nobel Prize for Literature: William Faulkner Fulton Oursler: "The Greatest Story Ever Told" Norman Vincent Peale: "A Guide to Confident *(contd)*	J. D. Bernal: "The Freedom of Necessity" Roy Lewis and Angus Maude: "The English Middle Classes" Erich Fromm: "Man for Himself" Paul Tillich: "The Shaking of the Foundations" Hungarian Cardinal Mindszenty is sentenced to life imprisonment for "high treason" Albert Schweitzer: "Hospital in the Jungle" The "Great Palindrome" solved: "Sator *(contd)*

D. VISUAL ARTS	E. MUSIC	F. SCIENCE, TECHNOLOGY, GROWTH	G. DAILY LIFE	
Churchill made Honorary Academician Extraordinary Fernand Léger: "Homage to David" Ben Shahn: "Miners' Wives" Jackson Pollock: "Composition No. 1" Henry Moore: "Family Group" (Stevenage New Town, Eng.) Lyonel Feininger: "The Lake" T. T. Heine, Ger. cartoonist of "Simplizissimus," d. (b. 1867) Films: "Hamlet," Academy Award (Olivier); "The Red Shoes" (Michael Powell); "Oliver Twist" (David Lean); "The Fallen Idol" (Carol Reed); "Bitter Rice" (de Santis); "The Naked City" (Jules Dassin); "The Bicycle Thief" (de Sica); "Louisiana Story" (Flaherty); "Macbeth" (Orson Welles); "The Young Guard" (Gerasimov) D. W. Griffith, Amer. director who produced 484 films, d. (b. 1875) Arshile Gorky d. (b. 1904)	Olivier Messiaen: "Turangalila-Symphony" Howard Hanson: "Piano Concerto No. 1" Bohuslav Martinu: "String Quartet" and "Seventh String Quartet" Britten: "Beggar's Opera," new version, Cambridge Arnold Schönberg: "Survivor from Warsaw" Franz Lehár d. (b. 1870) Werner Egk: "Circe," opera Richard Tauber d. (b. 1891) Ermanno Wolf-Ferrari, Ital. operatic composer, d. (b. 1876) Richard Strauss: "Vier letzte Lieder" Umberto Giordano, Ital. operatic composer, d. (b. 1867) Cole Porter: "Kiss Me, Kate," musical comedy, New York Popular songs: "Nature Boy"; "All I Want for Christmas Is My Two Front Teeth"; "Buttons and Bows"	Lajos Jánossy: "Cosmic Rays and Nuclear Physics" The antibiotics aureomycin and chloromycetin prepared Long-playing record invented by Peter Goldmark (U.S.) Orville Wright, aircraft pioneer, d. (b. 1871) Charlotte Auerbach's studies begin the science of chemogenetics The price of uranium rises to $1,600 per ton Ferdinand Porsche (Germany) builds the "Porsche 356" car First port radar system introduced in Liverpool, England In U.S. tests in New Mexico, rocket missiles reach 78 mile altitude and 3000 miles per hour 200-inch Mount Palomar reflecting telescope dedicated Idlewild Airport on Long Island, N.Y., dedicated by President Truman (renamed Kennedy Airport in 1963) Alfred C. Kinsey: "Sexual Behavior in the Human Male" Ruth Benedict, U.S. anthropologist, d. (b. 1887)	Brit. railroads nationalized First World Health Assembly meets in Geneva Bread rationing ends in Britain Brit. Electricity Authority established Prince Charles, the Prince of Wales, b. Babe Ruth d. (b. 1895) Glamorgan, youngest of cricket county clubs, wins championship London Olympiad: Fanny Blankers-Koen wins four gold medals for the Netherlands Joe Louis retires from the ring after fighting 25 title bouts since 1937 Federal rent control bill passed in U.S. Selective Service Act in U.S. provides for continued military draft (—1973) "Citation," Eddie Arcaro up, wins Belmont and Preakness Stakes and Kentucky Derby (fourth Derby win for Arcaro) Davis Cup tennis matches won by the U.S. team against Australia Michigan defeats Southern California 49—0 to win Rose Bowl football game U.S. team is high scorer in Olympic Games held in London "Pancho" Gonzales wins Men's Singles championship of U.S. Lawn Tennis Association; Mrs. Margaret O. du Pont wins Women's Singles Willie Turnesa wins U.S. Golf Association Amateur championship; Ben Hogan wins Open Cleveland (AL) wins World Series, 4—2, over Boston (NL)	**1948**
Graham Sutherland: portrait of W. Somerset Maugham Kenneth Clark: "Landscape into Art" Jacob Epstein: "Lazarus" Chagall: "Red Sun" James Ensor, Belg. painter, d. (b. 1860) Kokoschka Exhibition at N.Y. Museum of Modern Art Films: "The Third Man" (Carol Reed); "La Macchina Ammazzacattivi" (Rossellini); "Manon" (H. G. Clouzot); "The Winslow Boy" (Asquith); "All the King's Men," Academy Award *(contd)*	Richard Strauss d. (b. 1864) Arthur Bliss: "The Olympians," opera, London Britten: "Let's Make an Opera," Aldeburgh Hans Pfitzner, Ger. composer, d. (b. 1869) The samba comes into fashion Carl Orff: "Antigonae," opera, Salzburg Theodor W. Adorno: "Philosophie der neuen Musik" Kurt Weill: "Lost in the Stars," musical tragedy, New York Rodgers and Hammerstein: "South Pacific," musical play, New York Leonard Bernstein: "The Age of Anxiety," symphony for piano and orchestra Peter Racine Fricker: Symphony No. 1, Op. 9 *(contd)*	Philip Hench discovers cortisone Neomycin isolated by Selman Waksman U.S.S.R. tests its first atomic bomb Friedrich Bergius, Ger. chemist and industrialist, d. (b. 1884) R. W. G. Wyckoff: "Electronic Microscopy" Nobel Prize for Chemistry; W. F. Giague for his work in chemical thermodynamics U.S. Air Force jet flies across U.S. in 3 hours 46 minutes U.S. launches guided missile 250 miles, *(contd)*	British Gas Industry nationalized Charlemagne Prize for European understanding established at Aix-la-Chapelle Geoffrey de Havilland: "Comet" (airplane) Clothes rationing ends in Britain "Pancho" Gonzales wins U.S. Lawn Tennis Association Men's Singles; Mrs. Margaret O. du Pont wins Women's Singles Charles R. Coe wins U.S. Golf Association Amateur; Cary Middlecoff wins Open "Capot," T. Atkinson up, wins Belmont and Preakness Stakes Rose Bowl football game won by Northwestern defeating California 20—14 Ezzard Charles named world heavyweight boxing champion after match with "Jersey" Joe Walcott *(contd)*	**1949**

	A. HISTORY, POLITICS	B. LITERATURE, THEATER	C. RELIGION, PHILOSOPHY, LEARNING
1949 contd	Jordan Vietnam state established at Saigon U.S. completes the withdrawal of its occupying forces in South Korea Apartheid program is established in South Africa UN warns of danger of civil war in Korea Theodor Heuss elected President, Konrad Adenauer Chancellor, of West Germany which becomes a full participant under the Marshall Plan Britain devalues the pound sterling from $4.03 to $2.80; most European nations follow Berlin airlift ends after 277,264 flights Democratic Republic established in East Germany with Pieck as President and Grotewohl as Minister-President Eleven U.S. Communists are found guilty of conspiracy to overthrow the government India adopts constitution as federal republic Holland transfers sovereignty to Indonesia; France to Vietnam Pandit Nehru becomes Prime Minister of India President Truman appoints Tom C. Clark (—1967) and Sherman Minton (—1956) to Supreme Court	Living" Colette: "Le Fanal bleu" Nelly Sachs: "Sternverdunklung," poems Robert E. Sherwood: "Roosevelt and Hopkins," Pulitzer Prize biography Edith Sitwell: "The Canticle of the Rose," poems Sigrid Undset, Norw. novelist, d. (b. 1882) Carson McCullers: "The Member of the Wedding," drama Edward Streeter: "The Father of the Bride" J. P. Marquand: "Point of No Return" Eleanor Roosevelt: "This I Remember"	Arepo Tenetopera Rotas" (Arepo - Rex et Pater between A and O is God) Rabbi Stephen S. Wise d. (b. 1874) Building of Lomonosov University, Moscow, begins (—1953)
1950	Britain recognizes Communist China; U.S.S.R. and Communist China sign 30-year pact; Chiang Kai-shek resumes presidency of Nationalist China; Communist China's forces occupy Tibet; Tibet appeals to UN, but China rejects UN appeal for cease-fire Senator Joseph McCarthy advises President Truman that State Department is riddled with Communists and Communist sympathizers Alger Hiss, a former U.S. State Department official, sentenced for perjury Riots in Johannesburg against apartheid Truman instructs U.S. Atomic Energy Commission to develop hydrogen bomb Klaus Fuchs found guilty of betraying Brit. atomic secrets to U.S.S.R. and imprisoned; Harry Gold, his American confederate, sentenced to 30 years in prison London dock strike Britain recognizes Israel West Germany joins Council of Europe N. Korean forces invade S. Korea June 25 and capture Seoul; Douglas MacArthur appointed commander of UN forces in Korea; UN forces land in S. Korea and recapture Seoul; S. Korean troops cross 38th parallel; UN troops forced to withdraw; state of emergency declared in U.S. following Korean reversals; Chin. forces cross 38th parallel U.S. recognizes Vietnam, capital at Saigon; supplies arms and sends mission to instruct in their use; signs military assistance pact with France, Cambodia, Laos, and Vietnam King Leopold III returns to Belgium after six years' exile; Socialists demonstrate against him; he abdicates in favor of his son Baudouin Indonesia admitted to UN King Gustavus V of Sweden d.; succeeded by his son Gustavus VI (b. 1882) Poland and E. Germany proclaim Oder-Neisse line as frontier Attlee visits Washington Nobel Peace Prize: Dr. Ralph J. Bunche (U.S.) Henry L. Stimson, U.S. political figure, d. (b. 1867) Congress passes McCarran Act over presidential veto; it calls for severe restrictions against Communists, particularly in sensitive positions during emergencies, *(contd)*	Ray Bradbury: "The Martian Chronicles" Ernest Hemingway: "Across the River and into the Trees" Budd Schulberg: "The Disenchanted" Francis Parkinson Keyes: "Joy Street" Thor Heyerdahl: "Kon-Tiki" Ezra Pound: "Seventy Cantos" C. P. Snow: "The Masters" Anouilh: "La Répétition" Henry Morton Robinson: "The Cardinal" George Bernard Shaw d. (b. 1856) William Cooper: "Scenes from Provincial Life" Nobel Prize for Literature: Bertrand Russell Nigel Balchin: "The Anatomy of Villainy," essays Hedwig Courts-Mahler, Ger. novelist who wrote 192 romances, d. (b. 1867) Christopher Fry: "Venus Observed," verse play, and "The Lady's Not for Burning" John Hersey: "The Wall," novel about the Warsaw Ghetto Sidney Kingsley: "Darkness at Noon" Heinrich Mann, Ger. novelist, d. (b. 1871) Evelyn Waugh: "Helena" Emil Jannings, Ger. actor, d. (b. 1887) Robert Penn Warren: "World Enough and Time" The Library of Congress, Washington, D.C., consists of 8.6 million books, 128,000 yearly newspaper vols., 11 million manuscripts, 2 million maps, 76,000 microfilms, 2 million musical scores, and 4 million miscellaneous items Nevil Shute: "The Legacy," novel Tennessee Williams: "The Roman Spring of Mrs. Stone" Edgar Rice Burroughs, creator of "Tarzan," d. (b. 1875) Edna St. Vincent Millay, U.S. poet, d. (b. 1892) Edgar Lee Masters, U.S. poet, d. (b. 1869) Al Jolson d. (b. 1886) Carl Van Doren d. (b. 1885) Gwendolyn Brooks: "Annie Allen," Pulitzer *(contd)*	A. L. Rowse: "The England of Elizabeth" Boswell: "London Journal, 1762—1763" Nikolai Berdyaev: "Dreams and Reality" R. A. Knox: "Enthusiasm" Margaret Mead: "Social Anthropology" Gilbert Ryle: "The Concept of Mind" Sartre: "La Mort dans l'âme" Pope Pius XII proclaims the dogma of the bodily assumption of the Virgin Mary International Exhibition of Ecclesiastical Art in Rome 25 Protestant and four Eastern Orthodox Church groups organize National Council of the Churches of Christ in the U.S.: 32 million members

D. VISUAL ARTS	E. MUSIC	F. SCIENCE, TECHNOLOGY, GROWTH	G. DAILY LIFE	
(Rossen); "Les Enfants terribles" (Jean Melville) Walter Kuhn d. (b. 1880) José Orozco d. (b. 1883)	George Antheil: "Symphony No. 6" Béla Bártok: "Viola Concerto" Paul Hindemith: "Concerto for Flute, Oboe, Clarinet, Bassoon, Harp, and Orchestra" Darius Milhaud: "Quartet No. 5" and "Quartet No. 14" Popular songs: "Bali Ha'i"; "Some Enchanted Evening"; "I'm in Love with a Wonderful Guy"; "So in Love"; "Riders in the Sky"; "I Love Those Dear Hearts and Gentle People"; "Diamonds Are a Girl's Best Friend"; "Rudolph, the Red-Nosed Reindeer"	highest altitude ever reached by man Edward L. Thorndike, U.S. psychologist, d. (b. 1874)	New York (AL) defeats Brooklyn (NL) 4—1 to win World Series	**1949 contd**
Chagall: "King David" Bernard Berenson: "Aesthetics and History" Giacometti: "Seven Figures and a Head," sculpture UN Building, New York, completed Eugenio Montiori designs new railroad station in Rome Pani and del Moral design University City, Mexico Max Beckmann, Ger. expressionist painter, d. (b. 1884) Kokoschka: portrait of Theodor Heuss Matisse begins work on the Vence Chapel Eliel Saarinen, U.S. architect, d. (b. 1873) Films: "La Beauté du Diable" (René Clair); "Orphée" (Cocteau); "La Ronde" (Ophuls); "Sunset Boulevard" (Wilder); "Rashomon" (Jap.); "All About Eve," Academy Award	Gian Carlo Menotti: "The Consul," Pulitzer Prize, opera, New York International Bach Year honors Johann Sebastian Bach (d. 1750) Kurt Weill d. (b. 1900) "Cool jazz" developed from bebop Frank Loesser and Abe Burrows: "Guys and Dolls," musical comedy, New York Popular songs: "If I Knew You Were Comin' I'd've Baked a Cake"; "Ragg Mopp"; "Sam's Story"; "A Bushel and a Peck"; "C'est Si Bon"; "Good Night, Irene"; "Tzena, Tzena, Tzena, Tzena"; "Music! Music! Music!"; "Mona Lisa" Howard Swanson: "Short Symphony," New York Benny Goodman and the NBC Symphony Orchestra premiere "Clarinet Concerto" by Aaron Copland	Plutonium separated from pitchblende concentrates G. T. Seaborg discovers element 98 (californium); berkelium discovered Einstein: "General Field Theory" (attempt to expand Theory of Relativity) Miltown, a meprobamate, comes into wide use in the U.S. as a tranquilizer Nobel Prize for Medicine and Physiology: Philip S. Hench (U.S.), Edward C. Kendall (U.S.), and Tadeusz Reichstein (Swiss, born in Poland) for their work in hormones Antihistamines become popular remedy for colds and allergies Brooklyn-Battery Tunnel opens in New York	World population is approximately 2.3 billion U.S. population 150,697,999; illiteracy is 3.2 per cent City populations (in millions); London, 8.3; New York, 7.8; Tokyo, 5.3; Moscow, 4.1 Jan Smuts d. (b. 1870) 1.5 million Germans are still missing UN reports that of the 800 million children in the world, 480 million are undernourished 30,000 varieties of roses catalogued 1.5 million TV sets in U.S. (one year later approx. 15 million) Nobel Prize winners by nation: 49 Germans, 40 Britons, 45 Americans, 30 Frenchmen Heavy earthquake damages Assam European Broadcasting Union formed World record crowd of 199,854 attends World Cup soccer game (Brazil versus Uruguay) in Rio de Janeiro "Hap" Arnold, General of the U.S. Air Force, d. (b. 1886) Arthur Larsen wins U.S. Lawn Tennis Men's Singles championship; Mrs. Margaret O. du Pont is winner of Women's Singles Sam Urzetta wins U.S. Golf Association Amateur; Open is won by Ben Hogan Australian tennis team wins Davis Cup from the U.S. team Ohio State wins Rose Bowl football classic, 17—14 against California New York (AL) wins World Series, 4—0, against Philadelphia (NL)	**1950**

	A. HISTORY, POLITICS	B. LITERATURE, THEATER	C. RELIGION, PHILOSOPHY, LEARNING
1950 contd	and for registration of all Communist organizations and individuals, and forbids entry into U.S. of aliens who have belonged to totalitarian organizations Assassination attempt against Truman made by two Puerto Rican nationalists; one is killed, the other sentenced to death, later commuted to life imprisonment Léon Blum d. (b. 1872)	Prize for poetry A. B. Guthrie, Jr.: "The Way West," Pulitzer Prize novel Clifford Odets: "The Country Girl"	
1951	N. Korean forces break through at 38th parallel, take Seoul, and reject Amer. truce offers; Seoul retaken; General MacArthur relieved of Far East command; new N. Korean offensive; further attempts to negotiate an armistice fail; UN forces capture "Heartbreak Ridge" north of Yanguu; armistice negotiations at Panmunjom begin, but fail Ben-Gurion's new government dissolved in Israel; a new coalition formed Czechoslovak Communist Party purged Mossadegh becomes Prime Minister of Iran De Valera returns to power in Eire Brit. diplomats Burgess and Maclean, who have been spying for the Russians, escape to the U.S.S.R. King Abdullah of Jordan assassinated in Jerusalem Peace treaty with Japan signed in San Francisco Brit. Conservatives win General Election; Churchill forms government Perón reelected President of Argentina Adenauer visits Paris, Rome, and London Maxim Litvinov, former U.S.S.R. Foreign Minister, d. (b. 1876) 22nd Amendment to the U.S. Constitution passed by Congress: provides for maximum of two terms (eight years) service as president and one term for vice presidents succeeding to the presidency who have already served more than two years Henri Pétain d. (b. 1856) Julius and Ethel Rosenberg are sentenced to death for espionage against the U.S.; their confederate, Morton Sobell, to 30 years imprisonment	Robert Frost: "Complete Poems" Conrad Richter: "The Town," Pulitzer Prize novel Carl Sandburg: "Complete Poems," Pulitzer Prize Nicholas Monsarrat: "The Cruel Sea" J. D. Salinger: "The Catcher in the Rye" Herman Wouk: "The Caine Mutiny," Pulitzer Prize novel (1952) Anouilh: "Colombe" Christopher Fry: "A Sleep of Prisoners" Sartre: "Le Diable et le bon Dieu" Foundation stone of Brit. National Theatre laid at South Bank, London André Gide d. (b. 1869) Louis Bromfield: "Mr. Smith" Camus: "L'Homme révolté" John Van Druten: "I Am a Camera" William Faulkner: "Requiem for a Nun" Graham Greene: "The End of the Affair" James Jones: "From Here to Eternity" Louis Jouvet, Fr. actor and producer, d. (b. 1887) Nikos Kazantzakis: "The Greek Passion" John Erskine, Amer. author, d. (b. 1879) Bernhard Kellermann, Ger. novelist, d. (b. 1879) Fanny Brice d. (b. 1891) Sinclair Lewis d. (b. 1885) Thomas Mann: "Der Erwählte" François Mauriac: "Le Sagouin" Best seller: "Desirée," by Annemarie Selinko Tennessee Williams: "The Rose Tattoo" Harold Ross, "New Yorker" editor, d. (b. 1892) William Styron: "Lie Down in Darkness" Catherine Marshall: "A Man Called Peter" Rachel Carson: "The Sea Around Us"	Theodor W. Adorno: "Minima moralia," essays Georg Katona: "Psychological Analysis of Economic Behavior" Ludwig von Mises: "Socialism, an Economic and Sociological Analysis" Ortega y Gasset: "Man as Utopist Creature" Ludwig Wittgenstein, Neo-Positivist Aust. philosopher, d. (b. 1889)

D. VISUAL ARTS	E. MUSIC	F. SCIENCE, TECHNOLOGY, GROWTH	G. DAILY LIFE	
				1950 contd
Salvador Dali: "Christ of St. John on the Cross" Graham Sutherland: "Lord Beaverbrook," portrait Gerald Barry and Hugh Casson: Festival of Britain on London South Bank Basil Spence designs new Coventry Cathedral Matisse completes Vence Chapel Picasso: "Massacre in Korea," painting Otto Dix: "Peasant Girl with Child" Films: "The African Queen" (John Huston); "Le Plaisir" (Ophuls); "Miracle in Milan" (de Sica); "An American in Paris," Academy Award (Gene Kelly, Minnelli); "Viva Zapata" (Elia Kazan); "Strangers on a Train" (Hitchcock); "A Streetcar Named Desire" (Brando) Brit. Film Censors introduce "X certificate" classification Fred Waller (U.S.) invents Cinerama Ludwig Mies van der Rohe designs Lake Shore Drive apartment building, Chicago Frank Lloyd Wright designs Friedman House, Pleasantville, N.Y. Marcel Breuer designs dormitory at Vassar College, Poughkeepsie, N.Y. John Sloan d. (b. 1871)	Britten: "Billy Budd," opera, London Stravinsky: "Rake's Progress," opera, Venice R. Vaughan Williams: "The Pilgrim's Progress," opera, London Arnold Schönberg d. (b. 1874) Constant Lambert, Eng. composer and conductor, d. (b. 1905) Fritz Busch, Ger. conductor, d. (b. 1890) Robert Matthew builds the Royal Festival Hall, London Sergei Koussevitzky, Russ.-Amer. conductor, d. (b. 1874) William Mengelberg, Dutch conductor, d. (b. 1871) Arthur Schnabel, Aust. pianist, d. (b. 1882) Rodgers and Hammerstein: "The King and I," musical play, New York Arthur Honegger: "Je suis compositeur," autobiography Popular songs: "Hello, Young Lovers"; "Getting to Know You"; "Shrimp Boats"; "Come On-a My House"; "Cry"; "In the Cool, Cool, Cool of the Evening"; "Kisses Sweeter Than Wine" Douglas Moore: "Giants in the Earth," opera, Pulitzer Prize Gian Carlo Menotti: "Amahl and the Night Visitors," opera written on commission for NBC-TV Huddie Ledbetter ("Lead-belly"), folk singer and composer, d. (b. 1888)	Krilium developed from acrylonitrile for use in fertilization Electric power produced from atomic energy at Arcon, Idaho J. Andre-Thomas devises a heart-lung machine for heart operations Charles F. Blair flies solo over the North Pole Ferdinand Sauerbruch, Ger. surgeon, d. (b. 1875) Approx. 400,000 pounds of penicillin and 350,000 pounds of streptomycin produced in the U.S. during the year Nobel Prize for Medicine and Physiology: Max Theiler (U.S.) for his work on a yellow fever vaccine Nobel Prize for Chemistry: Edwin M. McMillan (U.S.) and Glenn T. Seaborg (U.S.) for their discovery of plutonium	Hank Marino elected Amer. Bowler of the Half Century J. S. Coxey, U.S. businessman who led "Coxey's Army" to Washington, D.C., to protest against unemployment, d. (b. 1854) William Randolph Hearst, Amer. newspaper proprietor, d. (b. 1863) 46 per cent of the population works in commerce and industry in Great Britain, 41 per cent in Germany, 30 per cent in the U.S., 29 per cent in Italy, 20 per cent in Japan, and 10 per cent in India Color television is first introduced (in U.S.) Gordion, the Phrygian capital 4000 to 3000 B.C., is excavated Crown Prince William of Prussia, eldest son of William II, d. (b. 1882) New York defeats Brooklyn in play-off of tied American League pennant race, then goes on to lose World Series, 4—2, to New York (NL) "Citation" wins Hollywood Gold Cup horserace bringing his total winnings to more than $1 million "Jersey" Joe Walcott knocks out Ezzard Charles in seventh round to win world heavyweight boxing title Michigan defeats California to win Rose Bowl football game 14—6 Australia wins Davis Cup against U.S. Billy Maxwell wins U.S. Golf Association Amateur championship; Ben Hogan wins Open Frank Sedgman wins U.S. Lawn Tennis Association Men's Singles; Maureen Connolly wins Women's Singles	**1951**

	A. HISTORY, POLITICS	B. LITERATURE, THEATER	C. RELIGION, PHILOSOPHY, LEARNING
1952	Anti-Brit. riots erupt in Egypt; Aly Maher Pasha appointed premier in Jan.; resigns Mar. 10; General Mohammed Naguib seizes power and forms a government; King Farouk abdicates in favor of his infant son, Fuad; constitution of 1923 abolished Franco-Ger. crisis over Saar administration King George VI of England d.; succeeded by his daughter, Queen Elizabeth II Churchill announces that Britain has produced an atomic bomb; Truman announces H-bomb tests in the Pacific Dwight D. Eisenhower resigns as Supreme Commander in Europe; elected President of the U.S. European Defence Community Treaty signed in Paris Hydroelectric plants in N. Korea bombed by U.S. planes; UN General Assembly adopts Indian proposal for Korean armistice; China rejects plan Ruiz Cortines elected President of Mexico Honolulu Conference of three-power Pacific Council (Australia, U.S., and New Zealand) During the month of August 16,000 people escape from E. to W. Berlin Prince Hussein Ibn Talal (b. 1935), grandson of King Abdullah, proclaimed King of Jordan Chou En-lai visits Moscow China and Mongolia sign 10-year agreement U.S.S.R. Communist Party Congress meets in Moscow State of emergency proclaimed in Kenya following Mau Mau disturbances In Czechoslovakia Rudolph Slansky and Vladimar Clementis are accused of high treason and executed Chaim Weizmann d. (b. 1874); Yizhak Ben-Zvi elected President of Israel Israel and Germany agree on restitution for damages done to Jews by the Nazis Nobel Peace Prize: Albert Schweitzer Philip Murray, U.S. labor leader, d. (b. 1886) William Green, U.S. labor leader, d. (b. 1873)	Truman Capote: "The Grass Harp" Ralph Ellison: "The Invisible Man" Ernest Hemingway: "The Old Man and the Sea," Pulitzer Prize novel (1953) Joseph Kramm: "The Shrike," Pulitzer Prize drama F. R. Leavis: "The Common Pursuit" Doris Lessing: "Martha Quest" Marianne Moore: "Collected Poems," Pulitzer Prize Paul Osborn: "Point of No Return," based on J. P. Marquand's novel Dylan Thomas: "Collected Poems" Evelyn Waugh: "Men at Arms" Angus Wilson: "Hemlock and After" Agatha Christie: "The Mousetrap," London (celebrates 22nd year in 1974) Clifford Odets: "Winter Journey" Nobel Prize for Literature: François Mauriac Anouilh: "The Waltz of the Toreadors" Albert Bassermann, Ger. actor, d. (b. 1867) Samuel Beckett: "Waiting for Godot" Jan de Hartog: "The Fourposter" Norman Douglas, Eng. author, d. (b. 1868) Leonhard Frank: "Links wo das Herz ist," novel Knut Hamsun, Norw. novelist, d. (b. 1859) Ferenc Molnár, Hungarian dramatist, d. (b. 1878) Cesare Pavese; "Il Mestiere de Vivere," Ital. diary John Steinbeck: "East of Eden" Louis Verneuil, Fr. dramatist, d. (b. 1893) Edna Ferber: "Giant" Thomas B. Costain: "The Silver Chalice" G. B. Shaw: "Don Juan in Hell"	Alan Moorehead: "The Traitors" (Klaus Fuchs, Nunn May, Pontecorvo) Harold Nicolson: "King George V," biography Reinhold Niebuhr: "Christ and Culture" Martin Buber: "The Chassidic Message" John Dewey, Amer. philosopher, d. (b. 1859) C. G. Jung: "Antwort auf Hiob" George Santayana, Span.-Amer. philosopher, d. (b. 1863) St. Stephens Cathedral, Vienna, reopened Benedetto Croce, Ital. philosopher, d. (b. 1866) Norman Vincent Peale: "The Power of Positive Thinking" The "Revised Standard Version" of the Bible, prepared by 32 scholars over 15 years, published for Protestants
1953	London Conference of Northern and Southern Rhodesia and Nyasaland Churchill visits Eisenhower New constitution proclaimed in Yugoslavia; Marshal Tito elected president Eisenhower inaugurated as President of the U.S. Gen. Naguib is voted dictatorial powers in Egypt for three years; republic proclaimed U.S.S.R. severs relations with Israel in Feb.; resumed again in July Stalin d. (b. 1879); succeeded by G. M. Malenkov; L. P. Beria dismissed and executed; Khrushchev appointed First Secretary of the Central Committee of the Communist Party Tito visits London Dag Hammarskjöld (Swed.) elected Secretary- General of the UN U.S. Congress creates new cabinet post of Secretary of Health, Education, and Welfare Adenauer visits New York and London Jomo Kenyatta and five other Kikuyu convicted of managing Mau Mau Vietnamese rebels attack Laos Queen Elizabeth II crowned London Conference of Commonwealth prime ministers *(contd)*	Ian Fleming: "Casino Royale" C. Day Lewis: "An Italian Visit" T. S. Eliot: "The Confidential Clerk" N. C. Hunter: "A Day by the Sea" Arthur Miller: "The Crucible" Hilaire Belloc, Eng. author, d. (b. 1870) Nobel Prize for Literature: Winston S. Churchill Ivan A. Bunin, Russ. poet, d. (b. 1870) Eugene O'Neill d. (b. 1888) Dylan Thomas d. (b. 1914) Julian Green: "South," Fr. drama Gerald Hanley: "The Year of the Lion" Graham Greene: "The Living Room" Lee Shubert, U.S. theater owner, d. (b. 1875) George Axelrod: "The Seven-Year Itch" Robert Anderson: "Tea and Sympathy" Archibald MacLeish: "Collected Poems," Pulitzer Prize John Steinbeck: "Sweet Thursday" Tennessee Williams: "Camino Real" Saul Bellow: "The Adventures of Augie March" Leon Uris: "Battle Cry" *(contd)*	Karl Jaspers: "Tragedy Is Not Enough" J. B. Rhine: "The New World of the Mind" B. F. Skinner: "Science and Human Behavior" Allan Bullock: "Hitler," biography Martin Heidegger: "Introduction to Metaphysics" Richard von Mises, Aust. mathematician and philosopher, d. (b. 1883) Gunther Weisenborn: "The Silent Revolt," report on Ger. anti-Nazi resistance Simone de Beauvoir: "The Second Sex"

D. VISUAL ARTS	E. MUSIC	F. SCIENCE, TECHNOLOGY, GROWTH	G. DAILY LIFE	
Chagall: "The Green Night" Raoul Dufy: "The Pink Violin" Barbara Hepworth: "Statue," Eng. abstract sculpture Jackson Pollock: "Number 12" Georges Rouault: "End of Autumn" Art nouveau (Jugendstil) exhibition in Zurich Augustus John: "Chiaroscuro," autobiography Jacob Epstein: "Madonna and Child," Cavendish Square, London Lionel Brett designs Hatfield New Town, England Films: "This is Cinerama"; "Limelight" (Chaplin); "Othello" (Orson Welles): "Umberto D." (de Sica); "Moulin Rouge" (José Ferrer); "Don Camillo et Peppone" (Fernandel, Duvivier); "The Greatest Show on Earth," Academy Award (C. B. de Mille); "High Noon" (Gary Cooper, Grace Kelly) Lever House, New York City, designed by Skidmore, Owings, and Merrill, completed	Boris Blacher: "Preussisches Märchen," opera-ballet Adolf Busch, Ger. violinist, d. (b. 1891) Alfred Einstein, Ger. musicologist and critic, d. (b. 1880) Hans Werner Henze: "Boulevard Solitude," opera, Hanover Hindemith: "Cardillac," new version of 1926 opera Rolf Liebermann: "Leonore 40/45," Swiss opera Heinrich Schlusnus, Ger. baritone, d. (b. 1888) Elisabeth Schumann, Ger. soprano, d. (b. 1888) Popular songs: "I Saw Mommy Kissing Santa Claus"; "Jambalaya"; "It Takes Two to Tango"; "Your Cheatin' Heart"; "Wheel of Fortune" Gail Kubik: Symphony Concertante, Pulitzer Prize Paul Creston: Symphony No. 4 Alexei Haieff: Piano Concerto Roy Harris: Symphony No. 7 Gardner Read: "The Temptation of St. Anthony" Leonard Bernstein: "Trouble in Tahiti," opera, Waltham, Mass. Arthur Kreutz: "Acres of Sky," opera, New York City Alexandre Tcherepnin: "The Farmer and the Fairy," opera, Aspen, Colo.	Isotopes in use in medicine and industry Contraceptive pill of phosphorated hesperidin is produced Brit. first atomic tests in Monte Bello Islands, W. Australia First hydrogen bomb (U.S.) exploded at Eniwetok Atoll, Pacific, Nov. 6 Cyram and Becker statistically demonstrate a connection between death frequency and weather Sven Hedin, Swed. explorer, d. (b. 1865) Nobel Prize for Physics: Felix Bloch (U.S.) and Edward M. Purcell (U.S.) for their work on magnetic fields in atomic nuclei Nobel Prize for Medicine and Physiology: Selman A. Waksman (U.S.) for the discovery of streptomycin	The last London trams are retired Jericho excavated Eva Perón d. (b. 1922) Rocky Marciano wins world heavyweight boxing championship from "Jersey" Joe Walcott Germany becomes a member of the World Bank S.S. "United States" (U.S.) wins Blue Riband, crossing the Atlantic in 3 days, 10 hours and 40 minutes Christian Dior gains influence on Paris haute couture Helsinki Olympics: 43 gold medals for U.S., 22 for U.S.S.R., 22 for Hungary; Zatopek (Czechoslovakia) wins 5,000 meters, 10,000 meters, and Marathon in record time John Cobb killed while establishing a water-speed record of 206.89 mph on Loch Ness, Scotland Frank Sedgman (Australia) wins U.S. Lawn Tennis Association Men's Singles; Maureen Connolly wins Women's Singles Australian tennis team defeats Americans to retain Davis Cup U.S. Golf Association Amateur championship won by Jack Westland; Open by Julius Boros Rose Bowl football game is won by Illinois, defeating Stanford 40—7 Eddie Arcaro rides "Hill Gail" to his fifth Kentucky Derby win New York (AL) wins World Series 4—3 against Brooklyn (NL)	**1952**
Jean Bazin: "Chicago," Fr. abstract Georges Braque: "Apples" Chagall: "Eiffel Tower" Raoul Dufy, Fr. painter, d. (b. 1877) John Marin d. (b. 1872) Eric Mendelsohn, Ger.-born Eng. architect, d. (b. 1887) Francis Picabia, Fr. surrealist painter, d. (b. 1879) Picasso exhibition in Rome B. W. Tomlin: "No. 10–1952/3," Amer. abstract Henry Moore: "King and Queen," sculpture at Antwerp Eero Saarinen wins award for design of General Motors Tech. Center in Warren, Michigan Films: "I Vitelloni," *(contd)*	"Kismet," musical, based on Borodin's music for "Prince Igor" Britten: "Gloriana," opera, London Vaughan Williams: "Sinfonia antartica," No. 7, Manchester Gottfried von Einem: "The Trial," opera, based on Kafka's novel, Salzburg Hindemith: "A Composer's World" Emmerich Kálmán, Hungarian-Viennese operetta composer, d. (b. 1882) Eduard Künnecke, Ger. operetta composer, d. (b. 1885) Bohuslav Martinu: "What Men Live By," comic opera Sergei Prokofiev, Russ. composer, d. (b. 1891) Karlheinz Stockhausen: "Electronic Study I" Arnold Bax, Eng. composer, d. (b. 1883) *(contd)*	Nobel Prize for Medicine and Physiology: F. A. Lipmann (U.S.) and H. A. Krebs (Brit.) for their work on living cells Mazel discovers Cave Cougnac, near Gourdon containing prehistoric paintings R. A. Millikan, Amer. physicist, d. (b. 1868) Fourth International Astronautic Congress meets in Zurich Cosmic ray observatory erected on Mount Wrangell, Alaska U.S.S.R. explodes hydrogen bomb W. Le Gross Clark proves the Piltdown *(contd)*	Queen Mary of England d. (b. 1867) London Stock Exchange opens public galleries William T. Tilden II (Amer.), tennis world champion, d. (b. 1893) Murder of the Brit. Drummond family at Provence, France, by farmer Gaston Dominici Maureen Connolly, U.S. tennis player, wins women's Grand Slam–all four major championships Ben Hogan, U.S. golfer, wins Masters, U.S. Open, and Brit. Open championships Jim Thorpe, U.S. athlete, d. (b. 1888) Tornadoes in Texas, Michigan, and Massachusetts kill 350 people Controls on wages, salaries, and on some consumer goods are lifted (Feb. 6) in U.S.; all price controls removed (Mar. 17) "Native Dancer," E. Guerin up, wins Belmont and Preakness Stakes but loses Kentucky Derby to *(contd)*	**1953**

	A. HISTORY, POLITICS	B. LITERATURE, THEATER	C. RELIGION, PHILOSOPHY, LEARNING
1953 contd	The Rosenbergs, first sentenced as atomic spies in 1951, are executed Joseph Laniel elected Premier of France Korean armistice signed at Panmunjom July 27; U.S. and S. Korea sign mutual defense treaty Royalist coup d'état in Persia; Premier Mosaddegh arrested and sentenced to three years imprisonment Austrians stage protest strike against occupation Churchill, Eisenhower, and Laniel meet in Bermuda Ben-Gurion resigns; Moshe Sharett elected Prime Minister of Israel René Coty elected President of France Churchill named Knight of the Order of the Garter Nobel Peace Prize: Gen. George C. Marshall Robert A. Taft, U.S. Senator and public servant, d. (b. 1889)	Peter Ustinov: "The Love of Four Colonels"	
1954	Brit., Fr., U.S., and U.S.S.R. foreign ministers meet in Berlin; Russians reject the idea of Ger. reunification Col. Nasser seizes power in Egypt; becomes premier and head of state St. Lawrence Seaway project approved by Eisenhower U.S.-Jap. defense agreement Malenkov becomes Premier of U.S.S.R. Dien Bien Phu taken by Vietnamese Communists; Indo-China armistice signed in Geneva; Communists occupy Hanoi Queen Elizabeth II and Prince Philip begin Commonwealth tour U.S. Supreme Court rules that segregation by color in public schools is a violation of the 14th Amendment to the Constitution Marshall Tito visits Greece and India Eisenhower and Churchill meet in Washington and sign Potomac Charter Theodor Heuss elected President of W. Germany Southeast Asia Treaty Organization (SEATO) established U.S. and Canada agree to build radar warning stations across northern Canada (Distant Early Warning, "DEW" Line) to give warning of approaching aircraft or missiles over the Arctic France and W. Germany sign cultural and economic agreement Burma and Japan sign treaty U.S. signs pact with Nationalist China Emperor Haile Selassie of Ethiopia in Bonn Senator Joseph R. McCarthy continues his witch-hunting activities culminating in a nationally televised hearing seeking to prove Communist infiltration into the U.S. Army; his formal censure and condemnation by Senate resolution follow	Nobel Prize for Literature: Ernest Hemingway Jacinto Benavente, Span. dramatist, d. (b. 1866) Colette, Fr. novelist, d. (b. 1873) Aldous Huxley: "The Doors of Perception" Mac Hyman: "No Time for Sergeants" Thomas Mann: "Felix Krull" W. Somerset Maugham: "Ten Novels and Their Authors" Mauriac: "L'Agneau," Fr. novel Montherlant: "Port-Royal," Fr. play Martin Andersen Nexö, Dan. poet, d. (b. 1869) Theodor Plievier: "Berlin," novel John Patrick: "The Teahouse of the August Moon" J. B. Priestley: "The Magicians" Giraudoux: "Ondine" Terence Rattigan: "Separate Tables" Tennessee Williams: "Cat on a Hot Tin Roof," Pulitzer Prize drama (1955) Thornton Wilder: "The Matchmaker" Kingsley Amis: "Lucky Jim" William Golding: "Lord of the Flies" John Masters: "Bhowani Junction" Françoise Sagan: "Bonjour Tristesse" C. P. Snow: "The New Men" J. R. R. Tolkien: "The Lord of the Rings" Dylan Thomas: "Under Milk Wood" (posth.) Enid Bagnold: "The Chalk Garden" Christopher Fry: "The Light is Dark Enough" Lionel Barrymore d. (b. 1878) Bruce Catton: "A Stillness at Appomattox," Pulitzer Prize for history Charles A. Lindbergh: "The Spirit of St. Louis," Pulitzer Prize for biography Theodore Roethke: "The Waking: Poems 1933—1953," Pulitzer Prize for poetry	Richard Wright: "Black Force" Mortimer Wheeler: "The Indus Civilization" Gilbert Ryle: "Dilemmas" Billy Graham holds evangelistic meetings in New York, London, and Berlin C. E. Raven: "Natural Religion and Christian Theology" Isaac Deutscher: "The Prophet Armed" (first volume of Trotsky biography) Ritchie Calder: "Men against the Jungle" Pope Pius X proclaimed a saint by Pope Pius XII World Council of Churches convened at Evanston, Ill.

D. VISUAL ARTS	E. MUSIC	F. SCIENCE, TECHNOLOGY, GROWTH	G. DAILY LIFE	
(Fellini); "Roman Holiday" (Audrey Hepburn); "From Here to Eternity," Academy Award (Zinnemann); "The Robe" (Richard Burton): "The Living Desert" (Disney); "Julius Caesar" (Mankiewicz) Most U.S. movie theaters are adapted for CinemaScope film projection Yasuo Kuniyoshi d. (b. 1892)	Leonard Bernstein: "Wonderful Town," musical, New York Ernest Bloch: "Suite Hebraïque" George Antheil: "Volpone," opera Bohuslav Martinu: "The Marriage," opera, New York William Schuman: "Mighty Casey," opera, Hartford Popular songs: "Doggie in the Window"; "I Believe"; "Baubles, Bangles, and Beads"; "Ebb Tide"; "Stranger in Paradise"; "I Love Paris"	Man to have been a hoax Hillary and Tenzing become the first to climb Mount Everest Austro-Ger. expedition climbs Nanga Parbat in Himalayas Alfred C. Kinsey: "Sexual Behavior in the Human Female" E. P. Hubble, U.S. astronomer, d. (b. 1889) A rocket-powered U.S. plane is flown at more than 1,600 mph Lung cancer reported attributable to cigarette smoking	"Dark Star," a 25—1 long shot Australia retains Davis Cup, defeating U.S. tennis team Southern California wins Rose Bowl football game 7—0 over Wisconsin Boston Braves baseball club (NL) moves to Milwaukee; St. Louis Browns (AL) move to Baltimore, become the Baltimore Orioles New York (AL) wins fifth consecutive World Series, 4—2, over Brooklyn (NL)	**1953 contd**
Roger Bissière: "Composition," Fr. abstract painting Massimo Campigli: "Diavolo Player," Ital. cubist painting Lynn Chadwick: "Two Dancing Figures," Eng. sculpture Chagall: "The Red Roofs," surrealist painting André Derain, Fr. painter, d. (b. 1880) Dubuffet: "Les Vagabonds" Max Ernst: "Lonely" Fernard Léger: "Acrobat and Horse" Henri Matisse d. (b. 1869) Picasso: "Sylvette" GPO Tower, London, designed by Eric Bedford (—1965) Graham Sutherland: "Portrait of Churchill" Films: "Diabolique" (Clouzot); "La Strada" (Fellini); "On the Waterfront," Academy Award (Kazan); "Rear Window" (Hitchcock); "The Seven Samurai" (Jap.) Reginald Marsh d. (b. 1898) "Herblock" wins second Pulitzer Prize for cartoons (also 1942)	Lennox Berkeley: "Nelson," opera, London Britten: "The Turn of the Screw," opera, Venice Aaron Copland: "The Tender Land," opera, New York Schönberg: "Moses and Aaron," opera, Hamburg Gian Carlo Menotti: "The Saint of Bleecker Street," opera, New York, Pulitzer Prize (1955) William Walton: "Troilus and Cressida," opera, London Wilhelm Furtwängler, Ger. conductor, d. (b. 1886) Clemens Krauss, Aust. conductor, d. (b. 1893) Oskar Straus, Viennese operetta composer, d. (b. 1870) Toscanini retires Charles Ives d. (b. 1874) Julian Slade: "Salad Days" Sandy Wilson: "The Boy Friend" Adler-Ross: "The Pajama Game," New York First (annual) Jazz Festival held at Newport, R.I. Popular songs; "Hernando's Hideaway"; "Mister Sandman"; "Young At Heart"; "Three Coins in the Fountain"; "Hey, There" Quincy Porter: Concerto for Two Pianos and Orchestra, Pulitzer Prize Stravinsky: "Septet"; "Three Songs from Shakespeare"; "In Memoriam: Dylan Thomas"; "Four Russian Peasant Songs" David Diamond: "Ahavah," symphonic eulogy, Washington, D.C. Roy Harris: Symphonic fantasy, Pittsburgh, Pa. Alan Hovhaness: Concerto No. 5, New York City Ernest Krenek: Violoncello concerto, Los Angeles	U.S. atomic physicist J. Robert Oppenheimer is dismissed from government service, his security clearance withdrawn U.S. tests hydrogen bomb at Bikini U.S.S.R. Central Observatory near Leningrad opened Concern in Europe and America about fallout and disposal of radioactive waste Hugo Eckener, Ger. aeronaut, d. (b. 1868) Enrico Fermi, Ital. physicist, d. (b. 1901) Fritz London, Ger.-Amer. physicist, d. (b. 1900) Known chemical elements at the time of birth of Christ: 9; around 1500, 12; around 1900, 84; in 1954, 100 U.S. submarine "Nautilus" converted to nuclear power; U.S.S. "Forrestal," 59,650 ton aircraft carrier, launched at Newport News, Va. Dr. Jonas E. Salk, U.S. developer of antipolio serum, starts inoculating schoolchildren in Pittsburgh, Pa. Nobel Prize for Medicine and Physiology: J. F. Enders, T. H. Weiler, and F. Robbins (all U.S.) for their work on polio virus Nobel Prize for Chemistry: Linus Pauling (U.S.) for study of molecular forces	1,768 U.S. newspapers publish 59 million copies daily Swiss musical clown Grock retires Seebohm Rowntree, Brit. philanthropist, d. (b. 1871) Independent Television Authority established in Britain Eurovision network formed 29 million U.S. homes have TV Temple of Mithras excavated in the City of London Roger Bannister runs a mile in 3 minutes 59.4 seconds Gordon Richards becomes the first professional jockey to be knighted The U.S. contains 6 per cent of the world's population but has 60 per cent of all cars, 58 per cent of all telephones, 45 per cent of all radio sets, and 34 per cent of all railroads Desert locust plague in Morocco: within six weeks citrus crops valued at approx. $14 million destroyed Vic Seixas wins U.S. Lawn Tennis Association Men's Singles; Doris Hart wins Women's Singles Arnold Palmer wins Amateur championship of U.S. Golf Association; Ed Furgol wins Open Philadelphia Athletics baseball club moves to Kansas City Rose Bowl football game is won by Michigan State over U.C.L.A., 28—20 World Series is won by New York (NL) 4—0 over Cleveland (AL)	**1954**

	A. HISTORY, POLITICS	B. LITERATURE, THEATER	C. RELIGION, PHILOSOPHY, LEARNING
1955	U.S.S.R. decrees end of war with Germany Malenkov resigns; succeeded by N. A. Bulganin Italy, W. Germany, and France establish European Union Churchill resigns; succeeded by Anthony Eden Chou En-lai visits Rangoon Giovanni Gronchi elected President of Italy Germany becomes NATO member The Vienna Treaty restores Austria's independence Bulganin and Khrushchev visit Yugoslavia and E. Germany Railroad and dock strikes in Britain Perón resigns from Argentinian presidency President Eisenhower suffers heart attack Attlee retires from leadership of Brit. Labour Party and is succeeded by Hugh Gaitskell Raids on Israel—Jordan border increase The Shah of Persia and Empress Soraya visit Germany Cordell Hull d. (b. 1871) Walter White, U.S. civil rights leader, d. (b. 1893) U.S. Air Force Academy opens, modeled after West Point and Annapolis A.F.L. and C.I.O. merge; new president George Meany Blacks in Montgomery, Ala., boycott segregated city bus lines President Eisenhower appoints John M. Harlan to the Supreme Court Mary McLeod Bethune, Amer. educator and civil rights leader d. (b. 1875)	Anouilh: "Ornifle ou le courant d'air" Paul Claudel, Fr. dramatist, d. (b. 1868) T. E. Lawrence (d. 1935): "The Mint" (posth.) Sean O'Casey: "The Bishop's Bonfire" Theodor Plievier, Ger. novelist, d. (b. 1892) Alfred Polgar, Aust. essayist and critic, d. (b. 1875) Sartre: "Nekrassov," Fr. drama Evelyn Waugh: "Officers and Gentlemen" Thomas Mann d. (b. 1875) 8,420 public libraries in U.S. Mackinlay Kantor: "Andersonville," Pulitzer Prize novel (1956) Joyce Cary: "Not Honor More" Agatha Christie: "Witness for the Prosecution" Richard Church: "Over the Bridge" Julian Green: "The Enemy" Graham Greene: "The Quiet American" John Lehmann: "The Whispering Gallery" Vladimir Nabokov: "Lolita" Kay Thompson: "Eloise" Ugo Betti: "The Queen and the Rebels" (posth.) Arthur Miller: "A View from the Bridge" and "A Memory of Two Mondays" Ilya Ehrenburg: "The Thaw" Jean Genet: "The Balcony" James Agee, U.S. critic, playwright, and author, d. (b. 1909) Robert E. Sherwood d. (b. 1896) S. N. Behrman and Harold Rome: "Fanny" (based on Marcel Pagnol short stories) J. Lawrence and R. E. Lee: "Inherit tne Wind" William Inge: "Bus Stop" Christopher Fry: "Tiger at the Gates," based on Giraudoux's play Sloan Wilson: "The Man in the Gray Flannel Suit" John O'Hara: "Ten North Frederick" Herman Wouk: "Marjorie Morningstar" Rudolf Flesch: "Why Johnny Can't Read"	C. Hoffmann: "The Man Who Was Shakespeare," attempts to identify Shakespeare with Marlowe Walter Lippmann: "The Public Philosophy" H. J. Paton: "The Modern Predicament" Werner Keller: "Und die Bibel hat doch recht" Ortega y Gasset, Span. philosopher, d. (b. 1883) Klein and Goldberger: "An Economic Model of the U.S. 1929—52" Edmund Wilson: "The Dead Sea Scrolls"
1956	Sudan proclaimed independent democratic republic Tito meets Nasser in Cairo and visits Moscow Jordan and Israel accept UN truce proposals; King Hussein of Jordan dismisses Brit. Gen. J. B. Glubb; cease-fires arranged between Israel and Lebanon-Syria-Jordan; Israeli troops invade Sinai Peninsula; Anglo-Fr. ultimatum to Egypt and Israel calls for cease-fire; U.S. sends aid to Israel Eisenhower and Eden issue Declaration of Washington At the 20th Soviet Communist Party Conference Khrushchev denounces Stalin's policy Pakistan becomes Islamic republic Archbishop Makarios transported from Cyprus to the Seychelles Bulganin and Khrushchev visit Britain Nasser elected President of Egypt; U.S. and Britain inform Egypt that they will not participate in financing Aswan High Dam; Nasser seizes Suez Canal; Brit. and Fr. nationals leave Egypt; Dulles plan on Suez rejected by Nasser; Anglo-Fr. forces bomb Egyptian airfields Oct. 31; U.S. and U.S.S.R. pressures effect cease-fire Nov. 6; Fr. and Brit. *(contd)*	Anouilh: "Pauvre Bitoz," Fr. comedy John Hersey: "A Single Pebble" John Osborne: "Look Back in Anger" Terence Rattigan: "Separate Tables," opens in New York Angus Wilson: "The Mulberry Bush" English Stage Company at Royal Court Theatre, London Brecht's Berliner Ensemble visits England Max Beerbohm d. (b. 1872) Walter de la Mare d. (b. 1873) H. L. Mencken d. (b. 1880) Angus Wilson: "Anglo-Saxon Attitudes," novel Bertolt Brecht d. (b. 1898) Louis Bromfield, Amer. novelist, d. (b. 1896) Felicien Marceau: "L'Oeuf," Fr. comedy Malaparte: "Maledetti toscani," novel Lucie Höflich, Ger. actress, d. (b. 1883) Goodrich and Hackett: "The Diary of Anne Frank," Pulitzer Prize drama Gottfried Been, Ger. poet, d. (b. 1886) Lampedusa: "The Leopard" *(contd)*	Leo Baeck, Jewish theologian, d. (b. 1873) Alfred Kinsey, Amer. biologist, d. (b. 1894) Toynbee: "A Historian's Approach to Religion" Pollock and Weber: "Revolution of the Robots" Norman St. John-Stevas: "Obscenity and the Law" W. H. Whyte: "The Organization Man" Wilkins and Moore: "The Moon" *(contd)*

D. VISUAL ARTS	E. MUSIC	F. SCIENCE, TECHNOLOGY, GROWTH	G. DAILY LIFE	
Bernard Buffet: "Circus" De Chirico: "Italian Square" Lucien Contaud: "En souvenir d'un peintre" Joseph Glasco: "Salomé" George Grosz: "Ein kleines Ja und ein grosses Nein," autobiography Karl Hofer, Ger. painter, d. (b. 1878) Fernand Léger, Fr. painter, d. (b. 1881) Max Pechstein, Ger. painter, d. (b. 1881) Picasso exhibition in Paris, Hamburg, Munich Yves Tanguy, Fr. painter, d. (b. 1900) Maurice Utrillo, Fr. painter, d. (b. 1883) "The New Decade" Exhibition of Modern Art, New York Pietro Annigoni: "Queen Elizabeth II," portrait Salvador Dali: "The Lord's Supper" Kokoschka: "Thermopylae Triptych" London Airport Buildings designed by Frederick Gibberd Films: "Smiles of a Summer Night" (Ingmar Bergman); "Les Grandes Manoeuvres" (René Clair); "Marty," Academy Award (Ernest Borgnine); "The Rose Tattoo" (Anna Magnani); "The Seven Year Itch" (Billy Wilder); "Rififi" (Jules Dassin); "Richard III" (Laurence Olivier)	Werner Egk: "Irische Legende," opera, Salzburg Frieda Hempel, Ger.-Amer. singer, d. (b. 1885) Arthur Honegger, Swiss composer, d. (b. 1892) The rebuilt E. Ger. State Opera House opens Prokofiev: "Fiery Angel," opera, Venice Michael Tippett: "The Midsummer Marriage," opera, London Papal encyclical: "Musicae sacrae" Rolf Liebermann: "School for Wives," opera, Louisville Adler and Ross: "Damn Yankees," musical comedy, New York Charlie "Bird" Parker, U.S. jazz musician, d. (b. 1920) Cole Porter: "Silk Stockings" Ernst Krenek: "Pallas Athene Weint," opera, Hamburg George Antheil: "The Wish," opera, Louisville Popular songs: "The Yellow Rose of Texas"; "Davy Crockett"; "Rock Around the Clock"; "Love Is a Many-Splendored Thing"; "Whatever Lola Wants"; "Sixteen Tons" Darius Milhaud: Symphony No. 6, Boston Walter Piston: Symphony No. 5, Boston	Ultra high frequency waves produced at the Massachusetts Institute of Technology Atomically generated power first used in the U.S. (Schenectady, N.Y.) Dorothy Hodgkin discovers a liver extract for treating pernicious anemia (vitamin B12) Frederick Sanger determines the molecular structure of insulin Albert Einstein d. (b. 1879) Alexander Fleming d. (b. 1881) Bundy, Hall, Strong, and Wentorf report on the artificial manufacture of diamonds at 2,700 degrees C	Jacques Fath, Fr. fashion designer, d. (b. 1912) Gordon Pirie, with a time of 29.19 minutes, wins 10,000-meter run against Zatopek "Sugar" Ray Robinson wins world boxing championship from Carl "Bobo" Olson 82 die in a disaster at the Le Mans car race Deutsche Lufthansa Airlines resumes service Commercial TV begins broadcasting in Britain U.S. golf statistics show that the game is played by 3.8 million people on approximately 5,000 courses encompassing 1.5 million acres Duke of Edinburgh announces his award scheme for young people Universal Copyright Convention takes effect U.S. and U.S.S.R. announce that they will launch earth satellites in the International Geophysical Year 1957—58 U.S. Gross National Product rises to $397.5 billion Harvie Ward wins U.S. Golf Association Amateur; Jack Fleck defeats Ben Hogan to win Open Tony Trabert wins U.S. Lawn Tennis Association Men's Singles; Women's Singles won by Doris Hart Ohio State wins Rose Bowl football game from Southern California, 20—7 "Nashua," Eddie Arcaro up, wins Preakness and Belmont Stakes Brooklyn (NL) wins World Series, 4—3, over New York (AL)	**1955**
John Bratby: "A Painter's Credo" Lynn Chadwick: "Teddy Boy and Girl" Barbara Hepworth: "Orpheus," sculpture Richard Lippold: "Variation within a Sphere, No. 10: The Sun," sculpture Eero Saarinen designs U.S. Embassy, London Jorn Utzon designs Sydney Opera House Bernard Buffet: "Self-portrait" Lyonel Feininger, Amer. painter, d. (b. 1871) Jackson Pollock, Amer. painter, d. (b. 1912) Fabrizio Clerici: "Complesso di tre templi dell' Uovo," Ital. surrealist painting *(contd)*	Jean Martinon: "Hécube," Fr. opera Humphrey Searle: "Noctambules," ballet Guido Cantelli, Ital. conductor, d. (b. 1920) Walter Gieseking, Ger. pianist, d. (b. 1895) Alexander Gretchaninoff, Russ. composer, d. (b. 1864) Hans Werner Henze: "König Hirsch," opera, Berlin Herbert von Karajan becomes musical director of the Vienna State Opera Erich Kleiber, Aust. conductor, d. (b. 1890) Stravinsky: "Canticum sacrum ad honorem Sancti Marci nominis" Bernstein: "Candide," musical comedy, New York *(contd)*	Neutrino, an atomic particle with no electric charge, produced at Los Alamos Laboratory, U.S. Antineutron discovered by Cork, Lambertson, Piccioni, and Wenzel "Dido" reactor opened at Harwell, England F. W. Müller develops the ion microscope Bell Telephone *(contd)*	Brit. bank interest rate raised to 5.5 per cent, the highest since 1932 The first C.N.D. Aldermaston march Prince Rainier of Monaco marries Grace Kelly "Rock and Roll" dance is in vogue Olympic Games at Melbourne; Vladimar Kuts, U.S.S.R., wins 5000 meters in 13 minutes 39.6 seconds and 10,000 meters in 28 minutes 45.6 seconds The palace of Emperor Diocletian is excavated at Split, Yugoslavia "Andrea Doria," Ital. liner, sinks after collision with "Stockholm" off Nantucket Island Mildred "Babe" Didrikson Zaharias, U.S. athlete and sportswoman, d. (b. 1914) Thomas J. Watson, U.S. founder of IBM, d. (b. 1874) Cornelius McGillicuddy ("Connie *(contd)*	**1956**

	A. HISTORY, POLITICS	B. LITERATURE, THEATER	C. RELIGION, PHILOSOPHY, LEARNING
1956 contd	troops withdraw; UN fleet clears Suez Canal Cardinal Wyszynski released from prison Cardinal Mindszenty released Soviet troops march into Hungary; UN Security Council's request vetoed by U.S.S.R.; UN General Assembly censures U.S.S.R.; martial law and mass arrests in Hungary Dwight D. Eisenhower reelected President of the U.S., with Richard M. Nixon as vice president; Congress is Democratic Anthony Eden leaves London to recuperate in Jamaica; R. A. Butler named Deputy Prime Minister Japan admitted to UN Nehru visits Bonn; Nehru-Tito-Nasser conference held at Brioni, Yugoslavia King Paul I and Queen Frederika of Greece visit Bonn Tito and Khrushchev meet in the Crimea President Eisenhower appoints William J. Brennan to the Supreme Court Martin Luther King emerges as leader of campaign for desegregation Fidel Castro lands in Cuba with small armed force intent on the overthrow of dictator Fulgencio Batista Victor Riesel, U.S. labor columnist, is blinded by acid thrown by a gangster; four months later, labor racketeer Johnny Dio is indicted for conspiracy with six others	William Brinkley: "Don't Go Near the Water" Grace Metalious: "Peyton Place" John F. Kennedy: "Profiles in Courage," Pulitzer Prize biography (1957) Edwin O'Connor: "The Last Hurrah" Talbot F. Hamlin: "Benjamin Henry Latrobe," Pulitzer Prize biography Paddy Chayevsky: "Middle of the Night" Patrick Dennis: "Auntie Mame"	Harold Acton: "The Bourbons of Naples" Lord Beaverbrook: "Men and Power, 1917" W. S. Churchill: "History of the English-Speaking Peoples" A. J. Ayer: "The Revolution in Philosophy" Jean Mouroux: "The Christian Experience" Colin Wilson: "The Outsider" Karl Mannheim: "Essays on the Sociology of Culture"
1957	Chou En-lai visits Moscow Anthony Eden resigns as Prime Minister of Great Britain and is succeeded by Harold Macmillan President Eisenhower formulates "Eisenhower Doctrine" for protection of Middle Eastern nations from Communist aggression Israeli forces withdraw from Sinai Peninsula and hand over Gaza strip to UN forces; Hammarskjöld visits Nasser; UN reopens Suez Canal to navigation; U.S. resumes aid to Israel; King Hussein proclaims martial law in Jordan Gromyko becomes U.S.S.R. Foreign Minister; Molotov, Malenkov, Spekilov, and Zhukov sacked Eisenhower and Macmillan hold Bermuda Conference "The Six" sign Rome Treaty; beginning of the Common Market Archbishop Makarios released Britain explodes thermonuclear bomb in central Pacific Franco announces that the Span. monarchy will be restored on his death International Atomic Energy Agency established King Haakon VII of Norway d.; succeeded by his son Olaf V Queen Elizabeth visits Canada and the U.S. and addresses UN General Assembly Nicolaus von Horthy, ex-Regent of Hungary, d. (b. 1868) Edouard Heriot, Fr. statesman, d. (b. 1873) Joseph M. McCarthy, U.S. Senator, d. (b. 1908) Teamsters Union is expelled from AFL-CIO when Jimmy Hoffa refuses to expel criminals and union refuses to expel Hoffa President Eisenhower appoints Charles E. Whittaker to the Supreme Court (—1962)	Richard Mason: "The World of Suzie Wong" Nobel Prize for Literature: Albert Camus Sholem Asch, Jewish novelist, d. (b. 1880) Kathe Dorsch, Ger. actress, d. (b. 1889) Jonathan Griffin: "The Hidden King," verse drama William Faulkner: "The Town" Curzio Malaparte, Ital. author, d. (b. 1898) Dorothy L. Sayers, Eng. author, d. (b. 1893) Sacha Guitry, Fr. actor and dramatist, d. (b. 1885) Nevil Shute: "On the Beach" John Braine: "Room at the Top" James Gould Cozzens: "By Love Possessed" C. Day Lewis: "Pegasus" Ketti Fring: "Look Homeward, Angel," drama adapted from Thomas Wolfe's novel Jack Kerouac: "On the Road" Iris Murdoch: "The Sandcastle" Roger Vailland: "The Law" Samuel Beckett: "Endgame" Robert Bolt: "The Flowering Cherry" John Osborne: "The Entertainer" Sir Laurence Olivier receives honorary doctor's degree from Oxford University Pulitzer Prize to Kenneth Roberts Eugene O'Neill: "Long Day's Journey into Night" (posth.), Pulitzer Prize play Richard Wilbur: "Things of This World," Pulitzer Prize poetry William Saroyan: "The Cave Dwellers" Gore Vidal: "A Visit to a Small Planet" William Inge: "The Dark at the Top of the Stairs" Dr. Seuss: "The Cat in the Hat" *(contd)*	Trevor Huddleston: "Naught for Your Comfort" V. P. Menon: "The Transfer of Power in India" Richard Hoggart: "The Uses of Literacy" Kathleen Kenyon: "Digging up Jericho" New Cambridge Modern History begins publication Arthur Bryant: "The Turn of the Tide" A. J. Ayer: "The Problem of Knowledge" Fred Hoyle: "Man and Materialism" Walther Hofer: "Der Nationalsozialismus" (3 vols.)

D. VISUAL ARTS	E. MUSIC	F. SCIENCE, TECHNOLOGY, GROWTH	G. DAILY LIFE	
Films: "The Seventh Seal" (Ingmar Bergman); "Baby Doll" (Elia Kazan; "Nuit et Brouillard" (Resnais); "War and Peace" (King Vidor); "The Man with the Golden Arm" (Preminger); "Romeo and Juliet" (ballet film, Bolshoi Theater); "Around the World in 80 Days," Academy Award (Mike Todd); "The King and I"; "The Ten Commandments"; "Lust for Life" Emil Nolde d. (b. 1867)	Alan Jay Lerner and Frederick Loewe: "My Fair Lady," musical, New York Popular songs: "Blue Suede Shoes"; "Around the World in 80 Days"; "Hound Dog"; "I Could Have Danced All Night"; "On the Street Where You Live"; "Que Sera, Sera"; "Don't Be Cruel"; "Poor People of Paris" Gian Carlo Menotti: "The Unicorn, the Gorgon and the Manticore," opera, Washington, D.C. Douglas Moore: "The Ballad of Baby Doe," opera, Central City, Colo. William Bergama: "The Wife of Martin Guerre," opera, New York Maria Callas, U.S. soprano, makes debut in Bellini's "Norma," Metropolitan Opera, New York Elvis Presley gains in popularity	Company begins to develop "visual telephone" Transatlantic cable telephone service inaugurated M. D. Ross and M. L. Lewis (U.S.) reach the stratospheric height of 22.8 km. in a balloon Four new antibiotics are tested in the U.S. Oral vaccine developed by Albert Sabin against polio	Mack") d. (b. 1862) Fred Allen, U.S. comedian, d. (b. 1894) New York Coliseum, with nine acres of exhibit space, opens Harvie Ward wins U.S. Golf Association Amateur championship; Cary Middlecoff wins Open Ken Rosewall wins U.S. Lawn Tennis Men's Singles; Shirley Fry wins Women's Singles "Needles," D. Erb up, wins Belmont Stakes and Kentucky Derby Michigan State defeats U.C.L.A. to win Rose Bowl football game 17—14 World Series is won by New York (AL), 4—3, over Brooklyn (NL) Rocky Marciano retires undefeated from boxing, and Floyd Patterson, at 21 the youngest boxer to win the heavyweight crown, knocks out Archie Moore in title fight	**1956 contd**
Constantin Brancusi, Rum. sculptor, d. (b. 1876) Chagall: "Self-portrait" Carlo Levi: "Anna Magnani," portrait Diego Rivera, Mexican painter, d. (b. 1886) Kenneth Clark: "The Nude (A Study of Ideal Art)" Graham Sutherland: "Princess Gourielli" H. G. Adam: "Beacon of the Dead" (in Auschwitz) Le Corbusier: Tokyo Museum of Art (—1960) Films: "A King in New York" (Chaplin); "The Bridge on the River Kwai," Academy Award (David Lean); "The Prince and the Showgirl" (Olivier, Monroe); "Bonjour Tristesse" (Preminger); "Love in the Afternoon" (Billy Wilder); "Twelve Angry Men" (Henry Fonda) Max Ophuls, Fr.-Ger. film director, d. (b. 1902) Charles Pathé, Fr. film pioneer, d. (b. 1863) Erich von Stroheim, Aust. actor and director, d. (b. 1885) Pavel Tchelitchev d. (b. 1898) Frank Kupka d. (b. 1871) Humphrey Bogart, U.S. actor, d. (b. 1899)	Ralph Benatzky, Aust. composer, d. (b. 1884) Werner Egk: "Der Revisor," comic opera, Schwetzinger Wolfgang Fortner: "Blood Wedding," opera, Cologne Erich Wolfgang Korngold, Aust. composer, d. (b. 1897) Carl Orff: "Comoedia de Christi Resurrectione," Easter oratorio Othmar Schoeck, Swiss composer, d. (b. 1886) Jean Sibelius d. (b. 1865) William Walton: Concerto for Cello and Orchestra Beniamino Gigli, Ital. opera singer, d. (b. 1890) Arturo Toscanini d. (b. 1867) Hindemith: "Harmonie der Welt," opera, Munich Benjamin Britten: "The Prince of the Pagodas," ballet, London Ildebrando Pizetti: "Assassinio della cathedrale," opera, based on the drama by T. S. Eliot, Milan Francis Poulenc: "Dialogues des Carmélites," opera, Milan Stravinsky: "Agon," ballet, Paris John Gardener: "The Moon and Sixpence," opera, based on Maugham's novel, London Leonard Bernstein: "West Side Story," musical, New York Meredith Willson: "The Music Man," New York Benjamin Britten: "The Turn of *(contd)*	U.S.S.R. lanches Sputnik I and II, first earth satellites Giberellin, a growth-producing hormone, is isolated Nobelium (element 102) discovered in Stockholm Frederick Lindemann, Lord Cherwell, d. (b. 1886) Kiyoshi Shiga, Jap. bacteriologist, d. (b. 1871) John Von Neumann, U.S. mathematician, d. (b. 1903) Irving Langmuir, U.S. physicist, d. (b. 1881) Admiral Richard E. Byrd, U.S. polar explorer, d. (b. 1888) International Geophysical Year is proclaimed by 67 cooperating nations Mackinac Straits Bridge, Michigan, world's longest suspension bridge, opens	Cities with over one million inhabitants number 71 as against 16 in 1914 Fort Salmanassar in Nimrud-Kalash (dating from 840 B.C.) is excavated Christian Dior, Paris fashion designer, d. (b. 1905) The Aga Khan d. (b. 1875) Wolfenden Report on homosexuality and prostitution published in Britain Brit. bank interest rate raised to 7 per cent Regular London—Moscow air service inaugurated Desegregation crisis in Little Rock, Ark.; President Eisenhower sends paratroopers to forestall violence Tidal wave follows hurricane Audrey into coasts of Texas and Louisiana, leaving 530 dead and missing Major John Glenn, Jr. (later an astronaut) sets speed record from California to New York in a jet: 3 hours 23 minutes 8.4 seconds Carmen Basilio defeats "Sugar" Ray Robinson to win middleweight boxing championship New York Giants baseball club moves to San Francisco; Brooklyn Dodgers to Los Angeles Malcolm Anderson wins U.S. Lawn Tennis Association Men's Singles; Althea Gibson wins Women's Singles Iowa wins Rose Bowl football game from Oregon State, 35—19 *(contd)*	**1957**

	A. HISTORY, POLITICS	B. LITERATURE, THEATER	C. RELIGION, PHILOSOPHY, LEARNING
1957 contd		Robert Paul Smith: "Where Did You Go? Out. What Did You Do? Nothing." Ayn Rand: "Atlas Shrugged" Bernard Malamud: "The Assistant"	
1958	European Common Market comes into being West Indies Federation in force Egypt and Syria join to form the United Arab Republic with Nasser as president England and Spain sign trade pact Khrushchev succeeds Bulganin as Chairman of Council of U.S.S.R. Ministers Fidel Castro begins "total war" against the Batista government in Cuba Vice President Nixon, on good-will tour of S. America, is received with open hostility; Eisenhower sends troops to Caribbean De Gaulle forms government; meets Adenauer; is elected President of France Imre Nagy executed in Hungary after secret trial Alaska becomes 49th state of the U.S. Khrushchev visits Peking U.S.S.R. grants a loan to the United Arab Republic for building Aswan Dam Ayub Khan elected Prime Minister of Pakistan Nelson A. Rockefeller elected Governor of New York Tension grows in U.S. as desegregation of schools is attempted in the South; Governor Orval Faubus of Arkansas defies Supreme Court by closing schools in Little Rock, reopening them as private, segregated schools President Eisenhower appoints Potter Stewart to the Supreme Court	Nobel Prize for Literature: Boris Pasternak Johannes R. Becher, Ger. poet, d. (b. 1891) Ferdinand Bruckner, Aust. dramatist, d. (b. 1891) Truman Capote: "Breakfast at Tiffany's" Shelagh Delaney: "A Taste of Honey," Eng. play Mazo de la Roche: "Centenary at Jalna" Lawrence G. Durrell: "Balthazar" Rumer Godden: "The Greengage Summer" Harry Golden: "Only in America" T. S. Eliot: "The Elder Statesman" Graham Greene: "The Potting Shed" J. Edgar Hoover: "Masters of Deceit" James Jones: "Some Came Running" Kafka: "Letters 1902—1924" Nevil Shute: "The Rainbow and the Rose" The complete works of Tolstoi published in U.S.S.R. in 90 vols. Boris Pasternak: "Dr. Zhivago" Angus Wilson: "The Middle Age of Mrs. Eliot," novel Harold Pinter: "The Birthday Party" Leon Uris: "Exodus" James Branch Cabell d. (b. 1879) George Jean Nathan d. (b. 1882) Friedrich Dürrenmatt: "The Visit" Lorraine Hansberry: "A Raisin in the Sun" Robert Penn Warren: "Promises: Poems 1954—56," Pulitzer Prize Archibald MacLeish: "J. B.," verse drama, Pulitzer Prize (1959) William Humphrey: "Home from the Hill" Dore Schary: "Sunrise at Campobello" Eugene O'Neill: "A Touch of the Poet" (posth.) Lion Feuchtwanger, Ger. novelist and dramatist, d. (b. 1884)	Pope Pius XII d.; Cardinal Roncalli elected Pope John XXIII J. K. Galbraith: "The Affluent Society" J. D. Stewart: "British Pressure Groups" Stephen Runciman: "Sicilian Vespers" J. Wheeler-Bennett: "King George VI," biography R. S. Peters: "The Concept of Motivation" Supreme Religious Center for World Jewry dedicated in Jerusalem Ruth Fischer: "The Re-formation of Soviet Society" Golo Mann: "German History in the 19th and 20th Century" Cyril N. Parkinson publishes his satirical exposition of the growth of bureaucracy ("Parkinson's Law") Leopold Ziegler, Aust. philosopher, d. (b. 1881)

D. VISUAL ARTS	E. MUSIC	F. SCIENCE, TECHNOLOGY, GROWTH	G. DAILY LIFE	
	the Screw," Stratford Hilding Rosenberg: "The Portrait," opera, Stockholm Popular songs: "Love Letters in the Sand"; "Young Love"; "Tonight"; "Maria"; "Seventy-Six Trombones"		Milwaukee (NL) wins World Series, 4—3, over New York (AL) Bobby Fischer, 13 years old, emerges as chess champion "Beat" and "beatnik" take hold as new words to describe the "Beat Generation" first treated in Kerouac's "On the Road"	**1957 contd**
Ludwig Bemelmans: "My Life in Art" James Brooks: "Acanda," Amer. painting Serge Poliakoff: "Composition in Blue-Yellow-Red-Brown" Maurice de Vlaminck, Fr. painter, d. (b. 1876) Henry Moore: "Reclining Figure," UNESCO Building, Paris Oscar Niemeyer designs President's palace, Brasilia Arthur Ling designs Belgrade Theater, Coventry, England Films: "Mon Oncle" (Jacques Tati); "Touch of Evil" (Orson Welles); "Me and the Colonel" (Danny Kaye); "Cat on a Hot Tin Roof" (Elizabeth Taylor); "Marjorie Morningstar" (Gene Kelly); "Ashes and Diamonds" (Andrej Wajda); "Gigi," Academy Award Mike Todd, Amer. film producer, d. (b. 1907) Olaf Gulbransson, Ger. painter and caricaturist, d. (b. 1873) Guggenheim Museum, New York, designed by Frank Lloyd Wright, opens Fire at Museum of Modern Art, New York, causes $320,000 damage Georges Rouault d. (b. 1871)	W. C. Handy d. (b. 1873) Ralph Vaughan Williams d. (b. 1873) Benjamin Britten: "Noye's Fludde," opera Van Cliburn (U.S.) wins Moscow Tchaikovsky piano competition Hans Werner Henze: "Ondine," ballet, London Pierre Boulez: "Le Visage Nuptial," cantata Menotti: "Maria Golovin," opera, Brussels Sviatoslav Richter, the Russ. pianist, appears in Western countries Florent Schmitt, Fr. composer, d. Cha Cha Cha is the new dance vogue Stravinsky: Threni–id est Lamentationes Jeremiae Prophetae Popular songs: "Chanson d'Amour"; "Chipmunk Song"; "The Purple People Eater"; "Volare"; "Catch a Falling Star"; "A Certain Smile" Robert Dhery and Gerard Calvi: "La Plume de ma Tante" Samuel Barber: "Vanessa," opera, Pulitzer Prize Rodgers and Hammerstein: "Flower Drum Song"	U.S. artificial earth satellite Explorer I (31 pounds) is launched from Cape Canaveral U.S.S.R. Sputnik III (3,000 pounds) launched U.S. nuclear submarine "Nautilus" passes under icecap at North Pole Stereophonic recordings come into use The Rotocycle, an aerial motor scooter, invented Ernest O. Lawrence, U.S. physicist, d. (b. 1901) John Broadus Watson, U.S. psychologist, d. (b. 1878) U.S. establishes National Aeronautics and Space Administration (NASA) to administer scientific exploration of space U.S. launches first moon rocket; it fails to reach moon but travels 79,000 miles from earth Nobel Prize for Medicine and Physiology: J. Lederberg, G. W. Beadle, and E. L. Tatum (all U.S.) for their discoveries of chemical reactions in living cells Space probes reveal Van Allen radiation belts around earth that *(contd)*	Pakistani cricket team tours U.S. World's Amateur Golf Council organized Eddie Arcaro becomes (after Sir Gordon Richards and Johnny Longden) the third jockey to attain over 4,000 wins First parking meters appear in London London bus strike The "Beatnik" movement, originating in California, spreads throughout America and Europe Brussels World Exhibition First life peerages in Britain Prince Charles created Prince of Wales The last debutantes are presented at the Brit. court Arnold Palmer, U.S. golfer, wins his first Masters' tournament Unemployment in U.S. reaches almost 5.2 million "Columbia" defeats "Sceptre" to win America's Cup for U.S. over England Charles F. Kettering, U.S. industrialist, d. (b. 1876) "Sugar" Ray Robinson regains middleweight boxing championship for fifth time by defeating Carmen Basilio Nathan Leopold, jailed in 1924 for the kidnapping and murder of Bobby Franks (with Richard Loeb, who was killed in prison), is paroled Charlie Coe wins U.S. Golf Association Amateur championship; Tommy Bolt wins Open "Tim Tam," Ismael Valenzuela up, wins Preakness Stakes and Kentucky Derby U.S. Lawn Tennis Association Men's Singles championship is won by Ashley Cooper; Althea Gibson wins Women's Singles Ohio State wins Rose Bowl football game against University of Oregon, 10–7 New York (AL) wins World Series, 4—3, against Milwaukee (NL)	**1958**

	A. HISTORY, POLITICS	B. LITERATURE, THEATER	C. RELIGION, PHILOSOPHY, LEARNING
1958 contd			
1959	Cuban President Batista flees to the Dominican Republic; Fidel Castro becomes Premier of Cuba; expropriates U.S.-owned sugar mills Belgium grants reforms in Congo De Gaulle proclaimed President of the Fifth Republic in France Disturbances in Nyasaland; Hastings Banda arrested Macmillan visits U.S.S.R., France, Germany, Canada, and the U.S. Archbishop Makarios returns to Cyprus; Cyprus becomes a republic Hawaii becomes 50th state of the U.S. New York City Council appoints a committee to study possibility of its becoming 51st state Khrushchev visits Albania and the U.S. De Valera becomes President of Eire Heinrich Lübke elected President of W. Germany Eisenhower visits W. Germany, England, India, and eight other nations Bandaranaika, President of Ceylon, assassinated European Free Trade Association ("The Seven") ratify treaty Britain and United Arab Republic resume diplomatic relations Nobel Peace Prize: Philip J. Noel-Baker John Foster Dulles d. (b. 1888) George C. Marshall d. (b. 1880)	Saul Bellow: "Henderson the Rain King" Ivy Compton-Burnett: "A Heritage and Its History" Norman Mailer: "Advertisements for Myself" James Thurber: "The Years with Ross" Laurence Housman, Eng. poet, d. (b. 1865) Ionesco: "Les Rhinocéros" Werner Krauss, Ger. actor, d. (b. 1884) Robert Penn Warren: "The Cave" Jean Louis Barrault becomes head of the Théâtre de France, Paris Günter Grass: "Die Blechtrommel" (The Tin Drum), Ger. novel William Faulkner: "The Mansion" Colin MacInnes: "Absolute Beginners" V. S. Naipaul: "Muguel Street" Muriel Spark: "Memento Mori" Brendan Behan: "The Hostage" Arnold Wesker: "Roots" Françoise Sagan: "Aimez-vous Brahms?" Vance Packard: "The Status Seekers" Allen Drury: "Advise and Consent," Pulitzer Prize (1960) Graham Greene: "The Complaisant Lover" Maxwell Anderson d. (b. 1888) Ethel Barrymore d. (b. 1879) John Updike: "Poorhouse Fair" Robert L. Taylor: "The Travels of Jamie McPheeters," Pulitzer Prize Stanley Kunitz: "Selected Poems: 1928—1958," Pulitzer Prize William Gibson: "The Miracle Worker" James Michener: "Hawaii" Nobel Prize for Literature: Salvatore Quasimodo (1901—68), Ital. novelist Moss Hart: "Act One" Ian Fleming: "Goldfinger" Philip Roth: "Goodbye, Columbus" Lillian Hellmann: "Toys in the Attic" Peter Schaffer: "Five Finger Exercise"	C. Wright Mills: "The Causes of World War III" Garrett Mattingly: "The Defeat of the Armada" Karl Barth: "Dogmatics in Outline" Pope John XXIII announces calling of the first Ecumenical Council since 1870 Pierre Teilhard de Chardin: "The Phenomenon of Man" G. M. Mure: "Retreat from Truth" Anti-Semitisn. flares at Cologne, Germany Abraham Flexner, U.S. educator, d. (b. 1866)

D. VISUAL ARTS	E. MUSIC	F. SCIENCE, TECHNOLOGY, GROWTH	G. DAILY LIFE	
		might imperil travel outside atmosphere; later, protective shielding proves adequate		**1958 contd**
André Beaudin: "La Lune de Mai," Fr. abstract George Grosz, Ger. painter, d. (b. 1893) Yuichi Inoue: "Fish," Jap. painting Frank Lloyd Wright d. (b. 1869) Barbara Hepworth: "Meridian," State House, London Basil Spence designs Thorn House, London Stanley Spencer, Eng. painter, d. (b. 1891) Norman Bluhm: "Chicago" Chagall: "Le Champ de Mars" Alfred Kubin, Aust. artist, d. (b. 1877) Ben Nicholson: "February 1959," Eng. abstract John Bratby: "Coach-House Door" Joan Miró: murals for UNESCO building, Paris Bernard Berenson d. (b. 1865) Jacob Epstein d. (b. 1880) Alfred Munnings, Eng. painter, d. (b. 1878) Films: "Le Testament d'Orphée" (Cocteau); "Anatomy of a Murder" (Preminger); "Our Man in Havana" (Carol Reed); "Hiroshima, mon amour" (Resnais); "Orfeu negro" (Marcel Camus); "La Dolce Vita" (Fellini); "Suddenly Last Summer" (J. L. Mankiewicz); "Ben Hur," Academy Award (William Wyler) Cecil B. De Mille d. (b. 1881)	The anniversaries of Handel (d. 1759), Haydn (d. 1809), and Purcell (d. 1659) celebrated Eduard van Beinum, conductor, d. (b. 1901) Karl-Birger Blomdahl: "Aniara," Swed. science fiction opera Mario Lanza, Amer. tenor, d. (b. 1921) Bohuslav Martinu, Czech composer, d. (b. 1890) Artur Rodzinski, Pol.-Amer. conductor, d. (b. 1894) Heitor Villa-Lobos, Brazilian composer, d. (b. 1881) Richard Rodgers: "The Sound of Music" Theodor W. Adorno: "Klangfiguren" (Theory of Modern Music) Billie Holiday d. (b. 1915) Julie Styne: "Gypsy," musical Popular songs: "He's Got the Whole World in His Hands"; "Tom Dooley"; "Everything's Coming Up Roses"; "Mack the Knife"; "Personality"; "The Sound of Music"; "High Hopes" Henry Cowell: Symphony No. 13, Madras Alban Berg: "Wozzeck," opera, revived in New York (original premiere 1934, Berlin) Hugo Weisgall: "Six Characters in Search of an Author," musical Jerome Weidman, George Abbott, Jerry Bock, and Sheldon Harnick: "Fiorello!" musical, Pulitzer Prize (1960)	U.S.S.R. launches rocket with two monkeys aboard U.S. artificial planet Pioneer 4 at Woomera U.S.S.R. Lunik reaches moon; Lunik III photographs moon Grantly Dick-Read, Eng. gynecologist, d. (b. 1890) First International Congress of Oceanography held in New York Alvarez discovers the neutral xi-particle De Beers (Johannesburg) manufactures a synthetic diamond Nobel Prize in Physics: E. G. Segrè (b. 1905) and Owen Chamberlain (b. 1920) (both U.S.) for their discovery of antiproton Nobel Prize for Chemistry: Jaroslav Heyrovsky (1890—1967) (Czech) for his development of polarography Nobel Prize for Medicine and Physiology: S. Ochoa (b. 1905) and A. Kornberg (b. 1918) (both U.S.) for their synthesis of RNA and DNA First U.S. nuclear-powered merchant vessel, "Savannah," is launched	World Refugee Year proclaimed TV coverage of Brit. General Election Louis S. B. Leakey finds the skull of "Nutcracker Man" in Tanganyika (approx. 600,000 B.C.) First section of London—Birmingham Motorway (M1) opens Printing strike in Britain Bowling: Ed Lubanski (Detroit) scores 700 pins for his five-men team in the ABC all counts Ingemar Johansson defeats Floyd Patterson to win world heavyweight boxing championship Surrey wins cricket championship for record seventh successive time Grock, the Swiss music clown, d. (b. 1880) Rudolf Caracciola, Ger. car racing champion, d. (b. 1901) Total U.S. auto accident death toll more than 1.25 million–more than have died in all U.S. wars combined Bill Mauldin wins the Pulitzer Prize for the second time (first was 1945) for his cartoons U.S. Postmaster General Summerfield bans D. H. Lawrence's "Lady Chatterley's Lover" from the mails on grounds of obscenity; ruling is reversed in 1960 by Circuit Court of Appeals President Eisenhower invokes Taft-Hartley Act to halt 116-day-old steelworkers' strike; longshoremen's strike halted the same way Australia wins Davis Cup tennis match over U.S. team Los Angeles (NL) defeats Chicago (AL), 4—2, to win World Series Jack Nicklaus wins U.S. Golf Association Amateur championship; Billy Carper wins Open Iowa defeats California, 38—12, to win Rose Bowl football game Neale Fraser (Australia) wins U.S. Lawn Tennis Association Men's Singles championship; Maria Bueno (Brazil) wins Women's Singles Edward B. Elliott lands a 97-pound blue catfish at Missouri River, S. Dak.; Heinz Wichmann lands a 92-pound Chinook salmon at Sheena River, British Columbia; Alfred Dean lands a 2,664-pound shark at Ceduna, South Australia	**1959**

1960

A. HISTORY, POLITICS

U.S. protests against Cuban expropriations
Khrushchev in India, Burma, and Indonesia
Brezhnev becomes President of the U.S.S.R.
U.S. admits to aerial reconnaissance flights over U.S.S.R. when a U-2 airplane is shot down and its pilot, Francis Gary Powers, confesses
Khrushchev, Macmillan, Eisenhower, and de Gaulle meet in Paris but the summit talks fail
Former Gestapo chief Adolf Eichmann arrested
Belgian Congo granted full independence
Aneurin Bevan, Brit. socialist politician, d. (b. 1897)
Cyprus becomes independent republic with Archbishop Makarios as president
Historic TV debates between John F. Kennedy (Democrat) and Richard M. Nixon (Republican), presidential candidates
John F. Kennedy elected President of the U.S.
King Baudouin of Belgium marries Dona Fabiola of Spain
Adenauer visits the U.S.
Ex-King Amanullah of Afghanistan d. (b. 1892)
W. E. B. DuBois, Amer. civil rights leader, d. (1868)
Students protest segregation by nonviolent sit-ins at whites-only lunch counters in Greensboro, N.C.

B. LITERATURE, THEATER

Boris Pasternak, Russ. author, d. (b. 1891)
John Betjeman: "Summoned by Bells," autobiography in verse
Robert Bolt: "A Man for All Seasons"
Terence Rattigan: "Ross"
William L. Shirer: "The Rise and Fall of the Third Reich"
John Updike: "Rabbit, Run"
Errol Flynn: "My Wicked, Wicked Ways" (posth.)
Arnold Wesker: "I'm Talking about Jerusalem"
Albert Camus, Fr. author, d. (b. 1913)
Alberto Moravia: "La Noia"
John O'Hara: "Ourselves to Know"
Ezra Pound: "Thrones"
Armand Salacrou: "Boulevard Durand"
Lawrence Durrell: "Clea"
Harper Lee: "To Kill a Mockingbird," Pulitzer Prize (1961)
Allan Sillitoe: "The Loneliness of the Long Distance Runner," novel
John Mortimer: "The Wrong Side of the Park"
Harold Pinter: "The Caretaker"
Vicki Baum, Austro-Amer. novelist, d. (b. 1888)
Curt Goetz, Swiss actor and dramatist, d. (b. 1888)
C. P. Snow: "The Affair"
John Hersey: "The Child Buyer"
Vance Packard: "The Waste Makers"
Richard Wright d. (b. 1908)
Nobel Prize for Literature; St.-John Perse (Fr.)
Gore Vidal: "The Best Man"
Zora Neale Hurston, Amer. author and folklorist, d. (b. 1891)

C. RELIGION, PHILOSOPHY, LEARNING

Sartre: "Critique de la raison dialectique"
Gavin de Beer: "The Sciences Were Never at War"
A. J. Ayer: "Logical Positivism"
Archbishop Fisher of Canterbury visits Jerusalem, Istanbul, and Rome
Three women admitted to the ministry of the Swed. Lutheran Church
Lewis Namier, Brit. historian, d. (b. 1888)

1960

D. VISUAL ARTS

Picasso exhibition at Tate Gallery, London
Oscar Niemeyer: museum and Congress Building at Brasilia opened
Le Corbusier: Monastry La Tourette at Eveux, near Lyons, France
John Bratby: "Gloria with Sunflower"
Oskar Kokoschka and Marc Chagall receive Dutch Erasmus Prize
Karel Appel wins Guggenheim award for abstract painting, "Woman with Ostrich"
Minoru Yamasaki: Pavilion of Sciences, Seattle, U.S.
Films: "Last Year at Marienbad" (Alain Resnais); "Exodus" (Preminger); "Psycho" (Hitchcock); "Saturday Night and Sunday Morning" (Karel Reisz); "Rocco and his Brothers" (Visconti); "The Entertainer" (Olivier); "The Apartment," Academy Award; "La Notte" (Antonioni)
Henny Porten, early Ger. film star, d. (b. 1890)
Hans Albers, Ger. film and stage actor, d. (b. 1892)
Clark Gable d. (b. 1901)
Mack Sennett d. (b. 1880)

E. MUSIC

Pierre Boulez: "Portrait de Mallarmé"
Hans Werner Henze: "Der Prinz von Homburg," opera
Paul Abraham, Hungarian operetta composer, d. (b. 1892)
Hugo Alfvén, Swed. composer, d. (b. 1872)
Boris Blacher: "Rosamunde Floris," opera
Ernst von Dohnányi, Hungarian pianist and composer, d. (b. 1877)
Edwin Fischer, Ger. pianist, d. (b. 1886)
Dimitri Mitropoulos, Greek-Amer. conductor, d. (b. 1896)
Karlheinz Stockhausen: "Konstakte" (for electronic sounds)
Jussi Bjoerling, Swed. tenor, d. (b. 1911)
Leonard Warren, Amer. baritone, d. (b. 1911)
Benjamin Britten: "A Midsummer Night's Dream," opera, Aldeburgh
Lionel Bart: "Oliver!"
Oscar Hammerstein, II d. (b. 1895)
Popular songs: "Itsy Bitsy Teenie Weenie Yellow Polka Dot Bikini"; "Let's Do the Twist"; "Never on Sunday"; "Calcutta"
Elliott Carter: String Quartet No. 2, Pulitzer Prize

F. SCIENCE, TECHNOLOGY, GROWTH

U.S. launches a radio-reflector satellite
Nobel Prize for Physics: D. A. Glaser (U.S.) for his invention of the bubble-chamber for the study of subatomic particles
Nobel Prize for Medicine and Physiology: F. M. Burnet (Australian) and P. B. Medawar (Brit.) for their discovery of acquired immunity against foreign tissue
Optical microwave laser constructed
R. L. Mössbauer (U.S.) makes important gamma ray discoveries
Strell and Woodward independently synthesize chlorophyll
K. H. Hofmann (Ger.) synthesizes pituitary hormone
G. N. Robinson (Brit.) discovers methicillin
"Triton," U.S. nuclear submarine, completes first circumnavigation of the globe under water
Walter Baade, Amer. astronomer, d. (b. 1893)
Maurice de Broglie, Fr. physicist, d. (b. 1875)
A. B. Joffe, Russ. physicist, d. (b. 1880)
A. L. Kroeber, U.S. anthropologist, d. (b. 1876)
U.S. scientists develop laser device (light amplification by stimulated emission of radiation)
Lt. Don Walsh (U.S. Navy) accompanies Jacques Piccard, Fr. bathynaut, on dive of the bathyscaphe "Trieste" to record 35,800 feet in the Pacific near Guam
American Heart Association issues a report attributing higher death rates among middle-aged men to heavy smoking of cigarettes
Nobel Prize for Chemistry: W. F. Libby for his work in archaeological dating techniques using radioactive carbon 14
U.S. experimental rocket-powered airplane travels at almost 2200 mph
First weather satellite, Tiros I, launched by U.S. to transmit TV images of cloud cover around the world

G. DAILY LIFE

Caryl Chessman, convicted rapist, executed in San Quentin gas chamber after 12 years of futile appeals
Washington defeats Wisconsin, 44—8, in Rose Bowl football game
Paul Pender wins middleweight boxing championship from "Sugar" Ray Robinson
Bobby Fischer, 16, defends U.S. chess title successfully
Neo-Nazi political groups banned in Germany
Brasilia (designed by Lucio Costa) replaces Rio de Janeiro as capital of Brazil
Churchill College, Cambridge, founded
Prince Andrew born to Elizabeth II and Prince Philip (first birth to a reigning monarch since 1857)
Pittsburgh (NL) wins World Series, 4—3, against New York (AL)
Princess Margaret marries Antony Armstrong-Jones
Olympic Games held in Rome–Herb Elliott, Australia, runs 1500 m. in 3 minutes 35.6 seconds
Floyd Patterson regains world heavyweight boxing title from Johansson
T.V. sets: U.S., 85 million; Britain, 10.5 million; W. Germany, 2 million; France, 1.5 million
Dr. A. Cordeiro lands a 296-pound yellowfin tuna off Mexico
Sylvia Pankhurst, suffragette leader, d. (b. 1882)
Franklin Pierce Adams ("FPA"), U.S. humorous columnist, d. (b. 1881)
Montreal Canadiens win Stanley Cup hockey championship for fifth consecutive year
Neale Fraser (Australia) wins U.S. Lawn Tennis Association Men's Singles; Darlene Hard (U.S.) wins Women's Singles; Neale Fraser wins Wimbledon championship
Emily Post d. (b. 1873)
U.S. population at 179,323,000; Gross National Product $502.6 billion
Arnold Palmer wins U.S. Open golf championship; D. R. Beman wins Amateur
Charles Van Doren is among 13 contestants on TV show "21" arrested for perjury in testifying that answers to questions were not given them in advance
Australia defeats Italy to win Davis Cup (tennis)
R. C. Webster lands a 410-pound blue shark off Rockport, Mass.

	A. HISTORY, POLITICS	B. LITERATURE, THEATER	C. RELIGION, PHILOSOPHY, LEARNING
1961	Queen Elizabeth II tours India, Pakistan, Persia, Cyprus, and Ghana U.S. breaks off diplomatic relations with Cuba John F. Kennedy inaugurated as 35th (and youngest) President of the U.S.; establishes Peace Corps; meets Harold Macmillan at Key West, Fla.; visits Paris, Vienna, and London; meets Macmillan again in Bermuda Activities of reactionary John Birch Society are a concern of the U.S. Senate Adenauer visits London UN General Assembly condemns apartheid Elizabeth Gurley Flynn succeeds Eugene Dennis as Chairman of the U.S. Communist Party Cuban exiled rebels attempt an unsuccessful invasion of Cuba at the Bay of Pigs; they were trained and supplied by U.S.; a week later, President Kennedy acknowledges his full responsibility for the fiasco Austria refuses application of Archduke Otto of Hapsburg to return Kennedy and Khrushchev meet in Vienna to discuss disarmament, Laos, and Germany Berlin Wall constructed; Vice President Johnson visits Berlin Dag Hammarskjöld killed in air accident (b. 1905) Nobel Peace Prize: Dag Hammarskjöld Ben-Gurion forms new coalition government in Israel Edward Heath, Lord Privy Seal, begins negotiations for Brit. entry into Common Market Adolf Eichmann found guilty in Jerusalem trial Rafael Trujillo, dictator of Dominican Republic, assassinated; succeeded by his son Ex-King Zog I of Albania d. (b. 1895) Sam Rayburn, elected Speaker of the House of Representatives for 10 terms, d. (b. 1882); succeeded by John McCormack	Jean Anouilh: "Becket" Leonhard Frank, Ger. novelist, d. (b. 1882) Max Frisch: "Andorra," Swiss play Christopher Fry: "Curtmantle," Eng. historical play Graham Greene: "A Burnt-out Case," novel Ernest Hemingway d. (b. 1898) Hermann Hesse: "Stufen," poems J. D. Salinger: "Franny and Zooey" John Osborne: "Luther," play Bernard Malamud: "A New Life," Amer. novel Thomas Mann: "Letters 1889—1936" François Mauriac: "Le Nouveau bloc-notes" Qualtinger and Merz: "Der Herr Karl," Viennese farce Henry Morton Robinson, Amer. novelist, d. (b. 1898) Dorothy Thompson, Amer. author, d. (b. 1894) Richard Hughes: "The Fox in the Attic" Iris Murdoch: "A Severed Head" Harold Pinter: "The Collection" John Whiting: "The Devils" Henry Miller: "Tropic of Cancer," first legal publication in U.S. (published in Paris, 1934) John Steinbeck: "The Winter of Our Discontent" Irving Stone: "The Agony and the Ecstasy" Jean Kerr: "Mary. Mary" G. A. Mosel, Jr.: "All the Way Home," Pulitzer Prize drama T. H. White: "The Making of the President: 1960," Pulitzer Prize (1962) Mark Schorer: "Sinclair Lewis: An American Life" Mackinlay Kantor: "Spirit Lake" Dashiell Hammett d. (b. 1894) George S. Kaufman d. (b. 1889) James Thurber d. (b. 1894) Shelagh Delaney: "A Taste of Honey" Harold Robbins: "The Carpetbaggers" Joseph Heller: "Catch-22" Robert Heinlein: "Stranger in a Strange Land," science fiction James Baldwin: "Nobody Knows My Name" Nobel Prize for Literature: Ivo Andric (Yugoslav)	Leon Radzinowycz: "In Search of Criminology" Michael Ramsey appointed Archbishop of Canterbury Raymond Williams: "The Long Revolution" New English Bible appears on 350th anniversary of Authorized Version Stephen Neill: "Christian Faith and Other Faiths" Meeting of World Council of Churches in Delhi Moscow synagogues closed Gordon W. Allport: "Pattern and Growth in Personality" Frank N. D. Buchman, founder of Moral Re-Armament, d. (b. 1878) Carl Gustav Jung, Swiss psychiatrist and philosopher, d. (b. 1875) Learned Hand, U.S. jurist, d. (b. 1872)
1962	U.S. military council established in S. Vietnam Georges Pompidou forms government in France Adolf Eichmann hanged Attempt on the life of Charles de Gaulle U.S.S.R. agrees to send arms to Cuba; establishes base for fishing fleet in Cuba; Kennedy announces installation of U.S.S.R. missile base in Cuba; Khrushchev offers to withdraw it if U.S. removes bases from Turkey; Kennedy rejects offer and announces that U.S.S.R. will dismantle bases in Cuba and withdraw bombers; blockade ends Ahmed Ben Bella named Premier of Algeria Uganda and Tanganyika become independent U Thant elected UN Secretary-General Kennedy and Macmillan meet in Nassau Nobel Peace Prize: Linus Pauling (U.S.), who was awarded 1954 Nobel Prize for Chemistry U-2 pilot Frances Gary Powers is traded by *(contd)*	John Steinbeck: "Travels with Charley: In Search of America" Nobel Prize for Literature: John Steinbeck Frank Loesser and Abe Burrows: "How to Succeed in Business without Really Trying," Pulitzer Prize drama Albert Camus: "Notebooks 1935—1942" Martin Esslin: "The Absurd Theater" William Faulkner: "The Reivers," Pulitzer Prize (1963) Uwe Johnson: "Das dritte Buch über Achim," Ger. novel Boris Pasternak: "In the Interlude," poems Alexander Solzhenitsyn: "One Day in the Life of Ivan Denisovich," Russ. novel Edward Albee: "Who's Afraid of Virginia Woolf?" James Baldwin: "Another Country" Philip Roth: "Letting Go" BBC starts the satirical revue: "That Was the Week That Was" e. e. cummings d. (b. 1894) William Faulkner d. (b. 1897) Hermann Hesse d. (b. 1877) Robinson Jeffers d. (b. 1887) *(contd)*	Anthony Sampson: "The Anatomy of Britain" Second Vatican Council opens in Rome F. W. Deakin: "The Brutal Friendship" (Mussolini and Hitler) G. M. Trevelyan, Eng. historian, d. (b. 1876) Franz Alexander: "The Scope of Psychoanalysis 1921—61" Cardinal Augustin Bea: "The Christian Union" *(contd)*

D. VISUAL ARTS	E. MUSIC	F. SCIENCE, TECHNOLOGY, GROWTH	G. DAILY LIFE	
Augustus John d. (b. 1878) Eero Saarinen, Amer. architect, d. (b. 1910) Goya's portrait of the Duke of Wellington stolen from National Gallery, London Anna Mary Moses ("Grandma Moses"), d. (b. 1860) Museum of the Chinese Revolution opened in Peking Sir Edward Maufe completes Guildford Cathedral, England Films: "Jules et Jim" (Truffaut); "Boccaccio '70" (Fellini); "Viridiana" (Span. film by Buñuel); "Too Late Blues" (Cassavetes); "West Side Story," Academy Award; "Judgment at Nuremberg"; "The Hustler" (Rossen) Gary Cooper d. (b. 1901)	Sir Thomas Beecham d. (b. 1880) Hans Werner Henze: "Elegy for Young Lovers," opera Luigi Nono: "Intoleranza," opera Royal Ballet visits U.S.S.R. Deutsche Oper, W. Berlin, rebuilt Henri Barraud: "Lavinia," Fr. opera buffa Renzo Rosselini: "Uno Sguardo Dal Ponte," Ital. opera (based on Arthur Miller's play "A View from the Bridge") Walter Piston: Symphony No. 7, Pulitzer Prize Popular songs: "Love Makes the World Go Round"; "Moon River"; "Where the Boys Are"; "Exodus"	Yuri Gagarin (U.S.S.R.) orbits the earth in six-ton satellite Alan Shepard makes first U.S. space flight Leucotomy operations and operations for deafness Atlas computer installed at Harwell Erwin Schrödinger, Aust. physicist, d. (b. 1887) Otto Loewy, Ger.-Amer. physiologist and pharmacologist, d. (b. 1873) Percy Bridgman, U.S. physicist, d. (b. 1882) Lee De Forest, U.S. electrical engineer and inventor of the vacuum tube, d. (b. 1873) Nobel Prize for Physics: R. Hofstadter (U.S.) for his study of nucleons and R. L. Mössbauer (U.S.) for work with gamma rays Nobel Prize for Chemistry: M. Calvin (U.S.) for determining the reactions in photosynthesis Nobel Prize for Physiology and Medicine: George von Békésy (U.S.) for his study of the mechanism of the inner ear	Trans-Siberian Railroad electrified between Moscow and Irkutsk Farthings no longer legal tender in Britain Spy trials in London: Gordon Lonsdale, George Blake, and the Krogers University of Sussex founded Tanganyika conference moves to protect African wildlife Last journey of "Orient Express" (Paris—Bucharest) World population (in millions): China, 660; India, 435; U.S.S.R., 209; U.S. 179; Japan, 95; Pakistan, 94; Brazil, 66; W. Germany, 54; Great Britain, 53 Ty Cobb, Amer. baseball player, d. (b. 1886) U.S.S.R. trade fair held in London Floyd Patterson retains heavyweight boxing crown against challenger Ingemar Johansson with a K. O.; later in year knocks out Tom McNeeley in fourth round Bobby Fischer, 17, wins U.S. chess championship for fourth time, defeating Paul Benko, Hungarian Grand Master Washington wins Rose Bowl football game against Minnesota, 17—7 "Freedom Riders," White and Black liberals loosely organized to test and force integration in the South, are attacked and beaten by White citizens (including women) in Anniston and Birmingham Australia trounces Italy, 5—0, to win Davis Cup (tennis); since 1946, Australia has won 10 times, U.S. 6 Roy Emerson (Australia) wins U.S. Lawn Tennis Association Men's Singles; Darlene Hard (U.S.) wins Women's Singles Jack Nicklaus wins U.S. Golf Association Amateur; Gene Littler wins Open; Gary Player wins Masters "Carry Back," J. Sellers up, wins the Preakness Stakes and the Kentucky Derby New York (AL) defeats Cincinnati (NL), 4—1, to win the World Series Lynn Joyner catches a 680-pound giant sea bass off Fernandina Beach, Fla.; W. C. Timm lands a 69-pound 1-ounce albacore off Hudson Canyon, N.J.; Tony Burnand catches a 141-pound 1-ounce Atlantic sailfish off the Ivory Coast, Africa	**1961**
National Gallery, London, buys from Royal Academy Leonardo da Vinci s cartoon "The Virgin and Child" Oskar Kokoschka: "Ringed with Vision," autobiography Franz Kline, Amer. action painter, d. (b. 1910) Jean Renoir: "Renoir, My Father," reminiscences New Festival Theater, *(contd)*	Michael Tippett: "King Priam," opera Kirsten Flagstad, Norw. opera singer, d. (b. 1895) Georges Auric appointed general manager of the Fr. National Opera Houses Britten: "War Requiem" Alfred Cortot, Fr. pianist, d. (b. 1877) Norman Dello Joio: "Blood Moon," Amer. *(contd)*	U.S. spacemen Glenn, Carpenter, and Schirra orbit separately Telstar satellite launched from Cape Canaveral Mariner 2 launched by U.S. as Venus probe Advances in molecular biology Rachel Carson: "Silent Spring" Russ. scientist Chudinov revives fossil algae, aged 250 million years U.S. has 200 atomic reactors in operation; Britain, 39; U.S.S.R., 39 Thalidomide causes children to be born with malformations Royal College of Physicians *(contd)*	Ex-Queen Wilhelmina of the Netherlands d. (b. 1880) James Meredith, Black applicant, is denied admission to University of Mississippi by Governor Barnett; U.S. Court of Appeals finds Barnett guilty of civil contempt and threatens him with arrest and fines; U.S. marshals and 3,000 soldiers suppress riots when Meredith arrives on campus to begin classes Commonwealth Immigrants Act passed in Britain to control immigration "The Sunday Times" issues its first color supplement Sonny Liston becomes world heavyweight boxing champion, knocking out Floyd Patterson in the first round Eleanor Roosevelt d. (b. 1884) Of the world's adult population of 1.6 billion, approx. 44 per cent are illiterate Total world population approx. 3.1 billion Rod Laver (Australia), wins Grand Slam of tennis–all four major championships An earthquake in northwestern Iran kills 10,000 *(contd)*	**1962**

	A. HISTORY, POLITICS	B. LITERATURE, THEATER	C. RELIGION, PHILOSOPHY, LEARNING
1962 contd	U.S.S.R. for U.S.-held Soviet spy Rudolf Abel President Kennedy appoints Byron R. White and Arthur J. Goldberg (—1965) to the Supreme Court	James Jones: "The Thin Red Line" Charles Laughton d. (b. 1899) Katherine Anne Porter: "Ship of Fools," novel Robert Shaw: "The Sun Doctor" Mario Tobino: "Il Clandestino" Arthur Kopit: "Oh Dad, Poor Dad, Mamma's Hung You in the Closet and I'm Feeling So Sad," drama Arnold Wesker: "Chips with Everything" Tennessee Williams: "The Night of the Iguana" Robert Bolt: "A Man for All Seasons," New York premiere Charles M. Schulz: "Happiness Is a Warm Puppy" E. Burdick and H. Wheeler: "Fail-Safe" Ken Kesey: "One Flew Over the Cuckoo's Nest"	Coventry Cathedral consecrated Protestant Episcopal Church consecrates J. M. Burgess, a Negro, as Suffragan Bishop of Massachusets
1963	De Gaulle objects to Britain's entry into Common Market; Britain rejected Hugh Gaitskell, leader of Brit. Labour Party, d. (b. 1907); Harold Wilson elected as his successor Profumo crisis: the Secretary of State for War makes a personal statement in Commons; he resigns, admitting untruthfulness of statement; Stephen Ward found guilty of living on immoral earnings of Christine Keeler and others, commits suicide Winston Churchill becomes honorary citizen of the U.S. Riots, beatings by Whites and police, and maltreatment by officials mark civil rights demonstrations in Birmingham, Ala., culminating in arrest of Martin Luther King and in President Kennedy's calling out of 3,000 troops United Arab Republic, Syria, and Iraq agree to Union Fidel Castro in U.S.S.R. U.S. and U.S.S.R. agree on "hot line" from the White House to the Kremlin Kennedy visits Macmillan Nuclear testing ban is signed by U.S., U.S.S.R., and Great Britain Brit. journalist H. A. R. Philby, who disappeared from Beirut, is granted asylum in the U.S.S.R. 200,000 "Freedom Marchers," Blacks and Whites, descend on Washington to demonstrate Adenauer resigns as W. Ger. Chancellor and is succeeded by Ludwig Erhard Buddhist-led military coup overthrows *(contd)*	Robert Frost: "In the Clearing" Robert Frost, Amer. poet, d. (b. 1874) Günter Grass: "Dog Years," Ger. novel Jessica Mitford: "The American Way of Death" Iris Murdoch: "The Unicorn" John Updike: "The Centaur" Rolf Hochhuth: "The Deputy" Montherlant: "Le Chaos et la nuit" Ramòn Gómez de la Serna, Span. author, d. (b. 1891) Gustaf Gründgens, Ger. actor and producer, d. (b. 1899) Jean Cocteau d. (b. 1889) Aldous Huxley d. (b. 1894) Mary McCarthy: "The Group" John Arden: "The Workhouse Donkey" Ionesco: "Exit the King" Oliver La Farge d. (b. 1900) Theodore Roethke d. (b. 1901) William Carlos Williams d. (b. 1883) Van Wyck Brooks d. (b. 1886) Clifford Odets d. (b. 1906) Jacob Shubert, theater owner, d. (b. 1880) Tristan Tzara, Rum. author, d. (b. 1896) Morris L. West: "The Shoes of the Fisherman" John Le Carré: "The Spy Who Came in From the Cold" Hannah Arendt: "Eichmann in Jerusalem: A Report on the Banality of Evil" Monty Woolley, Amer. actor, d. (b. 1888) Bernard Malamud: "Idiots First" Ford Foundation donates $7.7 million to the development of ballet in the U.S. Barbara Tuchman: "The Guns of August," Pulitzer Prize nonfiction William Carlos Williams: "Pictures from Brueghel," Pulitzer Prize poetry	Pope John XXIII d.; succeeded by Cardinal Montini as Pope Paul VI John G. G. Wootton: "The Politics of Influence" Edward Crankshaw: "The Fall of the House of Habsburg" Isaac Deutscher: "The Prophet Outcast: Trotsky, 1929—1940" Theodor Heuss: "Erinnerungen," autobiography

D. VISUAL ARTS	E. MUSIC	F. SCIENCE, TECHNOLOGY, GROWTH	G. DAILY LIFE	
Salzburg, Austria Films: "Les séquestrés d'Altona" (Sartre, Fredric March); "Vivre sa vie" (Godard); "La Steppa" (Lattuada); "Lawrence of Arabia," Academy Award (David Lean); "Freud" (John Huston); "The Trial" (Orson Welles); "Cleopatra" (Taylor, Burton); "Phaedra" (Dassin); "The Manchurian Candidate" (Frankenheimer) Marilyn Monroe d. (b. 1926)	opera Hanns Eisler, Aust. composer, d. (b. 1898) Jacques Ibert, Fr. composer, d. (b. 1890) Fritz Kreisler, Austro-Amer. violinist, d. (b. 1875) Shostakovich finishes his twelfth symphony Bruno Walter, Ger.-Amer. conductor, d. (b. 1876) Robert Ward: "The Crucible," Pulitzer Prize Popular songs: "Days of Wine and Roses"; "Go Away, Little Girl"; "Blowin' in the Wind"	issues its report on smoking and health Niels Bohr d. (b. 1885) Charles William Beebe, Amer. biologist, d. (b. 1877) Arthur H. Compton, Amer. physicist, d. (b. 1892) Auguste Piccard, Swiss physicist, d. (b. 1884) Nobel Prize for Physics: Lev D. Landau (U.S.S.R.) for his studies of condensed gases, liquid helium in particular Nobel Prize for Chemistry: M. F. Perutz (Brit.) and J. C. Kendrew (Brit.) for discovering the molecular structure of myoglobin and hemoglobin Nobel Prize for Medicine and Physiology: F. H. C. Crick (Brit.), M. H. F. Wilkins (Brit.), and J. D. Watson (U.S.) for determining the molecular structure of DNA	Nine New York daily newspapers are struck from Dec. 8, 1962, until Apr. 1, 1963 Arnold Palmer wins his second British Open golf championship in a row; he also ties with Jack Nicklaus for U.S. Open, but Nicklaus wins playoff, his first major professional title; Palmer also wins Masters third time; he becomes leading money winner for the year ($81,448.33) Minnesota defeats U.C.L.A. to win Rose Bowl football game 21—3 New York (AL) defeats San Francisco (NL) 4—3 to win World Series Toronto Maple Leafs win Stanley Cup hockey championship "Weatherly" (U.S.) defeats "Gretel" (Australia) 4—1 to win America's Cup yacht race	**1962 contd**
Leonardo da Vinci's "Mona Lisa" exhibited in New York and Washington, D.C. Goya exhibition at Royal Academy, London Berlin Philharmonic built by Hans Scharoun Georges Braque d. (b. 1882) David Low, Brit. cartoonist, d. (b. 1891) Museum of Modern Art, New York, holds retrospective exhibit of works by Hans Hofmann Richard Lippold: "Orpheus and Apollo," sculpture Renewed world-wide interest in the Art Nouveau (Jugendstil) period Andy Warhol, Robert Rauschenberg, Jasper Johns, and other artists are represented in New York's Guggenheim Museum show of Pop Art, featuring soup cans, comic-strip-style silk screens, inflatable sculpture, etc. Films: "The Silence" *(contd)*	Michael Tippett: Concerto for Orchestra Francis Poulenc d. (b. 1899) Paul Hindemith d. (b. 1895) Ferenc Fricsay, Hungarian conductor, d. (b. 1914) Edith Piaf, Fr. chanteuse, d. (b. 1916) Winfried Zillig, Ger. composer, d. (b. 1905) Popular songs: "Those Lazy, Hazy, Crazy Days of Summer"; "Danke Schoen"; "Call Me Irresponsible"; "Eighteen Yellow Roses" Menotti: "Labyrinth" and "Death of the Bishop of Brindisi" Joan Baez and Bob Dylan lead in popularity as *(contd)*	Anti-xi-zeno discovered Russ. Valentina Tereshkova makes a three-day flight in space, becoming the first female astronaut U.S. astronaut Gordon Cooper completes 22 orbits in Atlas rocket Hodgkin and Eccles: work on the transmission of nerve impulses Friction welding invented J. Robert Oppenheimer receives Enrico Fermi medal for his work as atomic scientist, despite his declassified status since 1954 Nobel Prize for Physics: E. P. Wigner (U.S.) for his contributions to nuclear and theoretical physics; Maria Goppert-Mayer (U.S.) and J. H. D. Jensen (Ger.) for their discoveries in the shell structure of atomic nuclei Nobel Prize for Chemistry: K. Ziegler (Ger.) and G. Natta (Ital.) for producing complex molecules from simple carbons T. A. Matthews and A. R. Sandage discover quasars Dr. Michael De Bakey (Amer.) first uses an *(contd)*	Earthquake in Skopje, Yugoslavia, kills about 1,100 Glasgow—London mail train robbery nets £2.5 million Hilton Hotel, Park Lane, London, opened Greek liner Lakonia sinks in North Atlantic; 150 lives lost Coldest Jan. and Feb. since 1740 strikes Britain Major religions: 890 million Christians; 200 million Buddhists; 365 million Hindus; 13 million Jews Jack Nicklaus, U.S. golfer, wins his first Masters' Tournament, then the Tournament of Champions (Las Vegas) and the World Series of Golf (Akron) Arnold Palmer is–for the fourth time in six years– top money winner in golf with a total of $128,230 "Credibility gap" becomes evident between the truth and official reports of events in Cuba, Vietnam, and elsewhere By Feb., U.S. unemployment reaches 6.1 per cent Rogers ("Rajah") Hornsby, champion U.S. baseball batter (.424 in 1924), d. University of Southern California wins the Rose Bowl football game, defeating Wisconsin 42—37 Stanley Cup hockey championship is won by the Toronto Maple Leafs "Chateaugay," B. Baeza up, wins the Belmont Stakes and the Kentucky Derby U.S. tennis team wins the Davis Cup for the first time in five years, defeating Australia 3—2 *(contd)*	**1963**

	A. HISTORY, POLITICS	B. LITERATURE, THEATER	C. RELIGION, PHILOSOPHY, LEARNING
1963 contd	government of S. Vietnam; U.S. sends financial and economic aid Macmillan resigns as Brit. Prime Minister and is succeeded by 14th Earl of Home (Sir Alec Douglas-Home) President John F. Kennedy assassinated by Lee Harvey Oswald in Dallas, Tex., Nov. 22; Lyndon B. Johnson sworn in as president Lee Harvey Oswald shot and killed by Jack Ruby as America watches on TV Kenya becomes independent republic within Commonwealth		
1964	Zanzibar declared a republic; sultan banished; Zanzibar unites with Tanganyika to form Tanzania; Julius Nyerere president; Kenneth Kaunda becomes President of Northern Rhodesia; which becomes independent republic of Zambia 24th Amendment to the U.S. Constitution is ratified, abolishing the poll tax King Paul I of Greece d.; succeeded by his son Constantine II Jack Ruby, found guilty of killing Lee Harvey Oswald, the alleged assassin of President Kennedy, is sentenced to death; he dies of cancer in Jan. 1965 UN peace force takes over in Cyprus; Makarios abrogates 1960 treaty between Greece, Turkey, and Cyprus; Greece rejects direct talks; Turk. planes attack Cyprus; Gen. Grivas named commander of Greek Cypriot forces Douglas MacArthur, Amer. general, d. (b. 1880) Ian Smith elected Premier of Southern Rhodesia Pandit Nehru d. (b. 1890); succeeded as Prime Minister of India by Lal Bahadur Shastri Maxwell William Aitken, Lord Beaverbrook, d. (b. 1879) A U.S. destroyer is allegedly attacked off N. Vietnam; U.S. aircraft attack N. Vietnam bases in reprisal; escalation of war, heavy fighting Nyasaland becomes the independent country of Malawi within the Commonwealth Moise Tshombe becomes Premier of the Congo; declares People's Republic Winston Churchill makes last appearance in the House of Commons shortly before his 90th birthday Commission, appointed by President Johnson under Chief Justice Earl Warren, finds that Lee Harvey Oswald, alone, was responsible for assassinating President Kennedy De Gaulle tours S. America Malta becomes independent within the Commonwealth Queen Elizabeth visits Canada Nobel Peace Prize: Martin Luther King Alec Douglas-Home resigns as Brit. Prime Minister and is succeeded by Harold Wilson Khrushchev replaced as Soviet Prime Minister by Kosygin and as Party Secretary by Brezhnev Ex-President Herbert Hoover d. (b. 1874) King Saud of Saudi Arabia deposed; his son Faisal *(contd)*	Shakespeare Quatercentenary Exhibition at Stratford-upon-Avon and Edinburgh The Windmill Theatre, London ("We Never Close"), closes as nonstop vaudeville John Osborne: "Inadmissible Evidence," play Peter Schaffer: "The Royal Hunt of the Sun" Brendan Behan, Ir. author, d. (b. 1923) Ian Fleming, Eng. thriller writer, d. (b. 1908) Edith Sitwell d. (b. 1887) Harold Pinter: "Homecoming," play Peter Weiss: "Marat-Sade," play Saul Bellow: "Herzog" William Golding: "The Spire" Isherwood: "A Single Man" Sartre: "Les Mots" C. P. Snow: "Corridors of Power" Gore Vidal: "Julian" Arthur Miller: "After the Fall" and "Incident at Vichy" Sean O'Casey, Ir. author, d. (b. 1880) Elizabeth Jennings: "Recoveries," poems Hans Moser, Viennese actor, d. (b. 1880) Ernest Hemingway: "A Moveable Feast" (posth.) Louis Auchincloss: "The Rector of Justin" Terry Southern and Mason Hoffenberg: "Candy" S. N. Behrman: "But for Whom Charlie" Richard Hofstadter: "Anti-Intellectualism in American Life," Pulitzer Prize nonfiction Ben Hecht d. (b. 1895) Eric Berne, M.D.: "Games People Play" John Lennon: "In His Own Write" Martin Luther King, Jr.: "Why We Can't Wait"	Randolph Churchill: "The Fight for the Leadership of the Conservative Party" François Mauriac: "De Gaulle" A. H. M. Jones: "The Later Roman Empire" Alexander Werth: "Russia at War" Pope Paul VI makes pilgrimage to the Holy Land

D. VISUAL ARTS	E. MUSIC	F. SCIENCE, TECHNOLOGY, GROWTH	G. DAILY LIFE	
(Ingmar Bergman); "The Cardinal" (Preminger); "Tom Jones," Academy Award (Richardson); "The Leopard" (Visconti); "Irma La Douce" (Wilder); "The Birds" (Hitchcock); "Dr. Strangelove" (Kubrick and Sellers) Zasu Pitts, Amer. film actress, d. (b. 1900) Adolphe Menjou, Amer. film actor, d. (b. 1890)	singers Samuel Barber: Piano Concerto No. 1, Pulitzer Prize	artificial heart to take over the circulation of a patient's blood during heart surgery	Mikhail Botvinnik (U.S.S.R.) loses the world chess championship to Tigran Petrosian, his countryman; Petrosian retains title until 1969 Sonny Liston retains his heavyweight boxing crown when he (again) knocks out Floyd Patterson in the first round Los Angeles (NL) wins the World Series 4—0 over New York (AL) Elsa Maxwell, internationally known party-giver, d. (b. 1883) A hurricane and resulting tsunamis leave about 22,000 dead in E. Pakistan; an estimated 4,000 die in Cuba and Haiti in a hurricane	**1963 contd**
Stuart Davis, Amer. artist, d. (b. 1894) Cézanne's "Les Grandes Baigneuses" acquired by National Gallery, London "Art of a Decade" Exhibition, Tate Gallery, London Basil Spence: library and swimming pool at Swiss Cottage, London Alexander Archipenko, Russ. sculptor, d. (b. 1887) Gallery of Modern Art, built by Huntington Hartford, opens in New York Allen Jones: "Green Girl," Eng. painting Picasso: "The Painter and His Model" Films: "Lord of the Flies" (Peter Brook); "The Passenger" (Munk); "A Hard Day's Night" (The Beatles); "Goldfinger" (James Bond film); "Zorba the Greek" (Cacoyannis); "Mary Poppins" (Stevenson); "My Fair Lady," *(contd)*	Gustav Mahler: Symphony No. 10 (posth.), completed by Deryck Cooke Cole Porter d. (b. 1893) Benjamin Britten: "Curlew River" Luigi Dallapiccola: "Parole di San Paola" Karlheinz Stockhausen: "Plus/Minus" Roger Sessions: "Montezuma," performed for the first time (composed 1947) Jerry Herman: "Hello Dolly," musical comedy, New York Jerry Bock: "Fiddler on the Roof," musical play, New York Marc Blitzstein d. (b. 1906) Popular songs: "Hello, Dolly!"; "I Want to Hold Your Hand"; "From Russia with Love"; "Chim Chim Cheree"; "Fiddler on the Roof"	Nobel Prize for Chemistry: Dorothy Hodgkin (Brit.) Fundamental particle omega-minus discovered using Nimrod-cyclotron Hoyle and Marlikar (Cambridge) postulate a new theory of gravitation Ranger VII, launched from Cape Kennedy, returns close-up photographs of the moon's surface "Brain Drain"–Brit. scientists emigrate to U.S. in great numbers Britain grants licenses to drill for oil and gas in the North Sea Hans von Euler-Chelpin, Swed.-Ger. chemist, d. (b. 1873) Norbert Wiener, founder of the science of cybernetics, d. (b. 1894) Rachel Carson d. (b. 1907) Verrazano-Narrows Bridge, the world's longest suspension bridge, opens to traffic in New York	Major earthquake in Alaska–114 die; $500 million in property damage Brit. government changes August Bank Holiday to last Monday in month Easter outbreak of Mods versus Rockers disturb Brit. sea resorts Sentences totaling 307 years passed on 12 mail-train robbers in England 300 spectators are killed in riots at soccer match in Lima Race riots erupt in Harlem, New York, and in many other U.S. cities as reaction against enforcement of civil rights laws "Daily Herald," London, ceases publication Olympic Games in Tokyo: U.S.S.R. wins 41 gold medals; U.S., 37; Japan, 16; Germany, 13; Britain, 5; Peter Snell, New Zealand, wins 800 meters and 1500 meters Cassius Clay wins world heavyweight boxing championship from Sonny Liston Sir Jack Hobbs, Brit. cricketer, d. (b. 1882) Princess Irene of the Netherlands marries Span. Prince Carlos Hugo of Bourbon-Parma Arnold Palmer wins his fourth Masters' Tournament (since 1958) World's Fair in New York Gracie Allen, Amer. comedienne (with her husband, George Burns), d. (b. 1905) James Hoffa, president of Teamsters Union, found guilty of jury tampering (in 1962) and sentenced to eight years' imprisonment and payment of $10,000 fine; later, another jury convicts him of fraud and conspiracy and he is sentenced to five years and $10,000 fine The Watusi, Frug, Monkey, Funky Chicken, and other varieties of the Twist drive many people to discothèques, where go-go girls set the pace "Constellation" (U.S.) outsails "Sovereign" (Brit.) 4—0 to win America's Cup Australian tennis team defeats Americans to win the Davis Cup Eddie Cantor, Amer. comedian, d. (b. 1892) Toronto Maple Leafs win Stanley Cup hockey trophy third year "Northern Dancer," Willie Hartack up, wins the *(contd)*	**1964**

	A. HISTORY, POLITICS	B. LITERATURE, THEATER	C. RELIGION, PHILOSOPHY, LEARNING
1964 contd	proclaimed King Lyndon B. Johnson elected President of the U.S. Chou En-lai visits Moscow Brit. bank interest rate increased to 7 per cent Harold Wilson visits Washington Kenya becomes republic with Jomo Kenyatta as president Arafat takes over leadership of Arab guerrilla force Al Fatah		
1965	Lyndon Baines Johnson inaugurated as 36th President of the U.S. Winston Spencer Churchill d. (b. 1874) Gambia becomes independent Malcolm X, Black Muslim leader, shot in New York (b. 1925) Seretse Khama becomes first Premier of Bechuanaland Outbreaks of violence at Selma, Ala.; Martin Luther King heads procession of 4,000 civil rights demonstrators from Selma to Montgomery, Ala. to deliver Negro petition; Ku Klux Klan shootings in Selma N. Vietnamese MIG aircraft shoot down U.S. jets; students demonstrate in Washington against U.S. bombing of N. Vietnam; U.S.S.R. admits supplying arms to Hanoi; further Amer. demonstrations against the war; Ho Chi Minh rejects peace talks with U.S. 750th anniversary of Magna Carta; 700th anniversary of Brit. Parliament Queen Elizabeth II visits W. Germany Revolution in Algeria; President Ben Bella deposed Medicare bill becomes law upon President Johnson's signing; it was first proposed by President Kennedy in 1960 Edward Heath elected leader of Brit. Conservative Party Severe race riots in Watts district of Los Angeles result in 35 dead, 4,000 arrested, and $40 million in property damage New U.S. immigration law classifies applicants by family condition, refugee status, and skills, replacing 1921 law based on nationality Six former Auschwitz prison officials sentenced to life imprisonment Talks on Rhodesia–Ian Smith in London; Harold Wilson later goes to Salisbury; Rhodesian Unilateral Declaration of Independence (UDI); Britain imposes oil embargo on Rhodesia Podgorny replaces Mikoyan as President of the U.S.S.R. De Gaulle wins election to Fr. presidency The Shah of Iran visits Moscow President Johnson appoints Abe Fortas to the Supreme Court (—1969) Bernard M. Baruch, U.S. financier, philanthropist, and public servant, d. (b. 1870) Felix Frankfurter, U.S. jurist, d. (b. 1882) Joseph C. Grew, U.S. diplomat, d. (b. 1880) Frances Perkins, first woman cabinet member, Secretary of Labor under F. D. Roosevelt, d. (b. 1882) Adlai E. Stevenson d. (b. 1900) Henry A. Wallace d. (b. 1888) Gambia, Singapore, and Maldive Islands join the UN	Norman Mailer: "An American Dream" Enid Bagnold: "The Chinese Prime Minister" John Osborne: "A Patriot for Me" Frank Marcus: "The Killing of Sister George" Nobel Prize for Literature: M. A. Sholokhov With 24,009 performances, Shakespeare is the most produced author in Ger. theaters this year, followed by Schiller with 17,860 and Shaw with 11,200 T. S. Eliot d. (b. 1888) Robert Lowell: "Union Dead" John Arden-Armstrong: "Last Good Night" Jacques Audiberti, Fr. poet, d. (b. 1899) William Somerset Maugham d. (b. 1874) Percy H. Newby: "One of the Founders" Robin Moore: "The Green Berets" Arthur Schlesinger, Jr.: "The Thousand Days," Pulitzer Prize biography (1966) Ian Fleming: "Thunderball" Ralph Nader: "Unsafe at Any Speed" Frank D. Gilroy: "The Subject Was Roses," Pulitzer Prize drama Shirley Ann Grau: "The Keepers of the House," Pulitzer Prize novel John Berryman: "77 Dream Songs," Pulitzer Prize poetry	Pope Paul VI visits New York Britain celebrates Westminster Abbey's 900th anniversary Albert Schweitzer d. (b. 1875) Max Born: "On the Responsibility of Scientists" Martin Buber, Jewish philosopher, d. (b. 1878) Herbert Marcuse: "Culture and Society" Paul Tillich, Ger.-Amer. theologian, d. (b. 1886)

D. VISUAL ARTS	E. MUSIC	F. SCIENCE, TECHNOLOGY, GROWTH	G. DAILY LIFE	
Academy Award; "Topkapi" (Peter Ustinov) Elizabeth Taylor divorces Eddie Fisher and, 10 days later, weds Richard Burton Peter Lorre d. (b. 1905)			Preakness Stakes and the Kentucky Derby Ken Venturi wins the U.S. Open golf championship Jack Nicklaus is top golf money-winner of the year, with a total of $113,284.50 Peter Simons lands a 149-pound amberjack off Bermuda; B. C. Bain, at Cape Brett, New Zealand, lands a 415-pound striped marlin St. Louis (NL) defeats New York (AL) 4—3 to win the World Series	**1964 contd**
Goya's portrait of the Duke of Wellington, stolen in 1961, returned to National Gallery, London Rembrandt's "Titus" sold at Christie's, London, for 760,000 guineas Josaku Maeda: "Mystagogie d'espace," Jap. abstract painting Laura Knight: "Autobiography" Giacometti exhibition in London "Op" art becomes the rage: nonobjective art directed at optical illusions based on use of color and form and perspective in unusual ways Le Corbusier d. (b. 1887) Picasso: "Self-Portrait" Films: "Help!" (The Beatles); "Cul-de-sac" (Polanski); "Othello" (Olivier); "Dr. Zhivago" (David Lean); "The Sound of Music," Academy Award Charles Chaplin and Ingmar Bergman awarded the Dutch Erasmus Prize	Malcolm Williamson: "Julius Caesar Jones," opera, London Leonard Bernstein: "Chichester Psalms," oratorio Private commercial stations like "Radio Caroline" are established off the Brit. coast Nat "King" Cole, jazz singer and pianist, d. (b. 1919) Boris Blacher: "Tristan und Isolde," ballet Jean Françaix: "La Princesse de Cleve," opera Wieland Wagner stages a new production of the "Ring" in Bayreuth Verdi, with 20,631 performances, is the most produced operatic composer on the Ger. stage this year; followed by Mozart with 18,064; Johann Strauss with 15,555; and Puccini with 12,794 performances Popular songs: "King of the Road"; "It Was a Very Good Year"; "Downtown"; "A Hard Day's Night"	Soviet astronaut Leonov leaves spacecraft Voskhod II and floats in space for 10 minutes U.S. astronaut Edward White walks from Gemini 4 for 21 minutes First Fr. satellite launched The "Vinland Map" proves, according to Yale University Press statement, that Leif Ericson discovered America in the 11th century (map discredited as forgery in 1974) Rare earth complexes first separated by gas chromatography Legislative momentum gains for anti-pollution laws on a national scale in the U.S First flight around the world over both poles	Ex-King Farouk of Egypt d. (b. 1920) Herbert Morrison, Brit. Labour politician, d. (b. 1888) Earthquake shakes Chile Tornadoes strike Midwestern U.S. Cyclones ravage E. Pakistan; 12,000—20,000 die Universities founded in Kent and Warwick, England General Post Office Tower, London, opened U.S. spends more than $26.2 billion for public school education; $654 per student Out of 3.52 million, 2.63 million 17-year-olds are high school graduates in the U.S. Out of 709,332 degrees conferred 551,040 are Bachelors, 140,055 are Masters, and 18,237 are Doctors Circulation figures of Brit. daily newspapers: "Express" 3,400,000, "Mail" 2,400,000, "Mirror" 5,000,000, "Telegraph" 1,300,000, "Times" 250,000 10 Brit. professional soccer players found guilty of "fixing" matches Jim Clark becomes world motor-racing champion Helena Rubinstein, Amer. cosmetician, d. (b. 1870) World production of diamonds totals 342,000 carats When a relay switch in Ontario malfunctions, the entire northeastern U.S. and parts of Canada lose electrical power: blackout affects 30 million people; noticeable increase in birth rate nine months later Edward R. Murrow, U.S. journalist and commentator, d. (b. 1908) Amos Alonzo Stagg, Amer. football coach, d. (b. 1862) The average union hourly wage scale in the U.S. has doubled for workers in the building trades since 1949, at least doubled in the trucking industry and among transit workers, and has increased by about 75 per cent for those in the printing trades Los Angeles (NL) defeats Minnesota (AL) 4—3 to win the World Series Michigan 34, Oregon State 7 in the Rose Bowl football game The Montreal Canadiens win the Stanley Cup hockey trophy Gary Player wins the U.S. Open golf championship, Jack Nicklaus, the Masters; Nicklaus is again top money winner with $140,752.14 Australia defeats Spain to win the Davis Cup	**1965**

	A. HISTORY, POLITICS	B. LITERATURE, THEATER	C. RELIGION, PHILOSOPHY, LEARNING
1966	De Gaulle inaugurated for his second seven-year term as President of France; visits U.S.S.R.; requests removal of NATO forces from France Mrs. Indira Gandhi, Nehru's daughter, becomes Prime Minister of India; tours Europe Harold Wilson visits Moscow International Days of Protest (against U.S. policy in Vietnam) Abdul Rachman Arif elected President of Iraq Economic and technical pact signed by Italy and U.S.S.R. Meeting between Pope Paul VI and Soviet Foreign Minister Gromyko 2,000 Madrid University students battle with police in demonstrations Chou En-lai visits Rumania H. Kamuzu Banda inaugurated as President of Malawi Brit. Prime Minister Wilson announces "standstill" in wages and prices Red Guard demonstrates in China against Western influences B. J. Vorster named Prime Minister of S. Africa Nkrumah government in Ghana is removed by military coup; Nkrumah goes into exile Pope Paul VI issues encyclical on Vietnamese war Nazi ministers Albert Speer and Baldur von Schirach released after 20 years' imprisonment President Johnson goes on Far East tour Israeli and Jordanian forces fight battle in Hebron area Pakistani President Ayub Khan visits London Kurt Georg Kiesinger elected W. Ger. Chancellor Wilson and Smith agree to a partial settlement of the Rhodesian question at a conference aboard HMS "Tiger"; settlement later withdrawn 48-hour Christmas truce observed in Vietnam British Guiana becomes the independent nation of Guyana Chester W. Nimitz, U.S. admiral, d. (b. 1885)	Truman Capote: "In Cold Blood" Bernard Malamud: "The Fixer" Adela Rogers St. John: "Tell No Man" Fletcher Knebel: "The Zinkin Road" Kingsley Amis: "The Anti-Death League" Jacques Borel: "L'Adoration" Erwin Piscator, Ger. theatrical producer, d. (b. 1893) Peter Ustinov: "Halfway Up the Tree" Georges Duhamel, Fr. author, d. (b. 1884) C. S. Forester, Eng. novelist, d. (b. 1899) Evelyn Waugh, Eng. novelist, d. (b. 1903) Günter Grass: "Die Plebeier proben den Aufstand," Ger. play Françoise Sagan: "Le Cheval évanoui" Abe Burrows: "Cactus Flower" Jacqueline Susann: "Valley of the Dolls" H. M. Petrakis: "A Dream of Kings" Allen Drury: "Capable of Honor" Iris Murdoch: "The Time of the Angels" Graham Greene: "The Comedians" Martin Walser: "Das Einhorn" Nobel Prize for Literature: S. J. Agnon (Israeli) and Nelly Sachs (Swed.) Russel Crouse, Amer. playwright and producer, d. (b. 1893) Billy Rose, Amer. showman, d. (b. 1899) Sophie Tucker, "Last of the Red-Hot Mamas," d. (b. 1888) Clifton Webb, Amer. actor, d. (b. 1893) Ed Wynn, comedian, d. (b. 1887) Charles Dyer: "Staircase" David Mercer: "Belcher's Luck" Peter Shaffer: "Black Comedy" Katherine Anne Porter: "Collected Short Stories," Pulitzer Prize Edward Albee: "A Delicate Balance" William Manchester: "The Death of a President" Kathleen Norris d. (b. 1880) Anne Nichols, author of "Abie's Irish Rose," d. (b. 1891) Lillian Smith, author of "Strange Fruit," d. (b. 1898) A. E. Hotchner: "Papa Hemingway" Robert Blake: "Disraeli" John Barth: "Giles Goat-Boy" Robert Heinlein: "The Moon Is a Harsh Mistress," science fiction Mao Tse-tung: "Quotations of Chairman Mao"	Cambridge Medieval History: "The Byzantine Age" Max Braubach: "Prinz Eugen von Savoyen" (five vols.) G. and M. Beadle: "The Language of Life" Raymond Williams: "Modern Tragedy" James Cameron: "Witness," on the war in Vietnam W. G. Runciman: "Relative Deprivation and Social Justice" Alfie Hinds: "Contempt of Court" (on penal system of South Africa) R. T. de George: "Patterns of Soviet Thought" L. S. Dembro: "Conceptions of Reality in Modern American Poetry" Billy Graham conducts his Greater London Crusade World Jewish Congress in Brussels attempts to promote Jewish-Christian understanding The Archbishop of Canterbury visits Pope Paul VI The United Brethren and Methodist Churches vote to merge (in 1968) as United Methodist Church with combined membership of almost 11 million Roman Catholic bishops rule that U.S. Catholics need no longer abstain from eating meat on Fridays except during Lent

1966

D. VISUAL ARTS

Kumi Sugai: "Mer soleil," Jap. abstract painting
"Les Plus Belles Gravures Du Monde Occidental, de 1410 à 1914," exhibition at the Bibliothèque Nationale, Paris
A small oil painting, "St. George and the Dragon," by Hubert van Eyck or Rogier van der Weyden auctioned at Sotheby's, London, for £220,000 ($616,000)
Van Gogh's portrait of Mlle. Ravoux sold at Christie's, London, for 150,000 guineas ($441,000)
The temples and statuary of Abu Simbel, Egypt, moved to save them from the rising waters of the Aswan High Dam
Marc Chagall's mural "Le Triomphe de la musique," in the Metropolitan Opera House, New York
Carlo Carrà, Ital. painter of the "peintura metafisica," d. (b. 1881)
Alberto Giacometti, Swiss sculptor, d. (b. 1901)
Maxfield Parrish, Amer. painter, d. (b. 1870)
Gino Severini, Ital. painter, d. (b. 1883)
"Vicky" (Victor Weisz), Brit. political cartoonist, d. (b. 1913)
Hans Hofmann, Ger.-Amer. painter, d. (b. 1880)
Paul Manship, Amer. sculptor, d. (b. 1885)
Malvina Hoffman, Amer. sculptress, d. (b. 1887)
William Zorach, Amer. sculptor, d. (b. 1887)
Films: "Torn Curtain" (Hitchcock's 50th film); "The Bible" (John Huston); "Fahrenheit 451" (Truffaut); "Modesty Blaise" (Losey); "Alfie" (Lewis Gilbert); "Masculin-Féminin"
(contd)

E. MUSIC

Hermann Scherchen, Ger. conductor, d. (b. 1891)
Mahler's "Song of the Earth," produced at Stuttgart as ballet, choreographed by Kenneth MacMillan
Mitch Leigh: "Man of La Mancha," musical play, New York
William Schuman: "The Witch of Endor," ballet, New York
Harry Freedman: "Rose Latulippe," the first full-length Canadian ballet, Stratford, Ontario
40th World Music Festival of the ISCM held in Stockholm
Debut of Maxim Shostakovich, conducting his father's Symphony No. 1 in Moscow
Josef Matthias Hauer: "Die Schwarze Spinne," opera, Vienna (posth.)
The new Metropolitan Opera House opens in New York City's Lincoln Center
Samuel Barber: "Antony and Cleopatra," opera, New York
Wieland Wagner, Wagner's grandson and an opera producer, d. (b. 1917)
Burton Lane: "On a Clear Day You Can See Forever," musical play, New York
Leslie Bassett: "Variations for Orchestra," Pulitzer Prize
Anthony Wesker: "The Kitchen"
Douglas Moore: "Carrie Nation"
Deems Taylor
(contd)

F. SCIENCE, TECHNOLOGY, GROWTH

Michael E. De Bakey (Houston, Tex.) implants plastic arteries leading to an artificial heart which function throughout 3.5-hour valve replacement operation on a 37-year-old woman, who 19 days later returns home
Fourth World Congress of Psychiatry held in Madrid
Soviet spacecraft Luna 9 makes successful soft landing on the moon
U.S. spacecraft Surveyor 1 makes soft landing on moon and transmits more than 11,000 TV images of the terrain
Two male dogs sent into orbit aboard Soviet satellite Cosmos 110
Edwin E. Aldrin, Jr. (U.S.) steps out of the Gemini 12 spacecraft for 129 minutes
Peter Debye, Dutch physician, d. (b. 1884)
Otto Hahn, Lise Meitner, and Fritz Strassmann awarded Enrico Fermi Prize
Nobel Prize for Medicine and Physiology: C. B. Huggins (U.S.) for his study of hormonal treatment of cancer of the prostate and F. P. Rous for his discovery of a cancer virus
(contd)

G. DAILY LIFE

In London Cassius Clay wins two title fights against British and Empire Champion Henry Cooper
Boris Spassky defeats Mikhail Tal (both U.S.S.R.) at a Tbilisi Tournament for the world Chess championship
Italian Bridge team wins world championship for eighth successive time at Saint Vincent
Floods ravage northern Italy; thousands of art treasures ruined at Venice and Florence
W. Ger. autobahn system totals more than 2,000 miles
Miniskirts come into fashion
Elizabeth Arden d. (b. 1884)
Supermarket retailing expands in Europe and the Far East
England defeats W. Germany to win the soccer World Cup
"Buckpasser," three-year-old Thoroughbred, is the sensation of the U.S. turf season
New York "Herald Tribune" ceases publication
Prince Rainier of Monaco and Greek shipowner Aristotle Onassis feud over control of the Société des Bains de Mer, Monte Carlo
Margaret Sanger, vigorous Amer. advocate of birth control, d. (b. 1883)
Jack Brabham (Australia) becomes first man to win world driving championship in a car of his own construction
A Ger. team makes the first ascent of the direct route on the north face of the Eiger
Ivanitski (U.S.S.R.) wins world heavyweight wrestling championship
Manuel Santana (Spain) wins men's tennis singles title at Wimbledon
The Salvation Army (approx. 27,000 members) celebrates its centenary
U.S. car registrations total 78 million passenger cars and 16 million trucks and buses
Color TV becomes popular
Approx. 126 million vacationists are tourists (estimated by International Union of Official Travel Organizations)
U.S. population totals 195,827,000
President Johnson's younger daughter Luci marries Patrick J. Nugent
Lebanese Intra Bank fails
Brit. yachtsman Francis Chichester arrives in Sydney, Australia, 107 days after sailing alone from London
The "Times" of London changes its format, putting news instead of advertisements on the front page
Swed. newspaper "Stockholm Tidende" ceases publication
Archduke Otto von Habsburg obtains Aust. passport after 47-year exile
Princess Beatrix, heir to the Dutch throne, marries Ger. diplomat Claus von Amsberg
U.S. jockey Johnny Longden retires with over 6,000 victories
Consumer expenditure for alcoholic beverages in U.S. for 1966 totals $17,400 million
Dick Weber wins his fourth open U.S. Bowling championship in five years
Jim Ryun, Amer. college student, sets world record for mile run of 3 minutes 51.3 seconds
Baltimore (AL) wins World Series 4—0 over Los Angeles (NL)
U.C.L.A. defeats Michigan State 14—12 to win the Rose Bowl football game
(contd)

	A. HISTORY, POLITICS	B. LITERATURE, THEATER	C. RELIGION, PHILOSOPHY, LEARNING
1966 contd			

1967

A. HISTORY, POLITICS

Harold Wilson reduces Brit. cabinet from 23 to 21 members
Israeli forces use tanks against Syria in worsening border conflict
Jeremy Thorpe elected leader of Brit. Liberal Party
Podgorny makes official visit to Italy; meets Pope Paul VI
W. Ger. Foreign Minister Brandt visits U.S.
Soviet Union and Britain pledge to make every possible effort to obtain peace in Vietnam
France launches its first nuclear powered submarine, "La Redoutable"
Israeli Mirage fighter planes shoot down six Syrian Air Force MIG-21s
Konrad Adenauer d. (b. 1876)
Svetlana Alliluyeva, Stalin's daughter, arrives in U.S. from Switzerland
5,000 persons riot in Hong Kong; 700,000 persons march down Fifth Avenue, N.Y., in support of U.S. soldiers fighting in Vietnam
Hanoi attacked by U.S. bombers
Nasser and Hussein sign mutual defense pact
Israeli Gen. Moshe Dayan appointed Defense Minister
Six-Day War between Israel and Arab nations begins; Israeli forces move into Sinai Desert and Jordan; capture old city of Jerusalem, gain control of Sinai Peninsula approaches to Suez Canal; Nasser decides to resign, but U.A.R. National Assembly rejects his decision; Israeli forces penetrate into Syria; U.S.S.R. severs diplomatic relations with Israel; Israel and Syria agree to ceasefire; Arab nations reject Israeli proposal for negotiations; Nasser names himself Prime Minister of U.A.R.; Jerusalem proclaimed united city under Israeli rule
Queen Elizabeth and Prince Philip arrive in Canada to take part in centennial celebrations
Arab refugees begin returning to their homes on West Bank of Jordan
Nasser vows to continue struggle against Israel
Black Power conference held in Newark, N.J.
De Gaulle, on state visit to Canada, makes his "free Quebec" speech
Pope Paul VI makes a "peace pilgrimage" to Istanbul
Britain rejects Chinese ultimatum demanding three pro-Communist Hong Kong newspapers; Brit. chancery in Peking sacked and burned
Amer. Nazi Party leader G. L. Rockwell is shot to death in Arlington, Va.
King Hussein of Jordan visits the U.S.S.R. in state
Ernesto ("Che") Guevara, Cuban revolutionary leader, d. (b. 1928)
Clement Attlee d. (b. 1883)
50,000 persons demonstrate against Vietnam war at
(contd)

B. LITERATURE, THEATER

National Library in Ottawa, Ontario, opened
Federal aid to U.S. libraries during fiscal year 1966—67 totals $76 million
Gore Vidal: "Washington D.C.," novel
Sarah Gainham: "Night Falls on the City"
Isaac Bashevis Singer: "The Manor"
W. H. Auden: "Collected Shorter Poems, 1927—1957"
Stephen Birmingham: "Our Crowd"
Ira Levin: "Rosemary's Baby"
Thornton Wilder: "The Eighth Day"
Leon Uris: "Topaz"
Svetlana Alliluyeva: "Twenty Letters to a Friend"
Harold Pinter: "The Homecoming"
Walter Greenwood: "There was a Time"
Emlyn Williams: "Beyond Belief"
William Golding: "The Pyramid"
Angus Wilson: "No Laughing Matter"
Christopher Isherwood: "A Meeting by the River"
Charles de Quintrec: "Stances du verbe amour," Fr. poetry
Dutourd: "L'Amour de l'art"
Günter Grass: "Ausgefragt"
Aldo Palazzeschi: "Il doge"
Robert Shaw: "The Man in the Glass Booth," play
Tom Stoppard: "Rosencrantz and Guildenstern Are Dead," drama
Rolf Hochhuth: "Soldaten"
Robert K. Massie: "Nicholas and Alexandra"
Studs Terkel: "Division Street"
Martin Walser: "Zimmerschlacht"
Cornelia Otis Skinner: "Madame Sarah," biography of Sarah Bernhardt
Jules Feiffer: "Little Murders"
William Styron: "The Confessions of Nat Turner"
Samuel Beckett: "Têtes mortes"
Marguerite Duras: "L'amante anglaise"
Heinz Hilpert, Ger. theatrical producer, d. (b. 1890)
Arthur Miller: "The Price"
165 W. Ger. theaters receive government and municipal grants of DM 340 million
Mischa Auer, Russ.-Amer. actor, d. (b. 1900)
Charles Bickford, Amer. actor, d. (b. 1889)
Martine Carol, Fr. actress, d. (b. 1920)
Alice B. Toklas d. (b. 1877)
Ilya Ehrenburg, Soviet writer, d. (b. 1891)
Pamela Frankau, Eng. novelist, d. (b. 1908)
Sir Victor Gollancz, Eng. publisher, d. (b. 1893)
Vyvyan Holland, Eng. writer, Oscar Wilde's son, d. (b. 1886)
Langston Hughes, Amer. Negro poet, d. (b. 1862)
(contd)

C. RELIGION, PHILOSOPHY, LEARNING

Isaac Deutscher, Pol.-Brit. historian, d. (b. 1907)
Cardinal Francis Spellman, Archbishop of New York, d. (b. 1889)
J. K. Galbraith: "The New Industrial State"
Gertrude E. Gunn: "The Political History of Newfoundland 1832—1864"
Carl J. Burckhardt: "Richelieu"
Arthur J. May: "The Passing of the Habsburg Monarchy"
G. H. N. Seton-Watson: "The Russian Empire 1801—1917" (Oxford History of Modern Europe)
Gilles Perrault: "L'Orchestre rouge" (on the Soviet Secret Service)
Bertrand Russell: "Autobiography, 1872—1914"
Michael Holroyd: "Lytton Strachey: A Critical Biography" (first of two vols.)
Hugh Trevor-Roper: "Religion, the Reformation and Social Change"
Anthony Sampson: "Macmillan, a Study in Ambiguity"
George Steiner: "Language and Silence"
Aurel David P.
(contd)

D. VISUAL ARTS	E. MUSIC	F. SCIENCE, TECHNOLOGY, GROWTH	G. DAILY LIFE	
(J. L. Godard); "A Man for All Seasons," Academy Award; "Who's Afraid of Virginia Woolf?" (Elizabeth Taylor) Eric Pommer, Ger. film producer, d. (b. 1889) Walt Disney d. (b. 1901)	d. (b. 1885) Gunther Schuller: "The Visitation," Hamburg State Opera Popular songs: "Born Free"; "Eleanor Rigby"; "Strangers in the Night"; "Ballad of the Green Berets"	Salazar Suspension bridge, fifth longest in the world (3,323 feet), opens in Lisbon A U.S. B-52 crashes near coast of Spain and four unarmed hydrogen bombs are dropped –three on land and one in the sea; last is recovered after three months	"Kauai King," D. Brumfield up, wins the Preakness Stakes and the Kentucky Derby Jack Nicklaus wins the Masters golf tournament second year in a row Billy Casper wins playoff against Arnold Palmer in U.S. Open making him biggest money-winner for the year with $121,944.92 Maria Bueno (Brazil) wins U.S. Lawn Tennis Association Women's Singles, her fourth victory in past eight years Australian tennis team wins the Davis Cup, defeating India 4—1	**1966 contd**
Three Paris exhibitions: Picasso, Ingres, and the treasures from the tomb of Tutankhamen Ad. Reinhardt, U.S. painter, d. (b. 1913) Monet's painting "La Terrasse à St.-Adresse" sold at Christie's, London, for £588,000 ($1.65 million) Picasso's "Mother and Child" sold for $532,000 Leonardo da Vinci's portrait of Ginevra de Benci acquired by National Gallery, Washington, D.C., for $6 million from Prince Francis Joseph II of Liechtenstein René Magritte, Fr. surrealist painter, d. (b. 1898) Marc Chagall: "The Blue Village" Charmion von Wiegand: "The Secret Mandala," Amer. abstract painting Edward Hopper, U.S. painter, d. (b. 1882) Films: "Blow-Up" (Antonioni); "Belle de Jour" (Buñuel); "Bonnie and Clyde" (Penn); "The Countess from Hong Kong" (Chaplin); "El *(contd)*	André Prevost: "Terre des hommes," symphonic poem, composed for the inaugural concert of Expo 67, Montreal Willard Stright: "Toyon of Alaska," opera, Anchorage; commissioned to celebrate the centenary of the purchase of Alaska from Russia Hans Werner Henze: concerto for double bass and orchestra, Chicago M. D. Levy: "Mourning Becomes Electra," opera, New York Gaetano Zuffre: "Hiroshima," cantata William Walton: "The Bear," one-act comic opera Barbra Streisand sings in Central Park, New York, for 135,000 listeners Sandie Shaw wins Eurovision Song Contest for Britain with "Puppet on a String," Vienna Eng. singer Gerry Dorsey changes his name to Engelbert Humperdinck, and gains world fame Marius Constant: "Paradise Lost," ballet, choreographed by Roland Petit Harriet Cohen, Eng. pianist, d. (b. 1901) O. E. Deutsch, Austro-Brit. music historian, d. (b. 1890) Mischa Elman, U.S. violinist, d. (b. 1891) Nelson Eddy, singer and film star, d. (b. 1901) Geraldine Farrar, U.S. *(contd)*	J. Robert Oppenheimer, U.S. nuclear physicist, d. (b. 1904) Bela Schick, U.S. pediatrician, d. (b. 1877) Soviet cosmonaut Vladimir M. Komarov killed during reentry of Soyuz 1 Stanford University biochemists produce synthetic version of DNA, the substance that controls heredity Seventh International Congress of Biochemistry meets in Tokyo; special symposium held to honor Sir Hans Krebs on his retirement from Oxford Low temperature irradiation of hydrogen iodine mixtures carried out by J. H. Sullivan, Los Alamos, N. Mex., leads to reassessment of the mechanism of this reaction The People's Republic of China explodes its first hydrogen bomb Dr. Christiaan N. Barnard performs the world's first human heart transplant operation at Groote Schuur Hospital, Cape Town, S. Africa Dr. Irving S. Cooper (U.S.) develops cryosurgery as a means of treating *(contd)*	Expo 67 opens in Montreal Heavyweight boxing champion Muhammad Ali (Cassius Clay) indicted in Houston, Tex., for refusing to be inducted into U.S. armed forces Primo Carnera, Ital. boxer, d. (b. 1906) Jacques Heim, Fr. couturier, d. (b. 1900) Ilse Koch, Ger. war criminal, the "beast of Buchenwald," found hanged in prison cell (b. 1907) Henry R. Luce, U.S. publisher, founder of "Time," "Life," and "Fortune," d. (b. 1898) Goose Tatum, U.S. basketball player, d. (b. 1921) Mickey Mantle (New York Yankees) hits his 500th career home run Boston wins its first baseball pennant since 1946 Soviet team, headed by Nona Gaprindashvili, wins Women's International Chess Tournament at Oberhausen, W. Germany Australian cricket team under R. B. Simpson loses in S. Africa by three matches to one, with one draw Albert H. de Salvo (35), the "Boston Strangler," who admitted 13 murders, is sentenced to life imprisonment Tropical rains and cloudbursts inundate eastern Brazil Lake Point Tower, Chicago–645 feet, 70 stories–becomes the world's tallest reinforced concrete apartment building Lost Creek Dam, Utah, completed 12 billion cans of beer and 5.3 billion cans of soft drinks consumed during the year in U.S. Toronto Maple Leaf hockey team wins the Stanley Cup Peggy Fleming (U.S.) wins world championship for women's figure skating, Vienna Increases in cost of living range between 1.8 per cent (U.S.) and 5.8 per cent (New Zealand) 100 million telephones are in service in the U.S. John Newcombe (23) of Australia wins Wimbledon and U.S. singles tennis titles 3.6 million births registered in the U.S. Sweden changes from left- to right-side driving Francis Chichester finishes his single-handed voyage around the world in 226 days David Frost (b. 1939) emerges as "Television Personality of the Year"; his program "Frost over England" wins the Golden Rose of Montreux Twiggy, a Brit. model, takes U.S. fashion by storm "Damascus" wins the Preakness and Belmont Stakes Jimmy Foxx, baseball player, d. *(contd)*	**1967**

	A. HISTORY, POLITICS	B. LITERATURE, THEATER	C. RELIGION, PHILOSOPHY, LEARNING
1967 contd	Lincoln Memorial, Washington, D.C. The Shah of Iran crowns himself and his wife, Empress Farah, at Teheran King Constantine and his family flee from Greece to Rome after failing to overthrow military government President Johnson appoints Thurgood Marshall to the Supreme Court 25th Amendment to the U.S. Constitution is ratified; it provides for presidential appointment of vice president if that position is vacated and for appointment of the vice president as acting president in the event of an inability of the president to perform his duties Martin Luther King leads anti-Vietnam war march in New York; another protest march takes place in San Francisco Negro riots in Cleveland, Newark, and Detroit	Margaret Irwin, Eng. novelist, d. (b. 1889) Margaret Kennedy, Eng. author, d. (b. 1896) Bert Lahr d. (b. 1895) Vivien Leigh, Eng. actress, d. (b. 1913) André Maurois, Fr. author, d. (b. 1885) John Masefield, Eng. poet, d. (b. 1878) Carson McCullers d. (b. 1917) Paul Muni, U.S. actor, d. (b. 1895) Dorothy Parker, U.S. writer, d. (b. 1893) Claude Rains, Anglo-Amer. actor, d. (b. 1890) Basil Rathbone, U.S. actor, d. (b. 1892) Elmer Rice, U.S. author, d. (b. 1892) Carl Sandburg, U.S. poet, d. (b. 1878) Siegfried Sassoon, Eng. writer, d. (b. 1886) Spencer Tracy, U.S. actor, d. (b. 1900) Anton Walbrook, Aust.-Brit. actor, d. (b. 1900)	Auserve: "Vie et mort de Giraudoux"
1968	U.S. Navy intelligence ship, "Pueblo," is captured by N. Korea on charge of violation of N. Korean waters; her crew is finally released in Dec. upon admission by U.S., instantly repudiated, that violation of waters took place Alexander Dubcek named First Secretary of Czechoslovak Communist Party Talks between Israeli Prime Minister Eshkol and U.S. President Johnson Israel and the U.A.R. agree to general exchange of prisoners of war Protests in Warsaw against governmental interference in cultural affairs Brit. colony Mauritius becomes independent state within Commonwealth Brit. Foreign Secretary George Brown resigns; succeeded by Michael Stewart Senator Robert F. Kennedy announces his candidacy for Democratic presidential nomination Antonin Novotny forced to resign as President of Czechoslovakia; succeeded by Gen. Ludwik Svoboda President Johnson announces that he will not seek another term Rev. Martin Luther King, Jr., leader of Negro civil rights movement and winner of 1964 Nobel Peace Prize, is assassinated in a Memphis motel; Scotland Yard arrests James Earl Ray in London; he is extradited to U.S. to stand trial "Action Program" with freedom of press and expression of minority views issued in Czechoslovakia by First Secretary Dubcek Pierre Elliott Trudeau sworn in as Canadian Prime Minister King Olav V of Norway on state visit in Washington, D.C. Student rioting in Paris De Gaulle arrives on state visit to Rumania; returns to Paris and asks Fr. nation to give him a personal vote of confidence *(contd)*	Nobel Prize for Literature: Yasunari Rawabata (Jap.) Charles Portis: "True Grit" Meyer Levin: "Gore and Igor" Richard Bradford: "Red Sky at Morning" S. N. Behrman: "The Burning Glass" Peter Beagle: "The Last Unicorn" John Updike: "Couples" Phyllis McGinley: "Wonders and Surprises," verse anthology Arthur Hailey: "Airport" George E. Condon: "Laughter from the Rafters" Kingsley Amis: "I Want It Now" John Braine: "The Crying Game" Paul Morand: "Monplaisir" Roger Peyrefitte: "Les Américains" Marguerite Yourcenar: "L'Oeuvre au noir" Bernard Clavel: "Les Fruits de l'hiver," awarded Prix Goncourt Montherlant: "La Rose de sable" Simone de Beauvoir: "La femme rompue" Françoise Sagan: "La Garde du coeur" Gunter Eich: "Maulwürfe" John Hersey: "The Algiers Motel Incident" C. Day Lewis appointed Eng. poet laureate Adam Smith: "The Money Game" Frederick Rolfe: "Hadrian VII" Gore Vidal: "Myra Breckinridge" Peter Weiss: "Vietnam Diskurs" Tom Wolfe: "The Electric Kool-Aid Acid Test" Aleksei Arbusov: "Confession at Night" William Douglas-Home: "The Secretary Bird" Enid Bagnold: "Call Me Jacky" Matt Crowley: "The Boys in the Band" *(contd)*	Worldwide confusion in university life created by student unrest Sabatino Moscati: "The World of the Phoenicians" R. W. Stallman: "Stephen Crane," biography Walter S. Ross: "The Last Hero: Charles A. Lindbergh" John Kobler: "Luce, His Time, Life and Fortune" Will and Ariel Durant, authors of "The Story of Civilization," receive Pulitzer Prize for general nonfiction Han Suyin: "Birdless Summer" Edward H. Madden: "Civil Disobedience and Moral Law" Yehuda Leib Levin, chief rabbi of Moscow, visits *(contd)*

D. VISUAL ARTS	E. MUSIC	F. SCIENCE, TECHNOLOGY, GROWTH	G. DAILY LIFE	
Dorado" (Howard Hawks); "Accident" (Losey); "The Chelsea Girls" (Warhol); "Portrait of Jason" (Shirley Clarke); "La Prise de la pouvoir par Louis XIV" (Rossellini); "In the Heat of the Night," Academy Award; "Guess Who's Coming to Dinner" (K. Hepburn, S. Tracy); "The Taming of the Shrew" (Schlesinger) Jayne Mansfield, U.S. film actress, d. (b. 1933) G. W. Pabst, Ger. film director, d. (b. 1885)	operatic soprano, d. (b. 1882) Woody Guthrie, Amer. folk singer, d. (b. 1912) Zoltán Kodály, Hungarian composer, d. (b. 1882) Sir Malcolm Sargent, Eng. conductor, d. (b. 1895) Paul Whiteman, U.S. "King of Jazz," d. (b. 1890) Alexander Goehr: "Arden muss sterben," opera, Hamburg Herbert von Karajan begins his Easter Music Festival at Salzburg, Austria Victor de Sabata, Ital. conductor, d. (b. 1892) J. Masteroff, J. Kander, and F. Ebb: "Cabaret," musical, opens in New York	Parkinson's disease U.S. has 74 nuclear-powered submarines in commission Seven new mesons are discovered (Cern, Geneva) Robert J. Van de Graaff, U.S. physicist, d. (b. 1901) H. J. Muller, U.S. geneticist, d. (b. 1890) Guggenheim Astronautical Award: J. E. Blamont (Fr.) Russia launches Luna 13 toward moon Desmond Morris: "The Naked Ape" U.S. manned space flights are suspended after death of three astronauts in fire on launching pad	"Intrepid," U.S. defender of America's Cup yachting trophy, defeats Australian "Dame Pattie" 4—0 Mrs. Billie Jean King wins almost every American and international tennis match open to women Lynda Bird Johnson, President Johnson's older daughter, marries marine Capt. Charles Robb St. Louis (NL) defeats Boston (AL) 4—3 to win World Series For the third consecutive year and the sixth time in eight years, the Green Bay Packers, coached by Vince Lombardi, win the National Football League National Conference championship, then go on to win NFL championship Purdue defeats Southern California 14—13 to win Rose Bowl football game Martha C. Webster lands a 410-pound blue shark at Rockport, Mass., to tie record of Richard C. Webster set in 1960, also at Rockport	**1967 contd**
U.S. architect R. Buckminster Fuller awarded Gold Medal by Royal Institute of Brit. Architects Tate Gallery, London: retrospective exhibition of Brit. sculptor Barbara Hepworth's 40-year career (April—May) Sotheby's of London sells 400 impressionist and modern pictures in three days (Apr.); highest price paid, £125,000 for Picasso's "La Pointe de la lite" The columns of the Parthenon in Athens in danger of collapsing as result of weathering and erosion of foundation Exhibition: "Dada, Surrealism and Their Heritage" at the Museum of Modern Art, New York Peter Arno, U.S. cartoonist, d. (b. 1904) Roy De Maistre, Australian painter, d. (b. 1894) René d'Harnoncourt, former director of the Museum of Modern Art, New York, d. (b. 1901) Marcel Duchamp, Fr.-Amer. *(contd)*	Oliver Knussen, 15-year-old Eng. schoolboy conducts first performance of his Symphony No. 1, London Symphony Orchestra Jerome Rosen: Concerto for Synket (electronic instrument) and Orchestra, Seattle Ital. composer Luciano Chailly appointed artistic director of La Scala, Milan Jean Louis Barrault produces "Carmen" at the Metropolitan Opera Robin Orr: "Full Circle," Scot. opera, Perth Angelo Musco: "Il gattopardo," opera, Palermo Laci Boldemann: "The Hour of Folly," Swed. opera, Malmö Gary Burton, 25-year-old jazz vibrophonist, popular Michael Stewart and John and Fran *(contd)*	58-year-old retired dentist Philip Blaiberg of Cape Town, S. Africa, becomes the third recipient of a transplanted heart; operation performed by Dr. Christiaan N. Barnard U.S. spacecraft Surveyor 7 lands successfully on the moon Two unmanned Soviet satellites find each other by radar while in earth orbit U.S. explodes experimental hydrogen bomb underground 100 miles northwest of Las Vegas Apollo 7 spacecraft with three astronauts aboard, launched from Cape Kennedy, Fla.; (11-day) orbiting flight with splash-down in Atlantic Ocean Intelsat 3A, first of new series of communication satellites, launched Apollo 8, with three astronauts aboard, *(contd)*	World production of wine in 1968: 269.3 million hectoliters A 28-million-year-old skull of an ape found by Elwyn L. Simons in the Fayyum region of the U.A.R. World heavyweight boxing championship in dispute U.S. gross national product at almost $861 billion Brit. government abandons £55 million plan to build London's third airport at Stansted Bridge team Olympiad at Deauville, France, won again by Italy Eng. cricket team under M. C. Cowdrey wins W. Indies series Crimes of violence in the U.S. have increased 57 per cent since 1960 Hugh Porter (Brit.) wins world cycling championship, Rome Yearly Brit. market for prepared potatoes (French fries and mashed) amounts to approx £360 million Population of Europe (excluding U.S.S.R.) is 455 million people; (the Soviet Union, 239 million) 78 million TV sets in U.S.; 25 million in U.S.S.R.; 20.5 million in Japan; 19 million in Great Britain; 13.5 million in W. Germany; 10 million in France Mexico City Olympic Games host more than 6,000 competitors from 112 countries; Bob Beamon (U.S.) long-jumps 29 feet 2.5 inches; U.S. team takes 45 gold medals; the U.S.S.R. takes 29 *(contd)*	**1968**

	A. HISTORY, POLITICS	B. LITERATURE, THEATER	C. RELIGION, PHILOSOPHY, LEARNING

1968 contd

A. HISTORY, POLITICS

Senator Robert F. Kennedy assassinated in Los Angeles immediately after his victory speech upon winning the California Democratic primary; a Jordanian, Sirhan Sirhan, is arrested, charged, and, later, convicted of the crime

Queen Elizabeth II invests her eldest son, Prince Charles, with the Order of the Garter

Riots and police brutality and bullying mark the Democratic convention in Chicago; Hubert H. Humphrey wins the nomination

Leadership of Czech Communist Party wins endorsement of Central Committee for its policy of resisting pressure from U.S.S.R.; Soviet Union announces maneuvers under way in areas near Slovak border; Dubcek vows in radio address that Czechoslovakia will continue on the road it has chosen and that the country's sovereignty is not threatened; Yugoslav President Tito arrives in Prague to show his support for Czech liberation drive; Czechoslovakia invaded at night by Soviet and Warsaw-Pact troops; Dubcek arrested; U.S.S.R. justifies invasion, claiming the Czech government "had requested assistance"; National Assembly declares the country's invasion illegal and demands withdrawal; government guarantees all its people "personal security and freedom"; direct press censorship reestablished in Czechoslovakia; Dubcek appeals to nation not to provoke occupying forces; "Pravda" article appears on the "necessity" of protecting socialist countries from outside attacks; Czech leaders accede in Moscow to Soviet demands to abolish liberal policies and agree that foreign troops will stay indefinitely; Kosygin visits Prague; Czech and Slovak autonomy established within a two-state federation; anti-Soviet demonstrations held in Prague; Czechoslovak Defense Minister announces that all occupation troops will be withdrawn; summit meeting of Soviet and Czech leaders held in Kiev

Brit. Prime Minister Wilson and Rhodesian leader Ian Smith confer aboard Brit. warship "Fearless"; they fail to reach agreement

Brit. government restricts immigration from India, Pakistan, and the W. Indies

Richard M. Nixon, promising to end the Vietnam War, elected 37th President of the U.S. by the narrowest margin since 1912

Queen Elizabeth II on state visit to Brazil and Chile

Israeli Defense Minister Moshe Dayan meets president-elect in New York

Norman Thomas, one of the founders of the American Civil Liberties Union and six times (1928—1948) candidate for president of the U.S. on the Socialist Party ticket, d. (b. 1884)

B. LITERATURE, THEATER

Arthur Kopit: "Indians"

Peter Nichols: "Joe Egg"

Joe Orton: "Loot"

Giorgio Strehler resigns from Milan Piccolo

Howard Sackler: "The Great White Hope," Pulitzer Prize play (1969)

Edward Albee: "Box-Mao-Box"

Gerome Ragni and James Rado: "Hair"

Neil Simon: "Plaza Suite"

Muriel Spark: "The Primc of Miss Jean Brodie"

Russ. authors Galanskov, Ginsburg, and Dobrovolski sentenced to two-to-seven years' imprisonment; Vera Lashkova, one year

Tallulah Bankhead, U.S. actress, d. (b. 1903)

Max Brod, Aust. author, d. (b. 1884)

Edna Ferber, U.S. novelist, d. (b. 1885)

Dorothy Gish d. (b. 1898)

Giovanni Guareschi, Ital. author, d. (b. 1908)

Fanny Hurst, Amer. author, d. (b. 1889)

Howard Lindsay d. (b. 1889)

Sir Harold Nicolson, Eng. diplomat and author, d. (b. 1868)

Salvatore Quasimodo, Ital. poet, d. (b. 1901)

Conrad Richter d. (b. 1890)

Upton Sinclair d. (b. 1878)

Ruth St. Denis d. (b. 1878)

John Steinbeck d. (b. 1902)

Sir Donald Wolfit, Eng. actor-manager, d. (b. 1902)

Arnold Zweig, Ger. author, d. (b. 1887)

Leo Rosten: "The Joys of Yiddish"

C. RELIGION, PHILOSOPHY, LEARNING

New York

Ulster civil rights campaign leads to fighting between Protestants and Roman Catholics

Pope Paul VI: encyclical "Humanae Vitae" against all artificial means of contraception

Cardinal Augustin Bea d. (b. 1881)

Herbert Marcuse: "Psychoanalysis and Politics"

Helen Keller, U.S. blind and deaf educationist, d. (b. 1880)

Terence J. Cooke succeeds Francis Spellman as Catholic Archbishop of New York

Thomas Merton, Trappist monk and author, d. (b. 1915)

D. VISUAL ARTS

painter, d. (b. 1887)
Lucio Fontana, Ital. painter and sculptor, d. (b. 1899)
Foujita, Fr.-Jap. painter, d. (b. 1886)
John Heartfield, Ger. pioneer of photomontage, d. (b. 1891)
Kees Van Dongen, Dutch-Fr. painter, d. (b. 1877)
Wassenaar Bonies: "Red-White Blue 68" Dutch abstract painting
Light show at the Whitney Museum, New York
Eero Saarinen: Gateway Arch in St. Louis, Mo., is dedicated
Valerie Solanis, an actress in one of his films, shoots and wounds Andy Warhol
Norton Simon pays $1.55 million for "Le Pont des Arts," by Renoir
Films: "The Thomas Crown Affair" (Jewison); "Star!" (Julie Andrews); "Funny Girl" (Streisand); "The Odd Couple" (Lemmon, Matthau); "In Cold Blood" (Richard Brook); "The Comedians" (Peter Glenville); "The Lion in Winter" (K. Hepburn, O'Toole); "Je t'aime, Je t'aime" (Resnais); "2001: A Space Odyssey" (Kubrick); "Oliver!" Academy Award (Sir Carol Reed)
Anthony Asquith d. (b. 1902)
Carl Dreyer, Dan. film director, d. (b. 1889)
Dan Duryea d. (b. 1906)
Lilian Harvey, Ger. film star, d. (b. 1907)
Mae Marsh d. (b. 1895)
Franchot Tone d. (b. 1905)
Walter Wanger, U.S. film producer, d. (b. 1894)
Mickey Mouse celebrates his 40th birthday

E. MUSIC

Pascal: "George M!"
Popular songs: "Congratulations"; "Cinderella Rockefella"; "Hey Jude"; "Mrs. Robinson"; "Stoned Soul Picnic"
Harold Kreutzberg, Ger. dancer and choreographer, d. (b. 1902)
Mathilda Kchessinska, former prima ballerina assoluta of the Russian Imperial Ballet, celebrates her 96th birthday, Dame Adeline Genee her 90th, and Dame Marie Rambert her 80th
Michael Carr, Eng. pop-song composer, d. (b. 1904)
Joseph Keilberth, Ger. conductor, d. (b. 1908)
Charles Münch, Fr. conductor, d. (b. 1891)
Ildebrando Pizzetti, Ital. composer, d. (b. 1880)
Tullio Serafin, Ital. conductor, d. (b. 1878)
Luigi Dallapiccola: "Odysseus," opera, Berlin
Hans Werner Henze: "Das Floss der Medusa," oratorio
Aretha Franklin ("soul" music) and Jimi Hendrix (hard rock music) compete for popularity

F. SCIENCE, TECHNOLOGY, GROWTH

launched on flight to the moon, orbits the moon and splashes down in Pacific Ocean
Pulsating radio sources (Pulsars) discovered by Hewish and Bell, Mullard Observatory, Cambridge, England
Sir Bernard Lovell: "The Story of Jodrell Bank"
James D. Watson: "The Double Helix"
"The Second Ten Years of the World Health Organization" traces achievements and difficulties of WHO in last decade
Chester Carlson, inventor of xerography, d. (b. 1906)
Sir Henry H. Dale, Brit. physiologist, d. (b. 1878)
Yuri A. Gagarin, Soviet cosmonaut, d. (b. 1934)
Otto Hahn, Ger. nuclear chemist, d. (b. 1879)
Lev D. Landau, Soviet physicist, d. (b. 1908)
Charles Mayo of the Mayo Clinic, Rochester, N.Y., d. (b. 1898)
Lise Meitner, Aust. scientist, d. (b. 1878)
Benjamin Masar (Jerusalem University) discovers foundations of the Temple of Herod, destroyed 70 A.D.

G. DAILY LIFE

U.S. takes Davis Cup (tennis) away from Australia for the first time since 1963
Mrs. Jacqueline Kennedy marries Aristotle S. Onassis
Thomas Bridges, U.S. baseball player, d. (b. 1906)
Randolph Churchill, Brit. author and politician, d. (b. 1911)
James Clark, Scot. car racing champion, d. (b. 1936)
George Hackenschmidt, Brit. wrestler, d. (b. 1877)
Princess Marina, the former Duchess of Kent, d. (b. 1906)
Jess Willard d. (b. 1882)
Aswan Dam (Egypt) completed
Earthquake strikes Iran, killing 12,000
Between Aug. and Oct. some 27,000 Czech refugees enter Austria
The "midi" fails to replace the "mini"
Harold Gray, creator of the comic strip "Little Orphan Annie," d. (b. 1893)
R. Dirks, creator of the comic strip "The Katzenjammer Kids," d. (b. 1876)
Julie Nixon, daughter of the president-elect, weds Dwight David Eisenhower, grandson of the former president
Southern California defeats Indiana, 14—3, to win the Rose Bowl football game
Figure skater Peggy Fleming wins the only U.S. gold medal at the Winter Olympics
"Forward Pass" is named the winner of the Kentucky Derby when "Dancer's Image" is disqualified; "Forward Pass" wins the Preakness Stakes
Lee Trevino defeats Jack Nicklaus to win the U.S. Open golf championship
Julius Boros wins the Professional Golf Association championship, defeating Arnold Palmer
Detroit (AL) defeats St. Louis (NL) 4—3 to win the World Series
An Atlantic blue marlin weighing 845 pounds is caught by E. J. Fishman at St. Thomas, Virgin Islands

	A. HISTORY, POLITICS	B. LITERATURE, THEATER	C. RELIGION, PHILOSOPHY, LEARNING
1969	New Czech federal government inaugurated Violent fighting in Northern Ireland between Protestants and Roman Catholics Sirhan Sirhan tried and convicted of the murder of Senator Robert Kennedy Jan Palach, a Czech student, publicly burns himself to death in Prague in protest against Soviet occupation Richard M. Nixon inaugurated as 37th President of the U.S. De Gaulle states he will serve full presidential term London School of Economics and Political Science closes for several weeks because of student disorders Red Cross flies relief airlifts into Biafra Al Fatah leader Yasir Arafat elected Chairman of Executive Committee of Palestine Liberation Organization; shifts his main guerrilla forces to Jordan; Arab terrorist bomb explodes in Jerusalem supermarket Caribbean island of Anguilla votes to break all ties with Britain Levi Eshkol, Israeli Prime Minister, d. (b. 1895) Nixon makes eight-day tour of western Europe Gustav Heinemann elected President of W. Germany James Earl Ray sentenced to 99 years in prison for assassination of Rev. Martin Luther King, Jr. Mrs. Golda Meir becomes Israel's fourth Prime Minister Pakistani President Ayub Khan resigns and is succeeded by Aga Muhammad Yahya Khan The "Chicago Eight," indicted for violating the antiriot clause of the Civil Rights Act in connection with the demonstrations during the 1968 Democratic convention in that city, are found not guilty after boisterous trial Dwight D. Eisenhower d. (b. 1890) Alexander Dubcek sacked as Czechoslovak Communist Party First Secretary De Gaulle resigns as President of France James Chichester-Clark succeeds Terence O'Neill as Prime Minister of Northern Ireland New Party guidelines established in Czechoslovakia, based on strict Marxist-Leninist principles Nixon meets S. Vietnamese President Thieu on Midway Island U.S. and Japan agree on the return to Japan of the Ryukyu Islands (including Okinawa) in 1972 Brit. Conservative M.P. Enoch Powell proposes that the government finance the repatriation of Black and Asian residents Franz von Papen, Ger. politician, d. (b. 1879) Georges Pompidou elected President of France Queen Elizabeth II invests Prince Charles at Caernarvon Castle as Prince of Wales First U.S. troops withdrawn from Vietnam; by the end of the year, 75,000 have been sent home Senator Edward Kennedy, driving a car at Chappaquiddick Island, Mass., plunges into a pond; body of woman passenger Mary Jo Kopechne found in car Pope Paul VI meets Nigerian and Biafran representatives in Uganda Ho Chi Minh, President of N. Vietnam, d. (b. ?1892) Golda Meir and Nixon meet in Washington, D.C. Dubcek dropped from Czechoslovak Communist Party Central Committee Brit. army sends 600 troops into Belfast to quell rioting Willy Brandt elected Chancellor of W. Germany; revalues the mark Hundreds of thousands of people in several U.S. cities demonstrate their protests against war in Vietnam More than 100 U.S. combat deaths reported in one week in *(contd)*	Philip Roth: "Portnoy's Complaint" Mario Puzo: "The Godfather" Lillian Hellman: "An Unfinished Woman," autobiography "Penelope Ashe": "Naked Came the Stranger" (written as a jest by 24 journalists from a Long Island, N. Y., newspaper) Leonard Woolf: "The Journey Not the Arrival Matters" Henry Williamson: "The Gale of the World" (15th and last novel of the "Chronicle of the Ancient Sunlight") J. P. Donleavy: "The Beastly Beatitudes of Balthazar B." William Trevor: "Mrs. Eckdorf in O'Neill's Hotel" Nathalie Sarraute: "Entre la vie et la mort" P. Bourgeade: "New York Party," novel Anna Seghers: "Das Vertrauen" Siegfried Lenz: "Deutschstunde" Alberto Moravia: "La vita è gioco" John Mason Brown, U.S. critic, d. (b. 1900) Gabriel Chevalier, Fr. novelist, d. (b. 1895) Ivy Compton-Burnett, Eng. novelist, d. (b. 1892) Judy Garland d. (b. 1922) Boris Karloff, Brit.-Amer. actor, d. (b. 1887) Jack Kerouac d. (b. 1922) Erika Mann, Ger. writer, daughter of Thomas Mann, d. (b. 1905) Eric Portman, Eng. actor, d. (b. 1903) Stephen Potter, Eng. humorist, d. (b. 1900) Sir Osbert Sitwell, Eng. author, d. (b. 1892) Robert Taylor, Amer. film actor, d. (b. 1911) B. Traven, Ger.-Amer. writer, d. (b. 1900) Jay Richard Kennedy: "The Chairman" (appears first as a film, then as a paperback, and finally in hardcover) Harold Robbins receives a $2.5 million advance for his novel "The Inheritor" Joe Orton: "What the Butler Saw," play (posth.) George Hulme: "The Lionel Touch" Félicien Marceau: "Le Babour" Agatha Christie's play "The Mousetrap" celebrates its 7,000th performance at London's Ambassadors Theatre; enters its 18th year New York sex revue "Oh! Calcutta!" Nobel Prize for Literature: Samuel Beckett Soviet novelist Alexander Solzhenitsyn expelled from Soviet Writers' Union *(contd)*	René Dubos: "So Human an Animal," Pulitzer Prize nonfiction Alain Ollivier: "Otton III, empereur de l'an mille" R. R. Betts: "Essays in Czech History" (posth.) Lady Antonia Fraser: "Mary, Queen of Scots" Ragnhild Hatton: "Europe in the Age of Louis XIV" R. F. Delderfield: "Imperial Sunset" G. Roux: "Napoleon III" Carlos Baker: "Ernest Hemingway; a Life Story" Dean Acheson: "Present at the Creation, My Years at the State Department," Pulitzer Prize history Theodore H. White: "The Making of the President 1968" Joe McGinniss: "The Selling of the President 1968" William L. Shirer: "The Collapse of the Third Republic" Cecil Harmsworth King: "Strictly Personal" Harold Macmillan: "Tides of Fortune" H. Montgomery-Hyde: "Henry James at Home" Pope Paul VI names 33 new cardinals and eliminates over 200 saints from the liturgical calendar Karl Jaspers, Ger. philosopher, d. (b. 1883) Kingsley Martin, Eng. journalist, d. (b. 1897) Theodor W. Adorno, Ger. philosopher and musicologist, d. (b. 1903) Hedwig and Max Born: "The Luxury of Conscience" Robert D. Cumming: "Human Nature and History" Louis O. Mink: "Mind, History and Dialectic" Debabrata Sinha: "Phenomenology" Sir Allen Lane, founder of Penguin Books, retires after 50 years in publishing Gallup Poll shows that 70 per cent of those questioned feel that the influence of religion is declining in the U.S.

1969

D. VISUAL ARTS

Museum of Modern Art, New York, purchases art collection of the late Gertrude Stein for $6 million

Walter Gropius, Ger. architect, d. (b. 1883)

Boston's new city hall designed by Kallmann, McKinnell, and Knowles

Ben Shahn d. (b. 1898)

300th anniversary of the death of Rembrandt

200th anniversary of the founding of the Royal Academy, London

A self-portrait by Rembrandt sold at Christie's, London, for $1,256,000, a ceiling painting by Tiepolo for $1,063,400

Sir William Russell Flint, Brit. painter, d. (b. 1880)

Ludwig Mies van der Rohe, Ger.-Amer. architect, d. (b. 1886)

Films: "Midnight Cowboy," Academy Award; "Justine" (Cukor); "MacKenna's Gold" (Foreman); "Easy Rider" (Hopper); "Bullitt" (Yates); "If" (Lindsay Anderson); "Battle of Britain" (Guy Hamilton); "Oh! What a Lovely War" (Attenborough); "Butch Cassidy and the Sundance Kid" (Hill); "Z"; "They Shoot Horses, Don't

(contd)

E. MUSIC

Stockhausen: "Stimmung" (for six voices)

Luciano Berio: "Sinfonia"

At the Musicki Biennale in Zagreb, Yugoslavia, 150 works by 120 composers from 24 countries are performed

Pierre Boulez conducts 16 concerts with the New York Philharmonic

Olivier Messiaen: "The Transfiguration," oratorio

Humphrey Searle: "Hamlet," opera, London

Panderecki: "The Devils of Loudun," opera, Hamburg

Malipiero: "Gli Eroi di Bonaventura," opera, Milan

Duke Ellington celebrates his 70th birthday; President Nixon presents him with Medal of Freedom

Woodstock Music and Art Fair, near Bethel, N.Y., attracts more than 300,000 enthusiasts

Mary Hopkin emerges as bright new singing star

Menotti: Triple Concerto

Dame Margot Fonteyn's 50th birthday

Schönberg's "Pelleas and Melisande" choreographed by Roland Pettit for Fonteyn and Nureyev, New York

Ernest Ansermet, Swiss conductor, d. (b. 1883)

Michael Tippett: "Knot Garden," opera, London

Wilhelm Backhaus, Swiss pianist, d. (b. 1884)

Irene Castle, U.S. dancer, d. (b. 1894)

Vernon Duke, U.S. composer, d. (b. 1903)

Amparo Iturbi, Span.-

(contd)

F. SCIENCE, TECHNOLOGY, GROWTH

The Concorde, Anglo-Fr. supersonic aircraft makes its first test flight

Apollo 10 astronauts bring lunar module within 9.4 miles of the moon's surface

Apollo 11, launched from Cape Kennedy, lands lunar module on the moon's surface July 20; Neil Armstrong steps out on the moon July 21, and Apollo 11 returns with its crew July 24

U.S. astronauts Charles Conrad and Alan L. Bean land on moon in Apollo 12 lunar module; return to Earth with samples of material from the lunar surface

Philip Blaiberg, who lived with a transplanted heart for 19 months, d.

Sadao Otani, U.S.-Jap. pathologist, d. (b. 1894)

C. F. Powell, Eng. physicist, d. (b. 1903)

Amos de Shalit, Israeli nuclear physicist, d. (b. 1927)

In Thailand a new species of swallow, the white-eyed river martin (Pseudochelidon sirintarae) is discovered

Lease sale in Alaska for oil fields brings in one single day the sum of $900,220,590

J. Weber of the University of Maryland observes gravitational waves, first postulated by Albert Einstein in 1916

U.S. government, heeding the results of laboratory experiments linking food additives to cancer, removes cyclamates from the market and limits use of monosodium glutamate

Two Mariner space probes send back pictures of surface of Mars

U.S. government takes steps to ban

(contd)

G. DAILY LIFE

"Saturday Evening Post," founded 1821, suspends publication

Suffragan Bishop Matthias Defregger, Munich, is identified as the subject of a Nazi war crimes investigation in Italy

Camille, the strongest hurricane to strike the U.S. since 1935, devastates Mississippi Gulf coast

Rains in California cause mud slides that destroy or damage 10,000 homes and kill 100

New York Mets defeat Baltimore Orioles 5—3 to win World Series

Joseph Patrick Kennedy, U.S. financier and father of the Kennedy brothers, d. (b. 1888)

Rocky Marciano, U.S. boxer, d. (b. 1924)

Ohio State wins Rose Bowl football game, defeating Southern California 27—16

George Archer wins the Masters golf tournament

Robert A. Rolfe, U.S. baseball player, d. (b. 1908)

1792 vintage wine auctioned at Christie's, London

General Motors recalls almost five million cars for adjustment of mechanical defects

Three Brit. boxing champions retire: heavyweight Henry Cooper, middleweight Johnny Pritchett, and featherweight Howard Winstone

18th Chess Olympiad in Lugano, Italy, won by U.S.S.R. team

Representatives of 39 nations meet in Rome to survey pollution of the seas

The Sydney-to-Hobart sailing race won by "Morning Cloud," owned and skippered by Edward Heath

Bandits hijack a trunk in Central London and escape with bullion worth £75,000

Brit. cycling champion Peter Buckley d. following a training accident

Inflation becomes a worldwide problem

Lillebaelt suspension bridge (Denmark) and Newport Bridge (U.S.) completed

Trouser outfits become acceptable for everyday wear by women

Bodies of actress Sharon Tate (wife of Roman Polanski) and four others found at her Los Angeles home; Charles Manson, leader of hippie commune nearby, indicted for the crime with several others

World and European amateur hockey titles won by U.S.S.R. in Stockholm

Annual sales of glass and glasswear in Britain total £172.2 million

Soviet spies Helen and Peter Kroger exchanged for Brit. lecturer Gerald Brooke

World population growing by about 2 per cent annually, estimated at 3.5 billion

Approx. 225 million telephones are in service all over the world, 114 million of them in the U.S.

Prince Philip maintains that Britain's royal family will have to ask Parliament to increase the queen's allowance

U.S. tennis team retains Davis Cup, defeating the Rumanians 5—0

Walter Hagen, Amer. golf champion, d. (b. 1892)

Off Cuttyhunk, Mass., E. J. Kirker lands a 72-pound striped bass; A. J. Bielevich, fishing off Isle of Shoals, Mass., catches a 98-pound 12-ounce oceanic bonito; G. D. Perez brings in a 1153-pound Pacific blue marlin near Guam

Boris Spassky defeats Tigran Petrosian to win the world chess championship

(contd)

A. HISTORY, POLITICS | **B. LITERATURE, THEATER** | **C. RELIGION, PHILOSOPHY, LEARNING**

1969 contd

A. History, Politics

Vietnam

U.S. Army Staff Sgt. David Mitchell and Lt. William Calley ordered to stand trial on murder charges for massacre of civilians at Mylai, Vietnam

John L. Lewis, Amer. labor leader, d. (b. 1880)

Abe Fortas, Supreme Court justice, resigns after disclosure of questionable dealings with convicted financier

President Nixon appoints Warren Burger Chief Justice of the Supreme Court

B. Literature, Theater

Günter Grass: "Ortlich Betaubt," Ger. novel

Michael Crichton: "The Andromeda Strain"

Kurt Vonnegut: "Slaughterhouse-Five"

Laurence Peter and Raymond Hall: "The Peter Principle"

Vladimir Nabokov: "Ada"

Jacqueline Susann: "The Love Machine"

Peter Maas: "The Valachi Papers"

Gay Talese: "The Kingdom and the Power"

Norman Mailer: "Armies of the Night," Pulitzer Prize nonfiction

1970

A. History, Politics

Biafra capitulates to federal Nigerian government; end of civil war which began 2.5 years ago

Albania and the People's Republic of China conclude a trade agreement

Wilson and Nixon meet in Washington, D.C.

President Pompidou of France visits Washington

Dubcek becomes Czechoslovak ambassador to Turkey; later suspended from Communist Party membership and dismissed from his post

Gambia proclaimed a republic within Brit. Commonwealth

General Election in Britain won by Conservative Party; Edward Heath succeeds Harold Wilson as prime minister

Israel and the U.A.R. agree to a 99-day truce along Suez Canal

U.S.S.R. and W. Germany sign a friendship treaty in Moscow

King Hussein of Jordan escapes assassination attempt in Amman

Arab commandos hijack three jets bound for New York from Europe

U.S. strength in Vietnam is reduced to below 400,000 men

Student protests against Vietnam War result in killing of four by the National Guard at Kent State University in Ohio

Yugoslav President Tito announces that he will be succeeded by a collective leadership

Gamal Abdel Nasser d. (b. 1918)

Golda Meir visits London

Haile Selassie embarks on his first official visit to Italy since the Ital. takeover of Ethiopia in 1935

(contd)

B. Literature, Theater

Nobel Prize for Literature: Soviet novelist Alexander Solzhenitsyn

Maggie Smith, Eng. actress (b. 1934), emerges as a stage and film personality

Saul Bellow: "Mr. Sammler's Planet"

Eudora Welty: "Losing Battles"

Thomas Berger: "Vital Parts"

Ernest Hemingway: "Islands in a Stream" (posth.)

Philip Kunhardt: "My Father's House"

William Saroyan: "Days of Life and Death and Escape to the Moon"

William Meredith: "Earth Walk," poems

Iris Murdoch: "A Fairly Honorable Defeat"

Michael Arlen: "The Exiles"

Muriel Spark: "The Driver's Seat"

C. P. Snow: "Last Things" (the 11th and concluding volume of "Strangers and Brothers")

Pamela Hansford-Johnson: "The Honors Board"

Storm Jameson: "Parthian Words," a survey of the present state of fiction

Romain Gary: "Chien blanc"

Michel Tournier: "Le Roi Des Aulnes," wins Prix Goncourt

F. Nourissier: "La Crève Femina"

Zoë Oldenburg: "La Joie des pauvres"

Peter Weiss: "Trotzky im Exil," Ger. drama

Rolf Hochhuth: "Guerrillas"

Galsworthy's "Forsyte Saga," televised by the BBC, gains worldwide popularity

Christopher Hampton: "The Philanthropist"

David Mercer: "Flint"

Ronald Millar: "Abelard and Heloise"

Peter Schaffer: "The Battle of Shrivings"

Antony Schaffer: "Sleuth"

Robert Bolt: "Vivat! Vivat Regina!"

William Douglas-Home: "The Jockey Club Stakes"

Ionesco: "Jeux de massacre"

John Mortimer: "A Voyage Round My Father,"

(contd)

C. Religion, Philosophy, Learning

Fifth centenary of the birth of Erasmus of Rotterdam

Roland Bainton: "Erasmus of Christendom"

Miles Copeland: "The Game of Nations"

Jon Kimche: "The Second Arab Awakening"

George Christian: "The President Steps Down"

James MacGregor Burns: "Roosevelt, the Soldier of Freedom 1940—1945," Pulitzer Prize (1971)

Theodore Roszak: "The Making of a Counter-Culture"

Angus Wilson: "The World of Charles Dickens"

Christopher Hill: "God's Englishman"

Anthony Grey: "Hostage in Peking"

Charles de Gaulle: "Mémoires d'espoir"

A. J. Ayer: "Metaphysics and Common Sense"

Eliot Deutsch: "Between Philosophy and History"

R. Klibansky: "Contemporary Philosophy, a Survey"

"Life" magazine serializes what are purportedly the authentic reminiscences of former Soviet Premier Nikita S. Khrushchev

In Mont El Dore, Guatemala, archaeologists unearth a

(contd)

D. VISUAL ARTS	E. MUSIC	F. SCIENCE, TECHNOLOGY, GROWTH	G. DAILY LIFE	
They?" (Jane Fonda); "Satyricon" (Fellini); "Isadora" (Vanessa Redgrave); "M A S H" (Robert Altman); "Women in Love" (Ken Russell) Lilian Gish: "The Movies, Mr. Griffith and Me," autobiography Leo McCarey, U.S. film director, d. (b. 1898) Nicholas M. Schenck, U.S. film executive, d. (b. 1881) Josef von Sternberg, U.S. film director, d. (b. 1894)	Amer. pianist, d. (b. 1899) Giovanni Martinelli, Ital.-Amer. operatic singer, d. (b. 1885) Gladys Swarthout, U.S. operatic mezzo-soprano, d. (b. 1904) Frank Loesser, U.S. composer, d. (b. 1910) Popular songs: "A Boy Named Sue"; "Hair"; "Aquarius"; "In the Year 2525" "1776," musical based on signing of Declaration of Independence Katherine Hepburn in "Coco," musical, New York City Menotti: "Help! Help! The Globolinks!," opera, Santa Fe, N. Mex.	use of the insecticide DDT Nobel Prize for Economic Science: R. Frisch (Norw.) and Niko Tinbergen (Dutch) for their development of econometrics Nobel Prize for Physics: Murray Gell-Mann (U.S.) for work on the theory of elementary particles Nobel Prize for Medicine and Physiology: M. Delbrück, A. D. Hershey, and S. E. Luria (all U.S.) for work on the genetic structure of viruses	The Montreal Canadiens win the Stanley Cup hockey championship For the fourth year in a row–and for the eighth year out of the past 10–Wilt "The Stilt" Chamberlain leads as the rebound leader in the National Basketball Association; Chamberlain also holds most of the other NBA records Rod Laver, 31, wins Grand Slam of tennis for second time "Majestic Prince," Willie Hartack up, wins the Preakness Stakes and the Kentucky Derby Lew Alcindor emerges as one of the greatest stars of basketball, playing for UCLA Professional Golfing Association names Orville Moody "Golfer of the Year" after his winning of the U.S. Open Westbrook Pegler, Amer. journalist, d. (b. 1894)	**1969 contd**
Ada Louise Huxtable wins Pulitzer Prize for criticism Minoru Takeyama designs Tokyo's new department store Ichi-Ban-Kan Henri Matisse exhibition at Grand Palais, Paris Giacometti's bronze "Femme de Venise" sold at Parke-Bernet, New York, for $150,000 Works of art, valued at over £25 million, sold during 1969—70 season at Sotheby's, London Velázquez's portrait of Juan de Paraja sold at Christie's in London for $5,540,000 Mark Rothko, Amer. painter, d. (b. 1903) *(contd)*	Burt Bacharach (b. 1929) emerges as a personality in the realm of popular music (two Academy Awards: for the musical score of "Butch Cassidy and the Sundance Kid" and the song "Raindrops Keep Falling on My Head") Mikis Theodorakis (b. 1925), Greek composer, arrested and rearrested in Greece for his political activities since 1964, lands at Paris The New York City Ballet marks its 500th performance of Tchaikovsky's "Nutcracker" Sir Frederick Ashton retires as artistic director of the Royal Ballet and is succeeded by Kenneth MacMillan and John Field Pablo Casals (b. 1876) conducts a rehearsal of an all-cello ensemble in his honor at New York's Philharmonic Hall Klemperer conducts Mahler's "Lied von der Erde" at his 85th-birthday concert Kripps conducts William Walton's "Improvisations on an Impromptu of *(contd)*	Apollo 13 launched from Cape Kennedy 448 U.S. universities and colleges are closed or on strike The first complete synthesis of a gene announced by scientists at the University of Wisconsin Luna 16, unmanned Soviet spacecraft, returns from moon with rock samples; Luna 17 lands a self-propelled eight-wheel vehicle on the moon Venera 7, unmanned Soviet spacecraft, lands on Venus P. I. Belyayev, U.S.S.R. astronaut, d. (b. 1925) Hans Kronberger, Brit. physicist, d. (b. 1920) A. I. Mikoyan, Soviet aircraft designer, d. (b. 1905) O. H. Warburg, Ger. physiologist and biochemist, d. (b. 1883) *(contd)*	Price of gold on the free market falls below official price of $35 an ounce Japan World Exhibition, Expo 70, opens in Osaka Brazil defeats Italy, 4—1, and wins the ninth World Cup soccer championship in Mexico City Baltimore Orioles (AL) defeat Cincinnati Reds (NL) to win World Series 4—1 Stanley Benham, U.S. bobsled champion, d. (b. 1913) Lilian Board, Brit. Olympic athlete, d. (b. 1948) Heinrich Brüning, Ger. Chancellor 1930—1932, d. (b. 1885) Edouard Daladier, Fr. politician, d. (b. 1884) A. F. Kerenski, Russ. politician, d. (b. 1881) Ted Lewis, Brit. boxer, d. (b. 1894) Ian Macleod, Brit. politician, d. (b. 1913) Peter II, ex-King of Yugoslavia, d. (b. 1923) Jochen Rindt, Aust. racing driver, d. (b. 1942) James Bouton: "Ball Four" (best seller about baseball) Joe Frazier of Philadelphia becomes official world heavyweight boxing champion Cancellation of S. African cricket tour of England World cycling championship race held in Leicester, England, won by Hugh Porter of Great Britain Dance hall fire in Saint-Laurent-du-Pont, France, kills 146 young people Tony Jacklin becomes the first Brit. golfer to win U.S. Open championship in 50 years World crude steel production in 1970 reaches 595 million metric tons World's most valuable stamp, the 1856 Brit. Guiana one cent, sold at a New York auction for $280,000 The world bear market in the U.S. in eight years touches bottom; Dow-Jones industrial average drops to 631 *(contd)*	**1970**

	A. HISTORY, POLITICS	B. LITERATURE, THEATER	C. RELIGION, PHILOSOPHY, LEARNING
1970 contd	De Gaulle d. (b. 1890) Assassination attempt on Pope Paul VI in the Philippines Gomulka, Pol. Communist Party First Secretary, resigns after 14 years in office Paris peace talks end their second full year without progress toward peace in Vietnam Salvador Allende, a Marxist, is elected President of Chile President Nixon appoints Harry A. Blackmun to the Supreme Court Walter P. Reuther, Amer. labor leader, d. (b. 1907)	biographical play David Storey: "Home" Neil Simon: "Last of the Red Hot Lovers" S. Y. Agnon, Israeli novelist, d. (b. 1888) Billie Burke, U.S. actress, d. (b. 1886) John Dos Passos, U.S. novelist, d. (b. 1896) E. M. Forster, Eng. novelist, d. (b. 1879) Erle Stanley Gardner, Amer. writer, creator of "Perry Mason," d. (b. 1889) Francis Parkinson Keyes, Amer. writer, d. (b. 1885) Gypsy Rose Lee, Amer. dancer and writer, d. (b. 1914) François Mauriac, Fr. author, d. (b. 1885) John O'Hara, Amer. author, d. (b. 1905) Erich Maria Remarque, Ger.-Amer. novelist, d. (b. 1898) Max Lincoln Schuster, U.S. publisher, d. (b. 1897) Nelly Sachs, Ger. poet, d. (b. 1891) Louise Bogan, Amer. poet, d. (b. 1897) Jean Giono, Fr. novelist, d. (b. 1895)	five-foot Buddha-like statue, estimated to date from 700—300 B.C. Pope Paul VI declares priestly celibacy to be a fundamental principle of the Roman Catholic Church Roman Catholic and Jewish leaders confer in Rome Rudolf Carnap, U.S. philosopher, d. (b. 1891) Cardinal Richard Cushing, Archbishop of Boston, d. (b. 1895) John Gunther, journalist and author, d. (b. 1901) Bertrand Russell d. (b. 1872) Hjalmar Schacht, Ger. financier and politician, d. (b. 1877) Joseph Wood Krutch, Amer. critic and essayist, d. (b. 1893)
1971	U.S. planes bomb Vietcong supply routes in Cambodia; fighting in Indochina spreads to Laos and Cambodia; U.S. conducts large-scale bombing raids against N. Vietnam Canada and the People's Republic of China exchange diplomatic envoys; Mainland China hosts the U.S. table tennis team, beginning a new era of U.S.-Chin. détente; Henry Kissinger secretly visits China to arrange Nixon visit; Mainland China admitted to the UN Maj.-Gen. Idi Amin establishes himself as Ugandan strongman Women granted right to vote in Switzerland Whitney Young, Amer. civil rights leader, d. (b. 1922) *(contd)*	"No, No, Nanette" revival; Burt Shevelove director Gilbert M. ("Bronco Billy") Anderson, actor who made his screen debut in "The Great Train Robbery," d. (b. 1883) St. John Ervine, Eng. playwright, author, and critic, d. (b. 1884) Erich Segal: "Love Story," novel Tyrone Guthrie, Eng. author, director, and producer, d. (b. 1901) Alexander I. Solzhenitsyn: "August 1914," novel (circulated secretly in U.S.S.R.) Sylvia Plath: "The Bell Jar," *(contd)*	Gyorgy Lukacs, Hungarian Marxist philosopher, d. (b. 1885) A synod of Roman Catholic bishops, meeting in Rome, reaffirms the role of celibacy for the clergy The Church of England and the Roman Catholic Church end a 400-year-old dispute when they agree on a definition of the "essential meaning of the Eucharist" John Marshall Harlan, Amer. jurist, d. (b. 1899) *(contd)*

D. VISUAL ARTS	E. MUSIC	F. SCIENCE, TECHNOLOGY, GROWTH	G. DAILY LIFE	
Reuben L. Goldberg ("Rube"), U.S. cartoonist, d. (b. 1883) Films: "Catch-22" (Mike Nichols); "Paint Your Wagon" (Joshua Logan); "True Grit" (John Wayne); "Topaz" (Hitchcock); "Woodstock" (Wadleigh) Boris Karloff: "The Man with Nine Lives," autobiography U.S. actor Elliot Gould emerges as most successful film star of the year Almost all the great old Hollywood companies are being taken over by conglomerates	Benjamin Britten," San Francisco Eugene Ormandy conducts the first U.S. performance of Shostakovich's Symphony No. 13, Philadelphia Benjamin Britten conducts the first Eng. performance of Shostakovich's Symphony No. 14 Hans Werner Henze: "El Cimarron," Aldeburgh "Waldmärchen," first part of Mahler's "Das Klagende Lied," London Duke Ellington gives a concert of sacred music at the Saint-Sulpice Church in Harlem, New York City Musical plays on Broadway: "Company" (Sondheim); "Applause" (with Lauren Bacall) Sir John Barbirolli d. (b. 1899) Dame Adeline Genee, Dan.-born ballerina, d. (b. 1878) Alfred Newman, prolific composer of film scores, d. (b. 1901) George Szell, Aust.-Amer. conductor, d. (b. 1897) Kerstin Thorborg, Swed. opera singer, d. (b. 1896)	James Finley of St. Paul, Minn., sues federal government for $500,000 in damages after treatment in a veterans' hospital changes his skin color from black to white In France and Britain nuclear-powered heart pacemakers are successfully implanted in three patients to correct a condition called "heart block" The 150-inch reflecting telescope at Kitt Peak Observatory, Tucson, Ariz., and the 150-inch instrument at the Inter-American Observatory, Cerro Tololo, Chile, are completed	TV sets in use throughout the world estimated at 231 million The U.S. Open Tennis Championship at Forest Hills, N. Y., awards a record $160,000 in prize money; Margaret Smith Court (Australian) wins Grand Slam of Women's tennis The United Kingdom £50 travel allowance replaced by an allocation of £300 per person per trip U.S. census shows smallest number of men (94.8) in ratio to women (100) in history Cyclones and floods kill 500,000 in E. Pakistan; 30,000 die in earthquakes, floods, and landslides in Peru U.S. tennis team defeats W. Germany 5—0 to win the Davis Cup Ken Rosewall of Australia wins the U.S. Lawn Tennis Association Men's Singles championship Billy Casper wins the Masters The Boston Bruins win the Stanley Cup hockey championship Southern California wins the Rose Bowl football game over Michigan, 10—3 Baltimore defeats Dallas to win the National Football League championship; winners' share is $15,000 per player, losers' $7,500 World populations: People's Republic of China, 760 million; India, 550 million; U.S.S.R., 243 million; U.S., 205 million. U.S. has population of 85 people per sq. mi.; China, 305/sq. mi.; India, 655/sq. mi.; Japan, 1,083/sq. mi. Hospital care costs in U.S. reach average of $81 per patient per day, $664.28 per average patient-stay U.S. yacht "Intrepid" defeats Australian "Gretel II" 4—1 to win the America's Cup At Great Bear Lake, Canada, L. Daunis catches a 65-pound lake trout; D. R. White lands a 42-pound 2-ounce rainbow trout at Bell Island, Alas.; J. B. Penwarden lands a mako shark weighing 1,061 pounds at Mayor Island, New Zealand; a record bluefin tuna weighing 1,065 pounds is caught off Cape Breton, Nova Scotia, by R. G. Gibson	**1970 contd**
Rockwell Kent, painter, d. (b. 1883) Harold Lloyd, Amer. film star of the 1920s, d. (b. 1894) Paul Terry, creator of "Mighty Mouse" and other cartoon characters, d. (b. 1887) Kennedy Center for the Performing *(contd)*	Igor Stravinsky d. (b. 1882) Louis Armstrong, Amer. jazz trumpeter, d. (b. 1900) "Fiddler on the Roof" becomes the longest running musical in Broadway history, surpassing the 2,844 performances of "Hello Dolly" Leos Janácek: "The *(contd)*	U.S. Apollo 14 and 15 crews become the third and fourth groups to explore the moon's surface Nobel Prize for Medicine: Earl W. Sutherland (U.S.) Nobel Prize for Physics: Dennis Gabor (Brit.) U.S. satellite, Mariner 9, orbits *(contd)*	Cigarette advertisements are banned from U.S. television Baltimore Colts defeat Dallas Cowboys, 16—3, to win football's Super Bowl Gabrielle (Coco) Chanel, Fr. fashion designer, d. (b. 1884) Rolls-Royce, Ltd., declares bankruptcy William G. Wilson, founder of Alcoholics Anonymous, d. (b. 1896) Joe Frazier outpoints Muhammad Ali to retain world heavyweight boxing championship James Cash Penney, department store founder, d. (b. 1876) Audie Murphy, Amer. World War II hero, d. (b. 1925) Montreal Canadiens defeat Chicago Black Hawks to win hockey's Stanley Cup Milwaukee Bucks defeat Baltimore Bullets to win *(contd)*	**1971**

	A. HISTORY, POLITICS	B. LITERATURE, THEATER	C. RELIGION, PHILOSOPHY, LEARNING

1971 contd

A. History, Politics

Lt. William L. Calley, Jr., found guilty of premeditated murder in Mylai massacre
Thomas E. Dewey, Amer. politician, d. (b. 1903)
François Duvalier, Haitian dictator, d. (b. 1907)
First segments of "Pentagon Papers" appear in "The New York Times"
The 26th Amendment to the U.S. Constitution, allowing 18-year-olds to vote, ratified
Violence worsens in Northern Ireland after Britain institutes policies of preventive detention and internment without trial
Nixon orders 90-day freeze on wages and prices and announces other economic measures designed to curb domestic inflation and strengthen the U.S. balance of payments position
Lewis F. Powell, Jr., and William H. Rehnquist named to U.S. Supreme Court
Nobel Peace Prize: Willy Brandt, W. Ger. Chancellor
India (fighting on the side of the Bengali rebels) and Pakistan go to war
Mao's heir-apparent Lin Piao, fleeing after an unsuccessful coup, dies in a mysterious air crash
Kurt Waldheim, Aust. diplomat, chosen UN Secretary General
Dean Acheson, Amer. diplomat, d. (b. 1893)
Wladyslaw Gomulka, former Pol. Communist Party boss, suspended from Party's Central Committee
U.S. and U.S.S.R. sign treaty banning nuclear weapons on the ocean floor
Algeria seizes majority control of all Fr. oil and gas interests within its borders but promises restitution
U.S. Congress votes to end funding of the supersonic transport project
Korean President Chung Hee Park reelected to a third term
Erich Honecker succeeds Walter Ulbricht as head of E. Germany's Communist Party
Japan announces a self-imposed quota on its textile exports to the U.S.
A cyclone and tidal wave kill an estimated 10,000 people in Bengal

B. Literature, Theater

autobiographical novel (posth.)
Nobel Prize for Literature: Pablo Neruda, Chilean poet
Bennett Cerf, Amer. author and founder of Random House, d. (b. 1898)
John Updike: "Rabbit Redux," novel
E. M. Forster: "Maurice," novel (posth.)
Herman Wouk: "The Winds of War," novel
Edward Albee: "All Over," play, New York
Paul Zindel: "The Effect of Gamma Rays on Man-in-the-Moon Marigolds"
Alwin Nikolais: "Structures" and "Scenario," dances
Bernard Malamud: "The Tenants," novel

C. Religion, Philosophy, Learning

William Irwin Thompson: "At the Edge of History"
"The Jesus Movement" becomes a much-publicized element of religion in America
Federal and state aid to parochial schools is ruled unconstitutional by the U.S. Supreme Court

1972

A. History, Politics

U.S. returns Okinawa to Japan
Bangladesh (E. Pakistan) established as sovereign state; Sheik Mujibur Rahman named prime minister
King Frederick IX of Denmark d. (b. 1900)
Llewellyn E. Thompson, Jr., Amer. diplomat, d. (b. 1905)
President Nixon visits China and Russia
District of Columbia police arrest five men inside Democratic National Headquarters in the Watergate complex–beginning of the "Watergate" affair; Republicans deny Democratic charges that the raid was sanctioned by Nixon campaign officials; John N. Mitchell resigns as director of CREEP (Committee to Reelect the President); cover-up continues as trial of original defendants begins before Judge John J. Sirica
Gov. George C. Wallace of Alabama, a contender for the Democratic presidential nomination, is shot by Arthur Bremer and partially paralyzed
Republican Richard M. Nixon reelected President of the U.S. in a near-record landslide; Spiro T. Agnew reelected vice president; Democrats Sen. George S. McGovern and R. Sargent Shriver defeated (Shriver replaced the Democratic convention's nominee, Sen. Thomas Eagleton, when the latter was shown to have a history of mental depression and resigned); Democrats win majorities in both houses of Congress
Lon Nol takes complete control of Cambodian government
(contd)

B. Literature, Theater

John Berryman, Amer. poet, d. (b. 1915)
Marianne Moore, Amer. poet, d. (b. 1889)
Bronislav Nijinska, Russ.-born choreographer and ballerina, d. (b. 1891)
"Fiddler on the Roof," longest running Broadway show in history, closes after 3,242 performances
Cecil Day Lewis, Brit. poet laureate (1968—1971), d. (b. 1904)
Edmund Wilson, Amer. literary and social critic, d. (b. 1895)
R. F. Delderfield, Eng. novelist, d. (b. 1912)
Jules Romains, Fr. novelist, dramatist, and poet, d. (b. 1886)
Charles Correll, cocreator of "Amos 'n' Andy" comedy series, d. (b. 1890)
Mark Van Doren, Amer. man of letters, d. (b. 1895)
Henri de Montherlant, Fr. author and critic, d. (b. 1896)
(contd)

C. Religion, Philosophy, Learning

Eugene Cardinal Tisserant, Fr. Roman Catholic churchman, d. (b. 1891)
Athenagoras I, Eastern Orthodox Patriarch, d. (b. 1886)
Joseph Fielding Smith, 10th President of the Mormon Church, d. (b. 1877)
Dimitrios I elected Patriarch of the Faith of the Eastern Orthodox Church
Lord Fisher of Lambeth, Archbishop of Canterbury (1945—1961), d. (b. 1887)
"A Supplement to the Oxford English Dictionary," Vol. I, A-G, published
Rabbi Abraham Joshua Heschel, Amer. theologian, d. (b. 1907)
A U.S. Supreme Court ruling effectively prohibits capital punishment,
(contd)

1971 contd

D. VISUAL ARTS

Arts, Washington, D.C., opens
Academy Awards (for 1969)–best picture: "Patton"; best actor: George C. Scott ("Patton"); best actress: Glenda Jackson ("Women in Love")
"Conceptual" art becomes a major new craze in America
The Metropolitan Museum of Art pays a record $5,544,000 for a portrait by Velázquez
Films: "A Clockwork Orange" (Stanley Kubrick); "Claire's Knee" (Erick Rohmer); "The French Connection" (William Friedkin); "The Conformist" (Bernardo Bertolucci); "Investigation of a Citizen Above Suspicion" (Elio Petri)

E. MUSIC

Makropoulos Affair," opera
Krzysztof Penderecki: "Utrenja," symphony, New York
Karlheinz Stockhausen: "Hymnen," symphony, New York
Rock impresario Bill Graham closes Fillmores East and West

F. SCIENCE, TECHNOLOGY, GROWTH

Mars
Three Russ. cosmonauts die when their Soyuz 11 capsule develops an air leak while reentering the earth's atmosphere
U.S.S.R. soft-lands a space capsule on Mars
The 372,400-ton tanker "Nisseki Maru" is launched in Japan, the largest ship built to date
Dr. Choh Hao Li, at the University of California, synthesizes the hormone that controls human growth
Amer. astronomers discover two "new" galaxies adjacent to earth's own galaxy, the Milky Way
The U.S. Atomic Energy Agency explodes a hydrogen bomb beneath Amchitka Island, Alas.

G. DAILY LIFE

National Basketball Association championship
Hank Aaron hits his 600th career home run, the third baseball player ever to reach that mark
Pittsburgh Pirates win World Series from Baltimore Orioles, 4—3
U.S. devalues dollar; Japan and most European countries revalue their currencies upwards
"Canonero II" wins Kentucky Derby and Preakness but loses Belmont Stakes
Robert Tyre ("Bobby") Jones, Amer. golfer, d. (b. 1902)
Tennis star Mrs. Billie Jean King becomes first woman athlete to win $100,000 in a single year
Charles Manson and three codefendants found guilty of Sharon Tate murder
Los Angeles earthquake kills 60 and causes $1 billion in damage
Postal strike leaves Britons without mail for 47 days
Legalized offtrack betting introduced in New York
Amtrak begins to operate U.S. passenger railroads
Tricia Nixon marries Edward Finch Cox
"Look" magazine folds
Twenty bodies discovered buried in Yorba Linda, Calif.; Juan Corona, a farm labor contractor, accused of the murders
10 guards and 32 prisoners are killed when police storm Attica prison following a five- day uprising

1972

D. VISUAL ARTS

Maurice Chevalier, Fr. actor, d. (b. 1888)
Jane Morgan, radio and television star, d. (b. 1881)
Wesley Ruggles, film director, d. (b. 1888)
Jerome Cowan, film and television actor, d. (b. 1898)
Betty Blythe, silent screen star, d. (b. 1900)
Brian Donlevy, film star, d. (b. 1903)
Michelangelo's "Pietà" is seriously damaged by a hammer-wielding fanatic
Asta Nielsen, European film and stage star, d. (b. 1882)
Dame Margaret Rutherford, Eng. actress, d. (b. 1892)
George Sanders, Brit.-born film actor, d. (b. 1907)
Brandon de Wilde, Amer. film actor, d. (b. 1942)
John E. Costigan, Amer.
(contd)

E. MUSIC

Robert Casadesus, Fr. pianist and composer, d. (b. 1899)
Jean Claude Casadesus, pianist, son of Robert, killed in automobile accident (b. 1928)
Mahalia Jackson, Amer. gospel singer, d. (b. 1912)
Stefan Wolpe, Amer. avant-garde composer, d. (b. 1903)
Shostakovich: Symphony No. 15, Moscow
Oscar Levant, Amer. composer and
(contd)

F. SCIENCE, TECHNOLOGY, GROWTH

Apollo 16 astronauts, John Watts and Charles Duke, spend 71 hours on the surface of the moon; Apollo 17 crew, Eugene Cernan and Dr. Harrison Schmitt, later stay a record 74 hours, 59 minutes
The Tasadays, a Stone Age tribe, are discovered living in caves in the southern Philippines, subsequently revealed to be hoax
Richard Leakey and Glynn Isaac discover a 2.5-million-year-old human skull in northern Kenya
Dr. Louis S. B. Leakey, Eng. archaeologist and anthropologist, d. (b. 1903)
Nobel Prize for
(contd)

G. DAILY LIFE

Dallas Cowboys defeat Miami Dolphins, 24—3, to win football's Super Bowl
Strict antihijack measures are instituted at U.S. airports
11th Winter Olympics held at Sapporo, Japan; U.S.S.R. team wins eight gold medals
Summer Olympics held in Munich; U.S.S.R. takes 50 gold medals; Amer. swimmer Mark Spitz captures record seven gold medals; deaths of 11 Israeli athletes mar event
Clifford Irving concocts his Howard Hughes "biography"
A 47-day coal strike cripples Great Britain
Professional baseball players strike over pension rights, delaying season's opening by 13 days
"Pie" Traynor, baseball great, d. (b. 1900)
Harold S. Geneen, chairman and president of ITT, receives total annual compensation exceeding $1.6 million
The Star of Sierra Leone, the largest diamond (969.8 carats) ever discovered, is unearthed in Sierra Leone
Militant Angela Davis is acquitted of murder-conspiracy charges
Hurricane Agnes causes an estimated $1.7 billion damage to the eastern U.S.
(contd)

	A. HISTORY, POLITICS	B. LITERATURE, THEATER	C. RELIGION, PHILOSOPHY, LEARNING
1972 contd	Following years of violence between Catholics and Protestants, Britain imposes direct rule on Northern Ireland; 467 Northern Irish killed during the year "ITT-Dita Beard memo," suggesting that the Justice Department settled an antitrust suit in exchange for a campaign contribution, surfaces in Jack Anderson's newspaper column Phase II economic measures continue to control U.S. wages, prices, and profits Kwame Nkrumah, Ghanaian independence leader, d. (b. 1910) J. Edgar Hoover, F.B.I. Director since 1924, d. (b. 1895) Canada moves to establish limited control over foreign investments in Canadian resources and industry Vietnam: Paris peace talks continue; U.S. mines N. Vietnamese ports; Henry Kissinger makes his "peace is at hand" statement shortly before the November election Ireland, Britain, and Denmark agree to full membership in the European Economic Community (Common Market); Norw. voters reject entry Ceylon becomes a republic and changes its name to Sri Lanka Duke of Windsor, former King Edward VIII of Great Britain (1936), d. (b. 1895) Kakuei Tanaka elected Premier of Japan Paul Henri Spaak, Belg. Premier and a founder of the Common Market, d. (b. 1899) Arab terrorists kill two Israeli Olympic athletes in Munich; take nine others hostage; all nine killed during a shoot-out with W. Ger. police and soldiers Sporadic Arab-Israeli violence continues to erupt throughout the Middle East Philippine President Ferdinand Marcos declares martial law in response to what he calls a "Communist rebellion"; Marcos assumes near-dictatorial powers Chilean Marxist President, Salvador Allende Gossens, continues a policy of nationalizing large industrial concerns In Canadian elections Prime Minister Pierre Elliott Trudeau's Liberal Party wins popular vote plurality, but fails to win overall majority of seats in the House of Commons; Trudeau continues in office New Zealand's Labour Party, led by Norman E. Kirk, unseats National Party, ending 12 years of rule Australian Labour Party, led by Gough Whitlam, ends 23 years of Liberal-Country Party rule At year's end fewer than 24,000 Amer. troops remain in Vietnam Harry S. Truman, 33rd President of the U.S. (1945—1953), d. (b. 1884) Managua, Nicaragua, earthquake kills 10,000 U.S. petroleum products shortage first becomes apparent	Nobel Prize for Literature: Heinrich Böll (Ger.) Alexander Solzhenitsyn: "August 1914," novel, published in U.S. Sylvia Plath: "Winter Trees," poetry (posth.) Ezra Pound, Amer. poet, d. (b. 1885) Compton Mackenzie, Eng. playwright and biographer, d. (b. 1883) Joseph Papp (producer): "Two Gentlemen of Verona," "Sticks and Bones," by David Rabe, and "That Championship Season," by Jason Miller Tom O'Horgan (director): "Jesus Christ, Superstar" Tom Moore (director): "Grease," New York	pending new legislation from the states

D. VISUAL ARTS	E. MUSIC	F. SCIENCE, TECHNOLOGY, GROWTH	G. DAILY LIFE	
landscape artist, d. (b. 1888) Max Fleischer, cartoonist who created "Popeye," d. (b. 1883) William Boyd, "Hopalong Cassidy," d. (b. 1898) Mitchell Leisen, movie director, d. (b. 1898) Norton Simon pays $3 million for a painting by Raphael, a "Madonna and Child" Academy Awards (for 1971)–best picture: "The French Connection"; best actor: Gene Hackman ("The French Connection"); best actress: Jane Fonda ("Klute") Films: "Cabaret" (Liza Minnelli, Bob Fosse); "The Godfather" (Marlon Brando, Francis Ford Coppola); "Frenzy" (Alfred Hitchcock); "Play It Again, Sam" (Woody Allen); "The Discreet Charm of the Bourgeoisie" (Buñuel)	pianist, d. (b. 1900) Lale Anderson, Ger. cabaret singer, d. (b. 1913) Richard Crooks, star tenor of the Metropolitan Opera, d. (b. 1900) Mezz Mezzrow, Amer. jazz clarinetist, d. (b. 1899) Rudolf Friml, Amer. operetta composer born in Bohemia, d. (d. 1880) Goeran Gentele, newly appointed general manager of the Metropolitan Opera, d. (b. 1919) Leonard Bernstein: "Mass," Washington, D.C.	Physiology and Medicine: Gerald M. Edelman (U.S.) and Rodney R. Porter (Eng.) Nobel Prize for Chemistry: Stanford Moore, William Howard Stein, and Christian B. Anfisen (all U.S.) Nobel Prize for Physics: John Bardeen, Leon N. Cooper, and John Robert Schreiffer (all U.S.) Andrei N. Tupolev, Russ. aviation pioneer, d. (b. 1888) Igor I. Sikorsky, Russ. aviation pioneer who did much of his work in the U.S., d. (b. 1889) Soviet space craft, Venus 8, soft-lands on Venus	National League wins All-Star game, 4—3, over American League Howard Johnson, Amer. restaurateur, d. (b. 1897) Bobby Fischer (U.S.) wins world chess title from Boris Spassky (U.S.S.R.) The military draft is phased out in the U.S.; armed forces become all-volunteer U.S. tennis team wins Davis Cup for fifth straight time Oakland Athletics win World Series, 3—2, over Cincinnati Reds Roberto Clemente, Pittsburgh Pirate superstar, becomes 11th player to reach 3,000 base hits; later dies in plane crash (b. 1934) Jackie Robinson, first Black to play major league baseball, d. (b. 1919) The Dow-Jones Index for industrial stocks closes above the 1,000 mark for the first time "Team Canada" defeats Soviet Union for world hockey championship "All in the Family" leading TV show in U.S. "Life" magazine ceases publication Charles Atlas, promoter of body-building, d. (b. 1893)	**1972 contd**

A. HISTORY, POLITICS

1973 Great Britain, Ireland, and Denmark formally join the Common Market

President Nixon ends wage-price controls except in the food, health care, and building industries

Watergate: the five original defendants plead guilty before Judge John J. Sirica; before he is sentenced conspirator James W. McCord, Jr., begins to implicate Republican party officials; on Apr. 17 President Nixon, who has previously maintained that there is no official involvement in the affair, announces "major developments" arising from his own investigation; his aides H. R. Haldeman and John Ehrlichman are forced to resign; the Senate Watergate committee, chaired by Sen. Sam J. Ervin, Jr., hears former White House and campaign officials, one of whom, John Dean, attempts to implicate the president; John Mitchell and Maurice Stans indicted by grand jury for obstruction of justice and perjury; Nixon appoints Archibald Cox special Watergate prosecutor but discharges him when Cox insists that Nixon turn over tape recordings of conversations Nixon had with aides about Watergate; Attorney-General Elliot L. Richardson resigns; serious talk of impeachment begins; Nixon names Leon Jaworski to replace Cox as Watergate prosecutor; White House releases tape recordings, although there are "gaps" in crucial conversations and some subpoenaed tapes are declared to be nonexistent

Spiro T. Agnew, U.S. Vice President since 1969, resigns and pleads "nolo contendere" to one count of income tax evasion

Gerald Ford, Republican leader in the House of Representatives, named vice president to replace Agnew; takes office Dec. 6

War in Indochina: U.S.-S. Vietnam/N. Vietnam-Vietcong cease-fire agreement signed Jan. 23; Amer. losses 1965—1973–combat deaths 45,948, wounded 303,640, deaths from noncombat causes 10,298; S. Vietnamese losses–deaths 184,546, wounded 495,931; Vietcong and N. Vietnamese losses–combat deaths, 937,562; civilians killed, 415,000 (est.); civilians wounded, 935,000 (est.); maximum Amer. troop level during war, 543,000 (1969); total U.S. expenditures 1965—1973, $109.5 billion; fighting continues after cease-fire agreement; second four-party pact signed in June; fighting continues

Lyndon B. Johnson, 36th President of the U.S. (1963—1968), d. (b. 1908)

U.S. devalues dollar for second time in two years

President Georges Pompidou's Gaullist alliance wins reelection in France

Shah Mohammed Reza Pahlavi nationalizes all foreign-operated oil firms in Iran

Fighting breaks out in the Middle East between Arabs and Israelis; after initial gains the Arabs are pushed back, although at great cost to both sides; an unstable cease-fire remains in force as peace talks are begun and broken off several times

Arab oil-producing nations move to embargo shipments to the U.S., western Europe, and Japan in retaliation for their support of Israel; the cutoff precipitates an energy crisis in the industrialized world

E. and W. Germany establish diplomatic relations, formally acknowledging their post-World War II separation for the first time

"Pentagon Papers" defendants Daniel Ellsberg and Anthony Russo freed

Premier George Papadopolous announces the abolition of the Greek monarchy; months later he is ousted in a bloodless coup; Gen. Phaedon Gizikis becomes

(contd)

B. LITERATURE, THEATER

William Douglas-Home: "The Jockey Club Stakes," play, New York

U.S.S.R. agrees to abide by the terms of the Universal Copyright Convention

Elizabeth Bowen, Ir. novelist, d. (b. 1900)

Fyodor V. Lopukhov, Russ. choreographer and ballet director, d. (b. 1887)

Pearl Buck, Amer. author of books on China, d. (b. 1892)

David Storey: "The Changing Room," play, New York (named best play of season by New York Drama Critics)

"Irene" revival, New York

Noël Coward, Eng. author and playwright, d. (b. 1899)

Arna Bontemps, Black poet, leader of the 1920s "Harlem Renaissance," d. (b. 1903)

William Inge, Amer. playwright, d. (b. 1910)

Nobel Prize for Literature: Patrick White (Australian)

Conrad Aiken, Amer. poet, d. (b. 1889)

Pablo Neruda, Chilean poet, d. (b. 1904)

J. R. R. Tolkien, Eng. author and scholar, d. (b. 1892)

Kurt Vonnegut, Jr.: "Breakfast of Champions," novel

Thomas Pynchon: "Gravity's Rainbow," novel

Malcolm Cowley: "A Second Flowering," criticism

W. H. Auden, Eng.-born Amer. poet and essayist, d. (b. 1907)

Taha Jussein, Egyptian author, d. (b. 1888)

C. RELIGION, PHILOSOPHY, LEARNING

U.S. Supreme Court rules that individual states may not prohibit abortions during the first six months of pregnancy

Pope Paul VI names 30 new cardinals

Three Cypriot bishops attempt to unfrock Archbishop Makarios after he refuses to resign as President of Cyprus

Frances Fitzgerald: "Fire in the Lake: The Vietnamese and the Americans in Vietnam"

Jacques Maritain, Fr. Roman Catholic philosopher, d. (b. 1882)

Helen Parkhurst, innovative Amer. educator, d. (b. 1887)

Alfred Kazin: "Bright Book of Life"

David Halberstam: "The Best and the Brightest" becomes best seller

Gabriel Marcel, Fr. Roman Catholic philosopher, d. (b. 1897)

Catherine Drinker Bowen, Amer. biographer, d. (b. 1897)

Charles Evans Whittaker, associate justice of U.S. Supreme Court (1957—1962), d. (b. 1901)

Harold B. Lee, 11th President of the Mormon Church, d. (b. 1899)

D. VISUAL ARTS | **E. MUSIC** | **F. SCIENCE, TECHNOLOGY, GROWTH** | **G. DAILY LIFE**

1973

D. Visual Arts

Edward G. Robinson, Amer. film actor, d. (b. 1894)
Chic Young, creator of "Blondie" comic strip, d. (b. 1901)
Carmine Gallone, Ital. film director, d. (b. 1886)
Academy Awards (for 1972)–best picture: "The Godfather"; best actor: Marlon Brando ("The Godfather"); best actress: Liza Minnelli ("Cabaret")
A New York Criminal Court judge rules the motion picture "Deep Throat" "indisputably and irredeemably obscene"
Pablo Picasso, influential and controversial Span. artist, d. (b. 1881)
Edward Steichen, Amer. photographer, d. (b. 1880)
Joseph Coletti, Amer. sculptor, d. (b. 1892)
Jacques Lipchitz, Lithuanian-born Amer. sculptor, d. (b. 1892)
Jack Hawkins, Eng. stage and film star, d. (b. 1911)
Betty Grable, Amer. film star, d. (b. 1917)
Lon Chaney, Jr., Amer. actor famous for monster roles, d. (d. 1906)
Joe E. Brown, Amer. comedian, d. (b. 1893)
John Ford, Amer. film director, d. (b. 1895)
Laurence Harvey, Eng. actor, d. (b. 1928)
Sessue Hayakawa, Jap. actor, d. (b. 1889)
Walt Kelly, creator of "Pogo" cartoon strip, d. (b. 1913)
Lila Lee, silent screen star, d. (b. 1914)
Constance Talmadge, silent screen star, d. (b. 1900)
Films: "Sleeper" (Woody Allen); "Last Tango in Paris" (Marlon Brando, Maria Schneider, Bernardo Bertolucci)

E. Music

Walter E. Rollins, Amer. popular songwriter, author of "Frosty the Snowman," d. (b. 1907)
Ted Koehler, Amer. popular songwriter, author of "I Got the World on a String," d. (b. 1895)
Edward "Kid" Ory, Dixieland jazz trombonist, d. (b. 1887)
Lauritz Melchior, Dan.-born Wagnerian tenor, d. (b. 1891)
Paul Keltzki, Pol.-born Amer. conductor, d. (b. 1901)
Elmer Snowden, jazz banjo player, d. (b. 1901)
Karel Ancerl, Czech-born conductor of the Toronto Symphony Orchestra (1968—1973), d. (b. 1908)
Francesco Malipiero, Ital. composer, d. (b..1882)
Otto Klemperer, Ger. conductor and composer, d. (b. 1885)
Eddie Condon, jazz guitarist, d. (b. 1906)
Pablo Casals, Span. cellist, d. (b. 1876)
Benjamin Britten: "Death in Venice," Aldeburgh, England
Gene Krupa, Amer. jazz drummer, d. (b. 1909)
Rosetta Tharpe Morrison, Amer. gospel singer, d. (b. 1916)
Istvan Kertesz, music director of the Cologne Opera, d. (b. 1933)
Bruno Maderna, Ital. composer and conductor, d. (b. 1923)
Henri Busser, Fr. composer, former director of Paris Opéra, d. (b. 1872)

F. Science, Technology, Growth

Andrei Belozersky, Russ. biochemist, d. (b. 1906)
Amer. Skylab I (unmanned), II and III (manned) space missions completed successfully; Skylab II astronauts spend 28 days in space; Skylab III, 59.5 days; Skylab IV sets out for record flight
Nobel Prize for Medicine: Konrad Lorenz (Aust.), Niko Tinbergen (Dutch), and Karl von Frisch (Aust.)
Nobel Prize for Physics: Leo Esaki (U.S.), Ivar Giaver (U.S.), and Brian D. Josephson (Eng.)
Nobel Prize for Chemistry: Ernst Otto Fischer (Ger.) and Geoffrey Wilkinson (Eng.)
Dr. Paul Dudley White, Amer. heart specialist, d. (b. 1886)
Amer. space probe Pioneer 10 transmits television pictures from within 81,000 miles of the planet Jupiter

G. Daily Life

Miami Dolphins defeat Washington Redskins, 14—7, to win football's Super Bowl
Baseball: American League allows a 10th player, the designated hitter, to bat in place of pitcher; Oakland A's defeat New York Mets, 5—2, to win World Series
George Foreman scores a technical knockout to win world heavyweight boxing championship from Joe Frazier
Frank Costello, Amer. underworld figure, d. (b. 1891)
"Secretariat" wins horse racing's Triple Crown: the Kentucky Derby, the Preakness Stakes, and Belmont Stakes
Irene Ryan, star of "Beverly Hillbillies" TV show, d. (b. 1903)
New York Nicks win National Basketball Association trophy; Indiana Pacers win American Basketball Association title
Marjorie Merriweather Post, Amer. businesswoman and philanthropist, d. (b. 1887)
Energy crisis: a petroleum products shortage of undetermined magnitude, coupled with Arab oil embargo, forces cutbacks in Amer., western European, and Jap. home heating and transportation services and fuel-consuming industries; by Dec. an additional 100,000 are unemployed in the U.S.
Brit. government orders three-day work week to conserve electricity following coal-workers' overtime ban
Halfback O. J. Simpson sets one-year rushing mark of 2,003 yards
Notre Dame, undefeated in 10 games, wins national collegiate football championship
In a tennis match billed as the "battle of the sexes" Mrs. Billie Jean King defeats Bobby Riggs, 6-4, 6-3, 6-3

	A. HISTORY, POLITICS	B. LITERATURE, THEATER	C. RELIGION, PHILOSOPHY, LEARNING
1973 contd	president Militant Amer. Indians occupy the S. Dakota hamlet of Wounded Knee for 70 days Soviet Communist Party General Secretary Leonid I. Brezhnev visits U.S.; Brezhnev and Nixon sign treaty to limit nuclear war Salvador Allende Gossens, Marxist President of Chile since 1970, is overthrown by a military junta and reportedly commits suicide Following three centuries of colonial rule, the Bahamas are granted independence from Britain The 10th Congress of the Chinese Communist Party meets in Peking Swed. King Gustav d. (b. 1883); Crown Prince Carl Gustav crowned King Carl XVI Gustav Edward "Capt. Eddie" Rickenbacker, World War I flying ace, d. (b. 1891) Walter Ulbricht, leader of East Germany (1950—1971), d. (b. 1893) Argentinian ex-President Juan Perón and his wife, Maria Estela Martinez, elected President and Vice President of Argentina Nobel Peace Prize awarded to Amer. Henry Kissinger and N. Vietnamese Le Duc Tho, who refuses the award India begins the release of 90,000 Pakistani prisoners of war held since 1971 David Ben-Gurion, Israeli founder and former premier, d. (b. 1886) Nelson A. Rockefeller, Governor of New York since 1959, resigns to head Commission on Critical Choices Violence continues in Northern Ireland; 250 people are killed during the year Span. Premier Luis Carrero Blanco assassinated (b. 1903)		
1974	Worldwide inflation helps to cause dramatic increases in the cost of fuel, food, and materials; oil-producing nations boost prices, heightening inflation; economic growth slows to near zero in most industrialized nations; Dow Jones stock exchange index falls to 663, the lowest level since the 1970 recession All price and wage controls, in effect since 1971, end in the U.S. Yitzhak Rabin is named to head the Israeli cabinet after Premier Golda Meir steps down W. Ger. Chancellor Willy Brandt resigns after a close aide is exposed as an E. Ger. spy; Helmut Schmidt succeeds Brandt Brit. Prime Minister Edward Heath resigns; Labour party leader Harold Wilson succeeds him Prime Minister Pierre Elliott Trudeau of Canada wins reelection A bloodless coup, led by the military, deposes Portuguese dictatorship and begins democratic reforms After marathon negotiating sessions, U.S. Secretary of State Henry Kissinger persuades Syria and Israel to agree to a cease-fire on the Golan Heights President Richard M. Nixon visits Egypt, Saudi Arabia, Syria, and Israel; later tours U.S.S.R. Mohammad Ayub Khan, ruler of Pakistan (1958—69), d. (b. 1907) Juan Perón, president of Argentina (1946—1955, 1973—74), d. (b. 1896); succeeded in office by his wife, María Estela Terrorism continues in Northern Ireland and spreads to England; the Tower of London and the Houses of Parliament are bombed Greek-led Cypriot rebels overthrow the government; *(contd)*	Author Aleksandr L. Solzhenitsyn is stripped of his Soviet citizenship and exiled Lydia Sokolova, ballerina, d. (b. 1897) Jack Cole, Amer. choreographer, d. (b. 1914) Patrick White: "The Eye of the Storm," novel Pär Lagerkvist, Nobel-prize-winning Swed. author, d. (b. 1891) Russian ballet dancers Valery and Galina Panov are granted permission to emigrate to Israel Marcel Achard, Fr. playwright, d. (b. 1899) Thomas Pynchon: "Gravity's Rainbow" and Isaac B. Singer: "A Crown of Feathers and Other Stories" (novel), win National Book awards Neither the Pulitzer prize for literature, nor the one for drama, is awarded this year Swed. writers Harry Edmund Martinson and Eyvind Johnson awarded Nobel prize for literature Anne Sexton, Amer. Pulitzer Prize-winning poet, d. (b. 1928) Cyril Connolly, Eng. literary critic and writer, d. (b. 1903) *(contd)*	Pope Paul VI canonizes Teresa Ibars, a 19th-century Spanish nun Jozsef Cardinal Mindszenty, exiled Roman Catholic Primate of Hungary, is removed by Pope Paul VI Dr. Frederick Donald Coggan, Archbishop of York, is named Archbishop of Canterbury to succeed the Most Reverend Michael Ramsey Dr. Horace Kallen, educator, founder of the New School for Social Research, d. (b. 1883) Jean Wahl, existentialist philosopher and poet, d. (b. 1885) Four U.S. Episcopal bishops defy church law and ordain 11 women as priests A Gallup Poll shows that 40 per cent of U.S. adults attend church services weekly. Roman Catholic attendance is down to 55 per cent from 71 per cent in 1963 Nima H. Adlerblum, Amer.-Jewish philosopher and historian, d. (b. 1892)

D. VISUAL ARTS	E. MUSIC	F. SCIENCE, TECHNOLOGY, GROWTH	G. DAILY LIFE	
				1973 contd
Samuel Goldwyn, pioneer Hollywood producer, d. (b. 1883) Louis I. Kahn, Amer. architect, d. (b. 1901) Academy Awards (for 1973)–best picture: "The Sting"; best actor: Jack Lemmon ("Save the Tiger"); best actress: Glenda Jackson ("A Touch of Class") Agnes Moorehead, stage, screen, and television actress, d. (b. 1907) David A. Siqueiros, Mexican muralist, d. (b. 1897) Katharine Cornell, Amer. actress, d. (b. 1893) Paul Mazursky (producer and *(contd)*	Tex Ritter, country and western singer, d. (b. 1907) Duke Ellington, jazz musician, d. (b. 1899) Darius Milhaud, French composer, d. (b. 1893) Cass Elliot, Amer. pop singer, d. (b. 1943) Ross Parker, Eng. lyricist and composer, d. (b. 1915) David Oistrakh, premier Russ. violinist, d. (b. 1908) Frank Martin, Swiss composer, d. (b. 1890) Josef Krips, Austrian symphony orchestra conductor, d. (b. 1902)	U.S. Skylab 3 astronauts spend 84 days in space, surpassing Skylab 2's record of 59 days Erret Lobban Cord, aviation and auto pioneer, d. (b. 1895) U.S. Mariner 10 satellite transmits detailed pictures of both Venus and Mercury; Venus is shown to be surrounded by a well-defined shell of haze; Mercury is found to have an atmosphere A U.S.S.R. space probe lands on Mars and detects more water vapor than scientists had previously supposed existed India becomes the sixth nation to explode a nuclear device; Great Britain, France, and Cnina conduct nuclear tests Edward U. Condon, Amer. physicist, d. (b. 1902) Jacob Bronowski, Brit. scientist, d. (b. 1908) Charles A. Lindbergh, aviation pioneer, d. (b. 1902) Sir James Chadwick (Eng.), discoverer of neutron, d. (b. 1891) Alexander P. de Seversky, Russ.-born Amer. scientist, d. (b. 1894) A U.S. Air Force SR-71 jet plane flies from New York to London in one hour 55 minutes and 42 *(contd)*	Gasoline shortage inconveniences Americans through winter months; year-round Daylight Saving Time is adopted to save fuel but law is later repealed Miami Dolphins defeat Minnesota Vikings in football's "Super Bowl" Muhammad Ali wins 12 round non-title decision over Joe Frazier; defeats George Foreman in Zaïre, reclaiming heavyweight championship of the world 170 die as fire sweeps through São Paolo, Brazil, high-rise bank building A Turkish jetliner crashes in a forest near Paris; 345 killed Patricia Hearst, kidnaped heiress, announces she has decided to join her captors, the Symbionese Liberation Army Henry Aaron betters Babe Ruth's record of 714 career home runs A smallpox epidemic kills 10,000—20,000 in India "Streaking" becomes a fad in the U.S. Boston Celtics win the National Basketball Association championship Philadelphia Flyers defeat Boston Bruins to win hockey's Stanley Cup World's population reaches 3.782 billion Little League Baseball, Inc., votes to allow girls to play on its teams Dizzy Dean, 1930s baseball great, d. (b. 1911) Golfer Johnny Miller establishes one-year money-winning record of $346,933 *(contd)*	**1974**

	A. HISTORY, POLITICS	B. LITERATURE, THEATER	C. RELIGION, PHILOSOPHY, LEARNING
1974 contd	Archbishop Makarios flees; Turkish forces invade the island and gain control of much of Cyprus Watergate and impeachment: several former White House aides are convicted and sentenced in Watergate cover-up and related matters; President Nixon agrees to pay $432,787.13 in back taxes; it is revealed that a grand jury secretly named Nixon as an unindicted co-conspirator; when made public, tapes of White House conversations damage the President's cause; the U.S. Supreme Court decides, unanimously, that the President must turn over additional tapes to the Special Prosecutor; the House Judiciary Committee recommends three articles of impeachment for consideration by the full House of Representatives; additional tapes reveal early Presidential involvement in the cover-up; Nixon resigns Aug. 9 and Vice President Gerald R. Ford becomes 38th U.S. president Nelson Rockefeller nominated by President Ford to be vice president The military government of Greece, in office since 1967, resigns; ex-premier Constantine Caramanlis returns from exile to become premier Marshal Georgi Konstantinovich Zhukov, World War II Russian hero, d. (b. 1897) Workmen begin clearing the Suez Canal, closed since the Arab-Israeli war of 1967 A drought-induced famine threatens millions throughout Africa Floods kill at least 2,500 in Bangladesh The U.S. and East Germany establish formal diplomatic relations, 25 years after the formation of the E. Ger. state New Zealand Prime Minister Norman E. Kirk, d. (b. 1915) Ethiopian Emperor Haile Selassie, ruler of Ethiopia since 1916, peacefully deposed President Ford grants former President Nixon a pardon for any criminal offenses committed while in office; widespread protest develops President Ford grants a limited amnesty to Vietnam War draft evaders and military deserters Brit. Prime Minister Harold Wilson's Labour Party wins second Brit. general election in eight months U Thant, Secretary General of the United Nations (1961–1971), d. (b. 1909) Nikolai Kuznetsov, commander of Soviet naval forces during World War II, d. (b. 1902) Creighton W. Abrams, U.S. Army General, d. (b. 1914) Portuguese Guinea, a colony of Portugal, is granted independence as Guinea-Bissau; Grenada, a former Brit. colony, declares its independence U.S. General Alexander Haig is appointed Supreme Commander of the North Atlantic Treaty Organization (NATO)	Eric Linklater, Eng. novelist, d. (b. 1899) David M. Jones, Welsh poet and painter, d. (b. 1895) John Le Carre: "Tinker, Tailor, Soldier, Spy," novel Peter Benchley: "Jaws," novel Carl Bernstein and Bob Woodward: "All the President's Men" W. H. Auden: "Thank You, Fog: Last Poems" (posth.) Aleksandr I. Solzhenitsyn: "The Gulag Archipelago: 1918–1956"	Walter Lippmann, Amer. political columnist, d. (b. 1889)
1975	U.S. government cuts off aid to Turkey Turkish Cypriotes set up separate state in northern Cyprus, which is denounced by Cyprus's President Makarios Margaret Thatcher becomes leader of the Brit. Conservative Party, succeeding Edward Heath Fierce fighting erupts between Ethiopian government troops and secessionist guerrillas in the province of Eritrea Maurice H. Stans, former U.S. Secretary of Commerce, pleads guilty to five misdemeanor charges of violating campaign laws during the 1972 Nixon re-election campaign; he is third member of Nixon cabinet convicted John N. Mitchell, John D. Erlichman, and H. R. Haldeman —powerful members of the Nixon Administration—are convicted and sentenced to two-and-a-half to eight years *(contd)*	John Updike: "A Month of Sundays," novel Richard Adams: "Watership Down" and "Shardik," novels Robert Stone: "Dog Soldiers" and Thomas Williams: "The Hair of Harold Roux," win National Book awards Per Wahloo, Swed. novelist, d. (b. 1926) Carlo Levi, Ital. writer and painter, d. (b. 1902) P. G. Wodehouse, Eng.-born *(contd)*	Anglican Church in Canada approves ordaining women to the priesthood James Joyce's unpublished work is found at the University of Padua Rugby, 408-year-old English public school accepts coeds Josef Mindszenty, exiled Hungarian Cardinal, d. (b. 1892) Daniel J. Boorstin, historian, becomes librarian of the U.S. Library of Congress, which celebrates its 175th birthday *(contd)*

D. VISUAL ARTS	E. MUSIC	F. SCIENCE, TECHNOLOGY, GROWTH	G. DAILY LIFE	
director): "Harry and Tonto," motion picture Roman Polanski (producer): "Chinatown," motion picture David W. Rintels (author) and John Houseman (director): "Clarence Darrow," starring Henry Fonda Vittorio de Sica, Ital. Oscar-winning film director, d. (b. 1902) Francis Ford Coppola (producer and director): "The Godfather, Part II," starring Al Pacino and Lee Strasberg Jack Benny, Amer. comedian and actor, d. (b. 1894) Pietro Germi, Ital. Oscar-winning film director, d. (b. 1914)		seconds, reaching speeds of 2,000 m.p.h. Albert Claude (Amer.), Christian Rene de Duve (Belg.), and George Emil Palade (Amer.) share Nobel Prize for Medicine for their work in ethnology Paul John Flory (Amer.) awarded Nobel Prize for Chemistry for his work with polymers Martin Ryle (Eng.) and Antony Hewish (Eng.) awarded Nobel Prize for Physics for their work in radioastronomy Amer. scientists detect a new subatomic particle, the psi or J meson; interpreted as a state composed of a charmed quark and a charmed antiquark John C. Garand, Can.-Amer. gun designer, inventor of the M-1 rifle used in World War II, d. (b. 1888) Nobel Prize for Economics: Gunnar Myrdal (Swed.) and Friedrich A. von Hayek (Eng.)	The net profits of 30 of the world's largest oil companies increased by an average of 93 per cent during the first half of 1974, according to the Chase Manhattan Bank Frank Robinson becomes the first Black to manage a major league baseball team, when the Cleveland Indians name him to head the team The Oakland A's defeat the Los Angeles Dodgers, 4 games to 1, to win the 1974 World Series The American Telephone & Telegraph Co., largest private employer in the U.S., bans discrimination against homosexuals Amy Vanderbilt, Amer. columnist on etiquette, d. (b. 1908) Jimmy Connors (U.S.) wins Wimbledon, Australian, and U.S. Open men's singles tennis championships; Billie Jean King (U.S.) captures her fourth U.S. Open women's singles championship; Chris Evert (U.S.) wins Canadian, French, and Italian Open women's singles championships; South Africa wins the Davis Cup, defeating India by default "Little Current" wins horse racing's Preakness and Belmont Stakes W. Germany wins the 10th World Cup soccer championship Gary Player (S. Afr.) wins his third British Open and second Masters golf championship Amer. sloop "Courageous" defeats the Australian sloop "Southern Cross" to retain the America's Cup	**1974 contd**
Frank Sully, Amer. character actor, d. (b. 1908) Rod Serling, Amer. TV writer and producer, d. (b. 1925) Academy Awards (for 1974)—best picture: "The Godfather, Part II"; best actor: Art Carney ("Harry and *(contd)*	Michael Bennett (director, choreographer), Marvin Hamlisch (music), and Edward Kleban (lyrics): "A Chorus Line," named best musical by New York Drama Critics Dimitri Shostakovich, *(contd)*	U.S. Viking unmanned spacecraft sets off on 500-million-mile journey to Mars to seek signs of life U.S. Apollo and Soviet Soyuz 19 spacecrafts link up 140 miles above earth; American astronauts Brig. General Thomas P. Stafford, Donald K. Slayton, and Vance D. Brand shake hands and share meals with Soviet cosmonauts Col. Aleksei Leonov and Valery N. Kubasov; the first interna- *(contd)*	Kidnappings by leftists, radicals, and terrorists in Argentina, West Germany, Italy, Somalia, Tanzania, and other countries Dr. Kenneth C. Edelin, a Boston obstetrician, is found guilty of manslaughter in the death of a male fetus in a "legal" abortion he performed in October, 1973 Charlie Chaplin and P. G. Wodehouse are knighted (January 1) by Queen Elizabeth II Pittsburgh Steelers defeat Minnesota Vikings, 16–6, to win football's Super Bowl Bobby Fischer gives up world chess championship; dislikes terms of Karpov match In U.S.'s first strike by doctors, 21 New York *(contd)*	**1975**

A. HISTORY, POLITICS

1975 contd

in prison for their roles in the Watergate cover-up; Robert C. Mardian, also convicted, is given a 10-month to three-year sentence; Judge John J. Sirica orders the release of three convicted Watergate figures—John W. Dean III, Herbert W. Kalmbach, and Jeb Stuart Magruder, who respectively, served four, six, and seven months in prison for Watergate-related offenses; Charles Colson and James W. McCord, Jr., both convicted and serving sentences, are released; Judge Sirica refuses to reduce the sentence of either E. Howard Hunt, Jr., or G. Gordon Liddy, both imprisoned for the Watergate break-in and conspiracy

Antonin Novotny, former First Secretary of Communist Party and President of Czechoslovakia, d. (b. 1904)

The military in Portugal imposes a constitution on the country that gives all essential power to the armed forces

Sarvepalli Radhakrishnan, former President of India, d. (b. 1888)

Nikolai Bulganin, former Premier of the U.S.S.R., d. (b. 1895)

Ivy Baker Priest, former Treasurer of the U.S., d. (b. 1905)

King Faisal of Saudi Arabia is assassinated by a nephew, who is beheaded; new king is Khalid, brother of Faisal

Cambodian President Lon Nol flees beseiged Phnom Penh before Communist takeover; U.S. Embassy closes and last Americans leave; Khmer Rouge insurgents set up headquarters in Phnom Penh following the surrender of government; Khmer Rouge force urban inhabitants on long, hard marches to the countryside as part of their "reform" program

Nguyen Van Thieu resigns as President of South Vietnam; Communist forces overrun South Vietnam; U.S. engages in immediate evacuation of troops, civilians, and refugees; Communists seize Saigon; U.S. ends two decades of military involvement in the Vietnam War; U.S. Congress approves $405 million for Vietnamese refugee aid and resettlement in U.S.

Nobel Peace Prize: Andrei D. Sakharov, Russ. physicist who developed the Soviet Union's hydrogen bomb

Sikkim abolishes its monarchy and becomes an Indian state

Egypt reopens the Suez Canal eight years after it was closed during the Arab-Israeli war of June, 1967

Daniel P. Moynihan is named U.S. Ambassador to the United Nations, succeeding John A. Scali

Cambodian naval ship fires on and seizes U.S. merchant ship "Mayaguez," which is retrieved by U.S. forces

Chiang Kai-shek, President of Nationalist China (1950–1975), d. (b. 1887)

Communist-led Pathet Lao take control of Laos

U.S. withdraws its last combat aircraft from Taiwan and reduces its military force there to 2,800

Eisaku Sato, former Premier of Japan and winner of the Nobel Peace Prize, d. (b. 1901)

Mayor Richard Daley of Chicago wins sixth term

Bloody fighting occurs between rival rightist Christians and leftist Moslems in Beirut, Lebanon; cabinet of prominent Christians and Moslems is formed to halt fighting

People of the northern Mariana Islands vote to become American citizens and to make the islands a commonwealth of the U.S.—the first territorial acquisition by the U.S. since 1925

Italy's Communist and Socialist Parties register large gains in local, provincial, and regional elections

Eamon De Valéra, President of Ireland (1959–1973), d. (b. 1882)

Emperor Haile Selassie, ruler of Ethiopia (1916–1974), d. (b. 1893)

The Greek cabinet commutes the death sentence of former President George Papadopoulos, who led the military coup in 1967, to life imprisonment

Leaders of 35 nations sign the charter of the Conference on

(contd)

B. LITERATURE, THEATER

Amer. novelist and humorist, d. one month after being knighted by Queen Elizabeth II. (b. 1881)

David Storey: "The Farm," play

Lanford Wilson: "The Mound Builders," play

Ed Bullins: "The Taking of Miss Janie," New York Drama Critics award as best American play

Peter Shaffer: "Equus," play, New York Drama Critics and Tony awards

Edward Albee: "Seascape," Pulitzer Prize drama

Michael Shaara: "The Killer Angels," Pulitzer Prize novel

Gary Snyder: "Turtle Island," Pulitzer Prize poetry

Sylvia Plath: "Letters Home: Correspondence 1950–1963" (posth.)

Iris Murdoch: "A Word Child," novel

St.-John Perse, Nobel Prize-winning Fr. poet and diplomat, d. (b. 1887)

Wallace Shawn: "Our Late Night," play

Athold Fugard, John Kani, and Winston Ntshona: "Sizwe Banzi Is Dead," "The Island," plays about South Africa's inhumanity to blacks

Ivo Andríc, Nobel Prize-winning Yugoslav writer, d. (b. 1892)

Peter Matthiessen: "Far Tortuga," novel

C. P. Snow: "Trollope: His Life and Art," biography

Nobel Prize for Literature: Eugenio Montale (Ital.)

Irving Stone: "The Greek Treasure," biographical novel

Aleksandr I. Solzhenitsyn: "Gulag Archipelago Two" and "Lenin in Zurich"

Agatha Christie: "Curtain," (death of nonpareil detective Hercule Poirot)

Pavel P. Virsky, Russ. choreographer, d. (b. 1905)

Rex Stout, Amer. writer and creator of the detective "Nero Wolfe," d. (b. 1886)

Thornton Wilder, Amer. novelist and playwright, d. (b. 1897)

Marguerite Steen, Eng. novelist, d. (b. 1894)

Thomas Mann's notebooks are opened 20 years after his death, as he directed

Émile Ajar: "La Vie Devant Soi," novel

Larry Woiwode: "Beyond the Bedroom Wall," novel

C. RELIGION, PHILOSOPHY, LEARNING

Elijah Muhammad (born Elijah Poole), leader of the Black Muslims, d. (b. 1897); succeeded by his son, Wallace Muhammad

Will and Ariel Durant: "The Age of Napoleon," 11th book in their monumental History of Civilization series

Hannah Arendt, Amer. political philosopher and writer, d. (b. 1906)

Robert Nozick: "Anarchy, State and Utopia," National Book award

Elizabeth Ann Bayley Seton (1774–1821) canonized; first Amer.-born saint

Ivan Maisky, Russ. historian and diplomat, d. (b. 1884)

Four women ordained to the Episcopal priesthood in Washington; previous ordination of 11 women in Philadelphia is invalidated by the House of Bishops

Fifth assembly of the World Council of Churches convenes in Nairobi, Kenya; call for a "radical transformation of civilization"

Lionel Trilling, Amer. writer and professor, d. (b. 1905)

Five saints canonized by Pope Paul VI

New York City's Council of Churches rejects the membership application of the Unification Church of Rev. Sun Myung Moon

D. VISUAL ARTS

Tonto''); best actress: Ellyn Burstyn (''Alice Doesn't Live Here Anymore'')

Six thousand life-sized pottery figures from the 3rd century B.C. are found in northwest China

Metropolitan Museum of Art pays $5.1 million for Packard collection of Japanese art

Susan Hayward, Amer. Oscar-winning actress, ''I'll Cry Tomorrow,'' d. (b. 1919)

Thomas Hart Benton, Amer. painter, d. (b. 1889)

Richard Conte, Amer. screen actor, d. (b. 1918)

Ethel Griffies, Eng. stage and screen actress, d. (b. 1878)

Michel Simon, Swiss-born Fr. stage and screen actor, d. (b. 1895)

Donald M. Oenslager, Amer. stage designer, d. (b. 1902)

George E. Marshall, Hollywood film director (1913–1975), d. (b. 1890)

Films: ''Jaws'' (Steven Spielberg); ''Nashville'' (Lily Tomlin, Robert Altman); ''Hearts of the West'' (Alan Arkin); ''The Story of Adele H'' (Isabelle Adjani); ''The Sunshine Boys'' (George Burns)

Josephine Baker, Amer. singer and dancer, d. (b. 1906)

George Stevens, Amer. Oscar-winning film director, d. (b.

(contd)

E. MUSIC

Russ. composer, d. (b. 1906)

Robert Stolz, Ger. composer, d. (b. 1882)

Leroy Anderson, Amer. composer, famous for ''Blue Tango'' and ''Sleigh Ride,'' d. (b. 1908)

Sarah Caldwell becomes first woman conductor of the Metropolitan Opera, New York

Sir Arthur Bliss, Eng. composer, d. (b. 1891)

Lionel Tertis, Eng. viola player, d. (b. 1876)

Richard Tucker, Amer. operatic tenor, d. (b. 1915)

The centennials of Charles Ives and Arnold Schoenberg celebrated in performances of their works

Charles Weidman, Amer. choreographer, d. (b. 1901)

Carman Moore: ''Wildfires and Field Songs''

George Rochberg: ''Concerto for Violin and Orchestra,'' premiered by Isaac Stern and the Pittsburgh Symphony Orchestra

Vittorio Gui, Ital. conductor, d. (b. 1885)

Musicians' strike closes 12 Broadway musicals for 25 days

Dominick Argento: ''From the Diary of Virginia Woolf,'' Pulitzer Prize music

Bernard Herrmann, Amer. composer, d. (b. 1911)

American premiere of Berlioz's ''Benvenuto Cellini,'' opera, Boston

Beverly Sills sings

(contd)

F. SCIENCE, TECHNOLOGY, GROWTH

tional manned space flight

Jakob A. B. Bjerknes, Nor. meteorologist, d. (b. 1897)

Julian Huxley, Eng. biologist and author, d. (b. 1887)

Sir Robert Robinson, Nobel Prize-winning Eng. chemist, d. (b. 1886)

William D. Coolidge, Amer. inventor of the X-ray tube (1913), d. (b. 1875)

The U.S.S.R.'s Tupolev-144 becomes the first supersonic airplane on a regularly scheduled mail-and-freight flight

Edward L. Tatum, Nobel Prize-winning Amer. biochemist, d. (b. 1909)

Linus C. Pauling receives the U.S. National Medal of Honor from President Ford

Gustav Hertz, Nobel Prize-winning Ger. physicist, d. (b. 1887)

George P. Thomson, Nobel Prize-winning Eng. physicist, d. (b. 1892)

Atlantic salmon, gone 100 years, return to spawn in the Connecticut River, which was restocked in 1973 after long effort to end pollution; sturgeon coming back to Hudson River

Nobel Prize for Economics: Leonid V. Kantorovich (U.S.S.R.) and Tyalling C. Koopmans (U.S.)

Nobel Prize for Chemistry: John W. Cornforth (Eng.) and Vladimir Prelog (Swiss)

Nobel Prize for Medicine or Physiology: David Baltimore, Howard M. Temin, and Renato Dulbecco (all U.S.)

Nobel Prize for Physics: James Rainwater (U.S.), Ben R. Mottelson (Dan.), and Aage N. Bohr (Dan.)

Alvin H. Hansen, Amer. economist, d. (b. 1887)

John R. Dunning, Amer. physicist who helped develop the method of isolating U-235, d. (b. 1907)

Ernst Alexanderson, Swed.-born Amer. electrical and radio engineer and inventor, d. (b. 1878)

Theodosius Dobzhansky, Amer. geneticist, d. (b. 1900)

G. DAILY LIFE

City hospitals reduce services until agreement is reached to shorten hours; doctors begin slowdown in some states as some malpractice insurance rates quadruple

New York City, needing cash to avert default, appeals to Federal government

London's worst subway crash leaves 41 dead and more than 90 injured

Ezzard Charles, former world heavyweight boxing champion, d. (b. 1921)

The U.S. marks the start of the American Revolution Bicentennial with ceremonies at the Old North Church in Boston

Mrs. Junko Tabei, 35-year-old Japanese, becomes first woman to climb Mt. Everest; 36th person to reach summit

American Air Force cargo jet carrying 243 Vietnamese orphans to the U.S. crashes and burns shortly after takeoff from Saigon; more than 100 children die

Sam Giancana, Chicago Mafia leader, d. (b. 1910)

Britain's inflation rate jumps 25%

The International Woman's Year World Conference in Mexico City adopts a 10-year plan to improve the status of women

Aristotle S. Onassis, Argentine (formerly Greek) shipping magnate, d. (b. 1906)

Philadelphia Flyers defeat Buffalo Sabres to win hockey's Stanley Cup

Golden State Warriors win National Basketball Association championship; Kentucky Colonels win American Basketball Association title

Unemployment rate in the U.S. reaches 9.2%, highest since 1941

Patricia Hearst, missing since Feb. 7, 1974, is caught by the F.B.I. in San Francisco; caught with William and Emily Harris, remnants of the Symbionese Liberation Army, who kidnapped Miss Hearst

John Walker (N.Z.) runs the mile in 3 minutes, 49.4 seconds, a new world's record

James R. Hoffa, former president of the International Brotherhood of Teamsters, disappears

Earthquake destroys Great Temples of Pagan in Burma

Mauna Loa erupts in Hawaii, first time since 1950

Eastern Airlines jet crashes at New York's Kennedy International Airport; 113 die in America's worst domestic airlines crash

Mirabel International Airport, the world's largest airport, is opened in Montreal

W. T. Grant stores, billion dollars in debt, files voluntary bankruptcy; only Penn Central failure was larger

Casey Stengel, former manager of the Brooklyn Dodgers, Boston Braves, New York Yankees, and New York Mets, d. (b. 1891)

Animal encephalitis outbreak rages in 16 U.S. states, worst in years

W. A. (''Tony'') Boyle, former head of the United Mine Workers, is sentenced to three consecutive life terms for ordering the murder of union official Joseph A. Yablonski

A federal jury in Cleveland exonerates Ohio Governor James A. Rhodes, 27 Ohio

(contd)

1975 contd

	A. HISTORY, POLITICS	B. LITERATURE, THEATER	C. RELIGION, PHILOSOPHY, LEARNING
1975 contd	Security and Cooperation in Helsinki, Finland (Helsinki accord) Forty Islamic nations meeting in Saudi Arabia vote to expel Israel from the United Nations Malcolm Fraser becomes Prime Minister of Australia Generalissimo Francisco Franco, chief of state of Spain (1939–1975), d. (b. 1892); Prince Juan Carlos de Borbón is sworn in as King Juan Carlos I, the first King of Spain in 44 years Oil prices are raised 10% by the Organization of Petroleum Exporting Countries (OPEC) Two assassination attempts are made on the life of President Ford in California Peru's President Juan Velasco Alvarado is ousted in a military coup and replaced by his Premier, General Francisco Morales Bermúdez King Savang Vatthana of Laos abdicates the throne; a people's democratic republic is established Justice William O. Douglas retires from the U.S. Supreme Court after serving 36½ years; John Paul Stevens takes Douglas' seat on the Court Portugal grants independence to its former African colonies of Angola, Mozambique, Cape Verde, and São Tomé and Príncipe; the Comoro Islands, a former French colony, declare their independence; Papua New Guinea becomes an independent nation; Surinam becomes independent of The Netherlands		
1976	Abdul Razak, Premier of Malaysia, d. (b. 1922); succeeded by Hussein Onn Chou En-lai, Premier of the People's Republic of China (1949–1976), d. (b. 1898) Venezuela nationalizes the petroleum industry María Estela Martínez de Perón, President of Argentina, is overthrown; Lt. General Jorge Videla becomes president of Argentina's military junta Field Marshal Bernard Law Montgomery, 1st Viscount, Brit. World War II hero who defeated the Germans at El Alamein, Egypt, d. (b. 1887) Spain relinquishes colonial control of Spanish Sahara; Morocco and Mauritania divide the territory, ignoring the Sahara nationalists' proclamation of independence Daniel P. Moynihan resigns as U.S. Ambassador to the United Nations; replaced by William W. Scranton René Cassin, Nobel Prize-winning Fr. jurist (1968), d. (b. 1887) U.S. and U.S.S.R. sign a treaty limiting the size of underground nuclear explosions set off for peaceful purposes; it provides, for the first time, some on-site inspection of compliance Lebanon's parliament elects Christian leader Elias Sarkis as President Brit. Prime Minister Harold Wilson resigns; James Callaghan succeeds him Khieu Samphan is named Chairman of the State Presidium of Cambodia, succeeding Prince Norodom Sihanouk as head of state; Pol Pot (Tol Saut) is appointed Premier The U.S. celebrates its Bicentennial with special events in Philadelphia, Washington, D.C., and across the country; more than six million people watch "tall ships" from 31 nations parade up the Hudson River North and South Vietnam are reunited as one country after 22 years of separation; called the Socialist Republic of Vietnam, with Hanoi as its capital; Saigon renamed Ho Chi Minh City Seychelles Islands, former Brit. colony, declare their independence General Antonio Ramalho Eanes is elected President in Portugal's first free presidential election in half a century; Mario Soares becomes Premier *(contd)*	William Sansom, Eng. short story writer and novelist, d. (b. 1912) U.S. copyright laws are revised for the first time in 67 years Paul Gallico, Amer. journalist and novelist, d. (b. 1897) Richard Hughes, Eng. poet and writer, d. (b. 1900) Stuart Cloete, South African novelist, d. (b. 1897) Paul Robeson, Amer. actor, singer, and political activist, d. (b. 1898) Margaret Leighton, Eng. stage and screen actress, d. (b. 1922) Dame Agatha Christie, Eng. novelist of detective fiction, d. (b. 1891) Saul Bellow: "Humboldt's Gift," Pulitzer Prize fiction; "To Jerusalem and Back: A Personal Account" Michael Bennett: "A Chorus Line," musical, Pulitzer Prize drama and Tony award John Ashbery: "Self-Portrait in a Convex Mirror," Pulitzer Prize poetry and National Book award Nobel Prize for Literature: Saul Bellow (U.S.) Paul Morand, Fr. novelist and diplomat, d. (b. 1889) Dame Sybil Thorndike, Eng. stage actress, d. (b. 1882) Henri Bosco, Fr. poet and novelist, d. (b. 1889) Enid Bagnold: "A Matter of Gravity," play William Luce: "The Belle of *(contd)*	Martin Heidegger, Ger. philosopher, d. (b. 1889) The Episcopal Church approves the ordination of women to be priests and bishops; the Anglican Church of Canada ordains six women as priests Samuel Eliot Morison, Amer. historian, d. (b. 1887) Fr. Archbishop Marcel Lefèbvre is suspended by Pope Paul VI for rejecting reforms by the Second Vatican Council in the saying of Mass; Lefèbvre continues to celebrate banned traditional Latin Mass and ordains 13 deacons at his seminary in Econe, Switzerland Lin Yutang, Chin. author and philologist, d. (b. 1895) Kathryn Kuhlman, Amer. evangelist and faith healer, d. (b. 1910?) Roman Catholic Church accuses the right-wing Brazilian military government of violating human rights Pope Paul VI asks 75-year-old Stefan Cardinal Wyszynski to continue as leader of Poland's 30 million Roman Catholics Rev. Moon ends U.S. ministry with rallies in New York and Washington, D.C.; parents protest the "brainwashing" tactics allegedly used by Moon's Unification Church to recruit and train its young members, known as "Moonies" Rudolf Bultmann, Ger. existen- *(contd)*

D. VISUAL ARTS	E. MUSIC	F. SCIENCE, TECHNOLOGY GROWTH	G. DAILY LIFE	
1905) Fredric March, Amer. Oscar-winning actor of stage and screen, d. (b. 1897) Francine Larrimore, Amer. stage actress, d. (b. 1897) Barbara Hepworth, Eng. sculptress, d. (b. 1903)	Rossini's "The Siege of Corinth" in her Metropolitan Opera debut George Crumb: "Makrokosmos II"		National Guardsmen, and the former president of Kent State University of any responsibility for the 1970 shootings at Kent State that left four students killed The cost of mailing a first-class letter in the U.S. increases from 10 cents to 13 cents Billie Jean King (U.S.) captures her 6th Wimbledon women's singles tennis championship; Chris Evert (U.S.) wins U.S. Open women's singles tennis championship; Manuel Orantes (Sp.) wins U.S. Open and Canadian Open men's singles tennis championships; Sweden takes the Davis Cup Cincinnati Reds defeat Boston Red Sox, 4 games to 3, to win World Series Jack Nicklaus wins his fifth Masters and his fourth Professional Golfers' Association championship First Women's Bank opens in New York City	**1975 contd**
Adolf Zuckor, Amer. film producer, d. (b. 1873) Alvar Aalto, Finnish architect, d. (b. 1898) Academy Awards (for 1975)—"One Flew Over the Cuckoo's Nest" swept all five major awards: best picture, best actor (Jack Nicholson), best actress (Louise Fletcher), best director, and best screenplay; the first film to win all since 1934 Max Ernst, Ger. painter, d. (b. 1891) Josef Albers, Amer. painter and art teacher, d. (b. 1888) Lee J. Cobb, Amer. actor, d. (b. 1911) Luchino Visconti, Ital. film director, d. (b. 1906) Mark Tobey, Amer. abstract painter, d. (b. 1890) Rosalind Russell, Amer. screen *(contd)*	Geza Anda, Hung.-born Swiss pianist, d. (b. 1921) Elisabeth Rethberg, Amer. soprano, d. (b. 1894) Alexander Brailowsky, Russ. pianist, d. (b. 1896) Meyer Davis, Amer. society bandleader, d. (b. 1895) Rudolf Kempe, Ger. conductor, d. (b. 1910) Jean Martinon, Fr. conductor and composer, d. (b. 1910) Lily Pons, Amer. operatic soprano d. (b. 1904) Percy Faith, Amer. conductor, d. (b. 1908) Guy Lombardo, Amer. bandleader, d. (b. 1902) Roland Hayes, Amer. concert tenor, d. (b. 1887) Benjamin Britten, Eng. composer, d. (b. 1913) Walter Piston, Amer. composer and teacher, d. *(contd)*	Nikolai I. Muskhelishvili, Russ. mathematician, d. (b. 1891) U.S.S.R.'s Soyuz spacecraft docks successfully with the orbiting Salyut space station Carl Peter Henrik Dam, Nobel Prize-winning Dan. biochemist, d. (b. 1895) Werner Heisenberg, Nobel Prize-winning Ger. physicist, d. (b. 1901) New atomic particle is detected by Amer. scientists, headed by Leon Lederman, at the Fermi National Accelerator Laboratory in Batavia, Ill.; known as "upsilon," the particle is thought to belong to a new family of atomic fragments, named psions, first observed in late 1974 George Hoyt Whipple, Nobel Prize-winning Amer. pathologist, d. (b. 1878) Lars Onsager, Nobel Prize-winning Amer. chemist, d. (b. 1903) Leopold Ruzicka, Nobel Prize-winning Swiss chemist, d. (b. 1887) The National Academy of Science reports that gases from spray cans can cause damage to the atmosphere's ozone layer First detailed radar observations of the surface of Venus are recorded at the Arecibo Observatory, Puerto Rico Landing vehicles from U.S. spacecrafts Viking I and II set down safely on Mars and *(contd)*	Montreal Canadiens defeat Philadelphia Flyers to win hockey's Stanley Cup Howard Hughes, Amer. reclusive billionaire and head of a vast business empire, d. (b. 1905) Officials of the Mormon church discover a handwritten will attributed to Howard Hughes; authenticity of "Mormon Will" questioned, particularly provision bequeathing one-sixteenth of Hughes's estate to Melvin Dummar, a Utah gas station operator Argentina devalues the peso 70%; the value of the Brit. pound sterling and Ital. lira fall to an all-time low against the U.S. dollar; Australia devalues its currency by a peacetime record of 17.5% 12th Winter Olympics held at Innsbruck, Austria; U.S.S.R. team wins 13 gold medals World's first scheduled supersonic passenger service is inaugurated when two Concorde jets take off simultaneously from London and Paris; Britain and France begin trans-Atlantic supersonic service to Washington Pittsburgh Steelers defeat Dallas Cowboys, 21–17, to win football's Super Bowl Roy Herbert Thomson, Canadian-born Brit. newspaper publisher d. (b. 1894) Israeli airborne commandos rescue 103 hostages held at Entebbe Airport, Uganda, by seven pro-Palestinian hijackers of an Air France jetliner; 31 persons die in the raid U.S. Air Force Academy admits 155 women, ending the all-male tradition at the U.S. military academies J. Paul Getty, Amer. oil billionaire, d. (b. 1892) Boston Celtics win National Basketball Association championship; New York Nets win American Basketball Association title; four ABA teams merge with the NBA when the ABA disbands *(contd)*	**1976**

1976 contd

A. HISTORY, POLITICS

Portuguese Timor votes to become the 27th province of Indonesia
Thailand's government falls in a coup by the military
Chancellor Helmut Schmidt wins reelection in West Germany
Blacks in South Africa battle armed policemen as waves of rioting and violence against apartheid and government policies spread from Soweto to Johannesburg and Cape Town in black townships and white areas
U. S. President Ford and Jimmy Carter, democratic candidate for President, debate social, political, and economic issues on national television three times
Sweden's Premier Olof Palme resigns after his Social Democratic Party suffers its first defeat in parliamentary elections in 44 years
The Republic of Transkei is proclaimed, the first of South Africa's black homelands to attain its independence
Syrian troops and Lebanese Christians battle Palestinian guerrillas and Lebanese Moslems in southern Lebanon; the Syrian army takes control of Beirut, Tripoli, Sarda, and the highways between the cities
Cearbhall Ó Dalaigh resigns as President of Ireland; succeeded by Patrick J. Hillery
Senators Walter F. Mondale and Robert J. Dole meet in a TV debate, the first ever between U.S. vice-presidential candidates
Mao Tse-tung, leader of the People's Republic of China (1949–1976) and founder of the Chinese Communist Party, d. (b. 1893)
Parti Québécois (PQ), formed in 1968 to promote Quebec independence, wins a majority of seats in the provincial parliament and raises the possibility of Quebec's secession from Canada; René Lévesque, leader of the PQ, becomes Premier of Quebec
Civil war in Angola causes more than 9,000 refugees to flee to Namibia (South-West Africa)
Jimmy (James Earl, Jr.) Carter is elected 39th President of the U.S., narrowly defeating President Ford; Senator Walter F. Mondale elected Vice-President
Hua Kuo-feng is appointed Premier of the People's Republic of China and Chairman of the Chinese Communist Party; a coup attempt by Mao Tse-tung's widow and three other counterrevolutionaries—the Gang of Four—is crushed
Takeo Fukuda is elected Prime Minister of Japan
Kurt Waldheim (Austria) wins approval for a second five-year term as Secretary General of the United Nations
José Lopez Portillo succeeds Luis Echeverría Alvarez as President of Mexico
East Germany issues new restrictions on emigration to the West, clamping down on dissidents and discontent
Richard J. Daley, Mayor of Chicago (1955–1976), d. (b. 1902)
The Central African Republic is renamed the Central African Empire by President-for-life Jean Bedel Bokassa
Marshal Ivan I. Yakubovsky, Soviet Chief of Armed Forces of the Warsaw Pact since 1967, d. (b. 1912)
Juscelino Kubitschek, President of Brazil (1955–1960), d. (b. 1901); João Goulart, President of Brazil (1960–1963), d. (b. 1918)

B. LITERATURE, THEATER

Amherst," play
Alan Ayckbourn: "The Norman Conquests," comedy
Eyvind Johnson, Nobel Prize-winning Swed. novelist, d. (b. 1900)
Mikhail K. Lukonin, Russ. poet, d. (b. 1919)
Tom Stoppard: "Travesties," New York Drama Critics and Tony awards for best play
David Rabe: "Streamers," play
William Gaddis: "J R," National Book award fiction
Patrick Grainville: "Les Flamboyants," novel
Lillian Hellman: "Scoundrel Time," nonfiction
Carl Bernstein and Bob Woodward: "The Final Days," nonfiction
Leon Uris: "Trinity," novel
John Hawkes: "Travesty," novel
Kurt Vonnegut: "Slapstick," novel
Alex Haley: "Roots," nonfiction
Gore Vidal: "1876," novel
Hedrick Smith: "The Russians," historical study
André Malraux, Fr. novelist, d. (b. 1901)
Dame Edith Evans, Eng. actress, d. (b. 1888)
Michel Henry: "L'Amour Les Yeux Fermes," novel
Donald Barthelme: "Amateurs," fiction

C. RELIGION, PHILOSOPHY, LEARNING

tialist theologian, d. (b. 1884)
Gilbert Highet: "The Immortal Profession"
Michael J. Arlen: "Passage of Ararat," National Book award for contemporary affairs
U.S. Lutherans split over interpretation of Bible and synod administration; new breakaway church founded
Arnold Toynbee, Eng. historian, d. (b. 1889)
Gilbert Ryle, Eng. philosopher and writer, d. (b. 1900)

1977

A. HISTORY, POLITICS

Brig. Gen. Teferi Bante, Ethiopian head of state, d. (b. 1921)
Ethiopia's ruling military council, the Dergue, names Lt. Col. Mengistu Haile Mariam head of state
President Carter grants a pardon to almost all American draft evaders of the Vietnam War era
Tom (Thomas Campbell) Clark, U.S. Supreme Court justice (1949–1967), d. (b. 1889)
New human rights manifesto signed by 241 Czechoslovak

(contd)

B. LITERATURE, THEATER

Konstantin A. Fedin, Russ. novelist, d. (b. 1892)
Vladimir Nabokov, Russ.-born Amer. novelist, d. (b. 1899)
James Jones, Amer. novelist, d. (b. 1921)
Jacques Prévert, Fr. poet and playwright, d. (b. 1900)
John Dickson Carr, Amer. mys-

(contd)

C. RELIGION, PHILOSOPHY, LEARNING

Ernst Bloch, Ger. Marxist philosopher, d. (b. 1885)
Bruno Bettelheim: "The Uses of Enchantment: The Meaning and Importance of Fairy Tales," National Book award
Rev. Martin Cyril D'Arcy, Brit. Jesuit philosopher, d. (b. 1888)

(contd)

D. VISUAL ARTS	E. MUSIC	F. SCIENCE, TECHNOLOGY, GROWTH	G. DAILY LIFE	
actress, d. (b. 1911) Man Ray, Amer. painter, sculptor, and photographer who helped found the Dadaist movement, d. (b. 1890) Jean Gabin, Fr. screen actor, d. (b. 1904) Fritz Lang, Austrian film director, d. (b. 1890) Alexander Calder, Amer. sculptor known for his "stabiles" and "mobiles," d. (b. 1898) Films: "All the President's Men" (Jason Robards, Alan J. Pakula); "Rocky" (Talia Shire, Sylvester Stallone); "Taxi Driver" (Robert De Niro); "Face to Face" (Liv Ullmann) Leo Kerz, Ger. theater producer and stage designer, d. (b. 1912) Alastair Sim, Eng. stage and screen actor, d. (b. 1900) Aquiles Badi, Argentinian semi-abstract painter, d. (b. 1893)	(b. 1894) Rosina Lhévinne, Russ.-born Amer. pianist and teacher, d. (b. 1880) Carlisle Floyd: "Bilby's Doll," opera, Houston Gian-Carlo Menotti: "The Hero," opera, Philadelphia Lotte Lehmann, Ger.-born Amer. soprano, d. (b. 1888) Gregor Piatigorsky, Russ.-born Amer. cellist, d. (b. 1903) Gina Bachauer, Eng. concert pianist, d. (b. 1913)	transmit to earth first closeup photos of the surface; scientific experiments remain inconclusive about the existence of life on Mars Scientists at M.I.T. announce construction of a functional synthetic gene, complete with regulatory mechanisms Discovery of viral cause of multiple sclerosis Archeologists discover in northern Syria the ancient civilization of Ebla that flourished 4,400 years ago Trofim D. Lysenko, Russ. geneticist, d. (b. 1898) Nobel Prize for Economics: Milton Friedman (U.S.) Nobel Prize for Physics: Burton Richter (U.S.) and Samuel C. C. Ting (U.S.) Nobel Prize for Chemistry: William N. Lipscomb (U.S.) Nobel Prize for Medicine or Physiology: Baruch S. Blumberg (U.S.) and Daniel C. Gajdusek (U.S.) Alexander S. Wiener, Amer. serologist and co-discoverer (with Karl Landsteiner) of the Rh blood factor, d. (b. 1907)	Britain fights worst drought on record Jerry Pate, a rookie on the PGA tour, wins the U.S. Open and Canadian Open golf championships "Bold Forbes" wins horse racing's Kentucky Derby and Belmont Stakes Hurricane Belle hits the east coast of the U.S.; estimated $23.5 million damage Summer Olympics held in Montreal; 32 African and Asian countries withdraw because of political issues; U.S.S.R. takes 47 gold medals, East Germany 40, and U.S. 34; 14-year-old Rumanian gymnast Nadia Comaneci wins three gold medals, gaining seven perfect scores, the first time such marks awarded in Olympic gymnastics Mysterious illness kills 29 persons who attend a state American Legion convention in Philadelphia; 151 others are stricken by "Legionnaires' disease" "Smokey the Bear," U.S. national symbol of fire prevention, dies at the National Zoo in Washington, D.C. Carlo Gambino, leader of New York's Mafia, d. (b. 1902) Cincinnati Reds defeat New York Yankees, 4 games to 0, to win World Series The Orient Express, the romantic train whose name conjured up beautiful women and sinister spies, ends its Istanbul-to-Paris run Two airliners collide over Yugoslavia killing all 176 persons aboard in aviation's worst mid-air collision Jimmy Connors (U.S.) wins U.S. Open men's singles tennis championship; Bjorn Borg (Swed.) captures Wimbledon men's singles tennis title; Chris Evert (U.S.) wins Wimbledon and U.S. Open women's singles tennis championships; Italy wins the Davis Cup Violent earthquakes strike northeastern Italy, Peking and Tientsin in China, Mindanao in the Philippines, eastern Turkey, Bali, and Guatemala; an estimated 780,000 die Henry ("Hank") Aaron retires as a baseball player, holding the U.S. major league record of 755 career home runs The manslaughter conviction of Dr. Kenneth C. Edelin in an abortion case (1975) is overturned by the Massachusetts Supreme Judicial Court Tanker "Argo Merchant" runs aground off Nantucket, Mass., spilling millions of gallons of oil	**1976 contd**
Roberto Rossellini, Ital. film director, d. (b. 1906) Joan Crawford, Amer. actress, d. (b. 1908) TV dramatization of "Roots" Henri-Georges *(contd)*	Leopold Stokowski, Amer. conductor, d. (b. 1882) Elvis Presley, Amer. singer known as the "King of Rock 'n' Roll," d. (b. 1935) Australians choose *(contd)*	U.S. space shuttle "Enterprise" makes its first manned flight Wernher von Braun, Ger.-born Amer. rocket expert, d. (b. 1912) George C. Cotzias, Amer. neurologist and developer of L-Dopa therapy for Parkinson's disease, d. (b. 1918) *(contd)*	Portland Trail Blazers win National Basketball Association championship More than 570 persons die in the world's worst aviation disaster when a KLM Royal Dutch Airlines Boeing 747 crashes into a Pan American World Airways Boeing 747 on the runway of Los Rodeos Airport on the Canary Island of Tenerife Bernard ("Toots") Shor, New York City res- *(contd)*	**1977**

	A. HISTORY, POLITICS	B. LITERATURE, THEATER	C. RELIGION, PHILOSOPHY, LEARNING
1977 contd	intellectuals and activists is published in West Germany; Czech police harass and arrest activists; U.S. charges Czechoslovakia with violations of the 1975 Helsinki accord; Russ. Andrei D. Sakharov appeals to Pres. Carter "to raise your voice" on behalf of persecuted political activists in the Soviet Union and Eastern Europe Sir Anthony Eden, former Prime Minister of Britain, d. (b. 1897) Kamal Jumblatt, Lebanese politician and hereditary Druse chieftain, d. (b. 1919) Forces from Angola, including Katangan exiles, invade Shaba (formerly Katanga) Province, threatening Zaire's rich copper industry Members of a Russ. Helsinki accord monitoring group, including Jewish human rights activists Alexander Ginzberg, Yuri Orlov, Anatoly Shcharansky, and Vladimir Slepak, are arrested by Soviet authorities President Carter warns that the energy crisis in the U.S. could bring on a "national catastrophe"; Americans must respond with the "moral equivalent of war," making "profound" changes in their oil consumption Tom Bradley, elected Los Angeles's first black Mayor in 1973, is reelected, defeating 11 white opponents Indira Gandhi resigns as Prime Minister of India after her ruling Congress party suffers defeat in national elections; Morarji R. Desai, head of the opposition Janata party, becomes India's Prime Minister The Palestine National Council calls for "an independent national state" on "national soil" Jacques Chirac, former Fr. Premier, is elected Mayor of Paris; municipal voting in France puts the leftists in control of more than three-quarters of the country's large cities Israeli Prime Minister Yitzhak Rabin resigns; Menahem Begin becomes Israel's sixth Prime Minister The French territory of Afars and Issas becomes independent as the Republic of Djibouti The U.S. Justice Department widens its investigation of alleged illegal South Korean lobbying to influence Congress to determine if there was a willful cover-up Ludwig Erhard, former Chancellor of West Germany, d. (b. 1897) U.S. Department of Energy is established Pakistan's army overthrows the government and imposes martial law Turkey's government internally divided: Premier Bulent Ecevit's ten-day-old minority government steps down after a no-confidence vote; Suleyman Demirel becomes Premier until his three-party coalition government falls on a no-confidence vote Archbishop Makarios III, President of Cyprus (1960–1977), d. (b. 1913) Communist Party Chief Leonid Brezhnev is elected President of the Soviet Union, becoming the first leader to combine both positions Ethiopians halt Somali-backed guerrillas in Ogaden to force a stalemate in the battle for the region; rebels fight for the independence of Ethiopia's coastal Eritrea Province Pol Pot is named Secretary General of Cambodia's Communist Party G. Gordon Liddy, credited with having devised the Watergate break-in, is released from prison; his 52½ months of imprisonment was longer than any other convicted Watergate figure Nobel Peace Prize: Amnesty International, a London-based human rights organization; the 1976 Nobel Peace Prize is belatedly awarded to two Irish women, Mairead Corrigan and Betty Williams President Carter and Brig. General Omar Torrijos, Panama's chief of government, sign the new Panama Canal treaties *(contd)*	tery novelist, d. (b. 1905) Anaïs Nin, Fr.-born Amer. novelist and diarist, d. (b. 1903) Carl Zuckmayer, Ger.-Swiss playwright and novelist, d. (b. 1896) Sir Terence M. Rattigan, Eng. playwright, d. (b. 1911) Mackinlay Kantor, Amer. writer, d. (b. 1904) Robert Lowell, Pulitzer Prize-winning Amer. poet, d. (b. 1917) Ethel Waters, Amer. singer and actress, best known for her roles in "The Member of the Wedding" (stage) and "Cabin in the Sky" (film), d. (b. 1900) Mark Schorer, Amer. literary critic and author, d. (b. 1908) Zero Mostel, Amer. actor, d. (b. 1915) Alfred Lunt, Amer. actor, d. (b. 1893) Richard Wright: "American Hunger," autobiographical fiction (posth.) Richard Eberhart: "Collected Poems: 1930–1976," National Book award Wallace Stegner: "The Spectator Bird," National Book award James Merrill: "Divine Comedies," Pulitzer Prize poetry Nobel Prize for Literature: Vicente Aleixandre (Sp.) Louis Untermeyer, Amer. poet, critic, and editor, d. (b. 1885) Dennis Y. Wheatley, Eng. mystery novelist, d. (b. 1897) Didier Decoin: "John l'Enfer," novel Jerzy Kosinski: "Blind Date," novel John Cheever: "Falconer," novel John Le Carre: "The Honourable Schoolboy," novel J. R. R. Tolkien: "The Silmarillion," novel (posth.) John Fowles: "Daniel Martin," novel Colleen McCullough: "The Thorn Birds," novel John Toland: "Adolf Hitler," biography Cyril Ritchard, Australian-born Amer. actor, d. (b. 1898) Simon Gray: "Otherwise Engaged," New York Drama Critics award Bert Brecht-Kurt Weill: "Happy End," musical Martin Charnin: "Annie," New York Drama Critics and Tony awards for best musical David Mamet: "American Buffalo," New York Drama Critics award for best American play Michael Cristofer: "The Shadow *(contd)*	Tanzanian black activist Bishop Josiah M. Kibira is elected head of the Lutheran World Federation John Neopomucene Neumann (1811–1860) canonized; first American male saint Jacqueline Means becomes the first woman ordained a priest in the Episcopal Church in America Scholastic Aptitude Tests of U.S. college-bound students show steady decline between 1963 and 1977 The Orthodox Church in America selects its first Amer.-born prelate, Archbishop Theodosius Raoul Berger: "Government by Judiciary" William L. Langer, Amer. historian, d. (b. 1896) Sir Charles Petrie, Eng. historian d. (b. 1895)

1977 contd

D. VISUAL ARTS

Clouzot, Fr. film director, d. (b. 1907)
Peter Finch, Eng. stage and screen actor, d. (b. 1916)
Henri Langlois, founder and director of the French Cinemathèque, d. (b. 1914)
William Gropper, Amer. painter and cartoonist, d. (b. 1897)
Jan Zrzavý, Czech painter, d. (b. 1890)
Uday Shanker, Indian classical and folk dancer, d. (b. 1901)
John N. Nash, Eng. landscape painter and illustrator, d. (b. 1893)
Naum Gabo, Russ.-Amer. sculptor, d. (b. 1890)
Academy Awards (for 1976)—best picture: "Rocky"; best actor: Peter Finch ("Network"); best actress: Faye Dunaway ("Network")
Groucho Marx, Amer. comedian, d. (b. 1890)
Joe Musial, Amer. cartoonist who for 25 years drew the Katzenjammer Kids, d. (b. 1905)
Films: "Star Wars" (George Lucas); "Annie Hall" (Woody Allen, Diane Keaton); "Julia" (Vanessa Redgrave, Jane Fonda, Jason Robards); "Saturday Night Fever" (John Travolta); "Oh, God!" (George Burns); "New York, New York" (Martin Scorsese)
Howard Hawks, Amer. director, d. (b. 1896)
Charles ("Charlie")
(contd)

E. MUSIC

"Advance Australia Fair" as national song
Nunnally Johnson, Amer. screenwriter and director, d. (b. 1897)
E. Power Biggs, Amer. organist, d. (b. 1906)
Sidney Foster, Amer. concert pianist, d. (b. 1917)
Rudolf Barshai, Russ. chamber orchestra conductor, emigrates to Israel
Erroll Garner, Amer. jazz pianist and composer, d. (b. 1921)
Thomas Schippers, Amer. conductor, d. (b. 1930)
Richard Addinsell, Eng. composer of film, television, and theater scores, d. (b. 1904)
Bing Crosby, Amer. singer and actor, d. (b. 1904)
Maria Callas, Greek-Amer. operatic soprano, d. (b. 1923)
Bruce Hungerford, Amer. concert pianist, d. (b. 1922)
U.S.S.R. adopts a new text for its national anthem, ending more than 20 years during which the anthem could not be sung because of its glorification of Joseph Stalin

F. SCIENCE, TECHNOLOGY, GROWTH

U.S. launches two spacecrafts to probe the atmosphere of Venus
U.S. scientists report that Uranus is encircled by at least five rings resembling those around Saturn
Brit. scientists report they have determined for the first time the complete genetic structure of a living organism
Rear Adm. George J. Dufek, Amer. polar explorer, d. (b. 1903)
Nobel Prize for Medicine or Physiology: Rosalyn S. Yalow, Roger C. L. Guillemin, and Andrew V. Schally (all U.S.)
Nobel Prize for Physics: John H. Van Vleck (U.S.), Philip W. Anderson (U.S.), and Sir Neville F. Mott (Eng.)
Nobel Prize for Chemistry: Ilya Prigogine (Belg.)
U.S. unmanned spacecrafts Voyager I and II begin journeys to explore outer solar system
Edgar D. Adrian, Nobel Prize-winning Eng. physiologist, d. (b. 1889)
U.S. confirms testing of neutron bomb which kills with massive radiation leaving most buildings intact
U.S. scientists announce the discovery of primitive microorganisms called methanogens, a separate form of life distinct from bacteria, plants, and animals
Peter C. Goldmark, Amer. inventor of the long-playing record and developer of the first practical color television, d. (b. 1906)
Jean Rostand, Fr. biologist and writer, d. (b. 1894)
Amer. scientists claim detection of a fundamental electric charge one-third that of the electron charge; possible detection of a quark
Jacob Marschak, Amer. economist who helped develop the field of econometrics, d. (b. 1898)
Nobel Prize for Economics: Bertil Ohlin (Swed.) and James E. Meade (Eng.)
The structure of the sun's magnetic field is determined for the first time from data returned by the U.S. Pioneer II spacecraft
The 2,300-year-old tomb of King Philip II of Macedon, father of Alexander the Great, is found in northern Greece
Discovery of a mini-planet
(contd)

G. DAILY LIFE

taurateur and confidante of celebrities, d. (b. 1903)
Oakland Raiders defeat Minnesota Vikings, 32–14, to win football's Super Bowl
General Lewis B. Hershey, director of the U.S. Selective Service System (1941–1970), d. (b. 1893)
Offshore Norwegian oil well in the North Sea is capped after blowing out of control for eight days; about 8.2 million gallons of crude oil spilled
U.S. seizes two Soviet fishing vessels, charging them with violating the new U.S. 200-mile fishing zone
Montreal Canadiens defeat Boston Bruins to win their 20th Stanley Cup
A massive blackout in New York City leaves 9 million persons without electricity for between 4½ and 25 hours; lightning bolts hit Consolidated Edison Co.'s two largest generating facilities; airports, tunnels, banks, and offices close down; rampant looting, vandalism, and other criminal activity leads to the arrest of 3,700 persons; at least 500 fires reported
Alice Paul, leader of women's movement in U.S., d. (b. 1885)
Magda Lupescu, Rumanian adventuress, d. (b. 1904?)
Oil flows through the 800-mile trans-Alaska pipeline from Prudhoe Bay on Alaska's North Slope south to the port of Valdez
Tom Watson wins the Masters and his second British Open golf championship
Queen Elizabeth II of England celebrates her Silver Jubilee
Volcanoes erupt in Japan, Italy, and Hawaii
Sadaharu Oh, Japanese first baseman, hits his 756th home run to become the most prolific home-run hitter in the history of professional baseball
"Seattle Slew" wins horse racing's Triple Crown
Lou Brock, St. Louis Cardinal outfielder, breaks Ty Cobb's base-stealing record
Steven Biko, South African black leader, d. (b. 1947)
Chris Evert (U.S.) wins her third consecutive U.S. Open women's singles tennis championship; Bjorn Borg (Swed.) captures his second consecutive Wimbledon men's singles tennis championship; Australia wins the Davis Cup
French is adopted as the official language of Quebec
New York Yankees defeat Los Angeles Dodgers, 4 games to 2, to win World Series
Cyclone kills 20,000 and leaves two million persons homeless in India; earthquake devastates northwestern Argentina; typhoons disrupt Taiwan and northern Philippines
Brazilian superstar Pele plays his last professional soccer game in a match between the Cosmos, his current team, and Santos of Brazil, the team he led to three world championships in the 1950s and 1960s
Amer. 12-meter sloop "Courageous" defeats "Australia" to retain the America's Cup
Canadian Cindy Nicholas becomes the first woman to complete a round-trip, nonstop
(contd)

	A. HISTORY, POLITICS	B. LITERATURE, THEATER	C. RELIGION, PHILOSOPHY, LEARNING
1977 contd	Egyptian President Anwar Sadat arrives in Israel on the first visit by an Arab leader to the Jewish state since it was founded in 1948 Edward I. Koch is elected Mayor of New York City Military junta seizes control of Thailand's government Kurt von Schuschnigg, Chancellor of Austria (1934–1938), imprisoned by the Nazis until liberated by the Allied Advance (1945), Amer. political science professor (1948–1968), d. (b. 1897) Rhodesian Prime Minister Ian Smith announces his government is prepared to work out a political settlement with Rhodesia's black majority The Socialist minority government of Premier Mario Soares falls when it loses a vote of confidence in Portugal's National Assembly President-for-life Jean Bédel Bokassa of the Central African Empire crowns himself Emperor Bokassa I during a $25-million gilded coronation South Africa declares the black homeland of Bophuthatswana independent David K. E. Bruce, former U.S. Ambassador to France, West Germany, and Great Britain, d. (b. 1898)	Box," Pulitzer Prize drama and Tony award	
1978	Violence sweeps Nicaragua in nationwide leftist campaign by the Sandinista guerrillas to overthrow the government of President Anastasio Somoza Prime Minister Junius Richard Jayawardene becomes President of Sri Lanka under new presidential governing system adopted by the National Assembly in 1977 Spyros Kyprianou, Cypriot lawyer, wins full five-year term as President of Cyprus Hubert H. Humphrey, U.S. Vice-President (1965–1969) and U.S. Senator (1949–1964, 1970–1978), d. (b. 1911) Bulent Ecevit is named Premier of Turkey Wadi Haddad, co-founder in 1966 of the Popular Front for the Liberation of Palestine and terrorist guerrilla leader who directed numerous airplane hijackings, d. (b. 1927) Former Italian Premier Aldo Moro is kidnapped and murdered by the Red Brigades, a revolutionary terrorist group A military junta seizes power in Afghanistan U.S. Senate ratifies new Panama Canal treaties Cearbhall Ó Dalaigh, former jude and President of Ireland, d. (b. 1911) Premier Chiang Ching-kuo is elected President of Nationalist China, replacing retiring President Yen Chia-kan (C. K. Yen) U.S. and the People's Republic of China announce establishment of full diplomatic relations Antonio Guzmán is elected President of the Dominican Republic, defeating his rival Joaquin Balaguer; first peaceful transfer of power between constitutionally elected governments in Dominican history Zaire's Shaba (Katanga) Province is invaded by secessionist rebels; Angolan, Cuban, and Russian backing is reported; French and Belgian paratroopers evacuate Europeans from region; U.S. airlifts troops from Morocco and other African countries that help repel invaders Philibert Tsiranana, President of the Malagasy Republic (1959–1972), d. (b. 1912) President Giovanni Leone of Italy resigns ; Socialist Alessandro Pertini elected President Nobel Peace Prize: Israeli Premier Menahem Begin and Egyptian President Anwar Sadat Julio César Turbay Ayala is elected President of Colombia, narrowly defeating Belisario Betancur President Ferdinand E. Marcos of the Philippines assumes the additional post of Premier Robert Gordon Menzies, former Prime Minister of Austral- *(contd)*	A Gutenberg Bible is sold at auction in New York for $2 million, the highest price ever paid for a printed book John Hall Wheelock, Amer. poet, d. (b. 1886) Faith Baldwin, Amer. author, d. (b. 1893) Harry E. Martinson, Nobel Prize-winning Swed. novelist and poet, d. (b. 1904) Freda Utley, Eng.-born Amer. author and journalist in Asia and Europe, d. (b. 1898) Leon Damas, Fr. Guianan poet who helped found the Negritude literary and cultural movement in Paris in the 1930s, d. (b. 1912) Phyllis McGinley, Amer. poet of light verse and essayist, d. (b. 1905) Sylvia Townsend Warner, Eng. novelist and poet, d. (b. 1893) James Jones: "Whistle" (posth.) Joyce Carol Oates: "Son of the Morning," novel Herman Wouk: "War and Remembrance," novel Mario Puzo: "Fools Die," novel Hugh Leonard: "Da," Tony award for best play Mary Lee Settle: "Blood Tie," National Book award, fiction Howard Nemerov: "Collected Poems," Pulitzer Prize and National Book award James Alan McPherson: "Elbow Room," Pulitzer Prize novel D. L. Coburn: "The Gin Game," play Michael Bennett: "Ballroom," musical William Manchester: "American Caesar: Douglas MacArthur 1880–1964" *(contd)*	Frank Raymond Leavis, Eng. professor and writer, d. (b. 1895) Mario Pei, Ital.-born Amer. linguistics professor and author, d. (b. 1900) Margarete Bieber, Ger.-born Amer. historian, archaeologist, and author, d. (b. 1879) Bergen Evans, Amer. language professor and author, d. (b. 1904) James B. Conant, Amer. educator, scientist, and diplomat, d. (b. 1893) Jacques Chastenet, Fr. historian, d. (b. 1893) Gilbert Highet, Amer. professor, critic, poet, and author, d. (b. 1906) Theodore H. White: "In Search of History: A Personal Adventure" Margaret Mead, Amer. anthropologist and author, d. (b. 1901) Étienne Gilson, Fr. historian and philosopher, d. (b. 1884) Pope Paul VI dies; his successor Cardinal Albino Luciani as Pope John Paul I dies; succeeded by Cardinal Karol Wojtyla who takes the papal name John Paul II (he is the first non-Italian to be elected Pope in 456 years and the first Pole chosen) Kuo Mo-jo, Chin. scholar, poet, and politician, d. (b. 1891) Hannah Arendt: "The Life of the Mind" (posth.), 2 vols.: I, "Thinking" (1977); II, "Willing"

1977 contd

D. VISUAL ARTS

Chaplin, Eng. actor, d. (b. 1889)

André Eglevsky, Russ.-born Amer. ballet dancer and producer, d. (b. 1917)

E. MUSIC

F. SCIENCE, TECHNOLOGY, GROWTH

circling the sun between Saturn and Uranus

U.S. National Institute of Health reports that for the first time a life-threatening viral infection—herpes encephalitis—has been successfully treated with a drug

G. DAILY LIFE

swim across the English Channel

Janelle Penny Commissiong, representing Trinidad-Tobago, is the first black woman to win the Miss Universe title

Gordie Howe becomes the first man in the history of hockey to score 1,000 professional career goals

Passenger service on the Concorde supersonic transport begins between New York and Paris and London

U.S. population reaches 216 million

1978

D. VISUAL ARTS

Charles Boyer, Fr. stage and screen actor, d. (b. 1899)

Edward Durell Stone, Amer. architect, d. (b. 1902)

U.S. television drama "Holocaust" viewed by more than 120 million persons

Art collection of Robert von Hirsch, Ger.-Swiss leather merchant, is sold at auction for $37.6 million

Duncan Grant, Eng. painter, d. (b. 1885)

Academy Awards (for 1977) —best picture: "Annie Hall"; best actor: Richard Dreyfuss ("The Goodbye Girl"); best actress: Diane Keaton ("Annie Hall")

Karl Wallenda, Ger.-born high-wire performer, d. (b. 1904)

Peggy Wood, Amer. stage, screen, and television actress, d. (b. 1892)

Ilka Chase, Amer. actress and author, d. (b. 1905)

(contd)

E. MUSIC

Alexander Kipnis, Ukrainian-born Amer. operatic basso, d. (b. 1891)

Aram Khachaturian, Russ. composer, d. (b. 1903)

Ray Noble, Eng. composer and conductor, d. (b. 1906)

Nicolas Nabokov, Russ.-born Amer. composer, d. (b. 1902)

Soviet Union rescinds the citizenships of composer-cellist Mstislav Rostropovich and his wife, soprano Galina Vishnevskaya

Alex Bradford, Amer. composer, gospel singer, and actor, d. (b. 1926)

Zubin Mehta, former conductor of the Los Angeles Philharmonic, becomes music director of the New York Philharmonic

Krzysztof Penderecki: "Paradise Lost," opera, Chicago

"Disco" music and dancing is in

(contd)

F. SCIENCE, TECHNOLOGY, GROWTH

Reinhold Messner (Ital.) and Peter Habeler (Aust.) make the first conquest of Mt. Everest without artificial oxygen supplies

Jap. explorer Naomi Uemura becomes the first to complete a solo journey to the North Pole

Jacques Leon Rueff, Fr. economist, d. (b. 1896)

Samuel A. Goudsmit, Dutch-Amer. physicist, d. (b. 1902)

Norwegian explorer-ethnologist Thor Heyerdahl sails on a reed boat from Qurna, Iraq, to the coast of Djibouti

Roy F. Harrod, Eng. economist, d. (b. 1900)

Armand J. Quick, Amer. doctor and expert on blood clotting and diseases, d. (b. 1894)

Kurt Gödel, Amer. mathematical logician, d. (b. 1906)

Soviet cosmonauts in orbiting Salyut 6 space station set an endurance record of 139 days and 15 hours

Isador Lubin, Amer. economist, d. (b. 1896)

"Test-tube baby" born in England: Lesley Brown gives birth to girl—first human baby conceived outside the body of a woman

Ronald G. W. Norrish, Eng. Nobel Prize-winning chemist, d. (b. 1897)

Mstislav V. Keldysh, Russ. mathematician, d. (b. 1911)

Oil drilling begins in the Baltimore Canyon region off the New Jersey shore

Nobel Prize for Economics: Herbert A. Simon (U.S.)

Nobel Prize for Physics: Arno A.

(contd)

G. DAILY LIFE

Dallas Cowboys defeat Denver Broncos, 27–10, to win football's Super Bowl

After 32 years in U.S. keeping, the crown of St. Stephen and its coronation regalia are returned to Hungary

John D. MacArthur, Amer. billionaire insurance and real estate magnate, d. (b. 1897)

Air India 747 crash kills 213 persons; India's worst air disaster

David R. Berkowitz, also known as the .44-caliber killer and the "Son of Sam," receives life imprisonment for six murders he committed before his arrest in August, 1977

New York Yankees defeat Los Angeles Dodgers, 4 games to 2, to win World Series

Montreal Canadiens defeat Boston Bruins to win their 21st Stanley Cup

Washington Bullets win National Basketball Association championship

U.S. dollar plunges to record low against the Japanese yen, the West German mark, and the Swiss franc; gold in London rises to record $243.65 an ounce; Canadian dollar falls to a 45-year low against U.S. dollar

Gary Player wins his third Masters golf championship; Jack Nicklaus wins his third British Open title

Longest U.S. coal strike ends on 110th day after miners approve agreement

The "Chicago Daily News" ceases publication after 103 years; new daily newspaper "The Trib" publishes for three months in New York City

Leon Spinks wins world heavyweight boxing championship; Muhammad Ali beats Spinks seven months later to regain title and to become the first boxer ever to win a heavyweight title three times

Argentina wins soccer's World Cup

The supertanker "Amoco Cadiz" breaks apart in heavy seas off France's Brittany coast, spilling a record 220,000 tons of oil which blackens more than 110 miles of coastline

Brig. General Margaret A. Brewer is the first female general in the U.S. Marine Corps

(contd)

	A. HISTORY, POLITICS	B. LITERATURE, THEATER	C. RELIGION, PHILOSOPHY, LEARNING
1978 contd	ia, d. (b. 1894) Solomon Islands, Tuvalu (formerly the Ellice Islands), and Dominica become independent nations Russ. human rights activists Yuri Orlov, Anatoly Shcharansky, and Alexander Ginzburg are convicted of "anti-Soviet agitation" and sentenced to 7, 13, and 8 years in prisons and forced labor camps respectively; Vladimir Slepak receives 5 years of internal exile for "malicious hooliganism" South Yemen's President is deposed and executed by pro-Soviet faction that seizes power; North Yemen's President is assassinated President Moktar Ould Daddah, ruler of Mauritania since its independence from France in 1960, is ousted Twenty-nine of the 46 Red Brigades members on trial in Turin, Italy, are convicted of intent to subvert the government and other charges Arab League uses military force to separate warring Syrian and Christian militia forces and to restore peace to Lebanon John Vorster resigns as Prime Minister of South Africa (afterward appointed President of South Africa); succeeded by Pieter Willem Botha Jomo Kenyatta, President of Kenya (1964–1978), d. (b. 1891?) A military junta takes control of Honduras U.S. House Committee on Standards of Official Conduct investigates the Korean lobbying scandal in Congress Discord between Portugal's political parties brings votes of no-confidence in the National Assembly Army officers oust Bolivia's President and seize control of the government—the 200th coup in Bolivia's 158 years of independent statehood The Soviet Union and Vietnam sign a 25-year treaty of friendship and cooperation Jap. Premier Takeo Fukuda and Chin. Deputy Premier Teng Hsiao-ping attend signing of Japanese-Chinese treaty of peace and friendship Israeli Premier Menahem Begin and Egyptian President Anwar Sadat agree on a framework for Mideast peace at Camp David summit talks arranged by U.S. President Carter; officials from Israel and Egypt negotiate in Washington, D.C., on drafting a bilateral peace treaty Houari Boumédienne, ruler of Algeria (1965–1978), d. (b. 1927) Golda Meir, Prime Minister of Israel (1969–1974), d. (b. 1898) Shah Mohammed Riza Pahlavi imposes martial rule to put an end to violent anti-government demonstrations in Iran; Iranian oil industry shut down by striking workers; self-exiled Moslem leader Ayatollah Ruholla Khomeini appeals for labor strife to topple the Shah	Graham Greene: "The Human Factor," novel Iris Murdoch: "The Sea, The Sea," novel John Updike: "The Coup," novel Barbara Tuchman: "A Distant Mirror: The Calamitous Fourteenth Century," history James A. Michener: "Chesapeake," historical novel Ignazio Silone, Ital. novelist, best known for "Fontamara" and "Bread and Wine," d. (b. 1900) Richard Maltby, Jr.: "Ain't Misbehavin'," Fats Waller musical, New York Drama Critics and Tony awards Janet Flanner, Amer. writer and foreign correspondent for "The New Yorker" under the pen name "Genêt," d. (b. 1892) Robert Shaw, Eng. author and actor, d. (b. 1927) Louis Zukofsky, Amer. poet, d. (b. 1904) Nobel Prize for Literature: Isaac Bashevis Singer (U.S.) James Gould Cozzens, Amer. novelist, d. (b. 1903) Bruce Catton, Amer. author and historian, d. (b. 1899) Betty Comden and Adolph Green: "On the Twentieth Century," musical Liza Minnelli wins her third Tony award for her performance in "The Act"	

1978 contd

D. VISUAL ARTS

Abraham Rattner, Amer. painter, printmaker, and teacher, d. (b. 1895)

Films: "Grease" (John Travolta, Olivia Newton-John); "National Lampoon's Animal House" (John Belushi); "Interiors" (Woody Allen, Maureen Stapleton, Diane Keaton); "Coming Home" (Jon Voight, Jane Fonda); "Autumn Sonata" (Ingmar Bergman, Ingrid Bergman, Liv Ullmann); "A Dream of Passion" (Jules Dassin, Melina Mercouri, Ellyn Burstyn); "The Deer Hunter" (Robert De Niro)

Dan Dailey, Amer. song-and-dance man, d. (b. 1917)

Giorgio de Chirico, Ital. painter, d. (b. 1888)

Edgar Bergen, Amer. ventriloquist, d. (b. 1903)

Norman Rockwell, Amer. illustrator and painter, best known for his covers for "The Saturday Evening Post," d. (b. 1894)

E. MUSIC

vogue

Carlos Chávez, Mex. pianist, conductor, and composer, d. (b. 1899)

Howard Swanson, Amer. composer, d. (b. 1906)

Tibor Serly, Hung.-Amer. composer and conductor, d. (b. 1902)

Twenty-nine Italian opera house managers, art directors, and agents are arrested in an investigation into alleged corruption in the opera world

William Steinberg, Amer. conductor, d. (b. 1899)

William Grant Still, Amer. black classical composer, d. (b. 1895)

F. SCIENCE, TECHNOLOGY, GROWTH

Penzias (U.S.), Robert W. Wilson (U.S.), and Pyotr L. Kapitsa (Russ.)

Nobel Prize for Chemistry: Peter Mitchell (Eng.)

Nobel Prize for Medicine: Daniel Nathans (U.S.), Hamilton O. Smith (U.S.), and Werner Arber (Switz.)

Karl M. G. Siegbahn, Nobel Prize-winning Swed. physicist, d. (b. 1886)

Willy Messerschmitt, Ger. aircraft designer and industrialist, d. (b. 1898)

Victor Hasselblad, Swed. inventor and industrialist, d. (b. 1905)

Discovery of a moon orbiting Pluto

Umberto Nobile, Ital. Arctic explorer and engineer, d. (b. 1885)

G. DAILY LIFE

Joseph Colombo, Sr., reputed Amer. Mafia leader, d. (b. 1923)

Lucius D. Clay, Amer. general and businessman, d. (b. 1897)

Trading on the New York Stock Exchange has record single-day volume of 63.5 million shares on April 17; the Dow Jones industrial average soars 35.34 points on Nov. 1, a record-breaking single-day advance

U.S. Congress extends the ratification of the Equal Rights Amendment from March 22, 1979 to June 30, 1982

U.S. Supreme Court affirms a lower court decision requiring the U. of California Medical School to admit Allan P. Bakke, who claimed the school's minority-admissions plan had made him a victim of "reverse discrimination"

Gene Tunney, world heavyweight boxing champion, d. (b. 1898)

Earthquakes rock Greece, Japan, Mexico, Iran, and central Europe

California's voters approve "Proposition 13" to cut property taxes 57%

King Hussein of Jordan marries Elizabeth Halaby; Princess Caroline of Monaco marries Philippe Junot; Princess Margaret of Britain and Anthony Armstrong-Jones (Earl of Snowdon) are divorced; Christina Onassis, Greek shipping heiress, and Sergei Kausov (Russ.) are married

Jetliner and single-engine plane collide over San Diego; 144 die in worst mid-air collision in U.S. aviation history

Chris Evert (U.S.) captures her fourth consecutive U.S. Open women's singles tennis title; Jimmy Connors (U.S.) wins his third U.S. Open men's singles tennis title; Bjorn Borg (Swed.) wins his third consecutive Wimbledon, his third French Open, and his second Italian Open men's singles tennis championships; U.S. wins Davis Cup

Americans Max Anderson, Ben Abruzzo, and Larry Newman complete the first transatlantic crossing by balloon; Naomi James (Eng.) becomes the first woman to sail around the world alone

Striking unions shut down the "New York Post" for 56 days and the "New York Times" and the "Daily News" for 88 days; "The Times" of London and the "Sunday Times" suspend publication because of chaotic labor relations

U.S. Rep. Leo J. Ryan and four other Americans are shot to death in Guyana by members of the Peoples Temple, a California-based religious cult; murder-suicide of 917, including Peoples Temple leader Jim Jones, occurs at the cult's Guyanese jungle commune

World's population stands at about 4.4 billion persons, with 200,000 being added daily

World chess champion Anatoly Karpov of the Soviet Union successfully defends his title against Viktor Korchnoi

"Affirmed" wins horse racing's Triple Crown

New York Yankees defeat Los Angeles Dodgers, 4 games to 2, to win their second consecutive World Series

A. HISTORY, POLITICS

1979

Shah of Iran is forced into exile and is replaced as Iranian leader by Ayatollah Khomeini, who heads Islamic fundamentalist government; nearly 100 U.S. Embassy staff and Marines are taken hostage

Vietnamese army invades Cambodia and installs new government under Heng Samrin; Chinese forces attack Vietnam; mass graves of up to 3 million victims of Khmer Rouge discovered

Colonel Chadli Benjedid is elected President of Algeria; former President Ahmed Ben Bella is released after 14 years detention

Nelson Rockefeller, U.S. Vice-President (1974–77) and Governor of New York (1959–73), d. (b. 1908)

St. Lucia, St. Vincent, and the Grenadines win independence from Britain; Maurice Bishop becomes leader in Grenada following coup overthrowing Eric Gairy

Idi Amin, President of Uganda, is overthrown by Tanzanian-backed rebels; new President is Yusuf Lule

U.S. President Jimmy Carter, Israeli Premier Menachem Begin, and Egyptian President Anwar Sadat agree on the Camp David peace treaty; Egypt is expelled from Arab League

José Mariá Velasco Ibarra, former President of Ecuador, d. (b. 1893)

Zulfikar Ali Bhutto, former Prime Minister of Pakistan, is hanged after international pleas for mercy are ignored by General Zia; mobs attack the U.S. Embassy and other U.S. posts in Islamabad

John Vorster, President of South Africa, resigns after "Muldergate" scandal involving allegations of government corruption

U.S. President Jimmy Carter and U.S.S.R. President Leonid Brezhnev sign SALT-2 arms limitation treaty in Vienna; Carter calls it "a victory in the battle for peace" but faces Congressional opposition

Direct elections to the European Parliament held for the first time

Margaret Thatcher becomes Conservative Prime Minister of Britain following "Winter of Discontent" and rejection of Labour Party's devolution plans for Scotland and Wales

Ferenc Nagy, former Premier of Hungary, d. (b. 1904)

Jeremy Thorpe, former Eng. leader of Liberal Party, is acquitted of conspiring to murder homosexual Norman Scott

Ignatius Acheampong, former President of Ghana, is executed

Pierre Trudeau, Prime Minister of Canada, ends his term when Joe Clark of the Progressive Conservative Party is elected new Prime Minister

General Alexander Haig, Chief of Allied Forces in Europe, survives terrorist assassination attempt

Nicaragua's President Anastosio Somoza is overthrown by Sandinistas after bloody civil war; a new Marxist government is installed

Gustavo Diaz Ordaz, former President of Mexico, d. (b. 1911)

Maria Pintassilgo becomes Portugal's first woman Prime Minister

Francisco Nguema, brutal dictator of Equatorial Guinea, is overthrown in coup

Commonwealth Conference reaches Lancaster House agreement on the future of Rhodesia as the independent state of Zimbabwe; Bishop Abel Muzorewa is elected first prime minister

John George Diefenbaker, former Prime Minister of Canada, d. (b. 1895)

Victor Raul Haya de la Torre, Peruvian elder statesman, d. (b. 1895)

Earl Mountbatten of Burma, cousin of Queen Elizabeth II of England, is murdered in continuing I.R.A. bombing campaign; another bomb kills prominent Conservative

(contd)

B. LITERATURE, THEATER

Victoria Ocampo, Arg. writer and editor, d. (b. 1891)

Allen Tate, Amer. poet, d. (b. 1900)

Emmett Kelly, Amer. clown, d. (b. 1899)

Rene Marques, Puerto Rican playwright and novelist, d. (b. 1920)

Jean Stafford, Amer. Pulitzer Prize–winning novelist, d. (b. 1926)

Jean Rhys, Eng. novelist, d. (b. 1895)

Anatoly Kuznetsov, Russ. novelist, d. (b. 1930)

Herman Shumlin, Amer. stage producer-director, d. (b. 1899)

William Styron: "Sophie's Choice," novel

William Wharton: "Birdy," novel

Joseph Heller: "Good as Gold," novel

M. M. Kaye: "The Far Pavilions," novel

Bernard Malamud: "Dubin's Lives," novel

William Golding: "Darkness Visible," novel

Patrick White: "The Twyborn Affair," novel

Kurt Vonnegut: "Jailbird," novel

V. S. Naipaul: "A Bend in the River," novel

Norman Mailer: "The Executioner's Song," biography

Henry Miller: "Letters to Anaïs Nin," autobiography

John Cheever: "The Stories of John Cheever," Pulitzer Prize fiction and National Book Critics Circle Award

Robert Penn Warren: "Now and Then: Poems, 1976–1978," Pulitzer Prize poetry

Sam Shepard: "Buried Child," Pulitzer Prize drama

Edward O. Wilson: "On Human Nature," Pulitzer Prize nonfiction

Bernard Pomerance: "The Elephant Man," play, New York Drama Critics and Tony awards

Peter Shaffer: "Amadeus," play

Brian Clark: "Whose Life Is It Anyway?" play

Arthur Kopit: "Wings," play

Stephen Sondheim: "Sweeney Todd: the Demon Barber of Fleet Street," musical

Neil Simon, Marvin Hamlisch, and Carole Bayer Sager: "They're Playing Our Song," musical

Nobel Prize for Literature: Odysseus Elytis (Greece)

Cornelia Otis Skinner, Amer. actress and playwright, d. (b. 1901)

(contd)

C. RELIGION, PHILOSOPHY, LEARNING

Pope John Paul II becomes first Pope to visit a Communist country when he visits his native Poland; subsequently he tours the U.S. and with U.S. President Jimmy Carter calls for universal peace

Talcott Parsons, Amer. sociologist, d. (b. 1903)

Eric Partridge, Eng. lexicographer, d. (b. 1894)

Herbert Marcuse, Ger.-born Amer. philosopher and guru of sixties revolutionary movements, d. (b. 1898)

John Wright, senior Amer. Roman Catholic administrator, d. (b. 1909)

Joel Teitelbaum, Amer. Judaic leader, d. (b. 1887)

Ivor Armstrong Richards, Eng. educationalist, d. (b. 1893)

Gunmen seize the Grand Mosque in Mecca, Saudi Arabia; Saudi troops recapture it after bloody battle

Nobel Peace Prize: Mother Teresa

D. VISUAL ARTS

Pier Luigi Nervi, It. architect, d. (b. 1892)
Jean Renoir, Fr. film director, d. (b. 1894)
Aaron Douglas, Amer. painter, d. (b. 1900)
Merle Oberon, Aus.-born Amer. actress, d. (b. 1911)
Léonide Massine, Russ. ballet choreographer, d. (b. 1896)
John Carroll, Amer. actor, d. (b. 1907)
Kurt Joos, Ger. ballet choreographer, d. (b. 1901)
Mary Pickford, Can.-born Amer. actress, d. (b. 1893)
Jack Haley, Amer. stage and screen actor who played the Tin Man in "The Wizard of Oz," d. (b. 1900)
John Wayne, Amer. actor known as "The Duke," d. (b. 1907)
Academy Awards (for 1978)—best picture: "The Deer Hunter"; best actor: Jon Voight ("Coming Home"); best actress: Jane Fonda ("Coming Home")
Films: "Manhattan" (Woody Allen); "Apocalypse Now" (Francis Coppola); "Kramer vs. Kramer" (Robert Benton); "Being There" (Hal Ashby)
Corrine Griffith, Amer. actress known as the "Orchid of the Silent Screen," d. (b. 1906)
Michael Wilding, Eng. stage and screen actor, d. (b. 1933)
George Seaton, Amer. Oscar-
(contd)

E. MUSIC

Charles Mingus, Amer. jazz bassist and composer, d. (b. 1923)
Sid Vicious, Eng. punk-rock singer, d. (b. 1957)
Guiomar Novaes, Braz. pianist, d. (b. 1896)
Lester Flatt, Amer. country singer, d. (b. 1915)
Arthur Fiedler, Amer. conductor of Boston Pops Orchestra, d. (b. 1895)
Minnie Ripperton, Amer. pop singer, d. (b. 1948)
Samuel Barber: "Third Essay for Orchestra"
Michael Tippett: "The Ice Break," opera
Ray Eberle, Amer. singer with Glenn Miller Orchestra, d. (b. 1919)
Stan Kenton, Amer. big band leader, d. (b. 1912)
James Galway, Ir. flautist, acclaimed on U.S. tour
Richard Rodgers, Amer. composer, d. (b. 1902)
Gracie Fields, Eng. entertainer, d. (b. 1898)
Joseph Schwantner: "Aftertones of Infinity," Pulitzer Prize
Howard Swanson, Amer. composer, d. (b. 1907)
Don Ellis, Amer. jazz trumpeter, d. (b. 1934)
Riccardo Muti succeeds Eugene Ormandy as music director of the Philadelphia Orchestra
Beverly Sills retires as soprano and becomes music director of New York
(contd)

F. SCIENCE, TECHNOLOGY, GROWTH

Hiram H. Merrit, Amer. neurologist, d. (b. 1901)
Heinrich Focke, Ger. aircraft designer, d. (b. 1891)
Discovery of ring around Jupiter by Voyager 1 spacecraft
Nuclear disaster is narrowly averted at Three Mile Island, Pennsylvania; reactor building is badly contaminated
Philippe Cousteau, Fr. oceanographer, d. (b. 1940)
Werner Forssmann, Ger. Nobel Prize–winning medical researcher, d. (b. 1906)
Shinichero Tomonaga, Jap. Nobel Prize–winning chemist, d. (b. 1906)
Robert Burns Woodward, Amer. Nobel Prize–winning chemist, d. (b. 1917)
Bertil Ohlin, Swed. Nobel Prize–winning economist, d. (b. 1899)
Feodor Lynen, Ger. Nobel Prize–winning biochemist, d. (b. 1911)
Ernst B. Chain, Eng. Nobel Prize–winning biochemist, d. (b. 1906)
Two Soviet cosmonauts in orbiting Salyut 6 space station return to earth after record-breaking 175 days in space
Sir Barnes Neville Wallis, Eng. air engineer, d. (b. 1887)
Nobel Prize for Physiology and Medicine: Godfrey Hounsfield (Eng.) and Allan Cormack (U.S.)
Nobel Prize for Physics: Sheldon Glashow (U.S.), Steven Weinberg (U.S.), and Abdus Salem (Pak.)
Nobel Prize for Chemistry: Herbert Brown (U.S.) and George Wittig (Ger.)
Nobel Prize for Economics: Theodore Schultz (U.S.) and Sir Arthur Lewis (Eng.)

G. DAILY LIFE

Pittsburgh Steelers defeat Dallas Cowboys, 35–31, to win football's Super Bowl
Conrad N. Hilton, Amer. hotel owner, d. (b. 1888)
Patty Hearst, Amer. heiress, is released from prison
Beattie Feathers, Amer. running back for the Chicago Bears, d. (b. 1910)
Pittsburgh Pirates defeat Baltimore Orioles, 4 games to 3, to win World Series
Montreal Canadiens defeat New York Rangers in hockey to win their fourth consecutive Stanley Cup
Seattle SuperSonics win National Basketball Association championship
273 persons die in America's worst aviation disaster when an engine falls off a DC-10 on take-off at Chicago Airport; 257 die when another DC-10 crashes into a mountain in Antarctica
Cyrus S. Eaton, Amer. millionaire industrialist, d. (b. 1884)
Barbara Hutton, Amer. Woolworth heiress known as the "poor little rich girl," d. (b. 1912)
A. Phillip Randolph, Amer. black civil rights leader, d. (b. 1889)
Karen Silkwood is posthumously awarded $10,500,000 damages for negligent exposure to atomic contamination in 1974
John McEnroe (U.S.) captures his first U.S. Open men's singles title; Martina Navratilova (Czech.) wins her second Wimbledon women's singles tennis championship; Bjorn Borg (Swed.) captures his fourth consecutive Wimbledon men's singles tennis championship; U.S. wins Davis Cup
James Crockett, Amer. horticulturalist, d. (b. 1916)
Carmine Galante, reputed Amer. gangland leader, d. (b. 1901)
Tony "Two-Ton" Galento, Amer. heavyweight boxer, d. (b. 1910)
Don C. Miller, Amer. right halfback who was one of the "Four Horsemen" of Notre Dame, d. (b. 1902)
Elizabeth "Bunny" Ryan, Amer. tennis player who won a record 19 Wimbledon titles, d. (b. 1892)
Ku Klux Klan stages 50-mile "white rights" march from Selma to Montgomery, Alabama
14 persons die when the Fastnet international yacht race between Cornwall and Ireland is hit by Atlantic storm
Sebastian Coe, Eng. middle-distance runner, becomes first to hold world records simultaneously in 800 m, 1500 m, and 1 mile events
Alvin Karpis, Amer. gangster known as "Public Enemy No. 1" in the 1930s, d. (b. 1908)
Sally Rand, Amer. fan dancer and striptease artist, d. (b. 1904)
Juan Pérez Alfonso, Ven. founder of OPEC, d. (b. 1904)
André Meyer, Fr.-born Amer. banker, d. (b. 1898)
Hurricanes Frederick and David hit Mobile, Alabama, and southern Florida; estimated $45 million damage
(contd)

1979

	A. HISTORY, POLITICS	B. LITERATURE, THEATER	C. RELIGION, PHILOSOPHY, LEARNING
1979 contd	politician Airey Neave; large arms shipment sent by U.S. sympathizers of the I.R.A. is seized by security forces in Ireland Agostino A. Neto, President of Angola, d. (b. 1923) Ludvik Svoboda, former President of Czechoslovakia, d. (b. 1896) Emperor Bokassa of the Central African Empire is overthrown; new President David Dacko abolishes Empire Carlos Romero, President of El Salvador, is overthrown in military coup President Park Chung Hee of South Korea is shot dead, allegedly by accident, by his Chief of Intelligence U.S. Embassy in Tripoli is attacked by mob Charles Haughey is elected Prime Minister of Ireland, replacing Jack Lynch Adolph Dubs, U.S. Ambassador to Afghanistan, is kidnapped by Muslim terrorists and killed in gun battle; Soviet army invades Afghanistan on Christmas Eve; new President is Babrak Karmal	Maxwell D. Geismar, Amer. critic and editor, d. (b. 1910) James T. Farrell, Amer. novelist, d. (b. 1904) Kurt Kasznar, Amer. stage and screen actor, d. (b. 1913) Nicholas Monsarrat, Eng. novelist, d. (b. 1910) Konstantin Simonov, Russ. novelist, d. (b. 1915) Preston Jones, Amer. playwright, d. (b. 1936) Max Gordon, Amer. stage producer, d. (b. 1892) Fay Compton, Eng. actress, d. (b. 1894)	
1980	Indira Gandhi's Congress I Party gains a massive victory in the general election in India; later her son Sanjay (b. 1947) dies in plane crash Soviet forces are engaged in fierce clashes with Mujaheddin guerrillas in the Hindu Kush mountains, Afghanistan; U.N. General Assembly calls for Soviet troop withdrawal from Afghanistan President Carter restricts grain sales to the U.S.S.R. in protest against the Soviet invasion of Afghanistan Saudi Arabia beheads 63 Islamic fundamentalists who had violently occupied the Great Mosque in November 1979 In the U.S.S.R., Andrei Sakharov, dissident and Nobel physicist, is stripped of honors and sent into internal exile in Gorky Pierre Trudeau defeats Joe Clark to regain his office as Canadian Prime Minister 10,000 Cubans seek political asylum in the Peruvian Embassy; later over 120,000 Cubans are allowed to emigrate to the U.S. President Carter breaks off diplomatic relations with Iran and announces trade ban because of the continued Iranian detention of U.S. Embassy hostages; airborne commando raid to rescue the hostages fails disastrously; several helicopters break down and eight Americans are killed and five wounded in an accidental collision; Secretary of State Cyrus Vance resigns in protest against the mission and is replaced by Senator Edmund Muskie William L. Patterson, Amer. Communist Party leader, d. (b. 1891) Master Sgt. Samuel Kanyon Doe seizes power in Liberia Zimbabwe (formerly Rhodesia) gains independence; Robert Mugabe becomes the nation's first Prime Minister Marshal Josip Broz Tito, President of Yugoslavia (1953–1980), d. (b. 1892) Terrorists seize the Iranian Embassy in London and take 19 hostages; after five days two hostages are killed and British Special Air Service personnel storm the building and rescue the hostages, killing three of the five gunmen Constantine Karamanlis is elected President of Greece; Giorgios Rallis replaces him as Premier Palestinian mayors of Ramallah and Nablus are severely injured in bomb attacks Vigdis Finnbogadottir becomes Iceland's first female President The Republican National Convention selects Ronald Reagan as its presidential candidate; George Bush is his vice presidential running mate Muhammad Reza Pahlavi, deposed Shah of Iran, d. of cancer (b. 1919) The Israeli Parliament proclaims that a united Jerusalem is *(contd)*	Jean-Paul Sartre, Fr. author and philosopher, d. (b. 1905) Henry Miller, Amer. author, d. (b. 1891) Nobel Prize for Literature: Czeslaw Milosz, a Polish-language poet resident in the U.S.A. William Golding: "Rites of Passage," Booker Prize Norman Mailer: "The Executioner's Song," Pulitzer Prize fiction Donald Rodney Justice: "Selected Poems," Pulitzer Prize poetry Lanford Wilson: "Talley's Folly," Pulitzer Prize drama Douglas R. Hofstadter: "Gödel, Escher, Bach," Pulitzer Prize nonfiction David Lodge: "How Far Can You Go?" Whitbread Prize Romain Gary, Fr. novelist, commits suicide (b. 1914) Maurice Genevoix, Fr. novelist, d. (b. 1890) Marshall McLuhan, Can. media author, d. (b. 1911) C. P. Snow, Eng. novelist, d. (b. 1905) Ben Travers, Eng. comic dramatist, d. (b. 1886) Kingsley Amis: "Russian Hide and Seek," satire Samuel Beckett: "Company," novel Anthony Burgess: "Earthly Powers," novel John Le Carré "Smiley's People," novel Bernard Crick: "George Orwell," biography J. P. Donleavy: "Schultz," novel Graham Greene: "Dr. Fischer of Geneva," novel Hammond Innes: "Solomon's Seal," novel R. B. Martin: "Tennyson: The Unquiet Mind," nonfiction *(contd)*	Theodore F. Adams, Amer., former President of the Baptist World Alliance, d. (b. 1898) Rev. Ernest Alexander, Eng., former President of the World Council of Churches, d. (b. 1902) Roland Barthes, Fr. philosopher, d. (b. 1915) Benedictos I, Greek Orthodox Patriarch of Jerusalem, d. (b. 1892) Sergio Pignedoli, Ital. Roman Catholic Cardinal, d. (b. 1910) John H. Randall, Amer. philosopher, d. (b. 1899) Oscar Romero (b. 1917), Archbishop of San Salvador in El Salvador, assassinated while celebrating mass; 39 others shot dead at his funeral Henry Knox Sherrill, Amer. Presiding Bishop of the Episcopal Church, d. (b. 1890) Robert Runcie becomes 102nd Archbishop of Canterbury Pope John Paul II visits six African nations, followed later in the year by journeys to France, Brazil, and West Germany Polish radio broadcasts a Mass for the first time under Polish communist rule Publication of the "Alternative Service Book 1980": the first fully authorized prayer book for the Anglican (Episcopalian) Church since 1662

D. VISUAL ARTS	E. MUSIC	F. SCIENCE, TECHNOLOGY, GROWTH	G. DAILY LIFE	
winning film producer, director, and screenwriter, d. (b. 1911) Andrew Darburg, Amer. painter, d. (b. 1887) Jean Seberg, Amer. actress who played Joan of Arc, d. (b. 1938) W. Eugene Smith, Amer. photojournalist, d. (b. 1918)	City Opera Oliver Messiaen's 70th birthday marked by renaming of a peak in Utah as "Mount Messiaen"		Grete Waitz (Nor.) breaks $2\frac{1}{2}$-hour barrier in women's marathon during New York Marathon Sir Anthony Blunt, Eng. art historian, is unmasked as "fourth man" in Burgess, Maclean, and Philby spy scandal; he is stripped of his knighthood by Queen Elizabeth II	**1979 contd**
Sir Cecil Beaton, Eng. photographer and stage designer, d. (b. 1904) Tex Avery, Amer. film animator, d. (b. 1909) Robert Brackman, Amer. portrait painter, d. (b. 1898) Eliot Candee Clark, Amer. landscape painter, d. (b. 1883) Jimmy Durante, Amer. comedian, d. (b. 1893) Philip Guston, Amer. artist, d. (b. 1913) Sir Alfred Hitchcock, Eng.-born Amer. film director, d. (b. 1899) David Janssen, Amer. actor, d. (b. 1930) Oscar Kokoschka, Aust. expressionist painter, d. (b. 1886) Mario Marini, Ital. sculptor, d. (b. 1901) Steve McQueen, Amer. actor, d. (b. 1930) George Raft, Amer. actor, d. (b. 1895) Peter Sellers, Eng. comic actor, d. (b. 1925) Jay Silverheels, Amer. actor *(contd)*	Don Banks, Austral. composer, d. (b. 1923) Adolph Deutsch, Amer. film composer, d. (b. 1897) John Lennon, Eng. musician, (b. 1940) shot dead in New York by Mark Chapman John Jacob Niles, Amer. folk singer and composer, d. (b. 1892) Allan Pettersson, Swed. composer and violinist, d. (b. 1911) Vladimir Vysotsky, Soviet folk singer, d. (b. 1938) Popular songs: "Sailing," "This Is It," "The Rose"	Joseph Banks Rhine, Amer. investigator of extrasensory perception, d. (b. 1895) Amer. author of the "Complete Scarsdale Medical Diet," Dr. Hermann Tarnower (b. 1911), shot dead by his lover Jean Harris The World Health Organization formally announces the worldwide eradication of smallpox India puts its first satellite into orbit, becoming the 7th country to do so In Mexico, a giant panda gives birth to the first cub born naturally in captivity The wreck of the "Titanic" is found 12,000 feet deep in the North Atlantic Japanese oceanologists find traces of the Chinese invasion fleet dispatched by Kublai Khan in 1274 but sunk by a hurricane or "divine wind" Nobel Prize for Economics: Lawrence Klein (U.S.) for advances in econometrics Nobel Prize for Physiology and Medicine: Dr. George Snell (U.S.), Dr. Jean Drausset (Fr.) and Dr. Baruj Benacerraf (U.S.) for contributions to understanding the body's acceptance and rejection of foreign cells Nobel Prize for Physics: James Cronin and Val Fitch (both U.S.) for research into subatomic particles Nobel Prize for Chemistry: Paul Berg and Walter Gilbert (both U.S.) and Frederick Sanger (U.K.) for their work on nucleic acids in DNA; Sanger had previously won the Nobel Prize in 1958 Soviet cosmonauts return to Earth after a record 185 days aboard the Salyut 6 space station *(contd)*	Pittsburgh Steelers beat the Los Angeles Rams, 31-19, to win football's Super Bowl Joy Adamson (b. 1910), Brit. author of "Born Free," is found murdered in the Meru National Park, Africa In Philadelphia, Mary Decker becomes the first woman to run a mile in under $4\frac{1}{2}$ minutes The latest census reveals that the U.S. population is 226,504,825 "Dallas" fever sweeps the world and everyone wants to know who shot J.R.; the program has the highest ratings ever for a regular television series (88.6 million viewers) The 13th Winter Olympics are held at Lake Placid, New York; U.S. speed skater Eric Heiden wins a record five gold medals A priceless 8th-century gold chalice and other gold and silver treasures are found in a field in Tipperary, Ireland, by a tourist with a metal detector President Anwar Sadat (Egypt) opens the reconstructed temples of Philae, which had been moved to avoid their flooding by the Aswan Dam Israel replaces the pound with a new currency named the "shekel" The "Alexander Kielland" oil platform capsizes in the North Sea, killing 147 Brit. and Norw. workers Patrick Depailler, Fr. racing driver. d. in a car crash (b. 1945) Mount St. Helens volcano, Washington State, erupts; a column of debris is sent 12 miles high and the explosion is heard 200 miles away; most residents had been evacuated but 36 die Tornadoes strike nearly 30 towns in a broad band from Nebraska to Pennsylvania and West Virginia; 37 die and damage is severe Boxing: Roberto Duran (Pan.) beats Sugar Ray Leonard (U.S.) for W.B.C.'s welterweight title, but loses the rematch; Marvin Hagler (U.S.) is the new world middleweight champion Bjorn Borg (Swed.) wins his fifth successive Wimbledon men's tennis title by beating John McEnroe (U.S.) in five sets; Evonne Cawley (Australia) defeats Chris Evert-Lloyd for the women's title New York Islanders defeat Philadelphia Flyers *(contd)*	**1980**

	A. HISTORY, POLITICS	B. LITERATURE, THEATER	C. RELIGION, PHILOSOPHY, LEARNING
1980 contd	the capital of Israel rather than Tel Aviv 84 people are killed and over 200 injured by a bomb planted in Bologna railroad station, Italy A strike at the Lenin Shipyard in Gdansk spreads to other factories in Poland and 500,000 stop work; Lech Walesa becomes chairman of the new independent trade union (Solidarity); Solidarity's demands include freedom of speech, the release of political prisoners, and new labor laws General Kenan Evren is appointed Turkish President following a military coup Border hostility erupts into war when Iraq invades Iran in an attempt to gain control of Abadan and the Shatt al Arab waterway; this war persists through the decade with many thousands of fatalities on each side Jamaican general election sees a decisive victory for right-winger Edward P. G. Seaga's Labor Party over Michael Manley's People's National Party Ronald Reagan becomes 40th President of the U.S. after a landslide victory over Jimmy Carter; Republicans control the Senate for the first time since 1964 Portuguese Premier Francisco Sá Carneiro dies in an air crash in Lisbon; Francisco Pinto Balsemátao replaces him Three Amer. nuns and a lay preacher are murdered in El Salvador; U.S. aid is suspended Karl Dáuonitz, Ger. former admiral and head of state, d. (b. 1891) Nobel Prize for Peace: Adolfo Pérez Esquivel, Arg. sculptor and human rights campaigner Milton Obote wins Ugandan presidential election John W. McCormack, former Speaker of the House of Representatives, d. (b. 1891) Charles B. Hoeven, former U.S. Congressman, d. (b. 1895) Joel Le Theule, Fr. Defense Minister, d. (b. 1930) Alexei Kosygin, former Soviet Prime Minister, d. (b. 1904) Michael Foot (b. 1913) replaces James Callaghan as leader of Brit. Labor Party	Iris Murdoch: "Nuns and Soldiers," novel Shiva Naipaul: "Black and White," nonfiction V. S. Naipaul: "The Return of Eva Peron," collected essays Mordecai Richler: "Joshua Then and Now," novel Tom Sharpe: "Ancestral Vices," novel Tom Wolfe: "The Right Stuff," nonfiction "Camelot," musical, revived on Broadway starring Richard Burton Athol Fugard: "A Lesson from Aloes," play Mark Medoff: "Children of a Lesser God," play Arthur Miller: "The American Clock," play Sam Shepard: "True West," play Neil Simon: "I Ought to Be in Pictures," play Tennessee Williams: "Clothes for a Summer Hotel," play In London, the Royal Shakespeare Company stages "The Greeks," a trilogy by John Barton and Kenneth Cavander, and David Edgar's "Nicholas Nickleby" starring Roger Rees Howard Brenton's "The Romans in Britain" is prosecuted for indecency Michael Frayn: "Make and Break," play Ronald Harwood: "The Dresser," play Tom Kempinski: "Duet for One," play Willie Russell: "Educating Rita," play	

D. VISUAL ARTS	E. MUSIC	F. SCIENCE, TECHNOLOGY, GROWTH	G. DAILY LIFE	
(most notably in "The Lone Ranger" TV series), d. (b. 1919) Graham Vivian Sutherland, Eng. painter, d. (b. 1903) Mae West, Amer. actress, d. (b. 1890) The Picasso retrospective exhibition at the Museum of Modern Art, New York, has over a million visitors to see the 1,000 works Jasper Johns's "Three Flags" is sold for $1 million—a record for the work of a living Amer. painter "Juliet and Her Nurse" by Turner is sold in New York for $4 million—a world record for a painting Academy Awards (for 1979)—best picture: "Kramer vs. Kramer"; best actor: Dustin Hoffman ("Kramer vs. Kramer"); best actress: Sally Field ("Norma Rae") Films: "The Amityville Horror" (Stuart Rosenberg); "1941" (Steven Spielberg); "American Gigolo" (Paul Schrader); "Coal Miner's Daughter" (Michael Apted); "The Empire Strikes Back" (Irvin Kershner); "Airplane!" (Jim Abrahams); "My American Uncle" (Alain Resnais); "Kagemusha" (Akira Kurosawa); "Ordinary People" (Robert Redford); "Raging Bull" (Martin Scorsese)		Voyager 1 space probe sends back spectacular photographs of Saturn, its moons and rings; six new moons are discovered The U.S. Supreme Court rules that a microbe created by General Electric to eliminate oil waste can be patented I.C.I. begins production of the world's first commercially available animal foodstuff to be made from micro-organisms Walter Alvarez (U.S.) and colleagues discover a worldwide layer of iridium-enriched clay; this may be the residue of a gigantic meteorite that struck the Earth and wiped out the dinosaurs Leslie Orgel and Francis Frick postulate the existence of "selfish DNA," that reproduces itself within the gene Jean Piaget, Swiss psychologist, d. (b. 1896) Stephen Kuffler, Amer. neurobiologist, d. (b. 1913) Willard F. Libby, Amer. nuclear chemist, d. (b. 1908) J. H. Van Vleck, Amer. physicist, d. (b. 1899)	to win hockey's Stanley Cup The 22nd Olympic Games begin in Moscow but are boycotted by over 50 nations, including the U.S., in protest against the Soviet invasion of Afghanistan; the U.S.S.R. wins 80 gold medals followed by East Germany (47); rival Eng. runners Steve Ovett and Sebastian Coe win golds in the 800 and 1500 meters, respectively Philadelphia Phillies defeat Kansas City Royals, 4 games to 2, to win World Series The severe summer heat wave in the southern U.S. causes 1,117 deaths in 20 states; Missouri declares a state of emergency Elston (Gene) Howard, Amer. baseball player and coach, d. (b. 1929) Finn Ronn, Amer. Antarctic explorer, d. (b. 1899) Colonel Harland Sanders, Amer. founder of Kentucky Fried Chicken, d. (b. 1890) A Lockheed Tristar crashes at Riyadh Airport, Saudi Arabia, killing 301 passengers Two violent earthquakes flatten the Algerian city of El Asnam, leaving 20,000 dead Jesse Owens, Amer. athlete, d. (b. 1913) Fire destroys the 26-story MGM Grand Hotel in Las Vegas; 84 die and 600 are injured Severiano Ballesteros (Sp.) becomes the youngest winner of golf's U.S. Masters National Basketball Association adopts three points for a field goal; Ann Meyers is the first woman to sign for the N.B.A., although she doesn't make the Indiana Pacers team Los Angeles Lakers win National Basketball Association championship	**1980 contd**

	A. HISTORY, POLITICS	B. LITERATURE, THEATER	C. RELIGION, PHILOSOPHY, LEARNING

1981

A. HISTORY, POLITICS

Greece becomes the 10th member of the European Community
Bernardette McAliskey (formerly Devlin) is shot and wounded by Protestant gunmen in Ulster
Ronald Reagan is inaugurated the 40th President of the U.S.
The 22nd Olympic Games begin in Moscow
Iran releases all 52 hostages
Four leading U.K. Labor politicians announce the creation of a breakaway party, the Social Democratic Party, which forms alliance with Liberals
China sentences to death for treason Mao Tse-Tung's widow, Jiang Qing; this is later commuted to life imprisonment
South African commandos enter Angola's capital city, Maputo, and kill 12 A.N.C. members
A border dispute leads to five days' fighting between Ecuador and Peru; a cease-fire is agreed upon after the Organization of American States intervenes
Labor leader Gro Harlem Brundtland becomes Norway's first female Prime Minister; later in 1981, a minority Conservative government is elected with Kare Willoch as Prime Minister
President Reagan's first budget proposes the greatest-ever tax and spending cuts
Spanish civil guards seize control of the Chamber of Deputies in a military coup, but resolute action by King Juan Carlos thwarts it
Lieut. Gen. Roberto Viola becomes Argentine President, but is later replaced by Gen. Leopoldo Galtieri
John Hinckley shoots President Reagan, Jim Brady (White House Press Secretary), and two others outside the Washington Hilton hotel
Civil war rages in Lebanon, with clashes between the Syrian Arab Deterrent Force, Saad Haddad's Israeli-backed militia, Islamic guerrillas, and the U.N. peacekeeping force
Bobby Sands, an I.R.A. hunger striker in the Maze Prison, is elected to the British Parliament for Fermanagh and South Tyrone; he dies in prison after fasting for 66 days
The U.S. grain embargo to the U.S.S.R., which was imposed after the invasion of Afghanistan, is ended
François Mitterand (Socialist) narrowly defeats the incumbent Giscard d'Estaing to become President of France; the Socialists later also win the national elections
In May, Pope John Paul II is shot twice by Mehmet Ali Agca in St. Peter's Square; the Pope has almost fully recovered by October
Jaime Aguilera, President of Ecuador, d. in an air crash (b. 1940); Vice President Osvaldo Larrea succeeds him
Scandal rocks Italy when Premier Arnoldo Forlani releases the names of 962 people allegedly linked to a secret Masonic lodge known as P2; influential figures in the government, army, and big business are on the list; Forlani resigns after other parties refuse to support his coalition and Giovanni Spadolini becomes Prime Minister
President Ziaur Rahman (Bangladesh) is assassinated; Vice President Abdus Sattar succeeds him
Israeli jets destroy an Iraqi nuclear plant near Baghdad; the U.N. Security Council unanimously condemns the attack
Garrett Fitzgerald (Fine Gael) becomes the new Irish Taoiseach (Prime Minister) in a coalition government with the Labor Party
The Iranian President, Prime Minister, and 29 others are killed in a bomb attack by leftist Mujaheddin guerrillas; in reprisal, over 2,000 Mujaheddin are executed before the year's end
Sir Dawda Jawara, Gambian President, is ousted by a military coup while at the U.K. royal wedding, but returns to power within a week with the assistance of 2,800 Senegalese troops; in November, Senegal and Gambia unite in a confederation to be known as Senegambia

(contd)

B. LITERATURE, THEATER

Nobel Prize for Literature: Elias Canetti, a Jewish Hungarian living in the U.K.
Salman Rushdie: "Midnight's Children," Booker Prize
John Kennedy Toole: "A Confederacy of Dunces," Pulitzer Prize fiction
James Schuyler: "The Morning of the Poem," Pulitzer Prize poetry
Beth Henley: "Crimes of the Heart," Pulitzer Prize drama
Carl E. Schorske: "Fin-de-Siècle Vienna: Politics and Culture," Pulitzer Prize nonfiction
Lucien Bodard: "Anne-Marie," Prix Goncourt
Maurice Leitch: "Silver's City," Whitbread Prize
The "Washington Star" daily newspaper publishes its final edition on August 7
A new English translation of the complete version of Marcel Proust's "Remembrance of Things Past" is published
The Royal Shakespeare Company's "Nicholas Nickleby" plays to packed houses on Broadway
A surprise London success is "Cats," a new musical based on poems by T. S. Eliot
Film stars who return to the New York stage include Anne Bancroft ("Duet for One"), Claudette Colbert ("A Taste for Murder"), Katharine Hepburn ("West Side Waltz"), Elizabeth Taylor ("The Little Foxes"), Joanne Woodward ("Candida"), and Susannah York ("Hedda Gabler")
Christy Brown, Irish novelist, d. (b. 1932)
Mary Chase, Amer. playwright best known for "Harvey," d. (b. 1907)
A. J. Cronin, Brit. novelist, d. (b. 1896)
Isabella Gardner, Amer. poet, d. (b. 1915)
Anita Loos, Amer. novelist and playwright, d. (b. 1893)
Lawrence Neal, Amer. poet, d. (b. 1937)
Boris Polevoi, Sov. author, d. (b. 1907)
William Saroyan, Amer. novelist, d. (b. 1908)
Gwyn Thomas, Brit. novelist, d. (b. 1913)
Yuri Trifonov, Sov. author, d. (b. 1925)
Thomas Valentin, W. Ger. novelist, d. (b. 1922)
Woody Allen: "The Floating Light Bulb," play
William Boyd: "A Good Man in Africa," novel

(contd)

C. RELIGION, PHILOSOPHY, LEARNING

A new translation of the Koran is printed in China
Susan Hurley is the first woman in 542 years to be elected a Fellow of All Souls College, Oxford
Iran releases three Anglican (Episcopalian) missionaries held captive since 1980
The Unification Church of Sun Myung Moon ("Moonies") loses its libel action against the "Daily Mail" Brit. newspaper
Cardinal Stefan Wyszynski, Roman Catholic Primate of Poland, d. (b. 1901); Josef Glemp succeeds him
The Salvation Army withdraws from the World Council of Churches in protest at the W.C.C.'s "political" support for guerrilla movements
Kelly Segraves (U.S.), a leading Baptist "creationist," argues in a Sacramento court against the teaching of evolution in state schools
The government puts Egyptian Coptic Pope Shenouda III under house arrest in a secluded monastery
Persecution of the Baha'i community in Iran continues, and thousands flee the country
The South African Presbyterian Church instructs its clergy that they can marry people of different races in defiance of the apartheid laws
Ethiopia's Marxist government closes Christian churches and Muslim mosques and especially persecutes the Ethiopian Lutheran Church; 600 Christian and Muslim leaders are executed
Deaconess Elizabeth Canham (U.K.) receives U.S. Episcopalian ordination as a priest in a ceremony in Trinity Cathedral, Newark, New Jersey
Reform Jews of the Union of American Hebrew Congregations decide to end its 400-year ban on proselytization
Muhammad Beheshti, Iranian Ayatollah, d. (b. 1929)
Metropolitan Ireney, Primate of the Russian Orthodox Church in America, d. (b. 1892)
C. Kilmer Myers, Amer. Episcopal Bishop of California, d. (b. 1916)
Yitzhak Nissim, Sephardic Chief Rabbi of Israel, d. (b. 1896)
Mohammed Ayoob: "The Politics of Islamic Reassertion"
Leslie Howard: "The Expansion of God"
Arthur Koestler: "Kaleidoscope"
Cyril Williams: "Tongues of the Spirit"

D. VISUAL ARTS

1981

The Museum of Modern Art, New York, donates Picasso's "Guernica" to the Prado Museum, Spain
The National Gallery, Washington, D.C., stages the largest-ever exhibition of Rodin's sculptures
Toronto Art Gallery stages an acclaimed exhibition on Turner
M-G-M takes over United Artists
Walter Cronkite retires from regular television broadcasting
South Africa's second television channel begins transmission; it is intended mainly for a black audience
"Brideshead Revisited" is shown on British television to great acclaim
Academy Awards (for 1980)—best picture: "Ordinary People"; best actor: Robert De Niro ("Raging Bull"); best actress: Sissy Spacek ("Coal Miner's Daughter")
Films: "An American Werewolf in London" (John Landis); "Arthur" (Steve Gordon); "Gallipoli" (Peter Weir); "An Officer and a Gentleman" (Taylor Hackford); "On Golden Pond" (Mark Rydel); "Raiders of the Lost Ark" (Steven Spielberg); "Reds" (Warren Beatty); "Time Bandits" (Terry Gilliam); "The French Lieutenant's

(contd)

E. MUSIC

The Houston Grand Opera premieres new operas by Philip Glass ("The Panther") and Carlisle Floyd ("Willie Stark")
Karl-Heinz Stockhausen's "Donnerstag aus Licht" is premiered at La Scala, Milan
The centennial of Bartok's birth and Mussorgsky's death are marked by productions of their works in several countries
The Metropolitan Opera House, New York, stages a triple bill of Stravinsky works with designs by David Hockney
The New York City Ballet stages a highly popular Tchaikovsky Festival
Soviet conductor Maxim Shostakovich and his son defect to the West
John Lennon and Yoko Ono win Grammy Award for best album, "Double Fantasy"
Karl Böhm, Aus. conductor, d. (b. 1894)
Tadeusz Baird, Pol. composer, d. (b. 1928)
Mike Bloomfield, Amer. rock guitarist and songwriter, d. (b. 1944)
Hoagy Carmichael, Amer. songwriter, d. (b. 1899)
Harry Chapin, Amer. songwriter, d. (b. 1942)
Carol Fox, Amer. founder of the Chicago Lyric Opera, d. (b. 1926)
Bill Haley, Amer. rock bandleader, d. (b. 1925)

(contd)

F. SCIENCE, TECHNOLOGY, GROWTH

The first U.S. space shuttle, "Columbia," successfully makes its maiden flight
The world's largest single-span bridge is opened by Elizabeth II; spanning the Humber Estuary, U.K., its main span measures 4,626 feet
Scientists identify Acquired Immune Deficiency Syndrome (AIDS)
The European rocket "Ariane" makes its first successful launch into space
NASA scientists announce that two unusual meteorites found in the Antarctic may have originated from Mars
The world's fastest train, the French TGV, enters service between Paris and Lyons
Voyager 2 flies by Saturn and provides data on the planet, its ring system and several of the moons
In September, the Salyut 6 space station completes four years in space, having made 23,029 orbits of the Earth
I.B.M. launches its "home" or "personal" computer (the P.C.)
Nobel Prize for Economics: James Tobin (U.S.)
Nobel Prize for Physiology and Medicine: Robert Sperry (U.S.) for work on "split brain" patients, and David Hubel and Torsten Wiesel (both U.S.) for cellular analysis of the brain's visual cortex
Nobel Prize for Physics: Nicolaas Bloembergen and Arthur Schawlow (both U.S.) and Kai Seigbahn (Swed.) for developments in laser and electron spectroscopy
Nobel Prize for Chemistry: Kenichi Fukui (Japan) and Roald Hoffman (U.S.) for a predictive framework for hypothetical chemical reactions
Surgeons at University of Denver, U.S., insert a valve into the skull of an unborn baby to drain off excess fluid from the brain and so prevent hydrocephalus
A new species of deep-water sea fish is washed up on a South African beach; scientists name it "Hexatrygon bickelli"
David Pilbeam determines that "Ramapithecus" was probably an early ancestor of the orangutan rather than of humanity
The most massive star known is discovered: "R136a" is 2,500 times larger than our Sun but only 10 times brighter
Chinese scientists are the first to clone a fish successfully (a

(contd)

G. DAILY LIFE

Oakland Raiders beat the Philadelphia Eagles, 27-10, to win football's Super Bowl
Peter Sutcliffe is arrested in Sheffield, U.K., and charged with the 13 "Yorkshire Ripper" murders; he is later jailed for life
A Baltimore court sentences former C.I.A. agent David Barnett to 18 years' imprisonment for selling secrets to the U.S.S.R.
Sir Ranulph Fiennes and two others (all U.K.) complete the longest and swiftest transit of Antarctica on foot, traveling 2,500 miles in 75 days
An Indonesian ferry sinks in the Java Sea, with the loss of 5,000 lives
Rupert Murdoch buys the "Times" (Newspapers Ltd) of London
Prince Charles and Lady Diana Spencer announce their engagement in February and are married in St. Paul's Cathedral on July 29
Hundreds die in riots in Kosovo, Yugoslavia
Great Train Robber Ronnie Biggs is abducted from Brazil to Barbados, but successfully appeals against extradition to the U.K. and returns to Brazil
Mike Hailwood, Eng. motorcycle racing star, d. in car crash (b. 1941)
Omar Bradley, Amer. five-star general, d. (b. 1893)
Sir Maurice Oldfield, head of MI6, d. (b. 1915)
Joe Louis, Amer. World Heavyweight Boxing Champion (1937-1949), d. (b. 1914)
Riots break out in several of the U.K.'s inner-city areas, including Brixton (London), Toxteth (Liverpool), and Moss Side (Manchester)
New Jersey Senator Harrison A. Williams is convicted of accepting bribes in the F.B.I.'s "Abscam" operation
The U.N. issues a blacklist of sportsmen and women who have competed in South Africa
A jet crashes onto the deck of the USS "Nimitz": 14 are killed and 45 are injured
A train crashes into the Bagmati River, India, with the loss of 268 lives
America's largest-ever naturalization ceremony is held at Memorial Stadium, Los Angeles, where 9,700 become U.S. citizens
Stephen Ptacek (U.S.) makes the first solar-powered flight across the English Channel in the "Solar Challenger"; the airplane flew the 180 miles from Paris to Manston, Kent, in 5½ hours
Major league baseball players in the U.S. strike from June 12 to August 9
Concrete roofing collapses in the Hyatt Hotel, Kansas, killing 111 and injuring 180
The South African international rugby team make a 2-month tour of New Zealand; anti-tour demonstrations are numerous and 1000 arrests are made
More than 12,000 U.S. air traffic controllers go on strike and are dismissed
Sandra Day O'Connor becomes the U.S. Supreme Court's first female judge
Walter Polovchak, a 12-year-old who remained in the U.S. after his parents returned to the U.S.S.R., is granted political asylum against the wishes of his parents

(contd)

	A. HISTORY, POLITICS	B. LITERATURE, THEATER	C. RELIGION, PHILOSOPHY, LEARNING
1981 contd	U.S. jet fighters shoot down two Libyan Su-22s over the Gulf of Sidra A Maryland court rules that former Vice President Spiro Agnew did take bribes and should repay them The A.N.C. launches a rocket attack on the Pretoria headquarters of the South African army; South African forces launch raids into Angola in pursuit of S.W.A.P.O. guerrillas Solidarity's first national conference is held in Gdansk, Poland Belize (population 150,000) gains independence; Elizabeth II is head of state and George Price is Prime Minister Antigua Barbuda (population 74,000) gains independence; Elizabeth II is head of state and V. C. Bird is Prime Minister Anwar Sadat, Egyptian President (1970–1981), is assassinated by soldiers while at a military parade; Vice President Hosni Mubarak succeeds him Moshe Dayan, Israeli soldier and statesman, d. (b. 1915) Bulgaria celebrates the 1,300th anniversary of the Bulgarian state The Greek national elections are a victory for Pasok (Socialist) over the New Democracy Party; Andreas Papandreou becomes Premier Nobel Peace Prize: U.N. High Commission for Refugees Gen. Wojciech Jaruzelski becomes Prime Minister of Poland and later also Communist Party Leader Urho Kekkonen, Finnish President (1956–1981), resigns On Dec. 17, U.S. Brig. Gen. James Dozier is abducted from his home in Verona, Italy, by Red Brigade terrorists, but is rescued in January Israel formally annexes the Golan Heights Flight Lt. Jerry Rawlings seizes power in Ghana	Martin Cruz Smith: "Gorky Park," novel Nell Dunn: "Steaming," play Tom Eyen: "Dreamgirls," musical Jules Feiffer: "Grown Ups," play Nadine Gordimer: "July's People," novel Simon Gray: "Quartermaine's Terms," play Beth Henley: "Crimes of the Heart," play David Henry Hwang: "Family Devotions," play John Irving: "The Hotel New Hampshire," novel Ian McEwan: "The Comfort of Strangers," novel Michael Moorcock: "Byzantium Endures," novel Brian Moore: "The Temptation of Eileen Hughes," novel Peter Nichols: "Passion Play," play Alan Paton: "Ah! But Your Land is Beautiful," novel Sylvia Plath: "Collected Poems," posthumous anthology Paul Theroux: "The Mosquito Coast," novel D. M. Thomas: "The White Hotel," novel Gore Vidal: "Creation," novel Arnold Wesker: "Caritas," play	
1982	Gen. Rios Montt becomes Guatemalan President after a military coup Lt. Gen. Mohammad Ershad seizes power in Bangladesh Argentine forces invade the Falkland Islands (Malvinas); the U.K. sends a task force while U.S. Secretary of State Alexander Haig unsuccessfully tries to mediate; Brit. forces land on the Falklands on May 21 and Arg. occupying forces surrender on June 14 Canada's Constitution Act comes into force, severing the nation's last legal ties to the U.K. Israel returns Sinai to Egypt in accordance with the Camp David agreement President Kaunda (Zambia) meets Prime Minister Pieter W. Botha (South Africa) and urges him to free Nelson Mandela and other A.N.C. leaders Sapin becomes N.A.T.O's 16th member Israeli troops invade southern Lebanon, occupy Tyre and Sidon, and besiege West Beirut, a P.L.O. stronghold; P.L.O. guerrillas leave Beirut under U.N. supervision Rebel troops led by Hissène Habre overthrow Chad's government The Colombian government declares a unilateral cease-fire against the insurgents and ends the 34-year-old state of siege Khalid Ibn Abdul Aziz al-Saud, King of Saudi Arabia, d. (b. 1914); his brother Prince Fahd succeeds him General Reynaldo Bignone replaces General Galtieri as Argentine President Alexander Haig resigns as U.S. Secretary of State and is replaced by George Shultz President Reagan extends Soviet sanctions to W. European companies with contracts on the Siberian gas pipeline, sparking an acrimonious dispute with the European Community *(contd)*	Okot p'Bitek, Ugandan poet, d. (b. 1931) John Cheever, Amer. author, d. (b. 1912) Frederic Dannay, Amer. mystery writer and half of "Ellery Queen," d. (b. 1905) Philip K. Dick, Amer. science-fiction writer, d. (b. 1928) John C. Gardner, Amer. novelist, d. (b. 1933) Dame Celia Johnson, Eng. actress, d. (b. 1908) Dame Ngaio Marsh, New Zealand detective writer, d. (b. 1899) Archibald MacLeish, Amer. poet, d. (b. 1892) Barbara Pym, Eng. novelist, d. (b. 1913) Ayn Rand, Amer. novelist, d. (b. 1905) Peter Weiss, Swed. playwright, d. (b. 1916) "USA Today" newspaper is published for the first time Elizabeth Taylor makes her London theatrical debut in "The Little Foxes" Centennial of the Yiddish Theater, New York Nobel Prize for Literature: Gabriel Garcia Márquez (Colombia) *(contd)*	The Ethiopian government closes the Addis Ababa headquarters of the Evangelical Church; Coptic Archbishop Mathias flees to the West John Paul II becomes the first Pope to visit the U.K.; in 1982 he also travels to Ireland, Argentina, West Africa, Spain, and Portugal The Vatican orders Czechoslovakian clergy to stop collaborating with the government An Anglican-Roman Catholic International Commission recommends that the Pope should be recognized as "universal Primate," but this is fiercely opposed by many Anglicans The General Assembly of the United Presbyterian Church merges with the Presbyterian Church, U.S., having split from them in the Civil War A Covenant of Unity is agreed between the Methodist, United Reformed, and Moravian churches Sun Myung Moon of the Unification Church ("Moonies") holds a mass wedding for 2,075 couples selected by himself at Madison Square Garden, New York *(contd)*

D. VISUAL ARTS	E. MUSIC	F. SCIENCE, TECHNOLOGY, GROWTH	G. DAILY LIFE	
Woman" (Karel Reisz); "Chariots of Fire" (Hugh Hudson) René Clair, Fr. film director, d. (b. 1898) Melvyn Douglas, Amer. actor, d. (b. 1901) Allan Dwan, Canadian film director, d. (b. 1885) Gloria Grahame, Amer. actress, d. (b. 1924) William Holden, Amer. actor, d. (b. 1918) Alfred Jensen, Amer. painter, d. (b. 1903) Robert Montgomery, Amer. actor, d. (b. 1904) Enzo Plazzotta, Ital. sculptor, d. (b. 1921) Theodore Roszak, Amer. sculptor, d. (b. 1907) Natalie Wood, Amer. actress, d. (b. 1938)	Yip Harburg, Amer. popular lyricist, d. (b. 1896) Bob Marley, Jamaican reggae musician, d. (b. 1945) Vera-Ellen, Amer. Hollywood dancer, d. (b. 1926) Harry Warren, Amer. songwriter, d. (b. 1893) Mary Lou Williams, Amer. jazz pianist and composer, d. (b. 1910)	golden carp) Carlton S. Coon, Amer. anthropologist, d. (b. 1904) Gustav Eckstein, Amer. physiologist, d. (b. 1890) Philip Handler, Amer. biologist and former President of the National Academy of Sciences, d. (b. 1917) Oddo Hassel, Norw. chemist, d. (b. 1897) Hans Helbaek, Dan. paleoethnobotanist, d. (b. 1900) Sir Hans A. Krebs, Eng. biochemist, d. (b. 1900) Rebecca Lancefield, Amer. bacteriologist, d. (b. 1895) Kazimierz Michalowski, Pol. archeologist, d. (b. 1901) Jerzy Neyman, Amer. mathematician, d. (b. 1899) John H. Northrop, Amer. aviation engineer, d. (b. 1895) Kenneth P. Oakley, Eng. anthropologist, d. (b. 1911) Aleksandr Oparin, Sov. biochemist, d. (b. 1894) Carl Siegel, W. Ger. mathematician, d. (b. 1896) Harold C. Urey, Amer. physicist, d. (b. 1893) L. Sterling Wortman, Amer. plant geneticist, d. (b. 1923) Hideki Yukawa, Jap. physicist, d. (b. 1907)	94 coal miners are killed in an accident in Yubari, northern Japan Muhammad Ali finally retires from boxing after losing on points to Trevor Berbick; Ali's career record is 56 wins and 5 defeats Los Angeles Dodgers defeat New York Yankees, 4 games to 2, to win World Series Boston Celtics win the National Basketball Association championship Bob Champion, riding Aldanti, wins Eng. Grand National, two years after Champion was given months to live as a result of cancer being diagnosed The New York Islanders win hockey's Stanley Cup for the 2nd year in succession	**1981 contd**
The U.K.'s fourth television channel ("Channel 4") begins broadcasting; it aims to cater to minorities Switzerland and the U.K. jointly stage the largest-ever exhibition of Jean Tinguely's sculptures Broadcasters and the U.S. Justice Dept. end restraints on the length and frequency of television commercials The Vietnam Veterans' War Memorial is dedicated in Washington, D.C.; the names of more than 58,000 dead are inscribed on the black granite memorial By the year's end, *(contd)*	New concert halls are opened in Toronto (Canada), Aarhus (Denmark), and the Barbican Center (London) The D'Oyly Carte Opera Company gives its last performance of Gilbert and Sullivan at the Adelphi Theater, London; subsequently the company is revived New operas include Luciano Beria's "La Vera Storia" (premiered at La Scala, Milan), Bernard Herrmann's "Wuthering Heights" (Portland, Oregon), Stephen Paulus's "The Postman *(contd)*	Nobel Prize for Economics: George J. Stigler (U.S.) for studies of the interaction between business and government Nobel Prize for Physiology and Medicine: John Vane (U.K.) for work on prostaglandins Nobel Prize for Physics: Kenneth Wilson (U.S.) for work on phase transitions Nobel Prize for Chemistry: Aaron Klug (U.K.) for analysis of the structure of viruses and DNA The U.N. Law of the Sea Conference adopts an international convention to supervise the exploitation of the world's sea beds as the "common heritage of mankind," but the U.S. and U.K. do not sign The centenary of Charles Darwin's death is marked by conferences throughout the world; "punctuated evolutionism" is a controversial new theory about the way life developed Karl Setter (W. Ger.) discovers a primitive bacterium that can live in boiling water around undersea volcanoes, geysers, etc. 20 million U.K. elm trees (66%) are killed by Dutch Elm disease Soviet spacecraft Venera 13 and *(contd)*	San Francisco 49ers beat Cincinnati Bengals, 26-21, to win football Super Bowl American Telephone and Telegraph ("Ma Bell") agrees to sell 66% of its assets after a seven-year antitrust suit A Boeing 737 crashes into the Potomac River in Washington, D.C, killing 78 Braniff Airlines (U.S.) and Laker Airways (U.K.) both file for bankruptcy The U.S. and U.K. return 18.5 tons of Czechoslovakian gold held since World War II; its current value is $250 million The Indian government institutes a pollution-free zone around the Taj Mahal by banning all nearby pollutant industries Salisbury, capital of Zimbabwe (formerly Rhodesia), is renamed Harare 15 English cricketers join a "rebel" tour of South Africa and are banned from the English national team The 1982 World's Fair is held at Knoxville, Tennessee El Chichón volcano, Mexico, erupts cataclysmically, sending dust and gases into the stratosphere Gilles Villeneuve, Can. racing driver, d. (b. 1950) The Indianapolis 500 ends in the closest finish in 66 races; Gordon Johncock beats Rick Mears by just 0.16 second Satchel Paige, Amer. baseball pitcher, d. (b. 1906) A Pan Am Boeing 727 crashes on takeoff from New Orleans, resulting in 153 deaths *(contd)*	**1982**

A. HISTORY, POLITICS

1982 contd

Miguel de la Madrid Hurtado is elected Mexico's new President

Antonio Guzmán, Dominican President, d. (b. 1911); Vice President Jacobo Majluta succeeds him

Gerald Tuite is sentenced by an Irish court to 107 years in jail for possessing illegal gunmaking apparatus in London; this was the first time an Irish court had tried an Irish citizen for a crime committed in the U.K.

Yasser Arafat, P.L.O. leader, signs a document accepting U.N. resolutions on Israel's right to existence, but the U.S. government still refuses to recognize the P.L.O as a legitimate body

Prince Sihanouk and supporters join the Khmer Rouge in a resistance coalition against the Vietnamese-backed Cambodian government

The world's longest reigning monarch, Sobhuza II of Swaziland, d. (b. 1899)

Bashir Gemayel (b. 1947) is elected President of Lebanon, but is assassinated before taking office; his brother Amin becomes President

Kristjan Eldjarn, President of Iceland (1965–1980), d. (b. 1916)

The Labor government is defeated in the Dutch national elections; a center-right coalition led by Ruud Lubbers takes power

Christian Falangist militia massacre 800 Palestinians in two Beirut refugee camps

Sweden's center-left government is defeated in a general election, and Olof Palme (Social Dem.) becomes Prime Minister

Helmut Kohl becomes West German Chancellor after unseating Helmut Schmidt

The Polish Parliament votes to ban Solidarity

Pierre Mendes France, Fr. statesman, d. (b. 1907)

Junius Richard Jayawardene remains President after Sri Lanka's first presidential election

Provisional Sinn Fein win 10% of the vote and 5 seats in elections for the new Northern Ireland Assembly

Felipe Gonzalez becomes Spain's first Socialist Prime Minister

Upper Volta's fourth military coup in 22 years of independence makes Maj. Jean-Baptiste Ouedraogo the new President

Geoffrey Prime (U.K.), formerly an employee at the Government Communications headquarters, is jailed for 35 years for Soviet espionage

Leonid Ilyich Brezhnev, Soviet Leader (1966–1982), d. (b. 1906); Yuri Andropov succeeds him

A bomb blast at the Israeli military headquarters, Tyre, Lebanon, kills 100

Lech Walesa (Pol.) is released from government detention; martial law is suspended

Nobel Peace Prize: Alva Myrdal (Swed.) and Alfonso Garcia Robles (Mex.) for services toward disarmament

Italy's 43rd government since 1945 takes power; Amintore Fanfani is the new Premier

B. LITERATURE, THEATER

Thomas Keneally: "Schindler's List," Booker Prize

John Updike: "Rabbit Is Rich," Pulitzer Prize fiction

Sylvia Plath: "The Collected Poems," Pulitzer Prize poetry

Charles Fuller: "A Soldier's Play," Pulitzer Prize drama

Tracy Kidder: "The Soul of a New Machine," Pulitzer Prize nonfiction

Dominique Fernandez: "Dans la Main de l'Ange," Prix Goncourt

John Wain: "Young Shoulders," Whitbread Prize

Margaret Atwood: "Bodily Harm," novel

John Barth:"Sabbatical," novel

Saul Bellow: "The Dean's December," novel

Heinrich Böll: "The Safety Net," novel

William Boyd: "An Ice Cream War," novel

Bruce Chatwin: "On the Black Hill," novel

John Cheever: "O, What a Paradise It Seems," novel

Carlos Fuentes: "Distant Relations," novel

Graham Greene: "Monsignor Quixote," novel

James Fenton: "The Memory of War," poetry

James Fox: "White Mischief," recent history

Roy Fuller: "Vamp Till Ready," autobiography

Henry Kissinger: "The Years of Upheaval," autobiography

Timothy Mo: "Sour Sweet," novel

Robert Middelkauf: "The Glorious Cause, The American Revolution," history

Laurence Olivier: "Confessions of an Actor," autobiography

John Osborne: "The Life and Crimes of Agatha Christie," biography

Edward Bond: "Summer," play

Caryl Churchill: "Top Girls," play

Hume Cronyn and Jessica Tandy: "Foxfire," play

Harold Pinter: "A Kind of Alaska," play

Tom Stoppard: "The Real Thing," play

C. RELIGION, PHILOSOPHY, LEARNING

Rev. Margaret Philimore (U.S.) becomes the first female priest to preach in Canterbury Cathedral, England

A federal court in Little Rock, Arkansas, declares it unconstitutional to teach "creationism" equally with the theory of evolution

The Pope meets Yasser Arafat in the Vatican despite strong Israeli protests

Islamic fundamentalists riot in Maiduguri, Nigeria, in protest at "westernization" of Nigerian Islam and demand fundamental reforms

The World Alliance of Reformed Churches suspends South Africa's two Dutch Reformed Churches for the "heresy" of racial segregation

Vinoba Bhave, Indian Hindu philosopher, d. (b. 1895)

Cardinal John Patrick Cody, Roman Catholic Archbishop of Chicago, d. (b. 1907)

John Collins, Eng. founder of Christian Action, d. (b. 1905)

Zvi Yehuda Kook, Israeli Zionist leader, d. (b. 1891)

Sybil Leek, Eng. "white witch", d. (b. 1917)

Muktananda Paramahamsa, Indian Hindu religious leader, d. (b. 1908)

Gershom Scholem, Israeli Jewish mystical scholar, d. (b. 1897)

Yefet Ben-Avraham Tsedaka, Samaritan leader, d. (b. 1895)

"Hymns for Today's Church" introduces new hymns and modernizes the wording of old ones

Robert Alter: "The Art of Biblical Narrative"

David Barrett: "World Christian Encyclopedia"

Elizabeth Isichei: "Varieties of Christian Experience in Nigeria"

Lord Longford: "Pope John Paul II: an Authorized Biography"

Morris Yanoff: "Where is Joe? Lost Among the Hare Krishnas"

D. VISUAL ARTS

28 million U.S. households have cable television
Sophia Loren spends one month in prison for tax evasion
John Belushi, Amer. film comedian, d. (b. 1949)
Ingrid Bergman, Swed. film actress, d. (b. 1915)
Aurel Bernath, Hungarian painter, d. (b. 1895)
Rainer Werner Fassbinder, W. Ger. film director, d. (b. 1946)
Marty Feldman, Eng. comedian, d. (b. 1934)
Henry Fonda, Amer. film actor, d. (b. 1905)
Grace Kelly, Princess of Monaco and film actress, d. in car crash (b. 1929)
Kenneth More, Eng. actor, d. (b. 1914)
Ben Nicholson, Eng. abstract painter, d. (b. 1894)
Kenzo Okadd, Jap. painter, d. (b. 1902)
Eleanor Powell, Amer. dancer and film actress, d. (b. 1912)
Romy Schneider, Aus. actress, d. (b. 1938)
Jacques Tati, Fr. comedian and film director, d. (b. 1908)
Jack Tworkov, Amer. painter, d. (b. 1900)
Fred Williams, Austral. landscape painter, d. (b. 1927)
Academy Awards (for 1981)—best picture: "Chariots of Fire"; best actor: Henry Fonda ("On Golden Pond"); best actress: Katharine Hepburn ("On Golden Pond")
Films: "E.T.
(contd)

E. MUSIC

Always Rings Twice" (St. Louis), and Robert Ward's "Minutes Till Midnight" (Miami)
Valeria Bettis, Amer. modern dancer, d. (b. 1919)
Sir Clifford Curzon, Eng. pianist, d. (b. 1907)
Lehman Engel, Amer. conductor, d. (b. 1910)
Glenn Gould, Can. pianist, d. (b. 1932)
Leonid Kogan, Soviet violinist, d. (b. 1924)
Thelonious Monk, Amer. jazz pianist and composer, d. (b. 1917)
Mario del Monico, Ital. operatic tenor, d. (b. 1915)
Carl Orff, W. Ger. composer, d. (b. 1895)
Art Pepper, Amer. jazz saxophonist, d. (b. 1925)
Marie Rambert, Eng. founder of Ballet Rambert, d. (b. 1888)
Marty Robbins, Amer. country-and-western singer, d. (b. 1925)
Artur Rubinstein, Pol.-born Amer. classical pianist, d. (b. 1887)
Humphrey Searle, Eng. composer, d. (b. 1915)
Leonid Utyosov, Soviet jazz musician, d. (b. 1895)
John Watts, Amer. composer, d. (b. 1930)
The U.S. Festival at San Bernardino, California, attracts an audience of 400,000; performers include Fleetwood Mac, Police, Pat
(contd)

F. SCIENCE, TECHNOLOGY, GROWTH

14 land on Venus and send back the first color pictures; they confirm the surface temperature to be 870°F (460°C)
Evidence grows that children living near traffic routes are more affected by lead poisoning
Jean-Loup Chrétien (Fr.) becomes the first Westerner to fly on a Soviet space mission
Svetlana Savitskaya (U.S.S.R.) becomes the second woman in space after flying on Soyuz T-7
The first magnetized tissues to be discovered in mammals are found in dolphins; they may assist navigation
Scientists at Groningen University, Netherlands, postulate the existence of a black hole at the center of our galaxy
W. Ger. scientists announce the creation of a single atom of element 109 (Unnilennium)
The first commercial product of genetic engineering appears when human insulin produced by bacteria is marketed
The first private space rocket (the Conestoga 1) makes a suborbital flight
Canada blames environmental damage to its forests on acid rain mainly from U.S. industry and calls for extensive antipollution measures
The Tudor warship "Mary Rose" is raised from the Portsmouth Harbor seabed where it sank in 1545
A naturally occurring chemical in the brain is discovered and named "tribulin"; tribulin is an antitranquilizer that stimulates alertness
Combined heart-lung and kidney-pancreas transplants are carried out successfully
Brazil and Paraguay begin construction of the Itaipú Dam, the world's largest hydroelectric project
E. H. Carr, Eng. historian, d. (b. 1892)
René Dubos, Fr. microbiologist, d. (b. 1901)
Anna Freud, Eng. psychoanalyst, d. (b. 1895)
William F. Giauque, Amer. chemist, d. (b. 1895)
Stanford Moore, Amer. biochemist, d. (b. 1913)

G. DAILY LIFE

1982 contd

Italy wins soccer's World Cup for the third time, defeating West Germany, 3-1, in the final
A motorway pile-up in France during summer vacation causes 53 deaths (44 of them children)
Salvador Sanchez, Mex. W.B.C. featherweight boxing champion, d. (b. 1959)
Bombay police riot for several days until the Indian army restores order; 4 die, 37 are injured, and there is widespread destruction
Alfred Bloomingdale, Amer. founder of "Diner's Club", d. (b. 1916)
In September, N.F.L. American football players go on strike for more money
Gen. Carlo Alberto Dalla Chiesa, Prefect of Palermo, Sicily, and his wife are assassinated by Mafia hitmen
Abuja is declared Nigeria's new capital
Disneyworld, Florida, opens EPCOT (Experimental Community of Tomorrow), a futuristic theme park
Neoli Fairhall (New Zealand) wins the gold medal for archery at the 12th Commonwealth Games; she is the first paraplegic to do so
In Texas, convicted murderer Charlie Brooks is executed by a lethal injection—the first time this method has been used
Jack Swigert, Amer. astronaut on Apollo 13, d. (b. 1931)
The World Boxing Council decides to reduce the length of world title fights from 15 to 12 rounds
St. Louis Cardinals defeat Milwaukee Brewers, 4 games to 3 in World Series
The New York Islanders win hockey's Stanley Cup for the 3rd year in succession
Boston Celtics win National Basketball Association championship

	A. HISTORY, POLITICS	B. LITERATURE, THEATER	C. RELIGION, PHILOSOPHY, LEARNING
1982 contd			
1983	The Irish govenment outlaws the Irish National Liberation Army The Strategic Arms Reduction Talks in Geneva continue through the year with both the U.S. and the U.S.S.R. making constructive proposals Nigeria expels 2 million Ghanian migrant workers Klaus Barbie, Nazi war criminal, is put on trial in Lyons, France, after extradition from Bolivia In the Australian General Election, Bob Hawke (Labor) defeats Malcolm Fraser (Liberal) to become Prime Minister West Germany's Christian Democrats under Chancellor Helmut Kohl are reelected; the Green Party gains their first seats Umberto, last King of Italy, d. (b. 1904) Belfast-born Chaim Herzog is elected Israel's President President Reagan dubs the U.S.S.R. the "Evil Empire" and proposes a revolutionary new antimissile defense system to be known as the Strategic Defense Initiative (nick-named "Star Wars") Harold Washington (Dem.) is narrowly elected mayor of Chicago; Wilson Goode and Harvey Gantt (both Dem.) become the first black mayors of Philadelphia and Charlotte, North Carolina In April, a bomb planted by Shiite Muslims destroys the U.S. Embassy in Beirut, Lebanon, and 87 people are killed; in Oct. two suicide attacks on the U.S. and Fr. peacekeeping forces kill 242 U.S. and 62 Fr. personnel President Reagan openly backs the Contra rebels against the Marxist Sandinista government of Nicaragua Jesse Jackson becomes the first black man to address the Alabama legislature In the U.K., the Conservatives under Margaret Thatcher are reelected with the largest parliamentary majority since 1945 Li Xiannian becomes President of China Bettino Craxi becomes Italy's first Socialist Premier in a five-party coalition government Ethiopia appeals for aid for 4 million drought victims Tensions between Sinhalese and Tamils in Sri Lanka erupt violently; hundreds are killed and thousands made *(contd)*	Fyodor Abramov, Sov. writer, d. (b. 1920) Desmond Bagley, Eng. thriller author, d. (b. 1923) André Chamson, Fr. author, d. (b. 1900) Owen Dodson, Amer. poet and playwright, d. (b. 1914) Lynn Fontanne, Amer. actress, d. (b. 1887) William Goyen, Amer. author, d. (b. 1915) Arthur Koestler, Eng. author, commits suicide with wife Cynthia (b. 1905) Richard Llewellyn, Eng. author, d. (b. 1906) Ross Macdonald, Amer. thriller author, d. (b. 1915) Sir Ralph Richardson, Eng. actor, d. (b. 1902) Mary Renault, Eng. author, d. (b. 1898) Gabrielle Roy, Can. author, d. (b. 1909) Vittorio Sereni, Ital. poet, d. (b. 1913) Dame Rebecca West, Eng. novel-ist, d. (b. 1892) Leonard Wibberly, Ir. author, d. (b. 1915) Tennessee Williams, Amer. play-wright, d. (b. 1911) "Der Stern," a leading West Ger-man magazine, announces the discovery and purchase of Hitler's personal diaries; they are soon revealed as for-geries fabricated by Konrad Kujau A 12th-century manuscript, titled *(contd)*	The Roman Catholic Church ends its automatic excommunication of Freemasons The Vatican and Sweden resume diplomatic relations after a break of 450 years The oldest college in Cambridge, England (Peterhouse), votes to admit female under-graduates The World Council of Churches reaches new levels of con-sensus on central aspects of Christian faith and worship; the Council holds a historic interdenominational Eucharist Pope John Paul II visits his native country of Poland and meets both President Jaruzelski and Lech Walesa Raymond Aron, Fr. philosopher, d. (b. 1905) Cardinal Mario Casariego, Archbishop of Guatemala, d. (b. 1909) R. Buckminster Fuller, Amer. philosopher and architect, d. (b. 1895) Eric Hoffer, Amer. social philoso-pher, d. (b. 1902) Christmas Humphreys, leading Eng. Buddhist and judge, d. (b. 1900) Sir Kenneth Clark, Eng. historian, d. (b. 1903) John D. Needham, Amer. National Commander of the Salvation Army, d. (b. 1917) Joan Robinson, Amer. economist, d. (b. 1904) *(contd)*

D. VISUAL ARTS	E. MUSIC	F. SCIENCE, TECHNOLOGY, GROWTH	G. DAILY LIFE	
The Extra-Terrestrial" (Steven Spielberg); "Fanny and Alexander" (Ingmar Bergman); "First Blood" (Ted Kotcheff); "48 Hrs." (Walter Hill); "Gandhi" (Richard Attenborough); "My Favorite Year" (Richard Benjamin); "Sophie's Choice" (Alan Pakula); "Tootsie" (Sydney Pollack); "The Verdict" (Sidney Lumet); "The World According to Garp" (George Roy Hill)	Benatar, and Talking Heads Popular songs: "Rosanna," "Truly," "Up Where We Belong"			**1982 contd**
"Two Women" by de Kooning is sold for $1,200,000—a record price for a living artist's work A portrait by Rembrandt is stolen from Dulwich College, London, for the fourth time in 15 years "The Day After," starring Jason Robards, is watched on U.S. television by half the adult population; it depicts the effects of a nuclear strike on a U.S. community The television comedy series "M*A*S*H*" ends after 251 episodes "Hill Street Blues" receives the Emmy Award for the best television dramatic series Robert Aldrich, Amer. film director, d. (b. 1918) Luis Buñuel, Span. *(contd)*	An unknown chamber symphony by Mozart is discovered in Odense, Denmark; the manuscript was written when he was nine The Bayreuth Festival, W. Ger., marks the centenary of Wagner's death with a new production of "The Ring" Oliver Messiaen's first opera, "Saint Francis of Assisi," is premiered in Paris Rudolf Nureyev becomes Director of the Paris Opera Ballet George Balanchine, Amer. ballet choreographer, d. (b. 1904) Karen Carpenter, Amer. singer, d. (b. 1951) Ira Gershwin, Amer. lyricist, d. (b. 1897) John Gilpin, Eng. ballet dancer, d. (b. 1930) Herbert Howells, *(contd)*	Nobel Prize for Economics: Gerard Debreu (U.S.) for analysis of price stabilization Nobel Prize for Physiology and Medicine: Barbara McClintock (U.S.) for contributions to genetics Nobel Prize for Physics: William A. Fowler and S. Chandrasekhar (both U.S.) for investigations into the development of stars Nobel Prize for Chemistry: Henry Taube (U.S.) for contributions to reactions in inorganic chemistry U.S. Space Shuttle "Challenger" is launched on its maiden flight and completes three missions in 1983; Sally Ride is the first Amer. woman in space; Guion Bluford is the first black astronaut An ancient fossil skull discovered in Pakistan may be from the missing link between whales and land animals; "Pakicetus" lived approximately 50 million years ago The world's first artificially made chromosome is created at Harvard University and grafted onto yeast cells In Kenya, Maeve Leakey discovers a 16-million-year-old fossil jaw of an early primate named "Sivapithecus" The U.S. government approves the use of aspartame as an artificial sweetener in soft drinks A gene marker that identifies *(contd)*	Washington Redskins beat Miami Dolphins, 21-27, to win football's Super Bowl Meyer Lansky, Amer. head of organized crime, d. (b. 1902) Bjorn Borg (Swe.) retires from tennis at the age of 26 Paul "Bear" Bryant, Amer. football coach, d. (b. 1910) A Congressional Committee formally condemns the internment of Japanese-Americans in World War II A two-year drought in Ethiopia brings famine to millions Persistent ethnic and religious riots in Assam, India, result in 5,000 deaths and 300,000 refugees The first person to receive an artificial heart, Barney Clark (U.S.), dies 112 days after its implantation The Rhine floods and swamps large parts of Bonn, Cologne, and Koblenz Argentina introduces a new set of bank notes; each new peso equals 10,000 old pesos People's Express airline begins a discount round-trip service from New York to London for $150 Jimmy Demaret, Amer. golfer, d. (b. 1910) Jack Dempsey, World Heavyweight Boxing Champion (1919–1926), d. (b. 1895) Ling Ling gives birth to the first panda to be born in the U.S., but the infant panda dies after three hours George Meegan (U.K.) reaches N. Alaska after walking a world record 19,000 miles from Tierra del Fuego, S. America Dame Mary Donaldson becomes the first woman to be elected Lord Mayor of London in the position's 800-year history Richard Noble (U.K.) in Thrust II breaks the world land speed record with a speed of 633.6 m.p.h. *(contd)*	**1983**

	A. HISTORY, POLITICS	B. LITERATURE, THEATER	C. RELIGION, PHILOSOPHY, LEARNING
1983 contd	homeless; the government adopts emergency powers A military coup in Upper Volta replaces Maj. Ouedrago with former Prime Minister Capt. Thomas Sankara The Council on Hemispheric Affairs nominates Guatemala as the Latin Amer. country with the worst human rights record Chad rebels and Libyan troops seize the northern Chad town of Faya-Largeau but are driven out after France, the U.S., and Zaire back the government; 3,000 Fr. troops are deployed in Chad Benigno Aquino (b. 1932), Philippine political opponent of President Marcos, flies home and is assassinated at Manila Airport Israel and Lebanon sign a peace treaty enabling Israel to withdraw its forces in stages; Syria opposes this and the Lebanese civil war continues Unemployment in the U.S. rises to over 12 million, the highest figure since 1941 A South Korean airliner is shot down over the U.S.S.R. while flying from New York to Seoul; all 269 on board are killed The European Conference on Security and Cooperation in Madrid ends with unanimous agreement on the final document The 10th anniversary of the military coup in Chile is marked by mass protests in which 40 die Menachem Begin resigns as Israel's Prime Minister; Yitzhak Shamir succeeds him 38 I.R.A. prisoners escape in a mass breakout from the Maze Prison, Northern Ireland U.S. warships shell Druze strongholds in Beirut's mountains Neil Kinnock replaces Michael Foot as the British Labor Party leader Nobel Peace Prize: Lech Walesa (Poland) Grenada's Prime Minister Maurice Bishop is killed in a military coup; 6,000 U.S. troops invade and institute civil rule Teddy Kollek, Mayor of Jerusalem, is attacked by ultra-orthodox Jews angered at archaeological excavations on religious sites in the city Bishop Abel Muzorewa, former Prime Minister of Zimbabwe, is arrested on charges of destabilizing the State South Africa adopts a new constitution giving limited political rights to "Colored" and "Asian," but not "Black," South Africans The first cruise missiles to be deployed in Europe arrive at Greenham Common U.S.A.F. Base; female peace campaigners begin a permanent picket W. Germany agrees to the deployment of Pershing missiles within its borders Raul Alfonsín becomes President of Argentina after eight years of military rule Yasser Arafat and 4,000 P.L.O. members are expelled from Lebanon to Tunisia President Shagari of Nigeria is replaced by Maj. Gen. Buhari in a bloodless coup Turkish-held North Cyprus declares itself to be an independent republic, but only Turkey officially recognizes it	"The Gospels of Henry the Lion"(Duke of Bavaria), is auctioned at Sotheby's for over $12 million, a world record Nobel Prize for Literature: William Golding (U.K.) J. M. Coetzee: "Life and Times of Michael K," Booker Prize Alice Walker: "The Color Purple," Pulitzer Prize fiction Marsha Norman: " 'Night, Mother," Pulitzer Prize drama Galway Kinnell: "Selected Poems," Pulitzer Prize poetry Susan Sheehan: "Is There No Place on Earth for Me?" Pulitzer Prize nonfiction William Trevor: "Fools of Fortune," novel, Whitbread Prize Peter Ackroyd: "The Last Testament of Oscar Wilde," novel Isaac Asimov: "Foundation's Edge," novel John Le Carré: "The Little Drummer Girl," novel John Fowles: "Mantissa," novel Martin Gilbert: "Winston Churchill: The Finest Hour," official biography Ian Hamilton: "Robert Lowell," biography Norman Mailer: "Ancient Evenings," novel Gabriel Garcia Marquez: "A Chronicle of Death Foretold," novel Iris Murdoch: "The Philosopher's Pupil," novel Ruth Prawer Jhabvala: "In Serach of Love and Beauty," novel Salman Rushdie: "Shame," novel Lisa St. Aubin de Terran: "The Slow Train to Milan," novel John Updike: "Bech: A Book," novel Gore Vidal: "Duluth," novel Kurt Vonnegut: "Deadeye Dick," novel Morris West: "The World Is Made of Glass," novel "A Chorus Line" becomes the longest-running show on Broadway after its 3,389th performance Dario Fo: "Mistero Buffo," play David Hare: "A Map of the World," play Percy Mtwa: "Woza Albert," play Peter Ustinov: "Beethoven's Tenth," play	Ruth Carter Stapleton, Amer. evangelist, d. (b. 1929) Alfred Tarski, Amer. philosopher, d. (b. 1902)

D. VISUAL ARTS	E. MUSIC	F. SCIENCE, TECHNOLOGY, GROWTH	G. DAILY LIFE	
film director, d. (b. 1900) Buster Crabbe, Amer. film actor best known as "Flash Gordon", d. (b. 1908) George D. Cukor, Amer. film director, d. (b. 1899) William Demarest, Amer. film actor, d. (b. 1892) David Niven, Eng. film actor, d. (b. 1910) Pat O'Brien, Amer. film actor, d. (b. 1899) Slim Pickens, Amer. film actor, esp. Westerns, d. (b. 1919) Norma Shearer, Amer. film actress, d. (b. 1901) Gloria Swanson, Amer. film actress, d. (b. 1899) King Vidor, Amer. film director, d. (b. 1896) Academy Awards (for 1982)—best picture: "Gandhi"; best actor: Ben Kingsley ("Gandhi"); best actress: Meryl Streep ("Sophie's Choice") Films: "The Big Chill" (Lawrence Kasdan); "Educating Rita" (Lewis Gilbert); "Flashdance" (Adrian Lyne); "Gorky Park" (Michael Apted); "National Lampoon's Vacation" (Harold Ramis); "Never Say Never Again" (Irvin Kershner); "Terms of Endearment" (James L. Brooks); "Trading Places" (John Landis); "Yentl" (Barbra Streisand); "Zelig" (Woody Allen)	Eng. composer, d. (b. 1892) Earl Hines, Amer. jazz pianist, d. (b. 1905) Harry James, Amer. jazz trumpet player and bandleader, d. (b. 1916) Elisabeth Lutyens, Eng. classical composer, d. (b. 1906) Sir William Walton, Eng. composer, d. (b. 1902) Muddy Waters, Amer. blues artist, d. (b. 1914) U.S. Festival in Southern California attracts 725,000 people; the performers include David Bowie, Judas Priest, U2, and Van Halen Popular songs: "Beat It," "Thriller," "Flashdance," "Every Breath You Take," "Can't Slow Down"	Duchenne muscular dystrophy is identified by Kay Davies and Robert Williamson; a gene marker for Huntington's Disease is identified by James F. Gusella A meter is officially redefined as the distance that light travels in $^1/_{299,792,458}$ of a second A method of obsidian dating is developed similar to that of carbon dating After 11 years in flight, Pioneer 10 becomes the first spacecraft to leave the solar system The Soviet satellite Cosmos 1402 makes an unguided return to Earth and crashes into the Indian Ocean France tests its neutron bomb A Soviet nuclear-powered submarine sinks in the North Pacific with the loss of all 90 lives The compact disc is launched The first fossil land mammal to be found in Antarctica is thought to be the remains of an ancient marsupial Felix Bloch, Amer. physicist, d. (b. 1905) Bart J. Bok, Amer. astronomer, d. (b. 1906) William Boyd, Amer. immunologist, d. (b. 1903) Sir Harry Massey, Austral. physicist, d. (b. 1908) Ivan M. Vinogradov, Soviet mathematician, d. (b. 1891) Edward Weidlein, Amer. chemist, d. (b. 1887)	An earthquake in Turkey kills 1,200 people President Reagan signs legislation to make Martin Luther King, Jr.'s birthday a national holiday from Jan. 1986 onward The U.S. loses yachting's America's Cup after 132 years of unbroken victory: "Australia II" beats "Liberty," 4 races to 3 Baltimore Orioles defeat Philadelphia Phillies, 4 games to 1, to win World Series Philadelphia 76ers win National Basketball Association Championship New York Islanders win hockey's Stanley Cup for the 4th year in succession An I.R.A. car bomb explodes outside Harrod's store in London during the pre-Christmas shopping period; 6 people are killed and 90 are injured D. Ferhardt, the former commanding officer of Simonston Naval Dockyard, South Africa, is convicted with his wife of spying for the U.S.S.R.; they receive sentences of life imprisonment	**1983 contd**

	A. HISTORY, POLITICS	B. LITERATURE, THEATER	C. RELIGION, PHILOSOPHY, LEARNING

1984

A. History, Politics

Brunei becomes an independent sultanate and the 159th member of the U.N.
A U.S. pilot shot down over Lebanon is released by Syria after Jesse Jackson intervenes
The National Bipartisan Commission on Central America, led by Henry Kissinger, recommends $8 billion in aid
The U.S. peacekeeping force is withdrawn from Lebanon followed by the rest of the U.N. force
Yuri Vladimirovich Andropov, General Secretary of the U.S.S.R. (1982-1984), d. (b. 1914); Konstantin Chernenko succeeds him
Pierre Trudeau resigns as Canadian Prime Minister and is replaced by John Turner; he loses an election to the Progressive Conservative Party led by Brian Mulroney
Brit. coal miners begin a bitter national strike against pit closures; the strike continues through the year
Members of the Maitatsine Islamic sect riot in Yola, Nigeria; 700 deaths reported
Ahmad Sekou Touré, President of Guinea (1971-1984), d. (b. 1922)
President Reagan visits China
Andrei Sakharov goes on hunger strike to obtain medical treatment abroad for his wife Yelena Bonner, who is later sentenced instead to 5 years' internal exile
The Ethiopian government appeals for further aid, stating that as many as 5 million people could be killed by the drought
Sikh extremists occupy the Golden Temple, Amritsar, India; it is recaptured by the army, with 250 deaths; many Sikh soldiers mutiny in protest at the government's action
President Reagan and other heads of state visit Normandy, France, to commemorate the 40th anniversary of the D-Day Invasion
Enrico Berlinguer, Ital. communist statesman, d. (b. 1922)
Walter Mondale becomes the Dem. Presidential candidate, with Geraldine Ferraro as his running mate
Upper Volta is renamed Burkina Faso ("the republic of honest men")
Shimon Peres (Labor) becomes Israeli Prime Minister of a coalition government
The U.K. and China agree that Hong Kong will revert to China in 1997
An I.R.A. bomb explodes at the Grand Hotel, Brighton, during the Conservative Party Conference; 5 die and 32 are injured, but Mrs. Thatcher is unhurt
Polish priest and Solidarity supporter Father Jerzy Popieluzko is beaten to death by secret policemen
Indian Prime Minister Indira Gandhi (b. 1917) is assassinated by her Sikh bodyguards; her son Rajiv becomes the new Prime Minister; anti-Sikh riots sweep India and over 1,000 die
In November, Israel begins "Operation Moses," a secret airlift of Ethiopian Jews (Falashas) from Sudan; this ends in January with 25,000 airlifted
President Reagan easily defeats Senator Walter Mondale in the Presidential election, winning every state except Minnesota (Mondale's home) and Washington, D.C.
Argentina and Chile settle their dispute dating from 1881 on sovereignty over the Beagle Channel
South African President Pieter W. Botha appoints two "colored" men to his cabinet (Rev. Allen Hendrickse and Amichand Rajbansi) for the first time
Nobel Peace Prize: Bishop Desmond Tutu, General Secretary of the South African Council of Churches
Nobel Peace Prize: International Physicians for the Prevention of Nuclear War
Dom Mintoff, Maltese Prime Minister (1971-1984) resigns and is succeeded by Carmello Bonnici

B. Literature, Theater

Vincente Aleixandre, Sp. poet, d. (b. 1898)
Sir John Betjeman, Eng., Poet Laureate, d. (b. 1906)
Sir Basil Blackwell, Eng. publisher, d. (b. 1890)
Richard Burton, Brit. actor, d. (b. 1925)
Truman Capote, Amer. novelist, d. (b. 1924)
Julio Cortázar, Arg. novelist, d. (b. 1914)
Eduardo de Fillippo, Ital. playwright, d. (b. 1900)
Lillian Hellman, Amer. playwright and screenwriter, d. (b. 1907)
Alfred A. Knopf, Amer. publisher, d. (b. 1892)
Liam D'Flaherty, Ir. novelist, d. (b. 1896)
J. B. Priestley, Eng. novelist and playwright, d. (b. 1894)
Dame Flora Robson, Eng. actress, d. (b. 1902)
Mikhail Sholokov, Sov. novelist, d. (b. 1905)
The Cambridge University Press celebrates its 400th anniversary
A corrected version of James Joyce's "Ulysses" is published with corrections to the 5,000 errors made by the original French printer
Ted Hughes becomes the new Poet Laureate after Sir John Betjeman's death
An unpublished collection of poems by William Faulkner is donated to the University of Mississippi
Dustin Hoffman appears on Broadway as Willy Loman in Arthur Miller's "Death of a Salesman"
Nobel Prize for Literature: Jaroslav Seifert (Czech.)
Anita Brookner: "Hôtel du Lac," Booker Prize
William Kennedy "Ironweed," Pulitzer Prize fiction
Mary Oliver: "American Primitive," Pulitzer Prize poetry
David Mamet: "Glengarry Glen Ross," Pulitzer Prize drama
Paul Starr: "Social Transformation of American Medicine," Pulitzer Prize nonfiction
Marguerite Duras: "L'Amant," Prix Goncourt
Whitbread Prize: "Kruger's Alp," Christopher Hope
Kingsley Amis: "Stanley and His Women," novel
Martin Amis: "Money," novel
J. G. Ballard: "Empire of the Sun," novel
Julian Barnes: "Flaubert's Parrot," novel
(contd)

C. Religion, Philosophy, Learning

The Texas Board of Education repeals a ruling from the 1970s that banned the teaching of evolution as a scientific fact
The U.S. and the Vatican establish full diplomatic relations after a hiatus of 116 years
The Vatican publishes a document on the "Theology of Liberation" warning against Marxism
The Pope pronounces 99 martyrs of the French Revolution to be "blessed," the first stage toward awarding sainthood
The largest demonstrations in Fr. history, with nearly a million marchers, force the government to abandon its challenge to the independence of church schools
York Minster damaged by fire after being hit by lightning
Roland H. Bainton, Amer. Protestant theologian, d. (b. 1894)
Ben Herbster, First President of the United Church of Christ, d. (b. 1904)
Martin Niemöller, W. Ger. Protestant pastor, d. (b. 1892)
Karl Rahner, W. Ger. Roman Catholic theologian, d. (b. 1904)
Cardinal Lawrence Sheehan, Roman Catholic Archbishop of Baltimore (1961-1974) d. (b. 1898)
Greg Bailey: "The Mythology of Brahma"
W. D. Davies and L. Finkelstein: "The Cambridge History of Judaism"
Kwesi Dickson: "Theology in Africa"
Amin Maalouf: "The Crusades through Arab Eyes"
Ian Wilson: "Jesus, the Evidence"

1984

D. VISUAL ARTS

The Motion Picture Association of America creates the PG-13 film rating

Johnny Weissmuller, Amer. actor especially noted for "Tarzan" films, d. (b. 1904)

71 drawings belonging to the Duke of Devonshire are sold for more than $30 million

Turner's painting "Seascape: Folkestone" is auctioned at Sotheby's for a new high price of $10 million

Ansel Adams, Amer. photographer, d. (b. 1902)

Jackie Coogan, Amer. actor, d. (b. 1914)

Jimmy Ernst, Amer. abstract expressionist painter, d. (b. 1920)

Carl Foreman, Amer. screenwriter and producer, d. (b. 1914)

Tom Keating, Eng. painter and forger, d. (b. 1917)

Lee Krasner, Amer. abstract expressionist painter, d. (b. 1908)

Joseph Losey, Amer. film director, d. (b. 1909)

James Mason, Eng. actor, d. (b. 1909)

Alice Neel, Amer. painter, d. (b. 1900)

Sam Peckinpah, Amer. film director, d. (b. 1925)

Walter Pidgeon, Amer. actor, d. (b. 1898)

Irwin Shaw, Amer. screenwriter and novelist, d. (b. 1913)

François Truffaut, *(contd)*

E. MUSIC

Band Aid launches a Christmas record titled "Do They Know It's Christmas?" in aid of Ethiopian famine relief; it tops the charts worldwide

Soul singer Marvin Gaye (b. 1939) is shot dead by his father

The New York Metropolitan Opera's centennial season is marked by its first U.S. production of a Handel opera ("Rinaldo")

John Scott wins the J. S. Bach International Organ Competition in Leipzig, E. Germany

1984 Pulitzer Prize for Music: "Canti del sole" for tenor and orchestra by Bernard Rands

William "Count" Basie, Amer. jazz pianist and bandleader, d. (b. 1904)

Tito Gobbi, Ital. operatic baritone, d. (b. 1915)

Alberta Hunter, Amer. jazz singer, d. (b. 1895)

Ralph Kirkpatrick, Amer. harpsichordist, d. (b. 1911)

Ethel Merman, Amer. popular singer, d. (b. 1909)

Judith Raskin, Amer. soprano, d. (b. 1928)

Leonard Rose, Amer. cellist, d. (b. 1918)

Arthur Schwartz, Amer. popular composer, d. (b. 1900)

Ernest Tubbs, Amer. country singer, d. (b. 1914)

Meredith Willson, *(contd)*

F. SCIENCE, TECHNOLOGY, GROWTH

Nobel Prize for Economics: Sir Richard Stone (U.K.) for work on national income accounting

Nobel Prize for Physiology and Medicine: Cesar Milstein (U.K.) and Georges Köhler (W. Ger.) for research on monoclonal antibodies, and Niels Jerne (Den.) for studies of the immune system

Nobel Prize for Physics: Carlo Rubbia (Ital.) and Simon van der Meer (Neth.) for their discovery of W and Z particles

Nobel Prize for Chemistry: R. Bruce Maxfield (U.S.) for work on peptides and proteins

The Apple Macintosh microcomputer with mouse is launched

Bruce McCandless and Robert Stewart (both U.S.) are the first to fly in space untethered and with back packs; on completion of the mission "Challenger" lands for the first time at Kennedy Space Center, Florida

The European Space Agency launches the world's largest telecommunications satellite

U.S. and Fr. teams independently discover the AIDS virus

A silicon microchip that stores four times more data than previously possible is developed

The Thames Flood Barrier, the world's largest, is officially opened

Soviet engineers drill $7^{1}/_{2}$ miles to reach the Earth's lower crust

Test-tube triplets and quadruplets are born in the U.K.

"Baby Fae," a 15-day-old Amer. baby, has a baboon's heart transplanted into her, but dies 20 days later

In the U.K. Dame Mary Warnock's committee of inquiry into human fertilization recommends controlling "test-tube" baby research and banning surrogate mothers

The space shuttle "Discovery" successfully makes its maiden flight

A 5-million-year-old jawbone of "Australopithecus afarensis" is discovered in Kenya; this is the earliest known ancestor of ours that is not also an ancestor of the apes

DNA analysis reveals that chimpanzees are more closely related to humans than to gorillas or other apes; the genetic difference is barely 1%

An undisturbed Mayan tomb is discovered in Guatemala

W. Ger. scientists announce the creation of three atoms of element 108 (unniloctium)

(contd)

G. DAILY LIFE

Ray Kroc, founder of McDonald's restaurants, d. (b. 1902)

Los Angeles Raiders beat Washington Redskins, 38-9, to win football's Super Bowl

Anna Anderson Manahan, who claimed to be the Grand Anastasia of Russia, d. (b.c. 1901)

Seven U.S. chemical companies agree to pay compensatison of $180 million to 15,000 U.S. Vietnam War veterans whose health had been impaired by "Agent Orange" pesticide

The U.S.S.R. and the Communist bloc boycott the Olympics in retaliation for the Western boycott of 1980; Carl Lewis (U.S.) becomes the first athlete to win gold medals in the 100- and 200-meter dashes, the 400-meter relay, and the long jump

Disney World, Florida, celebrates Donald Duck's 50th birthday

Viv Richards (W. Indies) scores 189 not out against England—the highest-ever innings in a limited-overs cricket international

The world's largest corporate merger is announced; Standard Oil of California acquires Gulf for $13.2 billion

A huge explosion in Severomorsk, U.S.S.R., destroys a third of the Northern Fleet's stock of surface-to-air missiles; the number of casualties is unrevealed

Robert Maxwell (U.K.) buys Mirror Group Newspapers for $170 million

A man shoots 20 dead and wounds 16 in a McDonald's restaurant in San Ysidro, California, before being shot dead himself

A typhoon in the Philippines kills 500 and leaves a million homeless

Walter Alston, Amer. manager of Brooklyn/L.A. Dodgers (1954-1977), d. (b. 1911)

Velma Barfield (who fatally poisoned her mother, boyfriend, and two others) is executed by lethal injection in North Carolina; she is the first woman to be executed in the U.S. since 1962

A toxic gas leak from the Union Carbide Plant, Bhopal, India, kills 2,500 people and injures thousands more

By the year's end, more than 70 U.S. banks fail, the highest rate since 1937

Detroit Tigers defeat San Diego Padres, 4 games to 1, in World Series

Edmonton Oilers win hockey's Stanley Cup

Boston Celtics win National Basketball Association championship

The U.S. Army awards 8,612 medals for the 1983 Grenada campaign, even though there were never more than 7,000 soldiers on the island

	A. HISTORY, POLITICS	B. LITERATURE, THEATER	C. RELIGION, PHILOSOPHY, LEARNING
1984 contd		Saul Bellow: "Him with His Foot in His Mouth," novel Angela Carter: "Nights at the Circus," novel Tony Harrison: "Selected Poems" Seamus Heaney: "Station Island," poetry Joseph Heller: "God Knows," novel Erica Jong: "Parachutes and Kisses," novel Milan Kundera: "The Unbearable Lightness of Being," novel Georges Simenon: "Intimate Memoirs," autobiography Isaac Bashevis Singer: "The Penitent," short stories John Updike: "The Witches of Eastwick," novel Gore Vidal: "Lincoln," novel Fay Weldon: "Life and Loves of a She-Devil," novel Peter Parnell: "Romance Language," play Harold Pinter: "One for the Road," play Stephen Sondheim: "Sunday in the Park with George," musical	
1985	Daniel Ortega is inaugurated President of Nicaragua In New Caledonia, agitation for independence from France continues; separatist leaders Eloi Machero and Marcel Nanaro are killed by security forces President Reagan begins his second term of office Spain reopens its frontier with Gibraltar after 16 years' closure Henry Cabot Lodge, Amer. statesman, d. (b. 1902) A civilian government takes office in Uruguay after 12 years' military rule; Julio Sanguinetti is the new President Konstantin Chernenko, General Secretary of the U.S.S.R. (1984-1985), d. (b. 1911); Mikhail Gorbachev succeeds him J.M.G.M. "Tom" Adams, Prime Minister of Barbados (1976-1985), d. (b. 1931); Bernart St. John succeeds him Israel partially withdraws from southern Lebanon; President Amin Gemayel is unable to end the country's civil war The Brit. coal miners' strike ends in failure in March; pit closures continue In Uitenhage, South African police fire on unarmed marchers commemorating the 25th anniversary of the Sharpeville massacre; 18 are killed and 36 injured President Nimeiri of Sudan is overthrown in a coup and replaced by General Suwar Al-Dhahab Mikhail Gorbachev unilaterally halts deployment of medium-range missiles in Europe Enver Hoxha, Albanian dictator (1945-1985), d. (b. 1908); Ramiz Alia succeeds him South Africa withdraws its troops from Angola Argentina puts on trial former military leaders for crimes against human rights; ex-President Jorge Videla receives life imprisonment, ex-President Viola is jailed for 17 *(contd)*	Julian Beck, Amer. theater director, d. (b. 1925) Heinrich Böll, W. Ger. novelist, d. (b. 1917) Abe Burrows, Amer. playwright and director, d. (b. 1918) Italo Calvino, Ital. novelist, d. (b. 1923) Robert Graves, Eng. novelist and poet, d. (b. 1895) Christopher Isherwood, Eng.-born Amer. author, d. (b. 1904) Philip A. Larkin, Eng. poet, d. (b. 1922) Lilli Palmer, W. Ger. actress, d. (1914) Merlo Pusey, Amer. author, d. (b. 1902) Sir Michael Redgrave, Eng. actor, d. (b. 1908) Axel Springer, W. Ger. newspaper publisher, d. (b. 1912) Theodore Sturgeon, Amer. science-fiction author, d. (b. 1918) "Times" of London celebrates its 200th anniversary The poet Lord Byron's only short story is discovered by his publisher, John Murray Jason Robards stars again on Broadway in "The Iceman *(contd)*	The Vatican imposes a year's silence on the Brazilian Francisan Leonardo Boff because of his writings on "liberation theology" The Pope summons an "Extraordinary Synod" of Bishops to celebrate the 20th anniversary of Vatican II Large crowds visit a statue of the Virgin Mary in Ballinspittle, County Cork, Ireland, which is said to move back and forth The Coptic Pope Shenouda III is released from banishment in Wadi Natroun Monastery and preaches reconciliation with Egypt's Islamic majority China releases the former Roman Catholic Bishop of Shanghai, Ignatius Kung (Gong Pinmei), after 30 years' imprisonment for his religious beliefs; Beijing's (Peking's) Roman Catholic cathedral is reopened Ruth Lawrence, aged 13, gains a first-class mathematics degree from Oxford University Spencer Kimball, Amer. President and Prophet (1973-1985) of the Church of Jesus Christ of Latter Day Saints (the Mormon Church), d. (b. 1895) *(contd)*

D. VISUAL ARTS	E. MUSIC	F. SCIENCE, TECHNOLOGY, GROWTH	G. DAILY LIFE	
Fr. film director, d. (b. 1932) Academy Awards (for 1983)—best picture: "Terms of Endearment"; best actor: Robert Duvall ("Tender Mercies"); best actress: Shirley MacLaine ("Terms of Endearment") Films: "Amadeus" (Milos Forman); "Beverly Hills Cop" (Martin Brest); "Ghostbusters" (Ivan Reitman); "Gremlins" (Joe Dante); "Greystoke" (Hugh Hudson); "The Killing Fields" (Roland Joffe); "Paris, Texas" (Wim Wenders); "Police Academy" (Hugh Wilson); "Romancing the Stone" (Robert Zemeckis)	Amer. popular composer, d. (b. 1902) Michael Jackson, pop singer, wins unprecedented eight Grammy Awards for his album, "Thriller," with sales over 37 million copies	A naturally mummified male body is found in an English peat bog; "Lindow Man" had been ritually sacrificed by Druid priests N.A.S.A. astronomers photograph a planetary system forming around the star Beta Pictoris There are currently 1,462 spacecraft and satellites in space as well as countless thousands of pieces of debris, according to the N.A.S.A. Goddard Spaceflight Center A world record total of 71,830 patents are filed in the U.S. Carl Ferdinand Cori, Amer. Nobel biochemist, d. (b. 1896) Paul Dirac, Eng. Nobel mathematician, d. (b. 1902) Piotr Leonidovich Kapitsa, Soviet Nobel physicist, d. (b. 1894) Alfred Kastler, Fr. Nobel physicist, d. (b. 1902) Sir Martin Ryle, Eng. Nobel Astronomer Royal, d. (b. 1918)		**1984 contd**
Mantegna's "Adoration of the Magi" is sold to the Getty Museum for a record $12 million The painting that gave the Impressionist movement its name, "Impression, Sun Rising" by Monet, is among the works of art stolen from the Marmottan Museum, Paris Christo, a Bulgarian artist, wraps the Pont Neuf bridge, Paris, in 40,000 square yards of canvas Laura Ashley, Eng. fashion designer, d. (b. 1925) Anne Baxter, Amer. actress, d. (b. 1923) *(contd)*	Events around the world mark the tercentenaries of the births of Handel and J. S. Bach Handel's "Tamerlano" has its U.S. stage premiere at the University of Indiana Canada's first International String Quartet Competition (at Banff) is won by the Colorado Quartet The U.K. Postal Service marks European Music Year by issuing four stamps depicting Delius, Elgar, Handel, and Holst U.S.A. for Africa record their Ethiopian benefit song, "We Are the World," written by *(contd)*	Nobel Prize for Economics: Franco Modigliani (U.S.) for analysis of corporate finance Nobel Prize for Physiology and Medicine: Michael S. Brown and Joseph L. Goldstein (both U.S.) for their study of cholesterol Nobel Prize for Physics: Klaus von Klitzing (W. Ger.) for his discovery of the quantized Hall effect Nobel Prize for Chemistry: Herbert A. Hauptman and Jerome Karle (both U.S.) for their mathematical analysis of molecular structure The U.S. and U.K. both resign from U.N.E.S.C.O. (the United Nations Educational, Science and Cultural Organization) Scientists at University of California, Berkeley, gain more evidence of a gigantic black hole in the middle of our galaxy Switzerland becomes the first European country to make catalytic converters, which need lead-free fuel, mandatory for private automobiles The earliest well-preserved amphibian skeleton is found *(contd)*	Gabriel "Flash" Elorde, Philippine world lightweight boxing champion (1960-1967), d. (b. 1935) The severe winter in Europe kills more than 100 people San Franciso 49ers beat the Miami Dolphins, 38-16, to win football's Super Bowl Bernhard Goetz, a vigilante who admitted shooting four black suspected muggers on the New York subway, is charged only with possession of an illegal gun The World Bank organizes a famine relief fund for Africa with contributions from 13 nations A Boeing 727 crashes at Bilbao, Spain, killing 145 The U.K. begins screening blood donations for the AIDS virus Robbers steal approximately $40 million from the Wells Fargo Bank, New York A fire at Bradford City Football Ground, U.K., kills 52 spectators Southern Bangladesh is devastated by a cyclone and tidal waves which kill 10,000 The European (soccer) Cup Final is held at the Heysel Stadium, Belgium, between Liverpool and Juventus of Turin, but a riot causes the deaths of 41 (mostly Ital.) spectators; English clubs are banned indefinitely from European soccer competitions John Ringling North, Amer. circus director, d. (b. 1903) Boris Becker (W. Ger.) becomes Wimbledon's *(contd)*	**1985**

	A. HISTORY, POLITICS	B. LITERATURE, THEATER	C. RELIGION, PHILOSOPHY, LEARNING
1985 contd	years A T.W.A. airliner is hijacked by Arab terrorists and 39 U.S. passengers are held hostage for 17 days (one is murdered) Zimbabwe's first general election ends in victory for Prime Minister Mugabe's Zanu (PF) Party Eduard Shevardnadze becomes Soviet Foreign Secretary; his predecessor, Andrei Gromyko, becomes President Fr. secret agents sink the Greenpeace flagship "Rainbow Warrior" in Auckland harbor, killing a crewman; two Fr. agents are later jailed in New Zealand and Fr. Defense Minister Charles Hernu resigns South Africa imposes a state of emergency in 36 districts Ugandan President Milton Obote is overthrown in a military coup Forbes Burnham, President of Guyana (1980-1985), d. (b. 1923); H. D. Hoyte succeeds him Bangladesh and Burma reach agreement on the location of their mutual border President Reagan announces limited sanctions against South Africa Israeli aircraft bomb the P.L.O. headquarters in Tunis and kill 60 in response to the murder of three Israelis in Cyprus The Portuguese Social Democrats defeat the ruling Socialists; Anibal Silva becomes President Palestinians hijack the Italian cruise liner "Achille Lauro," seize 450 hostages, and kill a U.S. passenger; subsequently they surrendered to the Egyptian government, which flies them to Tunis, but U.S. jets intercept the flight and force it to land in Italy where the hijackers are jailed Julius Nyerere retires as Tanzanian President; Ali Hassan Mwinyi replaces him The U.K. and Ireland sign the Anglo-Irish Agreement, which gives the republic a consultative role in Northern Ireland; Ulster Unionist Members of Parliament resign from the House of Commons in protest Mikhail Gorbachev and President Reagan meet for a two-day summit in Geneva A border dispute between Burkina Faso and Mali erupts into war; eventually a cease-fire is agreed upon and the matter is referred to the International Court of Justice	Cometh," in which he first appeared in 1961 Nobel Prize for Literature: Claude Simon (Fr.) Keri Hulme: "The Bone People," Booker Prize Alison Lurie: "Foreign Affairs," Pulitzer Prize fiction Stephen Sondheim and James Lapine: "Sunday in the Park with George," Pulitzer Prize drama Studs Terkel: "The Good War: An Oral History of World War," Pulitzer Prize nonfiction Carolyn Kizer: "Yin," Pulitzer Prize for poetry Yan Queffelec: "Les Noces Barbares," Prix Goncourt Douglas Dunn: "Elegies," Whitbread Prize Peter Ackroyd: "Hawksmoor," novel Simon Callow: "Being an Actor," nonfiction Peter Carey: "Illywacker," novel Donald Davies: "Elegies," poetry Lawrence Durrell: "Quinx," novel Alice Thomas Ellis: "Unexplained Laughter," novel Vassily Grossman: "Life and Fate," novel Alec Guinness: "Blessings in Disguise," autobiography John Irving: "The Cider House Rules," novel Garrison Keillor, "Lake Wobegon Days," novel Doris Lessing: "The Good Terrorist," novel Brian Moore: "Black Robe," novel Grace Paley: "Later the Same Day," short stories Bob Shacochis: "Easy in the Islands," short stories Anne Tyler: "The Accidental Tourist," novel Larry Kramer: "The Normal Heart," play Wallace Shawn: "Aunt Dan and Lemon," play Sam Shepard: "A Lie of the Mind," play	Willem Visser 'T Hooft, Dutch church leader, d. (b. 1900) Pinchas Lapide: "The Resurrection of Jesus" Emmanuel Sivan: "Radical Islam" W. S. Hatcher and J. D. Martin: "The Baha'i Faith"

D. VISUAL ARTS	E. MUSIC	F. SCIENCE, TECHNOLOGY, GROWTH	G. DAILY LIFE	
Louise Brooks, Amer. silent film star, d. (b. 1906) Yul Brynner, Amer. actor, d. (b. 1920) Marc Chagall, Fr. artist, d. (b. 1887) Jean Dubuffet, Fr. artist, d. (b. 1901) Sergei Gerasimov, Soviet film director, d. (b. (1906) Diego Giacometti, Swiss painter, d. (b. 1902) Chester Gould, Amer. cartoonist creator of "Dick Tracy," d. (b. 1900) Frank Hampson, Eng. cartoonist creator of "Dan Dare," d. (b. 1918) Rock Hudson, Amer. actor, d. (b. 1925) André Kertész, Hung.-born Amer. photographer, d. (b. 1894) Edmond O'Brien, Amer. actor, d. (b. 1915) Phil Silvers, Amer. comedian, d. (b. 1911) Sam Spiegel, Amer. film producer, d. (b. 1903) Orson Welles, Amer. filmmaker, d. (b. 1915) Tapio Wirkkala, Finnish sculptor, d. (b. 1915) Academy Awards (for 1984)—best picture: "Amadeus"; best actor: F. Murray Abraham ("Amadeus"); best actress: Sally Field ("Places in the Heart") Films: "After Hours" (Martin Scorsese); "Back to the Future" (Robert Zemeckis); "The *(contd)*	Lionel Richie and Michael Jackson The Live Aid Rock Concert in London and Philadelphia raises over $60 million for African famine relief and is beamed to a worldwide audience; the artists play for free and include Bob Geldof, Status Quo, Dire Straits, U2, David Bowie, Beach Boys, Paul McCartney, Phil Collins, The Who, Madonna, Bob Dylan, and Ultravox New York Theater's Tony Award for Best Musical: "Big River"; for the first time in its history no awards are made for best actor, actress, and choreographer in a musical because of the low overall standard Pulitzer Prize for Music: "River Run" for orchestra by Stephen Albert Elliot Carter, Amer. composer, is awarded the National Medal of Arts of the U.S. Grawemeyer Award for distinction in music composition: Witold Lutoslawski (Pol.) Xue Wei (China) wins the Carl Flesch International Violin Competition Beno Blachut, Czech. operatic tenor, d. (b. 1913) Emil Gilels, Soviet pianist, d. (b. 1916) Kay Kyser, Amer. *(contd)*	in Scottish oil shale and is 340 million years old The transputer is invented by Inmos, U.K., to enable a computer to manage parallel information processing Deep oceanic vents are found in the Mid-Atlantic Ridge The Brit. Antarctic Survey discovers a hole in the ozone layer over Antarctica The figure "1" written 1,031 times is proved to be a prime number Surgeons use lasers to clean out clogged arteries The space shuttle "Atlantis" makes its maiden flight "Discovery" makes the space shuttle's first exclusively military space mission Amstrad launches the PCW 8256 word processor Dian Fossey, Amer. zoologist, d. (b. 1932) Simon Kuznets, Amer. Nobel economist, d. (b. 1901) Charles Richter, Amer. seismologist and originator of the Richter earthquake scale, d. (b. 1900)	youngest Men's Singles Champion; Martina Navratilova (U.S.) wins the Women's Singles title Diver Andy Matroci discovers the wreck of the Spanish treasure galleon "Nuestra Señora de Atocha," which sank off Florida in 1622; its cargo of bullion is estimated to be worth $400 million The wreck of the "Titanic," lying deep in the North Atlantic, is photographed by a remote-controlled camera Europe defeats the U.S.A. $16\frac{1}{2}$-$11\frac{1}{2}$ in golf's Ryder Cup for the first time in 28 years Jock Stein, Scottish national soccer team manager, d. (b. 1922) Pete Rose of baseball's Cincinnati Reds makes the 4,192th hit of his career to break Ty Cobb's 1928 record An earthquake in Mexico City kills 7,000 Black rioters in Tottenham, London, hack to death Police Officer Keith Blakelock Ladislao José Biró, Arg. inventor of the Biro pen, d. (b. 1899) Gary Kasparov defeats Anatoly Karpov (both U.S.S.R.) to become the world's youngest chess champion at the age of 22 A U.S. court sentences Arthur Walker, head of a family spy ring, to life imprisonment with a $250,000 fine for passing military secrets to the U.S.S.R. for 18 years Johnny Blood, Amer. football player, d. (b. 1904) Roger Maris, Amer. baseball player, d. (b. 1934) The U.S. officially becomes the world's largest debtor nation, with a deficit of $130 billion Colombian town of Armero is destroyed in volcanic eruption; 20,000 lives lost Kansas City Royals beat St. Louis Cardinals, 4 games to 1, to win World Series Los Angeles Lakers win the National Basketball Association championship Edmonton Oilers win hockey's Stanley Cup	**1985 contd**

	A. HISTORY, POLITICS	B. LITERATURE, THEATER	C. RELIGION, PHILOSOPHY, LEARNING
1985 contd			
1986	Portugal and Spain enter the European Community Ugandan guerrillas capture Kampala and install Yoweri Museveni as President In the Philippines presidential election, President Ferdinand Marcos retains the Presidency by defeating Corazon Aquino, who alleges extensive ballot rigging; subsequently Marcos flees the Philippines and Corazon Aquino becomes the new President Haitian President Jean-Claude Duvalier flees to France after nationwide demonstrations against his rule In Berlin, Soviet dissident Anatoly Shcharansky and three others are exchanged for five East European spies James Eastland, Amer. Senator for Mississippi (1942-1978), d. (b. 1904) Mário Soares is elected Portugal's first civilian President in 60 years Olof Palme (b. 1930), Swedish Prime Minister (1969–1976 and 1982–1986), is shot dead by an unknown gunman; Ingvar Carlsson succeeds him 176 foreign hostages in Angola are handed over to the Red Cross Jacques Chirac (Gaullist) is elected Fr. Prime Minister under President Mitterand (Socialist) U.S. warplanes bomb Tripoli and Benghazi, Libya, in retaliation for Libyan missile attacks on U.S. aircraft and alleged terrorist attacks on U.S. servicemen Wallis Simpson (née Warfield), Duchess of Windsor, d. (b. 1896) The seven major Western economic powers hold a summit meeting in Tokyo, which is the target of five terrorist rockets; the conference agrees on proposals to combat terrorism and makes a statement on the Chernobyl nuclear disaster "Manny" Shinwell, Eng. politician, d. (b. 1884) Former Argentine President General Galtieri and two others are jailed for negligence in conducting the Falklands War South Africa launches combined air and land raids against alleged A.N.C. bases in Botswana, Zambia, and Zimbabwe, ending hopes of a truce between South Africa and the A.N.C. Jagjivan Ram, Indian politician, d. (b. 1908) Former U.N. Secretary General Kurt Waldheim is elected Austrian President, despite his alleged wartime Nazi connections; Franz Vranitzky replaces Fred Sinowatz as Austrian Chancellor South African President P. W. Botha announces a nationwide state of emergency, and 20,000 are held in deten- *(contd)*	Simone de Beauvoir, Fr. novelist, d. (b. 1908) Jorge Luis Borges, Arg. novelist, d. (b. 1899) John A. Ciardi, Amer. poet, d. (b. 1910) Abram Hill, Amer. theatrical director, d. (b. 1911) Jean Genet, Fr. novelist and playwright, d. (b. 1910) Bernard Malamud, Amer. novelist, d. (b. 1914) Jaroslav Seifert, Czech. poet, d. (b. 1901) Robert Penn Warren is appointed the first official Poet Laureate of the U.S. The final supplement (Se–Z) of the "Oxford English Dictionary" is published more than a century after the project's inception Two national newspapers are launched in the U.K. ("Today" and "The Independent") News International Ltd. moves the "Times" (of London) from Fleet St. to Wapping despite union strike action The U.K. government attempts to get an Australian court injunction to ban publication of "Spycatcher" by retired M.I.5 officer Peter Wright Ingmar Bergman's production of Strindberg's "Miss Julie" is shown at the Edinburgh International Festival Robert De Niro becomes the latest Hollywood star to act on Broadway when he stars in "Cuba and his Teddy Bear" Nobel Prize for Literature: Wole Soyinka (Nigeria) Kingsley Amis: "The Old Devils," Booker Prize Larry McMurtry: "Lonesome *(contd)*	John Paul II becomes the first Pope in recorded history to visit a synagogue and also leads a hundred world religious leaders (Christian, Buddisht, Hindu, Jewish, Muslim, Shinto, Sikh) in prayers for peace at St. Francis' Basilica, Assisi Convicted murderer James Nelson becomes a Protestant minister in Lanarkshire, Scotland Eva Burrows (Austral.) is elected world head of the Salvation Army Desmond Tutu becomes the first black Archbishop of Cape Town Israeli archeologists discover a 2,600-year-old biblical text South Africa's Dutch Reformed Church votes to open its membership to all races Church of England bishops publish "The Nature of Christian Belief," which reaffirms their belief in the Virgin Birth and the Resurrection Herbert Armstrong, Amer. fundamentalist founder of the Worldwide Church of God, d. (b. 1892) Christopher Butler, Eng. Anglican Bishop and leading theologian, d. (b. 1902) Mircea Eliade, Rom. religious philosopher, d. (b. 1907) Moshe Feinstein, Amer. Talmudic scholar, d. (b. 1895) L. Ron Hubbard, Amer. founder of Scientology, d. (b. 1911) Jiddu Krishnamurti, Indian religious philosopher, d. (b. 1895) Michele Pellegrino, Ital. Roman Catholic Cardinal, d. (b. 1903) Kazem Shariat–Madari, Iranian Ayatollah, d. (b. 1905) Cynthia Wedel, Amer. Episcopalian leader, *(contd)*

D. VISUAL ARTS	E. MUSIC	F. SCIENCE, TECHNOLOGY, GROWTH	G. DAILY LIFE	
Color Purple" (Steven Spielberg); "Desperately Seeking Susan" (Susan Seidelman); "Insignificance" (Nicholas Roeg); "Plenty" (Fred Schepisi); "Prizzi's Honor" (John Huston); "Rambo: First Blood, Part II" (George Pan Cosmatos); "Subway" (Luc Besson); "Witness" (Peter Weir)	bandleader, d. (b. 1906) Rick Nelson, Amer. rock singer, d. (b. 1940) Eugene Ormandy, Amer. conductor and violinist, d. (b. 1899) Efrem Zimbalist, Amer. violinist, d. (b. 1890)			**1985 contd**
Braque's "Woman Reading" is auctioned for $10 million Manet's "La Rue Mosnier aux Paviers" is auctioned for $12 million Philadelphia's Academy of Fine Arts acquires 1,000 works by Thomas Eakins The Museum of Contemporary Art (MOCA) opens in Los Angeles The Museeé d'Orsay, Paris, is opened inside the Gare d'Orsay, the defunct railroad station and will specialize in 19th-century art Rembrandt's portrait of Jacob De Gheyn III, which has been stolen four times from the Dulwich Gallery, London, is found in W. Germany and returned again. Controversy arises when film companies begin to "colorize" old black-and-white films *(contd)*	Barry Douglas (U.K.) wins the International Tchaikovsky Piano Competition in Moscow Andrew Litton (U.S.) becomes conductor of the Bournemouth Symphony Orchestra, U.K. An International Women's Festival of Music is held in Beer-Sheva, Israel, and is dedicated to cellist Jacqueline du Pré The most extensive festival ever to celebrate the career of Leonard Bernstein (U.S.) is mounted at the Barbican, London An unknown score by Edward Elgar is found in a drawer in Bournemouth, England The Musiktheater, Amsterdam (Netherland Opera's new home), opens with the premiere of Otto Ketting's "Ithaka" The Bolshoi Ballet successfully tours W. Europe *(contd)*	Nobel Prize for Economics: J. M. Buchanan (U.S.) for analysis of the role of governments in economics Nobel Prize for Physiology and Medicine: Rita Levi-Montalcini (Ital.) and Stanley Cohen (U.S.) for analyses of chemical growth factors Nobel Prize for Physics: Ernest Ruska (W. Ger.), Gerd Binning (W. Ger.), and Heinrich Rohrer (Switz.) for development of the electronic microscope Nobel Prize for Chemistry: Dudley Hersbach (U.S.), Yuan Lee (U.S.), and John Polanyi (Can.) for work on reaction dynamics Voyager 2 flies by Uranus and discovers 10 more moons The space shuttle "Challenger" explodes on take-off, killing all seven crew members In Egypt, archeologists uncover the 3,500-year-old tomb of Maya, Tutankhamen's treasurer Europe's "Giotto" space probe photographs the core of Halley's Comet The Netherlands delta works flood protection scheme is completed after 33 years construction at a cost of more than $4 billion Using a submarine, a W. Ger. scientist films living coelacanths in their natural habitat 600 feet (180 m) below the sea's surface U.S. scientists discover the first gene known to inhibit growth (in this case it inhibits the cancer retinoblastoma) A Dominican miner finds a 35-million-year-old frog encased in amber Dick Rutan and Jeanna Yeager in *(contd)*	Chicago Bears beat New England Patriots, 46–10, to win football's Super Bowl John Demjanjuk (U.S.) is extradited to Israel to stand trial for war crimes Brazil combats inflation by creating a new currency in which one cruzado equals 1,000 old cruzeiros An oil surplus forces its price below $10 a barrel (which equals 32 gallons) A bomb in a West Berlin discotheque kills 2 and injures 200; the target was U.S. military personnel Jennifer Guinness is kidnapped from her Dublin home by a gang demanding $3 million ransom, but is rescued by Irish police eight days later and three men are arrested Guinness takes over the Distiller's Company for $4 billion, but there are later prosecutions for illegal share dealing A Bangladeshi riverboat capsizes in the River Dhaleshwar, causing 600 deaths The world's worst nuclear accident takes place when a reactor blows up at Chernobyl Power Station, Kiev, U.S.S.R.; 133,000 are evacuated and clouds of fallout affect all Europe General Motors overtakes Exxon as the biggest company in the U.S. Sherpa Tenzing Norgay, Nepalese mountaineer and one of the first two to climb Everest, d. (b. 1914) Sudanese athlete Omar Khalifa brings a torch from Khartoum to New York to inaugurate the "Race Against Time" (fund-raising series of events for African famine relief; approximately $150 million is raised Live television coverage of U.S. Senate debates begins Bob Geldof is awarded an honorary Brit. knighthood for services for world famine relief Argentina defeats W. Germany, 2–1, to regain soccer's World Cup President Reagan celebrates Independence Day by unveiling a renovated Statue of Liberty A Los Angeles court sentences ex-F.B.I. agent Richard Miller to life imprisonment for *(contd)*	**1986**

A. HISTORY, POLITICS

1986 contd

tion centers; the European Community adopts sanctions against South Africa
Averell Harriman, Amer. statesman, d. (b. 1891)
The U.S. Senate approves a treaty allowing I.R.A. terrorists to be extradited to the U.K.
New Zealand refuses to admit nuclear warships into port and the U.S. and Australia then suspend their security alliance with New Zealand (ANZUS)
South Africa lists 8,501 people detained under the state of emergency
Mikhail Gorbachev announces the extension of the Soviet moratorium on nuclear tests until 1987
Urho Kekkonen, Finnish President (1956–1981), d. (b. 1900)
Israeli Prime Minister Peres visits Egypt for talks with President Mubarak
Panayiotis Kanellopulos, Greek politician, d. (b. 1902)
The Reagan-Gorbachev summit in Reykjavik, Iceland, ends without agreement
Samora Machel, first President of Mozambique (1975–1986), dies in an air crash; Joaquim Chissano succeeds him
Yitzhak Shamir becomes Israeli Prime Minister
Vyacheslav Molotov, Soviet politician, d. (b. 1890)
General Ershad ends five years martial law in Bangladesh
President Reagan admits secret arms deals with Iran in breach of the U.S. arms embargo (the "Irangate" scandal); Nataional Security Adviser John Poindexter and Lt. Col. Oliver North later plead the Fifth Amendment at congressional hearings about Irangate
Jean-Bedel Bokassa, former Emperor of the Central African Empire (now Republic), is put on trial for crimes including mass murder, cannibalism, and theft
President Reagan appoints Frank Carlucci as National Security Adviser
Harold Macmillan, Eng. Prime Minister (1957–1963), d. (b. 1894)
James Wright succeeds Tip O'Neill as Speaker of the House of Representatives
Andrei Sakharov and Yelena Bonner return to Moscow after several years internal exile in Gorky
Nobel Peace Prize: Elie Wiesel (U.S.), author and human rights campaigner

B. LITERATURE, THEATER

Dove," Pulitzer Prize fiction
Henry Taylor: "The Flying Change," Pulitzer Prize poetry
No Pulitzer Prize for drama awarded
Michael Host: "Valet de Nuit," Prix Goncourt
Joseph Lelyveld: "Move Your Shadow: South Africa Black and White" and J. Anthony Lewis: "Common Ground," Pulitzer Prize nonfiction
Kazuo Ishiguro: "An Artist of the Floating World," Whitbread Prize
Margaret Atwood: "The Handmaid's Tale," novel
Julian Barnes: "Staring at the Sun," novel
Truman Capote: "Answered Prayers," novel
John le Carré "The Perfect Spy," novel
Robertson Davies: "What's Bred in the Bone," novel
Carlos Fuentes: "The Old Gringo," novel
Bob Geldof: "Is That It?" autobiography
Ted Hughes: "Flowers and Insects," poetry
Primo Levi: "If Not Now, When?" short stories
Dame Alicia Markova: "Markova Remembers," autobiography
Timothy Mo: "An Insular Possession," novel
Anthony Powell: "The Fisher King," novel
Irina Ratushinskaya: "No, I'm Not Afraid," poetry
Vikran Seth: "The Golden Gate," verse novel
Patrick Sussking: "Perfume," novel
William Luce: "Lillian," play
Richard Nelson: "Principia Scriptoriae," play
Hugh Whitmore: "Breaking the Code," play

C. RELIGION, PHILOSOPHY, LEARNING

d. (b. 1908)
Mircea Eliade: "Encyclopedia of Religion" (16 vols.)
Martin Gilbert: "The Holocaust: The Jewish Tragedy"
Ioan Lewis: "Religion in Context Cults and Charisma"

1986 contd

D. VISUAL ARTS

Ronald and Nancy Reagan make a prime-time anti-drug television special
Joseph Beuys, W. Ger. sculptor, d. (b. 1921)
James Cagney, Amer. actor, d. (b. 1899)
Broderick Crawford, Amer. actor, d. (b. 1911)
Cary Grant, Amer. actor, d. (b. 1904)
Corita Kent, Amer. artist, d. (b. 1918)
Elsa Lanchester, Amer. actress, d. (b. 1902)
Ray Milland, Amer. actor, d. (b. 1905)
Henry Moore, Eng. sculptor, d. (b. 1898)
Anna Neagle, Eng. actress, d. (b. 1904)
Georgia O'Keefe, Amer. painter, d. (b. 1887)
Pat Phoenix, Eng. television actress, d. (b. 1923)
Otto Preminger, Amer. filmmaker, d. (b. 1906)
Donna Reed, Amer. actress, d. (b. 1921)
Rudy Vallee, Amer. singer-actor, d. (b. 1901)
Keenan Wynn, Amer. actor, d. (b. 1916)
Academy Awards (for 1985)—best picture: "Out of Africa"; best actor: William Hurt ("Kiss of the Spider Woman"); best actress: Geraldine Page ("The Trip to Bountiful")
Films: "Blue Velvet" (David Lynch); "Crocodile Dundee" (Peter

(contd)

E. MUSIC

The American Ballet Theater stages two new productions by Kenneth MacMillan ("Requiem" and "Sleeping Beauty")
Alun Hoddinot writes "The Silver Hound," a song-cycle for tenor and piano
Operas: "The Mask of Orpheus," Harrison Birtwhistle; "Hells Angels," Nigel Osbourne; "Goya," G. C. Menotti; "Voss," Richard Meale; "Troades," A. Reimann
"The Phantom of the Opera" musical makes its world premiere in London with Michael Crawford in the lead
"Les Miserables" musical wins eight Tony awards on Broadway
Rock star Ozzy Osbourne is unsuccessfully sued by Californian parents of a man who shot himself after listening to Osbourne's "Suicide Solution"
Harold Arlen, Amer. popular composer, d. (b. 1905)
Erik Bruhn, Dan. ballet dancer, d. (b. 1928)
Lucia Chase, Amer. ballet dancer, d. (b. 1907)
Pierre Fournier, Fr. cellist, d. (b. 1906)
Benny Goodman, Amer. clarinetist and bandleader, d. (b. 1909)
Arthur Grumiaux, Belg. violinist, d. (b. 1921)
Sir Robert

(contd)

F. SCIENCE, TECHNOLOGY, GROWTH

the aircraft "Voyager" make the first nonstop flight around the world without refueling and take nine days
25,000 AIDS cases are diagnosed in the U.S.
Brit. surgeons perform the world's first triple transplant (heart, lung, liver)
Glyn Daniel, Eng. archeologist, d. (b. 1914)
Deng Jiaxian, Chinese pioneer nuclear physicist, d. (b. 1924)
Edward Doisey, Amer. Nobel biochemist, d. (b. 1893)
Georges Dumézil, Fr. archeologist, d. (b. 1898)
Robert S. Mulliken, Amer. Nobel chemist, d. (b. 1896)
Marlin Perkins, Amer. zoologist and television host, d. (b. 1905)
Nikolai Semyonov, Soviet Nobel chemist, d. (b. 1896)

G. DAILY LIFE

espionage
Prince Andrew and Sarah Ferguson are married in Westminister Abbey and become the Duke and Duchess of York
Greg Lemond becomes the first American to win the Tour de France cycle race
Toxic gas from the volcanic Lake Nyos, Cameroon, kills almost 20,000 people
A government report reveals that a hydrogen bomb was accidentally dropped near Albuquerque, New Mexico, in 1957; luckily it did not explode
53 die in a mid-air collision in California
The Soviet cruise liner "Admiral Nakhimov" sinks in the Black Sea after colliding with a freighter and over 400 are killed
A Soviet nuclear submarine sinks in the Atlantic near Bermuda
Candido Jacuzzi, Ital. inventor of the whirlpool bath, d. (b. 1903)
Customs officials in Mombasa, Kenya, seize 1,100 elephants' tusks which were being smuggled to Dubai; their black market value is approximately $500,000
The London Stock Market is deregulated (the "Big Bang"), allowing computerized share dealing and the abolition of many trading restrictions
Ivan Boesky (U.S. financier) pleads guilty to insider share dealing
Mike Tyson, aged 20, knocks out Trevor Berbick to become W.B.C. world heavyweight boxing champion
Israeli engineer Mordechai Vanunu, who revealed details of Israeli's nuclear weapons development, is abducted from Rome and charged with treason and espionage
Parisian students riot for three days over proposed university reforms, which are later canceled
Philips auctioneers sell a $75 million oil rig for only $23 million as North Sea oil profits decline
New York Mets defeat Boston Red Sox, 4 games to 3, to win World Series
Boston Celtics win the National Basketball Association championship
Montreal Canadiens win hockey's Stanley Cup

1986 contd

1987

A. HISTORY, POLITICS

Gorbachev campaigns for "glasnost" (openness) and "perestroika" (reconstruction)
President Reagan announces the nation's first trillion-dollar budget
S. Africa bans all reports of A.N.C. activities
Terry Waite, the Archbishop of Canterbury's envoy, is kidnapped in Lebanon while seeking the release of Western hostages
The Soviet government releases 140 political prisoners
Syrian troops enter West Beirut to stop warfare between Shiite and Druze militia
Finns elect a coalition government of nonsocialists for the first time since World War II
Michael Dukakis (Massachusetts Dem. Governor) enters the Presidential race
The U.S. Senate approves $40 million in aid to Nicaraguan Contra rebels
French-supported Chad troops regain northern Chad from Libyan control
Three U.S. Marine guards at the U.S. Embassy, Moscow, are accused of espionage for the K.G.B.
Portugal and China agree on the return to China in 1999 of Macao, a Portuguese colony since the 16th century
In Sri Lanka, Tamil guerrillas engage in large-scale clashes with government forces throughout the year; an Indian peacekeeping force attempts to establish a cease-fire
Sen. Gary Hart (Dem.) temporarily withdraws from the Presidential race after reports of a liaison with model Donna Rice
E. F. Adams (Nationalist) is elected Malta's Prime Minister
The Indian government imposes direct rule on the Punjab in an attempt to defeat Sikh terrorists
In Fiji, Lt. Col. Sitiveni Rabuka takes power in a coup against the Indian-led coalition government
Two Iraqi Exocet missiles hit the USS "Stark" and kill 37 crew members
A W. Ger. teenager, Mathias Rust, lands his Cessna aircraft in Red Square, Moscow, after flying undetected from Finland; Rust is jailed for four years but freed in 1988 and the Soviet Defense Minister is dismissed
Rashid Abdul Hamid Karami, Lebanese Prime Minister, is killed by a bomb (b. 1921)
Margaret Thatcher becomes the first U.K. Prime Minister in this century to be elected three times after the Conservatives' overwhelming victory in the U.K. general election
President Reagan visits Berlin to mark the 750th anniversary of its foundation and calls on Gorbachev to tear down

(contd)

B. LITERATURE, THEATER

Jean Anouilh, Fr. dramatist, d. (b. 1910)
James Baldwin, Amer. novelist, d. (b. 1924)
Erskine Caldwell, Amer. novelist, d. (b. 1903)
Carlos Drummond de Andrade, Braz. poet, d. (b. 1902)
Hermione Gingold, Eng. actress, d. (b. 1897)
Joan Greenwood, Eng. actress, d. (b. 1921)
Irene Handl, Eng. actress, d. (b. 1901)
Primo Levi, Ital. author, d. (b. 1919)
Alistair MacLean, Eng. novelist, d. (b. 1922)
George Mikes, Eng. humorist, d. (b. 1912)
Emlyn Williams, Brit. playwright, d. (b. 1905)
Marguerite Yourcenar, Fr. novelist, d. (b. 1903)
The reputation of Boris Pasternak, author of "Dr. Zhivago," is posthumously rehabilitated by the Soviet Writers' Union
Richard Wilbur becomes the second U.S. Poet Laureate
The U.K. government fails to get an Austral. court injunction against the publication there of retired M.I.5 officer Peter Wright's memoirs ("Spycatcher")
Nobel Prize for Literature: Joseph Brodsky (U.S.)
Penelope Lively: "Moon Tiger," Booker Prize
Peter Taylor: "A Summons to Memphis," Pulitzer Prize fiction
David K. Shipler: "Arab and Jew," Pulitzer Prize nonfiction

(contd)

C. RELIGION, PHILOSOPHY, LEARNING

The centenary World Esperanto Congress in Warsaw, Poland, is attended by more than 6,000 delegates from 70 nations
Osel Hita (Sp.), aged two, is enthroned as the reincarnation of a Tibetan lama
The Church of England ordains the first female Anglican deacons
The Pope visits the U.S. and Canada
Amer. evangelist preacher Oral Roberts successfully raises $4.5 million after declaring that God would "call him home" if he failed to do so
Jim Bakker, head of the "Praise the Lord" television network, resigns after accusations of adultery
The Rev. Pat Robertson announces his Republican candidacy for the Presidency
Sikh high priests excommunicate the Punjab's Chief Minister for defying their call to resign
Bernardus Alfrink, Dutch Roman Catholic Archbishop, d. (b. 1900)
Kevin McNamara, Roman Catholic Primate of All Ireland, d. (b. 1926)
Valerian Trifa, Romanian Orthodox Archbishop, d. (b. 1914)
Leonardo Boff: "The Maternal Face of God"
Hans Küng: "Christianity and World Religions"
Russell Miller: "Bare-Faced Messiah: L. Ron Hubbard"

D. VISUAL ARTS	E. MUSIC	F. SCIENCE, TECHNOLOGY, GROWTH	G. DAILY LIFE	
Faiman) "Ginger and Fred" (Federico Fellini); "The Fly" (David Cronenberg); "Howard the Duck" (Willard Huyck); "The Mission" (Roland Joffe); "Mona Lisa" (Neil Jordan); "The Name of the Rose" (Jean-Jacques Annaud); "Out of Africa" (Sidney Pollack); "Ruthless People" (Jim Abrahams)	Helpmann, Austral. ballet dancer and choreographer, d. (b. 1909) Alan Jay Lerner, Amer. popular lyrcist, d. (b. 1918) Gordon MacRae, Amer. singer-actor, d. (b. 1921) Peter Pears, Eng. tenor, d. (b. 1910) Whitney Houston and Madonna reign as divas of popular music			**1986 contd**
The world's three most expensive paintings are auctioned this year and all are van Goghs: "Irises" is sold in New York for $49 million, "Sunflowers" is sold in London for $37 million, "The Bridge of Trinquetaille" is sold in London for $19 million Police raid art galleries in 12 U.S. states and uncover a $600 million fraud in fake Dali paintings The Tate Gallery, London, buys Picasso's "Weeping Woman" for $5 million Fred Astaire, Amer. film actor and dancer, d. (b. 1899) Mary Astor, Amer. film actress, d. (b. 1906) Jackie Gleason, Amer. comedian, d. (b. 1916) Rita Hayworth, Amer. film actress, d. (b. 1918) John Huston, Amer. film director, *(contd)*	The Amadeus String Quartet breaks up after the death of viola player Peter Schidlof A Mozart notebook containing symphonies 22–30 is auctioned for $4 million Stephen Sondheim's new musical "Into the Woods" is premiered on Broadway Grawemeyer Award: "The Mask of Orpheus," Harrison Birtwhistle Operas: John Adams, "Nixon in China" (Houston); Pompeyo Camps, "La Hacienda" (Buenos Aires); Flavio Testi, "Ricardo III" (La Scala, Milan) Michael Bennett, Amer. choreographer, d. (b. 1943) Morton Feldman, Amer. avant-garde composer, d. (b. 1926) Bob Fosse, Amer. choreographer, d. (b. 1927) Jascha Heifetz, Amer. violinist, *(contd)*	Nobel Prize for Economics: Robert Solow (U.S.) for work on the substitutability of labor and capital Nobel Prize for Physiology and Medicine: Susumu Tonegawa (Japan) for work on antibodies Nobel Prize for Physics: Karl Alex Müller (Swiss) and Georg Bednorz (W. Ger.) for the discovery of high temperature superconductivity Nobel Prize for Chemistry: Charles J. Pedersen and Donald J. Cram (both U.S.) with Jean-Marie Lehn (Fr.) for work on molecular chemistry 1987 is shortened by one second to adjust it to the Gregorian calendar The 25th anniversary of the launch of the Telstar communications satellite; 3.6 billion telephone calls have been relayed by communications satellites since then Paul Chu (U.S.) creates a superconducting ceramic at much higher temperatures than previously possible The nearest supernova detected since 1604 is observed in the Large Magellanic galaxy A South African gives birth to her own grandchildren (triplets) after her daughter's fertilized ova had been implanted in her uterus Sir Clive Sinclair launches the Z88 portable computer weighing under 2 pounds Spearpoints made by the first Americans (the Clovis) are found, dating from 11,500 years ago The last wild Californian Condor is trapped and sent for breed- *(contd)*	New York Giants beat the Denver Broncos, 39–20, to win football's Super Bowl Excavations begin on the Anglo-French Channel tunnel "Stars and Stripes" (U.S.) defeats "Kookaburra III," 4 races to 0 to regain yachting's "America's Cup" John Demjanjuk (U.S.) is convicted in Jerusalem of alleged mass murders as a guard in Treblinka concentration camp The "Herald of Free Enterprise" ferry sinks off Zeebrugge, Belgium, resulting in 187 deaths Woody Hayes, Amer. football coach, d. (b. 1913) Baroness Maria von Trapp, Aust. singer and author of "The Sound of Music," d. (b. 1905) The "Baby M" surrogate motherhood trial ends with the surrogate mother losing the case A Spanish court tries 38 people for preparing and selling contaminated cooking oil, which killed 9,584 people and injured 24,992 The late Duchess of Windsor's jewelry is auctioned for $45 million in aid of cancer research The new U.S. Embassy, Moscow, is found to be heavily bugged The World Health Organization reports 8% of all pregnant Zairean women and 17% of blood donors are AIDS-infected David Gates (U.S.), 32-year-old founder of Microsoft, becomes microcomputing's first billionaire A court clears subway vigilante Bernhard Goetz of attempted murder and convicts him of illegally owning a gun Dick Howser, U.S. baseball manager, d. (b. 1937) Cleveland Health Authority, U.K., takes more than 200 children into care because of alleged sexual abuse Klaus Barbie, the "Butcher of Lyons," is jailed for life for wartime crimes against humanity *(contd)*	**1987**

	A. HISTORY, POLITICS	B. LITERATURE, THEATER	C. RELIGION, PHILOSOPHY, LEARNING
1987 contd	the Berlin Wall Errol Barrow, Prime Minister of Barbados (1961–1976, 1986–1987), d. (b. 1920); Erskine Sandiford succeeds him The U.S.S.R. introduces limited choices between candidates in local government elections The Social Democrats become the first party to gain an overall majority in a Portuguese general election Giovanni Goria forms Italy's 47th postwar government 402 pilgrims, including 275 Iranians, die in riots in Mecca David Owen resigns as leader of U.K. Social Democratic Party after it votes to merge with the Liberal Party Rudolf Hess, Ger. Deputy Führer (1933–1941), commits suicide in Spandau Prison, Berlin (b. 1894) Three Iranian mine-laying speedboats are sunk in the Persian Gulf by U.S. helicopters Vice President George Bush announces his candidacy for the Presidency Thomas Sankara, Burkino Faso's President since 1983, is assassinated in a military coup (b. 1950) Alfred Landon, Rep. Presidential candidate in 1936, d. (b. 1887) Fr. police board the SS "Esklund" and discover 150 tons of arms destined for the I.R.A. Deng Xiaoping retires from the Chinese Politburo Caspar Weinberger resigns as Defense Secretary (1980–1987) and is succeeded by Frank Carlucci An I.R.A. bomb explodes at a Remembrance (Veterans) Day religious service in Eniskillin, Northern Ireland, killing 11 and injuring 63 Boris Yeltsin is dismissed as Moscow's Communist Party head after publicly criticizing Mikhail Gorbachev South Africa announces the withdrawal of its troops from Angola, where they were aiding Unita rebels Reagan and Gorbachev meet for three days in Washington and sign a treaty to ban all short- and medium-range nuclear weapons in Europe Nobel Peace Prize: President Oscar Arias (Costa Rica)	Rita Dove: "Thomas and Beulah," Pulitzer Prize poetry August Wilson: "Fences," Pulitzer Prize drama Tahar ben Jelloun: "La Nuit Sacré," Prix Goncourt Ian McEwan: "The Child in Time," Whitbread Prize Brian Moore: "The Colour of Blood," novel Chinua Achebe: "The Anthills of the Savannah," novel Bruce Chatwin: "The Songlines," novel Margaret Drabble: "The Radiant Way," novel Günther Grass: "The Rat," novel Thomas Keneally: "The Playmaker," novel Arthur Miller: "Timebends," autobiography Tom Wolfe: "The Bonfire of the Vanities," novel Caryl Churchill: "Serious Money," play Robert Harling: "Steel Magnolias," play Arthur Miller: "Danger, Memory!" play Alfred Uhry: "Driving Miss Daisy," play	

D. VISUAL ARTS

d. (b. 1906)
Danny Kaye, Amer. film actor, d. (b. 1913)
Rouben Mamoulian, Amer. director, d. (b. 1897)
Lee Marvin, Amer. film actor, d. (b. 1924)
André Masson, Fr. painter, d. (b. 1896)
Robert Preston, Amer. film actor, d. (b. 1918)
Randolph Scott, Amer. film actor, d. (b. 1903)
Douglas Sirk, Amer. director, d. (b. 1900)
Andy Warhol, Amer. painter and filmmaker, d. (b. 1928)
Academy Awards (for 1986)—best picture: "Platoon"; best actor: Paul Newman ("The Color of Money"); best actress: Marlee Matlin ("Children of a Lesser God")
Films: "Cry Freedom" (Richard Attenborough); "Dirty Dancing" (Emile Ardolino); "Empire of the Sun" (Steven Spielberg); "Fatal Attraction" (Adrian Lyne), "Full Metal Jacket" (Stanley Kubrick); "The Last Emperor" (Bernardo Bertolucci); "Lethal Weapon" (Richard Donner); "Little Dorritt" (Christine Edzard); "Tin Men" (Barry Levinson); "Wall Street" (Oliver Stone); "The Witches of Eastwick" (George Miller)

E. MUSIC

d. (b. 1901)
Nora Kaye, Amer. ballerina, d. (b. 1920)
Liberace, Amer. pianist, d. (b. 1919)
Vincent Persichetti, Amer. classical composer, d. (b. 1915)
Jacqueline du Pré, Eng. cellist, d. (b. 1945)
Buddy Rich, Amer. jazz drummer, d. (b. 1917)
Andrés Segovia, Span. classical guitarist, d. (b. 1893)
Popular Songs: "Graceland," "Bad," and "Higher Love"

F. SCIENCE, TECHNOLOGY, GROWTH

ing in a local zoo
The second nest of fossilized dinosaur eggs to be found is identified in Alberta, Canada
Alexander Arkhipov of Moscow's Radio Astronomy Institute identifies 9 out of 4,500 "sunlike" stars that may be the focus of intelligent life
The U.S.S.R. launches the new heavy-lift rocket "Energiya"
An airport opens in London's Dockland for short flights to W. Europe
The 2,000th satellite to be launched is the Soviet "Cosmos"
The world's most powerful wind-powered electricity generator comes into operation in the Orkney Islands; it produces 3 megawatts
Soviet cosmonaut Yuri Romanenko returns to Earth from the Mir space station after a record 326 days in space
Louis, Duc de Broglie, Fr. Nobel physicist, d. (b. 1892)
Albert Crary, Amer. geophysicist, d. (b. 1911)
Gilberto Freyre, Braz. anthropologist, d. (b. 1900)
Andrei Kolmogorov, Soviet mathematician, d. (b. 1903)
Sir Peter Medawar, Eng. Nobel biologist, d. (b. 1915)
Karl Gunnar Myrdal, Swed. Nobel economist, d. (b. 1898)
John H. Northrop, Amer. Nobel chemist, d. (b. 1891)
Georg Wittig, W. Ger. Nobel chemist, d. (b. 1897)

G. DAILY LIFE

A Yugoslavian baby boy is declared the world's five billionth inhabitant by the U.N. Secretary General
174 Asian illegal immigrants land on Canada's East Coast
A jet crashes on a highway near Detroit, resulting in 161 fatalities
Didier Pironi, Fr. Grand Prix racing driver, d. (b. 1952)
A gunman in Hungerford, U.K., shoots 16 people dead before killing himself
Bangladesh's worst floods for decades kill almost 700 people and make millions homeless
Californian forest fires make thousands homeless
A hurricane-force storm in the southern U.K. destroys 15 million trees and causes immense damage, but only 18 people die
"Black Monday": world stockmarket share prices crash; Wall Street's Dow Jones Index falls by 508 points (– 23%)
U.K.'s former champion jockey Lester Piggott is jailed for three years for a $4 1/2 million tax fraud
A N. Korean bomb kills 115 people on board a S. Korean airliner
A fire at King's Cross underground rail station, London, kills 30 passengers
The worst peacetime maritime disaster of this century occurs in the Philippines, where 2,000 die when a ferry sinks
Minnesota Twins defeat St. Louis Cardinals, 4 games to 3, to win World Series
Los Angeles Lakers win the National Basketball Association championship
Edmonton Oilers win hockey's Stanley Cup

	A. HISTORY, POLITICS	B. LITERATURE, THEATER	C. RELIGION, PHILOSOPHY, LEARNING
1988	Canada and the U.S. sign a comprehensive free-trade agreement Chiang Ching-Kuo, Tawiwan's President (1978–1987), d. (b. 1910) Sean MacBride, Irish politician and Nobel Peace Prizewinner, d. (b. 1904) A border dispute between Laos and Thailand results in several weeks' fighting before a cease-fire is agreed upon Palestinians in the Occupied Territories begin prolonged active resistance ("Intifada") to Israeli rule A U.S. court indicts Gen. Manuel Noriega, Panama's leader, on drug smuggling charges A historical commission clears President Kurt Waldheim (Aust.) of war crimes The U.K. government makes permanent the Prevention of Terrorism Act introduced as a temporary measure in 1974 U.N. executive Lt. Col. William Higgins (U.S.) is kidnapped in Lebanon by Islamic terrorists Soviet nationalist demonstrations take place in the Baltic states and the Caucasus; many deaths occur in fights between Azerbaijans and Armenians before the army enforces curfews The U.K. Liberal and Social Democratic parties merge to be known as the Social and Liberal Democrats A U.K. S.A.S. unit shoots dead three suspected I.R.A. bombers in Gibraltar; a Protestant gunman later kills 3 and wounds 50 at their funeral; two soldiers are later killed during a funeral of one of these victims President Ceauşescu (Rom.) announces plans to demolish many villages and forcibly resettle the population in new towns The Nicaraguan government and Contra rebels agree on a 60-day cease-fire Ethiopia and Somalia sign a peace treaty after 11 years of border disputes Governor Evan Mecham of Arizona is removed from office following his conviction for various misdemeanors P.L.O. military leader Abu Jihad is assassinated by Israeli secret agents New Caledonian separatists kill three Fr. policemen and take many hostages; Fr. peacekeeping forces later capture them; a referendum supports the Fr. government's administration Widespread strikes by Solidarity supporters take place in Poland; the Pol. government holds direct talks with Lech Walesa for the first time since 1981 France unilaterally repatriates Fr. agent Dominique Prieur, jailed for participating in the "Rainbow Warrior" sinking, despite forceful new Zealand protests H.A.R."Kim" Philby, Soviet spy, d. (b. 1912) Soviet troops begin to retreat from Afghanistan after nine-year occupation, but the Afghan communist government survives János Kádár, Hungary's leader since 1956, is replaced by Károly Grósz Vietnam begins to pull its troops out of Kampuchea Reagan and Gorbachev hold a three-day summit in Moscow and finalize the I.N.F. treaty Soviet dissident Andrei Sakharov gives a news conference at the Foreign Ministry attacking the Soviet abuse of human rights; he later visits the U.S. A million S. African black workers hold a three-day strike against new labor laws The USS "Vincennes" mistakenly shoots down an Iranian airliner over the Persian Gulf, resulting in 290 fatalities Iran and Iraq accept a U.N. peace plan and begin direct peace talks The Democrats choose Michael Dukakis and Lloyd Bentsen as their presidential candidates; the Republicans choose Vice President George Bush and Dan Quayle *(contd)*	John Ball, Amer. crime writer, d. (b. 1911) Raymond Carver, Amer. short story writer, d. (b. 1938) René Char, Fr. poet, d. (b. 1907) Andrew Cruickshank, Brit. actor, d. (b. 1907) Yuli Daniel, Soviet dissident author and poet, d. (b. 1925) Robert Duncan, Amer. poet, d. (b. 1919) Hamish Hamilton, Brit. publisher, d. (b. 1907) Robert Heinlein, Amer. science-fiction writer, d. (b. 1907) Geoffrey Household, Eng. novelist, d. (b. 1900) Louis L'Amour, Amer. westerns author, d. (b. 1908) Marghanita Laski, Eng. novelist, d. (b. 1915) Alan Paton, S. African novelist, d. (b. 1903) Clifford D. Simak, Amer. science-fiction author, d. (b. 1904) Howard Nemerov is appointed the third official Poet Laureate of the U.S. A script of the only play written by George Orwell is auctioned for $8,000 Sir John Gielgud acts on stage for the first time in ten years when he stars in "The Best of Friends" in London Peter Brook's nine-hour Hindu religious epic, "The Mahabharata," with an international cast, is staged in Glasgow The National Theatre celebrates its 25th anniversary Nobel Prize for Literature: Naguib Mahfouz (Egypt)—the first time that an African writer has won the award Peter Carey: "Oscar and Lucinda," Booker Prize Toni Morrison: "Beloved," Pulitzer Prize fiction Richard Rhodes: 'The Making of the Atomic Bomb," Pulitzer Prize nonfiction William Meredith: "Partial Accounts," Pulitzer Prize poetry Alfred Uhry: "Driving Miss Daisy," Pulitzer Prize drama Erik Orsenna: "L'Exposition Coloniale," Prix Goncourt Paul Sayer: "The Comforts of Madness," Whitbread Prize Isabell Allende: "Eva Luna," novel Ethan Canin: "Emperor of the Air," short stories Raymond Carver: "Elephant and Other Stories," short stories Penelope Fitzgerald: "The Beginning of Spring," novel *(contd)*	Salman Rushdie's latest novel, "The Satanic Verses," is attacked by Muslims for sacrilege and blasphemy The film "The Last Temptation of Christ," directed by Martin Scorsese, is condemned by many Christian religious leaders as blasphemous Eugene Antonio Marino becomes the U.S.'s first black Roman Catholic Archbishop (of Atlanta) A service is held at St. Paul's Cathedral, London, to celebrate the 250th anniversary of the conversion of John Wesley World religious leaders attend celebrations in Moscow to mark 1,000 years of Christianity in Russia The Pope excommunicates for the sin of schism the Fr. dissident archbishop Marcel Lefèbvre The Roman Catholic Cathedral in Vilnius, Lithuania, is reopened after 38 years' closure The decimal Lambeth Conference is attended by 524 Anglican bishops from throughout the world Rev. Barbara Harris is elected the first female Anglican Bishop (of Massachusetts) The N. Korean government allows a Roman Catholic mass to be celebrated in Pyongyang by two S. Korean priests Lord Mackay, the U.K.'s Lord Chancellor (head of the legal profession), is suspended as an Elder of the Scottish Presbyterian Church for attending Roman Catholic requiem masses for two dead colleagues Peter Hurkos, Dutch-Amer. clairvoyant, d. (b. 1911) Sylvester Mooney, Eng. monk and Abbot of Douai (1929–1969), d. (b. 1886) Michael Ramsay, Archbishop of Canterbury (1961–1974), d. (b. 1904) Paul Ramsey, Amer. Protestant theologian, d. (b. 1913) Alphaeus Zulu, S. African Bishop of Zululand (1966–1975), d. (b. 1905) Richard Gombrich: "Theravada Buddhism" John Rohmer: "Testament" Stewart Sutherland: "The World's Religions"

1988

D. VISUAL ARTS

Picasso's "Acrobat and Young Harlequin" is auctioned in London for $38 million
Jasper Johns's "False Start" is auctioned for $17.05 million, a record for a living artist's work
Andy Warhol's art collection is sold for more than $25 million
Hereford Cathedral decides to sell its "Mappa Mundi" medieval map of the world, but widespread protests negate the decision
Queen Elizabeth II opens the new "Houses of Parliament of the Commonwealth" in Canberra, Australia
The Australian television series "Neighbours" begins on B.B.C. television and is a phenomenal success; its stars include Kylie Minogue and Jason Donovan
Hollywood film writers strike for 22 weeks
Charles Addams, Amer. cartoonist and creator of "The Addams Family," d. (b. 1912)
Pietro Annigoni, Ital. portrait painter, d. (b. 1910)
Hal Ashby, Amer. director, d. (b. 1930)
Sir Frederick Ashton, Eng. ballet choreography, d. (b. 1904)
John Carradine, Amer. film actor, d. (b. 1906)
Divine (Harris Glen Milstead)
(contd)

E. MUSIC

Beethoven's unfinished Tenth Symphony is premiered by the Royal Philharmonic Society of London, which had originally commissioned it
Boston hosts an important festival of Soviet music
"The Fall of the House of Usher," an opera by Philip Glass, is premiered in Louisville, Kentucky; other operatic premieres include Brian Howard's "Whit Sunday" (Sydney); Karl-Heinz Stockhausen's "Montag aus Licht" (La Scala, Milan); and Peter Maxwell-Davies's "Resurrection" (Darmstadt)
Jean-Michel Jarre (Fr.) holds a concert in London's Docklands accompanied by fireworks and lasers
Andrew Lloyd Webber's "Phantom of the Opera" opens on Broadway
Chet Baker, Amer. jazz trumpeter, d. (b. 1929)
Annelies Burmeister, E. Ger. mezzo-soprano, d. (b. 1929)
Antal Dorati, Amer. conductor, d. (b. 1906)
Leon Goossens, Eng. oboeist, d. (b. 1897)
Lily Laskine, Fr. harpist, d. (b. 1893)
Frederick Loewe, Amer. popular composer,
(contd)

F. SCIENCE, TECHNOLOGY, GROWTH

Nobel Prize for Economics: Maurice Allais (Fr.) for analysis of market behavior
Nobel Prize for Physiology and Medicine: Gertrude B. Elion, George H. Hitchings (both U.S.), and Sir James Black (U.K.) for investigations into drug treatment
Nobel Prize for Physics: Leon M. Lederman, Melvin Schwartz, and Jack Steinberger (all U.S.) for the discovery of the mu-neutrino
Nobel Prize for Chemistry; Johann Diesenhofer, Robert Huber, and Hartmut Michel (all W. Ger.) for discovering the structure of proteins involved in photosynthesis
Stephen Hawking: "A Brief History of Time"
The world population is growing by 220,000 a day, according to the U.N.
U.S. surgeons implant the world's first plutonium-powered pacemaker
Japan's Seikan Railroad Tunnel connecting Hokkaido and Honshu is opened; it is the world's largest tunnel under sea
A U.S. survey concludes that a daily aspirin halves the risk of a heart attack
Both Soviet "Phobos" space probes to Mars fail during their flight
Australia unveils the most powerful radio telescope in the southern hemisphere
The first transatlantic optical fiber telephone cable to enter service links France, the U.K., and the U.S.; it can process 40,000 simultaneous conversations (almost five times more than a conventional copper cable)
Turkey opens a second bridge over the Bosphorus, linking Asia to Europe
Israel launches its first satellite, named "Horizon"
The space shuttle "Discovery," the first U.S. manned space mission since the "Challenger" tragedy 20 months before, is successfully launched
Carbon dating establishes that the Turin Shroud dates from about 1330 A.D. and so is not the burial cloth of Christ
"Internet" computer virus designed by a U.S. student jams over 6,000 military computers across the U.S.
Eight major toiletry companies, including Beecham, Gillette, and Reckitt and Colman, decide to phase out ozone-
(contd)

G. DAILY LIFE

Washington Redskins beat Denver Broncos, 42–10, to win football's Super Bowl
Drug traffickers kidnap and kill Colombia's Attorney General; gang warfare between the Cali and Medellín cocaine traffickers leads to almost a hundred deaths
Television evangelist Jimmy Swaggart admits visiting a prostitute
Zola Budd (U.K.) is banned from the world cross-country championships in New Zealand because of her S. African links
Crack, a cocaine derivative, is increasingly found in U.S. cities
Henry Armstrong, Amer. champion boxer, d. (b. 1912)
Enzo Ferrari, Ital. carmaker, d. (b. 1898)
Prince Charles escapes death from an avalanche while skiing in Switzerland, but a companion is killed
English pound notes cease to be legal tender
The 50th anniversary of the cartoon character Superman
U.S. airlines ban smoking on all flights of less than two hours' duration
Kanellos Kanellopoulos (Gr.) pedals his muscle-powered aircraft 74 miles from Crete to Santorini in 3 hours 54 minutes
McDonald's opens 20 restaurants in Moscow
In the Ural Mountains, a leaking gas pipeline along the Trans-Siberian railway exploded, killing 500 and injuring 723 people on two passing trains
Mariya Kalinina is crowned the first Miss Moscow
A fire on the Piper Alpha North Sea oil rig kills 167
Fires burn 88,000 acres of Yellowstone National Park, Wyoming
A New Jersey jury orders a tobacco company to pay $400,000 to a man whose wife died of lung cancer as a result of cigarette smoking
70 people are killed when three Ital. jets collide at a W. Ger. air show
The "Race Against Time" charity event against children's diseases has 50 million participants worldwide
Hurricane Gilbert (the Western Hemisphere's strongest ever recorded) kills hundreds in the Caribbean and Mexico
The S. Korean Olympic Games are the first without a boycott since 1980; winter Olympic stars include figure-skater Katerina Witt (E. Ger.) and ski jumper Eddie "the Eagle" Edwards (U.K.); Ben Johnson (Can.) breaks the 100 meter world record but is disqualified for drug-taking; Kristin Otto (E. Ger.) wins six swimming golds; other star performers are weightlifter Naim Süleymanoglu (Tur.), swimmer Matt Biondi (U.S.), diver Greg Louganis (U.S.), and runner Florence Griffith Joyner ("Flo Jo") (U.S.)
An earthquake in Yunnan, China, kills more than 700
U.K. pubs are allowed to stay open all day after 70 years of restricted hours
A tidal wave kills 3,000 in Bangladesh
An earthquake in Armenia, U.S.S.R., kills 80,000 and makes 500,000 homeless
34 die in a train crash at Clapham, London
(contd)

	A. HISTORY, POLITICS	B. LITERATURE, THEATER	C. RELIGION, PHILOSOPHY, LEARNING
1988 contd	Gen. Ne Win resigns as ruler of Burma after 26 years in power; Gen. Maung Maung takes power in a military coup shortly thereafter The U.S.S.R. begins to destroy medium-range nuclear missiles in accordance with the I.N.F. Treaty Angola, S. Africa, and Cuba agree on a cease-fire in Angola General Mohammad Zia al-Haq, Pakistan's President since 1978, dies in explosion on board his aircraft; sabotage is suspected (b. 1924) Mieczyslaw Rakowski becomes Prime Minister of Poland and promises reconciliation with noncommunist groups; he removes restrictions on private enterprise and allows foreign ownership of companies Mikhail Gorbachev becomes President of the U.S.S.R. A major financial scandal in the Bank of Crete severely damages the Greek government George Bush (Rep.) defeats Michael Dukakis (Dem.) for the U.S. Presidency John Mitchell, U.S. Attorney General (1969–1970), d. (b. 1913) Ethnic Albanians demonstrate for freedom from Serb rule in Yugoslavia's Kosovo province The Irish court refuses to extradite Father Patrick Ryan on terrorist charges to the U.K., ruling that a fair trial had been prejudiced by adverse publicity The U.S. refuses an entry visa to Yasser Arafat to address the United Nations in New York; instead the U.N. holds a special session in Geneva Benazir Bhutto is elected the first female Prime Minister of Pakistan Gorbachev announces unilateral troop cuts of 500,000 (10% of Soviet military personnel) phased out over two years Edwina Currie, U.K. government minister, resigns over her comments about salmonella which cause a crisis in the U.K. egg industry Ranasinghe Premadasa is elected President of Sri Lanka Nobel Peace Prize: the United Nations Peacekeeping Forces	Paul Kennedy: "The Rise and Fall of the Great Powers," nonfiction Alison Lurie: "The Truth about Lorin Jones," novel Gabriel Garcia Marquez: "Love in the Time of Cholera," novel Irina Ratushinskaya: "Pencil Letters," poetry H. C. Robbins: "1791: Mozart's Last Year," biography Salman Rushdie: "The Satanic Verses," novel Lee Smith: "Fair and Tender Ladies," novel Anthony Thwaite: "Philip Larkin: Collected Poems," poetry Anne Tyler: "Breathing Lessons," novel Heathcote Williams: "Whale Notion," poetry David Hare: "The Secret Rapture," play David Henry Hwang: "M. Butterfly," musical David Mamet: "Speed-the-Plow," play Tom Stoppard: "Hapgood," play Timberlake Wertenbaker: "Our Country's Good," play Nicholas Wright: "Mrs. Klein," play	

D. VISUAL ARTS	E. MUSIC	F. SCIENCE, TECHNOLOGY, GROWTH	G. DAILY LIFE	
Amer. film drag artist-actor, d. (b. 1945) Jimmy Edwards, Eng. film comedian, d. (b. 1920) Gert Fröbe, W. Ger. film actor, d. (b. 1913) Charles Hawtrey, Eng. comedian in "Carry On" films, d. (b. 1914) S. W. Hayter, Eng. artist, d. (b. 1901) John Houseman, Amer. actor and filmmaker, d. (b. 1902) Trevor Howard, Eng. film actor, d. (b. 1916) Raj Kapoor, Indian film actor, d. (b. 1924) Louise Nevelson, Amer. sculptor, d. (b. 1900) Isami Noguchi, Amer. sculptor and garden designer, d. (b. 1904) Henryk Stazewski, Pol. abstract painter, d. (b. 1894) Kenneth Williams, Eng. comedian in "Carry On" films, d. (b. 1926) Academy Awards (for 1987)—best picture: "The Last Emperor" (also eight other Academy Awards); best actor: Michael Douglas ("Wall Street"); best actress; Cher ("Moonstruck") Films: "Beetle-juice" (Tim Burton); "Big" (Penny Marshall); "Die Hard" (John McTiernan); "A Fish Called Wanda" (Charles Crichton); "Good Morning, Vietnam" *(contd)*	d. (b. 1901) James McCracken, Amer. operatic tenor, d. (b. 1926) Ernst Meyer, E. Ger. composer, d. (b. 1905) Nico, W. Ger. rock singer, d. (b. 1944) Sy Oliver, Amer. jazz composer, d. (b. 1910) Roy Orbison, Amer. rock singer, d. (b. 1936) Irmgard Seefried, Aust. soprano, d. (b. 1919) Popular songs: "Don't Worry, Be Happy," "Faith," and "Fast Car"	hostile aerosols by late 1989 Pluto is confirmed to have an atmosphere A new mirror system is devised that concentrates sunlight to 60,000 times its normal intensity; this has applications in laser technology Surgeons perform the first U.K. brain cell transplants The U.S. B-2 "Stealth" bomber is unveiled Luis Alvarez, Amer. Nobel physicist, d. (b. 1911) Raymond Dart, Austral. anthropologist, d. (b. 1893) Richard Feynman, Amer. Nobel physicist, d. (b. 1918) David Michaelton, Can. biochemist, d. (b. 1920) Nikolas Tinbergen, Dutch ethologist, d. (b. 1907)	A bomb believed planted by Syrian-backed terrorists blows apart a Pan Am 747 flying over Lockerbie, Scotland, and 270 people are killed Yugoslavia's annual inflation rate exceeds 250% Steffi Graf (W. Ger.) becomes only the fifth tennis player to achieve the "Grand Slam" Los Angeles Dodgers defeat Oakland Athletics, 4 games to 1, to win World Series Los Angeles Lakers win the National Basketball Association championship Edmonton Oilers win hockey's Stanley Cup	**1988 contd**

	A. HISTORY, POLITICS	B. LITERATURE, THEATER	C. RELIGION, PHILOSOPHY, LEARNING
1988 contd			

1989

A. History, Politics

U.S. fighters shoot down two Libyan jets over the Gulf of Sidra
Hirohito, Emperor of Japan since 1926, d. (b. 1901); Crown Prince Akihito succeeds to the throne
Ante Markovic becomes Yugoslavian Prime Minister
Western embassies withdraw from Kabul, Afghanistan, but the Mujaheddin do not capture the city; the last Soviet troops leave Afghanistan
President P. W. Botha (S. Africa) resigns and is succeeded by F. W. de Klerk
Alfredo Stroessner, Paraguayan President since 1954, is replaced in a military coup by Gen. André Rodriguez
Michael Manley's People's National Party defeats the incumbent Labor Party in the Jamaican general election
Ayatollah Khomeini announces a "fatwa" (death sentence) on Salman Rushdie for "blasphemy" in "The Satanic Verses"; the U.K. government protests and Rushdie goes into hiding
Vaclav Havel, Czech dissident playwright, is jailed by the government in Feb.; massive peaceful opposition continues; President Husak resigns on Dec. 10 and a mainly non-Communist government takes power; Havel becomes President on Dec. 29
The Tigré People's Liberation Front defeats the Ethiopian Army to take control of much of northern Ethiopia
China imposes martial law in Lhasa, Tibet, after anti-Chinese protests
The U.S. Senate vetoes the candidacy of John Tower for Defense Secretary and later approves Richard Cheney
Soviet electors have a choice of candidates for the Congress of People's Deputies for the first time ever
S.W.A.P.O. guerrillas break the Namibian cease-fire and 160 are killed by S. African troops, but the cease-fire endures; democratic elections later put S.W.A.P.O. into power
Hundreds die in Lebanon in shelling between Christian and Islamic militias
Japan has three Prime Ministers in 1989; Noboru Takeshita resigns after admitting links with the recruit bribery scandal; Sosuko Uno's credibility is weakened by involvement with a geisha and he is replaced by Toshiki Kaifu
Thousands of prodemocracy students occupy Tiananmen Square, Peking; the occupation lasts seven weeks until the government imposes martial law and uses tanks to disperse the students; thousands are believed to have died
Gen. Noriega annuls the presidential elections, which the opposition leader has won; U.S. invades and installs new government; Noriega to be tried in U.S.
Solidarity gains an overwhelming victory in the Pol. parliamentary elections
Andrei Gromyko, Soviet Foreign Secretary (1975–1985), d. (b. 1909)
János Kádár, Hungary's leader (1957–1988), d. (b. 1912)
Lt. Col. Oliver North is found guilty of crimes in the Iran-
(contd)

B. Literature, Theater

Salman Rushdie and his publisher, Penguin, are criticized by Muslims for publication of "The Satanic Verses"
Archeologists uncover the Elizabethan Globe Theater in Southwark, London
Samuel Beckett, Irish Nobel playwright, d. (b. 1906)
Bruce Chatwin, Eng. novelist, d. (b. 1940)
Birago Diop, Senegalese poet and author, d. (b. 1906)
Nicholás Guillén, Cuban poet, d. (b. 1902)
Beatrice Lillie, Can. actress, d. (b. 1894)
Daphne du Maurier, Eng. novelist, d. (b. 1907)
Mary McCarthy, Amer. novelist, d. (b. 1912)
Laurence Olivier, Eng. actor, d. (b. 1907)
Anthony Quayle, Eng. actor, d. (b. 1913)
Georges Simenon, Fr. novelist, d. (b. 1903)
Irving Stone, Amer. novelist, d. (b. 1903)
Robert Penn Warren, Amer. poet, d. (b. 1905)
Tony Awards: Best Play: "The Heidi Chronicles," Wendy Wasserstein; Best Musical: "Jerome Robbins's Broadway"; Best Actor: Philip Bosco, "Lend Me a Tenor"; Best Actress: Pauline Collins, "Shirley Valentine"
Nobel Prize for Literature: Sp. writer Camilo José Cela
Kazuo Ishiguro: "The Remains of the Day," Booker Prize
Anne Tyler: "Breathing Lessons," Pulitzer Prize fiction
Neil Sheehan: "A Bright Shining Lie," Pulitzer Prize nonfiction
Richard Wilbur: "New and Collected Poems," Pulitzer Prize poetry
Wendy Wasserstein: "The Heidi Chronicles," Pulitzer Prize drama
Jean Vautrin: "Un Grand Pas
(contd)

C. Religion, Philosophy, Learning

The Polish Parliament grants the Roman Catholic Church legal stature and renews diplomatic relations with the Vatican
Amer. television evangelist Jim Bakker is convicted of a $3.7 million fraud and is jailed for 45 years
Mikhail Gorbachev becomes the first Soviet leader to meet a Pope
Rev. Jerry Falwell (U.S.) announces that Moral Majority Inc. will be dissolved and states that it has achieved its aim of reactivating the religious Right
Indian Hindu fundamentalists attempt to demolish an important Islamic mosque sited on the alleged birthplace of the Hindu god Rama; this becomes an important controversy in the Indian national elections
Nobel Peace Prize: the Dalai Lama
Sir A. J. Ayer, Eng. philosopher, d. (b. 1910)
Sheikh Hassan Khaled, Lebanese Sunni Grand Mufti, assassinated (b. 1923)
Sayyed Ruhollah Khomeini, Shiite Ayatollah and Iranian spiritual leader, d. (b. 1902)
The Panchen Lama, Tibetan Buddhist leader, d. (b. 1938)
Fredrik A. Schiotz, first President of Amer. Lutheran Church, d. (b. 1901)
Julian Baldrick: "Mystical Islam"
William Charlton: "Philosophy and Christian Belief"
Susanne Heine: "Women and Early Christianity"
John Sparkes: "The Philosophy of Buddhism"

D. VISUAL ARTS	E. MUSIC	F. SCIENCE, TECHNOLOGY, GROWTH	G. DAILY LIFE	
(Barry Levinson); "Moonstruck" (Norman Jewison); "The Naked Gun" (David Zucker); "Rain Man" (Barry Levinson); "Twins" (Ivan Reitman); "Who Framed Roger Rabbit" (Robert Zemeckis)				**1988 contd**
A controversial glass pyramid by I. M. Pei (U.S.) is erected outside the Louvre, Paris Prices continue to soar for works of art: Pontormo's "Duke Cosimo de Medici" is auctioned in New York for $35.2 million—a record for an Old Master Tate's Turner Prize for Sculpture: Richard Long (U.K.) Sky Television, the U.K.'s first satellite station, begins transmission Mikhail Baryshnikov leaves the American Ballet Theater Lucille Ball, Amer. film and television actress, d. (b. 1911) Richmond Barthé, Amer. sculptor, d. (b. 1901) Mel Blanc, Amer. "cartoon voice" of Bugs Bunny and Daffy Duck, d. (b. 1908) John Cassavetes, Amer. film director and actor, d. (b. 1929) Graham Chapman, Eng. member of "Monty Python" comedy troupe d. (b. 1941) Salvador Dali, Span. surrealist *(contd)*	The new Bastille Opera House, Paris, due to open in 1990, stages special concerts on July 13 and 14 to commemorate the French Revolution; Myung-Whun Chung (S. Kor.) replaces Daniel Barenboim as the Bastille Opera's Musical Director Claudio Abbado is appointed chief conductor at the Berlin Philharmonic Orchestra New Operas: "Cristobal Colon," Leonardo Balada (Barcelona); "Der goldene Topf," Eckehard Mayer (Dresden); "New Year," Sir Michael Tippett (Houston) New Musicals: "Aspects of Love," Andrew Lloyd Webber (London); "Miss Saigon," Claude-Michel Schönberg (London) Irving Berlin, Amer. popular songwriter, d. (b. 1888) Kurt Böhme, Ger. bass, d. (b. 1908) Roy Eldridge, Amer. jazz trumpeter, *(contd)*	Nobel Prize for Economics: Trygve Haavelmo (Norw.) for pioneering work in economic forecasting Nobel Prize for Physiology and Medicine: J. M. Bishop and H. E. Varmus (both U.S.) for cancer research Nobel Prize for Physics: N. F. Ramsey, H. G. Dehmelt (both U.S.), and W. Paul (W. Ger.) for isolation of subatomic particles Nobel Prize for Chemistry: T. R. Cech and S. Altman (both U.S.) for analysis of RNA Voyager 2 reaches Neptune, currently furthest planet from the Sun, and its satellite Triton Florida and Virginia allow DNA genetic "fingerprinting" as admissible evidence in some rape cases Israeli archeologists discover a Neanderthal skeleton U.S. archeologists discover an ancient Assyrian city, Mashkanshapir, in Iraq The Large Electron-Positron Collider begins operation in Switzerland; it is the world's largest-ever scientific apparatus, with a circumference of 16½ miles R. S. Pons (U.S.) and M. Fleischmann (U.K.) announce that they have achieved "cold fusion," but most scientists are skeptical Toshiba produces the first commercial samples of 4-megabit DRAM computer chips Computer viruses infect computer networks worldwide; Lloyds of London insurers create a new policy to cover losses caused by computer viruses that is available everywhere except the U.S. because of the proliferation of viruses there Meteorologists pronounce 1989 the warmest on record; this may be a sign of the greenhouse effect *(contd)*	France celebrates the bicentenary of the French Revolution San Francisco 49ers beat Cincinnati Bengals, 20–16, to win football's Super Bowl A U.K. 747 airliner crashes on the M1 motorway, resulting in 46 deaths Serial murderer Theodore Bundy is executed in the electric chair in Starke, Florida 170 people die and 1,000 are injured when two Bangladeshi trains collide head-on A gunman shoots dead five children in a Californian playground before killing himself The "Exxon Valdez" causes the world's largest oil spillage (11 million gallons) when it runs aground in Alaska Time Inc. buys Warner Communications for $13 billion to create the world's largest entertainment group Michael Milken, New York stockbroker, is indicted for fraud Sugar Ray Robinson, Amer. champion boxer, d. (b. 1921) 95 die in the U.K.'s worst sports disaster when they are crushed in Hillsborough soccer ground during an F.A. Cup semifinal 47 crew die in an explosion on the USS "Iowa" A gas pipeline explosion destroys two trains in the Trans-Siberian railroad causing 400 deaths The wreck of the "Bismarck" (sunk in 1941) is found almost three miles beneath the surface of the North Atlantic Ronald Reagan is awarded an honorary knighthood by the Queen Boris Becker and Steffi Graff (both W. Ger.) win Wimbledon's tennis singles championships President Bush authorizes the allocation of $300 billion to prevent the collapse of the savings and loan industry ("thrifts"); he also inaugurates a $7.8 billion antidrug campaign 56 die when a pleasure boat sinks in the Thames Pete Rose is banned from baseball for life because of betting on games A Tennessee court, taking the position that life begins at conception, rules that a wife is entitled to custody of seven frozen embryos Hurricane Hugo devastates the Caribbean and South Carolina A complete ban on ivory trading is ratified worldwide; Kenyan President Daniel arap *(contd)*	**1989**

	A. HISTORY, POLITICS	B. LITERATURE, THEATER	C. RELIGION, PHILOSOPHY, LEARNING
1989 contd	Contra scandal and receives a suspended three-year prison sentence plus a fine of $150,000 U.K. junior minister John Major becomes Foreign Secretary in July; in Oct. he becomes Chancellor of the Exchequer Arab terrorists hang William Higgins (U.S.), taken hostage in Beirut in 1986 Colombian presidential candidate Luis Carlos Galán is shot dead by drug traffickers Gen. Colin Powell is the first black American to become Chairman of the Joint Chiefs of Staff An I.R.A. bomb at the Royal Marines School of Music, London, kills 10 Ferdinand Marcos, Philippines President (1956–1986), d. (b. 1917) Thousands of E. Ger. refugees escape to W. Germany via Hungary; President Erich Honecker and later the Communist government resign; free travel to the West is sanctioned and the Berlin Wall is demolished; a reform government takes power Pakistan rejoins the Commonwealth after leaving in 1972 The Senegambian Confederation of Senegal and Gambia is dissolved S. Africa frees from jail eight A.N.C. leaders, including Walter Sisulu and Wilton Mkwayi The U.K. Court of Appeals finds innocent the "Guildford Four" jailed as I.R.A. bombers in 1975 Deng Xiaopeng (China) retires from politics because of age Todor Zhivkov (Bulgaria's leader since 1954) is deposed and replaced by Petar Mladenov The Romanian Communist Party unanimously reelects Nicolae Ceauşescu as President; fighting breaks out between protestors and the secret police (Securitate) and the government is overthrown; Ceauşescu (b. 1918) and his wife are swiftly tried and executed Alexander Dubcek makes a public speech for the first time since 1968; he is elected Chairman of the Czechoslovakian Parliament V. P. Singh is elected Indian Prime Minister after Rajiv Gandhi's Congress Party loses national elections Luis Lacalle is elected President in Uruguay's first free elections since 1971 Presidents Bush and Gorbachev hold a two-day summit in Malta Margaret Thatcher easily defeats Sir Anthony Meyer in the Conservative leadership ballot The U.K. begins forcibly to repatriate to Vietnam boat people in Hong Kong Andrei Sakharov, Nobel Peace Prizewinner, physicist, and dissident, d. (b. 1921) Hungary proclaims a new constitution to create a multiparty democracy David Dinkins (Dem.) is elected New York's first black mayor	Vers le Bon Dieu," Prix Goncourt Richard Holmes: "Coleridge: Early Visions," Whitbread Prize Martin Amis: "London Fields," novel Paul Auster: "Moon Palace," novel Julian Barnes: "A History of the World in 10½ Chapters," novel John Banville: "The Book of Evidence," novel Saul Bellow: "The Bellarosa Connection," short stories E. L. Doctorow: "Billy Bathgate," novel Umberto Eco: "Foucault's Pendulum," novel Thomas Pynchon: "Vineland," novel Philip Roth: "The Facts," autobiography Alexander Stuart: "War Zone," novel Rose Tremain: "Restoration," novel Gore Vidal: "Hollywood," novel D. C. Watt: "Now War Came," history Ronald Harwood: "Barnaby and the Old Boys," play William Nicholson: "Shadowlands," play Aaron Sorkin: "A Few Good Men," play	
1990	Nobel Peace Prize to Mikhail Gorbachev (b. 1931, Northern Caucasus), who is unable to accept it personally due to the ongoing political crisis in the U.S.S.R. The Vienna Conference on multilateral reduction of conventional weapons, in session since 1973, ratifies agreement to reduce conventional weapons At a meeting in London, NATO changes its strategy in favor of "partnership" with Warsaw Pact states A summit meeting between Gorbachev and G.H.W. Bush leads to several agreements concerning disarmament, but leaves the question of Ger. unification open Lothar de Maizière (b. 1940, Nordhausen), the first freely elected Prime Minister, forms coalition government in E. Germany Secretary of State G. Krause (E. Germany) and Minister of the Interior W. Schäuble (W. Germany) negotiate a Unification Treaty with plans for the E.'s accession to the West Parliaments of W. and E. Germany agree by a large majority to the terms of the monetary, economic, and social union and a govern- *(contd)*	Collette Audrey, Fr. author and screen writer, d. (b. 1906) Juliette Berto, Fr. actress and director, d. (b. 1947) Roald Dahl, Brit. author, d. (b. 1916) Peter Diederichs, Ger. publisher, d. (b. 1904) Friedrich Dürrenmatt, Swiss dramatist, d. (b. 1921, Bern) Lawrence George Durrell, Brit. author, d. (b. 1912, India) Aldo Fabrizi, Ital. director and actor, d. (b. 1905) Malcolm S. Forbes, Amer. publisher, d. (b. 1919) Paulette Goddard, Amer. screen actress, d. (b. 1906) Prize for a Political Book is to Václav *(contd)*	Alexij, Metropolitan of Moscow and Leningrad, becomes Patriarch of the Russian Orthodox Church Louis Althusser, Fr. philosopher, d. (b. 1918) Bruno Bettelheim, Amer. psychoanalyst, also child psychologist and specialist in social psychology, d. (b. 1903, Vienna) Bhagwan Shree Rajneesh, controversial guru to sects in Pune, India (for many years prior, in the U.S.), d. (b. 1931, India) Norbert Elias, sociologist and cultural historian who wrote "The Civilizing Process" and in 1977 was the first recipient of the city of Frankfurt's Adorno Prize, d. (b. 1897, Breslau) *(contd)*

D. VISUAL ARTS	E. MUSIC	F. SCIENCE, TECHNOLOGY, GROWTH	G. DAILY LIFE	
artist, d. (b. 1904) Bette Davis, Amer. actress, d. (b. 1908) Maris Liepa, Soviet ballet dancer, d. (b. 1936) Academy Awards (for 1988)—best picture: "Rain Man"; best actor: Dustin Hoffman ("Rain Man"); best actress: Jodie Foster ("The Accused") Films: "Batman" (Tim Burton); "Dead Poets Society" (Peter Weir); "Driving Miss Daisy" (Bruce Beresford); "The Fabulous Baker Boys" (Steve Kloves); "Field of Dreams" (Phil Alden Robinson); "Look Who's Talking" (Amy Heckerling); "Steel Magnolias" (Herbert Ross); "Turner & Hooch" (Roger Spottiswoode); "Uncle Buck" (John Hughes); "War of the Roses" (Danny DeVito); "When Harry Met Sally" (Rob Reiner)	d. (b. 1911) Vladimir Horowitz, Russ.-born Amer. pianist, d. (b. 1904) Herbert von Karajan, Aust. conductor, d. (b. 1908) John Ogdon, Eng. classical pianist, d. (b. 1937)	80 nations adopt a declaration agreeing to stop producing by 2000 A.D. chlorofluorocarbons (CFCs), which damage the world's ozone layer N.A.S.A. launches the "Galileo" space probe to Jupiter Astronomers discover a large, thin "sheet" of galaxies with vast emptiness on either side; it is dubbed the "Great Wall" and is unexplained by current theories of gravitational attraction The U.S.S.R. launches its 2,000th Cosmos satellite Mysterious "crop circles" appear in U.K. cornfields U.S. mathematicians discover the largest known prime number (65,087 digits long) A lemur previously thought extinct ("Allocebus tricholis") is rediscovered in Madagascar The U.N. Population Fund predicts that world population will rise to 14.2 billion by 2100 A.D. (current population is over 5 billion) George W. Beadle, Amer. Nobel physiologist, d. (b. 1903) Valentin Petrovich Glushko, Sov. space engineer, d. (b. 1908) Sir John Hicks, Eng. Nobel economist, d. (b. 1904) Konrad Lorenz, Aust. Nobel naturalist, d. (b. 1903) Sir Peter Scott, Eng. naturalist, d. (b. 1909) Emilio Segré, Amer. Nobel physicist, d. (b. 1905) William Shockley, Amer. Nobel physicist, d. (b. 1910) Sir Thomas Sopwith, Eng. aeronautical engineer, d. (b. 1888) Alexander Yakovlev, Sov. aeronautical engineer, d. (b. 1906)	Moi publicly sets fire to 12 tons of ivory tusks captured from poachers to demonstrate his country's commitment to protect the African elephant; the tusks were worth $3 million A strong earthquake kills 67 and causes extensive damage in San Francisco Javier Sotomayer (Cuba) becomes the first high jumper to clear 8 feet 22 die on the Pacific Highway in Australia's worst road accident Mitsubishi buys Rockefeller Center in New York U.K. television begins to broadcast the House of Commons procedures A gunman shoots 14 women dead at Montreal University Oakland Athletics defeat San Francisco Giants, 4 games to 0 to win World Series Detroit Pistons win National Basketball Association championship Calgary Flames win hockey's Stanley Cup	**1989 contd**
Keith Haring, Amer. artist famous for his graffiti art, d. (b. 1958) Felix Klee, art historian and theatrical director, son of painter Paul Klee, d. (b. 1907) Georg Meistermann, post-1945 avant-garde modern art (also created masterful stained glass windows), d. (b. 1911, Solingen) Capucine (given name, Germaine Lefèbvre), Fr. actress, d. (b. 1928) Sergio Corbucci, Ital. film director, d. (b. 1927) Sammy Davis, Jr., Amer. *(contd)*	Pearl Bailey, Amer. jazz vocalist, d. (b. 1918) Siegfried Behrend, Ger. conductor, composer and guitarist, d. (b. 1933) Leonard Bernstein, conductor and composer, d. (b. 1908, U.S.) Art Blakey, Amer. drummer, d. (b. 1919) Jorge Bolet, Cuban pianist, d. (b. 1914) Aaron Copland, Amer. composer and songwriter, d. (b. 1900, New York) Maurice Fleuret, Fr. musical critic and former musical director of the French *(contd)*	Walter Bruch, pioneer of German television, d. (b. 1908) Robert Hofstadter, physicist who received the 1961 Nobel Prize for his research on molecular structure, d. (b. 1915, New York) Nobel Prize for Physics to Jerome Isaac Friedman (U.S.), Henry Way Kendall (U.S.), and Richard Edward Taylor (U.S.) for proving the existence of the so-called quark particles in atomic nuclei through inelastic scattering Nobel Prize for Chemistry to Elias James Corey (U.S.) for development of theory of organic synthesis of molecules Nobel Prize for Medicine to Joseph *(contd)*	Initiative to establish a Nobel Prize for environmental protection fails initially World economic volume sees a twenty-fold increase since 1900 (an annual increase of 3%) World economic power: 5.3 billion people generate a GNP of over $20,000 billion (=3,800 per person) in approximately 2 trillion labor hours Nations with the greatest world economic power (GNP) are: 1) U.S.; 2) Japan; 3) F.R.G.; 4) France; 5) Italy; 6) U.K.; 7) Soviet Union; 8) Canada; 9) Spain; 10) People's Republic of China U.S. surpasses Germany in export value Greece threatened with national bankruptcy U.S.S.R. opens the North Sea to maritime *(contd)*	**1990**

A. HISTORY, POLITICS

1990 contd

ment declaration concerning the Oder-Neisse-Line, thus ratifying the E.'s accession to the W. in accordance with Article 23 of the Basic Law, whereby the partition of Germany by the Four Powers is nullified with their consent

At midyear, despite warnings from the German Bank, the Ger. mark is introduced to the new states of the Republic "overnight," leading to considerable economic and social difficulties. Conversion rate W. Ger. mark to E. Ger. mark 1 to 1

Chancellor H. Kohl (W. Ger.) and Prime Minister H. Modrow (E. Ger.) receive reassurances from Moscow that Ger. unification would be accepted

H. Kohl is reelected National Party Chairman at the National Convention of the CDU and L. de Maizière from the former "Block"-CDU in the E. Ger. becomes its sole deputy Chairman

One immediately following the other, leaders of the Ger. government H. Kohl and L. de Maizière visit the U.S. President G. Bush

Richard von Weizsäcker, President of W. Germany, is awarded honorary citizenship by the cities of East and West Berlin

Herbert Wehner, prominent Ger. politician, considered to have paved the way for the 1959 Godesberg Program, d. (b. 1906, Dresden)

In the first election for an all-German Lower House, incumbent Chancellor H. Kohl defeats O. Lafontaine, who had warned against the difficulties of unification

H. Kohl succeeds in gaining Moscow's approval from M. Gorbachev for full sovereignty for a unified Germany; Gorbachev's decision paves the way for the Two-Plus-Four talks (2 German and 4 Allied states) on German unification. Ratification of the Two-Plus-Four Treaty in Moscow finalizes German unity in foreign politics; a sovereign Germany remains a member of NATO, the superior power of the Four Powers is at an end

In a ceremony before the Reichstag, the black, red, and gold flag of Germany is raised to commemorate a unity achieved in peace and freedom. The date is declared a national holiday

Arrest warrant issued for former E. Ger. Chief of State and Party Chairman Erich Honecker (b. 1912, Saar Region)

Jörg Haider's Freedom Party (Austria), with its xenophobic platform, gains over 20% of votes in local elections

Bruno Kreisky, 1970–83 Chancellor of Austria, former Foreign Minister, d. (b. 1911)

As a result of the negative impact of the poll tax, Conservative Party in U.K. calls for the removal of Margaret Thatcher, who has been rigorous in leading the government since 1979, and her replacement by John Major

U.K. and Argentina renew diplomat relations, which had been severed during the Falkland Islands War

Mary Robinson, an activist in the women's movement, becomes President of Ireland; stringent Catholic moral laws continue to prevail

I. Carlsson (in office since 1974) forms Social Democratic minority government in Sweden

Italy's Communist Party suffers substantial losses in local elections

Center and left wing governments of Norway and the Netherlands step down

U.S. and U.S.S.R. agree to reduce the number of troops stationed in Europe to 195,000

U.S. halts its 1½-year-long talks with Yasser Arafat

M. Gorbachev (b. 1931, Northern Caucasus) is booed from the stage by the on-lookers on May 1 at Red Square and ostentatiously walks away from the podium at the Lenin Mausoleum

U.S.S.R. votes to strike from its constitution the guarantee of SPSU (Supreme Soviet) rule

Congress of the People's Deputies in the U.S.S.R. votes to abolish the CPSU's (Communist Party) monopoly on political power by investing extensive powers in the office of the President

With his election to the office of President of R.S.F.S.R. (Russian Republic), Boris Yeltsin gains political ground against M. Gorbachev, in a lead he will widen until Gorbachev resigns from his posts in 1991

(contd)

B. LITERATURE, THEATER

Havel for the autobiographical work *Disturbing the Peace*

Tadeusz Kantor, Polish theater director, painter, author, and director, d. (b. 1915)

Arthur Kennedy, Amer. actor, d. (b. 1914)

Martin Kessel, Ger. writer, d. (b. 1901)

Alberto Moravia, Ital. writer of Moravian descent, d. (b. 1907, Rome)

Walker Percy, Amer. writer, d. (b. 1916)

Manuel Puig, Argentine writer, d. (b. 1932)

Jannis Ritsos, Greek lyric poet, d. (b. 1932)

Delphine Seyrig, Fr. actress, d. (b. 1932)

Philippe Soupault, Fr. lyricist and novelist, co-founder of Surrealism, d. (b. 1897)

Barbara Stanwyck, Amer. screen actress, d. (b. 1907)

Antoine Vitez, Fr. actor and director, director of Comédie Française, d. (b. 1930)

Irving Wallace, best-selling Amer. author, d. (b. 1916)

Patrick White, Australian writer; 1973 recipient of the Nobel Prize for Literature, d. (b. 1912)

Nobel Prize for Literature to Octavio Paz (b. 1914, Mexico), Mexican diplomat and lyric poet of "poesía concreta"

Translator and Director of the Polish Institute in Darmstadt, Karl Dedecius, is decorated with the Peace Prize of the German Booksellers' Association

Kleist Prize to Heiner Müller (b. 1929)

Brit. writer Antonia S. Byatt receives U.K.'s Booker Prize

Prix Goncourt to the Fr. writer Jean Rouaud

Following the death of Antoine Vitez, Jacques Lassalle steps up as his successor as director of the Comédie Française

Piscator Society established in Essen, named after the socialist film director Erwin Piscator (1893–1966)

Mario Vargas Llosa, Peruvian novelist and literary critic, makes a bid for the Peruvian presidency as a candidate of the former conservative coalition of FREDEMO, but is defeated by the independent Alberto Fujimori

Frankfurt Book Fair presents 382,000 books (the world's largest libraries have about 10 million titles)

Peter Handke's "Das Spiel vom Fragen oder die Reise zum Sonorenland," stage play

Marina Tsvetaeva (1892–1941): "Phoenix," stage play

C. RELIGION, PHILOSOPHY, LEARNING

Karl Dietrich Erdmann, historian who became famous for the statement "There will not be a second Noah's ark," d. (b. 1910, Cologne)

Pimen (given name Sergey Mikhailovech Isvekov), Patriarch of the Russian Orthodox Church, d. (b. 1910)

Kurt Scharf, Nazi-era member of the Confessional Church, evangelical Lutheran theologian, Evangelical Bishop of Berlin-Brandenburg from 1966–76 who was not permitted to enter the eastern sector of Berlin, d. (b. 1902, Landsberg)

Milan Simecka, Czech. philosopher, d. (b. 1930)

Hans Speier, Ger. sociologist who founded the University in Exile in New York after 1933, d. (b. 1905)

Shepard Stone, patron and honorary citizen of W. Berlin, Director of Berlin's Aspen Institute, d. (b. 1917)

John D. Barrow (b. London), "Theories of Everything: The Quest for Ultimate Explanation"

Pope John Paul II receives PLO chief Y. Arafat

Pope John Paul II is subject to public criticism on his trip to Africa (Tanzania, Burundi, Ivory Coast, Rwanda)

Pope John Paul II visits Mexico

Despite protests by local Catholics there, Pope John Paul II appoints the conservative Wolfgang Haas as Bishop of the Diocese in Chur (Switzerland)

H.H. Lamb: "Climate and Cultural History," meteorology's influence on history

Heiner Müller becomes President of the E. German Academy

U.S. rejoins UNESCO after having withdrawn based on policies critical of the U.S.

U.N.O. Summit in New York on the growing problems of children and youth (abuse, drugs, criminality, etc.)

At a meeting between Edgar Bronfman, President of the Jewish World Congress, and Polish Prime Minister Mazoviecki, conflicts are resolved over plans to build a Carmelite cloister at the site of the former concentration camp, Auschwitz. A Carmelite convent will be built outside the perimeters of the camp compound

Albania lifts ban on religion

Jewish World Congress holds a conference in Berlin—the first of its kind in Germany in the last 60 years

Desecration of a Jewish cemetery in France leads to fierce protests and the passage of a law against anti-Semitism and racism

Discovery of extensive burial grounds from the Chinese Han Dynasty, dated approximately 2,000 years ago

In southern Israel, a bronze sculpture in

(contd)

D. VISUAL ARTS

entertainer and actor, d. (b. 1925, New York)

Jacques Demy, Fr. film director, d. (b. 1931, Pont Château, France)

Greta Garbo, already a legendary Amer. screen actress during her lifetime; completed her film career in 1941, d. (b. 1905, Stockholm)

Ava Gardner, Amer. screen actress, d. (b. 1923, U.S.)

Rex Harrison, known for his role as Prof. Higgins in the musical "My Fair Lady," d. (b. 1908, U.K.)

Jim Henson, Amer. Muppet creator, television and film producer, d. (b. 1936)

Margaret Lockwood, Brit. screen actress, d. (b. 1916)

Michael Powell, Brit. film director, d. (b. 1905)

44th Venice Biennale, Ital. painter Giovanni Anselmo is awarded Grand Prize for painting

Director Gianni Amelio receives the "Felix" for the European film of the year for his film "Open Doors"

"Driving Miss Daisy," U.S. film by Bruce Beresford, wins 4 Oscars

At the 40th International Film Festival in Berlin, the Golden Bear is to Costa Gavras for his film "Music Box" and to Jiri Menzel for his film "Larks on a String"

Akira Kurosawa receives an honorary Oscar for lifetime achievement as a film director

"Wild at Heart," a film by David Lynch, wins the Cannes' "Golden Palm"

At the 47th International Film Festival in Venice, the film "Rosencrantz and Guildenstern are Dead" by Tom Stoppard receives the Golden Lion

Director Wim Wenders is awarded the Murnau Prize

In Leipzig, 97 of over 800 works by the Expressionist painter Max Beckmann (1884–1950) are placed on exhibit

Major exhibit of approximately 220 works by Marc Chagall at the Wilhelm Hack Museum in Ludwigshafen

(contd)

E. MUSIC

Ministry of Culture, d. (b. 1932)

Maurice Gendron, cellist, student and partner of Pablo Casals, d. (b. 1921, France)

Sir Reginald Goodall, Brit. conductor, d. (b. 1901)

Dexter Gordon, Amer. jazz saxophonist, d. (b. 1923)

Tony Holiday, Ger. pop singer, d. (b. 1952)

Oleg Kagan, virtuoso violinist from the U.S.S.R., d. (b. 1946, Sachalin)

Herbert Kegel, Ger. conductor, d. (b. 1920)

"Ulrike Meinhof" (a choreographed play about this terrorist's premature death) by Johann Kresnik (b. Carinthia) receives the Theatrical Prize of the City of Berlin

Ashley Lewis, conductor for the State Ballett of Stuttgart, d. (b. 1934)

Mel Lewis, Amer. jazz drummer, d. (b. 1929)

Karl Münchinger, Ger. orchestra director and conductor, d. (b. 1915)

Luigi Nono, composer of serial music, d. (b. 1924, Venice)

Johnnie Ray, Amer. pop singer, d. (b. 1927)

Paul Tortellier, Fr. cellist and composer, d. (b. 1914)

Joe Turner, Amer. jazz pianist, d. (b. 1907)

Stevie Ray Vaughan, Amer.rock guitarist, d. (b. 1956)

Maurice Béjart, "Pyramide-Suite Orientale," ballet

"Ring around the Ring," Richard Wagner's "Ring of the Nibelung" by Maurice Béjart (b. Marseille) choreographed as a ballet at the German Opera in Berlin

Opening of the original home of the family of composer Johannes Brahms in Heide

Alfredeo Catalani "La Wally," opera

The three tenors Placido Domingo (b. Madrid), José Carreras (b. Barcelona) and Luciano Pavarotti (b. Modena) give an open-air concert in Rome, under the direc-

(contd)

F. SCIENCE, TECHNOLOGY, GROWTH

E. Murray (U.S.) and E. Donnal Thomas (U.S.) for their work on transplantation medicine, with specific regard to suppressing the immune system to keep it from rejecting genetically foreign implants

Nobel Prize for Economic Sciences to Harry M. Markowitz (U.S.), Merton H. Miller (b. 1923 in U.S.), and William F. Shaipe (U.S.) for work in theory of financial economics

Two U.S. researchers receive the Paul Ehrlich Prize for their analysis of diphtheria

Micro machines only millimeters in size are developed

Study in molecular genetics concludes that only 20% of all existing bacteria are known

Genes that regulate the structure of an organism are discovered

Field experiments conducted by the Max Planck Society (MPG) with genetically altered petunias meet resistance from ecologists

Over 210 field experiments in genetic engineering registered worldwide

Programs for total sequencing of human DNA in the U.S., Japan, and the E.U. require calculation of the sequence of several billion molecular components (nucleotides)

New astronomic telescopes with computer-controlled multisegment mirrors surpass all instruments produced to date

High-powered 12-foot NTT telescope at the European Southern Observatory in Chile is set to operate at the touch of a button

In Oxford a galaxy survey is published containing 2 million galaxies, centered around empty "bubbles"

A Very Large Array radio telescope produces a detailed image of center of the Milky Way, which is thought to contain a so-called black hole

Intermittent ("chaotic") disturbances are discovered in periodic comets

Another moon of Saturn is discovered

There are only three different types of neutrinos, which means that in order to maintain symmetry, there are three families of elementary particles

A 16-megabyte chip presented in New York shrinks 1,600 pages of text to the size of a postage stamp

The first high-resolution images of DNA molecules are made using a scanning tunnel microscope

(contd)

G. DAILY LIFE

freight in summer, substantially shortening the naval route to Japan

ILO in Geneva announces that approximately 55 million jobs are dependent on military armament

Heinz Oskar Vetter, President of the Association of German Trade Unions 1969–82, d. (b. 1918, Bochum)

U.K. joins the European Monetary Union (EMU)

Following the monetary union with the West, the economic situation in E. Germany worsens as a result of business closures without investments to compensate for it and high unemployment

U.S.S.R. begins introducing a "regulated" market economy

U.S. deficit reaches $5.4 billion

Trade ban on ivory leads to slump in prices

Inflation rate in Argentina surpasses 14,000%

Extensive environmental damage caused by a faulty oil pipeline in Siberia

So-called Ozone Conference in London deliberates over environmental damage to the atmosphere and agrees to halt production of chlorofluorocarbons (CFC) by 2000 (setting an earlier date was vetoed by the U.S.A., U.S.S.R., and Japan)

International conference in Geneva on the environment demands the immediate reduction of CO_2 emissions

Over 40 deaths, and damages in the billions, result from hurricanes in northwestern Europe

Ground is broken for the Channel Tunnel between France and U.K.

Studies reveal radioactive contamination and incidences of cancer in the immediate vicinity of a U.S. nuclear power plant

Saudi Arabia discovers new crude oil reserves with the potential to increase its production by about 20%

Turkey completes construction on the Ataturk Dam in the border region near Iraq

First Nations people in Canada capitulate after a long, fierce battle over plans to build a golf course in their territory

Iraq executes Brit. journalist for alleged spy activity

100th birthday of Rose Kennedy, mother of J.F. Kennedy (d. 1963)

Summit meeting between presidents of the U.S., Bolivia, and Peru to deliberate on increase in drug trafficking

W. Germany develops anti-drug program in light of increasing number of drug overdoses; leads Europe in the number of drug overdoses: Drug-related deaths up 20% from 1989

The first known case of AIDS is traced back to 1959

AIDS congress in San Francisco estimates between 6 and 8 million people infected with AIDS

Number of abortions for every 1,000 live births: Netherlands 107; W. Germany 146;

(contd)

	A. HISTORY, POLITICS	B. LITERATURE, THEATER	C. RELIGION, PHILOSOPHY, LEARNING
1990 contd	Under President Boris Yeltsin, the R.S.F.S.R. declares its sovereignty as the core political unit of the U.S.S.R. Foreign Minister of the Soviet Union E. Shevardnadze resigns, citing the imminent threat of an overthrow of government in the Soviet Union. M. Gorbachev thus loses his greatest pillar of support Lithuania, Latvia, and Estonia renew the terms of Baltic Council as a way of coordinating their political efforts Non-Communist Vytautas Landsbergis is elected president of the Republic of Lithuania. U.S.S.R. sends tanks into the Lithuanian capital of Vilnius. U.S.S.R. places sanctions with economic boycott on Lithuania's efforts to gain independence U.S.S.R. threatens Latvia with retaliation for reinstating its 1922 constitution written prior to its annexation with U.S.S.R. Estonia, as the third of the Baltic States that became part of the U.S.S.R. in 1940 by the terms of the Hilter-Stalin Pact, demands the return of its independence Lech Walesa is elected President of Poland in a run-off election C.S.F.R. (Czech Republic) President V. Havel appoints Marián Calfa (b. Slovakia) Prime Minister of a coalition government formed with the Communist minority Student protests force the admission of independent parties in Albania Election defeat of the Panhellenic Socialist Movement (PASOK) led by Andreas Papandreou in Greece. Constantine Mitsotakis becomes Greek Prime Minister after a long governmental crisis Bulgaria's first non-Communist government since 1945 led by Dimitar Popov Romanian President I. Iliescu orders shots to be fired at anti-Communist demonstrators and calls in miners to forcibly disperse demonstrators; dissolves the infamous secret police organization, Securitate Petre Roman becomes Prime Minister of Romania Yugoslavia shows the first signs of collapse Slobodan Milosevic (b. Yugoslavia) becomes President of Serbia. He is responsible for the breakup of the Yugoslavian state Former Yugoslavian republic of Slovenia declares its sovereignty Reformist Communist Milan Kucan becomes President of Slovenia Under the civilian coalition government of József Antall (b. Budapest), the Communist-led government comes to an end in Hungary Georgia and Uzbekistan (former members of the R.S.F.S.R.) declare sovereignty Armenia lay claim to territories in the Nagorno-Karabakh region of Azerbaijan, an area populated primarily by Armenians, even though it belongs to Muslim Azerbaijan; following a pogrom against Armenians in reaction to their Nagorno-Karabakh claims, martial law is declared in portions of Azerbaijan The first free elections in the Mongolian People's Republic shatter Communist monopoly rule Governmental crisis in Israel over settlement policies U.N. General Assembly condemns Israel's policies in Palestine General strike in Arab-occupied territories in Israel Shiites in Lebanon release three hostages from France and Belgium three years after their capture; two U.S. hostages are also set free by Shiites in Lebanon after a long period of captivity Bloody conflict between pro-Syrian and pro-Iranian militia in Lebanon Michel Aoun, General of the Lebanese Christian military, capitulates to Syria In Australian elections the Labor Party under Robert Hawke (b. 1929) attains a slight parliamentary majority, and he becomes Chief of State Foreign ministers of Iran and Iraq meet for the first time since the cease-fire in the 1988 Iran-Iraq War Iraq concentrates troops on the Kuwaiti border, which is under protection by the U.S. Iraq invades and subsequently annexes Kuwait. U.N. Security Council approves the U.S. resolution to *(contd)*		the form of a calf is found and dated 1550 B.C. Archaeologists prove the 550 B.C. collapse of the Temple of Hera on Samos Island Structure of an ancient church from the third century is found in Trier Geologically significant fossils make their way into the U.S. as gifts from the U.S.S.R. Human race looks back on approximately 5,000 years of transmitting cultural history in written languages, most of which have since been deciphered Japan Art Association awards "Praemium Imperiale" to Antoni Täpies (Span. painter), James Stirling (Brit. architect), Arnaldo Pomodor (Ital. sculptor), Leonard Bernstein (Amer. conductor and composer) and Federico Fellini (Ital. director) 20% of all adult men and 33% of all adult women in the world's population are illiterate

D. VISUAL ARTS

Museum for works of artist Ernst Ludwig Kirchner (1880–1938) opens in Davos, Switzerland
Exhibit in honor of O. Kokoschka (1886–1980) in London
Completion of an architectural project in Atlanta underway since 1953 by the architect J. Portman (b. 1924, U.S.), which includes enormous "utopian" buildings with sweeping interiors in a sort of "city of the future"
Large Rubens exhibit in Padua (Italy)
Mark di Suvero: "Tenderness," red steel sculpture on the Fr. Riviera
Exhibition of works by Titian (1477–1576) in Venice
Amsterdam commemorates the 100th Anniversary of V. van Gogh's death by exhibiting 130 of his paintings
The van Gogh portrait, "Dr. Gachet," confiscated by H. Göring during the Third Reich and sold abroad, is auctioned off for 136 million DM
An almost complete collection of the works of Diego Velázquez (1599–1660, Spain) is placed on exhibit in Madrid
Mies von der Rohe Prize to Ger. architect Friedrich Wagner for designing a Center for Quality Control in Stuttgart
Exhibition of Japanese and Ger. stone sculptors in Berlin (with works by Hashimoto Yoshimi, Kuetani Kazuto, Gerson Fehrenbach, and Louis Niebuhr)
Missing cathedral treasures from Quedlingburg surface in Texas
"Voices of the Moon," film by Federico Fellini (b. 1920, Italy)
Shohei Inamura: "Black Rain," film about dropping the atomic bomb on Hiroshima
"A Comedy in May," film by Louis Malle (b. 1932, France)
Walter Sedlmeyr, amateur actor, d. (robbed and murdered; b. 1926)

E. MUSIC

tion of the conductor Zubin Mehta (b. Bombay)
Marcia Haydée (b. Brazil) is confirmed for another five years in her post as director of the State Theater in Stuttgart
Premiere performance of Werner Henze's opera "Das verratene Meer," an opera with Japanese stylistic elements, in Berlin
Conductor of Leipzig's Gewandhaus Orchestra, Kurt Mazur, conducts at the Salzburg Easter Festival
Kurt Masur of the Gewandhaus Orchestra in Liepzig, becomes director of the New York Philharmonic Orchestra
Gerard Mortier, director of the Brussels Opera and appointed head of the Salzburg Festival speculates that, as an art form, opera is in an "end stage," but doesn't necessarily preclude the possibility of additional high points to come
"Medea," (choreographed by John Neumeier) premieres at the State Theater in Stuttgart with Marcia Haydée in the leading role
Premier of the South African musical "Township Fever" by Mbongeni Ngema in Johannesburg
The planned new production of Carl Orff's "Trionfi" to open the Munich Opera Festival is cancelled
To commemorate the Year of Van Gogh (100th anniversary of his death), premiere performance of two operas about him: Einojuhani Rautavaaras (Finland). "Vincent" and Jan van Vlijmens (Holland), "Un malheureux vêtu de noir"
Cellist and conductor Mstislay Rostropovich (b. Baku) returns to the U.S.S.R. after having relinquished citizenship there in 1974
Premier of the rock-and-roll spectacle "The Wall" is performed at the Potsdammer Platz in Berlin before a live audience of 300,000 and televised to

(contd)

F. SCIENCE, TECHNOLOGY, GROWTH

The X-ray satellite ROSAT, manufactured in Germany, is launched in the U.S., carrying a telescope with an extremely smooth-surfaced mirror (with only atomic deviations from the ideal image)
The space probe Voyager I, launched in 1977 by the U.S., photographed the solar system at a distance of 3.7 miles from the sun
18 years after its launch, the U.S. space probe Pioneer reaches a distance of 46.5 billion miles beyond all planetary orbits
N.A.S.A in the U.S. has collected 90 billion pages of satellite observations in the form of magnetic tapes
The Magellan probe sends images of the surface of Venus, which indicate that there are no signs of terrestrial plate tectonics on its surface
The People's Republic of China launches the satellite Asia SAT I, built in the U.S.
U.S. House of Representatives cuts funding for the manned mission to Mars that President G.H.W. Bush had already announced
Paul Ehrlich Institute, a new center for immunization research, opens in Frankfurt
AIDS research corrects long-standing misconceptions about the human immune system
Genetically manipulated mice with immune systems similar to humans prove invaluable to AIDS research
A medical institute in France discovers a vaccine for AIDS that is effective in apes
A high degree of variability makes it difficult to determine the genealogy of the HIV-AIDS virus
A so-called "adoptive" cancer therapy is developed using genetically manipulated immune cells
Endoscopic procedures increasingly used to supplement conventional surgery (soft medicine)
A clinic in Munich succeeds in simultaneous transplant of liver, pancreas, and duodenum in a 43-year-old female patient
Geophysicists prove that there is a slow, imperceptible pulsation of the entire planet after earthquakes, which allows them to register "silent quakes"
Depletion of the ozone layer above the North Pole is discovered
An approximately 16 million-year-old genetic substance is discovered in a fossilized plant
It is proven that the embryonic devel-

(contd)

G. DAILY LIFE

Austria 179; U.S. 347; Italy 389; Soviet Union 2,063
Experts declare the Aral Sea (U.S.S.R.) "biologically dead" after high water losses from irrigation
International workers celebrate the First of May for the 100th time
Strike in Nicaragua ends with 100% increase in wages
Only about 90% of the population is registered by the U.S. census
U.S.A. withdraws chemical weapons (poison gas) from W. Germany
Riots erupt at the premier of *Phantom of the Opera,* musical by Andrew L. Webber based on the text of *The Beauty and the Beast* in Hamburg
44 people murdered by drug mafia in Bolivia
High-ranking Mafia member in Palermo arrested as suspect in 30 murders
Mass graves with victims of Stalinism from the post-war and occupation period found near Neubrandenburg
In a heist at the Isabella Stewart Gardner Museum in Boston (U.S.), 11 paintings valued at approximately $100 to 300 million are stolen from museum
After 40 years of being banned, opposition in South Africa holds mass demonstration
A.N.C. in South Africa calls for general strike
On the island of Sri Lanka, fighting with Tamils displaces ½ million people from their home
Following unrest in Tirana, Albania, many citizens flee to EU missions; approximately 5,000 are able to leave Albania
Egypt is charged with torturing political prisoners (mostly Islamic fundamentalists)
Captain responsible for the 1989 oil spill in Alaska is acquitted on decisive points in his indictment
Shiites in Lebanon release the Amer. hostage Robert Polhill after three years' imprisonment
Harsh penalties for violating restrictions on dress in Iran
Execution by lethal injection of two prisoners sentenced to death in U.S.
Since 1976, 122 executions have taken place in the southern states of the U.S.
In Argentina, several generals indicted on charges of human rights violations are granted amnesty
In the presence of 6 foreign ministers (U.S., U.S.S.R., U.K., France, and W. and E. Germany) the U.S. closes Checkpoint Charlie as crossover point to East Berlin (in 1961 U.S. and U.S.S.R. tanks stood opposite one another at this spot)
A total of 1.3 billion people worldwide (26%) are forced to go without sanitary water
The city of Chemnitz, called Karl Marx City since 1953, takes back its original name; the E. Ger. city celebrates the 825th anniversary of its founding
Burma changes its name to Myanmar

(contd)

	A. HISTORY, POLITICS	B. LITERATURE, THEATER	C. RELIGION, PHILOSOPHY, LEARNING

1990 contd

take military action against Iraq if it fails to comply with the U.N. ultimatum. The Arab League breaks under the strain of the Iraq-Kuwait conflict

Willy Brandt secures the release of 193 hostages in Baghdad in negotiations with S. Hussein, who was using the hostages as military shields

Islamic fundamentalists gain an election victory in Algeria, and are subsequently persecuted and oppressed

U.S.S.R. and Saudi Arabia resume diplomatic relations after many years

Student protests call for reforms in Ethiopia

After a fire in the Rabda, Libya chemical plant, the revolutionary leader Khadafi, suspecting sabotage on the part of the secret services of the West, called for a severance of diplomatic relations with W. Germany, U.K., and the U.S.

North and South Yemen reunite after 250 years of separation

Civil war in Afghanistan continues even after the 1989 withdrawal of Soviet troops, which had been suffering high casualties in battles against the Mujahiddin since 1979

Benazir Bhutto, after 20 months as Prime Minister of Pakistan, is fired by the President under charges of corruption

Led by Nawaz Sharif, Islamic opposition wins elections in Pakistan

Threatened with bloody uprisings, King Birendra of Nepal reinstates the multiparty system

Democrats in Burma are led by Aung San Suu Kyi to an election victory over the military junta

Prime Minister of the People's Republic of China, Li Peng, visits the Soviet Union for the first time since 1964 and meets with M. Gorbachev

In the People's Republic of China, Deng Xiao Ping (b. 1904) resigns from his last political post, but retains political influence

People's Republic of China declares its intent to remain a Communist country

Republic of China (Taiwan) recognizes the People's Republic of China

Le Duc Tho, 1973 Nobel Peace Prize Laureate, d. (b. 1912, Vietnam)

Despite numerous scandals, Japanese Liberal Democrats gain absolute parliamentary majority, with strongest opposition from the Socialists

Ascension to the throne of the 125th Emperor Akihito Tsugu-no-miya (b. 1933, Tokyo) in Japan is accompanied by civil unrest

Military putsch attempt against President C. Aquino in the Philippines

Seventeen years after his 1973 murder, S. Allende is laid to rest at a state funeral in Chile

Violetta Chamorro defeats the Sandinistas in the presidential elections to become head of state in Nicaragua. She succeeds in disarming the U.S.-backed Contras and putting an end to the civil war that had prevailed since 1981

José Napoléon Duarte, Christian-Democratic President of El Salvador from 1980–82, d. (b. 1926, San Salvador)

Alberto Fujimori is victor in Peru's presidential election

Samuel Kanyon Doe, Liberian National President, d. (b 1959), murdered by political opponent and succeeded by Charles Taylor

After approximately 15 years of bloody civil war supported by the U.S.A. and the U.S.S.R., warring parties in Mozambique declare a cease-fire

S.W.A.P.O. (South West Africa People's Organization) leader Sam Nujoma becomes first president of the newly established independent state of Namibia (formerly German Southwest Africa, later a protectorate of South Africa)

Intense fighting in Mogadishu forces out Somalian government, which for 21 years had been run almost exclusively by members of one family dynasty

South Africa's F.W. de Klerk administration begins talks with the A.N.C. over the abolishment of apartheid

D. VISUAL ARTS | E. MUSIC | F. SCIENCE, TECHNOLOGY, GROWTH | G. DAILY LIFE

1990 contd

over a billion viewers. This concert, produced by Roger Waters, is the largest in the history of rock music

The new opera house "Opéra Bastille" opens in Paris

The only piano sonata ever written by Clara Schumann (in G-minor) is premiered in E. Berlin's Theater

The original script of the Mozart opera "Cosi fan tutte" is found in Kiev

opment of various species of animals (worms, insects, vertebrates) is regulated by a similar gene

35 million-year-old bird of prey is found in the Messel Pit Fossil site

The diet of hominids that went extinct 3 million years ago can be analyzed electro-microscopically

Worldwide molecular biological studies conducted on mitochondria support the hypothesis that the genealogical origins of the human race can be traced to people living in Africa approximately 200,000 years ago (female fossil find)

Remains of homo habilis from 90,000 B.C. discovered in Israel (the oldest remains in Southeast Europe date back to 43,000 B.C.)

Hyoid bone of a 60,000-year-old Neanderthal fossil from Israel indicates that this species of man possessed linguistic capabilities

Using the physical luminescence method developed around 1953, scientists are able to date deposits from the Ice Age for the past 100,000–200,000 years

Thermo-luminescence and radiocarbon measurements reveal that Australia was already populated from New Guinea approximately 60,000 years ago, that is, approximately 20,000 years earlier than previously thought to be the case

Dendrochronological (tree-ring dating) dating determines that the end of the last Ice Age was 11,300 years ago

Near Krems in northern Austria, a 30,000-year-old female figurine is found (Venus of Galgenberg)

Nucleonic lead isotope analysis acknowledges Sardinia as home to the oldest bronze objects (third millenium B.C.)

An approximately 6,000-year-old "industrial sector" with flint mines is discovered in Lower Bavaria. The widespread use of tools throughout Europe can be proven

Isotopic analysis of ivory allows for conclusions to be drawn about the habitat of elephants and thus allows testing of illegal imports and exports

Viking trade center from the 8th to 9th century discovered at Birka near Stockholm, with some indications of human sacrifice

Population of Mexico City sees a tenfold increase over the last 50 years

Fire on a Norwegian tanker causes oil spill in the Gulf of Mexico

State of emergency declared in California due to heat, wildfires, and water shortages

Despite moratorium on commercial whaling, Japan catches 300 Greenland whales

Sonar location systems are used to discover that the krill population in the Antarctic are 10 times that previously known

IOC lifts prohibitions on professionals for the Olympic Games

Two Norwegians reach the Polar ice cap in 60 days on foot

Reinhold Messner and Arved Fuchs cross the Antarctic in three months without any exceptional means of assistance

Martina Navratilova (b. Prague, living in the U.S.) sets a record with her 9th Wimbledon victory

Stefano Casiraghi, husband of Caroline of Monaco since 1983, d. (in a high-speed boating accident; b. 1960, Milan)

New Zealand wins sailing's Whitbread Round the World race in 128 days

Ger. sports journalists elect Kartin Krabbe and Boris Becker athletes of the year

Postal trains near Vienna and Cologne robbed (1.6 million and 6 million DM looted, respectively)

87 dead after arson attack at a night club in New York

Two injured by IRA bomb in London's Carlton Club, central meeting place of the conservative party

178 dead in a mining accident in Yugoslavia

320 dead in a tornado in southern India

Typhoon devastates the Philippines; countless dead, injured, and homeless

Approximately 200 dead in flooding catastrophe in South China

Earthquake disasters in northwestern Iran claims over 50,000 lives, 100,000 injured, and about ½ million homeless

Approximately 1,400 dead in earthquake in northern India

Another powerful earthquake in the Philippines claims about 1,000 lives

Approximately 1,500 deaths in a panic outbreak in a pedestrian tunnel among people making pilgrimage to Mecca

Meir Kahane, reactionary right-wing Israeli, gunned down by Palestinians, d. (b. 1932, U.S.)

A. HISTORY, POLITICS

1991 Nobel Peace Prize to Aung San Suu Kyi (Yangon, Burma [Myanmar]), as peaceful fighter for democracy. Since she was placed on house arrest, her son accepted the prize on her behalf

Deputy Prime Minister of Egypt, Boutros Ghali is appointed U.N. Secretary General as successor to Perez de Cuéllar (b. Lima, Peru), thus becoming the first representative of an African nation to assume the post

U.N. accepts seven countries as new members (among others, three Baltic countries, and North and South Korea)

U.N. now includes 166 members (Switzerland and the Vatican not included)

C.S.F.R. (Czech Republic), Poland, and Hungary enter European Association Agreements with the EU

EU Summit in Maastricht vetoes Brit. resistance to future political and economic development (proposal for European Currency Unit [ECU] by 1999)

Dissolution of the Warsaw Pact (established 1955) and COMECON (established 1949)

Helmut Kohl is re-elected Ger. Chancellor. He runs the administration under a coalition which no longer holds a majority in Upper House

Detlev Karsten Rohwedder, president of the Treuhand Corporation for privatization of businesses in the former E. Germany, d. (murdered by R.A.F.; b. 1932, Gotha); Birgit Breuel becomes new President of Treuhand

Ger. Lower House votes 338 to 320 in favor of Berlin as the parliamentary and governmental seat

Boris Yeltsin seeks to extradite Erich Honecker to W. Germany (which has issued a warrant for Honecker's arrest); Mikhail Gorbachev protests against it

Alfons Goppel, 1962–78 Prime Minister of Bavaria, d. (b. 1905, Regensburg, CSU)

Germany signs border contract with Poland

Belgian Prime Minister Wilfried Martens, in office since 1979, resigns from office because of differences between the Flemish and the Walloons

U.K. eliminates the poll tax introduced in 1990 by Margaret Thatcher

Fr. Prime Minister Michel Rocard resigns; Edith Cresson (Socialist) becomes head of Fr. government

Government in Finland, under Esko Aho, Centrist without Communist and Social Democratic parties

Iceland is the first European nation to acknowledge the three Balkan states annexed by the U.S.S.R. in 1940

Giulio Andreotti forms the 50th Ital. government as a five-party administration without the Communists; Andreotti five-party Ital. administration resigns

King Olaf V of Norway, d. (b. 1903 as Danish prince in Great Britain, King since 1957)

Under the populist candidate Jörg Haider, conspicuous for his use of right-wing extremist slogans, the Freedom Party gains tremendous electoral victories in Austrian elections

59 years of social democratic dominance in Sweden comes to an end with a slight majority in popular vote. Carl Bildt forms new government in Sweden

At a meeting in Moscow, George H.W. Bush and Mikhail Gorbachev announce plans to sponsor a Middle East Peace conference

People's Deputies elect Mikhail Gorbachev to the newly established office of President and strike the leadership role of the Communist Party of the Soviet Union (CPSU)

Public opinion poll in U.S.S.R. shows 76% of population supports Gorbachev's proposal to retain the Soviet Union as a federation

Radical reformist Boris Yeltsin who withdrew from the CPSU is elected President of the R.S.F.S.R. (Russian Socialist Federated Republic) with a 57.4% majority

9 of 15 republics of the Soviet Union agree upon a new international treaty (otherwise, Gorbachev would have threatened to resign)

(contd)

B. LITERATURE, THEATER

Max Frisch, Swiss writer ("Andorra"), d. (b. 1911, Zurich)

Natalia Ginzburg, Ital. writer, d. (b. 1916, Palermo)

Graham Greene, narrator and journalist, d. (b. 1904, U.K.)

Wolfgang Hildesheimer, Ger. writer, member of the "Gruppe 47," d. (b. 1916, Hamburg)

Yusuf Idris, Egyptian writer, d. (b. 1927)

Hitori Igarishis, Japanese writer who translated S. Rushdie's "Satanic Verses,"—Islamic leaders had threatened the death penalty to anyone disseminating this work, d. (murdered; b. 1947)

Yasushi Inoue, Japanese writer, d. (b. 1907)

André Kaminski, writer, reporter in Africa, d. (b. 1923, Geneva)

Klaus Kinski, Polish-born Ger. actor, d. (b. 1926)

Robert Ian Maxwell (given name: Jan Ludvik Hoch), Brit. publisher, d. (b. 1923, Selo Slatina, Czechoslovakia)

Sir Laurence Olivier (Brit. actor, d. 1990) is laid to rest in Westminster Abbey in London

Harold Pinter: "Party Time," stage play

Isaac B. Singer, Yiddish-language writer, 1978 Nobel laureate, d. (b. 1904)

Michel Soutter, Swiss director, d. (b. 1932)

Gene Tierney, Amer. actress, d. (b. 1920)

Vercors (given name Jean Marcel Bruller), Fr. writer and publisher, d. (b. 1902)

Hans Weigel, Austrian literary figure, d. (b. 1908, Vienna)

Sir Angus Wilson, Brit. writer, d. (b. 1914)

Nobel Prize for Literature to Nadine Gordimer (b. near Johannesburg, raised in a multi-lingual household). The South African writer is a fierce opponent of apartheid

Peace Prize of the German Booksellers' Association to György Konrad (Hungary), writer and silenced critic of the system in communist Hungary

"Freiheitstafel" by Sebastian Brant (1457–1521) rediscovered as the first example of the so-called liberation poetry

Norman Mailer: "Harlot's Ghost," a novel about the C.I.A.

Salman Rushdie, threatened with death by Iran, makes a public appearance in New York

Robert Wilson's "The Black Rider" is performed as kick-off event for the 28th Berlin Theater Gathering

(contd)

C. RELIGION, PHILOSOPHY, LEARNING

Pedro Arrupe, since 1965 highest ranking General of the Jesuits, d. (b. 1907, Spain)

Henri de Lubac, Fr. theologian and Cardinal, d. (b. 1896)

Dimitrios I, since 1972 Patriarch of the Greek Orthodox Church, d. (b. 1914, Bosporus)

Felix Gilbert, historian, after 1933 in U.S., d. (b. 1906, Germany)

Ernesto Grassi, Ital. philosopher, d. (b. 1902, Milan)

Václav Havel receives the Karis Prize of the City of Aachen

Traugott König, translator of Sartre, d. (b. 1936)

Marcel Lefebvre, staunchly conservative, tradition-conscious Fr. Cardinal who was suspended from the Apostolic See for having performed an unlawful episcopal ordination, d. (b. 1905)

Richard Löwenthal, political scientist, advisor to his party as expert on Soviet Union; Brit. citizen since 1947, d. (b. 1908, Berlin)

63 sermons by the church father St. Augustine discovered in Mainz

Sarcophagis of the Prussian Kings Friedrich Wilhelm I and Friedrich II are moved from the fortress at Hollenzollern near Hechlingen to Potsdam, where they find their final resting place

Pope John Paul II's encyclical "Centesimus Annus" written for the 100th Anniversary of the "Rerum novarum" is the first social encyclical since 1891 to address the issue of the ecumenical council

Pope John Paul II visits Portugal on his 50th trip abroad

Legendary gold treasure of Priamos found by H. Schliemann that has been missing since end of WW II is probably somewhere in Moscow

Worldwide discussions about whether there is any future for socialism after the collapse of the Communist countries

Japan and U.S. refuse to grant reparations or official apologies for acts of cruelty (1941 Pearl Harbor, 1945 Hiroshima)

President de Klerk announces the end of apartheid in South Africa; conference in South Africa to begin negotiating terms of a constitution without apartheid

Approximately 1 million people flee Sri Lanka, where a bloody civil war has been raging since 1983 between Hindus and the Buddhist majority

New light shed on pre- and early history of humanity by proving biological analogies in genealogies and in congruencies and similarities in linguistic development and relationships

(contd)

D. VISUAL ARTS

Berenice Abbot, Amer. photographer, d. (b. 1898)
Otl Aicher, graphic artist, founder of the so-called "visual communication," d. (b. 1922)
Giacomo Manzu, Ital. sculptor and illustrator, d. (b. 1908)
Rufino Tamayo, Mexican mural painter, d. (b. 1900)
Jean Tinguely, built montages from found objects and junk. His estate was made into a so-called "Anti-museum," d. (b. 1925, Switzerland)
Irwin Allen, Amer. director and producer, d. (b. 1916)
Jean Arthur, Amer. screen actress, d. (b. 1908)
Dame Peggy Ashcroft, Brit. stage and screen actress, d. (b. 1907)
Lino Brocka, Filipino director, d. (b. 1939)
Heidi Brühl, internationally acclaimed Ger. screen actress, d. (b. 1942)
Frank Capra, socially critical film director, d. (b. 1897, Palermo)
Ken Curtis, Amer. actor, played Festus on "Gunsmoke," d. (b. 1916)
Michael Landon, Amer. television actor and director, d. (b. 1936)
Sir David Lean, director; his films received a total of 28 Oscars. Among his famous films are "Lawrence of Arabia," "A Passage to India," "The Bridge on the River Kwai," and "Dr. Zhivago," d. (b. 1908 in England)
Richard Maibaum, Amer. screenplay writer (James Bond movies), d. (b. 1910)
Yves Montand, Fr. screen actor and singer, d. (b. 1921 in Tuscany)
Tony Richardson, Brit. film director, d. (b. 1928)
"Homo Faber": film by Volker Schlöndorff; adapted from the novel by Max Frisch (d. 1991)
Don Siegel, Amer. film director, d. (b. 1912)
Luigi Zampa, Ital. film director, d. (b. 1905)
Amer. architect Robert Venturi receives the Pritzker
(contd)

E. MUSIC

Carlos Alexander, Amer. singer, conductor, and composer, d. (b. 1915)
Claudio Arrau, pianist, d. (b. 1903, Chile)
Charlie Barnet, Amer. saxophonist, d. (b. 1913)
Roy Black, made several gold records as a pop singer, d. (b. 1943, Augsburg)
James Cleveland, Amer. singer and composer, d. (b. 1931)
Carmine Coppola, composer best known for his film scores, d. (b. 1911)
Miles Davis, famous jazz musician of the cool jazz-style, d. (b. 1926, E. St. Louis, U.S.)
John Field, Brit. dancer, d. (b. 1921)
Margot Fonteyn, world famous dancer and prima ballerina; she achieved worldwide renown with her partner R. Nureyev, d. (b. 1919, Great Britain)
Zino Francescati, Fr. violinist, d. (b. 1902)
Lawrence "Bud" Freeman, Chicago-style jazz musician, d. (b. 1907)
Serge Gainsbourg, Fr. chanson singer and actor, d. (b. 1928)
Stan Getz (given name: Stanley Gayetyky), Amer. jazz tenor-saxophonist, d. (b. 1927)
Martha Graham, dancer and choreographer of the artistic style "free dance," d. (b. 1931)
Brit. Peter Jonas is appointed new director of the Bavarian State Opera (beginning 1993/94)
Freddie Mercury, Brit. singer of Iranian descent. Became famous with his group "Queen," d. (b. 1946, Zanzibar, Tanzania)
Alex North, Amer. film composer, d. (b. 1910)
Sir Andrzej Panufnik, wrote 10 symphonies and a cello concerto, among others "Katyn Epitaph," d. (b. 1914, Warsaw, since 1954 in U.K.)
Max Rostal, violinist and music educator, d. (b. 1905, Teschen, Austria)
Ahmed Adnan Saygun, Turkish composer, d. (b. 1907)
Salvatore Sciarrino: "Perseus
(contd)

F. SCIENCE, TECHNOLOGY, GROWTH

Carl Anderson, Amer. physicist, 1936 Nobel Prize, d. (b. 1905)
John Bardeen, Amer. physicist, Nobel Prize 1956 and 1972, d. (b. 1908)
James C. Fletcher, Amer. physicist and former director of the Amer. space administration N.A.S.A., d. (b. 1919)
Edwin H. Land, inventor of instant photography, d. (b. 1909, U.S.)
Salvador E. Luria, microbiologist who specialized in the scientific study of bacteriology, Nobel Prize 1969, d. (b. 1912)
Edwin M. McMillan, Amer. physicist, Nobel Prize for Chemistry 1951, d. (b. 1907)
George J. Stigler, Amer. economic scientist, 1982 Nobel laureate, d. (b. 1911)
Sir Richard Stone, Brit. economic scientist, d. (b. 1913)
Nobel Prize for Physics to Pierre-Gille de Gennes (Fr.) for research into polymers and "liquid crystals"
Nobel Prize for Chemistry to Richard Ernst (Switz.) for development of high resolution nuclear magnetic resonance spectroscopy (NMRS)
Nobel Prize for Medicine to Bert Sakmann and Erwin Neher (Germany) for research on single ion channels in nerve cells (of substantial significance to the discovery of several diseases)
Nobel Prize for Economics to Ronald H. Coase for his study of the development of social costs
Computer simulations of galaxies colliding with 100 billion stars facilitates insights into the observable development of stars and galaxies
Study of the strongest quasar to date from a distance of about 3 billion light years that emits as much energy as 1,000 galaxies, reveals that the source of its energy is a gravitational field in the vicinity of a "black hole" the size of about 2 billion solar masses
U.S. limits construction of new space shuttles
U.S. tests nuclear-powered rockets
X-ray satellite ROSAT damaged by solar emissions
U.S. space shuttle releases Gamma-Ray Observatory (GRO) into the earth's orbit
German research institute for aeronautics and astronautics does not expect global climate changes to result from the oil fields burning in Kuwait after the war
Air travel presumed to contribute to depletion of the ozone layer; this
(contd)

G. DAILY LIFE

1991

The G7 industrialized nations, with only 23% of the world's population, control 55% of global GNP
Increase in the world's population for the 21st century expected to be 1 billion per decade
The outbreak of the Gulf War causes worldwide spike in stock prices
After the experience of the Gulf War, Germany restricts arms exports
Household deficit in the U.S. climbs to $187.6 billion (= 4.8% of GNP)
U.S.S.R. becomes associate member of the International Monetary Fund (IMF)
Slight decrease in arms expenditures worldwide, by 5%
50% of India's population lives below the poverty line
Gulf War against Iraq cripples civilian air travel, which, for the first time since 1983, sees no increase
A fifty-year limited treaty on protecting the as yet largely untouched natural environment of Antarctica, to run through 2041
Alpine nations sign agreement to protect the Alps at Alpine Convention in Salzburg
Eskimos in Canada receive land and reparations
Tropical rainforest shrinks by 1% annually as a result of human activities
Warming and pollution of the oceans causes degradation ("paling") of coral reefs
Cypress trees die off in the Mediterranean as a result of a fungus brought from the U.S. through Europe around 1950
Decision to tear down all the nuclear power plants in the former E. Germany because of inadequate safety measures
5 years after the MCA (maximum credible accident) at Chernobyl, Russian experts estimate casualties at 10,000; ruins of the reactor from the MCA at Chernobyl still present a danger to the environment. Since the MCA at Chernobyl, an additional 27 nuclear power plants have gone into operation (for a total of 424)
Germany begins running the ICE (Inter City Express) trains
Ernst von Siemens, CEO of Siemens Corporation, d. (b. 1904)
Public opinion polls on the first anniversary of Ger. reunification reveal that only 21% of E. and 12% of W. Germans approve of unification
First private nuclear power plant in the People's Republic of China
In Alaska, an international expedition finds what is likely to be the grave of Vitus Bering (1680–1741)
Arctic ice cover decreased by 2% in the last decade
Since the start of the "green revolution" in agriculture about 25 years ago, hectare yields have increased at a slightly greater rate than the human population
EU postpones decision on accepting Austria, Sweden, Cyprus, Malta, and Turkey as members
(contd)

	A. HISTORY, POLITICS	B. LITERATURE, THEATER	C. RELIGION, PHILOSOPHY, LEARNING
1991 contd	Mikhail Gorbachev is deposed by a group of "old Stalinists." Vice President Gennady Ivanovich Yenayev, who had placed Gorbachev in office, assumes the office of the President Boris Yeltsin seeks to overturn the coup-like overthrow of Gorbachev. With widespread support of the populace and its active assistance, Yeltsin ultimately succeeds in his largely nonviolent defeat of the putsch Soviet State Council recognizes Lithuania's independence Following a referendum, Armenia becomes the 12th republic to secede from the Soviet Union Boris Yeltsin outlaws the CPSU in Russia Referendum in Ukraine demands declaration of the state's independence by a substantial majority After the dissolution of the U.S.S.R., Russia is transformed into a Commonwealth of Independent States (C.I.S.) seeking forms of cooperation. Mikhail Gorbachev is stripped of his offices In Moscow on December 31, the flag of the now-dissolved Soviet Union was removed for the last time from the Kremlin; the state was originally founded by Lenin (b. 1870) in the spirit of Marxism at the time of the Russian Revolution of 1917 Free elections with four parties are held in Albania; Communists win Albania becomes the last (35th) European state to be accepted into the C.S.C.E. (Council on Security and Cooperation in Europe) after it disassociated itself from Communism EU and U.S. recognize the three Baltic states that were annexed by the Soviet Union in 1940 on the basis of the Hitler-Stalin Pact Lithuania passes a referendum declaring itself an independent democratic republic Philip Dimitrov becomes Minister President of Bulgaria and joins with the Muslim minority government Last of Soviet troops leave Hungary and the Czech Republic, where they have been stationed since 1955 and 1968, respectively Slovenia and Croatia secede from Yugoslavia, where the Serbs, successors to Tito, exercise and seek to retain central power Bloody, civil war–like conflicts in Yugoslavia between Croats and Serbs, whereby the latter are supported by the ruling Communist Party's state army EU issues economic sanctions against Yugoslavia in an attempt to end the civil war All cease-fire agreements between the EU and Yugoslavia regarding the civil war are broken Initially, the U.N. rejects the deployment of peacekeeping troops in Yugoslavia Jan Olszevski (b. 1930) becomes Prime Minister of a right-wing coalition in the center of Poland, against the wishes of Lech Walesa Leader of the Polish workers' union Solidarity, Lech Walesa (b. near Bromberg), is elected President of Poland 16 years of civil war in Lebanon draw to a close with the dissolution of all militia. Israel continues its claim to a safety zone in South Lebanon Jordan, pushed by its Palestinian population, sides with Iraq (one of its primary economic partners) in the Gulf War, but remains passive After a month of uninterrupted air strikes, the U.S. prepares for the transition to ground offensive in Kuwait at the risk of high casualties In accordance with U.N. Security Council resolutions, the U.S. and its allies liberate Kuwait from Iraqi occupation in the military campaign "Desert Storm," forcing Iraq to accept conditions set by the U.N. U.N. Security Council outlines conditions for peace in Iraq, under protests from the Iraqi regime U.S.S.R. and Israel resume diplomatic relations that had been severed since 1967 Israel aggressively pursues its settlement policies in Arab-occupied *(contd)*	Opening of the Swiss Literary Archive in Bern. Prior to his death, Friedrich Dürrenmatt had bequeathed the archive a generous gift	Animal pictographs from the period c. 10,000 B.C. are found in France in a cave whose mouth now lies 130 feet beneath the ocean's surface A temple find from the period c. 7,000 B.C. in Eastern Turkey near Nevali turns up the oldest known stone sculpture of God Three approximately 6,500-year-old canoes are found during excavations in Paris An approx. 5,300-year-old corpse "Ötzi" from the Bronze Age is recovered from a glacier in Tyrol with clothing and equipment intact The season in which Pompeii was destroyed in 79 A.D. is determined to have been winter, not fall The location of the so-called Varus Battle (9 A.D.; the Cherusci prince Arminius defeated a Roman army) identified near Bramsche in the foothills of the Wiehengebirge Mountain Range In the Sultanate of Oman, 50 grave stones from the period c. 2,500 B.C. are discovered by observations from the air Islamic fundamentalism becomes increasingly influential in Turkey In the Sudan, Islamic fundamentalism becomes an ever more influential denomination 7th Assembly of the Ecumenical Council of Churches. Approximately 1,000 delegates from 311 member churches participate and call for an immediate ceasefire in the Gulf War 100th anniversary of the births of R. Carnap, H. Reichenbach, and E. Zilsel recalls the meaning of "logical empiricism" and "Viennese Circle"

D. VISUAL ARTS	E. MUSIC	F. SCIENCE, TECHNOLOGY, GROWTH	G. DAILY LIFE	

1991 contd

D. VISUAL ARTS

Prize for Architecture

Scandal surrounding the awarding of the Golden Palm at the French Film Festival in Cannes to the U.S. film "Barton Fink" by Joel and Ethan Coen (because of its horror scenes)

Kevin Costner's film "Dances with Wolves" wins 7 Oscars

At the Golden Globe Awards in Hollywood, Kevin Costner's film "Dances with Wolves" wins for best film, best screenplay, and best director

Venice's Golden Lion awarded to film director Nikita Mikhalkov for "Urga"

High honors for the film "Malina" by Werner Schroeter (adapted from the novel by Ingeborg Bachmann [d. 1973]): Golden Film Band, Gold for direction, Golden Film Band for best performance by an actress (to Isabelle Huppert) and for editing (to Juliane Lorenz)

Albrecht Dürer exhibit in Düsseldorf's Museum of Art with approximately 50 drawings and water color paintings by the artist

Large exhibit of Max Ernst's work at the Tate Gallery in London to commemorate the 100th Anniversary of the painter's birth

The largest retrospective exhibit of the Fr. painter Théodore Géricault's work at the Grand Palais in Paris on the occasion of the 200th anniversary of the artist's birth

Major exhibit in Paris of works by the Swiss sculptor Alberto Giaconetti

Exhibition of works by John Heartfield at the Altes Museum in Berlin on the occasion of the 100th anniversary of the artist's birth

"Five Decades" retrospective of the portrait photographer Arnold Newman

Major exhibit in London documenting the work of architect and painter Karl-

(contd)

E. MUSIC

and Andromeda," opera

Rudolf Serkin, pianist, d. (b. 1903, Eger, after 1939 in U.S.)

Emil Tchakarov, Bulgarian conductor, d. (b. 1948)

Hellmut Walcha, organist, famous for his interpretations of Bach, (b. 1908, Leipzig)

John Adams: "The Death of Klinghoffer," opera; problematizes the phenomenon of terrorism

Maurice Béjart: "Death in Vienna" ballet to music of W.A. Mozart

European premiere of the musical "Grand Hotel" by Luther Davis, Robert Wright, George Forrest, and Maury Yeston in Berlin's Theater des Westens

Complete works of W.A. Mozart on 180 CDs

36 years in the making, Mozart complete works edition finished for the 200th anniversary of his death, with 105 volumes of notes

John Neumeier: "Fenster zu Mozart," ballet

Krysztof Penderecki: "Ubu Rex," light opera

Herbert Rosendofer/Helmut Eder: "Mozart in New York," opera; Salzburg Festival

Opening of the new opera house in Seville

To kick off the Salzburg Festival, the ballet "Requiem" by John Neumeier (based on a composition by Wolfgang Amadeus Mozart) is premiered

Reopening ceremony of the Frankfurt opera after it was destroyed by fire

F. SCIENCE, TECHNOLOGY, GROWTH

is the opinion expressed at the assembly of the European Geophysics Society

The trouble-free operation of the $1.5 billion Hubble space telescope is called into question after several of its stabilizers malfunction

Discovery of a quasar that is older than all previously known celestial phenomena. Distance from the earth: more than 12 billion light years

DNA-like substances of a specific sequence are discovered which stabilize the genetic material dating back about 400 million years (since the evolution of fish)

Science succeeds in breeding transgenic cattle with improved genetic characteristics

Blue roses are produced through genetic engineering

Researchers in the U.S. apply controversial gene therapy to fighting cancer for the first time

AIDS vaccine successful in apes

World Health Organization (W.H.O.) counts the number of reported AIDS cases at 345,333 and estimates that there will be 40 million by the year 2000

At an international conference on genetic engineering in London, the number of known genes is set at 2,500

The Amer. Society for the Protection of Animals doubts whether conclusions can be drawn about the behavior of the human organism from animal experiments with mice

According to a Harvard University study, the regular ingestion of estrogen (female sex hormone) reduces the risk of cardiovascular diseases in women after menopause by 50%

Increased stress doubles susceptibility to viral infections (results of a study by Carnegie Mellon University and the Medical Research Council)

Spread of cholera reaches near epidemic proportions in almost all countries of Latin America (approximately 3,500 deaths). According to W.H.O. statistics, ½ million people worldwide are afflicted by the disease

Medical scientists aboard the space shuttle Columbia study the effect of weightlessness on the human organism

According to a cautionary U.N. report, the countries of the Maldives and Bangladesh are in acute danger as a result of the increased

(contd)

G. DAILY LIFE

The city of Leningrad changes its name back to St. Petersburg. The nephew of the last czar of the Romanov dynasty is present at the ceremonies

Soichiro Honda, Japanese industrialist, d. (b. 1906)

A monument to the founder of Soviet secret police, F. Dzerzhinsky (1877–1926) is demolished by a mob in Moscow

Italy prepares to fend off a second wave of refugees from Albania by forcibly repatriating refugees

Immediately following the currency union between E. and W. Germany, economic crimes and crimes involving property rise drastically in the new states

Amnesty International reports human rights violations in 141 countries

Klaus Barbie, imprisoned for war crimes, 1943–44, head of Gestapo in Lyon, d. (b. 1913, Bad Godesberg)

Winnie Mandela sentenced to six years in prison for child abuse

At 1,916, number of Mafia murders in Italy is up from previous year by 29%

More members of the 1989 democratic movement are executed in the People's Republic of China

Jeffrey Dahmer pleads guilty to 17 murders in Milwaukee, WI

In Poland mass graves are found containing the remains of Polish officers murdered in 1939 while held prisoner by the Soviet NKVD

In Lebanon, 11 of 13 Western hostages are released from control of radical Shiites

During the Gulf War, the U.S. Patriot missile defense system is successfully deployed in Israel against Soviet-produced Iraqi Scud missiles

Germany sharpens control of exports due to illegal arms exports to Iraq

Cost of the Gulf War estimated at $60 billion

Upon its retreat from Kuwait, the Iraqi army sets fire to countless oil fields and causes severe environmental damage as a result. After 9 months, the last of approximately 500 Kuwaiti oil fields set ablaze by Iraq are extinguished

During the Gulf War, Iraq dumps 275 million gallons of oil into the Persian Gulf, resulting in the worst oil spill in history

One to two million Kurds flee Iraqi troops to the north and to Turkey where deplorable conditions and privation await them despite efforts to provide assistance

Hunger and the risk of infectious disease cause the U.N. Security Council to loosen the trade embargo imposed on Iraq in response to the Gulf War

South Africa is admitted to the Olympic Games for the first time in 32 years

Boris Becker ranked number one tennis player in the world

With Boris Becker and Michael Stich, two Ger. tennis players compete in Wimbledon finals for the first time

(contd)

	A. HISTORY, POLITICS	B. LITERATURE, THEATER	C. RELIGION, PHILOSOPHY, LEARNING

1991 contd

territories and thus hinders the U.S. peace plan "Land for Peace"

In Madrid, the long-anticipated Middle East conference opens, in which all parties to the conflict gather round the same table for the first time since 1948 (delegations from Israel, Egypt, Jordan, Syria, and Lebanon)

Acting on U.S. initiative, the U.N. revokes by a substantial majority the Resolution of 1975 in which Zionism is described as a form of racism

Saddam Hussein reaches an agreement with the Kurd leader Jalal Talabani concerning Kurdish autonomy

Turkey uses armed force to combat Kurds in its eastern territories and lays claim to buffer and safety zones in northern Iraq, where there is also a Kurdish population. This is followed by Turkish attacks on the Kurdish population in this region

Persecution of Kurds by N.A.T.O. member state Turkey meets with international criticism

Süleyman Demirel forms coalition government with Erdal Inönö in Turkey

Shapur Bachtiar, last head of state (1979) in Iran under the Shah, d. (murdered in exile in Paris; b. 1914)

Dictatorships in Benin and Mali deposed by democratic movements

After 10 years in exile, the former President of Algeria Ahmed ben Bella returns to Algeria

Parties in the civil war in Angola reach peace agreement in a so-called proxy war; the U.S. and U.S.S.R. agree to end civil war in Angola that has claimed more than 200,000 lives since 1975

Regime of Marxist Gen. Mengistu Haile Mariam in Ethiopia is toppled by rebels from various regions of the country. It is succeeded by a multiparty government in Addis Ababa

After a struggle for power, Meles Zenawi becomes President of the People's Democratic Revolutionary Front of Ethiopia

Following political unrest, regime change in Madagascar

Kenneth Kaunda, President of Zambia, allows for free elections; following the elections in Zambia, peaceful regime change: Frederick Chiluba (leader of the union movement) becomes president after Kenneth Kaunda

Military putsch in Somalia topples dictator Siad Barre (in power since 1970)

U.S. President G.H.W. Bush and EU lift the trade embargo that has been in effect since 1986 against South Africa

A.N.C., after many years now free to meet again, elects Nelson Mandela as its President

Following fighting (approximately 1,000 dead) between adherents of the A.N.C. and the Zulu movement Inkatha, the leaders of both groups, Nelson Mandela and Mangosuthu Buthelezi meet to settle the conflict

The fact that the South African government offered substantial financial support to the Zulu organization Inkatha as opponents of the A.N.C. is revealed. Vehement protests on the part of the populace; as a consequence of the scandal unleashed by the South African government's support of the Inkatha through a secret fund, President Frederik Willem de Klerk restructures South African government

Military putsch in Togo, W. Africa

Australia's Labor Party replaces controversial Prime Minister Robert Hawke with Paul Keating

Jiang Quing, member of the "Gang of Four" sentenced to death in 1981, third wife of Mao Zedong, d. (suicide; b. 1914)

Rajiv Gandhi, son of Indira Gandhi, d. (assassinated in a bombing during election campaign; b. 1944)

The controversial Japanese Prime Minister Toshiki Kaifu, in office since 1989, announces the end of his term in office. Kiichi Miyazawa becomes new Prime Minister of Japan

After 12 years of civil war in Cambodia, the four parties involved agree to a cease-fire in the so-called proxy war between the U.S.S.R. and People's Republic of China

(contd)

D. VISUAL ARTS	E. MUSIC	F. SCIENCE, TECHNOLOGY, GROWTH	G. DAILY LIFE	

D. VISUAL ARTS

Friedrich Schinkel

Stadtmuseum Berlin (E.) tears down the colossal Lenin monument by the Russian artist Nikolai W. Tomski

Methods of modern science (computer assisted and nuclear spin tomography) are used to detect forgeries of artwork

Reopening of Paris's Jeu de Paume museum as a gallery for contemporary art. The works of impressionists that were on exhibit there are now hanging in the Musée d Orsay

Opening of the Museum of Contemporary Art in Sidney, Australia

Legendary treasures of the Quedlinger Cathedral, recently found in the U.S. after having been missing since the end of WWII, are returned to their home

"JFK": film by Oliver Stone about the Kennedy assassination

Wim Wenders: "Bis ans Ende der Welt," film

E. MUSIC

F. SCIENCE, TECHNOLOGY, GROWTH

sea level expected from the effects of global warming

A research team of scientists from Germany and U.S.S.R., using a crystal from germanium-76.2 determines the equivalent mass of an electron neutrino at less than 1.45 electron volts

Half-life time of decay of free (ultra-cold) neutrons is measured at 888 sec.

Construction of an electric switch by setting the charge of individual atoms with scanning tunneling microscope

Improvements made in the development of x-ray microscopes with higher resolution than optical microscopes

20% of the world's electricity is produced by nuclear energy

In Hessen, the remains of a 250 million-year-old living organism is discovered from which mammals originated in the course of evolution

Rapid progress in the development of eco-friendly fuel cells

Researchers at the European Nuclear Fusion project in Culham (U.K.) conduct the first ever controlled nuclear fusion

250 million-year-old reptile fossil found in South Africa

3 million-year-old human jaw found in Malawi, Africa; the status of dental development situates it between the australophithecus afarensis and homo habilis

Near Tiflis a 1.8 million-year-old human jaw of the species homo erectus is found and thus supports the speculation that the human race spread from southeast Africa through the Middle East to Europe

Scientific community increasingly convinced of the notion that human beings have populated Europe for more than 1 million years

Thermo luminescent experiments demonstrate that Neanderthals and Cro-Magnons lived together for much longer than previously thought

An expedition of researchers sets out from Peru in a reed raft and travels to the Galapagos Islands in order to prove that the early indigenous populations of Latin America were already capable of extended naval travel

Communication between ants increasingly deciphered

The number of species of life that have ever inhabited the earth is estimated to be between 5 and 50

(contd)

G. DAILY LIFE

Elizabeth Taylor marries for the 7th time

Typhoon in Bangladesh claims between 150,000 and 500,000 lives. Warning systems and security prove completely inadequate

Flooding in southeast Iran destroys 88 villages

People's Republic of China asks for international assistance following a flooding disaster with more than 1,500 dead

Several volcanic eruptions in the Far East cause heavy contamination of the upper atmosphere with dust and gasses. The "greenhouse effect" is accelerated as a result

Eruption of the Mt. Pinatubo volcano in the Philippines after 400 years of dormancy leads to catastrophic mud- and ash flows that also destroy a U.S. air base

Cholera epidemic in Peru claims more than 500 lives

Wildfires in San Francisco cause millions in damages

265 people making the pilgrimage to Mecca die in a plane crash in Saudi Arabia

Oil tanker accident near Genoa leads to oil spill and declaration of state of emergency

140 dead after two ships collide in Livorno, Italy

Over 100 dead and missing after a dam breaks in Romania

650 passengers rescued from a sinking cruise ship off the coast of South Africa

223 deaths in a plane crash over Thailand, cause of the accident technical defect

Earthquake in northern India claims over 100 lives and 1,000 injuries

Approximately 500 dead in an earthquake in Afghanistan

Earthquake in Central America claims around 100 lives in Costa Rica

An increasing number of elderly people take their own lives (according to the 16th World Congress of the International Association for the Prevention of Suicide)

A. HISTORY, POLITICS | B. LITERATURE, THEATER | C. RELIGION, PHILOSOPHY, LEARNING

1991 contd

A. History, Politics

Basic agreement between North and South Korea improves relations that have been hostile since 1950

Narrow victory of the Congress Party over the Communist Party in free elections in the congress of Nepal

Central American Conference in El Salvador accepts Panama as new member and deliberates on the creation of Central American free trade area

At the national convention of the Communist Party in Cuba, Fidel Castro demands "Socialism—whatever the cost"

One year after disarming the rebels, renewed fighting between the rebels and the army in Nicaragua

After the military dictatorship in Haiti, the left-wing Catholic liberation theologian Jean-Bertrand Aristide becomes President of Haiti. Just eight months after taking office, the freely elected President of Haiti, Jean-Bertrand Aristide, an opponent of the army's interests, is toppled by the military and flees the country

1992

A. History, Politics

Nobel Peace Prize to Rigoberta Menchú Tum (b. 1959, Guatemala, since 1981 in exile in Mexico, descendant of the Mayas) for her advocacy of indigenous rights

After 24 years of negotiations, the Geneva Disarmament Commission of the U.N. agrees on wording of a treaty for worldwide chemical weapons to be presented to the General Assembly

With its refusal to sign the U.N. Convention on Climate Change and Biological Diversity at the U.N. summit in Rio de Janeiro, U.S. subjects itself to widespread criticism, especially since the U.S. is considered one of the "primary contributors" in terms of climate change, environmental pollution, etc.

N.A.T.O. retains the right to preemptive strikes to divert war in the event that nuclear weapons are deployed

EU countries recognize the former constituent states of Yugoslavia, Slovenia and Croatia, both of which are at war with Serbia

The ground-breaking resolutions for an economic union in the European Economic Community (E.E.C.) drafted in 1991 in Maastricht are signed at a ceremony there

Deep crisis in the European Monetary System (EMS) causes U.K. and Italy to at least a temporary withdrawal from the union

Radical protests by farmers in Strasbourg to oppose trade agreements between EU and U.S.

Summit meeting of nonaligned countries in Jakarta, Indonesia condemns fighting in Yugoslavia (founding member)

Willy Brandt, German politician; since 1968 in his role as foreign minister introduced policies of reconciliation with the East; Nobel Peace Prize 1971; 1949–57 Mayor of Berlin (W.), 1969–74 Chancellor of W. Germany, d. (b. 1913, Lübeck). He was buried in a state ceremony attended by Mikhail Gorbachev in Berlin-Zehlendorf

Hans Dietrich Genscher resigns from the post he has held as Ger. Foreign Minister since 1974. He is succeeded in office by Klaus Kinkel

After nine months in exile at the Chilean embassy in Moscow, Erich Honecker is flown in a Russian plane to Berlin, where he is held accountable for his complicity in deaths at the East–West German border

On a state visit to Germany, Queen Elizabeth II visits Berlin, Dresden, Leipzig, and other cities and pays tribute to the casualties of WW II

Ger. Lower House ratifies by a strong majority the EU Treaties of Maastricht (though the Ger. population remains skeptical and complains about insufficient information)

Germany and France agree to form a joint corps of armed forces in N.A.T.O.

Republicans in the U.S. approve an extremely conservative campaign platform before again nominating George H.W. Bush as candidate for the presidential election

(contd)

B. Literature, Theater

Isaac Asimov, biochemist who paved the way for the science fiction novel, d. (b. 1920 near Smolensk, since 1923 in the U.S.)

Martin Camaj, Albanian poet, d. (b. 1925)

Sven Delblanc, Swedish author, d. (b. 1931)

William Douglas-Home, Brit. playwright, d. (b. 1912)

Alex Haley, Amer. journalist and writer, author of the successful family epic "Roots," d. (b. 1921)

Martin Held, Ger. stage, screen, and television actor, d. (b. 1908)

Garcia Hortelano, Span. author of socially critical works, d. (b. 1928)

Heinrich Maria Ledig-Rowohlt, Ger. publisher, d. (b. 1908, Leipzig)

Monika Mann, daughter of Thomas Mann, d. (b. 1911)

Robert Morley, Brit. actor, d. (b. 1908)

Kenji Nakagama, Japanese writer, d. (b. 1946)

Amos Oz: "Der dritte Zustand," (The Third Condition) novel

Luis Rosales Camacho, Span. lyric poet, Cervantes Prize 1982, d. (b. 1936)

Immy Schell, Swiss actress, sister to Maria Schell, d. (b. 1934)

Nobel Prize for Literature to Derek Walcott from the Caribbean Island of St. Lucia, literature professor in Boston, who also writes in Creole

Peace Prize of the German Booksellers' Assoc. to Amos Oz, controversial author in Israel, advocate of reconciliation with Palestinians (supporter of the peace movement "Peace Now")

Michael Ondaatje and Barry Unsworth receive Britain's prestigious Booker Prize

Writer John Richardson receives Britain's Whitbread Prize for biography, "A Life of Picasso"

Heinrich Böll (1917–85): "Der Engel schwieg," novel (posthumous)

(contd)

C. Religion, Philosophy, Learning

Günther Anders, writer, philosopher, and spokesman for the anti-nuclear power movement, d. (b. 1902)

Giulio Carlo Arlan, Marxist art historian and politician, 1973–78 Communist Mayor of Rome, d. (b. 1918, Milan)

Giovanni Colomba, Ital. Cardinal, d. (b. 1902)

Karl W. Deutsch, Ger. scholar of peace, d. (b. 1912 in Prague)

René König, sociologist of Fr.-Ger. descent, d. (b. 1906, Magdeburg)

Frantisek Tomasek since 1977 Archbishop of Prague who became a symbolic figure in church resistance to Communist rule, d. (b. 1899)

Theodor Heuss Prize to Vaclav Havel in C.S.F.R.

U.N.E.S.C.O. Prize to Frederik Willem de Klerk and Nelson Mandela for overcoming racial segregation in South Africa

John D. Barrow: "Theories of Everything: The Quest for Ultimate Explanation"

Epistemologist Karl Popper, whose theory of falsifiability formed the basis of his critical rationalism, receives widespread recognition amongst experts in the field

Ger. animal rights activists demand that equal protection for animal rights be added to the constitution

Despite vehement debate and concerns about the ethical admissibility of the experiment, doctors at a clinic in Erlangen insist on delivering the baby of a pregnant woman who was declared brain-dead after an automobile accident

Queen Elizabeth II attends reconciliation mass at the Kreuzkirche in Dresden to commemorate deaths in WW II

About 500 dead following religious conflicts between Hindus and Muslims in India

At a Latin American Bishops conference, Pope John Paul II celebrates 500 years of Christianizing Indians

(contd)

D. VISUAL ARTS	E. MUSIC	F. SCIENCE, TECHNOLOGY, GROWTH	G. DAILY LIFE	
		billion (only .001 of these still exist today) Using radio carbon dating, Dead Sea Scrolls are estimated to be about 2,000 years old		**1991 contd**
Francis Bacon, Brit. painter known for his depictions of human suffering, d. (b. 1909, Dublin) Pierre Culliford, Belgian comic artist, creator of Smurfs, d. (b. 1928) César Manrique, Span. painter, architect, and sculptor, d. (b. 1920) Jean Mitchell, Amer. painter, d. (b. 1926) James Sirling, opponent of "functionally neutral" architecture (especially for museums) who created impressive buildings, d. (b. 1926, Glasgow) Nestor Almendros, Span. cinematographer and director, d. (b. 1931) Arletty, actress, famous in particular for her role in the film "Children of Paradise" by Marcel Camé (b. 1903), d. (b. 1898, France) Richard Brooks, film director, d. (b. 1912) Marlene Dietrich, earned worldwide acclaim for her role in the film "The Blue Angel" (1929) by Josef von Sternberg (b. 1894, Vienna), d. (b. 1901 in Berlin, Amer. citizen since 1933); Marlene Dietrich is buried in the Friedenau Cemetery in Berlin, as per her request José Ferrer, Amer. actor, director, and producer, d. (b. 1912) Werner Kreindl, Ger. television actor, d. (b. 1928, Wels) Anthony Perkins, Amer. film ("Psycho") and stage actor, d. (b. 1932) *(contd)*	John Adams: "Nixon in China," musical theater; German premiere at the Frankfurt Opera Dominique Bagouet, Fr. choreographer, d. (b. 1951) Ed Blackwell, Amer. jazz drummer, d. (b. 1929) John Cage, student of Schoenberg and experimental composer, also called "Father of Minimalist Music," d. (b. 1912, Los Angeles); "Pro musica nova" in Bremen dedicated to composer John Cage Georges Delerue, Fr. composer of movie scores, d. (b. 1925) Willie Dixon, Amer. blues singer and composer, d. (b. 1915) Jorge Donn, Argentine ballet dancer, d. (b. 1947) Jack Dupree, Amer. singer and blues pianist, d. (b. 1910) Sir Geraint Evans, Brit. opera singer, d. (b. 1922) Severino Gazzelloni, flutist, interpreter of contemporary music, d. (b. 1919, Rosasecca, Italy) Hanya Holm, Germ.-Amer. dancer and choreographer, d. (b. 1893) Albert King, Amer. blues musician, d. (b. 1923) Dorothy Kirsten, Amer. opera singer, d. (b. 1919) Gustav Kneis, Ger. composer, d. (b. 1906) Kenneth MacMillan, leading ballet master and choreographer, d. (b. 1929 near Edinburgh) Nikita Magaloff, Russian-Swiss pianist, d. (b. 1912) *(contd)*	Daniel Bovet, received the Nobel Prize in 1957 for his pharmaceutical research, d. (b. 1907, Neuenberg, Switzerland) Gerd Meyer Schwickerath, optometrist who invented ophthalmic laser surgery, d. (b. 1920, Wuppertal) Barbara McClintock, discovered the so-called "jumping genes" in corn plants, Nobel Laureate 1983, d. (b. 1902, U.S.) Nobel Prize for Physics to Georges Charpak (b. Poland, living in France since 1931) for work on the precise detection of events in particle physics, which would form the basis for important research results in the future Nobel Prize for Chemistry to Rudolf A. Marcus (U.S.) for groundbreaking research results with reference to, among other things, the transfer of electrons, which provide valuable foundations for experimental chemists Nobel Prize for Medicine to Edmond H. Fischer (b. Shanghai) and Edwin Krebs (U.S.) for their research on enzymes in muscle cells, work first begun in the 1970s in the U.S. Nobel Prize for Economics to Gary S. Becker (U.S.) for application of economic laws to human behavior in all domains Research satellite ROSAT records 60,000 cosmic x-ray sources within 6 months Maiden voyage of the U.S. space shuttle Endeavor Using "swing by" technique (exploitation of the gravitational field of a celestial body as a way of correcting the course of spacecraft), the course of the space probe Ulysses (launched 1990) is successfully diverted from the planetary orbit and brought onto a *(contd)*	43 Nobel Prize laureates throughout the world protest the civil war in Yugoslavia Economic comparison of the wealthiest 20% and the poorest 20% nations—GNP 82.7% to 1.4%; commerce 81.2% to 1.0%; domestic investors 80.5% to 1.3%—reveals the stark imbalance in economic power between them U.N. publishes a report on comparative income of richest 20% and poorest 20% of the world's population: 1960, 30 to 1; 1970, 32 to 1; 1980, 45 to 1; 1990, 60 to 1 According to ranking by the U.N., Canada and Japan have the highest standard of living; U.K. and Germany follow in 10th and 12th place Of the fruits and vegetables harvested worldwide, about 25% perishes before they can be consumed (approximately 250 million metric tons) worldwide EU institutes duty-free domestic market, effective New Year's Day 1993 Lichtenstein votes in favor of the European Economic Area (EEA) consisting of the EU and the E.F.T.A. (European Free Trade Association) U.S., Canada, and Mexico sign a free trade agreement which, with a financially strong market (360 million people) and a GNP of $ 6 trillion, is more imposing than the EU A.S.E.A.N. conference in Singapore resolves to create a common preferential tariff union A strike in the Ger. steel industry already approved by union workers is averted at the last minute by tariff compromise In the U.S., increasing aversion to economic competitor Japan On his trip to Asia, U.S. President George H. W. Bush seeks to improve economic relations with Japan U.S. airline company TWA declares bankruptcy U.S. national deficit at $4 trillion Disney opens Disneyland in Paris, "Euro Disney" Spain's King Juan Carlos opens the largest world's fair to date at the Expo 92 in Seville; it is also the last world's fair of the millennium *(contd)*	**1992**

1992 contd

A. HISTORY, POLITICS

U.S. President George H.W. Bush and President Boris Yeltsin both announce sweeping reductions in nuclear defense budget (U.S. to reduce spending by $50 billion in 5 years)

After a long battle over protocol, Middle East peace conference enters new rounds in Washington (with an additional round scheduled for Moscow)

Democratic party in the U.S. picks Bill Clinton as its presidential candidate, and Albert Gore as its vice presidential candidate

What little remains of the CPSU expels Mikhail Gorbachev (since 1985 General Secretary)

President Boris Yeltsin wrestles with the People's Congress, still dominated by the CPSU, in Moscow over his position as Chief of State and special executive powers

After a tense election campaign, Democrat Bill Clinton wins the U.S. presidential election and replaces George H.W. Bush as President of the U.S.

Boris Yeltsin appoints himself as Russia's Defense Minister

N.A.T.O. Cooperation Council accepts former C.I.S. states. The committee now consists of 35 member states

The controversy between Russian and Ukraine over command of the Black Sea fleet remains a point of contention for the C.I.S. states

Election victory for the Democrats in Albania over Socialists (formerly Communists) liberates the country from the Communist regime in place since 1944 under Enver Hoxha

Salih Berisha becomes President of Albania

In U.K., despite substantial losses, the conservatives retain absolute majority; John Major remains chief of state

Estonian Parliament elects Lennart Merz, a candidate with no Communist party past, to the office of President

Finnish Parliament decides to join the EU

Edith Cresson, Prime Minister of France since 1991, resigns after the Socialists are defeated there. She is succeeded by Minister of Finance, Pierre Bérégovoy

Eduard Shevardnaze, former Foreign Minister of U.S.S.R., returns to his home in Georgia to help resolve the conflict with Russia and is elected chief of state there by a large majority

Parliament in Greece ratifies the EU Maastricht Treaties

Elections in Ireland result in a victory for the opposition Labor Party and a liberalization of stringently Catholic abortion laws

The Italian judge and Mafia opponent Giovanni Falcone and his body guards fall victim to assassination by bombing

Franjo Tudjman and his party win the first post-war election in Croatia, whose independence he had called for in 1991; Former Communist Milan Kucan is elected president of Croatia in free election

Milan Panic (U.S. citizen since 1963) new Prime Minister of Yugoslavia

Attempt on the part of all parties in the civil war to end fighting in Yugoslavia; peace plan negotiated by Cyrus Vance, former U.S. Secretary of State and David Owen, former Brit. Foreign Minister

In Lithuana, where large numbers of Russians are eligible to vote, old-school Communists unexpectedly crush Democrats led by Vytautas Landsbergis; Algirdas Brazaukas becomes Prime Minister of Lithuania

Thomas Klestil becomes Austrian President as successor to Kurt Waldheim

In the Polish governmental crisis, caused largely by the fragmentation of political forces into 29 groups, Hanna Suchoka is appointed Prime Minister in a coalition government by Lech Walesa

Ger. Foreign Minister Hans-Dietrich Genscher signs a Germ.-Romanian Cooperation Treaty in Bucharest (the last treaty of its kind was in COMECON areas)

In Romania's presidential election, Ion Iliescu (formerly Communist Party) beats E. Constantinescu, leader of the Democratic opposition

Swiss Federal Council decides to apply for membership in the EU

Alexander Dubcek, during the Prague Spring fought for "Socialism

(contd)

B. LITERATURE, THEATER

District of Berlin purchases the literary estate of Bertold Brecht (d. 1956, Berlin)

Veza Canetti: "Der Oger," dramatic work written in 1934, premieres in Zurich in the presence of Elias Canetti

Athol Fugard (South Africa): "Playland," one-act play about apartheid

Günter Grass: "Unkerufe," novel examining the "Wende" of 1989/90

Peter Handke: "Die Stunde, da wir nichts voneinander wussten," stage play

Swedish author of children's books ("Pippi Longstocking") Astrid Lindgren announces that she will not be writing any more books

Theater of the Freie Volksbühne (founding director Erwin Piscator [d. 1966]) in former West Berlin is closed

C. RELIGION, PHILOSOPHY, LEARNING

New official catechism of the Catholic church is introduced to the worldwide public in Paris

Bloody persecution of Islamic fundamentalists in Algeria

Syria loosens restrictions on Jews

After much debate, the Anglican church permits women to hold the office of Bishop

Desecration of Jewish memorials and monuments on the rise in Germany

The age of language as a method of human communication is estimated to be approximately 100,000 years

Remains of 6,000-year-old horse are found near Kiev

Ongoing debate surrounding the origin of the Laocoön statue in the Vatican continues among art historians

Coptic grave from c. 640 A.D. discovered near the Egyptian pyramids

Catholic Academy in Bavaria organizes a conference on the Qumran Scrolls dating from c. 100 B.C. to 100 A.D. that were found on the Dead Sea in 1947 and whose significance for early Christianity is still controversial

World exhibition in Seville under the theme "The Age of Discovery"

D. VISUAL ARTS

Satyajit Ray, founder of Indian cinematography (creator of "Apu Trilogy" 1955–60), d. (b. 1922, Calcutta)
Hal Roach, Amer. movie producer, d. (b. 1892)
John Sturges, director of westerns and action films, among others "Magnificent Seven," d. (b. 1910, Oak Park, IL)
Cannes's Golden Palm to "The Best Intentions," film by Bille August (b. Denmark)
Berlin Film Festival's Golden Bear to Lawrence Kasdan for the film "Grand Canyon"
5 Oscars to "Silence of the Lambs," by Jonathan Demme
European Film Award "Felix" to Director Billy Wilder (b. Krakow, emigrated to U.S. 1933) for lifetime achievement
At the 49th Biennale in Venice, Golden Lion to Chinese director Zhang Yimon for his film "The Story of Qi Ju"
Exhibit of works by Amer. painter Jean-Michel Basquiat (1960–88) in New York
Moscow's Pushkin Museum exhibits drawings by J. Beuys (d. 1986)
Exhibit of previously unknown water colors and drawings by the Germ.-Amer. artist Lyonel Feininger in Nuremberg
"Edward Hopper [b. 1882, d. 1967] and Photography," exhibit in Essen
City of Cologne exhibits works of Jean Ipoustéguy
Major exhibit of Renaissance painter Andrea Mantegna (1431–1506) in London
A preliminary study from around 1930 for Henri Matisse's (1869–1959) "La danse" discovered in Paris
Major exhibit of works by the Fr. Impressionist Claude Monet in Balingen
Pablo Picasso (1881–1973) is at the center of an art exhibit at the Olympic Games in Barcelona, where several stages of his artistic development
(contd)

E. MUSIC

Olivier Messiaen, Fr. organist and composer, d. (b. 1908)
Roger Miller, Amer. country music singer, d. (b. 1936)
Nathan Milstein, virtuoso violinist, d. (b. 1904, Odessa)
Astor Piazolla, Argentine jazz musician and tango composer, d. (b. 1921)
Sammy Price, Amer. jazz pianist, d. (b. 1908)
Alfred Uhl, Austrian composer, d. (b. 1909)
Eberhard Waechter, Austrian opera singer and director, d. (b. 1908)
Mary Wells, Amer. R&B singer, d. (b. 1943)
Atahualpa Yupanqui, world-renowned Argentine singer, d. (b. 1908)
Ernst von Siemens Prize to the Amer. musicologist H.C. Robbins Landon
Alexander von Zemlinksy (b. 1871, Vienna of Polish descent, d. 1942, U.S.): "King Kandaules," premiere performance of portions of the opera from the period around 1934
Daniel Barenboim (b. Buenos Aires, of Russ. descent) becomes executive musical director of the German State Opera
Michel Berger/Luc Plamondon: "Starmania," Fr. rock opera; German premiere
Rafael Frühbeck de Burgos becomes new executive musical director of the Ger. Opera in Berlin
Body of Jan Paderewski (b. 1860, Poland, d. 1941, New York), Polish pianist and politician, Prime Minister 1919, is returned to his home in Poland for burial
Peter Tchaikovsky: "Jolanthe," opera; produced by Peter Ustinov

F. SCIENCE, TECHNOLOGY, GROWTH

course that will take it over the sun's poles in 1994/95
After several failed attempts, rockets in the People's Republic of China are able to launch Australian-made satellites into orbit
U.S. space shuttle Columbia, on the 48th flight of a U.S. spacecraft, sets a record flight duration, with 10 days and 21 hours in space
Mission of the U.S. space shuttle Discovery to study weightlessness and its impact on human beings, 7 astronauts on board, among them Ger. Ulf Merbold
Images of cosmic objects sent by the malfunctioning Hubble space telescope are corrected using computer technology to improve their quality
U.S. astronomers, using a high performance 12-foot telescope at La Silla, Chile, discover satellites outside Pluto's orbit; astronomy focuses increasingly on space beyond planets of Pluto, which are farthest from the sun
First gene for olfactory receptors is isolated and identified
First successful sequencing (nucleotide sequencing analysis) of a whole yeast chromosome, seen as a preliminary stage of comprehensive genome analysis
Molecular biology analyzes the full DNA sequence of genes (genome) in important cultivated plants for the purposes of hybridization
By stimulating the organ milieu, scientists succeed in producing organ-specific cell structures that allow them to test pharmaceutical or other substances for their effect without testing on animals
Since 1990, a total of 10 methods for gene therapy have been developed with the potential for introducing a new era in medicine
European patent office issues the first patent for a genetically altered animal, the so-called Harvard cancer mouse
New research results anticipate the ability to restrict the spread of bilharziosis (tropical infectious disease caused by parasites)
Increasing insights into the molecular foundations of mood and mental disorders
U.S. researchers discover the "leukemia gene" and identify the position in the human genome of the gene whose mutation may lead to leukemia
Implantation of embryonic stem cells
(contd)

G. DAILY LIFE

The "lean production" model developed in the U.S. and Japan, which seeks to minimize storage costs by delivering parts needed directly prior to use, is becoming increasingly popular, especially in the auto industry
Privatization in Russia through the distribution of shares (stock) in state-sponsored businesses to the population
Newspaper "Pravda" in Moscow ceases production
Experimental sale of stocks in People's Republic of China is interrupted by tumultuous throngs seeking to purchase
EU places 48-hour limit on work week
After being in operation for 164 years, London's zoo is forced to close because of a sharp decrease in number of visitors
As a result of the so-called green revolution begun in 1970, the People's Republic of China is able to feed approximately 22% of its population with the yields from its own crops (approximately 7% worldwide)
The percentage of electricity generated by nuclear power is estimated to be 18% worldwide (compared to 10% in 1980)
Worldwide warnings about the computer virus "Michelangelo," but the anticipated mass destruction of data never occurs
France begins airlift operation to deliver supplies to the population of Sarajevo suffering under the confusion of civil war. The operation is supported by the deployment of U.N. peacekeepers. Germany also sends supplies
U.N. begins airlift operation for food distribution in Somalia. The operation is hindered by marauding bands of rebels
Number of air travel casualties in 1991 cited at 1,035
Amsterdam closes its city center to vehicular traffic
Border between Britain and France marked in the Channel Tunnel
Pakistan claims to be in possession of sufficient resources to build nuclear weapons
Italy passes anti-Mafia laws
Former SS leader Joseph Schwammberger (b. Innsbruck, fled to Argentina after the war) is sentenced to life in prison on numerous charges of murder in the Nazi concentration camps, in what is considered to be the last trial of Nazi criminals. Neo-Nazis protest the ruling
Indictment and arrest warrant against Erich Honecker for his complicity in fatal shots fired at the border to the former E. Germany
According to official declarations of Brazilian authorities, the former concentration camp doctor Josef Mengele is said to have died in a drowning accident
Head of Peruvian terror organization "Shining Path," A. Guzman, is sentenced by a military court to life in prison for conspiracy to commit mass murder (25,000 victims since 1980)
(contd)

	A. HISTORY, POLITICS	B. LITERATURE, THEATER	C. RELIGION, PHILOSOPHY, LEARNING
1992 contd	with a human face" in Czechoslovak Socialist Republic (C.S.S.R.), became President of Parliament in the C.S.F.R. in 1989, d. (from injuries sustained in a car accident; b. 1921, C.S.S.R.) Vaclav Havel (author and politician, President of Czech Republic since 1989), falls short of the majority for reelection in the C.S.F.R. Parliament as a result of moves toward Slovakian separatism. Consequently, a split in the nation that Havel sought to avoid becomes inevitable; C.S.F.R. Parliament passes a resolution to separate the Czech sectors of the nation from the Slovakian by 1993; Vaclav Havel responds to Slovakia's secession from the C.S.F.R. by resigning from his post as President of the C.S.F.R., an office he has held since 1989 Chadli Bendjedid, President of Algeria since 1979, d. (murdered; b. 1929) Mohammed Boudiaf, since 1988 President of the Algerian National Council, where he fought against Islamic fundamentalists (FIS), d. (murdered; b. 1919) Military seizes control in Algeria and suppresses rapidly growing Islamic fundamentalist movement Menachim Begin, Prime Minister of Israel 1977–83, when he signed a peace accord with then-President of Egypt Anwar el Sadat, Nobel Peace Prize, 1978, d. (b. 1913, Brest-Litovsk) After a devastating election defeat, Yitzhak Shamir of the right-wing Likud, in office since 1977, is replaced by Yitzhak Rabin of the Social Democratic Workers' Party, victor in the 1967 Six Day War Israel uses military force to close off the Gaza Strip, resulting in substantial deterioration of living conditions for the Palestinians Deportation of 418 Palestinians from Israel as retribution for a murder poses substantial obstacles for the Middle East peace talks Iraq continues to hamper the efforts of U.N. weapons inspectors, leading to U.S. military deployments in Iraq U.N. Security Council extends the embargo against Iraq because it has failed to adhere to the conditions of the cease-fire In the first election in Iran since the death of revolutionary leader Khomeini in 1989, victory for adherents of the moderate policies promoted by President Ali Akbar Hashemi Rafsanjani (from the moderate Islamic camp, chief of state since 1989), against Islamic fundamentalists Elections in Kuwait result in majority for oppositional group Germany ceases delivery of weapons to Turkey because these are also being deployed in the war against the Kurds In Afghanistan, the military successes of the Islamic Mujahaddin terminate the rule of socialist President Mohammed Nadjibullah, who was appointed to office in 1971 by the former Soviet government in Moscow Deng Xiao Ping, since 1989 without official party post, publicly demands liberalization of economics in China; this is later agreed upon at a party convention and allows China the possibility for opening a market economy Israel and People's Republic of China enter into diplomatic relations. China subsequently participates in the Middle East peace conference South Korea and the People's Republic of China enter into diplomatic relations In Pakistan, the former Chief of State Benazir Bhutto is arrested at a demonstration against the government of Nawaz Sharif and expelled from the country Japan passes a constitutional amendment in order to allow for U.N. deployment on peacekeeping missions In South Korea's elections, the opposition part of New Democratic Union beats the incumbent Democratic Liberal Party; with the election of Kim Young Sam, the first civilian in years is elected President Reformist Communists win election in Mongolia By evacuating the military installation at Subic Bay in the Philip- *(contd)*		

D. VISUAL ARTS | E. MUSIC | F. SCIENCE, TECHNOLOGY, GROWTH | G. DAILY LIFE

1992 contd

D. VISUAL ARTS

took place

"documenta 9" exhibit in Kassel, curated by Jan Joet (art history professor in Belgium), portrays modern art as increasingly in need of and dependent upon interpretation, but with few limits imposed on interpretation, includes around 1,000 works by 190 artists

The exhibit "Degenerate Art," assembled in the U.S. with works decried as "degenerate" during the Nazi period, is also on show in Berlin

Critical investigations underway since 1990 reveal that the number of authentic Rembrandts is around 300, not 900 (remaining paintings are those of his students)

At the World Exhibition in Seville, the largest ever exhibit of contemporary Latin American painting opens; 90 artists with about 400 paintings participate

"Shadows and Fog," film by Woody Allen

"The Player," film by Robert Altman

"Batman Returns," Amer. action film by Tim Burton, a comeback attempt for the Batman figure

"Naked Lunch," film by David Cronenberg (b. 1942, U.S.)

E. MUSIC

F. SCIENCE, TECHNOLOGY, GROWTH

produces positive results in treating Parkinson's disease

Discovery of so-called biosignals using high temperature superconductor improves EEG and EKG

Development of a contrast medium for ultrasound examinations broadens the scope of diagnostic potential of this method

Color sonography develops into a viable method of diagnostics

Amer. researchers develop a blood test to detect increased risk in mongolism during pregnancy

Report by the World Wildlife Fund (W.W.F.) determines that the greenhouse effect has already led to a decrease in species diversity on the planet

10-ton fungus mass traced in the state of Michigan below the surface of 37 acres of hardwood forest, making it the largest living organism in the world

According to a report by Amer. scientists, the eruption of the volcano on Mt. Pinatubo in the Philippines caused a worldwide cooling of between 0.2 and 0.3 degrees Celsius

Species homo habilis is determined to be 2.4 million years old (as opposed to 1.9 as previously assumed)

New finds of bird fossils in China cause scientists to classify the archaeopteryx as a subspecies in the evolution of birds (the archaeopteryx had thus far been considered the earliest known bird species)

164-foot-long dinosaur skeleton discovered in the U.S. Dinosaurs are considered by the current state of research to be the largest animal known to have inhabited the planet

Results of studies determine the age of "Ötzi," the Ice Age corpse found in the Oetztal Mountains in 1991, to be 5,300 years (older than originally assumed)

13 million-year-old human jaw discovered in Namibia

The lost city of Ubar, which disappeared 4,000 years ago, was discovered, based on satellite images

Computer networking allows for processing speeds of 1 billion bits per second

Transatlantic fiberglass cable connection completed between the U.S. and Germany. Plans underway for a fiberglass cable connection between the U.S. and Moscow

Construction of a writing computer that can transcribe spoken word

(contd)

G. DAILY LIFE

The first execution in California in 25 years, performed using lethal gas

Computerized speech recognition technologies used as a tool in criminal investigations

City of Berlin awards honorary citizenship to Mikhail Gorbachev, Helmut Kohl, and Ronald Reagan for their contributions to unifying the divided city

2 million refugees from the former Yugoslavia throng into western Europe

Paintings by Lucas Cranach the Elder valued at $7 million are stolen from a collection in Weimar

Terrorist attacks by separatists in Corsica claim over 20 lives

Sicily's Mafia murders three justice department officials and their successors who were considered a threat

Arson attack on an apartment in Möllin, Germany that had been home to a Turkish family for years leaves three dead; fiercely xenophobic rioting by right-wing extremists in Rostock, Germany

Mass grave containing remains of approximately 12,500 dead discovered at the site of the former Soviet concentration camp near Oranienburg

In Colombia, cocaine cartel boss Pablo Escobar (b. 1950) escapes from the "luxury prison" in which he was held after his voluntary surrender

Former dictator of Panama, Manuel Antonio Noriega, deposed by the U.S. with the help of military invasion, is sentenced by a U.S. court to 40 years' imprisonment

200 dead in the military's defeat of a prison rebellion in Brazil

Intense rioting by youth in the streets of Bristol and other cities in U.K.

Fierce racial unrest unleashed in Los Angeles by the acquittal of four police officers charged with beating a black man

Thousands of cult members in South Korea wait in vain for the apocalypse prophesied by the leader of their sect

Number of HIV (AIDS) infected people cited at 10 million (0.2% of the world population)

Nuclear power plant at Chernobyl, Ukraine is shut down, but remains a risk factor due to fallout. Several reactors of the same type remain in operation in the former Soviet Union

As a result of sinking costs, the use of solar energy with photovoltaic collectors is on the rise

Turkey inaugurates the Ataturk Dam System on the upper Euphrates, 118 million kW

So-called space junk left in recent decades presents a serious problem for future projects due to the risk of collision with spacecraft

François Mitterand opens the Olympic Winter Games, in Albertville, France, where 2,300 athletes from 64 nations compete for 171 medals. Medal results (listed in sequence by Gold/Silver/Bronze): 1. F.R.G. 10/10/6;

(contd)

	A. HISTORY, POLITICS	B. LITERATURE, THEATER	C. RELIGION, PHILOSOPHY, LEARNING
1992 contd	pines, the U.S. ends a nearly century-long military presence and relinquishes a major foreign military base Victor in the People's Elections for President in the Philippines is Fidel Ramos, who as Defense Secretary successfully supported his predecessor Corazon Aquino Parliament of Brazil strips President Fernando Collor de Mello of his office on charges of corruption End of the civil war in El Salvador that has been raging since 1980 and claimed approximately 40,000 human lives President of Peru, Alberto Kenya Fujimori uses military force to disable the democratic government In Angola, President José Eduardo dos Santos, in office since 1979, of Soviet-backed MPLA defeats Jonas Savimbi of the U.S.-backed UNITA movement Cease-fire in Mozambique after 16 years of civil war In a referendum on his policies of apartheid, Frederick Willem de Klerk, President of South Africa, receives a two-thirds majority from the white population		
1993	Nobel Peace Prize to Nelson Mandela and Frederik Willem de Klerk for laying the foundations for a new South Africa. New constitution and free elections designed to ensure equal rights between blacks and whites U.S. President George H. W. Bush and Russian President Boris Yeltsin sign the Start II Treaty, calling for a bilateral reduction of strategic nuclear weapons by two thirds over the next ten years In Bali, four-day meeting of representatives from 37 nonaligned states seeking dialogue between developing countries and industrialized nations In Paris, the Organization for the Prohibition of Chemical Weapons (OPCW) is established with the expressed mission of regulating bans on manufacture, possession, storage, acquisition, and deployment of chemical weapons U.S. agrees to drop the Strategic Defense Initiative (SDI) and to terminate its program for stationing missile defense systems in space In Vienna, for the first time in 25 years, a world conference on human rights is sponsored by the U.N. Erich Honecker (b. 1913), former head of state in E. Germany, admits political responsibility for the construction of the Berlin Wall, but rejects personal culpability in the deaths of fugitives. The case against him is dismissed because of his failing health and he emigrates to Chile Arson attack on a building with Turkish residents in Solingen. Three children and two women are killed. In response to the arson attack in Solingen and to changes in laws for asylum seekers, protests and demonstrations held throughout Germany to combat racism and xenophobia The first of a total of 1,700 U.N. peacekeeping troops from the German army arrive in Somalia EU is formally ratified in the Treaty of Maastricht. After fierce internal debates, Denmark and U.K. also join the Union Bill Clinton (b. 1946) inaugurated as President of the United States Thurgood Marshall, Amer. jurist and civil rights activist, fought for equal rights for blacks, d. (b. 1908) Canada's incumbent Progressive Conservative party elects Kim Campbell chair as successor to Brian Mulroney (b. 1939). She thus becomes Prime Minister of Canada Russia, Belarus, and Ukraine resolve to form an economic union as a way of coordinating the transition to a market economy Russian president Boris Yeltsin prevails in a months-long power *(contd)*	Anthony Burgess, British writer, author of "A Clockwork Orange," d. (b. 1917) William Golding, British writer, author of "Lord of the Flies," d. (b. 1911) Joana Maria Gorvin, Ger. actress, famous for her roles in films by director Jürgen Fehling, d. (b. 1922) Masuji Ibuse, Japanese author, considered one of Japan's best narrative writers, d. (b. 1898) Hans Werner Richter, Ger. author, founder of the "Gruppe 47," d. (b. 1908) Nobel Prize for Literature: Amer. writer Toni Morrison (U.S.), author of "Beloved" (1987) and "Jazz" (1992) Peace Prize of the German Booksellers' Association to Friedrich Schorlemmer, Ger. pastor and human rights activist, co-founder of the citizens' movement "Demokratischer Aufbruch" Günter Grass is awarded honorary doctorate by the university in his home town of Danzig as well as honorary citizenship. His most famous novel, "The Tin Drum" takes place in Danzig At the 60th international PEN-Club meeting in Santiago de Compostela, South African, later British dramatist Ronald Harwood is elected President of the organization Rolf Hochhuth (b. 1931): "Wessis in Weimar," play E. Ger. dramatist Heiner Müller admits to having maintained regular contact with the Stasi *(contd)*	Dominique Bozo, Pres. of Centre Pompidou in Paris, d. (b. 1935). He is succeeded by François Barré Leo Löwenthal, Germ.-Amer. sociologist, co-founder of Critical Theory, d. (b. 1900) Cyril Northcote Parkinson, Brit. historian, developed "Parkinson's law" on the growth of bureaucracy, d. (b. 1931) Botho Strauss: "Anschwellender Bockgesang," essay; vindication of conservative, right-wing extremist thought from the perspective of an intellectual, unleashes debate over "right-wing intellectualism" Opening of the United States Holocaust Museum in Washington in the presence of Pres. Bill Clinton. With this design, New York architect James Ingo Freed, who fled Nazi Germany himself, developed an architectural language that memorializes the concentration camps while at the same time seeks to criticize the rationality of annihilation 15th Philosophers' Congress in Berlin focuses on the theme "New Realities: Challenges for Philosophy" and includes presentations by 187 speakers on such topics as business ethics, technological ethics, and the philosophy of law An encyclical published by Pope John Paul II, "Veritatis Splendor" (The Splendor of Truth), forbids artificial birth control. Remarriage is permitted only if it is not consummated sexually Pope conducts mass at the Hill of Crosses near Siaulai, one of Lithuania's most *(contd)*

D. VISUAL ARTS	E. MUSIC	F. SCIENCE, TECHNOLOGY, GROWTH	G. DAILY LIFE	
		into written text (with a limited vocabulary) Element 109 in the Periodic Table is named meitnerium (symbol Mt) in honor of the nuclear physicist Lise Meitner (1878–1968) Development of nanotechnology for dimensions that are less than one billionth of a meter With the help of atomic friction microscopy, an extension of scanning microscopy, scientists succeed in rendering nuclear structure visible Erbium doping of fiberglass has increased the capacity for transmitting information by almost one million times that of 1975	2. C.I.S. 9/6/8; 3. Norway 9/6/5; 4. Austria 6/7/8; 5. U.S. 5/4/2; 6. Italy 4/6/4; 7. France 3/5/1; to 20. North Korea 0/0/1 At the Summer Olympic Games in Barcelona, 172 teams with 10,517 athletes in 25 categories, meet to compete for 260 medals; $700 million spent on rights for television coverage. Medal results (listed in sequence by Gold/Silver/Bronze): 1. C.I.S. 45/38/28; 2. U.S. 34/37/37; 3. F.R.G. 33/21/27; 4. Cuba 14/6/11; 5. Spain 13/7/2; 6. Hungary 11/12/7; 7. South Korea 11/5/12; 8. France 8/5/16; to 25. Thailand 0/0/1 "World Athlete of the Year" is awarded to high jumper Hoika Henkel by the club Bayer Leverkusen; her clear stance on doping is cited as laudable 200 dead and about 800 injured after an explosion (presumably in the sewage system) in Mexico 2,000–3,000 dead after a seaquake off the coast of Indonesia (near Bali) Worst earthquake since 1757 in the Rhine embayment region	**1992 contd**
Charles Moore, Amer. architect, d. (b. 1925) Stella Adler, actress, co-developed method acting with Lee Strasberg d. (b. 1901) Eddie Constantine, Fr. actor, d. (b. 1917) Audrey Hepburn, Amer. actress and special ambassador for U.N.I.C.E.F., d. (b. 1925, Brussels) Inoshiro Honda, Japanese director of monster movies, d. (b. 1911) Elmar Klos, Czech director "The Shop on Main Street," d. (b. 1910) Joseph L. Mankiewicz, Amer. director, "All About Eve," d. (b. 1909) Christian Metz, Fr. cinema studies scholar (semiotics of film), d. (b. 1931) Clint Eastwood, Amer. actor and director wins Oscar as best director for "Unforgiven" Berlin Film Festival Golden Bear to Xie Fei (People's Republic of China) for "The Women from the Lake of Scented Souls" and to Ang Lee (Taiwan) for "The Wedding Banquet" Cannes's Golden Palm to Jane Campion (Australia) for "The Piano" and Chen Kaige (People's Republic of China) for *(contd)*	Maurice Abravanel, Amer. conductor of Portuguese descent, d. (b. 1903) Paolo Bortoluzzi, Ital. dancer, known for leading roles in almost all of Maurice Béjart's ballets, d. (b. 1938) John Campbell, Amer. blues guitarist, d. (b. 1952) Jacques Chazot, Fr. ballet dancer, d. (b. 1928) Agnes de Mille, Amer. choreographer, d. (b. 1909) Christoph Detz, Swiss composer and pianist, d. (b. 1950) Hans Franzen, Ger. bass, d. (b. 1935) Dizzy Gillespie, Amer. jazz trumpeter and founder of bebop, d. (b. 1917, given name John Birks Gillespie) Szymon Goldberg, Polish conductor and violinist who made his debut at 12 years of age, d. (b. 1909) Erich Leinsdorf, Amer. conductor of Austrian descent, d. (b. 1912) Friedrich Meyer, Ger. composer, d. (b. 1915) Rudolf Nureyev, dancer and choreographer whose incredible virtuosity gave new impulses to classical ballet, d. (b. 1938) Gret Palucca, dancer, choreographer and dance instructor who incorporated *(contd)*	Albert Sabin, Amer. physician and inventor of the oral polio vaccine, d. (b. 1906) Nobel Prize for Medicine to Philip R. Sharp (U.S.) and Richard J. Roberts (U.K.) for fundamental contributions to the field of genetic research Nobel Prize for Chemistry to Kary Banks Mullis (U.S.) for the development of a polymerase chain reaction (PCR) for doubling DNA, a prerequisite for creating "genetic fingerprints," and to Michael Smith (Can.) for a procedure to exchange individual nucleotides in DNA strands in order to facilitate "site-directed mutagenesis" Nobel Prize for Physics to Russell A. Hulse (U.S.) and Joseph H. Taylor (U.S.) for the discovery of a new form of celestial body, the double pulsar Nobel Prize for Economics to Robert W. Fogel (U.S.) and Douglass C. North (U.S.) for the application of economic theory to the field of economic history American researchers believe to have discovered the outer edge of the solar system with the help of the Voyager I and II space probes. Theory is based on the observation that, at a distance of between approx. 8 to 11 billion miles from the sun, particles of the solar wind enter interstellar space Astronomers in Hawaii believe to have discovered light rays from *(contd)*	According to a study by the I.L.O. (International Labor Organization), approximately 200 million children are currently subject to abusive labor conditions and denied of their childhood and education Approximately 1.4 billion people live in complete poverty; another billion hover around the poverty line Approximately 700 million people worldwide are either un- or underemployed. As a result of various patterns of migration, 38 million more are added to that number annually More than 2.5 million people in Europe are homeless After 17 years of negotiations, 117 countries become signatories to the General Agreement on Tariffs and Trade (GATT) for worldwide elimination of tariffs and import quotas. For the first time, service industries like banks, insurance, and intellectual properties (patents, trademarks) are included. As a result of resistance from France, film, music, and television productions are not included in the agreement According to GATT statistics, the 1993 world trade volume is up 2.5% from 1992. Better-than-average increases in exports seen in North and South America and in Asia José Ignacio López, Vice Pres. of GM, joins the board of Volkswagen (VW). Auto manufacturer Opel accuses him of having released trade secrets, but there is no evidence to support the claim Chinese People's Congress approves reforms to move toward a "socialist market economy" In the wake of the Maastricht Treaty that established the EU farmers throughout the continent protest reductions in agricultural subsidies *(contd)*	**1993**

	A. HISTORY, POLITICS	B. LITERATURE, THEATER	C. RELIGION, PHILOSOPHY, LEARNING

1993 contd

A. History, Politics

struggle against the old-guard Communist forces in the Supreme Soviet and the Congress of People's Deputies. 59% give him the vote of confidence and approve his plans for economic reform

55% voter turnout in Russia's elections. The referendum on the new constitution with extended executive powers introduced by Yeltsin is approved by a narrow margin. But the reformist parties near the middle receive less than 25% of votes cast. Surprisingly, the ultra-nationalist and reactionary Liberal Democrat party represented by Vladimir Shirinovski is strongest with 24% and the Communist party comes in third with 13%

Conflict spreads in the Caucasus Republics of Georgia, Armenia, and Azerbaijan

Nabiyev, first democratically elected President of Tajikistan, d. (b. 1931)

Baudouin, King of Belgium, d. (b. 1930)

Belgium becomes a federal state. The regions of Flanders, Wallia, and the capital city Brussels receive greater autonomy

Fighting between Muslims and Croats in Bosnia

Warring parties agree to partition Sarajevo into Muslim and Serbian sectors and to allow for temporary U.N.-controlled central administration of the divided city

Airlift initiated by the U.S. from Frankfurt airport to Bosnia delivers supplies to besieged cities of Gorazde, Cerska, Zepa, and Srebrenica

Pierre Eugène Bérégovoy, former French Premier, takes his life four weeks after his resignation, d. (b. 1931)

In elections for the National Assembly in France, Socialist party under François Mitterrand wins only 18% of the votes and 54 seats down from its previous 260. New Premier is Edouard Balladur

In Greece's parliamentary elections PASOK wins with 48.8% of the vote. Andreas Papandreou is charged with forming a government

Joint declaration for peace in Northern Ireland signed by British Prime Minister John Major and his Irish colleague, Albert Reynolds

Jailed Mafia bosses reveal the intimate ties between politics, economics, and the mafia. Ongoing investigations against influential traditionalists like the former Prime Minister and socialist leader Bettino Craxi, Republican leader Ugo La Malfa, as well as against the seven-time Prime Minister Giulio Andreotti; neo-fascists and the New Left profit from the spirit of upheaval

Italians approve a referendum for changing the election system from a proportional system to "winner-takes-all" majority system

Italian Prime Minister Giuliano Amato resigns in order to facilitate a fresh start. President Oscar Luigi Scalfaro delegates the task of building the new administration to the independent Carlo Azeglio Ciampi

Early elections in Yugoslavia and the two constituent republics of Serbia and Montenegro; Socialists led by Slobodan Milosevic win in Serbia, but Democrat Momir Bulatovic, an advocate of equal rights for Serbia and Montenegro, remains President of Montenegro

U.N. General Assembly excludes Yugoslavia from U.N.

In Latvia, the prewar constitution is reinstated. Latvian parliament elects Guntis Ulmanis as President

Markus Püschel (Progressive Citizens' Party) is elected Premier of Lichtenstein, to succeed Hans Brunhart (Union for the Fatherland)

54 years after the invasion of Lithuania by the Soviet army, Russian soldiers leave the country

In parliamentary elections in Norway, the Social Democratic Workers' party of incumbent Prime Minister Gro Harlem Brundtland wins a relative majority with 36.9%

Brabo Pilar, Spanish resistance fighter, later parliamentary representative, chief of police and General Director of Civilian Security d. (b. 1943)

In parliamentary elections in Spain the Socialist Workers' Party wins; *(contd)*

B. Literature, Theater

Harold Pinter: "Moonlight," play

Screen actor Michel Piccoli steals the stage in Luc Bondy's celebrated production of Henrik Ibsen's "John Gabriel Borkman"

Amer. author and director Susan Sontag stages "Waiting for Godot" in occupied Sarajevo

Dutch writer Harry Mulisch gives the keynote address to open the Frankfurt Book Fair, the focus of which is the Netherlands and Flanders

C. Religion, Philosophy, Learning

significant memorials to victims in the fight for freedom from Czarist Russia, National Socialism, and Stalinism

World religions conference in Chicago, the first of its kind since 1893. 6,000 representatives of 125 religious denominations condemn violence and war and advocate respect and tolerance

In the U.S., a group of Adventists led by David Koresh sets fire to a fortress where they have barricaded themselves against the F.B.I. 86 people die in the blaze

Inauguration of the mosque named after King Hassan II in Casablanca, as a birthday present to him. It is considered the most spectacular religious structure in the world. Construction costs were generated from a special tax equal in amount to the annual budget for developmental assistance to Morocco

In a desert region in Egypt, a 20,000 year-old-cave is discovered with paintings depicting everyday life

In the south of Belize in Central America, ruins from four Mayan cities are discovered where an estimated 7,000 inhabitants are presumed to have lived

Terra cotta models of female soldiers are discovered for the first time in the People's Republic of China near the ancient imperial city of Xian. The figures are almost 2,000 years old

Off the coast of the Dalmatian port of Split, remains of a sunken city are found. Archaeologists assume that this may be the Greek city of Sircula

First two volumes of "A History of Women" are issued, edited by Fr. historians Georges Duby and Michelle Perrot

D. VISUAL ARTS	E. MUSIC	F. SCIENCE, TECHNOLOGY, GROWTH	G. DAILY LIFE	

1993 contd

D. Visual Arts

"Farewell, My Concubine"
Fr. Film Award César posthumously awarded Cyril Collard, director and actor in "Savage Nights"
Venice's Golden Lion to Robert Altman (U.S.) for "Short Cuts" and Krzysztof Kieslowski (Fr.) for "Blue"
To mark the 200th anniversary of the establishment of Paris's Louvre, a new museum tract is opened in the Richelieu wing, with President François Mitterand performing the ceremony
Bridge of Mostar, a world heritage monument from the 16th century, destroyed in the war in former Yugoslavia, devastated by a Croatian grenade
In honor of Georg Grosz's 100th birthday, Josef Albers Museum in Bottrop exhibits watercolors and drawings by the artist
Frankfurt's Max Beckmann Prize to the Russian avant garde artist Ilya Kabakov
City of Barcelona, hometown to painter Joan Miró, sponsors a large memorial exhibit with 500 works from his last years on his 100th birthday
A traveling exhibit with 448 previously unknown drawings by Amedeo Modigliani (1884–1920) makes its debut at Venice's Palazzo Grassi
At the international exhibition for the broadcast industry, video artist Nam June Paik shows his work "Turtle," consisting of 166 monitors set in a dome-shaped metal plate to resemble the shell of a turtle. The turtle is a symbol of inner reflection and meditation
45th Biennale in Venice under the motto "Cardinal Directions in Art" with 713 artists from 53 countries
"Malcolm X," a film by Spike Lee, enjoys tremendous success with African-American audiences
"Jurassic Park," with $868
(contd)

E. Music

elements of the Bauhaus movement in her dance, d. (b. 1902)
Lucia Popp, soprano, d. (b. 1939)
Frank Zappa, Amer. rock, jazz, and pop musician and composer, d. (b. 1940)
Hans Zanotelli, Ger. conductor, d. (b. 1928)
Six Grammies to singer and guitarist Eric Clapton
Theodor Adorno's study of Beethoven edited for the first time
Pina Bausch: "Tanzabend I," dance theater
Maurice Béjart: "La Nuit," dance
Jan Gabarek, jazz saxophonist, records the Medieval "Officium" with the Hilliard Ensemble, using saxophone as an additional voice
Philip Glass: "Orphée," opera
John Kander and Fred Ebb: "Kiss of the Spider-woman," musical (Ger. lang. premiere)
Johann Kresnik: "Francis Bacon," dance theater
Leipzig's Gewandhaus Orchestra celebrates its 250th birthday with a special concert conducted by Kurt Masur
Roland Petit: "Dix," opera
Steve Reich/Beryl Korot: "The Cave"
Karl/heinz Stockhausen: "Dienstag aus Licht," opera
Establishment of a documentary center for the life and work of Kurt Weill (1900–50) in his birthplace, Dessau
300-year anniversary of the Leipzig Opera
Heiner Müller's production of Wagner's "Tristan und Isolde" is the most spectacular contribution to this year's Bayreuth Festival

F. Science, Technology, Growth

the most distant galaxy known to man
Using a radar antenna, Amer. scientists captured the most precise images of an asteroid (4179 Toutatis) that came within 2.25 million miles of earth
U.S. space shuttle Columbia launches its D2 mission at Cape Canaveral. The scientific command for the operation is in the hands of 2 Ger. researchers, Hans Schlegel and Ulrich Walter
Amer. space shuttle Endeavor, with 6 astronauts on board, is able to recover the European research satellite EURECA
Japanese satellite makes a crash landing on the moon. Scientists hope to glean insights into landing conditions with the experiment
Physicists at Princeton succeed in producing the world's second largest nuclear fusion to date, producing a controlled fusion reaction whose temperature was three times that of the sun's core
Protozoologists meet in Berlin for their 9th International Congress on Protozoology, where they discuss the alarming spread of parasites and possible strategies for combating them
Bio 93, the first international specialist exhibition for environmental protection, organic food, ecologically sustainable agriculture, health, and hygiene convenes in Dresden
Researchers in Göttingen Germany determine that trees would need 100 years to recover from the effects of acid rain
Skeleton of the most primitive dinosaur to date (225 million years old), about the size of a dog, is found in Argentina
Conclusion of the Biosphere 2 experiment in the Arizona desert. Four men and four women spent two years in a 140 acre, hermetically sealed structure designed to determine whether or not the conditions for life on earth could be reconstructed and exported to other planets. Each of the eight researchers lost one-third their body weight because conditions were not adequate for growing sufficient food resources
For the first time in history, a human embryo is cloned. Americans Jerry Hall and Robert Stillman created two embryos with identical genetic blueprints in culture dishes, which were able to survive in a liquid medium. The ex-
(contd)

G. Daily Life

Limits on imports from South and Central America increase the price of bananas in Europe
Robert W. Kempner, jurist, Amer. deputy prosecutor at the Nuremberg War Crimes Tribunal, d. (b. 1899)
Federal Constitutional Court in Germany decision; homosexual couples have no right to marry
Defendants in the Rodney King beating trial in Los Angeles are found guilty on appeal
James Hunt, 1976 Formula 1 champion, d. (b. 1947)
Number-one ranked world champion women's tennis player Monika Seles is stabbed by a 38-year-old spectator. Steffi Graf moves to number one
Zambia's national soccer team is killed in a plane crash over Central Africa
For the first time, test drive of a passenger train through the 31-mile-long tunnel between U.K. and France
William Randolph Hearst, Jr., Amer. newspaper publisher, d. (b. 1908)
Joseph Pulitzer, Jr., Amer. magazine publisher and journalist, d. (b. 1913)
The most spectacular fall of the season occurs on the catwalk in Paris: Supermodel Naomi Campbell, wearing 10-inch platform shoes, loses her balance and tumbles from the catwalk
Unknown perpetrators commit bombing attack on the World Trade Center in New York. 7 people are killed, 1,000 injured
Massive brush fires devastate valleys near Los Angeles and spread to the city
70,000 people left homeless after flooding of the Mississippi River
The heaviest winter storms in 100 years bring snowfall, hurricanes, and flooding to the U.S., Canada, and the Caribbean; 200 lives lost
Major earthquake in south and west of India claims 10,000 lives
Following a seaquake off the coast of Japan's Okushiri Island, a tremendous wave hits the coast at 500 mph, killing many people
Worst brush fire in 50 years in Australia. The world's second largest national park, Royal National Park, is almost completely destroyed

	A. HISTORY, POLITICS	B. LITERATURE, THEATER	C. RELIGION, PHILOSOPHY, LEARNING

1993 contd

minority coalition government is formed under Prime Minister Felipe González

74 years after its formation, the C.S.S.R. is divided into the Czech and the Slovakian Republic. The first Presidents are Michal Kovác in Bratislava and Vaclav Havel in Prague

Turgut Özal, Turkish president, d. (b. 1927). Successor is Süleyman Demirel; Tansu Çiller, Chair of the True Path Party is charged with forming the government administration of Turkey

Turkish government steps up its efforts against Kurdish population and their political organizations

József Antall, Hungarian prime minister, d. (b. 1932)

Chile's President Patricio Aylwin Azócar retracts his proposal for legal amnesty for crimes committed under the military dictatorship

In Chile's elections, Christian Democrat Eduardo Frei Ruiz-Tagle emerges as victor for the political alliance of Democrat/CPPD, which has been in office since 1990

In Guatemala, Jorge Serrano Elias dissolves the parliament and dismantles portions of the constitution. He is crushed by the military. Parliament elects Ramiro de Leon Carpio as President

Last of Soviet troops leave Cuba

Juan Carlos Wasmosy becomes new President of Paraguay

Ezer Weizmann is sworn in as new President of Israel at the Knesset

Israeli Foreign Minister Shimon Peres and PLO-representative Mahmoud Abbas sign an agreement over Palestinian self-rule and formalize mutual recognition of Israel and the PLO. PLO chairman Y. Arafat and Israeli Premier Yitzak Rabin shake hands

Israel and the Vatican begin diplomatic relations

Newly elected President of Burundi Melchior Ndadaye is killed in a military putsch which reignites civil war

In a referendum in Eritrea, 99.8% of voters approve the Ethiopian independence

After failed attempts to reach a cease-fire between warring parties in Somalia, U.N. responds with military intervention. U.N. actions are met with international criticism, causing the U.S. and Germany to withdraw their troops

After nearly 10 years of military dictatorship, the first free elections in Nigeria. But the military ousts the civilian government after only five months

Oliver Tambo, South African resistance fighter, President of the A.N.C., d. (b. 1918)

Transitional government formed in South Africa from members of the incumbent National Party and the A.N.C.

U.N. General Assembly lifts all economic sanctions against South Africa

The bloody fighting between Hindus and Muslims in India continues. No debates within government

Kakuei Tanaka, Japanese politician, prime minister 1972–74, d. (b. 1918)

In Japan, a no-confidence vote against the administration of Prime Minister Kiichi Miyazawa. Parliamentary elections seat Mohiri Hosokawa as new Prime Minister. Liberal Democratic Party forfeits its absolute majority for the first time since 1955

In Cambodia, the first free elections in twenty years are held to determine the constitutional assembly with voter turnout at approximately 90%. In the constitutional session, Prince Sihanouk is formally named head of state in a transitional government

Following criticism directed at the government in Pakistan, Prime Minister Nawaz Sharif and President Ghulam Ishaq Khan resign. Pakistan Peoples Party wins new elections Benazir Bhutto returns to her post as chief of state after 17 years

President Ranasinghe Premadasa of Sri Lanka is assassinated in a bombing at a demonstration. He is succeeded by Dingiri Banda Wijetunge, former Prime Minister

Australian parliament abolishes the pledge to Queen Elizabeth II in its swearing-in ceremony for new citizens

D. VISUAL ARTS	E. MUSIC	F. SCIENCE, TECHNOLOGY, GROWTH	G. DAILY LIFE	
million in ticket sales, most successful film ever in the U.S.		periment is met with worldwide shock In the U.K., controversial genetic therapy is used for the first time to treat a child suffering from a fatal immune deficiency disease Luc Montaignier, Fr. discoverer of the AIDS virus, joins with U.N.E.S.C.O. to form an international foundation for the research and prevention of AIDS in Paris World Health Organization (W.H.O.) estimates that 14 million people worldwide are infected with the AIDS virus. Number of new HIV infections in developing nations could be reduced by one half with an investment of $1.5 to 2 million, according to the W.H.O. Span. Medical scientists attribute the spread of a mysterious eye disease that has afflicted 48,000 people in Cuba to environmental factors The first robot able to work .62 miles below the surface of water is developed in a joint venture between GKSS Research Center and Siemens Corporation. It is scheduled for use in discovering natural gas and crude oil reserves in Brazil In India, the largest dam project in the world is built in order to utilize the Narmada River for irrigation purposes, but the project also involves uprooting 100,000 people and ecological disasters such as flooding		1993 contd

	A. HISTORY, POLITICS	B. LITERATURE, THEATER	C. RELIGION, PHILOSOPHY, LEARNING

1994

A. History, Politics

Nobel Peace Prize to leader of the Palestine Liberation Organization (PLO) Y. Arafat, Israeli Prime Minister Yitzhak Rabin, and Israeli Foreign Minister Shimon Peres for their contributions to the Middle East peace process

In France, celebrations of the 50th anniversary of the Allied landing in Normandy and the end of the Second World War. As an expression of the desire for a united Europe, German tanks participate in the parade in Paris on July 14

Defense budgets for N.A.T.O. countries in 1994/95, in billions of dollars: Belgium 1.397; Denmark 1.125; F.R.G. 14.786; France 17.987; Greece—figures not available; U.K. 18.319; Italy 7.456; Canada 6.926; Luxembourg 0.065; Netherlands 3.837; Norway 1.955; Portugal .402; Spain—figures not available; Turkey 6.866; U.S. 202.934

N.A.T.O. ratifies "Partnership for Peace" program designed to encourage cooperation with Central and Eastern European nations on military and security issues

Trilateral Treaty between Presidents Clinton (U.S.), Yeltsin (Russia), and Kravchuk (Ukraine) on the destruction of all remaining 176 former Soviet missiles in Ukraine with a total of 1,800 nuclear warheads

U.S. and Russia sign a pact for closing all nuclear facilities by the year 2000. Weapons production from new plutonium is prohibited

José Ayala Lasso assumes his post as U.N. High Commissioner for Human Rights at the rank of U.N. Secretary General. His task is to monitor guarantees of individual rights to freedom and civil rights and to continue to advocate the realization of economic and social rights

Erich Honecker, last chief of state of G.D.R. (1976–89); charges against him for manslaughter, breach of public trust, and abuse of office were dropped in 1993 based on his failing health, d. (b. 1913). He died in Santiago, Chile

Manfred Wörner, former W. Ger. Defense Minister, Secretary General of N.A.T.O. until 1994, d. (b. 1934)

Federal Assembly in Bonn elects Roman Herzog to the office of President in Germany

First woman to assume the rank of General in German military history, V von Weymarn, accepts her post as Surgeon General of the Air Force

50 years after the Red Army marched into Germany, Russian troops leave Germany

Ger. Constitutional Court loosens restrictions on the use of hashish, determining that people experimenting with the drug and occasional consumers may be prosecuted only in exceptional cases

207 million eligible voters in the first direct election of a European Parliament for a total of 567 seats; K. Hänisch from Germany is elected president of European Parliament

Precursor to the European Central Bank, the European Currency Institute begins operations

Ukrainian President Kravchuk signs partnership and cooperation treaty with EU in Luxembourg

Richard Nixon, former Pres. of U.S. (1969–74), d. (b. 1913)

U.S. lifts the trade embargo against Vietnam, in place since 1964

U.S. congressional and gubernatorial races produce heavy losses for Bill Clinton's Democratic Party. Republican majority in both houses

Russia grants amnesty to participants in the 1991 putsch against M. Gorbachev and against Yeltsin in 1993

Withdrawal of the last remaining Russian troops in the Baltic states

Russia and People's Republic of China agree to establish a "constructive partnership"; in the future, nuclear missiles will be targeted at sea, not at each other

Air strikes and invasion of Russian troops in Chechnya to prevent the republic's secession from the federation

Georgia joins the Commonwealth of Independent States (C.I.S.)

Belarus signs treaty with Russia on currency union and thus becomes part of the ruble zone

(contd)

B. Literature, Theater

Jean-Louis Barrault, Fr. actor and director, d. (b. 1910)

Charles Bukowski, Amer. writer, d. (b. 1920)

Elias Canetti, Germ.-speaking writer of Spanish descent and Brit. nationality, wrote, among other things, "Auto-da-Fé," "Crowds and Power," "The Tongue Set Free," and "The Torch in My Ear"; Nobel laureate, 1981, d. (b. 1905)

Eugène Ionesco, Fr. author of Romanian descent, primary representative of the Theater of the Absurd, (plays, among others, "Bald Soprano," "The Chairs," "Rhinoceros,") d. (b. 1909)

Walter Janka, Ger. publicist, former CEO Aufbau publisher, d. (b. 1914)

Kurt Meisel, Ger. actor, d. (b. 1912)

John Osborne, Brit. dramatist, d. (b. 1929)

Russian writer A. Solzhenitsyn returns to his native Russia after 20 years in exile

Helen Wolff, Amer. publisher of European literature, d. (b. 1908)

Nobel Prize for Literature to Japanese writer Kenzaburō Ōe, author of, among other books, "A Personal Matter" and "Teach Us to Outgrow Our Madness"

Peace Prize of the German Booksellers' Association to Span. writer Jorge Semprun, author of, "Literature or Life," a treatment of his experiences in the concentration camp at Buchenwald

Franz Xaver Kroetz: "Der Drang," play

Jakob Michael Reinhold Lenz's (1751–92) long lost work published, "Philosophische Vorlesungen für empfindsame Seelen"

Physician and writer Taslima Nasrin leaves her native country of Bangladesh because she's been threatened by Islamic fundamentalists for her critical interpretation of the Koran. She finds refuge in Sweden

World's most comprehensive encyclopedia, "Encyclopedia Britannica," ceases to produce an annual edition in 30 volumes, 6 feet long and 120 pounds in weight, and switches instead to the CD format, 4¾ inches in diameter

C. Religion, Philosophy, Learning

Paul Feyerabend, scholar and theoretician, d. (b. 1924)

Robert Jungle, futurologist, d. (b. 1913)

Yeshayahu Leibowitz, Israeli philosopher, d. (b. 1902, Riga)

Karl Raimund Popper, philosopher, primary proponent of critical rationalism, d. (b. 1902)

Opening of a memorial in Port Bou, Spain, to philosopher Walter Benjamin (1892–1940), who committed suicide there while fleeing from the Gestapo

Louis Begley's "Lügen in Zeiten des Krieges" ("Wartime Lies"), a moving autobiographical report on children in Poland who were persecuted by the National Socialists

Raul Hilberg: "Unerbetene Erinnerung. Der Weg eines Holocaust Forschers," autobiographical treatment of the author's groundbreaking work on the extermination of the Jews

Pope John Paul II reiterates his adamant refusal to ordain women as priests

Pope visits Zagreb. A visit to the besieged city of Sarajevo is cancelled due to security concerns

An assembly of 86 Protestant churches throughout Europe publishes a document on "The Church of Jesus Christ," outlining the nature of the church, its social and ecumenical duties

Church of England begins ordination of women

D. VISUAL ARTS	E. MUSIC	F. SCIENCE, TECHNOLOGY, GROWTH	G. DAILY LIFE	
Max Bill, Swiss Bauhaus student, painter, sculptor, designer, architect, d. (b. 1908) Donald Judd, Amer. sculptor, his metal sculptures introduced new variations of minimalist art in 1965, d. (b. 1928) Rearrangement of pictures in Berlin's Neue Nationalgalerie provokes debate: Curator Honisch places works by 3 E. Ger. artists W. Sitte, W. Mattheuer, and W. Tübke beside those of Kapheck, Vostell, and Bacon rather than banning them from the gallery altogether, as expected Tengiz Abuladze, Georgian director ("Repentance"), d. (b. 1924) Lindsay Anderson, Brit. director ("If"), d. (b. 1923) Axel Corti, director of Ger. films, d. (b. 1933) Joseph Cotton, Amer. actor, d. (b. 1905) Dolly Haas, Brit. actress, d. (b. 1910) Derek Jarman, Brit. director, most recently, "Wittgenstein" and "Blue," d. (b. 1942) Burt Lancaster, Amer. actor ("The Leopard"), d. (b. 1913) Myrna Loy, Amer. screen actress ("The Thin Man"), d. (b. 1905) Giulietta Masina, Ital. actress ("La Strada"), d. (b. 1908) Fernando Rey, Span. actor ("The Discreet Charm of the Bourgeoisie"), d. (b. 1917) Telly Savalas, Amer. actor ("Kojak"), d. (b. 1924) Terrence Young, Brit. director (James Bond movies), d. (b. 1915) Mai Zetterling, Swedish actress and director, d. (b. 1926) Pepe Danquart, Ger. director wins an Oscar for his short film "Schwarzfahrer" ("Black Rider") Steven Spielberg's "Schindler's List" receives Oscar for best Amer. feature film After winning in 1990 and 1992, Ital. director Gianni Amelio takes home his *(contd)*	Aldo Baldin, Brazil. tenor, d. (b. 1945) Cab Calloway, Amer. jazz performer and band leader, d. (b. 1917) Kurt Cobain, Amer. Rock guitarist, lead singer of the group Nirvana and idol of his generation, d. (b. 1967) William Chappel, Brit. dancer, choreographer, and set designer, d. (b. 1908) Gottlob Frick, Ger. bass, d. (b. 1906) Lejaren Hiller, Amer. composer and computer music pioneer, d. (b. 1924) Antonio Carlos Jobim, Brazil. pianist, songwriter, singer; creator of the Bossa Nova, d. (b. 1927) Witold Lutoslavski, Polish composer, together with Penderecki, considered a leading figure in Polish contemporary music, d. (b. 1913) Henry Mancini, Amer. film composer ("Moon River," "The Pink Panther"), d. (b. 1924) Milton "Shorty" Rogers, Amer. jazz trumpet player, d. (b. 1923 or 1924) Harry Nilsson, Amer. singer and composer, d. (b. 1952) Vittorio Rieti, Amer. composer of Ital. descent, d. (b. 1898) Jule Styne, Amer. composer of musicals, d. (b. 1906) Tatiana Troyanos, Amer. (of Ger./Greek parents) mezzo soprano, d. (b. 1938) City of Frankfurt music award to Brit. musician Brian Eno Austrian conductor Nikolaus Harnancourt and Amer. jazz musician Quincy Jones awarded the Swedish Polar Music Award Ingomar Grünauer: "Winterreise," opera about Walter Benjamin's attempts to escape the Gestapo Johann Kresnik: "Ernst Jünger," dance piece depicting the author Ernst Jünger as someone who glorified war *(contd)*	Erik Erikson, Amer. psychologist of German descent, d. (b. 1902) Nobel Prize for Economics to John F. Nash (U.S.), John C. Harsanyi (U.S.), and Reinhard Selten (F.R.G.) for their analysis of equilibria in the theory of noncooperative games Nobel Prize for Physics to Clifford Shull (U.S.) and Bertram Brockhouse (Can.) a half-century after their discoveries in the field of neutron scattering techniques Nobel Prize for Chemistry to George Olah (U.S.) for his contributions in the field of carbocation chemistry Nobel Prize for Medicine to Alfred Gilman (U.S.) and Martin Rodbell (U.S.) for discovery of G-proteins and their significance in cells Astronomers observe as fragments of the comet "Shoemaker Levy 9" plunge into the atmosphere of Jupiter at a speed of about 124,000 mph German-Canadian team of astronomers discover a star with a luminosity of over 1 million suns, 6,000 light years from Earth Astronomic measurements provided by the Hubble space telescope indicate that the universe is only 8 billion years old, half what was previously assumed On its mission to study the magnetic field of the Sun, the European space probe Ulysses becomes the first artificial celestial body to fly over the south pole of the Sun 7 new moons discovered in a ring of Saturn At the Fermi Lab in Chicago, discovery of the top quark with a mass of 174 gigaelectron volts The heaviest elements (Nos. 110 and 111) to date are produced using the heavy ion accelerator in Darmstadt Record temperatures of 450 degrees C (842 degrees F) generated at a fusion reactor in Princeton (U.S.) After four years in operation, the continental drilling program in Windischeschenbach whose mission was to study the earth's crust, is halted. The drill hole is 5.6 miles deep For the first time ever, a robot in Alaska is able to produce photographs from inside an active volcano. The device should help to predict future eruptions with more precision In Ethiopia, the oldest prehistoric human bones (4.4 million years *(contd)*	Signing of the NAFTA treaty formalizes free trade zone between Canada, U.S., and Mexico. With 360 million consumers, it is the world's largest free trade zone For the first time since WW II, the U.S. dollar drops below the 100 yen mark in Tokyo Auto manufacturer BMW opens its first foreign production plant in Spartanburg, SC Farmers and consumers in the U.S. dump gallons of milk in the streets of major cities to protest use of bovine growth hormones (rBGH) in order to increase milk production Auto manufacturer VW introduces the 28.8 hour work week without full wage compensation for its employees in Germany Physician Manuel Patarroyo (Colombia) donates his patent on malaria vaccination to the W.H.O. (World Health Organization) After two decades of international pursuit, "Carlos" (Illich Ramírez Sánchez) is finally apprehended in the Sudan. He has been wanted in Germany as a suspect in the massacre of Israeli athletes at the Olympic Games in Munich 1972 and for the attack on a Fr. cultural center in Berlin 1983 Most spectacular criminal trial in history against the football star O.J. Simpson, who is suspected of murdering his wife and her boyfriend 10.5 ounces of nuclear grade plutonium-239 confiscated at the airport in Munich For the first time in their history, the Winter Olympic Games in Lillehammer take an ecologically conscious approach. From now on, summer and winter games will no longer be held in the same year, but separately in two year intervals Medal results of the Winter Olympic Games in Lillehammer (Gold/Silver/Bronze): Russia 11/8/4; Norway 10/11/5; Germany 9/7/8; Italy 7/5/8; U.S. 6/5/2; S. Korea 4/1/1; Canada 3/6/4; Switzerland 3/4/2; Austria 2/3/4; Sweden 2/1/0; Japan 1/2/2; Australia 0/0/1 Soccer match between U.K. and Germany scheduled to take place on Hitler's birthday is called off due to security concerns Colombian soccer player Andres Escobar is shot by a fanatic in Colombia after he scored a goal for the opposing team in a World Cup match against the U.S. 20 years after being defeated by Muhammad Ali, heavyweight boxer George Foreman regains his world champion title Jack Sharkey, former world champion boxer and 1930 opponent of Max Schmelling, d. (b. 1903) Opening by Fr. Prime Minister F. Mitterand and Brit. Queen Elizabeth II of the approx. 31-mile-long Eurotunnel beneath the English Channel, the first link between U.K. and continental Europe since the Ice Age. It is the world's second longest tunnel, following Japan's Seikan Tunnel which connects the islands of Honshu and Hokkaido *(contd)*	**1994**

	A. HISTORY, POLITICS	B. LITERATURE, THEATER	C. RELIGION, PHILOSOPHY, LEARNING
1994 contd	Serbs continue attacks on Bosnian cities N.A.T.O. fighter jets attack Serbian military aircraft and tankers in N.A.T.O.'s first combat mission since its establishment in 1949 Muslims and Croats form the Federation of Bosnia-Herzegovina with a federation government consisting of 10 Muslims, 6 Croats, and 1 Serb. Bosnian Croat Kresimer Zuback becomes President of the new state Bosnian government calculates the cost of civil war: 142,595 Muslim deaths, over 162,000 wounded. The number of deaths among Croats is estimated at 50,000 In the first direct election of the head of state in Finland, Martti Ahtisaari is elected new president Law for the preservation of Fr. language in France seeks to restrict the use of foreign language terms in the media and official government publications Melina Mercouri, Greek politician and actress, d. (b. 1925) After 25 years, IRA decides to halt violence. First peace talks with the Brit. government. Protestant terrorist groups in Northern Ireland also agree to a cease-fire In London, South Africa is solemnly sworn back into the Commonwealth Italian Prime Minister Carlo Azeglio Ciampi resigns in the interest of allowing a re-vote. Milan media tycoon S. Berlusconi and his right-wing extremist alliance of nationalist parties win absolute majority in Italy and he is sworn in as the country's 53rd Prime Minister after WW II. After only seven months, Berlusconi resigns in the wake of investigations of corruption Croatia and the Yugoslav Federation sign agreement on normalization of relations to end the war Surprising victory for the Democratic Agrarian Party (ex-communist) in Moldavia Moldavia joins the Commonwealth of Independent States (C.I.S.) Changes in the Netherlands' immigration laws allow for deportation of any persons applying for political asylum who enter through third world countries that are considered safe Frisian is adopted as second official language of the Netherlands For the first time since 1917, Christian Democrats are no longer the largest majority in Dutch parliament after the elections. Wim Kok (Labor Party) becomes new head of state J. Jorgen Holst, Norwegian politician, last held office as foreign minister; he and his wife, M. Heiberg, were negotiators in secret talks between Israel and the PLO that led to the Gaza-Jericho Treaty, d. (b. 1937) In Ukraine's first free parliamentary elections under the new winner-takes-all majority system, the independent Vital Massol becomes Prime Minister, and in the presidential election, Leonid D. Kutschma is chosen as head of state Socialist party wins in Hungary's parliamentary elections. Gyula Horn becomes Prime Minister 19 Latin American nations as well as Portugal and Spain consolidate efforts to integrate according to the European model in the "Declaration of Cartagena" In Argentina elections are held for a Constitutional Assembly to revise the terms of its 1853 constitution Protected by U.S. troops as requested by U.N., President Jean Bertrand Aristide returns to Haiti and resumes control of government after the military junta surrounding Gen. R. Cédras steps down. Aristide was forced into exile after a 1991 military putsch Number of Cuban refugees to Florida increases drastically, with many risking their lives in an attempt to flee. U.S. prohibits overseas payments by Cuban exiles and sets limits on Cuban immigration and refugees Uprisings on the part of the indigenous Zapatista National Liberation Army in Chiapas, Mexico, the poorest state in the country. Indigenous people of Chiapas demand an end to human rights violations against them First democratic parliamentary and presidential elections in 25 years *(contd)*		

D. VISUAL ARTS

3rd Felix (European film award), this time for his "Lamerica"
Berlin Film Festival's Golden Bear to Irish director Jim Sheridan for "In the Name of the Father"
Cannes's Golden Palm to Quentin Tarantino (U.S.) for "Pulp Fiction" starring J. Travolta
Fr. film award César to Alain Resnais's "Smoking/No Smoking"
Comprehensive retrospective of the photographic works of Richard Avedon
Bulgarian-born artist Christo and his wife Jeanne-Claude finally receive approval for the project to wrap the Reichstag, which they have been hoping to do since 1965
Major retrospective of the works of George Grosz, Ger. painter and illustrator, in Berlin
Comprehensive retrospective of the works of Dada artist Raoul Hausmann in Berlin
A painting by Caspar David Friedrichs on loan from the Hamburg Gallery as well as two paintings by William Turner on loan from London's Tate Gallery are stolen from an exhibit ("Goethe und die Kunst") in Frankfurt's Schirn Gallery
In Groningen (Netherlands), Queen Beatrix inaugurates a new art museum, which features a yellow tower sculpture designed by Milan's Allessandro Mendini protruding from an artificial island
Michelangelo's Sistine Chapel frescos emerge with fresh brilliance after 14 years of restoration
Works of Amer. pop artist Robert Rauschenberg on exhibit in Düsseldorf
Ger. Chancellor Helmut Kohl opens museum of German history in Bonn
Historical opera house in Barcelona, Gran Teatro del Liceo, is destroyed by fire
The Zisterzienserklosters cloister in Maulbronn, built in 1147 and consid-
(contd)

E. MUSIC

John Neumeier: "Trilogie M.R.," ballet
Richard Wagner's unfinished opera "Wahnopfer" is premiered in Rudolfstadt
Robert Wilson stages Puccini's "Madame Butterfly" in Paris, musical direction by Myung-Whun Chung
Long-standing, renowned music publisher Breitkopf & Härtel celebrates 275th anniversary at the Gewandhaus in Leipzig
The three tenors José Carreras, Placido Domingo, and Luciano Pavarotti attract over 1 billion television viewers with their concert in Dodger Stadium on the eve of the soccer World Cup in Los Angeles
Pop marriage of the year: Lisa Marie Presley (only daughter of Elvis Presley) marries pop star Michael Jackson in the Dominican Republic
25 years after Woodstock, the Woodstock Revival Festival takes place in Saugerties, NY

F. SCIENCE, TECHNOLOGY, GROWTH

old) are discovered. This contradicts the theory that the first humans originated in Asia
Scientists who discovered a human tibia in southern England estimate that the oldest European is 500,000 years old
U.S. permits the sale of genetically altered tomatoes
According to research results of the Univ. of Vienna, Alpine plants are growing at increasingly high altitude regions in the Alps, which is seen as an index of the greenhouse effect
An Australian researcher succeeds in freezing human ova in a nitrogen solution at -196 degrees C (–385 degrees F)
First laser surgery performed in Germany on an infant in the womb
Two Amer. research teams independently discover a gene that may be responsible for about a third of all hereditary forms of gastrointestinal cancer
New ceramic material for filling small dental cavities presented at the World Health Day in Geneva
Clinical experiments with the abortion pill RU-486 (morning after pill) begin in the U.S.
Amer. researchers develop a light-refracting plastic that could be used to develop high-performance computers powered by light instead of electricity

G. DAILY LIFE

1992 Rio de Janeiro Convention on Climate Change goes into effect
Based on financial difficulties and energy shortages, the nuclear power plant at Chernobyl in the Ukraine is not shut down as scheduled. The 1986 accident there resulted in 8,000 deaths and 30,000 permanently disabled. Incidence of cancer, infant deaths, deformities, and general mortality rate have increased drastically. The fate of 600,000 people who came to Chernobyl as "volunteer aides" is unknown
Supreme Court in Alaska orders Exxon oil corporation to pay billions of dollars in compensatory damages to fishermen adversely affected by the 1989 tanker disaster
100 people dead, 231 wounded after an attack on a Jewish center in Buenos Aires
Black Death epidemic returns to India; hundreds afflicted
Biggest accident in European waterways since WW II: Estonian ferry *Estonia* sinks in the Baltic Sea off the coast of Finland, over 900 dead
Brush fires lead to the biggest fire catastrophe in the history of Australia. Some fires caused by arson
Worst earthquake since 1971 in southern California; Los Angeles particularly hard hit, 60 dead
Flooding disaster in Nepal, over 1,000 people perish
Colombian earthquake claims 628 lives

	A. HISTORY, POLITICS	B. LITERATURE, THEATER	C. RELIGION, PHILOSOPHY, LEARNING
1994 contd	in Panama. Ernesto P. Balladares becomes head of state. Beginning of U.S. troop withdrawal from Panama First general elections since the end of civil war in El Salvador are monitored by the U.N. In the presidential election, Arena Party candidate A. Calderón Sol is victor Bombing of a mosque in Hebron by an Israeli settler. 29 Palestinians killed while at prayer, over 300 wounded. Dozens of Israeli settlers killed by Palestinian extremists in revenge In a "Declaration of Principles," Israel and Palestine agree on provisions for partial Palestinian autonomy in the Gaza Strip and the West Bank Withdrawal of Israeli troops from the occupied Gaza Strip. The first of Palestinian police take control. Palestinian leader Y. Arafat returns to his native land after 27 years in exile Vatican and PLO establish diplomatic relations Yitzhak Rabin is the first Israeli head of state to visit Moscow Israeli Prime Minister Rabin and Jordan's King Hussein sign peace agreement to end 46 years of animosity and war between the two countries 4 years after the start of the crisis in the Gulf, Iraq recognizes current borders of the Emirate of Kuwait and thus fulfills one of the primary prerequisites to lifting the U.N. embargo Civil war between North and South Yemen. Socialist government of S. Yemen declares independence from N. Yemen and founds the Democratic Republic of Yemen. Civil war ends when N. Yemen seizes the port city of Aden Change in election law in Kuwait. Kuwaitis born in Kuwait, but whose fathers were naturalized citizens are given the right to vote; but women are still not allowed to vote The Presidents of Rwanda and Burundi, J. Habyarimana and C. Ntaryamira, are assassinated when their plane is shot down. Civil war breaks out yet again as a result First free elections in Malawi. Victor is the Democratic Front led by B. Muluzi First free elections in Mozambique Over 250,000 people a day fleeing the deteriorating situation in Rwanda to Tanzania in one of the most extensive refugee movements in history. Aid organizations estimate ½ million people killed in the civil wars "Operation Turquoise": U.N. sends international intervention troops under Fr. leadership to protect the civilian population in Rwanda After seizing the capital Kigali and other cities, rebels in the Rwandan Patriotic Front declare an end to their war against government troops and install a transitional government. The ensuing withdrawal of U.N. troops unleashes another flood of refugees fleeing the country. Withdrawal of Amer. and Europ. military units sent in conjunction with the U.N. mission in Somalia Black South African Nelson Mandela elected President in first democratic elections in South Africa. ANC receives 62.7%, de Klerk's National Party 20.2%, and the Zulu Inkatha Movement 10.5%. New South African constitution goes into effect. It outlaws racial discrimination, calls for a dissolution of the homelands, replaces them with provinces, and establishes a human rights charter and a constitutional court. Vatican and South Africa enter diplomatic relations Election of a Constitutional Assembly in Uganda Japanese Prime Minister Hosokawa resigns after 8 months in office under bribery allegations. His successor T. Hata only remains in office for two months. For the first time since 1948, a Social Democrat, T. Murayama, is elected Prime Minister Kim Il Sung, North Korean head of state, d. (b. 1912) After 50 years, South Korea lifts trade embargo against North Korea In parliamentary elections in Sri Lanka, the left-leaning People's Alliance beats the United National Party. Ch. Kumaratunga first becomes Prime Minister; she subsequently becomes President		

D. VISUAL ARTS	E. MUSIC	F. SCIENCE, TECHNOLOGY, GROWTH	G. DAILY LIFE	
ered one of the best-preserved medieval cloisters in the world, is added to the U.N.E.S.C.O. list of world cultural monuments. The old city center in Bamberg is also added to the list as one of the best preserved old city centers in Germany Paris's Grand Palais museum exhibit: "Impressionism—the Origins 1859–1869" Censorship board in Brit. prohibits delivery of the D.W. Griffith classic "Birth of A Nation" on VHS because the film presents the U.S. Civil War from a racist perspective				**1994 contd**

	A. HISTORY, POLITICS	B. LITERATURE, THEATER	C. RELIGION, PHILOSOPHY, LEARNING

1995

A. HISTORY, POLITICS

U.N.E.S.C.O. Peace Prize to former U.S. president Jimmy Carter for his peace missions in Korea, Haiti, and Bosnia, and to Spain's King J. Carlos for his role in the transition from the Franco-dictatorship to democracy

180 nations represented at the World Summit for Social Development in Copenhagen agree to issue a "declaration" and develop an "action programme," both of which are more or less symbolic in nature. No one agrees to binding obligations

Günter Guillaume, E. German spy whose affiliations with Willy Brandt played a major role in Brandt's resignation as Chancellor, d. (b. 1929)

Schengen Treaty goes into effect, eliminating border controls between Germany, France, Belgium, the Netherlands, Luxembourg, Portugal, and Spain

New President of the EU Commission: J. Delors of Fr. is succeeded by Santer from Luxembourg

J. William Fulbright, U.S. Senator from Arkansas 1944–74, d. (b. 1905)

Les Aspin, Amer. military analyst and briefly U.S. Secretary of Defense, d. (b. 1939)

Negotiations between the U.S. and Cuba over Cuban refugees

Republican representatives' efforts to revitalize the SDI program are vetoed in the first round in U.S. Congress

Amer. Gulf War veterans file class action suit against several Ger. companies for compensatory damages because the companies made deliveries to factories producing poison gasses

20 years after the end of the Vietnam War, R. McNamara, then-U.S. Secretary of Defense, says that the war in Vietnam was a mistake

Russia struggles to deal with conflicts arising from a flood of Russian refugees from other countries into the former republics. The number of refugees and resettlements is estimated at 3 million

A referendum in Belarus shows clear majority in favor of closer ties with Russia

New Bulgarian cabinet led by the socialist Schan Widenow

In Finland's elections, Social Democrats, previously the opposition party, emerge as the strongest party

Christian Pineau, former Fr. Foreign Minister, d. (b. 1905)

In France's presidential election, J. Chirac wins by a slim margin over L. Jospin in the second round. In the first round, contender E. Balladur was surprisingly weak. Chirac will succeed F. Mitterand as President. Alain Juppé is named new Prime Minister of France and current Interior Minister Ch. Pasqua is replaced by Jean-Louis Debré

Konstantinos Stephanopoulos becomes President of Greece

Harold Wilson, former Prime Minister of Great Britain, d. (b. 1916)

Former Italian Prime Minister Andreotti is accused of having had Mafia ties

Milovan Djilas, Yugoslav. dissident, d. (b. 1911)

Jean-Claude Juncker (Christian Socialist People's Party) becomes Premier of Luxembourg

Swedish navy admits that what they thought were Russian submarines and had been pursuing as such for several years were in fact small furry animals: mink

Dispute between Spain and Canada over fishing rights off the coast of Canada

Spanish police in Catalonia and Basque regions apprehend 14 members of the separatist organization ETA

Turkish military actions against Kurds extend beyond the country's borders

Carlos Menem is reelected president of Argentina

Peru's incumbent President A Fujimori wins elections against his competitor, former U.N. Secretary General Pérez de Cuéllar

Mehdi Bazargan, former Prime Minister of Iran, d. (b. 1909)

Bloodbath after a bomb attack at a bus stop north of Tel Aviv in Israel

Following a massacre at a refugee camp in Rwanda, hundreds of thousands flee to the provincial capital of Butaré

Withdrawal of the last U.N. troops from Somalia

(contd)

B. LITERATURE, THEATER

Gustave Lübbe, Ger. publisher ("King of the dime novel"), d. (b. 1918)

Jean-Patrick Manchette, Fr. writer, credited with having given the detective novel a comeback, d. (b. 1942)

Azeddine Medjoubi, director of the Algerian national theater, presumably shot down by Islamic fundamentalists, d. (b. 1945)

Rachid Mimouni, Algerian writer, d. (b. 1945)

Onoe Baiko VII, star of Japanese Kabuki theater, d. (b. 1916)

Peace Prize of the German Booksellers' Assoc. to the Orientalist Annemarie Schimmel

The New Yorker names T. Stoppard's comedy "Arcadia" best drama of the year and T. McNally's "Love! Valour! Compassion!" as best new Amer. piece

Adonis, Lebanese lyric poet, and his Palestinian publicist are barred from the Syrian branch of the Arab writers' association. Both favored a cultural normalization of the "Zionist entity" (Israel)

The first play Samuel Beckett (1906–89) ever wrote in the Fr. language, "Eleutheria," which the author did not wish to have published, is published in Paris

Within days after its publication, the autobiography of South African President Nelson Mandela becomes the biggest success ever in South African publishing

Wei Jingheng, dissident and writer incarcerated in the People's Republic of China, receives Stockholm's Olof Palme Prize in absentia

Tom Stoppard's play "Indian Ink" premieres in London

New volume of Jean-Paul Sartre's (1905–80) war diaries discovered

Four of Amer. poet Walt Whitman's notebooks, which had disappeared from the Library of Congress during WW II, resurface at Sotheby's auction house

Lufthansa's human relations department writes an open letter defending its decision not to allow Salman Rushdie to fly with the airline. Rushdie's supporters had organized a boycott of the airline

The Iranian government indicates that it will no longer issue death threats to the author S. Rushdie

For the first time since the revolution, books from the U.S. are exhibited in Cuba

C. RELIGION, PHILOSOPHY, LEARNING

Joseph Bochenski, Dominican patriarch and philosopher, d. (b. 1903)

Ernest Borneman, student of Wilhelm Reich and sexologist, d. (b. 1915)

Margherita von Brentano, Ger. philosopher, d. (b. 1922)

Emilio Garcia Gomez, Span. historian, d. (b. 1905)

Wolfgang Harich, Marxist philosopher, d. (b. 1924)

Graduate School for Social Research in Warsaw receives the Hannah Arendt prize, awarded for the first time, for their "pioneering approaches to rejuvenating the institutional foundations of theory and research in Eastern European reformist nations"

Pope John Paul II embarks on a 10-day trip to Asia

Mother Mary MacKillop, founder of a Catholic order, is beatified by the Pope and thus marks the first time in Catholic history that a woman from Australia is beatified

Bishop of Trent Johann Nepomuk von Tschiderer (1777–1860) is beatified

Pope removes the Fr. Bishop Gaillot from his post at the Diocese of Evreux and reassigns him to Mauretania; Gaillot's opinions on abortion, homosexuality, AIDS-prevention, and celibacy had provoked the church leader

Director of the State Office of Religious Affairs in Turkey, Yilmaz, states that beating women is "justified under certain circumstances, if it is what keeps the family intact"

Egypt demands its art treasures, including a bust of Queen Nefertiti, from Berlin museums where they are currently housed

A Greek fisher pulls an early Hellenistic bronze female figurine from the sea near the Island of Calymnos. Greek archaeologists say it's the most significant find of the century

Paris's Museum of Science and Technology, La Villette, opens the music complex Cité de la Musique. The museum attracts 8.5 million visitors a year, almost as many as Euro Disney in Paris

D. VISUAL ARTS	E. MUSIC	F. SCIENCE, TECHNOLOGY, GROWTH	G. DAILY LIFE	

1995

D. VISUAL ARTS

Rudolf Hausner, Austrian painter and founder of the school of "fantastic realism," d. (b. 1915)

René Allio, Fr. film and theater director ("The Shameless Old Lady" 1965), d. (b. 1924)

Sir Donald Pleasence, Brit. theater and screen actor, d. (b. 1920)

Ginger Rogers, actress, dancer, and partner to Fred Astaire in countless movies, d. (b. 1911)

Lionel Stander, Amer. movie actor, d. (b. 1908)

Zaha Hadid wins architecture competition for the new opera house in Cardiff, but does not get the contract in the end

Ital. architect R. Piano, designer of the Pompidou Center in Paris, receives the highest cultural honor bestowed an artist in the Netherlands, the Erasmus Prize, and also wins the Art Prize of Berlin's Academy of Fine Arts

Amer. director Robert Zemeckis receives Oscar for best director for "Forrest Gump." Oscars for lifetime achievement to M. Antonioni and C. Eastwood

Berlin Film Festival's Golden Bear to Fr. film "L'Appât" by Bertrand Tavernier

Cannes's Golden Palm to Emeri Kusterica for "Underground" and Theo Angelopoulos for "Ulysses' Gaze"

Airport at Lyons, a building-as-work-of-art designed by Fr. arch. Santiago Calatrava reminiscent of Tatlin's architectural "bird-flight" structures

Christo wraps the Reichstag in Berlin for two weeks, just before reconstruction gets underway according to plans by Brit. architect N. Foster

Hermitage in St. Petersburg exhibits plundered loot from WW II under the title "Hidden Treasures Revealed"

To mark the 100th anniversary of the Venice Biennale, Ch. Boltanski etches the names of 15,000

(contd)

E. MUSIC

Reza Abdoh, choreographer and director of Iranian descent, d. (b. 1964)

Julius Hemphill, Amer. saxophonist, d. (b. 1938)

Arturo Benedetti Michelangeli, Ital. pianist, d. (b. 1920)

Jess Stacy, swing era–pianist and member of the Benny Goodman Orchestra, d. (b. 1905)

Heinrich Sutermeister, Swiss composer, d. (b. 1910)

Eric Wright, rap artist in the group "Niggaz with Attitude," d. (b. 1964)

The first Richard Strauss Festival in thirty years held at the Semper Opera in Dresden

F. SCIENCE, TECHNOLOGY, GROWTH

Gerald Durrell, Brit. conservationist, author, and wildlife cinematographer, d. (b. 1925)

William A. Fowler, Amer. astrophysicist, 1983 Nobel prize for physics with S. Chandrasekhar, d. (b. 1911)

Georges Kœhler, Ger. immunologist, 1984 Nobel Prize for medicine, d. (b. 1946)

Widukind Lenz, bio-geneticist who uncovered the thalidomide scandal in the mid-1960s, d. (b. 1911)

Research results indicate that several million years ago a violent explosion on Mars sent meteorites hurling through space, some of which even landed on Earth

Saturn's moon Titan, hidden by a dense atmospheric haze, is not, as previously assumed, completely covered by ocean

Distances in elevation on the Moon are as much as 30% greater than previously assumed

Russian cosmonaut Valery Polyakov sets a world flight endurance record with his 438-day stay in space

Amer. space shuttle Endeavor stays in flight for 17 days with 7 astronauts aboard

Astronaut Norman Thagard becomes the first Amer. to board the Russian space station Mir; he was also the first Amer. to lift off in the Russian Soyuz launch vehicle

Financial difficulties make the planned mission of an unmanned Russian spacecraft seem ever more unlikely

Argentina unveils its own satellite

Ger.-Japanese space mission falters after research satellite Express crashes

Amer. scientists succeed in cooling rubidium atoms to 200 billionths of a degree over absolute zero (200 nanoKelvins). This is the lowest temperature that's ever been reached

Chinese scientists develop an optically nonlinear single crystal that can convert visible laser beams into ultraviolet rays at twice the frequency

Australian biologist accidentally discovers a species of rabbit-sized kangaroo thought to have been extinct for 125 years, the Gilbert's Potoroo, last seen in 1869. Biologists tagged the male of the pair and put him back in the wild

A species of chicken capable of surviving effortlessly in high tropical temperatures are bred at a re-

(contd)

G. DAILY LIFE

According to statistics published by the World Bank, Switzerland is ranked number one in terms of per capita income ($36,410), followed by Luxembourg, Japan, Denmark, Norway, and Sweden. Last on the list of 209 countries is Mozambique at $80. A ranking of income on the basis of purchasing power parity places Luxembourg ahead of the U.S., United Arab Emirates, Qatar, Hong Kong, and Japan

At a meeting in W. Bengal, 2,000 castrated men in India demand recognition as physically disabled. The number of eunuchs in India is estimated to be 1 million

World championships in Alpine skiing in the Span. Sierra Nevada are cancelled due to warm weather. Event organizers take a $9 million loss

33-year-old Briton Alison Hargreaves is the first woman to climb Mt. Everest (29,028 feet) alone and without supplemental oxygen

Microsoft, the world's largest software manufacturer, enters a so-called strategic alliance with NBC broadcast network to develop a future online service

Brit. film director Peter Greenaway and Fr. philosopher Jean Baudrillard joint recipients of Siemens' International Media Award

"La Notte," one of only two remaining evening papers in Italy, ceases publication

The so-called greenhouse effect, a warming of the planet caused by human activity, has yet to produce any clearly measurable effects. Fr. and Amer. scientists say that the increase in natural temperature deviations may not be measurable until the year 2010

Worldwide tourism becomes the increasing focus of criticism because of its environmental impact. Tourist industry is concerned that today's tourism is depleting resources for the tourism of tomorrow

Water shortages in south. Spain, ongoing for the past 5 years, force continued rationing

International fashion show in Shanghai opens with a gala event co-organized by the Communist Party

In a poison gas attack on a Japanese subway in Tokyo, 12 people killed and 5,000 wounded. 300 injured in another poison gas attack on public transportation system in Yokohama

Nearly 200 dead in bombing of a federal building in Oklahoma City, OK

	A. HISTORY, POLITICS	B. LITERATURE, THEATER	C. RELIGION, PHILOSOPHY, LEARNING
1995 contd	South Africa abolishes the death penalty. For the first time ever, there are black generals commanding in South Africa's police force U Nu, first chief of state in Burma after the independence in 1948, d. (b. 1908) Morarji Desai, former Prime Minister of India, d. (b. 1896) Prince Souphanouvong, former president of Laos, d. (b. 1909) O Jin-u, North Korean defense minister and most important supporter of Pres. Kim Il-Sung who died last year, d. (b. 1918?) In peace talks with the government, Tamil Tigers, Sri Lanka's most powerful rebel liberation group, agree to drop demands for a sovereign state Vietnam becomes a full member of A.S.E.A.N. (Assoc. of Southeast Asian Nations)		

D. VISUAL ARTS | E. MUSIC | F. SCIENCE, TECHNOLOGY, GROWTH | G. DAILY LIFE

1995 contd

artists who've had the privilege of exhibiting here into the main building. Americans R. B. Kitaj and G. Hill are awarded the Golden Lion

The last major construction project of the Mitterand-era is completed, Paris's National Library, designed by Dominique Perrault. It has the capacity to house 12 million books

Exhibit of the work of Ger. painter Kurt Schwitters at the Pompidou Center in Paris

First biennale in Africa takes place in Johannesburg with 63 exhibits by South African artists, and 267 foreign artists from 61 countries

A subterranean installation in Berlin by Israeli sculptor M. Ullmann is designed as a reminder of the book burning that took place at the site on May 10, 1933

Marc Allégret's film "Zouzou" with Josephine Baker in the leading role finally plays in German theaters sixty years after it was first shown in France

Major exhibit of the work of Federico Fellini at the film museum in Potsdam

Japanese director Juzo Itami ("Tampopo") films short stories by Nobel laureate Kenzaburō Ōe about the life of a Tokyo family with its mentally handicapped son

Essen's Folkwang Museum joins with Paris's Pompidou Center to purchase 226 photographs from the estate of László Moholy-Nagy for an undisclosed amount

Steven Spielberg, Amer. director ("Schindler's List") and owner of the film and entertainment company Dream Works joins Bill Gates, owner of the software giant Microsoft, in a joint venture to establish a company that will develop interactive film and television products

search station in Berlin's Humboldt University. They are known as "hair lock chickens" because of the feather-line curls that keep them cool

W.H.O. is confident that polio will have been eliminated by the year 2000

More than 1 million people die annually from the effects of contaminated food

A blood test for tuberculosis that measures the capacity of white blood cells to induce production of the antigen interferon-gamma by stimulating the TB with protein cells is developed; it could replace the tuberculosis test that has been in use for the past 100 years

Recent outbreak of the Ebola virus in Africa in a broad swath of land along the Equator

In Italy, a child is born two years after the death of its mother. The child was artificially inseminated and frozen before the mother's death, then carried to term by the biological father's sister

Retrofitting of nuclear power plants in Eastern Europe has not led to any substantial improvements in reactor safety

The nuclear plant at Chernobyl is to be officially shut down by the year 2000

The Fr. research reactor in Grenoble resumes operation after it was shut down in 1991

First wind-powered desalination plant in Europe begins operation in the Baltic Sea

A. HISTORY, POLITICS

1996 Joint Nobel Peace Prize to Catholic Bishop of East Timor, Carlos Felipe Ximénes Belo, and the exiled leader of the opposition there, José Ramos-Horta, for their efforts toward peaceful and just resolution to the conflict in East Timor

Right Livelihood Award ("Alternative Nobel Prize") in Stockholm to the mothers of Russian soldiers, to the forum of scholarly writers from the Indian Kerala, and the Greek homeopath Vithoulkas

U.S. is largest arms supplier in the world. According to the Arms Control Assoc. of America, Amer. deliveries make up a 56% or $21.4 billion share of the market, exceeding half of all international weapons exports for the first time. Other countries: U.K. ($3.4 billion), Russia ($1.3 billion), France and China ($800 million each), Germany ($700 million). By far the biggest importer of weapons is Saudi Arabia, which imported armaments in the amount of $5.2 billion, followed by Egypt ($1.5 billion) and Israel ($1 billion)

Anti-terrorism summit in Sharm el Sheikh, Egypt, with leading politicians from western and Arab nations to save the peace process in the Middle East

Nuclear safety summit in Moscow with the G7 states and Russia

Organization for Safety and Cooperation in Europe (O.S.C.E.) convenes in Lisbon to discuss extending its network toward the East

Kofi Annan from Ghana becomes new U.N. Secretary General

Israeli President Weizmann joins Ger. President Herzog on a visit to site of the former concentration camp at Sachsenhausen

Conflicts between Germany and Czechoslovakia in negotiations over a Ger.-Czech declaration of reconciliation between the two nations

Ger. Chancellor Kohl in Moscow. Yeltsin is outraged by N.A.T.O.'s planned eastern expansion

Ger. Chancellor Kohl visits Argentina, Brazil, Mexico, and Asia

Parliamentary Assembly of the European Council accepts Russia as its 39th member

Meeting of European foreign ministers in Palermo

German MP Leni Fischer is elected Pres. of the Parliamentary Assembly of the European Council in Strasbourg, replacing Span. Miguel Martinez

Italy assumes presidency of European Council

European Commission places export ban on beef and live cattle from U.K. after Mad Cow Disease (BSE) surfaces there

European Commission demands that Brit. Prime Minister John Majors drop his campaign of obstruction in the ministerial council in Brussels

Administrator of the EU in Mostar, Hans Koschnick, resigns his post

European Parliament rejects legislation mandating uniform labeling of genetically altered foodstuffs

Spiro Theodore Agnew, Republican politician, former U.S. Vice Pres., d. (b. 1918)

U.S. reacts to the escalation of tensions between China and Taiwan with warnings to China and by sending military aircraft carriers to the region

U.S. President Clinton visits peacekeeping forces in Bosnia

Pres. Clinton and the Repub. congressional majority reach a compromise on the budget debate

U.S. Republican presidential candidate after primaries is Bob Dole. Gen. Colin Powell rejects nomination as V.P. candidate

Democrat Bill Clinton wins the U.S. presidential election by a slim margin of 50% of votes cast

Members of the Commonwealth of Independent States (C.I.S.) confirm Boris Yeltsin as President of the C.I.S. Executive Council

Russian Pres. Yeltsin and Belarussian Pres. Lukashenka sign a treaty over integration of the two countries

Following the resignation of Russian Foreign Minister Andrei Kosyrev former director of the anti-espionage task force, Yevgeny Primakov, is appointed successor

Boris Yeltsin runs for reelection in presidential elections; the Communists nominate party chairman Gennady Zyuganov. Yeltsin wins in

(contd)

B. LITERATURE, THEATER

Hervé Bazin, Fr. writer, Pres. of Académie Goncourt, d. (b. 1911)

Harold R. Brodkey, Amer. writer, d. (b. 1930)

Joseph Brodsky, lyric poet, essayist, and Nobel laureate, d. (b. 1940, Leningrad)

Marguerite Duras, Fr. writer, d. (b. 1914, Vietnam)

Emil Schukri Habibi, Arab writer, d. (b. 1922)

Robert Hersant, Fr. publisher, d. (b. 1920)

Claude Mauriac, Fr. author, d. (b. 1914)

Maria Casarés, Spanish-born Fr. actress, d. (b. 1922)

Claudette Colbert, Fr. actress, d. (b. 1903)

Denise Grey, Fr. actress, d. (b. 1896)

Vladimir Nabokov's "The Pole" in a Grüber production at Berlin's Schaubühne

Nobel Prize for Literature to the Polish lyric poet Wislawa Szymborska

Peace Prize of the German Booksellers' Assoc. to Peruvian writer Mario Vargas Llosa

Britain's Whitbread Prize to Brit. author Kate Atkinson for her debut novel, "Behind the Scenes at the Museum"

Seamus Heaney, Irish poet and Nobel laureate, receives France's highest cultural honor, the Commandeur des Arts et Lettres

Pedro Maestre receives Spain's Premio Nadal

Salman Rushdie receives the British Book Award for "The Moor's Last Sigh"

Publication of Peter Handke's work "Gerechtigkeit für Serbien," written on a trip to Serbia, elicits vehement reactions when it is published

After vehement protests by critics, Amer. publisher St. Martin's halts publication of Brit. author David Irving's biography of Goebbels

Yasar Kemal, Turk. writer convicted by State Security Court in Istanbul on charges of "inciting public disorder" based on his contribution to a volume about "Turkey and Freedom of Speech"

Protests over the confiscation of Palestinian author Edward Said's (currently living and teaching in New York) books in the Palestinian autonomous areas

Franz Xaver Kroetz: "Der Dichter als Schwein"

Heiner Müller: "Germania 3. Gespenster am Toten Mann"

Harold Pinter: "Ashes to Ashes"

Arthur Schnitzler: "Familie"

Robert Wilson produces "Time

(contd)

C. RELIGION, PHILOSOPHY, LEARNING

José Luis Aranguren, Span. philosopher, d. (b. 1910)

Harold W. Bailey, Brit. philologist and expert on Sanskrit, d. (b. 1899)

Hans Blumenberg, Ger. philosopher, d. (b. 1920)

Georges Duby, Fr. historian, d. (b. 1919)

Renzo de Felice, historian, d. (b. 1929)

Gadd al Haqq Ali Gadd al Haqq, Egyptian sheik, highest ranking scribe in Sunni Islam, d. (b. 1916)

Timothy Leary, Amer. psychologists known for LSD use, d. (b. 1921)

Johannes Papalekas, Greek sociologist, d. (b. 1924)

Daniel Poirion, Fr. historian, d. (b. 1927)

Jean Rudolf von Salis, Swiss historian, d. (b. 1901)

Anselm Strauss, Amer. sociologist, d. (b. 1916)

Leon Joseph Suenens, Belgian cardinal, d. (b. 1905)

450th anniversary of Martin Luther's death

Film director and producer Steven Spielberg works with the Survivors of the Shoah Visual History Foundation to create an online multi-media Holocaust archive that is slated to include interviews with some 50,000 Holocaust survivors

Pope John Paul II visits Latin America, Germany, and France

Pope John Paul II passes reforms regulating his successor. In the future, a vote of ⅔ majority of Cardinals in the Papal conclave will be needed to become pope

Turkey declares the ancient city of Troy a national park

Republic of South Africa asks European museums to return human remains so they can be given a dignified burial in their homelands

New pyramid tomb discovered in the Mayan city of Palenque in southern Mexico

In the north of Peru, near the coastal city of Trujillo, discovery of an ancient Mochica temple from the first peoples who lived here between the 3rd and 10th centuries

In Xuzhou, China discovery of the c. 2,170-year-old grave of Prince Liu Wu, a Han Dynasty regent

Discovery of a 10 million-year-old skeleton in Spain, obviously a hominoid (Dryopithecus laietanus); it is the missing link between the 18 million-year-old Proconsul and the 3.1 million-year-old Australopithecus

At the Lake Enspel fossil site, oldest fossil of a gliding rodent found in a 26 million-year-old layer of oil shale; even its pelt and soft tissues are dis-

(contd)

D. VISUAL ARTS

1996

Helen Chadwick, Brit. artist, d. (b. 1954)
Major retrospective of works by Robert Doisneau in Paris
Dan Flavin, Amer. artist, d. (b. 1933)
Tim Gidal, Amer. photographer, d. (b. 1909, Munich)
Felix Gonzales-Torres, installations in Santiago de Compostela, Berlin, and Paris, d. (b. 1957, Cuba)
Duane Hanson, Amer. sculptor, d. (b. 1925)
Burne Hogarth, Amer. illustrator, creator of the comic figure Tarzan, d. (b. 1912)
Knwarreye, important Australian aborigine painter, d. (d.o.b. unknown)
Kumi Sagui, Japanese graphic artist and illustrator, d. (b. 1919, Kobe)
Meyer Schapiro, Amer. art historian, d. (b. 1904, Lithuania)
Tomás Gutiérrez Alea, Cuban film director, d. (b. 1928, Havana)
Martin Balsam, Amer. actor, d. (b. 1919)
Marcel Carné, Fr. director, d. (b. 1906)
René Clement, Fr. film director, d. (b. 1913)
Frank Daniel, screenplay writer, head of cinema studies dept. at Columbia University, d. (b. 1927)
Joseph Green, Amer. film director, d. (b. 1900, Lodz)
Margaux Hemingway, Amer. actress, d. (b. 1955)
Krzysztof Kieslowski, Polish film director, d. (b. 1941, Warsaw)
Masaki Kobayashi, Japanese film director, d. (b. 1916)
Marcello Mastroianni, Ital. actor, d. (b. 1923)
Christine Pascal, Fr. screen actress and director, d. (b. 1954)
Jacobus Johannes Uys, South African director, d. (b. 1920)
Robert Frank, Amer. photographer and filmmaker, receives the Hasselblad Award for Photography
Japanese cultural award, Praemium Imperiale, to Amer. painter Cy Twombly; Fr. sculptor Cesar (Baldaccini); Japa-
(contd)

E. MUSIC

Sergiu Celibidache, Romanian conductor, d. (b. 1912)
Serge Chermayeff, dancer and architect, d. (b. 1901)
Gottfried von Einem, Swiss composer, d. (b. 1918)
Ella Fitzgerald, Amer. jazz vocalist, d. (b. 1918)
Gianandrea Gavazzeni, Ital. composer and conductor, d. (b. 1909)
Gene Kelly, Amer. dancer, choreographer, and director, d. (b. 1912)
Lincoln Kirstein, Amer. ballet director and author, co-founder with Balanchine, of the New York City Ballet, d. (b. 1907)
Rafael Kubelik, Czech. conductor, d. (b. 1914)
Harry Lewis, Amer. conductor, first African American conductor of the New York Met, d. (b. 1933)
Pilar Lorengar, Spanish singer, d. (b. 1928)
"Survival Songs" by David Moss and Bernd Noglik premieres in Leipzig
Gerry Mulligan, Amer. jazz saxophonist, d. (b. 1927)
Kurt Peters, dancer, dance instructor, and founder of the German dance archives, d. (b. 1915)
John Pfeiffer, Amer. music producer, known as "producer of the stars" (among others Heifetz, Horowitz, Landowska), introduced the first stereo recordings in 1958, d. (b. 1920)
Ital. pianist Maurizio Pollini receives the international music award of the Ernst von Siemens Foundation
Nicolas Slonimsky, composer, conductor, pianist and musicologist, editor of several important reference works, d. (b. 1894, St. Petersburg)
Peter Stadlen, Austrian pianist, musicologist, and critic, d. (b. 1910)
Toru Takemitsu, Japanese composer, d. (b. 1930)
Tiny Tim, Amer. rock singer, d. (b. 1932)
Richard Versalle, Amer. opera singer, d. (b. 1933)
Johnny "Guitar" Watson, Amer. musician, d. (b. 1935)
Ljuba Welitsch, Austrian singer, d. (b. 1913)
(contd)

F. SCIENCE, TECHNOLOGY, GROWTH

Walter Birkmayer, Austrian neurologist, developed the agent L-Dopa as a treatment for Parkinson's disease, d. (b. 1910)
Tadeus Reichstein, Swiss Nobel laureate in medicine, discovered cortisone, d. (b. 1897)
André-Georges Haudricourt, Fr. ethnologist, linguist, and historian of technologies, d. (b. 1911)
Nobel Prize for Physics joint award to Amer. scientists David Lee, Douglas Osherhoff, and Robert Richardson for their discovery of so-called superfluidity in liquid helium-3
Nobel Prize for Chemistry to Amer. Robert Curl, Jr. and Richard Smalley as well as Briton Sir Harold Kroto for discovery of fullerenes, a previously unknown form of carbon
Nobel Prize for Medicine to Australian Peter Doherty and Swiss Rolf Zinkernagel for discovering the way immune cells recognize virus-infected cells within the immune system
Nobel Prize for Economics to William Vickrey (Canada) and James A. Mirrlees (U.K.). The jury determined that the two of them, independent of one another, established and developed an economic theory of incentives under asymmetric information
Paul Ehrlich and Ludwig Darmstadt Prize to Australians J. Robin Warren and Barry J. Marshall for discovering that ulcers are usually caused by bacteria and not, as generally assumed, by stress and improper diet
Paul Ehrlich and Ludwig Darmstadt Prize to Pamela Bjorkman (U.S.), Jack Strominger (U.S.), and Hans-Georg Rammensee (Germany) for their work on cell research
The comet Hyakutake, named after an amateur Japanese astronomer, is visible to the naked eye from Earth. It is the first time since 1956 that a comet of this size has come comparably close to Earth
Hubble space telescope offers the most penetrating glimpse of space to date when it captures images of the weak light emitted by 1,500 previously undetected galaxies more than 10 billion light years away
A star in the constellation Sagittarius is discovered in the Final Helium Flash, a stage of development directly preceding the fusion to a white dwarf
(contd)

G. DAILY LIFE

Amer. company introduces instant dinners to the Ger. market
Dutch aircraft manufacturer Fokker declares bankruptcy after majority stockholder Daimler-Benz Aerospace (Dasa) withdraws its funds from the company
Swiss chemical corporations Sandoz and Ciba-Geigy merge to form Novartis and thus become the world's second largest pharmaceutical manufacturer, after Glaxo Wellcome
Collapse of Austria's third largest construction company, Maculan
Europe's largest shipbuilder, Bremer Vulkan, files for bankruptcy. The firm's former board chairman, F. Hennemann, is arrested under suspicion of misappropriation of large sums of money
The world's largest container vessel, the Regina Maersk, begins operation
José Ignacio López de Arriotúa voluntarily quits the board of directors at Volkswagen
Two Amer. aircraft manufacturers, Boeing and Douglas, announce agreement to pursue extensive collaboration
Carnival Destiny, world's largest passenger ship, sets sail from Triese
In Australia's Northern Territory, first doctor-assisted suicide performed under the country's new voluntary euthanasia laws
International Labour Organization (I.L.O.) meeting in Geneva demands reduction of child labor. Some 250 million children worldwide between the ages of 5 and 14 are forced to work
According to U.N.I.C.E.F. statistics, over 2 million children worldwide are exploited for prostitution
Public prosecutor in Mannheim charges Peter Graf, father of tennis player Steffi Graf, and the family's accountant, Eckardt, with tax evasion
Military court in Rome acquits former SS officer Erich Priebke on the charge of having participated in the execution of 335 hostages near Rome in 1944. Italy's highest court of appeals squashes the decision
A German man is sentenced to 43 years in prison in Thailand for sexually abusing underage prostitutes
Bombing in a Paris subway kills 2 and injures 128 people
Ger. real estate magnate Jürgen Schneider markets his computer version of the board game Monopoly from the prison cell where he was awaiting trial on charges of tax evasion and fraud
Ital. Mafia boss Guiseppe "Johnny" Gambino, notorious for his cruelty, hangs himself in a prison cell in Milan
120 square-yard AIDS Memorial Quilt remembering AIDS victims throughout the world is spread out between the capitol building and Washington Monument in Washington, DC
René Lacoste, Fr. tennis player, d. (b. 1904)
Olympic Summer Games in Atlanta (U.S.)
(contd)

1996 contd

A. HISTORY, POLITICS

a runoff election and remains President of Russia. Russian Pres. Yeltsin fires security advisor Lebed
Russia delivers fighter jets to China
Lithuanian Parliament elects Mindaugas Stankevicius Prime Minister to follow A. Slezevicius; he is replaced in December
Yahyo Azimov becomes successor to Karimov as Prime Minister of Tajikistan
Belgium is the last country in the European Union to abolish the death penalty
71-year old Alija Izetbegovic becomes first post-war Pres. of Bosnia-Herzegovina
With the seizure by the Muslim-Croatian federation of the last remaining sector of Sarajevo still under Serbian control, the capital of Bosnia is reunited after four years of separation
François Mitterrand, Fr. president 1981–95, d. (b. 1916)
President Jacques Chirac demands a smaller, more efficient Fr. army and pleads for eliminating compulsory military service
In Paris, French police units CRS brutally remove 300 African men, women, and children from a church where they have taken up residence
French truck drivers paralyze the country with blockades, demanding shorter hours, higher wages and an earlier retirement age
Critically ill Greek Prime Minister Papandreou resigns from office and is succeeded by K. Simitis; Andreas Papandreou, socialist politician and former Prime Minister of Greece, d. (b. 1919)
British Queen Elizabeth II visits Prague
After three years of separation, Princess Diana agrees to divorce from Charles, British successor to the throne
Following the resignation of Italian Prime Minister Dini, Antonio Maccanico is initially assigned the task of forming a new administration, but President Scalfaro dissolves the chambers and calls for new elections. An electoral alliance between the moderate left under the name "Uliva" (olive tree) wins the elections in both chambers in Italy. Romano Prodi becomes Prime Minister of Italy, who will preside over the 55th post-war Italian cabinet
Corruption trial begins against former Italian Prime Minister Berlusconi
Following the anticipated resignation of Norwegian Prime Minister Gro Harlem Brundtland, she is succeeded by chairman of the labor party, T. Jagland
Netherlands abolishes compulsory military service
Austrian national council revokes parliamentary immunity for right-wing faction leader Jörg Haider
António de Spinola, conservative politician in Portugal, d. (b. 1910)
Socialist Jorge Sampaio wins presidential elections in Portugal with a 10-point lead over liberal candidate Cavaco Silva
Conservative Emil Constantinescu becomes new Romanian Pres. in a runoff election against incumbent Ion Iliescu
Former Finance Minister Göran Persson succeeds Ingvar Carlsson as Prime Minister of Sweden
Protest movement in Serbia against Pres. Milosevic
International War Crimes Tribunal in the Hague indicts Serbian General Milan Djukic
People's Party wins elections in Spain with a slim 1.2 point lead over socialists. José Maria Aznar becomes Prime Minister
Socialist Basque politician Fernando Mugica Herzog is murdered in San Sebastian. Basque separatist group ETA claims responsibility
In Turkey, chairs of the two right-wing parties, Yilmaz and Çiller, sign an agreement to form a joint administration
More than 200 political prisoners on hunger strike in Turkey; six die
René Préval elected President of Haiti
Colombian Pres. Samper is charged with having accepted money from the drug mafia
On his visit to the Vatican, Cuban President Fidel Castro invites the Pope to visit Cuba
Two private planes carrying Cuban exiles are shot down by Cuban fighter jets
(contd)

B. LITERATURE, THEATER

Rocker" with Lou Reed at Hamburg's Thalia Theater
Martin Wuttke succeeds Heiner Müller as head of the Berliner Ensemble

C. RELIGION, PHILOSOPHY, LEARNING

cernable. The fossil, Eomys quercyi, belongs to the extinct species Eomydia

D. VISUAL ARTS	E. MUSIC	F. SCIENCE, TECHNOLOGY, GROWTH	G. DAILY LIFE	

1996 contd

nese architect Tadao Ando; Ital. composer Luciano Berio; and Polish director Andrzej Wajda

Berlin Film Festival's Golden Bear to Ang Lee for "Sense and Sensibility." Best actress to Anouk Grinberg in "Mon Homme," best actor to Sean Penn for "Dead Man Walking"

American Academy Award winners: best picture, Mel Gibson's "Braveheart"; best actress in a leading role, Susan Sarandon for "Dead Man Walking"; best actor in a leading role, Nicolas Cage "Leaving Las Vegas"

Venice Film Festival: Briton Neil Jordan takes the Golden Lion for best film with "Michael Collins." Best actress to Victoire Thivisol ("Ponette"), best actor to Liam Neeson ("Michael Collins"). Lifetime achievement awards to Michèle Morgan, Vittorio Gassman, Dustin Hoffman, and Robert Altman

Cannes Film Festival: Golden Palm to Briton Mike Leigh for "Secrets and Lies." Best actress to Brenda Blethyn ("Secrets and Lies"), best actor to Daniel Auteuil and Pascal Duquenne ("The Eighth Day")

European Film Award Felix to Lars von Trier for "Breaking the Waves," best actress to Emily Watson ("Breaking the Waves"), best actor Ian McKellan ("Richard III")

European Academy of Film and Television in Brussels selects Orson Welles's "Citizen Kane," Marcel Carné's "Children of Paradise," and Charlie Chaplin's "Gold Rush" as three best films in the world

Francis-Bacon work-in-review first in Paris, then in Munich

Jean Tinguely Museum designed by Mario Botta opens in Basel

Excavation of a Celtic statue from the ancient royal

(contd)

U.N.E.S.C.O. music award to Hungarian composer Györgi Ligeti, Argentine singer Mercedes Sosa, and to the Paul Sacher Endowment in Basel

Ger. composer Hans Zimmer receives Grammy for the musical score to "Crimson Tide." Additional Grammy winners: Alanis Morisette, Coolio, Hootie and the Blowfish, Kurt Cobain, and Annie Lennox

Karsten Witt, manager and director of Frankfurt's Modern Ensemble, becomes new Pres. of Deutsche Grammophon

Iannis Xenakis: "Koirani"

Venice's opera house La Fenice destroyed by fire

Gerd Albrecht, chief conductor of the Czech Philharmonic Orchestra, announces his resignation due to conflicts that have been ongoing since he first assumed the post in 1993. He is succeeded by Vladimir Valek

Premiere of Pina Bausch's dance piece "Nu du" in Wuppertal

Richard Cragun replaces Ray Barra as ballet director for the German Opera in Berlin

Premiere of Philip Glass's "Les Enfants Terribles" in Zug

The estate of Arnold Schoenberg goes to the composer's birthplace in Vienna, not to the Academy of Fine Arts in Berlin

A series of concerts held in Bonn to commemorate the 100th anniversary of the death of composer and pianist Clara Schumann

Karlheinz Stockhausen: "Welt-Parlament," a capella choir

Christian Thielemann succeeds Rafael Frühbeck de Burgos as general musical director of the German Opera in Berlin

Coronal mass ejections in the solar chromosphere, so-called flares, are discovered by an 31.2-inch telescope attached to a balloon 25 miles above Antarctica

E.S.A. (European Space Agency) solar research satellite SOHO (Solar Heliospheric Observatory) detects protuberances at a speed of 15,500 mph

Amer. space shuttle Columbia loses one of its research satellites during a power generating experiment

Ger. astronaut Thomas Reiter returns to earth after 6 months at the Russian space station Mir

Amer. space shuttle Atlantis docks at the Mir orbital station

Amer. orbiter spacecraft NEAR (Near-Earth Asteroid Rendezvous) is launched. After three years in space, it should enter the orbit of the asteroid Eros to conduct research

Amer. space probe Pathfinder launches its 310 million mile mission to Mars, where it is scheduled to land on July 4, 1997

After 2½ years in flight, a 300-pound Chinese satellite spins out of control and crashes to earth over the Atlantic Ocean

Russian space probe Mission Mars 96 crashes in the Pacific Ocean after a 28 hour flight. At first it was feared that the space capsule carrying 10 ounces of plutonium-238 would slam into Australia

N.A.S.A. probe Galileo observes a blue-colored volcanic eruption reaching up to 62 miles into space on Jupiter's moon Io

Scientists at the Jet Propulsion Laboratory (JPL) in California uses laser technology to succeed in the first mutual exchange of information between a satellite and ground station

European space launcher Ariane delivers two telecommunications satellites to space

European infrared satellite Iso begins the first of some 2,000 measurements that will contribute to researching processes in and between Milky Ways

For the first time ever, scientists at CERN (European Laboratory for Particle Physics) in Geneva produce atoms from anti-matter

Scientists at GSI lab (Society for Heavy Ion Research) in Darmstadt provide verification of Element 112, an element 227 times as heavy as an H_2O molecule and is created from the fusion of a

(contd)

with athletes from 197 countries. Bomb explodes in Olympic Park during the competition. German team brings home 20 gold medals, 18 silver, and 27 bronze, in third place after the U.S. and Russia

Executive Committee of the Union of European Football Associations (U.E.F.A.) decides to lift restrictions on allowing foreign players to join

Ger. boxer Henry Maske defends his world middle weight champion title against Duran Williams, but then loses the title in his defeat against Amer. Virgil Hill

American Mike Tyson regains his world heavyweight champion title from Briton Frank Bruno. The prize is $30 million

German national soccer team wins the European championship, in a 2-1 victory over Czechoslovakia at Wembley Stadium in London

South African national soccer team wins the African Cup of Nations with a 2-0 final victory over Tunisia

Danish cyclist Bjarne Riis wins the Tour de France just ahead of Ger. Jan Ullrich

Basketball player Magic Johnson returns to the NBA after nearly four years and begins playing for the LA Lakers

Briton Damon Hill wins racing's Formula 1 World Championship, defeating defending champion Michael Schumacher

24-year-old Cristina Sanchez becomes the first female matador in the history of bullfighting. Several fighters refuse to get in the ring with her

Germany's censorship of pornographic offerings on the Internet by the online service Compuserve unleashes heated debate in U.S.

Italy's only nationwide weekly satirical paper *Curore* goes out of business

Madrid's daily newspaper *Ya,* one of four political papers in the city goes out of business

The Ger. Bertelsmann subsidiary Ufa and the Luxembourg media concern Compagnie Luxembourеoise Télévision S.A. (CLT) prepare for merger

38 million acres of rainforest are destroyed annually by timber cutting

Ozone layer above the Arctic continues to thin

Bruno H. Schubert Award, the most prestigious private award for environmental protection and nature conservation in Germany, goes to the Amer. biologist Edward O. Wilson for his fight against the loss of species diversity

America's east coast hit by the worst snowstorms in decades

More than 825,000 gallons of oil spill into the ocean after a tanker accident off the coast of Rhode Island

Environmental contamination increases in Russia as a result of leaking oil from pipelines

All 176 passengers and 13 crew members killed in a plane crash over the Dominican Republic

(contd)

	A. HISTORY, POLITICS	B. LITERATURE, THEATER	C. RELIGION, PHILOSOPHY, LEARNING

1996 contd

23 members of the Peruvian guerrilla group Tupac Amaru take several hundred people hostage at the Japanese embassy in Lima

Bombing attacks in Algeria. Murder of Bishop of Oran, Claverie. General strike in Algeria

An Egyptian court sentences six members of an underground Islamic organization to death on charges of terrorism

Unrest in Bahrain. Members of Shiite opposition arrested

Sons-in-law of Saddam Hussein who had fled to Jordan return to Iraq. Despite promises of amnesty, they are murdered

Iraqi army intervenes in conflict between opposing Kurdish factions in northern Iraq. U.S. Pres. Clinton responds by increasing troops in the Gulf region

Iranian Pres. Rafsanjani condemns terror attacks in Israel, but expresses solidarity with the aims of Hamas. He declines invitation to participate in an antiterrorism summit

Following terrorist attacks in Israel, Prime Minister Peres orders the borders to the West Bank and Gaza Strip closed and severs contact with Palestinian government authority. Chair of the right-wing Likud party, Benjamin Netanyahu, defeats Prime Minister Peres

In the Palestinian autonomous areas, Yasser Arafat (PLO) wins election to President of the Palestinian National Council with 87.1% of votes

Foreign ministers from 49 African nations sign the Pelindaba Treaty in Cairo establishing a nuclear weapon–free zone in Africa

King Moshoeshoe II, chief of state in Lesotho, d. (b. 1936); his son, Letsie Mohato Seeiso is appointed King

Civil war in Liberia

Fara Aidid, politician in the Sudan, d. (b. 1936)

Leader of the Islamic fundamentalist regime in Sudan, Omar Hassan el Bashir, is reelected president of the country. In several districts, the election is cancelled because of the ongoing civil war

Constitutional assembly in the Rep. of South Africa ratifies new constitution. Former South African Prime Minister de Klerk apologizes for human rights violations during apartheid

Sec. Gen. of the African National Congress (A.N.C.), Ramaphosa, resigns from his post and is replaced by his deputy, Cheryl Carolus. Archbishop of Cape Town, Desmond Tutu, retires from office and is showered with honors from both church and state. South Africa's notorious Robben Island prison is scheduled to be transformed into a museum dedicated to the struggle for liberation

Jean Bedel Bokassa, Emperor of the Central Africa Republic, d. (b. 1921)

Incumbent administration under Prime Minister Khaleda Zia wins elections in Bangladesh. The opposition party under Sheikh Hasina boycotts the elections

Military junta in Burma (Myanmar) again imposes severe legal sanctions against adherents of the opposition party led by Aung San Suu Kyi

China cancels planned visit by Ger. Foreign Minister Kinkel after the Ger. Lower House ratifies a resolution on Tibet

Police in Hong Kong use tear gas against Vietnamese refugees in an internment camp who are demanding recognition of their status as political refugees

Dispute between Japan and South Korea over an island in the sea of Japan

Japanese Prime Minister Murayama resigns, and is succeeded by former Minister of Commerce, Hashimoto

Japan compensates women in South Korea and other Asian countries who were forced to work as prostitutes under the Japanese imperial regime during WW II; of between 100,000 to 200,000 "comfort women," about 300 are still alive

During a memorial service for North Korea's Pres. Kim II-Sung who died in 1994, his son, Kim Jong-II, is heralded as "Great Leader"

North Korea requests food aid from countries throughout the world. Last year's flooding disasters have destroyed substantial portions of the harvest

(contd)

D. VISUAL ARTS | E. MUSIC | F. SCIENCE, TECHNOLOGY, GROWTH | G. DAILY LIFE

1996 contd

burial grounds at Glauberg

Traveling exhibition of the works of French artist Jean-Baptiste Corot in Paris, Ottawa, and New York

Exhibit about the work of Alberto Giacometti in Vienna

Goya commemorative year in Spain to mark the 250th anniversary of the artist's birth. Exhibit in Prado

Jasper Johns retrospective at the Museum of Modern Art in New York

Exhibit of the late works by Willem de Kooning in Bonn's Art Museum

Max Liebermann exhibit in Bremen

Düsseldorf's Art Collection exhibits "The Art of Conversation," with works by René Margritte and his followers

Museum for the works of Georgia O'Keeffe opens in Santa Fe, NM

Rock and Roll Hall of Fame, designed by Amer. architect, I.M. Pei, opens in Cleveland, OH; American architect I.M. Pei receives contract for expanding the Museum of German History in Berlin (Dt. Historisches Museum)

Photographs from China by Marc Riboud in Paris

Exhibit of contemporary South African art in Berlin

Getty Communication Group in London purchases the Hulton Deutsch Collection, one of the world's most extensive photographic archives

Exhibit, "American Perspectives" at Stedelijk Museum in Amsterdam

Exhibit "Africa—the Art of a Continent" in Berlin and London

After 40 years, the scaffolding surrounding the world's tallest church steeple, on the Münster Kirche in Ulm, is removed after completion of masonry work

Peter Greenaway: "The Pillow Book"

Work of Leni Riefenstahl on exhibit in Milan

lead atom and a zinc atom

IBM Research Lab in Zurich builds the world's smallest abacus, with molecular-sized beads that move along a single atom at the tip of a scanning tunneling microscope (STM); scientists from France and Switzerland use an STM to move copper porphyrin molecules

Genome for the microbe Methanococcus jannaschii, a type of archaea, is sequenced. It is the third fully sequenced genome ever

Another breast cancer gene, BRCA2, is identified by an international research team

A Ger. scientist succeeds in identifying the gene responsible for pancreatic cancer

World Health Organization (W.H.O.) classifies the drug most frequently prescribed worldwide for treating breast cancer, Tamoxifen, as a cancer-causing substance

Research indicates that tcytokines, messenger substances activated by fever which activate the immune system, have an antidepressive effect

Scientists at the University of Technology in Berlin develop an electronic glove that registers the hand's movements and transmits them to a robot, which then performs the same movements

More than 100 lives claimed in China after an explosion in an illegal firecracker warehouse in the basement of a multistory residential building

Russian aircraft crashes into a marketplace in Kinshasa (Zaire), killing 350 people

400 dead after a ferry sinks off the coast of Sumatra

Over 3,000 dead and tens of thousands stricken by a meningitis epidemic in West Africa

In Dunblane, Scotland, crazed gunman shoots 16 elementary school children and their teacher before killing himself

All 123 people on board lose their lives when a plane crashes in the Peruvian Andes

150 dead after a fire in a discotheque in the Philippines

In the Australian state of Tasmania, deranged gunman goes on a shooting spree, leaving a trail of 35 murder victims

German army helicopter crashes during a civilian exercise in Dortmund. 13 people, mostly youth, are killed

Jumbo jet bursts into flames just after take-off and crashes into the ocean off the coast of Long Island. All 230 people on board die

6 million refugees on the run after heavy monsoons cause severe flooding in Bangladesh

Russian plane crashes in the mountains: 140 dead

Plane crash over a heavily populated neighborhood in São Paulo. 117 people perish, 22 of them neighborhood residents

Following the eruption of the Bardadunga volcano, Iceland is inundated by a huge volume of water from melting of the ice sheet

Midair crash of two planes at an altitude of 4,000 meters near New Delhi: 350 deaths

	A. HISTORY, POLITICS	B. LITERATURE, THEATER	C. RELIGION, PHILOSOPHY, LEARNING
1996 contd	Under widespread protest, Philippines begins forced repatriation of Vietnamese boat people Government of Sri Lanka declares martial law nationwide Pres. Kim Young-sam loses absolute majority in South Korean elections, but remains strongest faction in parliament South Korea masses troops on the border to North Korea after North Korea announced that it would no longer respect the demilitarized zone between the two countries In Australia, the Labour Party, 13 years in office, loses election. After winning an absolute majority, the Liberal Party forms new administration under Prime Minister J. Howard		
1997	Nobel Peace Prize to International Campaign to Ban Landmines and its spokesperson, Amer. Jody Williams who provided impetus for the initiative which was founded in 1992 Right Livelihood Award ("Alternative Nobel Prize") to Ger. Michael Succow for his efforts to save nature preserves in the east of Germany, to the historian Joseph Ki-Zerbo from Burkina Faso for his research on Africa, to Fr. Mycle Schneider and Jap. Jinzabure Takagi for their fight against plutonium trade and to Amer. Cindy Duehring for her work on pollutants International armaments trade continues to grow. In 1996, weapons sales increased by 8% over the previous year, climbing to nearly $40 billion. The U.S. remains the largest arms supplier in the world (with nearly 43% of the market), followed by the U.K. (a solid 22%), and France (14%). The largest arms importer remains Saudi Arabia N.A.T.O. decides to begin negotiations with Poland, Hungary, and the Czech Republic on their admittance to the military alliance France declares that is has no immediate plans to return to N.A.T.O. U.N. Convention chemical weapons ban goes into effect U.N. Sec. Gen. appoints Irish President Mary Robinson as High Commissioner for Human Rights Following an 11-year hiatus, U.K. resumes its participation in the United Nations Educational, Scientific and Cultural Organization (U.N.E.S.C.O.) Amer. entertainment industry executive Ted Turner announces plans to donate $1 billion to the U.N. U.N.I.C.E.F. (United Nations International Children's Fund) demands that Germany pursue more aggressive legal measures against German tourists who have sexually abused children while vacationing abroad Amnesty International accuses Ger. police of abuse against foreign citizens and immigrants Ger. Foreign Minister Klaus Kinkel and Czech Prime Minister Vaclav Klaus sign a declaration of reconciliation between the two nations Netherlands takes over the presidency of the EU's Council of Ministers; the Council is presided over by member states on a rotating basis; European Union conference in Malta Span. Christian Democrat José Maria Gil-Robles becomes new President of European Parliament Dutch Wim Duisenberg becomes new President of the European Currency Institute EU approves radioactive treatment of edible goods European Commission passes resolution mandating labeling of genetically altered corn EU again extends its sanctions against the military regime in Myanmar (formerly Burma) Summit meeting of the European Council in Strasbourg. Plan for action is designed to lend stronger support to human rights U.K. will not join the European Currency Union by 1999 Bill Clinton begins his second term as President of the U.S. U.S. President Bill Clinton and Russian President Boris Yeltsin meet in Helsinki to discuss N.A.T.O.'s eastern expansion and economic relations between Russia and the western industrial nations *(contd)*	Kathy Acker, Amer. author, d. (b. 1948) William Seeward Burroughs, Amer. author, d. (b. 1914) Allen Ginsberg, Amer. poet and singer, d. (b. 1926) Jarl Kulle, Swedish actor, d. (b. 1927) James Michener, Amer. author, d. (b. 1907) Hans Quest, Ger. actor and director, d. (b. 1915) Harold Robbins, Amer. author, d. (b. 1916) Maurice Roche, Fr. author, d. (b. 1924) Andrei Sinyavsky, Russian author, d. (b. 1925) Osvaldo Soriano, Argentine writer, d. (b. 1943) Nobel Prize for Literature to Ital. dramatist and actor Dario Fo as an author who "emulates the gestures of the Middle Ages in scourging authority and upholding the dignity of the downtrodden." This was the statement of the jury which failed to note the contributions made by Franca Rame to Fo's work Peace Prize of the Ger. Booksellers' Assoc. to Turkish author Yasar Kemal. In his speech introducing the award, author Günter Grass accuses W. Germany of pursuing ruthlessly racist immigration policies Whitbread Prize to Irish Nobel laureate Seamus Heaney Cervantes Award, the most prestigious literary award in the Spanish-speaking world, goes to exiled Cuban Guillermo Cabrara Infante Planet Prize, highest-paid prize in the Spanish-speaking world goes to Span. writer Juan Manuel de Prada for his novel "La Tempestad" Patrick Rambaud receives the Grand Prize for a Novel of the Académie Française and the Goncourt Prize for his novel "La Bataille." Pascal Bruckner receives the Renaudot Prize for his novel "Les voleurs de beauté" Indian writer Arundhati Roy receives Brit. Booker Prize for her debut novel "The God of Small Things" Herman Kesten Medal of the Ger. *(contd)*	Isaiah Berlin, Brit. philosopher, d. (b. 1909, Riga) François Furet, Fr. historian, member of the Académie Française, d. (b. 1927) Hannah Arendt Prize for political thought to Joachim Gauck, Freimut Duve, and the Invisible College in Budapest Carl Gustav Hempel, Amer. philosopher, d. (b. 1903, Oranienburg) Sabatino Moscan, Ital. archeologist, d. (b. 1922) Joseph Pieper, Ger. philosopher, d. (b. 1904) Mother Teresa, Catholic nun in Calcutta, d. (b. 1910, given name: Agnes Gonxha Bojaxhiu) A.L. Rowse, Brit. historian, d. (b. 1904) In O.E.C.D. (Organization for Economic Cooperation and Development) nations, an average of 5.9% of the GDP (gross domestic product) is spent on education; percentage in Germany is 5.8, placing Germany in 9th place. Canada, U.S., the Scandinavian countries, and France all have higher expenditures Worldwide decrease in illiteracy rates. Whereas in 1980, nearly ⅓ of the world's population under 15 years of age could neither read nor write, this number had been reduced to 23% by 1995. ⅔ of all illiterates are still women François Revel accepted as new member of the Académie Française In Egypt, 1,600 teachers with alleged ties to Islamic fundamentalist circles are forcibly removed from their jobs and given administrative positions 12th Catholic World Youth Day in Paris with over 1 million visitors from 130 countries Pope John Paul II visits Poland, Lebanon and Brazil Pope John Paul II proclaims St. Thérèse of Lisieux a Doctor of the Church Bishops of the Catholic Church in France express remorse for silence over the persecution of Jews in France during the Nazi era Austrian Protestant Church condones the blessing of homosexual couples. Peter Krömer, President of the Synod, resigns *(contd)*

D. VISUAL ARTS	E. MUSIC	F. SCIENCE, TECHNOLOGY, GROWTH	G. DAILY LIFE	
				1996 contd

1997

D. VISUAL ARTS

Shirley Clarke, Amer. filmmaker, d. (b. 1925)
Sam Fuller, Amer. film director, d. (b. 1912)
Hu King Hu, most important Kung Fu director in Chinese film, d. (b. 1931)
Juzo Itami, Japanese film director, d. (b. 1933)
Paul Jarrico, blacklisted Amer. screenwriter and film producer, d. (b. 1915)
Willem de Kooning, painter, lived in U.S., d. (b. 1964, Rotterdam)
Roy Lichtenstein, Amer. painter, d. (b. 1923)
Toshiro Mifune, Japanese screen actor, d. (b. 1920, China)
Robert Mitchum, Amer. screen actor, d. (b. 1917)
Jack Nance, Amer. screen actor, d. (b. 1943)
James Stewart, Amer. actor, d. (b. 1908)
Tomoyuki Tanaka, Japanese costume designer, creator of Godzilla, d. (b. 1911)
Bo Widerberg, Swedish film director, d. (b. 1930)
Fred Zinnermann, Amer. film director, d. (b. 1907, Vienna)
At the 47th Biennale of contemporary art in Venice, Golden Lion to Gerhard Richter and Mariana Abramovic
Golden Film Band lifetime achievement awards to Billy Wilder and Jennifer Jones
Milos Formann takes Golden Bear at the Berlin Film Festival for best picture with "The People vs. Larry Flynt," best actress to Juliette Binoche ("The English Patient"), best actor to Leonardo DiCaprio ("Romeo and Juliet")
Cannes' Golden Palm split
(contd)

E. MUSIC

Luther Allison, Amer. blues guitarist, d. (b. 1938)
Barbara, Fr. chanson singer, d. (b. 1930, given name Monique Serf)
Jacques Canetti, discovered and promoted Jacques Brel, d. (b. 1909, Bulgaria)
Adolphus "Doc" Cheatham, Amer. jazz trumpet player, d. (b. 1905)
John Denver, Amer. folksinger, d. (b. 1943, given name Henry John Deutschendorf, Jr.)
Jean Françaix, Fr. composer, d. (b. 1912)
Stéphane Grapelli, Fr. jazz musician, d. (b. 1907)
Fela Anikulapo Kuti, Nigerian musician and dissident, d. (b. 1939)
Nicolette Larsen, Amer. pop singer, d. (b. 1952)
Vincente "Tete" Montilou, Span. jazz pianist, d. (b. 1933)
Conlon Nancarrow, Amer. composer, d. (b. 1912)
Nusrat Fateh Ali Khan, Pakistani Sufi-singer, d. (b. 1948)
Laura Nyro, Amer. singer-songwriter, d. (b. 1947)
Sviatoslav Richter, Russian pianist, d. (b. 1914)
Sir Georg Solti, Hungarian conductor, d. (b. 1912)
Margarthe von Trotta stages Alban Berg's "Lulu" in Stuttgart
Jimmy Witherspoon, Amer. blues and pop singer, d. (b. 1923)
Narciso Yepes, Span. guitarist, d. (b. 1927)
Amer. choreographer Merce Cunningham receives the Grand Prize of the French Society for Authors' Rights
Bob Dylan releases his first new album in 7 years,
(contd)

F. SCIENCE, TECHNOLOGY, GROWTH

Jacques Yves Cousteau, Fr. oceanographer, d. (b. 1910)
Sir John C. Eccles, Australian neurophysiologist and Nobel laureate, d. (b. 1903)
Eugene Shoemaker, Amer. geologist and astronomer, d. (b. 1928)
Sir Alexander Todd, Brit, chemist and Nobel laureate, d. (b. 1907)
Nobel Prize for Physics to Amer. Steven Chu and William D. Phillips and to Fr. Claude Cohen-Tannoudji for the development of methods for cooling and "trapping" atoms with laser light
Nobel Prize for Chemistry to Paul D. Boyer (U.S.), John E. Walker (U.K.), and Jens C. Skou (Denmark) for work on elucidating the enzymatic mechanism underlying the synthesis of adenosine triphosphate and for the first discovery of an ion-transporting enzyme
Nobel Prize for Medicine to Amer. neurologist and biochemist Stanley B. Prusiner for his discovery of Prions—a disease-causing agent of such deadly brain diseases as BSE (mad cow disease), Alzheimer's, and Creutzfeld Jakob disease, unknown until he discovered them in the early 1980s
Nobel Prize for Economic Sciences to two Amer. economists Robert Merton and Myron Scholes for their method of calculating the value of options on the stock market
Australian medical scientists Barry James Marshall and John Robin Warren receive the Paul Erhlich and Ludwig Darmstadt Prizes for their research into gastrointestinal diseases
Mathematician Andrew Wiles receives the award money for proving Fermat's last theorem, a cash prize that was first offered in 1908
At 5,249 feet, the planetarium at Königsleiten opens to become the
(contd)

G. DAILY LIFE

U.N. Food and Agriculture Organization (F.A.O.) announces that 18 million people die annually in the Third World from hunger and undernourishment. The number of people suffering from hunger and undernourishment worldwide is about 80 million
There are six million millionaires (measured in dollars) in the world. More and more wealthy people in Asia and Latin America
This summer, the dollar reached its highest rate since 1989
Luxembourg is the richest country in the world, with an average per capita annual income of $41,210, followed by Switzerland and Japan
Ten largest industrial corporations in Europe: Royal Dutch Shell (Netherlands/U.K., oil, chemicals), Daimler-Benz (Germ., automobile, aircraft), British Petroleum (U.K., mineral oil), Volkswagen (Germ., automobile), Siemens (Germ., electronics), Unilever (Netherlands/U.K., foodstuffs, chemicals), Fiat (Italy, automobile), Nestlé (Switzerland, foodstuffs), IRI (I, holding), Elf Aquitaine (France, oil, chemicals)
German sporting goods manufacturer Adidas takes over the French company Salomon S.A. to become the second largest manufacturer in the business, following Nike
At an elevation of 8,209 feet, the highest-elevation construction site in Europe is located at Säntis in Switzerland
Woolworth, U.S.A., closes all its discount stores
Haribo's gummi bear is 75 years old
World's largest traffic control system, Tokyo's "Intelligent Traffic Guidance" begins operation with 14,000 sensors and 2,007 cameras
Jeanne Calment, Fr. woman, oldest person in the world, d. (b. 1875)
McDonald's has the world's largest profits from fast food
The number of fatal heart attacks in western industrial nations is decreasing. The tendency in the countries of eastern Europe has been the opposite since 1989
Worldwide increase in the number of AIDS-infected children. 590,000 children infected with the HIV virus in 1997. 30 million people of all ages infected worldwide. In Africa, 1,000 children die from AIDS every day
(contd)

	A. HISTORY, POLITICS	B. LITERATURE, THEATER	C. RELIGION, PHILOSOPHY, LEARNING

1997 contd

A. HISTORY, POLITICS

U.S. President Bill Clinton's visit to South America is accompanied by protests
China's President Jiang Zemin visits the U.S.
Scandal over political contributions brings difficulties for President Bill Clinton and Vice President Al Gore
In Canada, slim victory in parliamentary elections for the Liberal Party led by Prime Minister Jean Chrétien
Summit meeting of the C.I.S. states in Moscow. Economic integration should remain a priority
Nurlan Balgimbayev succeeds Akezhan Kazhegeldin as Prime Minister of Kazakhstan
Russian President Boris Yeltsin fires his Defense Minister Igor Rodionov and general staff chief Samsonov. New Defense Minister is Igor Sergejev
Declaration of martial law in Albania after civil war–like conditions break out in the southern region of the country
Nationwide strikes in Bulgaria
Mart Siimann becomes new Prime Minister of Estonia
In elections for France's National Assembly, ruling parties lose their majority and half of all mandates. Incumbent Prime Minister Alain Juppé resigns and is replaced by socialist Lionel Jospin. He forms a cabinet with members of Socialists, Communists, and Greens
Princess Diana (born Diana Spencer), former wife of Brit. Prince Charles, d. (b. 1961)
Britain's Queen Elizabeth II visits Pakistan and India
Heavy losses for Conservatives in elections for British Parliament. Tony Blair becomes new Prime Minister. John Major resigns from party leadership
Scots in U.K. vote to establish their own parliament
Brit. Parliament ratifies ban on handguns
Negotiations between all parties in the conflict in Northern Ireland to determine the country's future. Prime Minister Tony Blair confers with Sinn Féin leader Gerry Adams
Commonwealth meeting in London. Membership nominees Yemen, Rwanda, and the Autonomous Palestinian Areas are not accepted into the Commonwealth
Opposition party Fianna Fail wins in Ireland's elections. Mary McAleese wins the election to fill the vacant office of the President in Ireland
Governmental crisis in Italy, Prime Minister Roman Prodi remains in office
Serbian President Slobodan Milosevic becomes new President of the Federal Republic of Yugoslavia (Serbia and Montenegro); Prime Minister Djukanovic becomes President of Montenegro, succeeding Bulatovic in office
Clear swing to the right evident in parliamentary elections in Norway. Prime Minister Thorbjörn Jagland resigns. Kjell Magne Bondevik becomes new Prime Minister
Austrian Chancellor Vranitzky resigns from government office. Finance Minister Klima succeeds
With voter turnout at 47.9%, left-wing alliance loses its majority in elections for Poland's Lower House of Parliament, defeated by the union-movement Solidarity. Jerzy Buzek becomes new Prime Minister
Swed. government plans to investigate reasons for the forced sterilization of thousands of women declared mentally or racially inferior between 1936 and 1976
Sweden announces plans to shut down its first nuclear reactor in 1998
Milan Milutinovic wins presidential election in Serbia
Milan Kucan is reelected President of Slovenia
Former army chief of staff Aslan Maskhadov is elected new President of Chechnya
Alparslan Türkesch, Turkish politician, leader of the right-wing extremist Party of Nationalist Movement, d. (b. 1917)
Government crisis in Turkey. Following the failure of the coalition government, Pres. Süleyman Demirel charges opposition leader
(contd)

B. LITERATURE, THEATER

PEN-Center to Edward Said in recognition of his efforts "on behalf of persecuted and incarcerated writers and journalists"
International PEN-Center elects Mexican author Homero Aridjis new President of the organization
Ingmar Bergmann announces that he will be returning to the National Theater in Stockholm
Writer Günter Grass establishes a foundation to support the Roma people
Peter Handke: "Zurüstungen für die Unsterblichkeit"
Amer. actress Sharon Stone discovers a radio play manuscript co-written by Aldous Huxley and Christopher Isherwood
Best-selling Amer. author Stephen King closes on a contract with Simon & Schuster over his newest work "Bag of Bones" and two additional works for net royalties between 50 and 75%
Jack Lang, former Fr. Minister of Culture, becomes director of the Piccolo Teatro
Opening exhibit for the National Library in Paris themed "The Encyclopedia"
Russian Academy of Sciences accepts writer Aleksandr Solzhenitsyn as a new member
Frankfurt Book Fair: 306, 476 titles from 9,544 publishers or 106 countries. Increased admission fees lead to a decrease in attendance
The Amer. conglomerate John Wiley and Sons sells Berlin's Akademie Verlag to the publishing house R. Oldenbourg in Munich

C. RELIGION, PHILOSOPHY, LEARNING

Interfaith symposium at the Vatican to discuss Christian roots of anti-Semitism
Approximately 2,500-year-old mummy of a child found in a cave south of Mexico City
Oldest existing architecture in North America found in Louisiana in a complex of 11 mounds dating back 5,400 years
Brit. Geologists find bones of a previously unknown carnivorous dinosaur species in the White Chalk Cliffs of the Isle of Wight
Archeologists in Lower Saxony unearth three well-preserved wooden spears in a coal mine. Spears provide proof that the hunting techniques of early man were organized and utilized weapons
Israeli archeologists discover ruins of the Biblical city of Sanoach not far from what is now the city of Bet Schemech
Paleontologists in the Liaoning Province of northeast China find dinosaur fossils, including the first organs ever found of the creatures who went extinct some 65 million years ago
Extensive ruins of antiquity found in Eritrea

D. VISUAL ARTS

between Iranian Abbas Kiarostami for "A Taste of Cherry" and Japanese director Shohei Imamura for "Unagi"
Anthony Minghella's "The English Patient" wins 9 Oscars (best picture, best director, supporting actress, cinematography, original dramatic score, film editing, sound, costume, and art direction). Best foreign film went to "Kolya" by Jan Sverák, best documentary film to "When We Were Kings" by Leon Gast and David Sonnenberg
Alan Parker's screen version of the musical "Evita" and the singer-actress Madonna take home three Golden Globes
"Amours" at the Foundation Cartier in Paris
Arken, the new museum of modern art in Copenhagen, closes
Villa Borghese in Rome reopens
Work-in-review of the Mexican photographer Manuel Alvarez Bravo at the Museum of Modern Art in New York
Presentation of the Brueghel painting dynasty in an exhibit at the Villa Hügel in Essen
Major exhibit of Byzantine art at the Metropolitan Museum in New York
Mosaic confiscated by police in Bremen is presumed to have come from the legendary lost Amber Room of the Catherine Palace near St. Petersburg
Christie's in New York auctions off the modern art collection of Victor and Sally Ganz for $206.5 million, setting a record high for the sale of a private collection at auction
Christo and Jeanne-Claude announce that they will never wrap again
Drawings by Dürer, Holbein, and Grünewald at the Art Museum in Basel
"Exile, Flight and Emigration of European Artists 1933–1945" at the New National Gallery in Berlin
Major exhibit of Ger. Expres-
(contd)

E. MUSIC

"Time Out of Mind"
Morton Feldman retrospective in Gütersloh, Ger.
Philip Glass's opera based on a novel by Doris Lessing, "The Marriage between Zones Three, Four and Five" premieres in Heidelberg
Hans Werner Henze's choreographed opera "Adonis" premieres in Munich
David Hockney produces Wagner's "Tristan und Isolde" in Los Angeles
René Kollo resigns from his post as director of the Metropolitan Theater in Berlin. The operetta theater is forced to close
Rolling Stones release their 21st studio album "Bridges to Babylon"
Hans Werner Henze: "Tanzstunden" performed by the Berlin State Opera

F. SCIENCE, TECHNOLOGY, GROWTH

highest-elevation planetarium in Europe
Amer. scientists discover a new planetoid beyond Pluto circling the sun in a pronounced elliptical orbit
Astronomers at the Harvard-Smithsonian Observatory discover a new planet near a star 50 light years away, the ninth planet found outside the solar system
First "loner" stars found 300,000 light years away from the nearest galaxy
Astronomers in Canada and the U.S. discover two new moons of the planet Uranus. 15 moons have previously been counted around the planet
Hale-Bopp, the "comet of the century," first time a tail containing neutral sodium atoms is ever captured on film
Sojourner space probe lands on Mars. Pathfinder Mars rover begins probing the surface, but the mission is aborted after only four months when the rover loses contact
Problems continue to plague the Russian space station Mir
Over 500 images of the gray-black asteroid 253 Mathilde made by an Amer. space probe launched in 1996 on a mission for flyby study of asteroids
Amer. space probe Cassini launched on its mission to Saturn carrying the European probe Huygens. The probe will reach Saturn in 2004
European Space Observatory (ESO) extends its mission until April 1998
First burial in space launched with 24 lipstick-sized urns carrying the remains of, among others, Timothy Leary
Brazil's first attempt at launching a space rocket ends 65-seconds after liftoff when the rocket explodes
The Hipparcos Catalogue is published, gives astronomers specific coordinates of over 118,218 celestial objects
Amer. geneticists generate artificial chromosomes for the first time ever
A research group in Munich performs molecular genetic experiment to prove that Neanderthals are not the ancestors of modern day humans. Rather they were members of a now extinct but distinct species that split off from the hominid line
(contd)

G. DAILY LIFE

Aspirin, the world's most widely used analgesic, is 100 years old
Amer. F.D.A. (Fed. Drug Administration) approves the use of Thalidomide
Ger. firm "Maggi" celebrates its 100th birthday
Holocaust survivors and/or their heirs file class action suit in New York against 7 European insurance companies, charging them with failing to pay life insurance claims after WW II
Father of tennis player Steffi Graf, Peter Graf and the family accountant, Joachim Eckhardt, indicted on charges of tax evasion
Religiously motivated suicide of 39 people near San Diego
Swiss railways celebrate 150th anniversary
John Akii-Bua, Ugand. track and field star and Olympic medalist (1972), 400 m. hurdles, d. (b. 1950)
International Olympic Committee (I.O.C.) announces that 2004 Summer Olympic Games will be held in Athens
8th Pan-Arabic Games in Beirut. The Iraqi team is refused entry to Lebanon by immigration officials
Track and Field World Championship in Athens. In the unofficial ranking by country, Germany takes second place behind the U.S.
Brazilian Ronaldo is named 1996 Soccer Player of the Year
Canadian race car driver Jacques Villeneuve becomes world champion in Formula 1
Darius Michalczewski, Ger. professional light heavyweight boxer, holds the championship title in all three world boxing organizations
16-year-old Swiss tennis player Martina Hingis ranks number one in the world ranking list
U.S. tennis player Pete Sampras wins the ATP-World Championship for the fourth time
Thomas Hellriegel becomes the first Ger. to win Hawaii's iron man competition, the world's most important triathlon
World Champion chess player Kasparov is defeated by the IBM computer "Deep Blue" with a score of 3.5-2.5 points
Jan Ullfrich becomes the first Ger. to win the Tour de France
German Women's National Soccer team wins the European championship with a 2-0 victory over Italy
Shot Put World Champion Astrid Kumbernuss named European Track and Field Athlete of the Year
Brazilian soccer player Ronaldo named Soccer Player of the Year in Europe
Soccer team Borussia Dortmund wins European Cup to become European Champion with a 2-1 victory over Juventus Turin
Boris Becker replaces Nikola Pilic as head of the German National Tennis Team
Ger. tennis player Michael Stich ends his tennis career at the age of 28
(contd)

1997 contd

Mesut Yilmaz with the task of building a new administration. Yilmaz gains vote of confidence in parliament

Turkey threatens to annex northern Cyprus. Turkey makes military incursions into Iraq to fight pro-Kurdish rebel bases of the Kurdistan Labor Party (PKK)

Ibero-American Summit meeting on the Caribbean Island of Margarita off the coast of Venezuela

Hugo Banzer, former Bolivian dictator, becomes Bolivian President

The body of Che Guevara is discovered buried beneath a runway at the airport in Vallegrande, Bolivia. The Argentine-Cuban revolutionary was shot dead in 1967 near Vallegrande. His remains are laid to rest in Cuba

In Ecuador, Fabián Alarbi becomes new President

In Haiti, President René Préval appoints rector of the university at Port-au-Prince, Hervé Denis, Prime Minister

In Honduras, candidate for the ruling Liberal Party, Carlos Flores, claims victory in the presidential election

For the first time since 1969, Christmas Day is celebrated as official holiday in Cuba

5th Communist Party Congress in Cuba. Fidel Castro speaks for 7 hours

After 80 years of U.S. military presence in Panama, U.S. troops begin the withdrawal that was agreed upon in 1977, scheduled to be completed by 1999

Violent end to the more-than-four-month-long hostage crisis at the Japanese embassy in Lima, Peru

Islamic militants stage an attack on tourists at the Temple of Hatshepsut in Egypt; more than 60 dead. President Hosni Mubarak fires interior minister

Countless attacks on neighborhoods and villages in Algeria. Since 1992, more than 60,000 people have been killed in Algeria in politically motivated attacks

First parliamentary elections in Algeria since banning of the Islamic Salvation Front (FIS) in 1992. Majority for the National Democratic Rally Party (RND)

Iraq ousts U.N. inspectors

Chaim Herzog, Israeli politician, d. (b. 1918, Belfast)

Israel declares 8th of May, the day the German Reich collapsed, a national holiday

Israel releases founder of Hamas, Sheik Ahmed Yassin, from prison after many years in exchange for two Mossad agents. Prisoner exchange between Israel and Jordan

Israeli Prime Minister Benjamin Netanyahu and President of the PLO Yasse Arafat agree to hold regular talks

Jordan retracts on cooperation with Israel over security issues after learning of a failed assassination attempt by Mossad agents on a Hamas leader in Amman

On a visit to Libya, South African President Nelson Mandela speaks in favor of lifting U.N. sanctions against Libya

First-ever direct parliamentary elections in Morocco. Victory for the opposition parties

Conference on Species Preservation in Harare (Zimbabwe) approves restricted trade in ivory in Zimbabwe, Namibia, and Botswana

Paul Biya reelected Pres. of Cameroon

Safina Party of the white Kenyan politician Richard Leakey is outlawed

Civil war in the Congo (Brazzaville). Former Pres. Denis Sassou-Nguesso seizes power

Coronation of Letsie III as King of Lesotho

Hastings Kamuzu Banda, first Pres. of Malawi, d. (b. c. 1900)

Morocco and Polisario agree to the terms of referendum on the political future of the former Spanish colony in the western Sahara

Military intervention by Nigeria in Sierre Leone following a military putsch there

290 dead in a Hutu attack on a prison in the northwest of Rwanda

Military putsch in Zambia fails

(contd)

1997 contd

D. VISUAL ARTS

sionists in Venice's Palazzo Grassi

Museum dedicated to the work of Lyonel Feininger is opened in Quedlinburg, with the most comprehensive single collection of the illustrators' graphics in Europe

Works-in-review of French art at the Centre Pompidou in Paris, titled "Made in France: 1947–1997"

Getty Center in L.A. designed by Richard Meier opens

Guggenheim Museum in Bilbao designed by Frank O. Gehry opens

Largest Gilbert and George retrospective ever in Paris

Doubts surface about the authenticity of the Van Gogh painting "Sunflowers" sold at auction in 1987 to the Japanese company Yasuda

Hannah Höch retrospective at the Museum of Modern Art in New York

London celebrates the 300th anniversary of William Hogarth's birth with a retrospective at the British Museum

Jasper Johns retrospective in Cologne

Swiss capital city of Bern announces plans to establish a Paul Klee museum there

Major Fernand Léger retrospective in Paris's Centre Pompidou

Robert Mapplethorpe exhibit at the State Museum in Stuttgart

Egon Schiele Show at the Museum of Modern Art in New York

"Sensation," exhibit of recent Brit. art at the Royal Academy in London

Ger. art historian Werner Spies named director of the National Museum of Modern Art at the Pompidou Center in Paris

William Turner retrospective at Vienna's Art Forum

Vasarely Museum in Aix-en-Provence closes

The Weimar Hall, a work of Classical Modern architecture built in 1932 and the city's largest building from the period between 1919 and 1933, is demolished

(contd)

E. MUSIC

F. SCIENCE, TECHNOLOGY, GROWTH

Scientists at PPL Therapeutics outside Edinburgh succeed in cloning a sheep

First World Conference on Ethics Codes in Medicine and Biotechnology in Freiburg, Germany

Designed to measure the earth's rotation, the world's largest ring laser gyro is installed in a subterranean cave in New Zealand

A Brit. jet-engine car breaks the sound barrier on a stretch in the Nevada desert with a speed of 763.055 mph

German manufacturer manufactures the world's largest tunnel boring machine. It has a circumference of 47 feet and will be used to build the fourth tunnel under the Elbe River in Hamburg

The largest moveable storm surge barrier in the world is opened in Hoek van Holland, Netherlands

G. DAILY LIFE

British Soccer Team Manchester United establishes its own broadcast channel

30 days of national mourning in Bolivia to mourn the suicide of 31-year-old soccer star Ramiro Castillo

Flipper, television star dolphin, d. (b. c. 1947, given name Bebe)

Some 2 billion people worldwide suffer from lack of clean drinking water

World Convention on Climate Change in Kyoto. Industrial countries agree to reduce emissions of greenhouse gases by an average of 5.2% by the year 2012

Oil tanker disasters cause spills off the coast of Yokohama, Japan; the southern coast of the Philippines; in the Japan Sea; off the coast of Uruguay and near Singapore

Deformities found in North Sea fish decrease in number

Paris places restrictions on driving in Paris to curb pollution; free public transportation offered drivers forbidden from driving in the city

El Niño forms in the ocean between Australia and South America. Unstable weather conditions. Hurricanes and drought in the southern hemisphere, colder temperatures in the north

Ground ice in Alaska melting in spots as the result of the greenhouse effect

In China, work begins on construction of the largest hydroelectric dam in the world, spanning 375 miles of the Yangtze River

Gianni Versace, Ital. fashion designer, d. (b. 1946)

Major earthquake in Iran: 1,500 dead

Fire breaks out at a Hindu festival in the city of Mmadhuban in eastern India, killing 200 and injuring at least 500

Fire in the Cathedral at Turin; Shroud of Turin is rescued

Midair collision of Ger. Army aircraft and U.S. Air Force plane over Africa; 33 dead

Boating accident off the coast of Haiti: several hundred people drown

Huge forest fires resulting from slash-and-burn programs in Indonesia

Plane crash south of the Indonesian city of Medan: 234 dead

Heavy storms on the west coast of Mexico

Argentine passenger plane crashes over Uruguay, leaving 74 dead

Heavy storms sweep through Somalia

Cholera epidemic in Mozambique

Russian cargo plane crashes over the Siberian city of Irkutsk

	A. HISTORY, POLITICS	B. LITERATURE, THEATER	C. RELIGION, PHILOSOPHY, LEARNING

1997 contd

50th Convention of the African National Congress (A.N.C.). Nelson Mandela passes A.N.C. chairmanship to Thabo Mbeki

South Africa's former president, de Klerk, resigns as opposition leader in parliament and as chairman of the National Party

Steve Biko, the South African politician murdered in 1977, is honored throughout the country on the 20th anniversary of his death

Major hunger crisis in Tanzania caused by worst drought in 40 years. Requests for aid from western nations

Bloody overthrow in Zaire. Pres. Mobutu flees the country. His successor Laurent-Désiré Kabila changes the country's name to the Democratic Republic of the Congo

Mobutu Sese Seko, former President of Zaire, d. (b. 1930)

In the capital of the Central African Republic, Bungui, Fr. troops squelch soldiers' mutiny

Currencies of southeast Asian countries come under severe pressure

Association of Southeast Asian Nations (A.S.E.A.N.) denies Cambodia's application for membership

Asian-Pacific Economic Cooperation (A.P.E.C.) meeting in Vancouver, Canada. Russia, Vietnam, and Peru accepted as new members

Deng Xiaoping, Chin. politician, former President and secretary general of the Communist Party, d. (b. 1912)

Peng Zhen, Chin. politician, d. (b. 1902)

In Beijing Chinese President Jiang Zemin and Boris Yeltsin of Russia sign a document ending centuries-old tensions over demarcation of the Chinese border

China allows dissident Wei Jingsheng to leave the country

British imperial colony of Hong Kong becomes part of the People's Republic of China

Congress Party politician Kocheril Raman Narayanan is elected President of India. Inder Kumar Gujral is Prime Minister of India, heading up a 15-party coalition that only lasts for a few months

Japanese Prime Minister Ryntaro Hashimoto forms new administration

Cambodian gov. seeks asylum for Khmer Rouge leader Pol Pot in Laos, Thailand, and China

Aid agreement between North and South Korea over hunger crisis in the North

North Korea breaks ground for the construction of two nuclear reactors

Muslim League claims absolute majority in early parliamentary elections in Pakistan. Nawaz Sharif becomes Prime Minister

In South Korea, former Mayor of Seoul Koh Kun becomes new Prime Minister

D. VISUAL ARTS	E. MUSIC	F. SCIENCE, TECHNOLOGY, GROWTH	G. DAILY LIFE	
Altarpiece by the Baroque painter Josef Johann Baptist Zimmermann found in severely damaged condition in the depository of the diocese in Würzburg. It had been considered lost since the end of WW II U.S. House of Representatives votes to eliminate funding for the National Endowment for the Arts (N.E.A.) Woody Allen: "Everyone Says I Love You" (U.S. 1996) Robert Altman, Amer. film director, wins his battle against PolyGram studios and is allowed to show his own version of his film "The Gingerbread Man" in theaters Luc Besson: "The Fifth Element," at a cost of $90 million, is the most expensive European feature film production British Board of Film Classification finally approves the uncut version of David Cronenberg's film "Crash" Marlene Dietrich's New York estate brings some 1.8 million DM at auction Comprehensive retrospective of the works of Rainer Werner Fassbinder in New York Robert Rauschenberg retrospective at the Guggenheim Museum in New York Leon Gast: "When We Were Kings," documentary film (U.S. 1996) Brit. filmmaker Peter Greenaway announces his intent to produce his next film on CD-ROM and to distribute it on the Internet Mike Leigh: "Career Girls," feature film (U.K. 1997) Ken Loach: "Carla's Song," feature film (U.K., Germ., Spain, 1996) Twenty years after its first release, George Lucas's "Star Wars" is back in theaters David Lynch: "Lost Highway," feature film (U.S. 1996) Amer. director Adrian Lyne's film of "Lolita" goes for *(contd)*				**1997 contd**

	A. HISTORY, POLITICS	B. LITERATURE, THEATER	C. RELIGION, PHILOSOPHY, LEARNING
1997 contd			
1998	Nobel Peace Prize to John Hume, Pres. of the largest Catholic minority party in Northern Ireland (SDLP), and David Trimble, leader of the Ulster Unionist Party (UUP) for their efforts to end the conflict in Northern Ireland. They were both instrumental in negotiating a peace agreement Right Livelihood Award ("Alternative Nobel Prize") to the Croatian peace activists Katarina Kruhonja and Verena Terselic, to Samuel Epstein (U.S.) for his contributions to cancer prevention, to Juan Pablo Orrego (Chile) for environmental protection in Chile, and to the International Baby Food Action Network for helping young mothers in developing countries Vaclav Havel is first-time recipient of the Peace Prize of Westphalia, established on the occasion of the 350th anniversary of the Peace of Westphalia To commemorate the 50th anniversary of the U.N's Universal Declaration of Human Rights, Amnesty International protests that in 117 of 193 countries people are still being tortured Ratification of a U.N. Statute establishing an International Criminal Court. 120 countries approve, 7 disapprove (U.S. included), 21 abstain U.N.I.C.E.F. study reports: Over 130 million children worldwide do not attend school, four out of five classrooms do not have a chalkboard; approximately 250 million child laborers worldwide U.S. and U.K. conduct four nights of bomb attacks in Iraq. President Bill Clinton justifies the deployment of 415 cruise missiles based on "U.S. national interests" and protecting the Gulf Region. Iraq's President Saddam Hussein had manufactured weapons of mass destruction despite the U.N. ban Great Britain assumes presidency of the EU Council through the end of June, when the post rotates to Austria until the end of the year European Parliament in Strasbourg denies relief to the EU Commission for its 1996 budget due to allegations of corruption and fraud 19 of 40 European Council members agree to ban human cloning in a protocol to become part of the European Council's Convention on Human Rights and Biomedicine EU Commission outlines preconditions for expanding the Union to include Poland, Czech Republic, Estonia, Slovenia, and Cyprus in its "Agenda 2000" package of agricultural and structural policy reforms Establishment of the European Central Bank in Frankfurt; Wim Duisenberg (Netherlands) is President U.S. President Bill Clinton is confronted with allegations of having *(contd)*	Eric Ambler, Brit. spy novelist, d. (b. 1909) Carlos Castaneda, Amer. writer and new age guru, d. (b. 1925) Eldridge Cleaver, African American writer and civil rights activist, d. (b. 1935) Paul Flamand, Fr. publisher (Editions du Seuil), d. (b. 1909) William Gaddis, Amer. author, d. (b. 1922) Martha Gellhorn, Amer. journalist and war correspondent, d. (b. 1907) Julian Green, Fr.-Amer. writer, d. (b. 1900, Paris) Zbigniew Herbert, Polish lyric poet, dramatist, and essayist, d. (b. 1924) Ernst Jünger, Ger. author, d. (b. 1895) Hamid Mosaddegh, Iranian poet and attorney, d. (b. 1939) Octavio Paz, Mexican writer, lyric poet, essayist, and literary theorist; 1990 Nobel laureate, d. (b. 1914) Richard Plant, Amer. writer and translator, d. (b. 1910) Dorothy West, African American writer, d. (b. 1907) Nobel Prize for Literature to Portuguese writer José Saramago, who wrote, among other things, "The Memorial," "The Stone Raft," and "Blindness" Peace Prize of the Ger. Booksellers' Assoc. to writer Martin Walser for lifetime achievement Alexander Pushkin Prize to Vladimir Makanin, Russian author American University in Cairo's Nagib Majfuz Medal for Contemporary Arabian Literature to Algerian author Ahlam Mustaghanami France's Prix Goncourt to Paule *(contd)*	Henry Steele Commager, Amer. historian, d. (b. 1900) Nelson Goodman, Amer. philosopher, d. (b. 1906) Trevor Huddleston, Brit. Anglican Archbishop, d. (b. 1913) Mohammed Metwali Sharawi, Egyptian cleric, popular Islamic evangelist, d. (b. 1910) Benjamin Spock, Amer. pediatrician and child psychologist, d. (b. 1904) Telford Taylor, Amer. jurist, prosecutor in the Nuremberg Trials, d. (b. 1908) Vatican opens its once nearly inaccessible archive of documents from the Inquisition and allows access to the "Index of Banned Books" Pope John Paul II visit the Socialist Republic of Cuba Pope John Paul II issues his 3rd encyclical since the beginning of his 20th year in the papacy: "Fides et ratio" ("Faith and Reason") Vatican makes its first public apology for lack of resistance to the mass murder of Jews by the Nazis Pope John Paul II canonizes Edith Stein, a Benedictine nun murdered in Auschwitz, to sainthood. It is the first time that a Catholic woman of Jewish descent is canonized Erich Hobsbawm, Brit. historian, publishes "The Age of Exremes"

D. VISUAL ARTS	E. MUSIC	F. SCIENCE, TECHNOLOGY, GROWTH	G. DAILY LIFE	
months in the U.S. without distribution, but is quickly picked up in France, U.K., and Germany Anthony Minghella: "The English Patient," feature film (U.S. 1996) James Cameron: "Titanic," feature film (U.S. 1997) Pathé Albatros, the historical film studio in Montreuil near Paris, first built in 1904, is declared a historical preservation site Sally Potter: "Tango Lesson," feature film (U.K. 1997) Jan Sverák: "Kolya," feature film (Chechnya, U.K., France 1996) Turkey signs the European Convention on Cinematographic Co-Production				**1997 contd**
James Algar, Amer. documentary filmmaker ("The Living Desert" [1953]), d. (b. 1913) Eva Bartok, Amer. screen actress of Hungarian descent, d. (b. 1929) Ilse Bing, Ger.-Amer. photographer and art historian, d. (b. 1900) Lloyd Bridges, Amer. screen and television actor, d. (b. 1912) César, Fr. artist, d. (b. 1921) William Congdon, Amer. painter, d. (b. 1912) Lúcio Costa, Brazilian architect, d. (b. 1902) Armin Dahl, Ger. screen actor and Germany's first stuntman, d. (b. 1922) Lydia Delectorskaja, Russian emigrée, colleague, model, and muse to Henri Matisse, d. (b. 1909) Albert Frey, Swiss-Amer. architect, d. (b. 1903) Bob Kane, Amer. comic illustrator (Batman), d. (b. 1916) Keisuke Kinoshita, Japanese film director, d. (b. 1912) Akiro Kurosawa, Japanese film director ("Rashomon," "The Seven Samurais"), d. (b. 1910) Jean Marais, Fr. screen actor, d. (b. 1913) Maureen O'Sullivan, Amer. actress, d. (b. 1910) *(contd)*	Theodore Bloomfield, Amer. conductor, d. (b. 1923) Sonny Bono, Amer. singer and politician, ex-husband of Cher, d. (b. 1936) Miltiades Caridis, Greek conductor, d. (b. 1923, Danzig) Richard Cassilly, Amer. tenor, d. (b. 1927) Basil "Manenberg" Cotzee, South African saxophonist, d. (b. 1943) Roman Cycowski, member of the legendary "Comedian Harmonists," d. (b. 1901) Peter Diamand, Dutch musician and founder of the Holland Festival, d. (b. 1913) Todd Duncan, Amer. baritone, first black actor to play Porgy, d. (b. 1907) Horst Jankowski, Ger. jazz musician and composer, d. (b. 1936) Matoub Lounès, Algerian singer and representative of the Berbers, d. (murdered; b. 1956) Linda McCartney, Brit. musician and photographer, wife of Paul McCartney, d. (b. 1942) Hermann Prey, Ger. baritone, d. (b. 1929) Jerome Robbins, Amer. choreographer and ballet master, d. (b. 1918) Leonie Ryansek, Austrian soprano, d. (b. 1926) Alfred Schnittke, Russian- *(contd)*	Sir Derek K. Barton, Brit. chemist, d. (b. 1919) Kenichi Fukui, Japanese chemist, d. (b. 1918) George H. Hitchings, Amer. biochemist and pharmacologist, d. (b. 1905) Karl Mönkemeyer, Ger. chemist, d. (b. 1916) Ferdinand "Ferry" Porsche, Jr., Ger. auto manufacturer, d. (b. 1909) Vladimir Prelog, Swiss chemist, d. (b. 1905) Maria Reiche, Ger.-Peruvian mathematician, d. (b. 1902) Alan Shepard, Amer. astronaut, d. (b. 1923) Haroun Tazieff, Fr. volcanologist, author, and filmmaker, d. (b. 1914) Nobel Prize for Physics to German Horst Störmer and to the Americans Daniel C. Tsui and Robert B. Laughlin for discovery of a new form of quantum fluid that led to a breakthrough in understanding quantum physics Nobel Prize for Chemistry to the Amer. scientist Walter Kohn and Brit. scientist John Pople for models and computer programs for calculating the properties of molecules Nobel Prize for Medicine to Americans Robert F. Furchtgott, Louis J. Ignarro, and Ferid Murad for their discoveries concerning nitric oxide as a signaling molecule in the cardiovascular system Nobel Prize for Economics to the Indian philosopher of economics from Trinity College in Cambridge, Amartya Sen, for key *(contd)*	F.A.O. report (U.N. Food and Agriculture Organization): Denmark has the most food resources in the world, Somalia has the least U.N. study determines that there are 828 million people suffering from hunger worldwide, a decrease when seen in proportion to the world population, but an increase in absolute numbers (822 million in 1992) Japan, second largest consumer economy in the world, is stuck in a recession. Major impact on the entire Asian economy Expo 98 in Lisbon with the theme "The Oceans—A Heritage for the Future." 155 countries and organizations involved For the first time in history, Germany's DAX stock index exceeds the 5,000-point mark Merger between U.S. Citicorp Bank and the Travelers Insurance group produces the world's largest finance group: total assets $83 billion, 100 million customers in 100 countries Chairmen of the boards of directors for automobile manufacturers Daimler Benz and Chrysler, Jürgen Schrempp and Robert Eaton, announce plans for a merger of the two companies under the name Daimler-Chrysler AG Largest U.S. long-distance carrier AT&T takes over the most important U.S. cable television corporation TeleCommunications Inc. (TCI). $48 billion transaction British Petroleum (BP) and U.S. oil company Amoco Corp. agree to a merger. Stock exchange value: $110 billion The Deutsche Bank buys out the eighth largest banking company in the U.S., Bankers Trust, to create the largest bank in the world with total assets at $820 billion U.S. oil companies Exxon and Mobil merge to create the largest petroleum company in the *(contd)*	**1998**

	A. HISTORY, POLITICS	B. LITERATURE, THEATER	C. RELIGION, PHILOSOPHY, LEARNING

1998 contd

had an affair with a White House intern, Monica Lewinsky. Signed affidavits are filed and special prosecutor Kenneth Starr subsequently writes a 450-page report, which is also published on the Internet. House of Representatives initiates impeachment proceedings, for only the second time in U.S. history, based on charges of perjury and obstruction of justice

Ger. President R. Herzog on state visit in South Korea

In his acceptance speech for the Peace Prize of the Ger. Association of Publishers and Booksellers, writer Martin Walser criticizes the instrumentalization of the Ger. past. "It is not appropriate that Auschwitz should be used as a routine threat." He complains about the "constant presentation of our disgrace" in the media. His statements lead to a public debate in which Ignatz Bubis, Pres. of the Central Council of Jews in Germany, calls Walser an "intellectual arsonist" and which includes the involvement of Klaus von Donnanyi, former SPD minister and Hamburg's first mayor

Ger. Foreign Minister Joschka Fischer fails in his attempt to initiate a "no first use" of nuclear weapons policy at the N.A.T.O. conference in Brussels

Deutsche Bank and Dresdner Bank sued for billions in damages by victims of the Nazis now living in the U.S. Swiss Banks UBS and Crédit Suisse settle with Jewish plaintiffs in the U.S. and agree to pay $1.25 billion for retaining funds from Holocaust survivors' accounts on the pretense that account holders were unknown

Austrian President Thomas Klestil is reelected for a second term

Social Democratic candidate Ruth Dreifuss wins presidential election in Switzerland

Led by Poul Nyrup Rasmussen, Social Democrats in Denmark narrowly defend their majority

Escape and recapture of pedophile and child murderer Marc Dutroux leads to a government crisis in Belgium. Interior Minister Lanotte and Minister of Justice De Clerck resign

Italy's former prime minister Berlusconi sentenced to prison for bribing tax auditors

No-confidence vote for Prime Minister Roman Prodi in the Italian Lower House of Parliament leads to his resignation. He is succeeded by Massimo D'Alema. New administration consists of 27 members from 7 parties

Spanish Basque separatist organization ETA declares indefinite and total cease-fire

Basque Nationalist candidate Ibarretxe becomes Head of State in the Basque Region

Agreement reached in peace talks concerning Northern Ireland: constitutional amendment for the Republic of Ireland which modifies its claim to the northern province. The 1920 Northern Ireland Statute is changed accordingly

28 dead and over 200 injured in Omagh in the worst bombing attack in Northern Ireland yet

Serbian militia continues its ruthless attacks on Albanian villages in the southern province of Kosovo

EU and N.A.T.O. threaten military intervention unless Slobodan Milosevic, Pres. of Yugoslavia, withdraws his troops from Kosovo

Croatia regains control over East Slovenia and thus assumes complete territorial sovereignty

Vaclav Havel is reelected by the Parliament in Prague for another 5-year term as president. Milos Zeman new Prime Minister in a Social Democrat minority administration

Vladimir Meciar, Prime Minister of Slovakia, resigns after crushing defeat in the election

Bulgaria abolishes the death penalty

Lithuania abolishes the death penalty

Minority government under the new Prime Minister Kristopan in Latvia reaffirmed. Strongest faction of the People's Party rejects coalition

Albanian Prime Minister Fatos Nano resigns and is succeeded by Pandeli Majko

(contd)

Constant, Fr. author, for the novel "Confidence pour confidence"

National Book Award (U.S.) in fiction to Alice McDermott for "Charming Billy," in poetry to Gerald Stern for "This Time: New and Selected Poems," in nonfiction to Edward Ball for "Slaves in the Family." Honorary Award to John Updike

50th Frankfurt Book Fair: Protests against Turkey's refusal to allow Turkish publisher Ayse Nur Zarakolu to leave the country in order to accept the Human Rights Award of the International Publishers' Union. Brit. author Salman Rushdie appears as guest

Hans Magnus Enzensberger: "Wo warst Du, Robert?," novel

Martin Walser: "Ein springender Brunnen," novel

J. Paul Getty, Amer. billionaire and patron of the arts, auctions off the most expensive printed book ever, a first edition of Geoffrey Chaucer's "Canterbury Tales," issued in 1477, at Christie's in London for 4.6 million British pounds

Bertelsmann AG purchases the New York publisher Random House and becomes the largest seller of English-language books. Bertelsmann also takes over the academic publisher Julius Springer Verlag in Heidelberg, a leader in scientific and medical publishing

Three years after its inception, the Lit. Verlag in Berlin is taken over by Bertelsmann

Iranian President Khatami declares an end to the fatwa issued by the Ayatollah Khomeini calling for the murder of Brit. author Salman Rushdie because of alleged heresy

D. VISUAL ARTS

E. MUSIC

F. SCIENCE, TECHNOLOGY, GROWTH

G. DAILY LIFE

1998 contd

D. VISUAL ARTS

Alan J. Pakula, Amer. director, d. (b. 1928)
Antonio Saura, Span. painter and graphic artist, d. (b. 1930)
Reg Smyth, Brit. illustrator, d. (b. 1917)
J.T. Walsh, Amer. screen actor, d. (b. 1943)
Freddie Young, Academy Award-winning Brit. cinematographer, d. (b. 1902)
At the Amer. Academy Awards, the $200-million production "Titanic" wins Oscars in 11 categories: best picture; James Cameron for best director; cinematography, costume design, art direction, film editing, original song, original dramatic score, sound, sound effects editing, visual effects. Best actress to Helen Hunt and best actor to Jack Nicholson for their roles in James L. Brooks's "As Good As It Gets"
Golden Globes of Hollywood's Foreign Press Assoc.: Best picture (comedy/musical) to James L. Brooks's "As Good as It Gets"; best picture (Drama) to James Cameron's "Titanic." Best foreign film to Alain Berliner's "Ma Vie en Rose"
Berlin's Golden Bear to Walter Salles for "Central do Brasil" (Brazil 1998), Silver Bear for best actress to Fernanda Montenegro ("Central do Brasil"). French actress Catherine Deneuve receives honorary award for lifetime achievement
Cannes Golden Palm to Greek director Angelopoulos for "Eternity and a Day." Jury's Grand Prize to Ital. director Roberto Benigni for "Life Is Beautiful." Best Director to Brit. director John Boorman for "The General"
Venice's Golden Lion to Ital. director Gianni Amelio for "Coi ridevano." Festival director Felice Laudadio demands the elimination of the competition and complete overhaul of the festival
(contd)

E. MUSIC

Ger. composer, d. (b. 1934)
Frank Sinatra, Amer. singer, actor, and entertainer, d. (b. 1915)
Shinichi Suzuki, Japanese violinist, conductor, and music educator, d. (b. 1898)
Klaus Tennstedt, Ger. conductor, d. (b. 1926)
Sir Michael Tippett, Brit. composer, d. (b. 1905)
Haj Hocine Toulali, Moroccan folk musician, d. (b. 1924)
Galina Ulanova, Russian ballet dancer, d. (b. 1910)
Carl Wilson, Amer. rock musician, member and founder of the "Beach Boys," d. (b. 1947)
Attila Zoller, Hungarian-born Amer. jazz guitarist, d. (b. 1917)
Russian composer Sofia Gubaidulina receives the Praemium Imperale from the Japan Arts Assoc.
Prix Grand Siècle (France) to William Christie, Amer. conductor and harpsichordist
American Music Awards to the Spice Girls as most popular new band and most popular new album
Ernest Bloch: "Macbeth," opera, directed by John Dew
O. Messiaen, "St. François d'Assise," opera, Ger. premiere in Leipzig, directed by Gottfried Pilz
John Neumeier: "Bartók Bilder," 3 musical pieces by Bela Bartók, ballet
Puccini opera "Turandot" conducted by Zubin Mehta, directed by Zhang Yimou in Beijing. Total cost of production: $15 million, ticket prices as high as $1,250
"Lord of the Rings," fantasy musical staged in Berlin, music and direction by Bernd Stromberger

F. SCIENCE, TECHNOLOGY, GROWTH

contributions to research on fundamental problems in welfare economics
Kyoto Prize of Japan's Inamori Endowment to Swiss molecular biologist Kurt Wütherich for discovering a technique for analyzing the structures of protein, to Japanese mathematician Kiyosi Ito for research into stochastic probability theory, and to Korean video artist Nam June Paik for his contributions to contemporary art
Ger. scientists discover the oldest traces of animal fossils in a 1 billion year old rock in India. Oldest animal fossils previously found were 580 million years old
Amer. scientists discover nearly 100 million-year-old dinosaur eggs, fully intact, in Argentina
South African paleontologists find 3.5 million-year-old hominid skeleton
Oldest known writing, dated c. 3200 B.C., discovered in Egypt. It is 200 years older than the hieroglyphs
The sarcophagus of Emperor Friedrich II in the Cathedral at Palermo is opened. Microbiologists, pathologists, and other experts want to study the corpse and clothing of this and two additional skeletons of unknown persons also in the tomb
For the first time ever, complete genetic sequencing of a polycellular organism achieved by Brit. scientists at the Sanger Centre in Cambridge and by Amer. scientists at the Genome Sequencing Center in St. Louis
Amer. genetic scientist Richard Seed plans to open a cloning clinic in Chicago where as many as 500 human clones will be created annually
Scientists at Cambridge University succeed in producing electromicroscopic images of atoms at a distance of less than ten nanometers. Previously only distances twice the size were able to be made visible
Siemens and Motorola join to launch Europe's largest microelectronic project in Dresden
VW begins production of the "New Beetle" model in Puebla, Mexico
Inauguration of the Vasco da Gama Bridge over the River Tagus near Lisbon, Portugal. At 1.065 miles in length, it is Europe's longest bridge
Opening of the world's largest suspension bridge: the 1.234 mile
(contd)

G. DAILY LIFE

world
World's largest pharmaceutical manufacturer created with the merger between Germany's Hoechst corporation and France's Rhone-Poulene to form the new company Aventis
U.S. tobacco industry agrees to pay $206 billion in damages to 46 states in the U.S. for the treatment of smoking-related diseases
Richard McDonald, entrepreneur, founder of the original McDonald's fast food chain, d. (b. 1909)
Theodore W. Schultz, Amer. economic scientist, d. (b. 1902)
In the worst explosion in oil-industry history, over 700 people—mostly women and children—are killed in Nigeria
Environmental catastrophe: dam failure at a lead-zinc mine near Seville, Spain leaves 7 million tons of toxic tailings, slurries, and liquid to clean up
Wreck of the Italian freighter "Pallas" causes major oil spill affecting the islands of Amrum, Sylt, and Föhr in the North Sea
James Earl Ray, murderer of Martin Luther King, Jr., d. (b. 1928)
Avalanche in the Fr. Alps claims 11 lives, countless injured
4,500 die in the immediate aftermath of several earthquakes in northern Afghanistan, 4,000 additional deaths in the course of the year
At least 3,000 dead after tidal wave hits the West Sepik province in Papua New Guinea
Flooding catastrophe on the Yangtze River in central China: 6 million homes destroyed, 240 million people affected, 3,656 dead. Flood waters extend all the way to Russia. Japan reports 14 deaths due to severe weather conditions. 500 die in a monsoon in Bangladesh
Several tornadoes in Florida suspected to be caused by El Niño claim 39 lives
Heavy flooding in Central America in the aftermath of hurricane Mitch. Thousands dead in Nicaragua, Honduras, El Salvador, and Guatemala, several hundred thousand people left homeless. Heads of state in the region demand some sort of "Marshall Plan" to rebuild their countries after the widespread destruction
60 miners killed in a mining accident in the eastern Ukrainian coal region of Donbass
A low-flying U.S. military jet severs the cable on a ski lift at Italy's Cavalese ski resort, 20 people plunge 985 feet to their death
101 dead and 88 injured in a train accident in Eschede, Germany. An I.C.E. (InterCity Express) train slams into a bridge at 125 mph. Cause of the crash is wheel failure
Over 200 dead in an airbus crash near Taipei, Taiwan
Crash of a SwissAir flight over Canada claims the lives of 229 in the worst crash in the history of Swiss air travel
60 people killed at a fire in a disco in Göteberg, Sweden
Carla Tucker, indicted on two counts of mur-
(contd)

	A. HISTORY, POLITICS	B. LITERATURE, THEATER	C. RELIGION, PHILOSOPHY, LEARNING

1998 contd

Bella Abzug, U.S. jurist, women's rights activist, and member of Congress, d. (b. 1921)

José Maria de Areilza, Span. politician, d. (b. 1919)

Stokely Carmichael, U.S. civil rights activist, d. (b. 1940)

Barry Goldwater, U.S. politician, senator, former Republican presidential candidate, d. (b. 1909)

Konstantin Karamanlis, former Greek president and prime minister, d. (b. 1907)

Enoch Powell, Brit. politician, publicist, and historian, d. (b. 1912)

Tudor Schiwkow, Bulgarian former head of state, d. (b. 1911)

Maurice Schumann, Fr. politician, former Foreign Minister, d. (b. 1911)

Morris Udall, U.S. politician, d. (b. 1922)

George Wallace, U.S. politician, d. (b. 1919)

Russia's Duma names Sergei Kirijenko Prime Minister and successor to Chernomyrdin. Shortly thereafter, Kirijenko is replaced by Boris Yeltsin and succeeded by Yevgeny Primakov

80 years following their murder Czar Nicholas II and his family are finally buried in St. Petersburg in a ceremony attended by Boris Yeltsin

Russian Duma demands Yeltsin's resignation. Hundreds of thousands demonstrate in the streets against Yeltsin and call for his resignation. Government sources report 700,000 protestors, one representative of trade unions claims 10 million

Eduard Shevardnadze, President of Georgia, narrowly escapes assassination attempt in Tiflis

Belarus Pres. Alexander Lukashenko expels 11 diplomats from his country

Islamic Welfare Party is outlawed in Turkey

Turkish Prime Minister Mesut Yilmaz ousted by parliamentary no-confidence vote

Abdullah Öcalan, leader of the Kurdish Labor Party is apprehended in Rome. He is released and leaves Italy for an undisclosed location

Cyprus's President Glafkos John Klerides is confirmed in a runoff election against former Foreign Minister Jakovou

Bomb attacks on U.S. embassies in Nairobi, Kenya, and Dar es Salaam, Tanzania, claim over 200 lives and 500 injuries. Islamic fundamentalists claim responsibility for the attacks. U.S. retaliates by attacking targets in Afghanistan and the Sudan

Heavy rioting ensues after the death of opposition leader Moshood Abiola in Nigeria, at least 60 dead

In Sierra Leone, West African peacekeeping troop Ecomog topples the military junta led by Johnny Paul Koroma. Democratically elected Ahmad Tejan Kabbah returns from exile in Guinea

President of the South African Truth Commission Desmond Tutu submits his final report on crimes under apartheid to President Nelson Mandela

Israel celebrates 50th anniversary of its founding

Israel's President Ezer Weizman is confirmed by the Knesset for a second term

Israel's Prime Minister Netanyahu and leader of the Palestinian Authority Arafat sign an interim agreement in the U.S., mediated by President Bill Clinton and Jordan's King Hussein. The agreement is approved by Israeli Cabinet by only a slim margin

First international airport in the Gaza Strip opens 20 months after its completion

Bill Clinton becomes the first U.S. President to visit the Palestinian Autonomous Areas

Jordanian women in Amman organize their first public demonstration to protest domestic violence

In Iran, countless oppositional intellectuals are murdered

Algerian Prime Minister Ahmed Ouyahia resigns and is succeeded by Ismail Hamdani

Salima Ghezali, Algerian journalist and civil rights activist, receives the European Parliament's Andrei Dmitrievitch Sakharov Prize

Elias Freij, Palestinian politician, mayor of Bethlehem, d. (b. 1918)

(contd)

D. VISUAL ARTS | E. MUSIC | F. SCIENCE, TECHNOLOGY, GROWTH | G. DAILY LIFE

1998 contd

D. Visual Arts

Christo and Jeanne-Claude wrap 178 trees on the park grounds of the Beyeler Foundation in Basel, Switzerland and present them as "Wrapped Trees"

Two paintings by Egon Schiele on loan from Vienna at the Museum of Modern Art in New York are confiscated after the heirs to the former Jewish owner of the works sue for possession of works stolen by the Nazis

Russian President Boris Yeltsin signs the so-called looted art law mandating that all artistic treasures looted during WW II and still in Russia will be returned to their countries of origin

Completion of the 8-year restoration of the Sphinx in Egypt

Highest priced paintings at auction in 1998: Vincent van Gogh, "Portrait of the Artist without a beard," (1889), $65 million; Claude Monet, "Bassin aux Nympheas et Sentier au Bord de l'Eau," (1900), 18 million pounds; Andy Warhol, "Orange Marilyn," (1964), $15.75 million

Opening of the Felix Nussbaum Museum designed by Amer. architect Daniel Libeskind. It includes the first permanent exhibit of the complete collection of some 140 works by the Jewish artist who was murdered in Auschwitz

Three major exhibits in Germany commemorate the 150th birthday of Paul Gauguin

Jackson Pollock retrospective at the Museum of Modern Art in Berlin

Amer. pop artist Robert Rauschenberg retrospective (acquired from the New York's Guggenheim Museum) in Cologne at the Ludwig Museum is named exhibit of the year by the Ger. division of the International Art Critics' Association

Exhibit "1648. War and Peace in Europe" at the state museum of Westphalia to

(contd)

E. Music

F. Science, Technology, Growth

long bridge spans from the southern tip of Japan's mainland to the Island of Awaji

Danish catamaran "Cat Link V" (built by Scandlines), sets the record for fastest crossing of the North Atlantic (Blue Riband) from New York to Southampton; traveling at 41.2 knots (47.4 mph) it made the trip in 2 days, 17.59 hrs

An 18 ton piece of the Titantic's hull is hauled to the surface from the ocean floor off the coast of Newfoundland

Argentine and Amer. scientists discover a 12.4-mile-wide crater on the southeastern coast of Argentina and attribute it to an asteroid that hit the earth 3.3 million years ago

U.S. scientists conclude, based on images transmitted by the Lunar Prospector probe, that there are large amounts of frozen water at both of the Moon's poles

U.S. senator and space pioneer John Glenn completes his second flight in space and, at age 77, is the oldest astronaut alive

Plans for the International Space Station (I.S.S.) are finalized by U.S., Europe, Russia, Japan, and Brazil

U.S. satellite Endeavor delivers the Unity connecting module to the Russian Zarya module. Unity will take over the propulsion control and power supply to the International Space Station (I.S.S.)

The spectacular Leonid meteor shower from the tail of the comet Tempel-Tuttle reaches the Earth's atmosphere but does not damage satellites as had been feared

European Southern Observatory (ESO) completes its Unit Telescope 1, a component of the Very Large Telescope Array (VLT) at the Cerro Paranal Observatory in northern Chile, the telescope is 27 feet in diameter. First successful images produced by ESO's Unit Telescope include the Butterfly Nebula NGC 6302, gasses emitted by a dying sun

From a telescope in southern New Mexico, the Sloan Digital Sky Survey begins the most comprehensive survey of the universe yet. The aim is to produce an atlas of the universe

Japanese space probe Planet B, later renamed Nozomi ("Hope") on its way to Mars to study interactions between the atmosphere of Mars and solar winds

(contd)

G. Daily Life

der, is executed by lethal injection in Texas. She is the first woman to be executed in Texas since 1863

Already at the beginning of the Muslim month of fasting, Ramadan, several hundred people murdered in massacres in Algeria

Olympic Winter Games in Nagano, Japan, with over 2,330 athletes from 72 countries

Soccer World Championship in France: France takes its first victory (in a final match against Brazil 3-0), followed by Croatia and the Netherlands. The World Championship is marked by the violence of Ger. fans who critically injured a French police officer in the northern French town of Lens

Member of the Fr. national team Zinedine Zidane is named World Soccer Player of the Year

Federation of International Football Associations (F.I.F.A.) elects Joseph Blattner (Switz.) as president. He succeeds Joao Havelange (Brazil), who has held the post for 24 years

Gottfried Dienst, Swiss soccer referee, famous for the "Wembley goal" in the 1966 World Championship, d. (b. 1920)

Florence Griffith-Joyner, U.S. track and field, 100m world record, several Olympic medals and world championships, d. (b. 1960)

Archie Moore, Amer. professional boxer, d. (b. 1914)

Marco Pantani (Italy) wins the 85th Tour de France, followed by Germany's Jan Ulrich in second place. The race is tarnished by doping scandals and police investigations

Mika Häkkinen (Finland) wins Formula 1 World Championship, his McClaren-Mercedes team wins the Constructor's Championship. Ger. Michael Schumacher takes second place

Mickey Mouse celebrates 70th birthday

A. HISTORY, POLITICS | B. LITERATURE, THEATER | C. RELIGION, PHILOSOPHY, LEARNING

1998 contd

A. History, Politics

Nazem Kudzi, Syrian politician, former President of Syria, d. (b. 1907)
Hilla Limann, West African politician, former President of Ghana, d. (b. 1933)
Ferndando Henrique Cardoso reelected President in Brazil
Gen. Augusto Pinochet, former Chilean dictator, after extradition petitions filed in Spain, is arrested in London. Britain's highest judicial body decides initially that he cannot appeal to diplomatic immunity as head of state, but the judgment is overturned based on bias on the part of one of the Lords
In Guatemala, just two days after the publication of a human rights report by the Catholic Church, Bishop Juan Gerardi Conedera is murdered
In Colombia 240,000 people displaced by armed conflicts between the left-wing guerrilla groups and right-wing paramilitary groups and the army
In Venezuela, former putsch leader Hugo Chávez is elected President
Economic reformist Zhu Rongji succeeds Li Peng as Prime Minister of China
Unrest in Indonesia. President Suharto resigns under public pressure after more than three decades in office. He is succeeded by Bacharuddin Yusef Habibie
Japan's Prime Minister Ryutaro Hashimoto resigns and is succeeded by Foreign Minister Keizo Obuchi
North Korean rocket test leads to tensions in East Asia
Despite international protests, India conducts several underground nuclear explosions. Pakistan is fiercely critical of the tests and reacts by setting off five of its own nuclear warheads
Christians in India protest persecution by fundamentalist Hindus with strikes and demonstrations
After a bloodbath in Northern Afghanistan, the radical Islamic Taliban gains control of most of the country
Former screen actor and Vice President Joseph Estrada emerges as victor in elections in the Philippines. He will replace Fidel Ramos
Nikhil Chakravarty, champion of Indian independence, d. (b. 1914)
Chatichai Choonhavan, Thai politician, former Prime Minister, d. (b. 1922)
Gulzarilal Nanda, Indian politician, former Prime Minister, d. (b. 1898)
Nguyen Van Linh, Vietnamese politician, d. (b. 1916)
Manuel Pérez, Colombian guerrilla leader, d. (b. 1942)
Pol Pot, Cambodian politician, co-founder and leader of the Khmer Rouge, former Prime Minister, d. (b. c. 1928)
Mohammed Yussuf, Afghani politician, former Prime Minister, d. (b. 1916)

1999

A. History, Politics

Nobel Peace Prize to the Fr. aid organization "Médicins sans frontières" (Doctors without Borders)
Right Livelihood Award ("Alternative Nobel Prize") to Spanish attorney Juan Garces, to the Cuban organization GAO, and the Colombian "Consolidation of the Amazon Region" (COAMA). Juan Garces was the attorney leading the extradition case against Chilean dictator Pinochet; the GAO (Grupo Agricultura Orgánica) advocates organic agricultural practices in Cuba; and COAMA works for indigenous people's rights and preserving species diversity in the tropical rainforest. An honorary award was also given to Hermann Scheer for his efforts to encourage alternative energy with his company "Eurosolar"
Germany assumes presidency of the European Council
Tens of thousands of protesters gather in Bonn to demonstrate against N.A.T.O. air strikes in Yugoslavia
Commemorations of the 10th anniversary of the fall of the Berlin Wall
Ger. Chancellor Schröder on state visit to China. Discussions on the rule of law and strengthening economic cooperation between the two states
Bill Clinton remains Pres. of the U.S. as Senate acquits him on
(contd)

B. Literature, Theater

Paul Bowles, Amer. writer, d. (b. 1910)
Jose Luis Cano, Span. lyric poet, d. (b. 1910)
Jerzy Grotowski, Polish theater director, d. (b. 1933)
Joseph Heller, Amer. writer, d. (b. 1923)
Jacques Lecoq, Fr. theatrical educator, d. (b. 1921)
Victor Mature, Amer. actor, d. (b. 1912)
Brian Moore, Irish author, d. (b. 1921, Belfast)
Iris Murdoch, Brit. writer and philosopher, d. (b. 1919, Dublin)
Mario Puzo, Amer. author, d. (b. 1920)
Natalie Sarraute, Fr. writer of Russian descent, d. (b. 1902)
Susan Strasberg, Amer. actress, d. (b. 1938)
Festivals, symposia and exhibits to
(contd)

C. Religion, Philosophy, Learning

Aleksander Gieysztor, Polish medievalist, d. (b. 1916)
George L. Mosse, Ger.-Amer. historian, d. (b. 1918, Berlin)
Weimar is named cultural capital of Europe
Pope John Paul II opens the Holy Doors and begins preparations for the Jubilee Year 2000
Pope John Paul II beatifies the Capuchin Monk Padre Pio (1887–1968)
At a meeting in Bucharest, leaders of the Christian Orthodox and Roman Catholic churches enter into dialogue
U.K. bans the "flogging" of students as disciplinary measure in Britain

D. VISUAL ARTS	E. MUSIC	F. SCIENCE, TECHNOLOGY, GROWTH	G. DAILY LIFE	
commemorate 350th anniversary of the Peace of Westphalia Exhibit with works by Marcel Duchamp and Joseph Cornell on the relationship between the two artists at the Philadelphia Museum of Art James Cameron's "Titanic," with ticket sales over $1.8 billion, becomes the most successful movie in the history of film. In Germany, just over 18 million viewers "Mulan" is the 36th animated film produced by Disney. Production design by Hans Bacher "The Prince of Egypt" from the animation studios at Dreamworks, directed by Brenda Chapman, Steve Hickner, Simon Wells Exhibit on the life and work of Leni Riefenstahl at the Film Museum in Potsdam		First images of active outer regions of the solar atmosphere, the corona, made by N.A.S.A.'s solar satellite TRACE		**1998 contd**
Lucien Aigner, Amer. photographer, d. (b. 1901) Sir Dirk Bogarde, (given name Derek Niven Bogaerde), Brit. actor, d. (b. 1921) Bernard Buffet, Fr. painter and graphic artist, d. (b. 1928) Harry Callahan, Amer. photographer, d. (b. 1912) Leo Castelli, Amer. gallery owner, d. (b. 1907) Andreas Feininger, Amer. photographer and journalist, d. (b. 1906, Paris) Iron Eyes Cody, Amer. actor (Cherokee), d. (b. 1904) Garson Kanin, Amer. film *(contd)*	Lionel Bart, Brit. composer of musicals, d. (b. 1931) Lester Bowie, Amer. jazz trumpeter, d. (b. 1941) Jaki Byard, Amer. jazz pianist, d. (b. 1922) Charlie Byrd, Amer. jazz guitarist, d. (b. 1925) Gabor Carelli, Amer. tenor, d. (b. 1915, Budapest) Harry "Sweets" Edison, Amer. jazz trumpet player, d. (b. 1906) Lucien Aigner, Amer. photographer, d. (b. 1901) Indrani, Indian dancer, d. (b. 1930) Alfredo Kraus, Span. tenor, d. (b. 1928) *(contd)*	Daniel Nathans, Amer. microbiologist, d. (b. 1928) Nobel Prize for Medicine to Ger.-Amer. biologist Günter Blobel for his discovery that proteins have intrinsic signals governing their transport and localization in the cell Nobel Prize for Physics to Dutch physicists Martinus Veltman and Gerardus 't Hooft for their research on the theory of particle physics Nobel Prize for Chemistry to Egyptian chemist Ahmed H. Zewail for discovery of a "slow motion" camera that allows us to record chemical reactions Paul Ehrlich and Ludwig Darmstaedter Prize to Amer. AIDS re- *(contd)*	The euro is introduced as monetary unit to 11 European countries; it won't be used as hard currency until January 1, 2002 Merger between the world's second and fourth largest tobacco manufacturers, British American Tobacco and Rothmans International U.S. court orders tobacco company Philip Morris to pay $81 million to survivors of a deceased chain smoker U.S. automaker Ford acquires Volvo's passenger vehicle division for $6.45 billion Ger. automaker Adam Opel AG celebrates 100 years in business Joachim Milberg replaces Bernd Pischetsrieder as board chairman of BMW after the latter comes under fire Dow Jones Index surpasses the 10,000 mark for the first time *(contd)*	**1999**

A. HISTORY, POLITICS | B. LITERATURE, THEATER | C. RELIGION, PHILOSOPHY, LEARNING

1999 contd

charges of perjury and obstruction of justice in the impeachment proceedings

Prime Minister Zhu Rongji becomes the first Chinese head of state to visit the U.S. Agreements concerning the development of economic relations

U.S. brings serious charges of espionage against China. Beijing is said to have collected documents concerning nuclear weapons and space technology over a period of 20 years

For the first time since the end of the Vietnam War, diplomatic representation of the U.S. in Ho Chi Minh City (formerly Saigon)

U.S. and Canada sign treaty ending the 7-year-long "Salmon War"

In St. Louis, Pope John Paul II challenges Americans to abolish the death penalty

Comprehensive Land Claims Agreement in Canadian "Nanavut" (Our Land) territory establishes autonomous control and self-government for the Inuit

Heads of state and government of EU countries meeting in Berlin agree on reforms in agricultural and structural policies as well as on reorganization of EU financing. "Agenda 2000" forms the basis for the EU's eastern European expansion

Nicole Fontaine becomes new President of European Parliament

Over 20,000 Polish victims of the Nazi regime sue the Ger. government for damages in the amount of 2.4 billion DM

Austria's right-wing extremist Austrian Freedom Party wins state elections in Carinthia. Their top candidate Jörg Haider becomes head of provincial government

Switzerland extradites Nazi collaborator and former minister Maurice Papon to France

Russian President Boris Yeltsin fires Prime Minister Yevgeny Primakov and replaces him with Sergei Stepashin, who only remains in office four months before he is replaced by former head of the secret police Vladimir Putin

Bribery charges against Boris Yeltsin and his family

A series of bombings in Russia, presumably terrorist acts committed by Muslim rebels, kill over 300 people

Russian offensive against Chechnya. Missile attacks on the capital city of Grozny leave nearly 300 dead and hundreds wounded

President Boris Yeltsin resigns unexpectedly and is succeeded by Vladimir Putin

Carlo Azeglio Ciampi becomes new President of Italy

Seven-time Prime Minister of Italy, Giulio Andreotti, is acquitted on charges of murdering journalist Mino Pecorelli

The Coliseum in Rome becomes the site of an appeal to abolish the death penalty: each time an execution is commuted or suspended anywhere in the world, the Flavian amphitheater is lit up for 48 hrs

Despite heavy electoral losses sustained by Social Democrats in Finland, Paavo Lipponen remains in office

Ger. Chancellor Schröder and Czech Prime Minister Zeman agree to refrain from seeking redress against each other for expropriations and expulsions that occurred during WW II

Poland, Hungary, and the Czech Republic are accepted into N.A.T.O; the alliance now has 19 members. EU decides on the application status for Turkey and an additional 6 countries

Celebrations on the 50th anniversary of the Geneva Convention

EU Summit meeting in Cologne: Javier Solano, former Spanish Foreign Minister and current Sec. Gen. of N.A.T.O. becomes first high representative for General Foreign and Security Policy. He is succeeded by Brit. Defense Minister George Robertson in his office as Sec. Gen.

At the end of the first summit meeting of Latin American, Caribbean, and European countries in Rio de Janeiro, the "Rio Declaration" is signed. 48 signatories agree to opening world markets, improving the flow of financial currents, closer collaboration in combating terrorism, drug trafficking, and organized crime

At the O.S.C.E. (Organization for Safety and Security in Europe) summit in Istanbul, the 54 member nations agree to continue dis-

(contd)

commemorate the 250th birthday of Johann Wolfgang von Goethe

Nobel Prize for Literature to Günter Grass for his complete works. The jury stated in its decision that Grass's "frolicsome black fables portray the forgotten face of history"

Prix Goncourt to Fr. writer Jean Echenoz

Peace Prize of the Germ. Booksellers' Assoc. to Amer. historian and author Fritz Stern

Whitbread Poetry Award and T.S. Eliot Prize (England) to Brit. lyric poet Ted Hughes (posthumously) for the book of poems "Birthday Letters"

Franz Xaver Kroetz: "Der Eingeborene," directed by Achim Freyer in Vienna

D. VISUAL ARTS

director and author, d. (b. 1912)
DeForest Kelley, Amer. actor, d. (b. 1920)
Stanley Kubrick, Amer. film director, d. (b. 1928)
Charles Luckman, Amer. architect, d. (b. 1909)
Paul Mellon, Amer. arts patron, d. (b. 1907)
Kuzuo Miyagawa, Japanese cinematographer, d. (b. 1908)
George Moorse, Amer. film director, d. (b. 1936)
Oliver Reed, Brit. actor, d. (b. 1938)
Sam Shaw, Amer. photographer and film producer, d. (b. 1913)
Saul Steinberg, Amer. caricaturist, d. (b. 1914)
Praemium Imperale to Japanese architect Fumihiko Maki, Ger. Painter Anselm Kiefer, and Amer. sculptor Louise Bourgeois
Jay A. Pritzker Prize for Architecture to the Brit. architect Sir Norman Foster
Golden Bear at the Berlin Film Festival to "The Thin Red Line" by Terence Malick (U.S. 1998). Silver Bear for best director to Søren Kragh-Jacobsen for "Mifundes sidste sang" (Denmark 1998). Best actress to Juliane Köhler and Maria Schader for their roles in "Aimée und Jaguar" (Germany 1998, directed by Max Färberböck) and best actor to Michael Gwisdek in "Nachtgestalten" (Germany 1998, directed by Andreas Dresen)
Cannes Golden Palm to Luc and Jean-Pierre Dardenne for "Rosetta." Jury's Grand Prize to Bruno Dumont for "L'humanité"; best director to Pedro Almodóvar for "Todo sobre mi madre"; acting awards to Severine Caneele in "L'humanité," to Emilie Dequenne in "Rosetta," and to Emmanuel Schotte in "L'humanité"
Golden Globes for "Shakespeare in Love" by John Madden (best picture), "Saving Private Ryan" by Steven Spielberg (best di-
(contd)

E. MUSIC

Alexandre Lagoya, Fr. guitarist, d. (b. 1929)
Rolf Liebermann, Swiss composer and opera director, d. (b. 1910)
Sir Yehudi Menuhin, Brit.-Amer. violinist, d. (b. 1916)
Werner Müller, Ger. trombonist and orchestra director, d. (b. 1920)
Michel Petrucciani, Fr. jazz pianist, d. (b. 1962)
Red Norvo, Amer. jazz vibraphonist, d. (b. 1908)
Joaquin Rodrigo, Span. pianist and composer, d. (b. 1902)
Hank Snow, Amer. country music singer, d. (b. 1914)
Dusty Springfield (given name Mary Isobel Catherine O'Brian), Brit. pop singer, d. (b. 1940)
Ernie Wilkins, Amer. composer and saxophonist, d. (b. 1920)
Joe Williams, Amer. jazz vocalist, d. (b. 1908)
Orlandus Wilson, Amer. jazz singer, d. (b. 1916)
Amer. rap-singer Lauryn Hill wins 5 awards at the 41st Grammy Awards in Los Angeles. Madonna wins a Grammy for the best pop album ("Ray of Light"). Four Grammies to Celine Dion
Praemium Imperale to Canadian jazz pianist Oscar Peterson
Pina Bausch receives the Samuel H. Scripps American Dance Festival Award for lifetime achievement
Sir Simon Rattle slated to replace Claudio Abbado as director of the Berlin Philharmonic at the end of the 2001 season
Kent Nagano becomes new chief conductor and artistic director of the German Symphony Orchestra in Berlin, succeeding Vladimir Ashkenazy
New Director of New York's Carnegie Hall is director of the Cologne Philharmonic, Franz Xaver Ohnesorg
Christoph Eschenbach, chief conductor of the North German Radio Symphony Orchestra becomes new
(contd)

F. SCIENCE, TECHNOLOGY, GROWTH

searcher Robert Gallo for lifetime achievement
Remains of an approximately 40,000-year-old human skeleton unearthed in the Neandertal Valley near Düsseldorf
Discovery of a cemetery more than 2,000 years old in the Egyptian Bahariya Oasis, where presumably more than 10,000 are buried, with mummies and burial items
An approximately 23,000-year-old mammoth discovered by an international research team in the northern Siberian permafrost. Researchers investigate the possibility of cloning the animal
Almost twenty years after it was first discovered, scientists succeed in determining the volatility of Bohrium, Element 107. It is classified as a group 7b element in the periodic table—with technetium and rhenium
Based on a study of ocean sediments, Ger. and Amer. marine geologists suspect that a greenhouse effect caused a sudden surge in carbon dioxide in the air already 55 million years ago
Biologist Heide Schulz discovers a bacteria up to .75 mm in diameter. The "Sulfur Pearl of Namibia" was found in muddy ocean sediment and plays an important role in the ecosystem of oceans
Brit. scientists 97% successful in sequencing the DNA code of the human chromosome 22
Japanese, Amer., and Dutch researchers in Boston build a 78-atom molecular rotor engine
After four decades of research, it is finally possible to determine the structure of complete ribosomes at up to angstrom resolution
Brit. scientists at the John Innes Institute in Norwich develop virus-resistant African rice
Susceptibility to asthma may be increased by two genes on chromosome 5, according to Amer. researchers in Berkeley
Japanese researchers succeed in transplanting stem cells and thus allowing for the regeneration of corneal epithelial cells; this may lead to preventing blindness
Mathematician Thomas Hales succeeds in proving the so-called Kepler Conjecture, which has been considered unsolvable for nearly four centuries. According to this theorem, the densest packing of spheres in three-dimensional space is the face-
(contd)

G. DAILY LIFE

Duty-free sales regulations within the EU lifted
U.S. is the world's largest weapons supplier, with exports in the amount of $11.8 billion, followed by Russia ($4.8 billion) and Germany ($4.0 billion). Worldwide weapons sales at $30.3 billion
Ger. chemical manufacturer BASF and Swiss Roche-Holding forced to pay 1.3 billion DM in fines to the U.S. as the result of illegal price fixing: BASF $225 million, Roche $500 million
International Monetary Fund agrees to $4.5 billion stand-by arrangement with Russia
Merger of Japan's three leading banks, Dai-Ichi Kangyo, Fuji, and Industrial Bank of Japan. With total assets in the amount of $1.3 trillion, they form the world's largest financial institution
Third largest aerospace and aeronautics company created by merger between DaimlerChrysler Aerospace AG (Dasa) and Aerospatiale Matra SA to form European Aeronautic, Defense, and Space Company (EADS)
U.S. media company Viacom and leading television broadcast service CBS merge to form a new media giant
Most expensive corporate takeover in history: MCI (Worldcom, Inc.) takes over telecommunications company Sprint Corp. Westwood for $115 billion
Luise Piech-Porsche, co-founder of the Ger. sports car manufacturer, d. (b. 1903)
Mattel's Barbie doll celebrates its 40th birthday
Marriage of Princess Caroline of Monaco and Ernst August Prinz von Hannover, great-grandson of the last Ger. Emperor
Prince Charles, successor to the Brit. throne, and his girlfriend of many years, Camilla Parker Bowles, make their first public appearance together
Prince Edward, youngest son of Britain's Queen Elizabeth II, marries the PR manager Sophie Rhys-Jones
Total solar eclipse over Europe
Nearly 1,000 dead in an earthquake in Colombia
Bus accidents: 18 dead and 32 injured in southern Austria; 22 dead and 21 injured in Cairo, Egypt
In the worst avalanche ever in the Alps, 31 people die in the village of Galtür; avalanches claim a total of 70 victims
Disastrous fire in the Montblanc Tunnel claims 39 lives. The fire broke out on a moving truck
Two boys, 17 and 18 years old, go on a rampage at Columbine High School in Littleton, CO, killing 15
An international search team discovers the body of mountain climber George Mallory at an altitude of 26,903 feet on Mt. Everest. Mallory had been missing since 1924. To this day, it is not clear whether he succeeded in being the first to reach the top of
(contd)

	A. HISTORY, POLITICS	B. LITERATURE, THEATER	C. RELIGION, PHILOSOPHY, LEARNING

1999 contd

armament; Charter for European Security strengthens the role of the O.S.C.E. in resolving conflicts

New President of Slovakia is Rudolf Schuster. He wins in a run-off election against Vladimir Meciar

A London court rules in favor in Spain's petition to extradite former dictator Augusto Pinochet. The House of Lords had previously recognized diplomatic immunity for Pinochet

"Good Friday Agreement" establishes new regulations for relationships with Ireland and finally brings consensus over the Brit. province of Northern Ireland

In Northern Ireland, some 80,000 Protestants march in the traditional parades of the Orange Order

British Province of Northern Ireland regains its autonomy after 27 years. Head of the multidenominational gov. is Protestant David Trimble

Serbian troops massacre civilians in Kosovo. Kosovar-Albanians are systematically purged, and reports of cruelties mount steadily; a total of 750,000 flee to Albania and Macedonia

Deputy Prime Minister of Yugoslavia, Draskovic, is fired for criticizing the leadership in Belgrade

U.N. International Criminal Tribunal for the Former Yugoslavia charges Yugoslavian Pres. with crimes against humanity and issues a warrant for his arrest and the arrest of four members of his government

Negotiations in Rambouillet, France, between Serbs and Kosovar-Albanians over settlement of the Kosovo conflict fail

N.A.T.O. begins air strikes against Yugoslavia. N.A.T.O. planes accidentally bomb the Chinese embassy in Belgrade. Mass demonstrations in China

Yugoslav leadership agrees to a peace plan, which grants extensive rights of autonomy to the Kosovar-Albanian population. International peacekeeping forces (KFOR) monitor adherence to the treaty. The so-called Kosovo Liberation Army dissolves and turns in its weapons to KFOR

Alleged Bosnian war criminal Momir Talic is arrested

Acute government crisis in Athens after members of the government found involved in the affairs of Kurdish leader Öcalan. Three ministers and a Greek security service member resign

Iranian Pres. Mohammad Hatami is received by Pope John Paul II

Bülent Ecevit becomes new Turk. Prime Minister

Abdullah Öcalan, leader of the Turkish Labor Party is arrested in Nairobi, Kenya, and flown back to Turkey, where he is tried for high treason. Violent demonstrations erupt in cities throughout Europe as a result. 3 Kurds are shot while attempting to storm the Israeli embassy in Berlin. More demonstrations follow after Öcalan is sentenced to death. Enforcing the sentence will require parliamentary resolution

Georgia, Uzbekistan, and Azerbaijan withdraw from the collective security pact of the Commonwealth of Independent States (C.I.S.)

Leonid Kutschma, Pres. of Ukraine, is reconfirmed for another five-year term

End of the official midday siesta for state employees in Mexico

Fernando de la Rúa replaces Carlos Menem as President of Argentina

Luis González Macchi becomes new President of Paraguay. His predecessor, Raúl Cubas Grau, is held responsible for murdering the Vice President

3,000 landless farming families in northeastern Brazil occupy 15 farms to protest their situation. The gap between the poor and the wealthy ruling class continues to widen and violence toward landless farmers escalates

Young Tibetans storm the Chinese embassy in India and demand independence for Tibet

Heavy fighting in the contested Kashmir Region between Pakistan and India

Military putsch in Pakistan. Chief of State Nawaz Sharif ousted and General Pervez Musharaf is placed in power

(contd)

D. VISUAL ARTS

rector), and "The Truman Show" by Peter Weir (Jim Carrey and Ed Harris for best leading and supporting actor). Special Golden Globe to Jack Nicholson for lifetime achievement

Seven Oscars to "Shakespeare in Love," among others, best actress to Gwyneth Paltrow. Best director: Steven Spielberg for "Saving Private Ryan"; best actor to Roberto Benigni in "Life Is Beautiful," honorary Oscar to Elia Kazan for lifetime achievement

Golden Lion at the Venice Film Festival to Zhang Yimou for "Not One Less"

European Film Award to Pedro Almodóvar for "Todo sobre mi madre" and Wim Wenders for the documentary film "Buena Vista Social Club"

French film academy's César for the best Fr. film to "The Dreamlife of Angels" by Erick Zonca

Exhibit of late works by Claude Monet at the Royal Academy in London

Exhibit of nearly 50 works by the bronze sculptor Adriaen de Vries (1556–1626) at the Rijksmuseum in Amsterdam

Exhibit "Soul and Countenance," portraiture from Leonardo da Vinci to Francis Bacon at the Palazzo Reale in Milan

Opening of the Jewish Museum in Berlin, designed by architect Daniel Libeskind, ceremonial passing of the keys to museum director Michael Blumenthal

Opening of the Museum of Scotland in Edinburgh. It covers the country's history from its geological beginnings to the present

Monument by Russian sculptor Yevgeny Chubarov to the victims of Soviet terror in the sculpture garden behind the Tretyakov Gallery

Amer. photographer Cindy Sherman is given the Goslar Imperial Ring

(contd)

E. MUSIC

musical director of Orchestre de Paris

French harpist Julie Polloc becomes the first woman to pass an audition at the Viennese Philharmonic

Israeli conductor Eliahu Inbal becomes new director of the Berlin Symphony Orchestra

Significant music and art collection of Carl Philipp Emanuel Bach discovered in Kiev, includes as yet unpublished or unperformed works of his father Johann Sebastian Bach

John Cage: "108," violoncello and orchestra, premiere in Cologne

Tobias Picker: "Fantastic Mr. Fox," opera based on Raold Dahl, directed by Donald Sturrock at the Los Angeles Opera

Opera house in Barcelona Teatro del Liceo, 6 years after it was closed because of a devastating fire, reopens

Placido Domingo opens the opera season at the Metropolitan Opera in New York for his 18th time and thus breaks the 80-year-old record set by Enrico Caruso

Hans Werner Henze: "Fraternité," premieres in New York

Krzysytof Penderecki: quartet for clarinet and strings (saxophone version)

Frank Wildhorn (music), Leslie Bricusse (script), Melitta Edith (Ger. translation): "Dr. Jekyll and Mr. Hyde," Ger. premiere in Bremen, directed by Dietrich Hilsdorf

Alan Menken (music), James Lapine (script), Stephen Schwartz (song lyrics): "The Hunchback of Notre Dame," directed by James Lapine in Berlin

Jonathan Larson (music, script), Heinz Rudolph Kunze (Ger. translation): "Rent," Ger. premiere in Düsseldorf, directed by Martha Banta and Michael Greif

Henry Mancini: "Victor/Victoria," directed by Pavel Fieber in Karlsruhe

BeeGees (music and script):

(contd)

F. SCIENCE, TECHNOLOGY, GROWTH

centered cubic lattice arrangement

Siemens, Toshiba, and IBM have developed the world's smallest memory chip (DRAM) to date. The 64-megabit chip is 30 sq. mm in size

A new commercial space station "Sea Launch" is launched from a platform in the Pacific Ocean off the coast of California in a joint venture between U.S., Norway, Russia, and Ukraine

Very Large Telescope (VLT) begins operation at the European Southern Observatory (ESO) in Chile. At 200 sq. feet with all mirrors engaged, it will be the most powerful Very Large Telescope and will allow for observations of up to 12 billion light years into space

27th and final crew of the Russian space station Mir returns to Earth. For 13 years, the station served as a research laboratory in space

China's first unmanned spacecraft returns to Earth after 14 orbits

X-ray satellite BeppoSax registers a tremendous cosmic flash, called "gamma ray burst 990123," presumably the tails of a hypernova in the early stage of the universe. The burst was between 10 and 100 times brighter than any gamma ray burst observed to date. U.S. satellite Compton discovers the optical counterpart of a high-energy gamma flash emitted at the same time as the burst in which more energy was released in a minuscule amount of space than in the entire known universe at a distance of approx. 9 billion light years

N.A.S.A. space probe Mars Polar Lander is on its way to Mars to research the climate there and test space travel technology

N.A.S.A. space probe "Stardust" is launched; the mission is scheduled to fly by the comet Wild 2 in 2004 and collect dust particles, which it will bring back to earth

X-ray satellite Chandra is launched. It will look for black holes and deliver the first clear photographs of the filigreed structure of the Supernova remnant Cassiopeia A

N.A.S.A.'s first commercial satellite, Ikonos 2, observes climate, oceans, and terrestrial ecosystems

U.S. space probe Lunar Prospector lands on the Moon looking for evidence of "hidden water"

The object with the lowest density mass beyond the solar system is found in the constellation Orion

(contd)

G. DAILY LIFE

1999 contd

the world's highest mountain shortly before his death or not

47 people lose their lives when 76 tornadoes sweep through the Midwest (U.S.) in two days

Following a mass collision, fire breaks out in the Tauern Tunnel in Austria, killing 12 and injuring 49

Devastating floods in southern Germany, Austria, and Switzerland following heavy rains

U.S. stuntman Robbie Knievel jumps across a nearly 230-foot gorge in the Grand Canyon on a rocket-powered motorcycle

In one of the most devastating earthquakes of the century, 17,000 lose their lives in northwestern Turkey. Some 30,000 are injured and 600,000 left homeless. The center of the quake, which measured 7.4 on the Richter scale, was near the city of Izmir

Major earthquake (7.6 on the Richter scale) in Taiwan. Over 2,000 dead and 10,000 injured

285 die in a train wreck in the Indian province of West Bengal

69 people exposed to radioactive contamination after an accident at the uranium processing plant Tokaimura in Japan

Worst flooding in Mexico's history claims the lives of 600

31 dead in a train accident in London

Four people die after a 16 year old goes on a killing spree in Bad Reichenhall, Germany

Four hooligans convicted of critically injuring a Fr. police officer during the 1998 soccer world championship in Lens are sentenced to long prison terms

61 people killed when a five-story building collapses in Foggia, southern Italy, due to structural defect

Belgian Crown Prince Philippe marries 26-year-old Mathilde d'Udekem d'Acoz; civil ceremony held in three official languages: French, Flemish, and German

Worst weather catastrophe in the history of Venezuela claims over 30,000 lives in the north of the country. 150,000 left homeless

Oil tanker "Erika" sinks off the coast of Brittany (France), dumping 12,000 tons of crude oil into the ocean

John F. Kennedy, Jr., lawyer and son of slain U.S. president John F. Kennedy, d. (b. 1961)

Corruption scandal surrounding the selection of Salt Lake City as site of the 2002 Winter Olympic Games. Countless members of the I.O.C. resign

In Chicago, Michael Jordan, the most successful professional basketball player of all time, announces his plans to retire

Swiss tennis player Martina Hingis wins the Australian Open for the third consecutive time

At the Alpine World Skiing Championship in Vail, CO, Norwegian Lasse Djus takes home 5 medals, two gold and three silver, winning the World Cup

(contd)

	A. HISTORY, POLITICS	B. LITERATURE, THEATER	C. RELIGION, PHILOSOPHY, LEARNING
1999 contd	Head of India's government Atal Behari Vajpayee wins early elections with a new governing alliance China's government outlaws the Falun Gong sect. The cult movement, which combines Buddhist and Taoist doctrine with meditation practices, is said to have approximately 15 million adherents Mass assemblies and military parades in Beijing to celebrate 50th anniversary of the founding of People's Republic of China China joins the World Trade Organization (W.T.O.). China opens its markets; bilateral trade agreement with the U.S. Portugal returns the Special Administrative Region of Macao to China In the first free elections in Indonesia since 1995, Megawati Sukarnoputri's Democratic Party of Struggle wins and she becomes Vice President; the Islamic leader Abdurrahman Wahid becomes President Referendum in East Timor, which has been occupied since 1975 by Indonesia: 78.5% favor independence. U.N. International Force for East Timor (Interfet) called in to protect the population from Indonesian terrorism Amintore Fanfani, former Ital. Prime Minister, d. (b. 1908) Raissa Maximovna Gorbachev, former first lady of the U.S.S.R., d. (b. 1932) King Hassan II of Morocco, d. (b. 1929) King Hussein II of Jordan, d. (b. 1935). His son Abdullah is successor to the throne Julius Nyerere, former President of Tanzania, d. (b. 1922) Georgios Papadopoulos, former Greek military dictator, d. (b. 1919) Gideon Rafael, Israeli diplomat, d. (b. 1913, Berlin) Franjo Tudjman, Croatian President, d. (b. 1922)		

D. VISUAL ARTS

After 20 years, Giuseppina Brambilla Barcilon completes his restoration of Leonardo da Vinci's "Last Supper"
Auction of 250 objects from the art collection of Nathaniel and Albert Rothschild brings in 168.5 million DM; the sixteenth century Rothschild prayer book alone brings in 24.8 million
Reconstruction of the Reichstag in Berlin according to plans by Sir Norman Foster is completed. Main attraction is its walk-in glass cupola
Inauguration of the office and administration building designed by architect Frank O. Gehry in Düsseldorf
6,000 participants from over 100 countries at the congress of the International Union of Architects (U.I.A.) in Beijing
After ten years, the renovation of New York's Grand Central Terminal, under the direction of John Belle, is complete
Land link between Denmark and Sweden now complete with the 10-mile-long bridge over the Öresund
Christo and Jean Claude present their project "The Wall," a wall of 13,000 multicolored oil barrels 85 feet in height and 223 feet wide, at the IBA (International Bauausstellung) in Emscher Park
Amer. film director Steven Spielberg presents his "Shoah Foundation" in Berlin. The initiative "Partners in Tolerance," sponsored by publishing companies Axel Springer, Bertelsmann and Burda, supports the foundation's work. The first of the foundation's documentary films, "The Last Days," shown in conjunction with the Berlinale
Thomas Vinterberg: "The Celebration," Danish feature film
Robert Bresson retrospective at the Museum of Modern Art in New York
(contd)

E. MUSIC

"Saturday Night Fever," directed by Matthias Davids in Cologne
Brit. rock guitarist Eric Clapton sells 100 guitars at auction. The $5.01 million in proceeds will go to a drug and alcohol rehabilitation clinic
100th birthday of Duke Ellington

F. SCIENCE, TECHNOLOGY, GROWTH

U.S. scientists discover a one-day-old type II supernova in the galaxy NGC1673 only 25 million light years away

G. DAILY LIFE

Bertrand Picard and Brian Jones succeed in making the first nonstop flight around the world in a hot-air balloon. Almost 20 days after their start in the Swiss Alps, they land in the Egyptian desert
Canadian ice hockey player Wayne Gretzky ends his sensational career. His legendary number 99 is retired by the league
Turin, Italy, is selected as the site of the 2006 Winter Olympic Games
The Czech Republic wins the ice hockey world championship for the 8th time
Professional tennis player Steffi Graf wins the French Open in a dramatic final. Just a few months later, she ends her spectacular tennis career (22 grand slam titles)
Boris Becker, after an eighth final defeat at Wimbledon, ends his career as a professional tennis player. Career record: 49 titles, 6 of them grand slam victories
In Cairo, Sweden wins its fourth world championship in handball
World record: in Athens, Maurice Green (U.S.) becomes the first person ever to run the 100 meters in under 9.8 seconds, with a time of 9.79
At the track and field world championships in Seville, Michael Johnson (U.S.) sets a new world record in the 400 m at 43.18 seconds. Maurice Green (U.S.) wins the 100 m and 200 m and takes his third gold medal in the relay. Marion Jones and Inger Miller (both U.S.) win the 100 m (10.7 sec) and 200 m (21.77 sec), Cathy Freeman (Australia) wins the 400 m (49.67 sec)
Vitali Klitschko becomes the WBO World Heavyweight Champion. He defeats Herbie Hide with a knockout in the second round in London
U.S. cyclist Lance Armstrong wins the 86th Tour de France
Finnish driver Mika Häkkinen wins his 2nd consecutive world championship Formula 1. In his McLaren-Mercedes, he beats Eddie Irvine of Northern Ireland driving a Ferrari
Cyclist Jan Ullrich wins the Tour of Spain race and becomes world champion in individual time trial
Britain's Lennox Lewis becomes WBC Boxing World Heavyweight Champion, beating Evander Holyfield in Las Vegas
Tennis pro Pete Sampras (U.S.) becomes five-time ATP world champion
Former Brazilian national player Pelé named world soccer player of the century
Joe DiMaggio, Amer. baseball player, d. (b. 1914)

	A. HISTORY, POLITICS	B. LITERATURE, THEATER	C. RELIGION, PHILOSOPHY, LEARNING
1999 contd			
2000	Nobel Peace Prize to South Korean President Kim Dae Jung for his lifelong engagement on behalf of human rights and democracy as well as his policies of reconciliation with Communist North Korea Right Livelihood Award ("Alternative Nobel Prize") to the Indonesian civil rights attorney Munir, to Ethiopian biologist Tewolde Gebre Egziobher for his engagement on behalf of preserving biodiversity, to the Turkish political scientist Birsel Lemke for her civil resistance to cyanide-based gold extraction in the Bergama region. Honorary award to the biogeneticist Wes Jackson (U.S.) for his development of a highly productive and at the same time ecologically sustainable agriculture The European Court ruled the ban on women in combat unconstitutional Johannes Rau is the first Ger. President permitted to speak in the Israeli Parliament (Knesset); he begs for "forgiveness for what the Germans have done." Ger. Pres. Rau and Nobel Peace Prize laureate Elie Wiesel break ground on the Holocaust memorial in Berlin Joschka Fischer is the first Ger. Foreign Minister in the last 9 years to meet with Iranian leadership in Teheran. 7,000 people protest when Iranian Pres. Mohammad Hatami returns the favor and makes an official state visit to Berlin U.S. companies that had factories in Germany during WW II plan to establish their own fund for paying restitution to slave laborers Horst Köhler becomes new head of the International Monetary Fund (I.M.F.) Rising fuel costs throughout Europe lead to protests and blockades at oil refineries. In England, Prime Minister Tony Blair declares a national state of emergency First case of mad cow disease (BSE) in Germany discovered on a farm in Schleswig-Holstein is the start of the BSE crisis U.N. Human Rights Commission outlaws participation of minors in military conflicts Heads of state and administrative leaders of the G8 states agree to expeditious debt relief for the world's poorest nations U.N. Conference on Climate Change in The Hague produces no results; no concrete measures for reducing greenhouse gases *(contd)*	Steve Allen, Amer. entertainer, d. (b. 1921) Giorgino Bassani, Ital. writer, d. (b. 1916) Barbara Cartland, Brit. writer, d. (b. 1901) Richard Farnsworth, Amer. actor, d. (b. 1920) Sir John Gielgud, Brit. actor, d. (b. 1904) Anne Hébert, Canad. writer, d. (b. 1916) William Maxwell, Amer. writer, editor, 1936–76 editor at "The New Yorker," d. (b. 1908) Roger Peyrefitte, Fr. writer, d. (b. 1907) John Sladek, Amer. writer, d. (b. 1936) Nobel Prize for Literature to exiled Chinese writer Gao Xingjian. According to the jury's statement, "in the writing of Gao Xingjian literature is born anew from the struggle of the individual to survive the history of the masses" Pulitzer Prize in theater to Donald Margulies for the off-Broadway play "Dinner with Friends" Pulitzer Prize in fiction to Jhumpa Lahiri for her collection of short stories "Interpreter of Maladies"; Pulitzer in poetry to C.K. Williams for "Repair" Peace Prize of the Ger. Booksellers' Assoc. to Algerian writer Asia Djebar "Dibaxu, Debajo, Darunter," a cycle of 29 love poems by the Argentine poet Juan Gelman, is published in a tri-lingual edition (Shepardic, Spanish, and German) *(contd)*	Hajime Nakamura, Japanese philosopher, d. (b. 1912) Pope John Paul II beatifies two of his predecessors, John XXIII and Pius IX Vatican declares the primacy of the Catholic Church and unleashes vehement protests from other Christian denominations The oldest excerpt from St. Paul the Apostle's Book of Hebrews discovered in the Austrian National Library 100th birthday of philosopher Hans Georg Gadamer Papal visit to the Holy Land: Pope John Paul II meets with the Grand Mufti at the Aksa Mosque and asks for forgiveness at the Wailing Wall, for suffering inflicted on the Jews by Christians. It is the first time a pope has made the pilgrimage to Mt. Sinai, where, according to Biblical accounts, Moses was given the Ten Commandments In a historical move, the Pope, cardinals, and bishops in Rome admit to past transgressions and ask for forgiveness Brit. historian David Irving loses his case against the Amer. scholar who called him a "Holocaust denier." In the ruling, he is described as an "anti-Semite and racist" 100th birthday of philosopher Friedrich Nietzsche 400th birthday of Giordano Bruno Israel releases the diaries of Adolf Eichmann for research purposes Members of the Salvation Army will be *(contd)*

D. VISUAL ARTS	E. MUSIC	F. SCIENCE, TECHNOLOGY, GROWTH	G. DAILY LIFE	

1999 contd

D. Visual Arts

John Lasseter's Disney animated film "A Bug's Life" first ever completely computer generated film

New episode of the science fiction film series "Star Wars" by George Lucas becomes the blockbuster of the year in U.S. theaters

Robert Altman: "Cookie's Fortune," Amer. feature film

"Eyes Wide Shut," Stanley Kubrik's last film, receives mixed reactions from critics

Lars v. Trier: "Idiots," Danish feature film

Werner Herzog outlines the details of his relationship to his favorite actor, Klaus Kinski, in his book "Mein liebster Feind"

2000

D. Visual Arts

Carl Barks, Amer. comic book illustrator ("father" of Daffy Duck), d. (b. 1901)

Walter Dörfler, set-designer for productions by such directors as Ingmar Bergman, d. (b. 1921)

Douglas Fairbanks, Jr., Amer. film actor, d. (b. 1909)

Vittorio Gassman, Ital. actor, d. (b. 1922)

Sir Alec Guinness, Brit. actor, two-time Oscar winner, d. (b. 1914)

John Hejduk, Amer. architect, d. (b. 1929)

Friedensreich Hundertwasser, Austrian painter and graphic artist, d. (b. 1928)

Konrad Kujau, Ger. graphic artist, best known for his forged "Hitler diaries," d. (b. 1938)

Hedy Lamarr, Austrian-Amer. actress, d. (b. 1914)

Ring Lardner, Jr., Oscar-winning Amer. screenplay writer ("M*A*S*H," "Cincinnati Kid"), d. (b. 1915)

Jacob Lawrence, Amer. painter, d. (b. 1918)

Conrad Marca-Relli, Amer. painter, d. (b. 1913)

Don Martin, Amer. cartoonist ("Mad" magazine), d. (b. 1931)

Walter Matthau, Oscar-
(contd)

E. Music

Joachim Ernst Berendt, Ger. music critic and author (jazz expert), d. (b. 1922)

Walter Berry, Austrian singer, d. (b. 1929)

Milt Hinton, Amer. jazz bass player and photographer, d. (b. 1910)

Jack Nitzsche, Amer. songwriter and music producer, worked with Phil Spector and Rolling Stones, d. (b. 1937)

Baden Powell, Brazilian guitarist and composer, d. (b. 1937)

Tito Puente, Amer. Latin jazz musician, d. (b. 1927)

Ustad Alla Rakha Khan Qureshi, Indian musician, d. (b. 1911)

Jean-Pierre Rampal, Fr. flutist and conductor, d. (b. 1922)

"Screamin" Jay Hawkins, Amer. singer and pianist, d. (b. 1929)

Carl Sigman, Amer. jazz composer, d. (b. 1909)

Stanley Turrentine, Amer. jazz saxophonist, d. (b. 1934)

Sensational comeback for the 53-year-old guitarist Carlos Santana: he receives 8 Grammies and 3 Latin Grammies in the inaugural round of this award

Latin Grammy for the best new artist to 73-year-old
(contd)

F. Science, Technology, Growth

Konrad Emil Bloch, Amer. biochemist, d. (b. 1912, Silesia)

John Cooper, Brit. automobile designer, d. (b. 1923)

Rene G. Favaloro, Argentine surgeon, pioneer in bypass surgery, d. (b. 1923)

Michael Smith, Canadian chemist, Nobel laureate, d. (b. 1932, England)

German Titov, Russian cosmonaut, d. (b. 1935)

Nobel Prize for Physics to Herbert Kroemer and Jack Kilby (both U.S.), and to Zhores Alferov (Russia) for basic work in developing microelectronic components and microchips

Nobel Prize for Chemistry to Alan Heeger, Alan MacDiarmid (both U.S.), and Hideki Shirakawa (Japan) for their collaboration in developing conductive polymers

Nobel Prize for Medicine to Erick Kandel, Paul Greengard (both U.S.), and Arvid Carlsson (Sweden) for research on Parkinson's disease, schizophrenia, and other diseases of the nervous system

Nobel Prize for Economics to James J. Heckman and Daniel L. McFadden (both U.S.) for developing theories and methods for the empirical analysis of behavior in individuals

The oldest and most significant text of Archimedes (d. 212 B.C.), first discovered by Danish mathematician Johan Heiberg, is made
(contd)

G. Daily Life

First world exhibition in Germany, EXPO 2000, comes to a close in October with a deficit. Originally, 40 million visitors were expected, but the event actually attracted only 18.1 million

America Online (AOL) and the entertainment company Time Warner merge

New York entertainment firm Time Warner and Brit. EMI Group PLC merge to form the world's largest music conglomerate

Glaxco Wellcome and Smithkline Beecham merge to form the world's largest pharmaceutical concern

World Bank, Japan, and the Asian Development Bank support reforms in Indonesia with $4.7 billion in loans

U.S. Dept. of Justice orders break up of software manufacturer Microsoft into two separate companies based on violations of anti-trust laws

Fifth largest weapons producer in the U.S., Northrop Grumman (Los Angeles), acquires its competitor Litton Industries, Inc. (Woodland, CA) for $5.1 billion, to become the world's largest arms-producing company

"Life" magazine, established in 1936 as a weekly magazine, ceases publication

Deutsche Telekom acquires the U.S. mobile phone operator VoiceStream Wireless Corp. for $50.2 billion

Biggest price drop in the 3-year history of NASDAQ: technology index loses 10% of its value in one day on the U.S. market

Ger. reality television show *Big Brother* broadcast on the private channel RTLH captures enthusiastic media attention: it features a group of people living for three months under 24 hour video surveillance with video cameras following their every move
(contd)

A. HISTORY, POLITICS	B. LITERATURE, THEATER	C. RELIGION, PHILOSOPHY, LEARNING

2000 contd

Pacific island nation of Tuvalu is accepted as the 189th member nation of the United Nations

All death sentences in the state of Illinois are overturned after numerous false convictions are revealed

Despite international protests, two men are executed for murder in Texas. One of them was mentally retarded. Then-Governor and future U.S. President George W. Bush denied a stay of execution

Hillary Clinton becomes the first former First Lady elected to the U.S. Senate

George W. Bush defeats Al Gore in the U.S. presidential election. In the most dramatic election in history, Bush was able to secure 271 electoral votes, 4 more than Gore

Despite international criticism, the U.S. seeks to continue with its plans for building a missile defense system. Bill Clinton leaves the final decision to his successor

At the U.N. Summit in New York, U.S. President Bill Clinton and Cuba's head of state Fidel Castro shake hands—more by coincidence than by design; it is the first time in 38 years that the leaders of both countries meet. U.S. House of Representatives votes in favor of loosening sanctions against Cuba; among other things, the embargo on food and medical supplies is lifted and travel to Cuba made easier

Prime Minister Jean Chrétien and his Liberal Party defend their absolute majority in early parliamentary elections in Canada

EU Summit in Lisbon: government leaders seek to make Europe a leading world economic power

France takes over presidency of EU Council after Portugal

EU Summit in Nice regulates acceptance rules for new members. A treaty is signed in which the proportional representation in the Council of Ministers and the makeup of the Commission are restructured

Ministry of Health in London seeks to pass a law that will make hitting children with canes, belts or other objects a punishable criminal offense

Elizabeth Bowes-Lyon ("Queen Mum"), mother of Brit. Queen Elizabeth II, celebrates her 100th birthday

86 Protestant and Catholic terrorists are released from the maximum security prison in Antrim, Northern Ireland

I.R.A. opens its weapons arsenal to regular inspections

Jens Stoltenberg becomes new Prime Minister of Norway

In Spain's parliamentary elections, the People's Party wins an absolute majority of seats, placing Prime Minister Aznar in office

Heavy racial clashes in southern Spain (El Ejido). Thousands of residents attack the Moroccan population, destroying their apartments and personal property

Alleged leader of the Basque underground organization ETA, Ignacio García Arregui, apprehended in the south of France

Demonstrations throughout Spain to protest ETA following the murder of Socialist leader Fernando Buesa

Italy's Prime Minister Massimo D'Alema resigns and is succeeded by Giuliano Amato

Ali Agca, the Turkish man who attempted to assassinate the Pope, is pardoned and returned to Turkey where he will serve time for an unrelated murder

Poland's governing coalition falls apart after 30 months. The liberal Freedom Union cancels its cooperation with the right-wing alliance Solidarity. New Prime Minister is the conservative Jerzy Buzek. Aleksander Kwasniewski is elected new President of Poland

In Finland, Foreign Minister Tarja Haalonen becomes the first woman to win a presidential election there

In a referendum, Denmark vetoes the introduction of the euro as monetary unit

Dutch Parliament rules that physicians have the right to actively participate in assisted suicide for terminally ill patients

Andris Berzins is elected new Prime Minister of Latvia

Wave of demonstrations in Minsk against Belarussian Pres. Alexan-
(contd)

Childhood home of author Thomas Mann is converted into a literary center

Fourth volume of writing sensation J. K. Rowling, "Harry Potter and the Goblet of Fire," appears. By the end of the year, over 75 million copies of all four volumes have sold worldwide

Berlin's Theater am Schiffbauerdamm opens its new season with the Berliner Ensemble in "Brecht-Akte" by George Tabori, who directed the playwright himself

Brit. composer Andrew Lloyd Webber buys ten of London's top West End theaters

400th birthday of the Span. poet Pedro Calderón de la Barca

Franz Xaver Kroetz: "Das Ende der Paarung" directed by Claus Peymann at the Berliner Ensemble

Actor Sean Connery is knighted in Edinburgh by Queen Elizabeth II

able to marry outside the faith if they choose. For the past 130 years, only marriage within the faith has been permitted

D. VISUAL ARTS

winning Amer. actor, d. (b. 1920)
Adolf K. Placzek, Austrian-Amer. architectural historian, d. (b. 1913, Vienna)
Jason Robards, Oscar-winning Amer. film and stage actor, d. (b. 1922)
Claude Sautet, Fr. film director, d. (b. 1924)
Charles Monroe Schulz, Amer. cartoonist ("Peanuts"), d. (b. 1922)
George Segal, Amer. sculptor and graphic artist, d. (b. 1924)
Walter Stöhrer, Ger. painter, d. (b. 1937)
Roger Vadim (born R.B. Plemiannikov), Fr. film director, d. (b. 1928)
Loretta Young (born Gretchen Michaela Belzer), Oscar-winning Amer. actress, d. (b. 1913)
Golden Globes to "American Beauty" for best dramatic film, best director (Sam Mendes), best screenplay (Alan Ball); best foreign film "All about My Mother" ("Todo sobre mi madre") by Pedro Almodóvar
50th Berlin Film Festival: Golden Bear to Paul Thomas Anderson for "Magnolia," Silver Bear to Zhang Yimou for "The Road Home." Silver Bear to Milos Forman (best director), Bibiana Beglau and Nadja Uhl (best actress), Denzel Washington (best actor). "Jury's Award" to Wim Wenders for "Million Dollar Hotel." Polish director Andrzej Wajda's historical epic "Pan Tadeusz" is shown in honor of the director
Actress Elizabeth Taylor is made a Dame Commander of the Order of the British Empire by Queen Elizabeth II
At the 25th César Film Awards, "Vénus Beauté" by Tonie Marshall wins
Five Oscars for "American Beauty" including best picture, best direction (Sam Mendes), and best actor (Kevin Spacey). Best foreign film:
(contd)

E. MUSIC

Cuban singer Ibrahim Ferrer
"Sieben Horizonte," concert in Hamburg featuring seven works of e-music
After several last-minute cancellations by several opera stars, chaos breaks out at a gala dinner planned in honor of the recently deceased Span. tenor Alfredo Kraus at the Teatro Real in Madrid
250th anniversary of composer Johann Sebastian Bach's death
125th birthday of Maurice Ravel
Jonathan Miller stages Mozart's "Zauberflöte" ("The Magic Flute") in Zurich
Opera of Jean Genet's "The Screens," directed by Adriana Hölsky in Frankfurt
100th birthday of Kurt Weill
Wim Hendericks: "Triumph of Spirit over Matter," opera, premieres in Brussels
Premiere of the documentary opera "Das Gedächtnis von Wasser" ("The Memory of Water") composed by Gordon Sherwood and Uve Müllrich at the Danube Festival in Ulm
New production of Richard Wagner's "Ring of the Nibelungen" in Bayreuth
Sofia Gubaidulina: "St. John Passion," premieres in Stuttgart
Following its 18-year run as the most successful musical of all time, "Cats" closes on Broadway. Over 10 million viewers have seen the show in 7,844 performances. The production won seven Tony Awards
"Guys and Dolls" by Frank Loesser (music) and Damon Runyon (script) experiences a celebrated renaissance at the Arena Stage Theatre in Washington
Guest performances of New York's Paul Taylor Dance Company in Frankfurt
Pina Bausch brings to the stage in Wuppertal her
(contd)

F. SCIENCE, TECHNOLOGY, GROWTH

available for research purposes at Stanford University
Development of the world's smallest quantum dot laser by Alfred Forchel and colleagues at the microstructure laboratory in Würzburg: three of them could be placed in a diameter of a strand of hair—the nano-mirrors are 300 nanometers thick
Evidence of the tau-neutrino, the last missing elemental particle of matter, is discovered by scientists led by Byron Lundberg using the Tevatron accelerator at the Fermi Lab in Chicago
At the European Organization for Nuclear Research (CERN) in Geneva, an international research team succeeds in generating quark gluon plasma (QGP), a form of matter that must have been present immediately following the Big Bang
According to N.A.S.A., the hole in the ozone layer over Antarctica, at 17 sq. miles, has increased by more than .62 sq. mile since 1999. Experts fear an increase in skin cancer
Shut down of the nuclear weapons test site at Semipalatinsk in what is now Kazakhstan
Span. researchers discover the largest form of submarine landscape formed by glaciers off the Antarctic Peninsula
Skeletal remains of the longest dinosaur found in Patagonia. It must have been about 164 feet long and weighed 15 tons
Archeologists unearth evidence of a previously unknown pre-Columbian culture in Nicaragua
Palatial compound discovered in Central China, presumably the residence of Emperor Shi Huang-Di (259–210 B.C.), using a cadmium magnetometer
First museum for paleontology in China
Divers in the Baltic port of Härnösand discover a nearly 1,000-year-old Viking ship
Ger. archeologists find skull fragments in the Neander Valley, among others, a bone fragment from a face that matches the skull of a Neanderthal found in 1856
Archaeological team led by Franck Goddio discovers remnants of the ancient cities Herakleion and Menouthis in the Bay of Aboukir off the Egyptian coast
First successful double hand transplant performed in Lyon
Ger. and Japanese scientists sequence
(contd)

G. DAILY LIFE

Euro hits a record low at 0.86 to the U.S. dollar. In an attempt to break its rapid decline, the European Central bank raises interest rates by 0.25 to 4.25%
John Harsanyi, Amer. economist, Nobel laureate, d. (b. 1920, Budapest)
Merton Howard Miller, Amer. economist, d. (b. 1923)
Harry Frederick Oppenheimer, South African entrepreneur, d. (b. 1908)
200 die in a cold spell in India
169 die in Kenya Airlines airbus crash off the Ivory Coast
Environmental disaster in eastern Hungary after cyanide from tailings dam of a gold mining plant spills into the Szamos River
911 fishermen are rescued from an iceberg in a dramatic rescue on Lagoda Lake near St. Petersburg
Despite international aid, devastating floods in Mozambique destroy livelihoods for at least 1 million people
80 miners killed in a mining accident in Ukraine
Two Brit. soccer fans are stabbed in bloody riots in Istanbul preceding a UEFA Cup game there
Boeing 737 crashes on landing approach in the Philippines. All 131 passengers on board die in the crash
Mass hysteria breaks out in Seville during Good Friday processions, 60 people injured
110 tons of fireworks explode in a factory in Enschede (Netherlands), destroying a whole city neighborhood
58 illegal Chinese immigrants die in the refrigeration compartment of a freight truck in the Port of Dover
Brazil's worst environmental disaster: 1 million gallons of oil spill from a broken pipeline near a refinery into the Iguacu River
165 employees of the company Royal Dutch Shell are taken hostage and held on two Nigerian oil rigs; hostage takers demand jobs for the indigenous population and compensation from oil revenues in their country
Russian nuclear submarine "Kursk" sinks in the Bering Sea, 118 crew members die. After several days of hesitation, Russian government finally accepts offers for help from the West
200 people dead after a landfill collapses in Manila
79 die in a ferry accident off the Island of Paros in the Aegean Sea
155 die when fire breaks out in a train tunnel carrying skiers to the Kitzensteinerhorn Glacier at Kaprun, Austria
Darius Michalczewski, after defeating Graciano Rocchigiani, remains boxing world champion in the middle heavyweight class
New Zealand takes home the coveted Americas Cup sailing trophy in its second consecutive win
(contd)

	A. HISTORY, POLITICS	B. LITERATURE, THEATER	C. RELIGION, PHILOSOPHY, LEARNING
2000 contd	der Lukaschenko. 400 protesters and countless foreign journalists are arrested Ukrainian Parliament abolishes the death penalty Incumbent Pres. Eduard Shevardnadze is reelected by a large majority in presidential elections in Georgia Nearly 15 years after the nuclear catastrophe at Chernobyl, the last reactor block is finally shut down Vladimir Putin easily wins the Russian presidential election with a 52% majority Seven years after it was signed, Russian Parliament ratifies the Russian-American disarmament treaty on strategic nuclear weapons Start II. Russian Lower House approves treaty on the comprehensive ban on nuclear testing Russian Duma confirms Mikhail Kasyanov as Prime Minister After heavy fighting, Russian troops seize the Chechen capital of Grozny In Croatian parliamentary elections, the incumbent Democratic Union loses with 40 seats to the Social Democrats (44 seats), Social Liberals (24 seats), and other parties (43 seats) Yugoslavian Prime Minister Pavel Bulatovic is shot by unknown perpetrators at a restaurant in Belgrade Following parliamentary elections in Yugoslavia, nearly 1 million members of the opposition protest against Pres. Slobodan Milosevic Stipe Mesic wins in a runoff election to succeed Croatian head of state Franjo Tudjman N.A.T.O. accepts Croatia as the 26th member of its "Partnership for Peace" Following Serbian parliamentary elections, Zoran Djindjic is President-elect Following his electoral victory in Slovakia, Janez Drnovsek assumes office of Prime Minister In Greek parliamentary elections, incumbent Pres. Kostas Simitis retains his post, defeating the Nea Demokratia Party Greece becomes the 12th EU state to enter the Euro-Zone Suppression of prisoner uprisings in 20 Turkish prisons leaves 19 people dead. Brutal tactics on the part of the police elicit staunch criticism within Turkey and abroad Romanian Pres. Emil Constantinescu resigns and is succeeded in a runoff election by Ion Iliescu International Union of Roma People demands recognition as a nation, not merely as an ethnic group Uzbekistan's Pres. Islam Karimov is confirmed in office Over 100,000 Israelis demonstrate in Tel Aviv to protest the return of the Golan Heights to Syria Israeli air strikes on Hizbollah militia bases in southern Lebanon Former Prime Minister and entrepreneur Rafik Hariri wins Lebanese parliamentary elections in Beirut Middle East peace talks between Israeli Prime Minister Ehud Barak and leader of the Arafat mediated by U.S. Pres. Bill Clinton at Camp David fail. Foreign Minister David Levy resigns in protest of Barak's Palestinian policy. Parliament approves new election. Increased incidents of violence between Israelis and Palestinians jeopardize the Mid-East peace process. In December, Barak resigns, but intends to run in the new elections in 2001 Parliamentary elections in Iran. Reformers backing current head of state Hatami win with 67% of votes Moshe Katzav becomes new Pres. of Israel, defeating Shimon Peres. His predecessor, Ezer Weizmann, was forced out of office prematurely after accepting millions in private contributions Hans von Sponeck, Ger. diplomat, resigns from his post as U.N. Coordinator for Humanitarian Aid in Iraq, criticizing the U.N. embargo against Iraq as a "human tragedy" Nambaryn Enkhbayar becomes new Prime Minister of Mongolia Ricardo Lagos is the first Socialist Democrat to be elected Pres. of Chile since Salvador Allende. Former dictator Augusto Pinochet is allowed to return to Chile after 503 days of house arrest in *(contd)*		

D. VISUAL ARTS

P. Almodóvar's "All about My Mother"
Cannes Film Festival's Golden Palm to the melodramatic musical "Dancer in the Dark" by Lars von Trier
Venice Film Festival's Golden Lion to the Iranian director Jafar Panahi for "Dajareh"
49 years after it was created by Charles M. Schultz, the last of the original "Peanuts" comic strip appears
Span. gov. purchases one of the most prized paintings by Goya, the 1800 portrait of Condes de Chinchón
"Abstract Art in France and Italy from 1945–1975: The Milieu of Jean Leppin," exhibit in Strasbourg's Zollhaus Museum
"ModernStarts: People": LeWitt, Gauguin, Picasso, Munch, Steichen, and others; exhibit at the Museum of Modern Art in New York
Exhibit of the early illustrations of Ellsworth Kelly in Winterthur
Highly praised Cézanne exhibit in Vienna and Zurich
Donald Judd's colorful block sculptures on exhibit in Hannover
Famous portrait by Dosso Dossi missing from the ducal palace in Ferrara resurfaces in India. Portrait by Mexican muralist Diego Rivera that has been missing for 47 years resurfaces in Moscow
Previously unknown pioneer collection of works by Paul Klee in Zurich
Opening of a new concert and conference center in Lahti (Finland), built according to plans by architects Hannu Tikka and Kimmo Lintula exclusively from wood
"Face to Face" exhibit at the Museum of Fine Arts in Boston shows portraits by Vincent van Gogh
"Bremen Leaves Collection" of art works looted during WW II and returned by Russia are on exhibit at the Kunsthalle in Bremen; includes works by Dürer,

(contd)

E. MUSIC

1978 piece "Kontakthof" with "Damen und Herren ab 65/Ladies and Gentlemen over 65"

F. SCIENCE, TECHNOLOGY, GROWTH

Chromosome 21 responsible for Down's Syndrome
Human DNA is decoded. Craig Venter, chief scientific officer of the Amer. biotech company Celera Genomics, announced the complete sequencing of the human genome in Washington
Scientists in Japan succeed in cloning the first second-generation cow. Up until now, the cloning of cloned animals had only been possible with mice
Great Britain approves the use of cloned human embryonic cells for research purposes
John Heidelberg at the Institute for Genomic Research in Rockville, Maryland, releases the sequence of the genome for cholera (vibrio cholerae), consisting of more than 4 million base pairs
Minor Planet Center at the Smithsonian Astrophysical Observatory in Massachusetts finds evidence of a 17th moon around the planet Jupiter. The moon, named S/1999 J1, is only 3.1 miles in diameter and revolves around Jupiter at a distance of about 15.5 million miles
U.S. scientists discover the black hole closest to Earth in the universe, at a distance of 1,600 light years
Space probe Galileo's mission to deliver valuable data from space is extended by a year
U.S. space probe Mars Global Surveyor sends images of the surface of Mars which, according to scientists, show evidence of gullies hinting at the presence of water on Mars
International Astronomical Union (IAU) announces the discovery of nine additional planets circling other stars. This increases the number of known so-called exoplanets circling stars to 50, all of which have been discovered within the past 5 years
Concept has been drawn for a 328-foot telescope at the European Southern Observatory (ESO). The primary mirror will have 3,048 hexagonal segments, each 5.25 feet in diameter. The largest telescope to date is 27 feet
Russian service module Zwezda successfully docks at International Space Station (ISS), where it will provide early living quarters and early propulsive attitude control
Astronauts aboard the U.S. space shuttle Endeavor bring solar arrays to the ISS that will power the station

(contd)

G. DAILY LIFE

Record-setting Ger. national soccer player Lothar Matthäus transfers toward the end of his career to the New York MetroStars
Lance Armstrong (U.S.) takes his second consecutive win at the Tour de France, Ger. Jan Ullrich in second place
European Football (Soccer) Championships take place in two different countries for the first time in history: in Belgium and the Netherlands; France versus Italy after a 2-1 victory to become European Champion
Women's world record for deep sea diving, weighted and without supplemental oxygen, is set by Yasemin Dalkilic (Turkey) at 394 feet
Germany receives the go-ahead from the World Football Assoc. (FIFA) to host the 2006 World Soccer Championships in 2006
U.S. tennis pro Pete Sampras takes his 7th Wimbledon win
XXVII Olympic Summer Games in Sydney, Australia with 10,500 athletes from 199 countries; 28 sports with 300 competitions. Results (Gold/Silver/Bronze): 1. U.S.A. (39/25/17); 2. Russia (32/17/26); 3. China (28/16/15); 4. Australia (16/25/17); 5. Germany (13/17/26)
11th Paralympics in Sydney (Australia) with 3,838 athletes (976 of them women) from 122 countries; 18 sports with 550 competitions. Results (Gold/Silver/Bronze): 1. Australia (63/39/47); 2. Great Britain (41/43/47); 3. Spain (39/30/38); 4. Canada (38/33/25); 5. U.S.A. (36/39/34)
Michael Schumacher wins the Grand Prix of Japan at Suzuka and becomes Formula 1 World Champion
Vladimir Klitschko defeats title defender Chris Byrd from the U.S. to take home the WBO heavyweight championship title
Russian Vladimir Kramnik succeeds Garri Kasparov as reigning world chess champion
FIFA names Frenchman Zinedine Zidane (Juventus Turin) Footballer of the Year
Don Budge, Amer. tennis player, d. (b. 1915)
Gene Sarazen, Amer. golfer, d. (b. 1902)
Emil Zatopek, Czech. cross country runner, Olympic champion and world record holder, d. (b. 1922)

	A. HISTORY, POLITICS	B. LITERATURE, THEATER	C. RELIGION, PHILOSOPHY, LEARNING

2000 contd

London; Spain's petition for extradition is blocked by a medical affidavit; five months later the Supreme Court of Chile suspends immunity for Pinochet in order to facilitate charges against him for human rights violations during his 1973–90 reign

EU and Mexico enter into free trade agreement

Historical regime change in Mexico: For the first time in 71 years the President is installed by a party other than the ruling Institutional Revolution; opposition leader Vicente Fox becomes new head of state

Economic and political crisis in Ecuador: following nationwide demonstrations, a national state of emergency is declared. Non-violent overthrow of government puts Gustavo Noboa in power

Peruvian Pres. Alberto Fujimori resigns amid a corruption scandal and is succeeded by Valentin Paniagua. Former U.N. Sec. Gen. Javier Pérez de Cuellar becomes new Prime Minister

Hugo Chávez is confirmed for an additional 6 years in office as Pres. of Venezuela

Constitutional court in El Salvador allows for the possibility of taking legal action on crimes committed during the civil war between 1980–92, which had not been permitted under terms of the 1993 amnesty law

World Bank relieves Nicaragua of $4.5 billion in debt, nearly ¾ of the country's total foreign debt

Former head of state Jean-Bertrand Aristide wins presidential election in Haiti

After 8 months in office, the Algerian Cabinet under Prime Minister Ahmed Benbitour resigns. Pres. Abdelaziz Bouteflika charges Ali Benflis with the task of forming a new government

Kumba Yala wins presidential election in Guinea-Bissau

Peace Treaty signed between Uganda and Sudan

Border war between Eritrea and Ethiopia is brought to an end with a peace treaty signed in Algeria

In parliamentary elections in Zimbabwe, incumbent Pres. Robert Mugabe wins but, for the first time, faces staunch opposition

Opposition leader John Kufour is elected new Pres. of Ghana

Military assumes power in the Fiji Islands; Ratu Josefa Hoilo becomes new Pres.

Following the death of Keizo Obuchi, Yoshiro Mori becomes new head of government in Japan. In the parliamentary elections, ruling parties defend their leadership positions, but lose their ⅔ majority

At 12.7%, China's military budget is growing at a faster rate than the economy (7%)

Two leading members of the Falun Gong sect are sentenced to long prison terms in China

In Taiwan, opposition candidate Chen Shui-bian wins presidential election

Park Tae-joon becomes new South Korean head of state

For the first time since partition 55 years ago, heads of state from North and South Korea meet in Pyonyang and agree to improving relations between the two countries

After years of isolation, North Korea becomes a member of the Asian security forum, A.S.E.A.N. Regional Forum (A.R.F.)

Bill Clinton becomes the first U.S. Pres. to visit Communist Vietnam

84-year-old Prime Minister of Sri Lanka, Sirimavo Bandaranaike, resigns and is succeeded by Ratnasiri Wickramanayake

In Thailand's parliamentary elections, party backing the military leader Thanksin Shinawatra wins

Hafez al Assad, Syrian Pres. since 1971, d. (b. 1930)

Sirimavo Bandaranaike, former government head in Sri Lanka, d. (b. 1916)

Habib ben Ali Bourgouiba, first Tunisian Pres., d. (b. 1903)

Bettino Craxi, Ital. politician, former head of state, d. (b. 1934)

Jacques Chaban-Delmas, Fr. politician, former Prime Minister, d. (b. 1915)

Poul Hartling, Danish politician, d. (b. 1914)

Hassan II, King of Morocco, d. (b. 1929)

(contd)

D. VISUAL ARTS	E. MUSIC	F. SCIENCE, TECHNOLOGY, GROWTH	G. DAILY LIFE	
Delacroix, Manet, and Lautrec An exhibit at Strasbourg's Musée d'Art Moderne et Contemporain highlights the influence of exiled Surrealists on Amer. art in the 1940s based on 300 art works in the show Scientists at the University of Tübingen discover a 30,000-year-old horse head carved from ivory Following a ten-year effort to correct its dangerous lean, the Leaning Tower of Pisa is re-opened for visitors Renzo Piano and Richard Meier design department stores in Cologne and Düsseldorf Restoration completed on frescos by Piero della Francesca in Arezzo some of the most significant masterpieces of the early Renaissance The Öresund Bridge between Denmark and Sweden is opened for traffic Norway's King Harald V opens the world's longest road tunnel (15 miles) to traffic. It is the final stretch of highway between Oslo and Bergen Queen Elizabeth II opens the new Brit. Embassy in Berlin, designed by Michael Wilford Atom Egoyan's film "Felicia's Journey" with Bob Hoskins and Elaine Cassidy in the leading roles pays homage to Alfred Hitchcock "Boys Don't Cry," directorial debut for Kimberly Peirce with Hilary Swank (Oscar for best actress) After massive protests on the part of the local population, Canadian director Deepa Metha is forced to cancel filming in the famous place of pilgrimage, Varanasi, India Alan Parker films the novel "Angela's Ashes" by Frank McCourt with Emily Watson in the leading role Lasse Halström films "The Cider House Rules" based on the novel by John Irving *(contd)*		Crew of four launch in a Soyuz rocket and settle in to the ISS space station for the first long-term presence of humans in space The European Airbus Consortium in Paris decides to go ahead with plans for the world's largest passenger plane, the Airbus A3XX, scheduled to accommodate up to 656 passengers and go into service by 2004 Communications satellite Eutelsat VV1 goes into orbit. It is designed to be in service transmitting for television and Internet for the next 12 years 125th birthday of the automobile designer Ferdinand Porsche Destructive computer virus ILOVEYOU spread by e-mail with a self-sending attachment shuts down computers worldwide, destroys data, and causes some $15 billion in damage and lost productivity The computer date rollover to the year 2000 did not result in the chaos many had feared it would		**2000 contd**

	A. HISTORY, POLITICS	B. LITERATURE, THEATER	C. RELIGION, PHILOSOPHY, LEARNING
2000 contd	Ingrid, Queen Mother of Denmark, d. (b. 1910) Rudolf Kirchschläger, Austrian politician, former Pres., d. (b. 1915) Petar Mladenow, former Pres. of Bulgaria, d. (b. 1926) Keizo Obuki, head of gov. in Japan since 1998, d. (b. 1935) William P. Rogers, former U.S. Secretary of State, d. (b. 1913) Pierre Trudeau, former Canadian head of gov., d. (b. 1919) Saeb Salam, former Lebanese Prime Minister, d. (b. 1904) Son Sann, former Cambodian Prime Minister, d. (b. 1911)		
2001	Nobel Peace Prize to the U.N. and its Sec. Gen. Kofi Annan for work toward a better organized and more peaceful world. 100th anniversary of the Nobel Prize Ceremony in Oslo and Stockholm Right Livelihood Award ("Alternative Nobel Prize") to the Israeli peace group "Gush Shalom," founded by Uri and Rachel Avnery, to the Brit. opponents of nuclear weapons "Trident Plugshares," to the Brazilian liberation theologian Leonardo Boff and to the Venezuelan economic scientist and orchestra leader José Antonio Abreu Memorial ceremonies commemorate the 40th anniversary of the building of the Berlin Wall U.N.-sponsored conference on the future of Afghanistan in Bonn. Four delegations from Afghanistan, 30 representatives in all, agree on a transitional government. Head of State is Hamid Karzai U.N. Security Council votes unanimously in favor of sending multinational peacekeeping forces to Afghanistan. The troops, led by Great Britain, should protect the work of the Afghani transitional government EU finance ministers meet in Stockholm to outline the terms for forming a common financial market E.U. Parliament in Strasbourg sets tighter restrictions on tobacco: more serious warnings about the health risks of smoking, in a larger format, required on packaging George W. Bush becomes new U.S. Pres.; Richard Cheney Vice Pres., Colin Powell Sec. of State George W. Bush refuses to sign the Kyoto Protocol on Climate Change. Bush questions the treaty's approach; it is designed to reduce CO_2 gas emissions in 30 industrialized countries by the year 2008 and 2012 Collision between a U.S. army surveillance aircraft and Chinese fighter jet in the South China Sea leads to diplomatic crisis between the two countries U.S. Department of Defense confirms that the U.S. has been conducting secret experiments in biological warfare; this supposedly involves purely defensive programs congruent with the terms of the 1972 international ban on chemical and biological weapons In the worst terror attack in the history of the U.S., over 3,000 people perish on September 11, 2001, among them several hundred fire fighters and rescue workers: At almost the same time, four separate teams of assassins hijack commercial airlines filled with civilian passengers and fuel and slam them into their targets on kamikaze flights; two planes slam into the two towers of the World Trade Center in New York, which collapse later. 2,983 people perish. A third plane crashes into the Pentagon, home to the U.S. Department of Defense near Washington, claiming 289 lives. A fourth aircraft crashes near Philadelphia, killing all 45 on board. U.S. government and the F.B.I. declare that the internationally sought terrorist Osama bin Laden is the most likely mastermind behind the operation. Western politicians speak in terms of a "declaration of war on civilization." "Ground Zero" becomes a worldwide center of mourning. Officials and citizens from around the world visit the site to pay tribute to the victims In light of the attacks on the U.S., N.A.T.O. invokes Article 5 of the alliance's charter, enabling collective self-defense, for the first time in its 52-year history U.S. and British fighter jets attack military and strategic targets in *(contd)*	Douglas Adams, Brit. writer ("Hitchhiker's Guide to the Galaxy"), d. (b. 1952) Jorge Amado, Brazilian writer, d. (b. 1912) Gregory Corso, Amer. lyric poet, d. (b. 1930) Ken Kesey, Amer. writer, d. (b. 1935) Anne Spencer Morrow Lindbergh, Amer. writer, wife of Charles Lindbergh, d. (b. 1907) Robert Ludlum, Amer. writer, d. (b. 1927) Nobel Prize for Literature to West Indian writer V.S. Naipaul Praemium Imperiale (in Theater) to Amer. dramatist Arthur Miller Prix Goncourt to Jean-Christophe Rufin for the novel "Rouge Brésil" Booker Prize, Britain's most prestigious literary award, to Australian writer Peter Carey for his novel "The True Story of Ned Kelly and his Gang" T.S. Eliot Prize to Canadian lyric poet Anne Carson for "The Beauty of the Husband" National Book Award to Amer. author Jonathan Franzen for his novel "The Corrections" Pulitzer Prize to Amer. author Michael Chabon and to Amer. dramatist David Auburn The private archive of Norwegian author and Nobel laureate Knut Hamsun (d. 1952), presumed to have been lost, is discovered and purchased by the Norwegian National Archive for 125,000 euro Michel Piccoli is the first actor to be honored with the European Theater Award, which has been in existence since 1990	Ernst Gombrich, Brit-Austrian art historian, d. (b. 1909, Vienna) Otto Herding, Ger. historian, d. (b. 1911) The 2,000-year-old Qumran Scrolls can be read using a laser microscope developed for medical research. The device with its three-dimensional magnification is able to decipher characters whose ink has long since disappeared. The Qumran Scrolls, first found in 1948 in the Dead Sea, document the religious beliefs of a strictly orthodox Jewish sect before the destruction of Judea by the Romans Pope John Paul II closes the Porta Sancta, thus bringing the Jubilee Year to a close; approx. 30 million visitors and pilgrims made it to Rome during the Jubilee Year At the confluence of the Ganga, Yamuna, and Saraswati Rivers in India, 30 million Hindus celebrate the festival of Kumbh Mela over an 11-day period John Paul II beatifies Ger. Sister Crescentia Höss (d. 1682) Resistance fighter Nikolaus Gross and Sister Euthymia declared saints by Pope John Paul II Otto Hahn Peace Medal for outstanding contributions to peace and understanding between people to South African vocalist Miriam Makeba Theodor Adorno Prize of the City of Frankfurt to Fr. philosopher Jacques Derrida

D. VISUAL ARTS	E. MUSIC	F. SCIENCE, TECHNOLOGY, GROWTH	G. DAILY LIFE	
Photographic exhibit about the films of Luis Buñuel at the Instituto Cervantes in Munich				**2000 contd**
Maurice de Bevere, Belgian illustrator, creature of the cartoon character "Lucky Luke," d. (b. 1923) Budd Boetticher, Amer. director of westerns, d. (b. 1916) William Hanna, Amer. illustrator (creator of "Tom and Jerry" and "The Flintstones"), d. (b. 1910) Pauline Kael, Amer. film critic, d. (b. 1919) Balthazar Klossowski, Fr. painter, d. (b. 1908) Alberto Korda, Cuban photographer, d. (b. 1928) Stanley Kramer, Amer. film producer and director, d. (b. 1913) Jack Lemmon, Amer. actor, two-time Oscar winner, d. (b. 1925) Philippe Léotard, Fr. actor, d. (b. 1940) Jacques Lowe, Amer. photographer, d. (b. 1930, Cologne) Anthony Quinn, Amer. actor, d. (b. 1915, Chihuahua, Mexico) Francisco Rabal, Span. actor, d. (b. 1925) Four Césars to the directing debut of Agnès Jaouis for "Le goût des autres" and to the film by Dominik Moll, "Harry, un amie qui vous veut du bien" Ger. Gregor Schneider wins the Golden Lion at Venice's Biennale. Two additional Golden Lions to sculptor Richard Serra and painter Cy Twombly (both U.S.) Turner Prize, Britain's most significant award for contemporary art, to conceptual artist Martin Creed Pritzker Architecture Prize to Swiss architects Jacques Herzog and Pierre de Meuron for their conversion of the Bankside Power Station into the "Tate Modern" in London *(contd)*	Chet Atkins, Amer. guitarist and music producer, d. (b. 1924) Gilbert Bécaud (born François Leopold Silly), Fr. singer and pianist, d. (b. 1927) Victor Braun, Canadian opera singer, d. (b. 1935) Perry Como, Amer. singer and entertainer, d. (b. 1912) Tommy Flanagan, Amer. jazz pianist, d. (b. 1930) George Harrison, Brit. musician, member of the Beatles, d. (b. 1943) Johnny Lee Hooker, Amer. musician, d. (b. 1917) Paul Huber, Swiss composer, d. (b. 1918) J.J. Johnson, Amer. jazz trombonist, d. (b. 1923) John Lewis, Amer. jazz musician, d. (b. 1930) John Phillips, Amer. rock singer (The Mamas and the Papas), d. (b. 1935) Giuseppe Sinopoli, Ital. composer and conductor, d. (b. 1946) Isaac Stern, Amer. violinist, d. (b. 1920, Ukraine) Dame Ninette de Valois, Brit. dancer and choreographer, founder of the "Royal Ballet" in London, d. (b. 1898, Ireland) Iannis Xenakis, Greek composer, d. (b. 1922, Romania) Jap. Praemium Imperiale (in Music) to Amer. saxophonist Ornette Coleman Composer György Ligeti conducts the premiere of his horn concerto Philippe Manoury's Kafka opera "K" premieres in Paris Luis de Pablo: "Fräulein Christine," opera, premiere in Madrid 50th anniversary of Marlboro Music Festival, founded by Ger. emigré musician Adolf Busch and Rudolf *(contd)*	Christiaan Barnard, South African heart surgeon, d. (b. 1922) Nikolai Bassov, Russian physicist and Nobel laureate (founder of quantum electronics and co-inventor of the laser), d. (b. 1922) Donald J. Cram, Amer. chemist and Nobel laureate, d. (b. 1919) Claude Shannon, Amer. mathematician (inventor of binary code), d. (b. 1916) Herbert Alexander Simon, Amer. computer scientist, d. (b. 1916) Clifford Glenwood Shull, Amer. physicist and Nobel laureate, d. (b. 1915) Nobel Prize for Chemistry to Americans William Knowles and K. Barry Sharpless and to Ryoji Noyori (Japan) for their research on molecules that mirror each other Nobel Prize for Physics to Americans Eric Cornell and Carl Wiemann and to German Wolfgang Ketterle for achieving Bose-Einstein condensation in dilute gases of alkali atoms and for early fundamental studies of the properties of condensation Nobel Prize for Medicine to Amer. Leland H. Hartwell and to the Britons Tim Hunt and Paul Nurse for their discoveries of regulators in the cell cycle Nobel Prize for Economics to Americans George A. Akerlof, A. Michael Spence, and Joseph E. Stiglitz for their analysis of markets with asymmetric information Swiss agricultural company Syngenta and Amer. genetic engineering firm Myriad Genetics announce completion of DNA sequencing for the entire rice genome. The rice genome consists of 430 million genetic "bases" and, aside from the human genome, is the second largest genome to have been sequenced to date The Mir space station, now 15 years old, plunges into earth's atmosphere as planned and disintegrates almost completely, with only the last remains of debris dropping into the Pacific Ocean *(contd)*	Peter Blake, sailor from New Zealand, d. (b. 1948) Didi (born Waldir Pareira), Brazilian soccer player, d. (b. 1928) Donald Bradman, Australian cricket player, d. (b. 1908) Chung Ju Yung, Korean industry magnate (founder of Hyundai), d. (b. 1915, North Korea) Katharine Graham, Amer. journalist (former editor of the "Washington Post"), d. (b. 1917) William Hewlett, Amer. computer manufacturer, d. (b. 1913) Victor Kiam, Amer. business executive, d. (b. 1926) Michel Navratail, psychology professor and presumably the last living survivor of the "Titanic," d. (b. 1908) Media giants AOL Time Warner, Bertelsmann, EMI Group, and RealNeworks announce in London the founding of an online platform for selling music on the Internet, MusicNet Internet music file-sharing service Napster signs licensing agreement with U.S. music publishers and songwriters/composers Bayer corporation's cholesterol lowering drug Baycol/Lipobay is pulled from markets worldwide following the deaths of 31 patients using the drug Bayer AG takes over the agro chemical concern CropScience, a subsidiary of Aventis, for $8 billion Settlement in the antitrust suit against Microsoft: the world's largest software com pany must guarantee software developers and competitors access to information about its operating system so they can make products that are Windows-compatible Several European countries sign contract for delivery of 196 Airbus A 400 military transport aircraft in what is Europe's biggest military contract to date. Germany places the bulk of the order, with 73 planes, at a price of 116.67 million euros each Merger between U.S. computer companies Hewlett Packard and Compaq On the first day of trading on Wall Street following the terrorist attacks on the World Trade Center in New York, the Dow Jones Index for 30 top industrial stocks experiences its biggest one-day drop in points in history (-7.1%), bringing the world's most important index to 8921 points; Nasdaq's technology index falls 6.8% Following several major earthquakes in Central *(contd)*	**2001**

	A. HISTORY, POLITICS	B. LITERATURE, THEATER	C. RELIGION, PHILOSOPHY, LEARNING
2001 contd	Afghanistan. Two months later, the Taliban regime comes to an end A series of anthrax attacks spreads fear in the Amer. public and shut down Congressional operations. Several people are infected with the virus after handling contaminated letters. An anthrax-infected letter is sent to the office of Senator Tom Daschle in Washington. The F.B.I. suspects the attacks are the work of an individual perpetrator and are unrelated to the terrorists attacks on September 11 Media tycoon Michael Bloomberg becomes Mayor of New York and successor to Rudolph Giuliani David McTaggart, Canadian environmentalist (cofounder of the organization Greenpeace), d. (b. 1932) William P. Rogers, Amer. politician, d. (b. 1913) Referendum on joining the EU rejected by 76.7% of Swiss; 78% oppose dissolution of the Swiss army Bertrand Delanoe is elected first Socialist Mayor of Paris since the Paris Commune (1871) Netherlands law supporting same-sex marriage goes into effect Dutch Parliament passes legislation to legalize assisted suicide, making the Netherlands the first country in the world to do so. Surveys indicate that 86% of the population approves the move New head of the minority coalition government of Denmark is Anders Fogh Rasmussen New Prime Minister of Norway is Kjell Magne Bondevik New Prime Minister of Poland is Leszek Miller Moderate Protestant politician David Trimble is elected First Minister by the regional parliament of Northern Ireland. He had resigned in July in protest of the I.R.A.'s refusal to put down its arms The Independent International Commission on Decommissioning (Northern Ireland) led by Canadian General John de Chastelain confirms that the I.R.A. has begun destroying its weapons In Italy's parliamentary elections, a center-right alliance prevails, led by former Prime Minister Silvio Berlusconi Socialist President Jorge Sampaio is voted into office in Portugal with 55.8% Otmar Hasler becomes new Prime Minister of Lichtenstein Former Yugoslav. Pres. Slobodan Milosevic is arrested in Belgrade. Police turn up plans for a revolution and a weapons arsenal in his villa. He is handed over to the U.N. War Crimes Tribunal in The Hague, where he is to be tried for crimes against humanity Parliament in Sarajevo passes election reform law under which registered voters in Bosnia-Herzegovina will only be able to vote for candidates within their own ethnic group In Pristina, in the Yugoslavian Province of Kosovo, parliamentary representatives elected in a U.N.-administered vote convene. It is the first time since 1991 that Albanian and Serbian representatives have met in a joint people's assembly U.N. Security Council lifts the weapons embargo that has been in effect against Yugoslavia since 1998, putting an end to the last remaining international sanction against the country Albanian rebels engage in bloody skirmishes with Macedonian security forces. Angry demonstrators storm parliament building New Albanian Pres. is former general and Defense Minister Alfred Moisiu Macedonian Parliament passes constitutional amendment in favor of the Albanian minority, whereby not only the Slavic Macedonians will be protected by the constitution, but also other ethnic groups such as the Albanians, Turks, Serbs, and Roma. Any language spoken by at least 20% of the population is now considered an official language Runoff election for the presidency in Bulgaria; Socialist Georgi Parvanov defeats Petur Stoyanov with 56% of votes Ukrainian Parliament in Kiev: liberal, reform-oriented government of Prime Minister Viktor Yuschenko ousted by a majority formed from the Communist Party and the parties surrounding Pres. Leonid Kuchma *(contd)*		

D. VISUAL ARTS

Japanese Praemium Imperiale (in Painting, Sculpture, and Architecture) to Korean painter Lee Ufan, Hungarian sculptor Martan Pan, and Fr. architect Jean Nouvel

Mies van der Rohe Architectural Award to the Span. architect Rafael Moneo for the Kursaal Auditorium in San Sebastián. Emerging architect award to Ger. architect Florian Nagler

Patrice Chereau's film "Intimacy" wins the Golden Bear at the Berlin Film Festival. Other winners: Jury's Grand Prize to Wang Xiaoshuai for "Beijing Bicycle," Silver Bear to the Danish film "Italian for Beginners" by Lone Scherfig

Venice's Golden Lion goes to Indian director Mira Nair for her film "Monsoon Wedding"

Oscars: Best picture, "Gladiator" by Ridley Scott; best actor in a leading role, Russell Crowe; best actress, Julia Roberts in "Erin Brockovich"; Ang Lee's "Crouching Tiger, Hidden Dragon" wins Oscars in three categories, including best cinematography; best director to Stephen Soderbergh for "Traffic." Best short film "Quiero ser" by Ger. director Florian Gallenberger

Grand prize at the Sundance Film Festival to Henry Bean for "The Believer," the nonfiction history of a Jewish student, Daniel Burros, who becomes a militant anti-Semite and rises to stardom in the neofascist scene

Andy Warhol retrospective in Berlin, with 168 objects and 80 illustrations, some never before displayed publicly

The famed Amber Room, parts of which remain missing, is being reconstructed. 50 restoration experts, stonecutters and architects work on the collaborative Ger. and Russian project at the

(contd)

E. MUSIC

Serkin, and Fr. musicians Marcel, Blanche, and Louis Moyse

Worldwide celebrations commemorate the 100th anniversary of composer G. Verdi's death. The program for the whole year is devoted exclusively to works by this Italian artist at the Arena in Verona. A highlight of the Verdi commemorative year is the interpretation of the complete "Don Carlos" cycle by Peter Konwitschny and Ingo Metzmacher in the French original at the Staatsoper in Hamburg

Amer. pop singer Madonna launches her first world tour in seven years

F. SCIENCE, TECHNOLOGY, GROWTH

Japanese researchers discover a previously overlooked superconductor: magnesium diboride transitions into superconductive state when it is cooled to -234 degrees C (–453 F)

Optisphere Networks and WorldCom set a world record for transmission capacity of data, video, and voice traffic on single installed network fiber to 3.2 terabits per second, the equivalent of sending over 41 million telephone calls at the same time on one strand of glass fiber

Space shuttle Discovery takes its third crew to the International Space Station

Microsoft introduces its new Windows XP operating system. According to Microsoft founder Bill Gates, the launch of Windows XP is the beginning of a new era and the final end to the age of DOS (Disk Operating System)

U.S. Space Agency N.A.S.A. announces five new missions planned for the space probe Galileo. For the past five years, the probe has been studying the planetary system of Jupiter. Its mission has already been extended twice

With its Mars probe Odyssey, N.A.S.A. launches a new foray into exploration of neighboring planets

U.S. millionaire Dennis Tito makes a several-day venture to the International Space Station aboard the Russian Soyus Capsule. The first tourist in space paid $20 million for the trip

U.S. space shuttle Endeavor delivers the new long-term crew to the International Space Station: Russian commander Yuri Onufrienkov and the two Americans, Daniel Bursch and Carl Walz

First landing of a space probe on an asteroid. The Near space probe touches down safely on Eros, a chunk of rock from the beginning of the solar system

The unmanned solar aircraft Helios reaches a record height of over 18 miles above the island of Hawaii. The $15 million experimental machine is powered by solar energy. In the future, devices of this type are to replace satellites

Scientists develop a nanomicrophone capable of recording the frequency of sound waves in the interior of the body's cells. The device is designed to aid in early

(contd)

G. DAILY LIFE

America (7.6 on the Richter scale), in El Salvador alone, the deaths of over 1,000 are mourned. Strongest earthquake in decades claims at least 20,000 lives in western India

Brit. train robber 71-year-old Ronald Biggs voluntarily returns to England from Rio de Janeiro after more than 35 years in exile. A participant in "The Great Train Robbery" in 1963, he had escaped from jail in 1965

World's biggest oil rig sinks off the coast of Brazil following an explosion

While surfacing off the coast of Hawaii, the U.S. nuclear-powered submarine "USS Greenville" rams into the Japanese training vessel "Ehime Maru"; 9 sailors drown

Mass hysteria in a crowd of 40,000 gathered at a soccer stadium in Accra (Ghana) claims 126 lives

269 die in the crash of an Airbus A 300/600 in the New York residential district of Belle Harbor, Queens

In one of the worst accidents in the history of rail, 373 die just south of Cairo in Egypt

A series of strong tremors in northern Afghanistan claims the lives of thousands

More than 2,000 injured and 29 dead in an explosion in the chemical plant AZF near the Fr. city of Toulouse

Ger. Jutta Kleinschmidt becomes the first woman to win the desert Rally Paris-Dakar

Goran Ivanisevic wins the Wimbledon Tournament against Patrick Rafter (Australia) and celebrates his first victory in the 48th Grand Slam tournament

Former tennis pro Steffi Graf marries Amer. tennis player Andre Agassi and gives birth to a baby boy

Christoph Langen and Marco Jakobs become five-time world champions in two-man bobsledding in St. Moritz

Brit. sailor Ellen MacArthur places second in the 24,000 mile Vendée Globe Regatta and becomes the first woman to take home a medal for the most difficult nonstop race in the world

Lars Riedel makes track and field history with his fifth title in disc throwing at the Track and Field World Championships in Edmonton

Erik Weihenmayer becomes the first blind mountain climber to conquer Mt. Everest

Lance Armstrong (U.S.) wins the 88th Tour de France

Czech decathlete Roman Sebrle sets a new world record with 9,026 points, thus breaking the magical 9,000-point margin for the first time in the history of the sport

Beijing gets the go-ahead from the IOC to host the Summer Olympic Games in 2008

Michael Schumacher takes his fourth world championship title in Formula 1, his second in Ferrari. In a record season, he wins 9 of 17 races, for a total of 53 Formula 1 wins in his career, more than any other racer to date

(contd)

	A. HISTORY, POLITICS	B. LITERATURE, THEATER	C. RELIGION, PHILOSOPHY, LEARNING
2001 contd			

Communist politician and former police force General Vladimir Voronin is elected new Pres. of Moldavia

Incumbent Pres. Alexander Lukashenko wins with a 75.6% majority in Belarus. O.S.C.E. observers bring charges of election fraud and suppression of opposition voters

Francisco Costa Gomes, Portug. politician (former Pres.), d. (b. 1914)

Edward Gierek, Polish politician (former Pres.), d. (b. 1913)

Maria José di Savoia, Belgian daughter of the King and last Queen of Italy, d. (b. 1906)

Israeli army kills a high-ranking PLO leader in a missile attack on an office in Ramallah

Series of terrorist attacks and military strikes escalate conflict between Israelis and Palestinians. Israeli government severs all diplomatic contact with Palestinian Pres. Yasser Arafat

New Israeli government headed by right-wing Prime Minister Ariel Sharon. Shimon Peres becomes Foreign Minister

Reform-oriented Pres. Mohammad Hatami is elected to a second term by a large majority in Iran

Faisal al Husseini, Palestinian politician, d. (b. 1940, Baghdad)

Soraya Esfandiari Bachtiari, former Iranian empress, d. (b. 1932)

Radical Islamic Taliban regime in Afghanistan orders the destruction of the world's oldest statue of Buddha, the over thousand-year-old Buddha of Bamiyan

Ahmed Shah Masud, Afghan opposition leader and adversary of the ruling Taliban regime, is killed by a suicide bomber

Afghan Taliban regime refuses to extradite the internationally wanted alleged terrorist Osama bin Laden to the U.S.

Afghan troops in the so-called Northern Alliance seize Taliban-controlled territories with the support of N.A.T.O. air strikes; after the collapse of the Taliban regime, Hamid Karzai becomes head of the transitional government

Argentine Pres. Fernando de la Rúa resigns; interim Pres. Adolfo Rodriguez Saa remains in office only one week. Numerous deaths in weeks of unrest, demonstrations, and looting

Chile's former dictator Augusto Pinochet charged with crimes committed during his rule (1973–90) and placed on house arrest in Santiago. A half year later, the appeals court suspends proceedings against him on the grounds that he is unfit to stand trial

Conservative opposition candidate Ricardo Maduro wins presidential election in Honduras

Daniel Ortega, candidate for the Sandinistas, fails to regain power in his third attempt at the presidential election in Nicaragua. Candidate for the incumbent Liberal Party, Enrique Bolaños becomes new President

Former Peruvian Pres. Alberto Fujimori charged with murder. He is said to have paid bonuses to members of the death squad Grupo Colina who were behind a massacre that killed 15 people. Fujimori is being charged with the deaths of nine students and a professor in 1992 and for the death of a secret agent in 1997

Sitting Pres. Yahya Jammeh wins presidential election in Gambia with some 53% of votes

Pres. of the Congo, Laurent Kabila, is killed in an assassination. His son Joseph Kabila is appointed successor the very same day and is later confirmed by Parliament

Incumbent Pres. of Uganda Yoweri Museveni wins presidential election with 69.3% of votes

Léopold Sédar Senghor, Senegalese writer and politician, d. (b. 1906)

In parliamentary elections in Bangladesh, opposition leader Khaleda Zia wins and becomes new Prime Minister; fundamentalist Muslims also see significant gains

Reformist politician Junichiro Koizumi succeeds Yoshiro Mori as new Prime Minister in Japan after Mori resigns. He is the eleventh Japanese chief of state since 1988

Assassins storm the Indian Parliament in New Delhi; eleven people killed

World Trade Organization (W.T.O.) accepts China and Taiwan as *(contd)*

D. VISUAL ARTS	E. MUSIC	F. SCIENCE, TECHNOLOGY, GROWTH	G. DAILY LIFE	
Catherine Palace in St. Petersburg "Cast Away," by Robert Zemeckis, with Tom Hanks. The film is a modern version of the Robinson Crusoe story "Merci pourle chocolat," directed by Claude Chabrol, starring Isabelle Huppert "Traffic," by Steven Soderbergh, starring Michael Douglas "Hannibal," sequel to "Silence of the Lambs," directed by Ridley Scott; Anthony Hopkins returns to his role as the cannibalistic murderer Hannibal Lecter Nicole Kidman and Ewan McGregor star in the film musical "Moulin Rouge" by Baz Luhrmann "The Man Who Wasn't There" is the latest work by the Coen brothers (Joel and Ethan) The hero in Steven Spielberg's science fiction film "A.I." is a robot disguised as a young boy Science fiction film "Final Fantasy" is the first completely computer-generated film that strives for a realistic, as opposed to animated, cinematic portrayal Special effects in computer animation become ever more sophisticated. New standards are set by the completely computer-generated fairy-tale film "Shrek" and the war drama "Pearl Harbor" "Harry Potter and the Sorcerer's Stone," directed by Chris Columbus, breaks all box-office records Successful start for "Lord of the Rings—Fellowship of the Ring," the third installation in director Peter Jackson's filming of the Tolkien bestselling trilogy		detection of cancer. Cancer cells are more active and thus "louder" than healthy cells Ger. archaeologists discover the first-ever tomb of a Pharaoh from the 17th Dynasty (1625–1539 B.C.) in upper Egypt. The tomb of Nub Kheper-Re Intef is in the Theban necropolis, at the entrance to the Valley of the Kings Remains of what may be the oldest ancient human found in Ethiopia, estimated to be 5.5 million years old Scientists at the U.S. bio-tech company ACT (Advanced Cell Technology, Inc.) in Worcester, MA, announce the world's first cloning of human embryos. The aim is to harvest embryonic stem cells for developing treatments for such diseases as diabetes, cancer, AIDS, and Alzheimer's. U.S. Congress debates placing a ban on human cloning. Germany and France already spoke out in favor of a worldwide ban on human cloning in August Asteroid "2001 YB5," with a diameter of 984 feet, passes Earth at a closer distance than any celestial body in the last 65 years, 516,000 miles U.S. researchers use a weather satellite to observe the way a sheet of ice larger than the surface of the Saarland snaps off the Antarctic Ice Shelf and breaks into pieces in the Weddell Sea	Luis Figo (Real Madrid) and Michael Owen (FC Liverpool) are named "World Footballer of the Year" and "European Footballer of the Year," respectively	**2001 contd**

	A. HISTORY, POLITICS	B. LITERATURE, THEATER	C. RELIGION, PHILOSOPHY, LEARNING
2001 contd	members and thus expands by about one fourth the world's population For the first time since the dissolution of China in 1949, the nationalist Kuomintang Party is no longer the strongest faction in the Taiwanese parliament. The Democratic Progress Party under Pres. Chen Shui-bian wins Nonviolent people's revolt deposes Philippine Pres. Joseph Estrada after 2½ years in office. A court issues a warrant for his arrest and charges him with abuse of office and corruption. He is succeeded by his former Deputy, Gloria Macapagal Arroyo Party of billionaire Thaksin Shinawatra wins parliamentary elections in Thailand First parliamentary election in East Timor: Revolutionary Front wins with 57% under leadership of Xana Gusmao Some 11,000 inhabitants of the Pacific Island nation of Tuvalu are forced to leave their homes. They will be taken in by New Zealand beginning in 2002. Tuvalu is the first country that must be abandoned because of the rising sea level caused by climatic change. The island nation, situated in the Pacific Ocean between Australia and Hawaii, is the fourth-smallest country recognized by the U.N. Conservative government coalition led by Prime Minister John Howard wins parliamentary elections in Australia for the third consecutive time Four days after parliamentary elections in Sri Lanka, the former opposition leader Ranil Wickremesinghe is sworn in as Prime Minister Laisenia Quarase new head of state on the Fiji Islands Duong Van Minh, South Vietnamese politician (former Pres.), d. (b. 1916) Salahuddin Abdul Aziz Shah Alhaj, King of Malaysia (since 1999), d. (b. 1926)		
2002	Nobel Peace Prize to former U.S. Pres. Jimmy Carter for his efforts to advance democracy and human rights and to find peaceful solutions to international conflicts Right Livelihood Award ("Alternative Nobel Prize") to Paraguayan civil rights activist Martin Almada for his fight against human rights violations, to the organization Kvinna till Kvinna (Woman to Woman) founded in Sweden to help women, especially in the Balkans, to overcome the hardships and atrocities of war, and to the youth center "Centres Jeunes Kamenge" from Burundi for its work facilitating peace in the civil war torn country In response to the terror attacks against the U.S. on September 11, U.N. invokes Article 5 of its charter (the "self-defense clause") for the first time in its 52-year history. According to Article 5, an attack on a member state constitutes an attack on all N.A.T.O. member states Largest expansion in the history of N.A.T.O.: seven eastern and central European nations accepted as new members (Bulgaria, Estonia, Latvia, Lithuania, Romania, Slovenia, and Slovakia) European Parliament approves the largest expansion of the European Union to date; effective May, 2004, the following countries will join: Estonia, Latvia, Lithuania, Malta, Poland, Slovakia, Slovenia, Czech Republic, Hungary, and Cyprus Organization for African Unity (OAU) is dissolved 39 years after it was established. It will be replaced by the EU-backed African Union (AU). First Pres. of the organization is South African President Thabo Mbeki U.S. Pres. George W. Bush and Russian Pres. Vladimir Putin sign a nuclear disarmament treaty in Moscow In congressional elections in U.S., George W. Bush's Republicans increase their majority in the House of Representatives and regain control of the Democratic-controlled Senate Both Houses of U.S. Congress, House and Senate, give George W. Bush the authority to disarm Iraq by military means if necessary U.S. begins construction of a ground-based missile defense system southeast of Fairbanks, Alaska. Missile silos 115 feet beneath the *(contd)*	Camilo José Cela, Span. writer, d. (b. 1934, Galicia) Jesus Diaz, Cuban writer, d. (b. 1942) Alexander Ginsburg, Russian writer and civil rights activist, d. (b. 1937) Astrid Lindgren, Swed. writer, d. (b. 1907) Elizabeth Longford, Brit. writer and historian, d. (b. 1906) Walter Lord, Amer. writer, d. (b. 1918) Jerry Sohl, Amer. scriptwriter ("The Twilight Zone"), d. (b. 1914) José Ortega Spottorno, Span. writer and publisher, son of philosopher José Ortega y Gasset, d. (b. 1916) Nobel Prize for Literature to Hungarian Imre Kertész Prix Goncourt, France's most prestigious literary award, to Pascal Quignard for his collection of fragments "Les ombres errantes" Booker Prize, Britain's most prestigious literary award, to Canadian writer Yann Martel for the novel "The Life of Pi" Pulitzer Prize to the Amer. novelist Richard Russo for "Empire Falls" Remains of Fr. writer Alexandre Dumas are transferred, 130 years after his death, to the Panthéon in Paris	Pierre Bourdieu, Fr. sociologist, d. (b. 1930) Martin Esslin, Brit. literary scholar, d. (b. 1918) Thor Heyerdahl, Norw. ethnologist and antiquities scholar, d. (b. 1914) Ivan Illich, Amer. theologian and social reformer, d. (b. 1926, Vienna) Robert King Merton, Amer. sociologist, d. (b. 1910) John Rawls, Amer. philosopher, d. (b. 1921) David Riesman, Amer. sociologist, d. (b. 1909) Kurt Ruh, Swiss medievalist, d. (b. 1914) Peace Prize of the German Booksellers' Assoc. to Nigerian author Chinua Achebe Opening of the "Bibliotheca Alexandrina" in Egypt near the site of the legendary library erected by the Pharaoh Ptolemais I 2,300 years ago. The new structure is designed to house up to 8 million volumes 63 inscribed clay tablets from the 14th century B.C. found beneath the ruins of the ancient Syrian imperial city of Qatna with detailed descriptions of the political situation in the Near East at the beginning of the late Bronze Age Discovery of a 2,700-year-old temple on the Island of Kythnos in the Aegean; evidence to suggest an erstwhile significant religious center *(contd)*

D. VISUAL ARTS	E. MUSIC	F. SCIENCE, TECHNOLOGY, GROWTH	G. DAILY LIFE	
				2001 contd
James Coburn, Amer. actor, d. (b. 1928) Richard Harris, Irish actor, d. (b. 1930) George Roy Hill, Amer. film director ("The Sting"), d. (b. 1922) Kim Hunter, Amer. actress, d. (b. 1922) Chuck Jones, Amer. illustrator, d. (b. 1912) Hildegard Knef, Ger. actress, d. (b. 1925) Roberto Matta (Matta Echaurren), Chilean painter and sculptor, d. (b. 1912) Spike Milligan, Brit. actor and comedian, d. (b. 1918, India) Dudley Moore, Brit. actor, composer, and pianist, d. (b. 1935) Inge Morath, Austrian-Amer. photographer, d. (b. 1923) Gabriele Mucchi, Ital. painter, d. (b. 1899) George Nader, Amer. actor, d. (b. 1921) Niki de Saint Phalle, Fr.-Amer. sculptor and painter, d. (b. 1930) Karel Reisz, Czech.-Brit. film director, d. (b. 1926) Herb Ritts, Amer. photographer, d. (b. 1952) *(contd)*	Rudolf Baumgartner, Swiss violinist and director, d. (b. 1918) Otis Blackwell, Amer. composer, pianist, and singer, d. (b. 1932) Ray Brown, Amer. jazz musician, d. (b. 1926) Ray Conniff, Amer. orchestra director and arranger, d. (b. 1916) Lonnie Donegan, Brit. guitarist and singer, d. (b. 1931) John Entwistle, Brit. rock musician ("The Who"), d. (b. 1944) Adolph Green, Amer. librettist and lyricist, d. (b. 1915) Lionel Hampton, Amer. jazz musician (vibraphone), d. (b. 1908) Waylon Jennings, Amer. country music singer, d. (b. 1937) Peter Kowald, Ger. jazz musician, d. (b. 1944) Peggy Lee, Amer. singer and pop composer, d. (b. 1922) Lisa Lopes, Amer. pop singer, d. (b. 1972) Jimmy Maxwell, Amer. jazz musician, d. (b. 1917) *(contd)*	Stephen Jay Gould, Amer. evolutionary biologist, d. (b. 1942) Rudolf Hell, Ger. radio technician, inventor of the fax machine, d. (b. 1902) Heinz Kaminski, Ger. engineer and astronomer, d. (b. 1921) Elisabeth Mann Borgese, Ger. marine biologist, d. (b. 1918) Cesar Milstein, Argentine-Brit. molecular biologist, d. (b. 1927) Max Ferdinand Perutz, Brit. chemist, d. (b. 1914) Alexander Mikhailovitch Prochorov, Russian physicist, d. (b. 1916) Nobel Prize for Chemistry to John Fenn (U.S.), Koichi Tanaka (Japan), and Kurt Wüthrich (Switzerland) Nobel Prize for Physics to Raymond Davis (U.S.) and Masaatoshi Koshiba (Japan) for the detection of cosmic neutrinos and to Riccardo Giacconi (U.S.) for contributions to astrophysics leading to the discovery of cosmic x-ray sources Nobel Prize for Medicine to Brit. medical scientists Sydney Brenner and John Sulston as well as to Robert Horvitz for their discoveries in the field of genetic regulation of organ development and programmed cell death Nobel Prize for Economics to Daniel *(contd)*	According to reports by the U.N. food program, more than 800 million people worldwide suffer from hunger. While poverty decreased by 20% during the 1990s, hunger was only curbed by 5% Media giant Bertelsmann sells its stake in AOL-Europe to AOL for $6.75 billion United Airlines files for bankruptcy protection and thus becomes the biggest bankruptcy case in the history of U.S. airline industry Ruth Handler, Amer. business executive, inventor of the Barbie doll, d. (b. 1917) Alfred Heineken, Dutch business executive, CEO of the Heineken brewery, d. (b. 1923) James Tobin, Amer. economist, d. (b. 1918) Lew Wassermann, Amer. film industry tycoon, former CEO of MCA, d. (b. 1913) Rudolf Augstein, Ger. editor and co-owner of the newsmagazine "Der Spiegel," d. (b. 1923) U.S. Supreme Court declares the execution of mentally retarded death row inmates unconstitutional Two snipers in the Washington D.C. area kill 10 people and injure 3 more, spreading panic and fear in the region for weeks before they are caught Oil tanker Prestige, loaded with 77,000 tons of crude oil, in distress off the Galician Coast in northwest Spain, begins leaking oil before it splits in two and sinks, losing thousands of tons of oil. A 125-mile stretch of Spanish coast is heavily soiled from the spill An aircraft from Taiwan breaks into four *(contd)*	2002

	A. HISTORY, POLITICS	B. LITERATURE, THEATER	C. RELIGION, PHILOSOPHY, LEARNING
2002 contd	Earth's surface should be finished by 2004; costs for the ground-based interceptors: $325 million. The entire system is expected to cost $64 billion Approx. 82% of Fr. voters re-elect Pres. Jacques Chirac, in a clear vote against his right-wing extremist opponent Jean-Marie Le Pen. Prime Minister Lionel Jospin, after being eliminated in the first round, steps down from politics. Jean-Pierre Raffarin becomes new head of government Cyrus Roberts Vance, former Amer. Secretary of State, d. (b. 1917) Italy's former Premiere Guilio Andreotti sentenced by an appeals court in Perugia to 24 years in prison in conjunction with the murder of a journalist One day after the resignation of Dutch Prime Minister Wim de Kok, Parliament establishes a commission to investigate government policy surrounding the deployment of U.N. peacekeeping troops in the Bosnian town of Srebrenica. The Dutch soldiers sent to protect the population were unable to prevent the 1995 massacre of Muslim civilians by Bosnian-Serb soldiers In parliamentary elections in Portugal, victory for the oppositional conservative Social Democrats under former Foreign Minister Jose Manuel Durao Barroso Trial begins against former Yugoslavian president Slobodan Milosevic before the U.N. War Crimes Tribunal in The Hague Imangali Tasmagambetov becomes new head of government in Kazakhstan, succeeding Kasjmschomart Tokajev who resigned without stating his reasons Former president of the Central Bank in Latvia, Einars Repse, elected to head up new government Russian Pres. Vladimir Putin defends actions of Russian troops against Chechen rebels as measures to combat international terrorism Chechen rebels take 800 theatergoers hostage in Moscow and threaten to blow up the theater. Three days later, special forces storm the building. 128 hostages and 41 rebels are killed in the takeover, most of them by the poison gas intended to disable the Chechen rebels Slovenia's current Chief of State, Janez Drnovsek, becomes new President; Anton Rop becomes new Prime Minister Claus von Amsberg, Prince of Netherlands, d. (b. 1926, Hamburg) Elizabeth (Lady Elizabeth Angela Marguerite Bowes-Lyon, Britain's Queen Mother), d. (b. 1900) Alexander Lebed, Russian politician and General, d. (b. 1950) Margaret Rose, Princess of England, sister to Queen Elizabeth II, d. (b. 1930) New Pres. in Argentina is Eduardo Duhalde Luiz Inacio Lula da Silva elected first Socialist Pres. of Brazil Candidate for the ruling Christian Social Unity, Abel Pacheco, wins presidential election in Costa Rica Barely three years after his putsch attempt, the left-leaning Officer Lucio Gutierrez is elected new head of state in Ecuador In Colombia's presidential election, the conservative candidate Alvaro Uribe, advocating a hard-line policy against the left-leaning rebels, wins in the first round Just two days after his defeat, Venezuela's left-leaning Pres. Hugo Chavez resumes his post as head of state. He had resigned under pressure from the military after a general strike. Two days later, the transitional Pres. Pedro Carmona resigned after demonstrations by Chavez supporters in which dozens died. Chavez's return to office was followed by looting and new protests Israeli troops destroy the international airport in Gaza Following countless Palestinian suicide-bombings, Israeli army enters the Palestinian cities of Ramallah, Kalkilja, and Tulkarm as well as several areas in the West Bank, Bethlehem, and the neighboring refugee camp at Deheisheh. 200 Palestinians, some of them armed, occupy the Church of the Nativity in Bethlehem, Christianity's most sacred site Palestinian Pres. Yasser Arafat is surrounded by the Israeli army in his *(contd)*		Pope John Paul II beatifies Padre Pio and Josemaría Escrivá de Balaguer, founder of "Opus Dei"

D. VISUAL ARTS

Larry Rivers, Amer. painter, graphic artist, and poet, d. (b. 1923)
George Sidney, Amer. director, d. (b. 1911)
Heinrich Siepmann, Ger. painter, d. (b. 1904)
Rod Steiger, Amer. actor, d. (b. 1925)
Hans-Heinrich Thyssen-Bornemisza, art collector, painter, and sponsor of Ger.-Hungarian descent, d. (b. 1921)
André de Toth, Hung.-Amer. director, d. (b. 1913)
Billy Wilder, Amer. director, d. (b. 1906, Vienna)
Turner Prize to the Brit. painter Keith Tyson
Jap. Praemium Imperiale (in Painting and Sculpture) to Ger. painter Sigmar Polke and Ital. sculptor Giuliano Vangi
European Film Award to "Hable con ella" ("Talk to Her") by Pedro Almodóvar (Spain)
Oscars: Best picture and best director, "A Beautiful Mind" by Ron Howard. Best actor, Denzel Washington in "Training Day"; best actress, Halle Berry in "Monster's Ball"; best foreign film "No Man's Land" by Danis Tanovic (Bosnia-Herzegovina). Honorary Oscars to Sidney Poitier and Robert Redford for lifetime achievement
International Film Festival in Berlin: Golden Bear to "Bloody Sunday" by Paul Greengrass (Great Britain), to "Spirited Away" by Hayao Miyazaki (Japan). Jury's Grand Prize to "Halbe Treppe" by Andreas Dresen; Silver Bear to Fr. director Otar Iosseliani for "Lundi Matin" ("Monday Morning"); Silver Bear (in acting) to Fr. actor Jacques Gamblin and Amer. actress Halle Berry. Honorary Bear to Amer. director Robert Altman for lifetime achievement
Cannes Film Festival: Golden Palm for best film to "The Pianist" by Roman Polanski; Jury's Grand Prize to

(contd)

E. MUSIC

Norbert Schultze, Ger. composer ("Lili Marleen"), d. (b. 1911)
Mal Waldron, Amer. jazz pianist, d. (b. 1925)
Gösta Winbergh, Swedish tenor, d. (b. 1944)
Jap. Praemium Imperiale (in Music) to Ger. opera and concert singer Dieter Fischer-Dieskau
American Music Awards: Lenny Kravitz for best pop-rock artist, N Sync for best band, Janet Jackson best female pop-rock artist, the band Destiny's Child for best album, and Alicia Keys as best new female artist. Best R&B and soul artist awarded posthumously to Aaliyah who recently died in a fatal plane crash
Sir Simon Rattle assumes artistic directorship of the Berlin Philharmonic Orchestra as successor to Claudio Abbado
Polar Music Award of the Swedish Academy of Music to South African singer Miriam Makeba and the Russian-born composer, now living in Germany, Sofia Gubaidulina
Nicholas Maw: "Sophie's Choice," opera directed by Trevor Nunn, conducted by Sir Simon Rattle at the Royal Opera in London
Directing debut for Katharina Wagner, great-granddaughter of the composer and the person her father, Wolfgang Wagner, designated to succeed him as director of the Bayreuth Festival: she stages Richard Wagner's "The Flying Dutchman"
21 years to the day after its premiere, the musical "Cats," based on T.S. Eliot's "Old Possum's Book of Practical Cats," is performed for the last time at the New London Theater. More than 50 million theatergoers have seen the show, one of the world's most successful musicals ever
British Awards, most prestigious distinction for rock

(contd)

F. SCIENCE, TECHNOLOGY, GROWTH

Kahnemann (Israel/U.S.) and Vernon L. Smith (U.S.) for establishing laboratory experiments as a tool in economic analysis
Right Livelihood Award ("Alternative Nobel Prize") to Australian pioneer in solar photovoltaics for his efforts to make solar energy viable
Paul Ehrlich and Ludwig Darmstaedter Prize to Craig Venter (U.S.) for sequencing the genomes of microorganisms and his contributions to sequencing the human genome
Swedish researchers develop a method for measuring the presence of acrylamide in food stuffs; the carcinogenetic substance is formed in high concentrations in foods such as potato chips and French fries
The debate has lingered for nearly 20 years, but now there is no longer any doubt that Fr. immunologist Luc Montagnier, and not Amer. Robert Gallo, was the first to have discovered the virus HIV that causes the immune disease AIDS
After six years of research, an international team of scientists succeeds in deciphering the complete genome for the malaria parasite plasmodium falciparum and for the Anopheles mosquito that carries the disease
Inauguration of the "High Energy Stereoscopic System" (HESS) in Namibia for studying the gamma rays of galaxies or Supernova remnants
Launch of the Earth observation satellite Envisat for measuring greenhouse gases, ocean pollution, algae growth, and holes in the Ozone layer
15 member nations of the European Space Agency (ESA) agree on financing for the satellite project Galileo as an answer to the U.S. navigation system GPS. By 2008, 30 satellites should have been sent into Earth orbit in an effort to determine the exact positioning of the Earth. The cost for constructing Galileo will be more than 3 billion euro and the project will create 150,000 jobs
An approximately 660-pound meteorite plunges into Earth's atmosphere and explodes in a fireball over southern Bavaria; a piece of the meteorite is found and named Neuschwanstein after the famous castle not far from the site

G. DAILY LIFE

pieces en route to Hong Kong, plunging 225 people to their deaths
1,000 people die when the ferry Joola, filled beyond capacity, sinks off the coast of West Africa
According to the aid organization U.N. AIDS, 40 million people worldwide are infected with the HIV virus, 4 million more than the previous year. Africa remains hardest hit
After a major eruption of the Nyiragongo volcano in the Congo, the city of Goma is devastated and dozens of people are killed, more than 300,000 flee across the border to Rwanda
In the wake of severe weather conditions throughout Europe, heavy rainstorms cause flooding in the southern and eastern German states. The "flood of the century" leads to major evacuations in Bavaria, Thuringia, Saxony, and Brandenburg; most extensive evacuation in Germany since WW II; 9 billion euros in damages, 20 deaths. In the Czech Republic, whose economy is much weaker, the damages are around 3 billion euros
19th Olympic Winter Games in Salt Lake City (U.S.) with 2,399 athletes from 77 nations competing in 78 contests. German places number one with 12 Gold, 16 Silver, and 7 Bronze medals. The Paralympic Winter Games are staged at the same site immediately following the Games, with 416 athletes from 36 countries
Soccer World Championship in Japan and South Korea, German national team defeated by Brazil in a 0-2 final victory
Lance Armstrong wins his fourth Tour de France, coming in ahead of Spain's Joseba Beloki and Lithuania's Raimondas Rumas
Michael Schumacher becomes Formula 1 World Champion for the 5th time, winning 11 of 17 races
At the basketball world championship in Indianapolis, the Ger. team takes third place with its NBA pro player Dirk Nowitzki. U.S. team eliminated in preliminary rounds
On May 16, a total of 54 mountain climbers reach the top of Mt. Everest, more than ever before
Ger. supermodel Claudia Schiffer marries Amer. film producer Matthew Vaughn
Computer scientist Salma Bennani marries Moroccan King Mohammed VI. But she does not become Queen because this position does not exist. For the first time in the country's history, a photograph of the king's wife is published

	A. HISTORY, POLITICS	B. LITERATURE, THEATER	C. RELIGION, PHILOSOPHY, LEARNING
2002 contd	government compound in Ramallah, essentially placing the leader on house arrest After 25 years of civil war in Angola, a cease-fire agreement is reached between the left-leaning government and the rebel organization UNITA After four months of civil war in the West African nation of Ivory Coast, parties in the conflict agree to a peace plan at a meeting near Paris; the aim is to form a government of national reconciliation Mwai Kibaki succeeds Kenyan Pres. Daniel Arap Moi, who has held the office for 24 years. Kibak's National Rainbow Coalition thus brings to an end the 39-year rule of Moi's party, the Kenyan African National Union Following the controversial reelection of Robert Mugabe as Pres. of Zimbabwe, the Commonwealth suspends the country's membership for a year After 29 years in Italian exile, Afghanistan's former King Mohammad Zaher Shah returns to Afghanistan and opens the traditional national assembly (loya jirga); sitting chief of state Hamid Karzai is elected President United Nations extends the mandate for international security forces in Afghanistan (ISAF) by one year 192 people are killed in a bombing attack on the Indonesian Island of Bali, most of them foreign tourists on vacation. The perpetrators are thought to be connected to the terrorist organization Al Quaeda After more than 1½ years, military regime in Myanmar lifts house arrest against Nobel Peace Prize laureate and opposition politician Aaung San Suu Kyi Pakistan's Pres. Pervez Musharraf, according to official accounts, wins referendum to extend his term for another five years. Opposition charges him with election fraud Former independence fighter Xanana Gusmao is the clear victor in the first free presidential election in East Timor North Korea admits to the U.S. State Department that it has been working on developing nuclear weapons for years, which leads to a new crisis in relations between the two countries. North Korea committed to a freeze on its nuclear weapons program in a 1994 treaty with the U.S. Opposition leader Ranil Wickremesinghe is sworn in as Prime Minister of Sri Lanka as successor to Pres. Chandrika Kumaratunga Representatives from North and South Korea enter into political dialogue at a meeting in the North Korean capital of Pyongyang Abba Salomon Eban, Israeli politician, d. (b. 1915) Jonas Savimbi, Angolan rebel leader, UNITA, d. (b. 1934) Hugo Bánzer Suárez, Bolivian politician, d. (b. 1928) Fernando Belaunde Terry, Peruvian politician, d. (b. 1914)		
2003	Nobel Peace Prize to Shirin Ebadi (Iran) for her efforts to promote democracy and human rights, especially on behalf of women and children Right Livelihood Award ("Alternative Nobel Prize") to former Prime Minister of New Zealand David Lange for his efforts to free the world of nuclear weapons; to Philippine human rights activists Walden Bello and Nicanor Perlas as critics of globalization; to South Korean organization "Citizens' Coalition for Economic Justice," advocates for social justice and for reconciliation with North Korea; and to the Egyptian agricultural company SEKEM and its founder Ibrahim Abouleish for their efforts to develop biodynamic agricultural methods National Award of the Ger. Nationalstiftung to former Czech Pres. Vaclav Havel After over 20 years in development, the first Eurofighter jet goes into *(contd)*	Maurice Blanchot, Fr. writer and essayist, d. (b. 1907) Hans Boesch, Swiss writer and civil engineer, d. (b. 1926) Roberto Bolano, Chilean writer, d. (b. 1953) Ulrich Brecht, Ger. theater director, d. (b. 1928) Mohammed Dib, Algerian writer, d. (b. 1920) Howard Fast, Amer. writer, d. (b. 1914) Norman Lewis, Brit. travel writer, d. (b. 1908) Franco Lucentini, Ital. writer, d. (b. 1920) *(contd)*	Lewis A. Coser, Amer. sociologist, d. (b. 1913, Berlin) Donald Davidson, Amer. philosopher, d. (b. 1917) Emil Fackelheim, Ger.-Can.-Israeli philosopher, d. (b. 1916) Maurice Michael Otunga, Cardinal and Archbishop of Nairobi, most prominent church leader in East and Central Africa, d. (b. 1923, Kenya) Neil Postman, Amer. media scholar, d. (b. 1931) Edward Said, Palestinian literary scholar and cultural historian, d. (b. 1935, Jerusalem) *(contd)*

D. VISUAL ARTS	E. MUSIC	F. SCIENCE, TECHNOLOGY, GROWTH	G. DAILY LIFE	
"The Man without a Past" by Aki Kaurismäki (Finland). Best actor to Kati Outinen (Finland) in "Man without a Past," to Olivier Gourmet (Belgium) in "Der Sohn." Best director to Im Kwontaek (South Korea) for "Chihwaseon" and to Paul Thomas Anderson (U.S.) for "Punch-drunk Love" 59th International Venice Film Festival: Golden Lion to "The Magdalene Sisters" by Peter Mullan (Great Britain); Jury's Grand Prize to "House of Fools" by Andrei Konchalovsky (Russian) Jap. Praemium Imperiale (in Film) to Fr. director Jean-Luc Godard Praemium Imperiale (in Architecture) to Brit. architect Sir Norman Foster A recently discovered early work by Peter Paul Rubens "Massacre of the Innocents" sold at auction (Sotheby's) for $76.7 million. It is the third highest priced painting in the world, following Vincent van Gogh's portrait of "Dr. Gachet" ($82.5 million) and "Au Moulin de la Galette" by Auguste Renoir ($78 million) Comprehensive retrospective of surrealistic art in the period from 1919–45 under the title "La révolution surréaliste" at the Centre Pompidou in Paris, with works by de Chirico, Ernst, Dali, Magritte, Picasso, and Giacometti	and pop music in Britain: best singer in the international category: Eminem and Pink (both U.S.), best group: Red Hot Chili Peppers (U.S.); best album to Eminem, best newcomer to Norah Jones (U.S.), best pop act to Blue; best Brit. Singer to Robbie Williams and to Ms. Dynamite, best Brit. group to Coldplay. Lifetime achievement award to Tom Jones			**2002 contd**
George Axelrod, Amer. screenplay writer ("Breakfast at Tiffany's"), d. (b. 1922) Charles Bronson, Amer. screen actor, d. (b. 1921) Horst Buccholz, Ger. screen actor, d. (b. 1933) John Coplans, Amer. photographer, painter, and art critic, d. (b. 1920, London) Jacques Deray, Fr. director ("Borsalino"), d. (b. 1929) *(contd)*	Luciano Berio, Ital. composer, d. (b. 1925) Benny Carter, Amer. saxophonist, clarinetist, and composer, d. (b. 1907) Johnny Cash, Amer. country singer, d. (b. 1932) Celia Cruz, Cuban singer (Salsa interpreter), d. (b. 1924) Dave Dudley, Amer. country singer, d. (b. 1928) Maurice Gibb, Brit. pop musician ("Bee Gees"), d. (b. 1949) *(contd)*	Robert Atkins, Amer. cardiologist and nutritionist, d. (b. 1931) Edward Teller, Hungarian-Amer. physicist, counted among the "fathers of the American atomic bomb," d. (b. 1908) Nobel Prize for Physics to Alexei A. Abrikosov (U.S./Russia), Vitaly L. Ginzburg (Russia), and Anthony J. Leggett (U.K./U.S.) for their contributions to the study of superconductors Nobel Prize for Chemistry to Peter Agre (U.S.) and Roderick MacKinnon (U.S.) for their re- *(contd)*	The last VW Beetle rolls off the conveyer belt in Puebla (Mexico). 21.5 million Beetles have been manufactured over the last nearly 70 years, making it one of the most successful cars in the world Fed. Court in New York dismisses a case against fast food chain McDonald's charging it with seducing customers, especially children, into consuming fast food and thus contributing to obesity Giovanni Agnelli, Ital. business executive (Fiat company), d. (b. 1921) Charles Kindleberger, Amer. economic theorist, d. (b. 1911) *(contd)*	**2003**

A. HISTORY, POLITICS | **B. LITERATURE, THEATER** | **C. RELIGION, PHILOSOPHY, LEARNING**

2003 contd

service. In what is the biggest joint military effort in Europe, Germany, Great Britain, Spain, and Italy plan to purchase 620 of the machines

Heinz L. Krekeler, Ger. diplomat (first ambassador to the U.S. after WW II), d. (b. 1906)

Tino Schwierzina, only freely elected mayor of East Berlin 1990, d. (b. 1927)

U.N. Security Council cannot agree on a resolution that would legitimate war against Iraq

International Criminal Court in The Hague begins its work as the first permanent institution for punishing war crimes. It has the power to prosecute against genocide, crimes against humanity, and war crimes. Human rights organizations speak in terms of the biggest milestone in justice since the trial of Nazi war criminals following WW II. Among opponents of the Court are U.S., China, and Israel. The U.S. refuses to ratify the treaty because it fears cases will be brought against U.S. soldiers and has concerns about the encroachment of national sovereignty. First Chief Prosecutor elected to the International Criminal Court in The Hague is Argentine jurist Luis Moreno Ocampo

20 people killed in a suicide-bombing attack on the U.N. Headquarters in Baghdad, among the victims, U.N. special representative for Iraq, Sergio Vieira de Mello (Brazil), U.N.I.C.E.F. coordinator Christopher Klein-Beekman (Canada), and several employees of the World Bank

Carla del Ponte is replaced as Chief Prosecutor in the U.S. War Crimes Tribunal for Rwanda. The Swiss jurist is now only responsible for the Yugoslavian Tribunal. The Gambian judge Hassan Bucabar Jallow is appointed new Chief Prosecutor for Rwanda

N.A.T.O. takes command of the International Security Assistance Force (ISAF) in Afghanistan. It is the first N.A.T.O. deployment outside of Europe in the organization's history

Jaap de Hoop Scheffer (Netherlands) is elected N.A.T.O. Sec. Gen. as successor to George Robertson

W.T.O. Ministerial Conference in Cancun (Mexico) collapses over uncompromising position maintained by developing countries. Non-governmental organizations (NGOs) celebrate the break-up of the conference as a victory for poor countries

Jean-Claude Trichet (France) assumes his post as successor to Wim Duisenberg (Netherlands) as President of the European Central Bank

U.S. combat forces and their allies conduct all-out military campaign against Iraq as a continuation of the international war on terrorism. George W. Bush and Brit. Prime Minister Tony Blair jointly stand behind the invasion. After three weeks, dictator Saddam Hussein has been toppled and would later be captured. U.S. installs U.S. Gen. Jay Garner as head of an Iraqi transitional government, but soon replaces him with Paul Bremer

U.S. Pres. pushes through his supplemental budget request of some $79 billion to cover war costs; later, he asks Congress for another $87 billion for expenditures in Afghanistan, Iraq, and for the worldwide war against terrorism

U.S. Senate repeals ban on research and development of smaller nuclear bombs. Critics warn against potential for new nuclear arms build-up

As a measure in the war against terrorism, U.S. tightens border controls and security checks on people entering the country from abroad

Hollywood star Arnold Schwarzenegger (b. 1947, Austria) is elected Governor of California by a large majority

Strom Thurmond, Amer. politician, d. (b. 1903)

Following a BBC report accusing Brit. government of "sexing up" intelligence reports of weapons of mass destruction (WMD) in Iraq, government advisor David Kelly, who was clearly an informant to the report, commits suicide

In Finland, new Prime Minister Matti Vanhanen succeeds the first fe-
(contd)

Terenci Moix, Span. writer, d. (b. 1942)

Manuel Vazquez Montalban, Span. writer, d. (b. 1942)

Herbert Otto, Ger. writer, d. (b. 1925)

Bhisham Sahni, Iranian writer, d. (b. 1915)

Antonis Samarakis, Greek writer, d. (b. 1919)

Carol Shields, Canadian writer, d. (b. 1935)

Leon Uris, Amer. writer, d. (b. 1924)

Nobel Prize for Literature to South African author J.M. Coetzee

Pulitzer Prize in Fiction to Jeffrey Eugenidis for "Middlesex" and in Poetry to Paul Muldoon for "Sand and Gravel"

Pulitzer Prize in Theater to Cuban dramatist Nilo Cruz for "Anna in the Tropics"

Kyoto Prize (in Art) to Japanese puppet master Tamao Yoshida

Ariel Dorfman: "Purgatory," intimate play, premieres in Hamburg

Rainer Werner Fassbinder: "Warum läuft Herr R. Amok," premieres in Frankfurt

Sir Wilfred Thesiger, Brit. adventure tourist, d. (b. 1910)

Hugh Trevor-Roper, Brit. historian, d. (b. 1914)

Pierre Vilar, Fr. historian, specializing in Hispanic history, d. (b. 1906)

Bernard Williams, Brit., philosopher, d. (b. 1930)

Georg Henrik von Wright, Finnish philosopher, d. (b. 1916)

Hannah Arendt Award for Critical Thought to Canadian writer Michael Ignatieff

Peace Prize of the German Booksellers' Assoc. to Amer. writer and cultural critic Susan Sontag

Vatican officials (Congregation for the Doctrine of the Faith) issue drastic statements rejecting homosexuality as "detrimental to the development of human society." While the document was welcomed by some, it generated worldwide protests, even from Catholic politicians

Vatican beatifies Mother Teresa (d. 1998)

Exhibition on the life and works of Theodor Adorno in Zurich and Frankfurt

Discovery of Stone Age (Mesolithic) settlements from the period between 6,000 and 4,000 B.C. submerged in the North Sea

D. VISUAL ARTS

Sir Terry Frost, Brit. painter, d. (b. 1916)
David Hemmings, Brit. actor and director, d. (b. 1941)
Katharine Hepburn, Amer. actress ("The Lion in Winter," "African Queen"), d. (b. 1909)
Al Hirschfeld, Amer. caricaturist, d. (b. 1903)
Bob Hope, Amer. actor, comedian, and entertainer, d. (b. 1903)
Elia Kazan, Amer. director and producer, d. (b. 1909)
Gregory Peck, Amer. actor ("To Kill a Mockingbird"), d. (b. 1916)
George Rickey, Amer. sculptor, d. (b. 1907)
Leni Riefenstahl, Ger. screen actress, director, and photographer, d. (b. 1902)
John Schlesinger, Brit. film director, d. (b. 1926)
John Shearman, Brit. art historian, d. (b. 1931)
Alberto Sordi, Ital. actor and director, d. (b. 1919)
Marie Trintignant, Fr. actress, d. (b. 1962)
Kirk Varnedoe, Amer. art historian, director of the Museum of Modern Art, d. (b. 1946)
Jean Yanne, Fr. actor and director, d. (b. 1933)
Praemium Imperiale (in Painting, Sculpture) to Brit. painter Bridget Riley and Ital. sculptor Mario Merz
Praemium Imperiale (in Architecture) to Dutch architect Rem Koolhaas
Pritzer Architecture Prize to Danish architect Jörn Utzon; most significant work: opera house in Sydney
Oscars 2003, 75th anniversary: Best picture: "Chicago," by Rob Marshall. Best actor: Adrien Brody for "The Pianist"; best actress: Nicole Kidman for "The Hours"; best actress in a supporting role: Catherine Zeta-Jones for "Chicago"; best actor in a supporting role: Chris Cooper for "Adaptation." Best director: Roman Polanski (France) for "The Pianist." Best screenplay adaptation: Ronald Harwood ("The

(contd)

E. MUSIC

Ruben Gonzalez, Cuban pianist, d. (b. 1919)
Gregory Hines, Amer. dancer, d. (b. 1946)
Tony Jackson, rock musician ("The Searchers"), d. (b. 1940)
Hans Koller, Austrian saxophonist, d. (b. 1921)
Volker Kriegel, Ger. jazz guitarist, d. (b. 1943)
Herbie Mann, Amer. jazz flautist, d. (b. 1930)
Sergio Ortega, Chilean composer, d. (b. 1938)
Sam Phillips, Amer. music producer, "discovered" Elvis Presley, d. (b. 1923)
Noel Redding, Brit. musician, bass guitarist, d. (b. 1945)
Harold C. Schonberg, Amer. music critic, d. (b. 1916)
Company Segundo (given name, Francisco Repilado), Cuban musician and composer ("Buena Vista Social Club"), d. (b. 1907)
Nina Simone, Amer. vocalist, d. (b. 1933)
Edwin Starr (Charles Hatcher), Amer. singer, d. (b. 1942)
Rosalyn Tureck, Amer. pianist, d. (b. 1915)
Tibor Varga, Hungarian violinist, d. (b. 1921)
Barry White, Amer. singer, d. (b. 1944)
Warren Zevon, Amer. band leader, singer, pianist, composer, and songwriter, d. (b. 1947)
Inaugural Herbert von Karajan Music Award to Anne-Sophie Mutter. Recipients are obligated to invest award money into promoting young artists
Grammy Awards album of the year to "Come Away with Me" by Norah Jones, also named best new female artist; best rock vocalist to Sheryl Crow with "Steve McQueen," and to Bruce Springsteen with "The Rising." Song of the year, "Don't Know Why" by Norah Jones
Pulitzer Prize in Music to Amer. composer John Adams for "On the Transmigration of Souls," a requiem for the victims of September 11

(contd)

F. SCIENCE, TECHNOLOGY, GROWTH

search into channels in cell membranes
Nobel Prize for Medicine to Paul C. Lauterbur (U.S.) and Sir Peter Mansfield (U.K.) for the discoveries in magnetic resonance imaging
Nobel Prize for Economics to Robert F. Engle III (U.S.) and Clive W.L. Granger (U.K.)
Paul Ehrlich and Ludwig Darmstaedter Prize to Amer. medical scientists Richard Lerner and Peter Schultz for their discovery of catalytic antibodies
The International Human Genome Project involving researchers from the U.S., U.K., Germany, France, Japan, and China, has succeeded up to 99.99% in sequencing the complete human genome. Hundreds of researchers in 20 laboratories have collaborated on the project. All their results have been published in data bases
First cloned horse is born in Italy, a foal named "Protea," a Haflinger mare
Stem cell biologists Hans Schöler and Karin Hübner announce the formation of germ cells from embryonic stem cells of a mouse
U.N. fails in its efforts to introduce a world convention against cloning. Human cloning is generally regarded unacceptable, but not cloning for the purpose of creating "spare part" tissue
World's first marine current turbine, Project Seaflow, designed to utilize tidal energy, begins operation in Wales
Sluice gate on the Three Gorges Dam project goes into operation on the Yangtze River; the river's water level has been raised to 440 feet. By the time the dam is completed in 2009, 1 million people will have been displaced from their homes
Supersonic jet Concorde ceases passenger service after nearly 30 years in operation
Chemists in the U.S. develop tear-resistant fibers from nanoparticles
Construction begins on the world's longest trans-oceanic bridge connecting the cities of Shanghai and Ningbo
Wolfgang Ketterle and his colleagues at MIT in Cambridge, MA, achieve coldest temperature ever recorded: they cooled a sodium gas to half a nanodegree (½ of one billionth of a degree) above ab-

(contd)

G. DAILY LIFE

Rudolf Leiding, former CEO of Volkswagen ("father of the VW-Golf"), d. (b. 1914)
Entertainment companies Bertelsmann and Sony form a merger of their music subsidiaries, BMG and Sony Music
Subway blaze started by individual perpetrator kills 198 people in Daegu, South Korea
U.S. Fed. Court in San Francisco suspends over 100 death sentences decided by individual judges, not by jury, and changes them to life in prison
The highly infectious respiratory disease SARS (Severe Acute Respiratory Syndrome) spreads from China, Singapore, and Vietnam. World Health Organization (W.H.O.) confirms that the cause is a corona virus borne by air or waste water systems. Worldwide, nearly 9,000 people infected in 15 countries, most of them in Asia. Over 800 die from the effects of the disease. People speak in terms of the first new worldwide plague of the 21st century
Devastating fires caused by extreme heat in central and southern Europe, especially in Spain and Portugal. 5% of Portuguese national territory destroyed. Massive forest fires in Canada and the U.S. (Oregon) as well
Earthquake in southeastern Iran claims 35,000 lives. 90% of the historical city of Bam is destroyed
Earthquake in northern Algeria claims some 1,500 lives, over 7,000 are injured
Heavy storms in parts of Asia claim the lives of nearly 850 in a matter of weeks. Approx. 2.3 million people in China are evacuated from their homes. 160 people die in India, up to 4 million left on the run. Tidal wave in Bangladesh leaves 400,000 people homeless
Disastrous flooding south of Manila costs 300 people their lives
In the biggest power blackout in the history of North America, some 50 million people in the northeastern states of the U.S. and in southern Canada are without electricity for up to 48 hours. The cause is traced to computer error and poorly trained technicians
243 dead, over 9,000 injured in a gas explosion near the Chinese city of Chongqing
Special Olympic Summer Games with 7,000 mentally handicapped athletes in Dublin
International Olympic Committee selects Vancouver as host for the 21st Olympic Winter Games in 2010
Germany's women's soccer team win the world championship in the U.S., defeating Sweden
Pete Sampras resigns from pro tennis after 15 years in the game (64 individual titles in tennis, ranked number one in the world for six years)
Michael Shumacher wins Formula 1 World Championship for the sixth time
Lance Armstrong wins his fifth Tour de France, beating Ger. Jan Ullrich and Alexander Vinokourov (Kazakhstan)

(contd)

male head of state in Finland, Anneli Jäätteenmäki, who stepped down after only 63 days in office

2003 contd

Sweden's Foreign Minister Anna Lindh is the victim of a stabbing attack and later dies of injuries sustained

Voters in many countries approve joining the EU: Malta (53.65%); Estonia (66.9%); Latvia (67%); Lithuania (91%); Poland (77.45%); Slovakia (92.5%); Czech Republic (77.3%); Slovenia (89.6%; also membership in N.A.T.O.); Hungary (83.8%), but voter turnout was only 45.6%). The parliament of Cyprus unanimously approves EU membership

In a special referendum in Sweden, with 81.2% voter turnout, 56.1% of Swedes reject the introduction of the euro

Juhan Parts is elected new head of state in Estonia

In Lithuania, Rolandas Paksas, former head of state, is elected Pres. and steps up to replace Valdas Adamkus

Former U.S. president Bill Clinton inaugurates the memorial to 7,000 victims of the Srebrenica massacre

Yugoslavian Parliament in Belgrade dissolves the Fed. Rep. of Yugoslavia and establishes the new state of Serbia-Montenegro

Serbia's Prime Minister Zoran Djindjic is assassinated in an attack outside the government seat in Belgrade. Serbian Parliament elects reformist politician Zoran Zivkovic to succeed him

Svetozar Marovic is elected first Pres. of Serbia and Montenegro

Parliament of the Czech Rep. elects Vaclav Klaus to succeed Vaclav Havel as President

Moderate Islamic Party wins parliamentary election in Turkey. Recep Tayyip Erdogan replaces incumbent Prime Minister Abdullah Gül

In the Greek Rep. of Cyprus, conservative opposition leader Tassos Papadopoulos is elected Pres. and successor to Glafkos Klerides

Following heavy clashes in Georgia, Pres. Eduard Shevardnadze resigns. Former Pres. of Parliament Nino Burdzhanadze appoints herself President

Akhmad Kadyrov is elected Pres. of Chechnya with 81.1% of votes

Alija Izetbegovic, Bosnian politician, d. (b. 1925)

Roy Harris Jenkins, Brit. politician and author, d. (b. 1920)

Ramon Serrano Suner, Span. politician under Franco, d. (b. 1925)

Néstor Kirchner becomes new Pres. of Argentina after Carlos Menem withdraws his candidacy

Conservative business executive Oscar Berger becomes new Pres. of Guatemala

Alvaro Uribe, Conservative Party, wins the presidential election in Colombia

Candidate backed by the ruling conservative Colorado Party, Nicanor Duarte Frutos, wins presidential election in Paraguay

U.S. and Britain's military attack against Iraq, based largely on Iraq's suspected production of weapons of mass destruction, meets with worldwide condemnation, but some pockets of approval as well. Germany, France, Russia, and China are among the countries most deeply dismayed by the outbreak of war. Other countries—Japan, for example—are sympathetic to Washington's policies. And opponents of the war take to the streets worldwide. In his final report, U.N. Chief Weapons Inspector Hans Blix determined that they had found no evidence of weapons of mass destruction

Three weeks into the war, U.S. troops seize control of Baghdad's city center. A U.S. convoy of tanks rumbles into the capital undeterred and joins Iraqis in a highly symbolic act of toppling a larger-than-life sized statue of Saddam Hussein. Government offices and public buildings are looted and plundered by Iraqis

U.S. Security Council approves an immediate suspension of economic and financial sanctions imposed against Iraq 13 years ago. At the same time, the U.S. and Great Britain are recognized as occupying forces

Chief Administrator of the U.S. Coalition Provisional Authority, Paul Bremer, assembles a 25-member "transitional council" of Iraqis as the first step toward building an Iraqi transitional government. The council consists of 13 Shiites, 5 Sunnis, 5 Kurds, 1 Christian, and 1 Turkmeni

(contd)

D. VISUAL ARTS	E. MUSIC	F. SCIENCE, TECHNOLOGY, GROWTH	G. DAILY LIFE	
Pianist"); best original screenplay: Pedro Almodóvar. For the first time in 23 years, since Volker Schlöndorff's "Blechtrommel," a Ger. film wins an Oscar for best foreign film: Carline Link's "Nirgendwo in Afrika." Honorary Oscar to Peter O'Toole for lifetime achievement Hollywood Foreign Press Association's Golden Globes: Best film, "The Hours" by Stephen Daldry; best director, Martin Scorsese for "Gangs of New York"; best actor, Jack Nicholson in "About Schmidt"; best actress, Nicole Kidman in "The Hours"; best foreign film, "Habla con ella" by Pedro Almodóvar (Spain). In the musical/comedy category: best film, "Chicago" by Rob Marshall; best actress Renée Zellweger and actor to Richard Gere for their roles in "Chicago." Best film song: to U2 for "Gangs of New York." Cecil B. de Mille Award to Gene Hackman for lifetime achievement 53rd International Film Festival in Berlin: Golden Bear to "In this World" by Michael Winterbottom (U.K.); Jury's Grand Prize to "Adaptation" by Spike Jonze (U.S.); Silver Bear for best direction to Patrice Chéreau for "Son Frère"; Silver Bear for best actor to Sam Rockwell in "Confessions of a Dangerous Mind" by George Clooney; best actress to Nicole Kidman, Meryl Streep, and Julianne Moore in "The Hours"; Blue Angel for best European film to "Good Bye, Lenin!" by Wolfgang Becker. Honorary Bear to Fr. actress Anouk Aimée for lifetime achievement 56th Cannes Film Festival: Golden Palm for best film to "Elephant" by Gus Van Sant (U.S.), also cited as best director Brit. Film Award for best film *(contd)*	Praemium Imperiale (in Music) to Ital. conductor Claudio Abbado Claudio Abbado forms the Lucerne Festival Orchestra consisting of a series of international chamber music groups and highly acclaimed soloists and principals from 27 world-famous orchestras Hans-Werner Henze: "L'Upupa," opera, premieres in Salzburg Miles Davis: "Bitches Brew/Tacoma Narrows" choreographed by Anne Teresa de Keersmaeker in Brussels	solute zero, beating the previous record by a factor of six Following a two-week stay in space, the space shuttle Columbia explodes on its return to the atmosphere, killing all 7 astronauts on board. An investigation into the tragedy reveals serious errors on the part of the U.S. space agency N.A.S.A. Mars and Earth come as close to one another as they have in 60,000 years: nearly 35 million miles Mars Probe "Mars Express" is Europe's first planetary satellite boondoggle. Scientists fail to make contact with the landing vehicle "Beagle 2" N.A.S.A. launches two Mars missions with robots for geological experiments China sends its first "Taikonaut" into space. Yang Liwei orbits the earth 14 times in the space shuttle Shenzou 5 Space Infrared Telescope Facility (SIRTF) for observing the infrared universe, designed to reach deep into the universe, discovers galaxies trillions of light years away and does for the field of infrared astronomy what the Hubble space telescope did for the visible universe. SIRTF is N.A.S.A.'s fourth largest observatory, following Hubble, x-ray telescope Chandra, and the Gamma Ray Observatory Compton "Liverpool telescope," world's largest fully robotic telescope with primary mirrors 6 feet in diameter, begins operation in La Palma, designed to study objects whose position or intensity varies, such as asteroids, comets, and supernovas After traveling nearly 2.85 billion miles through space, the space probe Galileo makes a fiery dive into Jupiter's atmosphere. The mission, launched in 1989, was one of N.A.S.A.'s most successful projects	Herb Brooks, Amer. ice hockey trainer, coach for the Olympic team, d. (b. 1937) Valerie Brumel, former world record holder in high jump, d. (b. 1942)	**2003 contd**

	A. HISTORY, POLITICS	B. LITERATURE, THEATER	C. RELIGION, PHILOSOPHY, LEARNING

2003 contd

Both sons of Saddam Hussein, Uday and Qusay, are killed in a shootout with U.S. soldiers and their bodies placed on graphic public display. They belonged to the most intimate circle of leaders surrounding the toppled dictator

Leader of the Shiite ethnic majority in Iraq, Ayatollah Muhammad Baquir al Hakim and more than 80 others are killed in a bombing outside the Holy Shrine of the Imam Ali in Najaf (Iraq)

Iraqi dictator Saddam Hussein is captured by U.S. soldiers near Takrit, 8 months after his defeat

Women in Kuwait are given the right to vote in local elections, but they remain prohibited from voting at the parliamentary level

Iranian Pres. Mohammad Hatami admits for the first time to having enriched uranium reserves, but says that the nuclear program is designed to serve civilian purposes only

Parliamentary election in Israel: conservative incumbent Prime Minister Ariel Sharon wins with 37 of 120 mandates, followed by the Labor Party of Amram Mitzna which championed peace negotiations with Palestinians during the campaign, and suffered the heaviest loss in the party's history with only 19 mandates

By a slim majority, Israeli Cabinet approves international road map for peace calling for the establishment of a Palestinian state by the year 2005, marking the first time an Israeli parliament has recognized the Palestinian's right to their own state. The Palestinian Authority had already approved the plan

Mahmud Abbas, Deputy to Palestinian Pres. Yasser Arafat, becomes first head of government is the Palestinian Autonomous Areas, but soon resigns due to lack of support from Israel and the U.S. He is succeeded by Ahmed Qurei

The Israeli government's decision to remove Pres. of the Palestinian Authority Arafat from his headquarters meets with worldwide indignation and condemnation. Vice Prime Minister Olmert says that even killing Arafat would be "an option"

U.N. passes resolution condemning construction of an Israeli barrier "wall" in the West Bank

Syrian Pres. Bashar al Assad appoints Muhammad Nadshi al Otari Prime Minister following the resignation of Mustafa Miro

Military putsch in Guinea-Bissau; Pres. Kumba Yala is taken prisoner and a new transitional government installed

Liberia's Pres. Charles Taylor steps down and flees to Nigeria in exile

Libya assumes responsibility for the 1988 Lockerbie bombing and sets up a fund to compensate families of the 170 victims. In response, the U.N. Security Council lifts sanctions against the country

In the first free presidential election since Rwanda's independence, sitting Pres. Paul Kagame is declared the winner

Idi Amin, former Ugandan dictator, d. (b. 1925)

Walter Sisulu, South African politician, d. (b. 1912)

German and Dutch troops take over command of the International Security Force in Afghanistan (ISAF) for about six months

China's People's Congress elects Wen Jiabao as chief of state, to succeed Jiang Zemin; new Pres. is Hu Jiantau

In parliamentary elections in Cambodia, the party under incumbent Prime Minister Hun Sen is the clear winner over the opposition Sam-Rainsy Party and its coalition partner the Royalist Funcinpec Party

The military government in Myanmar takes opposition leader and Nobel Peace Prize-winning activist Aung San Suu Kyi into "protective custody" following clashes between progovernment demonstrators and her supporters in the opposition

Nepal's Prime Minister Lokendra Bahadur Chand steps down under pressure from the opposition; he is succeeded by Surya Bahadur Thapa, appointed by King Gyanendra

North Korea withdraws from the nuclear weapons ban treaty. The government is demanding a nonaggression pact from the U.S., but U.S. is looking for a multinational solution

Roh Moo-Hyun wins presidential elections in South Korea

D. VISUAL ARTS	E. MUSIC	F. SCIENCE, TECHNOLOGY, GROWTH	G. DAILY LIFE	
and best director to Roman Polanski for "The Pianist"; best foreign film to Pedro Almodóvar for "Habla con ella"; best actor to Daniel Day-Lewis (Ireland) for "Gangs of New York" and Nicole Kidman (Australia) for "The Hours" Venice Film Festival: Golden Lion for best actress to Katja Riemann in "Rosenstrasse" by Margarethe von Trotta; for best actor to Sean Penn in "21 Grams" by Alejandro Gonzalez; for best film to "The Return" by Andrei Zvyagintsev, Silver Lion for best direction to Takeshi Kitano for "Zatoichi," best direction to Michael Schorr for his debut "Schultze Gets the Blues" Praemium Imperiale (in Film) to Brit. film director Ken Loach Previously unknown and unsigned Van Gogh painting, the image of a peasant woman, auctioned for 510,000 euros in Japan. The painting had only been recently declared authentic "Vincent's Choice," exhibit at the Van Gogh Museum in Amsterdam, on the occasion of Vincent van Gogh's 150th birthday, exhibits over 100 works by other artists who may have been or were clearly identified as forerunners for the artist, including: Eugène Delacroix, Paul Gauguin, Paul Signac, and Georges Seurat 50th Art Biennale in Venice under the motto "Dreams and Conflicts: The Dictatorship of the Viewer" Completion and opening of the reconstructed Amber Room at the Catherine Palace in St. Petersburg Renovation of St. Stephan's Basilica in Budapest completed after 17 years Opening of the Disney Concert Hall in Los Angeles, designed by Amer. architect Frank O. Gehry The ancient Assyrian capital of Assur, located in what *(contd)*				2003 contd

	A. HISTORY, POLITICS	B. LITERATURE, THEATER	C. RELIGION, PHILOSOPHY, LEARNING
2003 contd			
2004	EU undergoes largest expansion in its history, accepting ten new states: Poland, Czech Republic, Estonia, Latvia, Lithuania, Slovakia, Hungary, Slovenia, Malta, and Cyprus. Highlight of the official ceremonies on May 1 is the flag ceremony with state and government leaders from 25 member states in Dublin. Seats in European Parliament increase from 626 to 788 Diplomat and former Dutch Foreign Minister Jaap de Hoop Scheffler succeeds George Robertson as N.A.T.O. Sec. Gen. Portugal's head of government José Manuel Durao Barroso becomes Chair of the EU Commission Record deficit in the U.S. at $521 billion, some 4.5% of the GDP Both U.S. Pres. George W. Bush and Brit. Prime Minister Tony Blair recant on their insistence that Iraq was in possession of weapons of mass destruction, an allegation that was used as primary rationale for the war in Iraq National Commission on Terrorist Attacks on the United States (9/11 Commission) releases a report that exposes a Saddam–Al Quaeda conspiracy as a farce, thus pulling the rug out from beneath George W. Bush's central justification for the war in Iraq U.S. Supreme Court rules—against the wishes of the U.S. federal government—that alleged terrorists being held at the military base in Guantanamo Bay, Cuba, have the right to challenge their detention in U.S. courts CIA chief George Tenet steps down in conjunction with the CIA's exaggeration of evidence of weapons of mass destruction in Iraq Ronald Reagan, Amer. screen actor and 40th Pres. of the U.S., d. (b. 1911) Following parliamentary elections in Greece, Kostas Karamanlis becomes new Prime Minister Ital. Prime Minister Silvio Berlusconi has now served the longest uninterrupted term in office in the postwar history Murderer of Swedish Foreign Minister Anna Lindh is first sentenced to life in prison, but then committed to a facility for psychologically impaired criminal offenders EU states scuffle with Switzerland over the introduction of a uniform dividend tax as a way of counteracting interstate tax evasion in the future Terror attacks on three suburban trains in Madrid leave 190 people dead and over 1,000 injured. Government of Prime Minister Aznar's first suspect is ETA Just days after the Span. elections, information surfaces to indicate that evidence of Al Quaeda involvement in the terrorist attacks in Madrid were systematically suppressed as part of a political *(contd)*	Olivia Goldsmith, Amer. writer, d. (b. 1949) Spalding Gray, Amer. actor and writer, d. (b. 1941) Hubert Selby, Amer. writer, d. (b. 1928) Roger W. Straus, Amer. publisher, d. (b. 1917) John Toland, Amer. writer, d. (b. 1912) Peter Ustinov, Brit. actor, writer, and director, d. (b. 1921) Peace Prize of the German Booksellers' Assoc. to Hungarian writer Peter Esterhazy Premio Nadal (Spain) to Span. writer Antonio Soler Amadou Hampate Ba (1901–91, Malían author): "Tierno Bokar," adapted for the stage and directed by Peter Brooks Yasmina Reza: "Une, pièce espagnole," premiere in Paris, directed by Luc Bondy	Dinu Adamesteanu, Romanian-Ital. archaelogist, d. (b. 1913) Daniel J. Boorstin, Amer. social historian, d. (b. 1915) Melvin J. Lasky, Amer. historian, d. (b. 1929) Maxime Rodinson, Fr. Orientalist, d. (b. 1915) Carl von Ossietzky Prize to Noam Chomsky, Amer. philosopher and linguist Ger. Pres. Johannes Rau intervenes in the debate concerning Muslim headscarves, placing the headscarf on a par with the traditional dress of Christian clergy and the Crucifix, which elicits vehement response from clergy

D. VISUAL ARTS	E. MUSIC	F. SCIENCE, TECHNOLOGY, GROWTH	G. DAILY LIFE	
is now Iraq, and the Bamiyan Valley in Afghanistan are placed on U.N.E.S.C.O. World Cultural Heritage List Amer. star-architect Daniel Libeskind is awarded the contract for rebuilding Ground Zero in New York. At the site of the terror attacks of September 11, 2001, which destroyed the World Trade Center, Libeskind's plan, "Gardens of the World," calls for the tallest building in the world: a 1740-foot spire, surrounded by five adjacent shorter towers and surrounded by a group of additional individual buildings				**2003 contd**
Marlon Brando, Amer. actor, d. (b. 1924) Frances Dee, Amer. actress, d. (b. 1907) John Hench, Amer. Disney animator, d. (b. 1908) Nino Manfredi, Ital. actor, d. (b. 1921) John Cullen Murphy, Amer. cartoonist ("Prince Valiant"), d. (b. 1919) Helmut Newton (given name, Helmut Neustädter), Amer. photographer, d. (b. 1920, Berlin) Tony Randall, Amer. actor, d. (b. 1920) Madeleine Robinson, Fr. actress, d. (b. 1916) Ingrid Thulin, Swed. actress, d. (b. 1929) Praemium Imperiale to Ger. painter George Baselitz, Amer. installation artist Bruce Nauman; Brazilian architect Oscar Niemeyer, Iranian film director Abbas Kiarostami, and to Polish composer Krzysztof Penderecki Pritzker Prize to Brit. architect of Iraqi descent Zaha Hadid Oscars: 11 Oscars to "Lord of the Rings 3: The Return of the King" by Peter Jackson, including best picture and best director; best actress to Charlize Theron in "Monster" by Patty Jenkins; best actor to Sean Penn in "Mystic River." Honorary Oscar to *(contd)*	Jan Berry, Amer. pop singer, d. (b. 1941) Iona Brown, Brit. violinist and conductor, d. (b. 1931) Ray Charles, Amer. singer, jazz pianist, and arranger, d. (b. 1930) Alvarez de la Fuente, Argentine composer, d. (b. 1953) Antonio Gades, Span. dancer and choreographer, d. (b. 1936) Nikolai Ghiaurov, Bulgarian opera singer (bass), d. (b. 1929) Elvin Jones, Amer. jazz drummer, d. (b. 1927) Arthur Kane, Amer. rock bass guitarist, d. (b. 1951) Barney Kessel, Amer. jazz guitarist, d. (b. 1923) Vilayat Khan, musician, sitar player, d. (b. 1922) Carlos Kleiber, Argentine conductor, d. (b. 1930, Berlin) Billy May, Amer. jazz trumpet player and composer, d. (b. 1916) Jost Michaels, Ger. clarinetist, pianist, and conductor, d. (b. 1922) Ann Miller, Amer. dancer and actress, d. (b. 1923) Czeslaw Niemen, Polish rock musician, d. (b. 1939) Boris Pergamenschikov, Russian cellist, d. (b. 1949) Robert Quine, Amer. guitarist and singer, d. (b. 1942) *(contd)*	Francis Crick, Brit. Physicist and biochemist, co-discoverer of DNA double helix, d. (b. 1916) Wilhelm Fresenius, Ger. chemist, founder of modern analytical chemistry, d. (b. 1913) Thomas Gold, Amer. astrophysicist, d. (b. 1920) Eugene Mallove, Amer. proponent of cold fusion, d. (b. 1947) William Pickering, Amer. aerospace specialist, d. (b. 1910) John A. Pople, Brit. chemist who discovered quantum chemistry, d. (b. 1925) John Meynard Smith, Brit. evolutionary biologist, d. (b. 1920) South Korean team of researchers led by Woo Sukhwang succeeds in using cloning technology to create human embryos and to harvest stem cells from them for generating tissue Doctors at Berlin's Charité succeed in Europe's first transplant of 8 vital organs at once. A 36-year-old female patient receives a liver, pancreas, stomach, duodenum, small intestine, partial large intestine, kidney, and adrenal gland in a 12-hour surgical procedure and is able to leave the hospital in good health A research team led by Adam Riess at STSCI in Baltimore, based on observations of supernovas, concludes that Earth will be uninhabitable in 600 million years and that the universe will no longer exist in about 30 billion years New measurements confirm that the 18 Scorpii star, 48 light years away, is almost an identical twin *(contd)*	Companies with the world's highest profits: Exxon Mobile (U.S.), $242,365 billion; Royal Dutch/Shell (Netherlands), 235,598; British Petroleum (U.K.) 232,571 Merger between the music subsidiaries of Japanese company Sony and Germany's Bertelsmann leads to the creation of the world's largest music corporation Debacle for airplane manufacturer Boeing: after the U.S. cancels a major contract for jet tankers, the Brit. air force also decides to go with the European Airbus manufacturer EADS with a nearly 19 billion euro contract EU Commission imposes a record-high fine on U.S. software company Microsoft, nearly a half billion euros, for illegally leveraging its monopoly position to its own advantage Toyota is the first Japanese company to turn a profit of over 1 billion yen, more than double what its U.S. competitors Ford and General Motors make combined Umberto Agnelli, Ital. business executive, CEO of Fiat corporation, d. (b. 1935) Estée Lauder, Amer. cosmetics executive, d. (b. 1908) Most spectacular celestial event of the year: Venus passes the Sun in an eclipse that is visible from Earth. The last Venus transit was visible in 1882, the next in 2125 According to a world AIDS report, there were about 5 million new cases of AIDS last year and about 3 million people died Avian influenza (bird flu) outbreak in 8 Asian countries. The outbreak led to the slaughter of millions of poultry birds. The virus can be transmitted to humans, and countless have been stricken and killed Collision of two trains carrying flammable chemicals in North Korea kills 161 people, among them 76 school children. Some 1,300 people are injured, 8,100 homes destroyed *(contd)*	**2004**

	A. HISTORY, POLITICS	B. LITERATURE, THEATER	C. RELIGION, PHILOSOPHY, LEARNING
2004 contd	campaign strategy deployed by the Span. government to focus attention on ETA as perpetrators of the attacks. The alleged mastermind behind the devastating attacks in Madrid, the Tunisian Serhane ben Abdelmadshid, blows up himself and three accomplices when police storm their hideout. The suicide bombings kill one police officer and injure eleven New Span. Prime Minister Zapatero orders the withdrawal of Spanish troops from Iraq Voters in Greek Cyprus vote against reunification with the Turkish north; thus, only half of the island of Cyprus joins the EU Princess Juliana, Queen of Netherlands 1948–80, d. (b. 1909) Croatia is acknowledged as an official candidate for EU membership Dr. Ivo Sanader to succeed Ivica Racan as Croatian Prime Minister Lithuanian Parliament ousts Pres. Rolandas Paksas. Former Lithuanian Premier Valdas Adamkus is elected to the office of Pres. for the first time Macedonian Pres. Boris Trajkovski dies in a plane crash. Head of the Social Democratic government Branko Crvenkovski succeeds him Just one day after Poland joins the EU, Prime Minister Leszek Miller resigns, as previously announced. Former Finance Minister Marek Belka succeeds him, but Parliament quickly retracts its support. Belka resigns, but is later confirmed in his post as head of government Russia's ambassador to the EU in Brussels, Mikhail Fradkov, is appointed new Prime Minister by Vladimir Putin. His cabinet is reduced from 30 to 17 ministers In the Russian presidential election, Vladimir Putin receives 71.2% of votes. O.S.C.E. election observers criticize the election process as undemocratic Reformist politician Boris Tadic is elected Pres. of Serbia Ivan Gasporovic is elected Pres. of Slovakia, running against former head of government Vladimir Meciar Social Liberal government under Prime Minister Vladimir Spidla steps down in the Czech Republic. Pres. Vaclav Klaus appoints Stanislaw Gross new Prime Minister Chechen Pres. Akhmad Kadyrov and the Commander of Russian troops are killed in a bomb attack in Chechnya, some 100 people injured. Prime Minister Sergei Abramov takes over government affairs. Rebel leader Shamil Basayev claims responsibility for the attack Kurdish separatists suspend their cease-fire against Turkey and warn tourists and businesses of renewed violence. Government in Ankara refuses to negotiate U.S. Defense Department declares Iraqi former dictator Saddam Hussein a prisoner of war U.S. and its allies transfer the bulk of power to the Iraqi transitional government; but its authority, as outlined in an addendum to the preliminary constitution and in U.N. Resolution 1546, is limited Car bomb kills Pres. of the Iraqi Governing Council Izzadin al Salim and 8 others Ghazi al Jawar, Sunni politician, is elected Pres. of Iraq, succeeding Saddam Hussein U.S. television broadcast station CBS covers the systematic torture of Iraqi prisoners in Iraq at the Abu Ghraib prison. Even high-ranking members of the U.S. military tolerated the sadistic abuses The International Court of Justice rules that Israel's construction of a wall in the occupied Palestinian territory of the West Bank is in violation of international humanitarian law Israeli Cabinet approves Prime Minister Ariel Sharon's plans to withdraw from the Gaza Strip, but explicitly refuses to address the issue of settlement Within just a few weeks Israel carries out the systematic liquidation of Hamas founder Sheikh Ahmed Yassin and his successor Abdel Asis Rantissi in Gaza City. More than 40 member states of the U.N. Security Council strongly condemn the military action U.S. accuses Syria of supporting international terrorism. Even though *(contd)*		

D. VISUAL ARTS | E. MUSIC | F. SCIENCE, TECHNOLOGY, GROWTH | G. DAILY LIFE

2004 contd

D. VISUAL ARTS

Blake Edwards for lifetime achievement

61st Golden Globes: Peter Jackson for best drama and best director, "Lord of the Rings"; best comedy and screenplay to Sofia Coppola for "Lost in Translation"; Bill Murray for best comic actor in "Lost in Translation"; best actor in a drama to Sean Penn in "Mystic River"; best actress in a drama to Charlize Theron for her leading role in "Monster"; best comic actress to Diane Keaton in "Something's Gotta Give"

César: best picture, best director, and best screenplay to the Canadian director Denys Arcand's "The Barbarian Invasions"; best European film to "Good Bye, Lenin!" by Wolfgang Becker; best foreign film to "Mystic River" by Clint Eastwood; best actor to Omar Sharif for his role in "Monsieur Ibrahim"; best actress to Julie Depardieu

54th International Film Festival Berlin: Golden Bear to "Gegen die Wand" by Faith Akin (Germany); Jury's Award to "El Abrazo Partido" ("Lost Embrace") by Daniel Burman (Argentina); Silver Bear to Korean director Kim KiDuk for "Samaritan Girl"

Amer. artist James Turrell presents the first elements of one of his most ambitious projects of "land-art" that has been in planning for nearly 30 years: the transformation of a natural cinder volcano in the Arizona desert into an observatory that allows visitors to see celestial phenomena with the naked eye

Sotheby's sells Pablo Picasso's painting "Garçon à la pipe" for $104,168 at auction, making it the most expensive painting sold in the history of auctioning

"The Passion of the Christ" by Mel Gibson is the most hotly debated film of the year. It includes scenes of

(contd)

E. MUSIC

Leonard Stein, Amer. pianist, d. (b. 1919)

At the 46th Grammy Awards, 5 Grammies to Beyoncé Knowles, member of singing trio "Destiny's Child," for her debut solo album "Dangerously in Love"; 4 Grammies to soul artist Luther Vandross. Other Grammy-winners include Christina Aguilera, Kylie Minogue, Pink, Eminem, Evanascence and "Coldplay" as well as the Ger. bass-baritone Thomas Quasthoff

"Tarde," orchestral piece for 130 instruments and a soprano, by Aribert Reimann, premiered by Claudia Barainsky and the musicians of the Staatsorchester Stuttgart under the direction of Lothar Zagrosek

Wilfried Hiller: "Wolkenstein," opera, premieres in Nuremberg

Brian Ferneyhough: "Shadowtime," opera

Michael Nyman: "Man and Body: Dada," premieres in Karlsruhe

Thomas Ades: "The Tempest," premieres in London, Convent Garden

Konstantin Wecker and Rolf Rettberg: "Hundertwasser," musical

Jiri Kylian: "Il faut qu'une porte," choreography, premieres in Paris, Palais Garnier

F. SCIENCE, TECHNOLOGY, GROWTH

to the Sun in terms of mass, size, and surface temperature

Using a Spitzer infrared space telescope, astronomers discover an object with a 1250-mile diameter in the Kuiper Belt. It is the largest celestial object to be discovered in the solar system since the planet of Pluto was discovered in 1930

Two N.A.S.A. space probes with the rovers Spirit and Opportunity land on the surface of Mars within 3 weeks of one another and send spectacular images as well as evidence of water on Mars back to earth

Mars rover Spirit sets new Internet record: in a 48-hour period, 513 million hits to the N.A.S.A. site, with 86 million downloads

European Space Agency (ESA) successfully launches its space probe Mars Express into the orbit of the red planet and thus determines the exact position and volume of ice and dry ice on its south pole. The probe also delivers spectacular images of Mars with a high resolution color stereo camera developed by Gerhard Neukum at the Ger. Center for Aeronautics and Aerospace Research

Space probe Cassini sends spectacular images of the Saturn moon Phoebe back to Earth before it eases into Saturn's orbit. After seven years, it has finally reached its destination and begins exploring the planet, its rings, and 7 of the 31 known moons of Saturn

European comet probe Rosette sets off on its 10-year flight through space to the comet 67P/Tschurjumov-Gerasimenko

After nearly 30 years in planning, a Mercury space probe is launched. N.A.S.A.'s Messenger space probe will take nearly seven years to cover a distance of 5 billion miles, in order to study the geology and magnetic field of the planet closest to the Sun

Scientists using a cyclotron at the Joint Institute for Nuclear Research in Dubna generate two new chemical elements, which have been assigned the atomic numbers 113 and 115

World's largest cruise vessel "Queen Mary 2" is christened by Queen Elizabeth II in Southampton

An international team of archaeologists in Abu Dhabi discovers the ruins of buildings presumed to be nearly 7,000 years old, older than the pyramids at Gizeh

(contd)

G. DAILY LIFE

Mass panic erupts during the annual Hajj pilgrimage in Mina, Saudi Arabia, leaving 244 dead and hundreds injured

Catastrophic fire in a shopping center on the outskirts of Asunción, Paraguay, kills over 460 people, more than 400 injured

17-year-old Maria Sharapova wins the Wimbledon Tennis Tournament; victor for the men is Swiss player Roger Federer

A. HISTORY, POLITICS | B. LITERATURE, THEATER | C. RELIGION, PHILOSOPHY, LEARNING

2004 contd

there is no evidence to prove the charge, U.S. imposes sanctions against Syria

Abu Abbas, Palestinian politician, PLO founder, d. (b. 1948)

Pres. Jean-Bertrand Aristide flees Haiti after a coup and nationwide revolts that claimed hundreds of lives. U.N. sends in international peacekeeping forces. Longtime U.N. diplomat Gérard Latortue is installed to head a transitional government

Abdelaziz Bouteflika confirmed as Algerian Pres.

After a 24-year hiatus, U.S. resumes diplomatic relations with Libya after Muammar Khadafi announces it has abandoned weapons of mass destruction

Macky Sall is Senegal's fourth Premier in four years

In parliamentary elections in South Africa, the ruling A.N.C. wins with 62.65% of the votes

U.N. High Commission on Human Rights—following the genocide in Rwanda—warns against genocide in western Sudan. 10,000 are already dead and a million people in Darfur are fleeing the Sudanese army and government-backed militia

Rebels opposing the Ugandan Pres. stage a massacre at a refugee camp in Northern Uganda, killing 192 people

The Council of Elders (loya jirga) in Afghanistan convenes to adopt a democratic constitution. The nation declares itself an Islamic republic, which grants women equal rights

Hundreds of thousands demonstrate to demand more democracy on the 7th anniversary of Hong Kong's return to China

Regime change in India: the opposition Congress Party defeats Prime Minister Atal Bihari Vajpayee. Despite the election victory, top candidate Sonia Gandhi declines the office of Prime Minister. Former Finance Minister Manmolian Singh becomes head of government

After talks concerning North Korea's nuclear policies fail, the International Atomic Energy Agency considers North Korea the most urgent threat to world peace

Pakistani nuclear scientist Abdul Qadeer Khan admits to having shared nuclear secrets with Iran, Libya, and North Korea

Philippine Pres. Gloria Macapagal Arroyo is declared winner of the presidential election

D. VISUAL ARTS	E. MUSIC	F. SCIENCE, TECHNOLOGY, GROWTH	G. DAILY LIFE	
brutal violence previously unprecedented in film Wolfgang Petersen's $200 million production "Troy," with Brad Pitt in the role of Achilles		Computer worm "My Doom" is considered the fastest worm ever to infect the Internet. Within four days, the virus spread to 211 countries throughout the world, causing damages in the amount of several billion euros N.A.S.A.'s supersonic combustion ramjet Scramjet sets a new world air speed record with a speed of nearly 7,000 mph at an altitude of 110,000 feet		2004 contd

INDEX

[Index entries refer the reader to a year and column, not to a page number.]

A

B

C

D

E

F

H

K

L

M

N

O

P

Q

R

S

T

U

V

W

X

Y

Z